C0-ASZ-764

125 Years Of Famous Pages From The New York Times 1851-1976

Introduction by James Reston

Edited by Herbert J. Cohen

ARNO PRESS
A New York Times Company

Distributed by Crown Publishers, Inc.
One Park Avenue
New York, New York 10016

Manufactured in the United States of America

Library of Congress Cataloging in Publication Data
Main entry under title:

125 famous pages from the New York times.

1. World politics — 19th century — Sources. 2. World politics — 20th century — Sources. I. Cohen, Herbert J. II. New York times.
D363.053 909.81 76-14532
ISBN 0-517-52791-X

INTRODUCTION

On the big clock of history, the newspaper is the second hand of time, ticking off with its headlines the first urgent reports of the news. This collection of "125 Years of Famous Pages From *The New York Times*" reminds us of how former pre-television generations learned of the events that shaped their lives, but it does more than that. It recalls the tragedies and triumphs of the human race, and somehow helps illuminate the problems of our own time.

What has been suffered and somehow overcome in these 125 years! What divisions, uprisings, insurrections, rebellions, wars, and natural disasters of famine and earthquake! And yet what endurance and even progress within the human family! Most of these front pages are an account of some catastrophe, but if you flip through them from beginning to end, you have to conclude that *homo sapiens* is a fairly tough breed.

In the years between 1851, when *The New York Times* was founded, until 1898, when it was purchased and transformed by Adolph S. Ochs, the western nations had achieved a remarkable ascendency in the world. Almost everywhere on the globe, western concepts of human society seemed dominant.

Yet the front pages of *The Times* reproduced here tell a great deal about the disasters and decline of western supremacy in the first three quarters of the 20th century. Thus, Arnold Toynbee, in the last volume of his retrospective histories, could write that perhaps "This ascendency was going to be as transitory as the previously less than world-wide ascendencies of the Mongols, Arabs, Huns, Romans, Greeks, Persians, Assyrians and Akkadians." This judgment may prove to be as inaccurate as many of the news judgments of editors, but the ensuing pages are startling glimpses at the blunders and misfortunes of the past few generations.

Some of the headlines from the old days, though printed in small type, sound like shrieks in the night. November 27, 1854: "Bloody Work at Sebastopol." On the Charge of the Light Brigade: "Gallant But Disastrous Cavalry Charge—A Thrilling Description." April 15, 1865: "Awful Event—President Lincoln Shot by Assassin, The Act of a Desperate Rebel."

But mainly in the 19th century, the headlines were modest labels in gray expanses of almost unreadable type, unrelieved by white space, photographs or graphics of any sort. June 13, 1854: "Japan Opened—Satisfactory Result of Commodore Perry's Visit." March 7, 1857: "Important Decision from Washington—Decision of the Supreme Court in the Dred Scott Case." April 13, 1861: "The War Commenced—The First Gun Fired by Fort Moultrie Against Fort Sumter."

Also on April 16, 1912: "Titanic Sinks Four Hours After Hitting Iceberg . . . 866 Rescued by Carpathia, Probably 1250 Perish . . . Ismay Safe, Mrs. Astor Maybe: Noted Names Missing." Nov. 9, 1917: "Revolutionists Seize Petrograd: Kerensky Flees . . . ," and adjoining this, a front page side-bar on the world reaction to the Soviet Revolution: "Hope Strong Man Will Rule Russia."

Some of the most interesting of these pages deal with the expansion of the nation by diplomatic negotiation and scientific or mechanical innovation. March 31, 1867: "Important Annexation . . . Russian America Purchased by the United States." May 11, 1869: "East and West . . . Completion of the Great Line Spanning the Continent." October 18, 1907: "Wireless Joins Two Worlds . . . Marconi Trans-Atlantic Service Opened With a Dispatch to *The New York Times*."

Increasingly after Adolph S. Ochs took over as proprietor of *The Times*, his conviction that science was transforming the world led him to pioneer, not only in reporting scientific events, but in promoting them to the benefit of the paper's circulation.

Thus he helped finance Admiral Peary's explorations of the polar regions. The front page of the paper on September 7, 1909 reports: "Peary Discovers the North Pole After Eight Trials in 23 Years." And Peary has a front page message exclusive to *The Times* proclaiming: "I Have the Pole."

These pages are also a history of American journalism, at least as seen in *The New York Times*. For example, the first front page illustrations recorded here appeared in the issue of March 10, 1862 on the "Desperate Naval Engagement in Hampton Roads" at the beginning of the War Between the States.

The first articles signed by correspondents in this collection appeared on January 9, 1918, beginning the era of by-lined journalism. And in this catalogue of front pages *The Times'* slogan, "All the News That's Fit to Print" appeared in the left hand "ear" for the first time on February 16, 1898, shortly after the newspaper was purchased by Mr. Ochs.

One of the interesting paradoxes of these pages is that while the United States followed a policy of political isolation from the struggles and wars of the rest of the world during the 19th century and the beginning of the 20th century, the news of the world dominated the front pages of the paper in the last quarter of the 19th and the first quarter of the 20th.

For example, the outbreak of the First World War dominates the entire front page of the issue of August 3, 1914, yet there is no page one dispatch recording the reaction from Washington, as if this were some foreign quarrel that didn't particularly shake the U.S. capital.

In recent years, there has been a great deal of discussion and criticism of "Personal Journalism" and "Investigative Reporting" in the American press, particularly since the Vietnam War and the resignation of President Richard Nixon. A glance through these pages, however, will remind us that the traditions of personal reporting and muck-racking against political corruption have been going on from the earliest days of the Republic.

Thus the reporting from the Civil War emphasized the dramatic and sometimes even lurid "Eyewitness Accounts" of *The Times'* reporters, and long before the days of Mr. Ochs, *The Times'* front page of July 22, 1871 is given over entirely to the "Secret Accounts of Ingersoll and Company. Proofs of Undoubted Frauds Brought to Light," cries *The Times.*

Nevertheless, given the limitation on communications in the early first half of these 125 years, it is perhaps surprising that the major events that influenced our own time were so promptly recognized and boldly displayed.

The old editors, to judge by these pages, were almost unfailingly solemn. There is very little cultural news on these front pages, and except for the "Marriage of the President (McKinley) to Miss Folsom" (the first in The White House), there is very little of what we now call the "Personality" stories.

Nor was there anything like the separation of "News" from "Opinion" in the minds of these early editors of *The Times*. In fact, news stories often appeared on the Editorial Pages, and editorial opinions in the news stories. The same charge, of course, is still levelled against the press today, but the practice was much more prevalent in the early days of the century.

Nothing said here, however, is meant to suggest that these front pages were typical or even representative of the front pages of most of the other daily newspapers of the United States during these 125 years. While most papers were concentrating on reporting the events of their own communities, *The New York Times,* from Mr. Ochs' days on, was consciously trying to keep the record of the important events of the entire world.

Now in the last quarter of the 20th century, we can see much more clearly just how important these events were to the history and the private lives of the American people.

May, 1976 **JAMES RESTON**

New-York Daily Times.

VOL. I....NO. 1. NEW-YORK, THURSDAY, SEPTEMBER 18, 1851. PRICE ONE CENT.

New-York Daily Times.

THE NEW-YORK DAILY TIMES IS PUBLISHED EVERY MORNING (*Sunday excepted,*) at the office, No. 113 NASSAU-STREET, between Beekman and Ann, just behind the Old Park Theater, and delivered to subscribers in the city, Brooklyn, Williamsburgh and Jersey City for six cents a week, or, when they prefer, they can pay in advance at the Desk for six months or a year at the same rate. Single copies, ONE CENT. Mail subscribers, FOUR DOLLARS a year.

THE NEW-YORK EVENING TIMES IS PUBLISHED EVERY EVENING, (*Sundays excepted,*) on the same terms as the Morning Edition.

THE NEW-YORK WEEKLY TIMES, A VERY LARGE NEWSPAPER FOR THE COUNTRY is published every *Saturday Morning*, at the low price of $2 per annum. Ten copies for $15, or twenty copies for $20, will be sent to one address, and the paper in no case continued beyond the time for which payment is made.

Payment in all cases must be paid in advance.

RAYMOND, JONES & CO. Publishers.

New-York Daily Times.

THE NEWS FROM EUROPE.

ARRIVAL OF THE EUROPA'S MAILS.

AFFAIRS IN ENGLAND.

The Election in France—Arrests, &c.

APPREHENDED DISTURBANCE IN AUSTRIA.

SOUTHERN EUROPE.

The Royal Mail Steamer *Europa* arrived at Boston yesterday morning, at about 6 o'clock. Her mails were sent on by the New Haven Railroad train, which left at 8 o'clock, and reached this city at an early hour last evening.

By this arrival we have received our regular English and French files, with correspondence, circulars, &c., to Saturday, September 6th—the *Europa's* day of sailing.

The news by this arrival has considerable interest, though it is not of startling importance.

In ENGLAND, political affairs are quiet. The *Humboldt* arrived at Southampton on Thursday, the 4th, with the news of the execution at Havana of the fifty men under Col. Crittenden's command. The details of the news are given at length in the London papers.

In FRANCE attention is chiefly absorbed with speculations on the approaching Presidential election. The Prince de Joinville is clearly to be a candidate, and will doubtless be a more formidable opponent of Louis Napoleon than any other that could be selected.

Another "Conspiracy" has been discovered in Paris, forty-seven arrests have been made by the Police.

In AUSTRIA hostility to the government still smoulders under the surface with occasional outbreaks. An affray took place near Gross-Waradin, between a rustic wedding party and several *Gendarmes*, of the most brutal character.

In PORTUGAL attention is absolved by an accusation of a Cabinet Minister of bribery. He has resigned and come before the courts of law.

The news of KOSSUTH's release is confirmed, but the time is now said to have been the 13th of September. It is said that he proposes to go first to England and provide there for the education of his children and then proceed to the United States.

The money market presents no feature of marked interest.

GREAT BRITAIN.

The Queen was absent on her visit to Scotland where she had been very enthusiastically received. The Exhibition continues to attract numerous visiters. The attendance and receipts were:

Tuesday, ...	40,866 persons—	£2,407,15s.
Wednesday, ...	41,917 persons—	2,080,12s.
Thursday, ...	44,209 persons—	2,137,18s

The necessity of reducing prices is strongly urged.

In Dublin it is stated that the Government intend to send four additional regiments of infantry from England, to enforce obedience to the law. The correspondent of *The Times* denounces this as simply preposterous.

The Freeman's Journal announces the death of one of the celebrities of the memorable year 1843, namely, the Rev. Thomas Tierney, one of the two clergymen included in the monster indictment of the then Attorney General, Mr. A. B. C. Smith. Up to 1843 he was one of the most active supporters of the Repeal movement headed by O'Connell.

DUBLIN, Sept. 4.—The weather has been extremely fine during the present week, and the agricultural reports from all parts of the country are proportionably favorable. In the south, harvest operations are nearly completed, and the yield is said to be good, both as regards quantity and quality. Of the potato the reports continue conflicting, but, making every due allowance for the loss by the fatal epidemic, there appears to be no rational doubt that enough will be saved to supply the wants of a greatly diminished population. In the meanwhile the tide of emigration still rolls on.

A new feature in connexion with emigration has just manifested itself, in the departure, by the emigrant ship Celeste, for Quebec, of a number of comfortable families, of the farming class, from the neighborhood of Park, near this city. So fertile and remunerating were the lands of Park considered for the last 50 years, that they were designated "the golden gardens of the city," yielding as they did successive rotation crops (chiefly vegetables and prime feeding for milch cows) throughout the year. The scene is changed, and the result now is, that the greater portion of the people of Park, a most industrious and expert class of agriculturalists, are determined to endure no longer the hardships to which they were of late years subjected to meet solely the demands of "tax gatherers, poor rate collectors, and landlords," without being able to provide ordinary comfort for their families.

The performances of the American yacht continue to attract attention. Several writers in *The Times* and other papers are drawing attention to the peculiarities of her construction and recommending the imitation of her to English builders.

The American and English Yachts.

To the Editor of The Times:

SIR—It is always regarded in history as peculiar to the most distinguished generals, that they have best known how to turn disasters to profitable use, and have frequently converted the ruins of defeat into foundations of victory. We are now in circumstances which give full scope to the display of such qualities, if we possess them. We have been beaten—signally defeated—on our own element. Our yacht squadron, so long masters of the Solent, hitherto victorious in all sea fights, are completely routed—I had almost said, put to flight. For a long time, not one of the Solent Sea Kings could be found to face the enemy or accept his challenge, and the American would have returned without his gage being taken up, had not the little Titania, of only half the tonnage, and therefore no adequate match, been courageous enough to hazard a defeat. Even the Alarm, which had been so long the champion of the English waters, declined battle. The victory of the America is complete.

[The writer then goes on at considerable length to specify the peculiarities of the *America* and concludes thus:]

I have entered thus minutely into all these points, because I conceive it to be of great importance that we should wisely and in time prepare ourselves for the probable contest of next year. We are more likely to fail next year by a blundering imitation of the unessentials of our victor than by any other course. It is most undesirable that we should be driven by a sudden defeat to abandon any of the excellent points which our own long experience may have taught us to be unquestionably excellent. The roominess, the comfort, the excellent sea-going qualities, the ease of motion in bad weather, are points in our own yacht-building which we must on no account abandon. It is our duty, therefore, to see what we must do to win next year.

1. We must build yachts of the newest construction, of as large a size as may be likely to come against us—*i. e.* somewhat larger than the America, and not allow ourselves to be caught, as this year, with a vessel of half the tonnage only fit even to accept the challenge.

2. We must adopt the best scientific principles of construction for the build of our new yachts, instead of allowing old maxims of routine to govern us. The Americans have boldly adopted the wave system, and applied it to the America in an unmitigated form; we must as boldly adopt it, and give speed to our vessels by offering to the water that form which shall produce the least disturbance in it, and receive from it the least resistance.

3. We must not abandon such forms of midship section as have been found to give easy motion and good sea qualities to our own yachts.

4. We must thoroughly revise our system of rigging and cutting sails. The true theory of sails is that they are flat boards. All mechanical means must be adopted to give them that form, and make them keep it. The superior cut of American sails has long been matter of notoriety to seamen. Sail-cutters have long resisted the abandonment of cherished prejudices on this head. They must now at once adopt the true sail-theory of plane surfaces, and carry it out—whether with the use of booms or a new cut, or both, they must well consider.

5. As to rigging, the simpler the rigging, the fewer the ropes, the better. The Americans have long been distinguished in this respect for simplicity and efficiency. Multiplicity of ropes and blocks is an old-fashioned error, out of which we are rapidly escaping, and the America merely gives us a fresh impulse in this direction.

In conclusion, I have only to express a hope—one which has prompted this letter—that we shall not degenerate into vulgar imitation of our victor, a course in which we shall always be behind him, but rouse ourselves to apply more independently than hitherto the resources of our science and skill to the attainment of that superiority in yacht building, which we have hitherto fancied we possessed. I have the honor to be your obedient servant, A MEMBER OF SEVERAL YACHT CLUBS.

From The London Spectator, Aug. 30.

Off one of our great naval ports, the ship-building of England has been challenged by an alien vessel, and defeated totally. It is a remarkable incident, and not satisfactory to the national pride.

We may find solace in the fact that it is due to "accident." Strange as it must appear, it has only been in comparatively recent times that attempts have been made to reduce the water-cleaving power of the ship to scientific rule; and hitherto science has not been happy in its efforts. The victory of the America, if we are not mistaken, practically refutes the newest hypothesis in the search for the philosopher's stone in the science of shipbuilding. The principle of Mr. Scott Russell's plan, we believe, was based on the fact that water displaced by a body which is removed fills the cavity, not so much by falling in at the sides as by rising from below; hence it was calculated that if a vessel was built sharp and deep toward the bows, broad and shallow toward the stern, the very act of the water in rising to supply the displacement would aid the impetus on the body of the vessel; and experiment tended to justify that expectation. The make of the America, we understand, is quite the reverse of that just described: the bows are sharp, and the breadth of beam, which is considerable, is greatest about parallel to the mainmast, so far coinciding with the other model. But the draught of water at the bows is trifling—about three feet, and it deepens to three times as much toward the stern.

The make is not conducive to great freightage capacity, yet its origin is commercial. American shippers have inclined lately to prefer speed to large capacity; as they find that rapidity, by facilitating certainty of movement and a multiplicity of voyages within a given time, returns a larger profit than slower and more uncertain voyaging with greater bulk. The model of the America is the result.

The good luck of the discovery has first fallen to the United States; but there is no room either for chagrin or dismay. Ship-building in this country is not stagnant; a considerable number of ships are made annually, and there can be no doubt that any well-tested model will soon find its way to our docks. We shall not, therefore, be much behind in the practical progress of ship-building. Nor is it to be assumed, that because empiricism has beaten science, that the latter is to yield to despair. On the contrary, empiricism has always been the jackal to theoretic science, and every discovery by the working shipwright only brings us nearer to the desideratum—a scientific rule. We have heard an American express the hope that England, by beating America, would give the impulse for a new effort, which should again give his country a new triumph. Such friendly emulation is not rivalry; it is but the pride of him, who for the moment gets foremost in the search for the common good. A more invidious feeling would have kept the America at a distance from our waters: as it is, our friends hasten over, with a natural pride, to make us a party in the new idea.

From the London Examiner, Aug. 30.

The American challenge stipulating for at least a six-knot breeze, proves that the America must be a wholesome as well as a fast craft. A six-knot breeze with a dead beat in a head sea would be too much for many of our crack yachts, which, if they are brought to reducing sail, are overwhelmed by the excess of their masts and spars in a sea way.

The truth is, they are built for the inside of the Isle of Wight, and for owners who take to yachting for fashion's sake, knowing nothing about the matter, having no real taste for the sea, subject to sickness, and confining their trips to Hurst Castle to the west, Ryde and Portsmouth to the east, and preferring to them the Southampton water if a weather-tide raises a popple on the gentle Solent. The great pleasure of these gentlemen is to swagger about in sea-toggery, and to have boats'-crews in smart equipment dangling after them. Many a yacht hardly stirs from its moorings at Cowes in a whole season; but to make up for that inaction, there is plenty of boat-work, rowing backwards and forwards, hailing and signalling. There are exceptions; there are some score of the two hundred members of the Royal Squadron Club who are good seamen, ay, and competent navigators to boot; but the great majority are unskilled. The other Clubs contain a much larger proportion of seamen among their members, because with them it is not a matter of fashion so much as it is with the aristocratic Squadron. Some years ago a member of the Thames Club undertook to man his yacht (between 60 and 70 tuns) with gentlemen, members of the Club, exclusively, not employing a single working-man, and to sail her against any vessel of the Squadron, manned in like manner; but the challenge fell to the ground. And well it might, for though there are some few members of the Royal Yacht Squadron who know whether a gaff-topsail is properly set or not, we have our doubts whether there is one who could go aloft and lace it to the topmast. But no matter how shallow the taste is, or how much is mere fashion, the fashion is a good one, and has excellent consequences susceptible of further improvement, which we trust the present lesson of the America will stimulate.

The veteran yachter, the Marquis of Anglesea, upon seeing the America, is reported to have remarked, "If she is right, we are all wrong."

It is to be borne in mind, however, that something besides speed is to be considered in the yacht. A yacht must have stowage and accommodation, and both these points are in the America sacrificed to speed. Still we have no doubt that something may be learnt from a craft which requires a six-knot breeze, and beats our clippers; and it is her model, not her canvass, that must be looked to for the lesson.

Kossuth and Austria.

From The London Daily News, Sept. 2.

This is the day on which the Sultan promised to liberate Kossuth, Perczel, Bathyani, and the illustrious prisoners of Kutahia. Since the fact was first announced, as it was by us some weeks back, a regular fire of menace has been kept up by all the organs, or would-be organs of the great military governments. They would break with the Porte, the ambassadors should be withdrawn, retaliation taken by reëxciting the Bosnian insurrection; and the whole East was to be convulsed because Kossuth was allowed to receive visits at Bayswater instead of planting cabbages and defending himself against assassins at Kutahia.

The question is, in truth, one of mere sentiment and humanity, for no one hopes or thinks to work harm to the Empires of Austria and Russia, or to disturb their peace by liberating Kossuth. Admiration for the past, not intrigue for the future, is the sole motive with our Hungarian sympathizers. But the solemn politicians of St. Petersburg and Vienna cannot understand that the most practical of earthly races, the Anglo-Saxon, should simultaneously, in England and in America, have been taken with such enthusiastic sympathy for the Hungarian cause, and for its chiefs, unless some deep policy lay at the bottom of it. We need not say to English readers that neither Britons nor Americans have the the least admixture of policy in their love of Hungary and Kossuth. It is from sentiment, the unmingled homage paid to brave men struggling in a righteous cause.

The future fate of Hungary and its definitive connexion with Austria, are things, we believe, very much in Austria's own power. After the complete conquest it has effected, great wisdom, moderation, and liberality on her part might, we have no doubt, secure Hungary to the HAPSBURGS and to the Austrian power too firmly for KOSSUTH and all his influence to shake. But there is no wisdom, moderation, or liberality in the conduct of Austria.

Not only is barefaced tyranny the adopted principle of government, but it is the avowed one. Until now the Austrian ministers were supposed to be responsible to the nation, or to some imaginary States. Hopes of a constitutional system, at least for the future, were not at an end. The fiction of ministerial responsibility did not the least detract from the absolute power of the government. But the young Emperor would not tolerate the decorous fiction. And he has published a solemn decree, declaring that his ministers are only responsible to himself. Every one well knew such to be the fact. Why then declare it? In order to promulgate divine right in theory as well as practice, and to seek to establish it as a philosophic truth, what was already established in the only way it could be established, by force.

Such *doctrinaires* of despotism, such puerile politicians, monarchs whose sovereignty is unbounded by the horizon of their staff, and statesmen who have taken a personal pique to constitutions—such men as these cannot found an empire, re-attach defective provinces, or give that confidence and freedom, without which industry cannot breathe, nor prosperity be developed. The hope of consolidating such an empire as that of Germany, by denying in royal and imperial edicts, the *grundrecht* or national rights, voted by national assemblies, and promulgating instead the law of ministers, being only responsible to sovereigns, and sovereigns to GOD; this is the current mistake of seeking to pacify the nineteenth century by reducing it to the ignorantism and servility of the fifteenth.

The big children, who assert that political wisdom is the gift of Heaven, and who prove themselves possessed of it by governing in this way, may well dread Kossuth, as they must dread every independent man that wields a sword or a pen. Well may they tremble at every shadow. And yet they are wrong to dread individuals, and mean to move Heaven and earth to fetter down one political Prometheus like Kossuth. For their system of government soon converts a whole people into a tacit band of conspirators, biding their time to be insurgents, and only biding that opportunity from the certainty, that a fatuitous government cannot fail to afford it.

However, we may foresee all this in the inevitable course of things, we have no wish to interfere, to foment conspiracies, or keep alive a war of jealousy with a great European power, whatever the folly of its misgovernment. Such abuses always cure themselves without foreign intervention; and if we should hail with pure welcome and delight the coming of Kossuth to our shores it is with no desire to prompt or aid him to a renewal of that contest, which for the present epoch has been decided in the field.

FRANCE.

PARIS, Wednesday Evening, Sept. 3.

The announcement of the Prince de Joinville as candidate for the Presidency of the Republic has created a great sensation here, and affords the Paris papers ample food for comment. It would appear that a considerable portion of the Orleanists are dissatisfied with the appearance of the Prince de Joinville as a candidate. Some of them fear that he will be beaten, and that the defeat will have an injurious effect on the consideration of the Orleans family with the country. Others look on the candidateship with coldness, because it was started by *The Ordre*, the organ of M. Thiers. An article appears in *The Assemblée Nationale* of to-day, which has excited great surprise. That paper, which is the organ of M. Guizot and of the Fusionists, declares that if the Prince de Joinville should be so ill-advised as really to throw himself into the revolutionary conflict of 1852, "it would not hesitate to combat with all its force a candidateship which would be a serious injury to the Monarchical principle, and would throw the country into an ocean of difficulties and dangers." Upon the whole, the impression created among the Orleanists, by the announcement, appears to be that the policy of allowing a Prince of the House of Orleans to appear as a candidate for the Presidency of the Republic, is extremely doubtful in itself, and that, at all events, the announcement is premature. As regards the Legitimists, they declare their determined hostility to the "adventure," and treat the whole affair with ridicule. *The Univers*, the organ of M. de Montalembert and the clergy, also opposes the Prince de Joinville, and foretells that the result must be "the abasement, and probably the ruin, of the Orleans family, which has so long, so terribly, and so perseveringly erred."

It must be admitted that the Prince de Joinville is decidedly the most formidable opponent that Louis Napoleon has yet had to contend with. The friends of the President are fully alive to the danger, and are using every effort to meet it. None of Louis Napoleon's friends seem to think that the Prince de Joinville will have a majority of votes at the election, but they know that all the votes given to the Prince de Joinville will be taken from Louis Napoleon, so that the final choice of a President will probably be left to the Assembly, which is not by any means well-disposed towards the present President.

The number of councils-general, which up to the present time have recorded resolutions in favor of the revision of the Constitution amounts to about sixty. Out of this number about fifteen have declared themselves in favor of the prolongation of the Powers of the President.

The council of war of Marseilles has just pronounced judgment on five men belonging to the 11th regiment of dragoons, who were tried for having excited their comrades to insubordination and revolt, in June last, at Orange. Four of them have been condemned to death, and the fifth acquitted.

P. S. 6½ o'clock.—For several days vague rumors of a plot, discovered in Paris, have prevailed. Last night a number of arrests were made, in relation to which I have just heard the following account. It has for some time been known to the police that Ledru Rollin and Mazzini's Central European Committee were in correspondence, through the Central German Committee of London, with a German committee sitting in Paris. A man named Meir was the delegate employed to transmit instructions to the Paris committee from the two committees in London. Besides this, an advocate, named Maillard, formerly secretary to Ledru Rollin, was instructed by the latter to organize an insurrectional committee in Paris, ready to take arms at a signal to be given by the Central European Committee of London. Such was the activity of Maillard that he had formed the nucleus of a society that had put itself in communication with the departments, and had made such progress as to be able to send to London within the last few days to take Ledru Rollin's final instructions.

It was on the return to Paris of the emissary sent on this occasion that the Prefect of Police informed the authorities that the time had come for putting a stop to all these proceedings. Warrants were issued simultaneously to arrest persons designated at St. Amand. Forty-seven arrests have been made. All the prisoners have been sent to the prison of Mazas, and this explains the reason why the Prefect of Police has within these few days sent away several prisoners who were there, in order to have vacant cells at his disposition.

The most prominent among the persons arrested are M. Dalicau, the director of *The Voix du Proscrit*, and M. Maillard, the advocate. The rest are obscure individuals, principally journeymen, tradesmen, and mechanics. One of them named J. J. Cherval, a lithographer, is described as an "Irish subject." Last night, at about 9 o'clock, 60 "Sergens de Ville" marched to the Café de la Haute-Saône, Rue Grenelle St. Honoré, where they arrested a dozen persons. Several brigades of police were sent in the night to different quarters of Paris, with instructions to execute warrants of arrest. As many as 80 prisoners have already been sent to the Mazas prison.

It is said at the Palais de Justice that most important papers, emanating from the London Committees, have been seized.

Paris is absolutely quiet, and no alarm or even excitement has been produced in the public mind.

AUSTRIA.

VIENNA, Aug. 27.—The decrees of the Emperor on the responsibility of the ministers, and on the revision of the constitution, *octroyée* in March, 1849, amount to a complete retrogression to absolutism.

In Italy, Radetski fears an outbreak, and the army is said to be reinforced for the third time—ten thousand men are to march to the Piedmontese frontier. There is a report that the dissensions between the Croat and Hungarian soldiers are daily increasing, and that they led to a bloody conflict in the neighborhood of Verona. The papers remain silent on such events, but the letters from Italy mention it as a fact. In Hungary the gendarmerie had had several conflicts with the peasants, and a tragedy which in the month of June happened at Szent Maria, near Gross-Waradin, is soul-stirring, like an episode of a French novel. I relate it as I had it from an Hungarian gentleman of the Bihar county, who happened to be at Vienna.

At a peasant's wedding, when the procession of the betrothed was moving toward the church, the gendarme approached the bride and summoned her immediately to divest herself of the red, white and green ribbons which she had in her tresses, according to the custom of the country girls, saying that these colors were revolutionary. The bridegroom objected, saying that after the ceremony the bride would comply with the desire of the gendarme, but that now they could not keep the priest waiting at the altar. The gendarme retired, the procession proceeded to the church, but at the moment the bride was kneeling at the steps of the altar to receive the benediction, the gendarme rushed forward and cut her tresses and ribbons with scissors from her head. In Hungary it is considered a great insult to a female to cut her hair; it conveys the notion of infamy. Naturally an affray took place, the gendarme was assailed by the bridegroom, other gendarmes arrived in aid of their fellow-official, the people, though without arms, rushed upon them, and the result was the slaughter of seven men, three gendarmes and four peasants, amongst them the bridegroom and the brutal assailant of the bride.

The Preussische Zeitung says, that Austria has just obtained by negotiation a military right of way through Bavaria for the passage of troops to the federal fortress of Mayence.

A telegraphic dispatch from Ischl, received in Vienna on the 31st, announces that the Emperor of Austria will prolong his stay in that watering place until the 6th inst. Nothing has transpired relative to the interview between him and the King of Prussia.

SPAIN.

MADRID, Aug. 29.—The principal topic of the provincial journals is still the serious effects produced by the long drought and extraordinary heat. At Madrid we have now been four months without rain. The country is burnt up, and fires, extending in some cases over many leagues, are no doubt the result of this state of things. Great scarcity of water was felt at Saragossa, and throughout Aragon, and the most rigorous measures had been decreed by the authorities to preserve a supply for the most indispensable purposes.

A Gijon letter of the 25th says that five leagues of the railway there would shortly be open to public traffic, and speaks of the great natural difficulties overcome in constructing it.

TURKEY.

CONSTANTINOPLE, Aug. 16.—The liberation of Kossuth is now decided upon by the Sublime Porte.—In spite of all the threats of Russia and Austria, the porte stood her ground, and when reminded by the English government of its promise, the Divan replied, "We keep it." Kossuth is, therefore to be released on the 13th September. His intention, as far as I could ascertain, is to proceed first to England, to leave there his children, and to provide for their education, and after a stay of a fortnight, to sail to the United States, there to express his thanks to the Congress and the President.—But the Captain of the steam frigate Mississippi, which has waited for Kossuth since the month of June, objects to this arrangement; he wishes to carry Kossuth without delay to New-York. I do not know, therefore, whether you will have the pleasure of seeing the mighty man—who, even when in prison in Asia Minor, frightens the Czar and the Kaiser—before December.

The dismissal of the seraskier, Mehemet Ali Pasha, made here, for a moment a painful impression, for everybody knew that he, the brother-in-law to the Sultan, was the greatest enemy to Russia in the cabinet. But it soon became obvious that this step had no political importance whatever.

PORTUGAL.

LISBON, Aug. 29.—Public attention is chiefly directed towards the accusation of bribery preferred against Senhor Ferrao, which compelled him to retire from the Ministry. The accusation is of so serious and grave a nature that the Ministry had a meeting upon the subject (Senhor Ferrao not having been present at it), when, it is said, it was determined that he should be invited to resign and carry the accusation before the tribunals, he being accused of having received from the contract of tobacco 2,093,600 reis. This Senhor Ferrao has done.

The heat and the drought this year is without example. Accounts from the country say the small rivers are drying up.

The ports of Ceara in the Brazils are declared infected with the yellow fever, and those of Moroco with cholera.

The Government has advertised for proposals to complete the roads and form new ones in the Minho. The former contractors, conceiving it an infringement of their rights, protest against it, and say they shall have recourse to the tribunals. There is to be a new road from Oporto to Braga, and another from Oporto to Guimaraens.

It appears that several officers of the 14th, at Vizeu, endeavored to make their escape, but were prevented and placed in arrest. A general officer is implicated in the attempted insurrection.

Another serious conspiracy, that was to have broken out at Vizeu, and had extensive ramifications, has been rendered abortive.

The elections of the electoral Commissioners are in the gross in favor of Government and Septembristas.

BREMEN.

The treasurer of the head corporation school of Bremen, who held large sums of money in trust for that establishment, as well as for other institutions, has been arrested, charged with embezzling upwards of 120,000 thalers. The arrest of this man, whose name is Haase, who was an alderman of the city, and a most esteemed member of the corporation, created quite a sensation.

BAVARIA.

AUG. 29.—The sale of cavalry and artillery horses has suddenly been stopped, and new purchases are to be made by order of the Minister of War. We are told that the late movement of troops was in consequence of some possible eventuality in France. But the Munich correspondent of a Brussels paper, who is apparently well informed, says the military movements are nothing more than the ordinary garrison changes, consequent upon the manœuvres which take place in the autumn of every year.

FRANKFORT

The Frankfort Diet has taken its first resolution, says *The Augsburgh Gazette*, in commercial affairs. It has adopted as the basis of deliberation in these matters, the resolutions of the Dresden Conferences. *The Augsburg Gazette* says that the Diet has again called special men together, to give it special information on the subject.

The same journal affirms that the Diet have come to the formal resolution, that it has authority to establish a common principle on which to act in regulating the constitutions of the divers states.

PRUSSIA.

The provincial diets are beginning to meet. That of Brandenburg and Lusatia met on the 31st ult., sixty members being present, under the presidency of M. Von Flottwell, who made a speech in his capacity of royal commissioner. Count Arnim Boitzenburg, Marshal of the Diet, and chief of the party of the extreme right in the second chamber of Prussia, replied to M. Von Flottwell.

A letter from Berlin of the 29th ult., states that the minister of state, Von Thill, is dangerously ill. The Diet of the province of Prussia will meet on the 14th inst.

ITALY

The Genoa Gazette announces from Cagliari that the levy of recruits in the island of Sardinia has been effected without the slightest resistance, but that a serious affair occurred in the north of the island. It appears from this account that Major de Sant Elia, one of the recruiting commissaries, while on his way to Nulvi, with an escort of twelve dragoons, was attacked by a party of bandits, who fired four shots at him, his horse was wounded, and the flap of his coat pierced with a ball. Three of his escort were also wounded. The bandits have not been arrested.

The King of Naples, says *The Brussels Independent*, has just appointed a commission for the reform of the prisons in his kingdom. His Majesty, in order that the truth may be known, has requested several members of the *corps diplomatique* to follow the labors of this commission, and to visit, with its members, the different prisons in the city of Naples.

The Pope is about to erect the city of Hamburg into a bishopric.

The Opinione of Turin announces military evolutions on a large scale, representing the battle of Montenotte, which, in 1796, opened Italy to the invasion of the French. General La Marmora is entrusted with the general direction of the evolutions.

LOMBARDY

The Milan Gazette of the 29th ult. announces that the brigadier of carabineers, who, in 1849, arrested Ugo Bassi, (the priest who acted as chaplain to Garibaldi's troops, and was shot by the Austrians,) has been assassinated at Commachio.

TUSCANY.

The Tuscan Moniture publishes a series of regulations issued by the minister of worship at Florence on the 28th ult., concerning the right of censorship reserved to the bishops by the new concordat. By these regulations every bishop has the right of censorship over ecclesiastical works to be published within his diocese; a work rejected by one bishop cannot be approved by another, and there is no appeal from the decision of a bishop in such matters.

THE PAPAL STATES.

A dissolution of the Ministry has taken place, we learn, at Naples, and another Cabinet been formed. The names of the members of the new Administration had not been made public at the date of the last advices. [*Galignani.*

SWITZERLAND.

According to letters from Berne of the 29th ult., the damages caused in the canton by recent inundations are valued at 2,400,000 fr., or about £96,000. Subscriptions are open all over Switzerland to cover the losses of the inundation. The city of Berne has already subscribed 12,000fr.

ICELAND.

The Diet of Iceland was opened on the 5th July at Reikiavik. Amongst the bills presented was one enacting that from the 15th June, 1852, foreign vessels shall be allowed to enter the port of Reikiavik without passports of the authorities of the island, and shall be treated as Danish vessels.

Fugitive Slave Riot in Lancaster Co., Pa.

Our readers will be already advised of the occurrence of a lamentable riot and loss of life at Christiana, Lancaster Co., Pa., on the 9th inst.,—growing out of the attempted capture of two fugitive slaves by their owner.

In order to give the conclusion of this affair in an intelligible shape, a brief summary of the circumstances of the case may be necessary.

A party composed of Edward Gorsuch, of Baltimore county, Md., his two sons, Dickerson Gorsuch and Joshua Gorsuch, Dr. Thomas Pierce, Henry C. Kline, a Deputy Marshal, and two police officers from Philadelphia, started from Philadelphia, with a warrant issued by Edward D. Ingraham, United States Commissioner, to arrest two fugitive slaves belonging to Edward Gorsuch, who were supposed to be in the neighborhood of Christiana, in Lancaster county. After spending a day in Chester county, they arrived at break of the next day, at the place in which it was supposed the fugitives were harbored. This was a two-story stone building, on the farm of Levi Pownall, about three miles from Christiana. As the party approached the house, one of the fugitive slaves was identified, but took shelter in the house, and was followed by Mr. Gorsuch and his party. While in the house, an axe was thrown at the Deputy Marshal, and he fired. The negroes returned the fire, and the whites retreated outside of the house, where they were again fired upon.—Neither party being yet injured, a parley ensued, and the Deputy Marshal read aloud his warrant for the apprehension of the negroes.

In the midst of this parly, a horn was blown by some one in the house, when sixty or eighty armed blacks rushed upon the party from the adjacent woods and cornfields, and after a few words discharged a volley. At this fire, the elder MR. GORSUCH fell dead, and his son DICKINSON was shot in the breast and lungs. DR. PIERCE was also shot in several places, but succeeded in making his escape, together with the Marshal.

The matter rested, from some oversight, till Friday morning, when information of the unhappy event was given to the authorities of Lancaster County, and legal steps were taken for the arrest of the blacks. Nine of them were at once arrested. On Saturday morning, the United States Commissioner and the United States District Attorney proceeded to Lancaster County for the purpose of investigating the affair. Twenty-five arrests were made in the course of the day, and a large amount of arms was captured. Thirteen witnesses were examined, who testified that the firing was principally from the blacks. On Sunday, the party of U. S. authorities returned to Philadelphia, and ten prisoners, found guilty of participation in the riot, were confined in Moyamensing prison. Their names are as follows: Joseph Scarlet, (white) Wm. Brown, Ezekiel Thompson, Isaiah Clarkson, Daniel Caulsberry, Benjamin Pendergrass, Elijah Clark, George W. H. Scott, Miller Thompson, and Samuel Hanson, all colored. The three last-named, were placed in the debtors' department, and the others in the criminal department of the prison, to await their trial on the charge of treason and levying war against the United States.

The examination was resumed before United States Commissioner Ingraham, at Philadelphia, on Monday last. A number of additional arrests were made, and Henry Green, William Williams, John Halliday, Wm. Brown, Geo. Read, John Jackson, Thos. Butler, and Benjamin Johnson, were fully committed.

Hopes are entertained of the recovery of young Gorsuch.

On Monday, a proclamation was issued by Gov. Johnston, offering a reward of $1000, for the arrest of the guilty parties. The proclamation is strongly expressive of the energetic character of the Executive.

Gov. JOHNSTON has replied, in the following excellent letter, to a memorial addressed to him by a number of citizens of Pennsylvania, requesting him, as the Chief Executive, to "vindicate the laws and uphold the dignity" of the Commonwealth. The common-sense view of the subject which characterizes this production will commend it to the candid reader.

Letter from Gov. Johnston.

PHILADELPHIA, Sept 14, 1851.

To Messrs. John Cadwallader, A. J. Roumfort, Jas. Page, and others.

GENTLEMEN: Your letter, without date, was this afternoon put into my hands by one of the servants of the hotel. The anxiety which you manifest to maintain the laws of the land and the public peace, is fully appreciated, and I have great pleasure in informing you that more than twenty-four hours before the receipt of your letter the parties implicated had been, through the vigilance and decision of the local authorities, arrested, and are now in prison, awaiting an inquiry into their imputed guilt. The District Attorney and Sheriff of Lancaster County, acting in concert with the Attorney General of the State, deserve especial thanks for their prompt and energetic conduct. This was all done early on Saturday morning, and duly reported to me by the local officers.

The testimony taken by the United States Commissioner, who arrived at a later period on the ground, a printed copy of which has accidentally reached me this afternoon, confirms me in the belief that the State authorities had vindicated the law, and to a large extent arrested the perpetrators of the crimes.

The cruel murder of a citizen of a neighboring State, accompanied by a gross outrage on the laws of the United States, in the resistance of its process, has been committed; and you may be assured that so soon as the guilty agents are ascertained, they will be punished in the severest penalty by the law of Pennsylvania. I am very proud that the first steps to detect and arrest these offenders have been taken by Pennsylvania officers.

Permit me, gentlemen, having thus removed all just cause of anxiety from your minds, respectfully to suggest that the idea of rebellion or "insurrectionary movement" in the county of Lancaster, or anywhere else in this commonwealth, has no real foundation, and is an offensive imputation on a large body of our fellow citizens. There is no insurrectionary movement in Lancaster county, and there would be no occasion to march a military force there, as you seem to desire, and inflame the public mind by any such strange exaggeration. I do not wish our brethren of the Union to think that, in any part of this State, resistance to the law goes undetected or unpunished, or that there exists such a sentiment as treason to the Union and the constitution.

The alleged murderers of Mr. GORSUCH, whose crime is deep enough without exaggerating it, have been arrested and will be tried, and they and their abettors will be made to answer for what they have done in contravention of the law. But in the meantime, let me invite your cooperation, as citizens of Pennsylvania, not only to see that the law is enforced, but to add to the confidence which we all feel in the judicial tribunals of the land, by abstaining from undue violence of language, and letting the law take its course. Depend upon it, gentlemen, there is in Lancaster county a sense of duty to the laws of the land, manifested in the easy and prompt arrest of these offenders, which will on all occasions show itself in practical obedience.

The people of that county are men of peace and good order, and not easily led aside from the path of duty which the constitution prescribes. They and every Pennsylvanian love the constitution and the Union. They will detect, as they have done in this case, and arrest and punish all who violate the laws of the land. There is no warrant, depend on it, for representing the men of Lancaster county as traitors and participants in an "insurrectionary movement." You do them, unintentionally, I have no doubt, great injustice.

I am deeply indebted to you for affording me the opportunity of expressing my views. But for your communication, I might not have been able to do so. You, and my fellow citizens at large, may be assured of my firm determination at all hazards and under all circumstances, to maintain the supremacy of the constitution, and enforce obedience to the law, alike of the United States and of this commonwealth.

In order that I may be sure that my answer may reach its destination (your letter having but accidentally come to my hands,) I have requested Mr. White to put it in the hands of Mr. John Cadwallader, whose signature, I observe, is first. I am, with great respect,

your obedient servant,

WM. F. JOHNSTON.

The Baltimore Sun of yesterday, learns from a private source, that the Executive of Maryland, Gov. LOWE, will take immediate action upon the official information which he has received relative to the riot. A special messenger has already been despatched to the President with a communication on the subject.

A mulatto man, supposed to be the slave Pinkney, owned by Mr. Garsuch, was seen yesterday on the hills near Lancaster, and several citizens had gone in pursuit of him.

NEW-YORK CITY

☞ The weather was the theme upon which we hinged an item for our morning edition, but we have been forced to forgo the infliction of it upon the public, by the proceedings of the Boston Jubilee, which our special correspondent has forwarded us. Never mind, the President cannot always be lionising through the country, and as soon as he returns home, we shall endeavor to do this important subject full justice.

DEATH OF A BAPTIST MISSIONARY. We regret to announce the death of Rev. WM. T. BIDDLE, of this city, who departed this life yesterday morning, at the house of Rev. John Dowling, D. D., where he was making a temporary home, in anticipation of his early departure for his field of labor in Burmah, at or near the station lately occupied by Rev. Dr. Judson. The intelligence of Mr. Biddle's death will be received with deep regret by a wide circle of friends, who were looking to his future career with large hopes, warranted by the honor with which he acquitted himself at Hamilton University, where he has just graduated. He was married but a few weeks since, and in a few days was to have sailed for his future home in India. The funeral exercises were held at the Berean Baptist Church, cor. of Bedford and Downing streets, and were attended by a large and deeply affected audience. The body is to be taken, this morning, to Brookfield, Conn., the residence of his father, Rev. M. Biddle, where closing exercises will be held previous to interment.

EXECUTION OF THE TWO CONDEMNED MURDERERS.—Between the hours of 10 and 11 o'clock to-morrow morning, *Aaron Stookey* and *Henry Carnal* the Frenchman, are to undergo the penalty of death, for the murder of two fellow beings. Yesterday afternoon, each culprit seemed greatly troubled in mind, and they appeared to dread the awful fate that awaits them. The gallows will be erected in the City Prison yard, this afternoon, by direction of Sheriff Carnley, who, we understand, will hang the culprits simultaneously. The evidence of guilt was clearly proved against these murderers at the time of their trials, and, if any, very brief confessions will be made respecting their perpetrating the horrible deeds for which they are to suffer the extreme penalty of the law.

☞ The Board of Supervisors met yesterday, Mr. DELAMATER, of the XVIth Ward, in the Chair.—Eleven members were present, but neither the Mayor nor the Recorder. The minutes of the last meeting were read and approved. Several petitions for the correction of taxes were referred, but no other business transacted. The Board adjourned to Wednesday next.

FIRE IN HUDSON-STREET.—At an early hour on Tuesday evening, a fire was discovered in the upper part of a dwelling house at No 159 Hudson-st., occupied by Stuart F. Randolph, Esq., which originated from the soot in the chimney taking fire, and before it could be put out, the chimney burst, and set fire to the wood work of the attic rooms. Hose Company No. 24 and other companies of the fire department, were promptly on the ground, but before they could arrest the progress of the flames, the building was inundated with water, which damaged the furniture about $500.

FIRE IN SPRING-STREET.—At half-past 12 o'clock yesterday afternoon, a fire was discovered in the Cabinet shop of Mr. George Boyd, at No. 151 Spring-street, which originated from a quantity of sparks that were blown from an adjoining blacksmith's shop. The firemen were promptly on the ground and the fire was speedily extinguished, before any material damage was sustained.

RUN OVER BY AN ICE CART.—Yesterday afternoon, about 3 o'clock, a young man by the name of George Fuller was thrown from an ice cart, in Spring-st., the wheels of which passed over his body and severely injured him. Capt. Turnbull, of the 8th patrol district, had the injured man conveyed to the N. Y. Hospital, where he received medical aid.

DISTURBANCE BETWEEN RIVAL BLACKSMITHS.—For some weeks past, a feeling of jealousy has existed between a number of workmen employed in the smith shop of Messrs. Marshall & Townsend, Stage Proprietors and others in the employ of the 6th-avenue Omnibus line, whom the former parties charged with waylaying them in the night time for no good purpose. On Tuesday night, several of these rival mechanics met at the corner of 7th-av. and 22d-st., and angry words passed, which, no doubt would have resulted in a desperate and fearful conflict, had not a posse of the 16th ward Police reached the scene of disturbance, in a few minutes after the gangs had assembled. Three of the workmen (employed by Messrs. M. & T.) named John Green, Bernard Daly, and John Davie, made complaints against seven of their opponents, by the names of Bernard Matthews, Henry Malloy, Martin Kehoe, Patrick McCourt, John Mathews, Hugh Matthews, and Dennis Broderick, all of whom were immediately arrested, conveyed before Justice Blakely, and committed to prison upon charges of assaults with intent to kill. The latter prisoner was armed with two large knives, and a deadly weapon, known as a "slung shot," and he was accordingly committe for "felony."

STEAMERS.—The *Marion*, Capt. BERRY, arrived from Charleston, yesterday morning. She has experienced heavy northeasterly gales during the passage, and consumed all her fuel when thirteen days from the Delaware Breakwater, at which place she was obliged to put in for a supply. The *Marion* brings $30,000 in specie.

The *Alabama*, Capt. LUDLOW, from Savannah, arrived on Tuesday evening.

The *Winfield Scott*, Capt. COVILLARD, sailed for New Orleans at 3 o'clock yesterday afternoon.

"THEY COME."—Six vessels arrived at this port on Tuesday, bringing an addition of 1,200 to our population.

Ship Rajah, from Liverpool	27
Ship Duchesse d'Orleans, from Havre	379
Ship Philadelphia, from Liverpool	508
Bark Jason, from Bremen	184
Bark Scotland, from Newport, Wales	11
Brig Lulea, from Gottenburg	83
Total	1,192

☞ The packet-ship *American Congress*, sailed from this port, for London, yesterday. She took out $100,000 in specie.

☞ The Board of Assistant Aldermen closed their session for September, last evening. Our sketch of the proceedings is driven out by the Foreign News, but we are consoled by the reflection that our readers will find a full record of their doings in *The Evening Times*, which will be published at 1 o'clock this afternoon.

☞ The Fountain in Washington Square gets on towards completion with considerable speed. It is to be a very large circular basin, with a central jet and several side jets. The excavation is made, the wall around the border of the basin is nearly done, and the workmen were yesterday laying a bottom of hard plaster. The fountain will be a very fine one, and will increase greatly the attraction of this beautiful park.

NEW STEAMBOAT LINE.—The staunch little steamer, the C. Durant, has been placed on the East River, to run between this city and Flushing, touching at Astoria and Strattonport, by Mr. Flammer, the enterprising proprietor of the latter village. The fare has been reduced to one shilling, and the boat is to make two trips each way a day, and is to be a permanent arrangement. We hail with pleasure every new enterprise that will bind the Metropolis and the quiet and beautiful rural districts in its closer contact.

DEATH IN A CELL.—At a late hour on Tuesday night, policeman Coelter, of the Fourth Patrol District, found an unknown female, aged 35 years, lying in Madison-st., laboring under the effects of delerium tremens, and apparently lifeless. A dray was procured, and the poor woman was conveyed to the Station-house, where she seemed to somewhat revive, but was yet under the influence of strong drink, and was accordingly placed in a cell in the female department, where she was found a corpse in about two hours after. Yesterday morning the Coroner held an inquest on the remains, and the jury rendered a verdict of "Death by an apoplectic fit."

DEATH FROM CONVULSIONS.—The Coroner held an inquest yesterday, at the Bellevue Hospital, upon the body of a young woman named Sarah Carr, born in New-York, and aged 21 years, who, it appears, was admitted into the above institution on the 15th inst., in a fit of convulsions, and after lingering a few hours, died from the effects of the same. A verdict was rendered in accordance with the foregoing facts.

☞ A Bloomer Costume made its appearance in Sixth-avenue day before yesterday. A crowd of "Conservatives" manifested their hostility to this progressive movement by derision. "New ideas" are compelled to wage fierce battle in this world before they obtain recognition and favor. Two Bloomers appeared in Broadway and two in Washington square yesterday.

☞ It has been stated that Senator Douglass was too ill to fulfil his engagement, to deliver the oration at the State Fair. We understand that he has so far recovered from his indisposition, that he left for Rochester last evening.

FALSE ALARM.—The Hall bell rang an alarm at 9 o'clock last evening for the Sixth District, but our item gatherer failed to discover the first spark of a fire.

ANOTHER.—About 2 o'clock there was an alarm in the Second District—but the fire was not visible.

WOMAN POISONED.—Coroner Geer was called yesterday to hold an inquest on the body of a married woman by the name of Mrs. Eliza Knecht, lying dead at her late residence, No. 204 Seventh-street. A jury was empanneled, and the first witness sworn was Mr. Leonard Smith, a resident of the same house, who deposed that deceased had been married about nine months, and that the husband only lived with her the first four weeks after they were united, since which time he had been absent until Sunday afternoon last, at 4 o'clock, when he called upon his wife and remained with her during the night; he then states that she was seized with violent pains and cramps at 11 o'clock that (Sunday) night, and was in great distress; her husband remained with her till Tuesday morning and then left, at which time she was apparently beyond all hopes of recovery, and continued to labor under severe convulsions. Dr. Ruppenrecht, residing at No. 21 Avenue B., was next called, and deposed, in substance, as follows: I was called, on Tuesday morning, to visit deceased, and was informed that she was on the eve of confinement, but upon examination, found that no symptoms of that nature exhibited themselves, but discovered that she was laboring under severe and repeated convulsions, and all efforts to save her life proved of no avail, and she died at 5½ o'clock on Tuesday evening. I then made a *post-mortem* examination and found the stomach in a high state of inflammation, and all her internal organs exhibiting signs of poison. The medical gentleman then closed his testimony, by saying, that it was his opinion, that deceased came to her death by taking some corrosive poison in a fluid state, and there being no further evidence adduced, the jury rendered a verdict, "That the deceased came to her death by the administration of some corrosive poison given to her by some person, to this jury unknown." The deceased was a native of Germany, twenty-nine years of age, and had she lived a month longer, she would have undoubtedly been the mother of an offspring. As the case now stands, a strong suspicion rests upon the husband of deceased, and we trust our worthy coroner will cause a diligent search to be made for him or any other person who may be suspected of being in any way connected with the horrible affair.

ACCIDENT TO AN OMNIBUS-DRIVER.—Yesterday morning the driver of a Broadway omnibus, named John Ashbury, was severely injured by falling from the top of his vehicle and striking his head upon a curbstone, causing a dangerous fracture of the skull and other serious injuries to his limbs. He was conveyed to the N. Y. Hospital, by a citizen, and placed under the care of a skillful surgeon.

A SAD AND FATAL ACCIDENT.—About 8 o'clock yesterday morning, a brick layer named Patrick Halligan, residing at No. 27 West 17th-st., met with a sad and fatal accident, while at work upon the fourth story of a new brick building, in the course of erection in 14th-st., near the 6th-av. It appears that the unfortunate man was engaged in placing a row of bricks on the outside wall, and in consequence of missing his footing, he was precipitated to the ground and instantly killed.—His body was removed to the residence of his family to await a coroner's inquest.

ARREST OF AN ESCAPED PRISONER.—On the 29th of July last, a man by the name of William Clark made his escape from a cell in the City Prison, where he was confined upon a charge of Grand Larceny, in stealing a gold watch and several chains from a jewelry store at No. 4 Maiden-lane, for which he was subsequently indicted. Nothing was heard of the accused until yesterday, when a telegraphic despatch was received from the Chief of Police at New-Orleans, La., by Mr. William Edmonds, the efficient Keeper of the Prison in Center-st., which conveyed the intelligence of Clark's arrest in that City. Mr. Edmonds immediately telegraphed to the authorities of New-Orleans, requesting them to detain Clark in custody, until such time as a requisition could be obtained from Governor Hunt and forwarded to them by one of our Police officers, who will bring him back to this City.

COURT CALENDAR.—*Thursday.*—U. S. CIRCUIT COURT—Nos. 2, 18 to 36. CIRCUIT COURT—Nos. 577, 578, 583 to 586, 588 to 591, 280, 403, 286, 602. COMMON PLEAS—Nos. 281, 540, 563, 575, 582, 586, 594, 592, 601, 603, 605, 611, 639, 640.

BROOKLYN

BRIGADE INSPECTION AND REVIEW.—The annual parade and review of the Fifth Brigade, Gen. H. B. Duryea, comprising the thirteenth regiment, Col. Abel Smith, and fourteenth regiment, Col. Philip S. Crook, located in Kings County, will take place at Brooklyn on Monday, the 29th inst. The artillery and cavalry will parade on the east side of Henry-st, right on Pineapple-st.; the infantry of the 13th regiment on Orange-st., right on Hicks-st., the infantry of the 14th regiment on Cranberry-st., right on Hicks-st. The regiments will be formed at 8½ o'clock, A. M., precisely; and punctuality will be strictly required, so that the march may be taken up at the hour of 9 o'clock, A. M., precisely. Major General Aaron Ward and staff will be present at this Parade. The light artillery companies of Captains Olney, (Brooklyn City Guard,) Graham, (Ringgold Horse Guard,) and Taft, (Williamsburg Artillery,) will parade with their Batteries. Capt. Neely's Dragoons (Washington Horse Guard) will act as an escort to the Brigadier General. The companies of Capt. John Willse and Henry Willse will do duty as Light Infantry and foot Rifles. In addition to the companies above named, there are attached to this brigade the Pierson Light Guard, Capt. R. B. Clark, Putnam Continentals, Capt. J. H. Morgan; Washington Life Guard, Capt. Sharpe; 1st Continentals, Capt. B. F. Hoagland; 1st Sarsfield Guard, Capt. ——; 2d Sarsfield Guard, Capt. ——. Union Blues, Capt. Burnett, National Guard, Capt. Sprague, Franklin Guard, Capt. Baldwin. Steuben Guard, Capt. Schaffer; Emmet Guard, Capt. Dodge. Shields Guard, Capt. Smith; Kings County Troop, Capt. Suydam; and some three or four companies from Williamsburgh. It is anticipated that this will be the finest parade ever witnessed in Brooklyn, and preparations are making to give much eclat to the occasion. This ought to be the best disciplined brigade in the State.

PREPARING FOR MUSTER—OFFICERS' DRILLS.—Our gallant militia men are brushing up right smartly for training. We see that orders have been issued to the officers and non-commissioned officers of the 5th Brigade to assemble in Fatigue dress, white trowsers, armed and equipped for Battalion drill and practice, at the City Armory, in Henry-street, on yesterday, the 17th inst., and Wednesday, the 24th inst., at 9 o'clock, A. M., on foot. Gen. Duryea, the worthy District Attorney of Kings county, is the commander of this Brigade.

LONG ISLAND VEGETABLES.—The State of Long Island is some on tomatoes. We were shown the other day, a tomato raised by Mr. Frederick Rewland of Hempstead, one of those vegetables which measured 22½ inches around it, and weighed 2 pounds 2½ ounces. Who can beat it!

New-York Daily Times.

VOL. III....NO. 854. NEW-YORK, TUESDAY, JUNE 13, 1854. PRICE TWO CENTS.

THE NEW-YORK DAILY TIMES.

A VERY LARGE DAILY NEWSPAPER—each number comprising Eight Pages, or Forty-Eight columns, and giving more reading matter than any other Daily Newspaper in the United States—is published EVERY MORNING—(*Sundays excepted*,) at No. 138 NASSAU-STREET, corner of Beekman, and is delivered to subscribers in New-York, Brooklyn, Williamsburg and Jersey City, for TWELVE AND A HALF CENTS a week, payable to the Carrier; Single Copies, TWO CENTS. Mail Subscribers, FIVE DOLLARS a year; six months Two Dollars and a Half; three months One Dollar and a Half; Three Dollars in advance required in all exchanges with Country Newspapers.

POSTAGE ON THE DAILY TIMES sent to any part of the United States, paid in advance at the office where delivered —39 cents per quarter, or $1 56 per annum.

THE NEW-YORK EVENING TIMES

PUBLISHED EVERY EVENING, (*Sundays excepted*.) One edition will be issued at 1 and the other at 3 o'clock, P. M. It will be sent by mail, or sold at the same rates as the DAILY TIMES.

THE NEW-YORK WEEKLY TIMES.

A VERY LARGE NEWSPAPER FOR THE COUNTRY, is published every SATURDAY MORNING, at the low price of Two DOLLARS per annum. Two copies for THREE DOLLARS. Five copies for FIVE DOLLARS, will be sent to one address; and the paper in no case continued beyond the time for which payment is made. Postage on the WEEKLY TIMES sent by mail one year, is as follows:

Within the County..............................Free.
Within the State..............................13 cents.
Within the United States..............................26 cents.
Payments in all cases must be made in advance.

THE TIMES FOR CALIFORNIA.

A LARGE NEWSPAPER OF EIGHT PAGES, or Forty-eight Columns, made up expressly for circulation in *California, Oregon and the Sandwich Islands*, and containing only news of interest to readers in those sections of the country, is published on the departure of every Mail steamer. Price, 6¼ cents per copy.

RAYMOND, HARPER & CO., Publishers.

New-York Daily Times.

JAPAN OPENED.

Satisfactory Result of Commodore Perry's Visit.

Three Ports Opened to American Trade.

Agreement to Furnish Coal to American Steamers.

INTERESTING NARRATIVE.

Detailed Account of Commodore Perry's Second Visit.

The *Susquehanna* arrived at Hong Kong from Japan on the 2d (April), bringing the gratifying intelligence that Commodore PERRY had succeeded in the objects of his mission in a manner that will confer honor on his country and enduring fame on himself. The precise terms of a Commercial Treaty had not been definitively arranged when the *Susquehanna* left the Yedó on the 24th of March; but enough had been done to establish a friendly feeling between the two countries. *The opening of Three or more ports to the Commerce of America, and the furnishing of Coals for its Steamers, may be considered as matters settled*, and Captain ADAMS held himself in readiness to proceed in the *Saratoga* to bear the intelligence to the Government at Washington.

We are enabled to furnish our readers with a detailed narrative of the proceedings in Japan, from which it will be seen that nothing could have been better or more fortunate than the course pursued by Commodore PERRY. Indeed we feel pretty certain that the most skillful diplomatist in Europe could not have brought matters to so speedy, pacific, and successful an issue. Commodore PERRY was known as a brave as well as accomplished seaman, but it was thought he had rather a propensity for fighting, which indeed, with such means at his disposal, and such people to deal with as the Japanese were ignorantly presumed to be, was deemed inevitable by most people, though, as our pages show, not by every one. Here however he has disappointed the world; and perhaps not a few in his squadron; but he has done what we did not do in China, and it was not expected any one could accomplish in Japan,—he *has peacefully and amicably opened it to the intercourse of his countrymen, without firing a shot or using an angry word.*

Commodore PERRY, in the *Susquehanna*, left the harbor of Hongkong on the 14th of January, accompanied by the *Powhatan* and the *Mississippi*, the sailing vessels, *Vandalia, Southampton, Supply* and *Lexington*, having some time before proceeded to the rendezvous at Napakiang in Loo Choo, where the squadron met on the 21st of January. Nothing of importance occurred at Loo Choo beyond visiting the capital, Shuidi, with the temples and forts, and admiring, as others have done, the picturesque and surpassingly beautiful scenery of the island.

The sailing vessels were dispatched for Japan on the last day of January, under command of Captain ABBOT, the steamships following on 7th February, and, along with the sloop *Saratoga* from Shanghae, joining the sailing vessels in the waters of Japan on the 12th, without accident beyond the temporary grounding of the *Macedonian*, which was lightened and speedily got off. The whole squadron then proceeded and anchored in the bay of Yedó, passing Uraga, where last year the interview and the delivery of the President's Letter took place. A few small forts, mounting ten or twelve guns each, were observed, but made no hostile demonstrations. Boats were not allowed to come alongside until the vessels had taken their stations, and then Government officers were directed to the *Powhatan*, (to which the Commodore's flag had been removed,) where they had an interview on the 13th with the fleet Captain ADAMS, to whom, after the exchange of compliments, the Japanese stated that in a few days a special high officer would be sent to Yedó to meet the Commodore and arrange everything in a courteous, frank, and friendly manner; but they objected that the vessels had come too far up, and recommended their return to Uraga, where the Emperor desired the meeting should be held as before; and that point they considered as of more importance than talking about the weather, which subject would seem to be the *pis-aller* of conversation in Japan as in all the rest of the world. We believe this was nearly all that passed during the first interview, and the deputation took leave in good humor, which grew to merriment, upon Captain ADAMS suggesting, that instead of returning to Uraga, perhaps a more favorable anchorage might be found higher up, and nearer the capital, which would also be more convenient for the high officers to be sent from Yedó, as well as in accordance with the customs of other nations.

The following day (14th) another interview was held on board the *Powhatan*, when the Japanese renewed their urgency about the meeting being held at Uraga, where on the previous occasion everything had passed in so amicable and pleasant a manner, and to which the Commodore had said he would return. Finding that Uraga was still objected to, they then proposed Kamakura, where the *Macedonian* had got ashore, and which they held to be a much more convenient place than Kanagawa, between the present anchorage and Yedó, as suggested by Dr. S. W. WILLIAMS. But after much talk on the subject, the Japanese at length left it to the Commodore to select a place for the interview. Before taking leave, the deputation said if the ships needed water or provisions, boats would be sent with supplies; but they were told that, except water, nothing else was likely to be required.

After mature consideration, Commodore PERRY decided to send Captain ADAMS in the *Vandalia* to meet the Governor of the Province at Uraga. Captain ADAMS was there informed by the Governor that everything was ready for considering the terms of a treaty between Japan and the United States, and if the Commodore (or, as he was termed, the Admiral) *would come to Uraga, it would be concluded before the going down of the sun.* It is supposed, however, that what was here meant by a treaty, was a favorable reply from the Emperor to the President's Letter on the subject. But Captain ADAMS reiterated, that the Commodore would not come to Uraga, where he had found the anchorage to be indifferent, but would meet the Japanese Commissioners at Yokohama, off the present anchorage of the flag-ship, ten to twenty* miles from Uraga. Captain ADAMS rejoined the squadron on the 24th February, and the following day the Japanese officers visited the flag-ship to settle the place of meeting, when the Commodore, among other things, told them that, having been entrusted with so many ships, which were seventeen thousand miles from home, he was reasonably anxious about their safety, and experience had proved to him that Uraga did not offer so secure an anchorage as where they now lay. Some discussion ensued, but finally it was arranged that the meeting should be he held at Yokohama.

* Our present information does not enable us to be more precise about the distance.

Eleven days afterwards the meeting took place; and in the interval, entertainments were interchanged by the American and Japanese officers. At one of two given by Capt. BUCHANAN, the Governor of Uraga, as we have seen in KEYING and other high Chinese officials, at once fell in with foreign observances in toasting and speechifying. Captain BUCHANAN proposed the health of the Emperor of Japan, which was drunk standing "with all the honors," and was acknowledged by the Governors of Uraga, who in return similarly proposed the health of the President of the United States. The Japanese took their liquor freely, especially champagne and liqueurs, greatly admiring the glassware that contained them; and expressed a hope that the time was at hand when they would be at liberty to visit foreign countries in steamers and ships of three masts.

It was during this interval that an officer of the squadron approached Yedó, and if he did not actually enter it, at least was near enough to judge of its appearance, and to ascertain, what, however, we believe a surveying party had done before, that close to the shore there is five fathoms water, so that it can be approached by large ships. The city is in the form of a crescent, and stands on an extensive plain with a magnificent back-ground of the mountains and wooded country; but it seems to possess no striking public buildings, while the dwelling-houses are generally of one story, and, therefore, present nothing imposing in their appearance, except their vast numbers, and space they occupy. The population of the capital has, however, been greatly exaggerated, for though it is certainly great, the Japanese officers themselves placed Yedó third among the cities in the world, London, they said, being the first, and Paris the second.

On the 8th, the preparations were completed for the reception of the Commodore, who, by the bye, insisted upon the removal of the screen-work which extended from the shore to the hall, and which shut out the public gaze. Between 11 and 12 o'clock, the marines having been mustered by Major ZEILIN, and the sailors by Lieut. PEGRAM, the whole in twenty-nine boats under command of Captain BUCHANAN, who conveyed the cortège to the shore, and waited the arrival of the Commodore and suite, consisting of Captain ADAMS, the Secretary, Mr. O. H. PERRY, and the interpreters, Dr. S. W. WILLIAMS and Mr. J. L. C. PORTMAN, who landed about noon, under a salute of seventeen guns from the *Macedonian*, the men in the boats standing up, and the officers on shore being uncovered. The procession then moved forward, the band playing "Hail Columbia" and the "President's March."

On entering the hall, the Commodore was received by four Commissioners, appointed for the purpose. They were:

First, HAYASHI, with the title of *Daigaku no Kama*, or Prince Councillor.

Second, IDO, Prince of Tsus-sima, (the group of islands lying between Corea and Japan.)

Third, IDZUMA, Prince of Mimasaki, (a Principality lying west of Miaco.)

Fourth, UDONO, second assistant of the Board of Revenue.

The party being seated, the flag of Japan was run up on board the *Powhatan*, and saluted with twenty-one guns from the launches, after which another salute of seventeen guns was given to the Japanese High Commissioner, who through the interpreter presented his compliments and welcome to the Commodore and his officers, and particularly inquired about the health of the former. At a sign given the servants in attendance brought in laquered stands with tea and saki, sweetmeats and other conserves, and placed one beside each officer. The regalement seems to have been much the same as that which in China generally precedes the transaction of business with foreign officials; and while it was going on there was time to take a note of the place of meeting. The hall, which had been run up with great celerity, was about fifty feet long, forty wide, and twelve high, and surrounded with magnificent japonicas, some of them thirty feet in height, and in full bloom. Seats and tables about two feet high, covered with red cloth, extended the whole length of the apartment. The floor was covered with white mats, about three feet long by two wide; and the place was heated by highly ornamented braziers placed on beautiful Japan stands. The pillars supporting the erection were ornamented with purple crape, and the walls were richly adorned with paintings of birds and flowers. The hall was situated about five hundred yards from the landing-place, and was commanedd by the ships, which lay with their broadsides to it. Several native artists were present taking sketches of the strangers.

The refreshments being over, the Commodore and his personal staff were conducted by the Japanese Commissioners into another room in the rear, the entrance to which was covered with purple crape. The conference lasted three hours, and was carried on through the Dutch language, which the Japanese interpreters, MATS-NA-KI, and MICH-I-TASO, and Mr. PORTMAN, the Commodore's clerk, spoke fluently. *A very favorable answer was given to the President's letter*, which we presume was in terms a repetition of President FILLMORE's; and it is stated that Commodore PERRY was fully satisfied on all points suggested by him, which, we again presume, were in accordance with Mr. Secretary WEBSTER's letter of Instructions to Commodore AULICK accompanying the first letter to the Emperor. A draft Treaty, in English, Dutch, Chinese, and Japanese, was put into the hands of the Japanese Commissioners, who said that it would receive due consideration; but the old Emperor had died since Commodore PERRY was there last year, and his successor was a young man, who would require to consult his Council before coming to a determination; and the Commodore was reminded that Japanese did not act with the same rapidity as Americans did; which was thus illustrated: Should several Japanese meet together, desiring to visit the American ships, one would say: "It is a beautiful morning!" to which another would add, "How pleasant it is!" Then a third would remark, "There is not then a wave to be seen upon the water;" at length a fourth would suggest, "Come let us go and see the ships."

That the preliminaries of a treaty would be settled during the present visit was, however, more then probable. Its leading provisions, it is said, will be the opening of three or more of the ports of Japan to the commerce of the United States, and securing supplies of coals for the steamers of that country. In other respects the treaty, concluded or proposed, is understood to be nearly a counterpart of that with China, except, it is said, that the *Japanese objected to a clause admitting all other countries to the same privileges as America*; not like the Chinese, by whom, and not by Sir HENRY POTTINGER, as is generally supposed, the privileges of the English Treaty, were extended to all foreign countries. The Japanese would manifest more sagacity, and save themselves from incalculable vexation, were they to determine on allowing other nations to enjoy the same immunities as America, and no other, modeling all future treaties on precisely the same terms. But nothing can be as yet certainly known on the subject, for the *Susquehanna*, having been placed at the disposal of Mr. MCLANE, the Minister to China, and being under orders to be in Hong Kong in the beginning of April, was dispatched on the morning of the 24th March, the very day a Conference was to have been held for the purpose of considering the treaty.

As most of our readers may have forgotten the precise tenor of President FILLMORE's letter to the Emperor of Japan, and as it is not long, we here insert it, appending an outline of Mr. Secretary WEBSTER's instructions to Commodore AULICK, to whom the mission was originally entrusted:

"I send you, by this letter, an envoy of my own appointment, an officer of high rank in his country, who is no missionary of religion. He goes by my command to bear to you my greeting and good wishes, and to promote friendship and commerce between the two countries.

"You know that the United States of America now extend from sea to sea; that the great countries of Oregon and California are parts of the United States; and that from these countries, which are rich in gold and silver and precious stones, our steamers can reach the shores of your happy land in less than twenty days.

"Many of our ships will now pass in every year, and some perhaps in every week, between California and China. These ships must pass along the coast of your empire; storms and winds may cause them to be wrecked on your shores, and we ask and expect from your friendship and your greatness, kindness for our men and protection for our property. We wish that our people may be permitted to trade with your people; but we shall not authorize them to break any law of your empire.

"Our object is friendly commercial intercourse, and nothing more. You may have productions which we should be glad to buy, and we have productions which might suit your people.

"Your Empire contains a great abundance of coal; this is an article which our steamers, in going from California to China, must use. They would be glad that a harbor in your Empire should be appointed to which coal might be brought, and where they might always be able to purchase it.

"In many other respects commerce between your Empire and our country would be useful to both. Let us consider well what new interests may arise from these recent events which have brought our two countries so near together, and what purposes of friendly amity and intercourse this ought to inspire in the hearts of those who govern both countries."

The first half of Mr. Secretary WEBSTER's instructions is devoted to the subject of coals, that being apparently the leading object of the mission; but Commodore AULICK was to avail himself of any and every opportunity when brought in contact with Japanese officials—either in treating about coals, or in delivering over certain shipwrecked Japanese—to impress upon them "that the Government of the United States does not possess power over the religion of its own citizens, and there is therefore no cause to apprehend it will interfere with the religion of other countries." This point, not without reason, as afterwards appeared, was held to be of the first importance, for even the question of commercial intercourse was made subsidiary, its success being regarded as unpromising; but in order to provide for any "favorable contingency," the Commodore was invested with power to negotiate a treaty, and was furnished with copies of those of China, Muscat, and Siam, as models, "the two latter containing guarantees for the protection of American sailors and property which may be cast ashore," which WEBSTER held to be more important than opening "one or more of the ports of Japan." If however the Commodore should succeed in effecting a treaty, Mr. WEBSTER concludes by saying, "it would be prudent to fix the period for exchanging the ratifications at three years."

During the conference on the 8th, Commodore PERRY mentioned that one of the marines had died, and he was desirous to have a piece of ground pointed out where this man and any others of the squadron that might die in Japan could be buried. The Commissioners first suggested Nanasaki, and next Uraga, but on both being objected to, a spot near the place of meeting was fixed upon. An account of the funeral by Captain SLACK, the officer commanding the marines, is given in another column, and cannot fail to be read with interest. We have only to add, that before the funeral took place, the Japanese officials came on board to view the body, for which purpose the coffin was opened; and after the burial one of them remarked that, according to the inscription on the lid, the man was a native of Ireland, not of America; but the explanation that followed proved quite satisfactory. In the course of the arrangements for the funeral, the prudence of President FILLMORE's and Secretary WEBSTER's assurance on the subject of religion was shown. The Japanese said they had observed it with pleasure, and quite understood the distinction between Protestants and Roman Catholics. Before the interview broke up, the Commodore mentioned that he proposed to give his officers leave to go on shore for recreation. To this no great objection was made, and we believe that within a few days afterwards several the officers were taking exercise on shore. Rev. E. C. BITTINGER, the Chaplain, made several excursions among the villages and cornfields, which last he found in high cultivation. The houses were generally thatched, but those of the better sort were covered with tiles, having yards and small gardens within enclosures.

The following day, the same gentleman, finding the people neither unfriendly nor indisposed to receive him, and having obtained leave to go on shore, determined to visit two large cities some miles off, called Kanagawa and Kasacca, and with that view crossed an arm of the bay, which shortened the distance by several miles. He then proceeded through Kanagawa, supposed to contain from one to two hundred thousand inhabitants; and from the immense crowds that poured out everywhere to see the stranger, there can be no doubt of the population being very great. The crowds however, caused no inconvenience or impediment, for on a wave of the hand from the Japanese officials who accompanied Mr. BITTINGER, the people cleared a passage; and afterwards, a messenger having been sent forward for the purpose, the people packed themselves at the sides of the houses, and left the centre of the streets clear for the stranger. He entered some of the houses, which he found primitive in their furniture and arrangements; but, compared with other Oriental dwellings of the same class, neat, clean and comfortable. In some of them he observed clocks of Japanese manufacture. He also visited several temples, which though smaller than in China, have more gilding on their walls, and ornaments on their idols, and generally are in better order. The priests as well as the people were distinguished for their courtesy. The cities thus visited were not only very extensive, (estimated to be six miles long,) but with wide, well-formed streets. Kasacca is from fifteen to twenty miles distant, by land, from the ships; and Mr. BITTINGER being thus necessarily long absent, some anxiety was felt about him. As he was returning, a Japanese officer put into his hands an order from the Commodore for all officers to return on board, and shortly afterwards, a courier mounted on a splendid black horse, delivered a similar dispatch, and finding it was understood and acted on, turned round, and galloped back again to report the approach of the American officer, who concluded his journey by torch-light, and found on his arrival that everything that had occurred had been noted, even the number of buttons on his coat being recorded.

Four days after the interview, the presents were interchanged, time having been required to erect places for their reception. Those for the Emperor consisted of, among other things—

A Railway with Steam Engine—An Electric Telegraph—A Surf Boat—A Life Boat—A Printing Press—A fine Lorgnette—A set of Audubon's American Ornithology, splendidly bound—Plates of American Indians—Maps of different States of America—Agricultural implements, with all the modern improvements—A piece of Cloth—A bale of Cotton—A Stove—Rifles, Pistols, and Swords—Champagne, Cordials, and American Whisky.

And for the Empress, (presuming there is one,)—A Telescope—A Lorgnette in a gilded case—A Lady's Toilet-box, gilded—A Scarlet Velvet Dress—A changeable silk Dress, flowered—A splendid Robe—Audubon's Illustrated Works—A handsome set of China—A Mantelpiece Clock—A Parlor Stove—A box of fine Wines—A box of Perfumery—A box of fancy Soaps.

Of the other presents, perhaps the one most valued was a copy of WEBSTER's complete Dictionary to one of the Imperial interpreters. To the high officers were given books, rifles, pistols, swords, wines, cloths, maps, stoves, clocks, and cordials, the last of which they fully appreciated, and, as regards clocks, when it was proposed to bring an engineer from shipboard to set them going, the Japanese said there was no occasion for that, for they had clock-makers in Yedó who understood them perfectly. They were curious to know however about ERICSSON's caloric engine, of which they had heard, but, from the Commodore at any rate, we suspect they would not receive a very favorable opinion of its practical utility.

Whatever may be thought of some of the other presents, the Railway and Telegraph, at which the world at the time was disposed to laugh, were happy hits. The Rail is only about three hundred yards in all, but being formed in a circle, the carriage can be driven at the rate of forty miles or more. Just at first the Japanese were chary of venturing into the car, but after a single trial there was much good humored competition for places. The Telegraph still more astonished them, but they will speedily understand it, and may possibly by this time be laying down the wires for themselves.

Christian Burial in Japan.

One of the standing opinions about the Japanese, destined to be thrown down by Commodore PERRY, has been, that they were invincibly intolerant of Christianity in any form. Indeed this has generally been assigned as the main reason for their exclusiveness. To the emblem of the Cross they still object, but the story of the expelled Portugese, that every Christian landing in Japan was required to trample on it, or on a representation of the Virgin and Saviour, must, if true, have been almost entirely confined to themselves and their coreligionists. More recent writers, who have been able to deny that such is now the custom, tell us, that "the practice of religious rights is prohibited by irrevocable Japanese laws;" but the following narrative of the funeral of a marine of the United States squadron shows that there is as little foundation for the one statement as the other:

On the 9th of March, the day following the first meeting between Commodore PERRY and the Imperial Commissioner from Yedó, to negotiate the terms of a commercial treaty, a soldier's and a Christian burial was given to a Marine, ROBERT WILLIAMS, who had died a few days before on board the steamer *Mississippi*. The party detailed for this purpose, consisted of several officers, one of them the Chaplain in his gown, an escort of eight marines in charge of a corporal, and four marines as bearers of the corpse. Two boats left the ship; one containing the officers, and the other the body and escort. Upon reaching the shore the party was met by several Japanese Officials, ready to conduct them to the grave. The escort landed first, and received the body with the usual honors. The little procession was then formed; first the escort, followed by the music (drum and fife); next the body borne on the shoulders of four messmates; and then the Chaplain with the other officers, and a few sailors from the boats bringing up the rear. In this order, with the music playing a Dead March, the party moved to the grave, winding through the streets of a village, a distance of nearly half a mile. On either side of the road, and on the surrounding hills, at the foot of one of which the grave had been made, thousands of people, men, women, and children, could be seen, all manifesting eager curiosity to witness a sight so entirely novel in *their* land.

I could not but think as we passed along, how strange, not only the procession, but each of us individually, must appear to that eager throng, not one of whom probably had ever before looked upon the face of a stranger from a foreign country; and yet their was no undue noise made, or apparent alarm on the part of any of them,—only intense interest in observing what was passing before them. As we neared the grave (which occupied a very pretty spot) the voice of the Chaplain could be heard,—"I am the resurrection and the life, saith the Lord; he that believeth in me, though he were dead, yet shall he live; and whosoever liveth and believeth in me, shall never die." As we gathered round the grave, and the reading of the beautiful and touching burial service proceeded, the scene was one of unusual interest; for the time, and place, and circumstances, all conspired to make it, as an incident, honorable to our short sojourn in a land, where for centuries, it is said the symbol of our religion has been trodden under foot. The Church burial service ended, the escort fired three volleys over the grave. I had expected that on this there would have been some commotion among the crowd, but I noticed only, at the first discharge, that for a moment there was a slight movement as of surprise, and then all were again quiet and attentive observers.

Having now committed to the earth, with all due honor, the remains of our deceased shipmate, the procession was re-formed, and with music to the front, again passed through the village and the thousands of spectators, to our boats on the beach. Here we took leave of the officials, who throughout the entire ceremony had conducted themselves with great propriety, and extended to us every civility; and returned to the ship, pleased with the consciousness of not only having witnessed, but assisted in giving such honors, in such a place, to a deceased brother.

W. B. S.

The Resources of Japan.

Foremost among the resources of Japan are its fisheries. The sea and its productions, we believe, contribute fully as much to the sustenance of the natives, as do the fruits of the earth—rice, perhaps, excepted. One of their productions has a value which is not confined to the spot, but extends to us—to our enterprise, and our trade,—we mean the whale, or, as they call it, *kudsuri*. There is nothing of which such extensive use is made by the Japanese, both for rich and poor. It is found all around Japan, but particularly in the sea Keumano, which washes the Southern coast of the island Niphon, the most important territory of the Empire; and it also prevails in the islands of Tsussima and Goto, and upon the coasts of Omura and Nomo. These whales not only afford oil in great abundance, but their flesh, which is considered very wholesome and nutritious, is largely consumed. No part of them, indeed, is thrown away—all is made available to some useful purpose or another, excepting only the large shoulder bone. The skin, which is generally black; the flesh, which is red and looks like beef; the intestines, and all the inward parts; besides the fat or blubber, which is boiled into oil, and the bone which is converted to innumerable uses—all is made available to purposes of profit. We have gone into these few particulars respecting the whale, because it is that which has brought our countrymen into contact with Japan. Many of our ships have for some considerable time past frequented those seas for capturing the whale, an occupation which, it is found, might be pursued with great advantage, under a commercial treaty with the Government of Japan, whose inhuman laws at present not only prevent any assistance being rendered to shipwrecked mariners, but expose them to positive maltreatment, and even to violent death. To obtain redress in this respect was the primary object of Commodore PERRY's expedition.

Japan abounds in natural and artificial productions of great value. Its mineral riches are enormous, and include metals of various kinds, especially gold, silver, and copper. Sulphur and nitre are also found in large quantities;—there is no want of coal, and there are precious stones of almost every variety; agates, sapphires, jaspers, cornelians, and even diamonds; while pearls are found in great plenty among the shells upon the coast. Then the fertility of the soil is very great. The mulberry tree grows extensively and affords food for countless myriads of silk worms. The *Kadsi*, or paper-tree, serves innumerable useful purposes, including the manufacture of cloth, stuffs and cordage. The *urusi*, or varnish-tree, is another valuable production of the country, yielding large quantities of a milky juice which the natives employ to varnish, or *japan* as we call it, various articles. Then there are the bay-tree, the camphor-tree, the fig-tree, the cypress-tree, with very many more, all more or less valuable, and from which a great variety of useful things are made; and last, though not least, there is the tea-shrub, from the leaves of which the common drink of the people is brewed, and which is capable of yielding a valuable article of commerce. Trees growing nuts of various kinds are abundant; the maple is extensive and excellent; bamboos are very plentiful, and of great use, as they are everywhere in the Indies; they cultivate as much hemp and cotton as they can find room for in their fields: and as to rice, which is the main food of the natives, that grown in Japan is considered the best in all Asia, and it can be produced in almost any quantity. Their corns are of several sorts; besides the *komi* or rice, there are the *oomuggi*, a kind of barley; the *koomuggi*, their native wheat; and the *daidsen*, a species of bean,—all of which abound with superior farina.

The manufactures of Japan have hitherto been confined almost exclusively to their own domestic wants; but many of them are, nevertheless valuable as articles of export. Our adoption here and throughout Europe of the term *japan* as applied to certain kinds of varnished ware, indicates how well known has been their peculiar excellence in, if not their invention of that useful art. They make various articles from the paper tree, resembling our *papier-mache*, which they paint, and varnish, on paper, very highly—and these might form objects of considerable trade. Their silks, muslins, and cotton goods are most of them very superior, and some of them are calculated to become highly *recherche*; and their carvings in wood, ivory, pearl, and fish-bone, are most ingenious and elegant. These are but a few of the products of their handicraft; but they are sufficient to show, taken in connection with their natural productions, how varied and how valuable are the resources of the Japanese.

Progress of the Chinese Revolution.

From the Commercial.

HONG KONG, Saturday, April 8, 1854.

For many months we have known nothing of the movements of the Northern Army of the insurgents. After penetrating to within a hundred miles of Pekin, they went into Winter quarters, and no actions of any importance have since taken place. TAE-PING-WANG maintains his position; and when certain reinforcements reach him, which have been seen moving northward, he will probably march for the capital. There great distress prevails, and the poverty of the treasury leads to increased oppression.

The issue of paper money and the debasing of the copper currency have been resorted to by the Government, but these measures can afford it but little effectual aid. Pekin must fall; and then the army of the North will spread itself over the neighboring country, and take possession of Soo-Chow and Hong-Chow, and other rich cities, which it has only to attack. The districts for a considerable distance around Nankin have peacefully submitted to the insurgents, and the taxes for some months past have been collected by insurgent officers.

To the South and West more activity has prevailed. Nearly all the cities of Ngunhwei and many of Hupeh are occupied by the rebels, who do not merely capture and pass through as formerly; and lately we have heard of the capture of Wuchong and Hangkaw. Two days since, the powerful city of Changsha was reported lost. Although some part of this information may be erroneous, the tenor of it plainly indicates the total destruction of governmental power in the interior. Within a few days goods intended for the tea districts have been brought back, the owners finding it impossible to pass them through the country.

Warm weather is now rapidly approaching, and the camp at the North will soon be broken up. If Pekin falls, the power in those cities which have hitherto adhered to the Emperor must pass into the hands of the new party, and Canton can scarcely be exempt from such change. Looking at the history of the past year, and the rapid progress of the insurgents, it seems probable that the coming Summer will decide the fate of China, and it is very desirable that some result be reached. The exigencies of commerce demand it.

The Streets—Genin again in the Field.

To the Honorable the Common Council of the City of New-York:

The undersigned, a resident of the Sixteenth Ward, would respectfully inform your honorable body that the said Ward is, at present, in a filthy and disgraceful condition. Such is the state of the streets in certain localities, that, unless they are speedily purified, nothing short of Providential interference can save the inhabitants from pestilential disease.

The stench arising from the abominations which have been suffered to fester and rot in the thoroughfares and byways, is, in some places, almost overpowering; and as the heat increases, and additions are made to the pestiferous mass, fever and cholera may be looked for as the unavoidable results.

Under these circumstances, and they are notorious throughout the ward, prompt sanitary action is required. Experience has taught the undersigned the futility of looking for it from the Street Department. He therefore asks of you, as guardians of the public health, such an appropriation as will suffice for the periodical removal of the elements of danger in this quarter of the City; probably $400 per week would effect the desired object and save the ward from the visitation of disease. For the sake of his own family and the families of his neighbors, the undersigned would be willing to assume the task of cleansing the ward and keeping it clean during the Summer months, if sufficient funds should be appropriated for that purpose—he of course giving bonds for the faithful application thereof, and receipts and vouchers for all moneys expended. JOHN N. GENIN.

☞ We learn by a note from Mr. F. COOMBS, that he has commenced a suit against Messrs. GROVER, BAKER & Co., for having accused him of fraudulently disposing of Sewing Machines of their make. He pronounces the assertion false and malicious.

LATEST INTELLIGENCE

By Telegraph to the New-York Daily Times.

CONGRESSIONAL PROCEEDINGS.

Interesting Debate in the House on Fixing a Day for Adjournment.

Resolution Naming August 14 Passed.

Negotiations for the Purchase of Cuba—Our Relations with New-Granada.

Correspondence of the New-York Daily Times.

WASHINGTON, Sunday, June 11, 1854.

The statement is traveling over the country that WARREN WINSLOW, who went to Madrid with dispatches to Mr. SOULE, in relation to the *Black Warrior* affair, is about to return to that Court with a specific offer for the purchase of Cuba. As much credence is given to the rumor, I may as well say it is unfounded. It is not even probable that Mr. WINSLOW will go to Spain again at all at present, so far as I can learn.

Our Government continues to press its demand for some arrangement by which we shall be enabled to settle at Havana, and without reference to Madrid, disputes arising in the ports of Cuba between the Spanish authorities and American citizens. Spain has manifested, as yet, no disposition to yield this point; and thus a serious disturbing element in our relations with that country continues to exist. The President will send a Special Commission to Madrid to aid in settling this point by the purchase of Cuba, if the present manipulations of the public pulse shall show that such a Commission will be popular, but he has not determined on that point yet. The Mesilla difficulty was settled by swallowing the question up in the greater one of purchase; and so all our Spanish difficulties will be arranged, by buying up the Island Colony whence all of them flow.

Each successive arrival from Europe brings additional evidence that the Spanish Court is coming down to the plain matter-of-fact proposition for the sale of Cuba to the United States. The members of the Government now talk freely of that measure, as of any other;—at the same time that they avoid coming frankly to the point of saying that they *will* sell, and of making a definite statement of terms. In short, they see that to this complexion they must come at last; but they prefer a little coyness, in hope of enhancing the price. The wisest Statesmen of Spain fully appreciate the fact that they would derive great advantages from a sale of the island to us. One hundred millions of dollars would firmly establish the Government, and leave an ample sum for the construction of railroads and other works of internal improvement, calculated to develop the natural resources of the kingdom and convert its rich waste into a productive self-sustaining country. Notwithstanding her great agricultural resources, but a very small portion of Spain does or can live thereby, for want of means to get the crops to market. While famine rages at one point, frequently two or three years' crops of wheat are rotting at thirty miles distance, because there is no method of bringing them to the point where needed. With railroads intersecting the country and reaching the seaboard, Spain might soon recover much of her former power and greatness. She has within her the surest element of prosperity,—unsurpassed agricultural resources. Make these available, and she will not need an overtaxed and distant colony to support her Government. Her statesmen see this of late; and many of them are anxious to finger our millions, that they may exchange the gold for railroad iron. Such arguments as these will be far more effectual in securing us the possession of Cuba than all the bullets and cannon balls we can muster.

I understand that the President and Secretary of State have had under consideration the subject of the passenger tax levied by the New-Granadian Government on American citizens passing through Panama to or from the Pacific. Mr. GREEN, our Minister to Bogota, has earnestly remonstrated against this tax, as unjust and violative of express treaty stipulation; and steps are about to be taken by our Government to resist its collection at all hazards. For this purpose a vessel of war will probably be sent to Aspinwall, and another to Panama.

The absent members of Congress come in very slowly; but the general expectation is that to-morrow the business of both houses will be recommenced in good earnest. There is much to be done, if Congress will only take hold with a view of accomplishing it. S.

THIRTY-THIRD CONGRESS......First Session.

SENATE—WASHINGTON, Monday, June 12.

A message was received from the House communicating the proceedings of that body on the occasion of the death of Hon. J. F. SNODGRASS of Virginia.

Mr. MASON delivered a eulogy upon the virtues of the deceased, and offered the customary resolutions—when the Senate adjourned.

HOUSE OF REPRESENTATIVES.

WASHINGTON, Monday, June 12.

PROPOSITION FOR ADJOURNMENT.

The SPEAKER announced the first business in order to be Mr. WALBRIDGE's resolution providing for the adjournment of Congress on the 3d of July.

The rules were suspended by 104 against 38.

Mr. WALBRIDGE proposed to amend his resolution to adjourn July 17.

Mr. ORR offered a substitute—to adjourn the 14th of August. That would afford ample time for the transaction of other business.

Mr. HAVEN submitted the Senate's resolution for an adjournment from the 4th of July to the third Monday in October. He said, fix that time and all the necessary work will be done in the meantime. Congress had got into that kind of demoralization, so to speak, that they can do no valuable service till the members, after separating, shall come together at some future day.

Mr. ORR said his principle reason for voting for a suspension of the rules, was to defeat the Senate's resolution. He was opposed to taking a recess. It was unprecedented in the history of the Government. Congress should pursue the usual course.

Mr. HILYER proposed that Congress adjourn on the first Monday in August, and meet hereafter on the third Monday in October, in each year, instead of the first Monday in December.

Mr. MCMULLEN was opposed to fixing any day at present. Let Congress go to work, and transact the business before it, and then it would be time to provide for the adjournment.

Mr. HAVEN urged considerations why the Senate's resolutions should be adopted. He was satisfied if members stay here, they will keep the country in turmoil, without doing the public business. The private calendar has been taken up only twice. Disease is approaching us—the cholera is abroad. A quorum could only be maintained by the Sergeant-at-Arms scouring the city.

Mr. TAYLOR, of Ohio, said, if the 1st of August should be named, he would support the resolution. The business of Congress can be transacted in six weeks; the country demands it—we ought not to take recess.

Mr. HENN inquired whether if the Senate resolution should be adopted, members could not draw pay in recess; he understood that was the construction of the Comptroller.

Mr. HAVEN replied, the resolution was for adjournment, not recess; therefore members could not draw pay meantime.

Mr. CAMPBELL offered an amendment, which Mr. HAVEN accepted, providing no compensation shall be allowed members during recess.

Mr. DISNEY thought the whole matter premature, ill considered, and out of place. The Committees have their hands full of reports, and no one could say when Congress should adjourn.

Mr. JONES of Tenn. said the last ten days have been spent in idleness when there was not a working quorum in the House. He was opposed to recess, and thought all public business could be transacted by the 14th of August.

Mr. EWING could see no prospect of doing business if Congress remained here, and therefore was in favor of the earliest day of adjournment.

Mr. HILYER moved the whole subject be laid on the table. Negatived—56 against 97.

Mr. KEITT would prefer the 14th of September for adjournment. He understood the Democratic party came in power on a platform of principles many of which have not been carried out. (Laughter.) He wanted to give that party an opportunity to carry out their principles one of which he understood to be a modification of tariff and free trade.

Mr. WALBRIDGE and Mr. HAVEN's amendments were severally rejected.

Mr. ORR's was adopted, by 71 against 69.

The question recurring on the adoption of the resolutions thus amended, fixing the 14th of August for adjournment—motion made to lay it on the table negatived. The resolution was then adopted—82 against 68.

Mr. HOUSTON made an ineffectual effort to introduce a resolution, that the daily hour of meeting shall be 11 o'clock.

Mr. HILYER asked leave to introduce a bill fixing the annual meeting of Congress the first Monday in Nov.

Pending the motion to suspend the rules, the House adjourned.

Messrs. Riddle, Goode, Gerrit Smith, Elliot, Trout and Sollers, were appointed a Select Committee on the Memorial of 2,000 Citizens of Delaware, praying the Government to effect some arrangement with Peru, by which for a just and proper equivalent, the Peruvian Government will either cede to the United States Government one of the Guano Islands, or by removing the existing restriction on American vessels engaged in the guano trade, place the trade in the article on a more just and liberal commercial basis.

From Washington.

WASHINGTON, Monday, June 12.

The new City Government was inaugurated to-day, and the occasion was one of general rejoicing.

Mr. and Mrs. WM. F. RITCHIE arrived here this morning.

The New-York Light Guard in Boston.

BOSTON, Monday, June 12.

The New-York Light Guard, with Dodworth's Band, command much attention from our military and citizens generally. They are the special guests of the Boston Light Infantry, Capt. ROGERS, and this afternoon both companies were reviewed on the Common by Major General EDMANDS and staff.

In the evening the two companies, with numerous invited guests, partook of a sumptuous banquet in Faneuil Hall. Speeches were made by Governor WASHBURN, Mayor SMITH, Captains VINCENT and ROGERS, Lieut. CLAPP and others. It was a magnificently conducted affair throughout.

From Rio de Janeiro.

BALTIMORE, Monday, June 12.

The bark *Antelope* arrived here to-day with advices from Rio de Janeiro to the 1st of May. BREADSTUFFS were exceedingly dull with large receipts. No sales were reported, holders' views being above market rates. The COFFEE market opened at an advance upon previous rates, with sales during the week of 35,000 bags at 4$200@4$300 for lots, and 4$350@4$400 for good firsts and superiors. At the close of the market good firsts could not be had at less than 4$400. Stock in the market was small, and composed almost entirely of low qualities, the new crop being held. STERLING EXCHANGE, 27½@28d. FREIGHTS dull.

Arrived at Rio 28th April—Ship Amelia, New-York; 29th, bark Stamboul, Boston. Sailed—25th, ship Partar for Philadelphia; 27th, bark Nautilus, and 28th, ship Susquehanna, both for New-York.

Fugitive Slave Excitement in Manchester, N. H.—Fatal Affray.

MANCHESTER, (N. H.,) Monday, June 12.

Much excitement was caused here yesterday and to-day, by a report that two persons from Virginia had arrived in Lowell, in search of EDWIN MOORE, a colored barber, formerly resident in Lowell and now keeping shop here. MOORE is alleged to have escaped from Virginia, where he was a slave, twelve years since. A purse was made up for him to-day, and at noon he took the cars for Canada, accompanied by his wife and children.

JOHN MARSHALL, a stable-keeper of this city, killed MICHAEL COLLAMORE, one of his employés, last evening, during a quarrel about wages. MARSHALL has been arrested.

Philadelphia New City Councils.

PHILADELPHIA, Monday, June 12.

The New City Councils were organized this morning. JOHN P. VERREE was elected President of the Select Council, and JOHN H. DIEHL President of the Common Council. The vote in the latter body stood, DIEHL, Whig, 56; CRISPIN, Democrat, 10. A number of the seats of Democrats are contested, but they were sworn in by virtue of the certificates given by the Judges of Election.

New-Hampshire Legislature.

CONCORD, Monday, June 12.

Wednesday next has been assigned for the choice, in Convention of the two Houses, of Secretary of State, Treasurer and Public Printer.

A large number of bills for banks, five cent Savings Institutions, and for the increase of bank capital have been introduced, indicating that bank matters will be a prominent feature of the session.

Fatal Railroad Accident.

PATERSON, N. J., Monday, June 12.

A lamentable accident happened in this city this morning. A gravel train had stopped until some cattle were driven off the track, and two laborers on the cars were throwing stones to assist in driving them away, when the train suddenly started, and both men were precipitated on the track. The head of one of them was completely cut off, seven cars passing over him; and the other had the flesh torn from his legs. He is not expected to recover.

Fire at the White Mountains.

BOSTON, Monday, June 12.

The "Notch House" on the White Mountains was totally destroyed by fire on Friday last.

The Southern Mail.

BALTIMORE, Monday, June 12.

The Southern Mail as late as due is to hand, but the papers contain no news worth telegraphing.

THE TURF OF 1854.

Trotting Match at the Centreville Course—The Judges' Decision Disputed—Union Course Races.

The Centreville Course was attended yesterday by a large number of persons from the City, to witness a trotting match announced to come off as follows:

"Mile heats, best three in five, top wagons. I. Woodruff names b. g. Wedge; Wm. Wheelan names b. g. Frank.

The Judges were selected by the parties interested in the race, and took their seats on the stand. The horses scored several times, and on the second turn they received the word go, and the gelding of Mr. WOODRUFF was full one length ahead at the time the word was given, and having the pole, *Wedge* had advantage over his competitor. As the steeds glided around the lower turn of the track, the brown horse of Mr. WHEELAN's made a very bad break, and before he could be managed by his skillful driver, and compelled to settle down on a square trotting gait, he had made quite a run, but was checked as speedily as possible, and never made a skip or break after the first flurry. The horse under the management of Mr. WHEELAN exhibited most excellent speed under the existing circumstances, and with perfect ease he passed *Wedge* at the quarter pole, and left him in the rear for a long distance. ISAAC WOODRUFF urged *Wedge* to his utmost, but it was of no use, as he came very near being distanced at the first distance box, and only saved himself by making a desperate run on the back stretch, and thence homeward. Meanwhile, Mr. WHEELAN's steed made no break up, and at one period he trotted a 2:40 gait, and finally came to the Judges' stand nearly an eighth of a mile in advance of Mr. WOODRUFF. As the contestants returned to the stand, the decision of the Judges was announced, as here annexed: "We decide that Mr. WHEELAN is distanced, in consequence of making a run on the lower turn of the course." This decision appeared to astonish the spectators, and was disputed. They finally pronounced it to be entirely wrong, and a direct violation of the "rules of the track." The result caused quite a sensation among the spectators. The feeling was against the Judges' decision, and the majority were in favor of Mr. WHEELAN, who could have won the race without a struggle, provided he had been permitted to trot the balance of the heats. It was, however, a fixed fact that the brown horse was "shut out," and the only excuse given was "foul driving" by Mr. WHEELAN, which yet needs confirmation, to induce many of the audience to believe the Judges were right in their decision as above given. Appeal being out of the question, the owners and driver of *Frank* left the course, and the money was given over by the stakeholder to the owner of *Wedge*. The people on the track, were somewhat disappointed at the singular termination of the match, and they left quite equally divided on the subject. In this instance the Judges assured the [illegible] that they went in strict accordance with the *rules* and could not do otherwise. Only a few days ago a fine trotting match of two mile heats, came off on Long Island between *Fanny D* and *Whalebone*, when the Judges paid no attention to the "rules" and decided against the mare on the second heat, when she really won the heat if the time of *Whalebone* had been deducted when they came to the stand.

The entire ground on the inside enclosure of the Union Course is now plowed up, and yesterday the celebrated Southern horses of Mr. GIBBONS arrived at the course, and during the day they galloped around on the rough turf, and were exercised in various ways by the men in charge of them. The great races on the Union Course, Long Island, will commence on Tuesday, 20th inst., and subjoined we give a list of the liberal purses offered by the proprietors:

First day. Tuesday—Proprietor's purse $300, two mile heats. Same day—Purse $200, mile heats, best in five.

Second day. Wednesday—Proprietor's purse $700, three mile heats. Same day—Purse $100, mile heats; with $50 added.

Third day. Thursday—Proprietor's purse $1,500, four mile heats. Same day—Sweepstakes, mile heats; subscription $50 half forfeit, and $300 added by the proprietor, closed with the following entries: J. N. WHITTEN names ch. c. by imp. *Glencoe*, dam *Mary D*, by *Medoc*; R. TEN BROECK names gr. m. by *Glencoe*, out of *Belly Ward*, 4 years old; W. H. GIBBONS names b. f. by *Mariner*, dam *Cassandra*, 4 years old.

All the above mentioned purses and stakes are to be governed by the rules of the late New-York Jockey Club. N. B.—Entrances for the purses, five per cent. to be added, and two or more to start to make a race.

The track will be in fine running order, and no trotting will be allowed on the track until the races are over.

The challenge offered by Mr. RICHARD TENBROECK, of N. O., to run his horse against the best time over any course on the track, for a wager of $20,000, has been accepted by Col. GREEN and Capt. GREEN, of Baltimore. The forfeit money of $5,000, has been forwarded to Mr. MOREHEAD, Cashier of the Astor House, and the great race will probably take place on the Metaire Course, N. O., during the fall campaign. The acceptance of this challenge creates quite an excitement among the sporting men.

New-York Daily Times.

VOL. IV....NO. 996. NEW-YORK, MONDAY, NOVEMBER 27, 1854. PRICE TWO CENTS.

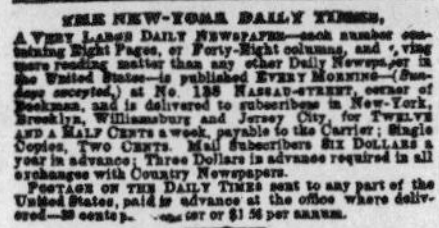

THE NEW-YORK DAILY TIMES,

A VERY LARGE DAILY NEWSPAPER—each number containing Eight Pages, or Forty-Eight columns, and giving more reading matter than any other Daily Newspaper in the United States—is published EVERY MORNING (Sundays excepted) at No. 138 NASSAU-STREET, corner of Beekman, and is delivered to subscribers in New-York, Brooklyn, Williamsburg and Jersey City, for TWELVE AND A HALF CENTS a week, payable to the Carrier; Single Copies, TWO CENTS. Mail Subscribers SIX DOLLARS a year in advance; Three Dollars in advance required in all exchanges with Country Newspapers.

POSTAGE ON THE DAILY TIMES sent to any part of the United States, paid in advance at the office where delivered—26 cents p[illegible] or $1 56 per annum.

THE NEW-YORK EVENING TIMES,

PUBLISHED EVERY EVENING, (Sundays excepted.) One edition will be issued at 1, and the other at 3 o'clock P. M. It will be sent by mail or sold at the same rates as the DAILY TIMES.

THE SEMI-WEEKLY TIMES

Is Published EVERY TUESDAY and FRIDAY, at $3 per year, payable invariably in advance. This paper is made up expressly for the mails, and contains all the reading matter of the Daily.

THE NEW-YORK WEEKLY TIMES.

A VERY LARGE NEWSPAPER FOR THE COUNTRY, is published every SATURDAY MORNING, at the low price of TWO DOLLARS per annum. TEN copies for FIFTEEN DOLLARS, will be sent to one address, and the paper in no case continued beyond the time for which payment is made. Postage on the WEEKLY TIMES sent by mail one year, is as follows:

Within the County.......................Free.
Within the State.......................13 cents.
Within the United States...............26 cents.

THE TIMES FOR CALIFORNIA

A LARGE NEWSPAPER OF EIGHT PAGES, or Forty-Eight columns, made up expressly for circulating in California, Oregon and the Sandwich Islands, and containing only news of interest to readers in those sections of the country, is published on the departure of every Mail steamer. Price 6 cents per copy.

RAYMOND, HARPER & CO., Publishers.

New-York Daily Times.

FOUR DAYS LATER FROM EUROPE

ARRIVAL OF THE BALTIC.

HIGHLY IMPORTANT NEWS

BLOODY WORK AT SEBASTOPOL.

A Charge of English Cavalry Repulsed with Loss 400 out of 600 Men.

Sanguinary Fights on the 4th and 5th November.

HEAVY LOSSES ON BOTH SIDES.

FOUR ENGLISH GENERALS WOUNDED.

Reported Storming of the Works on the 6th November.

Further Forces Demanded from Home by the French and English Generals-in-Chief.

Immense Preparations for Transporting Troops.

FALL IN THE FUNDS.

Later from China.

Markets, &c., &c.

The U. S. M. steamer *Baltic*, from Liverpool, afternoon of Wednesday, 15th November, arrived off Sandy Hook on Saturday night at 11:30, and came up to her dock, foot of Canal-street, early yesterday morning.

The steamship *Africa* arrived at Liverpool on the afternoon of Sunday, the 12th, at 4 o'clock.

The *Indiana* arrived at Southampton on the 14th, in thirteen days and a half—all well.

The Brazilian mail-steamer *Thames* arrived at Southampton on the 11th. Her dates were from Buenos Ayres to Oct. 3; Montevideo, 6; Pernambuco, 23; Madeira, Nov. 6; had about £25,000 in gold, silver and diamonds: news not important. At Montevido were the United States frigate *Savannah* and brig *Bainbridge*; at Rio the frigates *Germantown* and *Massachusetts*. The *Massachusetts* had been dismasted in a gale, 150 miles off Rio.

The news from the seat of war by this arrival is of very great interest and importance.

Our intelligence from Sebastopol is to the 5th of November;—and up to that time not only had the place not been taken, but *no attempt at storming had been made. Several desperate and bloody engagements had taken place,—a formidable attack of the Russians had been repulsed with difficulty and immense loss on both sides, and the opinion is freely expressed that such another victory, without additional reinforcements, would compel the allies to raise the siege!*

Under these circumstances, Generals RAGLAN and CANROBERT, the Commanders-in-Chief, have sent the most urgent demands for reinforcements. The haste manifested to transmit to the Crimea every available man,—Briton, Frenchman and Turk,—shows the importance attached to the demand. Seven first-class steamers are taken up for instant service, and others are wanted. The Cunard steamer *Alps* is withdrawn from the berth for New-York, and sailed on Sunday, the 11th, for Toulon, to embark Frenchmen. The Cunarder *Europa* would sail from Liverpool on the 18th for Kingston, Ireland, to ship drafts from the few regiments yet left in Ireland. The Peninsular and Oriental (Mediterranean) Company notify that they have received imperative orders to withdraw from the mail-service the steamers *Candia*, *Ripon*, *Manilla*, *Nubia* and *Rajah*, for immediate reinforcements to the Crimea. The steamer *Indiana*, just arrived from New-York, and the West India Mail-steamer *Thames* are also taken up.

The engagement of the Cunard steamers will not,—in the meantime, at least,—interfere with the weekly mail-service to America.

Our advices by the previous steamer enabled us to report the progress of the siege to the 23d—though details of the operations were lacking. We give below very copious extracts from the reports of the siege down to the 25th.

The most noticeable incident which occurred during this time was the terrible destruction of English cavalry, of which a rumor was brought by the *Canada* and telegraphed from Halifax, and of which a very graphic and spirited account is copied below from the London *Times*. It seems that the charge of cavalry that precipitated so many into certain destruction was the result of a mistake, or, at least, of a misconception of orders arising from the *esprit de corps* that induced the cavalry to attempt some brilliant exploit to retrieve the secondary part they played at the battle of Alma. In short, misconstruing an order from the commander-in-chief, conveyed by Captain NOLAN, Lords LUCAN and CARDIGAN rode the light horse over a plain a mile and a half in length, and exposed to a cross-fire, full at a Russian battery of 30 guns! The attempt was madness, and the result destruction. The troops were:

	Went into action.	Returned.
4th Light Dragoons	118	39
8th Hussars	104	38
11th Hussars	110	25
13th Light Dragoons	130	61
17th Lancers	145	35
Total	607	198

Not three hours, but *one quarter of an hour*, served to lay all these gallant fellows low, and every soul would have been cut off had it not been for the heavy dragoons, who charged as rapidly as they could in the track of the devoted "light." Of this latter charge, Lord RAGLAN says: "The charge of this brigade (heavy cavalry,) was one of the most successful I ever witnessed, was never for a moment doubtful, and was in the highest degree creditable to Brigadier General SCARLETT and the officers and men engaged in it." It, and the brave stand made by the Scotch Highlanders, and some assistance given by the French, certainly redeemed the day. After the action, it was resolved by the Allies to abandon the position at Balaklava, and to retire to the hills overlooking the town, in which case the dépôt would have been established at Arrow Bay or Cherson. But advices of the 27th state that it has been redecided to retain Balaklava.

The following, which comprises the most important news by this arrival, is also the

LATEST INTELLIGENCE.

The Attack upon the Allies by the Russian Army.

The London *Times* of the 15th gives the following dispatch from Vienna, received by Submarine and British telegraph:

VIENNA, Monday Evening.

The following is an epitome of several authentic dispatches of the 6th from the Crimea:

"Early on the morning of the 6th the garrison of Sebastopol and the army in the field made a violent attack on the right wing of the Allied army, composed of the English Foot Guards, and the Second, Third and Fourth Divisions.

"Gen. BOSQUET's division advanced to the support of the English, and subsequently other French troops, under Gen. CANROBERT, arrived.

"The battle lasted till the afternoon, when *the Russians retired*, having suffered a heavy loss and leaving several hundred prisoners in the hands of the English; the latter lost a great number of men. Gens. BROWN, BENTINCK, BULLER and TORRENS were more or less dangerously wounded.

"The prevalent opinion here is, *that if such another victory is obtained, the Allies will be obliged to raise the siege; but it is a good sign that the last Russian dispatch published only reaches up to the 5th.* Its sense is, that two sorties were made on that date—one against the right wing of the Allies, and the other against the left wing of the siege works. On the right wing of the army the guns of one battery were spiked, in the other 15 guns were spiked. The loss on both sides was very severe. *A French division, which pursued the Russians, and attempted to enter with them, was repulsed with great loss.*

"A terrific storm is raging here to-day.

"Prince GORTSCHAKOFF has officially announced to Count BUOL that *Russia is prepared to treat direct with Austria on the basis of the four conditions.*

"This is here considered a palpable attempt to *cause disunion between Austria and the Western Powers.*"

The French Official Report.

Gen. CANROBERT's official report of the battle of Nov. 5 is published in the *Moniteur* of the 13th. He says:

The Russian army, swollen by reinforcements from the Danube, as well as by the combined reserves of all the southern provinces, and animated by the presence of the Grand Dukes MICHAEL and NICHOLAS, attacked yesterday, Nov. 5, the right of the English position before Sebastopol.

The English army sustained the attack with the most remarkable firmness and solidity. I supported it by a portion of General BOSQUET's division,—as well as by the troops, which were nearest to the English position.

The enemy, who far outnumbered our force, beat a retreat, with a loss estimated at from 8,000 to 9,000 men.

The struggle lasted the whole day.

At the same time General FOREY was forced to repulse a sortie made by the garrison, and under his energetic command, the enemy were driven back into the place, with a loss of 1,000 killed and wounded.

This brilliant day, which was not purchased without considerable loss by the allies, does the greatest honor to our arms.

The siege continues with regularity.

(Signed) CANROBERT.

The Russian Account.

A telegraphic dispatch from St. Petersburg, dated November 12, states that Prince MENSCHIKOFF reports to the Emperor, under date the 6th November, from Sebastopol, that on the 5th the garrison made two sorties, one against the right flank, which was successful, and resulted in the capture of one of the enemy's batteries, the guns in which were spiked.

There was great loss on both sides.

The second sortie was also completely successful; the Russians having spiked 15 guns.

Immediately afterwards a French infantry division, pursuing the retiring Russians, attempted to mount to the assault, *but was thrown back with immense loss.*

Another Battle Next Day—Result Undecided.

The *Morgen Post*, of Vienna, has the following dispatch from

CZERNOVITZ, Nov. 11.—On the 6th the whole garrison of Sebastopol, amounting to 65,000 men, made a sortie.

A furious battle ensued, which was not ended when the messenger left, but the allies had the advantage.

This comprises all the reliable intelligence received of these operations. The Russian attack of the 5th is conceded on all sides to have been very formidable, and to have inflicted immense loss on the Allies, although they were victorious. The last dispatch published at Vienna, dated Nov. 11, reports *a sortie of the whole Russian garrison on the next day—the result of which was not known.* Nothing is more likely than that such an assault would be made; and in the condition of the Allied armies after the battle of the previous day, a disastrous result would not be very surprising.

THE SIEGE OF SEBASTOPOL.

Detailed History of the Operations.

From the Correspondence of the London Times.

HEIGHTS BEFORE SEBASTOPOL, Oct. 19.

The enemy scarcely fired a shot during the night of the 18th. Our batteries were equally silent. The French, on their side, opened a few guns on their right attack, which they had been working to get into position all night; but they did not succeed in firing many rounds before the great preponderance of the enemy's metal made itself felt, and their works were damaged seriously; in fact, their lines, though nearer to the enemy's batteries than our own in some instances, were not sufficiently close for the light brass guns with which they were armed. At daybreak the firing continued as usual from both sides. The Russians, having spent the night in repairing the batteries, were nearly in the same position as ourselves, and, unaided, or at least unassisted to the full extent we had reason to expect by the French, we were just able to hold our own during the day. Some smart affairs of skirmishers and sharp-shooters took place in front. Our riflemen annoy the Russian gunners greatly, and prevent the tirailleurs from showing near our batteries. On one occasion the Russian riflemen and our own men came close upon each other in a quarry before the town. Our men had exhausted all their ammunition; but as soon as they saw the Russians they seized the blocks of stone which were lying about, and opened a vigorous volley on the enemy. The latter either had empty pouches, or were so much surprised that they forgot to load, for they resorted to the same missiles. A short fight ensued, which ended in our favor, and the Russians retreated, pelted vigorously as long as the men could pursue them. The coolness of a young artillery officer named MAXWELL, who took some ammunition to the batteries through a tremendous fire along a road so exposed to the enemy's fire that it has been called "the Valley of Death," is highly spoken of on all sides. The blue jackets are delighted with Capt. PEEL, who animates the men by the exhibition of the best qualities of an officer, though his courage is sometimes marked by an excess that borders on rashness. When the Union Jack in the sailors' battery was shot away he seized the broken staff, and leaping up on the earthwork, waved the old bit of bunting again and again in a storm of shot, which fortunately left him untouched.

Our ammunition is running short, but supplies are expected every moment. Either from a want of cartridges or from the difficulty of getting powder down to the works our 12-gun battery was silent for some time. *The* Admiral (Sir E. LYONS,) on his little gray pony, is to be seen hovering about our lines indefatigably. To-day he rose out with Lord RAGLAN and his staff, and spent some time in examining the progress of our fire from a quarry in a hill overlooking the right attack. Two more 68-pounders were brought up to Captain GORDON's attack, and two more were ordered to be added to Captain CHAPMAN's attack last night, but they could not be got into position in time for the opening of the fire. We have to deplore the loss of Lieut.-Colonel ALEXANDER, R. E., a most energetic and indefatigable officer. On the death of Brigadier-General TYLDEN he succeeded to the command of the Engineers and the superintendence of the engineering operations, and when the works commenced before Sebastopol he devoted himself with such unrelenting zeal to his duties that he seriously injured his health. After the fatigues of a long day, he used to lie down in his clothes. Yesterday he complained of pains in his head; he retired to his tent as usual last night, and threw himself on his blanket with a leather stock on; an attack of apoplexy supervened, and ere morning he was no more. By his decease, Captain GORDON, R. E., than whom the service does not possess an abler, braver, or more devoted officer, succeeds to the command of the Royal Engineers, and his place in command of the left attack will be taken by Major TYLDEN, late Brigade-Major of Royal Engineers. Captain LOVELL succeeds to the post vacated by Major TYLDEN.

The smoke was so thick at intervals to-day that but little could be seen but its continual folds. The French fire slackened very much towards 1 o'clock, the enemy pitching shells right into their lines and enfilading part of their new works. The French fleet was said to be busy hammering about the forts, but as I did not see them I do not assert it to be a fact that they did so. Hour after hour one continuous boom of cannon was alone audible, and the smoke screened all else from view. At 3½ there was an explosion of powder in the tower opposite to our right attack. The Flagstaff Fort seemed much knocked about by the French. The Redan and Round Tower earthworks fire nearly as well as ever. As it was very desirable to destroy the ships anchored in the harbor below us, and to fire the dockyard buildings, our rockets were brought into play, and, though rather erratic in their flight, they did some mischief, though not so much as was expected. Wherever they fell the people could be seen flying up the streets when the smoke cleared. At 3 o'clock P. M., the town was on fire, but after the smoke had excited our hopes for sometime, it thinned away and went out altogether. At 3½ there was another explosion, but whether it occurred in the French or in the Russian lines I could not ascertain, as the whole of our left was covered with vapors of sulphur and "villainous saltpetre." As our seamen are rather prodigal of powder, and as our ammunition is not over abundant, they were again admonished to fire more carefully to-day, and our replies were much less frequent to the Russians than before, so that it almost seemed to one who did not know the truth that the enemy were overpowering our fire. They kept smartly at work from three guns in the Round Tower works, and from some four or five in the Redan, on our batteries. The Lancasters came out in force to-day. The men begin to understand them, and the true value of the arm is becoming apparent. There is a difficulty in ascertaining where the shot and shell from them strike, so great is the distance of range, but Mr. HOARE, R. N., speaks very highly of the gun under his charge, and I believe Colonel LAKE, R. A., has been enabled to send in a favorable report of the results. Our loss has been trifling. Yesterday, the 18th, the total of killed and wounded, as well as I can make it out, was as follows: Killed, 13; wounded, 45.

Lieut. SMITH, of the 95th, was slightly wounded in the trenches.

Some deserters came in from the enemy, and were forwarded to head quarters, where they were examined by the interpreters. They declared the town was in a very bad state, that sickness prevailed among the soldiery, and that there were great numbers of killed and wounded from our fire.

These men seemed glad at escaping, and their personal appearance was not nearly so good as that of the men who fought at the Alma. Admiral KORNILEFF is, they state, dead; he was wounded in the thigh, so severely while superintending the fire in the Round Tower battery that he had to undergo an amputation, from the effects of which he died. The Russians have suffered a severe loss in the death of this officer, whose name may be familiar to some readers in connection with the Sinope expedition.

OCT 20.—Two 68-pounders were mounted last night in our batteries, and the firing, which nearly ceased after dark, was renewed by daybreak. We are all getting tired of this continual "pound-pounding," which makes a great deal of noise, wastes much powder, and does very little damage. It is very hard to batter down earthworks. Most people about London have seen the Artillery butt at Woolwich. How long has it lasted our "heavy fire" of artillery? Then, again, the Russians have plenty of laborers. They easily repair at night what we destroy and damage during the day. It is difficult for us to do the same. Our men are worn out with fatigue; the daily service exhausts them, and the artillerymen cannot have more than five hours' rest in the twenty four. They are relieved every eight hours, but it takes them three hours to get down to their work and return from it to the camp. Our amateurs are quite disappointed and tired out. I fear so are people in England, but they must have patience. Rome was not built in a day, nor will Sebastopol be taken in a week. In fact, we have run away with the notion that it was a kind of pasteboard city, which would tumble down at the sound of our cannon as the walls of Jericho fell at the blast of Joshua's trumpet. The news that Sebastopol had fallen, which we received *via* England, has excited great indignation and ludicrous astonishment here. The whole army is enraged about it, as they feel the verity, whatever it may be and whenever it may be realized, must fall short of the effect of that splendid figment. They think, too, that the laurels of the Alma will be withered in the blaze of popular delight at the imaginary capture. In fact, people at home must know very little about us or our position. I was much amused at seeing in a recently-arrived journal a letter from an "Old Indian" on the manufacture of campaign bread *more Indico*, in which he advises us out here to use salt! milk! and butter! in the preparation of what must be most delicious food. Salt is a luxury which is rarely to be had unless in conjunction with porky fibre; and as to milk and butter, the very taste of them is forgotten. Lord RAGLAN was very glad to get a little cold pig and ration rum and water one night on our march here. However, the hardest lot of all is reserved for our poor horses. All hay rations for baggagers are rigidly refused; they only receive a few pounds of indifferent barley. There is not a blade of grass to be had—the whole of these plateaux and hills are covered with thistles only, and where the other covering of the earth goes I know not. The hay ration for a charger is restricted to six pounds daily. Under these circumstances horse-flesh is cheap, and friendly presents are being continually offered by one man to another of "a deuced good pony," which are seldom accepted.

When day broke this morning we saw the Russians actively engaged in throwing up new works at the rear of the Redan, to protect the ordnance stores and buildings. They were in readiness to open on us by the time we commenced fire, at 6 o'clock.

The Garden Battery is very troublesome to us and the French. The latter are pushing up zigzags and parallels close to the enemy's lines, and expect to be able to get their batteries to within 400 metres of the place. They are exposed to very heavy fire, and the Russians ply them with shell admirably. Every one is now talking of storming. We could have stormed with more chance of success when we first sat down before the place. Yes, we could, perhaps, but who was to know it? When we have reduced them to the state in which they were when we came up from Balaklava—*i. e.*, left Sebastopol minus the batteries, if we can—we shall only have done, it is said, what we could have done then, without going to all the labor of making our earth-works and trenches. However, I do not agree with this. No one could have calculated on the misfortunes of the French, and on the weakness of their attacks. The very work of silencing these Russian earth-works is productive of the best results, for by the time we have done so we shall have cowed the enemy, inflicted enormous loss on their troops, and have damaged the town and rendered it unfit for defence. So far, indeed, our shots anticipate our mission.

At 2:50 A. M., a fire broke out behind the Redan, caused by our rockets, shell, and red-hot shot. It looked very promising at one time, but died out towards sunset. From the column of smoke which rose it must have been considerable. At 3:15 P. M., a fire of less magnitude was visible to the left of the Redan, further in towards the centre of the town.

Lieutenant DAVIES, Grenadier Guards, received a severe wound in the right leg to-day while on duty in the trenches, and I regret to add that H. R. H. Prince EDWARD of Saxe Weimar, who is a universal favorite, and has behaved with the greatest gallantry throughout the campaign, was wounded a moment afterwards, close to the place where Lieutenant DAVIES had been. His wound is not at all serious, and need not cause the least anxiety to his friends. Our wounded officers are all getting on favorably. Our loss yesterday was 3 killed and 32 or 33 wounded.

Major YOUNG, R. A., was slightly wounded while in charge of his battery to-day.

I have just heard that the fires we saw to-day were most disastrous. We have unfortunately burnt the hospital, which, the deserters say, was full of wounded men from the Alma and from the batteries. We have also destroyed a small war steamer.

OCTOBER 21.—Any day is like another, and the scenes of yesterday are scarcely distinguishable from those of to-day. The enemy seemed more afraid of our Lancasters this morning, and we are told they are drawing over towards the French. The latter become more vigorous in their fire, and are doing marked damage on the left of their line. Their energy in working the new parallels is rapidly producing its results, and their works are creeping up hour after hour towards the enemy's walls. Sandbags have been placed on the top of most of the exposed public buildings, to prevent their taking fire. It is evident we must advance our works a little nearer. A trunnion was knocked off one of our new 68-pounders, and the gun rendered unserviceable in the right attack, where it was doing good service. The firing lasted on both sides, with short intermission, from sunset to sunrise. One's head aches with the repeated bursts of artillery. The Earl of SHAFTESBURY has come into Balaklava, with siege train and ordnance stores—just in time. The Russians slacken fire. There are only three guns from the Redan to-day worked vigorously. The Round Tower and Garden Battery are as strong as ever.

The enemy have got up a large gun to Inkermann, with which they pitch shot and shell into the camp of the Second Division merely to annoy them. They are still active and troublesome. There were two explosions—one in our own works, one in the Russians'—towards noon to-day.

OCTOBER 22.—Lord DUNKELLIN, Captain of the Coldstream Guards, and eldest son of the Marquis of CLANRICARDE, was taken prisoner this morning. He was out with a working party of his regiment, which had got a little out of their way, when a number of men were observed through the dawning light in the ravine in front of them. "There are the Russians," exclaimed one of the men. "Nonsense; they're our fellows," said his lordship, and off he went towards them, asking in a high tone, as he got near, "Who is in command of this party?" His men saw him no more. As they were unarmed, they retreated rapidly, but there is no fear of his lordship's safety, for the Russians fired no shot, and merely closed round and seized him ere he could get away. No doubt he will be well taken care of, and forwarded probably to St. Petersburg, for his father was Ambassador at the Court of the Czar, and is said to have once enjoyed his friendship.

The Russians opened a very heavy cannonade on us this morning; they have always done so on Sundays. Divine service was performed with a continued bass of cannon rolling through the responses and liturgy. The French are terribly cut up by the Garden Battery—more so, however, by their misfortune of last night. The Russians made a stealthy sortie towards morning, and advanced close to the French pickets. When challenged, they replied "Inglis, Inglis," which passed muster with our allies as *bona fide* English, they say; and before they knew where they were, the Russians had charged them, got into their batteries, and spiked five mortars. They were speedily repulsed; but this misadventure has mortified our brave allies exceedingly. The night before they fired on a party of men who used the same *passe partout*, and they turned out to be Russians. They were too confiding the second time. We are all liable to mistakes. There was a great alarm the other evening. Eleven battalions of Russians crossed the Tchernaya, and deployed towards Balaklava, but we were quite satisfied to leave Sir COLIN CAMPBELL to dispose of them. However, at night musketry and cannon opened along the rear, and woke us all up. It turned out that the officer of marines on the heights had been told he always would have a clear space left for his guns to play upon in case of attack, and that some newly-arrived Turks, unaware of this arrangement, had trenched on his space, with lanterns in their hands, whereupon, knowing the Russians were about, he blazed away at the poor "Bono Johnnies," all of whom he fortunately missed.

The French General sent over to-day to ask for assistance in silencing a new battery which tormented them excessively. We gladly rendered it, and silenced the battery ere sunset.

No incident of consequence occurred to-day. It was all filled up with volleys of artillery. A Pole and some Russians deserted last night. They tell us that the enemy have lost 3,000 killed and wounded, that the town is in a frightful state—the shops closed, the merchants fled, the goods placed underneath in the cellars, and that the "pointed" balls and shells (Lancasters) do frightful mischief. There are no longer *volunteers* to work the guns, as there were at first. The men have now to be forced to the batteries. Many poor women and children have lost their lives in this terrible cannonade. It seems incredible that the Russian authorities should have let them stay in the town when they could have easily sent them across by the bridge of boats to the north side. Provisions still continue plenty and water is abundant in the town.

There are now eighteen deserters at head-quarters including a woman, who was taken as she was going down to visit a cousin (sweetheart,) in the trenches. Two deserters leaped in through our embrasures. They were Circassian prisoners. They reported that all the *forçats* were let loose, as the Russians required the prisons for hospitals.

There was a fire in the town at 1 o'clock A. M. morning; it was speedily extinguished. The explosions in the Round Tower yesterday must have done some mischief. That which took place behind our 12-gun battery was harmless.

OCTOBER 24.—The return of the killed and wounded for the 22d of the month, during the greater part of which a heavy fire was directed on our trenches and battery attacks right and left, shows the excellent cover of our works and their great solidity. We only lost one man killed in the Light Division, and two men in the siege train; of wounded we had one in the First Division, two in the Second Division, two in the Third Division, six in the Fourth Division, five in the Light Division, and ten in the Siege Train. Lieutenant BROWN (of the 44th Regiment) lost his leg yesterday. Captain CHILDERS, R. A., was killed in his battery. He had just ordered a gun to be fired, and had run to look through an embrasure to watch the effect of the ball, when a shot came in and struck off his head. Mr. YOUNG, of the Artillery, who died on the 21st of cholera, was brother of Sir W. YOUNG, killed at the Alma, and was not the major of the same name in command of a company of artillery in the left attack. The latter was slightly wounded a couple of days ago, but is now quite well. The request made to us by the French that we would direct our fire on the Barrack Battery, which annoyed them excessively, was so well attended to that ere evening we had knocked it to pieces and silenced it. The Garden Battery is little better.

THE BRITISH CAVALRY.

GALLANT BUT DISASTROUS CAVALRY CHARGE.

A THRILLING DESCRIPTION.

From the London Times' Correspondent.

HEIGHTS BEFORE SEBASTOPOL, Wednesday, Oct. 25.

If the exhibition of the most brilliant valor, of the excess of courage, and of a daring which would have reflected lustre on the best days of chivalry can afford full consolation for the disaster of to-day, we can have no reason to regret the melancholy loss which we sustained in a contest with a savage and barbarian enemy.

I shall proceed to describe, to the best of my power, what occurred under my own eyes, and to state the facts which I have heard from men whose veracity is unimpeachable, reserving to myself the exercise of the right of private judgment in making public and in suppressing the details of what occurred on this memorable day. Before I proceed to my narrative, I must premise that a certain feeling existed in some quarters that our cavalry had not been properly handled since they landed in the Crimea, and that they had lost golden opportunities from the indecision and excessive caution of their leaders. It was said that our cavalry ought to have been manœuvred at Bouljanak in one way or in another, according to the fancy of the critic. It was affirmed, too, that the light cavalry were utterly useless in the performance of one of their most important duties—the collection of supplies for the army—that they were "above their business, and too fine gentlemen for their work;" that our horse should have pushed on after the flying enemy after the battle of the Alma, to their utter confusion, and with the certainty of taking many guns and prisoners; and, above all, that all Mackenzie's Farm first, and at the gorge near Inkermann subsequently, they had been improperly restrained from charging and had failed in gaining great successes, which would have entitled them to a full share of the laurels of the campaign, solely owing to the timidity of the officer in command. The existence of this feeling was known to many of our cavalry, and they were indignant and exasperated that the faintest shade of suspicion should rest on any of their corps. With the justice of these aspersions, they seemed to think they had nothing to do, and perhaps the prominent thought in their minds was that they would give such an example of courage to the world, if the chance offered itself, as would shame their detractors forever.

It will be remembered that in a letter sent by last mail from this, it was mentioned that 11 battalions of Russian infantry had crossed the Tchernaya, and that they threatened the rear of our position and our communication with Balaklava. Their bands could be heard playing at night by the travelers along the Balaklava road to the camp, but they "showed" but little during the day, and kept up among the gorges and mountain passes through which the roads to Inkermann, Simpheropol, and the southeast of the Crimea wind towards the interior. It will be recollected also that the position we occupied in reference to Balaklava was supposed by most people to be very strong—even impregnable. Our lines were formed by natural mountain slopes in the rear, along which the French had made very formidable entrenchments. Below those entrenchments, and very nearly in a right line across the valley beneath, are four conical hillocks, one rising above the other as they recede from our lines; the furthest, which joins the chain of mountains opposite to our ridges being named Canrobert's Hill, from the meeting there of that General with Lord RAGLAN after the march to Balaklava. On the top of each of these hills the Turks had thrown up earthen redoubts, defended by 250 men each, and armed with two or three guns—some heavy ship guns—lent by us to them, with one artilleryman in each redoubt to look after them. These hills cross the valley of Balaklava at the distance of about 2½ miles from the town. Supposing the spectator, then, to take his stand on one of the heights forming the rear of our camp before Sebastopol, he would see the town of Balaklava, with its scanty shipping, its narrow strip of water, and its old forts on his right hand; immediately below he would behold the valley and a plain of coarse meadow land, occupied by our cavalry tents, and stretching from the base of the ridge on which he stood to the foot of the formidable heights at the other side; he would see the French trenches lined with Zouaves a few feet beneath, and distant from him, on the slope of the hill; a Turkish redoubt lower down, then another in the valley, then, in a line with it, some angular earthworks, then, in succession, the other two redoubts up to Canrobert's Hill. At the distance of two or two and a half miles across the valley, there is an abrupt rocky mountain range of most irregular and picturesque formation, covered with scanty brushwood here and there, or rising into barren pinnacles and *plateaux* of rock. In outline and appearance this portion of the landscape is wonderfully like the Trosachs. A patch of blue sea is caught in between the overhanging cliffs of Balaklava as they close in the entrance to the harbor on the right. The camp of the Marines, pitched on the hill sides more than 1,000 feet above the level of the sea, is opposite to you as your back is turned to Sebastopol and your right side towards Balaklava. On the road leading up the valley, close to the entrance of the town and beneath these hills, is the encampment of the 93d Highlanders.

The cavalry lines are nearer to you below, and are some way in advance of the Highlanders, but nearer to the town than the Turkish redoubts. The valley is crossed here and there by small waves of land. On your left the hills and rocky mountain ranges gradually close in toward the course of the Tchernaya, till, at three or four miles' distance from Balaklava, the valley is swallowed up in a mountain gorge and deep ravines, above which rise tiers after tiers of desolate whitish rock, garnished now and then by bits of scanty herbage, and spreading away toward the east and south, where they attain the Alpine dimensions of the Tschatir Dagh. It is very easy for an enemy at the Balbek, or in command of the road of Mackenzie's Farm, Inkermann, Simpheropol, or Bakshiserai, to debouch through these gorges at any time, upon this plain from the neck of the valley, or to march from Sebastopol by the Tchernaya, and to advance along it towards Balaklava, till checked by the Turkish redoubts on the southern side, or by the fire from the French works on the northern side, *i. e.*, the side which, in relation to the valley to Balaklava, forms the rear of our position. It was evident enough that MENSCHIKOFF and GORTSCHAKOFF had been feeling their way along this route for several days past, and very probably at night the Cossacks had crept up close to our pickets, which are not always as watchful as might be desired, and had observed the weakness of a position far too extended for our army to defend, and occupied by their despised enemy, the Turks. I say "despised," because we hear from prisoners and from other sources, that, notwithstanding all the drubbings received on the Danube from the Osmanli, the Russians have the most ineffable contempt for the champions of the Crescent.

At half-past 7 o'clock this morning an orderly came galloping into the head-quarters camp from Balaklava, with the news that at dawn a strong corps of Russian horse, supported by guns and battalions of infantry, had marched into the valley, and had already nearly dispossessed the Turks of the redoubt No 1, (that on Canrobert's Hill, which is farthest from our lines,) and that they were opening fire on the redoubts Nos. 2, 3 and 4, which would speedily be in their hands unless the Turks offered a stouter resistance than they had done already.

Orders were dispatched to Sir GEORGE CATHCART and to H. R. H. the Duke of Cambridge, to put their respective divisions, the 4th and the 1st, in motion for the scene of action, and intelligence of the advance of the Russians was also furnished to Gen. CANROBERT. Immediately on receipt of the news the General commanded General BOSQUET to get the Third Division under arms, and sent a strong body of artillery and some 200 Chasseurs d'Afrique to assist us in holding the valley. Sir COLIN CAMPBELL, who was in command of Balaklava, had drawn up the 93d Highlanders, a little in front of the road to the town, at the first news of the advance of the enemy. The marines got under arms; the seamen's batteries and marines' batteries, on the heights close to the town, were manned, and the French artillerymen and the Zouaves prepared for action along their lines. Lord LUCAN's little camp was the scene of great excitement. The men had not had time to water their horses; they had not broken their fast from the evening of the day before, and had barely saddled at the first blast of the trumpet, when they were drawn up on the slope behind the redoubts in front of their camp to operate on the enemy's squadrons. It was soon evident that no reliance was to be placed on the Turkish infantry or artillerymen. All the stories we had heard about their bravery behind stone walls and earthworks proved how differently the same or similar people fight under different circumstances. When the Russians advanced the Turks fired a few rounds at them, got frightened at the distance of their supports in the rear, looked round, received a few shots and shell, and then "bolted," and fled with an agility quite at variance with commonplace notions of Oriental deportment on the battle-field. But Turks on the Danube are very different beings from Turks in the Crimea, as it appears that the Russians of Sebastopol are not at all like the Russians of Silistria.

Soon after 8 o'clock Lord RAGLAN and his staff turned out and cantered towards the rear of our position. The booming of artillery, the spattering roll of musketry, were heard rising from the valley, drowning the roar of the siege guns in front before Sebastopol. As I rode in the direction of the firing over the thistles and large stones which cover the undulating plain that stretches away towards Balaklava, on a level with the summit of the ridges above it, I observed a French light infantry regiment (the 27th, I think,) advancing with admirable care and celerity from our right towards the ridge near the telegraph house, which was already lined by companies of French infantry, while mounted officers scampered along its broken outline in every direction.

General BOSQUET, a stout soldierlike-looking man, who reminds one of the old *genre* of French generals as depicted at Versailles, followed, with his staff and a small escort of Hussars, at a gallop. Faint white clouds rose here and there above the hill from the cannonade below. Never did the painter's eye rest on a more beautiful scene than I beheld from the ridge. The fleecy vapors still hung around the mountain tops, and mingled with the ascending volumes of smoke; the patch of sea sparkled freshly in the rays of the morning sun, but its light was eclipsed by the flashes which gleamed from the masses of armed men below.

Looking to the left towards the gorge, we beheld six compact masses of Russian infantry, which had just debouched from the mountain passes near Tcharnaya, and were slowly advancing with solemn stateliness up the valley. Immediately in in their front was a regular line of artillery of at least 20 pieces strong. Two batteries of light guns were already a mile in advance of them, and were playing with energy on the redoubts, from which feeble puffs of smoke came at long intervals. Behind these guns, in front of the infantry, were enormous bodies of cavalry. They were in six compact squares, three on each flank, moving down *en echelon* towards us, and the valley was lit up with the blaze of their sabres and lance points and gay accoutrements. In their front, and extending along the intervals between each battery, were clouds of mounted skirmishers, wheeling and whirling in the front of their march like Autumn leaves tossed by the wind. The Zouaves close to us were lying like tigers at the spring, with ready rifles in hand hidden chin deep by the earthworks which run along the line of these ridges on our rear, but the quick-eyed Russians were manœuvring on the other side of the valley, and did not expose their columns to attack. Below the Zouaves we could see the Turkish gunners in the redoubts, all in confusion as the shells burst over them. Just as I came up the Russians had carried No 1 redoubt, the farthest and most elevated of all, and their horsemen were chasing the Turks across the interval which lay between it and redoubt No. 2. At that moment the cavalry under Lord LUCAN, were formed in glittering masses—the Light Brigade, under Lord CARDIGAN, in advance; the Heavy Brigade, under Brigadier-General SCARLETT, in reserve. They were drawn up just in front of their encampment, and were concealed from the view of the enemy by a slight "wave" in the plain. Considerably to the rear of their right, the 93d Highlanders were drawn up in line, in front of the approach to Balaklava. Above and behind them, on the heights, the marines were visible through the glass, drawn up under arms, and the gunners could be seen ready in the earthworks, in which were placed the heavy ships' guns. The 93d had originally been advanced somewhat more into the plain, but the instant the Russians got possession of the first redoubt they opened fire on them from our own guns, which inflicted some injury, and Sir COLIN CAMPBELL "retired" his men to a better position. Meantime the enemy advanced his cavalry rapidly. To our inexpressible disgust we saw the Turks in redoubt No. 2 fly at their approach. They ran in scattered groups across towards redoubt No. 3, and towards Balaklava, but the horse-hoof of the Cossack was too quick for them, and sword and lance were busily plied among the retreating herd. The yells of the pursuers and pursued were plainly audible. As the Lancers and Light Cavalry of the Russians advanced, they gathered up their skirmishers with great speed and in excellent order—the shifting trails of men, which played all over the valley like moonlight on the water, contracted, gathered up, and the little *peloton* in a few moments became a solid column. Then up came their guns, in rushed their gunners to the abandoned redoubt, and the guns of No. 2 redoubt soon played with deadly effect upon the dispirited defenders of No. 3 redoubt. Two or three shots in return from the earthworks, and all is silent. The Turks swarm over the earthworks, and run in confusion towards the town, firing their muskets at the enemy as they ran. Again the solid column of cavalry opens like a fan, and resolves itself into a "long spray" of skirmishers. It laps the flying Turks, steel flashes in the air, and down go the poor Moslem quivering on the plain, split through fez and musket-guard to the chin and breast belt. There is no support for them. It is evident the Russians have been too quick for us. The Turks have been too quick also, for they have not held their redoubts long enough to enable us to bring them help. In vain the naval guns on the heights fire on the Russian cavalry; the distance is too great for shot or shell to reach. In vain the Turkish gunners in the earthen batteries which are placed along the French intrenchments strive to protect their flying countrymen; their shot fly wide and short of the swarming masses. The Turks betake themselves towards the Highlanders, where they check their flight and form into companies on the flanks of the Highlanders.

As the Russian cavalry on the left of their line crown the hill, across the valley they perceive the Highlanders drawn up at the distance of some half mile, calmly waiting their approach. They halt, and squadron after squadron flies up from the rear, till they have a body of some 1,500 men along the ridge—lancers, dragoons and hussars. Then they move *en echelon* in two bodies, with another in reserve. The cavalry, who have been pursuing the Turks on the right, are coming up to the ridge beneath us, which conceals our cavalry from view. The heavy brigade in advance is drawn up in two columns. The first column consists of the Scots Greys and of their old companions in glory, the Enniskillens; the second, of the 4th Royal Irish, of the 5th Dragoon Guards, and of the 1st Royal Dragoons. The light cavalry brigade is on their left, in two divisions also. The silence is oppressive; between the cannon bursts, one can hear the champing of bits and the clink of sabres in the valley below. The Russians on their left drew breath for a moment, and then, in one grand line, dashed at the Highlanders. The ground flies beneath their horses' feet—gathering speed at every stride, they dash on toward that thin red streak, topped with a line of steel. The Turks fire a volley at 800 yards, and run. As the Russians come within 600 yards, down goes that line of steel in front, and out rings a rolling volley of Minié musketry. The Russians are not checked, but still sweep onwards with the whole force of horse and man, through the smoke, here and there knocked over by the shot of our batteries above. With breathless suspense, every one waits the bursting of the wave upon the line of Gaelic rock; but ere they came within 150 yards another deadly volley flashes from the leveled rifle, and carries death and terror into the Russians. They wheel about, open files right and left, and fly back faster than they came. "Bravo Highlanders! well done," shouted the excited spectators; but events thicken. The Highlanders and their splendid front are soon forgotten; men scarcely have a moment to think of this fact, that the 93d never altered their formation to receive that tide of horsemen. "No," said Sir COLIN CAMPBELL, "I did not think it worth while to form them even four deep!" the ordinary British line, two deep, was quite sufficient to repel the attack of these Muscovite chevaliers. Our eyes were, however, turned in a moment on our own cavalry. We saw Brigadier-General SCARLETT ride alon[g]

New-York Daily Times.

VOL. VI......NO. 1705. NEW-YORK, SATURDAY, MARCH 7, 1857. PRICE TWO CENTS.

LATEST INTELLIGENCE.

By Telegraph to the New-York Daily Times.

Magnetic Telegraph Co.'s Offices—4 Hanover-st., and 161 Broadway.

IMPORTANT FROM WASHINGTON.

Decision of the Supreme Court in the Dred Scott Case.

The Ordinance of 1787 and the Missouri Compromise Declared Unconstitutional.

MR. BUCHANAN'S CABINET.

WASHINGTON, Friday, March 6.

The opinion of the Supreme Court in the Dred Scott case was delivered by Chief Justice Taney. It was a full and elaborate statement of the views of the Court. They have decided the following important points:

First—Negroes, whether slaves or free, that is, men of the African race, are not citizens of the United States by the Constitution.

Second—The Ordinance of 1787 had no independent constitutional force or legal effect subsequently to the adoption of the Constitution, and could not operate of itself to confer freedom or citizenship within the Northwest Territory on negroes not citizens by the Constitution.

Third—The provisions of the Act of 1820, commonly called the Missouri Compromise, in so far as it undertook to exclude negro slavery from, and communicate freedom and citizenship to, negroes in the northern part of the Louisiana cession, was a Legislative act exceeding the powers of Congress, and VOID, and of no legal effect to that end.

In deciding these main points, the Supreme Court determined the following incidental points:

First—The expression "territory and other property" of the Union, in the Constitution, applies "in terms" only to such territory as the Union possessed at the time of the adoption of the Constitution.

Second—The rights of citizens of the United States emigrating into any Federal territory, and the power of the Federal Government there depend on the general provisions of the Constitution, which defines in this, as in all other respects, the powers of Congress.

Third—As Congress does not possess power itself to make enactments relative to the persons or property of citizens of the United States, in a Federal Territory, other than such as the Constitution confers, so it cannot constitutionally delegate any such powers to a Territorial Government, organized by it under the Constitution.

Fourth—The legal condition of a slave in the State of Missouri is not affected by the temporary sojourn of such slave in any other State, but on his return his condition still depends on the laws of Missouri.

As the plaintiff was not a citizen of Missouri, he, therefore, could not sue in the Courts of the United States. The suit must be dismissed for want of jurisdiction.

The delivery of this opinion occupied about three hours, and was listened to with profound attention by a crowded Court-room. Among the auditors were gentlemen of eminent legal ability, and a due proportion of ladies.

Judge Nelson stated the merits of the case. The question was whether or not the removal of Scott from Missouri with his master to Illinois, with a view to temporary residence there, worked his emancipation. He maintained that the question depended wholly on the law of Missouri; and for that reason the judgment of the Court below should be affirmed.

Judge Catron believed the Supreme Court has jurisdiction to decide the merits of the case. He argued that Congress could not do directly what it could not do indirectly. If it could exclude one species of property, it could exclude another. With regard to the Territories ceded, Congress could govern them only with the restrictions of the States which ceded them; and the Missouri act of 1820 violated the leading features of the Constitution, and was therefore void. He concurred with his brother Judges, that Scott is a slave, and was so when this suit was brought.

Several other Judges are to deliver their views tomorrow.

The following is Mr. Buchanan's Cabinet, as confirmed by the Senate to-day:

Secretary of State—General Cass.
Secretary of the Treasury—Hon. Howell Cobb.
Secretary of War—Hon. John B. Floyd.
Secretary of the Navy—Hon. Isaac Toucey.
Secretary of the Interior—Hon. Jacob Thompson.
Attorney-General—Judge Black, of Pennsylvania.
Postmaster-General—Hon. A. V. Brown.

Captain Pettigrew, of the U. S. Army, is dead.

Extra Session of the United States Senate.

WASHINGTON, Friday, March 6.

Mr. Seward presented the petition of certain British subjects, setting forth that as Lord Palmerston's act in surrendering the maritime rights of that Government is an act of high treason, those rights will revert to the British crown and nation as soon as the guilty party shall be impeached for that crime: that the petitioners have heard that the President of the United States is about proposing the terms on which the declaration of Paris will be agreed to by the United States; that such an act would be a connivance with Lord Palmerston in his attempt to possess himself of an arbitrary power foreign to the British Constitution and to the Constitution of the United States; and pray Congress to refuse their sanction to any convention with Great Britain founded on the illegal, treasonable and invalid declaration at Paris.

On motion of Mr. Seward the petition was laid on the table.

Mr. Bigler presented the protest of forty-four members of the House of Representatives, and the protest of fifteen members of the Senate of Pennsylvania, against the proceedings under which Mr. Simon Cameron claims to represent that State in the Senate.

Mr. Yulee presented the credentials of Mr. Mallory, elected Senator from Florida for six years from the 4th of March.

Mr. Mason was appointed to fill the vacancy in the Board of Regents of the Smithsonian Institution.

The Senate then went into Executive session, and afterwards adjourned till Monday.

The Inauguration Pageant—The Inaugural Address—Mr. Buchanan's Policy, &c.

Correspondence of the New-York Daily Times.

WASHINGTON, Thursday, March 5, 1857.

The event to which so many anxious thoughts were directed, and which, since November last, has engrossed so much attention, belongs now to history. At noon yesterday the Executive Administration of the Government passed quietly from the hands of Franklin Pierce into those of James Buchanan, and the latter is now established as President at the White House. The inauguration pageant was the most imposing in numbers, and the most brilliant in display, ever witnessed here. Facility of transportation from all the principal cities, North, South, East, and West, offered inducements which did not exist on any former occasion, and were gladly appropriated for a sort of national holiday at the Capital. The day itself was genial and bright, inviting everybody to participate in the spectacle, and a cheerful sun lighted up the scene with unusual splendor, until about the hour when the inaugural was delivered, when clouds portentously lowered over the head of the new President and the assembled thousands. Various military companies from distant points enlivened the turn-out, and relieved the heaviness of the black-coated throng.

In the evening, the inauguration ball attracted several thousands of both sexes, and is admitted to have been, in arrangement, style, and appointment, the most successful affair of the kind ever attempted. Some idea of the scale upon which it was conducted, may be imagined from the fact that the cost reached about $15,000. Mr. Buchanan was present for a couple of hours, but it was observed that his usual gracious manner was evidently forced, rather than natural, owing to the debilitating effects of an epidemic which has prostrated most of the guests of the National Hotel. This trouble has been aggravated too by mental perplexities and much physical exertion all which have conspired to shake the remaining energies of a frame already tried by age and its insidious infirmities.

Little if any impression has been made by the Inaugural. No paper of the sort has ever been less discussed in political circles. As an intellectual production, it has no claims to superiority, and is below the standard of many of the papers prepared by Mr. Buchanan when Secretary of State, and even more recently as Minister to England. In point of policy, its chief effort seems to be the conciliation of every shade of opinion; and the careful reader cannot fail to observe that while Squatter sovereignty is condemned in one breath, it is approved in another, and that the same rule of expediency is applied to every other embarrassing or controverted question. Mr. Buchanan wisely relieves himself from a serious cause of embarrassment by adopting the one-term principle at the start, by which he will be enabled to act with more independence of party shackles, and to feel more personal ease in administering the Government. The temptation of a second term, and the power which that inclination gave to flatterers and time-servers, were the active causes which led to the humiliating downfall of the late incumbent. The Union-saving sentiments uttered by Mr. Buchanan will, doubtless, be echoed by that class of patriots who rely more upon the shouts over empty phrases than they do on the principles implanted in the Constitution, and by which alone the Union can be maintained in its integrity and strength.

It is very well known that the Message as originally prepared, did not meet the concurrence of Gen. Cass, or the new editor of the *Union*, when submitted to their inspection on Tuesday night; and but for alterations which were here required and made at the last hour, both would probably have retired from the positions assigned to them. With all his love of office, Gen. Cass was tenacious of his Squatter Sovereign bantling, and even went so far as to threaten to throw up the seals which glittered so invitingly before his eyes. This little episode may serve to explain the "individual" opinion which Mr. Buchanan expresses, as to the point of time when the people of a Territory may undertake to decide upon the subject of Slavery.

Until Gen. Cass gets fully established as Secretary-of-State, there will be no positive indication as to his Assistant Secretary. Gen. Thomas, the present incumbent, whom Mr. Marcy advanced from personal partiality, is no favorite with Mr. Buchanan. The public will be greatly accommodated by any change that may be made in the Assistant Secretaryship of the Treasury Department, as it has been Mr. Washington's misfortune to acquire a general unpopularity with all parties, and with the people of the District, to whom he is peculiarly obnoxious, for some reason or other.

A great deal is said in reference to Mr. Buchanan's policy, as to the distribution of the patronage, but his mind is quite as liable to change in this respect as it did in regard to the principle of forming the Cabinet; and even more so, from the vast personal influences that will be brought to bear upon him in behalf of those who are in possession. OBSERVER.

The Inauguration Ball—Who were There and What was Done.

SPECIAL REPORT FOR THE NEW-YORK DAILY TIMES.

WASHINGTON, Thursday, March 5, 1857.

THE PREPARATIONS.

To the ladies who attend the quadrennial festival which marks the inauguration of a President, the Inauguration Ball is the great feature of the occasion, and it is certainly a most appropriate *finale*. Economical papas and departmental beaux thought that an X for a ticket, an X for a boquet, and an X for a carriage, was X-cessively X-travagant, and X-pensive, yet no X-cuse would be received, and they were forced to make the X-traordinary X-penditure. The ladies' tickets were huge enameled cards, bearing an engraved portrait of President Buchanan, surmounted by an arch, which rests upon emblematical pillars and a pedestal, completing the framework. These tickets were distributed with lavish profusion, and will probably be cherished by many a fair possessor as a *souvenir* of an occasion to be marked with a white-stone.

Provoking was it to several who had expected to be present, that "Old Winter lingering in the lap of Spring," so deranged the express and baggage-arrangements between your City and this metropolis, that their wardrobes remained in transit, somewhere on the road. Like the lady of whom we read in a recent Harper's *Journal of Civilization*, they had, of course, "nothing to wear" in the trunks which had possession of a good share of their rooms, and so remained at home. Among the brilliant luminaries of fashion who were thus embargoed was Mrs. W*****l, of New-York—she arrived in good season, but her baggage, including a *ravissante costume de bal* made for the occasion was detained on the way. Is there no torture that can be inflicted upon those baggage-masters?

THE PAVILION.

As there is no hall in the "city of magnificent distances" large enough to contain more than 600 people, the managers were forced to erect a building expressly for the ball. It was, accordingly, put up on Judiciary-square, extending nearly 300 feet from the City Hall, with which it was connected at one end. Without, it resembled a huge railroad-contractor's shanty, as it was to be used, only for this occasion and then demolished—so architectural beauty was not deemed requisite. But within, it presented a fine appearance. The walls were lined with alternate stripes of "red, white and blue" glazed cambric, with national emblems at intervals on the walls. A seat ran around the sides, on a raised platform, and at the end next the City Hall, the entrance door opened on a wide gallery, from which a broad flight of stairs led down into the hall. The ceiling was of white cloth, studded with golden stairs, which twinkled as they were moved in unison with the measure of the dancers below, and reflected the blaze of light from large gas chandeliers. These chandeliers were an improvement on the wax-dropping candle sconces of the "Rough and Ready" Inauguration Ball in 1849.

The mayor's office, in the City Hall was fitted up for the reception of the President, and some half-a-dozen other rooms were used by the committees. The spacious hall of the Common Council was used as the ladies' dressing-room, excellent accommodations for hats and coats were provided in the basement, and up in the second story was a room where large punch-bowls and a long array of decanters showed that "total abstinence" was not the order of the night.

THE ARRIVALS.

Before ten o'clock the guests began to arrive, and so delightful was the clear, moon-light evening, that many who resided near the City Hall preferred to walk there. On they came, and soon a gay and brilliant throng emerged from the dressing rooms, and entered the hall. The proportion of ladies was marked, for although in New England it does not appear strange to see the fair sex predominate, it is a novelty here. Moralists naughtily commented on the fact that while every gentleman present, (even "the press,") had to pay ten dollars for a ticket, the ladies came without charge!

THE MUSIC.

Hopes had been entertained by the lovers of sweet sounds that the managers would be able to secure the fine band of Dodworth or Gilmore, but they filled their orchestra with an impromptu conglomeration of musicians from the Navy-Yard, Baltimore and elsewhere, under the leadership of Mr. Weber. Considering the material, and the little time for rehearsals, he did well with them. Here is the

PROGRAMME.

1. Inauguration March.....Nutzer.
2. Quadrille, Charivari.....Strauss.
3. Quadrille, Stradella.....Strauss.
4. Waltz, Epionen Tanze.....Strauss.
5. Quadrille, My Mary Ann.....Weber.
6. Quadrille, Schafer.....Labitzky.
7. Polka, Redowa, Minna Haha.....Wagner.
8. Quadrille, Wiena Carnivals.....Strauss.
9. Quadrille, Constitution.....Bilse.
10. Waltz and Polka, Venus Riegen.....Gung'l.
11. Quadrille, Postillion.....Strauss.
12. Quadrille, Medley.....Weber.
13. Polka, Redowa and Scottische.....Bergman
14. Quadrille, (from opera Teufels Antheil)..Strauss.
15. Quadrille, Amorettan.....Strauss.
16. Waltz, Dreams on the Ocean.....Gung'l.
17. Quadrille, Concert Souvenir.....Strauss.
18. Quadrille, Almacks.....Strauss.
19. Polka, Redowa, Little Blossom.....Weber.
20. Quadrille, Sarah.....Strauss.
21. Quadrille, Louisen.....Strauss.
22. Waltz and Polka.....
23. Quadrille, Medley.....Weber.
24. Quadrille, Volsgarten.....Strauss.
25. Virginia Reel.

THE PRESIDENT'S ARRIVAL.

About eleven o'clock Mr. Buchanan arrived, accompanied by his niece, Miss Lane, who is to preside at the White House. He was received by Mayor Magruder, who very discreetly spared him the infliction of a speech, and as he descended the stairway from the gallery, the band announced his arrival by striking up "Hail to the Chief." The President looked well, although a shade of anxious thought appeared at times to cross his fine countenance. He wore, of course, the Lancaster-made suit, of which, with its hidden stitching, we have all heard. Miss Lane is rather below the medium height, but has a fine figure, and is of that blonde Saxon type of beauty so familiar to Christendom since the multiplication of portraits of Queen Victoria. She wore a white dress trimmed with artificial flowers similar to those which ornamented her hair, and clasping her throat was a necklace of many strands of seed pearls. She was escorted by Senator Jones, and behind her, in full uniform, walked the veteran General Jessup.

THE SCENE.

The pageant presented to the view of those in the gallery, as the President moved along the hall, was equal in magnificence to that witnessed at any European Court. The mass of humanity, "fair women and brave men," diplomatists, naval and military officers, opened to the right and left like the waves of the Red Sea, and reunited again as the President and his suite passed on, having saluted him with bow or curtesy. It was a rare scene to witness, and when, after having traversed the hall, the President received introductions to almost all present, there was no pushing or crowding. His presentations and conversations were of that unconstrained character which distinguishes refined society, Mr. Buchanan enlisting the good feeling of the ladies by his courteous demeanor and by his varied conversational powers.

THE NOTABLE GUESTS.

Mr. Breckinridge, the Vice-President, has many warm friends in Washington, who pressed around him to offer their congratulations. Ex-President Pierce was detained at home (he is at Mr. Marcy's) by the indisposition of his estimable lady, and the only representative of his Administration was his Private Secretary, Sidney Webster, Esq., who escorted the beautiful Miss F**e, whose father's term of Senatorial office also expired yesterday. Elegantly dressed in white, trimmed with flowers, and with a cluster of flowers trailing from her classically formed head, she was decidedly the most showy among the fair demoiselles present.

La Reine du Bal was Mrs. D*****s, who was dressed in bridal white, and commanded admiration. Senator Douglas escorted his niece, Miss G*****s, who is as fascinating as she is graceful. Senators Cameron and Dixon, with their ladies, were the only politically Northern members of the upper-house present, but there was no lack of those from sunnier climes, with their ladies, among whom Mrs. S*****l, who is somewhat an oracle in political circles, was conspicuous. Mrs. Senator T******n, of New-Jersey, in white with silver trimmings, is always admired.

Fain would we chronicle the New-York belles who were escorted by Mr. Crocker, the elegant costumes of the ladies of the diplomatic corps, among whom Madame de Sartiges is so prominent, and the other fair ones, many of whom mocked one's liveliest conceptions of Juno's regal beauty, and excited a regret that Phidias could not have immortalized them in marble. But as this report is to be sent by the early mails, we must pass them by—those who would have basked in the sunlight of their smiles and admired their toilettes, should have attended in person.

THE SUPPER.

A supper-room had been erected parallel with the large saloon, with which it communicated by several doors. Along one side of this room, opposite the entrances, was a buffet-table, nearly two hundred and fifty feet in length, behind which was an active body of waiters. The caterer was Monsieur Gautier, (the Delmonico of Washington,) who added to his high reputation by the gastronomic delicacies liberally provided. Prominent in the centre of the table, and visible from all parts of the room, towered a daintily decorated tower of confectionery, surmounted by a miniature American flag, bearing the National arms, and flanked by two banners, one inscribed with the name of the President, the other with that of the Vice-President. Lower down waved thirty-one flags, each one bearing the arms of a State. The designs for this exquisite and appropriate ornament were furnished by one of the first artists in the city—M. Bessau.

BILL OF FARE.
Paté Truffle.
Saddles of Venison and of Mutton.
Boar's Head, stuffed and decorated.
Boned and roasted Turkeys.
Spiced Rounds of Beef.
Filets de Beuf en Belle Vue.
Boned and Roasted Pheasants.
Tongues and Hams, decorated.
Aspic de Volaille.
Lobster, Chicken and Russian Salad.
Terrapins and Oysters.
Cream and Water Ices, in fancy moulds.
Marrons Glacés.
Charlotte Russe.
Meringues, Plombières, Bavaroises.
Jellies and Puddings.
Fancy Cakes, Preserved Fruits, Confectionery.
Roman Punch, Apple Toddy.
Wines, Liquors and Cordials.

An idea of the *quantity* provided of these delicacies may be formed from the fact that Monsieur Gautier used five hundred gallons of oysters, eight hundred chickens, one hundred gallons of ice-cream, one hundred pounds of bon-bons, &c.

Mr. Buchanan and suite were first admitted, with the Committee, to the table. They did not remain long, and then came that Balaklava charge which characterises the onslaught at every festive scene, when the doors of the supper room are opened. "Onward they rushed," yet any one who used to attend the balls of Louis Philippe can bear me witness that the Tuileries itself has witnessed some terrible scrambling. The action commenced by a running *feu de joie* from the champagne corks—forks were frantically demanded, and stupid youths would carelessly spill terrapin on ladies' dresses. Happy is your reporter to state that he saw no signs of intoxication nor rowdyism, and every one was good-natured, even the fair ones whose skirts were sadly stained by the negligence aforesaid.

Dancing was going on with unflagging spirit when your reporter was forced to leave, that he might transcribe his notes in season for the mail.

News from Kansas.

ST. LOUIS, Thursday, March 5.

A letter to the *Republican*, dated Westport, March 26, says that at a meeting of citizens at that place resolutions were passed to resist every effort and every movement intended or calculated to produce troubles similar to those of last year; extending hospitality and welcome to emigrants from all sections of the country; and pledging themselves to let the laws of Kansas and Missouri punish all violators of the law.

The Santa Fé mail arrived at Westport on the 26th ult. The party met no difficulty on the route, excepting from high streams and deep mud. The general news is unimportant. It is considered certain that Indian Agent Dodge was killed by the Apaches. All was quiet at Fort Bent.

ST. LOUIS, Friday, March 6.

The *Republican* contains a long communication signed by A. W. Jones, a resident of Lecompton, relative to recent affairs in Kansas; also, Governor Geary's letter and Sherrard's reply, together with the action of the Committee of the Judiciary in the Legislature on the matter, and the testimony taken before Judge Cato on the examination of Jones for shooting Sherrard. The version now presented differs somewhat from previous reports. The communication casts much blame on Governor Geary, and the Committee on Judiciary likewise censure his action Jones, who was held to bail in $5,000, has absconded.

Canal and Lake Navigation.

OSWEGO, Friday, March 6.

The schooner *Athenian*, which left Chicago last Fall with a cargo of 17,000 bushels of wheat for Oswego, and which was frozen in in the Welland Canal is now about two miles off this harbor. The Welland Canal is nearly free of ice.

The Missouri Legislature.

ST. LOUIS, Thursday, March 5.

Previous to the adjournment of the Missouri Legislature yesterday, a constitutional amendment limiting the State debt to $30,000,000 was passed.

Appointment of Commissioners to Remove Quarantine.

Special Dispatch to the New-York Daily Times.

ALBANY, Friday, March 6.

The Governor sent to the Senate this evening the names of Hon. George Hall, of Brooklyn, Hon. Egbert Benson, of New-York, and Hon. Obadiah Bowne, of Richmond, as Commissioners to remove Quarantine. The nominations were confirmed unanimously in open Senate. LEO.

NEW-YORK LEGISLATURE.

SENATE....ALBANY, Friday, March 6.

Mr. Richardson reported a bill appropriating $15,000 to the Commissioners of Emigration, to pay the debts due Counties for the support of emigrant paupers.

Mr. Noxon reported favorably on the bill to make certain the record of marriages.

Mr. Upham reported favorably on the concurrent resolutions forbiding contractors to let out the waters of the Canals, under a penalty of the forfeiture of the contract and all the money due them.

Mr. C. P. Smith reported favorably on the bill amending the pilot law.

The Governor sent to the Senate, in special executive session, the nomination of Egbert Benson, Geo. Hall and Obadiah Bowne as Commissioners under the act for the removal of Quarantine.

The bill for the relief of the wives and minor children of drunkards was passed. Also, the bill changing the name of the Broadway Baptist Church; the bill for the relief of destitute children of seamen; and the bill to amend the charter of the Manhattan Savings Institution.

ASSEMBLY....ALBANY, Friday, March 6.

The Assembly was occupied all the morning in debating a resolution against printing the Excise report.

BILLS REPORTED FAVORABLY.

Providing an appropriation for two State Lunatic Asylums, and making an appropriation for the support of the pauper insane.

To authorize the formation of a new Railroad Company in place of the present Northern Railroad Company.

The twice reported bill taxing dogs.

NOTICES OF BILLS.

By Mr. John J. Rielly, to amend the law for the recovery of debts against vessels.

By Mr. Mulligan, to amend the Brooklyn Police bills.

By Mr. J. J. Owen, to establish a State Printing office.

By Mr. Sluyter, for the advancement of agricultural science in the State.

The Assembly agreed to hold evening sessions hereafter, every evening in the week except Saturday.

The concurrent resolutions, amending the Constitution so as to confer the right of suffrage to colored persons, were debated, but no question was taken.

From Louisville.

ARRIVAL OF DR. KANE'S REMAINS—DESTRUCTIVE FIRE, ETC.

LOUISVILLE, Friday, March 6.

An imposing procession of Masons in regalia, firemen and citizens, received the remains of Dr. Kane on their arrival here, this morning, and, marching through the principal streets, attended them to the steamer *Telegraph*, which will leave with them for Cincinnati at noon to-day. John Scott, Agent of the Baltimore and Ohio Railroad, and William R. Patterson, of Adams' Express Company, will attend to the transportation of the remains between here and Philadelphia.

The river is falling slowly. The water in the Channel is 7½ feet deep. The thermometer is at the freezing point.

Bredden's planing mill, three new stores, and two dwelling-houses contiguous, on Main-street, were destroyed by fire last night. Mr. Bredden was the principal loser. Loss $30,000. Fully insured in Eastern offices.

New Jersey Legislature.

TRENTON, Friday, March 6.

The bill for the extension of the Morris and Essex Railroad to Jersey City passed the Senate today by 11 to 6. It now only requires the Governor's signature to become a law.

The bill to incorporate the Essex County Bank failed in the House by a vote of 26 to 28.

An attempt was made to reconsider the resolutions to meet the Committee of the New-York Legislature on the Quarantine question, but in consequence of a dispatch stating that Mr. Leavenworth's bill had passed the New-York Legislature, the matter was laid over till Tuesday.

The Governor sent in the name of William L. Dayton, for Attorney-General, and that of Senator Charles P. Smith, of Salem, for Clerk of the Supreme Court.

Markets by Telegraph.

NEW-ORLEANS, Friday, March 6.

Cotton—Sales to-day 7,000 bales. Prices stiffer but not quotably higher. Middling, 12¾c.@13⅛c. *Receipts to-day*, 5,250 bales. Sugar selling at 10c.; Molasses, 60c.; Mess Pork, (Eastern,) $22 50; Lard in kegs, $15c. Cotton freights to Liverpool, 15-32d. Sterling Exchange, 7⅞ ₩ cent. premium.

The Crowd in Broadway.

The Committee of the Board of Councilmen, to whom were deputed inquiry as to the practicability of some scheme to lessen the crowd in Broadway, met again yesterday in the City Hall Library, Councilman Haswell in the Chair. In the way of evidence little was reached.

Captain Hopkins, of the Third Ward, deposed to the fact that Broadway *is* obstructed, and that some of the causes of obstruction are susceptible of removal.

Mr. A. T. Stewart attended the meeting and offered some suggestions. He thought that the "snarl," or "jam," or "dead stand-still," was inevitably produced so often as the omnibus drivers are compelled to neglect their proper duty in giving change to passengers. He would advise the employment of a "cad" at the door of each omnibus. He thought better regulations would most materially abate the evil. He censured the Mayor for neglecting to employ his own servants in getting up informations against infractors of the street regulations, and for inviting the public to become informers. Mr. Stewart adverted to a proposed railroad in Broadway; he believed the scheme was not dead; another bill was in readiness, but of course it would have his opposition—parties at each end of such lines being the only people benefited—the property along such lines being always deteriorated in value. The Committee appeared to be of the same opinion. Mr. Stewart praised the low omnibuses drawn by 4 horses, common in many English cities, as peculiarly accessible, very convenient, and not so liable to block the streets.

The Chairman expressed to Mr. Stewart his anxiety to adopt a plan which would at once widen both the sidewalk and the roadway. The other members of the Committee thought any such widening would be nugatory and inefficacious; there would be a corresponding addition to the throng. Others thought that the formation of the proposed side avenue, and compelling all licensed vehicles to pass down that avenue, returning by Broadway, would remedy the evil.

ROAD OPEN ACROSS THE ISTHMUS OF TEHUANTEPEC.—The New-Orleans *Picayune* has later advices from Tehuantepec, bringing the important information that the preliminary carriage road across the Isthmus had been completed after the almost incessant labor of 200 to 300 men for a period of several months. The two first carriages passed over the road to the Pacific terminus, on the 4th of January; among their occupants were the American Consul at Vera Cruz, Señor Gutierrez, formerly Secretary of the Treasury of Mexico, and others. The carriages returned next day, when there was great rejoicing in consequence of the glorious achievement, all along the Isthmus. The contract with the Mexican Government is now fulfilled, and the privileges guaranteed by it are secured. The perfect completion of the road will be pushed forward as rapidly as possible, and it will probably be opened on the 1st of June to the traveling public.

A DISTRESSING ACCIDENT.—We regret to learn that yesterday, in Baltimore, Mr. Saml. Butterworth, the Superintendent of the Branch Mint in New-York, while on his way to attend the inauguration was severely wounded by the accidental discharge of a pistol in the overcoat pocket of his friend and traveling companion, Isaac V. Fowler, Esq., Postmaster of New-York City. The weapon went off as Mr. F. was taking off his coat, and the ball entering Mr. Butterworth's thigh ranged upwards. Though but a flesh wound, it is said to be severe.—*Washington Star.*

CALIFORNIA STEAMSHIP RUNNERS.

The Ticket-Swindlers' Own Story—Some of their Dodges—No Arrests made, and why it is hard to Punish them.

WARNINGS TO STRANGERS.

The ticket-swindlers are excited. They were very much stirred by our simple statement of a few of their villainous tricks upon unsophisticated countrymen who left in the *Illinois*. One who formerly was in the business and knows its workings volunteers a statement in extenuation of the abuses. He says the California steamship companies are more culpable than the runners, and he should like to see them bear a portion of the blame.

When the lines were first started, the steamship companies deemed it necessary to employ runners, at a regular salary, to go to the railway dépôts and hotels to solicit passengers. At that time there were no bogus offices. But the Companies soon found that the agent of one line would bribe the runners of the other. Then they adopted the plan of paying the runners a commission for each passenger they brought in. For a while it worked admirably. While the opposition ran strong between the Companies, both of them, weeks previous to the sailing of a boat, would extensively advertise and scatter handbills broadcast throughout the country, to the effect that the passage money was only $30, $40, or $50, as the case might be. Passengers for California flocked to the City, seduced by the prospect of so cheap a passage. Just previous, however, to the time of sailing, "as so many wanted to go," the price would be advanced to $100 or thereabouts. One boat started on the first of the month, the other on the 4th. It was of no use for the passengers to protest, and show the agent the advertisement, which stated that the fare was but $50, for the Company had the game all in their own hands. If, indignantly, the people refused to take passage in the first boat, it was their misfortune, as a still larger sum was asked on the next, the agent telling them that they should have gone in the first boat.

This method of the agents of the companies induced the runners to try a little speculation on their own risk. They reasoned thus: "If our employers advertise one price and charge afterwards what they please, let us by the same game turn a penny, too." At first they would buy four or five tickets at the low rate, and sell them at the advance. Respectable hotel-keepers furnished the necessary funds for the speculation, in return for which the runners sent countrymen to their hotels. This abuse has grown gradually into the outrageous system of ticket-swindling which is now practiced.

Most of the clerks in the regular offices, says our informant—a retired speculator in this line, remember—are aiders and abettors of the runners. They receive a large amount of the proceeds of the swindle. If they did not sell the runners the tickets by the quantity at $10 less per ticket than the regular price, the business would be stopped. But as things are managed now, the clerks in the genuine offices get the lion's share of the plunder, and the men who have to shoulder the infamy don't make such a large pile after all.

The clerks and runners are well acquainted. They drink together, and all that sort of thing. After the sailing of each steamer they adjourn to Delmonico's to dinner, and a division of the money.

This is the other side of the story; possibly there may be truth in it. At any rate it is all the ticket-swindlers have said to vindicate themselves.

It is positively denied, however, at the office of the United States Mail Steamship Company, that tickets are sold in large quantities to the runners, and none are sold below the regular price. It is impossible, they say, to keep the tickets out of the hands of these rascals, for if they refuse to sell them, the runners employ a stranger, who represents himself as about to emigrate with his family to California, and thus the tickets fall into their hands.

An instance was related us of the sharpness of these fellows in conducting their business. One of them who keeps a bogus concern in the vicinity of the Company's office, which is at No. 177 West-street, heard, just after the *George Law* sailed, that the price of passage by the *Illinois*, (the next steamer,) would be increased $25, as she was to carry out a company of United States Troops. His first thought was to obtain a large number of tickets at the low rate. But how could he procure them? He slipped off to Philadelphia, and bought them there, paying the money for 25 passages, at $100 each. But when he presented the agent's receipt at the New-York office, and asked for the tickets, Mr. Raymond refused to furnish them, on the ground that the Philadelphia agent had no authority to negotiate for passages, until he had been notified of any change in the price. The sharp ticket-swindler had the trouble and expense of his trip for nothing.

But unfortunately, the biters are not often bit—sorry statement as it is to make in this Christian age.

Upon the sailing of a steamer for California not long since, a party of five were met on the cars, as usual, while on their way to this City, by the man *going to California*. He knew exactly where Mr. Raymond's office was in the City, the strangers having been posted as to the existence of bogus establishments; he knew the best hotel to stop at. The addition of so accommodating a person to their crowd was regarded as auspicious, and everything went on smoothly. As the steamer was to sail on the following day, no time was to be lost, and *the* office was soon reached by the valuable aid of the guide. Entering it the strangers inquire if Mr. Raymond is in? The clerk behind a high mahogany desk answers, "No, gentlemen, but he will be soon." This is Mr. Raymond's office? they ask. "Yes, be seated gentlemen," is the courteous reply, "and make yourselves comfortable." A young man slips out of a side door, and in less than two minutes a dignified person enters at the front one. He has a business air, and scans the whole group with one eye as thoroughly as if his head were Argus', and every hair-pore were an eye. "There comes Mr. Raymond," says the clerk, as the portly gentleman makes a low bow and inquires—"What can I do for you, gentlemen?"

"W-a-ll, we're bound to the diggins, and want to know about the price of tickets. This is the true Californy ticket office of Mr. Raymond, isn't it?"

"Certainly, but there is a great crowd going, and I don't know as I can give you tickets by this steamer. How many are there of you?"

"Five, and—getting anxious—we must go if possible. There is no mistake neow, 'bout this office?" (looking round.)

"None whatever. Why, what makes you ask that?"

"Oh, we have been told that there is only one place in New-York where they sell the ginewine tickets, but that there are offices where strangers are sometimes taken in."

The guide reassures the company and points at the genuine poster on the wall. At this stage a young man enters quite out of breath, tips his hat, and addressing the bogus dignitary, hurriedly says:

"Mr. Raymond, there are so many passengers we shall want more blankets."

"How many do you want, Purser?"

"A hundred and fifty pairs."

"Very well—go down to the house of Hardhead, Snodgrass, & Bulwinkle, and get them,—and, mind you, get the very best they have. We don't want any more of those coarse things we had before."

[Exit Purser.]

This stroke is a settler; Mr. Raymond finally promises to squeeze out five first-class cabin tickets at $200 each. No sooner said than done. The five travelers give their names. A young man reaches out the side door, and by the time some brief conversation is disposed of the said young man returns and hands something to the Clerk. The tickets are now all ready. And the Californians depart tickled at their success. In the morning as they go down to board the steamer to inspect their quarters they are surprised to observe another California ticket office, into which curiosity leads them. The scales now fall from their eyes—they have now found the office of the genuine Raymond—discover they have steerage tickets, and have paid $75 more for each one than there was any occasion for; the company is minus $375. This case occurred on the sailing of the *George Law*, and is likely to recur when the next steamer sails.

Is there no remedy for such rascalities? The law is no sort of bar to these vagabonds. The police they ask out to take a drink if they present themselves. The press has some terrors for them. It will be a disgrace to our times if a journal of civilization is not privileged to report, at an early date, their wholesale apprehension and punishment.

THREE DAYS LATER FROM EUROPE.

ARRIVAL OF THE PERSIA.

Attacks on the Palmerston Administration.

Contradictory Rumors About Persian War.

Reported Destruction of Canton.

Aid from Russia to China and Persia.

DEATH OF THE EARL OF ELLESMERE.

COTTON QUIET—GRAIN DULL.

Consols 93 5-8@3-4.

The British Mail steamer *Persia*, from Liverpool about 8¼ o'clock A. M. of Saturday, the 21st, arrived yesterday afternoon.

The *Arago* arrived at Southampton morning of the 20th, and the *New-York* (S. S.) at Greenock, at 9¼ o'clock A. M. of the same day.

The news by this arrival has several features of interest. On the 20th, the night preceding the sailing of the *Persia*, Disraeli, as the leader of the opposition in the House of Commons, made an attack on the Government financial scheme. The scope of Disraeli's proposal was to adjust the estimates for a period of three years, instead of for one year, so as to permit the complete repeal of the income tax at the expiration of three years from the present date. The debate was postponed.

The Persian difficulty, which a few days since appeared in a fair way of settlement, has taken a new turn for the worse—it being reported that Ferouk Khan had, in consequence of the unexpected receipt of bellicose dispatches from his Government, broken off all negotiation with the British Minister at Paris, and would not now visit England. A statement opposed to this appears in a Paris Government journal.

The French Government has instructed its representatives at London, Vienna, St. Petersburg and Berlin to invite the Governments to which they are accredited to join in a Conference at Paris for the settlement of the Neufchatel affair. The Ministers of the above Powers resident at Paris will act as plenipotentiaries. The Conference will meet about the beginning of March, and it is believed will be protracted ere a satisfactory adjustment can be arrived at.

There is nothing nearer towards a settlement of the Danubian Principalities.

The London *Morning Advertiser* asserts that the Government has received a dispatch announcing the total destruction of Canton by the British.

After a long and painful illness the Earl of Ellesmere died, on the 18th, at Bridgewater House, London, in the 57th year of his age. Lord Ellesmere was distinguished as a munificent patron of art, as well as for his liberality of sentiment and his freedom from party fetters and rancor. As a poet he showed considerable talent, his works being a translation of Goethe's "Faust," and numerous translations of German lyrics, as also an original poem entitled "The Pilgrimage," descriptive of his travels in the East. He was the second son of the first Duke of Sutherland, was educated at Oxford, and afterwards took the name of Egerton, in place of his patronymic of Leveson-Gower. From 1820 to 1846 he was, for various terms, in the House of Commons; in 1827 was a Lord of the Treasury; from 1828 to 1830 was Chief Secretary for Ireland, and in 1830 was Secretary-at-War. He is succeeded in his titles and estates by his eldest son, Lord Brackley, who is in a precarious state of health.

An explosion took place on the 19th, at the Lund Hill Colliery, near Wombwell, on the South Yorkshire Railway. One hundred and sixty-six persons were in the pit at the time. Sixteen were drawn up alive, and the others remained for certain death, the interior of the pit having taken fire. Engines had arrived and the mouths of the shafts were being stopped up to extinguish the flames. Thirteen dead bodies had been found in the main tramways, but it would be some days before the pit could be safely entered to search for the rest. The pit had been worked but two years.

A report from the Russian Minister of War declares that the truce concluded with Schamyl, during the Turkish war, expired in May of last year, and that operations against the Circassians have been resumed along the whole line of the Caucasus.

Letters from St. Petersburg mention that it will be the beginning of April before the Emperor Alexander sets out on his journey to Nice, and either on his way or his return, he will visit Napoleon at Paris.

The ratifications of the treaty signed between Russia and Persia, on the 5th of January last, were exchanged at Teheran on the 18th of the same month. This treaty cedes to Russia a track of land on the frontiers of Turkey, and situate between Bayazid and Nakhshivan, giving to Russia a complete command of the strategic road from Trebizonde on the Black Sea to the Persian frontier by Erzeroum. Russia has been endeavoring since 1828 to obtain the concession which Persia now grants. It is added that orders were immediately sent from St. Petersburg to construct a line of fortresses on the ceded territory.

The Brussels *Nord* publishes the details of the concession granted by the Russian Government for the great network of Railways to be constructed within ten years at an outlay of £45,000,000 sterling. The conditions are substantially the same as those already announced. Among the contracting parties are Baring Brothers, of London, and Hope & Co., of Amsterdam.

We read in the Paris Correspondence of the London *Times:*

The last accounts received by the French Government from Persia announce that Ferhali Khan, who commands the advanced guard of the Persian army in Farsistan, had sent forward, on the 25th of December, a strong reconnoitering party of cavalry as far as 50 miles in advance of Shiraz. This demonstration, though so far from the British camp, had given rise to a report of an approaching attack on the English lines by the entire Persian army, but this is impossible, for the Persians, who have been joined by the Turcomans, have none but irregular cavalry in the province of Fars, with which it would be impossible to make an impression on the well-fortified position of the English army at Bushire.

Advices from the Principalities state that the Russian authorities had quitted Bolgrad, and surrendered the town to the commissioners sent from Jassy by the Moldavian Government. Col. Besson, the French Commissioner for fixing the boundary of the Principalities, charged with tracing the Upper Yalpuk, has written that his labors are so far advanced that Komrat may be handed over to the Russian authorities on the 15th February.

In the House of Lords, Lord Polwarth gave notice that he would move for any papers or correspondence relative to the cession of the islands of Haski, Gibleo, and Ghurzgoul by the Imaum of Muscat to Her Majesty, and their erection into a colony; and also to call the attention of the House to a license granted on the 20th of February, 1856, by the Commissioners of Emigration to John Ord and others, giving them the sole and exclusive right to raise and take away guano from these islands during five years.

It is announced that a commission is about to be appointed to choose a position to which to transfer the prisoners at Cayenne. Several places have been mentioned. One is New-Caledonia, and the other Algeria. Another idea suggested is to take possession of the Zephyrine Islands, opposite the coast of Africa, and which have the advantage of being detached from the continent or coast of Algeria.

W. H. Russell, the London *Times* correspondent, has entered into an engagement with Mr. Beale, of London, to deliver three lectures a week, on the Crimea, till April, 1858, for a sum which rumor calls £10,000.

LONDON NEWS AND GOSSIP.

Mr. Disraeli's Attack on the Government—Lord Palmerston's Chances—Lord Derby's Motion Against the War in China—The Persian War Not Terminated—Lord Napier—Relations with the United States—Non-Appointment of Consuls—The Railroad Hoax—Death of the Earl of Ellesmere—Miscellaneous, &c.

Correspondence of the New-York Daily Times.

LONDON, Friday Evening, Feb. 20, 1857.

This night week we were in the midst of financial ministerial uncertainty. To-night we are in the crisis of ministerial existence. A grand coup is in the act of being made on the Palmerston budget by Mr. Disraeli, the success of whose motion, if success it have, will be the knell of the present Administration. Whom that knell may summon to new official vitality

The New-York Times.

VOL. IX.—NO. 2520. NEW-YORK, TUESDAY, OCTOBER 18, 1859. PRICE TWO CENTS.

SERVILE INSURRECTION.

The Federal Arsenal at Harper's Ferry in Possession of the Insurgents.

GENERAL STAMPEDE OF SLAVES.

United States Troops on their March to the Scene.

Dispatches from our Special Correspondent.

WASHINGTON, Monday, Oct. 17.

The report that negroes have taken possession of Harper's Ferry, and now hold the Government Armory, has created great excitement here. It is said that troops from Fort McHenry, Baltimore, will be dispatched forthwith to the scene of disorder.

Dispatches to the President and Secretary of War confirm the report from Harper's Ferry. The President has telegraphed to Postmasters at Frederick and Baltimore for particulars. The train was fired into on the Bridge, and one man was killed. The insurgents have possession of the Bridge. A special train at Baltimore has been ordered to carry on troops. Frederick Volunteers have offered services.

WASHINGTON, Monday, Oct. 17.

The latest account says the insurgents are Government employes, headed by one ANDERSON, lately arrived there. It is believed to be an Abolition movement to protect runaways. A large number of negroes stampeded last evening from several localities. It is supposed that they are making for Harper's Ferry.

RELAY HOUSE BALTIMORE AND OHIO RAILROAD, Monday, Oct. 17.

Gov. FLOYD announced in the Cabinet meeting this morning that two months ago he received an anonymous letter stating that an Abolitionist movement was on foot, which would exhibit itself first at Harper's Ferry, about the middle of October, but he treated it with levity, and had not thought of it since. This seems to give the key to the insurrection.

A train has just arrived here with three companies, but without ammunition.

The eighty-five marines in company are fully equipped and supplied, and may divide. The marines were ready at Washington dépôt in one hour and twenty minutes from the first notice of the order.

BALTIMORE AND OHIO RAILROAD, PLANE NUMBER 4—9 P. M.

Our train of seventeen cars, with two hundred and ten Baltimore troops, eighty from Marines, and one hundred and twenty from Frederick, is just going on. Besides the above, there are one hundred and eighty Artillerymen from Fort Monroe. These constitute the whole force. Major REYNOLDS has command, until Major LEE, who is behind on a special train, with ammunition, comes up.

The insurgents have pillaged the pay-office. Gov. WISE has ordered out the Jefferson Regiment, and a horseman has been dispatched by the Baltimore and Ohio Railroad, with the Governor's orders. This messenger will endeavor to pass through the country, and deliver his message by three o'clock to-day. It is yet doubtful whether the troops will make an attack to-night or wait for daylight.

MONOCACY BRIDGE, Monday, Oct. 17.

A train has just returned from Harper's Ferry having been refused permission to pass. The insurgents are increasing. The baggage-master of the train was permitted to pass into the town, when he was marched into the Armory, where he found about six hundred runaway negroes. Mr. WASHINGTON, of Jefferson, also came down with his wife and servant. The latter was taken prisoner, and Mr. WASHINGTON and his wife were tied in their carriage. The place appeared to be deserted by the inhabitants. A few only remained. The baggage-master was permitted to return.

The same party reports about two hundred white men engaged in the insurrection. Everything had been plundered, and all appeared determined to fight. Mr. DIFFEY, master of trains, has telegraphed from Martinsburg, *via* Wheeling, that a body of armed men have taken possession of the Armory at Harper's Ferry and have planted guns in one bridge; they have stopped all our tonnage, and mail trains bound East are at the west end of the bridge. The telegraph wires are cut and there is no communication East. A body of armed men are getting ready to leave here at once to clear the bridge, that our trains can pass.

There is great excitement all through the neighborhood. It is now evident that the insurgents have fortified themselves and will make a desperate resistance. The Directors and families of the Pennsylvania Central Railroad are on an excursion, and have also been stopped at Harper's Ferry.

The following are the first dispatches received from the scene of disturbance, that were communicated to the Government:

"The express train east has been detained at Harper's Ferry in consequence of the railroad bridge and Armory being in the possession of an armed organized band of Abolitionists. They are 100, and perhaps more, in number. I took my baggage master and proceeded through the bridge, when I was stopped by three men having arms, who ordered me to halt or be shot down. I retired from the bridge and made my escape. I have been frequently shot at, and so have many others. All the watchmen of the bridge and Armory are under arrest. Moreover, every bridge around is guarded. HAYWOOD, the colored man, has been shot through the left side, greatly endangering his life. Inform the United States officials at once. There are some eight or ten men in the neighborhood of the Ferry in the greatest anxiety to know the issue of this dreadful affair. The captain of the band told me to notify you that no other trains should pass the bridge. Had you not better notify the Secretary of War of the circumstance?"

Our train is ordered to let Major LEE overtake us. The Frederick companies went at 3 o'clock, P. M., but have not since been heard from. We take on at this place two additional pieces of artillery, and an additional supply of ammunition from Frederick.

HARPER'S FERRY, Monday, Oct. 17.

Train arrived and halted below town, where runners communicated the state of affairs. Jefferson County Regiment had entered town, from Virginia side, and Frederick troops crossed the bridge; there had been a deal of firing. Some nine persons killed.

Mr. BECKHAM, Agent of the Railroad Company, was shot through, and his murderer fell almost at the same instant, pinned by a rifle ball from a friend of Mr. BECKHAM,

FROM THE REPORTER OF THE ASSOCIATED PRESS.

BALTIMORE, Monday, Oct. 17.

A dispatch just received here from Frederick, and dated this morning, states that an insurrection has broken out at Harper's Ferry, where an armed band of Abolitionists have full possession of the Government Arsenal. The express train going east was twice fired into, and one of the railroad hands and a negro was killed, while they were endeavoring to get the train through the town. The insurrectionists stopped and arrested two men, who had come to town with a load of wheat, and, seizing their wagon, loaded it with rifles, and sent them into Maryland. The insurrectionists number about two hundred and fifty whites, and are aided by a gang of negroes. At last accounts fighting was going on.

The above is given just as it was received here. It seems very improbable, and should be received with great caution, until confirmed by further advices.

BALTIMORE, Monday, Oct. 17.

A later dispatch received at the Railroad Office, says the affair has been greatly exaggerated. The reports had their foundation in a difficulty at the Armory, with which negroes had nothing to do.

BALTIMORE, Monday, Sept. 17—1 P. M.

It is apprehended that the affair at Harper's Ferry is more serious than our citizens seem willing to believe. The wires from Harper's Ferry are cut, and consequently we have no telegraphic communication beyond Moncacy Station. The Southern train, which was due here at an early hour this morning, has not yet arrived. It is rumored there is a stampede of negroes from this State. There are many other wild rumors, but nothing authentic as yet.

The Secretary of War has telegraphed to Fort Monroe for three companies of artillery, who are expected to be in Baltimore to-morrow morning. A company of marines will leave the Washington Navy-yard at 3:20 o'clock to-day for Harper's Ferry

BALTIMORE, Monday, Oct. 17—2 P. M.

Another account received by train says the bridge across the Potomac was filled with insurgents all armed. Every light in the town was extinguished and the hotels, closed in all the streets, were in possession of the mob, and every road and lane leading thereto barricaded and guarded. Men were seen in every quarter, with muskets and bayonets, who arrested the citizens, and pressed them into the service, including many negroes. This done, the United States arsenal and government pay-house, in which was said to be a large amount of money, and all the other public works were seized by the mob. Some were of the opinion that the object was entirely plunder, and to rob the government of the funds deposited on Saturday at the pay-house. During the night the mob made a demand on the Wager Hotel for provisions, and a body of armed men enforced the claim. The citizens were in a terrible state of alarm, the insurgents having threatened to burn the town.

The following has just been received from Monocacy, this side of Harper's Ferry: "The mail agent on the Western-bound train has returned to Monocacy, and reports that the train was unable to get through. The town is in possession of the negroes, who arrest every one they can catch, and imprison. The train due here at 3 P. M., could not get through, and the agent came down on an empty engine."

BALTIMORE, Monday, Oct. 17—2½ P. M

The Western train on the Baltimore and Ohio Railroad has just arrived here. Its officers confirm the statements first received touching the disturbance at Harper's Ferry. Their statement is to the effect that the bridge-keeper at Harper's Ferry, perceiving that his lights had been extinguished, went to ascertain the cause, when he was pursued and fired upon by a gang of blacks and whites. Subsequently the train came along, when a colored man, who acted as assistant to the baggage-master, was shot, receiving a mortal wound, and the conductor, Mr. PHELPS, was threatened with violence if he attempted to proceed with the train. Feeling uncertain as to the condition of affairs, the conductor waited until after daylight before he ventured to proceed, having delayed the train six hours. Mr. PHELPS says the insurrectionists number two hundred blacks and whites, and that they have full possession of the United States armory. The party is commanded or led by a man named ANDERSON, who had lately arrived at Harper's Ferry. Mr. PHELPS also confirms the statement in a previous dispatch, that the insurrectionists had seized a wagon, and loading it with muskets had dispatched it into Maryland. The military of Frederick had been ordered out.

Dispatches have been received from President BUCHANAN, ordering out the United States troops at this point, and a special train is now getting ready to convey them to the scene of disturbance. He has also accepted the volunteered services of Capt. SANICK's Company of Frederick, and has likewise ordered the Government troops from Old Point Comfort to proceed immediately to Harper's Ferry. This intelligence is authentic.

BALTIMORE, Monday, Oct. 17—3½ P. M.

The mail train going West got as far as Sandy, when Mr. HOOD, the baggage master, and another party started on foot to the bridge. They went through the bridge, and were taken and imprisoned, but subsequently went before the captain of the insurrectionists, who refused to let anything pass. All of the eastward bound trains laying west of Harper's Ferry, have been taken; persons from this side the river, tying them together, and taking off the slaves. The mail train bound West has returned to Monocacy. There are from five hundred to seven hundred whites and blacks concerned in the insurrection.

The United States marines at Washington are under orders for Harper's Ferry. There is great excitement in Baltimore, and the military are moving. Several companies are in readiness to take the train, which will leave soon.

BALTIMORE, Monday, Oct. 17—4 P. M.

An account from Frederick says a letter has been received there from a merchant at Harper's Ferry, sent by a boy who had to cross the mountain and swim the river, which says that all the principal citizens are imprisoned, and many have been killed; also, that the railroad agent had been shot twice, and that the watchman at the dépôt had been shot dead.

BALTIMORE, Monday, Oct. 17—5 P. M.

A train filled with military, including the Law Greys, City Guards, Shields' Guards, and other companies, left here at 4 o'clock for Harper's Ferry. Representatives of the press accompanied the military.

BALTIMORE, Monday, Oct. 17—7 P. M.

A dispatch from Martinsburgh, west of Harper's Ferry, received *via* Wheeling and Pittsburgh, confirms the report of the insurrectionists having possession of the arsenal at Harper's Ferry, and says they have planted cannon at the bridge. All the trains have been stopped. A body of armed men was getting ready to proceed thither to clear the road. There was great excitement at Martinsburgh, Va.

RICHMOND, Monday, Oct. 17.

It is reported and believed that the Governor of Virginia has ordered volunteer troops to Harper's Ferry.

WASHINGTON, Monday, Oct 17—4 P. M.

On the receipt of the intelligence from Harper's Ferry, orders were issued for three companies of artillery at Old Point and the corps of marines at Washington Barracks to proceed thither without delay. The marines, ninety-three in number, left in the 3:15 P. M. train, with two twelve-pound howitzers and a full supply of ammunition. It is reported that they are under orders to force the bridge to-night at all hazards. Col. FAULKNER accompanies them.

It is reported, on good authority, that some weeks ago Secretary FLOYD received anonymous epistles stating that about the 15th of October the Abolitionists and negroes, and other disaffected persons, would make an attempt to seize the arsenal and hold the place, but the statement was so indefinite and improbable as to cause no fears of such an outbreak.

WASHINGTON, Monday, Oct. 17.—9 P. M.

In view of the possibility of the disturbances at Harper's Ferry extending to this vicinity, the Mayors of Washington and Alexandria have taken precautionary steps for its suppression. The President, through the Mayor of Washington, ordered a strong detachment of volunteer Militia to be posted at the National and Company armories, which was promptly done. Two hundred stand of muskets and a supply of ammunition will also be placed in the City Hall, for emergency. It is suggested by well-informed persons that the cause of the insurrection is the reported fact that not long since the contractor for the construction of a Government dam, at the Ferry, absconded, largely indebted to several hundred employes, who have taken this step to indemnify themselves, by the seizure of the Government Funds, which it was supposed were transported thither on Saturday. A gentleman just in from Harper's Ferry, thinks the blacks participated in the outbreak only on compulsion.

RICHMOND, Monday, Oct. 17—9 P. M.

There is great excitement here. Company F with full ranks, has just left the Armory, expecting to take a special train to-night. There is a new company, with a similar uniform to the Greys.

The Greys leave for Harper's Ferry early in the morning. The Governor left to-night for Washington.

BALTIMORE, Monday, Oct. 17—9 P. M.

The *American's* special reporter telegraphs from Plane No. 4, 45 miles from Baltimore, and 31 from Harper's Ferry, at 8 o'clock, that the train consists of seventeen cars, with four hundred troops, under Maj. REYNOLDS, with a roadmaster and laborers to repair the track, and telegraphers to mend the lines. Three companies from Frederick were in an advance train. Col. HARRIS, of the United States Marines, commanding the expedition, follows in a special train. They will not reach Harper's Ferry before 10 o'clock.

MONOCACY BRIDGE, Monday, Oct. 17—10 P. M.

The train arrived here at 9 o'clock. LUTHER SIMPSON, baggage master of the mail train, gives the following particulars: I walked up the bridge; was stopped, but was afterwards permitted to go up and see the captain of the insurrectionists; I was taken to the armory, and saw the captain, whose name is BILL SMITH; I was kept prisoner for more than an hour, and saw from five hundred to six hundred negroes, all having arms; there were two or three hundred white men with them; all the houses were closed. I went into a tavern kept by Mr. CHAMBERS; thirty of the inhabitants were collected there with arms. They said most of the inhabitants had left, but they declined, preferring to protect themselves; it was reported that five or six persons had been shot.

Mr. SIMPSON was escorted back over the bridge by six negroes.

The train with the Frederick military is laying a Point of Rocks. A train with the directors of the Pennsylvania Railroad on board, is on the other side of Harper's Ferry. It was believed that the insurrectionists would leave as soon as it became dark. Orders have been received here that the train shall stop at Sandy Hook until Col. LEE, who is following in a special train, arrives. There are any amount of rumors, but nothing certain.

MONOCACY, Tuesday, Oct. 18—1 A. M.

The special train, with Col. LEE's command, passed this station at 11:30 P. M. It is supposed that there is difficulty in adjusting the breaks in the road this side of Harper's Ferry, as nothing has since been heard of the expedition.

Episcopal General Convention.

RICHMOND, Monday, Oct. 17.

Both houses have agreed to hold their next Convention in New-York.

The report of the Committee on typographical errors in the standard Bible has been adopted, and Dr. MASON, of Maryland, appointed typographical corrector.

The order of the day was the consideration of resolutions by the Committee on domestic and foreign missions. A long debate took place. It chiefly related to the extension of missionary operations in Japan, China, &c. All the Committee's resolutions were adopted except the last, which was to memorialize the President, asking him to address the Court of Spain respecting religious toleration in Cuba.

Pending the debate the house adjourned.

The Sunday Law in Pittsburgh.

PITTSBURGH, Monday, Oct. 17.

Chief-Justice LOWRIE, whose driver was fined twenty-five dollars for violating the Sunday laws in driving his family to church, has published a card, in which he says he was quite ignorant that he had been allowing a trangression of the law, though he had studied it carefully, and officially declines carrying the case further, because there may be suitors before the Supreme Court in other cases, and they ought not to be embarrassed by having one of its Judges pecuniarily interested.

J. F. Shepard of the People's Five Cent Savings Bank of Boston.

BOSTON, Monday, Oct. 17.

J. F. SHEPARD of the People's Five Cent Savings Bank of this city, was brought before the Police Court this morning on a charge of defalcation, and on waiving an examination was bound over in the sum of $12,000 to stand his trial at the Superior Court

Death of John Calhoun.

ST. LOUIS, Monday, Oct. 17.

JOHN CALHOUN, Ex-Surveyor-General of Kansas and Nebraska, and President of the Lecompton Constitutional Convention, died at St. Josephs on the 13th inst.

Murder on the High Seas.

BOSTON, Monday, Oct. 17.

The bark *Said Bui Sultan* arrived at Salem to-day from Zanzibar. On the passage, Capt. HENRY D. EDWARDS was stabbed by the cook, causing his death. The deceased was a passenger on the *Sultan*.

The Atlantic Monthly.

BOSTON, Monday, Oct. 17.

The *Atlantic Monthly* was to-day purchased by Messrs. TICKNOR & FIELDS, who will hereafter be the Publishers.

The Attempted Insurrection at Constantinople

From the correspondence of the Paris papers are derived the following particulars of the recent attempt to overthrow the reigning dynasty of Turkey:

It is not yet three months since a secret society was founded which had for its daring object to seize the Sultan and his Ministers, and to modify the form of Government. The principal personage, Sheik AHMED, a Kurd, born at Suleymanieh, inhabited the médreé (school) of the Mosque of Sultan BAJAZID. He is an enlightened man, free from fanaticism, much esteemed as a theologian and philosopher, and of incontestable honesty. Like most of the Turks, Sheik AHMED deplored the manner in which public affairs were conducted, the growing feebleness of the Empire, the administrative abuses, the financial disorders, the incessant and immoderate expenses of the palace; he severely criticised the acts of Ministers and the weakness of the Sovereign. He was listened to with deference, and his words derived great importance from the moral authority he enjoyed. Added to this, facts of daily occurrence confirmed those words, and increased the popular discontent. Around the Sheik were grouped men who shared his ideas, and frequently met. They comprised magistrates, clergy, military men, persons of the middle classes, and employes.

Among the Sheik's admirers and friends was the Circassian, HUSSEIN PASHA, a hot-headed, resolute man, distinguished, in 1855, in the Kars campaign. He was then Colonel of the First Regiment of Arabistan, and is said to have greatly distinguished himself in the repulse of the Russian attack. His conduct on that occasion won him a General's rank. Less fortunate last year in Montenegro, where his *corps d'armée* was roughly handled, and he himself had two horses killed under him, and escaped most narrowly he was removed from his command. He went to Constantinople to demand a court-martial, which was refused. Left without employment, and considering himself unjustly treated, he became a malcontent. He deemed himself dishonored and his character became soured. He fell in with Sheik AHMED, and readily joined in his plans. According to the version before me, he was the arm of the plot, as the Sheik was its head. About two months ago, however, HUSSEIN was appointed to the staff of the army of Roumelia. At first he refused to go, but at last yielded and departed. It is said to have been then agreed that, in his absence, the direction of the movement should be intrusted to HASSAN PASHA, General of Artillery and member of the Secret Society, who commanded the Bosphorous, with all his batteries and military posts. DJAFER PASHA was another conspirator. He is an Albanian of high family, who in former days was more than once in arms against the Porte, but who, during the campaign on the Danube, joined the Sultan's army with 200 of his countrymen armed and equipped at his own charge. After the war they promised him much, but performed nothing; they would not even let him return to his own country, but compelled him to live in Constantinople on his pay of about £7 sterling a month. The conspiracy made many other recruits, some of them men of much importance. They include a great number of officers, and even non-commissioned officers of Artillery, Engineers, and the Guard. The number of officers comprised is estimated at not less than 850. There was a regular organization. The society was divided into two classes, chiefs and associates. Only the chiefs knew each other; the associates knew only their chiefs, each of whom grouped around him 100 to 150 men. I believe I may affirm that this society reckoned scarcely less than 15,000 to 18,000 men. The following was the plan of the conspirators: When the Sultan should be returning from the mosque, or when at night he should leave his kiosk at Topkaneh, to return to the palace with his habitual escort of palace officials and domestics, he was to be allowed to reach the narrowest part of the street which runs parallel with the Bosphorus from Topkaneh to Dolma Bagtchi. In that part is the post of Cabutach. The officers and the soldiers were to carry off the Sultan. All had been gained over, or nearly so, and the officer answered for his men. The Sultan taken, rockets were to be thrown from the stairs of Cabutach, to serve as a signal for the regiment quartered at Kulalee, some distance up the Bosphorus, on the opposite side. This regiment was to go by detachments to arrest the Minister of War, RIZA PASHA, in his fall at Beglerbeg, and the Grand Vizier, AALI PASHA, and the Minister of Foreign Affairs, FUAD PASHA, at their falls at Canlidja.

Other Ministers and Presidents and Members of Councils were to be arrested, and, with the Sultan, were to be kept prisoners. According to one statement, the man who betrayed the plot, HASSAN PASHA, did so on account of a resolution taken to put them all to death, ABDUL MEDJID included. The general opinion in Constantinople, however, is said to be that there was no intention of proceeding to such extremities, and that HASSAN invented the story to extenuate his first fault. The conspirators had fixed (without consulting them) on a number of persons of distinction to replace the deposed dignitaries. The Sultan was to be declared deposed, and his brother or his eldest son (accounts vary) was to be put upon the throne. Everything was arranged. On Saturday, the 17th of September, the plot was to be carried out; but on the Wednesday night preceding HASSAN went to RIZA PASHA and told him all. Prompt measures were taken. In the night of Thursday, and on the Friday and Saturday, many arrests were made. The prisoners were sent to Kulalee, to Scutari, and to Doud Pasha.

NEWS FROM EUROPE.

LONDON PAPERS BY THE HAMMONIA.

THE SAN JUAN DIFFICULTY.

Kossuth on the Late War.

The screw-steamship *Hammonia*, of the Hamburg line, from Southampton on the 4th inst., arrived here last evening.

The advices thus received are not so late as those supplied by the *North Briton*; but we are placed in possession of London journals to the day of sailing, and from them derive additional news of interest.

According to the *Daily News*, it is said to have been decided that the *Great Eastern* is to leave Portland on the 8th and proceed to Holyhead. Under the provisions of the mercantile marine acts the *Great Eastern* would not be permitted to carry passengers, and the Directors would be liable to heavy penalties if they did so before receiving the certificate of the Marine Department of the Board of Trade. No passengers will, therefore, be conveyed on her trial trip.

The *Times* says: "During the past week no fewer than forty total wrecks have been posted on the books at Lloyd's. Among the more calamitous was the destruction by fire of the ship *Schah Jehan*, from Calcutta to the West Indies, with 300 coolie emigrants. Another heavy loss is the total wreck of the *Sovereign of the Seas*. There are, in addition, several missing vessels, respecting which the most painful forebodings are entertained.

The London papers announce the death of that eminent non-conformist divine and theological writer, JOHN ANGELL JAMES. The event occurred at Birmingham on the 1st inst.

The convict bankers, Sir JOHN DEAN PAUL and STRAHAN, now in prison under sentence, will be released from confinement on the 23d inst.

The British ship *Providence*, arrived at Falmouth, reports that she was fired into while passing Tarifa, on the 9th ult. One man was wounded, some stanchions and chain-plates carried away, and eight planks of the deck ripped up.

According to a Spanish Ministerial organ, the Government of Madrid intends to fortify Tarifa very strongly.

THE SAN JUAN BOUNDARY DISPUTE.

THE LONDON TIMES ON THE MISSION OF GENERAL SCOTT.

We are glad to learn by the last steamer from America that Gen. SCOTT has been sent to take the place of the bellicose Gen. HARNEY in the command of the Pacific coast. Such a step on the part of President BUCHANAN is only what we had a right to expect from a politician who is old, experienced, and has a knowledge not only of his own country, but of our own. We may say, without fearing the charge of timidity, that we trust this difficulty will be settled peaceably, and according to the just rights of either party. It is so usual for men in command of American detachments or ships of war to indulge in vagaries like those of Gen. HARNEY that we are not disposed to dwell on the discourtesy of this officer; but the notion of disputing our right to an island which has been in the possession of the Hudson's Bay Company for an indefinite time, and which has remained in their hands since the treaty of 1846, and of doing this simply because it was pretended that an American had been arrested for an outrage on the Company's property, is something new in the annals of military achievements. Gen. HARNEY has been beyond doubt merely the representative of a class sufficiently abundant in the unsettled regions of America. The choice spirits who flock to California and Oregon from the more civilized parts of the Union are too much accustomed to administer justice on one another with the rifle and bowie-knife to take much thought about legal tribunals and established jurisdictions. They flocked into British territory, refused to pay taxes levied by competent authority, gave Gen. DOUGLASS plenty of trouble, and at last were only brought to order by the determination of the Government, supported by the mass of British-born subjects. Having been foiled in attempting to subject British Columbia to the reign of rowdyism, they have since endeavored to nibble at the possessions of her Britannic Majesty. The Island of San Juan is the spot which, by a forced interpretation of a very simple treaty, it is attempted to make American ground. It is only within the last few days that anything has been heard of this island—that its very name has been known generally—in the British metropolis. But for some time the idea of contesting our rights has been cherished by the local patriots, and some two months or more since it was determined to try what boldness and affected contempt of British remonstrances would do. In Gen. HARNEY the promotors of this enterprise had a fitting leader. Under pretence that an American had been illegally arrested by the Hudson's Bay Company, he declared that the time was come to assert by force the rights of the United States. Oregon is not now at six months' distance from Washington, nor are the Atlantic States divided by any lengthened term of voyage from the shores of England. Three months might be sufficient to settle the question of the Gulf of Georgia by the two Governments, and in that time it could not be pretended that the citizens of the United States were likely to suffer any great injuries or indignities. But to send a dispatch home requesting the settlement of the dispute, and then to offer arrangements with the British authorities during the necessary interval, would be a tame way of proceeding. It suits neither the temper nor the interests of a republican commander. Such a man may be swayed by two desires—the first to show his resolution to foreigners, war with whom forms almost the whole history of his country; the second to gain popularity in his native State for the Union in general, and open the way for future professional or political success. It is, no doubt, a great thing for a General to have the admiration of such a race as peoples California, to be their leader in an aggression which they will all support, and to be able to count on the suffrages of them, or those like them in other States of the Union. We cannot tell what may have already happened in those distant regions, but it is quite certain that if blood has been spilt, it must rest on the head of the officer who bethought himself of settling by a *coup de main* the difference in the construction of a treaty between his own country and such an empire as England. The naval force which Governor DOUGLAS can call to his aid is far from small, and the resources of the two countries in this respect are so different that we need have no fear of the result, should the intemperance of Gen. HARNEY and his supporters carry matters further than the patience of the British authorities can bear.

The circumstances of the landing are already pretty well known. There had been petty disputes for a month or two, the island having always been treated as British, and the Americans guilty of any encroachment having been resisted by the Hudson's Bay Company, when in July the claim of the United States to the island was first put in force by the landing of a body of troops. This took place on the 27th, the United States' Boundary Commissioner accompanying the troops. Having thus put an end, as far as in them lay, to any discussion of the rights of England, the Americans then bethought themselves of a conference with the British Admiral. Not a single British ship of war had been at the place for weeks previously; but, the fact of the American aggression having become known to the Admiral, he repaired to San Juan, and on the 11th of August, a fortnight after the invasion, a Mr. CAMPBELL, the United States' Boundary Commissioner, and Col. CASEY, of the American army, arrived in a packet-ship, and requested that Admiral BAYNES would come on board their vessel, and confer with them. This request, it is needless to say, was at once declined.

So stood matters at the last dispatch of mails from California. We trust that nothing has since happened to complicate the dispute. Should things remain as they were, the arrival of Gen. SCOTT with instructions from Washington will, no doubt, tend to bring matters to an amicable conclusion. The principal work, however, is to be done in the two capitals, and we would counsel the American Government, in all friendship and sincerity, not to minister to the ambitious passions of any man or class, by contesting rights which seem to us too strong for sophistry to overturn. There can be no doubt that the treaty of 1846 gave, and was intended to give, to Great Britain and the United States the free navigation of the Gulf of Georgia, and that this could be alone effected by making the channel which divides the two empires what it was always considered to be—the broad estuary which flows to the eastward of San Juan. This was the channel in those days when California had not yet been colonized, when British Columbia was yet unknown and unnamed, and when Oregon itself was a wilderness, wandered over only by the hunter and the trapper. Nothing was thought of other channels between San Juan and Vancouver, passable indeed to the steamers of the present day, but never navigated in those times, and surely never present to the minds of the statesmen who, map in hand, negotiated the Treaty of 1846. This is the view of the matter according to the spirit of the treaty, but if we take the letter it bears out no less our claims. The express words are, that "the line shall be continued westward along the 49th parallel of latitude to *the middle of the channel which separates the Continent from Vancouver's Island*, and then southerly, through the middle of said channel and Fuca Straits, to the Pacific Ocean." On these words the British Government is content to rest its claim, and it is mere surveyor's work to determine whether the line southward from the middle point of the channel, in 49° north, and through the middle of Fuca Straits, does or does not give the Island of San Juan to the British Crown.

THE FATE OF HUNGARY.

INTERESTING LETTER FROM M. KOSSUTH.

The following letter, addressed to JOHN MCADAM, Esq., of Glasgow, is published in the *Bulletin* of that city:

LONDON, Sept. 26, 1859.

MY DEAR SIR: The fatal day of Villafranca prostrated my hopes at a moment when we had the deliverance of my country within sight; nay, almost within the reach of our hand, like a ripe fruit ready to be plucked; and here I am again, a poor exile, as I was four months ago, only older by ten years from the bitter pangs of disappointment.

I say designedly "disappointment," and not "deceit." Of deceit I cannot complain, for I took good care to guard myself and my country against even the possibility of deceit; but I feel my heart nearly broken by disappointment, unwarranted by circumstances, unaccounted and unaccountable.

Without that thunderbolt from a clear sky—the Villafranca arrangement—this moment at which I write, Hungary would have already filled a page in the annals of history than which none equal stands yet on record; because the whole nation was united, ready, and resolved as scarcely ever before. All the feelings which sometimes bring division into a national household—difference of religion, language, race, and distinction of classes—had melted into one great common resolution—to get rid of the banditti rule of the House of Austria as soon as the war would take its logical expansion.

And the positive knowledge of this fact only adds to the bitter pangs of my disappointment. To be thus stopped at the moment when we were stretching out our hand to pluck the ripe fruit of liberty is distressing beyond description.

Well, it is as it is, and must be borne. It shall be borne undespondingly, though not without grief. I feel tranquil in my conscience that I have done the duty of an honest man and of a good citizen, by not neglecting to try whether or not events might be turned, on a solid basis, to the profit of my native land.

And some consolation I have besides. I had occasion to get reassured on the point that no diplomatic tricks—in fact, nothing that the lying craft of despots may devise—will ever for a moment divert my nation from its unalterable determination to take advantage of every reasonable opportunity for reasserting its independence.

I have learned that this resolution can as little be broken by terrorism as it can be shaken by any concessions which the HAPSBURGS may devise in the hour of their need. I have learned that Hungary knows how to endure, how to wait, but never will change. I know that the nation is as well disciplined as it is determined.

I have been confirmed, together with my nation, in the conviction that no great European question can ever receive its definitive solution without us; nor can Europe be brought to a settled condition without the rights and legitimate claims of Hungary being taken into due account.

From this conviction we desire the certainty of our future. We believe in our future freedom, therefore we shall be free. The corresponding resolution has with the whole nation become a religious creed.

To have learnt all this is some consolation; and one more I have—I have the satisfaction to know that by insisting on the guarantee of irretractible facts preliminary to my giving the signal for rising, I have preserved my country from great misfortunes for aims which were not our own, and have preserved its future uncompromised—intact. This, at least, is a bright speck on the dreary horizon of my deep grief.

I was particularly careful to warn my fellow-countrymen in exile not to be led away by impatience, to throw up their positions which they may have gained by industry, before events take a turn which will warrant my calling on them. I even warned, in public papers, my countrymen in America to wait, and not to stir. Thanks to this precaution, no harm has accrued to any one on my account. But the prisoners of war from the Hungarian regiments flocked spontaneously to our banner.

We had already five battalions (upwards of 4,000 men) organized—alas! in three weeks more we should have had 25,000 of them. When the war was brought to an untimely end, I considered it a duty to guarantee the condition of the gallant band. I wished them to return home, rather than be scattered in misery over the face of the earth, provided I could secure to them a safe return.

I therefore insisted on a double stipulation for them—that of amnesty, and that of exemption (*congé définitif*) from further Austrian military service. I succeeded in both regards. France insisted peremptorily, and Austria felt obliged to yield—both points are guaranteed as far as stipulations can guarantee; it remains to be seen how Austria (false Austria) will execute them.

On this point I want to be kept in knowledge, accordingly I ordered * * * * * * *

He reports that some of our home-going braves may possibly write to me under your address.

Excuse this liberty, and should any such letters come to your hands, do me the favor to forward them to me. There will be nothing in them of a compromising character. We are no conspirators, nor do we want to be conspirators. Our national cause has long ago outgrown such poor swaddling clothes—where the whole nation is one conspiracies are useless, as they are unwise.

I am like the birds of the air; I had given up my house, and have yet none—in fact, have no spot on earth to rest my weary head upon; therefore, till further notice, please (occasion arising) to send letters to the care of FRANCIS PULSKY, Esq., No. 13 St. Alban's Villas, Highgate-rise, London, N. W.

Allow me to trust that your friendly feelings towards me and mine have undergone no change by late events; and believe me to be, with particular consideration, yours ever truly,

KOSSUTH.

JOHN MCADAM, Esq., No. 45 Hyde Park-street, Glasgow.

THE HUNGARIAN QUESTION AS EXPOUNDED BY KOSSUTH.

From the London Times.

M. KOSSUTH divides his attentions about equally between both sides, and after his chuckle over one monarch he proceeds immediately to make another as uncomfortable as possible. Hungary is represented as a simple volcano, only—and all the worse for that monarch—a most convenient and manageable volcano, ready to blow up whenever M. KOSSUTH tells it to do so. The concessions of the Austrian Court to the Protestants are dismissed with one contemptuous half-sentence, and Hungarian independence is described as biding its time, certain of the issue. He tells Austria that nothing but independence will satisfy Hungary, and that anything short of that will be accepted without thanks, as the forced gift of fear. We do not profess ourselves ready to take every word of M. KOSSUTH for gospel when he declaims and prophesies about Hungary. As a professed liberator he is, of course, bound to represent his country as aiming at a total rejection of the Austrian yoke, and never to be satisfied with anything else. At the same time, the facts which we all of us have before us are enough to show that Austria has but a weak and slippery hold of Hungary. She is somehow incapable of incorporating Hungary in her system, and making it feel at home in and a part of her Empire. How is this? Are we to take the pure unqualified "nationality" ground, and conclude that no people ever can be happy except under rulers of its own blood? Is it Austria's sole crime that Austria is not Hungary, and Hungary is not Austria? Nobody will, of course, deny the force of the nationality ground, and the liberation of Lombardy after five centuries of the German yoke will not weaken it; but the "nationality" ground is not everything or nearly everything. Nations have time after time been conquered by other nations, and have united afterwards with the conquerors, and the two have made one nation, and all the stronger and more powerful a one for the mixture. Look at the case of Ireland, so often quoted against us. Here there has not been that complete blending of races; but no one would for a moment say that Ireland was not incorporated into the English empire, and was not as substantial a part of us as Yorkshire, possessed of equal rights and privileges. The difference is, that liberty is a principle that incorporates, despotism is not. The process which incorporates a conquered nation with the conqueror is that of gradual concession, where disabilities are step by step removed, till after first yielding one point, and then another, there is at last produced a complete civil equality. But here lies the great difference between a free country and a despotism; the concessions of a free country are *trusted*, they are depended upon perfectly, because everybody knows that a free country *cannot* retrace a step of this kind; she is constitutionally incapable of it; it is not a matter of honor and keeping a promise, but of political nature; every concession is an advance in an order of things, and can no more be undone again than the course of the sun or the revolution of the seasons. But the concessions of a despotism cannot be trusted; they are not the gifts of an order of things, but of an individual will; they are given and taken away again as events dictate. This very case is one in point. The rights just conceded to the Protestants of Austria are only the same rights they enjoyed before the Revolution of 1848; they were then withdrawn; they are now granted again, but who can trust such a system of concession as this? Can the ruled nation feel any security in its position when it has only the will of an individual to depend upon? No, "Trust not in Princes nor in any child of man;" the individual's is a weak pledge indeed; an order of events is alone a sure security. Monarchs are censured for breaking their pledges, and they deserve the reproach, but the truth is they are men; they are individuals. Events take a turn, a prosperous crisis arrives, and they are immediately in the hands of the old party again. They can hardly, if they would, stand against the tide, and they forget their promises with their altered position. But the word of political nature is sure; the concessions of a free country advance and never can go back again, and they end in the complete incorporation of the conquered nation.

THE FRENCH ARMY—AN ORDER-OF-THE-DAY OF MARSHAL NEIL.

Marshal NEIL, on lately assuming his command at Toulouse, published the following order-of-the-day:

"SOLDIERS: The Emperor has deigned to confer on me the command of the sixth military arrondissement. In placing me at your head His Majesty accords me a proof his high confidence, of which I may well be proud. A recent and glorious war has shown once more what may be expected from the courage and devotion of the French soldier. At present, you are about to take advantage of the leisures of peace to improve your training and discipline, which are the first bases of the power of armies. The experience of the past will be turned to the advantage of the future, so that if war should again break out it may not be attended with less glory to our arms than in these later years, and that, under all circumstances, the Emperor may rely on your bravery and devoted loyalty. Unceasingly occupied in superintending and encouraging your labors, I shall always be happy to reward your services."

THE STATE OF ITALY.

CIRCULAR OF THE SARDINIAN GOVERNMENT.

Correspondence of the London Times.

PARIS, Sunday, Oct. 2—6 P. M.

A circular note has been sent by the Sardinian Minister of Foreign Affairs to the diplomatic agents of that country at the Courts of London, Paris, Berlin and St. Petersburgh, for the purpose of communicating it to those Governments. The document in question is couched, I understand, in lucid and earnest terms; and forcibly sets forth arguments in favor of the formation of a strong and independent Kingdom of Upper Italy, sufficiently powerful to counterbalance the influence of Austria, and keep in check her domineering tendencies. The constitution of such a State would, it is urged, dispel the apprehensions and tranquilize the mind of Europe, at the same time that it fulfilled the just wishes, so loudly and unanimously expressed, of those Italian countries which have lately shaken off tyranical governments. The note points out the impossibility of Piedmont's resisting Austria, should that Power, at any future time think fit to attack her, unless she be put in a more favorable position for so doing than has hitherto been secured to her. Intrenched in Venice and the quadrilateral, Austria will always press upon Italy, if there be not in that country a Power capable of inspiring her with respect. With Austria's fortresses overlooking her Lombard provinces, and with Austrian Dukes established by Austrian influence in the other countries adjacent, Sardinia would find herself hemmed in by hostile Governments, and her resistance to an attack might be desperate, but must be ineffectual. Signor DABORMIDA points out that peace, made on such bases, would be in reality only a truce, to be broken by Austria whenever she saw what she held to be a favorable opportunity. The people of Central Italy, with a true instinct of the necessities of the case, have shown—it is with great justice argued in the note—by their recent conduct how indispensable they deem the formation of the Kingdom of Upper Italy. Forgetting their long-standing feelings of rivalry, and discarding old jealousies, the different States voted, one after the other, with the utmost order and unanimity, their own annexation to Piedmont. Their wish, the note proceeds to say, has the strongest claim to respect; its realization would not be the sanction or introduction of a new and subversive principle, or of one opposed to European law and precedent, since the principle that would be recognized has already been acted upon in various European countries, in Greece, in Belgium, and in the Danubian Principalities, and since it is to its application that the present Emperor of the French owes his crown, and the present dynasty in England their first introduction as sovereigns of Great Britain.

PRESENT DIPLOMATIC ASPECTS OF THE QUESTION.

The *Journal des Débats* writes as follows on the difficultics of finding a solution for the Italian question:

"We do not pretend to give any solution of the difficulties which exist, and we should be greatly embarrassed to find one. Indeed, the annexation of the Duchies appears hardly possible without the coöperation of France, and hitherto France has declined to deviate from the engagements entered into at Villafranca. On the other hand, the restoration of the fallen Princes is impossible without the intervention of foreign aid, and both France and Austria have equally renounced that means of action. Even supposing the restoration accomplished, the question would not be settled. It must not be forgotten that the state of Central Italy before the war depended chiefly on Austrian domination in Lombardy and Austrian supremacy throughout Italy. The right of intervention attributed to Austria, and the possibility—or, to speak more correctly, the perpetual menace of that intervention, were the real bases of the thrones of the Archdukes and the indispensable condition of their maintenance. Now, that right of intervention, stipulated in private treaties between Austria and these Princes, it will be remembered, was one of the causes which led to the war; it has been destroyed by the French victories, and cannot be revived. And yet, not only the restoration, but also the maintenance of these Princes without the possibility of Austrian intervention, is hardly conceivable. Any one must be totally ignorant of Italy not to see that the Dukes would be at the mercy of every popular movement, and that as soon as it became known that no foreign Power would come to their aid they would not be able to stand. However, if we set aside these three solutions, the annexation to Sardinia, the restoration of the fallen Princes, and the erection of a new throne, what are we to look for in Central Italy? It is hardly too much to say, then, that the present state of affairs is a dead lock, extrication from which appears by no means easy. It is true, however, that everything has an end, that there is no drama or comedy without a conclusion, and that events, when human ingenuity is at fault, never leave embarrassing situations any great length of time without a solution."

DISTURBED CONDITION OF NORTHERN ITALY.

Correspondence of the London Times.

VIENNA, Friday, Sept. 30.

On the 22d inst., the anniversary of the day on which MANIN died, there were popular demonstrations at Venice and Verona. At Venice a kind of funeral procession went round the Place of St. Mark, and at Verona there was a promenade of the same description outside the walls of the fortress. Notwithstanding the introduction of drum-head law into the districts of Vicenza and Belluno, very many highway robberies are committed, and, as is said, by deserters from GARIBALDI's corps. On the 23d inst. twelve men in the uniform of the Sardinian volunteers attacked some travelers in the neighborhood of Verona, and several of the latter were severely wounded. Very many Austrian subjects cross the Po from the district of Rovigo, and join the Central Italian Corps, which has its outposts on the opposite side of the river. There is a brigade of Piedmontese Carabineers stationed at Vallegio, a small town near Villafranca, which gives great annoyance to the Austrians. The Piedmontese soldiers drill the fugitives from the province of Venetia, and when the latter have learned to handle their arms they join the abovementioned Central Italian Corps. There is also a dépôt of firearms at Valleggio, at which any Italian who is inclined to fight for the liberty of his country may purchase a very fine rifle for the sum of five francs (4s. 6d.) There are still about 4,000 Modenese soldiers in the Austrian territory, as not more than a score of the ducal troops have gone over to the National Party. The report that Austrian soldiers have recently been clothed in Modenese uniforms is so very absurd that it is not worth contradiction. The Lombards keep up the political agitation in Venice, and are to the inhabitants of that city what the Sardinians formerly were to the Milanese.

THE PAPAL STATES—SPEECH OF GARIBALDI.

On his arrival at Ravenna, Gen. GARIBALDI addressed the following words to the people who had assembled under the windows of the Governor's palace:

"We must arm while we are able to wield a weapon; independence is more difficult to preserve than to conquer. Armed as we are, our concord frightens our enemies; we shall always be united for the liberty and independence which Italy demands. When a whole people calls for it, it is God himself who inspires it with the thought, and in God's name we will defend it. To-morrow, at 6 o'clock, an enlistment-roll will be opened. Whoever writes his name in it shall be beloved by his country. I shall myself undertake the duty of conducting this chosen detachment of my fellow-townsmen—we shall be the stronger the more united we are. Ravenna is my native town, and its name shall remain engraven in my heart as long as I breathe."

The *Monitore* of Bologna publishes a letter from the Superieure of the Convent of Verrucchio, who declares that she has never seen a single soldier enter that building. This letter is signed "Fortunata Rinaldini," and legalized by "Pepoli." This declaration refers to a statement made by the clerical party, that the soldiers of the insurgents had entered the Convent and ill-treated the nuns.

MISCELLANEOUS.

The valedictory message of Gov. Hall, of Vermont, recommends economy in the State administration, and the abolition of State Attorney's fees, and the substitution of fixed salaries. The public institutions are in a prosperous condition, and the State Geological Survey is rapidly approaching completion. The Governor denounces the attempt to reopen the African Slave trade.

The recent failure of Henry Falls, carpet-dealer, in Cincinnati, is noticed by the Cincinnati *Times*. His liabilities are estimated at $50,000. It is stated that Mr. F. made collections of over $10,000 previous to his departure for parts unknown. The Sheriff levied on the establishment in satisfaction of a judgment in favor of Higgins & Co., of New-York, for $12,000.

The *Berliner Nachrichten* declares the story of the sale of Humboldt's library to Lord Bloomfield, to be altogether void of foundation; the more so as they have only just commenced to catalogue the collection—a task which is likely to consume a very considerable time, as it turns out to be far more extensive and valuable than was supposed.

A fire which occurred at Warsaw, N. Y., Oct. 14, destroyed property to the value of $13,000. It broke out in the planing mill of Gates & Hurd, and extended to Buxton's carriage factory. Loss on the former, $10,000; on the latter, $3,000. Insurance partial.

The *Critic* says: Mr. Robert Chambers is engaged upon a work that will excite much commotion in the literary world. He has a volume in the press refuting the antiquity of the Scottish Historical Ballads. We hear that he considers them to have been written in the early part of the eighteenth century.

A short time ago a cooper at Kierling, a village near Vienna, was sentenced to three months' imprisonment for having publicly found fault with the way in which the war was carried on in Italy.

THE ORIGIN OF SPECIES.

ON THE ORIGIN OF SPECIES BY MEANS OF NATURAL SELECTION OR THE PRESERVATION OF FAVORED RACES IN THE STRUGGLE FOR LIFE. By CHARLES DARWIN, M. A., etc. London, JOHN MURRAY: Reprint, D. APPLETON & Co.; 1860.

I.

It has been calculated, on data that may be considered as tolerably satisfactory, that the number of specific types of organic life at present existing on the globe considerably exceeds HALF-A-MILLION.

Enormous as this aggregation is, it is at the same time probable that each of the long suite of Geologic ages—all characterized by their own systems of animal and vegetable life—was at least as rich as at present in the number and variety of its organic structures.

Embracing in the imagination this vast *ensemble* of organisms—this ocean of forms amid which creative energy has sported—we realize the magnitude of the problem that seeks to account for the genesis of these millionfold incarnations of life. We touch, in fact, the grand and complex question of the Origin of Species—that mystery of mysteries, as one of our greatest philosophers has styled it.

With regard to this question the doctrine that has long prevailed is, that each species has been independently created. The idea of the *permanence of species* is, in fact, embodied in one shape or another in every definition of the term which has been framed. All the most eminent palæontologists, CUVIER, OWEN and AGASSIZ among them, and all our greatest geologists, LYLE, MURCHISON and the rest, have unanimously, often vehemently, maintained the immutability of species. No article of scientific faith is of more canonical authority, and though some bold speculator like LAMARCK, or some ingenious theorist like the author of the *Vestiges*, has ventured to question the soundness of its basis, yet it has given no outward sign of instability, and is commonly regarded as one of those doctrines which no man altogether in his right senses would set himself seriously to oppose.

Meanwhile, Mr. DARWIN, as the fruit of a quarter of a century of patient observation and experiment, throws out, in a book whose title at least has by this time become familiar to the reading public, a series of arguments and inferences so revolutionary as, if established, to necessitate a radical reconstruction of the fundamental doctrines of natural history.

Mr. DARWIN's mode of accounting for the diversity of the specific forms of organic life, differs alike from the doctrine of LAMARCK, (who made transmutation to depend mainly upon the efforts of the animal,) and from the hypothesis of the author of the *Vestiges* (who found the solution of the problem in the idea of consecutive development.)

It differs also, let us say, in having for its basis some undeniable facts.

Not by dubious speculations on the action of a "chemico-electric" operation on "germinal vesicles," but by the synthesis of a wide series of appreciable and daylight facts in the structure of animals and plants, does Mr. DARWIN sustain his startling theory. Rising from this synthesis, he ascends with the swoop and force of analogy to the august and audacious statement that "all the organic beings which have ever lived on this earth have descended from some one primordial form, into which life was at first breathed!"

It is clear that here is one of the most important contributions ever made to philosophic science; and it is at least behooving on scientists, in the light of the accumulation of evidence which the author has summoned in support of his theory, to reconsider the grounds on which their present doctrine of the origin of species is based.

II.

In the construction of his argument, Mr. DARWIN takes his *point de depart* from the striking modifications which animals and plants are susceptible of undergoing in domestication. The astonishing results achieved by English breeders in the modification of horses, dogs and cattle, furnish him fruitful exemplifications of the amazing versatility of animal structures. Indeed, breeders habitually speak of an animal's organization as something quite plastic, which they can model almost as they please.

But it is in the wonderful variations which domestic pigeons undergo that he finds his most striking illustrations of variation under domesticity. *In re* pigeons, Mr. DARWIN is immense. And really, the diversity of breeds is something astonishing: marked anatomical and physiological characteristics distinguish the various breeds; at least a score of pigeons might be selected which, if shown to an ornithologist, and he were told that they were wild birds, would certainly be ranked by him as well-defined species, and some even as distinct genera; and yet, great as the differences are between the breeds, it is the universal opinion of naturalists that all have descended from the Rock pigeon!

The key to this production of varieties under domestication is found in man's power of accumulative selection: nature gives successive variations: man *adds them up*—such is DARWIN's striking expression—in certain directions useful to him.

Is it not plain that this *capacity for undergoing such modifications* exhibits an elasticity of constitution which would equally tend to adapt these animals to varieties of natural conditions, and thus to originate diversified races which would perpetuate themselves without man's interference?

Species, then, are to some extent, and sometimes to a quite remarkable extent, variable—modifiable. There is a certain versatility in animal structures. They are more or less flexible—more or less plastic.

One of the chief powers in this tragedy of transmutation, this new diviner finds in the Struggle for Existence—an expression which he employs in a large and metaphorical sense.

A struggle for existence inevitably follows from the high geometrical ratio of increase which is common to all organic beings. There is no exception to the rule that every organic being naturally increases at so high a rate that, if not destroyed, the earth would soon be covered by the progeny of a single pair. Even slow-breeding man has doubled in twenty-five years, and at this rate, in a few thousand years, there would literally not be standing-room for his progeny. Of this prodigious capacity of increase Mr. DARWIN furnishes a copious series of illustration; but one of the most striking that has ever come under our notice is one which he does not give, and which we recall in LINNÆUS. The Aphides, or plant-lice, have been found to propagate so rapidly that in the course of a few months, if all interference were excluded, no fewer than 1,000,000,000,000,000,000 would be evolved from a single individual—an amount which only becomes conceivable when we learn that this mass of life would weigh somewhere about as much as *five hundred millions* of stout men!

Such is DARWIN's doctrine of the Struggle for Existence. Far more individuals being produced than can possibly survive, there must in every case be a struggle for existence, either one individual with another of the same species, or with the individuals of a distinct species, or with the physical conditions of life.

It is the doctrine of MALTHUS applied with manifold force to the whole animal and vegetable kingdoms.

The law of the Struggle for Existence Mr. DARWIN finds the key to many secret facts in the economy of nature. He records many striking instances of how complex and unexpected are the checks and relations between organic beings, which have to struggle together in the same country. By what a web of complex relations are plants and animals most remote in the scale of nature bound together! How, for example, could the domestic cats in any village be imagined to determine the frequency of certain flowers in that district? Mr. DARWIN shall make answer in his own words:

"I have reason to believe that humble-bees are indispensable to the fertilization of the heartsease. Hence I have very little doubt that if the whole genus of humble-bees became extinct or very rare in England, the heartsease and red clover would become very rare, or wholly disappear. The number of humble-bees in any district depends in a great degree on the number of field-mice, which destroy their combs and nests; and Mr. H. NEWMAN, who has long attended to the habits of humble-bees, believes that 'more than two thirds of them are thus destroyed all over England.' Now the number of mice is largely dependent, as every one knows, on the number of cats; and Mr. NEWMAN says, 'Near villages I have found the nests of humble-bees more numerous than elsewhere, which I attribute to the number of cats that destroy the mice!'"

One would think, in reading Mr. DARWIN's string of sequences, that the ingenious author of the "House that Jack Built" had intended to imbue the infant mind with a knowledge of high scientific truths: for the whole may be expressed, after the fashion of the immortal legend, in the following concise runic: "This is the old woman, that kept the cat, that ate the mouse, that killed the humble-bees, that fertilized the clover!"

In the midst of this constant and complex struggle for existence, there is a formative principle ever at work modifying the structure of organized beings. This, Mr. DARWIN calls the law of Natural Selection. The doctrine of Natural Selection is the radical thought of the book.

We have seen that there is something plastic in all organisms—a certain versatility, susceptible of producing varieties from species, susceptible of modifying the structure to a certain extent. We have also seen that man, by selection, can certainly produce great results, and can adapt organic beings to his own uses, through the accumulation of slight but useful variations, given to him by the hand of Nature.

Nature is constantly at work doing the same thing. Whatever variation occurring among the individuals of any species of animals or plants is in any way advantageous in the struggle for existence, will give to those individuals an advantage over their fellows, which will be inherited by their offspring until the modified variety supplants the parent species. By the steady accumulation, during long ages of time, of slight differences, each in some way beneficial to the individual, arise the various modifications of structure by which the countless forms of animal and vegetable life are distinguished from each other.

It may be said that Natural Selection is daily and hourly scrutinizing, throughout the world, every variety, even the slightest—rejecting that which is bad, preserving and adding up all that is good; silently and insensibly working, whenever and wherever opportunity offers, at the improvement of each organic being. We see nothing of these slow changes in progress, until the hand of time has marked the lapse of ages, and then so imperfect is our view into long past geological epochs, that we only see that the forms of life are now different from what they formerly were.

Through this long-continued course of modification, Mr. DARWIN has it that the slight differences characteristic of varieties of the same species tend to be augmented into the greater differences characteristic of species of the same genus.

But what are the real relations of varieties to species? Mr. DARWIN puts in the strongest light the fact that there is no absolute difference between these, but that they shade off into each other. Well marked varieties he regards as simply "incipient species." and species he looks upon as just strongly-marked and well-defined varieties. Few well-marked and well-known varieties can be named which have not been ranked as species by at least some competent judges. Certainly no clear line of demarcation has as yet been drawn between species and sub-species, and again between sub-species and well-marked varieties. These differences blend into each other in an insensible series: and a series impresses the mind with the idea of an actual passage.

From this point Mr. DARWIN advances to the examination of the Laws of Variation.

And here he frankly confesses our ignorance is profound. Not in one case out of a hundred can we pretend to assign any reason why this or that part differs, more or less, from the same part in the parents. But Mr. DARWIN maintains that, wherever we have the means of instituting a comparison, the same laws appear to have acted in producing the lesser differences between varities of the same species, and the greater differences between species of the same genus.

Among efficient causes, however, he numbers the external conditions of life, as climate, food, &c. Habit in producing constitutional differences, and use in strengthening, and disuse in weakening and diminishing organs, seem to have been more potent in their effects. Homologous parts tend to vary in the same way, and homologous parts tend to cohere.

Among the subtlest of the Laws of Variation is the principle of correlation of growth—a most important subject, most imperfectly understood. According to this doctrine the whole organization is so tied together during its growth and development, that when slight variations in any one part occur, other parts become modified. An instance of this is seen in the correspondence in length between the jaws and limbs, thus verifying the doctrine in transcendental anatomy that the lower jaw is homologous with the limbs. In monstrosities, the correlations between quite distinct parts are very curious, and many whimsical instances are given in GEOFFROY ST. HILAIRE's great work (*Anomalies*.) What can be more singular than the relation between blue eyes and deafness in cats, and the tortoise-shell color with the female sex; or again, the relation between the hair and teeth in the naked Turkish dog—though here probably homology comes into play?

"It is interesting," says Mr. DARWIN, "to contemplate an entangled bank, clothed with many plants of many kinds, with worms crawling through the damp earth, with birds singing on the bushes, and with various insects flitting about." In this doctrine all these elaborately constructed forms, so different from each other, and dependent on each other in so complex a manner, are looked upon as being produced by laws acting round us. These laws, taken in the largest sense, being Growth with Reproduction; Inheritance, which is almost implied by reproduction; Variability, from the indirect and direct action of the external conditions of life, and from use and disease; a rate of increase so high as to lead to a Struggle for Life, and as a consequence to Natural Selection, entailing divergence of character, and extinction of less-improved forms.

Such is Mr. DARWIN's theory. Easy enough to state, it is impossible to give within much less space than the author has himself employed any idea of the mass of argument and illustration by which this startling theory is sustained and defended. The book is indeed, as he declares, "one long argument," and the theory can only be fully appreciated by patiently following the many consecutive and collateral lines of evidence which he converges on the illustration of a doctrine which is with him manifestly a profound conviction.

III.

Shall we frankly declare that, after the most deliberate consideration of Mr. DARWIN's arguments, we remain unconvinced?

The book is full of a most interesting and impressive series of minor verifications; but he fails to show the points of junction between these, and no where rises to complete logical statement.

The difficulties, of course, are enormous. This he frankly acknowledges. "Some of them are so grave that to this day I can never reflect on them without being staggered." Such are his own *naive* and noble words.

He thinks, however, they are more apparent than real. We fear they are very real. To us insurmountable.

Ten times the space given to this article would not suffice for any adequate treatment of this vast and complicated subject. In a very general way, though, we may touch on a few topics. To this and every hypothesis which assumes the gradual transition from species to species, from genus to genus, geology opposes the irrefragable fact of the utter absence of all transitional links, and the clean and clear identity of specific forms. As on Mr. DARWIN's theory an interminable number of intermediate forms must have existed, linking together all the species in each group by gradations as fine as our present varieties, we have a perfect right to ask, why do we not see these linking forms all around us? Why are not all organic beings blended together in an inextricable chaos?

Mr. DARWIN answers this difficulty by urging the extreme imperfection of the geological record. That the geological record is imperfect all will admit; but few will be inclined to admit that it is imperfect to the degree Mr. DARWIN's doctrine requires.

This draft on the imagination of zillionfold transitional organisms to fill up the hiati between fossil species, is succeeded by a hypothesis still more startling. For, unhappily for the theory, when we go back even to the first apparition of life in the palæozoic rocks of the Silurian system, we find ourselves among organic structures specifically just as distinct as those our dredgers now take off our coasts. To obtain a background for this abrupt appearance of distinct types, his theory postulates that "before the lowest Silurian stratum was deposited, long periods elapsed—as long as, or probably far longer than, the whole interval from the Silurian age to the present day; and that during these vast but quite unknown periods of time, the world swarmed with living creatures."

To the question why we do not find records of these vast primordial periods, Mr. DARWIN fairly admits that he "can give no satisfactory answer," but tries to satisfy the inquirer by the assurance that his witnesses are all submerged! At a period immeasurably antecedent to the Silurian epoch, he affirms, continents may have existed where oceans are now spread out, and clear and open seas may have existed where our continents now stand. Nor should we be justified in assuming that if, for instance, the bed of the Pacific Ocean were now converted into a continent, we should there find formations older than the Silurian strata, and in those formations, one after another, throughout millions of ages, the successive forms of the primitive fauna and flora were silently entombed.

Amid this pile of unsupported conjecture there is but one consideration that we may profitably keep in mind—that it is an admission in Geology that the absence of all organic remains in a particular deposit is no proof whatever that animal life did not abundantly exist during the whole period of that deposit. An azoic *rock* is no necessary proof of an azoic *period*. It is even a doctrine of the most advanced school of English Geologists, that the fossils of the Silurian formation are by no means to be regarded as the first apparition of organic life, and the present writer had an opportunity last Summer, in company with Sir WM. LOGAN, of examining a fossil from the Laurentian rocks of Canada—far older than the Silurian strata—which if it holds its authenticity, must be the intimation of a new and elder world of organic forms, into which research and induction may yet be prolonged.

The fundamental limitation of Mr. DARWIN's theory springs from a fact in his own mental structure. He is but a *Naturalist*. Of that lofty series of speculations embracing the doctrine of Homologies, Embryology and Unity of Type, he seems ignorant in any profound sense. It is only, we apprehend, by converging the prophetic omens and intuitions from these grand reaches of science that light can be thrown on the mysterious problem of the Origin of Life. OKEN has profoundly remarked that "the animal system cannot be arbitrarily disposed of according to this or that organ, just as it may chance to meet the eye, but only in accordance with the rigid prescripts of the animal body's genesis."

The conception of the Unity of Nature passed like a new spirit into science, at the opening of the present century. It is one of those flaming thoughts the soul projects—plendid prophecies that become the light of all our science and all our day. Applied, within these few years, by St. HILAIRE, OKEN, CARUS, SERRES, OWEN, to Anatomy, it has revealed a sublime unity of design and composition throughout the whole hierarchy of animate organisms. GEOFFROY ST. HILAIRE formuled it in the grand conception that *there is but one animal*. Embryology has developed the doctrine that all animals resemble each other in their early stages, and Transcendental Anatomy reveals that the higher orders of animals pass through transitory embryonic stages, that are the permanent *states* of the lower classes. Polyp, mollusk, turtle, fish, bird, are successive incarnations of that divine idea that finds its latest vestment in the glorious garb of the human form.

IV.

But it would be to fail to extract the best uses of this book, to expect a finality. Its best suggestion is to show us how far we are from the possibility of any finality. Of how many things are we ignorant. "And we do not know how ignorant we are," adds Mr. DARWIN.

No one ought to feel surprise at much remaining as yet unexplained in regard to the origin of life. Think of the baffling problem it presents—the sphinx-riddle of life, the mother-mystery ever environing us! "It is good clearly to understand," said MALEBRANCHE, and with a very deep meaning, "that there are some things utterly incomprehensible." Indeed, considering the limitations of science, what is there for the wisest but to work in the spirit of the Shakspearean utterance:

"In Nature's infinite Book of Secrecy
A little I can read."

But while it seems to our apprehension that, in the very nature of things, the problem of life yet remains to receive epic statement, we at the same time look upon the contribution of Mr. DARWIN as a most legitimate and successful attempt to extend the domain of science—as, indeed, the most important of modern contributions to philosophic zoology.

And in respect of the great spinal thought of Mr. DARWIN's theory, we are persuaded that the doctrine of progressive modification by Natural Selection, will give a new direction to inquiry into the real genetic relationship of species, existing and extinct,—will, in fact, make a revolution in Natural History.

It will give a new and sure basis of classification. Indeed, this grand fact of the grouping of all organic beings seems inexplicable on any other theory. Read the interminable disputes of the naturalists as to what are species and what varieties, and you will see what a scientific chaos classification up to this day is. How the cumbersome catalogue of species increase! Meanwhile the difficulties increase, also, instead of diminishing with the extension of their researches.

That is a great fact, too, which Mr. DARWIN so impressively teaches—the imperfection of the geological record—and must go largely to modify existing palæontologic conceptions.

And what a vast background he lights up! What flowing æons mark the ascent from the Silurian Mollusks to man—gulfs of time over which the mind grows dizzy in the attempt to gaze, and we feel the shiver of eternity pass over us! It is well to feed the mind with this sense of the amplitude of time, as a counter-agent of our petty and contracted chronologies.

It is the leading idea of modern science that we need not go in search of any other causes than those which are at present in action, for an explanation of the phenomena of Nature. Modern geology has banished the notion of sudden cataclysms, by showing that the same agencies are now at work which have brought about all the wonders of the up-piling of the strata of the globe. We are thus introduced into the grand idea of growth—of the enormous effect of existing agencies, when spread over a great period of time.

DARWIN puts himself abreast these same tendencies. And just as LYELL has banished from Geology the notion of sudden cataclysms, DARWIN threatens to banish from Zoology the notion of sudden creations. Together, we feel justified in saying, they have laid the foundation of one of the mightiest changes in philosophical thought. It is certainly more in accordance with our ideas of the philosophy of causation to believe that the entire hierarchy of animate organisms are the result of the continuity of one mode of operation throughout the whole period that has elapsed since life was first introduced into our planet. It harmonizes better with our highest ideas of divine foresight, to believe that the scheme of evolution was originally made so perfect as to require no subsequent interference. We have no sympathy with those who, to use the admirable language of BADEN POWELL—"behold the Deity more clearly in the dark than in the light—in confusion, interruption and catastrophe, more than in order, continuity and progress."

V.

The most important contribution to modern thought is undoubtedly the indirect teachings of physical science. For, magnificent though the direct teachings be, the indirect are perhaps still more wonderful: the former have relation but to the material world, while the latter influence the whole of man's speculative activity. Indeed the only part of science that can ever profoundly touch the great laity are its glorious indirections—its grand out-croppings of truth. In this regard there is much for science yet to attain: science needs literature just as much as literature needs science. He is the master of science who makes his facts but initial, leading to heights where new vistas open in flashes of beauty and repose. It is a significant fact that certain propositions recommend themselves and find acceptance even though not fortified by authority. They seem to find metaphysical support and interior warranties. Who can fail to see that such doctrines as the Nebular hypothesis, the doctrine of Development, &c., aside altogether from their scientific validity, have an indirect import to the culture, far more potent than all their direct bearings?

It would seem as if the doctrine of "attractions proportioned to destinies" held equally true in science as in sociology. HARVEY's discovery of the circulation of the blood is recorded to have found acceptance from no physician over forty years old. Perhaps DARWIN felt that to his own theory some such elective affinities might apply. "I look," says he, towards the close of the volume, "with confidence to the future, to young and rising naturalists, who will be able to view both sides of the question with impartiality."

In that future to which he looks forward, he will not, we apprehend, be regarded as having drawn the cosmic circle of life, but rather as having indicated one of its arcs. At all events, it seems to be a historic law that the greater portion of truths in the theory of nature first appear as purple mirages—ruddy and auroral streaks gilding the matin of man's mind; but the appointed time duly brings up the perfect thought, fraught with the wealth of invisible climes, and flooding the age with the sunlight of science.

MONETARY AFFAIRS.

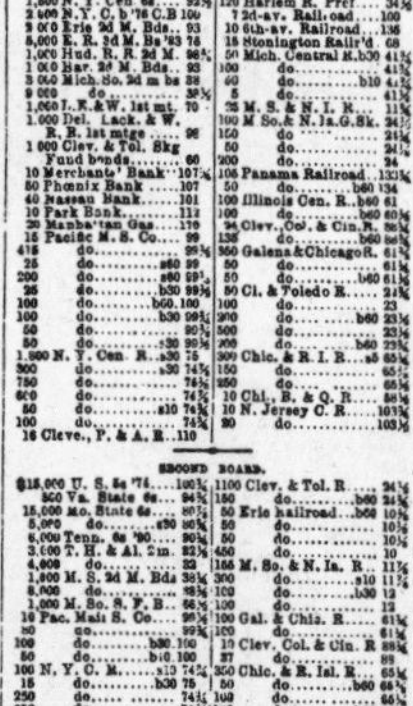

Sales at the Stock Exchange....MARCH 27.

6,000 M. S. 6s L. Bds..101
18,000 Mo. State 6s.....81
1,500 N. Y. Cen. 6s....92½
2,000 N. Y. C. b'76 C.B 100
3,000 Erie 3d M. Bds..93
5,000 E. R. 3d M. Bs '83 78
1,000 Hud. R. R. 2d M. 98½
1,000 Har. 2d M. Bds..93
3,000 Mich. So. 2d m bs 88
9,000 do..........38½
1,000 L. K. & W. 1st mt. 70
1,000 Del. Lack. & W. R. R. 1st mtge....96
1,000 Clev. & Tol. Skg Fund bonds.......60
10 Merchants' Bank..107½
50 Phœnix Bank.....107
40 Nassau Bank......101
10 Park Bank........112
20 Manhattan Gas....170
15 Pacific M. S. Co....99
415 do..........98½
25 do.......s60 99
200 do.......s60 99½
25 do.......b30 99½
100 do.......b60.100
100 do.......b30 99½
50 do..........99½
50 do.......s30 99½
1,800 N. Y. Cen. R..s30 75
300 do.......s30 74¾
750 do..........74½
600 do..........74½
50 do.......s10 74½
100 do..........74½
16 Cleve., P. & A. R..110
6 Erie Railroad.....10½
450 do..........10½
120 Harlem R. Pref....34½
7 2d-av. Railroad....100
10 6th-av. Railroad...136
15 Stonington Railr'd 68
50 Mich. Central R.b30 41½
100 do..........41½
60 do.......b10 41½
5 do..........41½
25 M. S. & N. I. R.....11½
100 M. So. & N. Ia.G.Sk. 24½
150 do..........24½
50 do..........24½
200 do..........24
108 Panama Railroad..133½
50 do.......b60 134
100 Illinois Cen. R..b60 61
100 do.......b60 60½
24 Clev., Col. & Cin. R. 88½
138 do.......b60 88½
350 Galena & Chicago R. 61½
50 do..........61½
50 do.......b60 61½
50 Cl. & Toledo R.....24½
100 do..........23
200 do.......b60 23½
500 do..........23½
200 do.......b60 23½
300 Chic. & R. I. R...s5 65½
150 do..........65½
250 do..........65½
10 Chi., B. & Q. R....88½
10 N. Jersey C. R.....103½
20 do..........103½

SECOND BOARD.

$15,000 U. S. 5s '74....100½
500 Va. State 6s.....94½
15,000 Mo. State 6s....80½
5,000 do.......s30 80½
6,000 Tenn. 6s '90.....90½
3,000 T. H. & Al. 2m..82½
4,000 do..........82
1,800 M. S. 2d M. Bds 38½
8,000 do..........38½
1,000 M. So. S. F. B...66½
10 Pac. Mail S. Co....99½
50 do..........99½
100 do.......b30.100
50 do.......b10.100
100 N. Y. C. R......s10 74½
15 do.......b30 75
250 do..........74½
250 do..........74½
50 Clev. & Tol. R.......24
1100 Clev. & Tol. R.....24½
150 do.......b60 24½
50 Erie Railroad...b60 10½
50 do..........10½
50 do..........10½
450 do..........10
165 M. So. & N. Ia. R...11½
300 do.......s10 11½
100 do.......b30 12
100 do..........12
100 Gal. & Chic. R.....61½
100 do..........61½
10 Clev. Col. & Cin. R 88½
27 do..........88
350 Chic. & R. Isl. R...65½
50 do.......b60 65½
100 do..........65½
100 do.......b60 65½

TUESDAY, March 27—P. M.

We have to report continued firmness on the Stock Exchange on most of the Share and Bond list. The principal exception to-day is New-York Central stock, which, under the pending decision at Albany on the tax question, is barely supported. Several considerable sellers came in to-day, at 75 @74¾ ℘ cent., and the closing quotations this afternoon fell off to 74½@74¾ ℘ cent., as against 75 yesterday afternoon. No definite information was received to-day from the Legislature, but an impression was attempted on the street to the effect that the decision on the pending tax-bill would be less favorable than anticipated. The Western Shares were higher by 2 ℘ cent. on Cleveland and Toledo, and ½@⅝ ℘ cent. on Michigan Southern than the advance reported yesterday, under a very large demand for the former, and a steady inquiry for the latter. Michigan Central, Galena, Illinois Central and Rock Island were steady. The last-named closed 65½ sales. The dividend question is yet undetermined, but a quorum of the Managers is expected to meet to-morrow, Wednesday, when a resumption of dividends upon the stock no doubt will be voted, and at a rate likely to be fully sustained, if not exceeded hereafter. The movement in the shares of the Michigan Southern Company, heretofore ascribed to the purpose of a new party to control the April election, is now continued and rather strengthened, from day to day, on the assured knowledge that the control in question has been secured, and that the new policy will be to reduce the whole incumbrance upon the property in Bonds and Shares to about twelve million dollars, equally divided, so as to secure after full reorganization 7 ℘ cent. on the former, and at least 8 ℘ cent. on the latter, on a minimum traffic of $1,900,000 ℘ annum, allowing one million dollars for all charges, exclusive of interest and dividends; that is:

7 ℘ cent. on $6,000,000 mortgage..........$420,000
8 ℘ cent. on $6,000,000 capital..........480,000
Together, a net income of..........$900,000

The amount of minor mortgage bonds, plain bonds, floating debt, guaranteed shares and common shares to be consolidated on an equitable scale into $6,000,000 capital stock, is something like twelve or twelve and a half millions. We are not advised of the particulars of the scaling process, which will be submitted by the new management in the event of their coming into the full control of the property, but presume that, as between the two classes of stock, the value of the guaranteed will be rated at about double the common shares. Pacific Mail shares advanced to par. The Panama shares were steady. The February traffic of the Company shows $163,500, against $92,000 same month last season. The State Stocks were steady. Missouris opened firm at 81, but fell off this afternoon to 80¾ ℘ cent. The advices from Jefferson City and St. Louis today are to the effect that the recent grant of aid to the Railways will become a law by the lapse of ten days after the presentation to the Governor for approval. Tennessee sixes are a fraction lower. The $300,000 new loan by the State of North Carolina, in renewal of an out-standing debt, has been taken at home, as the rate of 96 ℘ cent., the best bid from this City being about 93½ ℘ cent. The Railway Bonds to-day were generally firm, and but few parcels of the leading descriptions offered. City Bank Stocks also firm. The general market at the close quite steady.

The Exchange market for the *Asia* to-morrow, closes 108¾@109¼ ℘ cent. on London; f.5.18¾@f.5.17½ on Paris; a fair business done to-day with scarcely a shade of variation in the rates or tone of the market. In Discounts, we hear of August and September indorsed paper done as low as 5½ ℘ cent. outside of Bank, and October bills at 6 ℘ cent. Prime short acceptances, 5@5½ ℘ cent. Demand Loans, 5@6 ℘ cent. The steamer to-morrow will take a few hundred thousand dollars in Gold bars.

The following is a comparative statement of the Exports, (exclusive of Specie,) from New-York to Foreign Ports for the week and since Jan. 1:

	1858.	1859.	1860.
For the week	$1,344,083	$1,725,436	$1,688,836
Previously reported	12,547,127	11,547,852	17,089,024
Since Jan. 1	$13,891,210	$13,273,288	$18,777,860

The following was to-day's business at the Assistant Treasurer's Office:

Total receipts	$148,384 81
Payments	71,102 12
Balance	8,020,008 49

The receipts include $146,000 for Customs.

WEEKLY AVERAGES OF THE PHILADELPHIA BANKS.

BANKS.	LOANS. March 19.	LOANS. March 26.	SPECIE. March 19.	SPECIE. March 26.
Philadelphia	3,465,000	3,516,000	617,000	620,000
North America	2,797,317	2,814,785	538,814	617,473
Farm. & Mech.	3,890,895	3,972,254	806,698	754,914
Commercial	1,537,000	1,556,000	205,000	274,000
Mechanics'	1,765,330	1,800,803	276,170	215,625
N. Liberties	1,446,000	1,399,000	296,000	304,000
Southwark	962,636	979,055	204,654	204,270
Kensington	817,475	807,437	151,926	146,359
Penn Township	833,891	821,439	159,392	155,655
Western	1,425,880	1,474,281	396,046	388,850
Manuf. & Mech.	1,148,250	1,149,920	138,395	127,880
Commerce	588,176	619,291	191,730	213,493
Girard	2,134,749	2,142,869	319,017	344,239
Tradesmen's	589,192	574,119	103,229	107,468
Consolidation	495,049	505,072	88,79	184,413
City	796,611	812,334	170,910	179,989
Commonwealth	468,906	479,663	144,190	119,885
Corn Exchange	422,864	424,967	86,765	86,611
Union	530,842	546,930	89,917	107,873
Total	26,043,772	26,405,279	4,952,524	5,063,274

BANKS.	DEPOSITS. March 19.	DEPOSITS. March 26.	CIRCULATION. March 19.	CIRCULATION. March 26.
Philadelphia	1,662,000	1,685,000	269,600	297,600
North America	1,734,179	1,764,369	236,415	217,945
Farm. & Mech.	2,780,311	2,704,183	384,530	396,565
Commercial	737,000	772,000	143,800	146,900
Mechanics'	960,686	916,303	154,170	154,970
N. Liberties	947,000	904,000	142,000	151,000
Southwark	661,630	685,718	108,420	104,490
Kensington	565,835	555,240	129,830	136,445
Penn Township	566,260	552,311	90,810	87,075
Western	913,034	924,410	126,185	124,250
Manuf. & Mech.	618,000	603,455	112,380	116,210
Commerce	483,272	461,676	98,545	99,033
Girard	994,431	1,001,177	201,865	194,525
Tradesmen's	400,011	336,342	79,442	80,300
Consolidation	286,042	28,821	96,055	97,285
City	473,191	464,460	101,318	102,680
Commonwealth	333,425	316,516	123,045	130,970
Corn Exchange	297,869	292,690	107,831	124,569
Union	280,467	282,283	87,080	87,240
Total	15,893,622	15,543,269	2,784,773	2,859,812

The Supreme Court of the United States, in term at Washington, has affirmed, unanimously, as we learn, the judgment of the United States Circuit Court for the District of Ohio, in favor of the validity of the indorsement of the Cleveland, Columbus and Cincinnati Company on $400,000 of the 7 ℘ cent. Bonds of the Columbus and Piqua Company, now bankrupt. This final decision is, in every sense, a just and righteous one, though nothing more than the Cleveland and Columbus Company ought, in a proper spirit, to have anticipated, when at the instance of two or three of their repudiating stockholders, they attempted in 1856 to shirk this responsibility under color of an injunction before the Courts. The judgment of the Supreme Court is that the indorsement is valid, and that the overdue coupons must be paid and all subsequent coupons provided for, as though the obligation was an original undertaking by the Cleveland, Columbus and Cincinnati Company. The principal and accrued interest on the debt is (or will be on 1st April) about $540,000, and from our knowledge of the leading Directors of the Company we are inclined to believe that no further difficulty will be interposed to the full and prompt recognition of the obligation. The stock of the Company, which is a regular paying 10 ℘ cent. investment, has, in a certain sense, been under a cloud ever since the act of repudiation of their indorsement was resolved upon under pressure of the two or three stockholders who sued out the injunction, and has been selling at 88@90 ℘ cent., while the New-Jersey Transportation, New-Haven and Hartford, and other concerns paying no higher rate of dividend, have been and are considerably above par. We, therefore, look to see the *credit* of the shares of the Company, if not the price, improve on the final settlement of this vexed question, or as soon thereafter as provision is made for the arrearage of interest due on the indorsed Bonds.

The annual meeting of the Delaware and Hudson Company took place to-day, when Messrs. John Wurts, Silas Holmes, Wm. S. Herriman, Charles N. Talbot, Edward J. Woolsey, G. Talbot Olyphant, Robert Ray, Samuel B. Schieffelin, Abiel A. Low, Robert L. Kennedy, John Schenck, James M. Halsted and Le Grand B. Cannon were reëlected as the Board of Management for the ensuing year, and the General Balance Sheet and Annual Account for the year ending 15th instant were presented. It will be noticed that the net result of the account for the year, exclusive of interest on the moderate debt of the Company, is $618,210, equal to 8¼ ℘ cent. on the capital of $7,500,000, or one and a quarter ℘ cent. in excess of the cash dividends paid within the year.

DELAWARE AND HUDSON COMPANY, MARCH, 1860.

Canal		$6,184,615 72
Railroad and Equipment		1,792,829 40
Coal lands and other real estate		736,128 80
Canal boats, barges, steamboats, machinery, tools, &c.		362,870 93
Sinking Fund for redemption of Bonds		75,000 00
Mortgages receivable	$68,339 44	
Bills and accounts receivable	355,588 78	
Cash and demand loans	82,341 93	
Coal on hand at New-York, Rondout and Honesdale, with advances on business of 1860	669,677 95—	175,948 10
Total		$10,347,392 95
Capital Stock		$7,500,000 00
Seven per cent bonds		900,000 00
Mortgages payable	$141,723 09	
Bills payable	630,250 00	
Bills payable, 1861	264,928 49	
Due depositors	126,725 25—	1,161,625 83
Profit and loss account		785,766 12
Total		$10,347,392 95
To Coal on hand March 1, 1859		$221,611 30
To Mining Coal		435,006 73
To Railroad transportation and repairs		334,158 08
To Canal repairs and superintendance		227,505 41
To Freight of coal to Rondout		468,930 94
To Labor and expenses at Rondout		56,677 51
To Rent, salaries, current expenses, &c., New-York office		37,545 74
To Coal-yard and Harbor expenses, taxes, interest, &c.		223,141 49
Balance		618,210 76
Total		$2,624,886 96
By sales of coal to March 1, 1860		$1,831,050 15
By canal and railroad tolls collected		311,507 79
By Profits of barges, &c.		53,730 72
By Coal on hand at Honesdale, Weymart, Rondout and New-York		428,508 30
Total		$2,624,886 96
Balance		618,210 76

The Indiana State Auditor's report for 1859 shows an important increase in the taxable valuation of the State. The valuation is as follows:

The total valuation of all taxable as returned in 1859, is	$435,367,862
In 1856 it was	318,204,964
Total increase	$117,162,898
The number of acres appraised in the State is	22,149,396

The earnings of the Rock Island Railroad for the third week of March were:

1860	$19,699
1859	17,622
Increase	$2,077

The Exchange market at New-Orleans on Friday last, March 23, is thus noticed in the *Picayune*:

"Clear Sterling bills, 106@106¼@106¾; bills with shipping documents attached, 107@107¼@107¾; francs, f.5.17⅞@f.5.12½ ℘ dollar; sixty-day bills on New-York, &c., 1@1¼@1½ ℘ cent. discount; sight, 1-16@¼@⅜ ℘ cent. premium."

The *Commercial Advertiser* reports from Pennsylvania:

"The members of the Councils of Pittsburgh appeared before the Supreme Court yesterday, to answer a peremptory *mandamus*, commanding them to make provision for the payment of the interest upon the bonds issued as a subscription to the Chartreux Valley Railroad Company. Five of the members in their return stated their willingness to vote for the tax necessary to make the provision, but were afforded no opportunity to do so through the prevention of an opportunity by the majority. The other members state that they are not advised of the amount of interest due, and have no record or means of ascertaining the same; that, acting upon their several oaths of office, they cannot in conscience undertake to levy and assess a tax on their constituents against their own judgment, and without the consent of the people they represent. They express a willingness in case these opinions are supposed to be inconsistent with their duty to surrender their trust to their constituents, to be delegated anew at their pleasure, to such persons as may conscientiously accept of it, upon such terms as may enable them to conform to the order of the Court in the premises."

The earnings and expenses of the Watertown and Rome Railroad in February were as follows:

EARNINGS.

	1860.	1859.
Passengers	$9,082 83	$8,414 96
Freight	9,903 26	9,416 38
Mail and Miscellaneous	1,576 40	1,115 97
Total	$20,561 49	$18,947 30

The Anthracite Coal trade for the week shows a liberal increase in tonnage, so far as the various channels have been opened for the season, while the accounts of diminished stocks from last season and the growing preponderance of the New-York trade over that of Pennsylvania, are especially encouraging. We learn from the Pottsville *Miner's Journal* of Saturday that

"A letter from a coal-dealer in Boston states that the markets were never so bare of Coal as they now are, and predicts a fair business this year, if prices are maintained, which he thinks ought to be. He also states that but little is doing in the trade at present, owing to the high price of freights, which he thinks will soon come down. In the meantime those who are out are receiving small cargoes from New-York to supply their present wants. Such is also the state of the trade at New-York. Many of the dealers are receiving small supplies of from forty to sixty tons from Elizabethport, &c., until they have cleaned up their business for the last year. The Delaware and Raritan Canal is now open, and Coal will go forward from this region direct by water. The Toll and Transportation on the Lehigh Valley Railroad and Jersey Central has been fixed at $2 to Elizabethport. Last year it was $1 90. The rates of toll on the Lehigh Canal and Delaware Division, and also Morris Canals, were not promulgated up to yesterday, but it is understood that the rates will be advanced seven cents over last year's prices on the Lehigh and Delaware Division Canals."

The same authority—which, it will be borne in mind, is the organ of the Schuylkill Coal region—admits that "the Coal firm of VAN DUSEN, NORTON & Co., of Philadelphia, agents for the sale of Lehigh Coal, have been forced to take a wharf at Elizabethport, Bay of New-York, to sell Lehigh Coal, and open an office in New-York. *Nearly all the customers for Lehigh Coal were going to Elizabethport for their supplies*, which forced them into this measure. This, together with the abandoning of the shipping wharves at Bristol, on the Delaware, *shows the course of trade*."

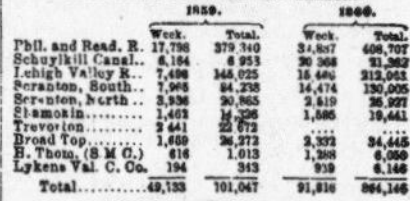

COAL TRADE FOR WEEK AND SEASON.

	1859. Week.	1859. Total.	1860. Week.	1860. Total.
Phil. and Read. R.	17,798	379,340	34,857	406,707
Schuylkill Canal	6,164	6,953	20,368	21,362
Lehigh Valley R.	7,496	145,025	15,446	212,062
Scranton, South	7,968	84,238	14,474	130,005
Scranton, North	3,936	20,865	2,619	26,927
Shamokin	1,461	14,326	1,586	19,441
Trevorton	2,441	22,672	....	....
Broad Top	1,659	26,272	2,332	34,445
H. Thom. (S M C.)	616	1,013	1,288	6,050
Lykens Val. C. Co.	194	343	939	6,146
Total	49,133	701,047	91,816	864,146

GENERAL MARKETS.

NEW-YORK, Tuesday, March 27, 1860—6 P. M.

The reported receipts of the principal kinds of Produce since our last, have been 90 bbls. Ashes, 6,851 bbs. Flour, 3,588 bbls. Corn Meal, 25,520 bushels Corn, 64 bushels Rye, 11,175 bushels Oats, 725 packages Provisions, and 636 bbls. Whisky.

ASHES—Sales have been reported to-day, of 42 bbls. at $5 25 for Pots, and $6 for Pearls, ℘ 100 lbs.

COFFEE—Sales have been reported to-day of 250 bags Jamaica at 13c., and 1,500 bags St. Domingo at 12c. ℘ lb., usual terms.

COTTON—About 1,500 bales were disposed of at unchanged prices.

NEW-YORK CLASSIFICATION.

	Upland.	Florida.	Mobile.	N. O. & Tex.
Ordinary ℘ lb.	8	8	8½	8½
Middling ℘ lb.	11½	11¾	11½	11½
Middling Fair ℘ lb.	12¼	12⅜	12¾	13¼

FISH—Dry Cod are in slack demand, chiefly at from $3 50@$4 ℘ cwt. Mackerel are inquired for, at steady rates. Salmon and Herring exhibit no noticeable changes.

FLOUR AND MEAL—State and Western brands of Wheat Flour have been freely offered to-day, and prices have tended downward. The demand, however, has been restricted. Sales have been reported of only 5,650 bbls., including superfine State at $5 15@$5 25, chiefly within the range; ordinary to choice extra State at $5 25@5 45; inferior to choice superfine Wisconsin, Indiana, Michigan and Ohio, at $5 10@$5 25; extra Iowa and Wisconsin, at $5 30@$6 25; extra Illinois, Indiana and Michigan, at $5 35@$6 40; inferior extra Ohio, at $5 75@$5 85; round-hoop extra Ohio shipping brands, at $5 90@$6 10, ℘ bbl.

Superfine State	5 15	@ 5 25
Extra State	5 25	@ 5 45
Superfine Western	5 10	@ 5 25
Extra Iowa and Wisconsin	5 30	@ 6 25
Extra Illinois, Indiana and Michigan	5 35	@ 6 40
Inferior Extra Ohio	5 75	@ 5 85
Extra Ohio, Round Hoop, shipping brds.	5 90	@ 6 10
Extra Ohio, trade brand	6 15	@ 6 90
Fancy Genesee	5 45	@ 5 60
Extra Genesee	6 00	@ 7 50
Inferior to choice Extra Missouri	6 20	@ 7 60

Southern Flour is heavy and drooping. The reported sales reach 2,250 bbls. in lots, at $5 85@$6 15 for poor to good superfine Alexandria, Baltimore, &c.; and $6 20@$7 50 for fancy to choice extra brands ℘ bbl. Canadian is in moderate demand, including inferior to very choice extra, chiefly at $5 35@$7 ℘ bbl. About 370 were sold within the range. Rye flour continues quiet at $3 60@$4 40 for fine and superfine ℘ bbl. Corn Meal is selling, in lots, at $3 55@$3 65 for Jersey; $4 05@$4 10 for Baltimore, and $4 15 for Brandywine, ℘ bbl. Buckwheat Flour $1 62½@$1 75 ℘ 100 lbs.

FOREIGN LIQUORS—Have been moderately inquired for, at unchanged prices.

FRUIT—Raisins have been in request,—including Layer, at $2 45@$2 47½, and Bunch, at $2 37½@$2 40 ℘ whole box. Other kinds have been quiet. Sales by auction: 3,500 boxes Palermo Oranges, and 1,380 boxes do. Lemons, at $2 15@$2 35 ℘ box.

GRAIN—Wheat is quiet, and prices are unsettled. Sales have been reported of only small lots, including white Western at $1 65; red do., at $1 50; and Canada Club on terms not ascertained, ℘ bushel. Corn is in moderate demand, at somewhat firmer prices. Sales have been made of 34,500 bushels, at 71c.@72c. for mixed Western, and 74c.@78½c. for inferior to good white and yellow Jersey and Southern ℘ bushel. Rye is in limited request, chiefly at 85c.@86c. ℘ bushel. Barley has been more freely sought after at previous quotations. Sales 30,000 bushels inferior to choice State, at 70c.@84c. ℘ bushel. Oats are in demand, including Canada at 42c.@43½; Western at 42½c @43c.; State at 43c.@44c.; Jersey and Pennsylvania at 39c.@41c.; Southern at 38c.@40c. ℘ bushel.

HAY—Sales have been reported of 650 bales North River at 87½c.@$1 06¼ for shipment and City use, ℘ 100 lbs.

NAVAL STORES—Crude Turpentine has been lightly dealt in at $3 55@$3 58 ℘ 280 lbs. Week's receipts, 1,551 bbls.; estimated stock at the close, 9,500 bbls. Spirits Turpentine has been freely offered, and has declined to 46c.@46½c. ℘ gallon. Week's receipts, 2,550 bbls. Estimated stock at the close 7,500 bbls. Tar has been in limited supply and moderate request at from $2 40@$2 81¼, here and to arrive, ℘ bbl. Week's receipts, 557 bbls. Estimated stock, 800 bbls. Resin, especially common, has been in less demand. We now quote common at $1 62½@$1 65; strained at $1 65@$1 70, and No. 2 at $1 75@$1 90, ℘ 310 lbs.; with No. 1 at $2@$4 ℘ 280 lbs. Week's receipts of Resin, 4,097 bbls. Estimated stock, 12,000 bbls. Messrs. LUCE & TURNER have prepared the following statement of the *Naval Store Trade of New-York, Jan. 1 to March 27, 1860.*

	Receipts.	Exports.
Crude Turpentine, bbls	18,802	14,709
Spirits Turpentine, bbls	27,580	14,928
Resin, bbls	124,304	84,828
Tar, bbls	9,616	2,076

OILS—A very moderate inquiry prevails for Crude Whale, at 46c.@50c., and Crude Sperm, chiefly at $1 40, and a fair demand for Linseed at 58c.@59c. ℘ gallon. Other descriptions are inactive.

PROVISIONS—Pork has been somewhat unsettled, to-day, sales having been reported of 3,100 bbls., in lots, at $18 for new Mess, here, and in part for future delivery; $17 25 for old Mess; $14 25@$14 37½ for new Prime, and $12 37@$12 75 for old Prime, ℘ bbl. Cut Meats are salable and steady, at 9c.@9½c. for Hams, and 7c.@7½c. for Shoulders, ℘ lb. Bacon is inactive, being scarce, and held at 9¾c.@11¾c ℘ lb. Lard is in demand, at, however, irregular prices; sales 475 tcs. and bbls., at 10½c.@11½c., with 450 kegs on private terms. Beef is quiet, at firmer rates; sales 385 bbls., at $9@$10 25 for repacked Western Mess; $11@$12 50 for Western Mess; $5@$6 for Country Mess, extra, and $4@$4 50 for Country Prime, ℘ bbl. Prime Mess, $16@$19 ℘ tierce. Beef Hams, $15@$16 ℘ bbl. Butter is inquired for, at 14c.@22c. for State, and 11c.@15c. for Ohio, ℘ lb. Cheese is in demand, at 9½c.@13c. ℘ lb.

PRINTING CLOTHS—Sales in Providence, during the week, 35,000 pieces, including 5,000 pieces, 64x64, 5⅞c.; 7,000 pieces, 64x64, private terms; 13,000 pieces, 60x64, 5½c.; 5,000 pieces, 60x64, private terms; 3,000 pieces, 60x60, 5¼c.; 2,000 pieces, 56x60, private terms.

SOAP—Sales have been reported of 500 boxes Castile, part at 9½c.@9¾c. ℘ lb.

SUGARS—Sales have been made, to-day, of 750 hhds., chiefly Cuba, at 6¼c.@7¼c.; 53 hhds. Melado, at 5c.; with 230 hhds. New-Orleans (by auction) at 6½c.@7⅝c.; and (reported) an invoice of bag Sugar on terms not ascertained.

TEAS—The public sale to-day was well attended, and the lots disposed of brought full prices. Importers withdrew several lines.

TOBACCO—Has been in fair request at uniform rates. Sales since Friday last, 40 hhds Kentucky at 5½c.@11¾c; 54 cases Seed Leaf at 4½c.@12½c.; 132 bales Havana at 28c.@38c; with 160 bales Yara and 260 bales Cuba on private terms.

WHISKY—Sales have been reported of 175 bbls., in lots, mainly at 22½c. ℘ gallon.

FREIGHTS—For Liverpool, the engagements included 150 bales Cotton at ¼d @9-32d. ℘ lb.; 100 pkgs. Lard on private terms; 100 boxes Bacon, part at 22s. 6d.; 50 tcs. Beef at 3s. 6d.; with, by steamer, 400 boxes Cheese at 40s., and 200 bbls. Resin at 2s. 10½d. For London, 400 boxes Cheese, by steamer, at 40s. For Bremen, 400 bales Cotton at ⅝d. ℘ lb.

The New-York Times.

VOL. X.—NO. 2850. NEW-YORK, THURSDAY, NOVEMBER 8, 1860. PRICE TWO CENTS.

THE ELECTION.

More of the Great Popular Pronunciamiento for Republicanism.

The Election of Abraham Lincoln Placed Beyond Doubt.

Bell and Conservatism Leading at the South.

New-Jersey the Only Free State Known to be Untrue to Freedom.

Delaware to be Represented in Congress by a Republican.

DEFEAT OF SPEAKER PENNINGTON.

Republican Losses and Gains on the Congressional Ticket.

How the News is Received North and South.

The returns received during yesterday entirely justified the enthusiasm with which the Republicans received the first intimations of victory. The fact that Mr. LINCOLN is to be the next President of the United States, if it needed confirmation, received it in each successive flash along the telegraph wires, until speculation settled down upon the mere calculation of his majority. But speculation was even here at a loss, so unexpectedly large were the majorities. We give in the subjoined table the estimates and actual figures, as far as they have been received from the States indicated. They will of course be modified hereafter:

THE PRESIDENTIAL VOTE.

MAJORITIES FOR LINCOLN.

Maine	20,000
New-Hampshire	9,000
Vermont	11,000
Massachusetts	55,000
Rhode Island	—
Connecticut	10,000
New-York	40,000
Pennsylvania	50,000
Michigan	25,000
Ohio	32,000
Indiana	27,000
Illinois	15,000
Wisconsin	12,000
Iowa	—
Minnesota	10,000

MAJORITIES FOR BELL AND BRECKINRIDGE.

New-Jersey	4,000

MAJORITIES FOR BELL.

Kentucky	12,000
Maryland	—

MAJORITIES FOR BRECKINRIDGE.

Delaware	2,000
North Carolina	—
Louisiana	—

MAJORITIES FOR DOUGLAS.

Missouri	5,000

From the Southern States our information is extremely scanty. Maryland is generally conceded to BELL; while Virginia remains in doubt, both parties claiming it. Delaware is secured to BRECKINRIDGE by 1,700; and North Carolina is also his by a small majority. The few returns received from Georgia and Arkansas place Mr. BELL in advance of his two competitors. Louisiana is regarded as safe for BRECKINRIDGE by a handsome majority. Mr. DOUGLAS is supposed to have Missouri, and Mr. BELL Kentucky.

The Congressional elections have resulted in the loss of one Republican member in Massachusetts; the gain of one and the loss of three in New-York; while three Anti-Lecompton Democrats have been replaced by Fusion Democrats. In New-Jersey, Ex-Gov. PENNINGTON has been defeated in the Fifth District, and a Straight Democrat has taken the place of an Anti-Lecompton Democrat, thus making a loss to the actual Opposition of two members. The delegations from the Western States appear to be without change. Delaware sends to Congress Mr. FISHER, the "People's Candidate," who was supported by the Republicans.

In this State the Assembly promises, from such data as we have before us, to give a good working Republican majority.

NEW-YORK.

THE PRESIDENTIAL ELECTION.

The latest returns received foot up as follows:

LINCOLN'S MAJORITIES.

County	Majority	County	Majority
Alleghany	3,749	Montgomery	264
Chemung	500	Monroe	3,525
Broome	1,672	Niagara	1,273
Chatauqua	5,000	Oneida	3,500
Chenango	1,950	Onondaga	4,209
Cattaraugus	1,500	Ontario	2,107
Clinton	400	Orleans	1,619
Cayuga	6,000	Oswego	3,750
Cortlandt	2,000	Otsego	1,000
Columbia	250	Rensselaer	25
Delaware	1,000	Saratoga	1,500
Dutchess	500	Schenectady	150
Erie	1,000	Schuyler	600
Essex	1,000	Steuben	3,000
Franklin	700	St. Lawrence	7,000
Fulton	500	Tioga	1,000
Greene	1,966	Tompkins	1,343
Genesee	2,000	Ulster	500
Herkimer	2,020	Warren	700
Jefferson	3,500	Washington	2,700
Lewis	925	Wayne	2,025
Livingston	1,955	Yates	1,500
Madison	3,330	[illegible]	—
Total			77,267

FUSION MAJORITIES

New-York	27,000
Albany	1,500
Kings	5,443
Queens	637
Richmond	1,833
Westchester	1,000
Putnam	90
Rockland	966
Wyoming	1,314—39,773
LINCOLN ahead	37,494

CONGRESSMEN ELECTED.

Dists.

1..E. H. Smith, Fusion, gain.
2..Moses F. Odell, Dem., majority 2000, gain.
3..Ben. Wood, Dem., plurality 1376.
4..J. E. Kerrigan, Dem., majority over Tuomey 1463.
5..William Wall, Rep., majority over Taylor 3381, gain.
6..—— Conkling, Rep., majority over Cochrane and Chanler 74, gain.
7..Elijah Ward, Dem., majority 1874, gain.
8..Isaac C. Delaplaine, Dem., majority 3,573.
9..Edward Haight, Dem., majority 1550.
10..D. B. St. John, Dem. (doubtful.)
11..P. H. Sylvester, Rep.
12..Stephen Baker, Rep., majority 800.
13..A. B. Olin, Rep., majority 400.
14..Erastus Corning, Dem. gain.
15..James B. McKean, Rep.
16..W. A. Wheeler, Rep.
17..S. N. Sherman, Rep.
18..S. H. Mix, Rep.
19..Richard Franchot, Rep.
20..Roscoe Conkling, Rep.—majority, 4,000.
21..R. Holland Duell, Rep.
22..Wm. E. Lansing, Rep.
23..A. W. Clark, Rep.
24..Charles B. Sedgwick, Rep.—majority, 4,000.
25..Theodore M. Pomeroy, Rep.—majority, 6,000.
26..F. B. Chamberlain, Rep.
27..A. J. Duen, Rep.
28..R. R. Van Valkenburg, Rep.
29..Alfred Ely, Rep.
30..Augustus Frank, Rep.—majority, 8,000.
31..R. Van Horn, Rep, long term; E. R. Reynolds, Rep., short term.
32..E. G. Spaulding, Rep.
33..R. E. Fenton, Rep.

The vote between St. John, Union, and Van Wyck, Republican, in the Tenth District, is very close, and the result can only be determined by the official returns.

In the Ninth District, Mr. Haight's majority over Nelson is 1,550.

CITY VOTE FOR CONGRESSMEN.

THIRD CONGRESSIONAL DISTRICT.

	Wood. Fusion.	Williamson. Rep.	Savage. Tam.
First Ward	1299	563	61
Second Ward	269	319	20
Third Ward	468	310	30
Fifth Ward	1516	1337	353
Eighth Ward	2347	1978	225
Total	5860	4507	689
Majority for Benj. Wood			673

FOURTH CONGRESSIONAL DISTRICT.

	Kerrigan. Mozart.	Tuomey. Tam.	Commerford. Rep.
Fourth Ward	1030	733	592
Sixth Ward	1382	1681	352
Tenth Ward	887	711	1600
Fourteenth Ward	1352	1297	809
Total	4672	3922	3353
Majority for Kerrigan			750

FIFTH CONGRESSIONAL DISTRICT.

	Taylor, Fusion.	Wall, Rep.	Duffy, Mozart.
Seventh Ward	2056	1350	1292
Fourteenth Ward	1524	1267	766
Brooklyn Vote	3247	4268	1016
Total vote for Taylor			6827
Total vote for Wall			6885
Total vote for Duffy			3074
Majority for Wall			58

SIXTH CONGRESSIONAL DISTRICT.

	Cochrane, Fusion.	Chanler, Tam.	Conckling, Rep.
Eleventh Ward	2053	2125	1878
Fifteenth Ward	1707	840	1734
Seventeenth Ward	2701	2006	2223
Total	6461	5571	6535
Majority for Conckling			74

SEVENTH CONGRESSIONAL DISTRICT.

	Ward, Dem.	Dow, Rep.	Letson, B. & E.
Ninth Ward	3524	3099	—
Sixteenth Ward	3187	2485	—
Twentieth Ward	4129	2795	—
Total	10,840	8380	—
Majority for Ward			2460

EIGHTH CONGRESSIONAL DISTRICT.

	Delaplaine, Dem.	Wakeman. Rep.	McCahill. Indpt.
Twelfth Ward	1,534	1,213	—
Eighteenth Ward	3,344	2,041	—
Nineteenth Ward	1,337	1,351	—
Twenty-first Ward	3,527	2,327	—
Twenty-second Ward	2,769	2,306	—
Total	12,811	9,238	—

Majority for Delaplaine, 3,573.

Nelson, Republican, for Congress, 7 majority.

Brewster, Republican, for Assembly, 59 majority.

JUDICIAL ELECTIONS.

More complete returns than those published in our yesterday's issue exhibit the following as the Judicial ticket elected:

Judge of Supreme Court—GEO. G. BARNARD, Union Dem.

Judge of Superior Court—MICHAEL ULSHOEFFER, Tammany.

Recorder—JOHN T. HOFFMAN, Tammany.

City Judge—JOHN H. McCUNN, Union Dem.

Surrogate—EDWARD C. WEST, Union Dem.

COUNTY OFFICES.

Supervisors—SMITH ELY, Jr., Dem., and Col. SCHWARZWAELDER, Dem.

Register—JOHN KEYSER, Rep.

ASSEMBLYMEN ELECTED.

NEW-YORK CITY.

The following is the result for Assemblymen in this City.

District.

1..John Callahan, Dem.
2..William Walsh, Dem.
3..Christopher Woodruff, Dem.
4..Lewis Hopps, Rep., (probable.)
5..John J. Shaw, Rep.
6..Samuel T. Webster, Dem.
7..Daniel Young, Dem.
8..Andrew Craft, Rep.
9..Horatio N. Sherwood, Rep.
10..Luke F. Cozzens, Dem.
11..John Hardy, Dem.
12..Andrew Smith, Dem.
13..E. C. Burdsall, Rep.
14..Robert C. Hutchings, Dem.
15..George W. Varian, Dem.
16..Henry Arcularius, Dem.
17..Jay J. Jones, Dem.

KINGS COUNTY.

The following gentlemen are reported elected:

Dist.

1..Andrew J. Provost, Dem.
2..Marquis D. Moore, Republican.
3..Theophilus C. Callicut, reported elected this morning, is now said to be defeated by Nathan Comstock, Rep., by 39 majority.
4..James Darcy, Democrat.
5..W. C. Jones, Democrat.
6..J. Nesbitt, Dem.
7..George H. Fisher, Republican.

WESTCHESTER COUNTY.

1..Ethan Flagg, Rep.
2..N. Holmes Odell, Dem.
3..Benjamin F. Camp, Rep.

ROCKLAND COUNTY.

W. R. Knapp, Fusion.

PUTNAM COUNTY.

—— Brewster, Rep.

DUTCHESS COUNTY.

1..John B. Dutcher, Rep.
2..John H. Otis, Dem.

ONONDAGA COUNTY.

1..J. Emerick, Rep.
2..A. Myers, Rep., (doubtful.)
3..Abner Chapman, Rep.

GENESEE COUNTY.

G. W. Wright, Rep.

SCHENECTADY COUNTY.

A. Macomber, Rep.

MONROE COUNTY.

1..Martin Roberts, Rep.
2..Lewis H. Morgan, Rep.
3..Benjamin R. Wells, Rep.

ALBANY COUNTY.

1..Jay Gibbons, Dem.
2..Lewis Benedict, Jr., Rep.
3..H. Lansing, Dem.
4..W. J. Wheeler, Dem.

OSWEGO COUNTY.

1..D. C. Littlejohn, Rep.

ALLEGHANY COUNTY.

1..Wilkes Angell, Rep.
2..Lucius L. May, Rep.

CHATAUQUA COUNTY.

2..Hiram Smith, Rep.

WARREN COUNTY.

Waller A. Paxon, Rep.

RENSSELAER COUNTY.

1..C. J. Saxe, Dem.
2..L. C. Ball, Rep.
3..Anson Brigham, Rep.

ESSEX COUNTY.

Martin Finch, Rep.

ORANGE COUNTY.

S. Fullerton, Jr., Rep.

The Albany *Journal* of last evening says:

As far as received, Members are elected as follows:

Republicans	69
Democrats	20

The Republicans will doubtless have two-thirds of the Assembly.

The SENATE—Largely Republican—holds over.

THE ELECTION IN BROOKLYN.

Great Gains for the Republicans.

The result in Kings County exceeds the expectation of the most sanguine Republican. In a total vote of about 38,000, the Union Electoral ticket received a majority less than 5,000, which, owing to the unpopularity of fusion, gives nearly every local office to the Republicans.

The following officers are elected:

CONGRESS.

Fifth District—Wm. Wall, Rep.
Second District—Moses F. Odell, Dem.
Sheriff—Anthony F. Campbell, Rep.
Supt. of the Poor—Jacob C. Dey, Rep.; Wm. M. Muchmore, Rep.
Justice of Sessions—Wm. H. Hoyt, Rep.
School Commissioner—Homer Bartlett, Rep.
City Judge—George G. Reynolds, Rep.
Police Justice—C. Perry, Rep.
Justices of the Peace—Wm. M. Boerum, Rep.; John Q. Adams, Rep.

ASSEMBLY.

First District—A. J. Provost, Dem.
Second District—M. D. Mone, Rep.
Third District—Nathan Comstock, Rep.
Fourth District—James Darcy, Dem.
Fifth District—L. C. Andrus, Rep.
Sixth District—George H. Fisher, Rep.
Seventh District—A. J. Spencer, Dem.

For several of the offices above named the vote is very close, and the official canvass may change the result given above.

The Fusionists full expected to obtain a majority of at least 10,000 in this County.

The vote cast exceeds that of any previous year by about 6,000, but it is no larger than was anticipated.

NEW-JERSEY.

The returns come in slowly. From the figures received it is thought the Fusion ticket is successful by about 4,000.

FUSION MAJORITIES.

The following are reported Fusion majorities:

Union County	300
Hunterdon County	700
Somerset County	130
Warren County	500
Middlesex County	500
Hudson County	1,282

CONGRESSMEN ELECTED.

The Congressional Districts will be represented as follows:

1—John S. Nixon, (Rep.)
2—John L. N. Stratton, (Rep.)
3—William G. Steele, (Dem.)
4—George T. Cobb, (Dem.)
5—Nehemiah Perry, (Dem.;) majority 440—a gain.

THE LEGISLATURE.

The Republicans have elected 11 Senators and the Democrats 10.

The Assemblymen at present foot up 33 Democrats and Union and 28 Republicans.

THE VOTE IN HUDSON COUNTY.

The majority in Hudson County of Perry, Dem., for Congress, is 797, which elects him.

The following were the successful candidates for County officers:

Members of Assembly—Franklin B. Carpenter, (Rep.,) First Assembly District. Theodore F. Randolph, (Fusion,) Second Assembly District. Michael J. Vreeland, (Rep.,) Third Assembly District.

Sheriff—John Francis, (Fusion,) reëlected.

Coroners—Thomas Gaffney, of Jersey City; Frederick W. Bohnstedt, Hoboken; and James H. Donnelly, Hudson City, (Fusion.)

CONNECTICUT.

TWENTY-SIX THOUSAND REPUBLICAN PLURALITY.

HARTFORD, Wednesday, Nov. 7.

Connecticut gives 10,180 Republican majority, and 26,000 plurality for Lincoln.

MAJORITIES FOR LINCOLN.

County	Majority	County	Majority
Hartford County	1888	New-Haven County	996
Litchfield County	1442	Fairfield County	1761
Middlesex County	261	New-London County	1486
Tolland County	856	Windham County	1619
Total			10180

MASSACHUSETTS.

SEVENTY THOUSAND REPUBLICAN PLURALITY.

BOSTON, Wednesday, Nov. 7.

The Presidential vote of Massachusetts, with the exception of nine small towns, foots up—Lincoln 104,467, Douglas 34,007, Bell 22,017, Breckinridge 6,072.

MAJORITIES FOR LINCOLN.

County	Majority	County	Majority
Hampshire Co	3,609	Plymouth Co	3 274
Franklin Co	2,674	Duke's Co	105
Norfolk Co	1,834	Barnstable Co	1,482
Hampden Co	2,620	Essex Co	6,451

FUSION MAJORITY.

Boston	926

THE VOTE FOR GOVERNOR.

The vote for Andrew, Republican, for Governor falls 2,626 behind that of Lincoln.

CONGRESSMEN ELECTED.

Dist.

1..Thomas D. Elliott, (Rep.)
2..James Buffinton, (Rep.)
3..C. F. Adams, (Rep.)
4..A. H. Rice, (Rep.)
5..Appleton. (Union Dem.)
6..J. B. Alley, (Rep.)
7..D. W. Gooch, (Rep.)
8..C. R. Train, (Rep.)
9..G. F. Bailey, (Rep.)
10..Charles Delano, (Rep.)
11..H. L. Dawes, (Rep.)

The Fourth Congressional District gives Rice, Republican, 7,293; Bigelow, Douglas, 6,599.

The Fifth Congressional District gives Appleton, Union, 8,015; Burlingame, Republican, 7,756.

The vote of the Ninth Congressional District gives Bailey 8,784; Thayer, 7,183.

The Republican candidates for Congress in all the other Districts are elected by large majorities.

THE LEGISLATURE.

STATE SENATE—Thirty-eight Republicans and two Democrats elected.

HOUSE—Twenty-three Republicans and seventeen Opposition elected.

PENNSYLVANIA.

LINCOLN MAJORITIES.

Philadelphia (over all)	873
Philadelphia (over Fusion Ticket)	17,884
Philadelphia (over Fusion and Douglas)	7,791
Franklin County	1,100
Snyder County	650
Union County	1,000
Mifflin County	260
Chester County	3,200
Westmoreland County	200
Centre County	700
Lancaster County	7,500
Huntington County	1,500
Alleghany County	10,000
Wyoming County	200
Wayne County	200
Indiana County	2,500
Delaware County	1,660
Cumberland County	400
Luzerne County	1,000
Carbon County	500
Bedford County	100
Blair County	1,800
Cambra County	tie.
Clinton County	200
Dauphin County	1,600
Erie County	4,000
Lebanon County	2,116
Lehigh County	100
Lycoming County	600
Montour County	50
Northumberland County	50
Perry County	500
Schuylkill County	1,500
Susquehanna County	2,000
York County	100

FUSION MAJORITY.

Monroe County	1,200
Berks County	1,000
Columbia County	200
Fulton County	150
Northampton County	1,000

DELAWARE.

PHILADELPHIA, Wednesday, Nov. 7.

Breckinridge's majority in the State is 1,700. Fisher, (People's Party,) for Congress, has 363 majority. Breckinridge local tickets are elected in Kent and Sussex Counties, and "People" in Newcastle.

MARYLAND.

The latest returns from Maryland indicate that Bell has probably carried the State. Howard County gives Bell a gain of 419.

VIRGINIA.

THE RESULT STILL DOUBTFUL.

Special Dispatch to the New-York Times.

RICHMOND, Wednesday, Nov. 7—P. M.

Returns received since morning show a gain of 2,000 for Breckinridge. It is a close contest between Breckinridge and Bell.

The Bell Party claim the State, but the leading Democrats express the utmost confidence that Breckinridge has a small majority.

The Democrats are encouraged by gains in the Seventh District. They are now anxiously awaiting the returns from the "Tenth Legion." The returns from Rockingham last night were unreliable. Both parties are still confident.

REPORTED MAJORITIES.

Taylor County—Bell, 50 majority.
Lewis County—Breckinridge, 300 majority.

NORTH CAROLINA.

WILMINGTON, N. C., Wednesday, Nov. 7.

The indications are that Breckinridge has carried the State, as he gains as far as heard from. New-Hanover gives him 1,000 majority.

GEORGIA.

But few counties have been heard from. Fifteen counties (official) give Bell 6,665; Breckinridge, 5,267; Douglas, 4,260. The returns come in exceedingly slow, and the result is uncertain.

LOUISIANA.

Special Dispatch to the New-York Times:

RICHMOND, Wednesday, Nov. 7.

A special dispatch from New-Orleans says that Bell carried the city, but Breckinridge will carry Louisiana.

ARKANSAS.

BELL TAKES THE LEAD.

ST. LOUIS, Wednesday, Nov. 7.

FORT SMITH—Bell, 250; Breckinridge, 231; Douglas, 164.

FAYETTEVILLE—Bell, 355; Breckinridge, 336; Douglas, 70.

MISSOURI.

MISCELLANEOUS RETURNS.

ST. LOUIS, Wednesday, Nov. 7.

KANSAS CITY—Douglas, 487; Bell, 368; Lincoln, 185; Breckinridge, 131.

LEXINGTON—Bell, 617; Douglas, 311; Breckinridge, 135.

ST. JOSEPH—Douglas, 1,064; Bell, 721; Lincoln, 410; Breckinridge, 226.

BOONEVILLE—Bell, 312; Douglas, 303; Breckinridge, 105; Lincoln, 11.

INDEPENDENCE—Bell, 449; Breckinridge, 342; Douglas, 369; Lincoln, 1.

SPRINGFIELD—Bell, 115; Breckinridge, 183; Douglas, 182; Lincoln, 21.

MINNESOTA.

ST. PAUL, Min., Wednesday, Nov. 7.

The entire Republican ticket is elected in St. Paul and Ramsay County. The City of St. Paul gives 186 majority for Lincoln; St. Anthony, 221 majority for Lincoln; Minneapolis, 278 majority for Lincoln; Brooklyn, 113 majority for Lincoln. Wabash County—Eight towns give Lincoln 137 majority. Goodhue County—About 800 majority for Lincoln. Dacotah County—Five towns give Lincoln 125 majority. Winona County gives 500 majority for Lincoln.

WISCONSIN.

MILWAUKEE, Wednesday, Nov. 7.

Walworth County, thirteen towns, give Lincoln 1,490 majority. Rock County gives 3,300 majority for Lincoln. Waukesha County, complete, Lincoln 458 majority. La Crosse County, 750 majority for Lincoln. Sauk County, 12 towns, 778 majority for Lincoln. Milwaukee City and County, complete, give Douglas 1,808 majority, a Democratic loss of 1,700 since 1859. The Republicans gain, in all parts of the State, as far as heard from. Dane County is estimated about 400 majority for Lincoln. The State has doubtless gone by 10,000 for Lincoln. All the Republican Congressmen are elected.

OHIO.

CLEVELAND, Wednesday, Nov. 7.

Twenty-three counties in Ohio show a Republican gain of 7,551 over Murray's vote in October, when he had over 25,000 majority. Corresponding gains elsewhere will give Mr. Lincoln 40,000 majority.

KANSAS.

ST. LOUIS, Wednesday, Nov. 7.

Returns from Atchinson, Kansas, elect all the Democratic members of the Legislature and all the County officers, by about 200 majority. Large Democratic gains are reported.

ILLINOIS.

FIFTEEN THOUSAND REPUBLICAN MAJORITY.

The latest returns from the Republican State Committee at Chicago show that the Republicans have carried the city by 3,092, and the State by 15,000 majority.

The Republicans carry four of the doubtful Legislative Districts in the central part of the State, thus giving them a majority of five in the House and one in the Senate.

The Congressional delegation will probably be unchanged.

HOW THE RESULT IS RECEIVED.

AT THE WEST.

From the Home of Mr. Lincoln—How He Received the News—Speculation as to His Course, &c.

Special Dispatch to the New-York Times.

SPRINGFIELD, Ill., Wednesday, Nov. 7—6 P. M.

Mr. LINCOLN has not yet given any public intimation as to the policy of his Administration. I have every reason to believe that he will not depart from the usual custom of newly-elected Presidents. In answer to all inquiries as to what will be his course, he asks, "Have you read my speeches?" If the question is still pressed, he quietly hands over one of the pamphlet publications of his speeches in the late controversy with Mr. DOUGLAS.

The general opinion here is, that something more serious than the present state of affairs will be required to elicit from Mr. LINCOLN at present, any further declaration of principles, or an assurance that the South need fear nothing from his policy. The idea is that he will deal out equal and exact justice to all sections of the country, and that it would be admitting just cause for suspecting his honesty if he should reutter at this time any professions of loyalty to Union, or disavow any design of infringing upon the rights of the South. It is regarded as a matter of course that he believes what he has said, therefore it would be superfluous for him after his conservative record as member of Congress, his frequently expressed belief in regard to the States rights doctrine, and above all his strictly constitutional elevation to office, to put himself out of the way to allay the groundless fears of his bitter opponents, at the risk of being deemed a coward by his friends.

That Mr. LINCOLN is a man of sufficient ability and nerve to meet any exigency, is conceded by all who know him. I believe, from what I see of him here, that he will prove a second JACKSON—only more so. When he thinks proper to make a *pronunciamiento*, you may depend upon it he will do so.

Mr. LINCOLN has been about town all day, and accessible to all who choose to speak with him. He has occupied the room of the Executive in the Capitol, and has been freely congratulated by his fellow-townsmen.

Mr. LINCOLN spent most of election-night in the Telegraph-office, where he heard returns and received private dispatches with a most marvelous equanimity. Those who saw him at the time say it would have been impossible for a bystander to tell that that tall, lean, wiry, good-natured, easy-going gentleman, so anxiously inquiring about the success of the local candidates, was the choice of the people to fill the most important office in the nation. Even during election day and night, Mr. LINCOLN was about town attending to his business as usual. Many of his Springfield acquaintances will long remember how he sat in a social circle at the Cheny House, while the returns were coming in, and indulged alike in pleasant chat and his propensity for story-telling.

So far as the Cabinet is concerned, there are so many conflicting rumors afloat, that I cannot credit any. Mr. LINCOLN is not at all anxious to gabble, and I don't believe he has told any one his intentions in this regard. It seems to be generally conceded that Mr. SEWARD will be tendered the mission to the Court of St. James, and that Mr. BELL will be offered the department of the Interior, or some other seat in the Cabinet.

SPRINGFIELD, Ill., Wednesday, Nov. 7—P. M.

Mr. LINCOLN was this evening captured by a number of his friends who carried him to the Hall of the House of Representatives, where about three hundred citizens spontaneously collected and earnestly but vainly pressed him for a speech. They finally got him in the Speaker's chair, and speeches were made by Messrs. SWETT and ORME, of Bloomington, FARMER, JOAB, WILKINSON and others.

A dispatch was received by Mr. LINCOLN, stating that Indiana had given twenty thousand Republican majority.

Mr. LINCOLN finally made the following speech—his first public address since his election:

"The representation of Coles and Douglas Counties is elected on the Republican side. We expected it would be so—and so it is pretty generally these times." [Applause and laughter.]

Mr. LINCOLN finally, in a jocular way, took advantage of his position as Chairman, to say that it was customary for the presiding officer to call some distinguished member to the Chair. He accordingly called Mr. KENT to take his place, and retired through a side door, in spite of vociferous calls for him to speak.

O., JR.

AT THE SOUTH.

The Feeling in Maryland—Conservative Sentiments—A General Acquiescence in the Result.

Special Dispatch to the New-York Times.

BALTIMORE, Wednesday, Nov. 7.

Excited crowds have been congregated around the newspaper offices and the head-quarters of the different parties all day. The election of LINCOLN was generally anticipated, and the people express no surprise.

The general tone of public sentiment is consistent with acquiescence with the result. Many say they worked hard and honestly to prevent the election of LINCOLN, but now, as he is to be President, they will see all his acts carried out, and at every hazard support the Constitution.

Embittered feelings have already greatly subsided, and not a solitary disunion sentiment has been heard from any one. The Breckinridge and Bell men and the Douglasites seem determined to abide by the decision of the people. The anxiety, indeed, appears greater than ever to counsel moderation on the part of the sister Southern States, and to avert any hasty acts—all denouncing secession unanimously, and disapproving of the hot haste of South Carolina towards interrupting the harmony of the Confederacy.

There is a willing confidence in Mr. LINCOLN's conservative purposes and a determination with very many to give him a fair trial. A large body of conservative people are content to take a fresh start, in the hope of a better state of things henceforward.

Such is the real condition of affairs. The people want the Old Hunkers supplanted by better men, and if they could not get it done by BELL, they are willing that LINCOLN shall be the man, and are glad that the corrupted Democracy is wiped out. The Unionists and the opponents of the

[*Concluded on Eighth Page.*]

THE COMING ADMINISTRATION.

Views, Opinions, Sentiments and Purposes of Abraham Lincoln.

HIS POSITION ON SLAVERY.

Is he Sectional and Ultra, or Conservative and National?

Now that ABRAHAM LINCOLN is to be President of the United States during the next term, all parties are equally interested in understanding his precise position on the great question by which the country has been, and still is, so profoundly agitated. During the canvass it suited the purposes of his opponents to represent him as an Abolitionist—as a man utterly reckless of the rights and interests of the Southern States, and disposed to make war upon Slavery, wherever it exists, regardless of its effect upon the prosperity of the country and the stability of the Union. It was to little purpose that his friends denied the truth of these representations; what they said was charged to the natural zeal of political partisans. But now that the election is over, and the result fixed, we have all one common interest in ascertaining upon what principles his Administration will probably be conducted.

Fortunately his public speeches, made long before his name had ever been mentioned in connection with the Presidency, afford ample material for such a judgment. And we are quite sure we shall do the public an essential service by publishing the following extracts from those speeches, giving his views upon each of the prominent points to which the Slavery agitation has given rise:

MR. LINCOLN'S DECLARARATION OF THE IRREPRESSIBLE CONFLICT.

From Mr. Lincoln's Speech at Springfield, June 17, 1858.

MR. PRESIDENT, AND GENTLEMEN OF THE CONVENTION: If we could first know where we are, and whither we are tending, we could better judge what to do, and how to do it. We are now far into the fifth year, since a policy was initiated with the avowed object, and confident promise, of putting an end to Slavery agitation. Under the operation of that policy, that agitation has not only not ceased, but has constantly augmented. In my opinion, it will not cease, until a crisis shall have been reached and passed. "A house divided against itself cannot stand." I believe this Government cannot endure *permanently* half slave and half free. I do not expect the Union to be dissolved—I do not expect the house to fall—but I do expect it will cease to be divided. It will become all one thing, or all the other. *Either the opponents of Slavery will arrest the further spread of it, and place it where the public mind shall rest in the belief that it is in the course of ultimate extinction*; or its advocates will push it forward till it shall become alike lawful in all the States, old as well as new—North as well as well as South.

MR. LINCOLN'S EXPLANATIONS OF HIS MEANING IN THIS DECLARATION.

From Mr. Lincoln's Reply to Douglas, July 10, 1858.

In this paragraph which I have quoted in your hearing, and to which I ask the attention of all, Judge DOUGLAS thinks he discovers great political heresy. I want your attention particularly to what he has inferred from it. He says I am in favor of making all the States of this Union uniform. He draws this inference from the language I have quoted to you. He says that I am in favor of *making war by the North upon the South for the extermination of Slavery*; that I am also in favor of inviting (as he expresses it) the South to war upon the North, for the purpose of nationalizing Slavery. Now, it is singular enough, if you will carefully read that passage over, that I did not say that I was in favor of anything in it. I only said what I *expected would take place*. I made a prediction only—it may have been a foolish one perhaps. I did not even say that I desired that Slavery should be put in course of ultimate extinction. I do now, however, so there need be no longer any difficulty about that. It may be written down in the great speech.

Gentlemen, Judge DOUGLAS informed you that this speech of mine was probably carefully prepared. I admit that it was! I am not master of language; I have not a fine education; I am not capable of entering into a disquisition upon dialectics, as I believe you call it; *but I do not believe the language I employed bears any such construction as Judge Douglas puts upon it.* But I don't care about a quibble in regard to words. I know what I meant, and I will not leave this crowd in doubt, if I can explain it to them, what I really meant in the use of that paragraph.

I am not, in the first place, unaware that this Government has endured eighty-two years, half slave and half free. I know that I am tolerably well acquainted with the history of the country, and I know that it has endured eighty-two years, half slave and half free. I *believe*—and that is what I meant to allude to there—I *believe* it has endured, because during all that time, until the introduction of the Nebraska bill, the public mind *did* rest in the belief that Slavery was in course of ultimate extinction. That was what gave us the rest that we had through that period of eighty-two years; at least, so I believe. I have always hated Slavery, I think as much as any Abolitionist—I have been an Old Line Whig—I have always hated it, but I have always been quiet about it until this new era of the introduction of the Nebraska bill began. I always believed that everybody was against it, and that it was in course of ultimate extinction. [Pointing to Mr. BROWNING, who stood near by.] BROWNING thought so; *the great mass of the nation have rested in this belief that Slavery was in course of ultimate extinction.* They had reason so to believe. The adoption of the Constitution and its attendant history led the people to believe so; and that such was the belief of the framers of the Constitution itself, why did these old men, about the time of the adoption of the Constitution, decree that Slavery should not go into the new Territory, where it had not already gone? Why declare that within twenty years the African Slave-trade, by which slaves are supplied, might be cut off by Congress? Why were all these acts? I might enumerate more of these acts—but enough. What were they but a clear indication that the framers of the Constitution intended and expected the ultimate extinction of that institution? And now, when I say, as I said in my speech that Judge DOUGLAS has quoted from, when I say that I think the opponents of Slavery will resist the further spread of it, and place it where the public mind shall rest in the belief that it is in course of ultimate extinction, *I only mean to say, that they will place it where the founders of this Government originally placed it.*

I have said a hundred times, and I have now no inclination to take it back, that *I believe there is no right, and ought to be no inclination in the people of the Free States to enter into the Slave States, and interfere with the question of Slavery at all.* I have said that always; Judge DOUGLAS has heard me say it—if not quite a hundred times, at least as good as a hundred times; and *when it is said that I am in favor of interfering with Slavery where it exists, I know it is unwarranted by anything I have ever intended, and, as I believe, by anything I have ever said.* If, by any means, I have ever used language which could fairly be so construed, (as, however, I believe I never have,) I now correct it.

So much, then, for the inference that Judge DOUGLAS draws, that I am in favor of setting the sections at war with one another. *I know that I never meant any such thing, and I believe that no fair mind can infer any such thing from anything I have ever said.*"

THE RIGHTS OF THE STATES.

From Lincoln's Reply to Douglas, Sept. 15.

LADIES AND GENTLEMEN: There is very much in the principles that Judge DOUGLAS has here enunciated that I most cordially approve, and over

The New-York Times.

VOL. X....NO. 2983. NEW-YORK, SATURDAY, APRIL 13, 1861. PRICE TWO CENTS.

THE WAR COMMENCED.

The First Gun Fired by Fort Moultrie Against Fort Sumpter.

THE BOMBARDMENT CONTINUED ALL DAY.

Spirited Return from Major Anderson's Guns.

The Firing from Fort Sumpter Ceased for the Night.

Hostilities to Commence Again at Daylight.

The Correspondence which Preceded the Bombardment.

The Demand for a Surrender and Major Anderson's Refusal.

THE RELIEF FLEET OFF THE HARBOR.

How the News is Received in Washington.

OUR CHARLESTON DISPATCHES.

CHARLESTON, Friday, April 12.

The ball has opened. War is inaugurated.

The batteries of Sullivan's Island, Morris Island, and other points, were opened on Fort Sumpter at 4 o'clock this morning.

Fort Sumpter has returned the fire, and a brisk cannonading has been kept up. No information has been received from the seaboard yet.

The military are under arms, and the whole of our population are on the streets. Every available space facing the harbor is filled with anxious spectators.

CHARLESTON, Friday, April 12.

The firing has continued all day without intermission.

Two of Fort Sumpter's guns have been silencod, and it is reported that a breach has been made in the southeast wall.

The answer to Gen. Beauregard's demand by Major Anderson was that he would surrender when his supplies were exhausted, that is, if he was not reinforced.

Not a casualty has yet happened to any of the forces.

Of the nineteen batteries in position only seven have opened fire on Fort Sumpter, the remainder are held in reserve for the expected fleet.

Two thousand men reached this city this morning and embarked for Morris Island and the neighberhood.

CHARLESTON, Friday, April 12.

The bombardment of Fort Sumpter continues.

The Floating Battery and Stephens Battery are operating freely, and Fort Sumpter is returning the fire.

It is reported that three war vessels are outside the bar.

CHARLESTON, Friday, April 12.

The firing has ceased for the night, but will be renewed at daylight in the morning, unless an attempt is made to reinforce, which ample arrangements have been made to repel.

The *Pawnee*, *Harriet Lane*, and a third steamer are reported off the bar.

Troops are arriving by every train.

LATER DISPATCHES—HOSTILITIES STILL PRODEEDING.

CHARLESTON, Friday, April 12.

The bombardment is still going on every twenty minutes from our morters. It is supposed that Major Anderson is resting his ment for the night.

Three vessels of-war are reported outside. They cannot get in. The sea is rough.

Nobody is hurt. The floating battery works well. Troops arrive hourly. Every inlet is guarded. There are lively times here.

CHARLESTON, Friday, April 12.

The firing on Fort Sumpter continues.

There are reviving times on the "Palmetto coast."

CHARLESTON, Friday, April 12—3 A. M.

It is utterly impossible to reinfofce Fort Shmpter, to-night, as a storm is now raging.

The mortar batteries will be playing on Fort Sumpter all night.

FROM ANOTHER CORRESPONDENT.

CHARLESTON, Friday, April 12.

Civil war has at last begun. A terrible fight is at this moment going on between Fort Sumpter and the fortifications by which it is surrounded.

The issue was submitted to Major Anderson of surrendering as soon as his supplies were exhausted, or of having a fire opened on him within a certain time.

This he refused to do, and accordingly, at twenty-seven minutes past four o'clock this morning Fort Moultrie began the bombardment by firing two guns. To these Major Anderson replied with three of his barbette guns, after which the batteries on Mount Pleasant, Cummings' Point, and the Floating Battery opened a brisk fire of shot and shell.

Major Anderson did not reply except at long intervals, until between 7 and 8 o'clock, when he brought into action the two tier of guns looking towards Fort Moultrie and Stevens iron battery.

Up to this hour—3 o'clock—they have failed to produce any serious effect.

Major Anderson has the greater part of the day been directing his fire principally against Fort Moultrie, the Stevens and Floating Battery, these and Fort Johnson being the only five operating against him. The remainder of the batteries are held in reserve.

Major Anderson is at present using his lower tier of casemate ordnance.

The fight is going on with intense earnestness, and will continue all night.

The excitement in the community is indescribable. With the very first boom of the guns thousands rushed from their beds to the harbor front, and all day every available place has been thronged by ladies and gentlemen, viewing the spectacle through their glasses.

The brilliant and patriotic conduct of Major Anderson speaks for itself.

Business is entirely suspended. Only those stores open necessary to supply articles required by the Army.

Gov. Pickens has all day been in the residence of a gentleman which commands a view of the whole scene—a most interested observer. Gen. Beauregard commands in person the entire operations.

It is reported that the *Harriet Lane* has received a shot through her wheelhouse. She is in the offing. No other Government ships in sight up to the present moment, but should they appear the entire range of batteries will open upon them.

Troops are pouring into the town by hundreds, but are held in reserve for the present, the force already on the island being ample. People are also arriving every moment on horseback, and by every other conveyance.

CHARLESTON, Friday, April 12—6 P. M.

Capt. R. S. Parker brings dispatches from the floating battery, stating that up to this time only two have been wounded on Sullivan's Island. He had to row through Major Anderson's warmest fire in a small boat.

Senator Wigfall in same manner bore dispatches to Morris Island, through the fire from Fort Sumpter.

Senator Chesnut, another member of the staff of Gen. Beauregard, fired a gun, by way of amusement, from Mount Pleasant, which made a large hole in the parapet.

Quite a number have been struck by spent pieces of shell and knocked down, but none hurt seriously. Many fragments of these missiles are already circulating in the city.

The range is more perfect than in the morning and every shot from the land tells.

Three ships are visible in the offing, and it is believed an attempt will be made to-night, to throw reinforcements into Fort Sumpter in small boats.

It is also thought, from the regular and frequent firing of Major Anderson, that he has a much larger force of men than was supposed. At any rate, he is fighting bravely.

There have been two rain storms during the day, but without effect upon the battle.

Everybody is in a ferment. Some of those fighting are stripped to the waist.

IMPORTANT CORRESPONDENCE PRECEDING THE BOMBARDMENT.

CHARLESTON, Friday, April 12.

The following is the telegraphic correspondence between the War Department at Montgomery and Gen. Beauregard immediately preceding the hostilities.

The correspondence grew out of the formal notification by the Washington Government, which is disclosed in Gen. Beauregard's first dispatches.

[No. 1.]

CHARLESTON, April 8.

L. P. Walker, Secretary of War:

An authorized messenger from President Lincoln, just informed Gov. Pickens and myself that provisions will be sent to Fort Sumpter peaceably, or otherwise by force.

(Signed,) G. F. Beauregard.

[No. 2.]

MONTGOMERY, 10th.

Gen. G. T. Beauregard, Charleston:

If you have no doubt of the authorized character of the agent who communicated to you the intention of the Washington Government to supply Fort Sumpter by force, you will at once demand its evacuation, and if this is refused, proceed in such manner as you may determine, to reduce it.

Answer.

Signed, L. P. Walker, Sec. of War.

[No. 3.]

CHARLESTON, April 10.

L. P. Walker, Secretary of War:

The demand will be made to-morrow at 12 o'clock.

Signed, G. F. Beauregard.

[No. 4.]

MONTGOMERY, April 10.

Gen. Beauregard, Charleston:

Unless there are especial reasons connected with your own condition, it is considered proper that you should make the demand at an early hour.

(Signed) L. P. Walker, Secretary of War.

[No. 5.]

CHARLESTON, April 10.

L. P. Walker, Secretary of War, Montgomery:

The reasons are special for 12 o'clock.

(Signed) G. F. Beauregard.

[No. 6.]

CHARLESTON, April 11.

L. P. Walker, Secretary of War:

Demand sent at 12 o'clock. Allowed till 6 o'clock to answer.

(Signed) G. F. Beauregard.

[No. 7.]

MONTGOMERY, April 11.

Gen. Beuregard—Charleston:

Telegraph the reply of Maj. Anderson.

(Signed,) L. P. Walker, Secretary of War.

[No. 8.]

CHARLESTON, April 11.

To L. P. Walker, Secretary of War:

Maj. Anderson replies:

"I HAVE THE HONOR TO ACKNOWLEDGE THE RECEIPT OF YOUR COMMUNICATION DEMANDING THE EVACUATION OF THIS FORT, AND TO SAY IN REPLY THERETO, THAT IT IS A DEMAND WITH WHICH I REGRET THAT MY SENSE OF HONOR AND MY OBLIGATIONS TO MY GOVERNMENT WILL PREVENT MY COMPLIANCE" He adds: "Probably I will await the first shot, and if you do not batter us to pieces, we will be starved out in a few days."

Answer. G. F. Beauregard.

[No. 9.]

MONTGOMERY, April 11.

Gen. Beauregard—Charleston:

We do not desire needlessly to bombard Fort Sumpter, if Major Anderson will state the time at which, as indicated by him, he will evacuate, and agree that, in the meantime, he will not use his guns against us unless ours should be employed against Fort Sumpter. You are thus to avoid the effusion of blood. If this or its equivalent be refused, reduce the fort as your judgment decides to be the most practicable.

(Signed) L. P. Walker, Secretary of War.

[No. 10.]

CHARLESTON, April 12.

L. P. Walker, Secretary of War:

HE WOULD NOT CONSENT. I write to-day.

G. F. Beauregard.

MR. FOX'S VISIT TO FORT SUMPTER.

CHARLESTON, Friday, April 11.

Intercepted dispatches disclose the fact that Mr. Fox, who had been allowed to visit Major Anderson on the pledge that his purpose was pacific, employed his opportunity to devise a plan for supplying the fort by force, and that this plan had been adopted by the Washington Government, and was in progress of execution.

THE KENTUCKY VOLUNTEER REGIMENT.

LOUISVILLE, Friday, Apr.l 12.

Dispatches have come here to hold the Kentucky Volunteer Regiment in readiness to move at a moment's notice from the War Department at Montgomery.

EXCITEMENT IN MOBILE.

MOBILE, Friday, April 12.

There is intense excitement and rejoicing here. Fifteen guns have been fired in honor of the attack on Fort Sumpter

THE CONFEDERATE STATES CONGRESS.

MONTGOMERY, Friday, April 12.

An extra session of the Confederate States Congress has been called for April 29.

THE NEWS IN WASHINGTON.

WASHINGTON, Friday, April 12.

The town was thrown into intense excitement to-night by the report of the commencement of hostilities at Charleston this morning at 4 o'clock. The more so because of the previous news of peace and landing of provisions at Fort Sumpter. The news came to-night from the Associated Press agent at Charleston, giving all the particulars of the correspondence between Beauregard and Major Anderson, the commencement of the attack by the Secessionists, and Anderson's response from his batteries.

The news was posted at once in all the hotels, and the wildest scene of excitement ensued. Among the Union men here there was general rejoicing that an issue was made at last, while no advocates of Southern rights were to be found.

Major Anderson's fame is on every one's tongue about the hotels and streets. The news was at once taken to the White House. All visiters will be excluded, and the Cabinet summoned to await further information and act upon it. One thing I am certain of, from positive knowledge—that if this last information proves true, the Administration will support Anderson and his course, with the whole power and means of the Government, at all hazards.

A crowd assembled at the telegraph office to await further news.

Everyone had been waiting anxiously all day for the report of an attack upon the Government supply vessels, which it was ascertained last evening would probably approach Charleston harbor some time during the night or this morning. The surprise occasioned by the report from repeated dispatches that they had entered the harbor without molestation, and were landing the supplies without any difficulty, present or apprehensive, created nearly as great an excitement as the later reports of battle. The President was informed by dispatches to three different parties, announcing the safe landing, until he finally concluded that they must be correct, and that better counsels were prevailing among the Southern men.

CABINET COUNCILS.

Mr. Lincoln summoned the Cabinet together the second time to consult. They had met once at 10 A. M., and now convened again at 1 o'clock P. M. There was general rejoicing at the prospects of peace and final adjustment of our national difficulties, dampened somewhat, however, by fear that it would prove false. Lincoln said to a friend that if these advices were correct, the crisis had been passed, and the whole question settled without firing a gun. He added that he did not consider the Government at war with the South, and did not intend it should by his act. It was in this view that the provisioning of the fort was ordered to be attempted, unaccompanied by armed demonstration. The President further said, while assuming that the supplies had been landed, that he did not consider maintaining supremacy of the Federal Government any victory over the South, but simply a vindication of the faith he had always reposed in the ultimate good sense, and sense of justice among the American people. The War Department did not place any reliance to-day on the peace dispatches. Secretary Cameron declared that he saw no escape from conflict at both Forts Sumpter and Pickens.

Later.—Notwithstanding a violent rain-storm, people are still thronging the streets, anxious to get the details of the fight at Charleston, but very little has leaked out except the leading statement that the fight has begun. The last rumor on the streets is that a breach has been effected in the walls of Fort Sumpter. Military men here say if this statement is part of the Associated Press news, it throws discredit on the whole story, as Fort Sumpter is too strong to be thus speedily reduced by any battery in the possession of the enemy. The motive of the statement that a breach has been effected, is supposed to be to discourage the President from sending additional forces there on the idea that the whole affair would be ended before reinforcements could arrive. This surmise is strengthened by the failure to get news of the arrival of the transports at Charleston, as there can be no doubt that some of them reached there before this. The President is anxious but calm at this trying hour of responsibility, confident in the rectitude of his course, and its approval by the people.

FOREIGN ASPECT OF SECESSION.

Mr. Seward and the President have consulted frequently with the foreign diplomats here concerning the present condition of our national affairs and the course of their respective Governments. On the part of the representatives of England and France, it is well understood that there is no sympathy whatever for the South. Lord Lyons says that he sees no benefit to be derived by the English Government, or any foreign Power, from the subremacy of its people; that there is, of course no prospect of foreign supremacy on this continent in any event; while England and the United States have become so strongly united in mutual interests, that misfortune to one is disaster to the other in all points of material interests. The Southern Commissioners had reason to discover these facts while in Washington, and have probably given Davis and his compatriots some new ideas not at all flattering to their vanity and visions of ultimate success.

VIRGINIA TRAITORS.

The report that R. A. Pryor, of Virginia, has joined the staff of Beauregard, gives color to the rumor that several companies had left Richmond for Charleston, to join the rebel forces. Under the circumstances, the Virginia Committee who arrived to day, will get only cold comfort from Mr. Lincoln, although they will be treated courteously, as the Administration cannot disclose its purposes while a rebellious army is opposing its power.

THE TRAITORS' MAILS TO BE STOPPED.

Should the news of to-night be confirmed, the Postmaster-General will suspend at once all mail communications with the rebel States.

THE DEFENCE OF WASHINGTON.

Two companies of the Second Cavalry are ordered to this city, to be selected by the officer in charge of the corps. Although Washington is not under martial law, all possible precautions are taken to guard against surprise. Mounted videttes are stationed at all the approaches to the city, at a distance of several miles, to give notice of any coming hostile force.

FROM ANOTHER CORRESPONDENT.

ANOTHER ACCOUNT OF THE NEWS AT WASHINGTON.

The first dispatches from the seat of war were received in this city about 7 o'clock this evening. The excitement caused by the meagre intelligence was most intense. Bulletins were posted at the principal hotels, where immense crowds gathered to discuss the probable results. It is almost needless to say that while there was but one opinion as to the end, there was an infinite variety of conjectures as to the *modus operandi*. The public sentiment is very decided that in the war inaugurated to-day the Government will prove to be the victor.

NEVER THOUGHT OF EVACUATION.

There is no foundation for the long stories told of the original purpose of the Government to evacuate Fort Sumpter. Mr. Lincoln has not entertained any such purpose. He has entertained no purpose but to maintain possession of the Government property and enforce the laws. All statements that negotiations were entered upon for the departure of Major Anderson's command were mere *canards* got up for the purpose of covering political defeats. The policy of the Administration never depended upon the contingency of evacuation. It was fixed within ten days after Mr. Lincoln's inauguration. If evidence were wanting of this, it would be found in the fact that the Government was prepared to dispatch such quantities of men and material as left the port of New-York within four days.

FORETHOUGHT OF THE ADMINISTRATION—ITS EFFECT.

The rapid shipment of supplies, men and munitions was the result of forethought and previous preparation—the end of means long before matured. The Government continues to receive assurances of the popularity of the measures it has inaugurated. These come from all quarters, and from men of all parties. I was talking with a gentleman from Maryland this evening, who assured me that the steps taken to maintain the supremacy of the General Government had done more to stifle secession in his State than all the compromise propositions. He was at home yesterday when a dispatch was received that a conflict had taken place in the harbor of Charleston. About forty persons were present, including Republicans and "very few" Douglas Democrats and Bell-Everett men. There was a universal expression of hope that the Government would succeed. This feeling pervades the Border States to an extent that surprises all. The stern realities of an actual conflict appear to have sobered the people and brought them to realize the duties of the Government and their own responsibility as citizens.

DEMOCRATIC INDORSEMENT OF MR. LINCOLN'S POLICY.

I met a Democrat to-day, whom I have known all through the excitement of the last election as an out-and-out friend of the Southern Secessionists. He is a New-Yorker, and widely connected with its business, he himself being one of the heaviest dealers in sugars in your City. I was astonished to hear him proclaim unguardedly his approval of the policy of the Administration, his hope that the vigor displayed in the beginning would continue to the end, and his willingness to make all the sacrifices which war imposes upon commercial enterprise. He says that the prominent Democrat of the State of New-York who shall venture to give his aid and comfort to the Southern Confederacy is doomed to political oblivion. I could multiply a dozen such instances in my experience of to-day.

NO EXTRA SESSION OF CONGRESS.

There is little probability of an extra session of Congress. As was telegraphed you yesterday, there is no necessity for such a session. The Government has all the power which Congress could confer, except the money.

MONEY PLENTY.

Until the limit of Treasury Notes is reached, the Government has as much means at its disposal as its wants are likely to exhaust before the regular period for the assembling of the National Legislature. Were it to be called together now, it could do nothing more to maintain the national honor than Mr. Lincoln is now doing, while it might seriously jeopardize the early success of the Government forces by needless but exciting debates. In the hands of a prudent, just and decided President, and an intelligent and harmonious Cabinet, the national honor and the national integrity is much safer than experience has proved it would be in the keeping of Congress.

LEO.

GENERAL WASHINGTON NEWS.

THE MORRILL TARIFF NOT SO BAD.

The alleged imperfections and imprudences of the Morrill Tariff, upon which an extra session has been defended, are found to be largely exaggerated, if not entirely unfounded. Mr. Barney assures me that he will find no difficulty in executing the law with his present force, and that its provisions are quite as explicit as such laws are usually made, and that the changes from the previous system are not so violent and general as is supposed. A gentleman from Maryland told me today that the new tariff was doing much to keep that State loyal. He represents the iron and coal interests of the State, and he thinks the same beneficial influences will be felt in Virginia and North Carolina, in both of which States the mining interests are fast becoming paramount.

FINANCES OF THE CONFEDERATE STATES.

The financial embarrassments of the "Confederate States" are betraying themselves at every turn. Yesterday's Times exposed some of the evidences of the pecuniary troubles of secession by calling public attention to the fact that the $5,000,000 of the $15,000,000 loan of the Confederate States are being "apportioned among" (that is, *forced* upon) the Banks of New-Orleans, Mobile, &c. Have you noticed, also, that the very first of the $1,000,000 Treasury Notes, issued by the Provisional Government of the seceded States, were taken "by the Secretaries of War and the Treasury in payment of their quarter's salaries." The significance of this fact is apparent when it is remembered that the test of financial soundness in any Government consists of its ability to pay all Government dues in gold.

An old Clerk of the Treasury Department, who was South last week on private business, met there Ex-Secretary Howell Cobb, with whom he had some conversation relative to the financial condition of the Government of the United States. Mr. Cobb's experience in the Southern Confederacy does not seem to have improved his judgment at all in the matter of financial estimates, for he continues to come as wide of the mark as ever. In the conversation referred to, he expressed the opinion that the revenues of the Treasury would be only about $1,000,000 per month; that, under this state of facts, the funds would be speedily exhausted, and that, as there is authority to borrow only $27,000,000, which, with the $1,000,000 per month for the ensuing year, would foot up only $39,000,000, while the expenses of the Government must be about $65 000,000, the Treasury must be bankrupted inevitably.

The figures in the Department show, in fact, an increase of revenue over last year, and the revenue is coming in at the rate of $3,000,000 per month, instead of $1,000,000, which Mr. Cobb graciously allows. During the two weeks ending April 9, 1860, the receipts in the Treasury were $1,471,241 48. The receipts during the corresponding fortnight of 1861 were $1,500,667 34; increase in 1861 $29,425 81.

It should be remembered, too, that these results are attained at a time when the new Tariff is operating unfavorably towards the Treasury, because goods are withdrawing from bond for consumption in cases where the duty is less under the old Tariff than under the new, while merchandise which can be taken out of bond at *reduced* duties under the new Tariff are allowed to remain. Unless a war shall occur, Government is likely to have abundant means during the coming year.

SUMPTER AND PICKENS CANNOT STAND BOMBARDMENT.

Gentlemen skilled as engineers, and whose judgment is usually sound, express the opinion that neither Pickens nor Sumpter can withstand bombardment, if their assailants are not operated against by land forces. The forts in question were not constructed to sustain a siege, but to defend harbors against hostile fleets. For the latter purpose they are admirably adapted; no "wooden walls" could withstand the fire from their batteries, or do themselves harm; but a well-sustained fire from different points on the adjacent shores, it is maintained, will reduce them both in time,—unless they have men enough and guns enough to promptly demolish the assailing forts.

SWAGGERING NAVAL OFFICERS.

An agent of the Navy Department might be profitably employed in an occasional stroll through the hotel lobbies at Washington, to notice the language and deportment of some who wear the naval buttons, and yet constantly and publicly swagger about the folly of the Government undertaking to bring the "Southern Confederacy" to terms. It is not often that a naval officer thus dishonors the button,—but when he does, if he has not the manliness to resign, it would be advisable to ship him to sea somewhere where he could do no harm if he should take the notion to turn traitor.

A. B. Dickinson, on Thursday, formally accepted the mission to Nicaragua.

GUARD DUTY BY THE CLERKS.

It is suggested that the Secretaries of the various departments call upon the clerks to perform guard duty at each Department where they are stationed. In this way all the loyal employes will be very easily discovered, and the shakey ones detected. I have the assurance that the experiment is to be tried in connection with the present military movements in the city.

AFFAIRS IN NEW-GRANADA.

The Government of New-Granada has no force with which to render effective its recent decree of blockade of the forts of Rio Hacha, Santa Marta, Carthagena and Zapote, in the Atlantic, these forts being in the complete possession of the revolutionists, So far as the Pacific is concerned, the forts of Buenaventura, Tumaco, etc., have been partially blockaded for the past six months or more, by small vessels fitted out at Panama—but I believe this does not directly much concern American interests, although it does so indirectly, as the business of the Panama Railroad is somewhat lessened by any disturbances affecting the trade of the Pacific.

UNABATED RUSH FOR OFFICE.

There was a great rush at the White House again to-day of office-seekers. Most of them failed to gain admittance on account of the exciting news. The entire remainder of the Boston appointments were made, to-day, as follows:

Surveyor, Charles A. Phelps.

Navy Agent, Eugene L. Norton.

United States District-Attorney, Richard H. Dana.

Marshal, John S. Keyes.

A strong, but unsuccessful effort to defeat this slate was made.

The crowd of New-York office-seekers is increasing. Charles A. Stetson denies that he is a candidate for Marshal, or any other office.

CALIFORNIA APPOINTMENTS.

The following additional appointments have been made for California:

Appraiser, John P. Zane.

Collector at Monterey, John T. Porter.

Collector at Stockton, S. W. Sperry.

Collector at Benicia, S. M. Swain.

Collector at San Diego, Joshua Sloane.

Collector at San Pedro, Oscar Macy.

Wm. Bell has been appointed Postmaster at Great Salt Lake City, Utah Territory.

DISPATCH TO THE ASSOCIATED PRESS.

WASHINGTON, Friday, April 12.

The Virginia Commissioners arrived in this City, this morning, and during the afternoon they visited the President, not in their official capacity, and were received by him directly after the Cabinet meeting adjourned.

The President has made the following Massachusetts appointments:

Chas. A. Phelps, Surveyor of the Port of Boston in place of Fletcher Webster, who was removed at the earnest request of the Massachusetts Congressional delegation; Eugene L. Norton, Navy-Agent at Boston: Richard H. Dana, District-Attorney; John S. Keys, Marshal; John A. Goodwin, Postmaster at Lowell.

C. C. P. Baldwin, Marshal, and George Howe, Attorney for Vermont.

James C. Aiken, Marshal, and Ed. G. Bradford, Attorney for Delaware.

Lansing G. Vance, Postmaster at Morristown, Pennsylvania.

Harmon Bennett, Postmaster at Norwich, New-York.

THE NEWS IN NEW-YORK.

Yesterday was a day of excitements. Rumors apparently well grounded concerning the progress of affairs at Charleston flitted through Wall-street, pervaded the thoroughfares and produced sensations of surprise, indignation and rejoicings, according to the nature of the mind to which they were brought. Dispatches were received stating that President Davis had, after consultation with his Cabinet, directed Gen. Beauregard to allow unmolested passage of the Federal transports with their loads of supplies for Fort Sumpter, thereby obviating immediate hostilities; others that Maj. Anderson and Gen. Beauregard were consulting together, and the probabilities were that the Fort would be surrendered so soon as its supplies were exhausted; and still others announcing that the war had actually begun. The first-mentioned dispatch was generally credited, and the feeling was almost universal that a great moral victory had been achieved by the United States Government.

At 5 o'clock in the afternoon, however, all uncertainty was set at rest. The telegraphic wire brought the long looked-for intelligence that WAR HAS BEGUN, and that the forces of the Confederated Traitors have struck the first blow. Expected as was the news, it produced a most remarkable and wide-spread sensation. Many had hoped the contest might yet be avoided; others thought the Federal Government would back down rather than shed blood; and others were certain that a Divine Providence would interfere to prevent so fratricidal a strife. The bulletin boards were surrounded; the streets near them were blockaded, and the fast-gathering multitude were only satisfied when the self-appointed reader had read himself hoarse in the frequent repetition of the brief announcement of the facts. Hundreds of anxious inquirers besieged the telegraph and publication offices, confident that there might yet be some item of information which was withheld from the masses, and they were only appeased when told that they were in possession of all, and that until this morning's papers were out they could have no more.

"Good, good," exclaimed many a one, as he read the statement, or as it was repeated to him by a friend, "at last we have reached a crisis; something *must* be done." The feeling of rejoicing was everywhere to be met, that Major Anderson had not lowered his flag, and that President Lincoln had determined to sustain, even at so fearful a cost, the honor of the country. Of the very many with whom we conversed, and from whom we heard the freest expression of opinions, we did not find a single individual who did not respond heartily to the sentiment, "Thank Heaven we have a Government." Speculations and wagers of all kinds were the order of the night, as to the probable effect of this or that battery, of the arrival and probable action of the fleet, and of the result of this first contest; and very long odds were offered and taken that Sumpter would silence Moultrie, and that the fleet, on arrival, would find but little to do. However that may be, the war has begun—the aggressors were the Confederated forces, the Federal post has returned vigorously the fire, and the entire moral support of the North stands about the President in this trying moment, as will the entire physical force stand at his side if a more trying hour should come.

THE PENNSYLVANIA WAR BILL.

HARRISBURGH, Friday, April 12.

The War bill passed both Houses to-night, without amendment. Gov. Curtin waited at the Executive office to sign it. It is signed.

The Charleston dispatches about hostilities were announced in both Houses, and produced a profound sensation.

Mr. Smith, a Democratic member of the House, after the Charleston dispatches were received, changed his vote to aye on the War bill. All the Democrats of both Houses voted against it. The bill appropriates $500,000 for the purpose of arming and equipping the militia; authorises a temporary loan; provides for the appointment of an Adjutant-General, Commissary-General, and Quartermaster-General, who, with the Governor, are to have power to carry the act into effect.

EFFECTS OF THE WAR IN BALTIMORE.

BALTIMORE, Friday, April 12.

The Charleston news was not generally promulgated here until after midnight. It produced a profound sensation, and general expressions of regret at

[*Continued on Eighth Page.*]

The New-York Times.

VOL. XI—NO. 3264. NEW-YORK, MONDAY, MARCH 10, 1862. PRICE TWO CENTS.

HIGHLY IMPORTANT NEWS.

Desperate Naval Engagements in Hampton Roads.

Attack Upon our Blockading Vessels by the Rebel Steamers Merrimac, Jamestown and Yorktown.

The Frigate Cumberland Run Into by the Merrimac and Sunk.

Part of Her Crew Reported to be Drowned.

SURRENDER OF THE FRIGATE CONGRESS.

Engagement of the Rebel Steamers with the Newport's News Batteries.

The Minnesota and Other Vessels Aground.

CESSATION OF FIRING AT NIGHT.

Opportune Arrival of the Iron-Clad Ericsson Battery Monitor.

A Five Hours' Engagement Between Her and the Merrimac.

The Rebel Vessel Forced to Haul Off.

THE MONITOR UNINJURED.

FORTRESS MONROE, Saturday, March 8.

The dullness of Old Point was startled to-day by the announcement that a supicious looking vessel; supposed to be the *Merrimac*, looking like a submerged house, with the roof only above water, was moving down from Norfolk by the channel in front of the Sewell's Point batteries. Signal guns were also fired by the *Cumberland* and *Congress*, to notify the *Minnesota*, *St. Lawrence* and *Roanoke* of the approaching danger, and all was excitement in and about Fortress Monroe.

There was nothing protruding above the water but a flagstaff flying the rebel flag, and a short smoke-stack. She moved along slowly, and turned into the channel leading to Newport's News, and steamed direct for the frigates *Cumberland* and *Congress*, which were lying at the mouth of James River.

As soon as she came within range of the *Cumberland*, the latter opened on her with her heavy guns, but the balls struck and glanced off, having no more effect than peas from a pop-gun. Her ports were all closed, and she moved on in silence, but with a full head of steam.

In the meantime, as the *Merrimac* was approaching the two frigates on one side, the rebel iron-clad steamers *Yorktown* and *Jamestown* came down James River, and engaged our frigates on the other side. The batteries at Newport's News also opened on the *Yorktown* and *Jamestown*, and did all in their power to assist the *Cumberland* and *Congress*, which, being sailing vessels, were at the mercy of the approaching steamers.

The *Merrimac*, in the meantime, kept steadily on her course, and slowly approached the *Cumberland*, when she and the *Congress*, at a distance of one hundred yards, raised full broadsides on the iron-clad monster, that took no effect, the balls glancing upwards, and flying off, having only the effect of checking her progress for a moment.

After receiving the first broadside of the two frigates, she ran on to the *Cumberland*, striking her about midships, and literally laying open her sides. She then drew off, and fired a broadside into the disabled ship, and again dashed against her with her iron-clad prow, and, knocking in her side, left her to sink, while she engaged the *Congress*, which laid about a quarter of a mile distant.

The *Congress* had, in the meantime, kept up a short engagement with the *Yorktown* and *Jamestown*, and having no regular crew on board of her, and seeing the hopelessness of resisting the iron-clad steamer, at once struck her colors. Her crew had been discharged several days since, and three companies of the Naval Brigade had been put on board temporarily, until she could be relieved by the *St. Lawrence*, which was to have gone up on Monday to take her position as one of the blockading vessels of the James River.

On the *Congress* striking her colors, the *Jamestown* approached and took from on board of her, all her officers as prisoners, but allowed the crew to escape in boats. The vessel being thus cleared, was fired by the rebels, when the *Merrimac* and her two iron-clad companions opened with shell and shot on the Newport's News batteries. The firing was briskly returned. Various reports have been received, principally from frightened sutler's clerks. Some of them represent that the garrison had been compelled to retreat from the batteries to the woods. Another was that the two smaller rebel steamers had been compelled to retreat from their guns.

In the meantime the steam-frigate *Minnesota*, having partly got up steam, was being towed up to the relief of the two frigates, but did not get up until it was too late to assist them. She was also followed up by the frigate *St. Lawrence*, which was taken in tow by several of the small harbor steamers. It is rumored, however, that neither of these vessels had pilots on board them, and after a short engagement both of them seemed to be, in the opinion of the pilots on the Point, aground. The *Minnesota* either intentionally or from necessity, engaged the three steamers at about a mile distance, with only her two bow guns. The *St. Lawrence* also poured in shot from all the guns she could bring to bear, and it was the impression of the most experienced naval officers on the point that both had been considerably damaged. These statements, it must be borne in mind, are all based on what could be seen by a glass at a distance of nearly eight miles, and from a few panic-stricken non-combatants, who fled at almost the first gun from Newport's News.

In the meantime darkness approached, though the moon shone out brightly, and nothing but the occasional flashing of guns could be seen. The *Merrimac* was also believed to be aground, as she remained stationary, at a distance of a mile from the *Minnesota*, making no attempt to attack or molest her.

Previous to the departure of the steamer for Baltimore, no guns had been fired for half an hour, the last one being fired from the *Minnesota*. Some persons declared that immediately after this last gun was fired, a dense volume of vapor was seen to rise from the *Merrimac*, indicating the explosion of her boiler. Whether this is so or not, cannot be known, but it was the universal opinion that the rebel monster was hard aground.

Fears were of course entertained for the safety of the *Minnesota* and *St. Lawrence* in such an unequal contest; but if the *Merrimac* was really ashore, she could do no more damage. It was the intention of the *Minnesota*, with her picked and gallant crew, to run into close quarters with the *Merrimac*, avoid her iron prow, and board her. This the *Merrimac* seemed not inclined to give her an opportunity to do.

At 8 o'clock, when the Baltimore boat left, a fleet of steam-tugs were being sent up to the relief of the *Minnesota* and the *St. Lawrence*, and an endeavor was to be made to draw them off the bar on which they had grounded. In the meantime the firing had suspended, whether from mutual consent or necessity, could not be ascertained.

The rebel battery at Pig Point was also enabled to join in the combined attack on the *Minnesota*, and several guns were fired at her from Sewall's Point as she went up. None of them struck her, but one or two of them passed over her.

The Baltimore boat left Old Point at 8 o'clock last night. In about half-an-hour after she left the wharf, the iron-clad Ericsson steamer *Monitor* passed her, going in, towed by a large steamer. The *Monitor* undoubtedly reached Fortress Monroe by 9 o'clock, and may have immediately gone into service; if not, she would be ready to take a hand early on Sunday morning.

The foregoing are all the facts as far as can be at present ascertained, and are, probably, the worst possible version of the affair.

THE LINE OF THE POTOMAC FROM HARPER'S FERRY TO CHETANK POINT.

Map Showing the Cockpit Point Batteries, Yesterday Evacuated by the Rebels, and Taken Possession of by Our Troops; Leesburgh, from Which the Rebels were Driven on Saturday Morning by Col. Geary, and All Other Important Points.

LATER AND BETTER NEWS.

A Five Hours' Engagement Between the Ericsson Battery and the three Rebel Steamers.

The Rebel Vessels Driven Off—The Merrimac in a Sinking Condition.

WASHINGTON, Sunday, March 9—6:45 P. M.

The telegraph line to Fortress Monroe is just completed, and a message from there states that after the arrival of the *Monitor*, last night, she was attacked by the *Merrimac*, *Jamestown*, and *Yorktown*. *After a five hours' fight they were driven off, and the Merrimac put back to Norfolk in a sinking condition.*

OFFICIAL.

[BY TELEGRAPH FROM FORTRESS MONROE.]

WASHINGTON, Sunday, March 9—7 P. M.

The *Monitor* arrived at Fortress Monroe last night.

Early this morning she was attacked by the three vessels—the *Merrimac*, the *Jamestown* and the *Yorktown*.

After five hours' contest they were driven off—the *Merrimac* in a sinking condition.

The above is official.

DISPATCH AUTHORIZED BY GEN. WOOL

FORTRESS MONROE, Sunday, March 9.

The *Monitor* arrived at 10 P. M., last night, and went immediately to the protection of the *Minnesota*, lying aground just below Newport's News. At 7 A. M. to-day the *Merrimac*, accompanied by two wooden steamers, the *Yorktown* and *Jamestown*, and several tugs, stood out toward the *Minnesota*, and opened fire. The *Monitor* met them at once, and opened fire, when the enemy's vessels retired, excepting the *Merrimac*. *The two iron-clad vessels fought, part of the time touching each other, from 8 A. M. till noon, when the Merrimac retreated.* Whether she is injured, or not, it is impossible to say.

Lieut. J. L. WORDEN, who commanded the *Monitor*, handled her with great skill, assisted by Chief-Engineer STIMERS.

The *Minnesota* kept up a continuous fire, and is herself somewhat injured. She was moved considerably to-day, and will probably be off to-night.

The *Monitor* is uninjured, and ready at any moment to repel another attack.

[Sent by order of Gen. WOOL.]

WASHINGTON, Sunday, March 9.

The following was received to-night by Major-Gen. McCLELLAN from Gen. WOOL, dated Fortress Monroe, at 6 o'clock this evening:

"Two hours after my telegraphic dispatch to the Secretary of War last evening, the *Monitor* arrived. She immediately went to the assistance of the *Minnesota*, which was aground, and continued so until a few moments since. Early this morning she was attacked by the *Merrimac*, *Jamestown* and *Yorktown*. After a five hours' contest they were driven off, the *Merrimac* in a sinking condition. She was towed by the *Jamestown*, *Yorktown* and several smaller boats toward Norfolk, no doubt, if possible, to get her in the dry-dock for repairs. The *Minnesota* is afloat and being towed toward Fortress Monroe."

THE VESSELS ENGAGED.

THE ERICSSON BATTERY MONITOR.

The new Ericsson battery, or, as she is now called, the *Monitor*, which left this port for Southern waters last Wednesday, has already had her first engagement with the enemy, and has come out victor. It appears that she arrived in Hampton Roads last Saturday night, just after the rebel battery *Merrimac* had been playing havoc with our blockaders. She came to the rescue precisely at the right moment. Yesterday morning she was set upon by the *Merrimac*, the *Jamestown* and the *Yorktown*. After a five hours' fight she drove them all off, the *Merrimac* putting back to Norfolk in a sinking condition. As the public will now be anxious to know something of the style and power of this iron-clad vessel, which has thus routed the famous rebel iron-clad floating battery, we append a full account of her, furnished by our correspondent, who accompanied her on a recent trial trip from this harbor.

DESCRIPTION OF THE VESSEL.

The designer and builder of the *Monitor* was Capt. ERICSSON, famous in connection with the invention of a mode of propelling vessels and working engines by the motor-power of caloric, or heated air. Capt. ERICSSON is a Swede by birth, but his remarkable and persevering scientific efforts have been carried on principally in this City for the last ten years.

By an act of Congress passed last Summer, the Secretary of the Navy was authorized to advertise for proposals to build one or more iron-clad vessels, all proposers to furnish their own plans. An appropriation of $1,500,000 was made to build such vessels, providing that the plans met with the approval of three commanding officers of the navy. The Board appointed consisted of Commodores JOSEPH SMITH, HIRAM PAULDING, and Capt. CHAS. H. DAVIS. Capt. ERICSSON sent in a plan which was accepted, with the understanding that the vessel was to be finished in one hundred days. The contract bears date the 4th of October, 1861.

The keel of this vessel was laid on the 25th of October, and so rapidly was the work performed, that the engines were put into the vessel and operated on the 31st of December last. The construction of the vessel was under the superintendence of Engineer ALBAN C. STIMERS, and Assistant Engineer ISAAC NEWTON, who were detailed from the frigate *Roanoke*, by Government, for that purpose. Annexed are the dimensions of the *Monitor*:

	Feet.	Inches.
Length of upper vessel	172	—
Beam of upper vessel	41	—
Depth of upper vessel	5	—
Length of lower vessel	124	—
Beam of lower vessel at junction with upper	34	—
Beam of lower vessel at bottom	18	—
Depth of lower vessel	6	9
Diameter of turret, interior	20	—
Height of turret	9	—
Diameter of pilot-house	6	—
Height above deck	5	—
Draught forward	7	3
Draught aft	8	1
Draught with armament, coals and provisions on board	9	9
Height above the water line	—	21

THE ARMAMENT.

The armament consists of two 11-inch Dahlgren guns, which are the heaviest now used by the navy. The lower part of the gun-carriages upon which the upper part slides when the gun is run in or out, consists of solid, wrought iron beams, extending the whole diameter of the turret, with their ends secured to it in such a manner that they essentially form a part of it. These beams are planned perfectly true, are seven inches deep by four inches wide, and are placed perfectly parallel in the turret, both guns pointing in the same direction. This permits the officer working the guns to take his aim by sights fixed with the turret instead of with the guns, in the usual way, which requires personal exposure when taking the aim. The ports through the side of the turret are only sufficiently wide to permit of the passage through them of the muzzle of the guns, and with just enough addition, vertically, for the elevation required. Inside of these swing iron pendulums, which close them against the enemy as soon as the gun recoils. The whole is made to revolve by a pair of steam engines placed beneath the deck, the handle which governs them passing up into the turret convenient to the hand of the officer who aims the gun.

HER AMMUNITION.

At the Novelty Iron Works a quantity of solid wrought iron shot was forged for the *Monitor*; each one weighing 187 pounds. These were intended for perforating and sinking iron clad vessels of the enemy whose sides are the ordinary height above the water line. Besides these she carries a quantity of cast iron shots, weighg 175 pounds each, and one hundred round of shells, in weight 155 pounds each.

THE MACHINERY.

Mr. C. H. DELAMATER fitted this vessel with machinery. It consists of two horizontal tubular boilers containing 3,000 square feet of fire surface, and two horizontal condensing engines, of forty inches diameter of cylinders, by twenty-two inches stroke of pistons. The propeller is nine feet diameter, sixteen feet pitch, and has four blades. Her speed is about six and a half knots an hour. All her machinery is below water-line.

THE MONITOR'S OFFICERS.

The following were the officers of the *Monitor* when she left this port, six days ago:

Lieutenant Commanding—JOHN S. WORDEN.
Lieutenant and Executive Officer—S. D. Green.
Acting Masters—L. N. Stodder and J. W. Webber.
Acting Assistant Paymaster—Wm. F. Keeler.
Acting Assistant Surgeon—D. C. Logue.
Chief Engineer—A. C. Steiners.
Engineers—First Assistant, Isaac Newton; Second Assistant, Albert S. Campbell; Third Assistants, R. W. Sands and M. T. Sunstron.
Acting Master's Mate—George Frederickson.

THE SCIENTIFIC PLAN OF THE MONITOR.

Capt. ERICSSON's idea in building the *Monitor* was to give the greatest buoyancy to the vessel, and as small a target as possible to the enemy, so as to enable him to completely protect every part, all its attachments and every person on board, when under the fire of an enemy. He conceived that to do this was to build a broad flat-bottomed vessel with vertical sides and pointed ends, so that it requires but a shallow depth to displace water sufficient to buoy itself up, though loaded with an impregnable armor upon its sides, and a bomb-proof deck upon which is placed a shot-proof revolving turret containing two of the heaviest Dahlgren guns. To insure such a vessel the power of locomotion, it was only necessary to suspend beneath it a vessel of ordinary strength, sufficiently narrow and sloping at the sides, that if, as actual experiment has proven possible, the enemy's missile should pass below the shot-proof upper vessel, these sides can only be hit at such an acute angle that little harm is likely to ensue, and in its length approaching the bow only so nearly that its raking stem may receive the shot fired from directly ahead in the same way, and at the stern giving sufficient space to permit the dipping shot coming from directly aft to pass under the shot-proof end, directly on its course, without hitting the rudder, which is placed abaft the propeller.

The sides of the upper vessel are first formed of plate-iron, half an inch thick, outside of which is attached solid white oak, twenty-six inches thick, which again receives the rolled iron armor of five inches thickness. The bomb-proof deck is supported by well-stanchioned and diagonally braced oak beams, ten inches square, placed with their faces twenty-six inches apart, upon which is laid planking seven inches thick, covered with rolled plate-iron one inch thick. As the bottoms of these beams are on a level with the water-line, the armor above water is supported by a backing of forty-one feet in depth. The lower vessel is of iron, one-half inch thick, made in the usual manner, and contains, in its after part, the steam machinery and coal, and in the forward part—the poop being divided by a wrought iron bulkhead—the quarters for the officers and crew, and the ammunition and stores. In describing the upper and lower vessel, it must not be imagined that they are constructed separately; they form, together, one vessel; it is only as respects form that they can be regarded as two.

The Pilot-House and Anchor.

The pilot is protected by a shot-proof pilot-house which alone weighs 22,000 pounds. The house stands five feet above the level of the deck. The anchor is suspended from a circular well, open at the bottom, situated in the extreme bow of the upper vessel, and connected with the capstan in the bow of the lower one. An arrangement is also provided for taking soundings below the water line.

The Turret.

The turret spoken of above is for the protection of the men while working the guns; in fact, no one is exposed or seen by the enemy. The turret revolves, and consists, first, of a rolled plate iron skeleton, one inch thick, to which is riveted two thicknesses, of one inch each, of rolled iron plates. Outside of these riveted plates are six thicknesses, of one inch each, of rolled iron plates. Outside of these riveted plates are six thickness, of one inch each, of rolled plates bolted firmly to the first two thicknesses with screw bolts, having deep countersunk heads on the outside and nuts within, so that if in action the enemy's shot should loosen any of the plates they can easily be refastened. The seams are vertical, and these break joints with each other, consequently no shot can strike the seam of more than one thickness. The top is covered with a bomb-proof roof, placed six inches down within the turret, and perforated with holes. In addition to the above the gunners are protected by a shield, within the turret, of one and a half inch thickness.

FOR WHAT THE MONITOR WAS INTENDED.

The Ericsson Battery was not intended for an ordinary cruiser, but for the defence of our harbors and coast, and for operations such as those in which she has just achieved such a signal success. She is enabled to carry eight days' fuel, and thus can proceed easily from port to port along our seaboard. Provisions for three months can be stowed away in her, and a condensing apparatus for supplying fresh water to the officers and crew is fitted up on board.

THE LAST TRIAL TRIP OF THE MONITOR AND ITS RESULTS.

Last Monday the *Monitor* went on a trial trip down the Bay, about five miles beyond Fort Lafayette. Her steering qualities were found to be all that could be desired.

The guns were fired to test the question which had been mooted, of whether the concussion within the turret would not be so great as to injure seriously the ears of the men. First, a blank cartridge was fired, with the hatches in the roof open. Then a charge of canister, weighing 135 pounds, with 15 pounds of powder, with the hatches still open, and finally the same charge with the hatches closed, as they will be under the fire of the enemy. It was found that in every case the concussion in every part of the interior of the turret was considerably less than when standing near such a gun fired in the open air. The sailors stationed at the guns, and who expected to handle them shortly against the enemy, all expressed themselves delighted at the success of the trial. The speed of the vessel by the chip log was 6½ knots, the engines making 65 revolutions.

The last heard of the *Monitor* previous to this news of her success, was by a bark which arrived here yesterday morning. The bark reported that, on the 7th inst., at 10 P. M., off Barnegat, she passed the *Monitor* in tow, bound for Fortress Monroe.

This magnificent success in her first trial, will settle all questions as to her efficiency.

LIEUT. WERDEN.

Lieut. J. R. WERDEN, it will be recollected, at the commencement of the rebellion was captured by the rebels, after having conveyed dispatches from the Government to the National fleet off Pensacola, and imprisoned several months at Montgomery. He was exchanged a short time ago, and was immediately assigned to the *Monitor*, in which, as will be seen from the dispatches, he has done most efficient service.

THE MERRIMAC.

The *Merrimac*, the iron-plated rebel steamer which attacked the Ericsson Battery, was formerly the United States screw-frigate of the same name. She was built at the Navy-Yard at Charlestown, Mass., in 1855; and her last active service was in the Pacific Squadron. At the time of the rebel attack on the Norfolk Navy-Yard, she was lying there in ordinary, as a store and receiving ship. She was a ship of 3,200 tons burden, and was pierced for forty guns. When the Navy-yard was assailed, she was set fire to, scuttled and sunk, by the National officers, in preference to letting her fall into the hands of the rebels. A recent official report on the subject, made to the rebel authorities, stated that she was sunk and burned to her copper line and down through to her berth-deck, which, with her spacious gun-decks were also burned. After the rebels had got possession of the Yard, they proceeded to raise the hull of the *Merrimac*, and to convert her into a vessel of war for their own purpose. Her hull was cut down to within three feet of her water-work, and a bomb-proof house built on her gun-deck. She was then iron-plated, and her bow and stern steel clad, with a projecting angle of iron for the purpose of piercing a vessel. She had no masts, and there was nothing to be seen over her gun-deck, with the exception of the pilot-house and smoke-stack. The bomb-proof was three inches thick, and made of wrought iron. Altogether she looked like a most formidable war-ship. But when her iron sheathing was half on, it was tested by columbiads and found inefficient. She was then additionally strengthened, until she was so heavy that she bade fair to become unmanageable, and even to sink by her own weight. In a description published some two or three months ago, her armament was stated as consisting of four 11-inch navy guns on each side, and two 100-pounder Armstrong guns at the bow and stern. But no doubt great changes have been made in her armament before this time. The Norfolk *Day Book* of the 4th ult. had an article describing the attempt to convert the *Merrimac* into an impregnable iron plated man-of-war as a failure. It began thus:

"We have scarcely patience enough left to condemn in temperate language the reckless impropriety of two of our cotemporaries, who have seen fit, in their thirst for notoriety, to thrust before the public the fact that the *Merrimac* has proved an abortion."

It was further said, that

"The calculation in displacement was erroneous. An error amounting to more than two hundred tons was discovered when the ship was floated off. The chief subject of regret is, that when she was shored up again the ship caught upon the blocks and received a considerable strain; consequently, some parts of the machinery have been taken up, and a quantity of dead-wood will have to be introduced to correct the

[Continued on Eighth Page.]

The New-York Times.

VOL. XI—NO. 3432. NEW-YORK, TUESDAY, SEPTEMBER 23, 1862. PRICE TWO CENTS.

HIGHLY IMPORTANT.

A Proclamation by the President of the United States.

The War Still to be Prosecuted for the Restoration of the Union.

A DECREE OF EMANCIPATION

All Slaves in States in Rebellion on the First of January Next to be Free.

The Gradual Abolition and Colonization Schemes Adhered to.

Loyal Citizens to be Remunerated for Losses' Including Slaves.

WASHINGTON, Monday, Sept. 22.

By the President of the United States of America:

A PROCLAMATION.

I, ABRAHAM LINCOLN, President of the United States of America, and Commander-in-Chief of the Army and Navy thereof, do hereby proclaim and declare, that hereafter, as heretofore, the war will be prosecuted for the object of practically restoring the constitutional relation between the United States and the people thereof in which States that relation is, or may be suspended or disturbed; that it is my purpose, upon the next meeting of Congress, to again recommend the adoption of a practical measure tendering pecuniary aid to the free acceptance or rejection of all the Slave States so called, the people whereof may not then be in rebellion against the United States, and which States may then have voluntarily adopted, or thereafter may voluntarily adopt, the immediate or gradual abolishment of Slavery within their respective limits; and that the efforts to colonize persons of African descent with their consent, upon the Continent or elsewhere, with the previously obtained consent of the governments existing there, will be continued.

That on the first day of January, in the year of our Lord one thousand eight hundred and sixty-three, all persons held as slaves within any State, or any designated part of a State, the people whereof shall then be in rebellion against the United States shall be then, thenceforward, and forever, free; and the Executive Government of the United States, including the military and naval authority thereof, will recognize and maintain the freedom of such persons, and will do no act or acts to repress such persons, or any of them, in any efforts they may make for their actual freedom.

That the Executive will, on the first day of January aforesaid, by proclamation, designate the States and parts of States, if any, in which the people thereof, respectively, shall then be in rebellion against the United States; and the fact that any State, or the people thereof, shall on that day be in good faith represented in the Congress of the United States by members chosen thereto at elections wherein a majority of the qualified voters of such State shall have participated, shall, in the absence of strong countervailing testimony, be deemed conclusive evidence that such State and the people thereof have not been in rebellion against the United States.

That attention is hereby called to an act of Congress entitled "An act to make an additional article of war," approved March 13, 1862, and which act is in the words and figure following:

"Be it enacted by the Senate and House of Representatives of the United States of America in Congress assembled, That hereafter the following shall be promulgated as an additional article of war for the government of the army of the United States, and shall be obeyed and observed as such.

ARTICLE—All officers or persons in the military or naval service of the United States are prohibited from employing any of the forces under their respective commands for the purpose of returning fugitives from service or labor who may have escaped from any person to whom such service or labor is claimed to be due, and any officer who shall be found guilty by a Court-martial of violating this article shall be dismissed from the service.

SECTION 2. And be it further enacted, that this act shall take effect from and after its passage."

Also to the ninth and tenth sections of an act entitled "An act to suppress insurrection, to punish treason and rebellion, to seize and confiscate property of rebels, and for other purposes," approved July 17, 1862, and which sections are in the words and figures following:

SEC. 9. And be it further enacted, that all slaves of persons who shall hereafter be engaged in rebellion against the Government of the United States, or who shall, in any way, give aid or comfort thereto, escaping from such persons and taking refuge within the lines of the army; and all slaves captured from such persons or deserted by them and coming under the control of the Government of the United States, and all slaves of such persons found on (or being within) any place occupied by rebel forces and afterward occupied by the forces of the United States, shall be deemed captives of war and shall be forever free of their servitude and not again held as slaves.

SEC. 10. And be it further enacted, That no slave escaping into any State, Territory or the District of Columbia, from any of the States, shall be delivered up, or in any way impeded or hindered of his liberty, except for crime or some offence against the laws, unless the person claiming said fugitive shall first make oath that the person to whom the labor or service of such fugitive is alleged to be due, is his lawful owner, and has not been in arms against the United States in the present rebellion, nor in any way given aid and comfort thereto, and no person engaged in the military or naval service of the United States shall, under any pretence whatever, assume to decide on the validity of the claim of any person to the service or labor of any other person, or surrender up any such person to the claimant, on pain of being dismissed from the service.

And I do hereby enjoin upon and order all persons engaged in the military and naval service of the United States, to observe, obey and enforce, within their respective spheres of service, the act and sections above recited.

And the Executive will in due time recommend that all citizens of the United States who shall have remained loyal thereto throughout the rebellion, shall (upon the restoration of the constitutional relation between the United States and their respective States and people, if the relation shall have been suspended or disturbed,) be compensated for all losses by acts of the United States, *including the loss of slaves.*

In witness whereof, I have hereunto set my hand, and caused the seal of the United States to be affixed.

Done at the City of Washington, this Twenty-second day of September, in the year of our Lord one thousand eight hundred and sixty-two, and of the Independence of the United States the eighty-seventh.

ABRAHAM LINCOLN.

By the President.
WILLIAM H. SEWARD, Secretary of State.

GENERAL NEWS FROM WASHINGTON.

OUR SPECIAL WASHINGTON DISPATCHES.

WASHINGTON, Monday, Sept. 22.

THE PRESIDENT'S PROCLAMATION.

The great event of the day here is the proclamation of the President ordering the execution of the war measures of the last Congress, and promising freedom to the slaves in all States that persist in the rebellion against the Government. This act, so long expected, so long delayed, bids fair to simplify at once the issues of the war, and immediately to array against each other the unconditionally loyal and the rebellious of all shades and grades. If the cause of the Union and free institutions is strongest, this test will show it, and the only question of its triumph will then be the power in the Government to execute its policy with courage and vigor.

THE NEWS FROM KENTUCKY.

A special private dispatch, just received from Cincinnati, announces that BRAGG is marching on Louisville, Ky., and that Gen. NELSON has ordered the women and children to leave the city. BUELL is believed to have been outgeneraled, and to be several hours behind. The dispatch closes—"A General wanted for the West."

THE OLD ISSUE OF TREASURY NOTES.

I have the following statistics in regard to the old issue of United States Treasury Notes, receivable for duties, of the $60,000,0000 issue: $28,420,000 have been returned to the Department and burned; $43,000 have been returned, and are not yet burned; $4,000,000 have been redeemed, but not yet returned to the Department, leaving $27,537,000 yet outstanding. As only about half the whole issue has yet been redeemed, and as the Government will be able to get no gold in payment of duties, so long as any of these notes remain in possession of the public, it is plain that the specie required to pay the interest falling due on Oct. 1—$4,000,000—as well as that falling due Jan. 1—$5,000,000—must be procured by the Government by purchase or loan.

Thirty thousand dollars of small currency notes were to-day paid out at the Treasury Department, and were all taken within an hour.

CONDITION OF GEN. HOOKER.

Gen. HOOKER is now with his friend, Dr. NICHOLS, at the United States Insane Asylum Hospital, near Washington. His wound is a rifle ball through the left foot. Although the wound is painful, it is not considered dangerous; yet it is sufficient to disable him for active service.

THE CONVALESCENT CAMP.

The Convalescent Camp, under the regulations of Gen. BANKS, is becoming an institution of very great utility. All stragglers and convalescents are immediately sent there, as are officers who have been absent without leave, or have overstayed their leave under circumstances that entitle them to lenity. Soldiers are classified according to the corps to which they belong, and are placed in charge of officers belonging to the same corps, who subject them to the daily drill of camp instruction. When the accumulation becomes sufficient to justify their removal, they are sent to their regiments and commands.

PENSIONS.

The Commissioner of Pensions has commenced making appointments of surgeons to make examinations and give certificates in cases of applications for pensions. The fees will make the offices desirable. The following are the appointments already made: Cincinnati, James H. Oliver; Indianapolis, Geo. W. Mears; Leavenworth, Kansas, Selden W. Jones; New-Philadelphia, Ohio, Wm. G. Smith; Terre Haute, Ind., Geo. W. Clippinger; Lafayette, Ind., O. L. Clark; Boston, Geo. S. Jones; Bangor, Me. Ralph J. K. Jones; Rochester, N. Y., Harvey F. Montgomery; Oswego, N. Y., Chas. C. P. Clark; Lyons, N. Y., Nelson Peck; Norridgewock, Me., Uno Robbins, Jr.

ACTING REAR-ADMIRALS.

The following naval officers have been made Acting Rear-Admirals and assigned to the command of the following squadrons, respectively: C. H. BELL, Pacific Squadron; CHAS. WILKES, "Flying Squadron;" T. L. LARDNER, Eastern Gulf Squadron; C. H. DAVIS, Mississippi Flotilla.

From Salt Lake.

SALT LAKE, Monday, Sept. 22.

CHARLES MCBRIDE, from Virginia City, arrived here yesterday, one of a party of fifteen bound for the States. He says:

"The party were attacked by the Snake Indians at the City of Rocks, on the Humboldt route, 150 miles north. They fought the Indians for 20 miles, losing six killed and two wounded, and all of their outfit. JOHN CONNER, JOHN SHARPP, BENJAMIN WHITE, JAMES SHAW, WM. DAVIS and MR. GOODMAN were killed. JOHN FOSTER and SAM. KELLY had their arms broken."

Reports of Indian depredations northward are coming in daily, and much trouble is expected to emigration.

THE LATEST WAR NEWS.

A Raid of Stuart's Cavalry Across the Potomac at Williamsport.

NO DAMAGE DONE.

The Reoccupation of Maryland Heights by Our Forces.

THE REBELS CONTINUING THEIR RETREAT

No Further Collisions at Last Accounts.

LATEST REPORTS FROM HEADQUARTERS.

HEADQUARTERS OF THE ARMY OF THE POTOMAC,
Saturday Evening, Sept. 20, 1862.

The firing heard last evening in the direction of Williamsport, turns out to have been a raid of STUART's rebel cavalry. He crossed the Potomac on Friday night into Maryland, at that point, with his cavalry, one regiment of infantry, and seventeen pieces of artillery. The force sent up to drive him back, arrived near the town late in the afternoon. The firing heard was principally from the rebel guns. During the night they recrossed into Virginia and this morning they had disappeared from the opposite shore. No one was hurt.

The work of burying the dead is still continuing. They average about one thousand per day. To-morrow will probably finish it.

The Maryland Heights were yesterday occupied by a National force.

The indications are that the rebels are continuing their retreat into Virginia, leaving the line of the Potomac.

Divine worship was held at headquarters this evening, Bishop WHIPPLE, of Minnesota, officiating.

HEADQUARTERS, ARMY OF THE POTOMAC,
Monday Evening, Sept. 22.

The following is the official report of loss in SUMNER's corps at the battle of the Antietam:

GEN. RICHARDSON'S DIVISION.

Killed	212
Wounded	899
Missing	24

GEN. SEDGWICK'S DIVISION.

Killed	335
Wounded	1,577
Missing	321

GEN. FRENCH'S DIVISION.

Killed	293
Wounded	1,321
Missing	203
Total loss in Gen. SUMNER's Corps	5,208

The loss in missing may be somewhat reduced by stragglers returning.

A train of cars crossed the Monocacy this morning. The road is now open to Harper's Ferry, where there is a sufficient Federal force for all purposes.

The rebels, in their hasty retreat from Maryland, left between 1,100 and 1,200 wounded between Sharpsburgh and the river. They are being paroled.

Twenty-six stands of colors were taken during the battle of the Antietam, and have been received at headquarters. Eleven more are known to have been captured, and are in the hands of the different regiments which captured them.

OUR LATEST WASHINGTON DISPATCHES.

WASHINGTON, Monday, Sept. 22.

A special dispatch from Frederick states that some surgeons, just arrived from the army, report rebels still falling back from the Potomac. Not even their pickets are now to be seen.

Another dispatch states that our losses in the last fight are not nearly as great as at first reported, especially in SUMNER's Corps. In the California Regiment only one commissioned officer was killed (Lieut. WILEY) and one hundred and fifty privates killed and wounded.

The last reports from headquarters represented "All quiet along the lines."

THE WAR IN MARYLAND.

Another Account of the Great Battle of Antietam.

LETTERS FROM THE BATTLE-FIELD.

The Strong Position Chosen by the Enemy—How the National Forces were Arranged—Desperate Character of the Fighting—The Results, &c.

ON THE FIELD NEAR SHARPSBURGH, MD.,
Wednesday Evening, Sept. 17, 1862.

This day will be memorable for one of the bloodiest fought battles on the American Continent. The combined forces of the enemy, under JACKSON, LEE, LONGSTREET, and the whole rebel set, have made a stand near Sharpsburgh, and all day long, from 5 o'clock in the morning until now, (8 o'clock P. M.,) have been contesting with the Union Army under MCCLELLAN, led by BURNSIDE, HOOKER, SUMNER, KEYES, and the other heroes of the war. Nothing, I am sure, since the battle of Pittsburgh Landing, can compare with this day's fight, either in its collossal proportions, or in the bloody character of the struggle. Our advance overtook the rebel forces, apparently in full retreat toward the Shepherdstown ford of the Potomac, yesterday morning, and a temporary halt was ordered near Kedysville, a little village three miles north from Sharpsburgh. The enemy had taken possession of the Antietam Hills, on the right of the creek by that name, with Sharpsburgh in their rear. They were attacked yesterday by our batteries across this creek, for the purpose of occupying them until our whole force should come up, but no general engagement ensued. The rebels were evidently preparing for a last desperate stand, before the final attempt to cross the Potomac. Their failure to check our advance here they knew would be fatal to their whole army, for they could not escape safely into Virginia with our artillery and infantry assailing their rear.

The day closed without any decisive results, except that in every encounter our artillery practice was found to be too accurate and terrible for them, and they doggedly yielded every position which they took up.

Meantime, LONGSTREET, who had succeeded in obtaining possession of Maryland Heights the day before, *having paroled the entire force found there,* (excepting the cavalry, which cut their way through and escaped,) abandoned the position, and was hurrying forward to reinforce the rebel troops at this point.

Thus the two armies, wearied by a harassing march over mountain ranges, and of four days' running fight from beyond Frederick, came together on this memorable field.

The enemy having chosen a strong position on the hills just beyond Kedysville, began a sharp cannonade at 5 o'clock in the morning. He found our boys wide awake, who replied firmly and steadily to the attack.

Gen. FITZ-JOHN PORTER had thoroughly examined the field on the previous day, and a council of the Generals had made a disposition of the various army corps for the grand contest. It will be sufficient, for the present purpose, to state that Gen. BURNSIDE took command of the extreme left, while the other Generals occupied the enemy's front and right. BURNSIDE, with Gens. RODMAN, WILCOX, COX and STURGIS Brigades, extended his lines as far as to the southeast of Sharpsburgh, with the stone bridge across the Antietam Creek in his front. Between their position and that of the enemy, who lay toward the village at the northwest, is a succession of hills running nearly north and south, the highest and most abrupt of which is that rising from the bed of the creek. Gens. HOOKER's and SUMNER's corps have been conspicuous throughout the bloody day, the early part of the fight being over their part of the field, while a fierce and protracted struggle was going on at the Stone Bridge, where Gen. BURNSIDE commanded in person. In the latter place we lost, in the forenoon, several brave officers and men. Gen. HOOKER is reported wounded; Lieut. Col. THOMAS BELL, of the Fifty-first Pennsylvania Volunteers, was mortally wounded while leading his men to the attack at this place, and died soon after. Lieut. BEAVER, of the same regiment; Capt. MALCOLM WILSON and Sergeant HARRY H. STEWART, of the Second Maryland Regiment, Co. A, were also killed. Col. KINGSBURY, of the Eleventh Connecticut, was mortally wounded; and Adjutant ANDREW FOWLER, of the Fifty-first New York, is dead. Sergeant DAVIS, acting Lieutenant in the Twenty-first Massachusetts, had a leg badly shattered; Capt. MARTIN, Co. E, Second Maryland, lost a leg; and Color Sergeants OSBORN and HOOVER, of the Second Maryland, are both severely wounded; also Capt. NEILL, Thirty-fifth Massachusetts. I saw all these lying at a barn near the Stone Bridge, while the battle was progressing, having visited the spot for the purpose of obtaining a list (which is only partial,) of the killed and wounded.

I also saw lying dead on the field the following privates: James Kirby, Co. A, Second Maryland; Peter Daily, Co. I; Wm. Kelly, Co. H; Sergt. Jas. Clark, Co. H; John Q. Adams, Co. C; Daniel Fisk, Co. F, Sixth N. H.; Corp. Chas. M. Noyes, Co. K, Ninth N. H.; S. H. Case, Co. B, Seventeenth Mich.; Sergt. Howard Rand, Co. K, Sixth N. H.; Michael Bolund, Co. G, Second Md.; —— Connerty, Co. G, Fifty-first N. Y.; Corp. Keefe, Co. I, Fifty-first N. Y.; Thomas N. Stockwell, Co. I, Fifty-first N. Y.; Robert C. Dale, Co. G, Fifty-first N. Y.; Geo. Summerlock, Co. A, Fifty-first Penn., and Thos. Davis, Co. I, Fifty-first Penn. I saw some half-dozen others on the east side of the bridge, whose names I could not learn, lying on the field. It was not safe to cross the bridge, but I was told several others lay on that side. It is impossible, in the present state of affairs, to obtain anything like an estimate of the numbers killed and wounded, but our losses have been very heavy.

The Irish Brigade, Gen. MEAGHER, in SUMNER's corps, occupied a very prominent position, and the brave General, I am told, had a horse shot under him. Some report him killed, but I cannot now learn that it is true. He rode in front of his brigade, and waving his flashing blade in the air, beckoned on his men to the attack. Wherever they made a charge the rebel lines were seen to waver and fall back.

The rebels kept as much as possible under cover of the ravines, and seldom advanced to the attack, but there has never been a battle, probably, where there was so little of woods for the rebels to conceal themselves in. The fighting has been mostly in the open field, with the exception of the sharp contest at the stone bridge, where woods (not dense) line both sides of the stream—and a considerable block of trees occupying nearly the centre of the right, where HOOKER was engaged.

The rebels have been driven back at least two miles since the fight began, so that Sharpsburgh has been, during the afternoon, about the centre of the rebel lines.

Three times the rebel caissons have been blown up by our shells. Five different conflagrations have occurred on the field of barns and houses which were set on fire by exploding shells, or purposely fired by the enemy. While I write the whole heavens are lighted up by burning barns and wheat stacks. It is an immense conflagration.

I made the following memoranda of events while overlooking the field:

Capt. COOK's Parrot Battery, Eighth Massachusetts, occupies the east hill opposite Sharpsburgh and the bridge, and does excellent practice on the enemy's position. Lieut. BENJAMIN, in charge of CARLISLE's Battery, also doing splendid execution. Twice the enemy's battery of six guns had been silenced or compelled to withdraw from the opposite hill.

The musketry firing down at the stone bridge, where WILCOX and STURGIS are engaged, is sharp and continuous. At 11 o'clock squads of rebels are seen "getting up" the hill. Our batteries are playing on them, which hurries their time. Shells burst, and solid shot plow up the ground all around them. Cheers from the ravine. The Seventeenth Michigan (new regiment and all brave boys) are charging down to the help of WILCOX. Our infantry are seen charging up the hill, and our batteries are ordered to cease firing to avoid hitting them. They are turned on the rebel batteries, which now open on the hill to the right of Sharpsburgh. Our infantry advance, and are shelled by the rebel batteries, and compelled to lie down and finally retire under cover of the next ravine. Our 20-pounder Parrots upset the rebel guns. Splendid shots by BENJAMIN. The Forty-fifth New-York come to the rescue, and are pressing by us toward the bridge. Gen. BURNSIDE has just sent orders for Gens. WILCOX and COX to cross the bridge with their brigades and occupy the hills south of the town. Our troops again advance, and as soon as they show themselves a new rebel battery of four guns, on the hill at the left opens upon us. At 12 o'clock a rebel caisson is blown up, the third one since morning.

Sharpsburgh is now the centre of the action in our front, while HOOKER is actively at work on the right. The firing in that part of the field is terrific and unceasing. The rebel lines are seen drawn up along the ravines at the northwest, and occasionally at tempting to advance. In each instance they are met and driven back.

At 1 o'clock the fighting at the Stone Bridge has ceased, and WILCOX and COX have all passed over. We now have a large force on the hills confronting the rebel lines. They keep up a constant cannonade upon the Union troops. At 1½ P. M. a squad of seventeen rebels are brought to Gen. BURNSIDE as prisoners, who orders them sent to the rear. The spokesman of the party says: "I don't think there is a man of us who doesn't want to get out of the fight." Gen. COX is ordered to move up and occupy the hills south of Sharpsburgh. At 2½ P. M. there is a temporary lull of the firing, but it is very short. At 4½ P. M. our troops push up the hill (the rebels always continue to have us on the down-hill side of the fight) and a large force appears at their extreme left, advancing toward them over the hill. A perfect storm of shot and shell now greet the advance of our boys from a half dozen different batteries at once. On the right of our advance our troops push up toward the rebel lines and are met half way, at a ravine, where a fierce musketry fight continues for half an hour. The balls strike up the dust in the plowed fields in all directions. The fight thickens, and so many batteries are in play, from so many different quarters, it is difficult to distinguish friend from foe. Dust and smoke completely envelope the battle-field.

On the left of the town the Union forces have now gained the crest of the hill, the rebels giving back under their steady fire, and cheers and shouts ring along the line. The rebel flag waves sulkily in the heavy air, in close proximity to the cheerful Red, White and Blue, borne into the thickest of the fight by our brave boys. The Union troops hold their position at the Sharpsburgh road for half an hour, while a deadly contest is going on. Our artillery, which has crossed the bridge, now takes up a position at the left, to check the advance of the rebels, who are trying to flank us, and open a brisk fire. On come the rebel hosts in overpowering numbers, to flank the force on the hill, and WILCOX's Brigade, which has stood their ground for over an hour, now retire part way down the hill. A tremendous onset was now made from the south, the enemy apparently having received reinforcements, and our left is pressed back. The sun has set, but the contest only thickens with the close of the day. The enemy's shell begin to burst over our hospital near the bridge, and the horses at BENJAMIN's Battery are shot at the guns. He is ordered by Gen. BURNSIDE to withdraw them. Stragglers come in from the field, some wounded, some *tenderly* escorting comrades who are wounded—it generally takes two or three to perform this service for one man, and all hands wear a gloomy countenance and limp. Gen. BURNSIDE orders them back to their regiments, with a sharp reprimand. Among these delinquents is a Lieutenant of the Sixteenth Connecticut Regiment, whom the General reprimands, and orders his name to be taken. He goes limping, and says a ball hit him in the leg. "But you walked all the way from the field—why did you come here to exhibit your cowardice? You had better remained at home," said the General sharply. At the same instant a youth, not over fifteen, who had his arm torn by a shell or ball, came up, holding the bleeding member in his other hand. "Look at that boy, Lieutenant, he has some excuse for leaving the field," but you have none. Shells now began to hum and burst all over the ground where we stood, and your correspondent began to think there might be danger in remaining longer in *that* place, so he *quietly* mounted his horse and *slowly* moved to the rear.

The rebels received a check soon after dark, and the contest ended for the night. It has been a most sanguinary fight. Our dead lie mingled with the rebel corpses on every part of this wide field—over a space of three or four miles. Many a poor fellow will lie on the cold, damp earth to-night, and pray for death to relieve him of his sufferings.

I shall endeavor to send fuller particulars of the fight than I am now enabled to do, as soon as they can be procured.

Both armies encamped on the field. To-morrow the dead must be buried, and possibly a renewal of the contest be had.

We shall have reinforcements of COUCH's Division this evening, from Harper's Ferry. E. S.

Events Succeeding the Great Battle—The Rebel Retreat Foreseen—Heavy Losses—Some of the Killed and Wounded—Incidents, &c.

ON THE FIELD, NEAR SHARPSBURGH, Md.,
Thursday, Sept. 18, 1862.

There has been no engagement to-day—only occasional firing between the pickets, who continue to confront each other on substantially the same field where the contest closed at sundown yesterday. The body of the enemy—if there be any body remaining—are at least three miles further toward the river than they were at the beginning of the battle yesterday morning. Competent judges, with whom I have conversed, among whom is Gen. GRIFFIN—a careful observer, and well versed in the ways of the rebels—believe that they are merely amusing us by these exhibitions of force, while the army proper is really on the retreat to the river, and should this hypothesis prove correct, we shall have a most mortifying result for all the labor, loss and bloodshed of this Maryland campaign. The rebel leaders have drawn after them from Washington an immense army, with its enormous train, which has marched, toiled, fought, and been dragged for fifty miles, over three mountain ranges, at an untold outlay of strength, expense and suffering; they will have supplied their starving army with all it needed; slaughtered and wounded thousands of our brave Union soldiers, and then have escaped back to Virginia to laugh in their sleeve at our laggard way of following up our successes. The old-fashioned way of waiting for the rebel army to make the first move to attack; to choose their own field of operations to fight us; lie still or retreat as suits *their convenience,* seems to be the humor of the hour.

What motives of "strategy" or mysterious plans requiring *time* for development, explains this failure to attack the rebels to-day, a mere novice in warfare has no right to draw in question. But one thing seems apparent to me, the Union army are eager to be "up and at them," and make an end of this rebel *canaille,* and of the rebellion, while we have them and it in our power. The humblest Union soldier will feel the mortification of permitting this ragged and wolfish lazaroni to escape our clutches, by crossing again into Virginia.

In order to ascertain the number of the killed and wounded, as near as might be, so soon after the battle, and to obtain such names of prominent persons who have suffered, I passed over the field to-day, and went to nearly all the hospitals where the wounded are being gathered in.

While the wounded are still on the field, and no official returns are made, it is, of course, impossible to obtain anything like a correct list of the killed and wounded. Lists will soon be prepared, however, and full accounts be sent forward. Every house and large barn contiguous to the field, is occupied by the wounded, where, I am happy to say, provision has very promptly been made for dressing wounds and rendering them comfortable.

The troops in HOOKER's, SUMNER's and RICHARDSON's corps have suffered greatly. Some officers of the General Staff estimate the number of wounded at 13,000, and say there are 5,000 on the field. My own judgment, after going pretty well over the ground is, that this estimate is greatly exaggerated, and that they do not amount to half that number, while the killed is very small in proportion to the wounded. I think six to eight hundred will cover the *killed,* and twenty-five hundred to three thousand the wounded, making a total of not to exceed *four thousand of killed and wounded.*

Gen. Rodman was shot through the body, the ball passing through the lung. Gen. Mansfield was instantly killed. Gen. Hooker was wounded in the foot. Gen. Hartsuff, of Rickett's Division, wounded in the right iliac region; a serious wound. Col. Beal, 10th Maine, in the thigh. Col. Richard Oakford, of Scranton, Penn., (132d Penn. Vol.,) was killed. Robert A. Abbott was seriously wounded in the lower jaw. Lieut. Jno. C. Dolan, injured in the hip by a shell. First Lieut. Sawyer, 7th Maine, killed, and about 100 privates of the same regiment wounded. Lieut.-Col. Fillebrown was thrown from his horse and injured, but not seriously. Gen. Max Weber was wounded seriously in the arm, and amputation may be rendered necessary. The Lieutenant-Colonel of the 49th New-York Volunteers, was dangerously wounded. Col. Kingsbury, of the Eleventh Connecticut, who was shot through the body twice and wounded in both feet, died this morning. Col. Childs, of the 4th Pennsylvania Cavalry, was killed while leading a charge on the right of the field. Gen. Richardson was wounded, and Gen. Hancock takes his command. Capt. Kelley, of the 6th Illinois Cavalry, was badly wounded on Monday in the mountain fight. Gen. Pleasanton's command, his cavalry division and four batteries of horse artillery lost severe other officers and men, whose names I cannot now obtain.

In Gen. King's Division the loss has been heavy. Col. H. A. V. Post, of the Second United States Sharpshooters, was wounded; also, Lieut. Chas. E. Cushing, Co. E, 22d New-York; Lieut. Whitman, Co. B, had his leg shot off—dead; Capt. Myers, Co. I, 14th Brooklyn—dead; Capt. O'Brien, Co. I, 24th Brooklyn—dead; Adgt. Parmele, 2d U. S. Sharpshooters—dead; Lieut. Seabury, 2d U. S. Sharpshooters—wounded; Lieut. Guest, 2d U. S. Sharpshooters—wounded; Capt. Chase, Co. A, 2d U. S. Sharpshooters—wounded; Sergeant-Major Shoot, 2d U. S. Sharpshooters—wounded.

In Caldwell's Brigade the loss was severe. The Fifth New-Hampshire Regiment have 119 killed and wounded, among which are fourteen officers. Some of these wounded are the following: Col. Cross, wounded in the head, slightly; Capt. Long, Co. G, wounded in the arm; Capt. Ranlet, Co. E, wounded in the thigh; Lieut. Graves, Co. H, forearm, slight; Lieut. Bean, Co. H, severely; Lieut. Gay, Co. H, mortally; Lieut. Parks.

KILLED IN MICHIGAN SEVENTEENTH REGIMENT.

Phelix Randall, Co. B.	Israel Colf, Co. C.
Andrew Saller, Co. C.	John A. Troy, Co. C.
Samuel Hunt, Co. D.	S. H. Hooley, Co. D.
Martin V. Moore, Co. D.	Daniel McMartin, Co. D.
Benjamin Ward, Co. D.	Almeron Palmeter, Co. D.
H. A. Smith, Co. D.	Henry Tomlinson, Co. D.
Wm. Woodward, Co. E.	Alex. McKinnon, Co. D.
Robert C. Irvin, Co. E.	Corp. Miron Hawley, Co. D.
Ephriam Micks, Co. F.	Silas Gardner, Co. D.
Delos Vandeberg, Co. H.	Mason Kearney, Co. I.
Frank Belknap, Co. I.	Wm. Clay, Co. K.
Oliver Chesney, Co. K.	Leonard Ives, Co. K.
David D. Tompkins, Co. K.	Total, 26.

Mr. IVES, of Providence, an Aid of Gen. RODMAN received a severe flesh wound in the thigh by a piece of shell. Probably not mortal. Mr. IVES is a brother of Capt. J. POYNTON IVES, who commanded the *Picket* in North Carolina, under Gen. BURNSIDE.

The Seventh Maine regiment (Third Brigade, SMITH's Division,) commanded by Major HYDE, went into the fight with 175 men and 14 officers, and came out with only 65 men and four officers unhurt.

Lieut. Butler, Co. A, was wounded and is missing; Capt. Jones, Co. B, wounded slightly; Adjt. Haskell was shot through both legs and his horse was killed; Lieut. Beason, Co. C, wounded in leg; Lieut. Goodman, Co. D, killed; Lieut. Emery, Co. E, wounded slightly; Lieut. Shorey, Co. F, wounded in the leg; Lieut. Warren, Co. H, wounded and missing; Capt. Cook, Co. I, wounded in leg; Lieut. Brown, Co. I, supposed killed; Capt. Cochran wounded in foot; Major Hyde wounded in hand and horse shot under him; not serious.

This regiment is now the body-guard of Gens. FRANKLIN and SMITH. The loss in this regiment is said to have been heavier than any regiment engaged, in proportion to numbers, since the beginning of the war. Their colors with "Williamsburgh" inscribed on them, were riddled with bullets. Capt. J. W. CHANNING has three bullet-holes through his clothes, and both he and Major HYDE came off the field with their clothing all bespattered with the blood of their comrades.

THE TURNER RIFLES.

Officers Killed.

Capt. Gustav A. Loreng, Co. C.
First Lieut. Jacob Pabst, Co. D.
Second Lieut. —— Krano, Co. G.

Some of the Wounded.

Capt. Robert Meikle, Pauls (?) Frick, —— Lohman, Capt. Weber, Lieut. Voelker.

Of enlisted men, there were twenty-six killed and eighty wounded.

THE FIRST DELAWARE—*Complete.*

Killed.

Capt. Watson, Co. A.	Corp. John Brierly, Co. A.
Capt. Leonard, Co. B.	Benjamin Lee, Co. A.
Capt. Richards, Co. C.	Minus J. Nelson, Co. B.
Ed. Moseley, Co. A.	Thomas Oskins, Co. A.

Wm. McCoy, Co. D—shot in both hands.
Emanuel Delasse, Co. F—left elbow.
Thos. G. Chance, Co. F—right knee.
Sergt. Chas. F. Holland, Co. E—right side.
Sergt. J. Spearsley, Co. H—left foot.
James E. Clark, Co. K—right thigh.
John Marshall, Co. A—left leg.
H. L. Savage, Co. G—little finger and right hand.
Geo. R. Ellis, Co. E—left leg.
Thos. Y. McCullen, Co. B—right shoulder.
Clarkson Cloud, Co. K—right shoulder.
Jos. Windser, Co. A—left leg.
Robt. Brierly, Co. A—abdomen.
James P. Dickerson, Co. F—abdomen.
Perry Wright, Co. D—right hand.
Wesley Freeman, Co. G—ball through right shoulder.
Wm. Porter, Co. H—bayonet thrust in hip.
Jesse Hurd, Co. K—struck by shell in the breast.
James Forgsum, Co. I—ball through right leg.
James Hilleyard, Co. F—right hand.
James Ross, Co. F—hand.
Ed. Ingham, Co. A—spent ball in breast.
Albert Nelson, Co. A—ball in back.
Corp. Geo. Camperson, Co. D—left knee.
Thos. Thornton, Co. I—flesh wound in left arm.
Corp. Patrick McClusky, Co. C—arm.
Jesse D. Furle, Co. A—wrist.
Sergt. J. Martin, Co. A—hand.
J. J. Kerbaugh, Co. A—right hand and one thumb amputated.
David M. Johnson, Co. E—left shoulder.
Henry Morris, Co. F—leg.
Patrick McGarraty, Co. C—right eye.
Corp. Henry Vinning—spent ball.
Jos. Fitzsimmons, Co. F—hip and back.
John Barton, Co. F—flesh wound in leg.
Thomas Workman, Co. F—neck.
Wm. Veach, Co. A—flesh wound in hand.
H. S. Chaffer, Co. I—flesh wound in left ear.
Sergt. M. Hill, Co. C—right foot.
Lieut. C. Tanner, Co. H—breast.
Jno. Walker, Co. H—left leg.
Jno. Curry, Co. H—left hand and right thigh.
Corp. Jos. Booth, Co. H—groin and leg.
Anthony Cheevers, Co. H—shoulder and leg.
Color Corp. Lewis Corell, Co. H—flesh wd. finger.
Daniel Reed, Co. H—flesh, left shoulder.
Jno. Shepherd, Co. A—left shoulder.
Wm. Wahl, Co. G—flesh wound in finger.
Patrick O'Brien, Co. E—flesh wound in left breast.
C. Platt, Co. A—hit by butt of a musket in breast.
Corp. Duley, Co. H—head and breast.
John Sweeney, Co. A—left side.
Jasper Calhoun, Co. A—left wrist.

In Gen. BURNSIDE's Corps there has been severe losses in officers and men. The great conflict culminated on the left, where he commanded, and a desperate effort was made to outflank WILCOX and COX's Divisions, which had gained the summit of the hills and were fast turning the tide of battle. The contest here was desperate and bloody. To-day I can see our dead scattered over the hill side up which our gallant boys fearlessly charged the enemy. Nothing in modern warfare could exceed the steadiness and courage of the troops, who fought on this part of the field. To-day they occupy the hill, only a quarter of a mile in rear of the position which they took yesterday. The enemy's batteries of seven guns on the left of Sharpsburgh and about the same number on the right of the town continue to threaten our front lines. No material change has occurred since last evening in the position of the forces, but *we occupy the field of battle.*

Gen. BURNSIDE and Staff have remained constantly on or near the field, watching intently every movement of the rebels, who keep themselves habitually out of sight. We ought to learn a lesson from them in this respect. This afternoon the General and his Staff and his Aids might all have been seen lying on the ground, under the shelter of a large wheat stack during a heavy rain. Let those who covet the glory and labors of the battle-field follow the march, and share the toils of our *working Generals,* and they will soon have enough of war.

On the right, in the extreme front, I found General COCHRANE, this morning, with his entire brigade engaged in picket service. Two hundred yards in advance of where he and Adjutant ROOME were, our lines of sharpshooters were lying along the ground, within short rifle range of the enemy's pickets. Every two or three minutes the sharp crack of rifles, and the "bim-m-m" of the bullet was heard, in some cases passing directly overhead or on either side. Behind them, in a large plowed field, the rebel dead lay very thickly scattered about, in every conceivable position, while muskets, bayonets and the *debris* of the previous day's battle covered the ground. Beside the fence of a small square burying-ground I counted

[*Continued on Eighth Page.*]

The New-York Times.

VOL. XII—NO. 3676. NEW-YORK, MONDAY, JULY 6, 1863. PRICE THREE CENTS.

THE GREAT BATTLES.

Splendid Triumph of the Army of the Potomac.

ROUT OF LEE'S FORCES ON FRIDAY

The Most Terrible Struggle of the War.

TREMENDOUS ARTILLERY DUEL.

Repeated Charges of the Rebel Columns Upon Our Position.

Every Charge Repulsed with Great Slaughter.

The Death of Longstreet and Hill.

Our Cavalry Active on the Enemy's Flank.

THE REBEL RETREAT CUT OFF

Chambersburgh in Our Possession.

Advance of the Militia under Gen. Smith to Important Positions.

The Rebel Pontoon Bridge at Williamsport Destroyed.

The Contents of the Captured Dispatches from Jeff. Davis to Lee.

A Peremptory Order for the Rebel Army to Return to Virginia.

OFFICIAL DISPATCHES FROM GEN. MEADE.

WASHINGTON, Saturday, July 4—10:10 A. M.

The following has just been received:

HEADQUARTERS ARMY OF POTOMAC, NEAR GETTYSBURGH, Friday, July 3—8½ P. M.

Major-Gen. Halleck, General-in-Chief:

The enemy opened at 1 P. M., from about one hundred and fifty guns, concentrated upon my left centre, continuing without intermission for about three hours, at the expiration of which time, he assaulted my left centre twice, being, upon both occasions, handsomely repulsed, with severe loss to him, leaving in our hands nearly three thousand prisoners.

Among the prisoners is Brig.-Gen. ARMSTEAD and many Colonels and officers of lesser rank.

The enemy left many dead upon the field, and a large number of wounded in our hands.

The loss upon our side has been considerable. Maj.-Gen. HANCOCK and Brig.-Gen. GIBBON were wounded.

After the repelling of the assaults, indications leading to the belief that the enemy might be withdrawing, a reconnoissance was pushed forward from the left and the enemy found to be in force.

At the present hour all is quiet.

My cavalry have been engaged all day on both flanks of the enemy, harassing and vigorously attacking him with great success, notwithstanding they encountered superior numbers both of cavalry and infantry.

The army is in fine spirits.

GEORGE G. MEADE,
Maj.-Gen. Commanding.

WASHINGTON, Sunday, July 5—4 P. M.

The latest official dispatch received here, up to this hour, from Gen. MEADE, is dated at Headquarters Army of Potomac, 7 A. M., July 4, which merely states that the enemy had withdrawn from his position, occupied for attack, on Friday. The information in the possession of Gen. MEADE, at that hour, did not develop the character of the enemy's movement, whether it was a retreat or a manoeuvre for other purposes.

Reliable information received here to-day asserts that Gen. LEE's Headquarters were at Cashtown yesterday afternoon, and further represents that the rebels were fortifying at Newman's Cut, in the South Mountains, apparently to cover a retreat.

Later official dispatches are expected this evening.

SECOND DISPATCH.

HEADQUARTERS ARMY OF POTOMAC, July 4—Noon.

Maj.-Gen. Halleck:

The position of affairs is not materially changed since my last dispatch of 7 A. M.

We now hold Gettysburgh.

The enemy has abandoned large numbers of his killed and wounded on the field.

I shall probably be able to give you a return of our captures and losses before night, and a return of the enemy's killed and wounded in our hands.

GEORGE G. MEADE, Major-General.

THIRD DISPATCH.

HEADQUARTERS ARMY POTOMAC, July 4—10 P. M.

To Maj.-Gen. Halleck:

No change of affairs since my dispatch of noon.

GEO. G. MEADE, Major-General.

FOURTH DISPATCH.

WASHINGTON, Monday, July 6—12.30 A. M.

The following is the latest official dispatch:

HEADQUARTERS ARMY OF THE POTOMAC, Sunday, July 5—8:30 A. M.

MAJOR-GEN. HALLECK: The enemy retired under cover of the night and the heavy rain, in the direction of Fairfield and Cashtown.

Our cavalry are in pursuit.

I cannot give you the details of our captures in prisoners, colors and arms.

Upward of twenty battle-flags will be turned in from one corps.

My wounded and those of the enemy are in our hands. GEO. G. MEADE, Major-General.

THE PRESIDENT TO THE COUNTRY.

WASHINGTON, D. C., July 4—10:30 A. M.

The President announces to the country that news from the Army of the Potomac, up to 10 P. M. of the 3d, is such as to cover that army with the highest honor; to promise a great success to the cause of the Union, and to claim the condolence of all for the many gallant fallen; and that for this, he especially desires that on this day He, whose will, not ours, should ever be done, be everywhere remembered and reverenced with profoundest gratitude.

(Signed) A. LINCOLN.

THE GREAT BATTLE OF FRIDAY.

Our Special Telegrams from the Battle-Field.

NEAR GETTYSBURGH, Saturday, July 4.

Another great battle was fought yesterday afternoon, resulting in a magnificent success to the National arms.

At 2 o'clock P. M., LONGSTREET's whole corps advanced from the rebel centre against our centre. The enemy's forces were hurled upon our position by columns in mass, and also in lines of battle. Our centre was held by Gen. HANCOCK, with the noble old Second army corps, aided by Gen. DOUBLEDAY's division of the First corps.

The rebels first opened a terrific artillery bombardment to demoralize our men, and then moved their forces with great impetuosity upon our position. HANCOCK received the attack with great firmness, and after a furious battle, lasting until 5 o'clock, the enemy were driven from the field, LONGSTREET's corps being almost annihilated.

The battle was a most magnificent spectacle. It was fought on an open plain, just south of Gettysburgh, with not a tree to interrupt the view. The courage of our men was perfectly sublime.

At 5 P. M. what was left of the enemy *retreated in utter confusion*, leaving dozens of flags, and Gen. HANCOCK estimated *at least five thousand killed and wounded on the field.*

The battle was fought by Gen. HANCOCK with splendid valor. He won imperishable honor, and Gen. MEADE thanked him in the name of the army and the country. He was wounded in the thigh, but remained on the field.

The number of prisoners taken is estimated at 3,000, including at least two Brigadier-Generals—OLMSTEAD, of Georgia, and another—both wounded.

The conduct of our veterans was perfectly magnificent. More than twenty battle flags were taken by our troops. Nearly every regiment has one. The Nineteenth Massachusetts captured four. The repulse was so disastrous to the enemy, that LONGSTREET's corps is perfectly used up. Gen GIBBON was wounded in the shoulder. Gen. WEBB was wounded and remained on the field. Col. HAMMELL, of the Sixty-sixth New-York, was wounded in the arm.

At 7 o'clock last evening, Gen. MEADE ordered the Third corps, supported by the Sixth, to attack the enemy's right, which was done, and the battle lasted until dark, when a good deal of ground had been gained.

During the day EWELL's corps kept up a desultory attack upon SLOCUM on the right, but was repulsed.

Our cavalry is to-day playing savagely upon the enemy's flank and rear. L. L. CROUNSE.

FROM ANOTHER CORRESPONDENT.

GETTYSBURGH, Friday, July 3.

The experience of all the tried and veteran officers of the Army of the Potomac tells of no such desperate conflict as has been in progress during this day. The cannonading of Chancellorsville, Malvern and Manassas were pastimes compared with this. At the headquarters, where I write, sixteen of the horses of Gen. MEADE's staff officers were killed by shell. The house was completely riddled. The Chief of Staff, Gen. BUTTERFIELD, was knocked down by a fragment of case-shot. Col. DICKINSON, Assistant Adjutant-General, had the bone of his wrist pierced through by a piece of shell. Lieut. OLIVER, of Gen. BUTTERFIELD's Staff, was struck in the head; and Capt. CARPENTER, of Gen. MEADE's escort, was wounded in the eye.

While I write the ground about me is covered thick with rebel dead, mingled with our own. Thousands of prisoners have been sent to the rear, and yet the conflict still continues.

The losses on both sides are heavy. Among our wounded officers are HANCOCK, GIBBON and a great many others whose names I feel restrained from publishing without being assured that they are positively in the list of casualties.

It is near sunset. Our troops hold the field, with many rebel prisoners in their hands. The enemy has been magnificently repulsed for three days—repulsed on all sides,—most magnificently to-day. Every effort made by him since Wednesday morning to penetrate MEADE's lines has been foiled. The final results of the action, I hope to be able to give you at a later hour this evening.

S. WILKESON.

DISPATCH TO THE ASSOCIATED PRESS.

HEADQUARTERS ARMY OF THE POTOMAC, Friday, July 3—6 A. M.

The enemy's guns opened on our left wing at daylight, apparently to feel our position. They found us "at home," and soon suspended operations. They also endeavored to push forward their front on our right, but were driven back with loss.

9:40 A. M.—An hour ago, the enemy made a strong infantry attack on our right, and endeavored to break our line. The Twelfth corps, which formed our right, steadily drove them back for half an hour, when the enemy were reinforced, and a portion of the Sixth corps was sent to its support.

Failing in this, the enemy opened a heavy cannonade all along the line. The attack on the right is believed to have been a feint to cover a more formidable flank movement on the left. The cannonading is now heavy in that direction, and appears to be extending.

The Third Corps suffered greatly yesterday. The number of wounded is heavy, with a large number of officers. No estimate can be formed of the killed at this writing.

Heavy musketry has opened now on our right again and cannonading on our left is slackening. The enemy are fighting with the greatest desperation. Nothing can surpass the vigor and precision of our artillery.

Yesterday, the rebels took two of our guns, for want of horses and infantry support, but the division (HUMPHREY's, I think,) rallied and recaptured them. We took one from the enemy.

Comparatively few prisoners have been taken on either side up to this hour.

Ten o'clock A. M.—The cannonading has slackened.

Rebel prisoners say when their infantry charged our left-wing batteries yesterday, the massacre was beyond parallel. Some of the guns were masked, and did not open until the enemy were within canister range.

IMPORTANT SEMI-OFFICIAL DETAILS.

HEADQUARTERS ARMY OF THE POTOMAC, July 3, 1863.

The decisive battle has been fought to-day, and the enemy have been repulsed with terrific loss.

At daylight LEE's right wing batteries opened upon our left, and shortly after those of his centre followed. After half an hour's cannonading, doing but little damage to us, the fire slackened, and only occasional shots were exchanged.

Shortly afterward the enemy's left, composed entirely of infantry and sharpshooters, made an attack on our right wing. So sudden and impetuous was it accomplished that our skirmishers and front line were driven back from their intrenchments; but, by the aid of the batteries in the rear, and the indomitable bravery of the Twelfth corps, we regained the first position, capturing a considerable number of prisoners.

Several hours of ominous silence followed this repulse. At 1 o'clock the enemy fired two shots, apparently as signals for the grandest artillery fight ever witnessed on this continent. Before a moment had elapsed it is estimated that at least eighty guns opened upon us. Our batteries returned the compliment with interest. *The air seemed literally thick with iron*, and for more than an hour it seemed impossible that man or beast could live through it. Strange to say the enemy's accuracy of range, as exhibited on the two previous days, was wanting on this occasion. Most of their shells exploded far in the rear of our front, and generally missing our batteries.

Under cover of this *feu d'enfer*, LEE advanced his columns of infantry from the covers, and made several desperate attempts to carry the lines by assault; but each successive attempt was repulsed with terrible havoc to their ranks.

After an hour's incessant cannonading the fire grew less intense for a short time, but was again renewed for a little while, with great spirit. During this period, some of our batteries whose ammunition was expended and the men exhausted, ceased to fire, and on the approach of the reserve batteries, withdrew to the rear. The enemy only seeing the batteries withdrawing, and mistaking this for a retreat, made a massed infantry charge up the hill, and obtained a position in our lines, cutting to pieces and almost annihilating the small infantry supports; but before they had time to rejoice at their imaginary success, the fresh batteries poured in a deadly fire of canister and case-shot. The infantry reserves joined on either flank of the gap, charged them, and added greatly to their destruction. They were completely surprised; and *hundreds of them threw down their arms and asked for quarter.* Nearly the entire brigade of, Gen. DICK GARNETT surrendered, and GARNETT himself, wounded, barely made his escape.

Longstreet was mortally wounded and captured. He is reported to have died in an hour afterward.

About 4:30 P. M. the artillery of the enemy slackened and had entirely ceased at 5, the last shots which they fired being far beyond their original position, and the infantry columns had withdrawn to their covers.

We took upward of three thousand prisoners. The enemy captured but few if any of our men.

The rebel prisoners report that *Gen. A. P. Hill was killed outright upon the field*, and that their officers suffered far greater casualties than in any previous engagement.

So terrific was the enemy's fire that the small house where Gen. MEADE and Staff were quartered, was perforated by several shots. Many of the Staff horses were killed around the house.

Gen. BUTTERFIELD was struck in the breast, and it is feared internally injured, by a piece of shell which exploded in the building. Lieut.-Col. JOSEPH DICKINSON, of the Staff, had his left arm perforated by a flying fragment of shell, and it seemed a miracle that no greater damage was done to life or limb.

Several of our general officers were wounded in the engagement. Gen. HANCOCK was wounded in the leg. Gens. GIBBON, WARREN and HUNT were wounded. In consequence of the excitement and difficulty in ascertaining their locations, the names of many prominent officers reported as killed or wounded cannot be ascertained to-night.

Too much credit cannot be given to our artillerists, who for hours stood to their guns under a broiling sun, and surrounded by the missiles of death, retiring only to give their positions to others, when their caissons and limbers were exhausted of ammunition. The infantry engaged also nobly did their duty, and the enemy to-day at their hands *has received the greatest disaster ever administered by the Union forces.*

All officers award the highest honors to Gen. MEADE for the able generalship he has displayed since he assumed command, and particularly for his coolness, decision and energy on this memorable 3d of July.

Last night, believing it to be his duty to the cause, and to learn how far he would be supported in the approaching conflict, he summoned his corps and division commanders for consultation.

DETAILS FROM OUR SPECIAL CORRESPONDENT.

HEADQUARTERS ARMY OF POTOMAC, Saturday Night, July 4.

Who can write the history of a battle whose eyes are immovably fastened upon a central figure of transcendingly absorbing interest—the dead body of an oldest born, crushed by a shell in a position where a battery should never have been sent, and abandoned to death in a building where surgeons dared not to stay?

The battle of Gettysburgh! I am told that it commenced on the 1st of July, a mile north of the town, between two weak brigades of infantry and some doomed artillery and the whole force of the rebel army. Among other costs of this error was the death of REYNOLDS. Its value was priceless, however, though priceless was the young and the old blood with which it was bought. The error put us on the defensive, and gave us the choice of position. From the moment that our artillery and infantry rolled back through the main street of Gettysburgh and rolled out of the town to the circle of eminences south of it. We were not to attack but to be attacked. The risks, the difficulties and the disadvantages of the coming battle were the enemy's. Our were the heights for artillery; ours the short, inside lines for manoeuvreing and reinforcing; ours the cover of stonewalls, fences and the crests of hills. The ground upon which we were driven to accept battle was wonderfully favorable to us. A popular description of it would be to say that it was in form an elongated and somewhat sharpened horseshoe, with the toe to Gettysburgh and the heel to the south.

LEE's plan of battle was simple. He massed his troops upon the east side of this shoe of position, and thundered on it obstinately to break it. The shelling of our batteries from the nearest overlooking hill, and the unflinching courage and complete discipline of the army of the Potomac repelled the attack. It was renewed at the point of of the shoe—renewed desperately at the southwest heel—renewed on the western side with an effort consecrated to success by EWELL's earnest oaths, and on which the fate of the invasion of Pennsylvania was fully put at stake. Only a perfect infantry and an artillery educated in the midst of charges of hostile brigades could possibly have sustained this assault. HANCOCK's corps did sustain it, and has covered itself with immortal honors by its constancy and courage. The total wreck of CUSHING's battery—the list of its killed and wounded—the losses of officers, men and horses COWEN sustained—and the marvellous outspread upon the board of death of dead soldiers and dead animals—of dead soldiers in blue, and dead soldiers in gray—more marvellous to me than anything I have ever seen in war—are a ghastly and shocking testimony to the terrible fight of the Second corps that none will gainsay. That corps will ever have the distinction of breaking the pride and power of the rebel invasion.

For such details as I have the heart for. The battle commenced at daylight, on the side of the horse-shoe position, exactly opposite to that which EWELL had sworn to crush through. Musketry preceded the rising of the sun. A thick wood veiled this fight, but out of its leafy darkness arose the smoke and the surging and swelling of the fire, from intermittent to continuous, and crushing, told of the wise tactics of the rebels of attacking in force and changing their troops. Seemingly the attack of the day was to be made through that wood. The demonstration was protracted—it was absolutely preparative; but there was no artillery fire accompanying the musketry, and shrewd officers in our western front mentioned, with the gravity due to the fact, that the rebels had felled trees at intervals upon the edge of the wood they occupied in face of our position. These were breastworks for the protection of artillerymen.

Suddenly, and about 10 in the forenoon, the firing on the east side, and everywhere about our lines, ceased. A silence as of deep sleep fell upon the field of battle. Our army cooked, ate and slumbered. The rebel army moved 120 guns to the west, and massed there LONGSTREET's corps and HILL's corps, to hurl them upon the really weakest point of our entire position.

Eleven o'clock—twelve o'clock—one o'clock. In the shadow cast by the tiny farm house 16 by 20, which Gen. MEADE had made his Headquarters, lay wearied Staff officers and tired reporters. There was not wanting to the peacefulness of the scene the singing of a bird, which had a nest in a peach tree within the tiny yard of the whitewashed cottage. In the midst of its warbling, a shell screamed over the house, instantly followed by another, and another, and in a moment the air was full of the most complete artillery prelude to an infantry battle that was ever exhibited. Every size and form of shell known to British and to American gunnery shrieked, whirled, moaned, whistled and wrathfully fluttered over our ground. As many as six in a second, constantly two in a second, bursting and screaming over and around the headquarters, made a very hell of fire that amazed the oldest officers. They burst in the yard—burst next to the fence on both sides, garnished as usual with the hitched horses of aids and orderlies. The fastened animals reared and plunged with terror. Then one fell, then another—sixteen laid dead and mangled before the fire ceased, still fastened by their halters, which gave the expression of being wickedly tied up to die painfully. These brute victims of a cruel war touched all hearts. Through the midst of the storm of screaming and exploding shells, an ambulance, driven by its frenzied conductor at full speed, presented to all of us the marvelous spectacle of a horse going rapidly on three legs. A hinder one had been shot off at the hock. A shell tore up the little step of the Headquarters Cottage, and ripped bags of oats as with a knife. Another soon carried off one of its two pillars. Soon a spherical case burst opposite the open door—another ripped through the low garret. The remaining pillar went almost immediately to the howl of a fixed shot that WHITWORTH must have made. During this fire the houses at twenty and thirty feet distant, were receiving their death, and soldiers in Federal blue were torn to pieces in the road and died with the peculiar yells that blend the extorted cry of pain with horror and despair. Not an orderly—not an ambulance—not a straggler was to be seen upon the plain swept by this tempest of orchestral death thirty minutes after it commenced. Were not one hundred and twenty pieces of artillery, trying to cut from the field every battery we had in position to resist their purposed infantry attack, and to sweep away the slight defences behind which our Infantry were waiting? Forty minutes—fifty minutes—counted on watches that ran! Oh so languidly. Shells through the two lower rooms. A shell into the chimney that daringly did not explode. Shells in the yard. The air thicker and fuller and more deafening with the howling and whirring of these infernal missiles. The chief of staff struck—SETH WILLIAMS—loved and respected through the army, separated from instant death by two inches of space vertically measured. An Aide bored with a fragment of iron through the bone of the arm. Another, cut with an exploded piece. And the time measured on the sluggish watches was one hour and forty minutes.

Then there was a lull, and we knew that the rebel infantry was charging. And splendidly they did this work—the highest and severest test of the stuff that soldiers are made of. HILL's division, in line of battle, came first on the double-quick. Their muskets at the "right-shoulder-shift." LONGSTREET's came as the support, at the usual distance, with war cries and a savage insolence as yet untutored by defeat. They rushed in perfect order across the open field up to the very muzzles of the guns, which tore lanes through them as they came. But they met men who were their equals in spirit, and their superiors in tenacity. There never was better fighting since Thermopylae than was done yesterday by our infantry and artillery. The rebels were over our defences. They had cleaned cannoniers and horses from one of the guns, and were whirling it around to use upon us. The bayonet drove them back. But so hard pressed was this brave infantry that at one time, from the exhaustion of their ammunition, every battery upon the principal crest of attack was silent, except CROWEN's. His service of grape and cannister was awful. It enabled our line, outnumbered two to one, first to beat back LONGSTREET, and then to charge upon him, and take a great number of his men and himself prisoners. Strange sight! So terrible was our musketry and artillery fire, that when ARMSTEAD's brigade was checked in its charge, and stood reeling, all of its men dropped their muskets and crawled on their hands and knees underneath the stream of shot till close to our troops, where they made signs of surrendering. They passed through our ranks scarcely noticed, and slowly went down the slope to the road in the rear.

Before they got there the grand charge of EWELL, solemnly sworn to and carefully prepared, had failed.

The rebels had retreated to their lines, and opened anew the storm of shell and shot from their 120 guns. Those who remained at the riddled headquarters will never the crouching, and dodging, and running, of the Butternut-colored captives when they got under this, their friends, fire. It was appalling to as good soldiers even as they were.

What remains to say of the fight? It staggled surlily on the middle of the horse shoe on the west, grew big and angry on the heel at the southwest, lasted there till 8 o'clock in the evening, when the fighting Sixth corps went joyously by as a reinforcement through the wood, bright with coffee pots on the fire.

I leave details to my excellent friend and associate Mr. HENRY. My pen is heavy. Oh, you dead, who at Gettysburgh have baptised with your blood the second birth of Freedom in America, how you are to be envied! I rise from a grave whose wet clay I have passionately kissed, and I look up and see Christ spanning this battle-field with his feet and reaching fraternal and lovingly up to heaven. His right hand opens the gates of Paradise—with his left he beckons to these mutilated, bloody, swollen forms to ascend.

INCIDENTS OF THE BATTLE.

Capt. CUSHING, Company A, Fourth Regular artillery, was killed, and his battery suffered severely. The gallantry of this officer is beyond praise. Severely wounded early in the afternoon, he refused to leave his post beside his guns, but continued to pour grape and canister into the advancing columns of the rebels until they had reached the very muzzles of his pieces, and sure of their capture, were attempting to turn them upon our forces, when they were driven off by our infantry. At this moment Capt. CUSHING received his death wound, and fell lifeless to the earth. Heaps of corpses and wounded in front of his battery this morning, told a terrible tale of the effectiveness of its fire.

None of the company were taken prisoners by the rebels. After the battle but one gun of this battery remained uninjured—the rest having been dismounted or destroyed by the terrible fire of the enemy, which for the time was concentrated upon the batteries on this part of the field. In front of this position fell dead the rebel Gen. DICK GARNETT, who was courageously leading his men in this charge upon our batteries on Crow Hill. The rebel Gen. ARMSTEAD was also wounded here while advancing at the head of his brigade.

About fifty yards in front of our batteries was a stone wall, running from our centre in a southwesterly direction, behind which laid several of our regiments, picking off the enemy as they advanced up the slope of the hill. Notwithstanding the terrible fire poured into their ranks from our guns, so impetuous was the charge of the rebels that they drove our men from their position, and were advancing upon our batteries, several of which they captured, but the capture was only temporary. Gen. GIBBON's division, composed of Gens. WEBB's, HARRELL's and HALL's brigades, at the point of the bayonet, drove them back over the stone wall into the plain below.

Gen. GIBBON's division captured fourteen stand of colors and a large number of prisoners. Twenty-eight stands of colors in all were captured by the Second corps.

Gen. ARMISTEAD, when taken prisoner, asked immediately for Gen. MEADE, who was his classmate at West Point.

Col. WARD, of the Fifteenth Massachusetts, was killed.

Corp. HAYDEN, of the First Minnesota, was captured—escaped, seized a musket and seized a rare opportunity, and actually made ten rebels surrender. While marching them to Gen. GIBBON's quarters, a rebel behind a tree on the way drew a bead on him with his rifle. HAYDEN saw him in time to bring his piece to a level, and cry out, "Surrender." The fellow actually threw down his gun and joined the cavalcade, and HAYDEN came in with eleven captives.

Wounded prisoners taken in Gettysburgh this morning report that Gen. BRADLEY L. JOHNSON, of Maryland, was killed in Thursday's attack on our right. He was struck by a shell while charging our lines at the head of his division. Gen. HOOD is also reported to have had his let shot off, and from the effects of which he has since died.

Rebel officers with whom I have conversed frankly admit that the result of the last two days has been most disastrous to their cause, which depended, they say, upon the success of LEE's attempt to transfer the seat of war from Virginia to the Northern Border States. A wounded rebel Colonel told me that, in the first and second days' fight, the rebel losses were between ten and eleven thousand. Yesterday they were greater still. In one part of the field, in a space not more than twenty feet in circumference, in front of Gen. GIBBONS' division, I counted seven dead rebels, three of whom were piled on top of each other. And close by in a spot not more than fifteen feet square lay fifteen "graybacks," stretched in death. These were the adventurous spirits, who in the face of the horrible stream of canister, shell and musketry, scaled the fence wall in their attempt upon our batteries. Very large numbers of wounded were also strewn around, not to mention more who had crawled away or been taken away. The field in front of the stonewall was literally covered with dead and wounded, a large proportion of whom were rebels. Where our musketry and artillery took effect they lay in swaths, as if mown down by a scythe. This field presented a horrible sight—such as has never yet been witnessed during the war. Not less than one thousand dead and wounded laid in a *space of less than four acres* in extent, and that, too, after numbers had crawled away to places of shelter.

The enemy's infantry, saving a small force of sharpshooters, was wholly out of sight at daylight on Saturday morning. There was talk on Friday night, after the battle, of organizing a column of pursuit.

Before the fighting was over—before sunset, considerably—the Signal Officers reported that an immense train of army wagons was going out of Gettysburgh northwest, on the road to Cashtown. Oh! that they could have run against the stonewall of the Harrisburgh army.

PARTIAL LIST OF KILLED AND WOUNDED.

Lieut. Dayton L. Card, commanding Co. E, 169th New York, was killed instantly by a shell. His body presented a ghastly sight. He was struck in the middle of the breast by a missile which exploded and tore him literally in two. Half of his face was also torn away by a fragment of shell.

Charles P. Leclear, Co. E, 169th N. Y.—killed.
J. Wickham, Co. E, 169th N. Y.—wounded.
Sergeant A. B. Hadley, do. do.—wounded.
Sergt. M. C. Bryant, Co. E, 169th N. Y.—wounded.
J. D. Anstuk, Co. E, 169th New-York—wounded.

Cowan's New-York Battery—Killed.

Privates James Gray, Otis C. Billings, Jacob Y. McIlroy, Edmund Pete.

Wounded.

Lieut. Wm. P. Wright—right breast, probably mortally.

[*Continued on Eighth Page.*]

The New-York Times.

VOL. XIII—NO. 3794. NEW-YORK, FRIDAY, NOVEMBER 20, 1863. PRICE THREE CENTS.

IMPORTANT FROM EAST TENNESSEE

The Rebels Advancing upon Knoxville.

THE PLACE COMPLETELY INVESTED.

HEAVY SKIRMISHING YESTERDAY.

The Position Very Strongly Fortified.

THE REBEL FORCES UNDER LONGSTREET.

KNOXVILLE, Thursday, Nov. 17.

The enemy began skirmishing from their position on Kingston Road, at 10 this morning. Our advance alone, composed wholly of mounted infantry and cavalry, occupied the position, under command of Gen. SANDERS, and each man fought like a veteran. At noon the enemy opened with artillery at short range, their battery protected by a large house. BENJAMIN's battery was the only one which replied, occupying the chief fortification, half a mile in front of and to the right of the town. A desperate charge was made by the enemy about 3 P. M. Our men were protected by rail barricades on the crest of the hill. Gen. SANDERS was severely wounded, and was borne from the field.

We yielded the position, and fell back about a third of a mile to a stronger one. We have lost about one hundred, one quarter of whom were killed. The enemy had completely invested the place, but Gen. BURNSIDE will defend it to the last man, and it is believed successfully. The troops are in the best spirits. Every important point is fortified, and confidence prevails that we shall whip the enemy out.

A MORE DETAILED ACCOUNT.

KNOXVILLE, Tenn., Tuesday, Nov. 17.

Gen. LONGSTREET, after crossing the Tennessee on Saturday morning, 14th inst., was attacked in the afternoon by Gen. SCAMMON, who drove the advance guard back to within a mile of the river's edge by nightfall.

LONGSTREET crossed the remainder of his troops during the night, and on Sunday morning advanced in force.

Gen. BURNSIDE, finding it impossible to cope with him with the small force at his disposal, fell back to Lenoir, the rear guard skirmishing heavily with the enemy through the day.

Three desperate charges were made upon our positions during Sunday night, but they were handsomely repulsed.

On Monday morning Gen. BURNSIDE evacuated Lenoir, but owing to the energy with which the rebel pursuit was kept up, determined to give them a decided check, and accordingly came into line of battle at Campbell's Station, when a fight ensued, lasting from late in the forenoon until dark. Our first position commanding the road from both sides, the infantry deployed in front of this, and were soon attacked by the enemy, who made several gallant charges, and finally succeeded, by outflanking our men, in driving them to the cover of the batteries, which now opened a terrific and destructive fire. The rebels retired before it, gave way, and eventually fell back to the river.

It was now three o'clock in the afternoon. The rebels showing a desire to renew the attack, and having brought three batteries to their assistance, Gen. BURNSIDE fell back to a more desirable position and again gave them battle. The contest continued, closing at nightfall, with our troops in possession of their own ground.

The object of the fight having been attained, and as the detention of the rebels had enabled our trains to get all in advance, our troops fell back during the night and early Tuesday morning reached Knoxville, where a great battle is expected to be fought to-morrow.

Yesterday the rebel advance guard attacked our outposts upon the Louden and Clinton roads and heavy skirmishing continued all day.

This morning the attack was resumed when the fog which set in during the night had lifted. The rebels finding it impossible to drive our men with infantry, brought several guns into position, and poured in a flanking fire.

In the afternoon they brought forward a heavy force of infantry once more, and, after a brief skirmish, charged our position. A terrific hand to hand conflict occurred—both sabres and revolvers being used on both sides. Our men fought with the greatest gallantry; but at last were compelled to fall back about a third of a mile, to a strong line, which they hold to-night.

We have to regret the wounding of Gen. SANDERS and Capt. SIKES, of the cavalry, who commanded the outpost. His condition is critical. Lieut.-Col. SMITH, of the Twentieth Michigan, was killed at Campbell's Station. Our loss in that fight was between two and three hundred. Our loss to-day will not exceed one hundred and fifty.

Our men are in the best of spirits and perfectly confident of success to-morrow.

LATE FROM CHATTANOOGA.

Correspondence of the New-York Times.

CHATTANOOGA, Monday, Nov. 16, 1863.

The stream of deserters from the enemy continues to increase. Among them are some of the Vicksburgh paroled prisoners, who are much exercised regarding their *status*. From information which they bring it is now rendered certain that LONGSTREET is operating against BURNSIDE in East Tennessee.

The weather for the past few days has been very fine, and the roads are in excellent condition.

REPORTS FROM REBEL SOURCES.

ATLANTA, Friday, Nov. 13.

Nothing from the front this morning. A party of Georgia State troops and Indians killed the notorious BAYSON and thirty-four of his men, a short time since, on the line between Georgia and North Carolina.

A special to the *Register*, dated Sweet Water, Nov. 12, says: "*The Federals have removed all their supplies to Knoxville for safety*, and are living on half rations. Several deserters, recaptured, were executed here yesterday."

A special to the *Intelligencer* says: "Two Yankee officers who deserted and came into our lines, report that GRANT expects soon to assault Lookout. His army is on half rations.

THE ARMY OF THE POTOMAC.

Cavalry Skirmish at Germanna Ford—Great Scarcity of Contrabands—The Army Being Paid Off.

WASHINGTON, Thursday, Nov. 19.

The intelligence received to-night from the Army of the Potomac is to the effect that a cavalry skirmish between 200 rebels and part of the Eighteenth Pennsylvania cavalry took place yesterday morning at Germanna Ford, on the Rapidan. The rebels crossed the river, when our men fell back upon our infantry pickets. The loss was small. Some of our men were captured.

There are frequent reviews and division drills, the country and weather being favorable for such purposes.

Hundreds of contrabands could be profitably employed in the army as drivers, teamsters, &c. In one artillery brigade alone, a sufficient number of soldiers are employed as wagoners and teamsters, to man a six-gun battery, for want of negroes.

Yesterday evening some cannonading was heard in the direction of the Rapidan south of Culpepper, but no particulars had been received when the messenger this afternoon left the army.

No sutlers have yet been granted right of transportation for their stores to the army. A few occasionally succeed in passing goods, but they are liable to arrest and confiscation.

Paymasters are busily at work in the discharge of their duties in almost all, if not all, the army corps.

THE HEROES OF JULY.

A Solemn and Imposing Event.

Dedication of the National Cemetery at Gettysburgh.

IMMENSE NUMBERS OF VISITORS.

Oration by Hon. Edward Everett—Speeches of President Lincoln, Mr. Seward and Governor Seymour.

THE PROGRAMME SUCCESSFULLY CARRIED OUT

The ceremonies attending the dedication of the National Cemetery commenced this morning by a grand military and civic display, under command of Maj.-Gen. COUCH. The line of march was taken up at 10 o'clock, and the procession marched through the principal streets to the Cemetery, where the military formed in line and saluted the President. At 11¼ the head of the procession arrived at the main stand. The President and members of the Cabinet, together with the chief military and civic dignitaries, took position on the stand. The President seated himself between Mr. SEWARD and Mr. EVERETT after a reception marked with the respect and perfect silence due to the solemnity of the occasion, every man in the immense gathering uncovering on his appearance.

The military were formed in line extending around the stand, the area between the stand and military being occupied by civilians, comprising about 15,000 people and including men, women and children. The attendance of ladies was quite large. The military escort comprised one squadron of cavalry, two batteries of artillery and a regiment of infantry, which constitutes the regular funeral escort of honor for the highest officer in the service.

After the performance of a funeral dirge, by BIRGFIELD, by the band, an eloquent prayer was delivered by Rev. Mr. STOCKTON, as follows:

O God, our Father, for the sake of the Son, our Saviour, inspire us with thy spirit, and sanctify us to the right fulfillment of the duties of this occasion. We come to dedicate this new historic centre as a National Cemetery. If all the Departments of the one Government thou hast ordained over our Union, and of the many Governments which Thou has subordinated to the Union be there represented; if all classes, relations and interests of our blended brotherhood of people stand severally and thoroughly apparent in Thy presence, we trust it is because Thou hast called us, that Thy blessing awaits us, and that Thy designs may be embodied in practical results of incalculable, imperishable good. And so with thy holy Apostle and with the Church in all lands and ages, we unite in the ascription: Blessed be God, even the Father of Our Lord Jesus Christ, the Father of Moses, and the God of all comfort, who comforteth us in all our tribulation, that we may be able to comfort them which are in any trouble by the comfort wherewith we ourselves are comforted of God. In emulation of all angels, in fellowship with all saints, and in sympathy with all sufferers, in remembrance of Thy works, in reverence of Thy ways, and in accordance with Thy word, we love and magnify Thy infinite perfections, Thy creative glory, Thy redeeming grace, Thy providential goodness, and the progressive, richer and fairer development of thy supreme, universal and everlasting administration. In behalf of all humanity, whose ideal is divine, whose first memory is thy image lost, whose last hope is thy image restored; especially in behalf of our own nation, whose position is so peerless, whose mission is so sublime, and whose future is so attractive; we thank Thee for the unspeakable patience of thy compassion and for the exceeding greatness of thy loving kindness. In contemplation of Eden, Calvary and Heaven, of Christ in the God on the cross, and on the throne—nay, more—of Christ as coming again in all-subduing power and glory; we gratefully prolong our homage by this altar of sacrifice, on this field of deliverance, on this mount of salvation, within the fiery and bloody line of these mountains and rocks, looking back to the dark days of fear and of trembling, and the rapture of relief that came after, we multiply our thanksgivings and confess our obligations to renew and perfect our personal and social consecration to thy service and glory. O, had it not been for God! for our enemies, they came unresisted, multitudinous, mighty, flushed with victory and sure of success, they exalted on our mountains; they revelled in our valleys, they feasted, they rested, they slept, they awakened, they grew stronger, prouder and bolder every day, they spread abroad, they concentrated here, they looked beyond this horizon to the stores of wealth, to the haunts of pleasure and the seats of power in our Capital and chief cities, they prepared to cast the chain of Slavery around the form of freedom, and to bind life and death together forever. Their premature triumph was the mockery of God and man. One more victory, and all was theirs. But behind these hills was heard the feebler march of a smaller but still a pursuing host, onward they hurried, day and night, for their country and their God; footsore, wayworn, hungry, thirsty, faint, but not in heart; they came to dare all, to bear all, and to do all that is possible to heroes. At first they met the blast on the plain, and bent before it like trees; but then led by Thy hand to the hills, they took their stand on the these rocks, and remained as firm and immovable as they. In vain were they assaulted; all art, all violence, all desperation failed to dislodge them. Baffled, bruised, broken, their enemies retired and disappeared. Glory to God for this rescue! But, Oh! the slain, in the freshness and fullness of their young and manly life! with such sweet memories of father and mother, brother and sister, wife and children, maiden and friend. From the coasts beneath the Eastern star; from the shores of Northern lakes and rivers; from the flowers of the Western prairies; from the homes of the midway and the border, they came here to die for us and for mankind! Alas how little we can do for them! We come with the humility of prayer, with the pathetic eloquence of venerable wisdom, with the tender beauty of poetry, with the plaintive harmony of music, with the honest tribute of our Chief Magistrate, and with all this honorable attendance; but our best hope is in Thy blessings. O Lord, Our God, bless us. O, Our Father, bless the bereaved, whether absent or present. Bless our sick and wounded soldiers and sailors. Bless all our rulers and people. Bless our army and navy. Bless the efforts to suppress this rebellion, and bless all the associations of this day, and place, and scene, forever. As the trees are not dead, though their foliage is gone, so our heroes are not dead though their forms have fallen. In their proper personality they are all with thee, and the spirit of their example is here. It fills the air, it fills our hearts, and as long as time shall last it will hover in these skies and rest on these landscapes, and pilgrims of our own land and of all lands, will thrill with its inspiration, and increase and confirm their devotion to liberty, religion and God.

Mr. EVERETT then commenced the delivery of his oration, which was listened to with marked attention throughout. [The oration of Mr. EVERETT will be found on our second page.]

Although a heavy fog clouded the heavens in the morning during the procession, the sun broke out in all its brilliancy during the Rev. Mr. STOCKTON's prayer and shone upon the magnificent spectacle. The assemblage was of great magnitude, and was gathered within a circle of great extent around the stand, which was located on the highest point of ground on which the battle was fought. A long line of military surrounded the position taken by the immense multitude of people.

The Marshal took up a position on the left of the stand. Numerous flags and banners, suitably draped, were exhibited on the stand among the audience. The entire scene was one of grandeur due to the importance of the occasion. So quiet were the people that every word uttered by the orator of the day must have been heard by them all, notwithstanding the immensity of the concourse.

Among the distinguished persons on the platform were the following: Governors Bradford, of Maryland; Curtin, of Pennsylvania; Morton, of Indiana; Seymour, of New-York; Parker, of New-Jersey, and Tod, of Ohio; Ex-Gov. Dennison, of Ohio; John Brough, Governor Elect, of Ohio; Charles Anderson, Lieutenant-Governor of Ohio; Major-Generals Schenck, Stahel, Doubleday, and Couch; Brigadier-General Gibbon; and Provost-Marshal-General Fry.

PRESIDENT LINCOLN'S ADDRESS.

The President then delivered the following dedicatory speech:

Fourscore and seven years ago our Fathers brought forth upon this Continent a new nation, conceived in liberty and dedicated to the proposition that all men are created equal. [Applause.] Now we are engaged in a great civil war, testing whether that nation, or any nation so conceived and so dedicated, can long endure. We are met on a great battle-field of that war. We are met to dedicate a portion of it as the final resting-place of those who here gave their lives that that nation might live. It is altogether fitting and proper that we should do this. But in a larger sense we cannot dedicate. We cannot consecrate, we cannot hallow this ground. The brave men, living and dead, who struggled here have consecrated it far above our power to add or detract. [Applause.] The world will little note nor long remember, what we say here, but it can never forget what they did here. [Applause.] It is for us, the living, rather to be dedicated here to the refinished work that they have thus so far nobly carried on. [Applause.] It is rather for us to be here dedicated to the great task remaining before us, that from these honored dead we take increased devotion to that cause for which they here gave the last full measure of devotion; that we here highly resolve that the dead shall not have died in vain; [applause] that the Nation shall under God have a new birth of freedom, and that Governments of the people, by the people and for the people, shall not perish from the earth. [Long continued applause.]

Three cheers were then given for the President and the Governors of the States.

After the delivery of the addresses, the dirge and the benediction closed the exercises, and the immense assemblage separated at about 4 o'clock.

About 3 o'clock in the afternoon, the Fifth New York regiment of heavy artillery, Col. MURRAY, was marched to the temporary residence of Gov. SEYMOUR, where they passed in review before the Governor, presenting a handsome spectacle. Upon the conclusion of this ceremony, which attracted quite a crowd of sight-seers, Gov. SEYMOUR presented a handsome silk regimental standard to the regiment, accompanying the gift with the following speech:

GOV. SEYMOUR'S SPEECH.

SOLDIERS OF NEW-YORK: We love our whole country, without reservation. But while we do so, it is not inconsistent with that perfect and generous loyalty to love and to be proud of our own State This day, when I took part in the celebration that was to consecrate yonder battle-field, while I felt as an American citizen, proud of my own country, and proud of the gallant services of her citizens, in every State, nevertheless my eye did involuntarily wander to that field where lie the glorious dead of our good and great State, and when I returned, to see marching before me your manly and sturdy columns, not knowing you belonged to New-York, my heart did quicken and my pulse tingle, to learn that you were acting commissions issued by myself! I am most proud and most happy that I have this opportunity, on behalf of the merchants of the great commercial City of New-York, to present to you this glorious banner, which has been sent as a token of their confidence in your loyalty and your courage, and your fidelity in the hour of danger. Sergeant, I place these colors in your hands in the firm confidence that they will be borne through every field of triumph, of toil and of danger, in a way that will do honor to yourselves, to the great State which you represent, and the still greater country, to which we all belong. My God bless you as you serve your country in the distant field of danger We find in those glorious fields you left behind you are not indifferent to this conflict; are not indifferent to the welfare of the whole Union. I do not doubt, therefore, that when you shall return from your dangerous fields of duty, you shall bring back this standard to place among the archieves of our State with honorable mention of the services her sons have performed. I do not doubt that though it may perhaps be returned torn and stained, yet it will be still more glorious, and with glorious recollections clustering around it. In concluding these remarks, I ask in return of the men of New-York, to give three cheers for the Union of our country, and three cheers for the flag of our land.

Gen. SCHENCK followed in a short speech.

A subscription of $280 was made by the Marshals attending these ceremonies, to be devoted to the relief of the Richmond prisoners.

In the afternoon, the Lieutenant-Governor elect of Ohio, Col. ANDERSON, delivered an oration at the Presbyterian Church.

The President and party returned to Washingto at 6 o'clock this evening, followed by the Governors' trains. Thousands of persons were gathered at the depot, anxiously awaiting transportation to their homes; but they will probably be confined to the meagre accommodations of Gettysburgh till tomorrow.

DEPARTMENT OF THE GULF.

ARRIVAL OF THE CREOLE FROM NEW-ORLEANS.

The Attack upon Gen. Washburn's Column.

Our Entire Loss Six Hundred and Seventy-seven.

The steamship *Creole*, Capt. THOMPSON, arrived yesterday morning from New-Orleans, bringing dates to the 10th inst. Further accounts from the Teche country concerning the attack on WASHBURN's column represents our whole loss in killed and wounded and taken prisoners at 677. The Indiana Sixty-seventh was captured almost entire; the Sixtieth Indiana and Ohio Ninety-sixth lost largely. The rebel force was as five to one. We only excelled them in artillery, by means of which, at short range, it is thought, we killed a large number of the enemy. It is reported that the Thirteenth army corps, now in the Teche country, is ordered back to Memphis.

The attack was made by the enemy in force of 5,000 upon our rear guard, only 1,800 strong. The enemy captured two pieces of artillery, but one of them was subsequently retaken. The fight took place at Buzzard Prairie, on the east side of Bayou Teche.

Gen. PRICE was reported at Alexandria with 15,000 men, and for this reason, as well as the impossibility of getting supplies, it was deemed best to fall back.

Gens. THOMAS and WADSWORTH arrived in New-Orleans on the 10th inst.

THE DELAWARE ELECTION.

The Union Ticket Overwhelmingly Successful—Smithers, for Congress, Walked the Course.

WILMINGTON, Thursday, Nov. 19.

The election in this State passed off quietly. The Copperheads, seeing defeat staring them in the face, abandoned the contest. BROWN did not withdraw, but the leaders, knowing they would be compelled to proclaim themselves loyal men in order to vote, gave the key-note for the whole party to stay at home. SMITHERS walked the course. Newcastle County gives SMITHERS 4,014 votes, and BROWN 6 votes. In six Districts of Kent County, SMITHERS has 1,275 votes, BROWN none. In five Districts of Sussex County, SMITHERS has 844 votes, and BROWN 7 votes, showing a gain for SMITHERS over FISHER's vote of last year in this county.

J. T. HEALD,
Chairman State Committee.

GREAT BRITAIN AND AMERICA.

Welcome to Rev. Henry Ward Beecher.

Demonstration at the Brooklyn Academy of Music.

A GREAT SPEECH:

His Impressions of British Feeling Toward America.

An immense audience assembled at the Academy of Music, Brooklyn, last evening, to welcome and hear the Rev. HENRY WARD BEECHER. The meeting was under the auspices of the War Fund Committee, the entire proceeds to be devoted to the Sanitary Commission. Rev. Dr. STORRS made an eloquent address of welcome to Mr. BEECHER, who, on his appearance, was most enthusiastically greeted. When quiet was restored Mr. BEECHER spoke as follows:

MR. BEECHER'S ADDRESS.

I will not attempt to disguise the deep feeling with which your generous kindness, expressed in the words of my brother, affect me. I am more touched and more stirred by this sympathy than by all that I have seen and by all that I have experienced in the whole of my travel abroad; and I speak the simple truth, which has the witness in your hearts, that it is here in this city more than anywhere else that I desire to be so greeted. For as, when in England, it was my pride to be an American, so when I am in America, it is my pride to be a citizen of Brooklyn; and I accept your generous confidence, and this affecting testimony of it, in so far as it relates to me personally, with profound sensibility and with deep gratitude. I thank you; and yet I should be vain if I supposed that this was meant for me in my simple individuality. I am myself the effect of American institutions; I am made by them and if I have done any service to the public worthy of your regard, I owe it to this very public and the institutions which enrich it the power to do it any service. And I am glad that it is so—so deep are my feelings of patriotism, so profoundly am I impressed with the grandeur of this latest and ripest development of civil life, that I am more than willing to be sunk myself if my decadence and disappearance could add anything to the glory of my country. I would fain be as the oil in the lamp that gives its life, that the light may be bright which consumes it. And that which is my feeling is your feeling, and I know I bear your sympathy with me in this simple and artless expression of my feelings to-night. I am glad that you asked me to be present; and I am proud that it shall go abroad that when I came back to America, having witnessed as I could in Europe for the truth of our cause, the first place to greet me was my own home, where I am best known. It is, indeed, a wreath which I shall wear none the less because it is invisible. I went abroad, as you know, simply as a private citizen. It was tauntingly asked me, on my arrival in England, why, in the very height of paroxysm of our national agony, I abandoned the field to go abroad. I did not answer, but I now do answer. I foresaw that the Autumn and the Winter would require labors even greater than any period previous, and the excitement and the excessive labors of the two and a half years, or three years preceding, had not destroyed my health nor destroyed my constitution; but certainly I was jaded, and I feared to go into the labor of the Autumn and Winter, which required the best powers of every man, without my full strength; and since I could do nothing in the Summer, I took that opportunity, upon the generous invitation of my own people, to go abroad and rest, that I might come back to labor more assiduously. Allow me to say that this generosity of my own dear people was a comfort to me everywhere, and that in Great Britain—not because I disesteemed their kindness or undervalued their hospitality, but because it was something that I cherished with a secret pride—I refused to received their hospitality or, in the remotest degree, compensation in any form. I said to them, my own people sent me abroad, and it is their pleasure that I shall stand upon them for support, and I will not take one penny from the hand of an Englishman. [Applause.] You will not misunderstand me; it was not because I disdained their kindness, but because I valued yours. It was also said that I had come abroad sent by our Government. That would have spoiled it all. I had no official character, and would not have had one. I went simply as a private citizen, and I was there merely and only as an American citizen. And when, unsought and, indeed, against my feelings, if not against my judgment, I entered upon the labor of the past few weeks of my sojourn in England, I assumed the responsibility, I cannot say with trembling, for I am not accustomed much to tremble; but I assumed the responsibility with the gravest sense of what it was. I have felt the inspiration of nationality often, but I never before was placed between two such great people, where I saw them both in prospective, both in their present relations and in their future. I never before felt so much as I felt all the time, waking or dreaming, night or day, what it was to stand and plead for the unity of these two great nations, for the sake of struggling mankind; and it was at once an excitement to me and a support. But, after all, I did not know how my countrymen would regard my efforts. If you had disapproved, I should have been sorry that you disapproved, but not sorry for what I had done. I did the best I knew how to do, every time, everywhere disinterestedly, for the love I bear to the cause and to the principles which underlie it, and I had no word, could not have, from home whether my representations of policy, and of fact, and of history, and of the tendencies of things, would accord with yours, or whether I should not be caught up in the whirl of conflicting parties, my reasonings traversed, my arguments denied—nor till I landed in Boston did I hear one whisper—and then I learned for the first time that my services had been accepted by my countrymen. [Applause.] But to-night I meet you, a citizen returned among his friends, profoundly thankful that the labor and the service which I attempted for the public good have the seal of their approbation. It is my purpose not to trespass any further upon your time in matters that are personal to myself. I know that you will not think me vain for what I have said, and I desire now this evening to speak upon that which you all have come to hear—namely, my impressions and experiences in respect to the condition of things in Great Britain, as they relate to this struggle and this country. Among the wise things said by that wisest of modern political writers, DE TOCQUEVILLE, is this: "That it is impossible to judge of the affairs of one country by applying to them the experiences and the rules of another one." There are many reasons why one would have presumed beforehand that it was easy to understand British feeling and British policy. There was a similarity of institutions and a sameness of radical principles; but that very similarity, since it begets, by different institutions and different vehicles, different policies in the end, is liable to deceive us, and we are liable to come to many conclusions, because, upon the face, things look like those to which we are accustomed at home. I myself have experienced that, for I had judged of the condition of England from the impressions produced upon me by my first four weeks' tarry there in the Summer. I should have judged very wrongly, as judged by my present convictions. Nor do I feel myself now adequate to analyze or state either the causes or the results of my feeling; I am quite aware that I am imperfect in my views in many directions. Nor can I presume to say that I present you opinions. My nature gives intensity to my expressions, and yet I wish beforehand to ask you to consider that the statements that I make are impressions liable to mistake, subject to corrections that may afterward be made in them. And with these preliminary remarks I will tell you what I saw and found. You are aware that the original expression of our people was almost universal that in Great Britain we should find a sympathiser, ready and prepared. One thing we counted sure, and that was, that if all the other nations stood aloof, there was one that would stand by us in the hour of our peril, and that was Great Britain. And the sharpness of our retaliatory complaints was acuminated by that very disappointment of a very confident conviction. When I was asked in Great Britain why the American Press so severely inveighed against England, and was almost silent in respect to France, I said: "Because we in our deepest hearts care for England, and not much for France." [Applause.] "Because under anger, and lower down than prejudice, when you strike the deeper feelings, the Americans know that they have an English origin, and they are proud of their history; when it gets back further than the present generation, [laughter;] and it was this growing affection and sympathy in the best natures and in the best parts of the best natures—it was this that made the disappointment of public expectation so sharp and so hard to be borne when Great Britain fouled our expectations and gave us no sympathy. We never asked for help. We never asked that she should lend us anything or stretch out so much as the little finger of her right hand. We did ask simply the generous confidence and generous moral sympathy and that was all, and that we did not get, and we felt sharply, the conduct of England. The expression of public feeling had an effect of throwing her moral weight against the North and for the South. So I told them. I carefully discriminated between the intention and the result. What men intend has much to do with judging of their moral character; but what men do does not depend always on their intention. And when, therefore, the British people disclaimed sympathy with the South, or a disposition to go against their own principles as represented by the North, I said to them, "What your intentions are you can best judge, but what the effect of your attitude is we on the other side can best judge." and we know that the moral influence of Great Britain has substantially gone for more than two years to help the rebellion of the slavocracy of the South, and to hinder the progress of free institutions in the North. And if there is rescue or relief—if there is redemption finally, Great Britain must stand aside, and it must be said: "The nation that boasted of her free institutions and her sovereign sympathy with the welfare of the common peoples has had no part nor lot in the great work." [Applause.] The denial of moral sympathy in Great Britain was only interpreted by the active exertions of certain parts of the British people on behalf of the South, so much so that it, I think, will scarcely be denied by any man that if the shipyards, and foundries, and looms, and shops of Great Britain had refused their succor to rebellion, the rebellion would have died out in the nation long ago. I said in private what it did not seem altogether judicious to say in public, that in some sense I might bring this war and lay it at the feet of the British people, and say, not that you intended it, but that the course of conduct pursued, legal or illegal, was such that, but for you, the rebellion would have perished almost in the beginning of it. [Applause.] And no man but knows that there was also in England an extraordinary spectacle of men who, from sheer hatred of war, by misjudgment and mistake were left to foment it. There never was a misposition more signal than that of the British public, as represented in their leading intelligent classes, in this conflict. There never was a case where a nation, by its upper classes, went so unquestionably in favor of slavery at the same time that they occupied themselves in the intensest denunciations of slavery—that went against free society at the very time they were particularly praising free society and arrogating to themselves its highest claims and honors. Under such circumstances we were, you recollect, drifting right toward war. I told the British people that war was not our choice, and yet terrible and cruel as it was, there was something in this struggle so near to us, and so indispensable to national life, that rather than that there should be interference, rather than there should be disruption and dismemberment, rather than that this republican free Government should fall, we would stand war with Great Britain, with France, with Europe. [Applause.] It would have been difficult to say this without the appearance of threat; but that difficulty was itself dissolved by the iterated and reiterated charges brought against me of having been bellicose in my own country, and of having threatened all manner of desolation to Great Britain; and my reply was this, that I felt a part, and full part in proportion, of the deep indignation which my own people felt against Great Britain, and that I had never desired war, and abhorred it, but that I held the great principles of free Republican Government to be so precious that we would not give them up, not even at the threat nor infliction of war, no matter who brought it upon us. This being the cruel disappointment that we experienced in our expectation of sympathy from Great Britain, you will ask me, "What did you find to the facts and condition of things?" I found, in the first place, on going there, that every man I met was a Southern man, not literally born in the South, but this is the division they have themselves made. These are the terms applied. They are Southerners and Northerners even more than we are here. I found that on the railways, on the boats, in the hotels, wherever there was a traveling public, there was a public that sympathized with the South, and adverse to the North. It was not an uncommon thing to hear a gentleman who had talked freely and kindly with me on other matters say as the news was discussed, "Bad news we have got by the last steamer." "Ah, what is the news?" being a little troubled. "I understand," he would reply, "that MEADE has driven LEE entirely out of Pennsylvania." [Laughter.] "God send us much more bad news, then," said I. But coming from communities enthusiastic and almost homogeneous on this subject, it was strange to my ears to hear well-dressed and well-read men congratulate themselves on disasters to the North, and rejoicing in the success of the South; and such is the case. Nor will there return to your side one young man has been traveling that will not bring back to you this substantial account, that wherever he went almost every man whom he met, without exception, was against the North and in favor of the South; and you can well imagine the impression that would be made on the mind of such. They would say "There is no question about this matter—the whole British nation is against us." Go where you will, up or down, you will find it all the same, and that was the effect impressed upon my mind. On still further inquiry, I was disappointed to find that that body to which I myself belonged—the Congregationalists, known as Independents in England. I had supposed, since they are set for a testimony for freedom and have been arrayed almost invariably on the side of struggling peoples and struggling liberties, I supposed I should find them right, I did not. I do not mean that there is not a very large part of that power whose principles are right. They will be included under the head which I shall mention by and by, but I am sorry to say that I did not find the influential and leading clergymen of that denomination, nor the influential and leading laymen on our side. They said that they sympathized with liberty. Yes, they sympathized with liberty just exactly as the icicles sympathize with sunlight and Summer. [Laughter.] It chills you to come near them; and I said to them, I want no such sympathy, and I want nothing if it cannot come from enthusiastic hearts, it does no good and we do not want it. I found also the most profound ignorance of our affairs and of the operation of our institutions, and that, too, in quarters where I had a right to expect more intelligence. I found the most active and unscrupulous efforts made by Southern men to stir up animosity toward our country. And let me say that the bad cause was better served than a good one there, as to some extent it has been in our own land, for I am sure that the South, for a bad cause, has more nearly put forth every particle of strength that it has to put forth than we have for a good cause. And as it is at home, it was abroad. Where we sent one man to England to influence public opinion, they sent a score; where we print one book of information, they a library; where we touched one spring, they touched a hundred. They seemed to pervade England, and they seemed, with the unerring instinct of selfishness and despotism, to know just where to undermine the generous and better feelings—just where to invoke the influence of ignorance—just where to touch men so that principle should fall and profit take its place. [Applause.] You may then imagine the surprise and skepticism with which, under these circumstances, I received the assurance of friends on every side that the great heart of the British nation was on our side. I had found nobody except unconditional friends of emancipation in whose society I was thrown—I had found almost nobody that spoke kindly of us on that seemed to be in sympathy with us, and yet my ears were filled with these assurances day and night. "You are mistaken, you are mistaken, this great English people are sound at heart." I said where under heavens do the English people keep their hearts, then? [Laughter and applause.] And if I had spoken in my early visit to England in June, I could not have spoken as I now do and shall. Neither on my first return from the Continent in September could I have understood and felt what I understand now, in some measure, and entirely believe that they were right, and that, after all, the great heart of the British nation is with us of the North. [Great applause.]

Let me take up, then, one part of society after another, and state, as I understand them to be, the facts. First, there is the great commercial class of England, those that are making money and those that have made it; if you please, call them the plutocracy. They are against us. In the first place there is a large class of men that are actively employed in supplying the South with all its necessaries—except principle, [laughter,] and they are making on suppose that they are making large fortunes. We cannot doubt which side they take. The next is a very large class of men who, for precisely an opposite reason, somehow are opposed to the North and in favor of the South; namely, those who have been accustomed to make money, but found this interrupting war has stopped their profits; and men that want to make money, but do not; they are opposed to us. And between these two classes lies an intermediate one of men, who are bewildered and perplexed, and see that business is more or less affected, as it is over the whole continent, by its sympathetic relations with this continent. They say when will this war end? and as the offensive is on the northern side, they feel as though whenever the North will stop *aggressing* the Sout the war will stop. So in the main they are against us. It may be lowered down to this: that while there are very noble exceptions here and there all through England—men that stand out of their class above and against it, not speaking comprehensively, the commercial class of England are against the North, and in favor of the South. I have spoken of the religious people. It is very difficult for me to analyze the causes that have turned both the established churchmen and the dissenters in respect to their most influential men against us. I do not think so in respect to the laymen; but the influential layman and the influential clergymen, I think, are adverse to us as a body. The ground usually taken is this: that the North is not sincere; and secondly, that the war is a great sin. And nowhere else in this world is there so tender a conscience on the subject of the war as Great Britain—when she is not waging it herself. [Great applause.] She has, I believe, only three wars on hand now—in China, Japan, and, I believe, in Australia—no matter where it is, it is somewhere; and the rest of her leisure she occupies with a profound regret and horror for this American war. If it was for but a ship on the sea, she was ready to go to war with us; if it was for the territory of a remote island in the Antartic Ocean, she was ready to go to war with the savages; if it was but to beat down the cities of Japan, she had no objection to burn the seat of 160,000 inhabitants in it; but when a people are making war for their own life, for everything that dignifies humanity, they stand throwing out their hands that men will make war. [Laughter.] But I am sorry to say that, while from the Friends, who have always maintained as against their own countrymen a consistent testimony against war, it should have been expected, from those men, that had no particular objection to the Crimean war, none to the opium war in China, and none to the war that they now have, if not on their hands, on the tips of their fingers. I told them to their faces, in Exeter Hall, there was not a land on the face of the globe against which they had not dashed their bloody prows and that their flag was a symbol of their history—a cross inscribed on a field of blood. [Great applause.] The English nobility, as a class are also against us. I shall read some very noble exceptions by-and-by. But these exceptions do not alter the general statement that the nobility as a class are against us. For the most obvious reason we are not accustomed to estimate the effect of our example upon European institutions. When he takes his walk abroad, it is not the elephant that weighs and measures its own gravity as he treads on the field-mouse's tail. It is the mouse that meditates. [Laughter.] A gigantic nation as this, on such a continent as this, while we are treading on the steps of accomplishing history, we are not feeling the jar that we ourselves are making; but they that have thrones and aristocratic privileges do; and they are the best interpreters of the reactionary influence of American ideas and American institutions. And it was the *Saturday Review*, that scholarly, keen, brilliant, unprincipled paper of England; it was that paper that had the frankness to say that Americans must not think that their remarks were because they disliked us, but it was because they found our ideas and our example working in Great Britain, and they were obliged in order to defeat these ideas in England to attack us in America. They are there, fighting home battles; for there is an unerring instinct—there is this feeling—that if a Government con be so efficient, covering such a continent, and so ludicrously cheap, how can we maintain our expensive and complicated Government in our sphere? Lest they should not think of it themselves, millions of common people, who are being taxed perpetually, suggest it to their attention. Do you suppose they do not know it? Do you not know that the effect of our Revolution was to send revolution all through Europe? The causes of it were all prepared. It was the torch of our Revolutionary war that set fire to the trains that burned all over Europe. They don't forget it. They dread the reactionary influence of American ideas. Such prosperity—such power and at so little expense—with so few monopolies and prerogatives to the favored classes! Therefore, when they oppose us, it is not to be construed as malignant opposition to us—it is nothing more than another form of self-love, for it is self defending itself. If you had been born with a coronet on your head, you would have done just so. [Laughter.] In Parliament, if a vote were taken to-day according to the private thoughts, sympathies and wishes among members, I suppose they would vote five to one against the North and in favor of the South. It is believed, too, by those well informed, that at least a portion of the Government have been entirely willing to go into a rupture with the North, and that but for the unflinching restraints they would have done so long ago. It is the impression throughout the realm that the Sovereign of Great Britain has been from the first our judicious but our steadfast friend. [Prolonged applause.] It is believed and so represented to me that her never rightly estimated and lamented consort was our fast friend, and that among the last acts of his life were those which erased from documents presented to him sentences that would have inflamed the growing anger. [Renewed applause.] He died with the blessing upon his head, "Blessed are the peacemakers." [Applause.] All through in the British Government, as at present constituted, (and I shall read you their names bye-and-bye,) there are several that are known to be warm and disinterested in their regard for the North, as there are others in that Government who, it is known in England—at least it was so represented to me by those who ought to know—who would not hesitate to plunge the Continent in a war for the sake of disrupting this nation. And if you ask me what is the great underlying influence that has been at work upon the upper class of England, I answer thus:

1. Commercial interest and rivalry therein.
2. Class power and the *fear* of contagion and American ideas.
3. (I know not how I shall say it so that it shall be the least offensive to our friends on the other side, but they have not come and you have not come to the bottom of the conduct of Great Britain until you have touched that delicate and real foundation cause,) we are too large and strong a nation. [Laughter.]

This is, in my judgment, the right of the whole matter. A distinguished clergyman of London, personally kind and friendly to me, said to me in these very words: "Mr. BEECHER, you may just as well have it said to you; you have been growing so strong that we have felt for a good many years that we had got to take you down, and we were very glad when the job was taken from our hands by your own people." [Laughter.] When Mr. ROEBUCK—whose speech it was my great privilege to hear—[laughter]—declared that same fact in Parliament it was cheered immensely, but reprobated in the *Times* and in the other presses that sympathized with the South, not because he had not spoken the truth, but because it was a truth not best to be spoken. [Laughter.] It is said (and I intended to have brought here to-night to have read) in one of their recent publications—and it was the immediate cause of one of my speeches there—that we were a lawless and arrogant set of men; were proud of our sudden growth; and it is said that even Mr. BEECHER himself was regarded as a specimen of what they should have to deal with in the nation supposed to be composed of men breathing that sort of threats. [Laughter.] Now when men make such lamentable mistakes as to suppose that such a peaceful man as I am is so dangerous, [laughter] is it to be supposed that they would not make a mistake in estimating the whole nation? [Renewed laughter.] It is the sun that makes the seeds grow. It is the light that stimulates the seeds into growth; but under all this is the dunghill that makes the heat that causes the seeds to spring up under the genial influences of the sun. And it is just exactly that hot bed at the bottom, underneath, that works up and turns aside what would be otherwise insufficient to do so, the natural sympathies from the North. It is just that which has prepared them for this, that and the other prejudice and misinformation. With this state of facts you will ask how is it then that the English people have been restrained? How is it that they have not gone into overt belligerency? That is the very question that I propose to answer and in the statement that the English heart is on our side. [Applause.] The nobility is against us; the Government is divided and a part is against us. I think I may say that while the brains that represent progress in Great Britain are in our favor, yet the conservative intelligence of Great Britain is against us, and that all there is on the *surface* of society representing its dignities, its power and intelligence is Anti-American. And the question I propose to you is how with the papers, magazines and universities—how with their titled estates opposed to us, that they have been restrained from manifesting this in open hostility? It is because there is a great underlying influence that restrains them—it is the influence of that underlife, and to a very great extent of the non-voting English who have produced this effect. It is a thing I could not understand at first, and which it is very difficult for us to understand—for whenever in our country there is a majority of the votes there is sure to be a direction of affairs. But it is not so in England. I learned that the men who could not vote where they were united and determined had the power to control the men who do vote. This is not an anomaly, then. It would be in our institution, but it is not in English institutions—among other reasons, because in a nation where one class have a predominance and privilege and the underlying class have none, all the instinct of self-preservation teaches this favored class never to goad that great underlying class into madness. There is always that dragon of revolution coiled up that they are afraid to arouse. Therefore it is, that when the great under class of England is determined in one direction, they always carry their point, first or last, the upper classes have to give way. Men whose fortunes are made—men whose only thought of the future is to carry the rich freights of the present along into their future—that class are generally against us. Men who have no fortunes—men having very little in the present to care for, who are struggling for better fortunes for themselves and children—that class are on our side. They are in our favor, but they are a class who have not much voice—have very little expression, and they are therefore little heard. Their report is not wafted across, but their influence is felt on the other side of the sea. It seems to me that it is peculiarly fitting that we, who believe in the common people, should find ourselves opposed by the titled and strong, but should find our allies and fast friends in the emergency have been

[Continued on Eighth Page.]

The New-York Times.

VOL. XIV.....NO. 4167. NEW-YORK, WEDNESDAY, FEBRUARY 1, 1865. PRICE FOUR CENTS.

THE PEACE QUESTION.

ITS LATEST ASPECT.

Three Commissioners Coming from Richmond.

They Apply for Admission to General Grant's Lines.

A. H. Stephens of Georgia, R. M. T. Hunter of Virginia, and A. J. Campbell of Alabama.

A FLAG OF TRUCE AND A PARLEY.

General Grant in Communication with the Government.

Expected Arrival of the Commissioners at Annapolis.

Special Dispatch to the New-York Times.

WASHINGTON, Tuesday, Jan. 31.

In regard to the rebel Peace Commissioners, the following facts are known:

ALEXANDER H. STEPHENS of Georgia, R. M. T. HUNTER of Virginia, and A. J. CAMPBELL of Alabama, the latter formerly of the United States Supreme Court, arrived at Gen. GRANT's lines last Sunday afternoon and desired permission to come to Gen. GRANT's headquarters.

After considerable delay and parley they were allowed to come to Gen. GRANT's headquarters at City Point. It appears that Gen. GRANT immediately notified the Government of the fact, but up to this time we are not aware of the decision arrived at, though they are expected to reach Washington presently, via Annapolis.

FROM GEN. GRANT'S LINES.

The Commissioners Appear in Front of Petersburgh—Application for a Permit to Come Through—Scenes under the Flag-of-Truce—Excitement among the Soldiers.

From Our Special Correspondent.

HEADQUARTERS FIFTH ARMY CORPS, Sunday, Jan. 29, 1864—10 A. M.

For many days the weather has been intensely cold, and many cases of frost-bitten feet, ears, cheeks, &c., on our picket lines are reported. To-day the intense cold had moderated, and though the sun shone brightly and the air was calm, the roads were solid and travelers many.

In front of Col. HARRIMAN's brigade, of WILCOX's division, Ninth Corps, about noon to-day, a flag of truce was displayed on the parapet of the enemy's works, a few rods to the right of the crater. The bearer of the flag stated, that "Hon. ALEXANDER H. STEPHENS, Vice-President of the Southern Confederacy, and Hon. R. M. T. HUNTER, of Virginia, were desirous of proceeding to Gen. GRANT's headquarters; that they were expected, and would have approached our lines via the James River, but were unable to do so, owing to the ice in the stream."

The message sent by the bearer of the Confederate flag of truce was sent at once to the headquarters of the Ninth Corps.

The news that Messrs. STEPHENS and HUNTER were awaiting permission to enter our lines flew like wildfire through the camps. They were distinguished men; they had made names for themselves before the war began, before acquiescing in the severance of the Republic, and the Union soldiers, who are reading men, knew it. Curiosity is one of the failings of the Union soldier, and, as the news of the flag passed from camp to camp, tents were evacuated, from bomb-proofs temporarily-buried soldiers emerged, pickets brought their rifled-muskets to an "order," and all, not otherwise engaged, covered the parapets of the works of the main and picket lines. As you know, for many days there has been a tacit understanding along this part of the line that there should be no firing; but, until to-day, the members of the corps did not think it conducive to their health to exhibit themselves prominently.

The white flag, however, brought both Unionists and Confederates within plain, point-blank shooting range of each other, and waiting for a reply to the rebel request, they showed themselves in clouds on the works of the contending armies. "How are you Fort Fisher!" says the Yanks; "Good-bye, European importations;" "Have you heard from Hood?" "Did you know that your Virginian, THOMAS, had presented to Old ABE a 'worsted Hood'?" and many other remarks of a like nature.

The "Confeds" seemed to take it all in good part, and made, in some instances, quite happy replies, such as, "Fort Fisher may be gone up, but why don't you take Fort Crater?" "GWIN's a fool, and we don't care a d—n for anything more from Europe;" and "HOOD's hoodwinked old THOMAS, and you'll hear from him directly, I reckon."

So they passed the time intervening before the reply came. Men who, a few moments later, might be engaged in mortal combat, whiled away the closing hours of the beautiful Sabbath in seemingly friendly intercourse. But does any one dream that, if in the midst of this sort of national gathering, the order had been given, "Prepare for action," any of the soldiers, so jocose and free from care, would have disobeyed the command? No! But, shoulder to shoulder, they would have repeated the lesson they have been endeavoring to teach the foes of their country for these long years. In the soldier's life there is sunshine and shadow, but, alas! the shadow predominates. The Union soldier lives on in the hope that through the shadow will finally break the [illegible] of peace, reflecting against the bank of adversity's clouds a rainbow of victory, telling in unmistakable colors of a "Union" conquered and thereafter indivisible.

As the bright orb of day neared the western horizon, and glanced upon the lofty spires of the yet unconquered "Cockade City," an officer from the headquarters of the Ninth Corps neared our foremost line. All were on the tiptoe of excitement; but, soldierlike, the gallant Colonel kept his own counsel; and, improvising a flag of truce from a white handkerchief, proceeded to scale the works; and, with one companion, advanced to the neutral ground.

After some minutes' waiting, he was met by four officers of the Confederacy, and a conference was held within a stone's throw of the scene of the terrible tragedy of the 30th of July last. What the result of this interview was, was not made public; but, it is believed that no word had been received from Gen. GRANT, and as a consequence, the "distinguished gentlemen" from Georgia and Virginia would have to bide their time, perhaps until to-morrow.

As the flags receded from each other, the thousands who covered the works suddenly disappeared, walking into their tents, crawling into their holes and descending into their bombproofs, to speculate upon the meaning of such a seemingly urgent desire on the part of the Vice-President and Ex United States Senator to enter the Union lines. Speculation upon this subject is not only rife among the soldiers, but among other thinking men, and the most extravagant propositions are put forth. Of course it is useless to speculate. It may be that the visit of these noted Southern gentlemen will be productive of good; but time alone will tell.

G. F. WILLIAMS.

REPORTS FROM BALTIMORE.

BALTIMORE, Tuesday, Jan. 31.

The *American*, this afternoon, publishes the following dispatch:

"The report has been current on the street since last evening to the effect that the Richmond *Sentinel* has announced the departure of three Peace Commissioners for Washington.

Up to noon to-day, we have no official confirmation of the rumor, though the assertion has been varied this morning by an equally positive announcement that Peace Commissioners, consisting of the rebel Vice-President ALEXANDER H. STEPHENS, and Ex-Senator R. M. T. HUNTER and Judge CAMPBELL had arrived at City Point and were expected to reach Annapolis to-day.

They are not spoken of as commissioners representing the rebel Government, but as citizens representing the people, on their way to Washington to confer with President LINCOLN on the subject of peace, precisely in the same capacity that Mr. BLAIR visited Richmond.

SECOND DISPATCH.

BALTIMORE, Tuesday, Jan. 31.

The *American* has the following special dispatch from Annapolis this morning:

ANNAPOLIS, Tuesday, Jan. 31.

Col. TYLER, of the Second Maryland Regiment, who arrived here this morning, says that on Sunday, ALEX. H. STEPHENS, R. M. T. HUNTER and two others reached our lines, and requested to come within our lines at Fort Hell, but were refused, and were awaiting permission from Gen. GRANT, who was then absent.

N. B.—I think the Commissioners were admitted nevertheless, and are now on their way to Washington. Hope to have something definite soon.

REPORTS VIA PHILADELPHIA.

PHILADELPHIA, Tuesday, Jan. 31.

A special dispatch to the *Evening Telegraph* says:

WASHINGTON, Tuesday, Jan. 31.

It is known in the best informed circles here that a commission from JEFF. DAVIS, consisting of Vice-President STEPHENS, R. M. T. HUNTER, and Gen. G. W. SMITH, have arrived at Annapolis with full power to arrange a settlement of our national difficulties.

It is believed from the understanding between Mr. BLAIR and Mr. DAVIS that the terms will be entirely satisfactory to the Administration and to Congress, and will chiefly consist of an amnesty to all offenders, and a withdrawal of the confiscation proclamation.

The Departure of the Commissioners from Richmond.

BALTIMORE, Tuesday, Jan. 31.

There is reason to believe that the Richmond papers of Monday contain an explicit statement of departure of commissioners for Washington.

From the Richmond Sentinel, Jan. 28.

It was a matter of pleasurable remark on yesterday that the President and Vice-President *had been engaged in a long consultation on public affairs.*

No Arrival yet from the James at Annapolis.

BALTIMORE, Tuesday, Jan. 31.

A dispatch from Annapolis to-night, says there has been no arrival from the James River, and there is no prospect of one to-night.

The Rebel Peace Commissioners.

The history and personal character of the rebel Vice-President, ALEXANDER H. STEPHENS, as well as his strenuous exertions to preserve the South from the folly and crime of secession, are well known to our readers. A. J. CAMPBELL, of Alabama, formerly occupied a seat on the Bench of the Supreme Court of the United States. It will be remembered that just previous to the capture of Fort Sumter, Mr. CAMPBELL appeared in Washington with Mr. FORSYTHE, of Mobile, CRAWFORD, ex-member of Congress from Georgia, and Mr. STEPHENS, on a mission to obtain the peaceful separation of the South from the Union. Since the commencement of hostilities his name has not been prominently before the public. Mr. R. M. T. HUNTER was formerly United States Senator from Virginia. He served a short time as rebel Secretary of State.

Return of Mr. Singleton.

Special Dispatch to the New-York News.

WASHINGTON, Monday, Jan. 30, 1865.

Gen. SINGLETON arrived in this city this evening, and immediately waited on the President. During his stay at Richmond he had frequent interviews with Mr. DAVIS and other prominent Confederate leaders, including Gen. LEE. Gen. SINGLETON represents those with whom he had intercourse as well disposed toward any movement calculated to restore peace on an honorable basis.

The Southern people remain firm in their determination to resist subjugation. The leaders are not averse to negotiation, provided it is not based on degrading conditions. They will meet us on equal terms, but not otherwise. They will not lay down their arms and accept whatever we choose to give them. There is no despondency in Richmond, but all, from Mr. DAVIS to the least important citizen, are desirous to have the war brought to a close.

FROM WASHINGTON.

ABOLITION OF SLAVERY.

Passage of the Constitutional Amendment.

One Hundred and Nineteen Yeas against Fifty-six Nays.

Exciting Scene in the House.

ENTHUSIASM OVER THE RESULT.

THE PEACE MISSION IN THE SENATE

A Resolution Calling for Information.

Passage of Retaliation Resolutions in the Senate.

Special Dispatches to the New-York Times.

WASHINGTON, Tuesday, Jan. 31.

THE PASSAGE OF THE CONSTITUTIONAL AMENDMENT.

The great feature of the existing rebellion was the passage to-day by the House of Representatives of the resolutions submitting to the Legislatures of the several States an amendment to the Constitution abolishing slavery. It was an epoch in the history of the country, and will be remembered by the members of the House and spectators present as an event in their lives. At 3 o'clock, by general consent, all discussion having ceased, the preliminary votes to reconsider and second the demand for the previous question were agreed to by a vote of 113 yeas, to 58 nays; and amid profound silence the Speaker announced that the yeas and nays would be taken directly upon the pending proposition. During the call, when prominent Democrats voted aye, there was suppressed evidence of applause and gratification exhibited in the galleries, but it was evident that the great interest centered entirely upon the final result, and when the presiding officer announced that the resolution was agreed to by yeas 119, nays 56, the enthusiasm of all present, save a few disappointed politicians, knew no bounds, and for several moments the scene was grand and impressive beyond description. No attempt was made to suppress the applause which came from all sides, every one feeling that the occasion justified the fullest expression of approbation and joy.

PETITIONS OF THE NAVAL CONTRACTORS.

The House Naval Committee having received a reply from the Secretary of the Navy to-day, unanimously instructed their Chairman to report a joint resolution, referring to the Navy Department the petitions of contractors asking for relief for losses in building double-enders, marine engines, &c., to be settled upon the principle of equity and justice. This is all the petitioners for relief ask, and without some such legislation the department cannot act in the matter.

THE TAX BILL.

The Ways and Means Committee to-day nearly finished the amendments to the tax bill. They expect to get through with the bill this week, and will report it at once.

THE NAVAL DEPOT AT CLEVELAND.

The Senate Naval Committee heard the arguments to-day in favor of a naval depot at Cleveland. The committee will not act definitely in regard to the matter until other parties have been heard.

THE TRADE IN COTTON.

The House Committee on Commerce to-day examined a large number of witnesses who are understood to have permits to trade in cotton with rebel States. These gentlemen, however, were very reticent, and the committee failed to elicit the required information as to how and where they got their permits.

Dispatches to the Associated Press.

WASHINGTON, Tuesday, Jan. 31.

THE VOTE ON THE AMENDMENT.

Soon after the passage of the Anti-Slavery Constitutional Amendment this afternoon, a salute was fired in honor of that event. The vote last June, when it was defeated for the want of the requisite two-thirds majority, was yeas, 96; nays, 65; absent, 21. Those who at that time voted against the amendment, but who changed their votes and cast them in the affirmative to-day, are Messrs. Baldwin of Michigan, Coffroth, McAllister, Ganson, Herrick, Radford, Steele, King, Rollins of Missouri, and Hutchins. Those who were absent on the former occasion, and who now voted aye, are as follows; Messrs. Brown of West Virginia, Davis of Maryland, Davis of New-York, Grinnell, McBride, Nelson, Pomeroy, Randall Worthington and Yeaman. The following who were absent or not voting when the June vote was taken, voted nay: Messrs. Hall, Harris of Maryland, Harris of Illinois, Winfield, Ben. Wood and Townsend. Those who voted against the resolution last year, and were to-day absent or not voting, are Messrs. Lazear, Le Blond, McKinney, Marcy, McDowell and Rogers.

MR. WADE ON THE PEACE MISSION.

During the debate on the retaliation resolution, while Mr. WADE was speaking about Mr. BLAIR's mission to Richmond, Mr. JOHNSON asked how he came to go there. Mr. WADE replied: "I would like to know. Yes, Sir. I intend to know if there is power in the United States Senate to be informed on that subject. I intend to know why it was that any man was permitted to go with impunity through our lines, and confer with the arch traitor of the Confederacy, and come back here and go again." Mr. JOHNSON said he went in a Government vessel the last time. Mr. WADE responded: "Yes, I understand he went on a Government vessel. He had no more right to be on that vessel on a mission to hold communication with this arch traitor and devil, than he had to be on his road to the lower regions in a vehicle furnished by the Government."

THE CIVIL GOVERNMENT OF VIRGINIA.

The Alexandria (Va.) *Journal* says the civil government has been restored on the eastern shore of Virginia, and that in a few days civil government will be restored in every county where it was suppressed by the action of Gen. BUTLER.

THE SUBSCRIPTIONS TO THE SEVEN-THIRTY LOAN.

The financial arrangements just concluded between the Treasury Department and JAY COOKE contemplate the continuance of subscriptions to the seven-thirties through the national banks in New-York, Philadelphia, Boston and elsewhere, as heretofore.

THIRTY-EIGHTH CONGRESS.

SECOND SESSION.

SENATE.

WASHINGTON, Tuesday, Jan. 31.

PROTEST AGAINST THE BANKRUPT BILL.

Mr. WADE, of Ohio, (Union,) presented a joint resolution of the Ohio Legislature protesting against the passage of the bankrupt law, which was ordered to be printed and laid on the table.

THE DUTY ON IMPORTED PAPER.

Mr. WADE also presented a resolution of the Ohio Legislature in favor of the repeal of the duty on printing paper, which was ordered to be printed and laid upon the table.

EMPLOYMENT OF GENERALS.

Mr. WADE—I notice that the Secretary of War, in replying to a communication of the Senate about the employment of Generals, has made a mistake which I wish to correct. He says, among other things, that Gens. BANKS and LEE are before the Committee on the Conduct of the War. This is a mistake, and one which I wish to rectify, because it seems to be a standing one. I think it interferes with the disposition which the Executive wishes to make of those officers. Mr. WADE further stated that on the 14th of December, Gen. BANKS was before the committee for about two hours, to give testimony concerning the Red River expedition. One day in January the committee found him in the city, and called on him for a few minutes to explain some matters. Gen. LEE had not been before the committee since the 13th of January, when he gave testimony for about two hours. He (WADE) wished it to be understood that neither Gen. BANKS nor Gen. LEE were detained here by the Committee on the Conduct of the War.

CLERGYMEN AND THE DRAFT.

Mr. HARRIS, of New-York, (Union,) offered the memorial of certain ministers of the Gospel, asking that they be exempted from the draft. Which was referred to the Committee on Military Affairs.

THE SCHELDT DUES.

Mr. SUMNER, of Massachusetts, (Union,) from the Committee on Foreign Relations, reported a bill for the extinction of the Scheldt Dues. Which was ordered to be printed.

CONGRESSIONAL DIRECTORY.

Mr. ANTHONY, of Rhode Island, (Union,) introduced a resolution that a Congressional Directory be published hereafter, under the superintendence of the Joint Committee on Printing. Mr. ANTHONY explained that this would be more economical than the present arrangement, by which it was published under the auspices of the Postmaster of the House; but its chief benefit would be the appearance of the Directory at an earlier day in the Session than it now appears.

The resolution was adopted.

CALL FOR INFORMATION ON MR. BLAIR'S MISSION.

Mr. SUMNER offered the following resolution:

Resolved, That the President of the United States be requested, if not incompatible with the public interests, to furnish to the Senate any information in his possession, concerning any recent personal communications with the rebel JEFFERSON DAVIS, said to have been under Executive sanction, and also copies of any correspondence relating thereto.

Mr. CONNESS, of California, (Union)—I suggest to the Senator if it would not be better to leave out the verbiage, and make the resolution refer to the message of Mr. BLAIR.

Mr. SUMNER—I beg the Senator's pardon, but I prefer it as it is.

Mr. JOHNSON, of Maryland, (Union,) offered the following as an amendment by way of a substitute for Mr. SUMNER's proposition:

Resolved, That the President of the United States be requested, if not incompatible with the public interests, to inform the Senate if any person, and if any, who has, with his authority and assent, been in Richmond negotiating with the President of the so-called Confederate States, or with any other person or persons in that place, in relation to the termination of the present war, or with a view to ascertain from such persons upon what terms, if any, they would be willing to have said war terminated; and if so, to inform the Senate, also, what information he has obtained from such agent or person; also, if such person was in Richmond as aforesaid: whether he was authorized or permitted by the President of the United States to represent to the Confederate authorities upon what terms or conditions the President would negotiate in relation to peace, and, if so, what such terms and conditions were.

Mr. SUMNER said that the resolution he offered was much briefer and simpler than that of the Senator from Maryland. There were some words in Mr. JOHNSON's resolution which he did not like. He did not like to see the Senate adopt such a phrase as the Confederate authorities.

SEVERAL SENATORS—The resolution says "so-called Confederate authorities."

Mr. SUMNER said he preferred to speak of them as rebel authorities.

Mr. DOOLITTLE, of Wisconsin, (Union,) suggested that both resolutions be printed and called up to-morrow.

This was agreed to and it was so ordered.

SECRETARY WELLES INTERROGATED.

Mr. HALE offered a resolution calling upon the Secretary of the Navy for information as to whether the arguments of the Judge-Advocate in the trial of Mr. SMITH, of Boston, had been printed by order of the Navy Department? What edition of the same had been published? What use has been made of the copies thus published? Also, whether any detectives have been employed by the Navy Department since January, 1864, and if so, how many, and how much they have been paid? what instructions they got, either written or verbal, from the Secretary or Assistant Secretary of the Navy? And especially whether any instructions were given to inquire into the conduct and business transactions of any member of either House of Congress? How much expense was incurred in this way? From what sources the funds were drawn, and by what authority?

Mr. CONNESS—I suggest that the resolution of the Senator from New-Hampshire lie over until the return of the chairman of the Committee on Naval Affairs, who is now absent.

Mr. HALE consented to the proposition, and the resolution was ordered to be printed.

NEW-YORK AND PACIFIC MAIL.

Mr. ANTHONY introduced a bill relative to mail service between New-York and the Pacific coast, which authorizes the Postmaster-General to contract for the transportation of the mails upon such lines by steamers on the Atlantic and Pacific coast, and by land transit across the Isthmus, semi-monthly, tri-monthly, or weekly, as in his judgment the public interest may from time to time require; the compensation not to exceed $400,000 for a semi-monthly, $600,000 for a tri-monthly, or $800,000 for a weekly line.

The bill was referred to the Committee on the Post-office and Post Roads.

THE BILL TO BRIDGE THE OHIO.

Mr. POWELL, of Kentucky, (Dem.,) asked that the Senate take up the bill to build a bridge across the River at Louisville.

The motion was disagreed to.

THE PROPOSED COMMITTEE ON CORRUPTIONS.

Mr. HALE then moved that the Senate proceed to the consideration of the resolution of Mr. DAVIS for the appointment of a Standing Committee on Corruptions of the Government.

Mr. DOOLITTLE suggested that as the animadversions of the Senator from New-Hampshire on the conduct of the Navy Department were likely to lead to protracted discussion, it would be well to make this the special order for some day, as there was very little time of the morning hour remaining.

Mr. HALE insisted on his motion.

Mr. HENDERSON desired to take up the bill to reimburse the State of Missouri for the expenses incurred in calling out the militia of that State.

The Senate refused to take up this bill and proceeded to the consideration of the resolution of Mr. DAVIS, upon which Mr. HALE was entitled to the floor.

Mr. HALE said he was opposed to appointing any more committees to investigate corruptions until some action was taken on frauds already discovered. He read at length from a report made by Hon. JOHN SHERMAN, when a member of the House, on the subject of naval contracts, to show that, while Congress had heretofore gone to great trouble and expense to discover frauds, yet none of the guilty parties had ever been punished.

THE QUESTION OF RETALIATION.

The morning hour expired, and the Chair decided that the retaliation resolution was in order on the proposition to recommit the papers on the subject to the Military Committee.

The subject was discussed by Messrs. HENDRICKS, WADE, SUMNER, SPRAGUE and HOWE.

Mr. SAULSBURY, of Delaware, (Dem.,) said that if all the allegations against the rebels as to their treatment of our soldiers be true, it was but another argument for peace. He was not ashamed to stand up in the Senate and advocate peace. He was not in the habit of endorsing what the President did. But if, as he heard, commissioners were on their way here to treat for peace, and this was the result of promises held out to the Confederates by the President, he was willing to endorse him so far.

The question was then taken on the motion to recommit the subject, and the Senate refused so to do. Yeas 10, nays 26.

YEAS—Messrs. Carlile, Davis, Hendricks, Powell, Richardson, Riddle, Saulsbury, Sumner, Van Winkle, Wright.

NAYS—Messrs. Anthony, Chandler, Clark, Collamer, Conness, Cowan, Dixon, Foster, Hale, Harlan, Harris, Henderson, Howard, Howe, Johnson, Lane of Indiana, Morgan, Merrill, Nesmith, Pomeroy, Ramsay, Sherman, Ten Eyck, Wade, Wilkinson, Willey.

The question then recurred on the amendment making retaliation comformable to the law of nations.

Mr. SUMNER moved further to amend by making it conform also to the usages of war as practiced among civilized nations. Mr. SUMNER called for the yeas and nays on the amendment, and it was adopted by a vote of 25 yeas against 13 nays.

YEAS—Messrs. Carlile, Cowan, Davis, Doolittle, Foote, Foster, Harlan, Harris, Henderson, Hendricks, Lane of Indiana, McDougall, Morgan, Nesmith, Pomeroy, Powell, Richardson, Riddle, Saulsbury, Sherman, Sumner, Ten Eyck, Van Winkle, Willey, Wilson, Wright.

NAYS—Messrs. Chandler, Clark, Collamer, Conness, Dixon, Farwell, Hale, Howard, Howe, Ramsay, Trumbull, Wade, Wilkinson.

Mr. SUMNER moved to amend by striking out the following; "Congress does not, however, intend by this to limit or restrict the power of the President to the modes or principles of retaliation herein mentioned; but only advises or requires a resort to them as demanded by the occasion."

Mr. SHERMAN, of Ohio, (Union,) suggested that the amendment be modified so as to strike out the words "to the modes or principles of retaliation herein mentioned."

This was adopted.

Mr. HENDRICKS, of Indiana, (Dem.,) offered as an amendment an additional resolution, declaring the sense of the Senate to be in favor of an exchange of prisoners.

Mr. HOWARD, of Michigan, (Union,) thought the subjects were so different that they should not be incorporated in the same resolution.

The amendment was adopted.

Mr. HENDERSON, of Missouri, (Union,) offered an amendment, advising the appointment of Commissioners of Prisoners, to look after the condition of our prisoners in the future.

The yeas and nays were called for, and the amendment was adopted.

YEAS—Messrs. Carlile, Collamer, Cowan, Davis, Doolittle, Foot, Foster, Harris, Henderson, Hendricks, Johnson, Lane of Kansas, McDougall, Morgan, Nesmith, Pomeroy, Powell, Riddle, Sumner, Ten Eyck, Van Winkle, Willey, Wilson, Wright—24.

NAYS—Messrs. Chandler, Clark, Conness, Dixon, Farwell, Hale, Harlan, Howard, Howe, Lane of Indiana, Morrill, Ramsay, Sherman, Trumbull, Wade, Wilkinson—16.

The resolution as amended was then passed and the Senate adjourned.

HOUSE OF REPRESENTATIVES.

WASHINGTON, Tuesday, Jan. 31.

MR. WOOD OFFERS A RESOLUTION.

Mr. FERNANDO WOOD asked leave to offer the following resolution:

Resolved, That it is the duty of the President to maintain, in every constitutional and legal manner, the integrity of the American Union, as formed by the Fathers of the Republic, and in no event, and under no circumstances, to proffer or accept negotiations which shall admit, by the remotest implication, the existence of any other Federal or Confederate Government within the territory of the United States.

Mr. FARNSWORTH, of Illinois, (Union,) objected to the reception of the resolution.

Mr. FERNANDO WOOD gave notice that he would next Monday move a suspension of the rules to introduce the resolution.

THE PRESIDENTIAL VOTE.

The Speaker appointed Mr. Stevens of Pennsylvania, Mr. Washburne of Illinois, Mr. Mallory of Kentucky, Mr. Davis of Maryland, and Mr. Cox of Ohio, as a committee on the part of the House to examine and count the votes for President and Vice-President of the United States, on the second Wednesday of February.

THE ANTI-SLAVERY AMENDMENT.

The House resumed consideration of the Senate joint resolution, proposing amendments to the Constitution of the United States.

Mr. MCALLISTER of Pennsylvania (Dem.) said when this subject was before the House on a former occasion, I voted against the measure. I have been in favor of exhausting all the means of conciliation to restore the Union as our fathers made it. I am for the Union and utterly opposed to secession or dissolution in any way or shape. The result of all the peace missions, and especially that of Mr. BLAIR has satisfied me that nothing short of recognition of their independence will satisfy the Southern Confederacy. It must therefore be destroyed, and in voting for the present measure, I cast my vote against the cornerstone of the Southern Confederacy, and declare eternal war against the enemies of my country.

Mr. COFFROTH, of Pennsylvania, (Dem.,) addressed the House in favor of the amendment, not, however, speaking for or against slavery. He argued the power of Congress to submit the amendment to the Legislatures of the States; that the South could defeat the amendment; that it must be submitted to the seceded States, or it would be recognizing their independence; that if this was done, it would apply only to those which adopted it. He also argued that the South would not remain in the Union under the Constitution as it now is, and that they would not come back after four years' fighting. All relating to slavery should be stricken from our statute books, and then, when the people of the South were tired and sick of this barbarous and inhuman war, and demand a cessation of hostilities, until it be ascertained if peace cannot be obtained, there will be no obstacles in the way of giving new guarantees to every person who shelters himself under the American Constitution. He also argued that slavery was the fruitful theme for the opponents of Democracy. It breathed life and existence into fanaticism, and unless that which sustained and fed fanaticism be removed from the political arena, the country would remain stationary, when all the rest of the world is moving. Change is the universal law of nature. What he had heretofore regarded as impolitic had ceased to operate. Having at the last session voted against the proposed Constitutional amendment, he would now vote for it. He had no doubt of the power to make the amendment in the manner proposed. In amending it three-fourths of the States represent the whole. The time has arrived to exercise the power. He believed that if Democratic policy and measures had been adopted, we should not now be engaged in war; but in the late Presidential election the people had endorsed the anti-slavery issue. He was prepared to follow it. The question had been settled by the verdict of the people, and so far as the National Government was concerned, it was not now a political issue. The adoption of the amendment would tend to restore all that is desirable to the prosperity of the country. He believed the best good of the Democratic party would be enhanced by the passage of the proposition, and it will open up a way to its triumph in the future.

Mr. BROWN, of Wisconsin, (Dem.,) spoke of the dangerous abuse of the power of the amendment. He had never been the apologist for slavery. He never thought it could be entirely destroyed. He was in favor of removing it, and then the people would place in power the Democracy. He gave this vote after much consideration, and as a Democrat, and would constantly stand by the organization of his party. No power on earth should prevent him from voting for the candidates of his party. His desire was the triumph of the party which has made this country great.

Mr. MILLER, of Pennsylvania, (Dem.,) said he owed it to himself and his constituents to reply to the sentiments of his colleagues just uttered on this floor. He wished to so act that when he returned home he would not be found derelict to the duty with which he had been entrusted, having taken an oath to protect, defend and preserve the Constitution of the United States. Long as the matter had been discussed here, it was very strange that no man had answered the question, what was to be done with the freed people, should such an amendment to the Constitution prove effective? Gentlemen on the other side had failed to make out a case. During this Administration the Constitution had been violated in all its important features.

Mr. HERRICK, of New-York, (Dem.,) in the course of his speech, said it was inconsistent that it would be a permanent institution. If he lived in Missouri or Kentucky, he should vote for the abolition of slavery therein; but as to Congressional action on that subject, it might be different. The question of slavery under the Constitution was reserved to the States respectively wherein it exists. In conclusion, he caused to be read a substitute which he desired to submit, providing that hereafter every sale and transfer of slaves shall be void and the slaves shall become free, and from and after 1880 slavery shall cease, and Congress shall give compensation for the actual damage and loss suffered by loyal citizens of the United States.

Mr. HARDING, of Kentucky, (Dem.,) said truth and principle never change, but men change, and from time to time adopt opinions just as readily as they change their garments. But he would rather hold on to the Constitution, which was the only ark of safety. He denied that there was any constitutional power to deprive any State in the Union of its local self-government. Kentucky had been treated in bad faith. Not one of the pledges made to her had been fulfilled. She had been betrayed, and now it was sought suddenly to emancipate all her slaves. The policy would result in the destruction of the slaves, and the men who proposed to carry it out had no more love for the slave than Satan has for sinners.

Mr. KALBFLEISCH, of New-York, (Dem.,) opposed the proposition. He maintained that all our political misfortunes are attributable to a disregard of the Constitution. He had not learned his democracy from his inveterate enemies, and he would not be instructed by them now. This amendment, he contended, if adopted, would stand in the way of peace negotiations and a restoration of the Union. He said he should strive to uphold and carry out the pledges which he had made to protect and defend the Constitution. Apart from the question of power, this was not the time to attempt an amendment of the Constitution in the manner proposed. He denied that the result of the Presidential election was in favor of abolishing slavery everywhere. No such issue was made up in New-York.

The debate having closed, Mr. ASHLEY, of Ohio, (Union,) who had charge of the subject throughout, demanded the previous question, which was on the motion heretofore made by the gentleman, to reconsider the vote of last session, by which the constitutional amendment was lost for the want of the requisite two-thirds majority.

Mr. STILES, of Pennsylvania, (Dem.,) moved that the motion to reconsider be laid on the table.

This was decided in the negative. Yeas, 57; nays, 111.

The question was then taken on the motion to reconsider, and it was decided in the affirmative. Yeas, 112; nays, 57.

Mr. MALLORY, of Kentucky, (Dem.,) raised the question that a vote of two-thirds was requisite to reconsider; but the Speaker overruled the point, saying all motions of this kind were governed by the rules.

Mr. MALLORY suggested a postponement of the vote until to-morrow, saying that several gentlemen who wished to record their names were absent. Let the time for taking the question be fixed so that all could have a fair warning.

Mr. ASHLEY replied that it had been universally understood that the question was to be taken to-day. He had consented to the extension of the debate even against the protest of his friends. It came with a very bad grace to ask for a postponement of the vote, considering the courtesy he had extended to the other side and the fair notice given.

Mr. BROWN, of Wisconsin, (Union,) asked the gentleman to give way in order that he might offer a substitute.

Mr. ASHLEY said he had one himself, which he preferred to the Senate's proposition now before the House.

Mr. ELDRIDGE, of Wisconsin, (Dem.,)—Why do you not offer it?

Mr. ASHLEY—Because I will not protract the proceedings.

The question was then taken on the adoption of the following Senate joint resolution, submitting to the Legislatures of the several States, a proposition to amend the Constitution of the United States:

Be it resolved by the Senate and House of Representatives of the United States of America in Congress assembled, two-thirds of both Houses concurring, that the following articles be proposed to the Legislatures of the several States as an amendment to the Constitution of the United States; when ratified by three-fourths of said Legislatures, shall be valid to all intents and purposes as a part of the said Constitution, namely:

ART. 13.—SECTION 1. Neither slavery nor involuntary servitude, except as a punishment for crime, whereof the party shall have been duly convicted, shall exist within the United States, or any place subject to their jurisdiction.

SEC. 2. Congress shall have power to enforce this article by appropriate legislation.

There was much confusion throughout the proceedings, amid which the clerk proceeded to call the roll on the passage of the joint resolution.

The Speaker said, "Call my name as a member of this House."

The name was accordingly called.

When the Speaker answered to the name of SCHUYLER COLFAX, applause followed his response, and also burst out at other parts of the proceedings; which, however, the Speaker checked, and calling the House to order, said he hoped a better example would be set to preserve the decorum of the House.

Several members on the Democratic side of the House said those on the other side were as noisy as the persons in the galleries.

Mr. GANSON, of New-York, (Dem.,) had voted "no" on the question of reconsidering the vote by which the joint resolution was heretofore lost, now voted "aye," and Messrs. RADFORD and STEELE, (Dems.) of New-York, changed their votes in the same manner. These changes gave rise to applause, which was promptly checked.

The utmost interest was manifested throughout the calling of the roll, and there was strict attention on the part of the members to their responses; for, on the previous vote to reconsider, two-thirds of the members present had not voted in the affirmative, but a large majority of the members present had carried that question. It was therefore somewhat doubtful whether the pending joint resolution would be passed.

The votes of Mr. BALDWIN of Michigan (Dem.) and the gentlemen above mentioned however gave additional hopes to the friends of the measure.

When the calling of the roll was completed the Clerk proceeded to read the names, first of those who voted in the affirmative, and next of those who had voted in the negative. The House was now comparatively silent. The result of the vote was noted on a piece of paper and handed by the Clerk to the Speaker, who then announced the passage of the joint resolution by a vote of 119 yeas against 56 nays.

Thereupon rose a general shout of applause. The members on the floor huzzaed in chorus with deafening and equally emphatic cheers of the throng in the galleries. The ladies in the dense assemblage waved their handkerchiefs, and again and again the applause was repeated, intermingled with clapping of hands and exclamations of "Hurrah for freedom!" "Glory enough for one day," &c. The audience were wildly excited, and the friends of the measure jubilant. Never was a scene of such a joyous character before witnessed in the House of Representatives, certainly not within the last quarter of a century.

There was extensive hand-shaking and congratulation in every direction. The proceedings had attracted thousands of persons of both sexes, and having been brought to a close, those on the floor who had been admitted by the favor of the members, and the occupants of the galleries, hastily departed.

The vote on the passage of the joint resolution is as follows:

YEAS (DEMOCRATS IN ITALICS.)

Messrs. Allison, Iowa,
Ames, Massachusetts,
Anderson, Kentucky,
Arnold, Illinois,
Ashley, Ohio,
Bailey, Pennsylvania,
Baldwin, Michigan,
Baldwin, Massachusetts,
Baxter, Vermont,
Beaman, Michigan,
Blaine, Maine,
Blair, West Virginia,
Blow, Missouri,
Boutwell, Massachusetts,
Boyd, Missouri,
Brandagee, Connecticut,
Broomall, Pennsylvania,
Brown, West Virginia,
Ambrose W. Clark, New-York,
Freeman Clark, New-York,
Cobb, Wisconsin,
Coffroth, Pennsylvania,
Colfax, Indiana,
Cole, California,
Creswell, Maryland,
Davis, Indiana,
Davis, New-York,
Dawes, Massachusetts,
Deming, Connecticut,
Dixon, Rhode Island,
Donnelly, Minnesota,
Driggs, Michigan,
Dumont, Indiana,
Eckley, Ohio,
Eliot, Massachusetts,
English, Connecticut,
Farnsworth, Illinois,
Frank, New-York,
Ganson, New-York,
Garfield, Ohio,
Gooch, Massachusetts,
Grinnell, Iowa,
Griswold, New-York,
Hale, Pennsylvania,
Herrick, New-York,
Higby, California,
Hooper, Massachusetts,
Hotchkiss, New-York,
Hubbard, Iowa,
Hubbard, Connecticut,
Hubbard, New-York,
Hutchins, Ohio,
Ingersoll, Illinois,
Jenckes, Rhode Island,
Julian, Indiana,
Kasson, Iowa,
Kelley, Pennsylvania,
Kellogg, Michigan,
Kellogg, New-York,
King, Missouri,
Knox, Missouri,
Littlejohn, New-York,
Loan, Missouri,
Longyear, Michigan,
Marvin, New-York,
McAllister, Pennsylvania,
McBride, Oregon,
McClurg, Missouri,
McIndoe, Wisconsin,
Miller, New-York,
Morehead, Pennsylvania,
Morrill, Vermont,
Morris, New-York,
A. Myers, Pennsylvania,
L. Myers, Pennsylvania,
Nelson, New-York,
Norton, Illinois,
Odell, New-York,
O'Neill, Pennsylvania,
Orth, Indiana,
Patterson, New-York,
Perham, Maine,
Pike, Maine,
Pomeroy, New-York,
Price, Iowa,
Radford, New-York,
Randall, Kentucky,
Rice, Massachusetts,
Rice, Maine,
Rollins, New-Hampshire,
Rollins, Missouri,
Schenck, Ohio,
Scofield, Pennsylvania,
Shannon, California,
Sloan, Wisconsin,
Smith, Kentucky,
Smithers, Delaware,
Spalding, Ohio,
Starr, New-Jersey,
Steele, New-York,
Stearns, Pennsylvania,
Thayer Pennsylvania,
Thomas, Maryland,
Tracy, Pennsylvania,
Upson, Michigan,
Van Valkenburgh, New-York,
Washburne, Illinois,
Washburne, Massachusetts,
Webster, Maryland,
Whaley, West Virginia,
Wheeler, Wisconsin,
Williams, Pennsylvania,
Wilder, Kansas,
Wilson, Iowa,
Windham, Minnesota,
Woodbridge, Vermont,
Worthington, Nevada,
Yeaman, Kentucky—119.

NAYS (ALL DEMOCRATS EXCEPT CLAY.)

Messrs. J. C. Allen, Illinois,
W. J. Allen, Illinois,
Ancona, Pennsylvania,
Bliss, Ohio,
Brooks, New-York,
Brown, Wisconsin,
Chanler, New-York,
Clay, Kentucky,
Cox, Ohio,
Cravens, Indiana,
Dawson, Pennsylvania,
Denison, Pennsylvania,
Eden, Illinois,
Edgerton, Indiana,
Eldridge, Wisconsin,
Finck, Ohio,
Grider, Kentucky,
Hale, Missouri,
Harding, Kentucky,
Harrington, Indiana,
Harris, Maryland,
Harris, Illinois,
Holman, Indiana,
Johnson, Pennsylvania,
Johnson, Ohio,
Kalbfleisch, New-York,
Kernan, New-York,
Knapp, Illinois,
Law, Indiana,
Long, Ohio,
Mallory, Kentucky,
Miller, Pennsylvania,
Morris, Ohio,
Morrison, Illinois,
Noble, Ohio,
O'Neil, Ohio,
Pendleton, Ohio,
Perry, New-Jersey,
Pruyn, New-York,
Randall, Pennsylvania,
Robinson, Illinois,
Ross, Illinois,
Scott, Missouri,
Steele, New-Jersey,
Stiles, Pennsylvania,
Strouse, Pennsylvania,
Stuart, Illinois,
Sweat, Maine,
Townsend, New-York,
Wadsworth, Kentucky,
Ward, New-York,
White, J. W. Ohio,
White, C. A. Ohio,
Winfield, New-York,
Ben. Wood, New-York,
F. Wood, New-York—56.

ABSENT, OR NOT VOTING.

The absentees, or those not voting, were:

Messrs. Lazear, Penn.,
Leblonde, Ohio,
Marcy, New-Hampshire,
McDowell, Indiana,
McKinney, Ohio,
Middleton, New-Jersey,
Rogers, New-Jersey,
Voorhees, Indiana—8.

All Democrats.

A motion to adjourn was carried amid the greatest confusion, yeas 121, nays 24.

The New-York Times.

VOL. XIV......NO. 4225. NEW-YORK, MONDAY, APRIL 10, 1865. PRICE FOUR CENTS

HANG OUT YOUR BANNERS

UNION

VICTORY!

PEACE!

Surrender of General Lee and His Whole Army.

THE WORK OF PALM SUNDAY.

Final Triumph of the Army of the Potomac.

The Strategy and Diplomacy of Lieut.-Gen. Grant.

Terms and Conditions of the Surrender.

The Rebel Arms, Artillery, and Public Property Surrendered.

Rebel Officers Retain Their Side Arms and Private Property.

Officers and Men Paroled and Allowed to Return to Their Homes.

The Correspondence Between Grant and Lee.

OFFICIAL.

WAR DEPARTMENT, WASHINGTON, April 9, 1865—9 o'clock P. M.

To Maj.-Gen. Dix:

This department has received the official report of the SURRENDER, THIS DAY, OF GEN LEE AND HIS ARMY TO LIEUT.-GEN GRANT on the terms proposed by Gen. GRANT.

Details will be given as speedily as possible.

EDWIN M STANTON,
Secretary of War.

HEADQUARTERS ARMIES OF THE UNITED STATES, 4:30 P. M., April 9.

Hon. Edwin M. Stanton, Secretary of War:

GEN LEE SURRENDERED THE ARMY OF NORTHERN VIRGINIA THIS AFTERNOON upon the terms proposed by myself. The accompanying additional correspondence will show the conditions fully.

(Signed) U. S. GRANT, Lieut.-Gen'l.

SUNDAY, April 9, 1865.

GENERAL—I received your note of this morning, on the picket line, whither I had come to meet you and ascertain definitely what terms were embraced in your proposition of yesterday with reference to the surrender of this army.

I now request an interview in accordance with the offer contained in your letter of yesterday for that purpose.

Very respectfully, your obedient servant,
R. E. LEE, General.

To Lieut.-Gen. GRANT, Commanding United States Armies.

Sunday, April 9, 1865.

Gen. R. E. Lee, Commanding Confederate States Armies.

Your note of this date is but this moment, 11:50 A. M., received.

In consequence of my having passed from the Richmond and Lynchburgh road to the Farmville and Lynchburgh road, I am at this writing about four miles West of Walter's church, and will push forward to the front for the purpose of meeting you.

Notice sent to me, on this road, where you wish the interview to take place, will meet me.

Very respectfully, your ob'd't servant,
U. S. GRANT,
Lieutenant-General.

APPOMATTOX COURT-HOUSE, April 9, 1865.

General R. E. Lee, Commanding C. S. A.:

In accordance with the substance of my letters to you of the 8th inst., I propose to receive the surrender of the Army of Northern Virginia on the following terms, to wit:

Rolls of all the officers and men to be made in duplicate, one copy to be given to an officer designated by me, the other to be retained by such officers as you may designate.

The officers to give their individual paroles not to take arms against the Government of the United States until properly exchanged, and each company or regimental commander sign a like parole for the men of their commands.

The arms, artillery and public property to be packed and stacked and turned over to the officers appointed by me to receive them.

This will not embrace the side-arms of the officers, nor their private horses or baggage.

This done, EACH OFFICER AND MAN WILL BE ALLOWED TO RETURN TO THEIR HOMES, not to be disturbed by United States authority so long as they observe their parole and the laws in force where they reside.

Very respectfully,
U. S. GRANT, Lieutenant-General.

HEADQUARTERS ARMY OF NORTHERN VIRGINIA, April 9, 1865.

Lieut.-Gen. U. S. Grant, Commanding U. S. A.:

GENERAL: I have received your letter of this date, CONTAINING THE TERMS OF SURRENDER OF THE ARMY OF NORTHERN VIRGINIA, as proposed by you. As they are substantially the same as those expressed in your letter of the 8th inst., THEY ARE ACCEPTED. I will proceed to designate the proper officers to carry the stipulations into effect.

Very respectfully,
Your obedient servant,
R. E. LEE, General.

THE PRELIMINARY CORRESPONDENCE.

The following is the previous correspondence between Lieut.-Gen. GRANT and Gen. LEE, referred to in the foregoing telegram to the Secretary of War.

CLIFTON HOUSE, VA., April 9, 1865.

Hon. Edwin M. Stanton, Secretary of War:

The following correspondence has taken place between Gen. LEE and myself. *There has been no relaxation in the pursuit during its pendency.*

U. S. GRANT, Lieutenant-General.

APRIL 7, 1865.

Gen. R. E. Lee, Commanding C. S. A.:

GENERAL: The result of the last week must convince you of the hopelessness of further resistance on the part of the Army of Northern Virginia in this struggle. I feel that it is so and regard it as my duty to shift from myself the responsibility of any further effusion of blood, by asking of you the surrender of that portion of the Confederate States Army, known as the Army of Northern Virginia.

Very Respectfully,
Your obedient servant,
U. S. GRANT,
Lieutenant-General,
Commanding Armies of the United States.

APRIL 7, 1865.

General: I have received your note of this date.

Though not entirely of the opinion you express of the hopelessness of further resistance on the part of the army of Northern Virginia, I reciprocate your desire to avoid useless effusion of blood, and therefore, before considering your proposition, *ask the terms you will offer, on condition of its surrender.*

R. E. LEE, General.

To Lieut.-Gen. U. S. GRANT, Commanding Armies of the United States.

APRIL 8, 1865.

To Gen. R. E. Lee, Commanding C. S. A.:

GENERAL: Your note of last evening in reply to mine of same date, asking the conditions on which I will accept the surrender of the Army of Northern Virginia, is just received.

In reply, I would say that *peace being my first desire, there is but one condition that I insist upon*, viz.:

That the men surrendered shall be disqualified for taking up arms again against the Government of the United States until properly exchanged.

I will meet you, or designate officers to meet any officers you may name, for the same purpose, at any point agreeable to you, for the purpose of arranging definitely the terms upon which the surrender of the Army of Northern Virginia will be received.

Very respectfully, your obedient servant,
U. S. GRANT, Lieut.-General,
Commanding armies of the United States.

April 8, 1865.

GENERAL: I received, at a late hour, your note of to-day, in answer to mine of yesterday.

I did not intend to propose the surrender of the Army of Northern Virginia, but *to ask the terms* of your proposition. To be frank, I do not think the emergency has arisen to call for the surrender.

But as *the restoration of peace should be the sole object of all*, I desire to know whether your proposals would tend to that end.

I cannot, therefore, meet you with a view to surrender the Army of Northern Virginia, but *as far as your proposition may affect the Confederate States forces under my command, and tend to the restoration of peace*, I should be pleased to meet you at 10 A. M., to-morrow, on the old stage road to Richmond, between the picket lines of the two armies.

Very respectfully, your obedient servant,
R. E. LEE,
General, C. S. A.

To Lieut.-Gen. GRANT, Commanding Armies of the United States.

APRIL 9, 1865.

General R. E. Lee, commanding C. S. A.:

GENERAL: Your note of yesterday is received. As I have no authority to treat on the subject of peace, the meeting proposed for 10 A. M. to-day could lead to no good. I will state, however, General, that *I am equally anxious for peace with yourself*; and the whole North entertain the same feeling. *The terms upon which peace can be had are well understood. By the South laying down their arms, they will hasten that most desirable event, save thousands of human lives, and hundreds of millions of property not yet destroyed.*

Sincerely hoping that all our difficulties may be settled *without the loss of another life*, I subscribe myself,

Very respectfully,
Your obedient servant,
U. S. GRANT,
Lieutenant-General United States Army.

REJOICINGS.

WILMINGTON, Del., Sunday, April 9.

Wilmington is in an uproar and blaze of glory, rejoicing over the greatest of victories yet achieved by our arms. Guns are firing, bells are ringing, and a large procession is proceeding through the streets. Such an excitement was never before witnessed in this city.

ALBANY, Monday, April 10—1 A. M.

There is great rejoicing here over the news of the surrender of Gen. LEE and his army.

The news was received at about 10 P. M., and about midnight State and Pearl streets were filled with people anxiously awaiting the particulars.

The bells are ringing, cannon firing, while the multitude are indulging in fireworks.

The Governor was called up and briefly addressed the throng around his residence.

The State House and many private residences are illuminated.

PHILADELPHIA, April 9.

The glorious announcement of LEE's surrender was received here about nine o'clock. It was telegraphed to all sections of the city, and was announced in the several churches. The *Ledger* office was illuminated in five minutes. The bell of Independence Hall was rung by the order of the Mayor. The firemen immediately assembled and blocked up the streets. Salutes were fired, and the whistles of the steam-engines and the cheers of the assembled multitudes made the whole city ring.

WORCESTER, Mass., Monday, April 9.

The news of the surrender of LEE and his army created an intense excitement here to-night. The bells were rung, guns were fired, bonfires kindled, the fire companies turned out, and many stores and buildings were illuminated.

PITTSBURGH, Pa., Sunday, April 9.

The news to-night brought nearly the entire population into the streets. The recruiting booths were turned into bonfires, salutes were fired, speeches were made, and bands played.

TRENTON, N. J., Sunday, April 9.

The glorious news was received here with cheering and ringing of bells. The people are turning out *en masse* to receive and rejoice over the glad tidings.

PROVIDENCE, R. I., Sunday, April 9—Midnight.

Bells are ringing, cannon are firing, and the citizens are out rejoicing over the news of LEE's surrender. A large bonfire is burning on Weybosset bridge.

FROM THE PACIFIC COAST.

Juarez said to be Coming to Washington by way of San Francisco—French Forces in Sinaloa—French War Steamers in California Ports—The Overland Mails.

SAN FRANCISCO, Friday, April 7.

The steamer *John L. Stephens*, from Mazatlan, brings $93,000 in treasure and a thousand bags of silver ore.

The Mazatlan *Times*, the Imperialist organ, give the report that JUAREZ was en route for Cape St. Lucas, whence he would sail for San Francisco on his way to Washington.

A French naval expedition had sailed, it was supposed, for Guaymas.

An Imperial force has moved to Sinaloa.

A correspondent of the San Francisco *Bulletin*, writing from Mazatlan, March 4, says that JUAREZ is still at Chihuahua with his ministers raising troops, though money, arms, and ammunition are scarce.

The French war steamer *Victoria* and transport *Du Rhine* was at Santa Barbara, on the coast of California. They hope to obtain supplies of coal at San Francisco.

The daily Overland Mail, hence to Salt Lake, resumed its trips yesterday. The first mail this way since the interruption arrived last night.

The recent meeting in behalf of the Christian Sanitary Commission, resulted in remittances, by telegraph, within the past few days, of $30,000 in gold.

The scarcity of flour and wheat continues. Extreme prices are obtained, and consequently trade does not improve much.

The Union Convention of Washington Territory have nominated A. A. DENNY as Congressional Delegate.

Military celebrations for the national victories were held throughout the State to-day.

A mass meeting in aid of the Soldiers' Relief Association was held here to-night.

THE VICTORY.

Thanks to God, the Giver of Victory.

Honors to Gen. Grant and His Gallant Army.

A NATIONAL SALUTE ORDERED.

Two Hundred Guns to be Fired at the Headquarters of Every Army, Department, Post and Arsenal.

[OFFICIAL.]

WAR DEPARTMENT, WASHINGTON, D. C., April 9, 1865—9.30 P. M.

Lieut.-Gen. Grant:

Thanks be to Almighty God for the great victory with which he has this day crowned you and the gallant armies under your command.

The thanks of this Department and of the Government, and of the People of the United States—their reverence and honor have been deserved—will be rendered to you and the brave and gallant officers and soldiers of your army for all time.

EDWIN M. STANTON, Secretary of War.

WAR DEPARTMENT, WASHINGTON, D. C., April 9, 1865—10 o'clock P. M.

Ordered: That a salute of two hundred guns be fired at the headquarters of every army and department, and at every post and arsenal in the United States, and at the Military Academy at West Point on the day of the receipt of this order, in commemoration of the surrender of Gen. ROBERT E. LEE and the Army of Northern Virginia to Lieut.-Gen. GRANT and the army under his command. Report of the receipt and execution of this order to be made to the Adjutant-General at Washington.

EDWIN M. STANTON,
Secretary of War.

FROM RICHMOND.

Perils and Excitements of a Voyage Up the James—Scenes and Incidents Along the River.

From Our Own Correspondent.

RICHMOND, Va., Wednesday, April 5.

The inspiration of the scene and the scope of the theme before us are far beyond the feeble descriptive powers of of the pen of your correspondent. No brilliant rhetoric, no vivid word-painting, no oratorical eloquence can portray the sublimity and immensity of the great victory. It is almost beyond the power of the human mind to comprehend its extent, and when you begin to descend to detail, the task is simply appalling in its magnitude. Think of a line of operations, held defensively and operated from offensively with such success, *thirty-nine miles long from flank to flank, thoroughly fortified throughout its entire length*. Think of the cities captured, of the fortifications stormed and taken, with their hundreds of guns, great and small, of the material of war now in our hands, yet beyond the possibility of computation of the terrible battles, and the overwhelming defeat, and rout of the chief army of the rebellion of the prisoners captured. Counted by the tens of thousands, of the terrified flight of the arch-traitor and his few desperate minions; of the triumphant entry of ABRAHAM LINCOLN into treason's fallen capital. Let every lover of his country depict the vast scene in his own imagination for words to fitly discribe it fails altogether.

Through the courtesy of Provost-Marshal Gen. PATRICK, I enjoyed an exceedingly pleasant sail from City Point to the Richmond wharves this morning, on his fleet flag ship, the *Mattano*. Accompanying the General were Hon. C. H. DANA, Assistant Secretary of War, his wife and son, and Hon. ROSCOE CONKLING, member of Congress from New-York. The snake-like bends of the James between City Point and Varina Landing, were quickly passed, and at the latter place assurance was given that the river was clear for our vessel to the very docks of Richmond; but I can assure you that the navigation of the tortuous channel of the James thence to Richmond, thickly sown with obstructions and supposed torpedoes, was an exceedingly delicate task, and full of excitement. Our pilot knew the channel of old, but he knew not the warlike devices of the enemy.

We were, however, very fortunate, and the approach to the city, especially during the last eight miles from Drewry's Bluff, was full of the intensest interest, for over these waters the Union flag had never before floated during the war. When we leave Dutch Gap and that famous canal, which looks as though it might have been washed out by a billow, we at once enter upon the lines held by the enemy. Howlett House Battery, famous for its determined resistance to our engineering operations on the north side of the river, stands abandoned and gloomy, with its twelve large guns still in the embrasures, but all silent as we steamed rapidly by. Another long and large earthwork appears on the left bank, mounting eight or ten guns, and bearing directly upon the mouth of the canal. This, too, like the rest, is abandoned, with its armament unimpaired. We next pass the wreck of the rebel gunboat, blown up by our batteries during the effort made to run through our fleet some months ago.

The next point of interest is Fort Brady, on the north bank of the river, and the left of the position of our Army of the James. What strikes one as very remarkable here is the fact that owing to the intricate windings of the James there are two rebal batteries, Howlett House and another, absolutely in the rear of this former position of our army. Fort Brady is the point where Gen. GIBBON opened on the retreating rebel rams. Had there been larger guns at his disposal, the range is so good that they would have stood a poor chance of escape.

We are now fairly in that part of the river held solely by the rebels, and a knowledge of the channel and obstructions is absolutely necessary to a safe voyage. The gunboat *Monticello* is therefore hailed, and on asking for information, a pilot who has been up and down is tendered with much politeness. The obstructions sunk by our own fleet are soon passed, likewise the fleet of monitors, and the next object which greets the vision is a gaily dressed tug, with a guard of marines, having in tow Admiral PORTER's barge with the President, on his return from Richmond, complacently seated in the stern sheets. It looks very much like a pic-nic. Following a short distance after is the President's handsome flag-ship, the *River Queen*. Not far behind is the beautiful steel gunboat *Bat*, ex-blockade runner, now general convoy to distinguished guests, and one of the fastest vessels in the navy. The *River Queen*, which took the President up the river, proceeded no farther than the obstructions at Drewry's Bluff. We are soon abreast of this historic fortification, and eager eyes scan closely its formidable walls and positions.

Here is the chief line of obstructions sunk by the rebels early in the war, and located as they are, directly under the guns of Fort Darling, subjecting every approaching thing to a terrible plunging fire, it is readily admitted that this was the impassable barrier to the naval advance on Richmond. The river here is very narrow, and the movement of large vessels attended with much danger. The obstructions were placed directly across the river, and filled it completely with the exception of a gap of fifty or sixty feet, left for the passage of the rebel fleet and flag-of-truce boats. They consist of the hulls of two or three old steamships, that formerly plyed between Richmond and New York. The wheel-houses, fast crumbling to decay, still rise above the water, and present the appearance of a melancholy ruin.

We pass so hurriedly under the guns of Fort Darling, that we have no good opportunity to observe its construction. We know it looks very strong, and on the north side it has one or two small outlying works on its flank. Our naval companions tell us that it is a casemated fortification, and with its surrounding field works, all parts of the fort itself, mounts not less than forty guns. All these, like hundreds more, are our trophies without blemish or injury.

Not far above Fort Darling lies the wreck of one of the famous rebel fleet in the James, the iron-clad *Virginia*. Whether she has been blown up or simply scuttled and sunk, cannot be ascertained from looking at her as she lies. She sank in deep water, and is careened over on her side, leaving a portion of her overhang visible above the water-line. Of the other iron-clad, the *Richmond*, we find no trace.

In the immediate vicinity of Fort Darling we pass through a very substantial bridge with a draw, used by LEE for the speedy transfer of troops from the north to the south side of the James. Ere reaching Richmond we pass two more of the same kind, though hardly so well built as the first; but all demonstrating that LEE had no pontoon bridges across the James anywhere—probably, because the rapid current rendered them unsafe, and probably, too, because he had not any pontoons to spare, when something else would answer just as well.

We have now steamed safely by all obstructions and chances of torpedoes, and the very pardonable trepidation which we felt in view of our possible danger, gives way to a feeling that just now is a moment in our lives, the significance, importance and sublimity of which cannot be justly appreciated. The City of Richmond is in view. The spires pointing heavenward; the smoke still rising from the conflagration's awful ruin, and the Stars and Stripes floating from a hundred house-tops and mastheads, all form a picture so sublimely grand and inspiring, that the human mind is simply lost in mute contemplation.

In a few moments we land at the Rockets, and a brisk walk of a mile and a half brings us to the Spotswood House, where we find dinner and a very comfortable room, amid hundreds of loyal guests.

L. L. CROUNSE.

First Impressions of Richmond—The Great Conflagration in the City—Who Was Responsible for it?—The Libby and Castle Thunder—Suffering for Food—Distribution of Supplies—Lee's Family.

From Our Own Correspondent.

RICHMOND, Thursday, April 6, 1865.

So many thousand facts are presented to the mind of the visitor here in such a very short space of time, that to record them systematically is almost impossible. The great features of the evacuation, the entrance of our troops, the conflagration, the President's visit and reception, have already been forwarded to you in detail by your correspondents who came in with the troops, and I will, therefore, allude to them only in a general way.

Let me say, though, at the outset, that the best part of the city is a ruin. That the awful fire kindled by the enemy, and which at first promised to consume but a few buildigns, was so fanned by the rising wind, that before it could be got under subjection, *thirty squares, comprising not less than eight hundred buildings in the very best and most valuable business part of Richmond were in ashes.* What the pecuniary loss is no one can estimate. Nearly all the principal mills, factories, warehouses, stores, banks and insurance offices were destroyed, and the losses being so heavy, the insurance companies, perhaps insolvent already from their countenance of the rebel currency, are now more than bankrupted, and thousands of property owners, computed wealthy in their actual possessions three days ago, are now reduced to beggary. It is among the things easily discernable, that this ruin, wrought by their own friends, to whom they have given all, and to whose tyranny they have submitted, with even cheerfulness, is the cause of far deeper gloom among many than that produced by the loss of the city or the defeat of their army. It is apparent indeed that the transfer of the city to the Union flag was not only *not distasteful to a very large portion of the people, many of them among the best classes, but even highly gratifying.* No captured city, not even Savannah nor Columbia, can present the ruin apparent here in Richmond. It will carry its painful evidences for half a score of years, and the only thing which will speedily alleviate the dire distress that must prevail, and give the city a chance for a speedy recovery from its present stagnation, is immediate peace. It is Richmond's only salvation. The origin of the fire and the incendiaries are so well and positively known that no extended investigation on these points is required. It seems that *Gen. Lee was not responsible for it, but that Jeff. Davis and his Secretary of War, Breckenridge, were.* The destruction of the supplies and the arsenal involved the destruction of the city, and it was so decided by the leading citizens. Gen. EWELL and Maj. CARRINGTON both protested against it in the most earnest manner, as did also a committee of citizens, but BRECKINRIDGE, in reply, exclaimed *that he didn't care a d—n if every house in Richmond was consumed, the warehouse must be burned.* Thus this wretched rebel, hoisted into a powerful position with no constituents, is responsible for the dreadful ruin, and his master DAVIS is likewise responsible, because he silently countenanced it.

The fire was started in two places, among the supply warehouses near the wharves, and at the Danville Depot, where there were 1,500 hogsheads of tobacco belonging to the Confederate Government. This consumed the Danville Depot, also the Petersburgh Depot, and the bridge over the James to Manchester. The famous Libby Prison, and Castle Thunder, as I have already informed you, were not burned. They were reserved for a far more appropriate fate. I visited them yesterday, and found Castle Thunder used as a guard-house for factious and thieving negroes, caught in acts of plunder, while the Libby contained 700 rebel prisoners, officers and privates, temporarily shut up together. They looked through the iron gratings with gloomy countenances, while the Union guard outside seemed to richly enjoy the transition that the famous building had undergone, evidently having been there himself. The whirligig of time makes all things even, and the thousands of loyal officers and soldiers who have suffered the tortures and horrors of these dungeons may now contemplate their present uses with serene satisfaction, and yet without resentment.

A close inspection of Castle Thunder reveals one of the most hideous dungeons that can be conceived. We failed to see it, however, in all its filth and nastyness, for a strong force of men had been engaged two days in carrying out the accumulation of the past three years. The corporal of the guard who conducted us through, pointed out a spot on the floor on one of the main halls, not yet cleaned, where the dirt was three inches thick, and alive with vermin, *and yet on this floor, in this condition, prisoners were obliged to sleep either upon the dirt itself or upon pallets of decaying straw.*

But I will not descant farther upon this vile relic of the rebellion. Its career is too well known. The prisoners confined here, it will be recollected, were those against whom special vengeance was directed, prisoners of State, persons charged with harboring Union prisoners, Union officers charged with being spies, blockade-runners, &c. Well has it been said that a confinement in Castle Thunder is a foretaste of the tortures of the damned.

This building, together with the Libby, belongs to the estate of JOHN ENDERS, and was leased by the rebel Government. They were originally built for stores, but subsequently turned into tobacco manufactories. But their base uses are now at an end.

This is the fourth day of the Union occupation, and the confusion in the city necessarily attendant upon such an evacuation, and such an occupation, is gradually subsiding. Could the ruins of the fire be removed from sight, Richmond would present an attractive appearance, for it is really a handsome city; but, after all, the saddest scenes are at the headquarters of the Provost-Martial, the Commissioners of Subsistence, and the office of Sanitary Commission, the latter being already established here. Gen. WEITZEL had no sooner established his headquarters here than thousands of citizens besieged him for rations. And as the city is now shut out from all supplies from the country, the crowd of applicants for subsistence is rapidly increasing. This morning there was nothing in the markets but a few small fish caught by negroes. The Capitol, the City Hall and the Capitol-square are filled with a great throng of all classes, condition, sexes and ages, with basket in hand and an appealing expression of face. What the regulations yet are in regard to the issue of rations to the citizens, I do not know, but a limited quantity is being supplied them at present.

In order to study this peculiar social feature of the rebellion, I mingled with these crowds this morning for a short time, to observe their temper, desires and condition. They were, of course, largely made up of what appeared to be the poorer classes, and many negroes were among them, some for subsistence for themselves and some as servants of families. I found many whose intelligent expression of countenance, fair features and attempted gentility of dress, indicated that they were of the higher classes, on whom the demands of want and hunger were as insatiable as upon those of less position. I noticed several ladies approach the officer in charge at the City Hall, genteelly attired, and with their faces so closely veiled as to defy the gaze of the keenest eye. They spoke in such tremulous tones when giving their names as to cause us to suspect their names were as foreign to them as the hunger they now sought to appease had been in days gone by. Many of the wealthiest families, however, who had the means, have far larger supplies of provisions on hand than was consistent with the repeated appeals of Confederate officials for such to spare from their bounty to feed the army.

The exodus of prominent citizens was confined mainly to those connected with the rebel government, and a few who had made themselves very conspicuous in rebel politics—all the rebel Cabinet and their chief assistants, though not much of their clerical force, got away. The preparations for the evacuation began very quietly among the officials. At noon of Sunday the important records of the departments were boxed up and carted to the depot; but very little suspicion was excited among the citizens as to the real state of the case. A strong guard was stationed at the Danville depot, and four trains were got ready, the first of which left, with DAVIS on board, at seven o'clock in the evening, and the last at midnight. DAVIS' family had gone into the country on the Friday preceeding, but not because of any apprehension that the city was to be given up. Very few families left the city, and there are very few vacant houses, the mansions of JEFF. DAVIS and GOV. BILLY SMITH being among those now in want of tenants. The family of Gen. LEE, consisting of his wife, who is an invalid, and three daughters, are among those who remain. They occupy a stylish house on Franklin-street, and for their protection a well disciplined guard is placed at the dwelling, and the family are scrupulously protected from annoyance of any character, the staring gaze of the passer-by hardly being allowed. This is the second time that Mrs. Gen. LEE has been in our hands. She was once captured by our cavalry near White House, in 1862, and sent through our lines to Richmond under flag of truce, by order of Gen. McCLELLAN.

L. L. CROUNSE.

Union Sentiment in Richmond—Projects of Reconstruction—Distinguished Visitors—Recruiting Negro Troops—The Truth about Rebel Enlistment of Negroes.

From Our Own Correspondent.

RICHMOND, Friday, April 7, 1865.

I can give you news, to-day, which will gratify the heart of every loyal American. Virginia will return to the Union, and that right speedily. Desiring to ascertain the exact truth with reference to the alleged existence of a strong Union sentiment in the city, I availed myself of an opportunity to call upon certain gentlemen here whom I had heard alluded to by Secessionists as Union men, and I must say, that I spent two of the happiest hours of my life in full and free conversation with some of the most thorough and radical Union men in the country; men of wealth and position, whose faith has never wavered for an instant, and who, slaveholders, as they are, *demand that Virginia shall be taken back into the Union "under the Emancipation Proclamation;" that no vestige of the rebellion shall be tolerated; that the usurpation State, and Confederate, which has wrecked Virginia, shall not be recognized in a single respect;* that the State Government must be organized anew, by a convention of the people, as soon as that can be properly effected, and the State and its inhabitants thoroughly purged of treason in every shape.

Union sentiments, in this strong form exist here to a far greater extent than has yet been conceived; not alone among the poorer classes,—mechanics and laborers,—*but in wealthy and influential circles, where may be found men who have never lost faith in the Union;* who have confidently anticipated its triumph, and who greeted the old flag with tears of joy. They are men of the John Minor Botts school, and they are the leaven which shall leaven the whole lump here in this venerable old commonwealth of Virginia. They will delight to see the mass of the people treated with magnanimity, but they have felt too deeply the

Continued on Eighth Page.

The New-York Times.

VOL. XIV......NO. 4230. NEW-YORK, SATURDAY, APRIL 15, 1865. PRICE FOUR CENTS

AWFUL EVENT.

President Lincoln Shot by an Assassin.

The Deed Done at Ford's Theatre Last Night.

THE ACT OF A DESPERATE REBEL

The President Still Alive at Last Accounts.

No Hopes Entertained of His Recovery.

Attempted Assassination of Secretary Seward.

DETAILS OF THE DREADFUL TRAGEDY.

[OFFICIAL.]

War Department, Washington, April 15—1:30 A. M.

Maj.-Gen. Dix:

This evening at about 9:30 P. M., at Ford's Theatre, the President, while sitting in his private box with Mrs. Lincoln, Mrs. Harris, and Major Rathburn, was shot by an assassin, who suddenly entered the box and approached behind the President.

The assassin then leaped upon the stage, brandishing a large dagger or knife, and made his escape in the rear of the theatre.

The pistol ball entered the back of the President's head and penetrated nearly through the head. The wound is mortal. The President has been insensible ever since it was inflicted, and is now dying.

About the same hour an assassin, whether the same or not, entered Mr. Seward's apartments, and under the pretence of having a prescription, was shown to the Secretary's sick chamber. The assassin immediately rushed to the bed, and inflicted two or three stabs on the throat and two on the face. It is hoped the wounds may not be mortal. My apprehension is that they will prove fatal.

The nurse alarmed Mr. Frederick Seward, who was in an adjoining room, and hastened to the door of his father's room, when he met the assassin, who inflicted upon him one or more dangerous wounds. The recovery of Frederick Seward is doubtful.

It is not probable that the President will live throughout the night.

Gen. Grant and wife were advertised to be at the theatre this evening, but he started to Burlington at 6 o'clock this evening.

At a Cabinet meeting at which Gen. Grant was present, the subject of the state of the country and the prospect of a speedy peace was discussed. The President was very cheerful and hopeful, and spoke very kindly of Gen. Lee and others of the Confederacy, and of the establishment of government in Virginia.

All the members of the Cabinet except Mr. Seward, are now in attendance upon the President.

I have seen Mr. Sewrrd, but he and Frederick were both unconscious.

EDWIN M. STANTON, Secretary of War.

DETAIL OF THE OCCURRENCE.

Washington, Friday, April 14—12:30 A. M.

The President was shot in a theatre to-night, and is, perhaps, mortally wounded.

Secretary Seward was also assassinated.

SECOND DISPATCH.

Washington, Friday, April 14.

President Lincoln and wife, with other friends, this evening visited Ford's Theatre for the purpose of witnessing the performance of the "American Cousin."

It was announced in the papers that Gen. Grant would also be present, but he took the late train of cars for New-Jersey.

The theatre was densely crowded, and everybody seemed delighted with the scene before them. During the third act, and while there was a temporary pause for one of the actors to enter, a sharp report of a pistol was heard, which merely attracted attention, but suggesting nothing serious, until a man rushed to the front of the President's box, waving a long dagger in his right hand, and exclaiming "*Sic semper tyrannis,*" and immediately leaped from the box, which was in the second tier, to the stage beneath, and ran across to the opposite side, making his escape amid the bewilderment of the audience from the rear of the theatre, and, mounting a horse, fled.

The screams of Mrs. Lincoln first disclosed the fact to the audience that the President had been shot, when all present rose to their feet, rushing toward the stage, many exclaiming "Hang him! hang him!"

The excitement was of the wildest possible description, and of course there was an abrupt termination of the theatrical performance.

There was a rush toward the President's box, when cries were heard: "Stand back and give him air." "Has any one stimulants." On a hasty examination, it was found that the President had been shot through the head, above and back of the temporal bone, and that some of the brain was oozing out. He was removed to a private house opposite to the theatre, and the Surgeon-General of the army, and other surgeons sent for to attend to his condition.

On an examination of the private box blood was discovered on the back of the cushioned rocking chair on which the President had been sitting, also on the partition and on the floor. A common single-barreled pocket pistol was found on the carpet.

A military guard was placed in front of the private residence to which the President had been conveyed. An immense crowd was in front of it, all deeply anxious to learn the condition of the President. It had been previously announced that the wound was mortal; but all hoped otherwise. The shock to the community was terrible.

The President was in a state of syncope, totally insensible, and breathing slowly. The blood oozed from the wound at the back of his head. The surgeons exhausted every effort of medical skill, but all hope was gone. The parting of his family with the dying President is too sad for description.

At midnight, the Cabinet, with Messrs. Sumner, Colfax and Farnsworth, Judge Curtis, Gov. Oglesby, Gen. Meigs, Col. Hay, and a few personal friends, with Surgeon-General Barnes and his immediate assistants, were around his bedside.

The President and Mrs. Lincoln did not start for the theatre until fifteen minutes after eight o'clock. Speaker Colfax was at the White House at the time, and the President stated to him that he was going, although Mrs. Lincoln had not been well, because the papers had announced that Gen. Grant and they were to be present, and, as Gen. Grant had gone North, he did not wish the audience to be disappointed.

He went with apparent reluctance and urged Mr. Colfax to go with him; but that gentleman had made other engagements, and with Mr. Ashman, of Massachusetts, bid him good bye.

When the excitement at the theatre was at its wildest height, reports were circulated that Secretary Seward had also been assassinated.

On reaching this gentleman's residence a crowd and a military guard were found at the door, and on entering it was ascertained that the reports were based on truth.

Everybody there was so excited that scarcely an intelligible word could be gathered, but the facts are substantially as follows:

About 10 o'clock a man rang the bell, and the call having been answered by a colored servant, he said he had come from Dr. Verdi, Secretary Seward's family physician, with a prescription, at the same time holding in his hand a small piece of folded paper, and saying in answer to a refusal that he must see the Secretary, as he was entrusted with particular directions concerning the medicine.

He still insisted on going up, although repeatedly informed that no one could enter the chamber. The man pushed the servant aside, and walked heavily toward the Secretary's room, and was then met by Mr. Frederick Seward, of whom he demanded to see the Secretary, making the same representation which he did to the servant. What further passed in the way of colloquy is not known, but the man struck him on the head with a "billy," severely injuring the skull and felling him almost senseless. The assassin then rushed into the chamber and attacked Major Seward, Paymaster of the United States army and Mr. Hansell, a messenger of the State Department and two male nurses, disabling them all, he then rushed upon the Secretary, who was lying in bed in the same room, and inflicted three stabs in the neck, but severing, it is thought and hoped, no arteries, though he bled profusely.

The assassin then rushed down stairs, mounted his horse at the door, and rode off before an alarm could be sounded, and in the same manner as the assassin of the President.

It is believed that the injuries of the Secretary are not fatal, nor those of either of the others, although both the Secretary and the Assistant Secretary are very seriously injured.

Secretaries Stanton and Welles, and other prominent officers of the government, called at Secretary Seward's house to inquire into his condition, and there heard of the assassination of the President.

They then proceeded to the house where he was lying, exhibiting of course intense anxiety and solicitude. An immense crowd was gathered in front of the President's house, and a strong guard was also stationed there, many persons evidently supposing he would be brought to his home.

The entire city to-night presents a scene of wild excitement, accompanied by violent expressions of indignation, and the profoundest sorrow—many shed tears. The military authorities have dispatched mounted patrols in every direction, in order, if possible, to arrest the assassins. The whole metropolitan police are likewise vigilant for the same purpose.

The attacks, both at the theatre and at Secretary Seward's house, took place at about the same hour—10 o'clock—thus showing a preconcerted plan to assassinate those gentlemen. Some evidence of the guilt of the party who attacked the President are in the possession of the police.

Vice-President Johnson is in the city, and his headquarters are guarded by troops.

ANOTHER ACCOUNT.

Special Dispatch to the New-York Times.

Washington, Friday, April 14. 11:15 P. M.

A stroke from Heaven laying the whole of the city in instant ruins could not have startled us as did the word that broke from Ford's Theatre a half hour ago that the President had been shot. It flew everywhere in five minutes, and set five thousand people in swift and excited motion on the instant.

It is impossible to get at the full facts of the case, but it appears that a young man entered the President's box from the theatre, during the last act of the play of "Our American Cousin," with pistol in hand. He shot the President in the head and instantly jumped from the box upon the stage, and immediately disappeared through the side scenes and rear of the theatre, brandishing a dirk knife and dropping a kid glove on the stage.

The audience heard the shot, but supposing it fired in the regular course of the play, did not heed it till Mrs. Lincoln's screams drew their attention. The whole affair occupied scarcely half a minute, and then the assassin was gone. As yet he has not been found.

The President's wound is reported mortal. He was at once taken into the house opposite the theatre.

As if this horror was not enough, almost the same moment the story ran through the city that Mr. Seward had been murdered in his bed.

Inquiry showed this to be so far true also. It appears a man wearing a light coat, dark pants. slouch hat, called and asked to see Mr. Seward, and was shown to his room. He delivered to Major Seward, who sat near his father, what purported to be a physician's prescription, turned, and with one stroke cut Mr. Seward's throat as he lay on his bed, inflicting a horrible wound, but not severing the jugular vein, and not producing a mortal wound.

In the struggle that followed, Major Seward was also badly, but not seriously, wounded in several places. The assassin rushed down stairs, mounted the fleet horse on which he came, drove his spurs into him, and dashed away before any one could stop him.

Reports have prevailed that an attempt was also made on the life of Mr. Stanton.

Midnight.

The President is reported dead. Cavalry and infantry are scouring the city in every direction for the murderous assassins, and the city is overwhelmed with excitement. Who the assassins were no one knows, though every body supposes them to have been rebels.

Saturday Morning—1 O'clock.

The person who shot the President is represented as about 30 years of age, five feet nine inches in height, sparely built, of light complexion, dressed in dark clothing, and having a genteel appearance. He entered the box, which is known as the State box, being the upper box on the right hand side from the dress-circle in the regular manner, and shot the President from behind, the ball entering the skull about in the middle, behind, and going in the direction of the left eye; it did not pass through, but apparently broke the frontal bone and forced out the brain to some extent. The President is not yet dead, but is wholly insensible, and the Surgeon-General says he cannot live till day-break. The assassin was followed across the stage by a gentleman, who sprang out from an orchestra chair. He rushed through the side door into an alley, thence to the avenue and mounted a dark bay horse, which he apparently received from the hand of an accomplice, dashed up F, toward the back part of the city. The escape was so sudden that he effectually eluded pursuit. The assassin cried "*sic sempre*" in a sharp, clear voice, as he jumped to the stage, and dropped his hat and a glove.

Two or three officers were in the box with the President and Mrs. Lincoln, who made efforts to stop the assassin, but were unsuccessful, and received some bruises. The whole affair, from his entrance into the box to his escape from the theatre, occupied scarcely a minute, and the strongest of the action found everybody wholy unprepared. The assault upon Mr. Seward appeares to have been made almost at the same moment as that upon the President. Mr. Sewards wound is not dangerous in itself, but may prove so in connection with his recent injuries. The two assassins have both endeavored to leave the city to the northwest, apparently not expecting to strike the river. Even so low down as Chain Bridge, cavalry have been sent in every direction to intercept them.

Saturday, 1:30 o'clock A. M.

The President still lies insensible. Messrs. Stanton, Wells, McCulloch, Speed and Usher are with him, as also the Vice-President, the Surgeon-General, and other Surgeons.

There is a great throng about the house, even at this hour.

2 o'clock A. M.

The President still lives, but lies insensible, as he has since the first moment, and no hopes are entertained that he can survive.

The most extravagant stories prevail, among which one is to effect, that Gen. Grant was shot while on his was to Philaphia, of course this is not true.

Another is, that every member of Mr. Seward's family was wounded in the struggle with the assassin there. This also is untrue. Mr. Fred. Seward, the Assistant Secretary, and Major Clarence Seward, of the army, were wounded, neither of them dangerously.

THE CONDITION OF THE PRESIDENT.

Washington, April 15—2:12 A. M.

The President is still alive; but he is growing weaker. The ball is lodged in his brain, three inches from where it entered the skull. He remains insensible, and his condition is utterly hopeless.

The Vice-President has been to see him; but all company, except the members of the Cabinet and of the family, is rigidly excluded.

Large crowds still continue in the street, as near to the house as the line of guards allows.

THE SIEGE OF MOBILE.

Fierce Bombardment of the Spanish Fort—Mobile Papers Announce the Capture of Selma.

New-Orleans, Saturday, April 8, via Cairo, Friday, April 14.

A special dispatch to the New-Orleans *Times*, from the Spanish Fort, dated April 5, says:

"A furious fire was opened on the rebel forts last night from our entire line. During the bombardment a small magazine in the Spanish Fort exploded. The damage is unknown. Quiet prevailed on the 5th. Deserters report from 18,000 to 20,000 troops in and about Mobile, including all the State Reserves, and about 2,000 in the Spanish Fort. The loss outside the Spanish Fort up to the 4th instant amounted to about 500 killed and wounded. The rebel loss exceeds ours."

Adjt.-Gen. Thomas arrived at New-Orleans on the morning of the 7th.

Mobile papers of the 4th inst. announce the capture of Selma, Alabama, with 23 pieces of artillery, and a large amount of Government property.

Fort Sumter Celebration in Bangor.

Bangor, Me., Friday, April 14.

The restoration of the Old Flag to Fort Sumter was celebrated here to-day by a national salute at noon, by a display of all the flags on public and private buildings, and by the raising of the Stars and Strips one thousand feet above the city by means of a monster kite bearing the name of U. S. Grant.

The Madrid *Bolsa* says if the Pope should leave Rome, Spain would confer upon him the Balearic Isles.

The *Politica* says the Pope would rather inhabit the Montpensier Palace at Seville.

EUROPEAN NEWS

TWO DAYS LATER BY THE EUROPA.

The Insult to Our Cruisers by Portugal.

The American Minister at Lisbon Demands Satisfaction.

Dismissal of the Commander of Fort Belan Requested.

Further Advance in Five-Twenties.

FINANCIAL AND COMMERCIAL.

Halifax, Friday, April 14.

The steamship *Europa*, from Liverpool on the 1st, via Queenstown on the 2d inst., arrived here at 2 o'clock this morning. She has 43 passengers for this port, and 30 for Boston. Her dates are two days later than those already received.

The steamship *Cuba*, from New-York, arrived at Liverpool at noon on the 1st inst.

THE STONEWALL AFFAIR.

A Lisbon dispatch, of the 31st of March, says that the American Minister at Lisbon has demanded satisfaction of the Portuguese Government for the firing upon the *Niagara* and *Sacramento* by the Portuguese forts. He also requests the dismissal of the Commander of Fort Belan, and a salute of twenty-one guns to the American flag.

Nothing as yet has been decided in regard to the matter.

A PROPHECY FROM RICHMOND.

The correspondent of the London *Times*, writing from Richmond on the 4th of March, says:

"I am daily more convinced that if Richmond falls and Lee and Johnston are driven from the field, it is but the first stage of this colossal revolution which will then be completed. There will ensue a time when every important town of the South will require to be held by a Yankee garrison, when exultation in New-York will be exchanged for soberness and right reason, and when it will be realized that the closing scenes of this mightiest revolutionary drama will not be played out, save in the times of our children's children."

GREAT BRITAIN.

Parliamentary proceedings on the 30th ult. were unimportant.

In the House of Commons, on the 31st, Lord C. Paget said that the Admiralty had received no proposal for sanctioning or supporting any fresh attempt to reach the North Pole. He was, therefore, unable to say what course the government would take if such a proposal were made.

Mr. Newdegate put some questions as to the idea of the Pope taking up his residence in England, as indicated in some foreign journals.

Lord Palmerston replied that the government respected the Pope personally very much, but for him to come to England would be both an anacronism and a solecism.

The revenue returns for the financial year, ending March 31, show a net increase of over £104,000 on the year. Notwithstanding the great reductions in taxation, the revenue exceeds by nearly half a million sterling the estimates of Mr. Gladstone.

Messrs. Baring's circular says that large business has been done in 5-20 bonds, and that prices advanced early in the week to 57½@58, but have since relapsed to 56½@57—the demand being chiefly from the continent.

On Friday, the telegrams per the steamship *Cuba* were received, and 5-20s again advanced to 57¾@58¼. Erie and Illinois Central Shares have also attracted attention, and have again advanced.

The Bank of England on the 30th ult. reduced its rate of discount to 4 per cent., at which there is a fair demand for money. This movement strengthened the English funds, and Consols are buoyant and advancing.

Kelson, Tritton & Co., East India and general merchants, have suspended payment. Their liabilities are estimated at £900,000 sterling.

Another provincial bank has suspended, the Portsmouth and South Hants Banking Company. Their liabilities are about £170,000 sterling.

The Birmingham and Joint Stock Banking Company had agreed to take up the business of Atwood & Spooner's Bank, which lately suspended at Birmingham, and to pay the creditors 11s. 3d. on the pound.

The West India Mail steamer had arrived, with over two and a quarter millions of dollars in specie. She also brought several Captains of blockade-runners, whose occupations were gone.

THE ATLANTIC TELEGRAPH.

The French Government will probably send one or two steamers to accompany the two that are sent by the English Government with the *Great Eastern* across the Atlantic, at the time of laying the Atlantic cable, and it is hoped that the United States Government will do the same.

FRANCE.

Weekly returns from the Bank of France show an increase of cash on hand of over ten and a half millions francs.

In the French Chambers of the 30th, M. Jules Favre spoke upon the necessity for political liberty, but was interrupted by the President and declined to finish his speech. The amendment was rejected.

The amendment in favor of the liberty of the press was debated, but rejected by a large majority.

It is stated that Napoleon will leave Paris early in May, not returning until November. His physicians have recommended seven months' absence in the country air.

The Bourse is firm, 67.45.

SPAIN.

The *Epoca* states that the Minister of War tendered his resignation, and that Gen. Leorsundi refused to place him.

A later dispatch says the Minister of War resigned from ill health.

Gen. Rivera succeeded to the office.

DENMARK.

The King relieved M. Hellzen, Minister of Justice, of his functions. Hellzen represented the alliance between the Reactionary and extreme Democratic parties. It is supposed that all members of the late Cabinet will return to their posts.

ITALY

In the allocutions delivered at the last consistory the Pope expressed surprise and sorrow at the sad events which have recently taken place in Mexico. His Holiness hoped Maximilian would abandon the course upon which he had entered, and satisfy the just desires of the Holy See. The Pope further thanked the Bishops of the Catholic world, especially those of Italy, for defending the religion and liberties of the Church, despite the decrees of the secular authorities.

PRUSSIA.

In the Military Committee of Chambers, the Deputies amendment was introduced with the object of effecting a reconciliation between the government and chamber, and proposing a maximum strength of the army at 180,000 men, which was rejected by 11 to 8. The committee also rejected the general military estimates and navy estimates and amendments, thus refusing the whole military and naval proposals of the government.

AUSTRIA.

Count Mensdorff had made some ministerial explanation in the Lower House Reichsrath. He said the views of the government on the question of the Duchies would be communicated in the Federal Diet on the 6th of April.

As regards relations with Italy, he said the government desired to promote the material interests of the two countries, but that Italy maintained a hostile attitude to the government. He desired to economize, but must maintain the position of Austria as a great Power.

INDIA.

A private Calcutta telegram of March 27 reports commercial affairs in much the same state as on the 25th, when slight improvement had taken place.

BRAZIL.

London, Sunday, April 2.

The Brazilian mail has reached Lisbon, bringing the following dates:

Rio de Janeiro, Saturday, March 11.

Exchange 25⅞@26¼.

Coffee.—Sales of good firsts at 6$106. Shipments 100,000 bags. Stock, 100,000 bags. Freights 50@62½.

Bahia, Saturday, March 11.

Exchange 26¼.

Cotton nominal.

Pernambuco, Saturday, March 11.

Exchange 26⅞@27.

Montivedeo has surrendered to Gen. Flores. The Brazilians now occupy the city.

LATEST VIA LIVERPOOL.

Liverpool, Saturday Evening, April 1, 1865.

The *Times* to-day has an editorial on the amended tariff law of the United States. It says:

"It is impossible to find an excuse for it. Tried by the light of reason or by the results of experience it is alike condemned."

It ironically credits the framers of the scheme with peculiar wisdom in selecting the 1st of April for its inauguration.

The *Army & Navy Gazette* says: "The work of the United States Navy has now been accomplished, and it must be confessed that in the hands of Farragut and Porter the high reputation which the officers and seamen of that Power established soon after the national existence of itself, has been greatly enhanced."

LATEST VIA QUEENSTOWN.

London, Saturday, April 1.

There is no news of importance this morning.

Paris, Friday, March 31—P. M.

The Bourse is steady. The Rentes closed at 67f. 30c.

COMMERCIAL.

LIVERPOOL MARKET.

Liverpool, April 31.—Evening.

The Market report was received per *Moravian*.

Cotton—The stock of Cotton in port is 580,000 bales by actual count, being 13,000 bales below the estimates, of which amount 48,000 bales are American.

TRADE REPORT.

The Manchester market was firmer with an upward tendency.

Breadstuffs—The market is easier. Messrs. Richardson, Spence & Co., and others, report: Flour dull and easier. Wheat quiet and quotations are barely maintained; red Western 8s.@8s. 8d. Corn inactive; mixed 27s. 6d.

Provisions—The market is downward. Wakefield, Nash & Co., and others, report: Beef has a downward tendency. Pork heavy and declined 2s. 6d. Bacon firmer and holders demand an advance. Lard dull and easier at 58s.@61s. Butter flat and declining. Tallow downward.

Produce.—Ashes easier at 29s. 6d. for Pots, and 30s. for Pearls. Sugar, flat. Coffee, quiet and steady. Rice, quiet and steady. Clover Seed, firmer. Jute, 10s.@30s. lower. Cod Oil, quiet at 57s. Sperm Oil, no sales. Linseed Oil, steady. Resin, very dull. Spirits Turpentine, quiet at 65s.@66s.

Petroleum—Boult, English & Brandon report: Petroleum firm, at 1s. 11d.@2s. for refined; no crude in market.

LONDON MARKETS.

Flour firm; Wheat steady. Iron advancing; bars and rails, £6 10s.@£6 15s; Scotch pig, 52s. 3d. Sugar inactive. Coffee active at a decline of 1s.@2s. Tea steady at 10½d. for common Congou. Rice steady. Spirits Turpentine firm at 67s. Petroleum steady at £18 for crude, 2s. for refined. Sperm Oil nominal at £82. Tallow downward, at 40s @43s. Linseed Oil flat.

LATEST COMMERCIAL.

Liverpool, Saturday, April 1—Evening.

Cotton—Sales to-day 6,000 bales, including 2,000 bales to speculators and exporters. The market is less firm but quiet and unchanged.

Breadstuffs—The market is quiet and steady.

Provisions—The market is dull.

Produce—The market is quiet and steady. Petroleum firm at 2s.@2s. 0½d. for refined.

London, Saturday, April 1—Evening.

Consols closed at 89⅞@90 for money.

American Stocks—Illinois Central Railroad 61¾@62¼; Erie Railroad 36¼@36¾; United States Five-twenties 57⅜@58¼.

Gen. Lee in Richmond—The Oath of Allegiance.

Baltimore, Friday, April 14.

The Richmond *Whig* of yesterday contains little of importance. It announces the arrival of Gen. Lee on the night previous.

The *Whig* publishes the oath of allegiance, which it says citizens will be required to swear and subscribe to. The Provost-Marshal's office is crowded with people anxious to take it, and the only question among citizens seems to be who shall be first to renew their citizenship.

Rejoicings at Cincinnati.

Cincinnati, Friday, April 14.

Business was entirely suspended to-day. The city was universally decorated with flags, and great enthusiasm prevailed. The procession was an immense affair, comprising the entire police force, Gens. Hooker and Wallich, with their staffs, four regiments of National Guards, discharged veterans, ward organizations, the Fenian Brotherhood, the Fire Department, and a large number of colored citizens. All the bells in the city were rung, and salutes were fired at 6 o,clock this evening. To-night the city is brilliantly illuminated, and there is generally a display of fireworks.

Fire.

Rochester, N. Y., Friday, April 14.

The cabinet warehouse of James E. Haydon, of this city, was partially destroyed by fire this morning. The stocks of Humphrey Reedy & Co., stove dealers, Hastings & McVean, paper dealers, S. B. Roby, saddlery and hardware dealers, and the agency of the American Tract Society, were damaged. Total loss, $30,000; insurance, $20,000. The origin of the fire is unknown.

The Funeral of Gen. T. A. Smyth.

Wilmington, Del., Friday, April 14.

The remains of Brig.-Gen. T. A. Smyth arrived here to-day at 1 o'clock, and will be interred on Monday afternoon with appropriate ceremonies.

An Unseaworthy War Steamer.

To the Editor of the New-York Times:

United States Steamer Muscoota, Hampton Roads, Va., Wednesday, April 12, 1865.

This vessel has returned to this port, having made her fourth attempt to make a cruise to the Pacific. On each occasion she has proved herself to be an unsafe sea boat. On her last trial she narrowly escaped being lost in the Gulf Stream. Inclosed you will find a list of her officers; please publish. Respectfully, &c.,

ARTHUR BURTIS, Jr., Paymaster.

List of officers attached to the U. S. steamer *Muscoota*, one thousand tons, 10 guns:

Commander Geo. M. Ransom, Lieut. Thos. S. Spencer, Ass't Paymaster Arthur Burtis, Jr., Ass't Surgeon Danl. McMurtrie, Act'g Master Geo. R. Durand, Act'g Ensigns Robt. M. Clark, Jas. Courtney, John D. Thomas, Chas. A. Stewart, Second Ass't Engineers Robert H. Gunnell, Jas. H. Grasmer, Henry Snyder, Act'g Third Ass't Engineers Robt. L. Case, Geo. Taylor, Geo. Westinghouse, Jr., Masters Fred'k. A. Beatie, A. I. Spinney, Wm. Merrill, Captain's Clerk Geo. S. Dana, Paymasters Clerk P. B. Hathaway.

Arrivals in the City.

Gov. Jos. A. Gilmore, Concord, N. H., is stopping at the Fifth-avenue Hotel.

Hon. O. N. Shannon, Cincinnati; Gen. B. F. Stringfellow, Atchison; Dr. N. Greene, Louisville, and Wm. D. Griswold, Terre Haute, are stopping at the Metropolitan Hotel.

Collision.—The steamship *La Favorete*, while returning from a trial trip and passing up the East River, collided with the Catharine Ferry-boat *Manhassett*, as she was entering her slip on the Brooklyn side, doing considerable damage to the *Manhassett*, by tearing away a portion of the gentlemen's cabin, and somewhat injuring the hull. Fortunately nobody was hurt.

The New-York Times.

VOL. XV......NO. 4631. NEW-YORK, MONDAY, JULY 30, 1866. PRICE FOUR CENT

THE ATLANTIC CABLE.

Successful Completion of the Great Work.

The Old and New Worlds Joined Together.

Perfect Working Throughout The Line.

London Dispatches of Friday Received.

History of the Voyage Across the Ocean.

Wonderfully Fortunate Condition of the Weather.

Daily Record of Miles of Cable Laid.

Congratulatory Dispatches from Cyrus W. Field.

Dispatch to President Johnson and His Reply.

Dispatch to Secretary Seward and His Reply.

The Old Cable to be Taken Up and Finished.

The Line Soon to be Open to the Public.

[We announced in a postscript to the TIMES of yesterday morning the auspicious event here more particularly recorded—*the landing and successful working of the Atlantic Cable*. This news should have reached us on Friday afternoon, but there is a gap of 90 miles between Cape Breton and Newfoundland, where there is no telegraph cable, so that dispatches must be brought by steamer from Port au Basque to Aspy Bay. Below we give all that has been received, and as the news yacht returned last night to Port au Basque, we shall have nothing more until she arrives some time to-day.]

THE GREAT WORK ACCOMPLISHED.

The Atlantic Cable Laid, and in Working Order.

NEW-YORK, Sunday—3 A. M.

The following dispatch has just been received from CYRUS W. FIELD:

HEART'S CONTENT, Saturday, July 28.

We arrived here at 9 o'clock this morning, all well, thank God. The cable has been laid, and is in perfect working order. CYRUS W. FIELD.

America in Telegraphic Communication with Europe.

SECOND DISPATCH.

HEART'S CONTENT, Saturday, July 28.

We are in telegraphic communication with Ireland!

The Cable is in perfect order.

CYRUS W. FIELD.

Messages Sent and Received Constantly.

THIRD DISPATCH.

HEART'S CONTENT, Saturday, July 28.

England and America are again united by telegraph. The cable is in perfect order.

We have been receiving and sending messages through the whole cable ever since the splice on the 13th inst. off Valentia.

CYRUS W. FIELD.

Further Particulars—Miles Run and Miles of Cable Laid—The Weather.

HEART'S CONTENT, Friday, July 27, 1866—9:30.

The *Great Eastern* has just anchored opposite the telegraph office. The cable spliced two hours since on the Medway. Will be here in three or four hours. Whole distance run, 1,669 nautical miles. Cable paid out 1,864 miles; slack was little less than 12 per cent. absolute distance.

CYRUS W. FIELD says the weather was terribly rough; rain squalls and fogs nearly all the time. The signals never failed, but were perfect all the time. He sent a telegram to London a day or two since, and got a reply in eight minutes. Last night he got the following telegram:

A Dispatch from Ireland.

VALENCIA BAY, July 26, 1866.

BARLEY TO FIELD, GREAT EASTERN.

Congratulate you heartily. All well here.

HISTORY OF THE WORK.

Operations of the Fleet—Names and Duties of the Vessels.

HEART'S CONTENT, Sunday, July 29.

The steamship *Great Eastern* left Sheerness on Saturday at noon, June 30; arrived at Bear-Haven on Thursday morning, July 5, and received the balance of her coal and provisions.

The other steamers joined the *Great Eastern* at Bearhaven as follows: The *Wm. Corry* and *Terrible* on Friday, July 6th, and the *Albany* on the 7th, and the *Medway* on Tuesday, the 10th inst.

Laying of the Shore End on the Irish Coast.

On Saturday, the 7th of July, the end of the Irish shore cable was landed from the *William Corry*, and at 2:30 the next morning the laying was successfully completed and the end buoyed in 94 fathoms: latitude 51° 40'; longitude 11° 8'; distance from the telegraph house at Valentia, 27¼ miles; 29¼ miles of cable paid out.

WEDNESDAY, 11TH INST.—H. M. S. *Racoon*, arrived at Bearhaven to render all assistance in her power.

Prayers for Success.

THURSDAY, 12TH INST.—The *Great Eastern, Medway, Albany, Terrible* and *Racoon*, near one another. Services held at Valentia and prayers offered up for the successful laying of the cable.

Connecting the Shore End with the Main Cable on the Great Eastern.

FRIDAY, THE 13TH.—The shore end was connected to the main cable on board the *Great Eastern*, and at 2:40 P. M. the telegraph fleet started for New-Foundland, and the *Racoon* returned to Valentia.

The Start—Order of Sailing—Condition of the Weather.

The telegraph fleet sailed in the following order: The *Terrible* ahead of the *Great Eastern*, on the starboard bow, the *Medway* on the port, and the *Albany* on the starboard quarter. Weather thick and foggy, with heavy rains.

Signals Perfect through 2,440 Miles of Cable.

Signals sent through the cable on board the *Great Eastern*, and to the telegraph house at Valentia. Two thousand four hundred and forty nautical miles found perfect.

Distance Run and Miles of Cable Laid Each Day.

SATURDAY, 14TH.—Distance run, 108 miles; cable paid out, 116 miles.

SUNDAY, 15TH.—Distance run, 128 miles; cable paid out, 139 miles.

MONDAY, 16TH.—Distance run, 115 miles; cable paid out, 137 miles.

TUESDAY, 17TH.—Distance run, 118 miles; cable paid out, 138 miles.

WEDNESDAY, 18TH.—Distance run, 108 miles; cable paid out, 125 miles.

THURSDAY, 19TH.—Distance run, 122 miles; cable paid out, 129 miles.

FRIDAY, 20TH.—Distance run, 117 miles; cable paid out, 127 miles.

SATURDAY, 21ST.—Distance run, 122 miles; cable paid out, 136 miles.

SUNDAY, 22D.—Distance run, 123 miles; cable paid out, 133 miles.

MONDAY, 23D.—Distance run, 121 miles; cable paid out, 138 miles.

TUESDAY, 24TH.—Distance run, 121 miles; cable paid out, 135 miles.

WEDNESDAY, 25TH.—Distance run, 112 miles; cable paid out, 130 miles.

THURSDAY, 26TH.—Distance run, 128 miles; cable paid out, 134 miles.

FRIDAY, 27TH.—Distance run, 112 miles; cable paid out, 118 miles; which, with shore end off Valentia, distance 27 miles, cable paid out 29 miles, makes distance run 1,669 miles, and paid out, 1,864 miles.

Arrival at Heart's Content—Average Speed During the Voyage.

Arrived at Heart's Content at 8 A. M., Friday, July 27.

The average speed of the ship from the time the splice was made until we saw land was a little less than five nautical miles per hour, and the cable has been paid out at an average of five and one-half miles per hour.

The total slack was less than twelve per cent.

Remarkably Favorable Weather.

The weather has been more pleasant than I have ever known on the Atlantic at this season of the year.

We have had alternate days of rain, sunshine, fogs and squalls.

Copies of the Diary for the Press.

I have requested Mr. JOHN C. DEAN, Secretary of the Anglo-American Telegraph Company, to send you by the first opportunity, for the Associated Press, twenty-five copies of his diary, which will give you a detailed account of the ups and downs experienced in laying a cable across the Atlantic.

Communication Uninterrupted from the Moment of Starting.

We have been in constant communication with Valentia since the splice was made on the 13th inst., and have daily received news from Europe which was posted up outside of the telegraph office for the information of all on board of the *Great Eastern* and signaled to the other ships.

The Old Cable to be Recovered and Completed.

After taking in coals the telegraph fleet will sail for the spot where the cable was lost last year, recover the end and complete a second line between Ireland and Newfoundland, and then the *Medway* will proceed to lay the new cable across the Gulf of St. Lawrence.

The Line Soon to be Open for the Transmission of Business Dispatches.

The cable will be open for business in a few days, and all messages sent to Europe in the order they are received at Heart's Content.

Thanks to All the Men Engaged in the Great Work.

I cannot find words suitable to convey my admiration for the men who have so ably conducted the nautical, engineering and electrical departments of this enterprise so successfully amid difficulties which required to be seen to be appreciated. In fact, all on board of the telegraph fleet, and all connected with the enterprise, have done their very best to have the cable made and laid in a perfect condition, and He who rules the winds and the waves has crowned their united efforts with perfect success.

CYRUS W. FIELD.

CONGRATULATIONS.

Mr. Field to President Johnson.

HEART'S CONTENT, July 27.

To His Excellency President Johnson, Washington, D. C.:

SIR: The Atlantic Cable has been successfully completed this morning. I hope that it will prove a blessing to England and the United States, and increase the intercourse between our own country and the Eastern Hemisphere.

Yours faithfully, CYRUS W. FIELD.

PRESIDENT JOHNSON'S REPLY.

WASHINGTON, July 29.

To Cyrus W. Field, Heart's Content:

I heartily congratulate you, and trust that your enterprise may prove as successful as your efforts have been persevering. May the cable under the sea tend to promote harmony between the Republic of the West and the Governments of the Eastern Hemisphere.

ANDREW JOHNSON.

Mr. Field to Secretary Seward.

HEART'S CONTENT, July 27.

To Hon. Wm. H. Seward, Washington, D. C.:

The telegraph cable has been successfully laid between Ireland and Newfoundland. I remember with gratitude your services in the Senate of the United States in the Winter of 1857, and recollect with pleasure the speech you then made in favor of the telegraph bill. That you may never have reason to regret what you have done to establish communication across the Atlantic, is the sincere wish of your friend, CYRUS W. FIELD.

SECRETARY SEWARD'S REPLY.

WASHINGTON, D. C., July 29.

Cyrus W. Field, Heart's Content:

Acknowledgments and congratulations. If the Atlantic Cable had not failed in 1858, European States would not have been led in 1861 into the great error of supposing that civil war in America could either perpetuate African Slavery or divide this Republic. Your great achievement constitutes, I trust, an effective treaty of international neutrality and non-intervention. WM. H. SEWARD.

Mr. Field's Congratulations.

HEART'S CONTENT, July 27.

To the Honorary Directors of the Atlantic Telegraph Company:

I congratulate you on the successful completion of telegraphic communication between Ireland and Newfoundland, and hope within two weeks from this time to inform you that the cable lost last year has been recovered, and that a second line is in operation across the Atlantic. I assure you that all on board the telegraph fleet will do all that they can to accomplish this object. CYRUS W. FIELD.

HEART'S CONTENT, July 27.

To the Directors of the New-York, Newfoundland and London Telegraph Company:

We arrived this day. The cable has been laid across the Atlantic, and is in perfect working order. As soon as we have taken in coal we shall proceed to the spot where the cable was lost last year, and when recovered, splice it with the cable on board of the *Great Eastern*, and return to this place. Then the *Medway* will proceed to lay the cable across the Gulf of St. Lawrence. I cannot express to you how thankful I feel that you will now receive some return for the money that you have spent and the time that you have devoted during the last half year to connect by telegraph our own country with Great Britain.

CYRUS W. FIELD.

List of Directors.

The following is a list of the Directors of the New-York, Newfoundland and London Telegraph Company: PETER COOPER, CYRUS W. FIELD, MOSES TAYLOR, MARSHALL O. ROBERTS, WILSON G. HUNT. The officers of the Company are: PETER COOPER, President; CYRUS W. FIELD, Vice-President; MOSES TAYLOR, Treasurer; ROBERT W. LOWBER, Secretary.

LATEST FROM ASPY BAY.

No More Dispatches from the Cable—The News Yacht Returns to the Newfoundland Shore—She will Bring Later Advices on Monday Morning.

ASPY BAY, C. B., Sunday, July 29—8:30 P. M.

All dispatches from Europe via Heart's Content and Port au Basque, being merely relative to the successful laying of the cable, have been forwarded by telegraph from this point, and the News Yacht sailed this afternoon on her return to Port au Basque. Another vessel will arrive to-morrow (Monday) morning from Port au Basque with further advices from the cable and Europe. The telegraph lines are in good working order.

PAST HISTORY.

Early Ocean Cable—First and Second Atlantic Cables—Failures and Lessons for Improvement—Differences in Construction—Beginning of the Present Voyage—What and Where is Heart's Content.

The first successful submarine telegraph was laid between Dover and Calais, a distance of twenty-four miles, in 1850, since when a great have been built and successfully worked:

Of course, no one at that time dreamed of an Atlantic cable: that was further along—a younger brother, whose birth was as yet uncontemplated from the womb of time, whose prophecied coming even would have been received with shouts of "derisive laughter." In 1851 the columns of the London *Athenæum* contained a proposition from an adventurous speculator, who suggested that a wire, enveloped in a double coat of gutta percha and hemp, might easily be laid between the coast of Ireland and Newfoundland. The proposition met with no favor, but much discussion. The

SCIENTIFIC DIFFICULTIES.

in the way were such as to disarm the project of possible success. For instance: In the ordinary arrangement of the wires of the telegraph, where they are stretched upon posts, and insulated by glass and the surrounding air, the current runs along as a simple stream, and with a velocity almost inappreciable, while, when the wires are inclosed in a sheet of insulating substance, and placed in a metallic envelope or moist medium, the case is materially different. The influence of induction becomes a retarding power. As soon as the central wire becomes electrically excited, that excitement operates upon the adjoining layer of metal, or moisture, and calls up in it an electrical force of an opposite kind. Each of these forces holds fast an equivalent portion of the other, and the electricity of the central wire is thus prevented from freely moving onward. In other words, it was found that a submarine cable was virtually a lengthened Leyden jar, transmitting signals while being charged and discharged, instead of allowing the stream to flow dynamically and evenly along it. When used it must first be filled, then emptied, a very simple operation, of course, but one requiring time, and time, too, depending on the length of the line, as it was demonstrated that the length increased the time proportionately.

Electricians throughout the scientific world devoted themselves to a solution of the problem, and many interesting and instructive experiments were made, resulting in great benefit to the progress of science. In 1855, when more complete and perfect instruments were available, and when new lines of telegraph afforded facilities for experiments, it was found that a current required a second and a half to discharge itself after a movement through 1,146 miles of wire. This was a rate of speed which precluded the use of the wire for commercial purposes, and putting quite beyond the power of capitalists the making of a line for the sake of profit. Experiments were then tried with different kinds of electricity over the same wire, it being hoped that the following current might clear away the preceding. The result was a success, and by the alternate working of positive and negative currents, the electric equilibrium of the wire was continually restored, each current cleaning away the inductive influence of its predecessors which had been left behind, and the operator securing a perfect record of seven or eight currents in a single second. It was also found that successive charges of electricity, either of the same or opposite kinds, could travel along lengthened conducting wires simultaneously, following each other like waves of the sea. Alternate positive and negative signals were sent along 900 miles of wire at the rate of eight signals per second, and two signals reached the terminus after the act of transmission had ended. This, therefore indicated the overcoming of one of the difficulties, showing a way in which the rapidity of transmitting electrical currents along a submarine wire could be increased; it needed simply the use of opposite currents—positive and negative alternately.

It was also feared that a diminution of the currents' power to produce mechanical effects, and a loss of speed, would naturally occur, thereby materially interfering with the practical working of the wire. Experiments were made with the voltaic and magneto-electric currents, with large wires and small wires, and it was conclusively demonstrated that the loss of power was slight; that the maximum speed of the magneto-electric current was six times greater than that of the voltaic, and that small wires are infinitely preferable to larger ones.

These points settled, it was conceded that, theoretically, no farther difficulties stood in the way of a usage of an Atlantic telegraph, once laid; it was then necessary only to ascertain whether signals actually sent by currents through 2,000 miles of cable could be accurately recorded. Under the skillful manipulation of Mr. BRIGHT, the engineer, and Mr. WHITEHOUSE, the electrician, ten gutta-percha covered wires, each 200 miles in length, were connected, so that a continuous circuit of 2,000 miles was obtained. Through the whole length signals were distinctly and satisfactorily passed at the rate of 210, 241 and 270 per minute. Experiment having shown that the conditions present in insulated wires under the ground and beneath the sea are analogous, the result was regarded as establishing, beyond all reasonable doubt, the practicability of working the Transatlantic Telegraph.

This brief synopsis sweeps away the rubbish of time's delay, and brings us to the threshhold of the great undertaking of the age, the

LAYING OF THE ATLANTIC CABLE.

There need be no grand and lofty chirographicies at this point. The enterprise possesses all elements of moral and political grandeur, needing no trumpetuous heralding nor unseemly puffing. Should success crown the effort, whether it be to-day or a hundred years from to-day, the conception and undertaking of so grand an achievement can be surpassed in sublimity only by its completion. Of the Company which first determined to invest its capital in the hazardous enterprise, Messrs. CYRUS W. FIELD and PETER COOPER, both of New-York, were the prominent men. Having secured a charter in April, 1854, it appointed Prof. MORSE as electrician, and proceeded to connect St. Johns, N. F., with the lines already in operation in the British North American Provinces and the United States, by submerging thirteen miles of cable across the Straits of Northumberland, and eighty-five miles in the waters of the St. Lawrence. England and the Continent had already been connected with Ireland, irrespective of any design to extend the telegraphic communication toward the West, so that there then remained but a single gap to fill in—the Atlantic basin. The solution of the problem, where to cross and how to do it, thenceforth occupied the attention of the directors and the distinguished professionals retained in the service of the company. Without entering at all upon the discussions of many nice questions which came before them for determination—discussions which, in a scientific journal, would be both pertinent and interestingly instructive—we will state the results of the investigations. They taught

That gutta-percha covered submarine wires do not transmit as simple insulated conductors, but that they have to be charged as Leyden jars before they can transmit at all.

That, consequently, such wires transmit with a velocity that is in no way accordant to the movement of the electrical current, in an unembarrassed way, along simple conductors.

That magneto-electric currents travel more quickly along such wires than simple voltaic currents.

That magneto-electric currents travel more quickly when in high energy than when in low although voltaic currents of large intensity do not travel more quickly than similar currents of smaller intensity.

That the velocity of transmission of signals along insulated submerged wires can be enormously increased, from the rate indeed of one in two seconds to the rate of eight in a single second, by making each alternate signal with a current of different quality, positive following negative, and negative following positive.

That the diminution of the velocity of the transmission of the magneto-electric current in inductive-embarrassed coated wires, is not in the inverse ratio of the square of the distance traversed, but much more nearly in the ratio of simple arithmetic progression.

That several distinct waves of electricity may be traveling along different parts of a long wire simultaneously, and within certain limits, without interference.

That large-coated wires used beneath the waters or the earth are worse conductors than small ones, so far as velocity of transmission is concerned, and therefore are not so well suited as small ones for the purposes of submarine transmission of telegraphic signals; and

That by the use of comparatively small-coated wires and of electro-magnetic inductive coils for the exciting agent, telegraphic signals can be transmitted through 2,000 miles with a speed amply sufficient for all commercial and economic purposes.

With full faith in the power omnipotent of combined science and wealth, the celebrated Atlantic Telegraph Company was formed, mainly by the influence of Mr. CYRUS W. FIELD, who was sent by his American associates in 1856 to England with a view of effecting such arrangements as in his opinion promised best for the completion of the great enterprise. Three hundred and fifty shares of one thousand pounds each were taken, the charters, and grants, and privileges, and patents of the old companies were made over to the new, and everything that money could secure or science suggest was at its disposal.

THE ROUTE,

however, was yet to be selected. It's one thing to buy a horse and quite another thing to keep him; it's one matter to project a telegraph and buy the wire; it's quite another to lay the wire and run the machine. Several routes were proposed, but as they were rejected we need not allude to them. The one which gave the greatest satisfaction is known as the telegraphic plateau, which is only some 12,000 feet below the level of the sea, and extends in a continuous ledge from Cape Clear, in Ireland, to Cape Race, in Newfoundland; the greatest depth being in mid-ocean, whence it ascends imperceptibly to the shore on either side. To verify the information then in the possession of the scientific world, Lieut. BERRIMAN was twice dispatched in the *Arctic* to make soundings along the proposed line, while as a check upon his observations, Her Britannic Majesty's steamer *Cyclops* traversed the ground in an opposite direction. The knowledge thus obtained was conclusive. The plain was gently leveled, so deep as to be below the reach of disturbing superficial causes and composed of particles of shells, so minutely triturated as to render their character indetectible save with the aid of the microscope. The presence of these shells clearly showed by the light of science that for ages these profound depths had rested in undisturbed security, that for uncounted centuries unmoved by the warring elements or the flow of waters, entire quiet, absolute repose had reigned along the bottom of the deep. It encouraged also the hope that the cable, when once laid, might rest as tranquilly—perchance as long, while the tendency evinced by these infinitessimal fragments to agglutinate to metallic centres held out the probability that the submerged cable would soon be incrusted by them, and a fresh element—if things so old and salty can by any possibility evolve anything fresh—of obscurity so obtained.

If any illustration was needed to show the unflinching determination of the enterprising men in charge, no more signal example could be pointed out than the frequent attempts made to establish a permanent telegraph communication between this country and the Old World. In 1857 the first effort was made, and failed when about 300 miles from the Irish shore. In 1858 it was again attempted with the two halves of the cable stowed in the *Niagara* and *Agamemnon*, and the terrific hurricane which both vessels met with then, no doubt, did serious injury to their easily injured freight. Nevertheless, the effort was persevered with, and some 100 miles were laid and lost between the two ships. Again the "wire squadron," as it was called, returned to Ireland, to start again for another attempt, and, to the astonishment of all, the damaged cable was not only laid, but actually worked with clearness for some days, when it gradually become incoherent, then rambling with occasional gleams of intelligence, till at last it became utterly intelligible, and so died out. It is needless to say how unhappily the expedition of last year failed, and to this day it is not known whether the injury to the cable's insulation was caused by accident or wanton mischief. The commercial loss upon these failures has been great, but even out of the evil has come some good, for in the interim the science of making, testing and laying cables has so much improved that an undetected fault in an insulated wire has now become literally impossible, while so much are the instruments for signaling improved that not only can a slight fault be disregarded, if necessary, but it is even easy to work through a submarine wire with a foot of its copper conductor stripped and bare to the water. This latter result, astonishing as it may appear, was actually achieved for some days past with the whole Atlantic cable on board the *Great Eastern*. Out of a length of more than 1,700 miles, a coil was taken from its centre, the copper conductor stripped clean of its insulation for a foot in length, and in this condition lowered over the vessel's side till it rested on the ground. Yet, through this the clearest signals were sent—so clear, indeed, as at one time to raise the question whether it would not be worth while to grapple for the first old Atlantic cable ever laid, and, with these new instruments working gently through it for a year or so at least, make it pay its cost. Nothing, in fact can give a better idea of the change which has come over the science of submarine telegraphy than by the statement of the manner in which the three cables of 1858, 1865, and that of this year have been constructed. The actual constituents of each is as follows:

CONDUCTORS.

Conductor in 1858.—A copper strand, consisting of seven wires, (six laid round one,) and weighing 107 pounds per nautical mile.

Ditto, 1865.—Copper strand, consisting of seven wires, (six laid round one,) and weighing 300 pounds per nautical mile, embedded for solidity in Chatterton's compound. Gauge of single wire .049—ordinary 18 gauge. Gauge of strand .144—ordinary No. 10 gauge.

Ditto in 1866.—Same.

INSULATION.

Insulator in 1858.—Guttapercha laid on in three coverings, and weighing 261 pounds per knot.

Insulation in 1865.—Guttapercha, four layers of which are laid on alternately with four thin layers of Chatterton's compound. The weight of the entire insulation, 400 pounds per nautical mile. Diameter of core, .464; circumference of core, 1.392.

Insulator in 1866.—Same.

EXTERNAL PROTECTION.

External Protection in 1858.—Eighteen strands of charcoal iron wire, each strand composed of seven wires (six laid round one) laid spirally round the core, which latter was previously padded with a serving of hemp saturated with a tar mixture. The separate wires were each 22½ guage; the strand complete was No. 14 guage.

Ditto, 1865.—Ten solid wires of the guage .095 (No. 13 guage) drawn from WEBSTER & HORSFALL's homogeneous iron, each wire surrounded separately with five strands of Manilla yarn, saturated with a preservative compound, and the whole laid spirally round the core, which latter is padded with jute yarn, saturated with preservative mixture.

Ditto, 1866.—Ten solid wires of the gauge .095 (No. 15 gauge) drawn from WEBSTER & HORSFALL's homogeneous iron, and galvanized, each wire surrounded separately with five strands of white Manilla yarn, and the whole laid spirally round the core, which latter is padded with ordinary hemp saturated with preservative mixture.

WEIGHT IN AIR.

Weight in Air in 1858.—20 cwt. per nautical mile.

Weight in Air in 1865.—35 cwt. 3 qrs. per nautical mile.

Weight in Air in 1866.—31 cwt. per nautical mile.

WEIGHT IN WATER.

Weight in Water in 1858.—13.4 cwt. per nautical mile.

Weight in Water in 1865.—14 cwt. per nautical mile.

Weight in Water in 1866.—14½ cwt. per nautical mile.

BREAKING STRAIN.

Breaking Strain in 1858.—3 tons 5 cwt., or equal to 4.85 times its weight in water per knot; that is to say, the cable would bear its own weight in a little less than 5 miles' depth of water.

Breaking Strain in 1865.—7 tons 15 cwt., or equal to 11 times its weight in water per knot; that is to say, the cable would bear its own weight in 11 miles' depth of water.

Breaking Strain in 1866.—8 tons 2 cwt., or equal to 12 times its weight in water per knot; that is to say, the cable will bear its own weight in 12 miles' depth of water.

DEEPEST WATER TO BE ENCOUNTERED.

Deepest water to be encountered, 1858—2,400 fathoms.

Deepest water to be encountered, 1865—2,400 fathoms.

Deepest water to be encountered, 1866—2,400 fathoms.

CONTRACT STRAINS.

Contract strain, 1858—equal to 4.85 times its weight per nautical mile in water.

Contract strain, 1865—equal to 11 times its weight per nautical mile in water.

Contract strain, 1866—equal to 12 times its weight per nautical mile in water.

LENGTH OF CABLE SHIPPED.

Length of cable shipped, 1858, 2,174 nautical miles.

Length of cable shipped, 1865, 2,300 nautical miles.

Length of cable to be shipped, to complete both lines, 1866, 2,730 miles.

From the improvement which these comparative cables show, both in the increased strength of the rope, its increased conductivity by the enlarged copper wire, and, above all, by its increased and more carefully guarded insulation, any one will be able to see at a glance what strides have been made toward ultimate perfection. But it is chiefly in what cannot be seen, nor even easily explained to the general reader in the instruments for detecting faults, and for working through them when they are detected, that the main progress has been made, and in this the expedition which will start next week is as perfect as the present high condition of electrical science can make it.

THE FINAL ARRANGEMENTS.

All the final arrangements for the sailing of this great mechanical and scientific expedition were settled. The great ship received her last length of cable from the *Iris*, and every part of the *Great Eastern* was got into the most perfect order. The machinery by which in less than four minutes her paddles can be disconnected and made to work independently of each other, was tried and found to answer admirably, and this improvement is of the last importance in keeping the ship on the same spot while engaged in hauling up the cable laid last Summer. It was then attempted to put a very powerful wrought-iron guard over the screw, so that in backing astern full power there should not be the least risk of the screw fouling the cable. For this purpose the ship was trimmed down by the head considerably, in order to bring her stern well out of water. After a while, however, it was wisely decided not to affix such a guard, and those who remember the imminent risk of loss to which the *Agamemnon* was exposed in the storm of 1858, by a similar apparatus, will not be sorry to hear that the *Great Eastern* sailed without one this time.

THE SHORE END

on the other side was successfully laid by the squadron, after a voyage devoid of incident to Valentia, Folhunneram Bay.

The shore end of the cable then was laid on the afternoon of the 6th July, and the regular paying-out commenced on the 7th.

The following Directors of the various Companies concerned sailed in the *Great Eastern*: DANIEL GOOCH, Esq., M. P., Chairman of the Great Eastern Steamship Company; Director of the Anglo-American Telegraph Company; Director of the Telegraph Construction and Maintenance Company.

Mr. CYRUS W. FIELD, Director of the Atlantic Telegraph Company; Director of the Anglo-American Telegraph Company; Vice-President of the New-York, Newfoundland and London Telegraph Company.

Capt. A. F. HAMILTON, Director of the Atlantic Telegraph Company; Director of the Anglo-American Telegraph Company.

HEART'S CONTENT

Let any ordinarily well-educated man ask himself where Heart's Content is, what are its characteristics and peculiarities, and the probabilities are that he will admit that he don't know. He may have an indistinct remembrance of a statement made in the TIMES that one end of the great cable was to rest, after its wearying roll across the ocean, at the place with the pleasant name—but that's all. Newspapers are the prime educators of the people and the cyclopedia of the savant; hence these revelations. There are various ways of reaching Heart's Content, depending, of course, upon the place from which one starts, but Halifax is the common base from which all have finally to commence the journey. Newfoundland, as a whole, has a dreary, desolate significance throughout the world. Fogs, damp clouds of mystification, vast perils for mariners, and oceanic horrors, crowd upon the mind, which perforce dwells upon this island and its history. But as Heart's Content is by no means the gay and festive spot which its felicitous but treacherous cogomen would indicate, so Newfoundland is not all the dreary waste which most people imagine. The selection of a part of its domain as the hither terminus of the cable, will bring it more prominently than ever before the eyes of the civilized world, and it may be well for us to consider some of its good and desirable points. The extreme length of the island is 420 miles, its area 36,000 square miles, and its population not far from 150,000. It was discovered in 1497 by JOHN CABOT, and in honor of the Saint upon whose day the land was made, he called it St. John; subsequently in 1583, Sir HUMPHREY GILBERT styled the entire island Newfoundland, the point at which CABOT landed, retaining the name of St. John. It is calculated that at least one-third of the area is covered with fresh water, of which there are innumerable streams, none being of great size or available for purposes of navigation. The coast presents an aspect by no means inviting. Great, ragged, rugged, craggy cliffs frown along its entire length, chilly fogs surround it, never ending discomfort is shadowed forth to all who approach the coast. The climate on the island itself is by no means unpleasant, particularly at this season of the year it is delightful. Fruits of every kind are produced in limited quantities, and its mineral resources, of which more can be said hereafter, are but waiting the innovations of capital and enterprise of people from the States, to develop wonderfully. But let us go to Heart's Content, after which the general surroundings will be in order. It is much easier to start for it, than reach it. The route embraces a variety of land and water, and the chance of conveyance, always a hazard, is just now extra hazardous, requiring skill, patience, money and perseverance. From Halifax to Portugal Cove the trip is made in a lumbering coach, whose conveniences are nil, and whose charges are extortionate. Thence by a little steamer the route continues to Carbonear, some twenty-two miles distant. Thus far the trip is confined to public conveyance; thence, however, private enterprise must take the onus. There are no stages, for there is ordinarily no travel. Nothing but a long hilly stretch of unbroken country connects the dirty hamlet of Carbonear with the cramped and miserable settlement of Heart's Content. Horses are not numerous, nor are carriages abundant. Avarice does not seem to be a controlling element with the Carbonearse, for money will not always obtain either horse or wagon. If the day be fine, the air bracing, and the walking good, there is generally but little difficulty in obtaining a conveyance, but if one desires to travel at night, or if the day be wet, the walking bad, and the ill-made apology for a road knee-deep in mud, horses are no where, wagons are not to be found, and drivers are beyond the influence of shekels.

Assuming, however, that fortune favored our venture, the dozen or so miles being safely passed, the village or settlement of Heart's Content then looms up. Henceforth and forever the name of Heart's Content will stand side by side with the great names of the world. The cable may snap asunder; eternal fate may defy its success—that makes no difference—Heart's Content was selected as the American terminus of the international coil, and can never again be forgotten or buried deep in Newfoundland fog. In the first place, there are no buildings of note; in the second place there are no people of any consequence. Nothing in or of itself suggested its name nor secured its present prominence. The bay has done all that will hereafter make the name of the place famous. There may be a thousand people at Heart's Content, if one should count all the men, women, very small children and strangers; but we should say that seven hundred was a more rational number. These people fish for a living, and eat fish for sustenance. At the present time their chief source of amusement and profit is the great number of strangers who are accidentally thrown among them. Civilized men, with garments of modern cut, unsoiled and whole, are to these ingenuous people pregnant with curiosity. No man appears upon the narrow street from abroad without being surrounded and accompanied to his place of destination by a throng of men, women and children. These cheerful people may be honest, but their appearance belies their nature; they may be hospitable, but their infernal bills contradict their generosity. They have been accustomed to regard the magnificent harbor which swells temptingly from the neck of land, as a safe place for bathing and an excellent reservoir for fish. Now that it looms before the world as one of the two main points in the history of the age, they transfer their regard for the water to the strangers who discovered its merits, and in their anxiety to do them honor become boresomely omnipresent and pecuniously exacting. Hotels are unknown; boarding-houses, properly so called, do not exist: *ergo*, the honest inhabitants, seeing the great influx of people who need hotels and boarding-houses, have resolved themselves into a guard of swindlers, and adopting, with true British sagacity, the famous Wellingtonian fiction of "Up, guards, and at 'em," as their war cry, are plundering right hand and left, under the fashionable guise of "accommodating a few lodgers, not for their money, but entirely for their sake." These landlords and landladies are bad enough and grasping enough in all conscience; they furnish small rooms at big prices; they spread long tables with slim bills of fare; they complain of the difficulty of obtaining food, but charge as though they not only obtained but furnished it. Then, too, the musquitoes, or rather the musquito-gnat, are the most persistent biters and annoying musicians this side of the infernal band that sit in the gate of Hades. Scientific investigation discloses the startling and provoking fact that the female musquito of this latitude has, in addition to its stomach, a sucking stomach, into which the surplus blood drawn from a disturbed human is discharged; this bag, when full, relieves itself of the fluid, but is at once refilled, the insect seemingly indulging in the operation for the mere sake of doing it.

The grasping nature of the people, then, and the successive sucking establishments of the mosquitoes, would seem to be the two prominent traits of the inhabitants of Heart's Content. The place itself is surrounded by hills, and at its feet, some thirty miles from the former cable terminus, lies this magnificent harbor to which we alluded. Such a harbor must have a destiny. Like that at Acapulco, it would seem impossible for the Creator to fashion it by accident or without design. For purposes of ordinary commerce, it is and can be of no avail, for there are no avenues of trade here, but for the landing-place of the cable, for the safe anchorage of great ships of war, whose protectorate may some day be invoked, for all purposes of tonnage and cableistic facility, this bay is simply superb. Should success attend the present enterprise, should the laid cable be enabled to do its duty, this place will become one of the curiosities of the hemisphere. It cannot fail to grow and become a great resort. As the seat of fashionable society during the Summer months it would be without a rival. The broad deep basin, which sleeps in perfect tranquillity, leads directly from the little town; upon its dark bosom boating parties could emulate the pleasure of Lake George, while Waltons need seek no further for the paradise of piscatoria. The hills abound in trees of beauty and in groves of shadiest nature; drives could be made, walks could be laid—nature has done her best, and art could perfect the attempt.

A better place could not have been chosen for the safe landing of the cable. Its advantages over the former selection are obvious, and so far as mere still deep water and a quiet basin are concerned, no skilled engineer could have so well devised a harbor as did the Great Architect of this.

PACIFIC COAST.

Circular from the Japanese Government—Mining Operations in Arizona.

SAN FRANCISCO, Monday, July 23.

The steamer *Constitution*, from Panama, arrived to-day, bringing New-York dates of June 30, and $34,900 in treasure from Manzanilla.

The steamer *Constitution* has also arrived from the Mexican ports, with $57,500 in treasure.

The Japanese Government has issued a circular, dated May 23, giving subjects permission to go beyond the seas for the purpose of learning any art or science, or for purposes of trade, when the application is properly made.

Mining Shares dull. Imperial, $93; Yellow Jacket, $580; Chollar, $185.

Legal tender notes, 70½c.

A letter from Prescott, Arizona, reports that numerous quartz-mills are being erected in that vicinity, and represents mining operations there as flourishing.

Choice wheat, new crop, sold on Saturday at $1 85 per 100 pounds. All kinds of coffee closed with an upward tendency.

Arrived, bark *Siam*, from Calcutta, with a cargo of rice.

The French Man-of-War Rhine not Lost—Later from Sonora—Unimportant Fighting.

SAN FRANCISCO, Tuesday, July 24.

The French Consul says the report of the loss of the man-of-war *Rhine* is incorrect. She was at Guaymas at last advices.

Dates from Sonora to July 5, and Mazatlan to July 16, have been received.

The Imperial Consul of Mexico, at this city, reports that numerous significant fights had taken place between the opposing forces in Sonora, but he considers affairs on the western coast as substantially unchanged.

Mining Stocks weak. Yellow Jacket improving in view of the approaching dividend; Ophir, 255; Chollar, 185; Imperial, 93; Alpha, 100; Yellow Jacket, 898.

Legal Tenders, 71.

KENTUCKY.

Frauds on the Revenue—The Saengerbund—The Members Visit the Mammoth Cave.

LOUISVILLE, Ky., Saturday, July 28.

Four citizens of Sarne and Nelson Counties were held to bail to-day in $1,000 each, for making false returns of distilled spirits.

Various singing societies left for the Mammoth Cave to-night to close the Saengerfest with a grand concert there, in Echo Hall, to-morrow. A small portion of the New-York Leiderkranz Society were among the number. The residue left for home this afternoon.

All the societies will be represented.

The Saengerfest.

CAVE CITY, Ky., Sunday, July 29.

The Saengerfest wound up to-day with a grand excursion to Mammoth Cave. Over one thousand persons were present. Everything passed off quietly.

Owing to a disarrangement of the programme by those in charge of the Cave, the concert did not come off, but there was an abundance of extempore vocal and instrumental music.

BY OCEAN TELEG

EUROPEAN NEWS TO JU

HIGHLY IMPORTANT INTELL

Reported Close of War in Germany

A Treaty of Peace Sign Austria and Prussia

Important Naval Batt the Island of Lissa.

The Italian and Aus Fleets Engaged.

The Austrians Obta Decisive Victory

One of the Italian Iron-clad and Three Blown Up.

Severe Fighting in th cinity of Olmutz.

THE AUSTRIANS CLAIM A VI

Reported Conclusion of Pea

TRINITY BAY, N. F., Friday,

Received from the Valentia (Ireland)

A treaty of Peace has been signed betwee and Prussia.

Naval Engagement off the Isl Lissa—The Italian Navy Repu

LONDON, Friday,

The Italian fleet of iron-clad steamboats h fire on the Island of Lissa, on the coast of The result is not known.

LONDON, Saturday,

There was a severe engagement yesterday The Austrians claimed the victory. They Italian iron-clads, *running down one and b three.*

[London dispatches of the 20th, receive *Peruvian*, add that after several hours fighting on the 20th, Admiral PERSANO, w iron-clad vessels, silenced the fort of St. The powder magazine in the fort was b during the engagement. The Italians had and wounded. Vice Admiral ALBANI j squadron of Admiral PERSANO, who was give orders for a disembarkation, when b prised of an Austrian squadron approachi vent this design being carried out, and th fleet was soon afterward preparing for an en with the Austrian squadron. This is proba engagement reported in the above dispatch

The Armistice—More Fighting Austrians Claim a Victory

LONDON, Monday,

Five days' armistice between Austria an commences at noon to-day.

More fighting yesterday—Austria clain victory.

Affairs in England—Reform B London.

LONDON, Sunday,

Lord SHAFTESBURY protests against reform in the House of Commons.

Discussion on the Tariff—Sir JOHN PA admits that England is behind other nations

A dispatch from Hearts Content, date morning, says that Mr. FIELD had receive gence that there had been riots in London o of the refusal of Government to allow me Hyde Park about reform.

The Cable—Great Excitemen

LOUISVILLE, Sunday,

There was great excitement here to-da announcement of the reception of foreig through the Atlantic Cable.

POLITICAL.

The Philadelphia Convention—E at Petersburgh, Va.

FORTRESS MONROE, Friday,

A large and enthusiastic meeting was held in Petersburgh, which passed a series o tions inviting the citizens of the Second sional District to unite with them in a conve nominate delegates to the Philadelphia Con During the meeting, Mr. KELLY stated that h ceived a letter from a United States Senator, he states that in his estimation there wou test demanded at the Philadelphia Convent any Southern man, sincerely desirous of a re of the Union, could not conscientiously assai

Large Fire at Rome, N. Y.—$150,000.

ROME, N. Y., Sunday,

An extensive fire occurred here to-da ing a loss of $150,000. The following are th COLEMAN, of the Willet House, $1,500; sured. BENJAMIN V. HUNTINGTON, $500, WARD HUNTINGTON, $700; both insured. MARCH, of New-York, $45,000; insurance $1 WHITE, shoes, $1,200; insured. S. BREWER, shoes, $250. J. ROWLEY, grocer, $800; ORSON KNOWLTON, saloon and dwelling, CHARLES HEMANS, millinery, $1,200; STILE WARDWELL, grocers, $3,000; J. SAULPAUGH, $700; T. G. HALLEY, hats, $1,500; insured GREENE, druggist, $500; insured. JEPTHA son, cabinet-maker, $1,200; not insured.

The whole brick block owned by HENTER including the Post-office, was destroyed. ting in the Post-office was saved. About other stores were more or less damaged, a were burned.

From Charleston.

CHARLESTON, S. C., Sunday,

The four prisoners sentenced by militar mission, but reprieved by the President, wi tempted liberation on a writ of habeas corpu dispute between the conflict of authority between SICKLES and the United States District Cou quietly removed last night by a steamer guard from Castle Pinckney. The military refuse information concerning their whereabouts. The impression prevails that the sent North beyond the jurisdiction of the Court

Arrival of the Propontis.

BOSTON, Sunday,

The steamer *Propontis*, from Liverpo 14th, via Queenstown the 16th inst., arrived

IMPORTANT ANNEXATION.

Russian-America Purchased by the United States.

Half a Million of Square Miles Acquired.

Great Britain Surrounded on the North Pacific Ocean.

Bright Prospects for Our Japan and China Trade.

WASHINGTON, Saturday, March 30.

The President has communicated to the Senate in its Executive Session, a treaty with Russia, by which that Power surrenders to the United States the sovereignty over all of Russian America and the adjacent islands. It especially includes the strip four hundred miles long, which extends down the coast, thus excluding a large part of British America from the ocean. The treaty was laid on the table, and will be taken up next week.

The British diplomats are naturally highly excited, and object to this hemming in of the British American Territory by the United States.

This acquisition more than doubles the United States coast on the Pacific, which now extends from Lower California to Behring's Straits, with the exception of the narrow strip comprising British Columbia.

The territory ceded by Russia comprises the whole of the Continent of North America west of longitude 141°. It is bounded by British America and the Pacific and Arctic Oceans. It includes a great number of islands, and is of the highest importance as a naval depot, and for strategic purposes. It is a valuable fur country, and embraces a vast section of territory, the possession of which will influence in our favor the vast trade of the Pacific.

The fact that such a treaty has been entered into excites intense interest in all circles, and is hailed with delight by Americans. Influential parties regard it as significant of Russian policy, in view of impending European complications on the Eastern Question.

The English representatives here are deeply chagrined, and it is said that Sir FREDERICK BRUCE will telegraph to Earl DERBY for instructions to protest against its acceptance by our Government.

ANOTHER DISPATCH.

It is true, as reported, that the President communicated to the Senate to-day a treaty with Russia, by which that Power surrenders to the United States the sovereignty over all of Russian-America and the adjacent islands. The price to be paid for this territory is about seven million of dollars. The territory is about 394,000 square miles. It nearly, but not altogether, excludes British America from the ocean. Its chief value consists in its fisheries and fur trade. The treaty was signed early this morning, and sent to the Senate shortly afterward.

WASHINGTON NEWS.

To the Associated Press.

WASHINGTON, Saturday, March 30.

A MESSAGE FROM THE PRESIDENT.

The President, this morning, sent the following:

To the House of Representatives:

In giving my approval to the joint resolution "providing for the expenses of carrying into full effect the act to provide for the more efficient government of the rebel States," I am moved to do so for the following reason: The seventh section of the act supplementary to the act "for the more efficient government of the rebel States" provides that all expenses incurred under or by virtue of that act shall be paid out of any moneys in the Treasury not otherwise appropriated. This provision is wholly unlimited as to the amount to be expended, whereas the resolution now before me limits the appropriation to $500,000. I consider this limitation as a very necessary check against unlimited expenditures and liabilities. Yielding to that consideration, I am bound to approve this resolution without modifying in any manner my objections heretofore stated against the original supplementary acts.

(Signed) ANDREW JOHNSON.

EXTRA EXECUTIVE SESSION OF THE SENATE.

Owing to the large number of Executive appointments to be acted on, the President, to-day, issued the following proclamation, a copy of which was addressed to every Senator:

Whereas, Objects of interest to the United States require that the Senate should be convened at 12 o'clock on Monday, the 1st day of April next, to receive and act upon such communications as may be made to it on the part of the Executive.

Now, therefore, I, ANDREW JOHNSON, President of the United States, have considered it to be my duty to issue this my proclamation declaring that an extraordinary occasion requires the Senate of the United States to convene for the transaction of business at the Capitol, in the City of Washington, on Monday, the first day of April next, at 12 o'clock on that day, of which all who shall at that time be entitled to act as members of that body are hereby required to take notice.

Given under my hand and the seal of the United States, at Washington, the 30th day of March, in the year of our Lord 1867, and of the independence of the United States of America the ninety-first. ANDREW JOHNSON.

By the President:

WILLIAM H. SEWARD, Secretary of State.

AFFAIRS AT THE TREASURY DEPARTMENT.

The receipts from Internal Revenue to-day were nearly $6,000, making the total amount for the week ending to-day, $3,155,538 14; and the total for the month of March, $15,183,226 21. Since the beginning of the present fiscal year the amount of receipts has been $214,336,474 31.

The amount of National Bank currency issued during the week, $39,530: the amount in actual circulation at this date is $296,866,834; the currency returned, including worn-out notes, &c., to date, has amounted to $3,441,693. The fractional currency redeemed during the week amounted to $312,300; the amount of fractional currency issued during the week, $218,600; the amount of fractional currency forwarded during the week to the Assistant Treasurer at New-York, National Banks and others, amounted to $207,233, of which $100,000 was sent to the former. The following are the disbursements of the week: War Department, $3,456,133; Navy Department, $480,680; Interior, $987,234. Total, $4,874,047.

For the month of March the disbursements were as follows: War Department, $11,477,385; Navy, $3,996,674; Interior, $4,845,590. Total, $19,221,599. The Fourth National Bank of Nashville was organized to-day, with a capital of $100,000. There will be no circulation, as the present law for organizing National Banks provides for no circulating notes beyond the amount already in existence.

BILLS PASSED AND APPROVED.

It is believed that all the public bills which passed both Houses have become laws by the President's signature. Among those which he approved to-day are bills giving the American Atlantic Telegraph Cable Company of New-York the privilege to establish stations anywhere along the Atlantic coast, Florida excepted; appropriating $175,000 for the relief of RYAN, SECOR & Co., arising out of their contract for the building of the iron-clad *Comanche*, on the Pacific coast; appropriating $1,000,000 for the relief of the destitute of the South, and prohibiting payments under awards for slaves enlisted in the army.

ARMY MATTERS.

Major M. H. KIDD, of the Tenth Cavalry, has been granted thirty days' leave of absence.

Second Lieut. JOHN L. CHURCHILL, of the Twenty-fourth Infantry. Thirty days' leave.

First Lieut. DAVID FARLEY, of the Seventh Cavalry, Second Lieut. JOHN H. SULLIVAN, of the Thirty-seventh Infantry, and First Lieut. B. M. TAYLOR, of the Twelfth Infantry, have been granted thirty days' delay in joining their regiments.

Brevet Brig.-Gen. B. S. ROBERTS, Major of the Third Cavalry, has three months' extension of leave of absence.

Second Lieut. HENRY H. BURN, Forty-second Infantry, ten days' delay has been granted.

NOMINATIONS CONFIRMED.

The Senate, in Executive session to-day, confirmed the following nominations:

Collectors of Internal Revenue—Gen. James B. Steedman, of Ohio, First District of Louisiana; Henry A. Guernsey to the Eighteenth District of Pennsylvania.

Assessors of Internal Revenue—John W. Frazier to the First District of Pennsylvania; Calvin W. McLane to the Tenth District of Illinois.

Postmasters—Wm. Cromwell at Bloomington, Ill.; Samuel G. Smith, Peru, Ill.; Leroy S. Brown, Natchez, Miss.; Henrietta Davies, Columbus, Miss.; Louisa Cameron, Tallahassee, Fla.; George Phillips, Key West, Fla.

Register of Land Office—Nathaniel S. Goss, at Humboldt, Kansas.

Receiver of Public Money—David B. Emmert, of Humboldt, Kansas.

To be Colonel United States Infantry—Capt. Ranold S. McKenzie, of the Corps of Engineers.

To be Captain United States Infantry—Jacob H. Smith.

Collector of Customs—Patrick S. Slevin, District of Miami, Ohio.

Surveyor of Customs—Jesse M. Harrison, Dubuque, Iowa.

Appraiser of Merchandise—Lander Valentine, Portland, Me.

The Senate rejected the following nominations:

Paymaster United States Army—Wm. H. Johnston, late Paymaster of Volunteers.

Brigadier-General by Brevet—Brevet Col. James B. Fry.

Register of Land Office—Abram S. Wadsworth, at Traverse City, Mich.

Collectors of Internal Revenue—Charles W. Baker, Eighth District of New-York; Thomas McGrath, Fourth District of Pennsylvania.

United States Marshal—Ansel D. Wass, District of Massachusetts.

MISCELLANEOUS ITEMS.

S. P. HANSCOM has withdrawn from the *National Republican* and disposed of his interest in that establishment to his partner, WM. J. MURTAGH.

The President and his Cabinet were at the Capitol to-day in the Vice-President's room attending to public business.

Speaker COLFAX was in the chair to-day, his stepfather having passed the crisis of his disease yesterday, and is now regarded out of danger.

FORTIETH CONGRESS.

FIRST SESSION.

SENATE....WASHINGTON, Saturday, March 30.

The Senate met at 10 o'clock. The reading of yesterday's journal was dispensed with.

WATCHMEN AT THE CAPITOL.

The House bill to authorize the appointment of watchman of the Capitol by the Sergeants-at-Arms of the House and Senate was passed.

EXTENSION OF PATENT.

Mr. CONNESS introduced a resolution calling upon the Secretary of the Interior for all papers connected with the extension of the patent of THADDEUS HYATT, which was adopted.

UNION PACIFIC RAILROAD.

Mr. HOWARD offered a resolution calling upon the Secretary of the Interior for a copy of the last report of the Directors of the Union Pacific Railroad, which was adopted.

DEATH OF SENATOR RIDDLE.

Mr. SAULSBURY offered a resolution to extend the session of the two Houses until 3 o'clock.

Mr. DAVIS said the object of this was to take notice of the death of Mr. RIDDLE, of Delaware, which would be done at 12 o'clock.

After discussion the resolution was laid aside.

SOLDIERS AND SAILORS' ORPHAN HOME.

Mr. CORBETT called up the one appropriating $5,000 for the support in part of the Soldiers' and Sailors' Orphan Home of the District of Columbia, which was passed.

BALTIMORE AND OHIO RAILROAD.

Mr. CAMERON moved to take up the resolution offered by him yesterday, calling upon the Secretary of War for information as to how much money was paid to the Baltimore and Ohio Railroad by the Government during the war, what rates were charged, whether they were higher than were paid to other companies, if so, why? &c.

Mr. JOHNSON moved an amendment to include the Northern Central and Pennsylvania Central Roads.

The amendment was agreed to and the resolution was adopted.

NOMINATIONS BY THE PRESIDENT.

On motion of Mr. SHERMAN the rule of the Executive Session requiring nominations not acted upon to be returned to the President after the close of the session was suspended, so as to allow nominations now pending in the Executive Session to be continued until acted upon.

COMMITTEE ON ORDNANCE.

Mr. WILSON called up the House resolution for the appointment of a joint Standing Committee on Ordnance, and moved to amend by making it a Joint Special Committee, with power to send for persons and papers, and take testimony as to the best and latest improvements in firearms.

The amendment was agreed to, and the resolution was adopted.

HONORS TO SENATOR RIDDLE.

Mr. SAULSBURY offered a resolution for the appointment of a Joint Committee of three Senators and five Representatives, to accompany the remains of the late Senator RIDDLE to his home, which was agreed to.

UNIVERSAL SUFFRAGE.

Mr. SUMNER gave notice that on the first Wednesday in July he would call up the bill for universal suffrage throughout the United States. He had reason to believe, he said, that there would be a quorum present on that day.

AGRICULTURAL COLLEGES.

Mr. THAYER called up a bill to extend to the State of Nebraska the privileges of an act granting land to the State for the establishment of agricultural colleges, which was passed.

SALARY OF THE CHAPLAIN.

Mr. POMEROY called up the bill to allow the chaplain of the House of Representatives to draw his salary for the present year, which was passed.

At 10:45 the Senate went into Executive Session.

ADJOURNMENT OF THE SENATE.

At 12 o'clock the doors were reopened, and the President *pro tem.* declared the Senate adjourned under the resolution of yesterday until the first Wednesday in July.

HOUSE OF REPRESENTATIVES.

The House met at 10 o'clock this morning.

The number of members present was apparently less than a quorum.

PRAYER FOR PROSPERITY.

The Chaplain in his prayer returned thanks for the great public services which Congress had been enabled to perform in placing the liberties of the people on lasting foundations and elevating the human race. As the battle cloud had passed away, so he prayed the political battle-cloud would pass away, to be followed by a prosperous calm, and that when Congress next met it would look out on a country reunited chiefly through its labors.

A MEMORIAL FROM MARYLAND.

Mr. THOMAS presented a memorial from the Mayor and members of the City Councils of Baltimore, asking Congress to assist the people of Maryland to form a State Government republican in form and in unison with the spirit of the age. Referred to the Judiciary Committee.

GEN. SHERIDAN'S REMOVALS.

Mr. BENTON asked leave to offer a resolution tendering the thanks of this House to Major-Gen. SHERIDAN for the removal of the Louisiana officials—Messrs. HERRON, Attorney-General; MUNROE, Mayor of New-Orleans, and ABELL, Judge of the First District Court, from the offices which they disgraced, and the appointment of loyal men in their places.

Mr. WOOD objected, and the resolution was not received.

MESSENGERS OF THE HOUSE.

On motion of Mr. STEVENS, of Pennsylvania, the resolution authorizing the retention of the Doorkeeper's messengers during the recess was ordered to be construed so as to include those employed at $3 per day.

TRADERS AT MILITARY POSTS.

The House then proceeded to the consideration of the business on the Speaker's table, and disposed thereof, as follows:

REMOVAL OF INDIANS.

The Senate joint resolution to authorize the Commanding-General of the army to permit traders to remain at certain military posts.

After explanation by Mr. ASHLEY, of Ohio, Mr. STEVENS, of Pennsylvania, moved to lay it on the table.

Motion negatived.

The joint resolution was then passed.

COLORADO TERRITORY.

The Senate bill amendatory of the Organic Act of Colorado Territory.

After explanation by Mr. ASHLEY, of Ohio, the bill was passed.

The Senate joint resolution in reference to the removal of the Indian tribes.

After discussion by Messrs. WINDOM and DONNELLY in support of the bill, and by Mr. BURLEIGH, of Dakotah, in opposition to it, Mr. COVODE moved to lay the bill on the table.

Motion agreed to by 43 to 41.

UNION PACIFIC RAILWAY.

On motion of Mr. BOUTWELL, the Judiciary Committee was authorized to continue during the recess the investigation of the affairs of the Union Pacific Railway, with power to send for persons and papers.

The business on the Speaker's table was continued as follows:

PUBLIC GROUNDS IN WASHINGTON.

The Senate bill appropriating $20,000 to grade in part the public grounds in Washington.

Mr. HOLMAN objected that the bill must, under the rules, be first considered in Committee of the Whole.

The rules were, on motion of Mr. STEVENS, of Pennsylvania, suspended, and the bill was considered in the House, and passed.

It provides for the extension of the Capitol grounds north and south on the land belonging to the Government.

APPOINTMENT OF WATCHMEN.

The Senate amendment to the House bill to authorize the appointment of certain watchmen was concurred in.

COMMITTEE ON ORDNANCE.

The Speaker laid before the House the Senate amendment to the House resolution for the appointment of a Committee on Ordnance, which was concurred in.

It authorizes the appointment of a clerk and stenographer.

SENATOR RIDDLE, OF MARYLAND.

The House also concurred in the Senate resolution for the appointment of a Committee to accompany the body of Senator RIDDLE to his late home in Delaware.

PAYMENT OF THE CHAPLAIN.

The Senate's amendment to the joint resolution for the payment of the Chaplain of the House was taken from the Speaker's table and concurred in.

THE MILITARY ACADEMY.

Mr. SCHENCK asked leave to offer a resolution directing those members of the House who were members of the Committee on Military Affairs of the last House to prosecute, during the recess, the investigation ordered at the last session into the management of the Military Academy at West Point.

Mr. ROSS objected, and Mr. SCHENCK moved to suspend the rules, which was disagreed to by 37 to 47.

TAX SALES IN SOUTH CAROLINA.

The House disposed of business on the Speaker's table, as follows:

The Senate bill to confirm certain sales made by the Direct Tax Commissioners for South Carolina, to persons in the army, navy or marine corps. Referred, on motion of Mr. ROSS, to the Committee on Claims.

TRANSPORTATION OF TROOPS.

The Senate joint resolution relating to the transportation of troops by the Isthmus routes to the Pacific States and Territories. After a brief discussion between Messrs. FARNSWORTH and BROOKS the joint resolution was, on motion of Mr. BROOKS, referred to the Committee on Military Affairs.

SOLDIERS' AND SAILORS' ORPHAN HOME.

The Senate bill appropriating $5,000 for the Soldiers' and Sailors' Orphans' Home in the District of Columbia. Passed.

AGRICULTURAL COLLEGES.

The Senate bill to extend to Nebraska the provisions of the Agricultural College Bill. Passed.

GOVERNMENT PRINTING PAPER.

Mr. LAFLIN offered a resolution that the report of the Congressional Printer on the purchase of paper be taken from the table and referred to the Committee on Printing, with power to investigate the same, send for persons and papers, and sit during the recess.

Mr. HOLMAN objected to the last clause.

The Speaker stated that all committees now appointed are authorized to sit during the recess, as this was not an adjournment of the session, but a recess. The resolution was adopted.

POST ROUTES.

Mr. LYNCH, on leave, introduced a bill to establish certain post routes in Maine, which was passed.

RECONSTRUCTION EXPENSES.

The Speaker presented a message from the President, stating that in giving his approval to the joint resolution providing for the carrying into effect of the "act for the more effectual government of the rebel States," he did so because it limited the expenditures to $500,000, and not because he had modified his objections to the original and supplementary acts.

The message was laid on the table and ordered to be printed.

PAYMENT FOR NAVAL GUNS.

Mr. SCHENCK introduced a joint resolution to pay to NORMAN WIARD $42,186, in full of all his accounts against the Government for semi-steel 50-pounder guns made for the navy in 1861.

Mr. FERNANDO WOOD moved to refer it to the Committee on Claims. Disagreed to.

Mr. WINDOM moved to refer it to the Committee of the Whole. Disagreed to.

Mr. SCHENCK then withdrew the bill.

SELECT COMMITTEES.

The Speaker then announced Select Committees as follows:

Committee to accompany the body of Senator RIDDLE to Delaware—Messrs. Nicholson, Farnsworth, Grossbrenner, Kerr and Benton.

On Ordnance—Messrs. Schenck, Logan and Butler.

To Wait on the President—Messrs. Laflin and Brooks.

LIGHTING THE CITY OF WASHINGTON.

Mr. INGERSOLL asked leave to have the Senate joint resolution for lighting the City of Washington with gas taken up and passed.

Objection was made.

TESTING ORDNANCE.

Mr. SCHENCK asked leave to offer a resolution in relation to experiments for testing ordnance.

BILLS APPROVED BY THE PRESIDENT.

Its reading was interrupted by a message from the President announcing his approval of a few of the latest bills passed, and then as the clock indicated the hour of noon, the Speaker let the hammer fall and said:

ADJOURNMENT.

GENTLEMEN: The hour of 12 o'clock having arrived, I do now, in accordance with the concurrent resolution of both Houses, wishing each one of you a safe journey to his home, and a happy reunion with family and friends, declare the Fortieth Congress of the United States adjourned until the first Wednesday of July next, at noon.

Applause and clapping of hands on the floor and in the galleries greeted this little farewell speech.

The members and officers then exchanged parting expressions of good will, and separated.

AFFAIRS IN INDIANA.

Correspondence of the New-York Times:

LAFAYETTE, Tuesday, March 26, 1867.

The readers of the NEW-YORK TIMES will, perhaps, still remember the particulars of the mysterious Delaforet affair which will always rank among the most singular trials that ever took place before our criminal Courts, and the details of which I communicated to you in a letter published in the NEW-YORK TIMES some time in November last. On merely circumstantial evidence, which was developed mostly in a truly providential manner, DELAFORET, a Frenchman, was at that time convicted of having robbed and assassinated, in the Spring of 1866, a native of Switzerland by the name of CASPAR SOIER, and sentenced to the State Prison for life.

Some circumstances developed during his trial gave rise to the suspicion that DELAFORET had been assisted by an accomplice in perpetrating his horrible crime. He himself, who is even now solemnly protesting his innocence, refused to furnish the authorities any clue as to the whereabouts and identity of this supposed accomplice, and it was therefore no easy task for the detectives, who had been sent after him, to get hold of him.

After a great deal of trouble, they found his trail at last, but the guilty accomplice, who seems to be a very shrewd rogue, gave them a long chase, and it was only a few days ago that he was arrested by the Sheriff of this county in a small town in Iowa, where he had been living under the inoffensive name of CHARLES JOHNSON. He was immediately taken back to Lafayette, and made here a partial confession, which, though he still denies having had anything to do with the murder of SOIER, is yet highly important, inasmuch as it confirms all the circumstantial evidence on which DELAFORET was convicted. The name of his accomplice is FRANCIS PIO. Like DELAFORET, he is a Frenchman, and his trial, which will take place in a few days, is looked for by our citizens with the most intense suspense. The old saying that "murder will out" was rarely confirmed in a more striking manner. DELAFORET and PIO are believed to be desperate French criminals, and, perhaps, escaped convicts from Cayenne.

The campaign for the Spring elections is an unusually animated one, especially in the cities where the nominations of the Union Party have been contested in the most excited and bitter manner. The contest was chiefly between the leaders of the Grand Army of the Republic and the civilians aspiring to nominations. The former were victorious everywhere; not, however, without exciting considerable ill feeling among their opponents. While the masses of the Union Party are eager and willing to confer nominations on deserving soldiers, they commence growing somewhat restive under the dictatorial airs assumed by certain leaders of the "Grand Army of the Republic." Especially is this the case at Indianapolis, where this very fact has endangered the success of the Union ticket. Here in Lafayette the Democrats are counting confidently on a victory. Their standard-bearer for the Mayoralty will be Ex-Senator JOHN PETTIT, once of national reputation. In most of the other cities the prospects of the Democracy are decidedly gloomy, and the Union Party will sweep the State by no less than twenty thousand majority, as the new registry law must considerably reduce the Democratic vote on the Southern border. But even aside from this, the course pursued by the Democracy of Indiana is such as to swell the vote of their opponents. Most of their papers are still bewailing the repeal of the infamous Black Laws, and several organs of theirs are giving vent to sentiments of the most fiendish character. As an instance, I will mention the *Herald on the Border*, who sheds bitter tears "because no more than three hundred thousand Yankees were killed in the late war. W. C.

Legislation Against Bribery in New-Jersey.

The New-Jersey Senate on Tuesday passed a bill, supplemental to the law against bribery, under which, if passed by the House, joint meetings and caucuses will be impossible. The main feature of the bill is as follows:

"That it shall not be lawful for the members of the Legislature to agree or combine together in any manner, either by resolution or otherwise, to vote for or against any matter which may require their action, whether the same be any bill pending before either the Senate or General Assembly, or in relation to the confirmation of any nomination or making any appointment, either in joint meetings or otherwise, and any member of the Senate or General Assembly who shall in any manner violate any of the provisions of this supplement, shall be deemed guilty of a misdemeanor, and on conviction thereof shall be punished by imprisonment at hard labor for the period of two years, or fined in the sum of $1,000, as the Court may direct."

Mob Law in Alabama.

A band of forty or fifty armed men entered the Court-house at Columbiana, Ala., on the 18th inst., while the Circuit Court for Shelby County was in session, and demanded the keys to the jail. Having obtained these, they released from confinement two men who were held on a charge of murder, and with them left the town. The Selma *Messenger* says:

"It is said that the mob consisted of some at least of the men who during the last year of the war were banded together for the purpose of pillage and plunder, and who about the time of LEE's surrender perpetrated some of the most atrocious murders on record. If, as we suspect, the civil authorities are utterly powerless to protect the people of the county or themselves against this formidable combination of lawless and desperate men, here is a case in which the military power of the Government may be profitably employed. This is the first instance of defiance of the law, State or Federal, we have heard of in this province, and we trust steps will be taken to prevent a repetition of it."

THE CHICAGO TUNNEL.

A Perilous Experimental Voyage.

On Saturday, just before water was let into the lake tunnel at Chicago, a final tour was made by the Superintendent, Mr. CHESBROUGH, who took with him three newspaper reporters. After reaching the "crib" out in the lake, an uncomfortable descent of sixty feet took them to the horizontal shaft, where they found a leaky flat-bottomed boat awaiting them. "The only means of propelling the vessel," according to the *Tribune* reporter, "was by pushing against the walls; and this was a very unsteady process, fraught with danger to the boat and her little crew. The water at the crib end was exactly half-way up the sides of the bore, gradually deepening, of course, as we approached the shore. For a time it was comparatively plain sailing, and by the aid of the lamps we were enabled to examine minutely the condition of the cement, which was the principal object of the voyage. Not a flaw could be discovered, with the exception of a space here and there between the bricks, where an iron spike had been introduced to hold the ventilators. The top of the arch seemed to be perfectly dry, save in the places where the water, not from the lake, but from springs in the vicinity of the tunnel, oozes through the walls. The water was beautifully clear, as clear as crystal, and sweet to the taste. We were not long permitted, however, to enjoy the contemplation of the surrounding scenery, limited as the view was. The bricks were soon exhausted, every brick being so much like its neighbor as to become somewhat monotonous. The lamps, too, began to flicker out. The silence became oppressive; the distant growlings from the end of the cavern were magnified into the noise of a cataract and our hearts stood still as we thought how by some unforseen accident the flood-gates might be opened. To perish like rats in a hole, to be distributed in the course of time through the water pipes of Chicago, and be boiled in kettles—we were not prepared for such a sacrifice. To chase away these fears, we sang the "Star Spangled Banner," and listened to the echo of our own voices from the nearest chamber. In this way we reached the closing-stone, a white marble tablet, placed there by the Mayor's own hands. We paused to scrutinize this closing-stone, and here an unlucky incident occurred, to which may be attributed the disaster which was soon to follow. One of the crew, inspired by a frantic wish to "write his name in water," leaned over the edge of the flat-bottomed boat, which had took in a little more than it could conveniently carry. Then in the process of bailing the crew got unsettled in their positions and never quite regained an equilibrium. We succeeded, however, in pushing our way at considerable risk on to a point beyond the fifth chamber or nearly a mile and a half from the crib.

Our heads had been gradually approaching the top of the tunnel as we pursued our darksome journey to the shore. From sitting postures each member of the party had slowly subsided into reclining attitudes, and by and by they were changed into horizontal positions. This in a flat-bottomed boat half full of water was refreshing. Further progress was deemed a little too precarious. Still no one was willing to give out, and our leader manifested a readiness to go the whole length if desirable. It was not desirable. In fact, it was not practicable, seeing that the boat by this time was effectually wedged in between the bricks and the water.

The return necessitated a change of propellers, and the new hands not being well accustomed to the duty, the unsteadiness of our devoted bark was increased. The water came in on all sides, so we got on swimmingly after a fashion. Only two lights were left and those but struggled drearily with the darkness. They were entrusted to the man in the centre of the boat; another propelled, while the two at each end set to work to bale out the water. We had not gone far toward the crib end again, when symptoms of uneasiness began to manifest themselves. In spite of all efforts to bale out the water, the boat seemed to be filling rapidly. We were yet a mile at least from the shaft and the water was nearly breast deep. Suddenly the man at the stern raised a sharp cry of distress; his end was settling down, he said, and what was the use in baling out. The man with the lamp rose to his feet just as he felt the boat subsiding. The man with the bucket sprang overboard, and Mr. CHESBROUGH floundered. We were shipwrecked.

The last expiring lamplight had flickered out and all was confusion and darkness. There was no help for us but to raise the boat and haul it to the crib end. This was a task of considerable difficulty, but after a vigorous effort we succeeded. Winding through the chilly water with our limbs benumbed, and dragging an ungrateful flat-bottomed boat, which would not carry us, we toiled painfully, but as cheerfully as possible for the distance of a mile, shouting occasionally for help, which did not come, bewailing our sad fate, and thinking sorrowfully of the four small obituaries that would appear in the morning papers.

At last a faint light glimmered upon us from far end. We had been floundering in our watery dungeon for nearly three hours, and were pretty well exhausted. The light proved to be lamp in the hand of Capt. BENO, who, fearing from our prolonged absence that some disaster had overtaken us, had descended to the bottom of the shaft. And there he stood profoundly amused at our mischance, and laughing consumedly as the bedraggled wayfarers came one by one into view. But our worst danger was not over. We had to climb the shaft, sixty-eight feet in height, by means of the ladder. "Just go straight up," said Capt. BENO, "you cannot go out of the way." There was no possibility of reaching the upper air that night, except by climbing, and as there was no comfortable lodging to be had in the tunnel, we again ventured. Mr. CHESBROUGH ascended first, and by way of a parting salute, when half way up he emptied a gallon of water from each boot upon our heads. The remainder of the party were already exhausted by fatigue and cold. How the others succeeded is best known to themselves. The present writer, for his part, was just on the point of giving out as he reached a platform let down about 16 feet from the mouth of the shaft, hands stiffened with cramp, a dizzy sensation of 60 feet beneath him, a creeping of the flesh, powerless to move another step. One last shout for help, and he found himself seized by a friendly hand and laid out on the platform, then tied to a rope and hauled up to the mouth of the shaft.

The flood-gates of the crib were reopened immediately after our ascent, and the waters went down with a roar like that of an infant Niagara. What became of the flat-bottomed boat we did not know and did not care. The tug was waiting for us at 10 o'clock, and in a few minutes the party were fleeting merrily home again. And so ended the adventurous voyage—the last that will be made through the Lake Tunnel.

Destitution in the South—Letter from Gen. Thomas.

LOUISVILLE, Ky., March 22, 1867.

Mr. Carter H. Harrison, Chicago, Ill.:

DEAR SIR: I received your favor of the 17th inst. this morning, for which I am much obliged, as it will enable me to point out a locality in Georgia and Alabama where the people of both sides of the question at present dividing the country are in extreme want for provisions, and many who have means to do so will be compelled to quit their homes, unless they can get subsistence enough to enable them to make crops this year. The people of Carroll, Haralson, Polk, Paulding, Campbell, Corveta and Heard, Ga., and Randolph, Calhoun and Cherokee, Ala., are represented to me as not having provisions to last them until May next; and great numbers who have the means to move will be compelled to do so, unless they can procure provisions from abroad. All classes of the citizens are alike destitute, the rich as well as the poor, and both must starve if they remain in the country, unless provisions are sent to them. The rich are perfectly willing to purchase if any one will send them provisions, and wait for them to gather in their crops before demanding payment.

By aiding these people, I knew you will be doing good service in relieving distress which is common throughout the South, and will also be giving encouragement to people who will appreciate the relief afforded them in their time of need. I am, Sir, very respectfully, your obedient servant,

GEO. H. THOMAS.

P. S.—Corn and bacon are articles most essential, as the people absolutely need something to enable them to remain at home and cultivate their crops. Anything sent to Mr. W. H. McDANIEL, Carroll County, Ga., via Newman, Ga., on the Atlanta and West Point Railroad, will reach him safely. He is the authorized agent of the citizens of Carroll County. I can send you the names of agents for the other counties, should you desire them. It will be necessary to write to these counties, however, to get the other names. G. H. T.

The Insurance Companies and "Jew Risks."

Quite a spirited indignation meeting was held in Richmond on Thursday, to express indignation at the recent action of the insurance companies which resolved to take no more "Jew risks." Resolutions were adopted by those present, who were for the most part Jews, that they would not insure in the Companies which had taken this action. Mayor MAYO made a speech, stating that he had been in the insurance business many years in Richmond, had had most of his dealings with the Jewish people, and could bear testimony to the uprightness and honesty of their conduct. He had also been prosecuting attorney for a long time, and during his entire official life not more than three Jews had ever been brought before him. In the council he had sat with them, and in all the relations of life had found them trustworthy. He did not design making a speech, or discussing the question of fanaticism, for he did not believe there was any fanaticism in the case. It had its origin in a willful desire to tell a falsehood, and these Companies had accomplished their purpose in slandering a most worthy class of our fellow-citizens.

The Republican Convention in North Carolina.

The Raleigh (N. C.) *Standard*, of the 28th inst., gives a report of the first day's proceedings of the Republican State Convention in that city. The Convention was called by the loyal members of the Legislature, and was temporarily organized by the appointment of Gen. ALFRED DOCKERY as Chairman, and two Secretaries, one of whom was white and the other black. After an address by Gen. DOCKERY, the Committee on Organization reported Hon. A. H. JONES as President, with a list of Vice-Presidents and Secretaries, divided equally between whites and blacks. The *Standard* says:

"Mr. JONES was conducted to the chair by Dr. WILLIAM SLOAN, (white,) and JAS. H. HARRIS, (colored.) He returned his thanks for the honor, and spoke at some length in an eloquent strain upon the condition of the country, and the importance of the deliberations of the body over which he had been called to preside. Considerable discussion ensued on various motions, in which a number of members took part, after which the President announced the Committee on Resolutions, and the meeting adjourned. There were nearly one hundred white delegates in the meeting, and some forty or fifty colored. The utmost harmony and good feeling prevailed between the two races, meeting as they did on the ground of absolute political and civil equality. Perfect decorum and good order prevailed, not only in the meeting but in the dense mass of people of both races in the lobbies and galleries. It was such a scene as had never before been witnessed south of the Potomac, and never surpassed in interest or enthusiasm in any of the Northern States. The Republicans of North Carolina are *one* people in all that concerns the good and glory of the Republic, and they will keep even step together in the great work of reconstruction."

The Fenian Movement—Sympathy in Connecticut.

The following letters were read at a recent meeting of the Fenian Circle in Norwich, Conn.:

NORWICH, March 25, 1867.

Messrs. M. McQuirk and F. S. Burke, Committee:

Your favor of the 23th instant is just at hand. While I have engagements for this evening, I assure you of my sympathy for the oppressed in Ireland and in every land, and my earnest desire that all people may soon enjoy all the blessings which are to be secured under a Republican Government—a representative democracy. Yours truly,

WM. A. BUCKINGHAM.

NORWICH, Conn., March 26, 1867.

GENTLEMEN: Your very polite letter of this day, inviting me to be present this evening at a meeting of the Wolf Tone Circle, came into my hands on my return this afternoon. I deeply regret that a prior engagement to speak with Hon. EARL MARTIN at Lebanon will prevent my being present on so interesting an occasion, and from enjoying the pleasure of listening to the eloquent gentlemen who, I understand, are to address you.

I most cordially sympathize with every movement which has for its object the advancement and elevation of the Irish nation. Your cause is, indeed, a just one, and I trust that the efforts of your noble people to secure Irish independence may be successful, and that you may yet win back the rights of your country and insure to all your people public safety and political freedom.

Very respectfully,

H. H. STARKWEATHER.

Southern State Courts During the Rebellion.

A dispatch from Nashville, March 26, says:

"The Columbus (Ga.) *Enquirer* learns, verbally, on the authority of a distinguished lawyer, that Judge ERSKINE, of the United States District Court, has, during its present term at Atlanta, ruled, in effect, that the adjudications by our State Courts during the war are of no binding effect. The point, we understand, came up in this way: The plaintiff in the United States Court sued on a note, and Mr. HANSELL, counsel for the defendant, interposed a plea that it had already been sued upon in the State Court, and judgment rendered therein. Judge ERSKINE overruled the plea on the ground that there were no Courts in Georgia from the date of the Ordinance of Secession to the close of the war which the United States Court would recognize. The *Enquirer* adds: 'Though no mention of the case has been made in the Atlanta papers, the information comes through sources that do not allow a doubt of its substantial correctness.'"

A Word for a Useful and Charitable Organization.

The ladies of New-York, who, during the war contributed so greatly to the noble work of the Sanitary Commission, are still engaged, like ministering angels, in relieving the maimed and suffering men whose patriotism brought upon them personal misfortune. The "Ladies' Union Relief Association," composed as it is of the most earnest, devoted and public-spirited women of New-York, steps in to fill up the place in usefulness to disabled soldiers which was made vacant by the dissolution of the Sanitary Commission. Since the organization of their Society, in the Autumn of 1865, these good Samaritans of the fair sex have found their field of operations to be constantly growing, and hardly a day passes without the knowledge of some new case of a feeble man whose life is slowly wasting away in a tenement house, a garret or cellar, being brought to their attention. Human wrecks from Salisbury, Florence, Andersonville, the Tobacco Factory, Belle Island and other places of hateful memory, plead for the assistance which a grateful people know they have fully earned by their heroic sacrifices. These claims can only be met by seeing to it that the exchequer of the Relief Association is well supplied. The ladies disburse their charities discreetly and with care, personally visiting all their beneficiaries. Columns of incidents might be furnished which would show the good work that the Association has already accomplished in the preservation of the life, health and self-respect of men who have lost limbs, been sick from rough experiences, or been pining away under diseases contracted in the camp. In addition to the disbursement of the means intrusted to them, these ladies have the additional labor of collecting the funds, and procuring employment for those who are capable of helping themselves. They are instant in season and out of season in their arduous undertaking, sacrificing their own comforts to the necessities of the poor and needy. They do this cheerfully, and without expecting or desiring a word of credit for themselves. But they require the support of the community, and would be sorry to make known that the American people have forgotten altogether too soon the brave men who fought in the war for the Union. Only $9,000 was collected last year for this enterprise, and if the amount had been quadrupled every penny of it would have found its way to a deserving object—not a cent being given at random, but only after the fullest personal inquiry into the merits of the case. The Association is at present much straitened in its resources. It needs money, good clothing, and opportunities of employment for one-armed and one-legged men. Its claims upon the philanthropic are second to none at present before the public. Those who would assist it may communicate with the Managing Committee, at the rooms of the Young Men's Christian Association, No. 927 Broadway.

The Field and the Easel.

This was the subject of a lecture before the Brooklyn Academy of Design, at the Brooklyn Institute, last evening, by WILLIAM HART, the President of the Academy. A large and appreciative audience was in attendance. It was impossible, said the lecturer, by way of introduction, to reveal the soul of art in language, and he could attempt little more than to indicate the principal rules by which the study of art was to be guided. It was quite popular among artists to affect ignorance of theories and rules of art, and it might sometimes happen that an original art genius would attain to high excellence, in real ignorance of the theories and rules that governed his inspiration, but it was none the less true that art, like everything else, was founded on theory and governed by rule, and there were few artists who could afford to dispense with these rules, however ignorant they might profess to be of their existence. His remarks on the present occasion would be confined to landscape art exclusively. His object would be to take his hearers on a tour through the fields, and thence back to the studio, laden with the spoils of the campaign. And first the student was supposed to be able to sketch objects singly or in combination, and he desired to impress upon all students the importance of a thorough study of single objects as indispensable at the outset of his career as an artist. Having gone forth into the broad sunshine and the fields, his first question would be what subject he should select for his pencil. And here he would caution the student against the selection of any particular scene merely because "it looked like a picture." If he did, the chances were it would be tame; and however true he might be in the delineation of nature, he would incur the criticism of having imitated some ideal picture manufactured for the occasion. The more harmonious combination of the natural elements that go to make up a picture were not necessarily good. It were better to select a subject or scene as far removed from the conventional as possible. Try, if possible, to embody a sentiment or idea of your own, and one in unison with your own feelings. This sentiment might precede or succeed the subject. The artist might have a preconceived idea or sentiment which he wished to embody in a picture, or he might come upon a scene that suggested a sentiment. In the one case the sentiment preceded the subject; in the other the sentiment was the offspring, so to speak, of the scene. An artist might command success in either way, but there should always be an idea, either preceding or succeeding the subject, and that idea should be his own—an idea or sentiment in which he was interested, and which should be wrought out with his pencil in such manner as to interpret his own thought and soul, and not in imitation of another man's. Having found his subject, he is next to inquire how much of the picture or panorama, of which he is the centre, he can take in upon his canvass. With regard to this it was only necessary to say, as a rule, that he must give enough to represent all the combinations that go to make up the individuality of the scene. (The speaker here illustrated the subject by reference to one of the sketches, of which there were a dozen or more suspended in the rear of the desk.) The importance of studying the topography of a landscape, as distinct from color, was urged, and TURNER was instanced as a master artist who made this a prominent feature of his method. The student was cautioned not to alter or modify the scene at the expense of nature and truth. The lecturer then spoke of the different methods of sketching—whether with lead pencil, black and white crayon, charcoal, pen and ink, water colors, &c., and pointed out the advantages and disadvantages of each, giving the preference on the whole to pen and ink.

Returning from the field to the studio, the student's purpose must now be earnest. He must now seek to contract, intensify and subject the sentiment to the picture. Any subject could be rendered interesting if true to nature. As to "treatment," so called, it was the broadest and most vague word in the vocabulary of art. One thing, however, was now well established—that "sky treatment" was of the highest importance. Accessories should not be made to appear as the principal in the completed work. Care should be taken not to follow too closely a favorite artist. It was well enough for the student to admire a good model—better than to essay independence before one had grown out of childhood, but admiration should not be allowed to end in mere imitation. St. Paul once sat at the feet of Gamaliel, as his master, but St. Paul did not feel bound to carry Gamaliel's carpet-bag for the rest of his life. If one imitates at all, by all means let him imitate the excellencies and not the defects of his master. It was not the wart on CICERO's nose that made him an orator. Above all, let your picture tell something that you feel. If you feel nothing, keep silent until you do feel something, and not attempt to tell what you think you ought to feel or what you imagine somebody else feels.

The lecture, of which the above is but a brief sketch, was illustrated throughout by reference to pictures before the audience, and was well received and frequently applauded.

The next of the course of lectures on Art will be delivered at the same place the second Saturday evening in April by Col. JAMES FAIRMAN. Subject—"The Æsthetics of Art."

Destruction of St. Andrew's Church, Staten Island.

One of the few remaining church relics of the last century was on Friday morning destroyed by fire—the venerable church of St. Andrew, in the village of Richmond, Staten Island, erected in the year 1713, under a charter granted by Queen ANNE. This was one of the oldest church edifices in the United States, and its destruction will be much regretted by all who value these venerable memorials of another age, whose every stone is a page of history. The loss is said to be about $10,000, which is only partially covered by insurance for $4,000, and $800 on the organ, in the Richmond County Mutual Insurance Company. A few relics only, rescued from the vestry, remain with the charred walls to suggest the story of the labors of those who built, and of the piety of those who worshipped there a hundred and fifty years ago.

NEW-JERSEY.

NEWARK NEWS IN BRIEF.—A mendicant who was soliciting alms in Newark yesterday, perpetrated three petit larcenies, for which he was arrested and committed for trial....The Democrats of East Newark made their nominations for their charter election on Friday evening. Newark City has a total tax of $465,000 to raise....A new literary enterprise is about to be set on foot in Newark in the form of a monthly periodical, to be called the *New-Jersey Magazine*....The April terms of the Essex County Courts will commence on Tuesday next....The stable of SAMUEL TERRY, at Belleville, was broken into on Saturday morning, at an early hour, and a quantity of harness stolen. No clue to the thieves.

CHARGED WITH VIOLATING A CITY ORDINANCE.—A man named JAMES CASSIDY, master of the schooner *Mary*, was arrested in Jersey City yesterday afternoon, charged with violating a city ordinance by obstructing the access to the Paterson Dock and refusing to move his vessel out of the way. The accused was locked up for examination.

POLITICAL.—The charter election of Jersey City takes place on Monday, April 8. Neither party has as yet made any nominations, and a general apathy seems to prevail among both Democrats and Republicans.

ANNEXATION.—A bill has been introduced in the New-Jersey Legislature to annex the town of Bergen to Jersey City.

THE SUBMARINE CABLE FROM FLORIDA TO CUBA.—The steamship *Francis Wright*, Capt. BOLGER, sailed yesterday for Key West and the west coast of Florida, laden with telegraph material and stores for the International Ocean Telegraph Company. She also carries out a sufficient corps of men to assist in laying the coast and shore line of this important telegraph. It may be interesting to the public to know that the success of this new enterprise so far is due mainly to the energy and perseverance of Gen. WM. F. (Baldy) SMITH, MATTHEW DELAFIELD, Esq., and Capt. JAMES SCRYMSER, formerly of Gen. SMITH's staff. These gentlemen are officers of the Company, and the originators of this important line of communication between the United States, Cuba, and the other West India Islands. The successful termination of this work will give business facilities to merchants and others interested in the West India trade, greatly enhancing the value of it, and, in fact, bringing Europe and the West Indies into almost direct communication. The surveys for this line have revealed some important and interesting facts. The greatest depth of water found was 5,100 feet, and the singular discovery is stated that a mountain of 3,000 feet elevation lies in the proposed cable route—a mountain over whose summit vessels have passed and repassed trading between this City and Cuba. The cable is to be delivered in May by the English firm who contracted for it, and by the end of that month the preparatory work in Florida will be completed. It is expected that the line will be in active operation by the 1st of July. The engineer is Mr. W. H. EVERETT, of the Morgan Iron Works, who will accompany the cable from England, where he is now superintending its construction.

DIED.

BRADY.—Suddenly, at his residence, No. 109 East 4th-st., on Saturday evening, March 30, ARCHIBALD C. BRADY, aged 68 years and 8 days.

Notice of funeral hereafter.

HITCHCOCK.—On Saturday, March 30, GRACE FLORELLA, infant daughter of J. G. and Anna L. Hitchcock.

The funeral will take place at 1 o'clock P. M. this day, (Sunday,) from No. 236 West 22d-st.

KNIGHT.—On Saturday, March 30, BETSY KNIGHT, in the 74th year of her age.

The relatives and friends are respectfully invited to attend the funeral from the residence of Charles Elliott, No. 574 3d-av., on Monday, April 1, at 10 o'clock A. M.

Leicestershire, England, papers please copy.

MANNING.—In this City, on Saturday, March 30, LENA R. MANNING, daughter of the late George and F. W. R. Manning.

Funeral services will take place at the residence of her uncle, Mr. B. G. Ropes, No. 89 East 29th-st., on Monday, April 1, at 3½ P. M. Relatives and friends are invited to attend without further notice. The remains will be taken to Salem, Mass., for interment.

McCORKINDALE.—At Fordham, Westchester County, on Saturday, March 30, ARCHIBALD McCORKINDALE, of Campbeltown, Scotland, aged 55 years.

RADDE.—The remains of the late Charles H. S., son of William and Christina Radde, who died at Kirseikahmen, East Prussia, in July last, having arrived in this City, the funeral will take place on Sunday next, March 31, at 1½ o'clock, from St. Mathew's Church, Walker-st., near Broadway. The friends of the deceased and of the family are respectfully invited to attend.

Glasgow and Argyleshire papers please copy.

STORY.—At Glen Haven, Cortlandt County, N. Y., ROBERT R. STORY, Jr., of Brooklyn, in the 23d year of his age.

Notice of funeral hereafter.

VAN DYKE.—At Bergen Point, N. J., on Thursday, March 28, after a severe illness, LYDIA A., wife of Isaac Van Dyke, aged 30 years and 3 months.

The relatives and friends of the family, also the members of Acacia Lodge No. 327, F. & A. M., and the members of Warren Lodge No. 253, I. O. of O. F., are invited to attend the funeral from No. 32 Greenwich-av., on Sunday, the 31st inst., at 1 P. M.

MISCELLANEOUS.

THE NEW-YORK LADIES' SOUTHERN RELIEF ASSOCIATION beg to acknowledge the following donations:

Through Rev. Wm. F. Morgan, D. D., being half of collection of Grace Church	$573 85
Daniel M. Smith	15 00
Total	$588 85
Amount acknowledged previously	37,564 32
Total receipts to date	$38,153 17

ARTHUR LEARY, Treasurer.

NEW-YORK, March 28, 1867.

POLITICAL.

EXECUTIVE COMMITTEE OF THE UNION REPUBLICAN GENERAL COMMITTEE.—The regular monthly meeting will take place on MONDAY EVENING, April 1, 1867, at Union Hall, corner of 23d-st. and Broadway. Punctual attendance requested.

A. J. DITTENHOEFFER, Chairman.

C. H. HALL, A. JACKSON PLUMB, } Secretaries.

RELIGIOUS NOTICES.

The New-York Times.

VOL. XVIII.......NO. 5501. NEW-YORK, TUESDAY, MAY 11, 1869. PRICE FOUR CENTS.

EAST AND WEST.

Completion of the Great Line Spanning the Continent.

The Closing Work and Ceremonies at Promontory Summit.

The News Flashed by Telegraph Simultaneously Over the Country.

Rejoicings of the Metropolis at the Completion of the Enterprise.

Celebrations in Chicago, Philadelphia and Other Cities.

The Work Accomplished—Ceremonies at Promontory Summit.

Special Dispatch to the New-York Times.

PROMONTORY, Utah, Monday, May 10.

The long-looked-for moment has arrived. The construction of the Pacific Railroad is *un fait accompli*. The inhabitants of the Atlantic seaboard and the dwellers on the Pacific slopes are henceforth emphatically one people. Your correspondent is writing on Promontory Summit amid the deafening shouts of the multitude, with the tick, tick, of the telegraph close to his ear. The proceedings of the day are:

1. Prayer by Rev. Dr. TODD, of Pittsfield, asking the favor of heaven upon the enterprise.
2. Laying of two rails, one opposite the other—one for the Union Pacific Railroad, and one for the Central Pacific Railroad.
3. Presentation of spikes to the two Companies—on the part of California by Dr. HARKNESS, on the part of Nevada by Hon. F. A. FRITLE, and on the part of Arizona by Governor SAFFORD.
4. Response by Governor STANFORD on the part of the Central Pacific Railroad.
5. Response by General G. M. DODGE on the part of the Union Pacific Railroad.
6. Driving of the last spikes by the two Companies; telegraph to be attached to the spike of the Central Pacific Company, and the last blow to announce to the world by telegraph the completion of the Pacific Railroad.
7. Telegram to the President of the United States.
8. Telegram to the Associated Press.

Announcement in Washington of the Completion of the Road—Scene in the Telegraph Office.

Special Dispatch to the New-York Times.

WASHINGTON, Monday, May 10.

The completion of the Pacific Railroad has monopolized public attention here to-day to the exclusion of everything else. The feeling is one of hearty rejoicing at the completion of this great work. There were no public observances, but the arrangements made by the telegraph company to announce the completion of the road simultaneously with the driving of the last spike were perfect. At 2:20 this afternoon, Washington time, all the telegraph offices in the country were notified by the Omaha telegraph office to be ready to receive the signals corresponding to the blows of the hammer that drove the last spike in the last rail that united New-York and San Francisco with a band of iron. Accordingly Mr. TINKER, Manager of the Western Union Telegraph Office in this city, placed a magnetic bell-sounder in the public office of that Company, corner Fourteenth-street and the avenue, connected the same with the main lines, and notified the various offices that he was ready. New-Orleans instantly responded, the answer being read from the bell-taps. New-York did the same. At 2:27 o'clock offices over the country began to make all sorts of inquiries of Omaha, to which that office replied:

"*To Everybody:* Keep quiet. When the last spike is driven at Promontory Point they will say 'Done.' Don't break the circuit, but watch for the signals of the blows of the hammer."

At 2:27 P. M., Promontory Point, 2,400 miles west of Washington, said to the people congregated in the various telegraph offices:

"Almost ready. Hats off; prayer is being offered."

A silence for the prayer ensued. At 2:40 the bell tapped again, and the office at the Point said:

"We have got done praying. The spike is about to be presented."

Chicago replied:

"We understand; all are ready in the East."

Promontory Point: "All ready now; the spike will be driven. The signal will be three dots for the commencement of the blows."

For a moment the instrument was silent; then the hammer of the magnet tapped the bell, "One, two, three," the signal; another pause of a few seconds, and the lightning came flashing eastward, vibrating over 2,400 miles between the junction of the two roads and Washington, and the blows of the hammer upon the spike were measured instantly in telegraphic accents on the bell here. At 2:47 P. M., Promontory Point gave the signal, "Done," and the Continent was spanned with iron. The same ceremony was observed at the military telegraph office in the War Department, where were present Secretary RAWLINS, Generals SHERMAN, TOWNSEND, and others. The President was unavoidably kept away by an engagement. The bell-taps here, too, repeated the blows of the hammer, and the completion of the great enterprise was known here before the echoes of the last stroke had died out of the ears of those present at the ceremonies on Promontory Point.

Rejoicing in This City—The Booming of Cannon and Chiming of Bells—Magnificent Thanksgiving Services at Old Trinity—Address by Rev. Dr. Vinton—Congratulatory Dispatches to San Francisco by Mayor Hall and the Chamber of Commerce.

It was apparent everywhere throughout the City yesterday that an event of more than usual importance was taking place, and that there was an evident disposition among the people to be jubilant. Especially was this the case in Wall-street, and in Printing-house-square and its vicinity. Flags were displayed on the City Hall, on all the newspaper offices, and on the prominent hotels. Every countenance seemed to bear a look of supreme satisfaction, and all were apparently awaiting with anticipations of delight the receipt of most welcome news. At length, soon after the sun had left the zenith, it came—the last rail of the road connecting our opposite ocean-bound shores was laid; the last spike (a gold one, by the bye) was driven; and thereupon there was booming of cannon, peals from Trinity chimes, and general rejoicing over the completion of the great enterprise, in the success of which not only this country, but the whole civilized world, is directly interested. According to the announcement made in yesterday's TIMES, there were special services in Old Trinity, and particular notice of the event was taken by the Chamber of Commerce. At 10 o'clock A. M., the Special Committee appointed by the Chamber at its last meeting proceeded to the office of the Western Union Telegraph Company, where Mr. S. B. RUGGLES, its Chairman, on behalf of the organization, handed to the operator, to be sent to San Francisco, the following

CONGRATULATORY DISPATCH.

From the Chamber of Commerce of New-York to the Chamber of Commerce of San Francisco, on the Completion of the Pacific Railway:

NEW-YORK, May 10, 1869—10 A. M.

The Chamber of Commerce of the State of New-York desires to unite at noon to-day with the Chamber of Commerce of San Francisco, in grateful thanksgiving to Almighty God, the Supreme Ruler of the Universe, on the completion of the continental line of railway, spanning the territory of the American Union and commercially uniting two great oceans of the globe; and in solemn recognition of the manifold benefits and blessings, industrial and commercial, moral and political, national and international, of this great avenue of intercommunication.

The new highway thus opened to man will not only develop the resources, extend the commerce, increase the power, exalt the dignity and perpetuate the unity of our Republic, but in its broader relations, as the segment of a world-embracing circle, directly connecting the nations of Europe with those of Asia, will materially facilitate the enlightened and advancing civilization of our age. By order of the Chamber.

SAMUEL B. RUGGLES,
WILLIAM E. DODGE,
GEORGE OPDYKE,
A. A. LOW,
Special Committee.

In a few minutes' time the lightning carried the congratulations of the Chamber across the Continent.

Up to the hour of going to press, no response had been received to the telegram sent to San Francisco by the Chamber of Commerce of this City.

SERVICES AT TRINITY CHURCH.

Long before 12 M., the hour at which the special religious services in honor of the great event were to begin, Old Trinity was crowded with a congregation representing all conditions of our municipal society, anxiously awaiting the commencement of the exercises. At noon, after a voluntary on the organ had been performed, a long line of white-robed choristers and attendant clergymen emerged from the vestry and entered the chancel, all singing the following processional hymn:

"O come, loud anthems let us sing,
Loud thanks to our Almighty King,
For we our voices high should raise
When our salvation's rock we praise.

The depths of earth are in His hand;
Her secret wealth at His command;
The strength of hills that reach the skies
Subjected to His empire lies.

The rolling ocean's vast abyss
By the same sovereign right is His;
'Twas made by His Almighty hand,
That formed and fixed the solid land.

O let us to His courts repair,
And bow with adoration there;
Down on our knees devoutly all
Before the Lord our Maker fall."

Among the ecclesiastics in attendance were Rev. Drs. DIX, OGILVIE and VINTON, of Trinity; Bishop LITTLEJOHN, of Brooklyn; Rev. Drs. BURGESS and STUBBS, Rev. Mr. OBERLY, Rev. J. P. WHYTE, of Newport, R. I.; Rev. Professor JOHNSON, of the Episcopal Seminary, and many other clergymen of this City and Brooklyn.

When all had taken their places in the chancel, the Lord's Prayer was recited with great fervor by the clergymen and congregation in unison, Rev. Dr. OGILVIE leading. The collects for the fourth, seventh and eighth Sundays after Trinity were then read, and the following special prayer, set forth by authority of the Bishop of the Diocese, was recited by Rev. Dr. DIX:

"O God, the Creator of the ends of the earth, Who upholdest all things by the Word of Thy power, without Whom nothing is strong, nothing is holy; we bless and magnify Thy glorious name that by Thy goodness the great work which we commemorate this day has been accomplished, so that the extreme borders of our land have been joined and brought nigh together, and a pathway opened between remote parts of the earth, both for the commerce of the nations and for a highway and a way whereby Thy Gospel may have free course, and Thy holy name may be glorified. We thank Thee that the wilderness and the solitary place are made glad, and that the desert may rejoice and blossom as the rose. We come before Thee this day, in deep humility and thankfulness of heart, acknowledging that Thine, O Lord, is the greatness and power, and the glory and the victory and the majesty: for all that is in the heaven and in the earth is Thine. Thine is the kingdom, O Lord, and Thou art exalted as Head over all. Both riches and honor come of Thee, and Thou reignest over all; and in Thine hand is power and might; and in Thine hand it is to make great and to give strength unto all. Now therefore, our God, we thank Thee, and praise Thy glorious name, through Jesus Christ our Lord. Amen.

The *Te Deum Laudamus* was then sung, after which Rev. Mr. OBERLY read the lesson from the 7th chapter of Deuteronomy. The epistle was read by Rev. J. P. WHYTE, of Newport, R. I., and the ante-communion service by Rev. Dr. DIX, when the Nicene Creed was recited, and the anthem, "Great is the Lord, and greatly to be praised," was sung as an offertory selection.

ADDRESS BY REV. DR. VINTON.

Rev. Dr. VINTON then ascended the pulpit and delivered the following address:

FELLOW-CITIZENS AND BRETHREN: You have just listened to the anthem of praise and thanksgiving sent up from two separate and distinct organs, one in the chancel and the other in the loft; and yet so uniform were their strains that you could not distinguish the harmonies of one instrument from those emitted by the other. This intimate connection between these instruments is grandly typical of the great event we are here assembled to commemorate—the harmony of music and concord of one tune are practically illustrative of the joining of two oceans by railroad connection. In order to give impressiveness to the completion of a work so fraught with blessings to us as a people, the Chamber of Commerce of New-York have sent, by their Committee, a congratulatory dispatch to the Chamber of Commerce of San Francisco. [The reverend gentleman here read the dispatch, which may be found above.] This communication has probably reached its destination long since, even earlier than it is dated, owing to the difference in time between the two points; and about the time when we shall have closed these exercises, our strains of praise and thanksgiving will be taken up and reiterated on the shores of the mighty Pacific. This is indeed a great event of the world; it is one of the victories of peace—a victory grander than those of war, which leave in their track desolation, devastation, misery and woe. It is a triumph of commerce—a triumph indicating free trade as a future law of the nation. It is practically, in view of the results that will flow to the cause of Christianity in consequence of it, a fulfillment of the prophecy recorded in Holy Writ: "And the Lord shall be king over all the earth; in that day there shall be one Lord, and his name one."—Zachariah xiv., 9. We are told again that the Lord shall be king, and all the nations shall hear the voice of Zion. When we contemplate this achievement we can hardly realize its magnitude. Three thousand two hundred and eighty-five miles of continuous railway within four degrees of latitude and fifty degrees of longitude in the temperate zone. It begun when the nation was agitated by war, and is finished now when we enjoy a reign of peace. When the ocean route was discovered around the Cape of Good Hope, it was very properly regarded as a blessing to mankind—hence the designation by which it is known; but the completion of this mighty work, which connects the two oceans, is a still greater blessing. In the olden times, when camels—those ships of the desert—were the means used for transportation, for the furtherance of commercial traffic, it was found that wherever the caravans stopped there would spring up cities, and there would be evidences of civilization. So with this great work. It will populate our vast territory and be the great highway of the nations; their merchants will cross it to trade with us. But there is another aspect in which we view it as a blessing, and in connection with which we esteem it of still greater importance. It will preserve the Union of these States. Philosophers tell us, and we know it to be true, that where there are rivers which diverge in their courses, and have separate and distinct outlets, (as in Europe,) there the nations become diffused, and the peoples are separated and disunited. But where, on the contrary, the topography is such that the rivers all flow into one common central basin, there is necessarily a concentration of interests and of peoples, and that territory is marked out by God to be under one Government. By the operation of this natural law we must regard it as decreed that there shall ever be a unity of people and government in all that territory which lies between the Alleghanies and the Rocky Mountains. Beyond these lofty heights, however, we find the rivers diverging, as in Europe, and, following the rule that obtains in the Old World, there might be a diffusion of interests and a separation of governments in that section of the country divided from us by the Sierra Nevada and the Rocky Mountains. But this railway counteracts such natural tendency to disunion, has prevented a separation, and binds the States of the Atlantic and Pacific into one nation. Roman roads unified and consolidated the Roman Empire. They were made by the ambition of Emperors for the necessities of war and commerce; but, under Divine Providence, they were the highways along which the Apostles and the missionaries of Christ carried the good tidings of salvation to the tribes of the peoples. So this Pacific Railway is a means, under Divine Providence, for propagating the Church and the Gospel from this, the youngest Christian nation, to the oldest land in the Orient, now sunk in Paganism and idolatry, and so will revive the worship of the Triune God—the God of our salvation—in the farther East, the birthplace of Christianity. For this we celebrate this great event. Join with me, therefore, in singing an anthem of praise to God, "Glory to God in the highest; on earth peace, good will to men."

The choir then pealed forth the *Gloria* in MOZART'S immortal Twelfth Mass, the rendering throughout being superbly grand. Dr. DIX then offered up the prayer for the whole state of Christ's Church militant here on earth, and pronounced the benediction, after which the clergymen and choristers returned to the vestry, singing the recessional hymn, commencing:

"Bless'd be thou, the God of Israel,
Thou our Father and our Lord;
Bless'd thy Majesty forever,
Ever be thy name adored.

Thine, O Lord, are power and greatness,
Glory, victory, are thine own;
All is thine in earth and heaven,
Over all thy boundless throne."

The musical exercises throughout were of a superior order, and chained the attention of the immense congregation.

THE CHIMES.

When the religious services were ended, Mr. AYLIFFE struck up the chimes, beginning by ringing the changes on eight bells, and following with national and operatic airs. The ringing of the chimes attracted a large crowd to Broadway at the head of Wall-street, and it was not until the booming of cannon in the City Hall Park told of the receipt of an official dispatch by His Honor Mayor HALL, announcing the driving of the last spike in the last rail, that this crowd separated.

In Wall-street, and at the rooms of the Chamber of Commerce, the great event of the day was the subject of conversation and congratulation, and many announcements were made by the merchants of a determination to visit San Francisco, *via* the new route, during the coming Summer.

At the City Hall.

The flags on the City Hall were hoisted at an early hour, and preparations were made to fire one hundred guns as soon as the announcement was received that the last rail had been laid and the great work completed. At 3:16 P. M. the following dispatch was handed to the Mayor:

MAYOR BROWN, OF SAN FRANCISCO, TO MAYOR HALL.

PROMONTORY POINT, May 10, 1869.

To Hon. A. Oakey Hall, Mayor of New-York:

The last spike in the rail connecting the Atlantic and Pacific by rail has been driven at 3:10 P. M., (New-York time.)

A. S. BROWN, Mayor.

In a few minutes after the receipt of Mayor BROWN'S dispatch Mayor HALL sent the following:

MAYOR HALL'S REPLY.

EXECUTIVE DEPARTMENT, CITY HALL, NEW-YORK, May 10, 1869.

To the Mayor of San Francisco:

New-York rejoiced when, almost half a century ago, by the completion of the Erie Canal, the silver chain of Western inland seas was riveted upon the Atlantic Ocean. The metropolis of America exults to-day, because by the completion of the Pacific Railway two extremities and coasts of an immense continent are commercially welded together. Apart from the relations of this grand event to Christianity, political economy, civilization and patriotism, it justifies the metropolis in the pardonably selfish expectation to soon become the commercial exchange of the world. Her newspapers, which have so largely contributed to this day's result, must soon accustom our citizens to phrases like this one: "The Asiatic freight train has arrived on time." So our flags are now flying, our cannon now booming, and in Old Trinity, at the head of Wall-street, a *Te Deum* imparts thankful harmonies to the busy hum about her church walls. Can it, then, be necessary, by mere words, to tender you fuller magnetic sympathy? As for congratulations to you, phrases seem inadequate to foretell the full fruition to your golden-gated city of enterprise of this beginning of railway intercommunication. Therefore let this 10th of May pass into the annals of San Francisco, New-York, and of every hamlet, village, town and city along the new highway, as an anniversary day.

A. OAKEY HALL,
Mayor of New-York.

The Mayor also gave orders to fire 100 guns in the City Hall Park in honor of the event, and Mr. ROOME having kept guns and ammunition in readiness, the first discharge was fired within five minutes after the receipt of the dispatch. A large number of persons congregated in the Park to listen to the booming of the cannon, which told of another great enterprise completed, and to congratulate each other on the event. Flags were hoisted on the Astor House and most of the private buildings so soon as the news was made public.

Celebrations in Chicago, Philadelphia, Buffalo and Other Places.

CHICAGO, Monday, May 10.

The celebration of the completion of the great interoceanic railway connection to-day was the most successful affair of the kind that ever took place in Chicago, and probably in the West. It was entirely impromptu, and therefore almost every man and woman and child in the city did their part toward making it a success. The procession was unique in appearance, and immense in length, which at the lowest estimate was seven miles. During the moving of the procession Vice-President COLFAX received the following dispatch:

PROMONTORY SUMMIT, Utah, Monday, May 10.

To Hon. Schuyler Colfax, Vice-President:

The rails were connected to-day. The prophecy of BENTON to-day is a fact. This is the way to India. Signed

G. M. DODGE, JOHN DUFF,
SIDNEY DILLON, T. C. DURANT.

This evening Vice-President COLFAX, Lieutenant-Governor BROSS and others addressed a large audience at Library Hall, in which they spoke eloquently of the great era which this day marks in the history of our country.

During the evening there was also a general indulgence in fireworks, bonfires, illuminations, &c.

PHILADELPHIA, Monday, May 10.

At 2:30 o'clock precisely, Philadelphia time, the news was received of the driving of the last spike of the Pacific Railroad. Word was sent to the Mayor, and, in a few minutes, the bells on Independence Hall and various fire stations were rung, drawing a crowd into the streets, thinking a general alarm of fire was being rung. The people soon ascertained the reason of the ringing of the bells, and flags were immediately hoisted everywhere. A large number of steam fire-engines were ranged in front of Independence Hall, with screeching whistles, hose carriages, bells ringing, &c. Joy was expressed in every face at the completion of the great work of the century. The sudden flocking of the people to the State-house reminded one of the reception of the news of the surrender of LEE'S army, when a similar scene was enacted.

BUFFALO, N. Y., Monday, May 10.

A large crowd of citizens assembled at the Board of Trade rooms this afternoon, to hear the announcement by telegraph of the driving of the last spike in the rail connecting the Atlantic coast with the Pacific. The telegraph wire was attached to a large gong bell, and at 2:41 o'clock, city time, repeating strokes were simultaneously made. At the completion cheers were given, the "Star Spangle Banner" sung by the crowd, prayer offered and appropriate speeches made by Hon. D. S. BENNETT, HENRY A. RICHMOND and others.

SCRANTON, Penn., Monday, May 8.

Scranton celebrated the completion of the Pacific Railroad by the firing of cannons, ringing of bells, whistling of locomotives, and a general expression of joy by its citizens.

The Southern Pacific—Meeting of Directors at St. Louis.

ST. LOUIS, Monday, May 10.

Judge LEVI PARSONS, of New-York, President of the southern branch of the Union Pacific Railroad, running from Fort Riley, Kansas, down the Neosho Valley to Fort Smith, Ark., arrived here last night, accompanied by the following New-York directors: FRANCIS SKIDDY, ROBERT S. STEVENS, GEORGE DENNISON, THEODORE JOHNSON and H. H. JOHNSON. The party leave this afternoon for Junction City, for the purpose of making an inspection of the road. The road is a feeder to the Kansas Pacific Railroad. The survey was commenced in December last. Sixty miles will be built by next September, and the whole road is under contract. The Company have a grant of 1,350,000 acres of land, and $810,000 in county bonds have been subscribed toward the road by the counties through which it passes. Five thousand emigrants from Copenhagen have paid their passage, and 30,000 Swedes are expected during the season to settle on the lands belonging to the road.

WASHINGTON.

Minister Motley's Instructions—The Alabama Claims—The Belgian Mission—Case of the Mary Lowell.

Special Dispatches to the New-York Times.

WASHINGTON, Monday, May 10.

Mr. MOTLEY, the new Minister to England, is, it appears, to receive some written instructions of a general character in reference to the resumption of negotiations for the settlement of the pending questions between this country and Great Britain. It is stated that they will be very brief, and cover not so much what the present Administration would be willing to consider a satisfactory solution of the Alabama difficulty, as what it would be sure to reject. Mr. MOTLEY, whose return to Washington before he leaves is not looked for, will sail from New-York on the 19th inst.

THE ALABAMA CLAIMS.

A gentleman who arrived here to-day direct from London, and who is well acquainted with the leading statesmen there, says that Sir HENRY LYTTON BULWER had given notice that he would, on the evening of May 11, call up the *Alabama* Claims Treaty in the House of Commons. It was Sir HENRY'S intention to speak at some length, criticising the action of the British Ministry, and also taking exceptions to the course of Mr. SEWARD in precipitating action on this subject after the American people had condemned the Johnson Administration at the ballot-box. This speech from a man so strong in this nation as Mr. BULWER, will be looked for with much interest, and it is hoped here that the reception of Mr. SUMNER'S speech in England will not defer its delivery.

THE BELGIAN MISSION.

A large number of consular commissions were signed at the State Department during Saturday and to-day, and will be transmitted during the present week. The President visited the Department to-day, and rumor has it that it was in reference to the Belgian mission, and the making of some provision for J. RUSSELL JONES. It can be stated authoritatively, however, that there will be no immediate change in the representation of the United States at that Court.

THE MARY LOWELL.

The facts in the case of the *Mary Lowell*, that she was an American ship, seized while in British waters, under charge of a British officer, and condemned as a prize by the Spanish authorities, were officially communicated to the Foreign Office of Great Britain by the State Department some time ago. The claim has been presented by the English Government for settlement at Madrid, and here it is that another complication arises. It appears that the Spanish authorities insist that the vessel was not in British waters at the time, being more than three leagues from shore, which in the very nature of things will take some time to decide. The Spanish Government professes its ability to produce witnesses who will testify to this fact of locality at the time of seizure.

THE TAX QUESTION.

Two representatives of the New-York brokers' interest were here to-day, endeavoring to induce the reopening of the recent decision in the tax question, for the purpose of reviewing some of its points. In the absence of the Commissioner, Mr. DOUGLASS, Acting Commissioner, and Mr. SMITH, Solicitor, decided not to reopen the question. A communication was also presented from C. S. SLOANE, Esq., Chairman of the Executive Committee of the Stock Exchange, requesting that the time for making monthly returns for April should be extended, and that meanwhile a reconsideration of the original question should be had. Mr. DOUGLASS, for the Commissioner, assured the parties that the Department would not exercise any arbitrary power, but would exercise all the discretionary authority that seemed necessary to facilitate parties in accommodating themselves to the requirements of the recent decision.

THE NEW-YORK CUSTOM-HOUSE.

Considerable important information was, to-day, laid before the President with reference to irregular and fraudulent practices hitherto prevalent in the New-York Custom-house. The matters were referred to Special Agent HOWE for his investigation, and he will probably bring them to the attention of Collector GRINNELL.

PERSONAL.

JOHN CLEM, of Ohio, the famous drummer boy, who dropped his drum for a musket at Chicamauga, and shot a rebel Colonel who demanded his surrender, and was subsequently wounded in another engagement, has been appointed a cadet at large to West Point by the President. He was but 12 years of age when he beat his drum, and is scarce 17 now. He was cordially greeted by the President, General LOGAN and the Secretary of War, all of whom knew him well in the army.

Dispatches to the Associated Press.

WASHINGTON, Monday, May 10.

APPOINTMENTS.

THOMAS J. KINNEY has been appointed Assessor of Internal Revenue for the Ninth Illinois District, *vice* AMOS C. BABCOCK, who declined. JOHN P. TAGGART, of Galena, has been appointed Assessor of Utah, *vice* CAREY declined. No further appointment of Supervisors will be made until the return of Commissioner DELANO.

THE "JAR CASE."

The celebrated jar case of ROWLEY *vs.* MASON has assumed a new phase. Judge FISHER had decided in favor of ROWLEY, but on Saturday the same Judge granted a preliminary injunction staying the issue of a patent to ROWLEY, it being claimed that J. L. MASON was the original inventor, and reduced the article to practice.

DUTIES ON IRON TUBES AND FLUES.

The Secretary of the Treasury has decided that the tariff, as well as commercial usage, recognizes a distinction between wrought-iron tubes and wrought-iron flues, and that the former are liable to a duty of 3½ cents per pound, and the latter of 2½ cents per pound, under the existing laws.

ANNEXATION OF ST. DOMINGO.

Mr. FABENS, the confidential agent of the St. Domingo Government, recently had an interview with Secretary FISH. The subject of annexation will receive official consideration at an early day. The parties interested in the annexation movement furnish an extract of a letter from Professor GABB, who says he has prospected 200 miles of gold-bearing territory, surpassing in richness any known portion of California and Arizona.

REVENUE SUPERVISORS.

On the return of Commissioner DELANO several additional Supervisors of Internal Revenue will be appointed.

ARMY AND NAVY INTELLIGENCE.

Lieutenant-Commander A. P. Cooke has been ordered to the Naval Academy on the 1st of October next. Chief Engineer Henry Mason has been ordered to special duty in charge of the machinery at Providence. First-Lieutenant Moses Wiley, of the Sixth United States Cavalry, has resigned. Brevet Lieutenant-Colonel J. N. Benet, Major of the Ordnance Department, who has been assisting General Dyer while before the Court of Inquiry, has been ordered to return to his station and resume his duties as commanding officer of the Frankford Arsenal, Pennsylvania. Captain Edward Ball, of the Second Cavalry, has been ordered to join his company in the Department of the Platte.

ALBANY.

End of the Contest Over the Tammany Tax Levies.

A Reduction of About Two Millions at Length Made.

Final Adjournment of the Legislature at Midnight.

The Row About the New-York Tax Levies—The Republicans Stand Firm—So do the Democrats—A Dead Lock.

From Our Own Correspondent.

ALBANY, Monday, May 10, 1869.

The row about the Tammany tax levies still continues, with no better prospect of an adjustment than existed when the two Houses adjourned on Sunday morning. Tammany labored hard all day yesterday to buy over another Republican Senator, but without success. The new bribery bill (which, by the way, the Governor has not signed yet) looms up as a dark shadow in the future, and begins to strike terror to the hearts of men who have been trading their votes during this and previous sessions. It is important for the future moral effect of the law that an example should be made under it immediately, and the public will be glad to know that evidence is being collected for that purpose. In order that the imputation of partisanship may not attach to the movement, the law should be enforced against a Democrat and a Republican at the same time, and an example should also be made of one or more of the prominent lobbyists who have got rich by hanging around the Legislature during this and past years, disbursing the bribery funds. The influence of these scoundrels on the legislation of the State is even more than that of the members who sell their votes, for each one of them has corrupted scores of members, who, but for them, would never have thought of selling themselves.

At the opening of the Senate this morning Mr. FOLGER moved to take from the table several vetoes of the Governor, which was carried, and all were sustained. The Senate then resumed the consideration of the tax levies where they left off Sunday morning. Mr. TWEED moved that the Senate concur in the levies passed by the Assembly, whereupon Mr. FOLGER raised the point of order that both Houses having refused to agree through their respective Conference Committees in the levies as passed by the Assembly, the same were dead, and could receive no further action from the Senate. The President decided the point of order not well taken, and Mr. FOLGER appealed. After considerable discussion, in which Mr. CROWLEY sustained Mr. FOLGER, and Mr. MURPHY the President, a vote was taken on the appeal, which resulted yeas 16, nays 16—MATTOON voting, as usual, with the Democrats. The President gave the casting vote in the affirmative to sustain his own decision, whereupon Mr. FOLGER raised another point of order, that on an appeal from the decision of the President that functionary had no right to give the casting vote.

Lieutenant-Governor BEACH—The chair decides otherwise.

Mr. FOLGER—"Otherwise," (with emphasis;) that is nothing but a reiteration of the chair's decision.

A discussion then ensued as to the rights of the President in the case, Mr. MURPHY claiming that he had the right to give the casting vote, and citing a similar case on the part of the Speaker of the Assembly several years ago.

Mr. FOLGER said that was not a parallel case. The Speaker of the Assembly was a member-elect of that body, whereas the President of the Senate was not a member of the Senate, but merely the constitutional presiding officer. As a question of delicacy on the part of the President, he declined to say anything.

Mr. MATTOON here raised the point that no question was pending, and the discussion dropped.

Mr. TWEED'S motion to concur in the tax levies passed by the Assembly being again in order, Mr. MORGAN moved to strike out the clause in the City levy making an appropriation of twenty per cent. of the Excise fund (equal to about $300,000) for the support of private schools in New-York. He said these private schools were simply parochial schools, and as such were sectarian. The larger share of them were Catholic, but he was opposed to appropriating money for the support of any sectarian schools of any denomination. It was a stepping-stone to the destruction of the entire public school system of the State. Instead of encouraging these schools by giving them a share of the public money, the State ought to discourage them, and compel the children educated therein to come out and attend the public schools.

Mr. VAN PATTEN opposed the appropriation and every other scheme for perpetuating religious prejudice, by encouraging schools founded in opposition to the public schools of the State. If there were not accommodations sufficient for all the children in New-York, let them be increased; but if any religious denomination insisted upon educating its children in sectarian schools, let it support such schools by private aid, and not with the public fund.

Mr. MATTOON advocated the appropriation, because it would reach a class of children who would not otherwise be educated.

Mr. CREAMER also advocated it, and said that he had talked with leading men in other denominations besides the Catholic, and they were equally earnest with the Catholics in desiring an appropriation of this kind. He did not state who the "leading men" were, or to what denomination they belonged.

Mr. HUMPHREY protested against any further discussion of the School question at this time, as it would not make a particle of difference or change a single vote on this or any other item of the tax levies now under consideration.

Mr. MORGAN then withdrew his motion to strike out this clause, and Mr. TWEED withdrew his motion to concur; whereupon Mr. CREAMER moved that another Conference Committee be appointed, which was carried. Mr. O'DONNELL moved to instruct the Committee to adhere to the tax levies that passed the Senate—lost by the same party vote, Mr. MATTOON voting with the Democrats. During the discussion on this motion Mr. MORGAN informed the Democratic side of the Senate that the Republicans would not move a hair's breadth from the position they had taken, and that they could never pass the tax levies that were put through the Assembly by the Tammany Ring.

Mr. MATTOON took the occasion to deny the insinuations that had been thrown out about his deserting his party and going over to the Democrats. There was not a drop of Democratic blood in his veins and never would be. But he denied that this was, or ought to be regarded as a party measure. It was entirely a local measure that ought to be left to New-York. He had always been opposed to special legislation for the City of New-York, and was ready at any time to vote for the repeal of all the commissions that had been created for that City except the Police Commission, which he said he believed was satisfactory to both parties. On party questions he always voted with his party, and always should. He claimed to represent his constituents satisfactorily, and was perfectly willing to take their judgment on his course as a Senator.

The President announced the new Conference Committee on the part of the Senate to be Messrs. CREAMER and GENET, Democrats, and VAN PATTEN, Republican. Mr. VAN PATTEN declined to serve, as did also Mr. STANFORD and Mr. FOLGER. Mr. WILLIAMS was then appointed and accepted, but afterward changed his mind and withdrew from the Committee. On the part of the Assembly the Speaker appointed Messrs. CAMPBELL, GLEASON and LA BAR, Republicans, and Messrs. HITCHMAN and IRVING, Democrats. The only change in the two Committees, from those that were unable to agree before, is in the name of GLEASON on the Assembly Committee in place of TUTTLE.

The Committee went into session at noon, and the Senate adjourned to 3 P. M.

IN THE ASSEMBLY

the proceedings to-day were of little public interest. A few Senate bills of a local character were concurred in, and an attempt was made to concur in Swain's Two-tier Railroad bill, as it passed the Senate, but failed. Another mock session was held while waiting for the Senate's Conference Committee, and after that was agreed upon the House adjourned to 4 P. M. S.

The Tax Levies—Agreement of the Conference Committees—The Levies Reduced—Their Passage.

Special Dispatch to the New-York Times.

ALBANY, Monday, May 10.

The new Conference Committees on the tax levies, after being in session all day, came in at 9 o'clock this evening with a report that they had agreed unanimously on both the City and County levies. Senator WILLIAMS, who at first withdrew from the Committee, again changed his mind, and went back and took part in the deliberations, and signed his name to the report. The levies, as agreed upon, are in the aggregate $2,200,000 larger than those that originally passed the Senate—the increase on the City levy being $1,600,000, and on the County levy $600,000; but the items of the ring levies that passed the Assembly have been cut down in the aggregate about $2,000,000. The item appropriating 20 per cent. of the Excise income to private schools is retained, but the money is to be distributed under the direction of the Board of Education. On the whole, the Republican members of the Assembly Committee think they have got a pretty moderate levy.

It was ratified by the Assembly nearly unanimously, but in the Senate it met with a strong opposition. It had been agreed among the Republican members of the Senate, with the exception of MATTOON, who had gone over to the enemy, that they would adhere to the levies which passed their body; and when they saw WILLIAMS' name signed to the report of the Conference Committee they were satisfied that another of their members had gone over to the enemy, and the result proved that there were two more traitors in the camp; for, when the vote on concurring with the report of the Committee was taken, it was found that VAN PATTEN had also become a sudden convert to the Tammany levies. Both of these Senators tried to excuse themselves for the vote they gave, but it was done in such a stammering way and with such evidence of guilt as to become not only a mortifying but a sickening spectacle. MATTOON, who does his business boldly, was disgusted with his associates in treason, and did not hesitate to say he was ashamed of them. The vote stood 18 in favor of concurring with the Committee and 13 against. Mr. STANFORD was absent; but was prepared to vote with his party if his vote had been necessary. Had the report of the Committee been substantially in favor of the ring levies as they passed the Assembly, it was the design of the Republicans to leave the Senate, so that three-fifths would not remain to do business, and thus prevent a confirmation of the levies in case it could not otherwise be done. After finishing the two levies, both Houses passed concurrent resolutions to adjourn *sine die* at 12 o'clock midnight, which they did, and many of the members left in the early morning trains.

THE STATE LEGISLATURE.

SENATE....ALBANY, Monday, May 10.

The Senate met at 9 o'clock.

On motion of Mr. FOLGER, the veto messages of the Governor were taken from the table. The veto of the bill relative to filling the vacancy in the office of Justice of the Peace at Lowville was first considered. The veto was sustained, 28 to 1—Mr. MATTOON.

The veto of the bill to authorize the appointment of a President *pro tem.* of the Metropolitan Board of Police was sustained, 17 to 8.

The veto of the One Hundred and Twenty-fifth-street Railroad bill was sustained, 28 to 3—Messrs. CAULDWELL, GENET and MATTOON.

The veto of the Avenue C Railroad bill was sustained, 23 to 3—Messrs. CAULDWELL, GENET and MATTOON.

The veto of the bill in relation to filling the vacancies of Justices of the Peace in the several towns of the State was brought up. Mr. FOLGER thought the Governor partly right and partly wrong, and favored passing over the veto. The veto was sustained, 15 to 15—Messrs. Crowley, Folger, Hale, Kennedy, Mattoon, Morgan, Nicks, O'Donnell, Pulver, Parker, Stanford, Thayer, Van Petten, Chapman and Humphrey voting no. The veto of the bill to incorporate the Oswego Pier and Dock Company was sustained by 24 to 2, Messrs. MATTOON and VAN PETTEN voting no.

Under the order of messages from the Assembly, Mr. TWEED called up the question of concurring in the amendments to the Tax Levy bill. Mr. FOLGER raised the point of order that the Senate having agreed with the report of the Conference Committee, that they had failed to agree, and having discharged the Committee, no further action could be taken, and that the bill is dead.

The President overruled the point of order. Mr. FOLGER appealed from the decision. The Chair was sustained by 16 to 16—all the Democrats and Mr. MATTOON voting yea and the Republicans voting nay, the Chair giving the casting vote.

Mr. FOLGER raised the point of order that on a question of sustaining a decision of the Chair the President cannot give the casting vote. Mr. MURPHY took issue thereon. The Chair overruled the point of order. The question being on concurring with the Assembly amendment, Mr. MORGAN asked for a division of the question so as to vote separately on the proposition to appropriate twenty per cent. of the Excise fund for what he termed sectarian schools in New-York.

The proposition was discussed at some length by Messrs. MORGAN and MURPHY.

Mr. MORGAN withdrew his request for a division.

Mr. TWEED withdrew his motion to concur in Assembly amendments.

Mr. CREAMER moved that a new Conference Committee be appointed; which was carried, 17 to 15—Messrs. MATTOON and VAN PETTEN voting yea with the Democrats.

Mr. VAN PETTEN said he voted under a misapprehension, and moved to reconsider the last vote.

Mr. CROWLEY thought this idle, and said that it was evident the question must be compromised.

Mr. MORGAN said compromise was impossible. The Republican Senators have only to stand by the original Senate bill.

Mr. TWEED said there was no remedy for the dilemma except compromise.

Mr. FOLGER said the compromise must be in the Senate, and not with the Citizens' Association.

The motion to reconsider was lost, 16 to 16—the President voting no, and Mr. MATTOON voting no with the Democrats.

The President appointed the following as such Committee of Conference: Messrs. CREAMER, GENET, FOLGER.

The latter declined and Mr. STANFORD was appointed. Mr. STANFORD declined and Mr. VAN PETTEN was appointed. Mr. VAN PETTEN declined and Mr. WILLIAMS was appointed.

Mr. O'DONNELL moved to instruct the Committee to insist on the original Senate bill, or on the Assembly bill, as reported by its Committee. Lost, 16 to 16—Mr. MATTOON voting no, with the Democrats; the Chair also voting no.

The Senate took a recess until this afternoon, awaiting the Conference Committee's action.

AFTERNOON SESSION.

Mr. O'DONNELL introduced a bill, which immediately passed, protecting the fishing interests in Lake Ontario, bays, estuaries and River St. Lawrence.

Concurred in: The Assembly amendments to the bill for the construction of a new work and extraordinary repair on canals. The bill imposing a tax of three-quarters of a mill involves an expenditure of about one million and a half dollars.

The report of the Conference Committee on amending the General Excise law so as to retain the Senate amendments authorizing licenses to be granted for the sale of ale or beer for $10 was agreed to. Mr. MATTOON dissented.

The bill to incorporate the Brevoort Savings Bank, New-York, was passed.

On motion of Mr. VAN PETTEN, the Judiciary Committee, upon investigating the gun contract, was excused from reporting this session, and have leave to sit during the recess without expense to the State.

The report of the Conference Committee on the Tax Levies was received. The report of the City levy was concurred in—18 to 13—yeas all Democrats, and Messrs. VAN PETTEN, WILLIAMS and MATTOON; nays, all Republicans.

YEAS—Messrs. Banks, Beach, Bradley, Cauldwell, Creamer, Edwards, Genet, Graham, Hubbard, Mattoon, Morris, Murphy, Nichols, Norton, Pierce, Tweed, Van Petten, Williams—18.

NAYS—Messrs. Campbell, Chapman, Crowley, Folger, Hale, Humphrey, Kennedy, Morgan, Nicks, O'Donnell, Palmer, Parker, Thayer—13.

The report of the Committee of Conference on the County Levy was read, and concurred in by the same vote as the City Levy.

At 10:45, the levies being disposed of, a concurrent resolution was adopted to adjourn at 12 midnight.

On motion of Mr. THAYER, a new Committee of Conference on the Canal Appropriation bill was appointed, as follows: Messrs. THAYER, MORRIS and HUBBARD.

Recess for three-quarters of an hour.

EVENING SESSION.

Messrs. BRADLEY and CREAMER were appointed a committee to wait on the Assembly and inform them that the Senate was ready to adjourn. A committee was also appointed to wait on the Governor.

At 12 midnight, Lieutenant-Governor BEACH after a few words of farewell, declared the Senate adjourned *sine die*.

ASSEMBLY.

On motion of Mr. HARTMAN, it was resolved that, if the Senate concur, the Assembly will adjourn *sine die* at 12 o'clock to-day.

The Speaker appointed the following as the Committee of Conference on the Tax Levies: Messrs. LA BAU, W. W. CAMPBELL, HITCHMAN, GLEASON and IRVING.

The Assembly took a recess for half an hour.

Upon reassembling, the Assembly concurred in the report of the Committee of Conference on the Canal Appropriation bill; also, the State Excise law.

Recess till 4 o'clock.

EVENING SESSION.

BILL ORDERED TO A THIRD READING.

For the construction of a railroad on Twenty-third-street, the charter to be sold at auction.

Mr. FREAR asked and obtained unanimous consent that said bill have now its third reading and the bill passed—Mr. SELKREG alone voting nay.

Mr. W. W. CAMPBELL, of the Committee of Conference on the Tax Levies, made a unanimous report cutting down the City Levy $1,800,000, and the County Levy about $600,000. The report of the City Levy was concurred in, 94 to 11. The report on the County Levy was concurred in 86 to 15.

The Senate bill to protect the fishing interests on Lake Ontario, its bays and entrances, and the River St. Lawrence, was passed.

At 11:15 o'clock a message was received from the Governor, vetoing the bill relative to the assessment rolls in the town of Oswegatchie, St. Lawrence County. The Governor says the bill is a needless interference with the duties of the Town Assessors and Town Supervisors, which are regulated by the general laws. The City of Ogdensburg is a part of the town of Oswegatchie, and its citizens have their share in electing Supervisors of the town, whose jurisdiction extends over the city as well as the town for all town purposes. So long as the city continues a part of the town it is not right that any of the duties and powers should be devolved upon the Ward Supervisors, whose jurisdictions are much more limited. If the proposed change is necessary, there should be a general law passed.

The veto was sustained by a vote of 71 to 1.

Messrs. RICH, HUSTED and FERRIS were appointed a Committee to inform the Senate that the House was ready to adjourn; and Messrs. HIXON and MILLER were also appointed a Committee to inform the Governor of the same.

Mr. JACOBS called up his resolution instructing the Canal Board to inquire into the expendiency of the building for the State a grain elevator in Buffalo.

The resolution was adopted, 43 to 24.

The Committee of Conference on the Canal Ordinary Repair Appropriation bill reported their failure to agree. Laid on the table and the bill killed.

Farewell speeches were made by Mr. SELKREG, Judge CAMPBELL and Mr. JACOBS. The Speaker, Mr. YOUNGLOVE, made the closing speech, and at 12:20 declared the Assembly adjourned *sine die*.

THE BILLIARD TOURNAMENT.

Close of the Tie Games—Foster Wins Against Snyder—The Winner of the Match Game in the Evening.

The closing game of the tie series of the tournament was played yesterday afternoon between FOSTER and SNYDER. It was to decide the choice for third and fourth prizes. There was not a game in the tournament proper that at all compares with this. It was played out in the shortest time, was marked by the largest run, and foots up the highest average. Both parties played strongly, the loser making an average of twenty-nine, going four times above triple figures, and one of these reaching above 200. FOSTER, on the other hand, ran up the tremendous number of 492 in the thirteenth inning. It was regretted that such a game as was that of yesterday afternoon had not occurred in the tournament proper, as it would undoubtedly have nerved up all the players, and as a result would have run up the grand averages many points from the lowest to the highest on the list. Below is presented a very full and concise table of the play, which gives the result in better form than any words can depict:

FOSTER—0, 0, 3, 21, 48, 6, 1, 90, 0, 63, 21, 3, 492, 60, 84, 6, 27, 3, 36, 6, 6, 0, 15, 12, 30, 21, 3, 3, 12, 87, 92.

SNYDER—0, 3, 3, 24, 0, 15, 13, 12, 42, 3, 249, 13, 27, 117, 3, 0, 0, 3, 123, 9, 6, 1, 10, 27, 0, 9, 30, 120, 9, 0.

Referee—R. SCOFIELD.

CYRILLE DION and JOHN MCDEVITT last evening played a game of three ball caroms for $250 a side, which, for closeness of score, was never excelled. MCDEVITT at one time was 60 points ahead, and toward the close of the game stood 35 ahead of his opponent, and had only 8 points to make to win. DION struggled manfully, and, although he was all over a loser apparently, ultimately won the game, amid deafening applause, by one run. Below is given the full score:

DION—0, 0, 0, 1, 0, 3, 2, 3, 0, 2, 2, 0, 1, 6, 0, 2, 0, 0, 4, 5, 2, 0, 0, 0, 2, 4, 1, 4, 0, 0, 0, 1, 1, 4, 0, 2, 0, 0, 6, 2, 2, 1, 5, 1, 0, 0, 0, 0, 0, 0, 0, 4, 0, 4, 10, 2, 5, 1, 2, 0, 1, 2, 0, 0, 0, 0, 6, 0, 18, 0, 2, 0, 1, 0, 0, 2, 4, 0, 2, 0, 6, 0, 1, 6, 11, 9, 7, 1, 11, 0, 1, 5, 0, 0, 0, 0, 0, 0, 1, 1, 0, 0, 0, 1, 1, 6, 1, 19, 0, 2, 0, 0, 13, 0, 0, 15, 2, 0, 0, 0, 0, 6, 2, 0, 3, 5, 0, 3, 0, 15, 3, 2, 2, 1, 2, 3, 0, 1, 0, 1, 1, 14, 2. Total 300.

MCDEVITT—3, 1, 0, 1, 5, 6, 1, 0, 2, 0, 9, 0, 0, 0, 1, 1, 13, 0, 4, 1, 1, 0, 0, 0, 0, 13, 1, 3, 2, 5, 0, 7, 9, 1, 0, 0, 2, 2, 7, 5, 2, 5, 0, 0, 5, 0, 0, 0, 2, 0, 1, 0, 0, 1, 0, 1, 9, 0, 3, 2, 0, 1, 0, 0, 6, 3, 0, 7, 2, 1, 1, 0, 0, 0, 3, 0, 29, 0, 1, 2, 5, 4, 2, 0, 0, 2, 0, 1, 0, 0, 2, 0, 0, 0, 0, 1, 3, 0, 0, 0, 0, 6, 3, 6, 2, 0, 0, 7, 0, 5, 6, 3, 0, 0, 0, 0, 0, 2, 1, 6, 27, 0, 0, 0, 0, 1, 0, 1, 0, 0, 4, 0. Total, 299.

The Massachusetts State Billiard Tournament at Boston.

BOSTON, Mass., Monday, May 10.

The Massachusetts Billiard Tournament, for the championship of the State, commenced this afternoon at the Olympic Theatre. The games to be played are 500 points each, push shot barred; the counting to be the same as in the New-York Tournament games. The first game was between R. E. WILMARTH and WILLIAM A. TOBIN, and was won by the former, 500 to 484. The winner's average was 12, and his highest runs 39, 43, 75, 27. TOBIN'S highest runs were 30, 73, 45, 40.

The second game was between J. H. FLACK and J. F. MURPHY, and was won by the former, 500 to 406. The winner's average was 18½, and his highest runs 30, 90, 24, 64. MURPHY'S highest runs, 138, 80.

In the evening the first game was between FLACK and TOBIN, and was won by the former, 500 to 365. The winner's average was 11 1-4, and his highest runs 51, 27, 38. TOBIN'S highest runs, 60, 27, 33, 36.

The next game was between WILLIAMS and DAVIS, and was won by the former, 500 to 471. The winner's average was 9, and his highest runs 48, 60, 42. DAVIS' highest runs were 38, 45, 30.

The Chess Tournament.

The tilt of Knights, Bishops, Kings and Queens commenced yesterday, at LIEDER'S Café Europa, Nos. 13 and 14 Division-street, about twenty-five members having signed their names as contestants for the prizes. The books will remain open during the week for fresh accessions, after which time they will be closed peremptorily, and no new entries will be allowed. Among the prominent signatures on the books are the names of Captain MACKENZIE, Major WERNICK, Messrs. MASON, DELMAR, KOFF, and others. There are also some new names, never before entered for a tournament. Up to last night at midnight, but few games had been played. During the week, the billiard tables will be removed to the floor above, and the chess-room capacity will be more than doubled. The present tournament promises to be extremely interesting.

The New-York Times.

'OL. XIX.......NO. 5668. NEW-YORK, MONDAY, NOVEMBER 22, 1869. PRICE FOUR CENTS.

TELEGRAMS.

Arrival of the Inauguration Fleet at Suez.

Undisturbed Tranquillity at the Paris Elections.

A Fearful Tornado at Georgetown, Colorado.

Two More Victims of the Fall of a St. Louis Building.

Burning of a Propeller and Disappearance of the Crew.

THE SUEZ CANAL.

Arrival of the Fleet at Suez—The Enterprise a Success.

PARIS, Nov. 20—6 P. M.—Advices from Alexandria, just received, contain the gratifying intelligence that the Suez Canal is a success. The Imperial yacht *Aigle*, with Her Majesty the Empress on board, has arrived at Suez without accident.

PARIS, Nov. 21.—A dispatch from Ismailia announces that the Emperor of Austria has set out on his return from Suez.

The Fleet in the Harbor of Suez—Particulars of the Passage.

SUEZ, Nov. 21, *via* ALEXANDRIA.—The Inauguration Fleet, consisting of forty-five steamers, has arrived here. None were obliged to employ pilots. The only difficulty they had was owing to their numbers. Some were crowded upon the banks of the canal several times, but they got off without trouble, the sandy bottom neither holding nor hurting them. On leaving Ismailia several steamers fouled with each other, but no serious damage was done. The water in the canal, between this point and Ismailia, is full twenty feet deep at the shallowest spot, and in several parts it is less than twenty-five feet in depth; but at all these points the bottom can be easily deepened. Steamers drawing fifteen feet can navigate the canal from Port Said to Suez with ease in fifteen hours. The water does not wash away the banks as much as was apprehended. The complete success of the great work exceeds all expectations. The arrangements for transporting and taking care of the visitors here are generally excellent. All the rolling stock on the Alexandria, Cairo and Suez Railroad has been brought into requisition to transport the immense crowds of visitors. The mails to and from India have been much delayed in consequence. The Canal is now clear of shipping, the entire fleet having anchored in the harbor of Suez. To-morrow the statue of WAGHORN, the Englishman who first proposed the building of the canal will be erected here, and on Tuesday the fleet will start on its return to Port Said. There a statue of FERDINAND DE LESSEPS, the builder and President-Director of the canal, will be raised. With this last ceremony the *fêtes* of the inauguration will probably terminate. The Empress EUGENIE will return through the canal with the fleet, her yacht, the *Aigle*, taking the lead, as on the downward trip.

FRANCE.

The Elections in Paris—The Day Quiet—Decoration of M. de Lesseps.

PARIS, Nov. 21.—The supplementary elections for members of the Corps Legislatif from this city began to-day, and are progressing quietly. Up to this hour (6 o'clock P. M.) there has been no disturbance in any quarter of the city. The Emperor left Compiègne this morning, by special train for Paris, and arrived at the Tuileries at noon. M. DE LESSEPS has been decorated with the Grand Cross of the Legion of Honor.

SPAIN.

A Republican Denial of Complicity with the Cubans—The Portuguese Minister.

MADRID, Nov. 21.—In the Cortes yesterday, Admiral TOPETE presiding, the members of the Republican minority presented a protest declaring that there was no truth in the reports that they were implicated in a conspiracy with the insurgents in the Island of Cuba. Additional reinforcements of volunteers for service in Cuba sailed during the latter part of last week for Havana. The newly-appointed Ambassador from Portugal was received to-day by the Regent with great ceremony.

AUSTRIA.

The Political Situation at Vienna—Return of Prince Metternich to Paris—The Insurrection.

PARIS, Nov. 20.—Prince METTERNICH, who went to Vienna recently, has returned to his post in this city as Envoy Extraordinary from Austria. His stay at Vienna was shortened on account of the political situation here. The Prince was incorrectly reported to have arrived at Ismailia a day or two ago.

LONDON, Nov. 20.—It seems the recent dispatches announcing the suppression of the Dalmation insurrection were premature. News has just been received that the Austrian forces have captured a defile heretofore held by the insurgents near Fort Dragoly, with the loss of only thirty men.

HONOLULU.

Opposition to Coolie Immigration—Earthquakes and Eruptions.

SAN FRANCISCO, Nov. 19.—Honolulu advices to Nov. 2 have been received. Large meetings had been held to consider the subject of coolie immigration. Resolutions strongly condemnatory of the importation of coolies were passed. Reports had been received of earthquakes on the Keomar coast. A bright light was observed on the slope of Mauna Loa, and the tides at Hilo Bay and along the coast were very singular. The Hawaiian commercial news was unimportant.

THE LAST GALE.

Further Details of the Destruction Along the Hudson—A Woman Fatally Injured at Albany.

HUDSON, N. Y., Nov. 21.—A heavy gale of wind prevailed here yesterday, which was more severe in its effects in this immediate vicinity than that of last Wednesday, and the destruction of property in the surrounding country has been great. In this city, the spire of the Presbyterian Church was partially blown over, and a portion of it was carried some distance. The building on the public square, known as the Anable Block, was unroofed and damaged to a considerable extent. In different parts of the city chimneys and fences were blown down. In Athens, the stables of the Knickerbocker Ice Company were unroofed and the roof carried some two hundred yards. Other damage was done about the village. At Stockport, the Columbiaville bridge, a substantial structure 200 feet in length, was blown down. It will require $20,000 to replace it. There was a general sweeping of trees and fences throughout the town, and the damage in this respect will be great. In Claverack, the hay barracks of JOHN MILLER were demolished, and the contents scattered over a wide range of territory. A large number of trees were uprooted, and seven chimneys were blown from the Claverack Institute. A large number of fences were blown down.

ALBANY, N. Y., Nov. 21.—At least fifty buildings were damaged more or less by the gale on Saturday. A Mrs. MURPHY was fatally injured by a piece of timber striking her on the head.

A TORNADO.

Part of the City of Georgetown, Col., Destroyed—One Life Lost, and Several Persons Injured.

GEORGETOWN, Col., Nov. 20.—A terrific tornado occurred here on the 18th inst. Heavy winds arose about 5 o'clock in the morning, increased in violence, and almost totally destroyed a portion of the city known as Lower Georgetown. Houses were demolished in almost every direction. During the heaviest gale the air was filled with trees, lumber, small stones, and articles of most every description. Among the prominent buildings destroyed is the new Episcopal Church. Hardy pines, which have weathered the storms for years, were uprooted, and in many cases hurled a distance of several hundred yards. The lower portion of the city is in ruins, and a number of families are left homeless. One person was killed and several seriously injured. The loss to property is estimated at $50,000.

FIRES.

Burning of a Lake Propeller—Her Crew Missing—Machine Shop Burned at Rondout.

MILWAUKEE, Wis., Nov. 21.—The small propeller *Belle Seen* was burned to the water's edge off Port Washington last night. Nothing has been heard of her crew, but it is presumed that they escaped in a lifeboat. There were no passengers on board.

POUGHKEEPSIE, N. Y., Nov. 21.—The machine shop of the Cornell line of steamers at Rondout was destroyed by fire last night. Loss $15,000; no insurance.

THE PACIFIC COAST.

Immigration—Rains in Oregon—A Railroad Bridge Carried Away—Arrest of the Switchman who Caused the Recent Slaughter.

SAN FRANCISCO, Nov. 19.—The California Immigrant Union will soon appoint agents to the principal cities in Europe. Another tin mine has been discovered a few miles northeast of San Bernardino. The ore is pronounced superior to the San Jacinto. The line of the Virginia City and Truckee Railroad was inaugurated yesterday. Heavy rains have prevailed in Oregon, and great damage has been done. Rivers were overflowed and the country inundated. The Oregon Central Railroad bridge over Clackamas River has been carried away.

SAN FRANCISCO, Nov. 20.—BERNARD KANE, the switchman who caused the accident on the Western Pacific Railroad on Sunday, has been arrested and committed to jail. It is stated that the United States steamer *Newberne*, on her last trip from Alaska, arrived with an invoice of whisky, which was passed as coal oil, and the profits were shared by the Government officials. The revenue agents are investigating the matter. The Maury silver mines, in Arizona, which were closed for years in the hands of the military authorities, are about to reopen.

Another Victim of the Railroad Collision—Another Collision on the Same Road.

SAN FRANCISCO, Nov. 21.—Mr. RAWLINGS, Internal Revenue Collector of this district, who was recently injured by the bursting of a centrifugal sugar drying pan, has had his leg amputated, but he is not expected to survive the operation. M. L. TAYLOR, of De Kalb, Ill., who was wounded by the railroad accident on Sunday last, died on the 19th in the Alameda Hospital. Two construction trains on the Western Pacific Railroad collided yesterday near Lybantas Station. Two locomotives and five cars were demolished. No lives were lost. The dense fog caused the accident.

CANADIAN RECIPROCITY.

The Spirit of Retaliation—The Denial Reviewed—What Ministers of the Dominion Have Said.

WASHINGTON, D. C., Nov. 21.—A telegram from Ottawa, dated Nov. 18, published on Friday morning, states on what is termed "good authority, that there is no truth in the report from Washington that the Government of the Dominion had threatened retaliatory measures if the present restriction on commercial intercourse was continued by the United States." The report from Washington, as contained in the Washington telegram of the 14th inst., and to which the Ottawa dispatch refers, made use of no such words as "threatened" or "retaliation." The authority for the above statement is ample, and is contained in the budget speech of the Canadian Finance Minister in the Dominion Parliament on the 7th of May last, in which he said, speaking of the commercial relations between the United States and Canada:

> "We may now fairly say to our neighbors, (the United States,) this state of things has gone on for three or four years, but you must understand it cannot continue. The time may soon come when we may require to have a national policy of our own; when the exceptional interests to which I have alluded, which are now suffering with special severity, will have to be considered in this House. But I do not think that the time to do this is when we may be on the eve of opening up negotiations on the whole question."

These remarks were made in deprecation of the attempts by members of the House to impose duties on American products. With special regard to the fisheries, a return has just been published by the Dominion Government, in reply to an address of the House of Commons—and which is to be laid before that body in February next—containing reports of the Minister of Marine and Fisheries, which embody several strong declarations as to the temporary character of the fishery license system, and urged the Government to yield to the prayers of the Nova Scotia fishing interests by abandoning the license system, and thus excluding American fishermen from their waters. The Privy Council of Canada fully indorsed the Minister's views, saying, that the license system "was adopted on the distinct understanding that unless some satisfactory arrangement between the two countries be made during the course of the year this privilege will cease, and all concessions made in the treaty of 1854 will be liable to be withdrawn." And they continue:

> "The Privy Council cannot refrain from respectfully impressing upon His Excellency (the Governor-General) the urgency of communicating without further delay to the American Government the course decided on, as they feel, should this not be done, advantage may be taken to continue the present system for still another year. Already has decisive action been deferred, in the hope that certain indications of a returning disposition toward renewed commercial intercourse, which were perceptible in the United States, would lead to proposals obviating the necessity for any special policy on the fishery question. These, however, have not as yet led to anything definite, and the subject being on this instance more urgent than when, two years ago, it was pressed on the decision of the Canadian Government by Mr. Secretary CARDWELL, (the British Colonial Secretary,) it is of the highest importance that no further time should be lost." [Pages Nos. 8 and 9 of the pamphlet.]

The entire pamphlet is full of expressions of a similar character, including the following, from Mr. MITCHELL, the Minister of Marine and Fisheries:

> "Under all of these circumstances it is respectfully but earnestly submitted whether the system of licensing United States fishing vessels, avowedly a provisional one, and implying no principle, should now be absolutely discontinued, and that it shall, in the future, give place to a definite policy of exclusion, agreeable to colonial interests and consistent with national dignity and rights."

THE INDIANS.

Hostilities in Arizona—A Battle Imminent—The Snake Reservation.

SAN FRANCISCO, Nov. 19.—Advices from Arizona state that the expedition under Colonel BARNARD, recently repulsed by the Indians, was reinforced from Camp Bowie, and assumed the aggressive. The savages have concentrated their forces, and a battle is imminent.

SAN FRANCISCO, Nov. 20.—The Indian difficulties on Lower Klamath River have been settled by stationing a company of soldiers among the savages.

Trouble is anticipated in removing the Snake and Piute Indians from Camp Harney to Klamath Reservation, and force will be used, as another Indian war in that region is expected.

THE ST. LOUIS DISASTER.

Two More Bodies Discovered Beneath the Fallen Building—Danger in Removing Them.

ST. LOUIS, Mo., Nov. 21.—The labor of removing the *débris* of the building in Fifth-street was continued all last night and to-day. This afternoon two more bodies were discovered, but as a removal of timbers was necessary to their extrication, and would probably result in bringing down a portion of the adjoining wall, work was suspended.

WASHINGTON.

The New Circuit Judges—The Question of the New Appointments as Discussed at Washington—Considerations which Must Control in the Selections.

From Our Regular Correspondent.

WASHINGTON, Saturday, Nov. 20, 1869.

The question of the appointment of the nine new Circuit Judges is becoming very interesting here, and is engrossing the attention of a different, and, I may say, better class of men than that which usually participates in the pressure for office. This is because the class of talent called for is of a different, and of a higher order, but more especially because of the serious nature of the considerations involved in the selections. As a gentleman distinguished for his patriotism and upright public career remarked a few days ago, "there is more for the weal or woe of this country in this question than in any other act which President GRANT will be called on to perform during his term of office." From all I can learn, I believe the President concedes the very high importance of the matter of proper selections, and that he is determined to bring to bear his maturest judgment, and to weigh with great care all the considerations involved. He has given the repeated assurance that there will be no haste in the matter—no "snap judgment" in favor of any man—and that the friends of all the candidates will be patiently heard. There is, therefore, not the slightest warrant for the utterances of certain knowing persons—persons who, by the way, ought to know better than to indulge in such utterances—that this man will be, or that that man will not be appointed.

The national and political considerations involved in the matter have been brought out into leading prominence within the past ten days. During that time several of our ablest and most discreet public men—Republicans I mean—have presented to the President and to some of the Cabinet the vital necessity of providing for the future security of the Government, and for the preservation and permanency of the results of the war, in the appointment of these Judges. It is proper to say that there seemed to be danger that in some quarters the single element of judicial fitness would be permitted to outweigh and overrule all other considerations. But I think that danger has been dissipated. It never existed with the President, and I doubt if it exists anywhere now. The impropriety, not to say absurdity, of selecting a man for such an important position, simply on the ground of his ability as a lawyer or of his reputation among lawyers, could never exist long anywhere except in the brain of a man who never rose higher than the crotchets or technicalities of the law, and who, consequently, could only look with contempt upon politics—the very marrow of our Government. Judicial fitness, in an eminent degree, will be an indispensable condition, but with it must be what is even of greater importance, a thorough sympathy with the Government and its institutions as they stand to-day; a hearty concurrence and approval of the results which are the legacies of the war; and a sincere support of the Constitution *as it is*, rather than the Constitution as it was. It is in these respects that the new Judges will make their strongest impress upon our jurisprudence and our institutions, and it is in these respects that their qualifications and claims should be most thoroughly examined. The evil consequences to ensue to the country in the future by such mistakes as Mr. LINCOLN made in some of his appointments to the Supreme Court cannot be easily overestimated, and should—I have good reason to believe will—be avoided by President GRANT. Not, by any means, that politics, pure and simple, should control in these selections, but that sympathy with the idea of National Government as it exists to-day—and a belief in a strong central power as the only permanent safety of the Union—is a *political* and not a judicial consideration, and candidates should possess that qualification equally with the other, or stand aside.

Therefore, political considerations like these must largely rule in the selection, and it is a fact viewed with much satisfaction here, that the suggestions advanced by prominent men during the past week—not in favor of any particular man or men—but with a view to impress their importance upon the appointing power, have been favorably received.

Another consideration, very important, and enhancing both political and judicial fitness if combined with them, is the question of proper age. By the law, a Judge may retire upon reaching the age of seventy, if he has served ten years. A leading ex-member of Congress, who had much to do with the framing of the law, and who is therefore qualified to speak of its intent, recently expressed the opinion that no man over fifty years of age should be appointed. "To a man of sixty years or upward," he said, "the statute extends a strong invitation to retire at the end of ten years—an invitation which a man who goes upon the Bench for his ease, as many good lawyers do, will not hesitate to accept." The Government should be able to obtain, and the appointees should be able to render, from twenty to thirty years' service, before the pension feature of the law takes effect. Otherwise, what with the large number of the old District Judges legally ready to avail themselves immediately of the benefit of the law, and a number of Circuit Judges going out under it after a brief ten years' service, the statute will be apt to be brought into disrepute, and the system made a burden upon the people before its benefits have been realized.

The two circuits which are deemed most important to the material interests of the Government, and which are being most closely considered here, are the circuits which embrace the cities of New-York and New-Orleans. In these cities it is of the greatest necessity that the Courts should zealously aid the officers of the Government in the enforcement of the laws for the suppression of frauds upon, and for the collection of the revenue; without their earnest coöperation, all efforts of all other officers are well-nigh useless. There must be not only a *willingness* to try and punish offenders, but there must be a *desire* to see the laws enforced, and a thorough sympathy with and countenance of the efforts of the law officers, who bear the brunt of the work of detection and prosecution. Nowhere is this necessity more strongly felt than in the Treasury Department, and the magnitude of its interests gives Governor BOUTWELL abundant warrant for a free expression of his views, which he will undoubtedly improve. He can scarcely afford to permit technical courtesy to another Department to stand in the way of such an important duty.

The difficulty of finding a proper man for the Louisiana Circuit within its limits is proving so great that the propriety of selecting some able man from another section of the country is strongly suggested. This might prove a happy solution of the matter. The rival interests and cliques in Louisiana and Texas are so strong that it is doubtful if a perfectly clean and disinterested man could be selected from those States. A stranger sent among them could do justice to all.

These are the chief suggestions that occur here in the discussion of the question of the Judgeships. The current of talk, among leading Republicans, in and out of the Cabinet, runs about as I have depicted it. I have only to repeat, in conclusion, that political considerations of the nature above indicated will unquestionably have much to do with the final selection, any number of mere lawyers to the contrary notwithstanding.

CYMON.

The Remains of George Peabody—The Richmond and the Inconstant—The Rank of Staff and Line Officers in the Navy—General Spinner's Report.

Special Dispatch to the New-York Times.

WASHINGTON, Nov. 21.—In naval circles considerable interest attaches to the fact that the remains of the late GEORGE PEABODY are to be brought home in a British man-of-war, with an American man-of-war as a consort. The name of the British vessel is the *Inconstant*. Rather a significant appellation, in view of the brilliant history which attaches to her American companion, the *Richmond*. The latter ship was one of the most conspicuous in the naval battles of the rebellion. She passed the forts at New-Orleans, ran the batteries at Vicksburg, and led the attack, under the gallant Commodore ALDEN, at Mobile. In the latter engagement she was struck fifty-seven times. The *Inconstant* is an iron-clad, of excellent speed, and will, in that respect, have the advantage of the *Richmond*, which is slow.

STAFF AND LINE RANK IN THE NAVY.

The Board to take into consideration the question of rank between the staff and the line in the navy has been incorrectly given. It consists of ten officers, five of the line and five of the staff, as follows: Commodore M. Smith, Commodore James Alden, Commodore A. L. Case, Captain Ammen, Chief Engineer J. W. King, Surgeon Pinckney, Paymaster Dunn, Capt. Wm. Reynolds, Surgeon Wm. M. Wood and John Lenthall, Chief of the Bureau of Construction and Repairs. The Secretary of the Navy in his forthcoming report will recommend to Congress a plan for the settlement of this question of rank, and may submit a bill drafted with a view to meet the existing difficulties. The proposition is to give the members of the staff an assimilated rank as high as that of Commodore, which is an advancement of one grade beyond that which any staff officer has ever hitherto been able to achieve even after a lifetime service.

GENERAL SPINNER'S REPORT.

The annual report of General SPINNER, United States Treasurer, was completed yesterday afternoon. The amount of the entries made on the books of the Treasurer during his term of office, eight and a half years, will not fall short of $44,000,000,000. For this entire sum, General SPINNER has been responsible. It has all passed through his hands, and it is a remarkable fact that not a single cent of it has been lost, and that his accounts to-day are correct to the last farthing.

CUBAN MATTERS.

Mr. LEMUS of the Cuban Junta is to arrive here to-morrow. His secretary says that Cuban revolutionary matters are progressing favorably for the insurgents.

FEMALE SUFFRAGE.

The Female Suffrage Party in this city, who number about 100, have held a meeting here every Saturday night, to discuss the woman question. These assemblies have become remarkable for their riot and disorder, but the one on last evening eclipsed all the others in turbulence and rowdyism.

Dispatches to the Associated Press.

ARGENTINE AFFAIRS.

The Argentine Customs law reduces the tariff on some of the American imports and exports for 1870. Importers of lumber and plows to the Argentine Republic will be interested to learn that the reduction of duties on those articles is from twenty-three to fifteen per centum—a reduction equal to an average of $4 in gold per thousand feet on lumber, and 60 cents in gold on a plow. Export duties on unwashed wool and sheepskins have also been reduced from six to two and a half per cent. for 1870. A pamphlet has just appeared, entitled "Remarks concerning the means to reëstablish the declining state of commerce between the United States and the Argentine Republic, by the proper reduction of the present tariffs." The fact is stated that the quantity of Argentine wool purchased by the United States was only 8,100,000 pounds in 1867, having been nearly 26,500,000 previous to the adoption of the new tariff. The pamphlet concludes by pressing upon Congress the necessity and propriety of a reduction of some rates of duty, "on the ground that a reduction of import duties on wool and hides will be profitable to everybody interested in the commercial prosperity of the American manufactures and trade, as well as beneficial to national income and Argentine producers and consumers of American commodities."

TAX ON SALES OF MANUFACTURES.

The following correspondence explains itself:

UNITED STATES INTERNAL REVENUE, ASSESSOR'S OFFICE, FOURTH DISTRICT, NEW-YORK, Nov. 11, 1869.

SIR: I wish particularly to call your attention to what seems to me to amount to an inconsistency between the decision of the Department made Oct. 26, 1866, in relation to sales of manufacturers at their principal office—page 166, vol. 4, No. 1 of the *Internal Revenue Record*—and that made on the same subject in a letter to "MASURY and WHITON," dated May 19, 1866, printed copy of which, with the correspondence, is herewith inclosed.

It is determined in the decision of Oct. 26, 1866, that "wherever manufacturers keep their own products at their principal office—except as samples—their entire sales at such office, whether by sample or otherwise, are excluded from the benefit of the proviso, &c." while the decision in the case of MASURY & WHITON is to the effect that, although the larger portion of the goods of their own manufacture is delivered from the factory in Brooklyn, the goods of their own manufacture, sold at their principal office and delivered to purchasers directly from the factory, are not required to be included in their monthly returns as dealers. It appearing from the correspondence on both sides in the latter case that the larger portion of the goods of their own manufacture is delivered from the factory, it has naturally been inferred by taxpayers and officers when the existence of the letter was known, that it was understood that part of the goods was kept at the principal office for sale and sold from there.

A diversity of practice exists on account of the letter to MASURY & WHITON not having been published in the *Internal Revenue Record*. Those not being aware of it still insisting upon a dealer's tax on all the goods when any of them are kept for sale at the principal office, as determined in the first decision. While those acting under the letter disregard the fact of some of the goods being kept for sale and sold at the principal office, and accordingly in such cases have not held the sales when the deliveries are made from the factory as liable to dealer's tax. The cases of mixed sales of this description are very numerous and extensive. The Department will see the propriety of promulgating explicitly a definite ruling on the subject.

Please return printed correspondence. Very respectfully,

PIERRE C. VAN WYCK,
Assessor.

Hon. C. DELANO, Commissioner Internal Revenue, Washington, D. C.

TREASURY DEPARTMENT, OFFICE OF THE INTERNAL REVENUE, WASHINGTON, Nov. 15, 1869.

SIR: Your letter of the 11th instant has been received, and its contents carefully noted.

In reply, I have to say that under the Act of March 31, 1868, this office holds that every person, firm or corporation manufacturing goods, wares or merchandise, or engaged in such manufacture, or preparation, or putting up of goods in packages with their own name or trade mark, any articles, &c., where such goods, wares, merchandise or articles, are not otherwise specifically taxed, are liable to a tax of $2 per thousand on their annual sales in excess of $5,000; that where any person, firm or corporation is actually engaged in the manufacture of such goods, &c., their returns of sales are to be made, and the tax paid, in the district where such goods are manufactured. If any person, firm or corporation is required to pay this tax on account of being engaged in the manufacture or preparation, &c., of such goods, the goods being really manufactured by others on commission or otherwise, then the tax is to be paid in the district where such person, firm or corporation have their principal office or place of business.

Where any person, firm or corporation remove their goods before sale from the place of manufacture to a store or warehouse, where their goods are sold or from which they are delivered, such person is held liable, in addition to the tax on sales as manufacturers, payable in the district where the goods are made, to a tax as dealers with respect to their sales. But when such manufacturer and dealer makes no removal of the goods until after they are sold, but delivers the goods directly from the factory or place of manufacture to the purchaser, he is not held to a tax on his sales as dealer with respect to the sale of goods delivered directly from the factory to the purchaser. Any ruling or decision which may have been given heretofore inconsistent with this ruling, is hereby revoked. Very respectfully,

J. W. DOUGLASS, Acting Commissioner.

P. C. VAN WYCK, Esq., Assessor Fourth District, New-York.

SOUTH AMERICA.

Prolongation of the War—Privileges for the Paraguayans—National Exhibitions in the Immediate Future—The Preservation and Exportation of Meat—More Natural Phenomena.

From Our Own Correspondent.

BUENOS AYRES, Thursday, Oct. 14, 1869.

It would seem as if the "Triumvirate" had resolved never to put an end to the war; the news from up North is totally devoid of all interest—and even this uninteresting kind is scarce. LOPEZ is reported to have taken refuge in the woods beyond San Estanislao, with a force estimated between 3,000 and 4,000, chiefly old men or young boys, badly armed and even still worse off for provisions. The Allies certainly seem inclined to leave him alone, since the Count D'EU leaves next month for Rio Janeiro, his command being given to General POLYDORO. So it appears as if no active operations were thought of just yet.

The Provisional Government of Paraguay has issued a decree offering free grants of land along the Upper Parana for the importation of live cattle. These privileges are offered for twelve months to any who wish to accept them. The Government has also abolished the monopoly on yerba, the Paraguayan tea. This was the only tax imposed upon the people by the late Government, and it yielded an immense revenue, the tea being purchased by the Government at about twenty-five cents the twenty-five pounds, and sold to exporters at about $8.

The chief matters of local interest are the two international exhibitions about being held; one at Cordoba toward the end of 1870, and the second in Buenos Ayres about February, 1871. The latter is a sort of joint stock concern, with a capital of $400,000 in gold, in 20,000 shares of $20 each. Both are chiefly agricultural exhibitions, though they will also have departments for produce and manufactures from all countries.

Some time back the Government offered a prize of $8,000, gold, for the best method of preserving meat for exportation; thirty-five competitors came forward in the shape of thirty-five tins from various parts of the world. These were opened on the 1st inst., and of the contents of the whole number only the contents of six were found at all preserved. Of the six the best comes from a Glasgow firm, and this will most likely gain the prize, which, however, has not yet been awarded. Another way for preserving meat, certainly the surest, provided it will pay, is also proposed, and the sanguine promoters of the project seem confident of success. I allude to the exportation of the live animals. Some months back a few were sent to England on trial, and on landing might have been sold at $75, gold, the head. The promoters of the scheme, however, determined to try the experiment of a few months' fattening. If this proves equal in pecuniary results, as may very reasonably be expected, a company already formed will send out a large steamer, built expressly for this purpose, to try how exporting a thousand head at once will pay.

Expectation was on the alert, on the 5th inst., for an earthquake, announced as likely to take place on this coast, by the wise ones in Europe. During the night of the 7th a slight shock was felt in Buenos Ayres. It overthrew several old walls. On the 11th one of the severest storms known for years swept over the river. It lasted for about a day and a half, doing great damage to the shipping, thirteen vessels being reported aground and missing, and smaller craft to the number of fifteen or twenty. At Montevideo, also, some half-dozen sea-going ships are reported lost, but no American vessels have come to grief, chiefly German brigs, and several larger vessels, supposed to be French or Italian, with all hands, being reported lost. In the course of a week or ten days we shall hear whether this is but the finish of more destructive events on the West Coast, which appears always more or less in commotion.

E. G. W.

THE STORM ON THE LAKES.

Eight Lives Lost—Gallant Attempt to Rescue a Crew.

From the Chicago Post, Nov. 19.

On Wednesday the *Post* recorded the fact that three vessels were reported ashore at Gross Point, twelve miles from this city, and to-day further details have been obtained of the disaster to the schooner *Arrow*, which went ashore at that point on Tuesday night in the great storm. Her crew of seven men were driven from below by the heavy seas which dashed over and rocked the vessel, and they were compelled to lash themselves to the rigging to keep from being washed overboard. Thus exposed to the cold and storm, the crew remained until an early hour on Wednesday morning, when word was sent to this city. The tug *Mosher*, with a lifeboat and seven hardy and intrepid seamen, among whom were Captain S. E. ANDERSON, of the schooner *Tempest*; Captain E. M. GUNNISON, of the bark *Courser*; Captain JOHN FREAR, the Captain of the schooner *King*, of St. Joseph, and others started to their assistance. The *Mosher* arrived at the scene of the wreck about noon, and approached within a short distance of the *Arrow*, the sea running so heavy that she could not get close to the wreck. The lifeboat was lowered and the ten men jumped into it and made for the wreck. They went through the mountain waves safely until within a few feet of the wreck, when suddenly a huge breaker struck the boat and swamped it. Here ensued a terrible scene—the gallant fellows buoying themselves as best they could, and making for the shore, the breakers pitching them about like so many corks. Nearly perished by the cold, and suffering terribly, the men finally got safely upon *terra firma*, a few of them being helped by the people who had gathered on the beach to render what assistance they could in the absence of boats, lines, and other life-saving apparatus. The wet and half frozen men were sent to the station at Winetka and took the cars for the city. In the meantime the poor fellows of the *Arrow* clung to the rigging with the hope that they might yet be rescued. The *Mosher* returned to the city without being able to render any assistance.

On receipt of the news of the failure of the first crew to save the *Arrow's* men, another volunteer crew was made up, consisting of Captain G. H. CLARK, of the bark *Erastus Corning*; Captain JOHN FREAR, of the barge *East Saginaw*; the mate and wheelsman of the latter named vessel and THOMAS EMERSON, cook of the tug *Wood*. This tug took a yawl and the men on board, and departed for the wreck at 8 o'clock on Wednesday night. The *Arrow* was reached at 10 o'clock, and the *Wood* went as close to her as possible, a heavy sea still running. The yawl was lowered and the crew manned it. All pulled with strong arms in the hope of saving the unfortunate vessel's crew, and the schooner was reached safely. A thrill of joy ran through the gallant men who had risked their lives to save the seven half-dead sailors, and the hope of still retaining life gave the latter new courage. With great difficulty the *Arrow's* crew were got into the yawl, and when all seemed apparently safe, alas for poor humanity! a heavy breaker struck the yawl and swamped her, throwing all overboard. The seven nearly exhausted men of the *Arrow* sank immediately, they not having strength to swim. THOMAS EMERSON, of the *Wood*, also drowned. Captain CLARK, who is physically a powerful man, weighing no less than 240 pounds, swam to the vessel and held on to a stanchion. He managed to get hold of FREAR and the wheelman, and saved them. The mate of the *Corning* got ashore safely by his own exertions. Captain CLARK got upon the cabin, disrobed himself, and in the chilled atmosphere wrung out his drenched clothes. The storm abated toward midnight, and the three men were got off safely by a small boat from shore, and returned to the city. The *Wood* arrived in safety after the sad accident. Captain CRAWFORD was in command of her.

The *Arrow* left Muskegon on Friday morning last, with a cargo of lumber, for Chicago. Including her Captain, JAMES DURNING, her crew numbered seven, all told. She was 180 tons burden, carrying about 163,000 or 164,000 feet of lumber, and is owned by MICHAEL BRANDT, of this city. She is valued at $15,000, and is insured in the Equitable for $2,500, in the Republic for $6,000 and in the Merchants' for $4,500. The names of the six seamen on her could not be ascertained this forenoon.

The bodies of six of the drowned men were washed ashore at Evanston, and brought to this city on the Northwestern Railroad last evening. The scene at the depot was one to call up the most painful feelings. The widow of EMERSON, the unfortunate man who lost his life in the endeavor to save others, was at the depot when the train arrived, and evinced the most inconsolable sorrow. Her wails were pitiful in the extreme. The scene which ensued when the bodies were exposed for recognition brought tears to many eyes. EMERSON'S body was not among the number. It is probable that the other bodies will be found soon. Other disasters to shipping are reported, but thus far no loss of life.

A HORRIBLE AFFAIR.

Enoch Arden with a Variation—A Woman's Second Husband Stabs her Child and Attempts Suicide.

From the Sacramento (Cal.) Union, Nov. 13.

A shocking affair occurred on L-street, between Twentieth and Twenty-first streets, last evening. Some three or four years since a man named MITCHELL, a shoemaker, residing in this city, had a falling out with his wife, which resulted in their separation, Mrs. MITCHELL going to Austin, Nevada. While there she made the acquaintance of a man named B. J. JOHNSTON, and, having received information leading her to believe that MITCHELL was dead, she married him. After several months had passed, however, she found that her former husband was not dead. The parties meeting, she concluded to leave JOHNSTON, and carrying out her intention, came to this city with MITCHELL.

About three months ago her second husband came to Sacramento and made such threats and acted in such a manner that she had him arrested fearing that her life was not safe. After being released from custody, JOHNSTON returned to Austin.

On Thursday last he came back to the city, and last evening about 6 o'clock called at MITCHELL'S residence on L-street, near Twenty-first, where he met his wife, and, after a slight conversation with her begged that she would let him see his child, (a daughter about 6 months old, which was born shortly after her mother came back from Austin,) saying that he intended to leave for Scotland to-day and would like to look upon the babe before his departure. Mrs. MITCHELL brought him the child, which he received and held a moment, and then suddenly drawing a small bowie knife, inflicted a terrible cut on its abdomen, made a lunge at MITCHELL, which the latter parried, and fled. The child died a short time afterward in its mother's arms.

People in the vicinity raised the shout of "Murder!" and the perpetrator of the deed was quickly pursued by three citizens, who followed him up one street and down another six or seven blocks, at the top of their speed, and finally caught him in E. GRUHLER'S yard, Sixteenth and L streets, where he was engaged in conversation with another man who happened to be there, apparently innocent of any crime. Upon finding himself discovered, however, he said, "Well, you've got me, boys; you can can do what you want to with me."

About this time it was discovered that he had stabbed himself twice in the neighborhood of the heart. He also informed his captors that he had taken a large dose of muriatic acid, (probably having intended to take prussic acid,) and would be dead before they could get him to the Station House. They, nevertheless, after awhile, started for that place with him, when they met Chief MARTZ and Deputy Constable FAYLOR, who had been notified, and, together with other officers, had just started out to hunt for JOHNSTON. The latter was conveyed to Dr. SIMMONS' office, where his wounds were [illegible] found to consist of two cuts, one about three inches deep, slanting downward, and the other less than an inch in depth. He also complained of a burning sensation in the throat and stomach. After his wounds had been dressed he was taken to the County Hospital to await the result of his injuries, which are not necessarily fatal, an officer having been detailed to watch him meanwhile.

While being conveyed to the physician's office JOHNSTON gave Chief MARTZ the following document, which shows his feelings and intentions prior to the killing:

SACRAMENTO, Nov. 12.

I take my child with me in order that shame and disgrace may not fall on her. She, SARAH JOHNSTON, now SARAH MITCHELL, ran away with my child. I married her in Austin, Nevada State, and she took everything from me and left me in debt. Please bury my child with me. They were all Mormons. So good-by to my friends, and God bless them.

B. G. JOHNSTON.

I am from Nevada City, California, aged 36 years on the 28th day of December next.

Suicide of a Student in Rochester University.

From the Rochester Express, Nov. 19.

This morning our citizens were startled by the report that a young man named TAYLOR LEWIS MORGAN, a student in the Freshman Class of the University, and a brother of Rev. THOMAS J. MORGAN, of the Theological Seminary, had committed suicide. The body was found about 7:30 o'clock this morning. He was found lying with his head against a pillow, and a revolver with two chambers empty, lying on the floor a short distance off. It seems that he had prepared his pillow so that he would naturally fall against it before firing. The blood had oozed from his mouth, and it was at first supposed that he had placed the pistol to his mouth before firing, but a further examination showed that the ball had entered the left nipple, and passed crosswise through his body, coming out under the right shoulder blade, where it was found lodged under the skin. The back of young MORGAN'S head was warm where it lay against the pillow; but his body was rigid, and there was no means of ascertaining when the fatal shot was fired. It was evident from the nature of the wound that death was almost instantaneous. The ball passed through the lungs, and to this is doubtless due the clotted blood around the mouth.

Mr. MORGAN came to Rochester with his brother from Franklin, Ind., and was highly esteemed by all who knew him. He studied in SATTERLEE'S Collegiate Institute, and graduated last Summer with honor. Many will remember his oration on "John Bright" as being the best of any delivered by the class. He entered the University as a Freshman last September. For some time past he had been feeling melancholy and discouraged, and wanted to leave his studies and go into business.

Jeff. Davis' Welcome to Memphis.

From the Memphis Appeal, Nov. 17.

Hon. JEFFERSON DAVIS arrived in the city last night on the *Great Republic*, from Vicksburg, and is a guest of our townsman W. R. HUNT, Esq. In accordance with his own wish, he has no public reception. But he is not the less welcome to our homes and hearts. He is tried and true. If he has stood against the Union, it was because he loved liberty more than "the Union." What true man does not? When he fell, liberty, for the South at least, fell with him. It remains to be seen whether that of the North also, and of the whole Union of States, is to follow it. If to be true to constitutional liberty is to be true to the country, then DAVIS is no traitor. He never stood against "the Union," except as that was abused, and stood against the true liberty and right of the South. He never asked more; and these given, there was not a more determined Union man in the land. In this he was the true impersonation of the Southern people. Tried as a patriot, he has their enthusiastic and devoted love. Not all the misrepresentation and abuse he has suffered can mar the pages of history. His fame will be vindicated by the friends who have shared his misfortunes and suffered in sympathy with him. Such a man can never fall, and heroic virtue can not be blackened by calumny. When prejudice and virulence have passed away and the nation takes its sober second thought, DAVIS and his compeers will be owned and honored as among the heroes of the North American continent; less fortunate than its Washingtons, but not less truly a friend of liberty and the country than they.

Opposition to Confederation in Newfoundland.

From the Toronto Leader, Nov. 20.

The opinion of our eastern contemporaries is that the Anti-Confederates will have a majority of from five to seven in the new House of Assembly of Newfoundland. The City of St. Johns returned 6 Anti-Confederates, Ferryland 2, Placentia Bay 3, Fortune Bay 1 and Conception Bay 3, while the last named constituency also returned 4 Confederates, and Burgos and La Poile 1—making 20 members altogether elected as far as heard from. There was a very large majority against Mr. AMBROSE SHEA, the Confederate leader.

The New-York Times.

VOL. XX........NO. 6189. NEW-YORK, SATURDAY, JULY 22, 1871. PRICE FOUR CENTS.

THE SECRET ACCOUNTS.

Proofs of Undoubted Frauds Brought to Light.

Warrants Signed by Hall and Connolly Under False Pretenses.

THE ACCOUNT OF INGERSOLL & CO.

The following accounts, copied with scrupulous fidelity from Controller CONNOLLY's books, require little explanation. They purport to show the amount paid during 1869 and 1870, for repairs and furniture for the New Court-house. It will be seen that the warrants are drawn in different names, but they were all indorsed to "INGERSOLL & Co."—otherwise, J. H. INGERSOLL, the agent of the Ring. Each warrant was signed by Controller CONNOLLY and Mayor HALL. What amount of money was actually paid to the persons in whose favor the warrants were *nominally* drawn, we have no means of knowing. On the face of these accounts, however, it is clear that the bulk of the money somehow or other got back to the Ring, or each warrant would not have been indorsed over to its agent.

We undertake to prove whenever we are afforded the opportunity, that the following account is copied literally from the Controller's books, and forms a part of the documents to which the public is entitled to have access.

The dates given for the work done are obviously fraudulent. For example: On July 2, 1869, a warrant was drawn for furniture supplied for County Courts and offices, from Oct. 18 to Nov. 23, 1868, for $42,560 64. On July 16—fourteen days afterward—another warrant was drawn for $94,038 13 for furniture supplied to the same offices from Nov. 7 to Dec. 31. That is to say, the bill was fully paid by the *first* of these two warrants down to Nov. 23. And yet a fortnight afterward another warrant was drawn paying the bill over again from Nov. 7. It is obvious that the fictitious dates were not remembered by the City authorities when these warrants were drawn. Many similar cases will be observed in the figures given below.

It will be seen that on one day furniture is supposed to have been supplied to the amount of $129,469 48—at least a warrant for that sum was signed by HALL and CONNOLLY in favor of C. D. BOLLAR & Co., and indorsed by INGERSOLL & Co.

1869. INGERSOLL & CO. 1869.

Date of Warrant.	*Character of Work. Date on Which Work was Supposed to be Done.*	*Amount Drawn.*
July 2.	—Paid for Furniture in County Courts and Offices from Oct. 18 to Nov. 23, 1868	$42,550 64
July 16.	—Paid for Furniture in County Offices from Nov. 7 to Dec. 31, 1868	94,038 13
Aug. 4.	—Paid for Furniture in County Offices July 19, 1868	53,206 75
Sept. 7.	—Paid for Furniture in County Offices Aug. 30, 1868	60,384 71
Sept. 8.	—Paid for Furniture in County Courts and Offices Sept. 23, 1868	42,901 47
Oct. 22.	—Paid for Iron Railing, Cases, Stairs, &c., Check in name of M. W. Davis, indorsed by Ingersoll & Co., July 29, '68	63,201 16
Oct. 23.	—Paid for Carpets, &c., in Co. Courts and Offices, Check in name of J. A. Smith, indorsed by Ingersoll & Co., Aug. 10, '68	27,154 55
Oct. 28.	—Paid for Furniture in County Courts and Offices Dec. 28, 1868	28,032 11
Nov. 5.	—Paid for Carpets, &c., in Co. Courts and Offices, Check in name of J. A. Smith, indorsed by Ingersoll & Co., April 6, '68.	36,422 10
Nov. 17.	—Paid for Carpets, &c., in Co. Courts and Offices, Check in name of J. A. Smith, indorsed by Ingersoll & Co., Jan. 26, '68.	32,617 13
Nov. 16.	—Paid for Carpets, &c., in Co. Courts and Offices, Check in name of J. A. Smith, indorsed by Ingersoll & Co., July 29, '68.	32,185 20
Nov. 19.	—Paid for Furniture, &c., in County Courts and Offices, Oct. 18, 1868	10,494 61
Nov. 24.	—Paid for Furniture, &c., in Co. Courts and Offices, Check in name of C. D. Bollar & Co., in'd. by Ingersoll & Co., Aug. 17, '68.	82,826 81
Dec. 3.	—Paid for Furniture, &c., in Co. Courts and Offices, Check in name of C. D. Bollar & Co., in'd. by Ingersoll & Co., Nov. 9, '68.	32,682 38
June 8.	—Paid for Furniture, &c., in Co. Courts and Offices, Check in name of C. D. Bollar & Co., in'd. by Ingersoll & Co., May 8, '69.	129,469 48
June 15.	—Paid for Carpets, &c., in New Court-House, Check in name of J. A. Smith, indorsed by Ingersoll & Co., April 16, 1869	72,605 97
June 8.	—Paid for Furniture, &c., in New Court-House to April 8, 1869	90,923 40
Dec. 16.	—Paid for Furniture, &c., in County Court-rooms and Offices, April 26, 1868	54,243 57
Jan. 11.	—Paid for Furniture in Armories and Drill-rooms, Nov. 12, 1868	38,906 71
Jan. 19.	—Paid for Furniture in same, Dec. 3 and 22, 1868	31,801 95
Feb. 27.	—Paid for Furniture in same from Jan. 13, 1869, to Feb. 9, 1869	55,791 56
April 26.	—Paid for Furniture in same, March 11, 9186	39,844 68
June 5.	—Paid for Furniture in same, Nov. 17, 1868	26,325 26
Sept. 20.	—Paid for Furniture in same, May 26, 1869	30,116 26
Feb. 18.	—Paid for Shades, &c., Check in name of J. A. Smith, indorsed by Ingersoll & Co., Dec. 21, 1868	15,786 40
May 12.	—Paid for Shades, Curtains, Cornices, &c., Check in name of J. A. Smith, indorsed by Ingersoll & Co., April 6, 1869	19,163 65
June 7.	—Paid for Repairs, &c., Check in name of J. A. Smith, indorsed by Ingersoll & Co., March 13, 1869	22,496 33
May 12.	—Paid for Repairs, &c., Check in name of C. D. Bollar & Co., indorsed by Ingersoll & Co., April 9, 1869	21,969 13
June 5.	—Paid for Repairs, &c., Check in name of C. D. Bollar & Co., indorsed by Ingersoll & Co., to Feb. 3, 1869	38,907 43
Sept. 30.	—Paid for Fitting up Armories, Check in name of C. D. Bollar & Co., indorsed by Ingersoll & Co., Sept. 1, 1868	44,737 45
Sept. 20.	—Paid for Fitting up Armories, Check in name of C. D. Bollar & Co., indorsed by Ingersoll & Co., July 1, 1869	32,112 78

GEORGE S. MILLER, 1869—*All the Checks Indorsed by Ingersoll & Co.*

July 2.	—Paid for Repairs to Court of Common Pleas to Oct. 17, 1867	$905 51
July 2.	—Paid for Repairs to Courts and Offices from Aug. 1 to Oct. 20, 1868	6,089 24
July 28.	—Paid for Repairs to County Offices, Dec. 23, 1868	10,647 56
July 28.	—Paid for Repairs to County Offices and Courts, Nov. 20, 1868	11,349 54
Sept. 8.	—Paid for Carpenter-work, County Offices and Courts, from Nov. 12, 1868, to Dec. 12, 1868	48,833 23
Dec. 3.	—Paid for Repairs to County Offices and Buildings from Oct. 21 to Oct. 31, 1868	23,038 74
Dec. 29.	—Paid for Repairs and Alterations, County Offices and Buildings, July 21, 1868	27,885 04
Jan. 11.	—Paid for Repairs in Armories and Drill-rooms from Nov. 27 to Dec. 19, 1868	15,415 14
Jan. 19.	—Paid for Repairs in Armories and Drill-rooms from Oct. 23 to Dec. 4, 1868	14,691 78
Feb. 27.	—Paid for Repairs in Armories and Drill-rooms from Jan. 14 to Jan. 30, 1869	27,937 51
May 12.	—Paid for Carpenter-work in Various Armories from Jan. 30 to March 23, 1869	27,651 40
June 7.	—Paid for Carpenter-work in Various Armories from April 23 to May 18, 1869	38,676 50
June 7.	—Paid for Carpenter-work in Various Armories from March 30 to April 16, 1869	13,864 07
Sept. 20.	—Paid for Carpenter-work in Various Armories from May 25 to June 9, 1869	14.130 36
Oct. 11.	—Paid for Carpenter-work in Various Armories from May 25 to June 29, 1869	49,763 80

A. G. MILLER, 1869—*Checks Indorsed by Ingersoll & Co.*

Dec. 20.	—Paid for Repairs to County Offices and Buildings, March 8, 1868	$34,785 03
Dec. 20.	—Paid for Repairs to County Offices and Buildings, July 7, 1868	18,222 47
Sept. 28.	—Paid for Repairs to County Offices and Buildings, July 2, 1869	48,798 63

1870. INGERSOLL & CO. 1870.

Jan. 17.	—Paid for Furniture Furnished County Court-rooms and Offices, July 17, 1868	$20,655 72
Jan. 24.	—Paid for Furniture Furnished County Court-rooms and Offices, May 13, 1868	33,538 36
Feb. 7.	—Paid for Furniture Furnished County Court-rooms and Offices	11,186 92
Feb. 16.	—Paid for Furniture Furnished County Court-rooms and Offices, Aug. 21, 1869	29,404 48
Feb. 23.	—Paid for Furniture Furnished County Court-rooms and Offices, Sept. 23, 1869	51,813 77
Feb. 26.	—Paid for Furniture Furnished County Court-rooms and Offices, Oct. 6, 1869	26,981 90
Feb. 26.	—Paid for Furniture Furnished County Court-rooms and Offices, Sept. 3, 1869	33,037 15
May 6.	—Paid for Furniture Furnished County Court-house, Dec. 10, 1869	64,954 87
May 21.	—Paid for Cabinet-work County Court-house, July 23, 1869	70,117 59
May 21.	—Paid for Cabinet-work County Court-house, Oct. 17, 1869	64,984 82
May 28.	—Paid for Furniture County Court-house, Oct. 21, 1869	40,314 09
May 28.	—Paid for Furniture County Court-house, Nov. 3, 1869	39,844 19
May 30.	—Paid for Furniture County Court-house, Dec. 27, 1869	68,218 89
June 3.	—Paid for Furniture Furnished in County Buildings and Offices, Feb. 5, 1870	54,030 26
June 10.	—Paid for Furniture, Clocks, &c., Furnished in County Buildings and Offices, March 23, 1870	69,719 10
June 13.	—Paid for Furniture and Cabinet-work in County Court-house, April 18, 1870	98,259 07
June 20.	—Paid for Cabinet-work in County Court-house, Feb. 3, 1870	66,292 33
June 27.	—Paid for Cabinet-work and Furniture in Armories and Drill-rooms, Feb. 27, 1869	58,330 93
June 30.	—Paid for Cabinet-work and Furniture in Armories and Drill-rooms, Feb. 6, 1870	54,053 33
June 30.	—Paid for Cabinet-work and Furniture in Armories and Drill-rooms, March 26, 1870	29,129 99
Aug. 1.	—Paid for Furniture in Court-rooms and Offices, March 28, 1870	91,325 50
Mar. 14.	—Paid for Furniture in Armories and Drill-rooms, Nov. 3, 1869	58,937 60
April 16.	—Paid for Furniture in Armories and Drill-rooms, Sept. 11, 1869	28,608 68
Aug. 31.	—Paid for Fitting up District-Attorney's Office, Aug. 22, 1870	30,000 00
Aug. 30.	—Paid for Fitting up Commissioners of Taxes' and Receiver of Taxes' Offices, June 30, 1870	40,000 00
Aug. 30.	—Paid for Fitting up Register's Office, Aug. 3, 1870	10,000 00
Oct. 26.	—Paid for Fitting up Surrogate's Office, Sept. 3, 1870	12,000 00

C. D. BOLLAR & CO.—*Checks Indorsed by Ingersoll & Co.*

May 7.	—Paid for Furniture, &c., Furnished in County Court-house, Sept. 16, 1869	$39,260 17
May 7.	—Paid for Furniture, &c., Furnished in County Court-house, Oct. 18, 1869	35,114 08
May 13.	—Paid for Cabinet-work Furnished in County Court-house, July 18, 1869	89,370 00
May 2[illegible].	—Paid for Fitting up in County Court-house, March 6, 1870	39,950 18
[illegible] 21.	—Paid for Fitting up in County Court-house, Jan. 20, 1870	39,614 59
May 27.	—Paid for Cabinet-work Furnished in County Court-house, Aug. 23, 1869	125,830 56
June 10.	—Paid for Cabinet-work Furnished in County Court-house, April 16, 1870	67,487 21
June 30.	—Paid for Fitting up Armories and Drill-rooms, Jan. 7, 1870	49,208 14
June 30.	—Paid for Fitting up Armories and Drill-rooms, March 13, 1870	37,072 16
Aug. 1.	—Paid for Cabinet-work, &c., done in County Buildings and Offices, March 12, 1870	60,503 43

J. A. SMITH—*Checks Indorsed by Ingersoll & Co.*

May 6.	—Paid for Carpets Furnished in New Court-house, June 22, 1869	$34,082 25
May 7.	—Paid for Curtains and Shades Furnished in New Court-house, Sept. 23, 1869	36,083 80
May 21.	—Paid for Carpets and Shades Furnished in County Buildings and Offices, Feb. 21, 1870	34,515 73
May 28.	—Paid for Carpets and Shades Furnished in County Buildings and Offices, Feb. 21, 1870	73,602 46
June 3.	—Paid for Carpets and Shades Furnished in County Buildings and Offices, Dec. 27, 1869	63,173 51
June 6.	—Paid for Carpets &c., Furnished in County Court-house, Aug. 3, 1869	42,291 45
June 6.	—Paid for Carpets, &c., Furnished in County Buildings and Offices, June 21, 1869	44,259 23
June 6.	—Paid for Shades Furnished in County Buildings and Offices, Sept. 16, 1869	36,987 25
June 24.	—Paid for Carpets Furnished in Armories and Drill-rooms Dec. 22, 1869	36,441 42
June 30.	—Paid for Carpets Furnished in Armories and Drill-rooms, March 16, 1870	37,426 87
July 26.	—Paid for Carpets Furnished in County Court-house, April 17, 1870	72,819 81

GEORGE S. MILLER—*Checks Indorsed by Ingersoll & Co.*

Jan. 17.	—Paid for Carpenter-work in Court-rooms and Offices, Aug. 19, 1868, to Sept. 11, 1868	$20,291 44
Jan. 17.	—Paid for Repairs and Alterations in County Buildings, June 7, 1868	23,005 83
Jan. 24.	—Paid for Repairs and Alterations in County Offices, Aug. 5, 1868	26,952 99
Jan. 28.	—Paid for Repairs and Alterations in County Offices, Sept. 23, 1868	25,366 49
Mar. 21.	—Paid for Repairs and Alterations in County Offices, May 13, 1869	20,255 00
April 8.	—Paid for Repairs and Alterations in County Offices, Aug. 7, 1869	18,955 69
April 8.	—Paid for Repairs and Alterations in County Offices, July 23, 1869	29,494 74
April 8.	—Paid for Repairs and Alterations in County Offices, June 10, 1869	21,418 99
May 7.	—Paid for Carpenter-work in Court-house, May 13, 1869	42,126 47
May 13.	—Paid for Carpenter-work in Court-house, Sept. 29, 1869	38,902 22
May 21.	—Paid for Carpenter-work in Court-house, Dec. 15, 1869	34,990 66
May 28.	—Paid for Repairs in County Buildings and Offices, Aug. 31, 1869	39,361 21
June 3.	—Paid for Repairs in County Buildings and Offices, Sept. 22, 1869	37,326 02
June 6.	—Paid for Repairs in County Buildings and Offices, Dec. 18, 1869	32,381 73
June 6.	—Paid for Repairs in County Buildings and Offices, Oct. 25, 1869	35,663 82
June 10.	—Paid for Fitting up New Court-house, Jan. 12, 1870	44,474 30
June 17.	—Paid for Repairs in County Buildings and Offices, Jan. 25, 1870	48,768 21
June 20.	—Paid for Carpenter-work in Court-house, Feb. 9, 1870	40,965 41
June 27.	—Paid for Repairs in County Buildings and Offices, March 29, 1870	44,874 59
June 30.	—Paid for Repairs in Armories and Drill-rooms, Aug. 3, 1869	40,549 24
June 30.	—Paid for Repairs in Armories and Drill-rooms, Sept. 8, 1869	35,748 79
July 8.	—Paid for Repairs in Armories and Drill-rooms, Feb. 10, 1870	29,317 59
July 8.	—Paid for Repairs in Armories and Drill-rooms, March 2, 1870	46,947 32
July 26.	—Paid for Repairs in Armories and Drill-rooms, March 31, 1870	49,251 31
Aug. 9.	—Paid for Repairs in County Buildings, April 12, 1870	40,607 49
Aug. 12.	—Paid for Repairs in Armories and Drill-rooms, April 2, 1870	48,639 49
Aug. 12.	—Paid for Repairs in Carpenter-work in Court-house, March 28, 1870	46,343 45
Mar. 14.	—Paid for Repairs in Armories and Drill-rooms to Nov. 13, 1869	38,084 28
Mar. 31.	—Paid for Repairs and Carpenter-work in Armories and Drill-rooms, July 6 to July 31, 1869	45,266 04
April 16.	—Paid for Repairs and Alterations in Armories and Drill-rooms, Aug. 3 to Aug. 13, 1869	25,948 38
April 16.	—Paid for Repairs and Alterations in Armories and Drill-rooms	8,147 88

A. G. MILLER—*Checks Indorsed by Ingersoll & Co.*

June 24.	—Paid for Cabinet-work in Court-house, Jan. 9, 1870	$49,082 30
June 27.	—Paid for Cabinet-work in County Buildings and Offices, March 29, 1870	85,163 22
June 30.	—Paid for Cabinet-work in County Court-house, April 2, 1870	59,932 01
Aug. 1.	—Paid for Cabinet-work in County Court-house, Oct. 8, 1869	69,537 68
Aug. 9.	—Paid for Cabinet-work in Armories and Drill-rooms, April 16, 1870	77,949 58
Mar. 28.	—Paid for Repairs in Armories and Drill-rooms, Aug. 26, 1869	49,742 45
Mar. 31.	—Paid for Repairs in Armories and Drill-rooms, Oct. 20, 1869	38,818 84
April 16.	—Paid for Fitting up Armories and Drill-rooms, Oct. 2, 1869	22,612 10
	Grand Total	**$5,663,646 83**

WASHINGTON.

Clearing up a Muddle in the Revenue Department—Lively Work in the Pension Bureau—Imports of Australia—Immigration at New-York—Kuklux Investigation—National Bank Circulation.

Special Dispatch to the New-York Times.

WASHINGTON, July 21.—It will be remembered that over a year ago Congress tried to give an expression of its will concerning the reduction of a part of the income tax, but failed to find language to convey its purpose successfully in regard to the payment of certain income taxes for the last five months of 1870. Judge DOUGLAS, the acting Commissioner, had the question of how the law should be construed before him, and gave the Government the benefit of the doubt. Commissioner PLEASONTON reversed the decision, and the corporations paid their semi-annual interest without withholding the amount of the taxes, as they would otherwise have done. The Attorney-General in turn reversed PLEASONTON'S decision, putting the case back where Judge DOUGLAS placed it, and now the corporations resist collection, on the ground that they acted on the instructions of an agent of the Government in neglecting to retain the amount of the tax, and that they are not liable to sustain loss because of the reversal of the decision on which they acted. Solicitor BANFIELD has been considering their plea, and today handed the Secretary of the Treasury his opinion as to the legality of action for the collection of these taxes. The opinion will be made public to-morrow, together with the Secretary's decision based upon it. This is another case which must make Commissioner PLEASONTON aware that he is one of the Secretary's subordinates, and that he is so regarded by the President.

BRISK WORK IN THE PENSION OFFICE.

A statement was not long ago published which showed that there were about 100,000 pension claims unexamined on the files of the Pension Office. Those who are anxiously looking for action upon applications will be glad to hear that the daily average work of the Pension Office under the new Commissioner, Gen. BAKER, has been already about doubled. Yesterday 188 certificates for pensions were issued, the largest number ever issued from the office in one day. The first week in June, which was the first week after Gen. BAKER came into the office, 423 certificates were issued. Since then there has been a general constant increase and last week 915 were issued. This week the number is expected to reach 1,100, and during July 4,000 are expected to be signed. At this rate the office will be gaining on its work instead of falling further behind, and an effort will be made to bring the work up to time as soon as possible with the limited force which can be employed.

SECRETARY DELANO.

Secretary DELANO has written that his return will be delayed till Tuesday next.

Dispatch to the Associated Press.

AUSTRALIA'S IMPORTATIONS.

A statement has been compiled at the Treasury Department from the latest statistics, showing the imports into Australia and New-Zealand, as follows: From Great Britain, £17,924,420; from the United States, £1,354,385; all other countries, £3,812,478. Stated by per centage, they are as follows: From Great Britain, 77 6-10; from the United States, 5 5-10; all other countries, 16 6-10. The Parliament of New-South Wales has recently voted a subsidy of $75,000 to a monthly line of American steamers between San Francisco and Sidney. The imports of Australia and New-Zealand being largely manufactured goods, it is believed that a very large and profitable commerce will spring up with our Western Coast.

IMMIGRATION AT NEW-YORK.

The official returns received at the Bureau of Statistics show that during the quarter ending June 30, 1871, the total number of passengers arrived at the port of New-York from foreign countries was 107,114, of whom 64,213 were males and 42,901 females. Of the total number arrived, 101,015 were actual immigrants—males, 60,082; females, 40,933. Ages—Under fifteen, 9,812; fifteen and under forty, 71,056; forty and upward, 10,147. The deaths on the voyage were 92, of whom 54 were males and 38 females. The principal nationalities of the immigrants were as follows: England, 17,845; Scotland, 4,613; Wales, 399; Ireland, 26,149; Great Britain, locality unknown, 6,672; Germany, 30,814; Austria, 1,983; Sweden, 5,727; Norway, 1,286; Denmark, 1,143; France, 849; Switzerland, 1,305; Spain, 104; Italy, 8,671; Holland, 409; Belgium, 78 Russia, 295; Poland, 183; Cuba, 43; Bermudas, 7.

THE KUKLUX INVESTIGATION.

The Kuklux Committee, today, examined a witness named MCBRIDE, who testified that while a teacher of a colored school in Chickasaw County, Mississippi, a band of disguised men seized and whipped him, and insisted he should leave the country. Other colored schools were broken up in that section. Three witnesses from North Carolina are in attendance, and will testify relative to the existence of Kuklux organizations in that State. A telegram was read to the Committee from a citizen of Macon, that he telegraphed on the 11th of July he was ready to report, but received the next day a telegram from the Sergeant-at-Arms of the Senate, telling him he need not come, as the Committee had not time for more witnesses. The Sergeant-at-Arms being out of town could not explain, but at the instance of the Democratic members this Georgian and six or more others were resummoned by telegraph to appear before the Committee.

NATIONAL BANK CIRCULATION.

The total circulation issued to the national banks to date is $318,686,999. The act of July 12, 1870, authorized the issue of $54,000,000 additional circulation, and the establishment of gold national banks, to which circulation can be issued upon the deposit of United States bonds, at the rate of eighty per cent. upon the par value thereof. Since the passage of the act, circulation has been issued to the following States: Virginia, $744,000; Illinois, $3,065; West Virginia, $950,000; Michigan, $1,166; Kentucky, $2,200,000; Indiana, $1,174,000; Wisconsin, $534,000; Ohio, $760,000; Tennessee, $1,300,000; Iowa, $1,076,000; Louisiana, $1,300,000; Minnesota, $380,000; Georgia, $561,000; Kansas, $176,100; North Carolina, $609,000; Missouri, $1,290,000; South Carolina, $258,000; Nebraska, $212,000; Texas, $145,000; Colorado, $61,000; New-Mexico, $155,000; Oregon, $137,000; Alabama, $260,000; California, $3,205. The law requires that one-half of the increased circulation shall be apportioned among the States not having an excess already, according to population, and one-half according to the existing banking capital resources and business of such State and Territory. The census returns of the valuation of property and banking capital have not yet been received, and the proportion of circulation for the States of Ohio, Indiana and Illinois cannot probably be ascertained with any accuracy until about the 1st of October. It is probable, however, that there will be sufficient circulation for all of the Southern and Western States when the full census returns are received. No additional circulation can be issued to the Eastern and Middle States.

THE ABUSED CAR-HORSES.

Inspection of Stables by Henry Bergh—Sickening Sights—Comparative Views.

Yesterday, Mr. BERGH and Mr. A. H. CAMPBELL, the President and Superintendent of the Society for the Prevention of Cruelty to Animals, accompanied by Dr. LIANTARD, of the New-York Veterinary College, and a TIMES reporter, made a tour of inspection of the principle car companies' stables to examine the horses, the condition of the stables, the quality of feed, and the general order of the homes of the best servants of mankind. The first stables inspected were those of the Fourth-avenue line. The Superintendent, Mr. MESSEROE, received his visitors very politely, and showed them over the premises. This line had lost eighteen out of ninety-four cases with the new disease. Ninety out of the ninety-four affected were mares, and the eighteen that died of the disease were mares. The hospital yesterday had sixty disabled horses in it. Only a very small portion, however, were down with the malady, the others being sick with sore feet, quittors, sore backs, and otherwise disabled. Some of the poor creatures had fearful wounds on the fetlocks, caused by their injuring themselves in the numerous switches on the line. This is reckoned the hardest road for horses of any in the City. The feed given the horses of this line is half oats and half corn. The condition of the stables is tolerable. The open windows of the stable in which the sick horses were, looked into a yard belonging to the proprietors of the Fourth-avenue stage line, and the filth and mud in this place was knee-deep. The stench must be anything but conducive to the recovery of the sick horses. The feed was examined and found of medium quality.

The stables of Messrs. WILKINS & MARSHALL, the proprietors of the Fourth-avenue stage line, were next visited. The stables were three tiers deep, and the atmosphere of the lowest was very bad. The refuse besides ran through from the top to the lower stable, rendering it altogether quite unfit for the purpose, in addition to which it is quite underground, and excepting just at the entrances quite dark. In a dirty yard were fifteen horses turned out for exercise in course of recovery from the disease. The stock consisted of 330 horses. Eighty had been attacked, out of which number eleven mares had died. One of the proprietors drew Mr. BERGH's particular attention to one horse which had been kept from work two weeks simply because he had a sore back. Mr. WILKINS, one of the proprietors, said he felt certain that the disease was easily curable if attended to quickly. He said the first symptoms were swelling of the hind legs and running at the eyes, but Dr. LIANTARD did not at all agree with this view. The horses were fed on half corn and half oats.

The stables of the East Belt line, at Thirty-seventh-street and First-avenue, were next inspected. Here were found 400 horses, a great proportion of which were in appearance very unfit for the every day toil required of them. There were about seventy cripples in a deplorable condition, and many more with large sores and ulcers on the fetlocks. Superintendent TERRY was asked if the latter were worked, and replied that he was compelled to work such stock or he must stop the line; and besides, he thought such horses better working than standing idle. Mr. BERGH did not agree with him, and cautioned him not to use many of the suffering beasts which were noticed in the stalls. The horses go over eighteen miles every day, and the daily feed of each consisted of twelve pounds of meal and four and a half pounds of ground oats. The line had lost forty animals, principally mares, with the new disease. There were only six cases now under treatment.

The stables of the Second-avenue line were next overhauled. Mr. SHAW reported that they were now quite free of the disease, not having had a case for two weeks. They had lost eleven horses out of 135 stricken down with the malady. The stables were in pretty good condition, but there were no signs of bedding, and apparently the poor beasts, after toiling over sixteen miles every day, had nothing but the hard and damp boards to lie on at night. The stock consisted of 750 horses. Daily feed, ten pounds—half oats and half corn. The hospital had some twenty patients in, under the homeopathy treatment.

The stables of the Third-avenue line were visited. In them were 1,600 horses. In an extra stable were a number of "green horses," which the hard work of the road had crippled. In the hospital were several bad cases, the poor creatures being covered with blisters, and scars arising therefrom. Two or three appeared in a dying state. There were no signs of bedding in a large portion of the stables. The feed taken from some of the mangers was sour, and as poor as any that had been inspected. The stablemen stated that the animals did not like it, and no wonder.

The stables of the Sixth-avenue line were found in admirable order, or as Mr. BERGH said, they were "perfect models." Everything was in first-rate order—perfect system reigning throughout the establishment. The best of feed is supplied the horses, and their daily rations are seventeen pounds each horse. The night stock were all good, sound animals. They were lying in their stalls on clean bedding. Mr. BIDGOOD only reported four cases of the disease, all of which were slowly recovering. He said that the Company had decided not to use in future any kiln-dried corn. After being dried it was found to have lost its virtue, and when sown it would not grow. The horses of this line had seventeen pounds of feed per day supplied to each.

The stables of the Forty-second-street, or Cross-town line, which has of late given Mr. BERGH and his officers so much trouble, were next visited. The clerk was very civil, and called the stable-keeper, A. CHALMERS, to escort Mr. BERGH and his party over the premises, but CHALMERS recognized the visitors, kept out of the way, and was found only after great trouble. He said he had received strict orders from JOHN GREEN, the President, not to show any one over the stables, and especially Mr. BERGH nor any of his officers. The reason of this refusal was quite apparent, for a more filthy, dilapidated and unwholesome-looking place, even from the outside, is difficult to conceive of. The office is dirty, and a coke-dealer would hardly deign to use it. The waiting-room is an inch deep in dirt, and the seats covered. Some half-dozen dirty-looking ruffians were squatting inside the shed, who were pointed out to our reporter as drivers and conductors of the "line." Mr. BERGH told CHALMERS he knew perfectly well the reason he was refused admittance, for he had gone over the cellars, called stables, a year ago, and had found them in an awful condition. CHALMERS denied that the stables were in a bad condition. It is strange that Mr. BERGH and his party should be so cordially received and treated so well at every other stable that was visited, and invited to call at any time and point out such horses as he might feel justified in ordering to be relieved of work, and yet be refused even admission to the "sheds" of the Green line. Mr. BERGH begged that CHALMERS would request Mr. GREEN to go over the Sixth-avenue stables, and then "go and do likewise."

DESTRUCTIVE FIRE.

Several Buildings in West Forty-Seventh and Forty-Sixth Streets Destroyed or Damaged.

Another destructive conflagration occurred last evening, which was discovered at about 9 o'clock, in the two-story saw and planing mill of KINNEY & CLARK, Nos. 628 and 630 West Forty-seventh-street, and which, being first seen in the boiler-room, probably originated from the furnace. The flames spread with extraordinary rapidity, and almost before the engines arrived the entire building was enveloped, and the fire communicated to adjacent property. The mill was entirely destroyed with all its contents and the loss will probably reach $15,000. Next west was the lumber yard of JOHN W. STEVENS & BRO., where stock to the amount of about $5,000 was destroyed. Next east was a five story building, Nos. 622, 624 and 626 West Forty-seventh-street, occupied as a morocco factory, by C. P. Buckin, the top floor of which was reached by the flames and the loss will probably exceed $5,000. The fire even reached across the street to the two story dwelling of THOS. INO, whose loss is $500; also to the building No. 627, owned by JOHN DARRAGH, and the lower floor of which was occupied as a stable and the upper portion as a tenement. The Twenty-second Precinct Police got out a great portion of the furniture of the tenants and the thirty horses in the stable, so that the loss was chiefly confined to the building, which will require $1,500 for repairs. No. 629 was occupied as a stable by HENRY BENKIN, whose loss is $500, and the slaughter-house of RICHARD DONOVAN, in the rear, was also slightly damaged. The fire also extended from the rear of the houses on the south side of the street to the raw-hide establishment of WM. CARR, Nos. 641 and 643 West Forty-sixth-street, whose loss is chiefly confined to the building, which is damaged $1,500. The fire at one time threatened to destroy the entire block, and that result would have undoubtedly followed, but for the great exertions of the firemen, ably directed by Chief Engineer PERLEY and the district engineers.

Meeting of the Riot Relief Fund Association.

A meeting of the Twelfth of July Relief Fund Association was held last evening at No. 295 Third-avenue, Dr. J. C. HANNAN presiding. The General Committee already appointed was authorized to begin the collection of subscriptions, and was authorized to name a subcommittee to investigate cases of distress arising out of the late riot. The election of a treasurer was deferred to the next meeting, each member of the Committee being ordered to report to the Secretary all collections made in the meantime. The name of JAS. H. GOODMAN, attorney-at-law, was added to the General Committee, which will meet at No. 204 East Twenty-first-street next Friday evening. Our reporter was informed that the subscriptions already promised amount to $700.

AFFAIRS IN EUROP[E]

Mr. Gladstone's Sensational Fl[illegible] Movement Against the Lords.

The Constitution Declared to [illegible] Violently Wrenched.

Parliament Brought into Conte[mpt] Before the People.

German Troops Ordered to be W[ith]drawn from Amiens and Rouen.

Formation of a Spanish Cabi[net] by Marshal Serrano.

Tumultuous Scene on the Adjou[rn]ment of the Cortes.

GREAT BRITAIN.

The London Journals on the Recent [illegible] of the Government—The Queen's W[ar]rant Laid on the Table of the H[ouse] of Commons—The New Castle Strik[e].

LONDON, July 21.—The *Times* says th[e] [illegible] of the Ministers abolishing the syste[m] [illegible] purchase of army commissions by royal [war]rant is a violent wrench of the Constitu[tion] and a wanton setting aside of the wi[ll of] the House of Lords. The *Times* regrets [that] this grave issue has been raised, but [ex]presses the hope that the Lords will in [their] future action think of the effect upon [the] officers of the army rather than the [immu]nity to their own privileges. The *Daily* [illegible] approves the conduct of the Governme[nt in] making themselves the exponents of [the] popular will, and recommends that [the] Lords pass the bill abolishing the purc[hase] of Army commissions. The *Telegraph* is [ex]ultant over the action of the Ministry, [and] says that Mr. GLADSTONE will be the [illegible] popular for vindicating the dignity of [the] House of Commons, in securing the har[vest] of its laborious session, and for reorgani[zing] the defenses of the country and guar[ding] the interests of the Army. The *Post* [illegible] the course of the Government has [been] somewhat unconstitutional, bringing [illegible] believes, Parliament into conte[mpt] before the people. The *Stan[dard]* asserts that Mr. GLADSTONE has [illegible]ly violated the privileges of [Par]liament, wasting its time, and precipitat[ing a] constitutional crisis. In the House of C[om]mons, this afternoon, Mr. CARDWELL, S[ecre]tary of State for War, laid on the table [the] Queen's warrant abolishing the syste[m of] purchase of army commissions.

The engineers on strike at Newcastle [held] a meeting today, and resolved to mak[e no] compromise with their employers.

FRANCE.

The Paris Elections To-Morrow—[Ru]mored Resignation of the Orl[eans] Princes—German Evacuation of [the] Northern Departments Ordered.

PARIS, July 21.—The Radicals are acti[ve in] canvassing for the municipal election[s to] be held next Sunday. The contest g[rows] more and more exciting. In the Ass[em]bly, today, Minister LAMBRECHT expla[ined] that the state of siege was still m[ain]tained in Paris, because the reorg[an]ization of the Police had not [yet] been completed. Notwithstanding the [ad]verse report of the Committee of the As[sem]bly, M. THIERS intends to defend his p[olicy] of protection before the Assembly. It i[s ru]mored that the Duke D'AUMALE and Prince DE JOINVILLE have resigned [their] seats in the Assembly. President TH[IERS] will shortly leave Paris for one of the wa[ter]ing-places. *Le Monde*, the ultra Catholic [or]gan, demands that the Government sup[port] the Pope in the exercise of his temp[oral] rights. Criminal proceedings have b[een] commenced against the *Avenir Nationale* [for] calumniating the Government. The P[rus]sian troops have received orders from B[erlin] to evacuate the Cities of Amiens and Ro[uen] and the Departments of the Somme, L[ower] Seine and Euse. Rouen will be evacu[ated] to-morrow.

GENERAL EUROPEAN NEWS

Serrano Forms a New Ministry [in] Spain—Adjournment of the Cor[tes]—Alsace and Lorraine—A Fleet [pre]paring to Convey the Grand D[uke] Alexis to America.

MADRID, July 20.—Marshal SERRANO [has] been intrusted by King AMADEUS with [the] formation of a new Ministry, and has [al]ready designated the following memb[ers:] Minister of Justice, Señor GOMEZ; Mini[ster] of Foreign Affairs, Señor CAUDAN; Mini[ster] of Marine, Admiral MALCAMPO; Minist[er of] Finance, Señor CAMADIO. The Cortes [has] adjourned tumultuously amid the protes[ts of] the minority.

VIENNA, July 21.—Count AGENOR GO[LU]CHOWSKI has been appointed Governor [of] Galicia.

BERLIN, July 21.—Several decrees are [pub]lished today, organizing Courts of law [in] Alsace and Lorraine.

LONDON, July 21.—The Grand Duke C[ON]STANTINE, of Russia, has arrived in Engl[and.] A naval squadron is fitting out at Cronst[adt] to accompany the Grand Duke ALEXIS [to] America.

The "Reformed" Hackmen—Opposit[ion] to the Proposed New Regulations.

The Hackmen's Association met last ev[en]ing in Apollo Hall, in Prince-street, with a [very] large attendance. JOHN MARRION, the P[res]ident, occupied the chair, and J. PHILLIPS [as] Secretary. A dozen new members were elec[ted] and $149 50 was received for dues and fees.

A resolution was passed to expel any mem[ber] of the association who should take passen[gers] with the Transfer Companies' tickets. The [ini]tiation fee was changed to $5 for owners, an[d] [illegible] for drivers.

The Treasurer reported that the expenses [for] the past week had been $217, and the cas[h on] hand, previous to the meeting, was $215.

The new regulations proposed by Mayor H[ALL] did not meet the views of the hackmen. Sev[eral] members spoke in opposition to them. T[hey] considered them as unjust and unconstitutio[nal;] they would drive the men out of their busin[ess,] and the men who had new carriages would [get] all the business, while those who had sec[ond-]rate or middling carriages would have to g[o to] the wall. They deemed the clause which [pre]vents the hackmen from soliciting [pas]sengers as illegal, and they w[ill] contest it in Court if necessary. It [is] a job got up to benefit a few politici[ans] who are engaged in the business, who wis[h to] monopolize it and drive the poorer men o[ut] it altogether. A committee was appointed [to] visit the Mayor and explain the view [of the] hackmen, and request him to modify i[t].

The New-York Times.

VOL. XXI.......NO. 6257. — NEW-YORK, TUESDAY, OCTOBER 10, 1871. — PRICE FOUR CENTS.

A CITY IN RUINS.

The Terrible Devastation of Chicago.

Three Square Miles in the Heart of the City Burned

Twelve Thousand Buildings Destroyed---Loss $50,000,000

Every Public Building, Hotel, Bank and Newspaper Swept.

Appeals to Other Cities and a Noble Response.

Frightful Details of the Disaster from Our Own Reporters.

Special Dispatch to the New-York Times.

ENGLEWOOD, (seven miles south of Chicago,) 5 P. M. MONDAY EVENING.

It is impossible to give in any approach to detail the devastation of Chicago. The fire of Sunday, previously reported, began in the lumber and coal tract, along the west bank of the river, laying in waste several squares, as previously reported, but the total of preliminary destruction among the cheap tenement structures and frame planing-mills of Canal and Clinton streets is lost and inconsiderable in the frightful sequel. The fire, early this morning, crossed the ...

The Devastation of Chicago—Map of the Burned District as Far as Heard From.

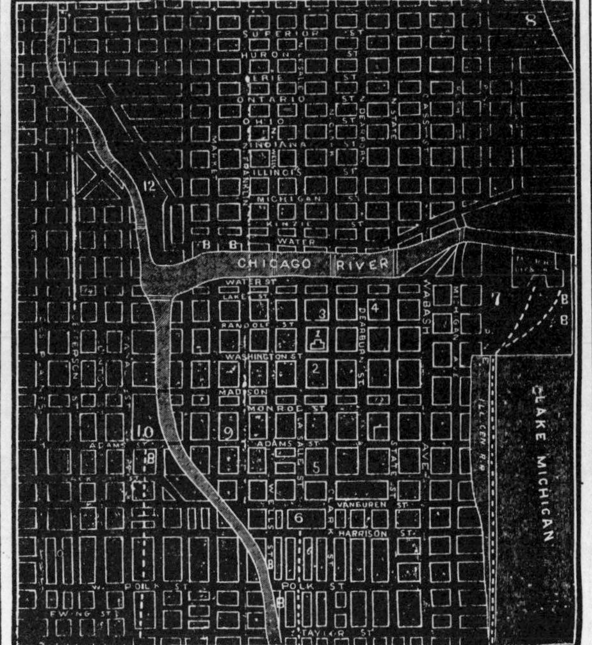

REFERENCES.

1. Court-house.
2. Chamber of Commerce.
3. Sherman House.
4. Tremont House.
5. Pacific Hotel.
6. Lake Shore and Michigan Southern, and Rock Island and Pacific passenger and freight houses.
7. Illinois Central, Michigan Central, and Chicago, Burlington and Quincy freight houses.
8. Chicago Water-works.
9. Chicago City Gas-works.
10. Pittsburg, Fort Wayne and Chicago, and St. Louis, Alton and Chicago Railroad passenger and sreight houses.
12. Chicago and North-western Depot grounds.
13. Chicago *Tribune* office.
14. Chicago Shot-tower.
B. B. B. B. Elevators.

present week. The building, receiving its interior finish, covered the entire square bounded by Jackson, Clark, Quincy and Jackson streets; $600,000 already expended. Just north on Clark, at the corner of Adams, the Lake-side Printing Company were completing their costly edifice, 100 by 100.

... gan-avenue, the elegant residence section extended, only recently begun, to be invaded by business. On Wabash, north of Madison to the river, on Randolph and Lake streets to the lake shore, was the solidly-built wholesale quarter, a large portion of which was rebuilt in costly style a season or two since.

The Chicago Court-house was a structure extending from Lasalle-street to Clark, 180 feet front on each street, and 325 feet in length, contained the Court rooms, Recorder's and municipal offices, the valable law library, and the jail in the basement. It had been recently rebuilt and enlarged. The structure cost not far from $1,000,000.

THE VERY LATEST.

Increased Spread of the Fire—The Southern Portion of Chicago Probably Destroyed—Telegraphic Communication with the City Cut Off.

Special Dispatch to the New-York Times.

CHICAGO, Oct. 10—1 A. M.—My associate in the city has been compelled to abandon his post, owing to the utter impossibility to keep up telegraphic communication. When he left the doomed City of Chicago the southern portion was threatened, in fact so great a hold had the flames obtained on the wooden buildings in that vicinity that the entire populace, men, women and children, were flying from their homes panic-stricken, ...

extension to State-street, occupied by SPEAR & CROFUT, carpets. The St. James Hotel, owned by Gen. W. L. STEWART, occupied the corner of State and Washington. The Third National Bank of J. IRVING PEARCE and others was in the costly marble McCormick Building on the north-west angle of the square, fronting on Dearborn and Randolph streets. Next south on Dearborn was the Rice Block, filled with offices and stores. South of this, on the same front, the Masonic Temple, built in ...

country is vividly lighted up by the glare of the burning city, and the scene even at this distance is appalling. The roads are thronged with fugitives who are vainly seeking shelter for the night. Vehicles of every description are constantly arriving, and I learn that all the roads leading from the city are in a similar condition. The agony and terror at present prevailing in the immediate neighbor- ...

... the entire loss, but it can scarcely fall below $150,000,000. Of course, but a fraction of this amount can be recovered from insurance.

Gen. SHERIDAN has today telegraphed to St. Louis, to the Missouri depot there, to send at once 100,000 rations. He has also telegraphed to Omaha for two companies of soldiers and 100 tents. He will also order another 100,000 rations.

Mayor MASON has issued a proclamation calling a meeting to-night in the West Division, to see what the citizens can do for the relief of the sufferers.

There are at least 150,000 people who know not where they can get enough provisions to satisfy their hunger.

A late rumor from the North Division says the devastation is less wide-spread than heretofore reported.

I hear of no deaths reported by the disaster as yet, but undoubtedly many have perished.

THE FEELING IN THE CITY.

The Effect Upon Wall-Street—Rapid and Extensive Decline in Western Stocks—A Panic in the Market, Followed by Failures.

The news of the extensive conflagration in Chicago did not reach Wall-street until after the commencement of the regular business yesterday, for the reason that the morning papers had very brief accounts of the fire and the occurrence was not regarded as of great importance. As the day wore on, however, the full details of the terrible catastrophe began to be received, and the news was posted on the telegraph and newspaper bulletins and made known by extras of the evening papers. The intelligence spread like wildfire, and reaching the stock market created the utmost consternation. Operators in stocks saw at once that such a terrible calamity must affect the values of the securities of all roads centering in or depending upon Chicago for business, and they immediately began throwing them over and selling short to a prodigious extent. The effect was electric. Stocks ...

... ther increase that which now overwhelms the great financial centre of the country. Thus the ruin attendant upon the fire in Chicago will not be confined to that city alone. Hundreds of homes all over the country will mourn losses consequent upon the fire, and the season which was believed to be the most prosperous for all classes known since 1865 may be made, by a single day's devastation, the most disastrous.

The panic in stocks was almost unparalleled. There was a universal depreciation of all values, and the extent of the decline will be seen by the following table:

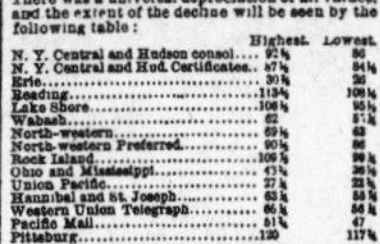

	Highest.	Lowest.
N. Y. Central and Hudson consol....	92½	86
N. Y. Central and Hud. Certificates..	87½	84½
Erie..............................	30½	26
Reading...........................	113¼	108½
Lake Shore........................	106½	95½
Wabash............................	62	57¾
North-western.....................	69½	62
North-western Preferred...........	90½	86
Rock Island.......................	109½	99½
Ohio and Mississippi..............	43¾	36½
Union Pacific.....................	27¼	22¾
Hannibal and St. Joseph...........	63¼	55½
Western Union Telegraph...........	66¼	56¼
Pacific Mail......................	51¾	47
Pittsburg.........................	120	117¾

The above table gives but a faint idea of the panic which prevailed in the market. The room was crowded all day, and throngs were hurrying to-and-fro, some with faces blanched with fear, and others flushed with excitement. Rumors of failures were circulated far and near, and as the day closed at least half a dozen firms were reported as having failed to meet their engagements. Some of the cooler operators made fortunes by going short of the market in the first flurry, and scarcely any would have failed in this respect who had sold short at any ...

THE THIEVES CONVICTED

Complete Exposition of the Ring Accounts.

Official Report of the Joint Committee of Investigation.

Nearly $75,000,000 Spent from the Appropriations in Three Years.

The Tax-Payers in Debt One Hundred and Twenty Millions.

Some of the Robbers Pointed Out by Name.

The Schuyler Fraud Traced Home to Tweed.

The Joint Board of Supervisors and the Committee of Citizens met at 3 o'clock yesterday, in the Supervisors' room, in the new Court-house, Alderman J. G. DIMOND presiding.

WM. A. BOOTH rose and said: This meeting, I believe, has been called, Sir, at the instance of the Committee of Sixteen, of which I have the honor to be Chairman That Committee, at last meeting, submitted their report in relation to the debt of the City, and also asked to be impowered to send for persons and papers. Since ...

[Continued on Eighth Page.]

The New-York Times.

VOL. XXI......NO. 6370. NEW-YORK, MONDAY, FEBRUARY 19, 1872. PRICE FOUR CENT

THE KUKLUX KLAN HYENAS.

Report of the Select Committee of Congress.

When, How and Why the Secret Order was Formed.

The Most Intelligent Negroes Selected for Immolation.

Extension of the President's Powers Recommended.

What the Minority of the Committee Have to Say.

WASHINGTON, D. C., Feb. 18.—The Joint Select Committee will, to-morrow, make their report on the condition of affairs in the late insurrectionary States. The Committee was organized April 20, and again met in Washington on the 17th of May last. On the 19th, a subcommittee of eight was appointed to proceed at once with the investigation, with authority to take testimony wherever they deemed it advisable, by a subcommittee of their own number, to be reported to a meeting of the full committee. Subcommittees were appointed to visit and take testimony in North and South Carolina, Georgia, Florida, Tennessee, Alabama, and Mississippi. The evidence taken in Washington and by a Subcommittee in South Carolina, having been reported to the Joint Committee, is now submitted and as an appendix to and part of the report is also submitted the report of the Subcommittee appointed to digest the reports of the Executive officers of the States. The testimony taken in Georgia, Florida, Alabama and Mississippi by the Subcommittees visiting these States is not yet prepared and will be submitted with a supplement or supplementary report.

SCOPE OF THE INVESTIGATION.

The proceedings and debates in Congress show that whatever other causes were assigned for disorders in the late insurrectionary States, the execution of the laws and security of life and property were alleged to be most seriously threatened by the existence and acts of organized bands of armed and disguised men known as Kuklux. Inquiring as our primary duty into the truth of these allegations in those States where such acts have most recently been committed, the investigation necessarily assumed a wider range. Not only has inquiry been made as to the commission of outrages, as to the execution of laws by the superior Courts and inferior Magistrates, but bad legislation, official incompetency, corruption, and other causes, having been assigned as accounting for, if not justifying, dis orders, they, too, have to a large extent entered into the statements and opinions of witnesses.

IMMUNITY OF DISGUISED CRIMINALS.

There is a remarkable concurrence of testimony to the fact that in those of the late rebellious States into whose condition the Committee have examined, the Courts and juries administer justice between man and man, in all ordinary cases, civil and criminal; and while there is this concurrence on this point, the evidence is equally decisive that redress cannot be obtained against those who commit crimes in disguise and at night. The reasons assigned are, that identification is difficult, almost impossible—that when this is attempted, the combinations and oaths of the Order come in and release the culprit by perjury either upon the witness-stand or in the jury-box; and that terror inspired by their acts, as well as public sentiment in their favor in many localities paralyzes the arm of civil power. That this organization may not be looked at in the exaggerated light of overriding all law and justice in the communities where it exists, and that the facility with which the well-disposed people of the South have adapted themselves to their changed circumstances may be seen, they introduce statements on this subject of a few prominent men from several of those States, including EX-GOV. ORR of South Carolina, EX-GOV. PARSONS of Alabama, Gen. CLANTON, C. D. FORSYTHE, Solicitor of the Rome, Ga., Judicial Circuit. While there is this general concurrence of evidence as to the efficiency of the administration of justice by the Superior Courts, there are complaints that in some instances incompetent Judges have been appointed. Numerous complaints of the incapacity of many of the inferior magistrates, and in several of the States the Governors are charged with an abuse of the pardoning power, especially in favor of the negroes, all of which assigned causes for disorder will be noticed when we come to consider those causes.

THE HITHERTO SECRET ORDER.

The inquiry into the present condition of the late insurrectionary States necessarily involved the history of the successive steps which have led to that condition as affected by the bands already referred to, and before proceeding to consider their present situation, the Committee trace so far as they are able to do so from the testimony, and from official reports, the origin, extent, purposes and modes of operation of this heretofore secret and mysterious organization, and the causes assigned for its existence and earlier actions. There are expressions of belief by United States military officers and others that secret organizations were formed in the insurrectionary States soon after the close of the war, hostile to and intended to embarrass the Government of the United States, and of the States, in the proper administration of the affairs of the country. Among these were the statements made by Major-Gen. THOMAS before the Reconstruction Committee in February, 1866, and by Gen. MEADE in his official report for 1868 as Commander of the Department of the South. Neither of the statements of these gentlemen refer by name to the Kuklux Klan, but they cover the period during which it made its appearance. Its gradual development may be traced by bearing in mind these facts, and taking up the evidence of Gen. N. B. FORREST, given before this Committee. As he fixes the earliest date for the existence of the Kuklux, assigns several motives for their organization, and possessed their confidence so far as to know their signs and passwords, and to be able, as he alleges, to disband them in 1868, we proceed to consider and compare his various statements. The time of the organization is thus fixed in 1866, and by reference to the proclamation of Gov. BROWNLOW, the report shows the extent to which outrage and crime were committed. The motives and means by which they were accomplished through Democratic clubs, Kuklux Klans and Knights of the White Camelia—different names for organizations shown to have worked for a common purpose—may be learned from the testimony, over 1400 pages of which was taken by the Subcommittee of the House Committee on Elections in the Louisiana contested election cases of 1868. Taking these statements from official sources showing the prevalence of this organization in every one of the late insurrectionary States and in Kentucky, it is difficult now, with the light which has recently been thrown upon its history, to realize that even the existence of the Kuklux Order has been so long a mooted question in the public mind. Especially is this remarkable, in view of the effects that are disclosed by some of this documentary evidence to have been produced by it. That it was used as a means of intimidating and murdering negro voters during the Presidential election of 1868, the testimony on the Louisiana and other contested election cases already referred to, clearly establishes.

OBJECT OF THE ORGANIZATION.

The report treats with minuteness on the occurrences in South Carolina; and Georgia, Mississippi and Alabama, are grouped together for the purpose of showing the existence of Kuklux and their practices. With the exception of the presence of Northern men in Southern States, and the establishment of Union Leagues to influence the political action of the negroes, none of these latter assigned causes for the origin of the Kuklux were themselves in existence in 1866 when it was established. The object of the Kuklux was to oppose and reject the principles of the Radical Party, as shown by the Constitution, to be accomplished by each member providing himself with a pistol, a Kuklux gown and signal instruments. If corroboration were needed upon this point it could be found in the expressions made by these bandits to their victims when inflicting their scourgings upon men and their outrages upon women. That testimony is uniform, and if "out of their own mouths we condemn them," it must be on the ground of their hostility to the Government, and to the enjoyment by the negro of the rights conferred upon him by the Amendments to the Constitution, and by the laws which they are organized to oppose.

ORIGIN OF THE CORRUPTION IN THE SOUTH.

The refusal of a large portion of the wealthy and educated men to discharge their duties as citizens has brought upon them the same consequences which are being suffered in Northern cities and communities from the neglect of their business and educated men to participate in all the movements of the people which make up self-government. The citizen in either section who refuses or neglects from any motive to take his part in self-government has learned that he must now suffer and help to repair the evils of bad government. The newly-made voters of the South at the close of the war, it is testified, were kindly disposed toward their former masters. The feeling between them, even yet, seems to be one of confidence in all other than their political relations. The refusal of their former masters to participate in political reconstruction necessarily left the negroes to be influenced by others. Many of them were elected to office and entered it with honest intentions to do their duty, but were unfitted for its discharge. Through their instrumentality, many unworthy white men, having obtained their confidence, also procured public positions. In legislative bodies, this mixture of ignorant but honest men with better educated knaves gave opportunity for corruption, and this opportunity has developed a state of demoralization on this subject which may and does account for many of the wrongs of which the people justly complain. It is apparent at the same time that the demoralization is not confined to race, nativity or political creed, but presents specimens alike in the negro, the carpet-bagger, and the white native citizens of both parties. These remarks are not applicable to all the reconstructed States. They are to several of them. Taking South Carolina as an illustration, and it is certainly as bad in these respects as any of the States, and there can be no doubt that venality and corruption in the Legislature prevailed largely. There, they are spoken of as existing by men of all parties, and seem to be conceded. Certainly, their existence is almost universally believed by the people of the State. With such material as the Legislature, and such views of virtue outside as are shown to have prevailed, corruption was inevitable. We point to the results of the opinion in South Carolina in the fact that the negroes in the nine counties of that State in which Kuklux violence prevailed to such an extent as to call for the suspension of the writ of habeas corpus in them, are, according to the testimony of Judge CARPENTER, much more intelligent than in any other part of the State. The fact they are so when placed alongside the list of men murdered and maltreated in these counties, demonstrates that it requires the strong arm of the Government to protect its citizens in the enjoyment of their rights, to keep the peace and prevent this threatened—rather to stay this initiated war of races until the experiment which it has inaugurated, and which many Southern men pronounce now, and many more have sworn shall be made a failure, can be determined in peace. The race so recently emancipated, against which banishment or serfdom is thus decreed, but which has been clothed by the Government with the rights and responsibilities of citizenship, ought not to be, and we feel assured will not be left hereafter without protection against the hostilities and sufferings it has endured in the past, as long as the legal and constitutional powers of the Government are adequate to afford it. Communities suffering such evils, and influenced by such extreme feelings, may be slow to learn that relief can come only from a ready obedience to, and support of constituted authority.

PATIENCE WITH THE SOUTH.

Looking to the modes provided by law for the redress of all grievances, that Southern communities do not seem to yield this ready obedience at once should not deter the friends of good government in both sections from hoping and working for that end. Northern communities, exasperated by the delay and insubordination, may be reminded that the elements of the two societies are widely different, composed of those who, a few years since ruled the State, and exacted obedience to their will from their slaves, and held absolute sway over the votes of their white dependents, but who are now reduced in influence and in wealth by the events of war, and of the poor white, who has found himself, as he supposes, degraded by the elevation of the negro to political equality with him, his vote before having been the chief badge of his superiority; of the negro, not only voting, but ruling the State, in office with, or over his former master, or struggling with the evils of poverty in beginning life for himself, after the best years of his life have been spent in the service of others. All these elements beget feelings, and result in disorders to which Northern communities are strangers. The strong feeling which led to rebellion, and sustained brave men, however mistaken, in resisting the Government which demanded their submission to its authority, the sincerity of whose belief was attested by their enormous sacrifice of life and treasure; this feeling cannot be expected to subside at once nor in years. It required full forty years to develope disaffection into sedition and sedition into treason. Should we not be patient if in less than ten we have a fair prospect of seeing so many who were armed enemies becoming obedient citizens? Should we not give encouragement to those who manifest a disposition now to become such, especially when it is that in many sections well-disposed men were deterred by fear of the power of an armed and desperate conspiracy from affording aid to the authorities in enforcing the law, but while we make this forbearance and conciliation, fully recognizing that from far the largest part of the Southern people a reluctant obedience is all that is to be hoped for, let it be understood that less than obedience the Government cannot accept. Obedient citizens they cannot be considered, who themselves complain of bad laws, excuse or encourage the masked and armed mobs that override all law. Brave and magnanimous enemies, even they cannot be reckoned who permit the remnants of rebellious feelings, the animosities of race or the bitterness of political partisanship to degrade the soldiers of LEE and JOHNSTON into the cowardly midnight prowlers and assassins, who scourge and kill the poor and defenseless. Against all such crime, as well as against incompetency and corruption in office, the power of an intelligent public sentiment and of the Courts of Justice should be invoked and united.

HOW TO CHANGE THE NEGRO VOTE.

Appealing for patience and forbearance in the North while time and these powers are doing their work, would, also, appeal to the good sense of Southern men, if they sincerely desire to accomplish political reforms through a change in the negro vote. If their theory is true that he votes solidly now with the Republican Party, and is kept there by his ignorance and by deception, all that is necessary to keep him there is to keep up by their countenance the Kuklux organization. Having the rights of a citizen and a voter, neither of these rights can be abrogated by whipping him. If his political opinions are erroneous he will not take kindly to the opposite creed, when the apostles continue to use the scourge upon himself and outrage his wife and children; if he is ignorant he will not be educated by burning his school-houses and exiling his teachers; if he is wicked he will not be made better by banishing to Liberia his religious teachers; if the resuscitation of the State is desired by his labor, neither will it be secured by a persecution which depopulates townships and prevents the introduction of new labor and of capital.

BENIFICENT EFFECT OF THE ACT OF 1871.

The law of 1871 has been effective in suppressing for the present, to a great extent, the operations of masked and disguised men in North and South Carolina. Bills have also been found by Grand Juries in Georgia, Alabama and Mississippi; but comparatively few, if any, of the defendants in the last-named States have yet been tried. The apparent cessation of operations should not lead to a conclusion that the community would be safe if protective measures were withdrawn. These should be continued until there remains no further doubt of the actual suppression and disarming of the wide-spread and dangerous conspiracy.

RECOMMENDATIONS.

The results of suspending the writ of habeas corpus in South Carolina shows that where the membership, mysteries, and power of the organization have been kept concealed, this is the most, and, perhaps, the only effective remedy for its suppression; and, in view of its cessation and resumption of hostilities at different times; of its extent and power; and that in several of the States where it exists the Courts have not yet held terms at which the cases can be tried, we recommend that the power conferred on the President by the fourth section of that act be extended until the end of the next session of Congress. In view, also, of the large number of indictments found in the several Courts under this act, which yet remain untried, and of the evident encouragement derived from the belief that the present United States Courts cannot possibly reach and try them within any reasonable time, we recommend such an increase of the Judiciary of the United States by districts and circuits, in the States shown to be affected by these disorders, as, in the judgment of Congress, will secure speedy and certain justice, to be administered, and leave no hope of impunity to criminals by the law's delay.

AS TO POLITICAL DISABILITIES.

The continuance of disabilities is the only cause not yet considered. No man under disabilities has avowed himself as either committing or encouraging outrages for that reason, and no member of the organization has justified their acts on that ground. It is one of the pretexts made by those who were willing to urge any plausible excuse for outrages which admit of none. But to remove alleged impediments to the local Government, encountered by the existence of disabilities to hold office, and being satisfied that there should be a general removal of them, with proper conditions and exceptions, we recommend the passage of a law for that purpose, agreeing in the recommendation made by the President to exclude from its benefits any great criminals distinguished above all others for the part they took in opposition to the Government. In this connection we wish to say that as disregard of law has been the evil so largely complained of, and so widely extended in the late insurrectionary States no encouragement should be given to those who have accepted office in defiance of the existence of these constitutional disabilities, or have elected to office men whom they knew to be excluded by them.

DEBTS AND ELECTION LAWS.

The report of Representative STEVENSON, from the Subcommittee on Debts and Election laws of the late insurrectionary States, says: Ex-Gov. BULLOCK, of Georgia, sent a letter more remarkable for argument against the proceedings of the Subcommittee as a breach of State Rights than for the facts furnished, and Gov. REED, of Florida, declined to answer at all, though he has forwarded to a member of the Subcommittee several of his messages. He protested against the invasion of the rights of the State of Florida. Generally where their inquiry has been resented, evaded, or ignored they discovered reasons for concealment which convince them that officials are more concerned about their own dignity than that of the State. In South Carolina the Governor has answered promptly, but sent such contradictory statements that they could give little weight to any. The report concludes with a statement of the general financial condition of the eleven States, as follows: Debts and liabilities in 1860, $102,536,778; in 1865, $222,848,132; increase since 1860, $120,331,354. When the late insurrectionary States entered the rebellion, they held in trust-funds, assets and balances, $70,147,747; these funds and assets were on deposit, or in stocks of banks, railroads, and other internal improvements; their contingent liabilities were secured by mortgages on lands, in stocks, banks, and interests in lien, or on turnpikes, railroads, and canals. The banks had a capital of over $61,000,000; coin, over $18,000,000; circulation, over $51,000,000; there were 8,944 miles of railway, which cost $237,376,097. The assessed value of property was $4,363,030,347: the estimated or assessed value of slaves, $1,634,105,341; value of property, exclusive of slaves, $2,728,825,006. According to the estimate of Secretary BELKNAP, the Confederate debt on the 1st of April, 1865, was about $2,345,297,823; the total ascertained loss by the rebellion in property assets and debts, State and Confederate, $5,262,303,554. There were debts due the merchants of the North from those of the South for goods purchased and consumed, and money loaned, estimated, when the war began, at $300,000,000. Add interest to 1866 and the sum would be $408,000,000; total State debt and disabilities existing, and prospective and Confederate debt and commercial debt, $2,976,145,965 90. Here was a burden which must have crushed the people of the South and reduced them to general bankruptcy. It was $218,456,384 47 greater than the national debt at its maximum; $247,320,949 85 more than the assessed value of all property in the States in 1860, less slaves, and $1,372,743,326 90 more than the assessed value of all property in the eleven States in 1865. They had neither money nor credit, nor sufficient means of subsistence.

HOW THE PEOPLE WERE FED.

If the Government had left the people of the South to their devices they must have fallen into anarchy and ruin. But before the war ended the Government had begun to feed, clothe, shelter and care for the destitute of both colors, and millions were distributed in supplies. In 1865 a bureau was organized for this purpose, and expended in relief, education and aid to the people of both colors and all conditions, $13,280,277 40. Millions more were donated by charitable associations and citizens of the North. The document concludes with a report of the Election laws of late insurrectionary States.

he Report of the Minority of the Committee.

The minority of the Committee say that although Tennessee was for some reason embraced among the States assigned to one of the Subcommittees, no evidence was attempted to be taken to show any lawlessness there. It follows, therefore, that five at least of the eleven Southern States, to-wit: Virginia, Tennessee, Arkansas, Louisiana and Texas, are free from even the suspicion of lawlessness on the part of the people, whatever may be the fact as to their rulers. These five States embrace greatly more than half the territory, and nearly half the population of the eleven Southern States, and it is hard to conceive why, if political or other combinations existed for any general purpose, they should be left out while the other six States, or part of them, were in combination for any such general objects. The minority do not deny that bodies of disguised men have in several States of the South been guilty of the most flagrant crimes—crimes which they neither seek to palliate nor excuse, for the commission of which the wrong-doers should suffer speedy and condign punishment. But they deny that these men have any general organization or any political significance, or that their conduct is indorsed by any respectable number of white people in any State.

CARPET-BAGGERS AND SCALLAWAGS.

The minority dwell at much length on carpet-bag, scallawag and negro rule, showing that while the assessed value of the taxable property in the eleven States of the South has been reduced from $4,333,757,942 in 1860, to $2,026,440,971 in 1870, being a loss of $2,307,306,971, or over $300,000,000 more than now remains, the State taxation on what those people now have was, in 1870, $12,813,615, while it was $6,165,486 in 1860, when their affairs were managed by their own people, and the county taxation in 1860 on all the property they then owned was only $3,115,184, while now, under carpet-bag and negro rule, it is $14,298,630, or $11,000,000 more on the remnant still in existence than it was on the whole property they owned when the war begun.

NO COMBINATION; NO CONSPIRACY.

The minority review these subjects at length and repeat they feel confident that they are sustained in the assertion that there is nothing in the evidence tending to show that there is either any combination, conspiracy, design or desire on the part of any respectable number of the people of the South to deprive the colored race of any of their civil or political rights, and there is certainly none either to subvert or interfere with the legitimate authority of the Federal or State Government. Appended to the views of the minority is the paper drawn up by Mr. VAN TRUMP, the minority member of the Subcommittee visiting State of South Carolina. He states the election in 1870 took place on the 19th of October. In looking over the official report of the Adjutant and Inspector General, it would be observed that, while the distribution of arms to the negro militia extends up to the very day of election, not a gun was placed in their hands after the day of election, and the expiration of the ten days allowed for the Republican Election Commissioners to retain the ballot-boxes in their possession. This was the exciting cause of whatever trouble and disturbance existed in South Carolina in 1870. It was there that Kukluxism showed its head, and even the miserable testimony of the negroes themselves showed that the principal object of the Kuklux visitation was to search for these very arms distributed among them by the Governor.

The report of the minority covers 300 printed pages.

The Latest Murder in Chelsea, Mass.

BOSTON, Mass., Feb. 18.—BARTHOLOMEW, who murdered STORER in Chelsea last night, was arrested; also, Dr. SYDNEY B. WEST and Mrs. GILBERT, the two latter as witnesses of the homicide. BARTHOLOMEW is a machinist, about sixty years of age, and a widower. STORER was forty-five years of age, and leaves a wife and four children. He was a builder, worth considerable property, and was respected in the community. STORER and the woman were partners in manufacturing medicated candy, and the tragedy took place in their rooms, where BARTHOLOMEW and STORER met, both, it is said, being enamored with Mrs. GILBERT.

The Fishing Bounties.

Gen. BUTLER has written a letter to Gloucester, Mass., in which he expresses the conviction that the hopes of the passage of a bill granting bounties to fishing vessels are illusory, and says that it seems very clear to him that if laws should be passed repealing our duties upon fish and opening our ports to the Canadian fishermen before any bounty or any relief to the fishermen shall be enacted, then we are, indeed, without remedy. He adds that he has still great hopes of relief to the fishing interest from a different source and in another way, which will be developed all in good time.

WASHINGTON.

The Ridiculous Failure of the Arms Sale Question.

Mortification of Sumner and Schurz—Bonded Warehouse Reform—Civil Service—Indian Matters—Pensions—Miscellaneous.

Special Dispatch to the New-York Times.

WASHINGTON, Feb. 18.—When the debate in the Senate on the French arms resolution closed on Friday both SUMNER and SCHURZ were sick of their work, and the former was reported as confessing himself deceived as to the merits of the case. That their object was thoroughly exposed and badly defeated was admitted on all hands, so to-morrow there will be no renewal of the debate unless they return to it. The malicious preamble will be killed, as it deserves to be, and the resolution of investigation will be adopted, with Mr. CONKLING's amendment, which is designed to show the contemptible origin of the matter. Had the resolution been brought into the Senate by Mr. SUMNER in the first instance, omitting the unnecessary and offensive preamble, and had he proposed to put it to a vote without speaking himself, it would have been unanimously adopted without a word of debate. But that was utterly foreign to their purpose. Every one here knows that they thought they had skillfully concocted a plan that was to blow GRANT's Administration out of the water. After Mr. SUMNER had prepared his resolution, and before he offered it, he handed it to his colleague, Mr. WILSON, and remarked in the hearing of several Senators, that ten days hence GRANT's renomination would not be spoken of, and yet Mr. SUMNER and Mr. SCHURZ, and their handful of adherents on the Press have the effrontery to say that they have not talked politics in this matter; that they have no political design in it. Such hypocrisy is as apparent as it is unparalleled. If they want people to believe what they say, let them hold their tongues to-morrow, and consent to the killing of the preamble to the resolution, which prejudges the case, and to the ordering of the investigation decently, and in silence.

THE BONDED WAREHOUSE REFORM.

The reform of the bonded warehouse and General Order business is proceeding in good earnest as rapidly as the details can be arranged. While the opponents of the Administration are recklessly charging it with all manner of culpability and negligence, the President and the heads of Departments proceed in an unostentatious, business-like manner to the correction of one evil after another, as fast as they are exposed. The rates of cartage and storage of the bonded warehouses have been fully revised by the three Committees of the Chamber of Commerce, Custom-house and warehouse-men, and Collector ARTHUR reports that the rates which have been unanimously agreed on are about fifteen to twenty-five per cent. advance on those which were fixed in 1867. The regulation of the General Order charges and the abolition of the present system of disposing of the business is now under consideration, and will be carried out as soon as the details can be arranged. The chief thing sought to be accomplished in this matter is the disposal of this business so that it cannot hereafter be a matter of political or personal control.

CIVIL SERVICE REFORM.

The Advisory Civil Service Board has almost completed its arrangements for carrying into effect the new civil service rules in their full extent. The Examining Boards for the Departments, provided for in the eighth rule, have not been designated yet by the President, but the appointments will probably not be delayed so as to embarrass or retard the execution of the plans of the Advisory Board. The operation of the general plan will be somewhat narrowed if Congress shall refuse to make an appropriation, without which some machinery much to be desired cannot be organized. With the instrumentalities that are now at the command of the President, the examination of Postmasters for instance, scattered all over the country, and the officers of the revenue service, cannot be made so effective and satisfactory as it might be. Then again it is desirable that there should be a representative in each of the Departmental Boards from outside the service. This would give an assurance of impartiality, and would relieve the executive officers of the Departments both from false charges of only formally supporting the system, and from any temptation to influence the Boards for political purposes. It may be remarked that the principles of the system will be applied as fully as possible in the offices for the collection of internal revenue and customs. The New-York Custom-house will be a group of itself, it is understood, and vacancies in the higher positions will be filled by promotions, and the vacant places in the lowest grades thus caused are to be filled by competitive examinations. The Custom-house at Philadelphia will form another group, and so on. In regard to the succession to Mr. FORNEY, it was remarked by a member of the Advisory Board that if any of the subordinates in the office at Philadelphia were fitted to discharge the duties of Collector, it would be filled by promotion. Otherwise the President would be compelled to select from persons outside the service without an examination. The manner of ascertaining the fitness of subordinates for promotion in such cases has been provided for by the Board.

THE INDIAN BOARD SECRETARYSHIP.

The resignation of VINCENT COLYER as Secretary of the Board of Indian Peace Commissioners did not occasion his retirement from the Board, as many supposed. He is still a member of the Board. The law says the Board shall appoint one of its own members Secretary, with such reasonable compensation as may be necessary. This clause was secured by the Commissioners especially for Mr. COLYER's benefit, and they deemed it reasonable to allow him $3,000 a year salary. When it became impossible for Mr. COLYER to continue longer in the position, the Board took advantage of another clause of the law, which was held to give discretion in the matter, and decided to appoint a Secretary, not one of their own number. Mr. THOMAS K. CREE, of Pittsburg, was some time since appointed. This is not considered to be what was contemplated by the law, which is mandatory in its terms as to the appointment of a Secretary, but practically it amounts to the same thing, for the Board could appoint one of its members Secretary, and authorize him to employ Mr. CREE as a clerk, to do the same duties now assigned to him.

THE LAND-OFFICE.

During the year ending Feb. 1, 1871, the General Land-office record about 45,000 letters on the business of the office. During the year succeeding that time, which is the year since Mr. DRUMMOND became Commissioner, the letters received numbered over 56,000. The number of letters received is not of itself an exact index of the comparative amount of the business, but still an approximately correct idea is to be gained of the increase of general business. There was a constant annual increase from 1854 to the beginning of the war, when there was a sudden falling off. Since the war the increase has been more rapid than ever. It would seem from the record of letters received that the increase during the last year has been about one-fourth. That is, the current business of last year is to that of this as four to five. There have been one-fourth more sales of land, one-fourth more lands surveyed, which has cost one-fourth more. In spite of this increase in the business, which causes a like increase in the clerical labor of the office, Commissioner DRUMMOND, with the same force which he found in the office, has not only kept up the current work, but made large gains upon work which he found in arrears. Among other things he found that the Agricultural College scrip had never been examined and canceled, which he has now nearly or quite completed. There is a prospect that for the year to come there will be double the amount of labor to be done in the office that there has been this year. A large share of the increase being expected from the special legislation of Congress last year designed to force pre-emptors of unsurveyed lands since surveyed and offered for sale, to come forward and make the payments which have been neglected. There are now surveyed and in the market 990,000,000 of acres of public lands.

POST-OFFICE COMPETITIVE EXAMINATION.

The Post-office Department has had another competitive examination—this time for lady applicants to a nine-hundred-dollar position. The examination was conducted by Mr. BLACKFAN, of the Civil Service Board; Mr. CHILDS, the Chief Clerk of the Department, and Mr. TERRELL, Third Assistant Postmaster-General. The examination papers were examined by these gentlemen separately. Mr. CHILDS and Mr. BLACKFAN arrived, independently of each other, at precisely the same result, each designating the same three in the same order. Mr. TERRELL only differed from them in regard to the third. All of those designated passed excellent examinations, the differences being very slight, the appointment has not been made, but will be soon. The officers of the Department are much pleased with their experience with competitive examinations thus far.

THE CHEROKEE LANDS.

The Secretary of the Interior is about to ask Congress to authorize the President to appraise all the lands of the Cherokee Nation west of the ninety-sixth meridian of west longitude. By the present treaty stipulations, it is to be appraised only as fast as friendly Indians are settled upon it. It will facilitate the settlement of friendly Indians to have it appraised previous to their occupancy of it, and therefore the authority of Congress will be asked to appraise it at once.

THE TARIFF QUESTION.

The high-tariff people are not contented with the action of the Ways and Means Committee, in reporting back the bill to place tea and coffee on the free list, and referring it to the Committee of the Whole, and so to-morrow they will try to secure a passage of the bill under suspension of the rules. The number of votes which the original resolution of instructions to the Committee to report the bill received, gives them some hope that a two-thirds vote may be had. Free coal and salt will doubtless be proposed on the other side, as a sort of counter-irritant to defeat the bill.

THE APACHE RESERVATIONS.

When the reservations were designated for the Apache Indians in Arizona last Fall, at the time Gen. CROOK was ordered to force those savages to accept the hospitality of the Government or be shot, the agencies were temporarily placed in the hands of military officers. It has now been determined to appoint civilians to the positions, in the usual way, to permanently supersede the military agents. There are three of these positions, and under the plans of the Peace Board they will be given to the Dutch Reform Church, the proper officers of which will be informed of their privilege to designate persons to be appointed.

GEN. ABBOTT'S CASE.

There now seems to be but little doubt that the Committee on Privileges and Elections will decide against the claims of Gen. ABBOTT to a seat in the Senate. The vote of the Committee has not yet been taken, however. If Mr. ABBOTT is rejected, then the case of Mr. RANSOM will be before the Committee, and not till then. The decision of the two cases will be made independently of each other.

ARMY AND NAVY PENSIONS.

A bill has been introduced in the House by Hon. W. L. SESSIONS, of New-York, allowing totally disabled soldiers and seamen increased pensions. Inasmuch as the sum involved is a very small one, and is in behalf of a very unfortunate class of cripples, it ought to pass. It provides that all persons who shall have lost the sight of both eyes, or both hands, shall be entitled to pensions at the rate of fifty dollars per month, and all persons who shall have lost both feet, or one hand and one foot, shall be entitled to pensions at the rate of forty dollars per month.

THE ALABAMA CLAIMS.

The Promise of the Parliamentary Session—Fresh Views of the English Press.

From the London Times, Feb. 6.

The Parliamentary Session of 1872 opens under circumstances which strangely illustrate the fallibility of political foresight. But a few weeks ago the whole atmosphere of politics appeared to be highly charged with that kind of electricity which is supposed to betoken the advent of dangerous storms, though it often passes off harmlessly enough after the meeting of Parliament. The warnings, however, which the Government received from all quarters had exclusive reference to domestic affairs. It is, indeed, a remarkable fact, and perhaps a proof of our insular simplicity, that two Cabinets have prematurely taken credit, in perfect good faith and without protest from their opponents, for the settlement of all outstanding differences between Great Britain and the United States. At the general election of 1868, the Conservative leaders pointed with a venial pride to the Stanley-Johnson Convention on the *Alabama* claims, as well as to that guaranteeing the neutrality of Luxemburg, as tangible achievements in foreign policy. Events which no one in England had foreseen showed how empty was the success thus discounted beforehand, and a similar fatality now threatens to disconcert the confident belief, so often expressed during the recess, that under Mr. GLADSTONE's Administration the *Alabama* question had at last been closed. Suddenly, that question looms upon us again in a new and wholly unexpected form, dwarfing and casting into the shade, for the present at least, all party interests, and calling for the exercise of the highest moderation and forbearance, not only on the part of the Ministry, but on the part of the Opposition and of independent members in both Houses of the Legislature. It is the pride, and the just pride, of public life in England that in grave national emergencies the voice of faction is hushed, that even legitimate criticism is reserved for a more convenient season, and that all who can speak with authority come forward to strengthen the hands of the Government. That such will be the prevailing spirit of this evening's debates we do not doubt for a moment. * * * Were it necessary to reinforce this paramount consideration by any other argument, we might remind the Conservative party that if they detected at first the weakness now disclosed in the Washington Treaty, it should have been pointed out in the debates of the last session. Now, a perusal of those debates will convince any one that nothing of the kind was then suspected. Lord RUSSELL's criticisms were founded almost entirely upon the impolicy of submitting to a retrospective operation of rules improvised for the occasion, and upon the "one-sidedness" of the bargain made about the Canadian fisheries. Lord DERBY fastened on the same points, especially on the former, complaining that, by assenting to rules framed upon American principles we had allowed the game to be played against us "with loaded dice." He also dwelt forcibly on the exclusion of claims in respect of the Fenian raids, which Lord CARNARVON regarded as the main flaw in the treaty. Lord CAIRNS, indeed, drew attention to important defects in its wording; and it must be confessed that, as a product of legal scholarship, it reflects little credit on any of the persons concerned in framing it. But Lord SALISBURY, who indulged his caustic humor without stint in pulling it to pieces did not find out what is now seen to be its vulnerable point. Not only so, but Lord GRANVILLE, answering Lord RUSSELL's assertion that no concession had been made by the United States, distinctly and emphatically specified the abandonment of claims for indirect losses as a substantial concession on their part, and a material advantage gained under the Washington Treaty as compared with the Clarendon-Johnson Convention. So far was this view from being challenged on the Conservative side, that it was strongly confirmed, in a subsequent debate of the House of Commons, by so competent a judge as Sir STAFFORD NORTHCOTE, whose acceptance of a seat on the Commission had been approved by Mr. DISRAELI, and who manfully assumed his full share of responsibility for its results. Sir STAFFORD NORTHCOTE, adopting the reasoning and almost the very language of Lord GRANVILLE, urged that, whereas, under former conventions, questions might have been raised "with regard to the consequential damages arising from the prolongation of the war," and other matters which England had never recognized as fit subjects for arbitration, all questions of that class had been effectually put aside. "The treaty, as actually concluded, narrowed the questions at issue very closely by confining the reference solely to losses growing out of the acts of particular vessels, and so shutting out a large class of claims upon which the Americans had heretofore insisted." But it is needless to accumulate evidence of what is beyond all denial—that, until the American case was published, no one in England had the least conception that it would or could revert to Mr. SUMNER's exorbitant demands. There is no doubt that our Commissioners should have guarded against the possible revival of these demands by an express provision in the treaty, and, when the proper time comes for discussing its history, explanations of this omission may fairly be demanded. At the present juncture the one duty of English statesmen is to say and do nothing which can prejudice the attempt to remove the misunderstanding which has unhappily arisen. Let us, then, once more state clearly what it is and what it is not to which Great Britain objects in the American case. It is the more necessary to do this because some of our New-York cotemporaries seem to be laboring under a strange confusion of thought as to the object and limits of the Geneva Arbitration, anticipating extravagant "counter-claims" on the part of Great Britain. We need hardly inform our readers that no counter-claim whatever has been made or could have been made in the British case. It was an essential condition of the Geneva Arbitration that it should only take cognizance of American claims against Great Britain, and the consent of Great Britain to place herself in this unfavorable position, without the power of pleading a set-off, was one of the main concessions made in consideration of "indirect losses" being struck out of the United States' account. There were, however, other concessions of equal importance, collectively amounting to a sacrifice, which it is absurd to suppose Great Britain could have made without any equivalent whatever. By deviating from all diplomatic tradition and precedent so far as to record an expression of national regret in the preamble of the treaty, by accepting rules for the decision of the questions to be brought before the arbitrators which Great Britain holds to be new in the law of nations, and by waiving altogether her right to indemnity for the Fenian invasions of Canada, the British Commissioners surrendered as much as it was possible to surrender without betraying the interests intrusted to them. Having cheerfully ratified their acts, Great Britain firmly declines to stand on her defense against claims the withdrawal of which she understood to be a condition of the whole agreement.

FRANCE.

Orleanists Accused of Intrigue—Paying the Indemnity—The Old Nobility and "Henry V."

PARIS, Feb. 18.—The Monarchists in the Assembly are canvassing with great activity to obtain signatures to their forthcoming manifesto and to organize a strong and compact party. The newspaper organs of M. THIERS and of the Legitimist Party accuse the Orleanists of intrigue and bad faith. The Subscription Committee in Nancy have already received 1,500,000 francs in contributions to the voluntary fund for the payment of the war indemnity. Many members of the old French nobility have visited Antwerp to pay their respects to the Count DE CHAMBORD.

SPAIN AND ITALY.

A Spanish Crisis—Gen. Sherman to be Feted at Pompeii.

MADRID, Feb. 18.—The Ministerial crisis continues. It originated in the opposition of Admiral TOPETE to certain promotions in the army and his demand for the dismissal of Señor GAMINDES from the Cabinet.

The Ministry has resigned. Señor SAGASTA will probably be intrusted with the task of forming a new Ministry. There is considerable agitation.

ROME, Feb. 18.—Major-Gen. SHERMAN leaves this city Tuesday, for Naples. The Americans there are preparing a fête at Pompeii in his honor.

THE SNOW BLOCKADE.

Thrilling Adventures of the Detained Passengers—The Railroad Badly Equipped.

SALT LAKE, Feb. 18.—Thrilling narratives are given by passengers just through the snow-blockade of the Union Pacific Railroad. There is said to have been much suffering among the passengers mainly from want of food, and but for relief from Fort Steele the situation would have been terrible. Many of the passengers scathingly condemn Superintendent SICKLES and his assistant, CLARK, for mismanagement and neglect. Others throw all the blame on CLARK, and declare that the passengers, when lying near Creston, would have lynched him had he made his appearance. The passengers are unanimous in the opinion that the road is not at all equipped for Winter travel, and that with proper appliances and management there would be no occasion for any serious interruption. It is now reported that the blockade is more rigorous than ever, and that altogether there are not over 200 men engaged in clearing the track.

A large party of our principal citizens intended to start for the East today, but became satisfied that they could not get through. The special cars for the Japanese Embassy, from Omaha, have not yet arrived, and the Embassy think it not prudent to start at present. The weather here is delightful, and the snow from the neighboring heights is rapidly disappearing.

Kansas Senatorial Bribery Investigation.

ST. LOUIS, Feb. 18.—A special dispatch from Topeka to the *Democrat* says: It is understood that the Senatorial Bribery Investigation Committee will report early this week the evidence taken, which makes a volume of four hundred pages. A number of prominent gentlemen, who were summoned to testify before the Committee, have kept out of reach by leaving the State.

Much evidence has been given that money was paid by Mr. SMITH, Senator CALDWELL's partner in railroad matters. It is also understood that the testimony will show as strong evidence of corruption against Ex-Congressman SIDNEY CLARKE, one of the defeated candidates for Senator, as against Senator CALDWELL.

Arrest of Liquor Dealers in Dakota Territory.

CHICAGO, Feb. 18.—A special from Fargo, Dakota Territory, says that Deputy United States Marshal LUTHER, assisted by a detachment of troops from Fort Abercrombie, yesterday arrested some twenty liquor-dealers charged with selling liquor on the Indian Reservation. The prisoners were arraigned before the United States Commissioner and committed to appear at the June term of the Court to be held at Pembina.

Telegraphic Brevities.

Preparations for the reception of the Grand Duke ALEXIS are actively going on at Havana.

The steamer *City of Mexico* arrived at Havana, yesterday, from New-York.

The residence of DAVID R. GOULD, at Quaker Hill, Dutchess County, with the furniture, was burned on Saturday. Loss, $8,000.

The Convention to frame a State Constitution for Utah, and apply for her admission, meets at Salt Lake City today.

Mr. GLADSTONE entertained the Hon. ROBERT C. SCHENCK, the American Minister, at dinner on Saturday evening.

The Kuklux trials at Jackson, Miss., commenced on Saturday. Two hundred cases are to be tried.

Thanksgiving services will be held in the Cathedral of St. Patrick, in Dublin, on the 27th inst.

In the case of JOSEPH D. SMITH, on trial at Bangor, Me., for the murder of THOS. S. JOSSLYN, the jury has found him guilty.

Dr. JOSEPH F. TROWBRIDGE, a physician of extended reputation, died at Syracuse, N. Y., last evening, aged eighty-one years, from paralysis.

The London Rowing Club accepts the challenge of the Atalanta Club, of New-York, to row a race with four-oared boats on the Thames in June.

Several buildings in Memphis were damaged by fire Saturday night. Loss, $10,000. HENRIETTA CONLEY, colored, was burned to death.

United States Deputy Marshal JOHN PEEKE, having in charge a man implicated in robbing the express at Muskogee, Indian Territory, was shot and mortally wounded by some teamsters, on the 15th.

Political Notes.

The Missouri regular Republican State Convention meets in Jefferson City on Thursday.

The Indiana Republican State Convention is to be held in Indianapolis on Thursday.

The Kansas Republican State Convention, to select delegates to the National Convention, meets in Lawrence, on Wednesday.

A delegate Convention of the National Labor Reform Party, to nominate candidates for President and Vice-President, meets in Columbus, Ohio, on Wednesday next.

GENERAL ORDER BUSIN

Why President Grant Did Abolish it Before.

Extracts from Official Correspondence on the Subject.

Letters from Messrs. Boutwell, nell and Murphy.

Consideration of the Steam-ship charge System.

The Treasury Department in F of Pier Warehouses.

Special Dispatch to the New-York Tir

WASHINGTON, Feb. 18.—The question been repeatedly asked during the Custom investigation, Why did not the Preside some attention to the representations merchants who wanted the General Order ness suppressed? The following correspon between Messrs. GRINNELL, MURPHY and WELL, covers the whole subject, and an the inquiry. These letters will be embra Secretary BOUTWELL's testimony next with others, on the same or kindred subje will be seen that the correspondence menced in June, 1870, and was continued the following October. These letters will of interest to New-York mercantile men:

TREASURY DEPARTMENT, June 1.

SIR: Upon full consideration of the papers r to the storage of goods upon delivery from the of the foreign steam-ship companies, I can see n objection to the use of the stores upon the comp piers, if those stores can be placed under the sive control of the officers of the Customs. By mean that the officers of the vessels, and the dinates of every kind, shall be excluded from storehouses. In fine, the storehouses upon th are to be treated and managed precisely as storehouses are treated and managed, and the stors of the steam-ships, and their servants, treated by the storehouse-keepers precisely other persons are treated. Should the manag the steam-ship consent to this arrangement, I good reason why the business of storage can restored to the warehouses on the piers.

Very respectfully,

GEO. S. BOUTWELL, Secret

Hon. MOSES H. GRINNELL, Collector of Cu New-York.

NEW-YORK, June 4,

Hon. Moses H. Grinnell, Collector of the Port of York:

DEAR SIR: When we had the pleasure of m you yesterday, on the subject of the General goods discharged from the lines of steamers of we are agents, you informed us that by followi course recommended by the honorable Secret the Treasury in his letter to you of 1st ins privilege of storing General Order goods were be restored to our bonded warehouses at Jerse and Hoboken unless our connection with said houses ceased, and unless they were managed i ties entirely disconnected from our respective ship lines.

You also proposed to us to name a rent at wh would be willing to lease our warehouses to parties, who, after binding them with consent, would carry on the storage ness, and receive the General Order from our lines. After due consideration proposal, we now beg leave to say that such rangement would not restore to the importe advantages they have enjoyed, and would exi der our management of the warehouse, and f are convinced that if by recommending the exc of officers of the vessels and subordinates of kind from said warehouses, the secretary d intend to disqualify us from carrying on the b of bonded warehousemen, and from enjoying a ileges connected therewith.

While we are, of course, perfectly willing to our bonded warehouses managed and treated pr as other bonded stores, and to leave them, always have been, under the complete control officers of the Customs, we respectfully remons against your construction of the Secretary's mendations, and solicit a reconsideration of th ject. Remaining very respectfully, dear Sir obedient servants,

OELRICHS & CO
KUNHARDT & C
Proprietors of the "Hoboken sto

NEW YORK, June 6,

Hon. Moses H. Grinnell, Collector of the Port of York:

DEAR SIR: When I had the pleasure of seei on Friday last with reference to the disposi General Order goods discharged from the C steamers, you informed me that by followi course recommended by the honorable Secre the Treasury in his letter to you of the 1s the privilege of storing General Order goods w be restored to the bonded warehouse at J City unless my connection with said wareh ceased, and unless it was managed by some who had no connection whatever with the C Company.

You also proposed that I should name a r which I would be willing to lease the warehou a third party, who, after binding it with my would carry on the storage business and r the General Order goods from the steamers.

After due consideration of your proposal, beg leave to say that such an arrangement wo restore to the importers the advantages the enjoyed, and would enjoy, under our manage the warehouse, and that I am convinced recommending the exclusion of officers of the and subordinates of every kind from said ware the Secretary did not intend to disqualify me carrying on the business of bonded warehous and from enjoying all the privileges con therewith.

While I am, of course, perfectly willing to bonded warehouse managed and treated pre other bonded stores, and to leave it, as it h been, under the complete control of the officers Customs, I respectfully remonstrate against construction of the Secretary's recommendatio solicit a reconsideration of the subject.

Remaining, very respectfully, your obedien vant,

CHAS. G. FRANCKL

TREASURY DEPARTMENT, June 9, 1

SIR: In reply to your letter of the 6th inst. ing remonstrances of Messrs. OELRICHS & CO., HARDT & CO. and CHARLES FRANCKLYN, Esq., I have to say that I can see no objection to storage of General Order goods in these wareh with the present proprietors, under the exclude the officers and subordinates of the em ployed by the steam-ship companies, but the prietors of the warehouses, though interested ships, may have custody of the houses subject check of the store-keepers equally with all ot houses. A sufficient number of reliable Customs must be assigned to each of these warehouses, at the expense of the proprietors, to e the safe custody of all merchandise deposited

With this precaution I am unable to perceive ample protection to the Government will not

I return herewith copies of the remonstran requested. I am, very respectfully,

GEO. S. BOUTWELL, Secret

MOSES H. GRINNELL, Esq., Collector of Cu New-York.

CUSTOM-HOUSE, NEW-YOR COLLECTOR'S OFFICE, June 13, 187

SIR: I beg leave to acknowledge the receipt letter of the 9th inst. in relation to the removal of Messrs. OELRICHS & CO., KUNHARDT & CO CHARLES FRANCKLYN, Esq., relative to their

The New-York Times.

VOL. XXV.......NO. 7742. NEW-YORK, FRIDAY, JULY 7, 1876. PRICE FOUR CENTS.

HE LITTLE HORN MASSACRE

ATEST ACCOUNTS OF THE CHARGE.

FORCE OF FOUR THOUSAND INDIANS IN POSITION ATTACKED BY LESS THAN FOUR HUNDRED TROOPS—OPINIONS OF LEADING ARMY OFFICERS OF THE DEED AND ITS CONSEQUENCES—FEELING IN THE COMMUNITY OVER THE DISASTER.

Special Dispatch to the New-York Times.

The dispatches giving an account of the ughter of Gen. Custer's command, pubhed in THE TIMES of yesterday, are conned and supplemented by official reports m Gen. A. H. Terry, commanding the expeion. On June 25 Gen. Custer's command ne upon the main camp of Sitting ll, and at once attacked it, charging thickest part of it with five companies, jor Reno, with seven companies attack- on the other side. The soldiers were ulsed and a wholesale slaughter ensued. n. Custer, his brother, his nephew, and brother-in-law were killed, and not of his detachment escaped. The dians surrounded Major Reno's comnd and held them in the hills ring a whole day, but Gibbon's command ne up and the Indians left. The number killed is stated at 300, and the wounded 31. Two hundred and seven men are d to have been buried in one place. The of killed includes seventeen commised officers.

t is the opinion of Army officers in Chio, Washington, and Philadelphia, inding Gens. Sherman and Sheridan, that n. Custer was rashly imprudent to atk such a large number of Indians, Sitg Bull's force being 4,000 strong. Gen. rman thinks that the accounts of the aster are exaggerated. The wounded diers are being conveyed to Fort Lincoln. ditional details are anxiously awaited oughout the country.

NFIRMATION OF THE DISASTER.

SPATCHES FROM GEN. TERRY RECEIVED AT SHERIDAN'S HEAD-QUARTERS—THEORIES OF THE BATTLE—PROBABLY TEN THOUSAND SIOUX IN POSITION—THE ATTACK CONDEMNED AS RASH BY OFFICERS OF EXPERIENCE—DISPOSITION OF THE WOUNDED.

CHICAGO, July 6.—At the head-quarters Lieut. Gen. Sheridan this morning, all was stle and confusion over the reported massa- of Custer's command. Telegrams were ing constantly received, but most of em were of a confidential nature and thheld from publication. It is known at the unfortunate command broke camp on e North Rosebud on June 22 for the purpose proceeding in a direction which would bring to the point named about the 25th, at which ace a bloody fight is reported to have taken ne. The following dispatch, the last reived at head-quarters in this city previous to news of the massacre, confirms the acunts given to the extent of showing that Cus- intended to go to that place.

CAMP ON THE NORTH ROSEBUD, June 21, 1876.
ent. Gen. P. H. Sheridan, Commanding Military Division of the Missouri, Chicago:

No Indians have been met with as yet, but traces large and recent camp have been discovered enty or thirty miles up the Rosebud. Gibbon's umn will move this morning, on the north side of Yellowstone, for the mouth of the Big Horn, where will be ferried across by the supply steamer, and ence it will proceed to the mouth of the Little rn, and so on. Custer will go up the Rosebud morrow with his whole regiment, and thence to head-waters of the Little Horn, thence down the tle Horn.

A. H. TERRY,
Brigadier General Commanding.

A dispatch received at the quarters of Gen. eridan this morning at 11 o'clock confirms first reports received. The dispatch states at the forces were falling back, and that the unded had been sent to Fort Lincoln. No tails were given, but the officers at headarters regard it as a full confirmation of the gagement reported. In reply to an inquiry to whether the attack was made by n. Custer of his own accord, or under ders from the department, an answer was ven that Custer made the charge of his own dition. A still later dispatch from Lieut. urie, of the Seventh Cavalry, was received, king that he be transferred from the departnt where he is now on duty to the scene of ion. This is also regarded as another conmation of the bloody massacre reported. Gen. ster's family are at Fort Lincoln, to which nt the wounded are being conveyed.

So far as an expression in regard to the wism of Gen. Custer's attack could be obtained head-quarters, it was to the effect that Cus- had been imprudent, to say the least. It is opinion at head-quarters among those who most familiar with the situation, that Cus- struck Sitting Bull's main camp. Gen. um, of Sheridan's staff, is of opinion at Sitting Bull began concentrating his ces after the fight with Crook, and that no ubt, Custer dropped squarely into the midst no less than ten thousand red devils and was erally torn to pieces. The movement made by ster is censured to some extent at military adquarters in this city. The older officers that it was brought about by that foolish de which so often results in the defeat of n. It seems that a few days before Gen. rry had offered four additional companies Custer, but that officer refused them.

The information at head-quarters further is the effect that Gen. Gibbon with his force known to be moving up to Custer for the rpose of reinforcing him, and that he [Cus-] knew of this, and knew that Gibbon would ive by the following day after the engagent. I have it on as good authority as one of leading officers at head-quarters, that Cus- had been ordered by Terry to make a march ward the Little Big Horn and to form a ction with a column of infantry that was ving diagonally across the country to the ne point. The two columns were then to operate and make an attack. Instead of rching from twenty to thirty miles per day, ordered, Custer made a forced march and ched the point of destination two or three ys in advance of the infantry; then finding self in front of the foe he foolishly attempted cut his way through and punish the red vils.

DISPATHES FROM GEN. TERRY.

RTICULARS OF THE PLAN OF THE MOVEMENT UNDER CUSTER AS AGREED ON BEFORE THE MARCH.

Special Dispatch to the New-York Times.

PHILADELPHIA, July 6.—This afternoon n. Sheridan received two dispatches from n. Terry relative to the Indian battle in ich Gen. Custer was killed, and this evening telegrams were handed to your corrependent. Gen. Sherman says that he thinks the first dispatch giving the details of the battle was mislaid, or else some enterprising newspaper correspondent bought up the messenger and sent the account East, thus keeping the War Department in ignorance of the occurrence. From what he knows of the occurrence he believes that Gen. Custer attempted a battle without reconnoitering the position, and that he was too bold. He does not think the slaughter so great as at first reported. The first dispatch received by Gen. Sheridan was as follows:

CAMP ON YELLOWSTONE, NEAR MOUTH OF BIG HORN, July 2.

On the evening of the 28th we commenced moving down with the wounded, but were able to get along but four miles, as the hard litters did not answer the purpose. The mule litters did excellently well, but they were insufficient in number; therefore, the 29th was spent in making a full supply of them. On the evening of the 29th we started again, and at 2 A. M. the wounded were placed on the steamer at the mouth of the Little Big Horn. The afternoon of the 30th they were brought down to the depot on the Yellowstone. I send them to-morrow by steam to Fort Lincoln, and with them one of my aids, Capt. E. W. Smith, who will be able to answer any questions which you may desire to ask. Col. Sheridan's dispatch informing me of the reported gathering of Indians on the Rosebud reached me after I came down here. I hear nothing of Gen. Crook's movements. At least a hundred horses are needed to remount the cavalrymen now here.

(Signed,) ALFRED H. TERLY,
Brigadier General.

The second dispatch was as follows:

CAMP BIG HORN, July 2.

I think I owe it to myself to put you more fully in possession of the facts of the late operations. While at the mouth of the Rosebud I submitted my plan to Gen. Gibbon and Gen. Custer. It was that Custer, with his whole regiment, should move up the Rosebud till he should meet a trail Reno had discovered a few days before, but that he should not follow it directly to the Little Big Horn; that he should send scouts over it and keep his main force further toward the south, so as to prevent the Indians from slipping in between himself and the mountains. He was also to examine the head waters of the Tollaska Creek, as he passed it, and send me word of what he found there. A scout was furnished him for the purpose of crossing the country to me. We calculated it would take Gibbons' column until the 26th to reach the mouth of the Little Big Horn, and that the wide sweep I had proposed Custer should make would require so much time that Gibbon would be able to co-operate with him in attacking any Indians that might be found on the stream. I asked Custer how long his marches would be. He said they would be at the rate of about thirty miles a day. Measurements were made and calculations based on that rate of progress. I talked with him about his strength and at one time suggested that perhaps it would be well for me to take Gibbon's cavalry and go with him. To the latter suggestion he replied: "That, without reference to the command, he would prefer his own regiment alone. As a homogeneous body, as much could be done with it as with the two combined. He expressed the utmost confidence that he had all the force that he could need, and I shared his confidence. The plan adopted was the only one which promised to bring the infantry into action, and I desired to make sure of things by getting up every available man. I offered Custer the battery of Gatling guns, but he declined it, saying that it might embarrass him, and that he was strong enough without it.

The movements proposed by Gen. Gibbon's column were carried out to the letter, and had the attack been deferred until it was up, I cannot doubt that we should have been successful. The Indians had evidently prepared themselves for a stand, but as I learned from Capt. Benton that on the 22d the cavalry marched twelve miles; on the 23d, twenty-five miles; from 5 A. M. till 8 P. M., of the 24th, forty-five miles, and then after night ten miles further, resting, but without unsaddling, twenty-three miles, to the battle-field. The proposed route was not taken, but as soon as the trail was struck it was followed. I cannot learn that any examination of Tallaska Creek was made. I do not tell you this to cast any reflections upon Custer, for whatever errors he may have committed Custer's action is unexplainable in the case.

A. H. TERRY, Brigadier General.

These dispatches were all that either Gens. Sherman or Sheridan received up to midnight, and were sent to the Secretary of War.

DETAILS OF THE BATTLE.

GRAPHIC DESCRIPTION OF THE FIGHTING—MAJOR RENO'S COMMAND UNDER FIRE FOR TWO DAYS—EVERY MAN OF CUSTER'S DETACHMENT KILLED EXCEPT ONE SCOUT—AFFECTING SCENES WHEN RELIEF ARRIVED.

Special Dispatch to the New-York Times.

CHICAGO, July 6.—A special to the *Times* to-night from Bismarck, recounts most graphically the late encounter with the Indians on the Little Big Horn. Gen. Custer left the Rosebud on June 22, with twelve companies of the Seventh Cavalry, striking a trail where Reno left it, leading in the direction of the Little Horn. On the evening of the 24th fresh trails were reported, and on the morning of the 25th an Indian village, twenty miles above the mouth of the Little Horn was reported about three miles long and half a mile wide and fifteen miles away. Custer pushed his command rapidly through. They had made a march of seventy-eight miles in twenty-four hours preceding the battle. When near the village it was discovered that the Indians were moving in hot haste as if retreating. Reno, with seven companies of the Seventh Cavalry, was ordered to the left to attack the village at its head, while Custer, with five companies, went to the right and commenced a vigorous attack. Reno felt of them with three companies of cavalry, and was almost instantly surrounded, and after one hour or more of vigorous fighting, during which he lost Lieuts. Hodgson and McIntosh and Dr. Dewolf and twelve men, with several Indian scouts killed and many wounded, he cut his way through to the river and gained a bluff 300 feet in height, where he intrenched and was soon joined by Col. Benton with four companies. In the meantime the Indians resumed the attack, making repeated and desperate charges, which were repulsed with great slaughter to the Indians. They gained higher ground than Reno occupied, and as their arms were longer range and better than the cavalry's, they kept up a galling fire until nightfall. During the night Reno strengthened his position, and was prepared for another attack, which was made at daylight.

The day wore on. Reno had lost in killed and wounded a large portion of his command, forty odd having been killed before the bluff was reached, many of them in hand to hand conflict with the Indians, who outnumbered them ten to one, and his men had been without water for thirty-six hours. The suffering was heartrending. In this state of affairs they determined to reach the water at all hazards, and Col. Benton made a sally with his company, and routed the main body of the Indians who were guarding the approach to the river. The Indian sharpshooters were nearly opposite the mouth of the ravine through which the brave boys approached the river, but the attempt was made, and though one man was killed and seven wounded the water was gained and the command relieved. When the fighting ceased for the night Reno further prepared for attacks.

There had been forty-eight hours' fighting, with no word from Custer. Twenty-four hours more of fighting and the suspense ended, when the Indians abandoned their village in great haste and confusion. Reno knew then that succor was near at hand. Gen. Terry, with Gibbon commanding his own infantry, had arrived, and as the comrades met men wept on each other's necks. Inquiries were then made for Custer, but none could tell where he was. Soon an officer came rushing into camp and related that he had found Custer, dead, stripped naked, but not mutilated, and near him his two brothers, Col. Tom and Boston Custer. His brother-in-law, Col. Calhoun, and his nephew Col. Yates, Col. Keogh, Capt. Smith, Lieut. Crittenden, Lieut. Sturgis, Col. Cooke, Lieut. Porter, Lieut. Harrington, Dr. Lord, Mack Kellogg, the Bismarck *Tribune* correspondent, and 190 men and scouts. Custer went into battle with Companies C, L, I, F, and E, of the Seventh Cavalry, and the staff and non-commissioned staff of his regiment and a number of scouts, and only one Crow scout remained to tell the tale. All are dead. Custer was surrounded on every side by Indians, and horses fell as they fought on skirmish line or in line of battle. Custer was among the last who fell, but when his cheering voice was no longer heard, the Indians made easy work of the remainder. The bodies of all save the newspaper correspondent were stripped, and most of them were horribly mutilated. Custer's was not mutilated. He was shot through the body and through the head. The troops cared for the wounded and buried the dead, and returned to their base for supplies and instructions from the General of the Army.

Col. Smith arrived at Bismarck last night with thirty-five of the wounded. The Indians lost heavily in the battle. The Crow Scout survived by hiding in a ravine. He believes the Indians lost more than the whites. The village numbered 1,800 lodges, and it is thought there were 4,000 warriors. Gen. Custer was directed by Gen. Terry to find and feel of the Indians, but not to fight unless Terry arrived with infantry and with Gibbon's column. The casualties foot up 261 killed and fifty-two wounded.

THE SCENE OF THE MASSACRE.

DESCRIPTION OF THE REGION BY MAJOR GRIMES, WHO REMOVED THE FORTS IN 1868, UNDER THE TREATY.

Special Dispatch to the New-York Times.

ST. LOUIS, July 6.—The news of the massacre of Gen. Custer with seventeen commissioned officers and 315 men, near the Little Big Horn River, has created an extraordinary sensation here. Subsequent advices received at military head-quarters in this city substantially confirm the terrible news. Your correspondent this evening had a conversation with Major J. W. Grimes, one of the military officers stationed here, and who is very familiar with Indian affairs in the West. He is well acquainted with the country where the fight took place. He was detailed by the Government in 1868 to remove all the forts on the Powder River route, in accordance with the provisions of the Fort Laramie treaty of 1868. The battle occurred about twenty miles from the mouth of the Little Big Horn River, which empties into the Big Horn, and the latter into the Yellow Stone. The fight took place on the Crow reservation, about forty miles east of Fort C. L. Smith, the most northern of the Powder River Road forts, removed by Major Grimes in 1868. The country is diversified by mountain ranges and deep cañons, with intervening plateaus of sage brush prairies.

Ex-Gov. Fletcher, who was a member of the Peace Commission that went out last Summer, stated to-night that the present desperate condition of affairs is only a legitimate result of the present peace policy pursued by the Government toward the Indians.

THE CAUSES AND CONSEQUENCES.

FRUITS OF THE ILL-ADVISED BLACK HILLS EXPEDITION OF TWO YEARS AGO—ABILITY OF THE ARMY TO RENEW OPERATIONS EFFECTIVELY DISCUSSED—THE PERSONNEL OF THE CHARGING PARTY STILL UNDEFINED.

Special Dispatch to the New-York Times.

WASHINGTON, July 6.—The news of the fatal charge of Gen. Custer and his command against the Sioux Indians has caused great excitement in Washington, particularly among Army people and about the Capitol. The first impulse was to doubt the report, or set it down as some heartless hoax or at least a greatly exaggerated story by some frightened fugitive. At the second thought the report was generally accepted as true in its chief and appalling incidents. The campaign against the wild Sioux was undertaken under disadvantageous circumstances owing to the refusal of Congress to appropriate money for the establishment of military posts on the upper Yellowstone River. Gen. Sherman and Gen. Sheridan both asked for these posts, which, in case of anticipated troubles would give the troops a base of supplies about four hundred miles nearer the hostile country than they could otherwise have. The posts desired would have been accessible by steam-boats on the Yellowstone, which would have conveyed men and supplies. The House Committee on Military Affairs unanimously recommended their establishment, but the Committee on Appropriations refused to provide in their bills the necessary means. This is regarded as the immediate cause of the disaster. The remote cause was undoubtedly the expedition into the Black Hills two years ago in violation of laws and treaties, authorized by Secretary Belknap and led by Gen. Custer. If there had been a post at the head of navigation on the Yellowstone the expedition would doubtless have proceeded thence against the Indians in one invincible column. The policy of sending three converging columns so many hundred miles against such brave and skillful soldiers as the Sioux has been the cause of some uneasiness here among the few who have taken the trouble to think about the facts and prospects. The Sioux seem to have understood clearly the plan of attack, and threw themselves with their whole force first against Gen. Crook's column and now against Custer's, and both times inflicted serious disaster. The feeling was common to-day that the campaign is a failure, and that there must follow a general Indian war, promising to be costly in men and money. The Sioux are a distinct race of men from the so-called Indians of the South-west, among whom the army found such easy work two and three years ago. The Sioux live by the chase and feed chiefly upon flesh. The Southern Indians are farmers and eat fruits and vegetables, the latter are at their worst cruel, cowardly robbers. The former are as much like the brave and war-like red men represented by the *Last of the Mohicans* as ever existed outside the covers of fiction and romance. This difference between the foes in the North and South-west seems not to have been well counted upon, nor provided for, and formed, as it might, prudently, no restraint upon the reckless fatal charge of the 300. If the tale told by the courier Taylor is true, the charge has scarce a parallel in the history of civilized or savage warfare. The massacre of Major Dade and his command in the Florida war is alone comparable with it in American history. The reason for an expedition against the Indians this Summer is not well understood, nor has any satisfactory explanation been published. The wild Sioux had never been willing to live upon the reservation marked out for them, and the understanding has been that they were to be whipped into submission, and compelled to live like Red Cloud and Spotted Tail, with their bands, about the Government agencies. The question of the policy and right of the war will now be renewed and discussed, and, indeed, is discussed to-day. Those who believe in the policy of the extermination of the Indians, and think the speedier the better its accomplishment, look upon the condition of war as inevitable, and are for pouring thousands of troops into the Indian country and giving them a terrible punishment. This class is small, even in the Army, where the policy of extermination is not popular save with a few high and restless officers. The invasion of the Black Hills has been condemned over and over again by the peace party, and there are very many who can truthfully say, "I told you so." From that unwarranted invasion the present difficulties have gradually sprung up, so that an expedition that originally cost a hundred thousand dollars perhaps, must lead to an expenditure of millions, which will advance civilization in no way, except by the destruction of the uncivilized. The Army, if the present campaign wholly fails, is in no condition to renew hostilities with sufficient force, and there is little reason to expect Congress will this session provide for an Indian war. Thus by force of circumstances a continuation of the war would probably be with the Government forces upon the defensive, protecting as far as possible agencies and settlements. There is another result that some hope for. It is the union of the three columns of troops and the delivery of a blow against the Indians that will place them at the mercy of the Army and compel them to sue for peace. The chances are, however, so far as the information now at hand may be relied on, that the Government forces are much too small in number, reduced as they are by two battles, to meet the powerful and exultant Sioux.

Until advised of the particular five companies of the Seventh Cavalry with which Custer charged the Sioux, with results so disastrous to his command, the War Department will not be able to furnish the list of casualties. From the dispatches printed to-day, based on the information furnished by Muggins Taylor, the scout, it is inferred that Capts. Thomas W. Custer and Myles Moylan, and Lieut. James Calhoun, of the Seventh Cavalry, and Lieut. A. B. Crittenden, of the Fourth Infantry, were among those killed. Capt. Custer was a brother of Gen. Custer, Calhoun was his brother-in-law, and Moylan was brother-in-law to Calhoun. Gen. Custer had but one brother in the Seventh Cavalry. The report that the General and his two brothers were killed doubtless arose from the relationship described between Custer, Calhoun, and Moylan. Crittenden was the son of Col. Crittenden, of the Seventeenth Infantry, and grandson of the late John J. Crittenden, of Kentucky. At his own request he was detailed for active service against the Indians and assigned to the Seventh Cavalry. The only dispatch received to-day at the War Department was one from Adjutant Gen. Crum, of Sheridan's staff, stating that Gen. Terry telegraphed from camp on Lone Horn River, under date of July 2, confirming the report of the fight on June 25 and the death of Gen. Custer. Terry's dispatches were sent to Sheridan at Chicago, and forwarded from there to Philadelphia, where Gens. Sherman and Sheridan now are.

VIEWS AT THE WAR DEPARTMENT.

THE CONFIRMATORY DISPATCHES FROM SHERIDAN'S HEAD-QUARTERS IN CHICAGO—FEELING AMONG CUSTER'S FRIENDS.

WASHINGTON, July 6.—Not until late this afternoon did the War Department receive confirmatory reports of the news published this morning of the terrible disaster in the Indian country. The absence of official advices in advance of the press reports, seemed to several Army officers, and to friends of those who are with Custer's command, fair grounds for arguing against the absolute correctness of the reports in the morning papers, but at the same time their was a profound anxiety to hear from Gen. Sheridan's Head-quarters, where it was considered certain that the earliest reports of any engagement that might have taken place would be forwarded. For this purpose Adjt. Gen. Townsend telegraphed early in the day for news from the Indian department, as also did Mr. Crosby, Chief Clerk of the War Department. In response to the latter the following came this afternoon from Chicago, signed by Assistant Adjt. Gen. Drum:

"Dispatches from Gen. Terry, dated from his camp, mouth of the Big Horn, July 2, confirm the newspaper reports of a fight on the 25th of June, on the Little Horn, and of Gen. Custer's death. Gen. Terry has fallen back to his present camp. I have sent full dispatches to the Lieutenant General, who will probably communicate them. I have not yet received Gen. Terry's report of the action, nor a list of the casualties."

In addition to the above a dispatch was received here to-day from Col. Ruggles, of Gen. Terry's staff, dated St. Paul, and addressed to Gen. Crittenden, announcing the death of his son, Lieut. Crittenden, in an Indian fight. There is the utmost anxiety in all quarters for additional news of the action, and the opinion is freely expressed among the officers of the Army that a war of considerable duration with the Indians seems inevitable, and these successes, it is feared, will have a very bad effect upon the Indians at certain agencies, particularly those at Red Cloud agency, who have been exhibiting a very uneasy spirit for some time past. Just at this time the Secretary of War and Gen. Sherman are both absent from Washington attending the celebration of the Army of the Cumberland in Philadelphia. The presumption is there will be an immediate conference upon the subject of the Indian war now fully inaugurated. It will be remembered that upon the ordering of the expedition into the Indian country, Gen. Custer was in this city and made an earnest application to join his command which had started while he was detained as a witness before a Congressional Investigating Committee.

Gen. Custer's old comrades in this city will hold a meeting on Saturday evening for the purpose of taking some action expressive of their esteem for him as a citizen and soldier, and adopting suitable resolutions regarding his death.

MISCELLANEOUS DISPATCHES.

A LIST OF OFFICERS KILLED—FEELING OVER THE DISASTER—A REGIMENT OF FRONTIERSMEN OFFERED FROM UTAH.

ST. LOUIS, July 6.—A telegram from Gen. Ruggles at St. Paul to Capt. Green Hale, commanding the cavalry at the arsenal here, gives the following as the names of the officers killed in the fight between the Sioux and Gen. Custer's command.

Gen. Custer,	Lieut. Smith,
Col. Custer,	Lieut. Porter,
Col. Yates,	Lieut. Harrington,
Col. Keogh,	Lieut. Calhoun,
Col. Cook,	Lieut. Reilly,
Lieut. McIntosh,	Lieut. Sturgis.
Lieut. Hodgson,	

Lieut. Harrington is missing.

Gen. S. D. Sturgis, in command of this post, received a telegram this afternoon from Assistant Adjt. Gen. Ruggles, at St. Paul, Minn., notifying him that his son was killed in the fight between the Sioux and Gen. Custer's command.

SALT LAKE, July 6.—The citizens here are very much excited over the Custer massacre, and several offers have been made to the Secretary of War to raise a regiment of frontiersmen in ten days for Indian service.

SAN FRANCISCO, July 6.—A dispatch from Virginia City reports great excitement at Custer's death. A meeting has been called to organize a company.

TOLEDO, July 6.—A special to the *Blade* from Monroe, Mich., the home of Gen. Custer, says the startling news of the massacre of the General and his party by Indians created the most intense feeling of sorrow among all classes. Gen. Custer passed several years of his youth at school in Monroe, and his parents have resided there many years. The town is draped in mourning, and a meeting of the Common Council and citizens was held this evening to take measures for an appropriate tribute to the gallant dead.

SKETCH OF GEN. CUSTER.

Major Gen. George A. Custer, who was killed with his whole command while attacking an encampment of Sioux Indians, under command of Sitting Bull, was one of the bravest and most widely known officers in the United States Army. He has for the past fifteen years been known to the country and to his comrades as a man who feared no danger, as a soldier in the truest sense of the word. He was daring to a fault, generous beyond most men. His memory will long be kept green in many friendly hearts. Born at New-Rumley, Harrison County, Ohio, on the 5th of December, 1839, he obtained a good common education, and after graduating engaged for a time in teaching school. In June, 1857, through the influence of Hon. John A. Bingham, then member of Congress from Ohio, he obtained an appointment to the United States Military Academy at West Point, and entered that institution on the 1st of July of the year named. He graduated on the 24th of June, 1861, with what was considered the fair standing of No. 34 in one of the brightest classes that ever left the academy. Immediately upon leaving West Point he was appointed Second Lieutenant in Company G of the Second United States Cavalry, a regiment which had formerly been commanded by Robert E. Lee. He reported to Lieut. Gen. Scott on the 20th of July, the day preceding the battle of Bull Run, and the Commander in Chief gave him the choice of accepting a position on his staff or of joining his regiment, then under command of Gen. McDowell, in the field. Longing for an opportunity to see active service, and determined to win distinction Lieut. Custer chose the latter course, and after riding all night through a country filled with people who were, to say the least, not friendly, he reached McDowell's head-quarters at daybreak on the morning of the 21st. Preparations for the battle had already begun, and after delivering his dispatches from Gen. Scott and hastily partaking of a mouthful of coffee and a piece of hard bread he joined his company. It is not necessary now to recount the disasters of the fight that followed. Suffice it to say that Lieut. Custer's company was among the last to leave the field. It did so in good order, bringing off Gen. Heintzelman, who had been wounded in the engagement. The young officer continued to serve with his company, and was engaged in the drilling of volunteer recruits in and about the defences of Washington, when upon the appointment of Phil Kearny to the position of Brigadier General, that lamented officer gave him a position on his staff. Custer continued in this position until an order was issued from the War Department prohibiting Generals of Volunteers from appointing officers of the regular Army to staff duty. Then he returned to his company, not, however, until he had been warmly complimented by Gen. Kearny upon the prompt and efficient manner in which he had performed the duties assigned to him. At the same time the General predicted that Custer would be one of the most successful officers in the Army. Nor were these predictions without a speedy realization. With his company Lieut. Custer marched forward with that part of the Army of the Potomac which moved upon Manassas after its evacuation by the rebels. Our cavalry was in advance, under Gen. Stoneman and encountered the rebel horsemen for the first time near Catlett's Station. The commanding officer made a call for volunteers to charge the enemy's advance post. Lieut. Custer was among the first to step to the front, and in command of his company he shortly afterward made his first charge. He drove the rebels across Muddy Creek, wounded a number of them, and had one of his own men injured. This was the first blood drawn in the campaign under McClellan. After this Custer went with the Army of the Potomac to the Peninsula and remained with his company until the Army settled down before Yorktown, when he was detailed as an Assistant Engineer of the left wing, under Sumner. Acting in this capacity he planned and erected the earthworks nearest the enemy's lines. He also accompanied the advance under Gen. Hancock in pursuit of the enemy from Yorktown. Shortly afterward, he captured the first battle-flag ever secured by the Army of the Potomac. From this time on he was nearly always the first in every work of daring. When the Army reached the Chickahominy he was the first man to cross the river; he did so in the face of the fire of the enemy's pickets, and at times was obliged to wade up to his armpits. For this brave act Gen. McClellan promoted him to a Captaincy and made him one of his personal aids. In this capacity he served during most of the Peninsula campaign, and participated in all its battles, including the bloody seven days' fight. He performed the duty of marking out the post on which was occupied by the Union Army at the battle of Gaines' Mills. He also participated in the campaign which ended in the battles of South Mountain and Antietam. Upon the retirement of Gen. McClellan from the command of the Army of the Potomac, Custer accompanied him, and for a time was out of active service.

He was next engaged in the battle of Chancellorsville, and immediately after that fight he was made a personal aid by Gen. Pleasonton, who was then commanding a division of cavalry. Serving in this capacity he took an active part in a number of hotly-contested engagements, and marked himself as one of the most dashing, some said the most reckless, officers in the service. When Pleasonton was made a Major General his first pleasure was to remember the valuable services of his Aid de Camp. He requested the appointment of four Brigadiers to command under him, and upon his recommendation, indorsed by Gens. Meade and Hooker, young Custer was made a Brigadier General and assigned to the command of the First, Fifth, Sixth, and Seventh Michigan Cavalry. He did noble service at the battle of Gettysburg. He held the right of line, and was obliged to face Hampton's division of cavalry, and after a hotly-contested fight, utterly routed the rebels and prevented them from reaching the trains of the Union Army, which they hoped to capture. Custer had two horses shot under him in this fight. Hardly had the battle concluded when he was sent to attack the enemy's train, which was trying to force its way to the Potomac. He destroyed more than four hundred wagons. At Hagerstown, Md., during a severe engagement, he again had his horse shot under him. At Falling Waters, shortly after, he attacked with his small brigade the entire rebel rear guard. The Confederate commander Gen. Pettigrew was killed and his command routed, with a loss of 1,300 prisoners two pieces of cannon and four battle flags. For some time after this fight he was constantly engaged in skirmishing with the enemy, and during the Winter which followed in picketing the Rapidan between the two armies. He participated in the battle of the Wilderness in 1864, and on the 9th of May of the same year, under Gen. Sheridan, he set out on the famous raid toward Richmond. His brigade led the column, captured Beaver Dam, burned the station and a train of cars loaded with supplies, and released 400 Union prisoners. Rejoining Grant's Army on the Pamunkey, he took an active part in several engagements. After the battle of Fisher's Hill, in which he did most important service, he was placed in command of a division and remained in that position until after Lee's surrender. At the ever-memorable battle of Cedar Creek his division was on the right, and not engaged in the rout of the morning, so that when Sheridan arrived on the field, after the twenty-mile ride, he found at least one command ready for service. His immediate order was "Go in, Custer!" The brave young General only waited for the word, he went in and never came out until the enemy was driven several miles beyond the battle-field. Nearly one thousand prisoners were captured, among them a Major General. Forty-five pieces of artillery were also taken. For this service Custer was made a Brevet Major General of Volunteers. Sheridan, as a further mark of approbation, detailed him to carry the news of the victory and the captured battle-flag to Washington. From this time on his fortune was made, and he continued steadily to advance in the esteem of his superiors and of the American people. When the rebels fell back to Appomattox, Custer had the advance of Sheridan's command, and his share in the action is well described in the entertaining volume entitled, *With Sheridan in His Last Campaign*. The book in question says: "When the sun was an hour high in the west, energetic Custer in advance spied the depot and four heavy trains of freight cars; he quickly ordered his leading regiments to circle out to the left through the woods, and as they gained the railroad beyond the station he led the rest of his division pell-mell down the road and enveloped the train as quick as winking. Custer might not well conduct a siege of regular approaches; but for a sudden dash, Custer against the world." After many another dash of the same kind as that described, Custer was mustered out of the volunteer service on the 1st of February, 1866, and on July 28 of the same year he was appointed Lieutenant Colonel of the Seventh United States Cavalry, and since that time has been almost constantly engaged in duty upon the frontier. Recently he has contributed several interesting articles to the magazines. Of his personal appearance, Col. Newhall, in *With Sheridan in His Last Campaign*, speaks as follows: "At the head of the horsemen rode Custer of the golden locks, his broad sombrero turned up from his hard, bronzed face, the ends of his crimson cravat floating over his shoulder, gold galore spangling his jacket sleeves, a pistol in his boots, jangling spurs on his heels, and a ponderous claymore swinging at his side. A wild, dare-devil of a General and a prince of advance guards." This description will be recognized by those who knew Gen. Custer as exceedingly true to nature. He was not a great General. He was a great fighter. His place in the Army will not easily be filled.

RECORD OF THE REGIMENT.

THE OFFICERS, AND WHAT THEY HAVE DONE—THE DATES OF THEIR PROMOTIONS.

The Seventh Regiment of United States Cavalry was organized by act of Congress July 28, 1866, and since then has been stationed at different posts until Nov. 27, 1868, when it was assigned to the Indian Territory. The following is a list of the regiment's officers: Colonel, Samuel D. Sturgis, of Pennsylvania, who entered the service on July 1, 1846, being then brevetted a Second Lieutenant in the Second Dragoons. He was promoted Second Lieutenant in the First Dragoons Feb. 16, 1847; First Lieutenant, July 15, 1853; Captain in the First Cavalry, March 3, 1855; Major, May 3, 1861; Lieutenant Colonel of the Sixth Cavalry, Oct. 27, 1863, and finally, to his present rank, May 6, 1869. Lieut. Col. George A. Custer, of Ohio, entered the Army June 24, 1861, as Second Lieutenant in the Second Cavalry; was promoted First Lieutenant in the Fifth Cavalry July 17, 1862; Captain, May 8, 1864, and Lieutenant Colonel of the Seventh Regiment, July 28, 1866. Major Joseph G. Tilford, of Kentucky, entered the service as Brevet Second Lieutenant July 1, 1851, and was elevated to the rank of Major Nov. 14, 1867.

Lewis Merrill, of Pennsylvania, entered the Army as Brevet Second Lieutenant in the First Dragoons July 1, 1855, and during the war served as Colonel of the Second Missouri Cavalry. He was brevetted Brigadier General of Volunteers and promoted Major of the Seventh Cavalry Nov. 27, 1868.

Marcus A. Reno, of Illinois, entered the service as Brevet Second Lieutenant in the First Dragoons July 1, 1857. During the war he was Colonel of the Twelfth Pennsylvania Cavalry, and was brevetted Brigadier General of Volunteers. He was made Major in the Seventh Cavalry Dec. 26, 1868.

Captains—Frederick W. Benteen, of Virginia, who entered the Army as Captain July 28, 1866, and served during the war as Captain, Major, and Lieutenant Colonel of the Tenth Missouri Cavalry; he obtained his present commission July 28, 1866. Myles W. Keogh, of the District of Columbia, was commissioned Second Lieutenant in the Fourth Cavalry May 4, 1866, and promoted Captain July 28, 1866. J. E. Tourtellotte, of Connecticut, was appointed Captain in the Twenty-eighth Infantry July 28, 1866; during the war he served as Captain, Lieutenant Colonel, and Colonel of the Fourth Minnesota Volunteers. Michael V. Sheridan, of Ohio, appointed Second Lieutenant in the Fifth Cavalry Feb. 23, 1866, and Captain in the Seventh July 28, 1866.

George W. Yates, of New-York, appointed Second Lieutenant in the Second Cavalry March 26, 1866, and Captain in the Seventh June 12, 1867. Thomas B. Weir, of Ohio, commissioned First Lieutenant July 28, 1866, and Captain July 31, 1867. Thomas H. French, of Maryland, commissioned Second Lieutenant in the Tenth Infantry May 15, 1864, and assigned to the Seventh Cavalry as Captain Jan. 1, 1871.

Owen Hale, of New-York, commissioned First Lieutenant July 28, 1866, and Captain March 1, 1869. Charles S. Ilsley, of Maine, appointed Second Lieutenant in the Sixteenth Infantry Feb. 23, 1866, and Captain in the Seventh Cavalry July 11, 1871. Miles Moylan, of Massachusetts, appointed Second Lieutenant in the Fifth Cavalry Feb. 19, 1863, and Captain in the Seventh Cavalry March 1, 1872. Thomas W. Custer, of Ohio, appointed Second Lieutenant in the First Infantry Feb. 23, 1866, and Captain in the Seventh Cavalry Dec. 2, 1875.

First Lieutenants—Thomas M. McDougall, of Wisconsin, appointed Second Lieutenant in the Fourteenth Infantry May 10, 1866, and First Lieutenant to the Seventh Cavalry Nov. 5, 1866. Henry J. Nowlan, of Corfu, appointed Second Lieutenant July 28, 1866, and promoted Dec. 3, 1866. James M. Bell, of Pennsylvania, appointed Second Lieutenant July 28, 1866, and promoted April 2, 1867. William W. Cooke, of New-York, appointed Second Lieutenant July 28, 1866, and First Lieutenant July 31, 1867. Henry Jackson, of Illinois, appointed Second Lieutenant July 28, 1866, and First Lieutenant July 31, 1867. Edward S. Godfrey, of Ohio, appointed Second Lieutenant June 17, 1867, and First Lieutenant Feb. 1, 1868. John F. Weston, of Kentucky, appointed Second Lieutenant Aug. 9, 1867, and promoted Nov. 27, 1868. Algernon E. Smith, of New-York, appointed Second Lieutenant Aug. 9, 1867, and promoted Dec. 5, 1868. Ed. G. Mathey, of Indiana, appointed Second Lieutenant Sept. 24, 1867, and promoted May 10, 1870. Donald McIntosh, of Oregon, appointed Second Lieutenant Aug. 17, 1867, and promoted March 22, 1870. James Calhoun, of Ohio, appointed Second Lieutenant in the Thirty-second Infantry July 31, 1867, and promoted Second Lieutenant in the Seventh Cavalry Jan. 9, 1871. Frank M. Gibson, of Pennsylvania, appointed Second Lieutenant Oct. 5, 1867, and promoted July 11, 1871. James E. Porter, of Maine, appointed Second Lieutenant June 15, 1869, and promoted March 1, 1872. William T. Craycroft, of Kentucky, appointed Second Lieutenant June 15, 1869, and promoted Dec. 2, 1875.

Second Lieutenants—Charles C. De Rudio, of New-York, appointed July 31, 1867. Charles Brewster, of Michigan, June 15, 1869. Benjamin H. Hodgson, of Pennsylvania, June 15, 1870. Winfield S. Edgerly, of New-Hampshire, June 15, 1870. Charles W. Larned, of New-York, June 15, 1870. Andrew H. Nave, of Tennessee, June 12, 1871. George D. Wallace, of South Carolina, June 14, 1872. Charles A. Varnum, of New-York, June 14, 1872. H. M. Harrington, of New-York, June 14, 1872. Luther R. Hare, of Indiana, June 17, 1874. James G. Sturgis, of New-Hampshire, June 16, 1875.

AN INTERVIEW WITH COL. CROFTON, COMMANDING GOVERNOR'S ISLAND—HIS RECOLLECTIONS OF GEN. CUSTER AND THE OFFICERS OF THE SEVENTH.

The massacre was of absorbing interest to the officers of Governor's Island, several of whom have served in the North-west and have been personally acquainted with Gen. Custer and all of the officers of the Seventh Cavalry. Col. Crofton, the commanding officer of the island, was connected with the service in the same detachment with Gen. Custer, leaving it in 1874. "Yes," he said in answer to an inquiry from a TIMES reporter, "I have seen a little Indian fighting, and I tell you that it is the worst business a man can engage in. Here is Gen. Custer, one of the bravest of men and one of the best Indian fighters that ever lived, after years of successful experience beaten and cut down and all of his command with him. He who had so often baffled the wiles of the Indian and over-matched them in cunning, at length falls a victim to Indian strategy. I can look at it in no other manner, and I am pretty sure that when we get official reports we shall learn that the unfortunate General fell into a trap. I knew Gen. Custer well. He was a daring man. I remember an instance of his courage: We were on the Yellowstone River, Gen. Custer in command, and we were preparing to go up the stream. We were of course accompanied by a train, and it was necessary that the train should go along the bluff instead of along the bed of the river. So the General dispatched the train upon the hills and the two companies of cavalry jogged along below. After a while the General ordered a halt so that the train might not get too far behind. The men unsaddled their horses and gave themselves up to rest. Suddenly they were attacked by Indians. There were at least three hundred of them to eighty soldiers. Gen. Custer was not dismayed, however. He ordered his men to return fire, and they fought till their ammunition was exhausted. Then the men were just giving themselves up for lost when Gen. Custer ordered a remount, the horses having already been saddled. The men obeyed. 'Now charge for them,' shouted Gen. Custer. The command charged, and, without a single bullet, they put the Indians to rout, and escaped what a moment before seemed certain death.

It may be that Gen. Custer was too brave, too daring. Possibly he has been too rash, but I almost think not. Indians never fight, except, first, when they are cornered, and, second, when they have the advantage. The most natural theory is that Gen. Custer's command reached its point of attack too soon and was forced to attempt alone what was originally intended for the two divisions acting in concert. I hope the reports of the massacre are exaggerated, but from what I know of Indian warfare I cannot indulge the hope that they are. I have no doubt that if the Indians were successful they murdered every man in the command. I do not know all of the officers of the regiment, but some of them I know, and I know them to be as fine officers as there are in the service."

A TILDEN ELECTIONEERING TRICK.

STATE ENGINEER VAN BUREN'S REPORT TO THE CANAL BOARD—WHAT IT REALLY IS AND WHAT IT PURPORTS TO BE.

Special Dispatch to the New-York Times.

ALBANY, July 6.—State Engineer Van Buren's report to the Canal Board on pending contracts for extraordinary repairs on the canals was taken up at the meeting to-day and practically shelved. But Mr. Van Buren was careful to have an abstract of the document sent beforehand to the newspapers. The whole purpose of this report is for political effect, and nothing else. The ambiguous language, and the numerous exceptions and conditions, are in themselves sufficient to show that there is nothing serious in this latest proclamation of "reform." Van Buren gives a list of some thirty-eight pending contracts on which he pretends he has reduced the prices, and will save to the State on each contract sums ranging from $1,000 to $30,000, and that by these reductions only a small portion of the $430,000 which the last Legislature appropriated to pay for this work will be needed. This is his statement, the object, of course, being to show how much is saved to the State under Mr. Tilden's canal reform, and at the same time to have a loop-hole of escape from what he knew to be nothing but an electioneering falsehood. Mr. Van Buren qualifies his statement with suggestions that owing to legal difficulties it may be advisable to effect compromises with contractors where fraud and collusion cannot be charged. Now, the simple truth in regard to these contracts, as Mr. Van Buren and Gov. Tilden very well know, is that many of them have passed beyond the purview of the courts, the work being done and officially certified to in some cases by Gov. Tilden's own appointees. The only effect of resisting payment of these certificates would be such litigation as there was in the Schaub case, and a like result. In fact, Mr. Van Buren will not deny that he had Schaub's case down on his list, and the $9,000 due there would have gone to swell the bogus list of savings had it not happened that the man fought his case so vigorously in the courts as to get judgment just before Mr. Van Buren was ready to publish his report. Mr. Van Buren is one of the Canal Investigating Commission, put into State office by Gov. Tilden, and naturally is anxious to assist the election of his patron.

An analysis of the report in detail will be given at another time. It is sufficient to say here that those who really have any knowledge of the matter say that this latest contribution to campaign literature carries in it nothing but the promise of expensive and disastrous litigation to the State, with no return except the assistance it may render Mr. Tilden in his electioneering.

MR. BLAINE'S ILLNESS.

NO CHANGE IN HIS CONDITION—A EUROPEAN TRIP RECOMMENDED.

AUGUSTA, Me., July 6.—Mr. Blaine has now been home eight days. So far there has been no special change in his case. The nervous prostration is still the marked characteristic of his illness. He is not able to leave his room, and is almost constantly confined to his bed. His physician thinks that it will be many weeks before he will resume active work. A European trip is strongly recommended as soon as his strength is sufficient.

THE DEMOCRATS IN WASHINGTON.

A WEAK RATIFICATION OF TILDEN—A FOUR-MINUTE TORCH-LIGHT PROCESSION.

Special Dispatch to the New-York Times.

WASHINGTON, July 6.—The Democracy held their ratification meeting to-night, their speakers occupying the same stand erected for the Republicans after Cincinnati. There was a great torch-light procession, numbering probably two hundred, which was exactly four minutes marching slowly past THE TIMES office in double file. A good proportion of the torch-bearers were boys about the size of the pages at the Capitol. The Democratic processions in Washington will be larger if Tilden should be elected.

FRENCH POLITICS.

DIFFERENCES AMONG THE REPUBLICAN DEPUTIES ON MUNICIPAL MATTERS—REPORTED ATTEMPT TO SHOOT THE DUC DE CHARTRES.

Paris, July 6.—Differences have arisen among the Republican Deputies over the Municipal bill. The members of the Left, who yesterday agreed to a compromise on the bill, form the group known as the "Republican Left." Another section of the Left called the "Republican Union," which is under the direct leadership of M. Gambetta, held a meeting to-day and passed a resolution rejecting the compromise.

The journals hostile to Republicanism are jubilant over these dissensions. They declare that confusion has taken possession of the Republican Party, for now both the Republican Left and the Irreconcilable Radicals are opposed to M. Gambetta.

VERSAILLES, July 6.—In the Chamber of Deputies to-day M. Moutjau, in view of the recent prosecution of *Les Droits de l'Homme* for publishing articles from the pen of Henri Rochefort, moved the abolition of the decree of 1852 prohibiting convicts from writing newspaper articles.

PARTY RECORDS REVIEWED

ADDRESS OF HON. L. BRADFORD PRINCE.

THE TWO POLITICAL PARTIES REVIEWED AND CONTRASTED—REDUCTION OF NATIONAL TAXATION BY THE PRESENT ADMINISTRATION—TILDEN'S RECORD EXAMINED AND CLEARLY DEFINED.

Hon. L. Bradford Prince addressed a Republican meeting in the village Hall, New-Brighton, Staten Island, on Wednesday night. Mr. J. W. Simonton, the President of the club under whose auspices the meeting was held, acted as Chairman, and introduced the speaker, who said: Mr. Chairman: In the political contest this year, as in other years, there are two great parties. These parties are not new parties; they are the same which have divided the country for twenty years. A candid man who desires to choose wisely will look at the history of the parties themselves and see what records they have made. And in looking over these records no candid man can have a doubt as to which of the parties deserves to have power intrusted to it. The Democrats say this is not a fair criterion this year. That these matters of history are all old issues, and that now there is a new state of affairs and but one issue, and that the issue of administrative reform. This is not the fair and proper way to judge of parties; but take this one issue, and if we find that Republican government has been marked by extravagance, and Democratic government by economy and reform, then let bygones be bygones and let us place the Democracy in power. What are the facts? We read in Democratic papers, and hear in Democratic speeches, a great deal about the weight of taxation under which the country has been placed by the Republican Party. I ask your attention to some events which have occurred within a few years. Ten years ago the internal revenue tax was upon everything you ate and drank and wore—there was no trade or profession not subject to it. In 1866 it amounted to $309,000,000, and it was reduced by Republican administration until in 1874 there remained but $102,000,000. Ten years ago there was an income tax which every man who had an income, and was willing to admit he had, was bound to pay. That also has been removed by the Republicans.

The speaker then showed by a long array of figures the immense reduction in the national debt which had been effected during the Republican administration, and compared this record with that of the Democratic Party in places in which it held power. In 1860 in New-York the debt was $18,000,000, and the Democrats reduced it in their own peculiar way until it was only $116,000,000. [Laughter.] In Brooklyn in 1860 the debt was $6,000,000, and there they reduced it—in their own peculiar way again—until it was only $38,000,000. Where can there be found in modern history, he asked, another instance in which an administration has succeeded (as the Republican Party has) in reducing the public debt and taxes at the same time? It seems to be impossible. How was it made possible? By a continual reduction in the expenses of Government and by the honesty of those who handled the funds. In 1869 the expenses of Government were $322,000,000; they have been reduced year by year under the administration of President Grant until the reduction has amounted to $63,105,000.

THE NATIONAL ADMINISTRATION.

The time which succeeded the war was a time of general demoralization. Defalcations in banking houses, in insurance companies, and in other branches of business, were frequent. Dishonesty seemed to be the rule and honesty the exception. This dishonesty, it might be supposed, would have existed in an extraordinary degree in the Government. What is the truth? We have had, within these last six or eight months, investigations by the score; they have probed to the bottom of everything which served to give an opportunity for developments. Every effort which partisan zeal or malice could suggest has been made. They sent for witnesses to the Pacific slope, to Europe, to the prisons, and, in one memorable instance, even to the lunatic asylum. What has been the result? It is such as to make us proud of the national honesty which has been developed. Instances of wrong doing have been discovered which are sources of national sorrow regret, and shame; they belong to no party; their discovery should not afford cause of congratulation or joy to any party. There is no true American, of any party, who does not feel the blush of shame at the fall of Belknap; who does not regret that Babcock was not more particular in his friendships. But these instances can be counted on the fingers of one hand. Beyond this these investigations have shown that there is a greater amount of national honesty and integrity in this country than in any other country on the face of the globe. During the twenty-five years before 1861 there was stolen out of every $1,000 that passed through the Treasury $9 02; during the war and after, the loss has been seventy-eight cents out of $1,000. In the time of Jackson it was $10 55; of Van Buren, $21 15; of Buchanan, $6 98; in the time of Abraham Lincoln, with all the war on his hands, but $1 41. [Applause.] In the first administration of Gen. Grant the amount lost out of every $1,000 was forty cents, and in his present administration only twenty-six cents. [Applause.] You may look through all history—you may go where you will over the face of the earth—to the most despotic country, where dishonesty on the part of an official would bring instant death—and nowhere will you find such another exhibit of absolute official honesty. Compare this state of things with that of New-York during the building of the new Court-house. Out of each thousand dollars there were stolen not only a few dollars or cents, but $650—sixty-five per cent.

TILDEN'S RECORD.

But Democrats will say, "That is not what we mean—we are a new party—the party of reform, the Tilden party. He is a reformer, and if elected to the Presidency he will control the Government." Now, that is not a fair way to do; no party has a right to put up one man and ask us to judge of them by him and to ignore the rest. Still, to accommodate them, let us take Tilden as the representative of the party and look at his record. Tilden made his record in the State of New-York; he never held office outside of the State. I do not, of course, allude to those little offices in railroads and iron companies. [Laughter.] He has held two offices—as a member of Assembly in 1872 and as Governor. The Legislature of 1872 was the first reform Legislature. No body of men ever had a better chance than they to distinguish themselves—they had to do the work of cleaning the Augean stables which had become filled during the administration of Tweed. No man could ask for a better chance to prove his character as a reformer than as a member of that Legislature. Tilden was a member of that Assembly. He was scarcely ever in his seat—scarcely ever took part in the debates, scarcely ever voted on a bill, absolutely neglected every duty which pertained to the office which he held. I have taken his record from the Journal of the Assembly. I had the roll-calls counted. There were 1,568 of them. Tilden voted on 107 and neglected to vote on 1,461. [Laughter.] "But," some Democrat will say, "Tilden was a member of the Judiciary Committee, and had to be absent in New-York attending to the cases of Cardozo and other Judges." That is true. He was absent with that committee part of the time, and I caused the roll-calls of the committee to be counted. There were 291 of them, and, giving him credit for every one of these, he still failed to vote on 1,170. Never has there been a case where a member, sick or well, made such a record of neglect. "But," they may say, "Mr. Tilden was a great man. He was interested in important reforms. So he picked out the 107 reform bills and voted on them, and did not take the trouble to vote on the others." I looked to see what bills he had voted on, and was astonished. Out of all the important sessions and meetings, Tilden voted on only one—and on that one he voted the wrong way. [Laughter.] That was on the bill of the Committee of Seventy to reform the charter of New-York. He voted no, and voted to continue in force the Tweed power, under which the City had been robbed. We hear a great deal of Tilden as a tax reformer, and you would suppose he would have availed himself of an opportunity to vote on bills designed for this object. Yet, on the Appropriation bill and the Supply bill, which call for millions of dollars, and on which from three to five votes are taken during their passage, he did not vote once. One of the first measures of reform was one to reduce the expenses of the Legislature itself, which had grown to enormous proportions through sinecures and other causes produced by the Tweed government. On the final passage of the bill on this subject Tilden was not present and did not vote. There were three reform bills to reduce the expenses of State prisons; Tilden did not vote on one of the three. "But," they say, "what he took interest in were the Canal bills; he did not want to fritter away his time with these minor matters." There were three Canal bills—the Ordinary, the Extraordinary, and the Seven-mill Tax bills. The Ordinary bill came up; Tilden was not there to vote—perhaps because it was an ordinary bill. [Laughter.] The Extraordinary bill came up. He was not there to vote—perhaps because it was an extraordinary bill. Then the Seven-mill Tax bill came up—a most important bill—on which there was a close vote, and on which we wanted the vote of every man to prevent what would undoubtedly prove to be a "steal;" but Tilden was not there. And the result was that during the 134 days—one of the longest sessions we ever had—Tilden did not vote on a single Canal bill.

THE CANAL RING.

We hear a good deal from the Democrats about Canal reform and tax reform. They are both dangerous matters, because the statements made in favor of Tilden contain half-truths. The Canal Ring has been broken and destroyed. Who did it? The people of the State, when, two years ago, they voted the amendment to the seventh article of the Constitution of the State. All the money that came to the Ring came in the way of "extra compensation." The amendment to the Constitution said in so many words, "Hereafter no extra compensation shall ever be paid to any contractor." When the people passed that, they destroyed the Canal Ring. This was in 1874; Tilden came into power in 1875. Tilden did a great deal that he deserves credit for. He made suggestions to the Legislature for the passage of certain laws, and the Legislature met him half way, and passed every bill he recommended. But it is an absurdity for Democrats to assert that he destroyed the Canal Ring, which had been destroyed by the people two months before he went into office.

In regard to the statement that Tilden reduced the taxes, the half-truth in that is that the taxes were actually reduced, but not by him. The reduction of the tax, Mr. Prince showed at length to have been brought about by several causes—by the previous payment of the last installment of the bounty debt; by results consequent upon the increased valuation of property in the State recommended by the State Assessors; by the previous payment of $293,000 of canal debt; by the appropriation of $200,000 less for the new Capitol than the previous year—all matters in which Tilden had no hand, but for which he received credit because the beneficial operation of these causes was not apparent until he came into office.

Mr. Prince concluded his address by reviewing the war record of Gov. Tilden and contrasting it with that of his competitor for the Presidency.

SPURGEON ON PREACHERS.

WHAT A LONDON PREACHER HAD TO SAY OF PREACHERS AND PEOPLE.

The London *Telegraph* of the 4th inst. says: Mr. Spurgeon took part yesterday in the proceedings in connection with the laying of the foundation-stone of a new hall in George street, Camberwell, in which Ned Wright proposes for the future to carry on the mission service, for which his present wooden and iron structure has become inadequate. There was a very crowded attendance, and Mr. Wright seemed to have many sympathisers, by one of the most liberal of whom, Mr. R. A. Gray, the stone was laid. I came here to-day, said Mr. Spurgeon, to help a neighbor. The time was when nobody would go inside any place of worship unless he agreed with all that was said and done there; but we have now come to rejoice in diversity of operations where we can see that they are directed to the service of the same Lord. I believe there is not half as much ground for the anxiety people feel when they look at the various denominations in the Church as they suppose. I have known one place in a town as dead as death could be, and another place was opened, and then both were filled. [Hear, hear.] For my part, if Ned Wright or anybody else can run away with my congregation—[a laugh]—they are uncommonly welcome; but it will take them all their time, for I always think that if there is a new coach put on the road the old coach should be horsed better, so as to keep customers. [Great applause.] What we want to do is by some means to get the great mass of our people to hear the Gospel. I am always hearing it said the great problem is to get the working classes to listen to the Gospel. I do not believe that to be the problem at all, and I deny altogether that the working classes of London attend less at the house of God than other classes in London. In proportion to their numbers they attend as well as any other class. At least that is my experience. People come to the Tabernacle, and when they see the congregation coming out they say no working classes go there, because they would not be so well dressed. But why should not a working man wear as good a suit of clothes as he possibly can get? Do you expect that on Sunday he would wear the same clothes in which during the week he is bricklaying or carpentering, in which he is up to his neck in dust, or in which he goes down a sewer? One of the first things I notice about a man when he turns from his evil ways is that he gets a decent suit of clothes and if ever he had such a thing before I am afraid he was in the habit of leaving them rather long at his uncle's. [Laughter.] I don't believe any one in Europe could tell the difference between a workman in his best clothes and any other swell. [Renewed laughter.] I suppose two-thirds of my congregation at the Tabernacle are working men, and whenever you have a vigorous, living church you will find that the bulk of it is made up of the very men whom it is said to be the problem to get to go to the house of God. There is a problem I should like to see solved, and that is how to get the people of the West End into church, because although there are many places in connection with the Church of England in which the gospel is truly preached, I must say I do not call it going to the house of God when a man goes to witness processions and pomps and shows. And I know there are hundreds of thousands of people living in the suburbs surrounding London, having large incomes and fine houses, who do not attend church any more than many of the workpeople do. Let us look at the objections people urge to going out on Sunday. Some say their clothes are not good enough, but they are good enough if they have been paid for. [Laughter.] I admit there are persons who should never go to church—those who wear boots that squeak, and ladies whose umbrellas are always falling down with a snap. Then you find people who say they don't go because of the heat and the bad air. I could indicate some places where they could have three pews to themselves if they liked [laughter] and plenty of air. To all sextons and chapel-keepers I would give this wrinkle—open your windows often. [Laughter.] I often preach in country chapels where the people get packed like herrings in a barrel [laughter,] and I have tried to get the windows opened, but they wouldn't, for they never had been opened. [A laugh.] I went into one of these places once, and it was so close and hot that I asked every gentleman near a window to smash a pane or two. [Laughter.] There was soon a very grand smash out then the beautiful fresh air streamed in. I paid the bill afterward like an honest man; but it was much better to do that than bear the cruelty of preaching in such an atmosphere or forcing people to listen when they were more disposed to sleep. There is a common complaint that the preacher can neither be understood nor heard, and there is some truth in it. I wish some preachers who mumble at a very great rate would get a new set of teeth. If men have anything worth being heard, they should speak out. I have heard of clergymen in Australia and Africa—I do not say in England—[a laugh]—of whom it is said that when you hear them once you hear as much of them as you want to hear. [Laughter.] Preachers use various kinds of English—one with many-syllabled words, the other the Saxon their mothers talked, and which they themselves began to use when they prattled as children. I heard a story once of a number of sailors who were playing cards up aloft, and had a light for the purpose. The captain sent a midshipman to tell them to put it out, and the midshipman told them to "extinguish that luminary." But the sailors did not understand him. Then the Captain called out, "Douse that glim"—and out went the candle. [Great laughter.] I should not have said that, but I should have taken a middle point, and said, "Put out that candle, old bers." [Laughter.] I believe "highfalutin" is too much used in the pulpit. We preachers should speak so that people could not misunderstand us even if they tried to do so. Some men occasionally stay away from communion because their wives have a large family, [a laugh,] and those poor women cannot leave the children. I should like to whisper in the ears of some Christian young woman that they might go and take care of the children for a Sunday and let the mother get out. [Applause.] As for the husbands, I don't think they always take their fair turn with their wives, for see some Christian men out on Sunday whose wives never get out for a month together. I think, too, that people have a good deal to do with the filling of the churches and that they might bring friends when they could, and certainly when they found it necessary to say the good man preaching had his wits a wool-gathering, they ought only to say it out in the country, when there was no one within a mile or so of them. [Laughter.] I'll tell you what I often find. When I go into a street and ask for a chapel I am told it is round the corner by the Duke of Prussia, or the Marquis of Granby, or the Mother Red Cap; but I don't find that the churches are conspicuous places. Don't let this happen to you. Advertise, distribute handbills, for the life of business is black ink. You ought to distribute tracts—I mean good ones—and if I knew where you could get good ones I should tell you, for they are generally soporific articles. [Laughter.] Mr. Spurgeon concluded, after an earnest exhortation, by remarking that as book numbers sold best when they were illustrated with plates, so in that meeting they were going to see what could be done with plates. A handsome collection was taken up, Mr. Spurgeon beginning it with £10.

HOW SOUTHERN INTERESTS WILL BE ADVANCED.

In his speech in Philadelphia, Thursday night, Hon. Jonathan Norcross, of Georgia, said: "Do you ask me which candidate for the Presidency is required to be elected by the best interests of the South? I answer, unhesitatingly, that they require the election of Rutherford B. Hayes and the continuance of Republican rule. If he is elected, all matters at the South will be quieted down. Under his administration capital and immigration will flow to the South to help build up our waste places. Under him we shall know precisely what to expect. We shall know that there will be no violent changes in the policy of the Government; there will be no working up of another rebellion, or something else equally bad and dangerous to our interests. But let Samuel J. Tilden be elected and the Democratic Party installed in power, then fear and trembling will take possession of every man. Everything would be thrown into suspense and uncertainty; and what is more significant, the great body of the Democratic Party being at the South, and only its tail here at the North, Mr. Tilden would be a mere puppet in the hands of the Southern Democracy, to dance to the tune of Ben Hill, Dr. Tucker, and Wade Hampton; and what is still worse for us, instead of capital and immigration going to the South to train under such leaders, thousands of Republicans would have to leave the South or be trampled into the dust. To tell you the plain truth, fellow-citizens, I can never believe that the people of the North can ever be so stupid and visionary as to hand the Government of the country over to the party and the men who risked everything and fought through four years to destroy that Government. I repeat, there is a strong element in the South, and, perhaps, a majority of the people, who have become reconciled to the new order of things, and who much prefer to have them remain as they are than to encounter the risks that would follow reaction, and the confusion that backward steps would produce."

GLEANINGS FROM THE MAILS

BOSS TWEED.

HIS RECEPTION ON BOARD THE GOVERNMENT STEAMER FRANKLIN—THE ARRANGEMENTS TO SECURE HIS SAFE PASSAGE "HOME."

Correspondence of the Baltimore Sun.

AT SEA, OFF CAPE ST. VINCENT, COAST OF PORTUGAL, Sept. 23, 1876.

Before this reaches you you will doubtless know that our ship has been awarded the flattering honor of conveying to the land of his birth no less noted a public celebrity than Boss Tweed. I say we have been thus honored, but as a few days must yet elapse ere we arrive at Vigo, the bulky, but slippery, old eel may again evade the clutches of the law and want to know "What we are going to do about it?" We arrived at Villefranche, from Spezia, on the 9th inst. A few days later the Marion joined us, and on the 14th the Admiral took official leave of us, together with the officers of his staff who remain out with him, and transferred his flag to the Marion. All this ceremony was done in due style—officers and crew in full dress on the quarter-deck. The old gentleman was very loath to leave the fine old ship, and displayed much emotion in his farewell speech. As his barge left the gangway, his flag was hauled down and saluted with thirteen guns, being hoisted with the same ceremony as he went on board the other ship. When the Admiral's flag came down, and the Franklin ceased to be the flag-ship, there was a man stationed at the main-truck who threw to the breeze a magnificent homeward-bound pennant 400 feet long, which rapidly unrolled itself and floated out far over the stern of the ship. The same afternoon at 4 o'clock we bade a final adieu to pretty Villefranche harbor, the grand old Alpes Maritimes that frown above, to Nice, the superb, the lovely, the nearest approach to paradise in Europe. We took a farewell view of this familiar scene of unsurpassed beauty, and felt a sorrow in doing so that even our homeward-bound pennant flying overhead was powerless for the moment to prevent. Many happy recollections cluster around Nice, and it is by far the most endeared of any place we have visited during the cruise. However, everything comes to an end, so we took our last glimpse with the setting sun on the evening of the 14th, and then turned our thoughts toward Gibraltar, America, and home. The run of five days down to the Rock was pleasant and uneventful, rather blue for us to miss a number of our messmates, but the homeward-bound feeling began to grow more real than it had been before. We expected to stop at Gibraltar only long enough to fill up with coal, and then set out at once across the ocean. We had heard before leaving Nice of the capture of Tweed at Vigo, where he came on a sailing vessel from Cuba, so upon our arrival, when the Captain received a telegram from the United States Chargé d'Affaires at Madrid, addressed to our Consul at Gibraltar, we immediately conjectured that the old thief was at the bottom of it. The telegram requested the Consul to detain any United States Government vessel passing out the straits until orders could come from Washington. A few hours later a dispatch from the Secretary of the Navy ordered us to remain at Gibraltar for further orders. The next day came telegraphic orders from Washington to proceed to Vigo, communicate with the United States Minister, and receive Tweed on board, place him under strict guard, allow him no communication with the crew, and upon arrival at New-York to allow no communication with the shore until instructions shall be received from the Navy Department as to his final disposal. We took in 500 tons of coal at Gibraltar in one day, pretty quick work, and at 9 o'clock yesterday morning left there en route to Vigo, where we expect to arrive on Monday. We have a head wind and a long, heavy, head sea which reduces our speed materially. If we get the Boss on board all right he will be given quarters in the Admiral's cabin, which is vacant now, and will have an officer on guard over him day and night in port. The cabin windows have been fitted with iron bars, which gives it a look of business and security to prevent him from falling overboard.

VIGO, Spain, Sept. 27.

We arrived on the bay on Monday evening, but too late to get a pilot, and the fog was too thick to run in without, so we had to stay outside until Tuesday (yesterday) morning. This is one of the handsomest bays in the world, and the view of the valley on both sides from the old castle on the hill overlooking the town is superb. The town itself does not amount to much. I was on shore yesterday afternoon for several hours, but devoted little time to the town. We climbed the hill to the castle, but admittance was denied us because the Governor had given orders to allow no communication with the prisoners. These prisoners guarded so closely were Boss Tweed and Hunt, a cousin of his. The people generally are opposed to giving up the old sinner, but the Government had no hesitation in gobbling him. Upon the arrival of the bark from Cuba with the fugitives on board the Governor of the Province went on board and found the Boss in his shirt sleeves, barefooted, in the midst of scrubbing deck. The Spaniards spoke no English and Tweed spoke nothing else, so the conversation was limited. Last night at 10 o'clock a boat came off, and the Secretary of the Governor delivered Tweed and Hunt on board. The former was at once placed in the quarters prepared for him and a sentry placed over him. Hunt was at once released, as we had no orders to keep him. The old Boss looks quite jolly and has brass enough to last him a hundred years. He will be confined to the cabin during the whole passage, and while in port an officer is always present with him. Last night a man died who has been ill a long time with consumption, and we put off sailing till to-morrow in order to bury him on shore. To-morrow we sail for home, and we ought to arrive at New-York by the 18th or 20th of October. We shall go by the southern passage by Madeira and West Indies in order to get the trade winds and save coal. I don't know whether we shall go out of commission at New-York or not. You will probably see me soon after you get this. I don't know whether you'll get this or not, as Spanish postal honesty is of a low order.

G. E. H. H.

PRODUCTION OF IRON IN GERMANY.

THE NUMBER OF BLAST FURNACES IN THE EMPIRE—QUANTITY OF IRON ORE USED—VALUE OF THE PRODUCTIONS—REACTION OF PRICES IN 1874.

The German Government has published some interesting statistics as to the production of iron in Germany for 1874. From these statistics it appears that during that year there were 394 blast furnaces, which worked for a total of 2,801 months, or, upon an average, for about eight months and twenty days each out of a possible total of twelve months. The quantity of iron ore used amounted to 4,342,184 tons, of which 4,130,090 tons were produced in Germany itself. The total quantity of pig iron and cast iron of the first quality produced was 1,660,208 tons. The mean working population employed in the trade was 22,765, of which number 853 were women. The positions held by the respective States of the Empire were as follows: Prussia stood first with 244 blast furnaces and a total production of 1,330,268 tons, valued at $28,106,313. Next come the Rhine Provinces, with a total production of 541,483 tons and a value of $11,723,078; in Westphalia, with 311,559 tons and $7,112,635; Silesia, with 276,258 tons and $5,936,109; Hanover, with 100,152 tons and $2,059,913; Hesse-Nassau, with 37,029 tons and $1,215,075, and Hohenzollern, with 238 tons and $18,012. None of the other States of the German Empire produced as much as the three Provinces of Prussia first mentioned; but Alsace-Lorraine follows close in the wake of Silesia, with 201,419 tons and a value of $3,716,374; and then come Bavaria, with 49,273 tons and $1,341,980; Saxony, with 22,059 tons and $637,892; Hesse, with 16,753 tons and $353,050; Brunswick, with 15,720 tons and $426,854; Wurtemburg, with 11,816 tons and $381,954; Saxe-Meiningen, with 12,213 tons and $257,887; Anhalt, with 634 tons and $32,095; Reuss, with 493 tons and $12,211 and Waldeck, with 124 tons and $5,429. A table is appended to these returns, giving the quantities and value of the pig and cast iron produced during the last ten years. From 960,879 tons and a value of $20,232,796 in 1865, the totals increased without interruption until 1871, in which year they were 1,420,830 tons and $29,135,286. In the following year, when the produce of Alsace-Lorraine was included for the first time, there was a further increase to 1,807,343 tons, and a value of $51,866,740, the rise in value, as will be seen, being considerably greater than the rise in quantity. There was an increase again in 1873 to 1,983,163 tons and $55,291,296; but a fall in 1874 to 1,660,208 tons, as stated above. The reaction of prices was also very considerable, as the 1,660,208 tons realized but $35,449,786, or about $19 per ton, as compared to nearly $29 per ton in 1873.

A METEOR.

The Hartford *Courant* of Thursday morning says: "Members of the Police force on night duty report a meteor of astonishing size and brilliancy at 1:53 this morning. All agree in describing the general direction of the meteor, as from the south-eastern to the north-western heavens. One of the officers speaks of the meteor as appearing as large as a half bushel, and of the light as having a bluish appearance, and of wonderful brilliancy. All observers speak of the remarkable size of the meteor, its brilliancy, and of its apparent bursting, filling a large space in the heavens with bright fragments, which, with a brilliant, irregular trail, having the appearance of sparks, could be seen for eight minutes by the watch before the light finally faded away. The illuminated path of the meteor had an irregular shape, like the milky way, or like clouds lighted up by a bright moon behind them, although the sky, before the passage of the meteor, was perfectly clear. It was evidently one of the most wonderful displays of the kind ever seen, and reports of observers in other parts of the country will be looked for with interest."

The New-Bedford (Mass.) *Mercury* of Thursday says: "At 2 o'clock this morning a magnificent meteor traversed the sky from south-east to north-west. It was so brilliant that objects were lighted up as if by a flash of sharp lightning. A long train, like that of a sky rocket, was left, and remained floating in the air more than fifteen minutes after the meteor had disappeared. The few who were fortunate enough to witness the spectacle report it as being extraordinary."

A Philadelphia paper says that about 2 o'clock Thursday morning a meteor passed over Camden, N. J. It appeared to the eye about three feet in diameter and passed from the south-east to the north-west. It was visible for about ten seconds, followed by a long trail similar to that of a comet. While passing it cast a light so great that persons on the street were led to suppose that there was a fire.

AUDIBLE SPEECH BY TELEGRAPH.

PROF. A. GRAHAM BELL'S DISCOVERY—SUCCESSFUL AND INTERESTING EXPERIMENTS BETWEEN BOSTON AND CAMBRIDGEPORT.

From the Boston Advertiser, Oct. 19.

The following account of an experiment made on the evening of Oct. 9 by Alexander Graham Bell and Thomas A. Watson is interesting, as being the record of the first conversation ever carried on by word of mouth over a telegraph wire. Telephones were placed at either end of a telegraph line owned by the Walworth Manufacturing Company, extending from their office in Boston to their factory in Cambridgeport, a distance of about two miles. The company's battery, consisting of nine Daniels cells, was removed from the circuit and another of ten carbon elements substituted. Articulate conversation then took place through the wire. The sounds, at first faint and indistinct, became suddenly quite loud and intelligible. Mr. Bell in Boston and Mr. Watson in Cambridge then took notes of what was said and heard, and the comparison of the two records is most interesting, as showing the accuracy of the electrical transmission:

BOSTON RECORD.	CAMBRIDGEPORT RECORD.
Mr. Bell—What do you think was the matter with the instruments?	Mr. Bell—What do you think is the matter with the instruments?
Mr. Watson—There was nothing the matter with them.	Mr. Watson—There is nothing the matter with them.
B.—I think we were both speaking at the same time.	B.—I think ... at the same time.
W.—Can you understand anything I say?	W.—Can you understand anything I say?
B.—Yes; I understand everything you say.	B.—Yes; I understand everything you say.
W.—The reason why you did not hear at first, was because there was a relay in the circuit.	W.—The reason why it did not work at first was because there was a relay in the circuit.
B.—You may be right, but I found the magnet of my telephone touching the membrane.	B.—You may be right, but I find ... that my ... touches the membrane.
W.—I cut this relay out, and then the sounds came perfectly.	W.—I cut the relay out, and then the sounds came out perfectly.
B.—I hear every syllable. Try something in an ordinary conversational voice.	B.—I hear every syllable. Try something in a conversational voice.
W.—Shall I connect their battery to the circuit?	W.—Shall I connect their battery in the circuit?
B.—No; there is no necessity to connect their battery in the circuit, for the sounds come out quite loudly.	B.—No; there is no necessity for putting their battery in the circuit, as the sounds come out quite loudly.
W.—I am now talking in quite a low tone of voice.	W.—I am now talking in quite a low tone of voice.
B.—The sounds are quite as loud as before, and twice as distinct.	B.—The sounds are quite as loud as before, and quite as distinct.
W.—Cut out the battery and then talk.	W.—Cut out the battery and then talk.
B.—All right. I will cut out the battery now if you will keep listening.	B.—All right. I will cut out the battery now if you will keep listening.
[Here an interruption occurred, and after a short time Mr. Bell said:]	
B.—I thought you were going to say something.	B.—I thought you were going to say something.
W.—Is the battery cut out?	W.—Is the battery cut out?
B.—No, but I will do it now.	B.—No, but I will do it now.
[Battery having been cut out, Mr. Bell continued.]	
B.—Do you hear anything now?	
[Battery replaced.]	
B.—Did you hear anything?	B.—Did you hear anything?
W.—No, not a sound.	W.—No, not a sound.
B.—Say something to me when I cut out the battery again.	B.—Say something to me when I cut out the battery again.
[Battery cut out.]	
W.—....	W.—I could not hear a sound when the battery was cut out.
[Battery replaced.]	
B.—I fancy I heard a trace of your voice.	B.—I fancied I heard a trace of your voice.
W.—Shall I put on our battery to see if it increases the effect?	W.—Shall I put on their battery to see if it increases the effect?
B.—I'll tell you what we'll do. We'll take off our battery and put on theirs, as before.	B.—I'll tell you what we'll do. We'll take off our battery altogether and put on theirs, as before.
[The company's battery having been placed in circuit faint and indistinct sounds were heard at the Boston end, and then came the intelligible sentence.]	
W.—Is our battery off?	W.—Is our battery off?
B.—Yes, our battery is off. What have you been doing? The sounds were quite soft at first, but now they are quite loud.	B.—[Very indistinct—unintelligible.]
B.—Shall I put on our battery again?	
W.—[Indistinctly heard.] That was very indistinct. Put on our battery.	W.—That was very indistinct. Put on our battery.
[Original battery replaced.]	
B.—We may congratulate ourselves upon a great success.	B.—We may congratulate ourselves on our great success.
W.—Both batteries are on now. [Another sentence heard indistinctly.]	W.—We deserve success. Both batteries are on now.
B.—Repeat the last sentence.	B.—Repeat the last sentence.
W.—Both batteries are on now.	W.—Both batteries are on now.
B.—I understood that before, but I thought you said something else.	B.—I understood that before, but I thought you said something else.
W.—Remove their battery, please.	W.—Reverse your battery, please.
B.—All right; our battery is the only one on now.	B.—All right; our battery is the only one on now.
W.—I have put battery cells on here.	W.—I have six Daniells cells on here.
B.—How many cells have you there?	B.—How many cells have you on there?
W.—S—i—x—six.	W.—S—i—x—six.
B.—Please whisper something to me.	B.—Please whisper something to me.
W.—[Sound of the whisper clearly audible, but the utterance unintelligible.]	W.—I am now whispering.
B.—I could hear you whispering, but could not understand what you said.	B.—I could hear you whispering, but could not understand what you said.
W.—Perhaps we have got the batteries opposed to one another. Had you not better reverse your battery and see what the matter is—or rather what the effect is?	W.—Perhaps we have got the batteries opposed to one another. Had you not better reverse yours; and see what the effect is?
B.—I will try the effect of reversing my battery.	B.—I will try the effect of reversing my battery.
[Battery reversed.]	
B.—Is this any better?	B.—Is this any better?
W.—That sentence was accompanied by that curious crackling sound.	W.—Much fainter, accompanied by that curious bubbling sound.
B.—Yes, I hear it too.	....
B.—What time is it by your watch?	....
[Battery again reversed.]	
W.—What are you doing? I have not heard anything except ... for quite a while.	W.—What are you doing? I haven't heard anything except that bubbling sound for quite a while.
B.—I asked you what time it was by your watch. Perhaps you hear me better now, because I have reversed the battery again.	B.—I asked you.... .... because I.... ....
W.—My battery is now cut out.	W.—My battery is now cut out.
B.—Don't you think we better go home now?	B.—Do you think we had better go home?
W.—Yes, but why does your talking come out so much fainter now?	W.—Yes, but why does your talking come out so much fainter now?
[Mr. Bell here placed the magnet of the telephone nearer to the membrane.]	
B.—Because I had moved the magnet further away from the membrane.	B.—Because I moved the magnet further away from the membrane.
W.—That was very much more distinct.	W.—That was very much more distinct.
B.—Will you try to understand a long sentence if I speak right on?	B.—Will you try to understand a longer question if I speak right on?
W.—I will.	W.—I will.
B.—A few minutes ago I heard a fire-engine pass by the door. I don't know where the fire is, but the number of the box is 196.	B.—A few minutes ago I heard a fire-engine go past the door. I don't know where the fire is, but the number of the box is 196.
W.—The time by my watch is five minutes past ten. Had I not better go into Boston.	W.—The time by my watch is five minutes past ten. Had I better not go into Boston.
B.—Yes; I think it is time to stop now.	B.—Yes; I think it is time to stop now.
W.—Shall I go to Exeter place?	W.—Shall I go to Exeter place?
B.—Yes; but look in here on your way in case I have not gone.	B.—Yes; but look in here on your way in case I have not gone.
W.—Let us talk conversationally without noting.	W.—Let us talk conversationally without noting.

Conversation was then carried on for about half an hour with the utmost freedom, and the experiment closed.

A MATRIMONIAL BROKER'S SUIT.

The Indianapolis *Journal* says: "A case was tried in a Justice's court at South Bend a few days ago which has some rather novel aspects, and involves some new principles of law. The plaintiff and defendant were both Germans, but we will call them A and B. A few months since B, the defendant, being a widower, expressed a desire to get married, as widowers have been known to do before. A, the plaintiff, so far sympathized with this laudable purpose as to propose to aid him in the matter, and proposed a junction with a certain young woman. This suited B exactly, and he accepted the proffered service. The young woman, however, proved to be intractable, as young women sometimes are, and the contract and negotiations were transferred to a widow whom the defendant expressed a perfect willingness to accept in lieu of anything better. The two were introduced, and after some brief and unimportant preliminaries, were married. The match, however, did not prove to have been made in heaven. After a month of wedded bliss they separated, and B drove his wife back to her old home in his wagon, like a good husband. But right then and there, and while his late spouse was in the very act of disembarking, his horses and wagon were levied upon by the officers of the law at the suit of A, who demanded $50 for his services in making the match. The case was tried before a jury. It does not appear that A warranted the marriage to be happy. B admitted the services, but denied that he had promised to pay anything for them. The jury heard the evidence, and after being out about an hour gave the plaintiff a verdict for $5."

LAW REPORTS.

DECISIONS.

SUPREME COURT—CHAMBERS.

By Judge Barrett.

McAndrew vs. Hyslop.—Motion granted, but without stay.

McDowell vs. Huntington.—Bailee exonerated.

Betts vs. Cobb.—Motion denied.

Barney vs. Barney.—Report confirmed.

In the Matter of Dupignac.—Motion granted.

By Judge Van Vorst.

O'Neil vs. Ford.—Default opened, and defendant allowed to answer on payment of $10 costs.

Harris Woolen Company vs. Hirsch, &c.—Motion granted on payment of costs. See memorandum.

By Judge Westbrook.

Murphy vs. Moses.—Order appointing Francis M. Bixby Receiver, &c.

By Judge Donohue.

In the Matter of Englis.—The petitioner stating her total inability to give the bond required, and disclaiming that she accepted the position of Trustee under the order, I think it my duty to vacate the order appointing her Trustee, and an order to that effect may be entered.

By Judge Lawrence.

Richards vs. Richards.—Memorandum for counsel.

COMMON PLEAS—SPECIAL TERM.

By Judge Robinson.

Busch vs. Abrahams.—Motion denied; $10 costs.

Manchester vs. Schappert.—Demurrer sustained and judgment for defendant Schappert, unless plaintiff amend on terms.

Coombs vs. Cantrell.—Motion denied; $10 costs. See memorandum.

SUPERIOR COURT—SPECIAL TERM.

By Chief Justice Curtis.

Brague vs. Lord et al.—Judgment secured on appeal.

Reference Ordered.—Stevins, Jr., vs. Armstrong et al.; Nuskey vs. Coolbaugh.

Hinckey vs. Smith.—Motion granted, with $10 costs to defendants.

Brown vs. Fisk, Jr.—Motion granted.

Pusey vs. The Orinoco Navigation Company.—Judgment and execution vacated.

Russell vs. Burgess.—Plaintiff's complaint dismissed conditionally.

Orders Granted.—Alexander vs. Bennetto; Wadsworth vs. Duncan et al.

By Judge Van Vorst.

Carleton vs. Winship.—Order resettled.

MARINE COURT—CHAMBERS.

By Chief Justice Shea.

Rathbun vs. Schrof.—Motion denied.

Motions Granted.—Ranney vs. Samuels; Herzig vs. Friday; Watt vs. Pottis; Harris vs. Boilet; Caldwell vs. Stolzenberg; Merwin vs. Casey; Ringe vs. Mittnacht.

Brounel vs. Cammeyer.—Motion denied.

Elder vs. Schwarzschild.—Defendant's appearance and demurrer are irregular and declared nullities; $10 costs to plaintiff.

Griswold vs. Tompkins.—Motion denied, with $20 to judgment debtor, to be deducted from judgment.

Marrin vs. Hall.—Motion granted, with $10 costs.

Herbst vs. Vichot.—Motion denied as to frivolousness and granted as to claim admitted.

Carpenter vs. Prince.—Motion denied; $10 costs to defendant.

Baxter vs. Carter.—Motion to open default granted.

McLarney vs. Devlin.—Motion granted.

Levi vs. Sinsheimer.—Demurrer to the first cause of action is overruled, with costs.

Duflocq vs. Daly.—Motion denied.

Westin vs. Shipman.—Motion granted.

Orders Granted.—Johnson vs. Conner; Gessner vs. Child; Neilson vs. Mackenzie; Hawley vs. Knap; Loughran vs. Matthews; New-York College of Veterinary Surgeons vs. Dickel; Railway Advertising Company vs. Elastic Truss Company; Fuller vs. Herbert; Lazard vs. Flammand; Kamena vs. Wegrun.

LARGE FEES TO ATTORNEYS.

The appeals in the suits of Brown against the Mayor, &c., were argued before the Supreme Court, General Term, yesterday. The case comes up on appeal from the order of the court below, made upon the report of a Referee, awarding fees to the attorneys prosecuting the suits against the City of John L. Brown, the deceased street-cleaning contractor. Oliver P. West was awarded $22,000, Stephen W. Fullerton $6,500, and John H. Strahan $3,500. The testimony showed that Brown in his lifetime had made a contingent agreement with West to pay the latter for his services $5,000, one-half of the interest, and the costs. The claim was for $86,000 and interest. The one-half of the interest amounted to $13,000, and the costs were somewhat over $4,000. These items, with the $5,000, made up the claim for $22,000. Brown had also employed Messrs. Fullerton and Strahan. Brown died before judgment had been obtained. The judgment finally had in the case amounted to $111,000. After it had been obtained John Ambrose, who acted as attorney for those interested in Brown's estate, without consulting the former counsel, compromised the claim on this judgment for $50,000, and compromised for $80,000 the other claims of Brown against the City. For this service he received $19,500; Sullivan, Kobbé & Fowler, the attorneys for Brown's widow, received $7,500; Field & Dovo obtained $5,500, and Mary Ann Brown, who had contested John L. Brown's will, received $2,500. These made up the sum of $35,000 for attorney's fees. The main ground of the present appeal, which is brought by the widow, is that where a counsel's bill is disputed the court has no power to make a compulsory reference to determine it, but the attorney or counsel must bring a suit. Decision was reserved. After the deduction of the total amount of the attorney's fees and costs, the widow of Mr. Brown will receive $53,000 out of the $130,000 recovered.

TRIAL OF A YOUTHFUL MURDERER.

The seventh homicide case taken up during the present term of the Court of General Sessions was commenced before Judge Sutherland yesterday in Part I. A youth of eighteen, named Michael McGinn, living at No. 223 Hudson street, was placed on trial for murder in the first degree, in having struck and killed Patrick Hayde, a brakeman on the Hudson River Railroad, who resided at No. 532 West Thirty-ninth street. The story of the murder, as testified to by the witnesses produced by Assistant District Attorney Lyon, is as follows: On Sunday morning, Sept. 3, Hayde, with two or three other employes of the railroad, was standing around the freight depot at Laight and Hudson streets, when McGinn and a number of other young roughs who frequent the locality came out of a lager-beer saloon, where they had been drinking. McGinn felt the pockets of Hayde, who was sitting asleep on a stoop, but, on being told by Hayde's companions to desist, went off. They shortly returned, however, and became involved in a fight, in which McGinn was seen to throw Hayde on the ground and beat him. After they had been separated McGinn drew a knife and pursued Hayde, but did not succeed in stabbing him. Hayde then moved off some distance and was pursued by McGinn, who picked up a heavy coupling-pin, with which he struck Hayde on the head, fracturing his skull. Hayde was taken up and conveyed to the Chambers Street Hospital, where he lingered until Sept. 27, when death ensued.

THE LAW OF INDORSEMENT.

The case of the Merchants' Exchange National Bank against Abraham Waitsfelder was brought to trial before Judge Donohue and a jury in Part II. of the Supreme Court yesterday. The action is brought against the defendant as indorser of a promissory note made by one Max L. Rau. A judgment was obtained by the bank against Rau, but Waitsfelder was not served with the papers in the suit at the time. The judgment obtained against Rau was assigned by the bank to a third party, and the bank now sues Waitsfelder on the note. The latter claims that the bank cannot recover, since it has, by the assignment, put it out of his power to become subrogated to its rights. The bank maintains, however, that under the law of 1841, authorizing compromises with joint debtors, they could sue Waitsfelder, even if they had released Rau. Waitsfelder's answer to this is, that though the statute allows the maker and indorser of a note to be sued jointly, it does not make them joint debtors, but they are as between themselves principal and surety. Judge Donohue reserved his decision on this point.

SEEKING TO SET ASIDE A MARRIAGE.

Chief Justice Curtis, in the Superior Court, Special Term, yesterday ordered a reference in the case of Caroline A. Nuskey against John Coolbaugh. From the plaintiff's complaint it appears that the parties were married in this City on Oct 16, 1873. In 1852, however, the defendant had been married at Wilkesbarre, Penn., to one Elizabeth Halleck, and subsequent to the latter date his first wife obtained a divorce from him in the Supreme Court of this State on the ground of his adultery. By the terms of the decree of divorce he was forbidden from remarrying during the lifetime of his first wife. The plaintiff alleges that the defendant's first wife is still living, and asks that the second marriage be set aside as void from the beginning. The defendant put in no answer to the suit.

THE ESTATE OF HOYT, SPRAGUES & CO.

An additional report of William P. Dixon, the Referee, passing on the accounts of the Receiver of Hoyt, Spragues & Co., was filed in the County Clerk's office yesterday. The Referee audits and allows twenty-two claims amounting to $170,666 43. Among the claims are one from the Merrimac River Savings Bank amounting to $34,907 99; another from the National Farmers and Planters' Bank of Baltimore for $11,479 85; a third from the National Exchange Bank of Newport for $5,004 90, and a claim from the Mechanics' Bank of Brooklyn for $5,759 64.

AN OLD EMBEZZLEMENT CASE.

A case of embezzlement and grand larceny, which has been pending for the past three years, was yesterday brought to trial before Judge Gildersleeve in Part II. of the Court of General Sessions. The accused is charged with having, on Nov. 20, 1873, while employed as clerk at the freight depot of the Erie Railway, in this City, appropriated to his own use a check for $200, given him by W. G. Miller & Co. in payment of freight. Although the case is a simple one, it will occupy several days in trial, an elaborate defense having been prepared. Ex-Recorder Smith and Dudley Field, on behalf of the Erie Railway, prosecute the case, and the accused is defended by John R. Fellows.

COURT NOTES.

Michael McGiven was yesterday committed at the Essex Market Police Court to answer for violently assaulting Officer Henry Bankars, of the Seventeenth Precinct.

John Adams, a book agent, residing at No. 153 Allen street, was yesterday arraigned at the Tombs Police Court and committed in default of $1,500 bail to answer for attempting to cash a forged check on Messrs. Sargent & Co., of No. 37 Chambers street, at the Importers and Traders' Bank, corner of Broadway and Murray street.

John C. Canning, a night watchman, residing at No. 495 East Houston street, was yesterday arraigned at the Essex Market Police Court and committed in default of bail to answer for pointing a revolver at Officer Kennedy, of the Seventeenth Precinct, when the latter ordered him to move from the front of a saloon in Eighth street, where he was conversing with some friends.

George L. Williams brought an action against the City to recover $90 for services rendered as one of the census enumerators in June, 1875. It appeared that at the time he was also employed as a laborer on the "big pipes" at One Hundred and Tenth street, and the City refused to pay him in both capacities. It was proved before Judge Joseph F. Daly yesterday that Williams had done his work on the census at night and on Sundays, when the classes he worked among could be best reached. A verdict was directed in his favor. John H. Strahan appeared for the plaintiff and E. L. Stetson for the City.

ST. PETER'S CHURCH AT ROME.

A BUILDING OF DISPROPORTIONS—FAULTY INTERIOR ARCHES—THE ARCHITECTS BLAMED.

Dr. Edward A. Freeman, in his book entitled *Historical and Architectural Sketches*, thus discusses the causes of the disappointment so frequently experienced when St. Peter's is first seen: "Let us premise that we are not going to maintain any such paradox as to deny either the real majesty of the interior of St. Peter's, the great triumph, both constructive and æsthetic, of its cupola, or the external grandeur of the cupola from without, wherever it can be seen—that is only when we have got a very long way off from it. But we must be allowed to hold that it is no triumph of art elaborately to hide such a structure when it is once made, and we think that Brunelleschi's cupola at Florence, rising boldly in the sight of all men above its supporting apses, is as far superior to St. Peter's without as it is inferior within. * * * But the point on which we wish specially to insist at St. Peter's is one which concerns the inside. Everybody who goes into the church complains that at first sight it does not look so large as he expected to find it, or as it really is. Everybody, learned or unlearned, makes the same remark. Now, the regulation answer is that it is the perfection of its proportions which makes the church look small. Such an answer is nonsense. Proportions which take off from the apparent size, and therefore from the dignity of a building, are in their own nature disproportions. It is certainly hard, on entering St. Peter's, to believe that we are in a church which is longer than St. Alban's and higher than Amiens. The reason is that the architects of St. Alban's and Amiens knew what to do with their length and their height, while the architects of St. Peter's did not know what to do with theirs. It is all the difference between the magnifying and the multiplying principle. At St. Peter's four arches of enormous height and enormous span occupy a length which, in an ancient basilica, would have been occupied by twenty arches. The necessary result is that, while both an ancient basilica and a mediæval church does full justice to its own length, St. Peter's looks a great deal shorter than it really is. So it is with the height; the space which a mediæval architect would have cut up into three or four stages makes only one stage at St. Peter's, therefore St. Peter's looks a great deal lower than it really is. Lofty pillars, with little or no triforium, and a low clerestory, will often give a great effect of height, as at Milan Cathedral and in many of our perpendicular churches. But at St. Peter's there are no lofty piers, only enormous piers. There is nothing to carry the eye vertically; there is nothing to carry it horizontally."

THE NEW-YORK MINE.

THE OPERATIONS OF TILDEN AND HIS CONFEDERATES—INDIVIDUAL HARDSHIPS RESULTING.

From the Big Rapids (Mich.) Pioneer.

The Democratic papers have labored assiduously to clear up and explain away Tilden's infamous record in regard to his connection with the villainous frauds perpetrated by the New-York Mine, near Marquette. They have published certificates from Tom, Dick, and Harry, together with a letter from Peter White, attempting to shift the responsibility for losses sustained by the laboring men and others from Tilden's shoulders. We have taken pains to inquire into the matter, and we publish below the substance of a statement made to us by L. C. Patterson, a gentleman residing in this city, and a man well known in this community as a man of truth and veracity.

Mr. Patterson worked in the New-York Mine in 1874, and when the concern collapsed they were indebted to him in the sum of $500, and still owe it to him. He will probably have that amount always coming to him from Tilden & Co. A Frenchman by the name of Sevasen worked with his son in the blacksmith shop at the mine, while his daughters kept a boarding-house. Sevasen drew as little money as possible from time to time, preferring, as a matter of supposed safety, to leave it in the hands of the company. When the company failed they owed him $5,000, which was all he had in the world. The poor man was almost insane over his loss, and his misery excited the warmest sympathy in the community, where he was highly respected as a worthy man and exemplary citizen. Ed. Morrison, a relative of Mr. Patterson's, who had been at work there for some time, also lost $5,000 by the failure. He is now at work in the silver mines in Nevada. Mr. Patterson states that whenever any of the men became dissatisfied and wanted to leave the company would pay them off in iron currency, and then employ men to go and buy it up at fifty cents on the dollar. He has seen $10 of this iron currency refused in payment for a three-cent postage stamp. And yet they say Tilden is not to blame for this state of affairs because he owns but $900 worth of stock. If that be the case, how does it happen that Samuel J. Tilden but a short time ago sent to the State Treasury his check for $710 as his share of the specific taxes on the New-York Mine?

Mr. Patterson stands ready to verify the statement made above whenever any person may call upon him; and, as he has been a life-long Democrat, his assertions cannot be denounced as Republican lies. The laboring men in the Upper Peninsula, and particularly those who have been swindled out of their hard earnings by Tilden & Co., don't take a cent's worth of stock—not even in iron currency—in Samuel J. Tilden as a reformer.

THE ENGLISH HOUSE OF LORDS.

The London *Times* says: "The recent elevations and new creations in the peerage have slightly affected the roll of the House of Lords, which now stands at a little over, instead of a little under, five hundred, as it did at this time last year. In January last the Earl of Erne was created a Baron of the United Kingdom, and Mr. J. R. Ormsby-Gore, Mr. Henry Gerard Sturt, Mr. John Tollemache, and Sir Robert Gerard were raised in a 'batch' to the upper house as Lords Harlech, Alington, Tollemache, and Gerard, while the Earl of Abergavenny was created a Marquis, and the Duke of Richmond had an additional Dukedom, that of Gordon, bestowed upon him. Since that time Lord Northbrook has been rewarded with an Earldom for his services in India, and the Earldom of Beaconsfield has also been bestowed upon Mr. Disraeli. The exact number of peerages, spiritual and temporal, including those enjoyed by members of the royal family, stands consequently at the present moment at 503, headed by his Royal Highness the Prince of Wales as Duke of Cornwall, and ending with 'Mortimer, Lord Sackville,' the junior Baron. The Dukes number 21, the Marquises 22, the Earls 132, the Viscounts 31, the Archbishops and Bishops, 26, and the Barons 265. The rest of the roll is made up by the Royal Dukes. There are one or two things to be noted in the present roll. Firstly, that the number of Peerages on it is slightly in excess of the actual total number of the Lords, spiritual and temporal; Lord Cairns being enumerated twice over, both as a Baron and as Lord Chancellor; the Duke of Richmond both as a Duke and also as Lord President of the Council; the Marquis of Hertford both as a Marquis and also as Lord Chamberlain; Earl Beauchamp both as an Earl and also as Lord Steward of the Household; and, lastly, the Earl of Erne both as an Irish Representative Peer and also as Lord Fermanagh. Again, it may be observed that the Buckhurst title has disappeared since last year as a separate entry, being merged in the superior honor of the Earldom of De la Warr, and that blanks are put against the names of the Earldom of Berkeley and the Barony of De Freyne. The name of the Earl of Beaconsfield also figures twice in the roll, firstly, in his own place at the end of the Earls, next after Lord Northbrook; and, again, as Lord Privy Seal, in which capacity his Lordship takes precedence above and before all Dukes, save after the members of the royal family, the two Archbishops, the Lord Chancellor, and the Lord President of the Council."

COTTON RECEIPTS.

The following were the total net receipts of cotton at all ports since Sept. 1:

	Bales.		Bales.
Galveston	96,510	Baltimore	1,352
New-Orleans	140,811	New-York	3,785
Mobile	40,395	Boston	6,159
Savannah	102,054	Providence	1,604
Charleston	101,249	Philadelphia	7,453
Wilmington	10,19[illegible]	Port Royal	3,000
Norfolk	64,807	Indianola	3,272
Total			[illegible]

POLITICAL MISCELLANY

LIVING WITHIN OUR INCOME.

HOW THE REPUBLICAN ADMINISTRAT[ION] HAVE DONE IT, AND THE DEMOC[RATS] DID NOT.

In a recent speech Hon. Edward McPhe[rson] said:

It is further charged against the Republicans [that] they have not kept the Government within its [in]come. On the other hand the official figures of [the] Treasury show that in no single year within [the] last eleven has the Government lived beyond it[s in]come. Not only have ordinary receipts paid [ordi]nary expenditures, but in each year a payment [has] been made upon the principal of the public d[ebt,] and in the last eleven years over six hundred [and] fifty-six million dollars have been paid upon [it,] and in the last fiscal year, which ended June [30,] 1876, $25,000,000 of debt were paid. These are s[am]ples of Republican keeping of the national ho[use]hold. What are the facts respecting the nati[onal] housekeeping during the last Administra[tion] chosen by the Democratic Party? If th[e] carping critics of us will study th[em]selves, they will find that during the [fis]cal years 1858, 1859, 1860, and up to March 4, 1[861,] when Mr. Buchanan left office, the annual expe[nses] of the Government were in excess of its annual [in]come nearly fifty-eight million dollars, to m[eet] which bonds and Treasury notes were issued to [the] amount of $68,425,900, and so bad was the credit [of] the United States in that time of peace that [the] Treasury notes were placed at a discount equival[ent] as to part of them, to twelve per cent. inter[est,] and a five per cent. bond of the [par] value of $100 brought only $89 10. [Con]trast such facts with the other undeni[able] fact that at this moment the Administration is [en]gaged in calling in six per cent. bonds, and rep[lac]ing them with four and a half per cents.; that [the] money-lenders of the world are freely offering [to lend] their money at those rates, and that, [on] the 4th of March next, $300,000,000 [of] six per cents. will be retired to the [an]nual saving, on interest account, of $4,500,[000.] Bad national housekeeping, indeed! During [the] last eleven years, not only has public debt paym[ent] gone on, and conversion of bonds of a higher [to a] lower rate of interest, with a resulting reducti[on of] annual interest account from $143,781,591 in 186[7 to] $100,243,271 in 1876, but there has been, concurr[ent]ly with this, a repeal of the war taxes, until no [cit]izen now pays a direct tax to the United Sta[tes] unless he consumes articles of foreign [ma]nufacture, or holds bank stock, or dri[nks] spirituous or malt liquors, or indulges [in] tobacco, or uses a few stamped articles. E[ven] the income tax has been abolished, to the relie[f of] such tender consciences as Gov. Tilden, who n[o] longer be distracted between the duty wh[ich] they owe the laws of their country and [the] "higher allegiance" they may deem due to th[e] Democratic prejudices and interests. Meanwh[ile] the number of civil officers employed has b[een] gradually reduced, except as new Post Offices h[ave] been created, chiefly on the frontiers, and the c[ol]lection and disbursement of the public moneys h[as] been made with less loss than at any time wi[thin] the last forty years.

SOUTH CAROLINA.

THE COLORED PEOPLE NOT LED AW[AY] FROM THE REPUBLICAN CAUSE.

In an article denying that the colored peo[ple] of South Carolina are disposed to go over to [the] support of Hampton, the Columbia *Union-He[rald]* of the 17th inst. says:

"In Edgefield County the advocates of the 'sh[ot-]gun' policy openly boast of their determinatio[n to] overcome the 1,600 Republican majority of [the] county, and yet of the 1,600 mounted and arm[ed] Democratic horsemen who paraded through [the] village last Saturday, under command of Gens. B[ut]ler and Gary, there were only nine colored men.

In Sumter, which is claimed as one of their stro[ng]holds, this 'shot-gun' Democracy could muster last Saturday but thirteen colored men to swell [the] 1,200 mounted cavalry drawn from the several [sur]rounding counties.

The Beaufort Democratic Convention has no[mi]nated a ticket largely colored, but there was [but] one negro in the convention. He was an alterna[te] and recently came from Georgia. The 'shot-g[un'] policy has not fifty advocates among the 8,000 [col]ored voters in the county.

In Barnwell County, where whippings and ass[as]sinations and every species of proscription have p[re]vailed, where colored men have been compelled [to] join the Democratic Clubs to keep starvation [from the door,] there will not be 100 colored votes cast for [the] 'shot-gun' ticket on the 7th of November.

In Charleston County there always have been every election barbers and lackeys who vote w[ith] Mr. Barnwell and Mr. Mitchell or some other le[ader] ere of the Broad street clique, but of the 17,600 c[ol]ored votes in Charleston County the Democr[ats] will scarcely get the odd 600.

In Richland there are several jail-birds whom [the] Democracy have liberated, several dram-drink[ers] whom the Democracy ply with bad whisky, an[d a] few fawning lackeys, barbers, and porters, whom an occasional dime is thrown—th[ese] characters are preaching 'Hampton and [Re]form;' but we challenge the Democr[ats] to name ten colored men, who have the respect [of] the community, who have even promised to v[ote] the 'shot-gun' ticket. They cannot do it. Of [the] 5,036 colored voters in the county our friends m[ay] confidently rely upon 5,000 for the Republi[can] ticket.

All this talk about colored Democrats is a bl[ind] to give color to the statements the 'shot-gun' [De]mocracy expect to make in the event of the de[feat] of the Republican ticket in this State. But th[anks to] heaven and Gov. Grant, their schemes have b[een] [illegible]

HOW THE DEMOCRATS CARRIED GEORG[IA].

Hon. Jonathan Norcross, [illegible]

HENDRICKS TRIES TO GET EVEN.

In his speech in Indianapolis Tuesday [illegible]

The New-York Times.

L. XXXV......NO. 10,843. NEW-YORK, THURSDAY, JUNE 3, 1886. PRICE TWO CENTS.

NATION'S FIRST LADY

IAGE OF THE PRESIDENT AND MISS FOLSOM.

CORATIONS, THE GUESTS, THE COS-MES, AND A VERY SIMPLE CERE-NY—DEPARTURE OF THE COUPLE R DEER PARK.

HINGTON, June 2.—The first wedding esident in the White House is over, and Cleveland and his charming young re speeding away to Deer Park, Mary- their wedding journey accompanied by gratulations of family and friends and l wishes of the entire Nation for their and happiness. The ceremony took the Blue Room at the appointed hour, presence of a small circle of relatives, and official guests, and while it was in s the bells of the city churches rang out greeting, and a salute of cannon an-d the union of the happy pair.

ad been decided and repeatedly an-d, it was a simple ceremony, held in the surroundings much less elaborate than at have been made for occasions when lomatic representatives have been in-meet the throng of legislators and lead-ers of the Government. The prepara-or the event were completed early in . The weather, while not perfect, was propitious. The sun shone when the d the groom plighted their vows, but it hrough passing shower clouds. A warm n breeze blew in at the windows of the House during the wedding service. The of the public was maintained respect-There were no crowds about the Executive n, none but kindly inquiries about the air, and there was an abundance of good d hearty good wishes for them as they hirled away to enjoy their short wedding At the Capitol during the day Senators presentatives talked of nothing so much approaching ceremony, and in the de-nts the preparations at the White House, ival of the bride, her reception by her nt lover, the toilets of the ladies, and the g presents were inquired about with ab-interest. During the wedding there unusual police precautions about the House, and there was no necessity for e small force of protectors on duty. The g presents, excepting only the superb d necklace presented by the groom to le, were not displayed.

THE ARRIVAL OF THE BRIDE.

bride's arrival in the city was as demo-as could be. She came only with her and cousin. No incident marked the When the long train rolled into the station at 5:30 o'clock rain was falling light and maiden's tears. The Folsom car, with curtains still drawn, brought up the rear rain, which had 11 coaches, besides sev-ggage cars. An engine backed down and d the private car to a track adjoining the treet sidewalk. Just then a carriage, he window of which protruded a bright awl around a woman's arm, rattled down treet. Drawing up near the favored car upant of the carriage, Miss Rose Cleve-lighted and entered the car. She was out t only a moment. Miss Folsom, clad in a ay jacket over her silk dress and with ack and white trimmings of her peaked t stirred gently by the wooing air, came ehind Miss Cleveland on her reappearance. heeks were tinged with soft color, and so m showing any trace of the cares of state oked as though she had gone to bed early, sensible young woman, and had had a ght's rest. The reach was long enough the lower step of the car to the walk to to the fraction of the score of spectators d about who were not all eyes for Miss rather more of the anatomy of the nt's sister than is usually to be seen in This mis-step did not escape the quick the bride, and with a dainty kick she d her skirts about her, and jumped to the ith only her boot tips protruding. While e cousin was helping Mrs. Folsom down ide tripped to the carriage. All of the were seated in a moment. Then the driver d the reins, swished his whip, and the swung smartly into the drive leading the Smithsonian building. The trees in the rk bent their boughs of rich and changing ike an arbor over the bride's pathway. he right and left stretches of wood and listened and sparkled under the sun, that me out to give a welcome befitting the s first lady. There had been no sudden g away of the clouds, only a gentle part-ch veiled the sky like wedding lace. It lover's June morning—the air laden with ss and the twitter of birds, and with no ound save the soft crunching of the car-heels over the gravel roadway. Proudly chman swished his whip, and the Presi-ays shot under the trees, a winding and ic course, past the agricultural grounds, into Monument Park. Then they turned y cityward, and in a moment were trot-er the cobblestones of the street between pillars of the Treasury and the wooded outh of the White House. The carriage the easterly gate on Pennsylvania-ave-The attendants who opened the carriage wed low before the radiant young woman epped out under the portico as lightly as girl.

s 6 o'clock to the minute when the nod-umes of her hat passed within the en-The attendants led the way to the glass screen that separates the public le from the private corridor. She may ipped lightly across the vestibule to hide citement, but excited or not she looked retty and blushed clear to her forehead as sident held out both hands to her at the e to the corridor. She let her hands fall rly in his. The obsequious attendants, their eyes, thought the prospect excel-r an old-fashioned American squeeze nd there, but by the time Mrs. and Mr. and Miss Cleveland had entered the at-s heard the joyful voices of the bride's atives and a good deal of kissing that sound quite robust enough to have pro-from the master of the house. Then fol-he usual prattle about how well the bride and she declared how well she felt. As teps grew faint down the corridor the fresh laughter could still be heard. It the solemn attendants as something to over, and it was a long time afterward their faces straightened out again.

bride had not only brought sunshine to y as her wedding day gift for the people when in the course of human events they awake, but she carried it straight into the ed old mansion and to the hearts of the ousehold there. The South Room, next library, on the second floor, which Gen. rs. Grant used to occupy, had been set for the bride's use. She uttered a little ation of delight as she stepped within the ower into which it had been transformed, ning to her mother put her arms around d led her to a lounge. Soon the voice was heard by those in the corridor g to a canary that was swelling his little in her welcome.

ours, if there were any, did not last long at e. Before 8 o'clock breakfast was served. athering at the family table had never large. Besides the President at the head able, there were Mrs. Folsom, Benjamin , Mr. and Mrs. Rogers, of Seneca Falls; dman and her daughter, of Detroit, and Mrs. Harmon, of Boston, all relatives of le; Miss Rose Cleveland at the foot of the ith the bride, charming in a suit of gray, ide; the Rev. W. N. Cleveland, the Presi-brother; Mrs. Hoyt, his sister, and W. S. of Buffalo, his former law partner. No ravenous, but all were happy. They about the wedding without much re-serve, the President chuckling over it good-naturedly and the bride looking prettier than ever in her blushes. When the company laughed most she joined them, fluttering the blue ribbons at her neck, although she was determined not to show confusion if she felt it. Every one liked her better for her pluck, and when breakfast ended, after an hour or so, she had proved her ability to carry herself under circumstances as trying, doubtless, as any that she will have to face.

Then the President went to his office, busy even on his wedding day, and the ladies made a leisurely inspection of the house. The bride showed a smiling and responsive interest in the decorations. It was hardly to be expected after her late ordeal and in anticipation of the events to come that she could be as demonstrative as under ordinary circumstances. She clung to her mother's arm and kept quiet except when addressed. The heightened color of her face told plainly, however, how glad the preparations made her and how proud she was that they were in her honor. As the morning glided away the party of ladies separated, several of them going out to drive. The bride and her mother then retired for rest.

Lunch hour found the bride refreshed. The President had finished his office work and had sought and obtained a quiet chat with her, which sweetened her smiles if it did not allay her nervousness. Mrs. Folsom had occupied herself meanwhile in directing the porters what to do with the bride's luggage, which comprised more pieces than any one had yet counted, and in picking out the pieces that were to go to the bride's chamber. When lunch was over all was thus ready for the up-stairs preparations for the evening's event. The ladies went in and out of the bride's room with offers of assistance, and as the offers were gratefully accepted, the wedding dress and all the other wonders of the bridal outfit were ready for the use for which they were to be put while the sun was yet high. It was the desire of Mrs. Folsom, seconded by the other ladies, that the bride should then rest herself thoroughly. Of course, she agreed with them; but as the ladies remained and talked and the bride wanted to listen rather than to try and sleep, a messenger from the library found her laughing and happy. She was wanted for a chat with the President and the Rev. Dr. Sunderland, who was to marry them. The clergyman and the bridegroom thought it important that all the parties should understand what forms of ceremony would be followed, and she was called to hear the minister rehearse what he would say and what she should say. She listened demurely and then went back to her room, almost ready to cry. From that time until the hour that she had to prepare for the great event she kept as still as a mouse and no one disturbed her.

THE PRESIDENT'S LAST DAY OF BACHELORHOOD.

It was a long and busy day for President Cleveland. He needed no one to awake him, even to be ready to receive Miss Folsom at 5:30 o'clock, and hours before the rest of Washington was awake he and the other agitated members of the White House family were exchanging happy greetings, and Miss Cleveland was preparing to go to the station to receive the bride. After breakfast he joined Col. Lamont in the library. The two close friends and companions looked with some concern at the heavy and mist-shedding clouds that rolled up from the southeast. Ominous thunder peals lurked along the horizon, and the leaves of the trees all turned their undersides to the light. There was too much work to be done to permit long study of the weather, and the President, with coat thrown back, bent himself to such official tasks as he was compelled to perform, with the perspiration rising in beads to his forehead. He kept Col. Lamont near by and all inquiries for the private secretary sent up by importunate newspaper representatives were answered by the statement by the messengers: "Too busy with the President; cannot be seen." While Mr. Cleveland was busily employed, he found time during the morning to stroll out into the upper hall and greet Miss Folsom as if to assure himself that his bride had really come. The President was in extremely good spirits, not flustered a bit, but calmer and more comfortable in spite of the heat of the day than those who were about him. He remembered all that he had undertaken to do in the way of absolutely necessary public business, and cleared it all off at an early hour. About 10:30 his old friend, Wilson S. Bissell, of Buffalo, climbed up the stairs to Col. Lamont's room. Under his arm he carried a small box with "Mrs. Grover Cleveland" written very plainly upon it. This was turned over to Mrs. Hindley to be added to a store of other packages of divers sizes and shapes that were securely put away. The two friends greeted each other most cordially, and after chatting together awhile in the library the President found an excellent opportunity for looking once more upon his bride so soon to be when he escorted Mr. Bissell to the group of ladies chatting together at the end of the hall, just over the conservatory. Later on Secretary Lamar called, and the President enjoyed his talk for half an hour. Mr. Lamar is one of the most warm-hearted of the President's official family, and he enters into the romantic side of the match with no effort whatever. After Mr. Lamar came Assistant Secretary Fairchild and Senator Van Wyck, who was specially privileged in being allowed to call on a business matter, but who did not lose the opportunity to comment upon the President's apparent good health and to extend hearty congratulations to him upon his good fortune in being able to enlist with the Benedicks. The Rev. Dr. Sunderland occupied the time of the President just before noon, and while he was present Col. Lamont was away from the White House. He had gone away in a carriage, and after an absence of perhaps half an hour he returned bearing a paper in his hand. This he unfolded and spread out before the President, who read it critically and then smiled, handed it back to his private secretary, and laconically remarked: "That's all right Lamont." It was the license, a paper absolutely necessary to be obtained before even the President could be legally married in the District of Columbia. It was on the usual printed blank, with the names and dates and places written in by the Clerk of the Supreme Court. It read as follows:

"To any minister of the Gospel authorized to celebrate marriage in the District of Columbia, greeting:

"You are hereby licensed to solemnize the rites of marriage between Frances Folsom, of Buffalo, N. Y., and Grover Cleveland, of Buffalo, N. Y., if you find no lawful impediment thereto; and having so done you are commanded to appear in the Clerk's office of the Supreme Court of said District and certify the same.

"Witness my hand and the seal of said court this 2d day of June, 1886. R. J. MEIGS, Clerk.

"By R. J. MEIGS, Jr., Assistant Clerk."

That decided the dispute as to what name Miss Folsom chose to be known by. She was to be married as Frances, not Frank. A form of return was added to the license, to be filled out by the officiating clergyman.

At noon the President's coupé was driven up to the door, and Mr. Cleveland went off for a ride alone, exciting great curiosity among the writers for the papers, who immediately concluded that he had gone away to complete arrangements for getting out of the city without being seen by the watchful and alert reporters. Of course he was upon no such business. He let Alfred Hawkins drive him out as far as Pretty Prospect, his house on the Tenallytown road, and back again to the White House. The trip gave him a chance to shake off all thoughts of further attention to business. The rest of the day was to be devoted to preparations for the wedding.

The lunch hour brought the family again together in the pretty family dining room, for possession of which Pinard was already clamoring, as the time was short for rearranging it, loading it with flowers, the elaborate fancies of the skillful caterer, and the dainties with which the palates of the wedding guests were to be tickled. All the morning the decorators had been busy in the Blue Room and the great East Room, putting the finishing touches upon their work. Over the asphalted drive leading up to the White House rolled now and then a hurried express wagon, bearing small and large packages that were handled with extreme care. A throng of persons who desired to be permitted to look at the flowers in the Blue Room, but who could not be allowed by the guards to penetrate further than the East Room were apparently very much gratified at being able to see four large floral shields carefully unloaded from a covered wagon and each carried in between two men. All the office attached to the White House were close-mouthed as to the programme for the evening. The most pathetic appeals by visitors for information as to what Miss Folsom wore at breakfast, or what she had eaten, or what name she had given to her pretty canary bird, or whether the bridal party were going on their wedding journey, were turned off with declarations of profoundest ignorance. Sidelong glances were cast up at the second-story windows by the disappointed ones in the hope that Miss Folsom's face might be seen behind the curtains that were swaying gently in the breeze. As most of these inquisitive looks were directed at the room of the President, and Miss Folsom was occupying a room on the opposite side of the house, they were all unrewarded.

A little stir was created when some large boxes, that were very light for their size and were supposed to contain the wedding cakes, were set down in the porch and quickly transferred to the dining room. Late in the afternoon an old farmer and his wife drove up to the White House in a dilapidated and ancient one-horse vehicle that looked as if it had been in use before the war. The farmer stopped in front of the house and called out to a policeman standing on the porch. Then his wife held up a big market basket filled with great blushing strawberries, each one of which looked as large as a teacup. The edges of the basket were wreaths of tastefully arranged flowers. "Give this to President Cleveland," said the farmer. "I'll call around for the basket some day." And then the couple started up the horse and drove quietly away.

All sorts of tricks and devices were resorted to by men and women whose devouring ambition was to get into the President's house and witness the marriage ceremony, or at least to catch a glimpse of the bridal party in the Blue Room. Of course, no effort was successful. One young man of more or less original ideas hunted up Prof. Sousa, leader of the Marine Band, this morning, and asked the musician if he didn't want to put a fifty-dollar greenback into his pocket. The leader remarked that he had no particular aversion to greenbacks of large or small denominations if honestly come by. "Well," said the young man, "I want you to lend me an old red coat and a triangle and let me go with you to the White House as a member of the band. It will be $50 in your pocket if you'll do this." The young man left Prof. Sousa without a red coat or a triangle, and the musician did not collect the $50.

It was nearly 6 o'clock when the President descended from the library and made a tour of the lower part of the house to examine the completed work of decoration. He found everything in order, the guards all at their posts, the throng of visitors gone, and the silence of rest pervading the whole place. There was nothing left to be done but to array himself in his wedding garments. He shook hands with Col. Lamont, who was about to go home, complimented him for the admirable manner in which he had performed the tasks assigned to him, and the two separated not to meet again until the wedding.

THE WHITE HOUSE IN WEDDING GARB.

The East Room was decked for the event with great skill, but without any attempt to outdo the decorations that have been seen on many occasions when the different circles of society have been invited to meet each other and pay their respects to the President. The central feature was a semicircular mass of palms and ferns of graded sizes at the east side of the room, the trees nearest the wall reaching to the ceiling, while those in front were so short that their leaves fell over the gilded bar that confined them. Palms, ferns, and other tropical plants were arranged in groups in the window spaces. The four great pillars were twined with garlands of roses of different hues, and upon each pillar, midway between floor and ceiling, was a shield about 4 feet in length, bent to the form of the pillar. The design of the shields was a representation of the national colors, with the stripes in red and white roses and a field of blue immortelles sprinkled with white roses. The four large mantels were banked with superb masses of cut flowers, roses, orchids, and lilies predominating, and fringes of maiden's hair fern depending from the front. Foliage plants filled the fireplaces and the crystal chandeliers were twined with smilax. Above the large mirrors were heavy festoons of roses.

The Green Room, adjoining the East Room, contained an abundance of palms and ferns, with cut flowers sprinkled among them, but it had been seen to quite as good advantage many times before, and those who saw it yesterday did not linger long. There were finer attractions in the private corridor, where trees of stately palm and arbor-vitae and sprays of fern were grouped with an artist's hand. The several groups were continuous, except at the doorways on either side, and produced the effect from a short distance of an avenue of green extending nearly the width of the mansion. One of these doorways, the one adjoining the Green Room door, opened upon the Blue Room. It was to this room that all the decorations led, in an artistic sense, and to which those fortunate enough to get an early view, as well as the evening's guests, turned their steps with the least possible delay.

Looking into the Blue Room from the corridor one saw the further wall a mass of green. It was dense enough to shut out the light from the two windows that overlook the south lawn, and presented a front in which were combined all shades of green. Some of the plants in this bank were in flower, but scarcely enough of them to relieve the prevailing color. This charm was saved for clusters of tall plants that flanked the mantelpieces at the sides of the room to the right and left as one entered from the corridor. Stepping within the room two candelabra stands spread their gilt branches within a few feet of the doorway. They were about far enough apart for two persons, one wearing a wedding veil, to pass safely between them. These ornaments were flanked clear to the entrance with potted plants in great variety and color, so graded that the loftiest of them were shoulder high above the floor. Having passed this mass of flowers, with the flowering plants still towering ahead on either hand and the dark-green mass in front, a sight was presented at the mantelpieces which is said to have been as fine as any floral display ever made at the White House. On the hearth under the east mantel lay a mass of begonia rubra, whose scarlet blossoms were designed to represent a glowing fire. Centauras scattered at the base were meant for ashes. Extending out from these designs was a mosaic of blossoms on a lower plane, which carried out the idea of the tiled floor of the hearth. Vines ran from the hearth to the mantel, on which reposed a bank of dark pansies with the inscription "June 2, 1886," in light blossoms, reaching nearly the mantel's width. The mantel was edged with a double border of golden selaginella and an overhanging drapery of green leaves. The west mantel, directly across the room, was built by the florist also from the bottom, in a design similar to the other. The mantel top, however, presented a brighter sight with its solid bank of choice red roses, growing darker toward the centre, where, in white moss and hybrid roses, was inscribed the monogram "C. F." All the mirrors in the room were draped, festooned, and garlanded with roses, which decorated as well the doorways to the Green and Red Parlors and to the corridor. Over the corridor door hung a scroll of immortelles in national colors, inscribed "E Pluribus Unum."

Some of the Cabinet officers and many others who called at the White House during the afternoon were permitted to look at these decorations after they were in place. The view to most of the visitors had to be a hurried one, however, for the afternoon was late and the attendants were getting out the stands for the musicians and making the last preparations for the great event. Before 6 o'clock people began to gather around the entrances to the White House, and found to their surprise and pleasure that none of the 24 policemen and detectives on duty about the mansion was at either of the gates. No obstruction in the shape of a policeman was encountered until the steps leading to the big covered porch was reached. There half a dozen officers saw that no one not bidden to the marriage went any further. The people came by twos and threes, most of them being women, and massed themselves on the sidewalks on either side of the porch and on the broad driveway in front. There were enough sightseers to make a good showing, but at no time were there more than 200 or 250 persons in the throng. Many persons drove through the grounds and passed the house with heads craned forward. All they could see were the masses of palms and other plants which filled the windows of the East Room. The windows of the private dining room and other rooms in the east end of the building were closed and the curtains tightly drawn. Inside blinds, carefully closed, shut out any view of the vestibule. Conspicuous among those who drove by in carriages was Congressman Frank Lawler, of Chicago, who came up in an open barouche and had the driver pull up the horses while he took in the scene. With him were two ladies and three children. For half an hour or more the crowd had to satisfy its curiosity by staring at the members of the Marine Band, who came stringing along at their leisure, each wearing the scarlet coat, blue trousers, and blue cap which, with a long straight sword and plenty of white and red cords and tassels, made up his regulation full-dress uniform.

THE ARRIVAL OF THE GUESTS.

The first carriage which drove up to the entrance brought Col. Lamont, who skipped into the house with a happy smile on his face. The carriage was driven at a rattling pace, and 10 minutes later returned with Mrs. Lamont. After this some of the servants brought out a long and narrow strip of carpet, which sadly needed sweeping, and spread it from the door to the driveway. Then Secretary Lamar, concealing his dress coat under a big light overcoat, rode up in a one-horse carriage, tipped his hat to the correspondents standing near, and hurried into the house. A moment later the Rev. Dr. Sunderland, who was to tie the marriage knot, stepped out of his carriage and handed out Mrs. Sunderland. Then the curiosity seekers waited five minutes before the Post Office Department carriage came up and left Postmaster-General and Mrs. Vilas at the door. Close behind them came Mr. W. S. Bissell, who had come down from Buffalo to see his old law partner married and who carried into the mansion a smile which left nothing else of his countenance to be seen. Then came Secretary of War Endicott and Mrs. Endicott, who had waited until the footman had descended slowly from his box and opened the carriage door. The Secretary and his wife had hardly disappeared from the porch before Secretary Bayard stepped out of the State Department carriage and walked into the house with an overcoat over his arm. A moment later Secretary of the Navy Whitney and his wife reached the house. Right behind them came the carriage of Secretary of the Treasury Manning, who was paying his first visit to the White House since he was stricken down with what everybody feared was a fatal stroke of apoplexy. The footman sprang down to help the Secretary from the carriage, and when he had reached the pavement Mrs. Manning followed. His wife took the Secretary by the left arm, while one of the department messengers helped him on the other side, and thus aided he walked slowly and with a perceptible limp into the mansion.

When the door closed on Mr. and Mrs. Manning it was just five minutes to 7 o'clock, the hour appointed for the ceremony to begin. The people had kept careful count of the arrivals, and they missed Attorney-General Garland. Those who knew his determination never to be seen in a swallowtail coat did not wonder at his absence, but many in the crowd expected him, and on all sides remarks were heard upon the tardiness of the Attorney-General, coupled with the wish that if he was not on time the President would not wait for him.

While the crowd was waiting for the absent Cabinet officer the hour hands of the White House clocks touched 7. Almost at the second the Marine Band struck up Mendelssohn's "Wedding March" from the "Midsummer Night's Dream," and everybody knew that the marriage ceremony had begun. Some of the people left, but most of the crowd staid in the grounds listening to the music, which floated out despite the closed windows, and waited to see the guests depart. While listening to the wedding march they heard the steady booming of a national salute, which was fired at the arsenal, more than a mile away, and the ringing of all the church bells.

The Secretary of State and Miss Bayard followed Miss Cleveland and Mr. Bissell to the Blue Room as soon as the ladies had put aside their wraps. Then came the others of the Cabinet and of the household as constituted to-day, who have already been named. When they had assembled there, and while the wedding march was ringing through the building, the Rev. Dr. Sunderland joined the party, followed shortly by the President and the bride, who had been waiting for the march in the private dining room at the west end of the corridor. The assembled company formed in semicircle as the happy pair advanced, the President trying to look solemn and the bride coyly dignified.

THE BRIDE'S DRESS.

A description of the wedding dress as a fashion-maker would call off its essentials would be utterly inadequate to give an idea of the warmth and glow that it diffused amid the romance and poetry of to-night's associations. Accustomed as were the ladies gathered in the Blue Room to the dazzle of rich costumes, they could barely restrain expressions of wonder and admiration at the beautiful picture presented by the bride, whom their eyes followed with an interest so tender as to be almost worshipful from the moment of her approach toward the bridal room. Nature did more to make the picture pretty than had the art of the costumer, for the delicate profile of the bride, her shapely head and self-reliant carriage, all subservient to the timid look of her eyes, the compression of her well formed lips, and the statuesque firmness of her face, made the fabrics she wore a simple and harmonious drapery. It was the woman at whom the women looked rather than the dress. The two together made as lovely a sight as ever graced the White House. Like its wearer, elegance and simplicity were the conspicuous charms of the dress. Every one knows that it was of corded ivory satin, heavy enough to stand without a woman in it. The drapery of India silk served the double purpose of softening the gloss of the heavier material and rounding the outlines of her tall figure, without detracting at all from her grace and shapeliness. Under the bright glow of the illuminated rooms the play of the satin through the drapery was like the motion of water gently moving in the moonlight and was deliciously remindful of all that poetry has dreamed of sweethearts and brides. A band of orange flowers outlined the delicate drapery from behind. In front the bosom was crossed by a filmy muslin in soft scarfs, which terminated beneath a heavy fold of satin at the hip. Orange blossoms and buds and leaves so small as to make a bare outline bordered the drapery of the skirt, also duplicating the neat effect obtained by the same means above the waist. The train was a marvel of graceful arrangement, and it was marvelous how she handled it in a small, well filled room, for it was nearly as long as the room itself, and would have reached easily during the ceremony from the spot where the vows were pledged into the corridor through which the bridal party had come but for the bride's deft management, whereby it lay in a glistening coil close to her feet. Its length, as officially stated, was 15 feet. Gloves were the bride's only adornment for the arm below the elbow, the sleeves reaching only to the elbow. They were disposed to be flowing sleeves, but this appearance was subdued by bands of India muslin extending across, forming a plisse. Blossoms, buds, and orange leaves were delicately embroidered upon the elbow points with charming yet modest effect. It should be said of the silk tulle veil that it was large enough almost to envelope the bride, and was held to the head by a coronet. Behind its folds the bride could hide her agitation, and in that respect it heightened the prettiness and took nothing from the solemnity of the effect.

The bride's mother, who followed her to the Blue Room and stood beside her for the ceremony, looked like an older sister in her violet satin dress. The dress was becomingly set off with trimmings of white and a dazzling profusion of violet crystal pendants.

Miss Rose Cleveland, who stood at the other side, wore a tasteful combination of Nile green and cameo pink duchesse satin. The low corsage was adorned with pink roses, and her fan was of pink egret feathers. Light tan gloves extended nearly the length of the arm. She wore ornaments of silver.

The President's other sister, Mrs. Hoyt, was dressed in the color of the room of honor—robin's egg blue of china crêpe. It was relieved with trimming of rare old lace, and she carried a bouquet of French roses with great curling petals. The bride's cousin, Mrs. Rogers, looked charmingly in a cameo pink brocaded dress of a most delicate shade.

Mrs. Cadman, an aunt, was attired in white satin, en train, relieved by draperies of black lace. Her bouquet was of choice Jacqueminot roses.

Miss Huddleston's fresh face smiled above a bewilderment of blue ribbons, which trimmed her pink silk dress.

Mrs. Harmon, completing the list of lady relatives of the bride, wore light orange satin.

The friend and guest of Miss Cleveland, Miss Nelson, had a dress of corn-colored satin. The dress was cut pompadour, and had elbow sleeves. It was beautified by an overdress of antique lace. She carried Jacqueminots.

The pastor's wife, Mrs. Sunderland, wore light gray satin, en train, with square neck and elbow sleeves. It was tastefully trimmed with lace.

Mrs. Lamont, wife of the private secretary, shone in ivory satin, demi-train, cut square in the neck, and with elbow sleeves. The dress looked charmingly with its pearl trimmings on one side and its edging of crystal and jet at the corsage.

The ladies of the Cabinet stood rather in the background, where they bloomed with matronly elegance. Mrs. Manning appeared in white satin, high in the neck, and with elbow sleeves. The front was soft and fluffy, with trimmings of duchesse lace set off with pearls.

Mrs. Endicott's dress was of the same shade and material, with which contrasted fine draperies of black Chantilly lace and trimmings of silver and sapphire. From her hair rose a scarlet pompon.

Mrs. Whitney's bodice of violet velvet made a handsome appearance above a skirt of white satin and tulle, the skirt being embellished with violets.

Mrs. Vilas wore a light blue silk dress, the front trimmed with crystal and pearls and with point lace. The dress was cut round in the neck, rising high behind. Daises of silver ornamented the train.

THE WEDDING CEREMONY.

The last notes of the wedding march floated in from the corridor. The chatter of the guests had ceased as they fell back toward the south end of the room, naturally arranging themselves in an irregular double line in front of the forest of palms and azaleas. The President, with the bride leaning on his left arm, advanced to about the centre, standing just beneath the chandelier. The groom was self-possessed and happy and the bride as charming in her look of love and confidence as the most exacting person could have hoped. Not far from the bride's left stood Mrs. Folsom, and Secretary Bayard and Mrs. Hoyt were just beyond them. Further along the semicircle were Secretary and Mrs. Whitney, with Secretary Endicott and Mrs. Endicott a few steps beyond. Miss Cleveland was about in the turn of the circle, standing a little forward and not far from Dr. Sunderland. Next to her was Secretary Lamar and separated from him by one or two ladies was Secretary Manning. On account of his invalid condition a chair had been provided for Mr. Manning, but he scorned its use and stood during the entire ceremony. Further around toward the President's right, beyond a group of the relatives of the bride, stood Postmaster-General and Mrs. Vilas, and beyond was Mrs. Sunderland. Closest to the President's right stood Col. Lamont and Mrs. Lamont. The circle was made up without prearrangement. The Rev. Dr. Sunderland and the Rev. William N. Cleveland stood a few feet in advance of the brilliant semicircle.

As the clocks were striking seven and the guns from the arsenal were heard, announcing that the wedding hour had come, the bride and groom advanced. The Rev. Dr. Sunderland stepped forward to meet them. With hands uplifted and head raised he began the simple service with a prayer, dignified and stately, not short, but of moderate length only, composed in entire good taste and appropriate. Then, addressing the bride and groom together, he asked that the persons contemplating the solemn vows of matrimony should join hands. The President and Miss Folsom had each come into the room with their right hands ungloved, carrying the unused gloves in their left hands. The right hands were extended, the President clasping the hand of his bride as it was held confidingly out. With much grace and dignity the officiating clergyman folded his hand over the clasped hands of the bride and groom, and in deliberate speech propounded the inquiries to the groom, addressing him: "Do you, Grover, take this woman to be your wedded wife," and in form closely resembling the Episcopal ritual, asking him if he would cleave unto her until death did them part. While he addressed these questions to the groom the bride fixed her eyes upon him, wearing an expression of superb happiness. She looked at her best at that moment. The President bore himself with manly composure, and when the question was finished he responded, not with any apparent effort at peculiar enunciation, but in his own sturdy, honest, sincere way, "I will." The bride listened in turn to a repetition of the question to her, and clearly and sweetly answered in a distinct voice "I will." The ring was then called for. The President promptly searched his waistcoat pocket and produced the ring. The bride's hand was extended and the groom deftly placed it upon her finger. The Rev. Dr. Sunderland pronounced them husband and wife, with the injunction: "Whom God hath joined together let no man put asunder." The Rev. Mr. Cleveland then stepped forward and concluded the ceremony with an invocation of blessing upon the pair.

There was a pause. Miss Cleveland was the first to step forward to offer her congratulations to the couple. She was very cordial to both, and the President embraced her affectionately as she spoke to him. The immediate relatives of the bride then came forward, and after them, without any order, followed the others. The solemnity of the occasion was over. The cheerfulness that had marked the assembling of the party returned. A few moments sufficed to give all a chance to speak their greetings. The ladies kissed the bride to their heart's content, but the gentlemen followed the example of the groom and refrained. With a glance around the clusters of friends and a consulting glance at his bride, which was answered by an arch look that expressed readiness to go, the President extended his arm. The bride took it, and the two turned and led the way through the door opening upon the corridor. The President and Mrs. Cleveland led the way to the west end of the corridor and into an open door, the company following. This was the first time any but the immediate household had seen the dining room.

THE WEDDING FEAST.

A revelation in floral art confronted the assembly. The ship Hymen, carrying white flags with the monogram "C. F.," was floating in the middle of the table. That, at least, was the illusion, owing to the mirror on which the ship rested. Everything in color composed the ship, the mirror was the lake, scarlet blossoms and bits of coral stood for shoals and rocks, and the banks were made of Jacqueminots. Vases of roses, smilax, garlands, festoons, and everything to afford variety of design in color were used to set off the tables. There were masses of green in the corners and bays and blooming plants banked against the walls. The florist's art revealed new possibilities in the decoration of the four sideboards and the mantels were banks of roses. There was no such profusion of plants and flowers as in the Blue Room, but the guests agreed that the effect was hardly less fine. Beside the main table, which stood midway in the room, were small tables placed amid nooks of green for the convenience of groups. The bride and groom took chairs at the north side of the big table. Secretary Whitney and Mrs. Whitney sat near them. The party divided into small groups, Secretary Manning choosing a small vine-sheltered table most remote from the centre of interest. All talked and laughed like a bridal party in unofficial life, while terrapin and a lot of dainty French dishes, of which no one knew the name, but which all thought delicious, were served. Then, as if by a common impulse, the company rose to pledge the bride's health. This little ceremony, entirely without formality, was pledged with the most cordial feeling on the part of all. The bride bowed her acknowledgments sweetly. After about an hour Miss Cleveland plunged a knife into the wedding cake and began to pass around the favors. While this went on the bridal pair retired to prepare for their journey. The boxes have been described. Everything promised was there, including the autographs which the bridegroom and bride had found time to write during the day. This was not all the writing done by the bride, for she had prepared for a friend during the day a description of her wedding dress.

OFF FOR DEER PARK.

The guests did not tarry long in the dining room after the President and the bride retired, but dispersed themselves in the various parlors. They were having a good time by themselves when a porter came staggering down stairs under a heavy trunk. That was about 9 o'clock. In a moment the President descended and walked along the corridor. Mistaking his intention, several hands were thrust out from the parlors, and he got a shower of rice and an old shoe or so went through the air after him. He laughed, and went on to the East room, the company following. Presently the bride joined him, attired in a traveling suit of deep gray cloth over a gray silk petticoat. She looked quite jaunty as she toyed with the steel buttons of her waistcoat and adjusted her neck to the high standing collar behind the band of velvet which clasped her neck. Her hat was of the suit's color, trimmed with velvet and surmounted with peacock ribbon and ostrich feathers. She looked every inch a happy bride, and if ever a husband looked prouder than the President there is no record of him. Farewells were then said, and, leaning on her husband's arm, the bride was escorted down the steps at the south porch, commonly but erroneously called the back porch, and to the carriage in waiting. Then the rice and old shoes were fired in earnest, and, amid hand-clapping and cheers from the company, the carriage rolled off in the darkness. Meanwhile, the band was playing from "Lohengrin," "Maritana," Mendelssohn's Spring song, "Bright Star of Hope," and other airs, and a crowd was waiting on the Pennsylvania-avenue side of the White House in hope of seeing and cheering the President.

While the band played and the crowd waited the President and Mrs. Cleveland were whirling swiftly toward the Baltimore and Ohio Railroad station. It was a drive of two miles. They went by a long course and reached the station at 9:15. President Garrett's car Baltimore, with another coach and a combination baggage car, had been waiting for him for half an hour, and a lot of baggage had been stowed away to his credit, as well as a retinue of servants. As soon as the bride and groom stepped aboard, the train moved out, bound for Deer Park, where they expect to stay for a week, having hired a cottage for that time. Two pairs of horses and two carriages went to Deer Park yesterday from a livery stable here for the President's use. The turnouts were the finest to be had. Deer Park is purely a Summer resort on the crest of the Alleghanies, about 200 miles from here. It is a night's run on the railroad. The hotel season will not open there for three weeks, and this fact, coupled with the comparative inaccessibility of the spot, led the President to choose it in the evident hope of anticipating Summer tourists and securing for himself and bride a honeymoon in solitude.

NOTES OF THE BRIDAL.

The gifts to the bride and groom were many and rich, but they were not extravagant in number or value. None of them, except the gift of the President to the bride, was shown. This gift was a beautiful diamond necklace, which the bride exhibited with natural delight. Secretary and Mrs. Whitney presented a diamond spray of antique pattern, very curious and beautiful. Secretary and Mrs. Endicott sent four large and elegant silver candlesticks, of Ionic pattern. The gift of Secretary Lamar was a gold smelling bottle, set with diamonds. The gift of Secretary and Mrs. Vilas was a beautiful diamond ornament, to be worn as a brooch or converted into a pin for the hair. Mr. Bissell gave a rarely beautiful diamond pendant. About 60 others, many of which have not been unpacked yet because they were received when there was not time for their examination, were put aside to be enjoyed hereafter.

The attachés of the White House, some of whom have been employed there for years, trooped into the corridor during the service and by invitation witnessed the ceremony from the doors opening into the Red and Green Rooms. Among them was Mr. Loeffler, who holds the door against the approach of all callers upon the President. Arthur Simmons, the colored man who stands at Col. Lamont's door, and who knows nearly everybody who comes to the White House, enjoyed the sight more than he is able to tell. He was married on June 2 23 years ago, and he says it is a lucky day, for he secured his position in the Executive Mansion in 1865, and has held it during the Administration of all Presidents for 21 years. Attorney-General Garland, the only member of the Cabinet who did not attend the wedding, sent in his place a note of regret.

Prof. Sousa felt so sure yesterday afternoon that the Marine Band's services would be wanted at the wedding this evening that he made up a programme before night and submitted it to Col. Lamont. The official order to play at the White House was not received by the leader until nearly noon to-day. It was in the regular official form and came with the signature of Secretary of the Navy Whitney, the band being a part of the naval establishment. Prof. Sousa's confidence that the order would be issued led him to call together the 38 musicians, who, with their leader, comprise the full strength of the famous band. They met early in the forenoon and for over two hours were drilled in the music they were to render in the White House vestibule. When the Secretary's formal order was read Prof. Sousa was a little surprised to find that he and his men were not to appear as an orchestra, and to wear the usual evening dress of civilians, but that were to present themselves as a full military band, and to be dressed in their regulation full dress uniforms, with the bright scarlet coats and profuse display of cords and tassels. The order called upon them to report at the Executive Mansion at 6:15 o'clock, but Prof. Sousa was given to understand that no music would be wanted until the bride and groom were ready to take their places in the Blue Parlor to listen to Dr. Sunderland. He was also warned to provide a programme long enough to keep the band at work until 10 o'clock, when it was intimated the musicians would be invited to enjoy a wedding luncheon prepared for them at the President's thoughtful suggestion, and would then be dismissed. Prof. Sousa spent a good deal of time yesterday in getting up the musical programme, and he took care to leave out all airs from comic operas as being inappropriate to the occasion. What he wanted was something light and graceful that would grate on no one's ears. When Col. Lamont looked over the eight numbers on the programme as finally arranged, his musical knowledge could suggest no criticism, and so he laid the document carefully away and cautioned the band leader not to talk about it to anybody.

BEGINNING THE JOURNEY.

WASHINGTON JUNCTION, Md., June 2.—No attempt was made by those in charge of the Presidential train to make unusually fast time. None could be made, as the special was only about 20 minutes behind the regular passenger train leaving Washington at 8:55 P. M. There were, of course, no demonstrations along the route, for nobody knew the train was coming except a few telegraph operators who had caught some of the telegraphic orders flashed over the wires regarding the movements of the special. The start from Washington was so quietly effected that nearly all of those interested in knowing how, when, and where Mr. and Mrs. Cleveland left the capital were left in ignorance until the train was well on its way to the mountains. Two or three urchins who were playing near the cars tried to jump on as the train pulled out, but these were all who had to be put off. The run from Washington to this place was entirely devoid of incident.

CONGRATULATIONS FROM ABROAD.

LONDON, June 2.—The Queen has sent the following cable message to President Cleveland:

Pray accept my sincere congratulations on your marriage and my best wishes for your happiness. VICTORIA.

At the banquet of the Cloth Workers' Company this evening a cable dispatch was sent to President Cleveland congratulating him upon his marriage. Mr. Gillig, replying to a toast to President Cleveland, said: "It is with great pleasure that I acknowledge this compliment paid to President Cleveland on the happiest day in his life. I know well his longing to visit this country as soon as he is freed from the trammels of his high office. On his behalf I thank you for your good wishes."

MONTREAL, Quebec, June 2.—The vessels in the harbor were to-day decorated with bunting in honor of the wedding of President Cleveland, and most of them carried the American flag at the foremasthead.

FASHIONABLE WEDDINGS.

BOSTON, June 2.—The marriage of Sherman Hoar, son of ex-Attorney-General Hoar, to Caroline Prescott Wood, took place in the old town of Concord this evening. The ceremony was performed in the Unitarian Church by the Rev. Grinnell Reynolds. At 7:30 o'clock the bride entered the church leaning on the arm of her father, Mr. James B. Wood, and proceeded to the altar, where she was met by the groom and best man, Samuel Hoar, the elder son of Judge Hoar. The ushers were John L. Gilmore, Frank E. Cutter, Rockwood Hoar, Henry E. Warner, Dr. William Prescott, R. M. Bradlee, and Herbert Blanchard. The bride was elegantly attired in white satin, waist cut low, and filled in with point lace. She carried a bouquet of roses. After the ceremony a reception was held at the residence of the bride's parents. Among those present were Samuel Bowles, of the Springfield *Republican*, who married a daughter of Judge Hoar; Col. William Forbes, Mrs. Ralph Waldo Emerson, Louisa M. Alcott, T. Quincy Brown, the family of William M. Evarts, Judge George M. Brooks, George Fred Williams, Judge John T. Keyes, and many others of prominence. Mr. and Mrs. Hoar left this evening for an extended wedding journey.

The marriage of Henry Luce to Louisa Davis, daughter of the late Admiral Davis, was solemnized in Christ Church, Cambridge, this afternoon. The ceremony was performed by the Rev. William Lawrence. A reception followed at the residence of the bride's mother, on Quincy-street. Mr. and Mrs. Luce will reside on Pinckney-street, this city, in a new house recently built for her by her brother-in-law, Henry Cabot Lodge.

ATLANTA, Ga., June 2.—Miss Lizzie, the daughter of Senator Alfred H. Colquitt, was married to-day at the residence of her father, in Edgewood, to Capt. William L. Marshall, United States Army. The ceremony was performed by the Rev. Clement A. Evans, of Augusta, who was formerly a Major-General in the Confederate Army. There were 22 bridesmaids, among whom were two daughters of the Rev. T. DeWitt Talmage, of Brooklyn. All the ladies carried large bouquets of daisies and were dressed in white. The bridal couple left for Washington to-night.

BOSTON, June 2.—J. G. Cupples, senior member of the book house of Cupples, Upham & Co., of the historic old corner bookstore, was married to-day to Miss Harriet E. Nichols, daughter of Dr. James R. Nichols, a leading citizen of Haverhill. The wedding ceremony took place at Haverhill, in the North Church, and a large party of Boston literary people and other friends of the bride and groom went down in a special train. The church was beautifully decorated. As the bridal party entered and passed to the front of the altar the wedding march from Lohengrin was performed by the organist. Robert Grant, one of the brilliant group of younger novelists, whose first book "The Confessions of a Frivolous Girl," was published by Mr. Cupples, served as best man. The bride was dressed in rich satin duchesse, trimmed artistically with rare old point lace. The front of the skirt was laid in plats, and the train fell in graceful folds, the whole being enveloped in a long white bridal veil. She wore orange blossoms in her hair. The Rev. N. Boynton performed the ceremony, and a brilliant reception followed at the home of Dr. Nichols, which was attended by over 500 guests. Many beautiful presents were received by the couple. They started early in the evening on a wedding tour to be absent two or three weeks, and upon their return they will make their home in Boston.

VESSELS IN COLLISION.

HALIFAX, Nova Scotia, June 2.—The schooner L. P. Churchill, Capt. Murray, arrived at Halifax to-day from Demerara. She reports having been in collision last Saturday with a steamship belonging to the State Line. A dense fog prevailed at the time. The vessels were in latitude 41° 18′, longitude 64°. Capt. Murray says that the steamer was going at full speed and came upon him suddenly out of the fog, bearing directly down on the schooner. Those on the steamer observed the Churchill just in time to avert a catastrophe. The only damage received by the sailing vessel was the loss of her jibboom. In answer to a call from the steamer's deck Capt. Murray cried out that his hull was damaged, but the steamer did not slacken her speed and was soon lost sight of. The steamer was made out as hailing from Glasgow and is believed to have been either the State of Virginia or the State of Alabama.

THE RIDING CLUB REACH SARATOGA.

SARATOGA, N. Y., June 2.—The eight members of the New-York Riding Club who left New-York May 22 and since then have been riding through Connecticut, Massachusetts, and Vermont, arrived here this evening. They were received outside the village by a committee of citizens, headed by Gen. W. B. French, Capt. B. F. Judson, and Dr. W. H. Hall, who escorted them to the Windsor Hotel, where an elaborate dinner was served. Capt. Judson toasted the New-Yorkers and Howard Carroll and George C. Clausen responded on behalf of the club. To-morrow Sir Joseph Fuller, who is one of the party, will give a dinner to a number of friends in Troy, which is the next stage of the club's journey.

THE SIBERIAN SAFE.

ST. JOHN'S, Newfoundland, June 2.—The Allan Line steamer Siberian, so long overdue, arrived here at 5 o'clock this morning. She had been delayed by fogs and ice. The Siberian reports that when the fog lifted the vessel was surrounded by 60 huge icebergs and she was within 100 feet of an enormous ice mountain.

RENOMINATED FOR CONGRESS.

ELGIN, Ill., June 2.—The Republican Congressional Convention for the Fifth District of Illinois has renominated A. J. Hopkins, the present representative of the district in Congress.

EXPORT DUTY REDUCED.

OTTAWA, June 2.—The export duty on pine logs has been reduced from $3 per 1,000 feet to $2.

POWDERLY'S MEN ROUTED

THE CONVENTION CAPTURED BY THE HOME CLUB.

WAR UPON TRADES UNIONS DECLARED AND A BIG VICTORY ATTAINED BY THE WORST MEN IN THE ORDER

CLEVELAND, Ohio, June 2.—The Knights of Labor are about to enter upon a new era. Hitherto the course of the order has been the marvel of the age. Its aims so far as known were lofty and pure. It has been welcomed far and near by the workingmen as its savior. Though not a secret organization, its affairs have been conducted so discreetly that the public has been compelled to depend for its information regarding the condition as well as the principles of the order upon the utterances of the General Master Workman. Though not uniformly successful in defending the attitude of the order, Mr. Powderly has succeeded in creating the impression that the Knights of Labor was an educational organization, and his excuses that it was young in years and that its growth was abnormal were accepted in good faith by the public as sufficient to account for all mistakes. His warning to the order to beware of labor men who do not labor, defined, it was generally supposed, not only his own position but that of the order on all matters relating to labor. His retention in power seemed strongly in favor of the assumption that the conservative element in the order was strongly in the ascendant. The errors of the order were condoned the moment it was discovered that Mr. Powderly was apparently most anxious to prevent their recurrence. His plans were shown to the order, and that they might be stamped with its approval the special assembly which convened here last Tuesday and is still in session was ordered. The assembly was informed at the outset that the situation was critical. Mr. Powderly said so, and the delegates knew that he spoke the truth. He said that other labor organizations were alarmed at the sudden and tremendous growth of the Knights. He counseled moderation and asked for peace. He championed the cause of trades unions against his own, knowing that the Knights were not in condition for war. He made the oft-repeated declaration that the Knights of Labor was an educational body, and then admitted that this object had been overlooked. He might have added, in view of the subsequent action of the assembly, by men who were greedy for personal gain and cared nothing for the principles of the order. He characterized the strike and the boycott as suicidal, and warned his hearers that the Knights did not constitute the population of the country. He advocated several other important reforms, and did not forget to add that politics and the Knights were as widely disconnected as the poles. He made a plea for the enlargement of the General Executive Board on the ground that the order had outgrown its working force. He asked for intelligent, conservative men as assistants.

By its action the assembly has willfully disregarded the principles of the order. It has derided Mr. Powderly's call for help. It has plunged the order into politics. It has declared war upon the trades unions. It has declared its approval of strikes by amending the proposition to give the General Executive Board the sole power to order a strike by giving that power to the district assemblies "in cases of emergency." But of all the blunders this special assembly has made the worst blunder was made to-day. The effect of it will be so serious that many Knights of Labor believe it will eventually smash the order, while some of the coolest heads among them admit that it will cast serious discredit upon it and make its immediate future at least troublous and uncertain. It is admitted on all hands that this has been the most disastrous week in the history of the order, and leading Knights confessed to THE TIMES's correspondent to-night that the convention had been captured by the worst element in the order. New-York Knights declared openly to-night that the doom of the order in New-York was sealed, and trade unionists who are still on the ground state that the unions might as well prepare for war.

The great blunder of the convention was its selection of additional members of the General Executive Board. The board is, as far as the order will allow it to be, the ruling power. Mr. Powderly has been handicapped by the men who form the present board. Mr. Bailey may have proved an efficient Chief of Police of Shawnee, Ohio, though not all of Shawnee's citizens will admit this; but he has not shown that he possessed executive ability of even the lightest calibre. He is a fighter, a native of Northumberland County, England, and is not averse to convincing an opponent by an exhibition of physical strength. His last official act of importance was to prolong the railroad strike in the Southwest until a majority of the men could not find employment, and the order is now asked to support them. In this work he was assisted by John W. Hayes, the retail tea merchant of New-Brunswick, N. J., another member of the board, and also to a slighter extent by Thomas B. Barry, of Saginaw, Mich. These with Secretary Turner and Mr. Powderly form the old board. Mr. Powderly is the only member of the board who has jumped out of obscurity. His assistants are mere routine workers. They have all been described by Knights of Labor here as "narrow waisted," though it must be said for Mr. Turner that he is almost as broad as he is long. The stock in trade of at least three members of the board is an amusing air of mystery and an air of thoughtfulness which fits badly. They opened the campaign here with mystery. The other delegates, with few exceptions, were infected. The assembly took extraordinary precautions to keep its work secret. Each delegate was warned not to disclose the business of the convention. A press committee was appointed, and it was so enwrapped in orders and obligations that it seldom had any news except of the baldest and most uninteresting character. The convention even appointed a committee to discover how the story of the Home Club's alleged methods obtained circulating outside of the charmed circle of the Knights. The latter are not yet aware that the circulars from which all this information was procured have appeared in the TIMES. The exposé created a profound sensation here. Only a comparatively small number of Knights outside of New-York knew anything about the scandal. New-York Knights say that the charges against the Home Club, so far as its attempt to seize the management of the order is concerned, are true. The accused Knights demanded an investigation and it has already begun and will be continued in New-York. They seem conscious of their power, and to-day demonstrated that they are not friendless and forlorn but powerful to a degree which has actually dazed the conservative element in the convention.

Secretary Turner denied a couple of nights ago that he was the candidate of the Home Club, yet to-day he left his place in the convention and lobbied for the candidates of the club. This morning the convention began balloting for the six additional members of the General Executive Board. It was decided that the additional members should be elected separately. The importance of the positions was well known and Mr. Powderly did not doubt that the men he favored would be chosen. He made a mistake. He made a discovery also. He found that he was not on the side of the majority in his own board. Barry was the only man in it who stood by him or seemed to appreciate the gravity of the situation. Turner, Bailey, and Hayes, in campaign language, threw off their coats for the men who are to be investigated for an alleged attempt to secure the management for their personal aggrandizement. The thoughtful men of the order were alarmed at the aspect of affairs and made a desperate effort to elect men who could be depended upon to act for the best interests of the order. They were almost panic-stricken and thoroughly disheartened at the result. They were routed; in spite of its reputation the Home Club won. But four new members were elected to-day, so much time was consumed in skirmishing.

The new members of the board are James E. Quinn, of New-York, who is spoken of so often and not so highly in Morrison's circular; Hugh Cavanaugh, of Cincinnati, W. H. Mullin, of Richmond, Va., and David R. Gibson, bricklayer, of Hamilton, Canada. Mullin's opponent was George H. Murray, of New-York, one of the most intelligent men in the convention. He was beaten by a vote of 66 to 65. Mullin is the editor of a labor paper at Richmond, and was the candidate of the Home Club. Cavanaugh is a shoemaker. He beat Joseph Buchanan, of Denver, editor of the *Enquirer*, an ex-member of the board and a man of some force of character. Buchanan was beaten by 25 votes. He and Murray were defeated by the Home Club and its allies on account of their conservative and conciliatory attitude toward the trades unions. They wanted peace with honor. Quinn was elected by one vote. His opponent was A. A. Carlton, of Boston, a general lecturer of the order and Past Master Workman of District Assembly No. 30 of Boston. Carlton has been considered one of the strong men of the order, and his defeat was a perfect knock-down to the Powderly men. Quinn lives in the building in which Justus Schwab has his saloon. He is a bookbinder. Some of the New-York delegates claim that he is an Anarchist. He masqueraded at a public meeting held on the square here last night as "Monroe." Mystery is the chief stock in trade

The New-York Times.

VOL. XXXVI.....NO. 11,007. NEW-YORK, SUNDAY, DECEMBER 12, 1886.---QUADRUPLE SHEET. PRICE THREE CENT

OLD WORLD NEWS BY CABLE

UNIONISTS THE CAUSE OF COERCION IN IRELAND.

DRIVEN TO IT BY THE LOGIC OF THEIR SITUATION—THE FUTURE OF THE LEAGUE—TOPICS TO COME BEFORE PARLIAMENT—NOTES ON MINOR AFFAIRS.

BY COMMERCIAL CABLE FROM OUR OWN CORRESPONDENT.

Copyright, 1886, by the New-York Times.

LONDON, Dec. 11.—It is nonsense, says Lord Salisbury, to talk of the tenants in the West of Ireland being oppressed or badly used. Nobody seeks to compel them to pay rents beyond their ability. If they can't pay they can go. A volume couldn't state more succinctly or describe more graphically the broad and lofty view of the Tory Premier on the Irish question. Since Marie Antoinette asked why the foolish people who were starving for want of bread did not eat cake there has been no other parallel for the grasp of the subject which Lord Salisbury shows. If he could put himself in the place of one of Lord Clanricarde's mountain cotters on a farm which never produced food enough for a family half fed and half clothed, with nothing but the leaking roof of a mud hut between them and the Winter storm, perhaps his easy phrase of pay or go would not strike him as such a complete and satisfactory settlement of the Irish problem. But Lord Salisbury is not wholly to blame for the fact that he learned nothing in the years when he earned his own living and is unable now to see any rights in the world save those of landed property. Why should the owner of Hatfield House be expected to have a keener eye for the dim and unfamiliar outlines of human rights than John Bright, George Trevelyan, and Mr. Chamberlain possess? I say nothing of Lord Hartington, who was bred to the purple, or of Banker Goschen, whose hereditary genius for the part of Shylock goes unquestioned. But if the Radicals, like others sprung from the people and trusted heretofore by the people, cannot see the right of the matter, it is not strange that Salisbury is blind.

The truth is, it is the Liberal Unionists who are pushing their Tory allies down the fatal incline toward the chaos of coercion. If they had the power all in their hands, the Tories would not be specially harsh toward Ireland. Indeed they might easily try and seek a compromise with the Parnellites, for they belong to the party whose principles—since Disraeli's time at least—are wholly opportunist; but the Unionists are under a cruel obligation to be logical. The necessity of justifying their secession weighs heavily on them. Hence it is that they feel forced to demand the most stringent measures of repression in Ireland. Hence it is that the *Chronicle*, which only a year ago was the organ of the democracy of London, leads all the Tory papers in the fierceness of its shouts for swift coercion. I doubt if, in the whole course of Irish history, more mean, cold-blooded, merciless things have been said about the country than were spoken at Tuesday's meeting and banquet. The old adage of the ferocity and bigotry of converts does not altogether explain the virulence of their attitude, for the bulk of them are not converts at all. In private confidences they deplore the miseries of Ireland as deeply as anybody, but they are filled with the idea that their public importance demands a consistent policy and are driven by the logic of their position to favor coercion, since it has become plain to all that theirs is no half-way house between that and home rule. So, alas, we have John Bright crying out for dragoons to cut down the starving peasantry, and Trevelyan framing excuses for rapacity on the part of rackrenting absentee landlords.

It is now that the full measure and importance of the fight which put Walsh in the chair of Laurence O'Toole becomes evident. If one of the English sycophants had been put in instead the League would now be crushed, with its leaders in prison and the whole island lying under martial law. If Rome is disposed to catechise Dr. McGlynn's views on land I wonder what it thinks of this higher prelate, who openly espoused and defends the *United Ireland* plan of campaign and outcrokes Croke in the firmness and frankness of his expressions of sympathy with the tenants. "Hereafter," says the *Saturday Review*, "as cheating on the turf is called welching, so the embezzlement of rents will be called walshing." The characteristic flout shows how grave a wound the Archbishop's arrow made. It is an open secret that the Government, which weeks ago, as I told you, resolved on proclaiming the League, still holds its hand because Walsh's attitude puts the whole Catholic Church in Ireland back of the League, and in case of attempted suppression would make every chapel in Ireland a meeting place for branches of the interdicted organization. The Ministry quite intelligibly shrinks from undertaking the thankless task against such odds. To suppress the League now means practically to re-enact the anti-Catholic penal laws of William and Anne. Ashbourne and Goschen perhaps do not object to this, but nobody else in or out of Parliament is ready to follow them; so the chances remain against a proclamation of the League. It still may be resorted to, but only on the Ministerial theory that it is better to do a thing foredoomed to be abortive than nothing at all.

As for the Irish, as I said last week, they are definitely confident that whatever might be the case with a genuinely strong Government it is no Hicks-Beach who will terrify them as a ruler, no little Hughie Holmes who will puzzle and trap them as a lawyer. They feel themselves to be both bolder and shrewder than the men opposed to them at the Castle, and have no fear as to the outcome of the game with them. There is less clearness of opinion regarding Irish legislation. At the commencement of the session here the Unionists, who have locked their minds on this subject and thrown the key away, can exert a malignant influence far beyond their proportionate numbers and weight, and there is no telling what this may not accomplish—that is to say, assuming that the prophets are right in believing Ireland to be the chief and sole topic of discussion during the coming session.

This is by no means certain. It is undoubtedly true, so far as domestic matters are concerned, but the foreign question is likely soon to claim a solitary place in Parliamentary attention. The Bulgarian delegation will probably time their leisurely tour of Europe so as to be here when the session begins. They are peculiarly qualified to enlist English sympathies, for the most of them speak English perfectly, being graduates of Roberts College. This ought also to interest Americans, for the assertion comes from both Alexander of Battenberg and the Turkish Minister here that the whole movement of Bulgarian independence is directly due to that distinctively American institution. There is scarcely a man identified with the present Regency Government who is not under 40, and an Alumnus of Roberts. They form a class by themselves and are practically the only educated class in Bulgaria, and from their American training have learned what the ignorant Bulgar peasantry do not realize, that Russian despotism is just as hateful as Moslem tyranny. When these resolute, brave, wise young patriots come to England and tell here in the English tongue of their trials and aspirations, there need be no fear that their words will fall on deaf ears.

I get a hint that Austria is quietly moving to have the Bulgarians elect Prince Ferdinand of Saxe-Coburg, who is a Lieutenant in the Eleventh Austrian Hussars. He was born in Vienna, his age is 25, he is unmarried, and is handsome, popular, and highly eligible. If this is done it is likely that Russia will veto it or get Turkey to do so, which would serve to put Russia still more in the wrong and give Austria further ground for quarrel. Kalnoky has formally recognized the legality of the Sobranje. Hence, for Russia to reject an Austrian subject elected to the throne on the pretext of the illegality of the Sobranje would be a clear affront.

I believe the plan to be, if Russia rejects Ferdinand, the Sobranje is to recall Alexander. Austria is reluctant to consent to this, but England greatly desires it, and it may be that Kalnoky will eventually yield rather than take the responsibility of the initiative of war for the sake of putting Ferdinand on the throne. Turkey continues to play the melancholy and despicable part of a courtesan striving to placate all parties to the fight. The Armenian Gadban is working hard at Sofia in the Russian interest, but I understand White's reports from Constantinople express confidence that the Sultan will be all right when the time comes.

When the time comes is the scare. This is the phrase which haunts all Europe. Moltke's grave words of warning have sent all the Bourses on the Continent down like quicksilver. Nothing has come to reassure them. From two private sources in the north of Germany I learn of general officers who have arranged to move their families to Holland and England this Winter, thus arranging affairs in the full conviction that there will be war in the Spring. More and more people, everywhere, are reluctantly coming to believe this. The Germans are especially nervous over the prospect, having everything at stake. The belief is that the next war will be one the brunt of which will be borne by the cavalry, mounted infantry, and light artillery. Both the French and Russians have been greatly developing these branches. The Russians are said to have 90,000 cavalry ready to burst into Gallicia and Silesia, while the French concentrations of horse at Chalons sur Marne, Besançon, Bourges, and Sedan, attract much attention. The Germans do not forget that 20 years after the death of the Great Fritz, the wonderful military machine he constructed was knocked all to pieces at Jena, largely because the French had a leader whom they liked. There is much anxiety lest Boulanger may exert the same magnetic power and contrive a dash in force which would break the German lines and carry the war into the Fatherland. Hence elaborate and earnest preparations are making on both sides of the Rhine for a combat which will be truly a battle of giants when it comes.

President Cleveland's and Secretary Manning's remarks on fiscal affairs have been read here with great attention, and are commended universally as above the average of official utterances. There is little or no feeling here discernible on the fisheries question. The English have no special regard for the Canadians at best, and just now are too busy with Ireland and Russia to take the smallest interest in the question of cod bait. If public feeling controlled Iddesleigh, instead of red-tape traditions, he would settle the matter promptly on any reasonable basis proposed from Washington.

The Campbell case wearies and disgusts everybody, but the stockholders of evening papers will reap a rich harvest. There is an understanding that next week, if Lady Colin's case seems likely to fail, her counsel will produce letters which will make it impossible for Lord Colin ever to live in Britain again, even if they do not send him to prison.

The Japanese Princes, one of whom is an uncle of the Emperor of Japan, visited "The Mikado" last evening, and gazed in rather mystified gravity at the burlesque for some time, but finally saw the section of a joke.

Mr. Gladstone's health is said to be perfect and his voice has been much strengthened. He intends personally to lead his party in the coming session, at least for the opening weeks, and is preparing a great speech, which later will be circulated as a pamphlet throughout the kingdoms.

Early in February "The Pickpocket" will be withdrawn from the Globe and succeeded by a new comedy by Brandon Thomas and M. Duveray.

Ellen Terry resumed the rôle of Margaret at the Lyceum last night.

It is now definitely settled that Mary Anderson will make a provincial tour, opening in the Autumn in London under the management of Michael Gunn.

H. M. Imans has been engaged by D'Oyly Carte to play Pooh-Bah in "The Mikado."

Camille Saint-Säens has been in London during the week. The celebrated French composer has taken great interest in the concert given exclusively of his works by Herr Peiniger.

The Carl Rosa season of English opera at Drury Lane will be begun on May 2. During the season Corder's new opera, "Nordisa," will be given.

Frank Thornton has arrived in London from Australia. His tour there with "The Private Secretary" has been one of the most successful ever played in the antipodes.

It is whispered in the highest theatrical circles that Wilson Barrett, on his return to London, will not resume his position as lessee and manager of the Princess's Theatre. No details are given, but the report is generally believed to be correct. H. F.

ON TRIAL FOR CONSPIRACY.

NEW-HAVEN, Conn., Dec. 11.—The City Court room was crowded again to-day when the trial of Superintendents Wallace and Opdyke, charged with conspiracy to injure Thomas T. Meaney by blacklisting him, was resumed. Peter E. Bowman, Freight Agent of the New-York, New-Haven and Hartford Railroad, was the first witness. He testified that both he and Wallace had the power to employ or discharge men. He declined to answer whether he discharged Meaney or not, but stated that Meaney was not exactly discharged, being simply sent away to get a letter from Superintendent Opdyke, of the Northampton Road, by whom he had been discharged the month before. The witness further testified that he had been told by Superintendent Opdyke that Meaney had acted in a mean way in leaving his work. He also said on cross-examination that Superintendent Wallace had never ordered him to discharge Meaney. Attorney Ely, for the defense, then asked for a discharge for his clients on the ground that no combination had been proved between Superintendents Wallace and Opdyke. Judge Pickett declined to discharge the prisoners. After setting Dec. 21 as the day for hearing argument, the court adjourned.

A POOR REPORTER.

LANCASTER, Penn., Dec. 11.—In the editorial room of the *New Era* office this afternoon Samuel M. Sener, the court reporter, was assaulted by Charles Macnay, a prominent young grocer of this city. Macnay claimed that Sener, in reporting the case of embezzlement against J. Slater Erb, in which he was prosecutor, did him an injustice by omitting important testimony and misrepresenting the case generally, and yesterday he demanded a correction, which was promised, but not given. This afternoon he visited the editorial room and asked Sener if he proposed to make the correction. Sener replied that he would not, and Macnay struck him twice in the face, knocking him from his chair. Sener made no attempt to defend himself, but crawled under the table and as he emerged on the other side Macnay struck him again. Then the news editor came to Sener's assistance and held Macnay until the compositors who were summoned by his calls for help entered the editorial room. After treating Macnay pretty roughly they allowed him to depart and he left without his hat, which had been lost in the mêlée. Neither of the men was much hurt, but Mr. Macnay will probably not attack a reporter in his own office soon again.

TALK OF THE DAY IN PARIS

GOBLET'S HARD TASK AND THE NEW PLAY BY SARDOU.

BOULANGER COMING TO THE TOP—THE POINT HE HAS CARRIED—SARDOU TALKS ABOUT HIS PIECE.

By Commercial Cable from Our Own Correspondent.

PARIS, Dec. 11.—The *Lanterne* seems to give expression to the general impression of M. Goblet and his Ministry when it says: "We give the little Minister from Amiens 60 days." This extreme Radical prophecy of short life is matched by the sullen opposition of the organs of the Right, which shows that Goblet will not be able to break the mischievous and unnatural union of these two factions. Of course epigrams on the situation abound. It has already occurred to almost every Parisian journalist to say the new Ministry is the play of "Hamlet" with the Prince (who is M. de Freycinet) omitted. One jibe runs that M. de Freycinet was always liable to be tipped out by fortuitous chance, but it is only by such a chance that Goblet can stay in. To-day, however, badinage is yielding to a more serious view, as the difficulty had in filling the Foreign Office begins to shed significance on the situation. M. Floquet would have accepted the Premiership—nay, he did accept on condition the step was approved at St. Petersburg—but M. Laboulaye wired back that the Czar had not forgotten that M. Floquet was the man who publicly insulted his martyred father by the famous cry of "Vive la Pologne, Monsieur," and that Russian friendship would be impossible with him at the head of affairs. Hence the final selection of Goblet, who has offended nobody but the priests, actors, and Anarchists. But when Goblet tried to get a Foreign Minister the fat was in the fire. M. de Freycinet laughed at his request that he take the place. M. Duclerc was much obliged to him, but had other engagements; besides his selection would create a rupture with Germany.

M. Courcel was invited, but he refused unless the Duc d'Aumale was invited to return to France. This Boulanger overruled on a threat of resignation, so Courcel was impossible. How the place will be filled is not yet known, but the hitch suffices to show the public how delicate and dangerous the country's foreign relations are.

It shows even more clearly how like a colossus Gen. Boulanger bestrides the situation. The only man in the past Cabinet who dwarfed him was M. de Freycinet. In the new Cabinet he will be head and shoulders over all the rest, including the Premier. It is everywhere known that he decreed the refusal of the Council's offer and himself entered the new Cabinet on the onerous condition that the Ministry should adopt as its own his demand for an immediate extra vote of $60,000,000 for arming the French soldiers with the new repeating rifle and strengthening the Savoyard defenses. Whoever else may suffer, his position seems sure as long as the Goblet Ministry survives. He is the biggest man in it, and when it falls, either he will dictate its succession, or, if there is a dissolution of the Chamber, his name will be the strongest in France to conjure with in the elections, and the new Chamber will contain a large party ready to rally round him as the savior of the country.

A new piece by Sardou is always a chief event of the Paris theatrical season. "Crocodile" is to be a tremendous affair in five acts and three times five tableaus, thirty-four characters (not supers, any of them) and a heap of money to be spent on scenic effects without precedent and wondrous costumes. Sardou is a stickler for scenery. He sets his face against dress rehearsals before even a select few and often makes a radical change at the last moment. He is the scene shifter, stage manager, and pantomimist of his own characters, and he has even been known to dance in the front row at a rehearsal one of his own incidental ballets. At home at Marly he sits in his study like an alchemist in a laboratory. It may be said, indeed, that his plots are often mere experiments flung aside mercilessly if the philosopher's stone of a Famille Benoiton, a Théodora, or a Rabagas is not seen at the bottom of the crucible or in the transparent balloon of the report.

I managed to have an interview with Sardou to-day on the coming presentation of "Crocodile," about which Paris that enjoys itself is now itching with curiosity, but I fancy that Paris will have to wait a few days still before knowing anything of the production, and I only owe my own knowledge to the fact that I made Sardou furious by hinting that "Crocodile," in the opinion of some people, was only a warmed-up edition of "Foul Play" and "The Overland Route."

"What!" cried the pallid dramatist, throwing off his black velvet smoking cap, "are these accusations of plagiarism never to cease? Because there is a steamer in 'The Overland Route,' and a desert island in 'Foul Play' am I to be accused of going to modern English authors for my pieces? The British stage has done me the honor to knock at my door, but I have never ventured to pay them a return visit."

"I should like to be able to lay low this ghost, *cher maître*, by having some notion of 'Crocodile.'"

"Well I will do enough to satisfy the English-speaking world on that score. You may find one or two characters dead and buried when the first night comes on, for I kill, marry, acquit, and condemn ruthlessly as I go on; but of this you must take your chance. The 'Crocodile' in question is a ship in the Dutch service trading to Batavia, having on board a goodly show of passengers. Let me say something of my passenger list, for all have their say in the first act. In the first place we have Richard Kolt, the leading part, played by Marais. Richard is in love with Liliane, (Mlle. Legault.) Mlle. Leriche is an Englishwoman of a very flaring pattern. The daughters of America are represented by Miss Olivia, (Mlle. Baretty,) who is equally overcharged with national qualities rarely seen off the stage and so cool that in every emergency she takes notes. M. Jimmy (M. Berton) is the doctor of the ship, in love with Olivia. We have besides Mme. Jordaens, (Mlle. Claudia,) a widow; Peter Becque, (M. Frances,) a voluble French lawyer; a grotesque clergyman, (M. Boudier;) and two married couples who have left France to make their fortunes somehow. The wife of one of these, Gabrielle Bertholin, is played by the handsome Jeanne Delorme. I pass over the sailors and one Strapoulos (M. Herbert) who will become prominent further on. The 'Crocodile' is steaming on gayly and the audience is enjoying the social satire with which the dialogue literally reeks when crack! the vessel catches fire and the passengers are rescued. The boats are seen taking them away. It is not quite certain yet whether the Captain is to die in the wreck or not. This may cast a shadow over the piece, but we must only wait and see. And now, so far, do you see anything like 'Foul Play,' or your 'Overland Route'?"

"Oh, dear, no. I retract not only in my own name, but in the name of your accusers."

"The second act," continued Sardou, getting animated, "is upon an island where we find our passengers reduced to expedients. The stylish Widow Jordaens does the cooking; the handsome Gabrielle turns to washing, and we see the elements of modern society brought back to their original roughness. Here we dip into politics. A President is elected. This is Richard Kolt. The glib lawyer Peter Becque has his say all round, and, with the exception of Gabrielle, who puts in a blank voting paper, all share in the hope of a form of government worthy of the name; but alas! the sailors, ship carpenters, and others take the same view that M. Jules Grévy did many years ago—that no President is wanted. In the third act the Executive is at work when the curtain rises. Gabrielle and the widow have a tremendous lawsuit. Peter Becque is of course to the front. He pleads as if he were at home in court. As far as I can judge from the rehearsals, M. Frances will be wonderful in this part. At the end of the act comes a resolution worked up by Strapoulos, who urges the sailors to overthrow the President, and indeed the whole Government.

"I need scarcely tell you," continues Sardou, "that my passengers are rescued by a passing vessel, and that the love element of the piece now becomes in the ascendant. There is a big love scene between Kolt and Liliane, admirably rendered by Marais and Legault. The dénouement is humorous. Apart from the serious interest attached to the obtaining of a fortune by Kolt and his marriage to Liliane, one marriage was solemnized by a clergyman on the island, who now turns out to be a fraud; he is really a drummer for Cologne water. So much for my 'Crocodile.'

"Oh, by the way," added Sardou, as he was shaking hands, "I forgot to tell you that M. Massenet is providing music to accompany the new work. French pieces have always lacked the support of music, and this, at least, we borrow from your own 'Macbeth' and 'Midsummer Night's Dream.' There the piracy begins and ends. Au revoir."

To-night's dinner gathering of English-speaking journalists in Paris is the first step toward organizing a club on the basis of the Savage, of London, and the Lotos, of New-York. The project is an old one. Hitherto it has failed through rivalries and jealousies. To obviate the vexed questions of precedence, to-night's dinner will have no Chairman.

More elaborate preparations than usual are made for the celebration of the holidays. The shops are sumptuous with displays, and have an encouraging amount of patronage. It seems as if the shows of Paris had turned a corner from the path of depression so long traveled.

HEMMED IN BY FIRE.

TERRIBLE EXPLOSION IN A STEAM SUPPLY STATION.

BOSTON, Dec. 11.—Shortly before 7 o'clock this morning a terrible explosion occurred in the steam supply station of Hazlett & Underwood, at East Cambridge, by which several men were seriously wounded and two were probably injured fatally. On First-street are several large furniture factories which receive their power from Haslett & Underwood's station. The power station was a building about 40 feet square, three stories in height, and was scarcely more than a wooden shell. In the boiler room was an immense bin piled high with shavings, which were the fuel used under the boilers. There was a number of workmen in the engine room this morning when the explosion took place, men who were employed in the neighboring factories and who had stopped on their way to work. The explosion occurred without a moment's warning, and the unfortunate men present were shrouded in one great sheet of flame. There was no way of escape until outside assistance was rendered. The building was soon a mass of fire, and the cries and shrieks of the imprisoned men were heart-rending. The southerly wall soon fell outward, and as soon as possible the unfortunate men were dragged from the ruins.

Harry Newhall, the engineer, was standing near the shaving bin when the explosion occurred, and was fairly covered with burning shavings. He managed to rush out, a mass of flames, and threw himself into the snow, rolling over until the fire was extinguished. He was fearfully burned, the flesh hanging in bloody strings from his arms, while his hair was completely burned off. He may possibly recover, although at a late hour to-night his case was considered critical. Fireman Albert Murray was badly scorched on the head and body, but will recover. Joseph Sears was badly burned, but his injuries are not considered fatal. Joseph Livenzca, 19 years of age, was horribly burned about the face, hands, and neck, and the hospital surgeons say he cannot possibly recover. The cause of the explosion is a mystery. It may have been caused by a spark in the shaving bin, or, as the room had no ventilation, it may have been caused by the generation of inflammable gas from the great pile of sawdust. The loss to the building will be fully $2,000.

WOODBRIDGE'S POSTMASTER.

WOODBRIDGE, N. J., Dec. 11.—James Freeman received his commission as Postmaster of this place yesterday and thus ended one of the most exciting and bitter personal contests that ever stirred the hearts of the people of this normally quiet village. The fight has been entirely Democratic in name and nature, and it all arose over the removal of the office from its long established position in the Masonic Hall building by D. P. Carpenter, who was appointed only a short time ago to succeed a Republican, and who now has to step down and out for his action in removing the office. The friends of the Masonic Hall position, led by ex-Assemblyman Savage, a son of George W. Savage, Consul to Belfast, had been using every means to have the office brought back, but without avail. Finally the ex-Assemblyman laid out plans to have Carpenter removed, and how successful he has been was seen yesterday, when his man Freeman took charge of the office, which is now in Main-street, and many of the most interested business men think it by far the best situation. The office will undoubtedly be brought back to the hall.

THE INDIANA ELECTION CASES.

INDIANAPOLIS, Dec. 11.—Judge Ayers, of the Civil Circuit Court, was expected to give his decision in the Lieutenant-Governorship case to-day, but has postponed it until Monday. The case will go to the Supreme Court in any event.

The examination of Messrs. Coy, Bernhamer, Spaan, and Counselman, charged with complicity in the Marion County election frauds, was begun to-day, but the defense interposed a demurrer that the facts stated did not make a crime against the United States, upon which the day was consumed in argument, the proposition being that the fraud must affect a Federal candidate in order to give the Commissioner jurisdiction. The Commissioner announced that he would give his decision on Monday. In his charge to the Grand Jury Judge Woods interpreted the law to give the Federal court jurisdiction of the offense, following the law as adjudicated in the Mackin case in Chicago. The case for the disbarment of Bernhamer for his complicity in the crime comes up before Judge Woods on Monday.

SENECAL'S APPEAL DISMISSED.

MONTREAL, Dec. 11.—A special cable dispatch says the appeal of L. A. Senecal, in the case of Hatton against Senecal, has been dismissed by the Privy Council. Action was taken by Mr. Hatton for the restoration of 35 bonds of the Montreal, Portland and Boston Railway Company, of the nominal value of $1,000 each. In default of producing the bonds it was asked that the defendant be condemned to pay $35,000, together with the amount of the interest coupons, &c. In the Superior Court the pretensions of the plaintiff, Mr. Hatton, were fully maintained, and Mr. Senecal was ordered to return the bonds or pay the amount claimed. Mr. Senecal appealed from the decision to the Privy Council.

THE COMSTOCKS DOWN.

SAN FRANCISCO, Cal., Dec. 11.—Mining stocks were all better this morning, excepting Consolidated Virginia, Sierra Nevada, and Utah. The first named opened at $37, the same as it closed last night, but dropped to $34 50, recovering to $36, to finally close at $33. Sierra Nevada opened 25 cents lower, closing at $8, a loss of 75 cents. Utah was weak at $9, at which it closed. The other stocks were strong, the advance ranging from 75 cents to $2 25 a share.

A LARGE BUILDING FALLS.

THE RUINS TAKE FIRE AND THREE MEN SUPPOSED TO BE LOST.

ST. LOUIS, Dec. 11.—About 2:30 o'clock this afternoon the roof of Shapleigh & Cantwell's hardware store, No. 414 to No. 420 North Main-street, fell in, carrying the four floors beneath it to the basement. The fourth floor was loaded with agricultural implements, the third with shelf goods, and the second with sample goods. Immediately after the crash the ruins caught fire from the boiler in the basement, and a general alarm was sounded, summoning the entire Fire Department. The water thrown on the Shapleigh building seemed to have no effect, and the firemen directed their attention to saving the adjoining buildings. A report quickly spread that at least a dozen men had been buried in the ruins, and the enormous crowd which had gathered in the vicinity looked on with horror. Men stood within 20 feet of the burning mass with the huge lines of hose emptying their contents into the roaring furnace. Shortly after the fire started the north wall of the building fell in, which materially lessened the danger to the firemen and made easier the work of saving the adjoining buildings, and by 3:30 the fire was under control. During the fire there was a constant fusillade of cartridges which were stored in the burning building, but the walls prevented the bullets from injuring any one. Most of the inmates of the building escaped with slight bruises, and as far as can be learned to-night only three are missing. They are John Mahan, porter; Arthur W. Palmer, clerk; Charles E. Reid, clerk.

Fireman Russell says that when he arrived on the scene he saw a man in the third story with the flames all around him. When he looked up an instant afterward the man had disappeared, and he supposes he must have fallen back into the burning building and perished. There were several narrow escapes. Walter B. Kincaid was standing in the archway between Nos. 416 and 418 when the first crash came and was struck by some of the débris, but escaped into the street. Joseph Furlong, an employe, was on the fourth floor, and was carried with the débris to the second floor, from whence he escaped with a broken leg. A man named Carpenter was assisted out badly injured and taken to a doctor's office. Fireman Jack Sheehan, of Hose Carriage No. 33, was struck on the head by falling timbers, and was taken away in a carriage. Joseph Chambers, foreman of engine No. 6, was struck on the head by falling bricks, and was seriously injured. Many others received slight cuts or bruises.

The Shapleigh Cantwell Hardware Company was one of the largest houses in the West. Their stock was valued at about $500,000, and is a total loss. The loss on building and stock, including the damage to adjoining buildings, will amount to $600,000; insurance, $400,000.

HORSEMEN AT ODDS.

THE TROUBLE IN THE NATIONAL TROTTING ASSOCIATION.

CHICAGO, Dec. 11.—The re-election of T. J. Vail as Secretary of the National Trotting Association was a surprise to many Chicago turfmen. Whether there will be an immediate break in the National Association as the result of his re-election is a question involved in considerable doubt. There is every probability of the organization of a Western association, but it is an open question whether the clubs that will form it will withdraw from or retain their membership in the National Association. The old association contains a considerable amount of money, and any member that withdraws forfeits all claim to that money. A desire to cut loose from Mr. Vail and his friends is expressed by a majority of the persons identified with trotting tracks of the West, but they have no desire to give their interest in the National Association's funds to the Vail side. It is claimed that St. Louis and Detroit will at once join hands to organize a new association. If this is true a Western association will be in existence inside of 60 days.

The St. Louis and Detroit Associations are enterprising and independent, and will come pretty near making a success of any project they embark in. If the telegraphic reports from New-York are correct, Judge Grant in an interview last night denounced as an unmitigated lie a statement that he had misrepresented his position toward Vail to H. V. Bemis, proprietor of the *Horseman*. He also said he went to the meeting of the board intending to sustain Vail. Mr. Bemis's reference to Judge Grant's position was made on information imparted by Messrs. Abercrombie, Hall, and Davis. Speaking of the Judge's remarks, Mr. Abercrombie said to-day: "I have sacredly withheld his expressions to me from the public, but now that he has seen fit to make such a furious and abusive denial of Mr. Bemis's statement I have nothing further to withhold. Judge Grant must now abide the consequences of his declarations and his rash denial. His action is beyond comprehension."

WALKING ON WATER.

A MAN TAKES A SHORT STROLL ON THE NIAGARA RIVER.

BUFFALO, Dec. 11.—An attempt was made to-day to outrival the feats of Donovan, Graham, Haslitt, Potts, and Allen in braving the terrors of Niagara, which, though a failure in one way, was a success in another. Mr. Alphonse King, who is the inventor of a water shoe, gave exhibitions some years ago in this country and Mexico and not long ago in Europe. He gave one in the Crystal Palace in London, and while there attracted the attention of Harry Webb, an old-time manager, who made him an offer of a year's engagement to come to this country. While here some time ago Mr. King had looked over Niagara River below the Falls and believed that he could walk across the channel on his patent shoes. He came to this country four weeks ago and has since that time been in New-York City practicing for the trip. While there, Thomas Bowe, hearing of King's determination to attempt the trip, made a wager of $1,500 with Webb that King could not walk 100 feet in the current. The money was deposited with a New-York newspaper, and on Friday afternoon Messrs. King and Webb, accompanied by A. C. Poole, of Poole's Eighth-Street Theatre, reached the Falls.

The trip to-day gave King two cold water baths, and demonstrated that while he could walk with or against the current all right it was impossible to walk across the river because of the eddies, which twice upset him. He retired confident that what he set out to do could not be done. King's "shoes" are of tin, 32 inches long, 8 inches wide, sloping at the top, and 9 inches deep. Each weighs 30 pounds. They are air-tight and have in the middle an opening large enough to admit the feet of the wearer. At the bottom are a series of paddles, which operate automatically as fins.

A TEMPERANCE MUDDLE.

DES MOINES, Iowa, Dec. 11.—While Mr. Kidd was considering whether to establish his big distillery here the constitutional prohibition amendment was pending in the Legislature. In order to facilitate the new manufacturing enterprise leading Republicans and temperance men lobbied a resolution through the Legislature that the amendment would not apply to spirits made for export beyond the State borders. The amendment failed in the courts, and the prohibitory laws followed. Recently a suit was brought under the law of last Winter to enjoin the distillery as a nuisance. The case was elaborately argued last week before Judge Given, of this city, who to-day in a long opinion denied the writ. In the arguments the defense relied on commercial comity between the States as establishing their right to do business, but Judge Given passes this by. He holds that the distillery began business under the law of 1857, and thinks none of the latter statutes interfere with this right. The prohibition question becomes daily more muddled in view of this decision, that of Judge Shiras, the straddling opinion of the Pharmacy Board, and the injunction issued against the latter body yesterday restraining them from canceling Sunday permits.

THE MINNEAPOLIS MILLERS.

ST. PAUL, Minn., Dec. 11.—The story regarding a scheme to consolidate the milling interests of Minneapolis is an "antique chestnut." The rumor was started some time ago and created some talk for one day, but investigation proved it to be without any foundation in fact. It is true that some such arrangement has been talked of for a long time in certain milling circles as one of the possibilities of the future, but there is no reason to believe that the matter has ever passed beyond the bounds of mere conjecture. When the rumor was revived some time ago leading millers declared that such a consolidation would be impracticable and out of the question. All of the big mills could not be induced to come in, and so the scheme could not be made to work. [The story alluded to is printed on the fourth page of this paper, and was sent out in substance by a press association.]

THE FEDERATION OF LA

TRADES UNIONISTS FOR NEW ORGANIZATION.

THE KNIGHTS OF LABOR IGNORE A CONSTITUTION FOR THE NEW ADOPTED—OFFICERS ELECTED.

COLUMBUS, Ohio, Dec. 11.—It will less prove a trifle galling to Terence Powderly and his old Executive Board that the trades unionists, who have been sion here for the best part of a week, hav ed as President of their new organizati American Federation of Labor, Samue pers, the man he so vilified in the " circular that was printed in to-day's The fact that Mr. Gompers was elected opposition may give Mr. Powderly an ide estimation in which he is held by trades ists. The latter are now prepared to own way. They did not invite interferenc position, in the first place, and if Mr. Pow lieutenants with his knowledge had not their powers so grossly there would be p day between organizations that are vals. The new organization has no the Knights, for its membership existence long before they were though begins life with 25 trades unions as a There is reason to suppose that as man will join the fold before another conve held. Its primary object is to secure bers every trade and labor union in the c and some of the steps it has taken to att object show the shrewdness of the builde

Heretofore the Knights have been ena enroll all the workers in small communit glance at the Federation's constitutio show that such a field will no longer be clusively to the "noble order." The have been enabled to secure many mem a promise of general assistance in ca strike or lockout. Such assistance has pr experience but a broken reed. The Fede constitution provides that, under cert cumstances, assistance of a general ch will be given in case of strikes or locko unionists know that their treasuries are empty, and that among them a prom usually amounted to fulfillment. The bers of the Federation will be allowed ernment. As among the Knights, a ciga will not, among trades unions, be to march into a silk mill and strike. The leaders of the new mo are tried men. The work is not new t They are acquainted with the weak spot "noble order" as well as in trades uni they have labored hard to construct suc ganization that will not need constant ti They think they have succeeded, and t like men who have satisfactorily accomp difficult task, upon adjournment late thi noon.

The salient points in the constitutio new organization are as follows:

This association shall be known as the Federation of Labor, and it shall consist trades unions as shall conform to the rules ulations.

The objects of the Federation shall be couragement and formation of local trades unions and the closer federation of such throughout the organization, of central tr labor unions in every city, and the further o of such bodies into State, Territorial, vincial organizations, to secure State legis the interests of the workingmen.

The establishment of national and inter trades unions based upon a strict recognitio autonomy of each trade.

To secure national legislation in the int the working people and influence public op peaceful and legal methods.

The basis of representation in the convent be from national and international unions than 4,000 members, one delegate; 4,000 two delegates; 8,000 or more, three delegates or more, four delegates, and so on, and fr local trade district or union not connecte national head, one delegate.

No organization which has seceded from a national, or international organization sh lowed representation or recognition in the tion.

The officers shall be an Executive Coun power to watch legislative measures directl ing the interests of working people and to whenever necessary, such legislative actio convention may direct.

This council shall use all possible means t ise new national and international and local unions, and to connect them with the Federa

While we recognize the right of each manage its own affairs, it shall be the dut Executive Council to secure the unificati labor organizations so far as to assist each any justifiable boycott, and with voluntar cial help in the event of a strike or boycott proved by the Executive Council. When has been approved by the latter, the particu difficulty, even if it be a lockout, shall be in a circular issued by the President of the tion. It shall then be the duty of all affi cieties to urge their local unions and me make liberal financial donation in aid of the people involved.

The revenue of the Federation shall be from a per capita tax of ½ cent per mon each member in good standing.

The salary of the President shall be $1, year, with mileage and expenses.

Whenever the revenues shall warrant it ecutive Council shall authorize the employ speakers in the interest of the Federation.

The remuneration for loss of time by the tive Council shall be $3 per day and travel incidental expenses.

Any seven wage-workers of good chara favorable to trades unions, and not member body affiliated with this Federation, who scribe to the constitution, shall have power a local body to be known as a Federal Labo and they shall have power to form their own conformity with the constitution, and granted a charter by the President of the tion, provided the request for a charter be by the nearest local or national trades un cers connected with this Federation.

This constitution shall go into effect 1887.

The committee that conferred with the of Labor who had been sent here by Mr. ly made the following recommendation:

"That the Executive Council of the newly ized Federation shall issue an address to th upon the subject of our differences with the of Labor. We might have terminated the ence the first half hour of the meeting, for it dent the Knights of Labor committee had n to act. In the interests of harmony we de wiser to spend three hours in a friendly di with the hope of coming to an understandin

The Federation elected as its President Gompers, of New-York. He is Vice-Presi the International Cigarmakers' Union, considered one of the cleverest leader trades unions of the country. He was London of Dutch parents. He has bee dent of this country since his thirteen and worked at his trade, cigarmaking, was 10 years old. He is now 37, and has member of his union since its organiz 1864.

George Harris, of Reynoldsville, Pen elected First Vice-President. He was England in 1853. In 1883 he was electe dent of the Miners and Laborers' Amalg Association of Pennsylvania, and still office. His association has, he said membership of over 35,000. The Knig thought, should not organize with "unf terial or in districts in which unions were take care of workingmen's interests.

J. W. Smith, the Second Vice-Preside member of the National Tailors' Unio resident of Springfield, Ill.

Gabriel Edmonston was elected Treasu is a member of the Brotherhood of Car and Joiners, and resides at Washington, I

The Secretary of the Federation is P Guire, who occupies a similar office Brotherhood of Carpenters and Joiners. a man of brains as well as of in the labor movement, and t more than to any other singl is due the successful organization of the ation. Secretary McGuire is a most su organizer, and is at the head of a union th few equals. He believes the Federatio bright future. He will not invite a conte the Knights, but if it comes he will be th cipal opponent.

Adolph Strasser, President of the Inter Cigarmakers' Union, expressed himsel lows, after adjournment:

"Our work will result in amalgamating tional and international trades unions. The of Labor are defunct; it's no use talking corpse. They have lost 75 per cent. of the Massachusetts since Oct. 1 through the c the Peabody strike."

J. R. Winders, San Francisco, said:

"I think the difficulties existing betw Knights and trades unions could be satis settled if No. 49, of New-York, was thrown ocean. Some of our radicals might be dispo the same way without causing a national los

Henry Emerich, of the National Fu Makers, said:

"We have laid the foundation of a gre movement."

George Block, National Bakers' Union,

"We will soon have all the trade and labor of the country in the Federation."

Christopher Evans, President of the fe of Miners and Mine Laborers, said:

"The convention could not have acco more."

Among the unions which were repres the convention and are now members Federation are the Brotherhood of Car and Joiners, organized in 1881 with a m ship of 2,342; its membership now is 26, has obtained an advance in wages o

Thursday
January 16-1896

The New-York Times.

Part Two
Pages 9-16

OMEN WIN MR. WURSTER

Says He Will Enforce Excise Laws When He Gets All the Statistics.

RECEIVES 200 W. C. T. U. CALLERS

nounces the Spy System of Work Against Saloons and Talks About Brooklyn's Lack of Policemen.

wo hundred women, with 200 arguments d confidence and perseverance sufficient r an army of 2,000, marched on the office Mayor Wurster of Brooklyn yesterday rning and spent an hour requesting, en-eating, and imploring that he see that the cise laws are properly enforced during administration.

The women represented the Women's ristian Temperance Union, the headquar-s of which are in Myrtle Avenue. They thered a few minutes before the time they ought the Mayor would reach his office, d, with Mrs. Emma F. Pettengill of the ard of Education commanding, started double files for the City Hall.

The trolley lines were tied up while the 200 re swinging across Fulton Street, and ousands of hurrying pedestrians forgot at there was anything in life but the tisfaction of curiosity.

Mayor Wurster had not arrived when the ty Hall was reached. He was late—lit-ally caught napping. When he arrived, teen minutes after the time named in his lf-constructed and self-announced rule official life, Mrs. Pettengill advanced, tched him dispose of his hat and coat, d then, smiling, said:

"Good morning, Mr. Mayor."

"I'm pleased to see the ladies of Brook-n," replied the Mayor.

"I don't believe he means a word of it," appingly whispered a determined-looking oman in the rear rank to a companion.

Then Mrs. Pettengill began to unmask the tteries of her army.

"Mr. Mayor," she said, "we come to u this morning as the representatives of arly a thousand women of the Woman's ristian Temperance Union of Kings unty, organized to labor for the sup-ession of the manufacture and sale of in-xicating liquors, the mitigation of the ils that result therefrom, and the deliv-ance of victims of intemperance from the ndage into which it has drawn them.

"There should be no uncertain sound to r position. We are organized against emperance, impurity, the saloon and mbling house, and Sabbath desecration. e are not voters, but we are citizens, and are mothers and wives and sisters of ters. We are a Christian organization, united to discuss the theory of the Gos-, but to prosecute our work on practical ristian lines. The interests of our city very near our hearts, and we come to u in this way because you have been cted by the people to the highest office this municipality, an office which is ecutive and administrative rather than dicial or legislative.

"You have not been elected to lead a ople of whose habits of life and manners u are ignorant, for you have been ought up among us, our ways have been ur ways and our people your people and r laws your laws. As a citizen you have en familiar with the statutes which affect ooklyn and Kings County. Your intelli-nce and your position as a business man tablished that fact.

"The moral condition of our city and its eds of reform on many lines to bring it to a Christian ideal have been within ur knowledge. And you have, therefore, t been unaware that good laws, laws that ke for prosperity and morality, have en notoriously and flagrantly violated re. And with all this knowledge of the w and of its open violation, you have ac-pted this office profferred to you by the ople, and you have taken the oath which s pledged you to us and to God, whom u have as publicly avowed to be your wgiver and king, to execute or cause to executed the laws which the people have ade for the protection of our rights.

"In Brooklyn to-day there is a licensed uor saloon to every forty-three voters, en seven days in the week and twenty-r hours in the day. The traffic legalized in certain hours of six ys in the week, but we are here ask you to do that which you ve voluntarily pledged yourself to —to make the Sunday sale of intox-nts in Brooklyn an impossibility. You y say that public opinion is mightier an law. But if you shall find that pub- opinion is in line with the law, what en? We believe it is in this matter of nday liquor selling, else how does it me about that, although year after year voice and force of greed has tried modify and overthrow this law, it still nds in January, 1896, practically un-anged in its provisions, and the Sunday e of intoxicants is still absolutely for-den by statute.

"We are not here this morning because enjoy this sort of thing; we are here cause our convictions are deep and ong that intemperance is sapping the rality and prosperity of a large part of r population, and because Sunday liquor ling is a peculiar menace in that robs a man's family so often of his esence at home on Sunday and of his ekly wage. And we know that you, nored Sir, and you alone, in all this city, d the power to right this wrong and eck this plague of defiance of law at expense of those who have a right to im your protection. And we appeal to u as a Christian gentleman, who has ed in our city with eyes and ears open, d who, therefore, needs no suggestion om us as to the noblest and most benefi- course to pursue to stop the sale of in-icants in Brooklyn on Sunday.

"We have a right to assume that you ve no particular axes to grind, that ur only desire is to serve the people thin the lines of the law. You have en pleased to say publicly as to one law ich has thus far been an untried one, the w which provides for scientific temper-ce instruction in our public schools, that shall be enforced. We have a right to sume, and we will assume, that as u feel the strength of public opinion on side of the law and its enforcement, u will carry our city to the high place ich it should occupy among the cities the world, even to the very top."

When Mrs. Pettingill had finished, her mpanions began to applaud, but she opped the demonstration by a wave of r hand.

Mrs. Baldwin then asked Mayor Wurster fulfill the solemn oath he had taken to force the laws, especially the law forbid-g the opening of saloons on Sunday.

While Mrs. Baldwin was speaking the ayor stood with his head bowed and his nds clasped. Then Mrs. Cora E. Seberry rced her way to the front and appealed the Mayor in this language:

"We trust you will, as a Christian gentle-an and Christian churchman, permit us, also members of the Church and Chris-an women, to remind you that the en-rcement of righteous laws and the protec-on of the homes often depend upon indi-duals alone. You have the power to act r us."

Mrs. Martin caused hearty laughter in r address, in which she said:

"If the men of my family were doing eir duty, of all our families, we could be home attending to other matters. But omen have had a strange influence over an from the first woman in the Garden of den. If the Delilahs and the Cleopatras another age could move men we should ove men for good in this. But why should oquence be used in this plea that all right-us and right-thinking Christian men ould respond as readily to as we do?"

Mayor Wurster had to smile when he ard Mrs. Martin's reference to the fall Adam.

Mrs. Mary E. Newton, State Superintend-t of Scientific Instruction, was heartily ceived. She said:

"We thank your Honor very heartily for e pledge you have given to the Christian en who waited on you last Monday morning at you will enforce the temperance edu-tion law. When the press sent out that ord it was received with joy and hope the mothers and Christian citizens of ooklyn. More than $2,000,000 and 100,000 ildren are placed in our public schools, at the State may turn out from these ctories good citizens. It is a cruel thing educate a boy without a warning knowl-ge of the dangers that beset his path. It is a cruel thing to educate our boys without a warning and a thorough scientific knowledge of the effect that alcoholic drinks have upon the human body. The law is very pacific."

At this part of the proceedings Mrs. Pettengill read these resolutions:

Whereas, The statutory law of our State and municipality for the Sunday closing and other restrictions of the saloon is being notoriously and flagrantly violated to our city's dishonor and a detriment of its morality;

Resolved, That in the general interest of home protection and Sabbath observance, and in the special interests of an impartial and righteous enforcement of existing law, we, the representatives and guardians of the home, urge your Honor to exercise the full authority vested in you as Mayor of the City of Brooklyn, and in accordance with the solemn oath of that office by which you are pledged to maintain the law, we urge you to demand of the Police Commissioner such vigilant and faithful execution of the excise law as shall compel absolute conformity to all legally prescribed limitations of the liquor traffic, making removal from office the penalty for willful laxity in the performance of sworn duty on the part of any official of the law. In brief, we ask that the illegal sale of liquor on the Sabbath and to minors be stopped; that the side door of the saloon, as well as the front door, be closed on that day, and that the voice of the law-abiding and Christian community be heard and the name of our loved city be redeemed.

That ended the women's part of the proceedings. Mayor Wurster took a long breath, "pulled himself together," and delivered a short address, in which he denounced the spy system. He said:

"I feel more than honored that you have been here this morning. I think that Brooklyn certainly should feel honored that it has among its citizens such a splendid deputation as has come here this morning to appeal in this cause. It is well, indeed, for a city that it should have a body of noble women of this imposing size to look after its morals. This question, however, is not a new one. It is one that has existed for a great many years. Just why it has not been carried out in the past I do not know. I am new here. I have been but a few days a representative of the City Government.

"Until waited upon the other morning by the gentlemen here for the same cause I had given but little thought to the subject as it now stands. Since then I have made inquiries into the matter. I have called upon the Police Commissioner and discussed with him. I have examined statistics and gained information, by whatever means I could, and I will do whatever I can to suppress this evil. I want to do what is right.

"Brooklyn and New-York differ in physical aspect upon this question. Brooklyn has over 700 miles of streets and has but one-third the number of police New-York has. It is impossible for us to put a policeman in front of every saloon. And I do not think you would ask me to make our policemen sneaking spies, to send in and buy drinks themselves. You certainly would not wish your boys or husbands to be made to do this in the saloons of the city. We must adopt some other way. I am going to co-operate with you, in any way I can, just as soon as I get all the statistics."

The women applauded this speech, especially that part in which the Mayor said he would do whatever he could "to suppress this evil." Then they departed as they had come, marching back to their hall.

SUPPORTED A FAMILY OF SEVEN

Twelve-Year Old Emma Albert Arrested for Selling Papers, but Discharged—Father and Mother Ill.

Agent Barkley of the Gerry society arraigned in Jefferson Market Police Court yesterday a twelve-year-old girl, Emma Albert, whom he had arrested Tuesday night for selling papers at a late hour along Broadway. Barkley said that the girl deserved praise rather than punishment, and asked that she be discharged.

Investigation showed that she was the oldest of five children, who lived with their father, Charles Albert, and their mother in two rooms at 342 West Thirty-seventh Street. The father was slowly dying of consumption and the mother had met with an accident that left her deaf. The father's illness had made it impossible for him to speak above a whisper, and he and his wife could only communicate by writing.

To save the family from starvation, Emma had taken to selling papers, and the money she earned was all they had had for some time. Barkley said that the father had been industrious till he became too weak to work.

Albert accompanied his daughter to court yesterday, but was hardly able to stand. Magistrate Flammer discharged the prisoner and a little purse was raised for her. Barkley said that in his experience with the Gerry society he had never seen a case where charity could be better applied.

ANNUITIES FOR HIS EMPLOYES

Liberal Provisions in the Will of William Fowler Foster.

The will of William Fowler Foster, who died at his residence at Riverside Drive and One Hundred and Second Street, on Dec. 3, 1895, was filed for probate in the Surrogate's office yesterday.

The will is dated Nov. 1, 1895, and, according to the petition, the real estate is valued at $50,000, and the personal property at $1,000,000.

The entire estate is directed to be turned into annuities to be purchased from the Equitable and Mutual Life Insurance Companies. The only absolute bequest is one of $10,000 to the testator's widow, Bertha M. Foster, and she is also to get an annuity of $10,000.

The will then gives annuities of $1,000 each to the testator's two brothers, his four sisters-in-law, three sisters of his wife, and to John P. Woodbury, his former partner. Annuities of $500 each are to be given to the children of each of his brothers, the children of his two deceased sisters, to his mother-in-law, and to several relatives and friends.

It is with his former employes that the deceased millionaire's will is liberal beyond parallel. To eleven of the employes of Foster, Paul & Co., the will gives annuities of $500; to thirteen more it gives annuities of $300, among these latter being two ladies, Miss Gussie Seeley and Mrs. James Wallace, and to twenty-seven other employes and five domestic servants in Mr. Foster's household are given annuities of $100 each.

The testator directs that if the estate cannot supply these annuities, then his wife shall first be provided for, and the balance of the estate shall be used to pay the annuities to the persons named, pro rata. If, however, there is a residue when the annuities are provided for, then this residue is to be divided into two equal portions, and with it from one part there shall be purchased an extra annuity for his widow and annuities from the other part for Livingstone Gifford, Samuel F. Paul, Thomas W. Foster, George A. Foster, C. T. Newall, Robert W. King, John Steele, and F. W. Quans, all of whom, with his widow, are named as executors.

MILK DEALERS NOT HEAVILY SENTENCED

William H. Deere, However, Forced to Pay a Two-Hundred-Dollar Fine.

A number of persons were arraigned before the Justices in the Court of Special Sessions yesterday, charged with selling adulterated milk. In most of the cases the Justices were lenient, and in some even suspended sentence.

William H. Deere, a farmer on the Boston Road, who sold milk to grocerymen and small dealers that was found upon examination to be adulterated 12 per cent. was sentenced to pay a fine of $200 or go to the city prison for thirty days.

Other cases where fines were imposed were: Lewis Street, $25; Abram Robinson, 45 Forsyth Street, $25; Barnard Subin, 21 Forsyth Street, $50; Max Blachman, 56 Forsyth Street, $50; Hyman Klein, 48 Chrystie Street, $25; Betsy Seiderman, 57 Forsyth Street, $25; Henry Jungerman, 186 Sixth Avenue, $25; Theodore Hildebrandt, 842 East One Hundred and Thirty-eighth Street, $35; Joseph Garibaldi, 173 Bleecker Street, $50; Henry Koehler, 27 Barrow Street, $100; Elizabeth Damm, 3,601 Third Avenue, $50; Michael Stemmerman, 939 Trinity Avenue, $50, and Henry Fuchs, 48 Oak Street, $15.

In all of the cases the fines were paid.

Excursions to the Quebec Carnival.

Quebec is busy with preparations for a Winter carnival, which will be opened Jan. 27.

The programme promises a week of merriment, with healthy outdoor sports, a magnificent ice palace, fancy-dress balls, torchlight parades, and other attractions. The Governor General and many other notables of the Dominion Government expect to attend. The New-York Central Railroad offers excursion tickets at $15 for the round trip, good from Jan. 24 to Feb. 15, with choice of routes and a stop-over at Montreal.

NO JUST CLAIM TO BARIMA

British Government Shown to be Wrong by One of Its Agents.

A LETTER WRITTEN BY R. K. PORTER

Venezuela's Ownership of Land Now in Dispute Clearly Acknowledged by Englishmen Sixty Years Ago.

Venezuelans are accumulating proofs showing that the British claim to a large section of their territory is an unjust one. In the tract which the British Government claims is the valuable island of Barima at the mouth of the Orinoco River. There is the best of proof—convincing to an unprejudiced mind—that the English do not own the island and did not pretend to own it sixty years ago.

The letter which is given below was written May 26, 1836, by Robert Ker Porter, the British agent at Caracas. He complained of the dangers encountered by mariners in entering the mouth of the Orinoco River, and requested, in a peremptory manner, that the Venezuelan Government place a conspicuous beacon on Cape Barima "without further delay."

Mr. Porter also declared that British merchants could effect no insurance on vessels bound for the Orinoco River without a considerable advance of premiums "and in many cases not at all." The Venezuelan Government was also asked to place buoys in the Orinoco River.

The letter shows that in 1836 the British Government did not own Cape Barima, and hence did not own the island of Barima. If it had owned this island, it would not have asked Venezuela to build a beacon on it. The beacon, which Mr. Porter said was needed to insure the safety of British ships, would have been built by the English if the island had not belonged to Venezuela.

The Schomburgk line is so drawn as to give the English control over the mouth of the great Orinoco River. Mr. Porter asked the Venezuelans to place buoys at the river's mouth, acknowledging that it belonged to the South Americans.

A copy of Mr. Porter's letter was sent in 1886 to F. R. St. John, the British Minister to Venezuela, as proof that the South American Republic owned the island of Barima.

Mr. St. John replied briefly. He could not deny that Mr. Porter was the authorized representative of England, but he declared the letter was written without the knowledge or authority of the British Government. Mr. St. John said Mr. Porter made no report regarding the letter to the home Government. To this assertion Mr. St. John added: "A doctrine that a Government is bound by every act or word of its diplomatic agent is entirely at variance with international law, it being perfectly well-known that even a formal treaty concluded and signed by a plenipotentiary is not valid unless it shall have been ratified by the Government of such plenipotentiary."

If, as stated by Mr. St. John, England is not bound by its agents' acts, yet Mr. Porter's letter shws that the merchants and British Consul at Angostura, now Ciudad Bolivar,) believed that Caracas was the place to apply in order to secure the beacon on Barima.

The Porter Letter.

A copy of the Porter letter is here given:

British Legation.

CARACAS, May 26, 1836.

Sir: From a recent correspondence I have held with his Majesty's Consul in Angostura, I have to request the serious attention of the Executive to a representation I am about to make relative to the more safe navigation for vessels on entering the principal mouth of the Orinoco, situated to the southwest of the Island of Trinidad. Being particularly induced to address the Government on this subject, in consequence of the very imminent danger vessels are exposed to, not only for want of proper land and water marks to guide them, but likewise on account of the inefficient state of the pilot establishment on the Island of Pagayos, a considerable distance up the river.

In proof of the results from what I have just mentioned, allow me to state that on the 7th of January last the British brig Coriolanus, coming from St. Thomas to Angostura, ran on shore a little to the leeward of the grand mouth of the Orinoco, and totally for want of a beacon to point out the proper entrance. Every effort was made on the part of the master and crew, assisted by some Indians, to get her off, but without success. She soon bilged and became a wreck. On the 29th she was totally abandoned, and on the 6th of February the Captain and crew reached Angostura, when he duly reported his misfortune, and the cause of it, to the British Consul in that city.

A second circumstance of the like nature (from similar causes) took place but a very few weeks afterward, namely: The British vessel The Sir Walter Scott, bound outward with a cargo of cattle for use of the troops in the English colonies, ran aground (and for want of a pilot) in crossing from the point of Crab Island to Cape Barima, where she remained in the greatest distress during three days. The Consul, in reporting this circumstance to me, adds: "Here is an additional instnace of ruinous tendency, arising out of the present imbecile pilot system of the Orinoco, and although the misfortune was known at the station of the pilots in Pagayos, no assistance whatever was rendered. The vessel and cargo must have sustained considerable injury, the particulars of which I have not yet had, as the Captain, the moment he got off, proceeded on his voyage." Let me here refer you for the present to the enclosed copy of a letter addressed to the Governor of the Province of Guiana by the Consul in illustration of the great neglect, as also disobedience to the pilot regulations:

Asks for a Beacon in Barima.

From what I have already said, it becomes my official duty to represent to the Executive of this republic, the indispensable necessity (and that without further delay) of placing a conspicuous beacon on Cape Barima, the point forming the grand mouth of the Orinoco to the south-southeast, where I am given to understand it could be done with the greatest facility and to the greatest advantage. This object would effectually prove a sure mark, as also a safeguard to all vessels seeking for the proper entrance into this vast river; and it becomes the more to be required, from the great difficulty experienced by all navigators in finding the entrance, as the coast presents the at this day has not a single mark to denote it. same appearance for many leagues together, and The Island of Cangrejos forms the other side of the great mouth, situated at a distance of about eighty leagues from the cape to the west-northwest, whose dangerous sandbanks reduce the only navigable channel to scarcely three miles in width, which commences on passing the Bar, (just without Cape Barima,) soon becoming difficult and intricate; particularly so, after ascending for about three leagues, where the channel frequently changes its course, on account of shifting sands. In fact, it cannot be denied but that the whole navigation up to the Island of Pagayos (eleven leagues from the cape) is extremely dangerous and uncertain, requiring to be well surveyed and carefully sounded by some one thoroughly acquainted with that part of the Orinoco and its probable casualities. Buoys ought to be forthwith laid down at those particular points which either mark the channel or show where sandbanks or sunken rocks lay, both being numerous, impeding the navigation and increasing the dangers of the river, to the great risk of lives and property.

The next subject of my representation regards the actual, and, I may say, almost useless system of the Orinoco pilotage. I am well aware that a pilotboat was intended to have gone out every day from Point Barima to cruise for vessels bearing toward the entrance of the river, but a shameful want of proper arrangement, attended by neglect, rendered abortive this wise and well-intended plan on the part of the Department of Marine. And it does not exist at this day. The only pilot station on the Orinoco is at the Island of Pagayos, forty miles distant from the entrance at the great mouth of the river. And it appears very clear that great difficulties and perils must be encountered in reaching it.

Condition of the Orinoco.

The amicable bearing at all times manifested by this Government in its foreign relations, not only political, but commercial, assures me that it is vividly alive at all times to whatever may either augment that friendly feeling, or increase the mercantile prosperity of the country. Under this firm belief, as well as from a sense of my duties in watching over that of my own country, I therefore seize the present occasion in endeavoring to impress on the Executive the imperious necessity of promptly taking stable and energetic measures in the regulation of that, which is of such vital importance to the growing trade of Angostura, whose increase or diminution cannot but very materially affect that of the whole of the neighboring provinces of the republic, and, consequently, influence the public revenue. Allow me to add, (as materially connected with the subject in question,) being a well-known fact, that not only in England, but in many of her colonies, the merchants are afraid to speculate, or even send their vessels to the Orinoco, in consequence of the dangers to which both property and life are exposed from the causes I have already set forth, thus corroborating what I have stated touching the total abandonment in which the navigation of the Orinoco at present is left. Indeed, so deep is the impression of risk on the British mercantile mind, that at Lloyds, in London, no insurance can be affected to that river without a very considerable advance on the premium, and, in many cases, not at all.

His Majesty's Consul at Angostura (as the preceding inclosure would show you) found it his indispensable duty to call the observance of the Governor of the Province of Guiana to the subjects I now write upon; under the full hope that he might be able by his authority and remonstrance to check in future the pursuance on the Orinoco of a system truly prejudicial to the interests of individuals as well as to general commerce. I have had the honor of just laying before you that gentleman's officio to the Governor, which, together with his answer, as also other documents connected with the present representation, was forwarded to me, mentioning at the same time that such had been duly sent officially to his Government for its knowledge and guidance. These papers, I cannot doubt, will further show the Executive how absolutely useless the present pilot establishment is on the Island of Pagayos, being rather detrimental than advantageous to the intent and use of the Legislature; hence demanding a most radical reform in some way or other.

Before I close this dispatch, I must once more repeat my solicitude that the Minister of the Marine be directed to investigate and correct the abuses which have frustrated the good intent of the Government and the department, and likewise that he be directed to attend to the recommendation I now have the honor of making by placing a proper beacon on the Barima Cape, as also the appropriate buoys in the Orinoco, for the safer navigation of it, so that I may be enabled in a very short time (and I trust the urgency will be seen) to have the satisfaction of officially communicating to his Majesty's principal Secretary of State for Foreign Affairs (for the information of the merchants interested at Lloyds) the measures that have been taken by this Government, rendering the great entrance to the Orinoco perfectly perceptible, as also the navigation of the river up to the Angostura perfectly safe.

I have the honor to remain, Sir, with the highest consideration, your most obedient, humble servant, ROBERT KER PORTER.

The Hon. Senor José E. Gallegos, &c.

A copy of this letter is included in one of the pamphlets issued by the Venezuelan Government in support of its claim to territory which England professes to own.

WILL HELP LAKE VESSELMEN

Deepening of the Erie Canal Regarded Favorably by the Carriers' Association—Officers Chosen.

DETROIT, Jan. 15.—The annual meeting of the Lake Carriers' Association was called to order by President Livingstone shortly after 11 o'clock this morning in Whitney's Music Hall, more than 200 members being present. The first business to come before the session was the report of the Board of Managers.

The annual report of the Board of Managers was read by Secretary Keep. The report shows that the membership of the association increased nearly 30,000 tons during the present year, and outside of ferry lines and passenger lines there are not twenty important vessels on the great lakes which are not now on the rolls of the association.

Shipping offices of the association have been maintained during the year at Cleveland, Chicago, South Chicago, Buffalo, Ashtabula, and Toledo. The total number of seamen shipped at these ports was 13,973, an increase of 3,918 over 1894.

The deepening of the Erie Canal will result in lowering the through rate on grain destined for the seaboard and will tend to the development of the business and the successful competition on the part of the water route with other methods of transportation. The Board of Managers say it would be a desirable thing to have the jurisdiction of the Government engineers in charge of the improvements in St. Mary's River extended to cover all that portion of St. Mary's River in which navigation is difficult, and necessary authority should be placed in their hands to enable them to make rules and regulations to govern all kinds of vessels as well as rafts while navigating such parts of the river.

President Livingstone, in his annual address, congratulated the members upon the success of the association during the past year as well as on the accomplishments of the various committees.

The election of officers resulted as follows:

President, J. J. B. Brown, Buffalo; Secretary, Henry Keep, Buffalo; Treasurer, George P. Mackay, Cleveland; General Counsel, Harvey D. Goulder, Cleveland; Vice Presidents, H. H. Brown, Cleveland; James Millen, Detroit; W. P. Henry, Toledo; J. G. Kent, Chicago; G. A. Tomlinson, Duluth; C. A. Eddy, Bay City, Mich.; C. C. Hadley, Toledo; James McBrier, Erie; Conrad Starke, Milwaukee; F. J. Firth, Philadelphia; Frank Owen, Ogdensburg.

THE BRONX RIVER VALLEY SEWER

Mount Vernon Wants It and More—Objection in Yonkers.

MOUNT VERNON, N. Y., Jan. 15.—At the meeting of citizens Monday in the Common Council Chamber, to discuss the proposed Bronx River Valley sewer, a resolution was passed unanimously in approval of the proposed Bronx River sewer, and asking that the Bronx River Commissioners incorporate in this sewer one along the valley of the Hutchinson River.

The branch sewer, which the people of Mount Vernon and Pelham are considering, would start in near the head of East Chester Creek, in Pelham, and would join the main sewer below Pelham Bay Park. It would be about two miles and a quarter long.

The estimated cost of the branch sewer would be $160,000. This sum would be shared by the City of New-York, the City of Mount Vernon, the town of Pelham, and possibly the town of New-Rochelle.

YONKERS, N. Y., Jan. 15.—The Common Council has adopted a resolution against the proposed scheme of building the sewer in the Bronx River Valley on the ground that to build the sewer would lay a heavy burden of taxation on the people of the city, and really about ruin those who own the farm lands along the line of the proposed sewer.

WHITE PLAINS, N. Y., Jan. 15.—The Westchester County Board of Supervisors has adopted a resolution that it is the sense of the board that the County of Westchester pay no portion of the expense of the building of the proposed Bronx River Valley sewer. Its idea is, that the expense should be assessed upon the property benefited, and that towns ten or twelve miles from it should not be called upon to pay anything toward its cost.

The Sewer Commission Reports.

The Bronx River Sewer Commission met in the Mayor's office yesterday and received the deport of the sub-committee appointed to devise a financial scheme to raise funds to pay for the building of the improvement. The sewer will be about twenty-one miles long, the village of White Plains being at the extreme northern terminus, and it will cost about $3,500,000.

The sub-committee reported that the improvement should be paid for in bonds of New-York and Westchester Counties, to be issued as the proper officials of either county shall determine, and that of the expense, New-York shall pay 60 per cent. and Westchester 40 per cent. It is also provided that the money shall be paid back to the counties by assessing the property tributary to the sewer.

The commission will make up its report some time during the month, and then it will be submitted to the Legislature for their action as to whether the scheme proposed is feasible.

Cripple Creek Mines Listed.

Several Cripple Creek mines, some of them dividend payers, were listed at the Consolidated Exchange yesterday. The list, with the capital of each mine, is as follows:

Alamo Mining Company, $1,000,000; Anaconda Gold Mining Company, $1,000,000; Cripple Creek Consolidated Mining Company, $2,000,000; Creede and Cripple Creek Mining and Milling Company, $800,000; Croesus Gold Mining and Tunnel Company, $1,000,000; Favorite Gold Mining Company, $1,200,000; Gold and Globe Hill Mining Company, $750,000; Mount Rosa Mining, Milling and Land Company, $1,000,000; Pharmacist Mining Company, $1,000,000; Rubicon Gold Mining Company, $1,000,000; Specimen Gold Mining and Milling Company, $1,200,000; Union Gold Mining Company, $1,250,000; Work Mining and Milling Company, $1,250,000.

Golden Fleece stock was called yesterday for the first time. The listing is significant because it occurs at the time set for the opening of a so-called Mining Exchange here.

HIDDEN SOLIDS REVEALED

Prof. Routgen's Experiments with Crookes's Vacuum Tube.

BULLETS FOUND BY USING LIGHT

Opaque Bodies Covered by Other Bodies Photographed — Views of Profs. O. N. Rood and Halleck of Columbia.

Men of science in this city are awaiting with the utmost impatience the arrival of European technical journals, which will give them the full particulars of Prof. Routgen's great discovery of a method of photographing opaque bodies covered by other bodies, hitherto regarded as wholly impenetrable by light rays of any kind.

Prof. Routgen of Würzburg University has recently discovered a light which, for purposes of photography, will penetrate wood, paper, flesh, and nearly all other organic substances. Thus, the bones of the human frame can be photographed in relief without the flesh which covers them, or metals inclosed in a box covered with a woolen cloth can be photographed as if the cloth and the wood did not exist.

In one sense, it is a misnomer to call the process photography, as now understood, because no lens is employed to project the image. It also seems, from the brief accounts of the process which have already been sent by cable, that the new images of concealed bodies resemble rather the old-fashioned daguerreotypes than the modern finished photographs, inasmuch as they appear only in outline.

Briefly, the new images are obtained by the energy given out in a Crookes's vacuum tube. The object to be photographed is placed behind the tube, and a dry plate is placed behind the object. If the object be, say, a hand, the image on the dry plate will be the bones in it, without any flesh covering whatever.

Prof. Routgen has already used his process to detect the exact location of bullets in gunshot wounds, and one of its first practical uses is expected to be a transformation of modern surgery by enabling the surgeon to detect the presence of foreign bodies of whatever kind in any part of the human body.

The germ of Prof. Routgen's discovery is to be found in an experiment made a few years ago by Prof. William Crookes. He found that when a glass bulb from which all the air possible has been extracted has a current of electricity passed through it, a beautiful light in the interior of the bulb is the result. If now a body, whether transparent or opaque, is placed between the poles between which the current passes in the vacuum, sharply defined shadows of these bodies are projected on the wall of the bulb behind the negative pole.

"It seems," says Prof. Sylvanus Thompson in his recent work on electricity, "as if the transparent or opaque bodies stopped the way for some of the flying molecules and prevented them from striking the opposite wall."

Hertz, the great electrician, better known in connection with the Panama scandals, discovered that while these rays will not pass through glass, mica, or any transparent substance, they will pass through a thin sheet of metal foil.

Lenard, by using a window of aluminium foil at one end of the bulb, succeeded in making the rays pass out into the atmosphere, where they excited phosphorescence. Hertz made the shadows appear in ordinary air by covering the negative pole of an electrical machine with silk, on which the shadows were thrown.

Prof. O. N. Rood, who occupies the Chair of Physics in Columbia College, was asked yesterday by a reporter for THE NEW-YORK TIMES if this discovery was in line with the previous anticipations of men of science. Although the information which the reporter was able to give Prof. Rood was of the briefest character, he kindly consented to explain the analogies which occurred to him as having any bearing on the new discovery.

"The phenomenon which we call light," said the professor, "is a peculiar manifestation of energy in the ether which pervades all substances. It consists of short vertical waves, roughly speaking, from one-forty-thousandth to one-sixty-thousandth of an inch in length. These waves are visible, to our eyes only for the length of the spectrum, which displays the component parts of white light, from red to violet.

"The most familiar example of the spectrum which we have is the rainbow. Men of science have been long aware that there are rays of light imperceptible to the senses. For example, in that part of the spectrum beyond the violet rays there are rays which, though imperceptible to our eyes, can be seized by the sensitive plate of a photographic apparatus. It so happens that the violet and ultra-violet rays are those which are chemically the most active. At the red end of the spectrum we have every reason to believe that there are other rays imperceptible to our senses, and which we have hitherto not been able to measure or detect directly for want of a suitable apparatus.

"The modern theory of light presumes that light, heat, and even electricity are merely different forms or manifestations of the same energy. The only difference between light and heat is in the length of the waves, those of light being much shorter than those of heat. If we call light and heat, therefore, radiant energy, we shall have a general term to express the subtle force which acts through the ether.

"Now, when we want to examine light we pass it through a prism or through a transparent substance, which polarizes it, such as tourmaline. Hertz showed by substituting a large prism of melted pitch that heat rays could be polarized in the same manner as light rays. The quantity of these heat rays can be actually measured by delicate electrical instruments, known as thermo-piles.

"I can quite readily conceive how heat rays could be passed through organic substances in the manner you describe. It is also quite conceivable to me that these heat rays would be stopped by a bullet or any substance which was a good electrical conductor. Eighty or ninety per cent. of the rays would be reflected, and the remaining 10 or 20 per cent. would be absorbed by the metallic substance."

Prof. Rood then introduced the reporter to his colleague, Prof. Halleck, who was greatly interested in the discovery, and who spoke of another aspect of it.

"The tenuous substance, which we can hardly call matter, because it is so foreign to our ideas of anything palpable," said Prof. Halleck, "is supposed to pervade the universe, and everything it contains.

"The modern theory of matter presumes that that no two atoms—an atom being the smallest possible particle of matter—touch each other. In spite of the close adhesion of even steel, each separate atom has a kind of spiral motion impelling it to fly away from its neighbor. Between these atoms is the all-pervading ether which transmits the rays of light or heat, as the case may be.

"Nothing is more familiar to our minds than that all substances transmit heat more or less perfectly according to their degree of conductivity. Now, as we believe that heat and light are simply manifestations of radiant energy, there is nothing impossible in the idea that this radiant energy may be conveyed so as to cast shadows, as it were, according to the relative permeability of the different parts of the same substance.

"There is only one point in the statement you make which seems a little confusing. If Prof. Klupathy of Pesth University has succeeded in making this invisible light or radiant energy pass through aluminium, what becomes of the theory that metals should reflect it in proportion to their electrical conductivity? Aluminium, though not heavy, is still a regular metal in its behavior, and is a relatively good conductor of electricity. These points, I hope, will be cleared up when we get the full reports of the experiments."

Dr. Daniel M. Stimson, when seen at his house, 11 West Seventeenth Street, last night, showed great interest in the new discovery. Without committing himself as to any of the details of the experiments, he expressed the opinion that the new discovery, when perfected, would doubtless lead to an immense revolution for good in the progress of modern surgery.

Dr. Stimson first showed the reporter how a tiny incandescent light covered with a short piece of rubber tubing exhibited one of the fingers of his hand as a completely translucent body. He proved that the bone of the finger transmitted the light equally as well as the less solid parts. In connection with this little experiment, Dr. Stimson told how he had once seen the stump of a needle embedded in the top of a woman's finger, the metal showing itself as an opaque body, while the rest of the finger was translucent.

By another small incandescent lamp, arranged so that it could be placed in the mouth of a patient, Dr. Stimson showed how the presence of an abscess in one of the upper jawbones could be detected. The light in this case shone at unequal heights through the right and left cheeks, proving that the fluid was turbid in one side and clear in the other.

"Imagine," said Dr. Stimson, "that when this discovery has been brought to perfection, we shall be able to detect foreign substances in any part of the body. It will take some time to get accustomed to the appearance of normal healthy tissue, but starting from that we shall be able to make all kinds of differentiations.

"It seems, from what has already been demonstrated, that with different strengths or gradations of the radiant energy, we shall be able to bring different substances or structures into view. Thus, with one strength, we shall detect metals; with another, bones or bony tumors; with a third, the various kinds of degeneration to which the structures of the body are liable.

"We may thus detect solidified portions of the lung, or parts of the lung where the structure has shrunk away, leaving a cavity. In the heart we may be able to detect the difference between fatty degeneration and brown or amyloid degenerations.

"In the abdominal cavity, we may be able to detect tumors, abscesses, hardened parts of the liver, or other abdominal organs, and very possibly calcareous deposits in all parts.

"What it may do for gunshot wounds, I am unable, from my own personal experience, which has been comparatively limited in such matters, to say. But the benefits which are likely to be derived from a discovery of such first-class importance will not dawn upon us fully until its use has become familiar all over the civilized world."

BROKER CHAPMAN ON HIS DEFENSE

His Refusal to Answer Questions of the Senate Sugar Committee Not Intended as a Contempt.

WASHINGTON, Jan. 15.—Following up his opening argument for the defense of Elverton H. Chapman for refusing to answer questions put by the Senate committee regarding the sugar clauses of the last tariff law, Counsel Jere Wilson this morning offered the Senate Journal to show that the Senate took no action on the committee's report and did not determine whether the questions asked by the committee were pertinent. The District Attorney's objection that this was immaterial was sustained by the court, and an exception noted.

W. B. Hibbs, a Washington broker, was the first witness put on the stand, being introduced to prove that the tariff legislation of 1894 did not affect the price of sugar or of the American Sugar Refining Company's stock. He produced quotations in great detail to demonstrate that there was a close parallel between ranges of stock in 1892 and 1894, the periods when the McKinley and Wilson bills respectively were under Congressional consideration. In January, 1892, the price was 75⅝, in August of the same year 114⅞. In January, 1894, it was 78¼, and in August following 115⅞. Taking stocks unaffected by the tariff, he showed by quotations that they acted much the same as sugar stocks for similar periods.

When asked as to the cause of variations in prices of stocks, Mr. Hibbs said that the prices were governed by the supply and demand at the hands of people trading on the floor at the time of sale. Prices were also affected by manipulation of "longs" and "shorts," or by reports of facts and fancies put in circulation, which sometimes, however, sent stocks in an opposite direction to expectation.

In reply to the District Attorney, he said that values were to some extent affected by earnings of business and by legislation, but the market could easily be manipulated in various ways.

Stenographer Prentiss, who took Mr. Chapman's testimony before the committee, was put on the stand and asked whether he heard any Senator say to the committee that he had been dealing in sugar stocks.

Judge Cole doubted the material bearing of this question on the case, and Mr. Dittenhoefer declared that he wished to show that the Senate investigation had not been made in good faith. In the Kilbourn case it had been ruled that the Constitution did not allow such an inquiry, except for the purpose of expelling a Senator or for legislation. Neither purpose was shown here. The questioning of Mr. Chapman was unnecessary if it could be shown that Senators admitted they had been speculating in stocks.

Judge Cole ruled that the court could not inquire into the good faith of the Senate. Mr. Prentiss was permitted to testify that Mr. Chapman stated to the committee that his business was confidential, and that to reveal its private affairs would injure it. He was not allowed to read Mr. Chapman's whole testimony from his notes.

Messrs. Shellabarger and Dittenhoefer, of counsel, were put on the stand to prove that Mr. Chapman had taken the precaution to secure their services before refusing to answer the questions put to him. This evidence was ruled out by the court.

The defendant, Elverton H. Chapman, was then sworn on his own behalf. He testified that he declined to answer the questions of the committee in good faith and in pursuance of the advice of Messrs. Shellabarger and Dittenhoefer, and with no intention to defy the committee, but to discharge his duty and to maintain his rights under the Constitution of the United States.

The case for the defense here closed, and the court adjourned till to-morrow.

Consecration of Dr. Satterlee.

It was announced yesterday that the consecration of the Rev. Dr. Henry Y. Satterlee of this city as Bishop of the new Diocese of Washington would take place on March 25 next, in Calvary Church, Fourth Avenue and Twenty-first Street, of which Dr. Satterlee has been many years the rector.

The consecrators will be the Right Rev. Bishops Williams of Connecticut, Potter of New-York, and Paret of Maryland. The presenters will be the Right Rev. Bishops Coxe of Western New-York and Dudley of Kentucky.

Bishop-elect Satterlee has written to his standing committee in Washington that he will hold his first services as Bishop in St. John's Church and the Church of the Epiphany, in that city, on Palm Sunday.

IN THE NEW QUARTERS

Clearing House Association Holds Dedication Ceremonies.

ATTENDANCE OF REPRESENTATIVE MEN

Prayer by Bishop Potter, Presentation by J. Edward Simmons, Acceptance by W. A. Nash—Mr. Orr for Chamber of Commerce.

Members of the Clearing House Association had abundant reason to be gratified yesterday with the successful dedication of their new building in Cedar Street. The attendance included representatives of the banks and financial associations, of all the Exchanges, of the Chamber of Commerce, and men prominent in the professions. It was a company that could be assembled only on an occasion pre-eminently great and memorable.

New-York Clearing House.
Ceremonies of Dedication Were Held Yesterday.

Fine weather displayed the new building to excellent advantage and enabled its visitors to pass upon the claims made for it that it is the finest banking house in the world. The general verdict sustained this estimate of its quality.

Architectural description of the building had prepared the visitors to see a substantial marble structure of unique design. Surprises awaited them in the superb interior fittings and decorations. They found that the work of the architect, R. W. Gibson, and of the builder of the massive vaults, J. M. Mossman, had been artistically supplemented by the decorator, D. S. Hess.

In mounting to the spacious clearing room, on the upper floor, where the ceremonies of dedication were to be performed, visitors were attracted by glimpses of rooms for accounts and for board and committee meetings which had been thrown invitingly open. They furnished a picture of rich fittings and construction which no other business building down town can match. Ceilings deeply paneled in gold, cornices supported by marble pilasters, doorways and windows framed in polished marble, a library with walls of mahogany and exquisite frescoing, were revealed to the passing glance.

The clearing room is spacious enough to accommodate 700 persons. Groups of flags, hung from the walls, furnished tasteful and ample adornment. The platform was occupied by the officers of the association and a few special guests, among them Bishop Potter, ex-Gov. Flower, Assistant Treasurer Jordan, and Alexander E. Orr. Close to the appointed hour of noon the ceremonies began with prayer by Bishop Potter, who wore his episcopal robes. A dedication glee by the Bank Clerks' Club followed, and then Frederick D. Tappen, in behalf of the Building Committee, of which he was Chairman, made the following statement:

I have been requested by the Building and Clearing House Committees to state the object of this gathering of bank officers and business men, which I will do as briefly as possible. This building was designed especially for the use of an association which has always stood for the soundest and best in finance, and which has many times interposed its united powers at periods of financial disturbance to prevent disaster and ruin, not only to the business interests of this great city, but to those of the State and the Nation. When this site was purchased, and the plans for the structure adopted, it was thought eminently proper that a cornerstone should be laid with appropriate ceremonies. On that occasion we requested the assistance of the Bishop of this diocese, who opened and closed the ceremonies with prayer. This building being now completed and ready for occupancy, we have again asked the services of the Bishop on its dedication. In concluding its labors, the committee congratulates the association on the possession of a building which is not only an ornament to the city, but a monument to the public spirit of the associated banks of New-York.

The oration and delivery of the building were assigned to J. Edward Simmons, who chose as his subject, "Sermons in Stones," and spoke with such force and skill that the company frequently commended him with hearty and prolonged applause. He said:

The spirit which called into existence the new Clearing House is the same public spirit that created the immortal masterpiece of the Athenian Acropolis, the same public spirit that built the wonderful structures of the Eternal City, the same public spirit that brought forth the grand municipal buildings and cathedrals of mediaeval Europe. The men who erected these marvels of architectural art were ready to sacrifice, yea, often did sacrifice, their treasures and their lives for their country. On the rich and tasteful façade of the new Clearing House are emblazoned the arms of our Nation, our State, and our city; these are meant to be a declaration that the bankers and the merchants of New-York are ready at their country's call to risk their fortunes for their country's sake. This is no idle boast. Well may the New-York Clearing House Association be proud of its record for wise and splendid patriotism. During the civil war, was it not our association that enabled the bankers of the metropolis to provide the vast sums by which the credit of the National Government was maintained? And since its formation, has not our association been a tower of strength in the succession of panics through which the Nation has passed?

Again and again has it been demonstrated that the great battles of the world are not always won by the soldier. There are Generals in finance as well as in war, and the intrepidity of the one is equal to the heroism of the other.

Mr. Simmons described the Clearing House operations of 1893, which averted panic, and said:

Such was the patriotic spirit that animated the old Clearing House. With such effect did this association step into the breach when our country was threatened with the direst of perils! The beauty and the glory of the new Clearing House are but the expression of the same spirit; and now that new dangers assail the nation let us declare that our new building stands for a pledge that never will the New-York Clearing House Association shrink from doing its full duty; ever will it stand in the front rank of our country's defenders.

Turning our eyes again to the façade, who is not struck by the cunning distribution of its members? Parts project, parts recede, and thus create a just proportion of light and shade. Has not our architect symbolized thereby the

"All the News That's Fit to Print."

The New York Times.

THE WEATHER. Rain or snow, followed by fair; much colder, with a cold wave.

COPYRIGHTED, 1898, BY THE NEW YORK TIMES COMPANY.

VOL. XLVII...NO. 15,008. NEW YORK, WEDNESDAY, FEBRUARY 16, 1898.—TWELVE PAGES. PRICE THREE CENTS

THE NEWS CONDENSED.

Stock market strong.

Cash wheat, No. 2 red, $1.05⅝; cash corn, No. 2 mixed, 37⅝c.; cash cotton, 6¼c.

CONGRESS.—The Senate yesterday adopted a resolution calling on the Attorney General for information as to the coming sale of the Kansas Pacific Railroad. The Attorney General promptly furnished the information called for. The House passed a bill regulating loans to officers of National banks.—Page 3.

FOREIGN—Lord William Nevill, fourth son of the Marquis of Abergavenny, was sentenced in London to five years' penal servitude for forgery. The Indian frontier war was discussed in the House of Commons. The Russian chargé at Pekin discussed the question of the Southern Manchurian Railway with the Tsung-li-Yamen. The Ambassadors at Constantinople are trying to arrange for the Autonomous Government of Crete without a provisional Governor. S. W. Rudolph of Philadelphia, an artist, expired at sea on the Aller, and was buried at Gibraltar. The British battleship Victorious is still aground at Port Said.—Page 7.

Page 1.

Fire of unknown origin destroyed the West End Hotel and seven cottages at Rockaway Beach.

The Classis of Kingston removed the Rev. Chandler A. Oakes as pastor of the Fair Street Reformed Church.

C. H. Rutherford of New York was arrested on the American Line steamer St. Louis at Newport News for passing a spurious check for $75 drawn on the Chemical Bank of New York.

Handwriting experts at Zola's trial in Paris expressed the opinion that Count Esterhazy was the author of the bordereau for writing which Dreyfus is serving a life sentence on Devil's Island.

It is reported that the Canadian Government has dispatched a note to Washington threatening to exclude Americans from the Klondike in case of hostile legislation by the United States.

A. J. Bowie, a mining engineer in the employ of James R. Keene, draws a dark picture of the outlook at the Klondike. Supplies, skilled miners, and machinery are wanting, he says, for successful work this year.

The proposed law taxing bachelors in New Jersey has brought to light a unique bachelors' club, which has hitherto been unknown to all but the initiated. Its objects are to promote gallantry toward the fair sex and discourage matrimony.

Señor Dupuy de Lome, the ex-Minister to the United States from Spain, with his family, reached the city last night en route for Spain. He declined to talk for publication, and was driven at once to the Hotel St. Marc. Two detectives from the Central Office met him as he landed from the Pennsylvania Railroad's ferryboat and remained on duty at the hotel all night. Señor de Lome and his party will sail to-day on the Britannic.

Page 2.

The Grand Trunk Railway is said to have purchased land near Toledo, which will give it an entrance into that city.

Contracts are said to have been made with the railroads to carry the greater part of Leiter's wheat holdings from Chicago to the seaboard. The Chicago market was strong yesterday.

It was said yesterday that the first of the four vessels being constructed for the American Mail Steamship Company will be ready in August, and that the new line will engage in the fruit trade between Jamaica and other West Indian points and the United States.

Page 3.

Arguments in favor of woman's suffrage were presented to the Senate and House committees in Washington by leading members of the National Woman Suffrage Association.

James B. Angell, United States Minister to Turkey, has announced his intention to resign in time to resume his duties as President of the University of Michigan next Fall.

Pay Director Luther G. Billings, United States Navy, has been convicted by a court-martial of falsehood and scandalous conduct and sentenced to dismissal from the navy.

Addresses to the silver men of the country urging united action in coming elections have been issued by the Democratic and Populist and Silver Republican National Committees.

Proposals were opened in Washington for carrying the mails to Jamaica. The American Mail Steamship Company of New Jersey proposes to furnish four new American twin-screw vessels for 66 2-3 cents per statute mile.

Commissioner Evans admitted the justice of THE NEW YORK TIMES's account of the abuses in the Pension Office. Reform in the selection and employment of clerks as well as a transfer of the bureau to the War Department have been proposed, but are not popular with Congress.

Page 4.

The old steamboat Narragansett, which has been fitted as a houseboat for detained immigrants, arrived at Ellis Island yesterday from Groton, Conn.

It is understood at Albany that the Democratic leaders propose next Fall to separate the State and Congressional campaigns, so that the fight for State officers and the Legislature shall be made on State issues and the fights in the Congressional districts on issues drawn to suit the conditions in each district. On the other hand, it is stated that the Republican leaders propose to make their fight chiefly on the financial issue.

The State Senate yesterday dicussed the proposed Constitutional amendment providing for biennial sessions of the Legislature. There was a hearing before the Senate Cities Committee on the Brush bill relating to the Board of Health. Many bills of local interest were introduced in both houses, and others were reported favorably by committees. The Judiciary Committees of the Senate and Assembly will hold a joint meeting to-day to begin the preparation of a primary election bill.

Page 5.

A waiter's version of the story told by Beck of loaning $10 to Noonan, taking his cuff as security, tended to discredit the testimony given by Beck.

The twelfth annual convention of the American Newspaper Publishers' Association will begin its sessions at the Waldorf-Astoria this morning.

The Executive Committee of the Insurance Tariff Association will meet to-day and frame its recommendation in reference to the maintenance of rates.

Mrs. Clara Baldwin, daughter-in-law of William S. Baldwin, has had him committed for examination as to his sanity. He imagines, she says, that he is Napoleon's son.

George Richards, an old man, was killed at a Newark crossing by a fast train. He had warned the railroad previously that the place was inadequately guarded and dangerous.

Serious trouble was narrowly averted at a game of basket ball between a team of New Rochelle players and Connecticut Guardsmen. A rival local club annoyed the home team.

A girl from Rockland Lake died of rabies in Roosevelt Hospital. She said last Summer to have fondled a dog afflicted with the disease, the saliva coming in contact with her chapped hands.

There was a large attendance yesterday at the auction sale of trotters and pacers in progress at Madison Square Garden, but the bidding lacked spirit, and a number of well-bred and speedy animals were knocked down at low prices.

The Board of Home Missions of the Presbytery held a special meeting yesterday, at which the Rev. Charles L. Thompson of the Madison Avenue Presbyterian Church was formally accepted as Secretary, to succeed the Rev. William C. Roberts.

John Moje, a Third Avenue saloon keeper, was fleeced of $200 in Philadelphia by three men. He says that he and his manager came up with one of the men and walked him about for six hours before he found a policeman, who arrested the man. Mr. Moje says a cigar he smoked dazed him.

Patrick Vaughan, the policeman who shot and wounded John Lawler, was discharged yesterday in Morrisania Police Court. Lawler pleaded for the officer. He said it was all his own fault, and vowed that he would live a better life in future, whereupon he was also discharged.

Nearly 700 covers, it is expected, will be laid at the banquet of the Merchants and Manufacturers' Board of Trade of New York, which will be held at the Waldorf-Astoria on Tuesday. The various industries and trades will be grouped at separate tables. Several United States Senators and Representatives will be present. A Reception Committee was appointed last night.

Page 7.

Charles L. Tiffany, who was eighty-six years old yesterday, received the congratulations of many old employes, some of whom have been with him for over forty years.

At a meeting of musical people at the home of Mr. and Mrs. A. W. Drake yesterday afternoon it was decided that the project to establish here a permanent orchestra should be energetically carried out. A committee will be appointed to raise the necessary amount, $1,000,000. There is already $115,000 in hand.

Page 9.

Opposition to the proposed combination of Western tin-plate manufacturers is developing in several quarters. New York dealers regard the scheme as impracticable.

A meeting of committees representing the Rapid Transit Commissioners and the Manhattan Railway Company was held, but a strict silence was maintained as to their proceedings.

Page 12.

Frank Moss denied yesterday the statement that the Society for the Prevention of Crime contemplates legal action against the promotion of William S. Devery to be Deputy Chief of Police.

The model tenement houses on Sixty-eighth and Sixty-ninth Streets, west of Amsterdam Avenue, were opened yesterday for inspection. One is ready for occupancy, and the first tenant will move in to-day.

Chairman Maxwell of the Brooklyn Committee of the Board of Education appeared before the Board of Estimate yesterday and asked for an allowance to pay the teachers for January. They will probably be paid Friday or Monday.

At the third monthly conference held under the auspices of the Charity Organization Society yesterday, the conditions of life of poor children in the city were discussed and the work done and in progress in their behalf was described. The necessity for more small parks in the congested districts was insisted upon, and examples were cited demonstrating the beneficial effects of rural surroundings upon health and morals.

Miss Dellaripha Richardson, daughter of the "Spite House" millionaire, appeared in Surrogate Fitzgerald's court yesterday during the hearing of the contest of her father's will brought by her brother and herself, made mysterious charges of murder and conspiracy, including the Surrogate in her accusations, and then went away. The evidence regarding Mr. Richardson's sanity when he made the will in dispute was conflicting.

At yesterday's meeting of the City Council a resolution was introduced to compel department stores to pay a license of $500 a year for each department; another to investigate the price and quality of gas in various parts of the city, and a third contained a protest against the usurpation of municipal functions by the State Legislature. All were referred to committees. A protest from Queens against the centralization of all municipal power in Manhattan received scant courtesy from the Aldermen at their meeting.

FIRE AT ROCKAWAY BEACH.

The West End Hotel and Seven Cottages Destroyed by Flames of Unknown Origin.

The West End Hotel and seven cottages at Rockaway Beach were destroyed by fire which started shortly after 11 o'clock last night in the hotel. The hotel was a four-story frame structure at the corner of Grove, Hammells, and Ocean Avenues. It contained 200 rooms and was owned by Paul Hauk, who lives in Seventy-fifth Street. He purchased it three years ago, paying $70,000 for it. He has since made extensive repairs and largely refurnished it.

The building was being repainted, and painters were at work in the building during the day. There was no one in the building when the fire started. The flames appeared to have spread through a large portion of the frame building when discovered. The fire was seen simultaneously by two policemen and a life saver.

When the volunteer firemen of Arverne, Hammells, and Rockaway Beach reached the building it was a mass of flame, and they turned their attention to the cottages, some of which were even then burning. Nothing was saved from the hotel. Four of the cottages were partially saved.

KINGSTON PREACHER REMOVED.

The Rev. C. A. Oakes No Longer Pastor of the Fair Street Reformed Church—He Will Appeal.

KINGSTON, Feb. 15.—The Classis of Kingston, after a special session which began yesterday morning and ended this afternoon, decided to dissolve the relations existing between the Rev. Chandler A. Oakes, Ph. D., and the Fair Street Reformed Church. Charges had been brought against Dr. Oakes by the consistory to the effect that the spiritual and financial condition of the church would be bettered by his dismissal. The case was summed up this afternoon for the consistory by the Rev. Dr. Oggel and by Dr. Oakes for himself. The Classis then retired, and after a deliberation of half an hour returned a verdict that the pastoral relations between Dr. Oakes and the church be dissolved on March 1. The vote of the Classis was 15 to 4.

Dr. Oakes is to be allowed to occupy the parsonage until April 1, and will be paid his salary up to June 1. The verdict was received in silence. Dr. Oakes announced his determination to appeal to the Synod, and said that he considered the offer of salary until June 1 as adding insult to injury.

"It is trying to bribe a man for a few hundred dollars, when life, honor, and justice are at stake," he said. This statement was received with applause. Moderator Davis stated that it would take twenty days for an appeal, and until that time the decision of Classis would stand and be in force.

A committee, composed of Dr. Oggel, the Rev. Mr. McNair, Dr. Oakes's counsel, and the Rev. Herman Hageman, was appointed to revise the stenographer's minutes for the appeal. Dr. Oakes says he will preach in the church.

MISS DEANS'S CLAIM ON TRIAL.

Aged Witness Heard in the Suit for a Share of the Stewart Estate.

The actual trial of the suit brought by Miss Euphemia Deans against ex-Judge Henry Hilton to recover a one-sixth interest in the old A. T. Stewart property at Thirty-fourth Street and Madison Avenue, was begun before Justice Scott.

Miss Deans, who is a school teacher, claims that through her mother she is one of the next of kin to the late A. T. Stewart. Her mother, Mary Bailey Deans, she contends, was an aunt of the dead millionaire. Judge Hilton denies the relationship.

The most important witness was James Bailey, eighty-six years old, who said he came to this country from Ireland on May 4, 1838. He said that when he came to this city in 1838 he met Mr. Stewart, to whom he had a letter of introduction from his mother, Mrs. Martin, and that Mr. Stewart spoke of him as the son of "his Aunt Mary." This testimony was intended to show the relationship between the plaintiff and her relatives in Europe. The case will go on.

ESTERHAZY IN THE TOILS

Handwriting Experts at Zola's Trial Affirm that He Was the Author of the Bordereau.

MME. DE BOULANCEY A FACTOR

She Received Letters from Esterhazy Animadverting on France and the Army—His Statements Startle the Court.

PARIS, Feb. 15.—The Zola trial will be concluded this week, according to programme, although it is expected that at least one night session will be necessary to get through on Saturday. So successful have been the efforts of M. Zola and his counsel, M. Laborie, to shatter the position taken by the Ministry on the Dreyfus case that already there are many who feel that Zola's acquittal is certain. When it is taken into consideration that the court was convened for the express purpose of securing a conviction, and that this seemed to be a foregone conclusion at the start, some idea may be obtained of the effect which the trial has had on public opinion in Paris. Even the Court itself, so bitterly hostile at the start, shows every day more and more evidence of being favorably disposed toward Zola. But this, of course, is no assurance that he will not be convicted by the Court.

It was rumored in the lobbies of the court to-day that MM. Laborie and Clemenceau are prolonging the examination of the witnesses in order to extend the trial, in the hope that the question of a revision of the Dreyfus trial will come before the Chamber of Deputies, now that it is generally admitted that Dreyfus was convicted on a secret document, and in the hope that something will happen in their favor.

While the examination of the experts proved rather tiresome, the flimsiness of their methods has turned favor toward Zola, and the mute sulkiness of the Advocate General is a strong indication of how matters are going.

To-day Col. Picquart seemed to come in for the hostility hitherto reserved for M. Zola. Mlle. Comminge's deposition tended to show that Lieut. Col. Paty du Clam wrote the telegrams, signed "Speranza," which were sent to Col. Picquart while he was in Tunis, with the intention to frighten him from following the Esterhazy trial. Prof. Grimand's testimony created a deep impression.

It is said to-night that Commandant Ravary, who compiled the unsatisfactory report for the Esterhazy trial, has had a sudden attack of congestion of the brain.

There were several quarrels outside the court to-day. In one case two barristers had a hand-to-hand fight.

High Prices Paid for Seats.

The visible excitement caused by the trial has greatly abated, but the real interest is absorbing and grows daily. The courtroom is packed, although the price of seats paid to those ready to wait all night to secure places has risen from 5f. to 25f.

Count Esterhazy will be examined to-morrow, so that the interest will be still higher, just as to-day's evidence exceeded yesterday's in exciting qualities.

When the trial is finished the discussion will be moved to the Chamber of Deputies and the Senate, where the Cabinet will be on its trial. There are still thirteen witnesses to be examined, and then will come the addresses of the Advocate General, M. Van Cassel; M. Laborie, and M. Clémenceau. M. Laborie is expected to speak four or five hours. M. Zola will speak very briefly.

The crowd present at the opening of the trial to-day was not so large as yesterday, and Zola's arrival at the court was not marked by any incident.

At the opening of the proceedings the Presiding Judge, M. Delagorgne, disallowed the request of counsel for M. Zola, M. Laborie, that the experts heard at the Esterhazy court-martial should be called to testify.

Gen. Gonse reappeared on the witness stand and protested against the assertion made by M. Jaures, the Socialist Deputy, on Saturday last, that the General Staff had refused to enlighten the Dreyfus affair.

M. Laborie, replying to Gen. Gonse, said that if he desired to throw light upon the case he could ask the War Minister's permission to do so.

To this Gen. Gonse answered that it was not within his province to transmit such a request to the Minister for War.

M. Crepieux Janin, a handwriting expert, was the next witness. He strenuously denied M. Teyssonnières's statement, made by the latter, who is also an expert in handwriting, yesterday, that he had attempted to bribe M. Teyssonnières to modify his reports of the Dreyfus bordereau.

M. Teyssonnières, M. Crepieux Janin added, had declared that it was on his (M. Teyssonnières's) report alone and not on M. Bertillon's that Dreyfus was convicted. This statement created a sensation.

M. Janin added that it was because M. Teyssonnières was angry with the witness for not sharing his opinion in regard to the Dreyfus case that he tried to compromise the matter. The witness further said he was a Frenchman and a Catholic, and exercised the profession of a dentist, and did not exercise the profession of an expert in handwriting.

M. Laborie Overruled by the Court.

Director Meyer of the French Record Office opened his testimony by affirming himself a Catholic. He declared that the published fac similes of the bordereau were as exact as possible, and he thought that Gen. Pellieux's contention that the fac similes looked like forgeries was an exaggeration. The witness added that he only desired an enlightenment of this sad affair, and if he was allowed to compare the fac similes with the original, if mistaken he would loyally say so. Continuing, the witness admitted that he had acted wrongly in intrusting the examination of the bordereau to M. Bertillon, who, the witness asserted, had acted in a manner devoid of all sense.

M. Meyer concluded with saying that the handwriting of Major Esterhazy resembled that of the bordereau.

M. Laborie then asked permission to examine the experts Couard, Belhomme, and Varinard, but the Court refused the request, upon which M. Laborie drew up conclusions, asking the Court to take cognizance of the fact. But the Presiding Judge, before even hearing the question, refused to let it be put, after which the Court retired to deliberate and decided that the Presiding Judge was right in refusing to allow questions "the only effect of which would be uselessly to prolong the proceedings."

Prof. Ernest Molinier of the College of France testified that Major Esterhazy's handwriting absolutely resembled that of the bordereau.

M. Clémenceau, counsel for the Aurore, read letters from Mme. de Boulancey admitting the possession of letters which Major Esterhazy wrote her between 1881 and 1894, and containing serious animadversions on France and the French Army. Major Esterhazy, it appeared, asked that the letters be returned to him; but Mme. de Boulancey refused to do so, in order to be able to prove that she had not committed forgery.

M. Clémenceau urged the Court to appoint a magistrate to ask Mme. de Boulancey if, among the letters, there was not one containing the following expressions:

"First—'Gen. Saussier [then the Commander in Chief of the French Army and Military Governor of Paris] is a clown. In our country the Germans would not show him in a circus.' [Uproar in court.]

"Second—'If the Prussians got as far as Lyons, they might throw away their guns and keep only their riding whips to drive the French in front of them.'" [Prolonged sensation.]

Blackboard for Demonstration.

Three amateur experts in handwriting testified that the fac simile was an exact reproduction of Major Esterhazy's handwriting, statements which caused further sensations in court.

M. Felix Frank, a lawyer of Brussels, testified that in order to demonstrate his evidence it would be necessary to have a blackboard, and that it would require an hour to demonstrate his theory.

Amid an uproar in court the session was suspended while a blackboard was procured and placed on an easel, after which M. Frank traced on the blackboard a fac simile of the bordereau and of Major Esterhazy's handwriting, and commenced his demonstration.

M. Frank made some long technical demonstrations and said:

"The majority of the experts started on the false idea that the writer of the bordereau had disguised his handwriting. The bordereau, however, was written naturally and in a running hand, which is identical with that of Major Esterhazy.

The latter, continued the witness, had recognized the bordereau as being his own handwriting, but had declared it had been traced by a forger. M. Frank proceeded technically to demonstrate the improbability of this explanation, showing how recurring words presented certain divergencies.

The lengthy demonstration of the witness caused impatience among the public in court, culminating in open murmurs, when M. Frank affirmed that the bordereau was written by one person alone, and added that this person was Major Esterhazy.

Annoyed at the murmurs, M. Frank turned and cried:

"I intended to end here, but since I am interrupted I will continue."

The Presiding Judge here remarked:

"I will ask you to use different language than that, which is discourteous."

M. Laborie thereupon intervened, asking the Presiding Judge to order silence in the court, pointing out that the lawyers were following the evidence with the closest attention.

"I am convinced," M. Frank resumed, "that the writer of the bordereau has a German mind."

The witness concluded with predicting that some day it would be recognized that the bordereau was not written by Dreyfus, which remark was greeted with murmurs.

The blackboard was then removed, and Prof. Grimand of the Polytechnic School deposed that he signed the protests against the conduct of the Dreyfus affair because he was convinced that respect for the law, honor, and the fatherland was involved. The whole procedure struck this witness as being extraordinary. He added:

"In spite of the disguised threats and acts of intimidation of which I have been the victim, I here affirm that a revision of the case is a crying necessity, and I intend to do my utmost to obtain it."

The witness concluded with asserting his rights as a patriot and his love for the army, which brought forth hearty applause.

Prof. Havelt of the College of France said he examined, as an expert, the bordereau and the letters of Major Esterhazy and Dreyfus, as well as a letter written by Dreyfus since his condemnation. The latter, the witness continued, was devoid of resemblance to the bordereau, of which he was convinced Major Esterhazy was the author.

Court was then adjourned. The crowd made no demonstration, and the officers, including Major Esterhazy and Gen. Pellieux, left amid silence.

At the Cabinet council to-day the trial of M. Zola and the publisher of Aurora was under discussion.

ARRESTED ON THE ST. LOUIS.

C. H. Rutherford in Custody at Newport News for Passing a Spurious Check on the Chemical Bank.

NEWPORT NEWS, Feb. 15.—A man representing himself to be C. H. Rutherford of New York, was arrested by Chief of Police Harwood on board the American Line steamship St. Louis this afternoon, charged with passing a spurious check for $75. Rutherford has been staying at the Hygeia Hotel, at Old Point, for a week or two. He spent money freely, mingling among the guests of the hotel and the officers at Fort Monroe and soon became well acquainted. Saturday he requested Harry Phoebus, a druggist at Old Point, to cash a check for $75, drawn on the Chemical National Bank of New York. After giving the money to Rutherford Phoebus became suspicious, and telegraphed to the bank for information as to his responsibility.

He received a reply pronouncing the check worthless. Rutherford came to this city, and to-day he went to the shipyard where the St. Louis is tied up for repairs, and requested permission to inspect the vessel. While walking about the big liner he was confronted by the Chief of Police. He attempted to elude the officer, but was soon arrested. Rutherford is now in jail at Hampton. He will be tried as soon as the check is returned from New York. The incident has created a sensation at the hotel, where Rutherford made himself quite popular. It is understood that he swindled several military officers at the fort out of small sums of money.

A UNIQUE JERSEY CLUB.

Its Object Is to Promote Gallantry Toward the Fair Sex and Discourage Matrimony.

TRENTON, N. J., Feb. 15.—The bill introduced by Assemblyman Weller of this city to tax bachelors has brought to light the Bachelors' Club of Trenton. Although the club is one of the oldest in the State, it was not known that such an organization existed until it was forced to announce itself and to formally protest against the passage of the bill now pending. The object of the club as disclosed by its by-laws is rather unique. It is to widen the scope and increase the possibilities of gallantry, and at the same time discourage the seemingly inevitable result of the law of association between persons of opposite sex, namely, matrimony.

Article VII. of the constitution sets forth the principles upon which the club is founded, and is as follows:

"Section 1. No member of the Bachelors' Club shall call upon any one friend among the gentler sex, nor escort her to entertainments or social functions, except in case of formal invitation, oftener than once a month; and it is hereby made mandatory that each member shall call upon, escort to entertainments or social functions, or show some direct gallantry to friends of the gentler sex upon at least three separate and distinct occasions in each month.

"Sec. 2. Violation or disregard of the preceding section shall, after due hearing before the Executive Committee, be deemed sufficient cause for dismissal from membership."

The rigidity of this regulation has had the effect of depleting the membership from time to time, and has, to an extent, discouraged new acquisitions, but, despite this fact, the club has flourished and become popular. John Hartpence of the Supreme Court office has been President of the club since its organization, early in 1891, and J. Harry Woodruff has been Secretary and Treasurer. It is authoritatively stated that Senator Edward C. Stokes of Cumberland will be added shortly to the membership of the club.

MR. HOYT SUED FOR $10,000.

E. G. Bates Asks Damages in Boston as a Result of a Word War.

BOSTON, Feb. 15.—The trial of a suit for $10,000 damages against Charles H. Hoyt, playwright and ex-member of the New Hampshire Legislature, was begun before Judge Sherman and a jury in the Second Session of the Suffolk Superior Court this afternoon.

The suit is brought by Edwin G. Bates, a member of the firm of Bates & Bendix, music publishers, for alleged injuries to character and reputation. Mr. Bates is also musical director of the Castle Square Theatre. Mr. Bates alleges in his bill that in the Park Theatre one night Mr. Hoyt called him a liar and in an uncontrollable fit of passion added a boisterous, loud, and blasphemous tirade of words. He adds that this took place before a large concourse of people and in the presence of ladies, and that Mr. Hoyt after exhausting his vocabulary spit upon him.

It was alleged that Mr. Hoyt continued his talk at the bar of the Hotel Reynolds when Mr. Bates was not present. Mr. Bates says that he has been greatly injured in his feelings and put to great mental suffering, and asks $10,000 damages.

The trouble grew out of a controversy over the song "Sweet Daisy Stokes," which was sung by Otis Harlan in the play "The Black Sheep."

Mr. Hoyt says that any words spoken to the plaintiff were not publicly uttered or published, and were justified and proper, in that they were true.

Mr. Hoyt was in the court room accompanied by Fred Wright, his managed.

DARK TALE FROM KLONDIKE

A. J. Bowie, James R. Keene's Engineer, Says There Are Few Miners There.

EXORBITANT PRICES FOR FOOD

Many Men Drowned in the Ice Floe on the Way—Famine Sure to Kill Many Laborers—Corporations Needed for Good Work.

SAN FRANCISCO, Feb. 15.—A letter has been received from Augustus J. Bowie, a mining engineer sent to the Klondike by James R. Keene in the interests of a New York syndicate, dated at Dawson Jan. 3. After stating that the cold is 20 degrees below zero, with no wind, he says meat is sold at $1.50 per pound wholesale, and flour at $135 for a sack of fifty pounds. Men are paid $1.50 an hour who are not worth that much per diem. "Without exception," he says, "there are fewer mining men than in any other place I was ever in. They have not the slightest conception of mining. The only wonder to me is the fact that the place has been able to exist as long as it has under the terrible prices demanded for everything.

"People in San Francisco and elsewhere cannot conceive the condition of affairs here. Absolutely nothing is to be obtained, and it will be fully two years before the mines can be handled as they should be, on account of the want of ordinary essentials for work, let alone living. Wood sells at $50 per cord. There is plenty of it, but no means for quick or easy transportation. The mines are certainly extraordinarily rich, but the present system of work must be largely or entirely abandoned.

"Corporations must take hold and clean out the crowd of good-for-nothings." A new era will dawn. The Alaska Commercial Company and North American Transportation and Trading Company are the only two business concerns here, where there is ample room for more, if transportation lines were established. Situated as these companies are, they will throw every obstacle in the way of any and every body coming in to compete with them, and thus keep up their sales. They will slowly but surely absorb all the gold output by charging infamous prices for supplies. The Alaska Commercial Company during the present famine has never raised prices on any staple article and has been very just, but when the North American Transportation and Trading Company finds that the Alaska Commercial Company has sold out any article, it raises the price 300 per cent. or more. Coal oil is $40 per gallon, candles fetch $1 each, and are esteemed a luxury. The restaurants are all closed, as are the bakers, and choice bacon is a thing of the past. The poorest whisky, made on the spot, commands $5 a bottle, and you can buy but little at that figure.

"Light just now is the most important thing. One cannot buy candles or oil now for love or money. I have spent only one night in town, as the place is absolutely too disgusting for anything. Gin mills, women, dance houses, and gambling dens are everywhere.

"There is not the slightest doubt that many a poor fellow died en route here, and will never more be heard of. A man who came in the other day by way of Dyea told me that on the way down he saw men's arms sticking up out of the ice. Their bodies were out of sight. They were grasping oars, planks, and pieces of wood, which they had grabbed as they were drowning in the ice floe. The famine here cannot be pictured in too awful form. Soon the fuel will give out. Men cannot work without food, and there is no food for wood cutters. Some large sales have been made to Eastern parties, $324,000 having been paid for three claims on Bonanza Creek, and $24,000 for two others. Twenty have been bought on Eldorado Creek for $100,000.

"Sulphur and Dominion Creeks now offer the best advantage for the money. The yield of all claims will, I think, be less than last year, as there are no supplies here, labor or materials to work with, and famine is sure to kill off many laborers. If I do not starve to death I shall be very lucky."

CANADA WILL RETALIATE.

Hostile Washington Legislation to be Met by Exclusion of Americans from the Klondike.

MONTREAL, Feb. 15.—A special dispatch from Ottawa says that the Dominion Government this afternoon dispatched a communication to Washington stating the determination of Canada, in the event of the passage by Congress of the bill introduced in the House by Mr. Payne and in the Senate by Senator Frye, to issue a proclamation barring all but British subjects from the right to mine in the Klondike or other Canadian territory in the Yukon region. The contents of the note, it is added, probably will be laid before the American Government by the British Ambassador, Sir Julian Pauncefote.

No official announcement has been made by the Government of the dispatch of such a note, but neither is it denied, and the general belief is that the step has been taken. There has been considerable agitation in favor of a move of this nature by the Canadian Government, and for some days the Government press has been hinting that it might have to come to that.

Sir Wilfrid Laurier and his Cabinet have been much annoyed at the threatened blocking of the "all Canadian Railroad" project by legislation at Washington, and the taunts of the opposition in Parliament probably have determined the Government to carry its plans through at any cost. It is now stated that in view of the disposition shown by the United States in its customs regulations at Fort Wrangell, the Canadian Government may abandon the proposed Stickeen River route and build the railroad from Port Simpson, which will bring it all in Canadian territory.

KLONDIKE RELIEF DELAYED.

SEATTLE, Washington, Feb. 15.—The three-masted ship Lucille, chartered by the Government to convey to Alaska the army pack train of twenty-two officers and men and 110 animals, was libeled for $6,000 to-day by the Alaska Forwarding Company of San Francisco. Five officers of this company boarded the Lucille at San Francisco with 44 animals and 50 tons of freight. A contract was entered into with Havner & Co., owners of the Lucille, to land the expedition at Skaguay, where the company intends to establish a pack train to be used over White Pass.

On the arrival of the Lucille at this port, Havner & Co. contracted to take the Government expedition, which is the advance detachment of the Klondike relief party. One thing after another delayed the departure of the Lucille, culminating to-day, when the San Francisco company libelled the ship because it was found that there was no room for both parties, and that the private expedition was to be left on the dock. A deputy marshal was put in charge of the ship. It is expected that the matter will be settled so that the Lucille can sail some time to-night or in the morning.

LOSS OF THE CLARA NEVADA.

SEATTLE, Washington, Feb. 15.—No further news has been received concerning the reported loss of the steamer Clara Nevada in Alaskan waters. Owing to the many conflicting rumors, hope for her safety has not yet been abandoned. Unless some unexpected steamer arrives, no definite news is expected before next Thursday.

The latest report was brought down by the steamer Excelsior, which arrived to-day. Capt. Donnellson said that just before he left Juneau the steamer Coleman arrived and reported that wreckage and bedding marked "Hassler" had been washed ashore at Seward. He said: "The Clara Nevada was formerly a Government vessel, known as the Hassler, and I have no doubt that she is at the bottom of the sea, at least such part of her as was not burned, for the Seward citizens report having seen a blazing vessel on the water."

The Excelsior arrived at Juneau five hours after the steamer Rosalie, which reported passing the Clara Nevada.

LAKE FISHERMEN LOST.

Carried Off on the Ice into Lake Erie—Between Twenty and Thirty in the Party.

BUFFALO, Feb. 15.—A number of men, estimated at between twenty and thirty, who were fishing through the ice on Lake Erie several miles up the lake, are believed to have lost their lives or to be adrift on the ice on the lake.

A heavy wind blowing from the east caused the ice to break away from the shore, and nothing can now be seen or heard of the men.

A large rescue party is on the way through a blinding snowstorm up the lake shore, but will not return before morning.

TALE OF MURDER MYSTERY.

A Jamaica (L. I.) Contractor Arrested as a Result of a Child's Strange Story.

Robert Brower, a contractor of Jamaica, L. I., was arrested last night by the police of Queens Borough on the strength of a story told by Mrs. Eliza Jackson of 102 Smith Street and her daughter Helen, aged seven years. The daughter says that on the morning of July 11 of last year she saw Brower and a young man employed by him place the body of a colored man in a box and bury it in his back yard.

Brower at first denied to the police that he had a colored man working for him at the time, but later admitted it, and said the man had gone away. Mrs. Jackson said that a son of Brower told her some time after the alleged interment that their colored man, named John, had been kicked by a horse, and had died and was buried in the yard.

RIOTERS KILLED IN HUNGARY.

Village Held Against Troops Sent to Restore Order—The Agrarian Socialist Movement.

VIENNA, Feb. 15.—The Agrarian Socialist movement in Hungary is becoming most serious. At Kistarkany, in the Kaschau District, a thousand peasants are in open revolt. They have murdered the local magistrate, and are holding the village against the troops sent to restore order.

At Agrad, in the same district, in a desperate fight between the gendarmes and the peasants, four were killed and twenty wounded.

At Karasz the Socialists tried to liberate their imprisoned comrades, and the gendarmes were obliged to prevent an onset with leveled bayonets. A woman tried to wrest his rifle from a gendarme, and the latter stabbed her in the breast. She fell dead.

There have been many arrests and much disorder in other districts. At Szathmar a rioter has been killed. The sale of gunpowder has been prohibited in the disturbed localities, and nobody is allowed out of doors after 7 in the evening without a special permit. There is talk of proclaiming a siege.

HANNA BRIBERY CHARGES.

C. C. Shayne Declines to Go to Ohio as a Witness.

C. C. Shayne, who was asked to appear as a witness before the committee of the Ohio Senate, which is investigating the bribery charges in connection with the election of Senator Hanna, has sent the following reply:

New York, Feb. 15, 1898.

Hon. Newman H. Burke, Chairman Senate Committee, Columbus, Ohio:

Engagements until after the London fur sales in March will prevent me from accepting your kind invitation. If, however, you desire a chapter for your Ohio political history, I refer you to my statements already published in the leading journals; or you can send a committee here, to whom every courtesy will be extended.

C. C. SHAYNE.

WEDDING OF MISS HANNA.

The Ohio Senator's Sister Married to a Young Man of Cleveland.

THOMASVILLE, Ga., Feb. 15.—Miss Lillian C. Hanna, the sister of Senator Hanna of Ohio, was married here this evening to S. Prentiss Baldwin of Cleveland.

The ceremony was performed at the country residence of Mrs. J. Wyman Jones, a sister of Miss Hanna, by the Rev. Mr. Whitney, rector of St. Thomas's Church of this city.

In addition to the family, those present were Gov. and Mrs. Merriam of Minnesota, Mr. and Mrs. Arthur Ely and M. J. C. Morse of Chicago, and Mr. and Mrs. Haskell of Cleveland.

Mr. Baldwin is twenty-eight years old; his bride is forty-five.

Glut of Money in Louisville.

LOUISVILLE, Ky., Feb. 15.—Owing to the money plethora the Louisville Clearing House Association has decided to reduce interest paid country correspondents from 2½ to 2 per cent. after March 1. The average balances of Louisville banks held for country correspondents is $10,000,000. Two years ago the banks paid 3 per cent. for country balances.

THE WEATHER.

The local forecast may be found at the top of this page to the right of the title.

The storm of Monday night in Illinois has moved very rapidly to New Jersey, increasing in intensity, a pressure of 29.34 inches being reported from Block Island and a northwest wind of sixty miles an hour from Norfolk. This storm has caused snow or rain from the Middle and Upper Mississippi Valley to the Atlantic Coast, and violent gales in the lower lake region. A second storm of considerable intensity has appeared to the north of Montana. It has grown colder from the interior of the Middle and North Atlantic States to the Rocky Mountains.

The record of temperature for the twenty-four hours ended at midnight, taken from THE NEW YORK TIMES's thermometer and from the thermometer of the Weather Bureau, is as follows:

	Weather Bureau. 1897.	Weather Bureau. 1898.	TIMES. 1898.
3 A. M.	38	33	36
6 A. M.	37	33	36
9 A. M.	41	34	41
12 M.	30	36	42
4 P. M.	36	35	42
6 P. M.	36	35	39
9 P. M.	38	36	39
12 P. M.	32	32	39

THE TIMES's thermometer is 6 feet above the street level; that of the Weather Bureau is 285 feet above the street level.

Average temperatures yesterday were as follows:

Printing House Square.....39¾
Weather Bureau.....36
Corresponding date 1897.....36
Corresponding date for last 20 years.....32

The maximum temperature yesterday was 40 degrees at 1 P. M.; the minimum was 32 degrees at 4 A. M. The humidity at 8 A. M. was .73, and at 8 P. M., .93.

THE MAINE BLOWN [UP]

Terrible Explosion on Board United States Battleship in Havana Harbor.

MANY PERSONS KILL[ED] AND WOUNDED.

All the Boats of the Spanish Cr[uiser] Alfonso XII. Assisting in the Work of Relief.

None of the Wounded Men Ab[le to] Give Any Explanation of th[e] Cause of the Disaster.

HAVANA, Feb. 15.—At 9:45 o'clock [this] evening a terrible explosion took pla[ce on] board the United States battleship [Maine] in Havana Harbor.

Many persons were killed or wounde[d. All] the boats of the Spanish cruiser A[lfonso] XII. are assisting.

As yet the cause of the explosion is n[ot ap]parent. The wounded sailors of the [Maine] are unable to explain it. It is believed [that] the battleship is totally destroyed.

The explosion shook the whole city. [The] windows were broken in nearly al[l the] houses.

The correspondent of the Associated [Press] says he has conversed with several [of the] wounded sailors and understands from [them] that the explosion took place while [they] were asleep, so that they can give no [par]ticulars as to the cause.

WHAT SENOR DE LOME S[AYS]

He Declares That No Spaniard W[ould] Be Guilty of Causing Such [a] Disaster.

Señor de Lome, the departing ex-Mi[nister] of Spain to this country, who arrived i[n this] city last night, and went to the Ho[tel St.] Marc, at Fifth Avenue and Thirty[-ninth] Street, was awakened on the receipt [of the] news from Havana.

He refused to believe the report at [first.] When he had been assured of the tr[uth of] the story he said that there was no [possi]bility that the Spaniards had anything [to do] with the destruction of the Maine.

No Spaniard, he said, would be gui[lty of] such an act. If the report was tr[ue, he] said, the explosion must have been [caused] by some accident on board the warsh[ip.]

THE MAINE'S VISIT TO HAVA[NA.]

First American Warship to Visit [Cuba] Since the Struggle Began.

The Maine was ordered to Havar[na] Jan. 24 last, and was the first Ame[rican] warship to visit that port since the [out]break of the Cuban rebellion. In exp[lana]tion of the visit of the American batt[leship] to Cuba Secretary Long issued the f[ollow]ing statement:

"So far from there being any found[ation] for the rumors yesterday of trouble a[t Ha]vana, matters are now in such con[dition] that our vessels are going to resume [their] friendly calls at Cuban ports and go [in and] out just as the vessels of other natio[ns do.] The Maine will go in a day or two o[n] such a visit. The department has issu[ed or]ders for vessels to attend the public ce[lebra]tions in Mobile and the Mardi Gras at [New] Orleans, and for the torpedo flotilla t[o go to] Galveston, Texas."

The Maine was commanded by [Capt.] Charles D. Sigsbee. Her other officer[s were] Lieut. Commander Richard Wainw[right,] Lieuts. G. F. Holman, John Hood, a[nd] W. Yungen, Lieuts. (junior grade) [G.] Blow, J. T. Blandin, F. W. Jenkins, [Ensigns] J. H. Holden, W. T. Cluverius, Amos [Bron]son, and D. F. Boyd, Jr.; Surgeon [L. G.] Heneberger, Paymaster C. W. Litt[lefield,] Chief Engineer L. G. Howell, Passe[d As]sistant Engineer E. C. Bowers, As[sistant] Engineers J. R. Morris and D. R. M[errit,] Cadet Engineers Pope, Washington[,] Arthur Grenshaw, Chaplain J. P. Chi[dwick,] and Lieutenant of Marines A. W. Ca[tlin.]

The commander of the Maine, Capt. [Sigs]bee, is a favorite in the Navy Depart[ment.] For four years he was Chief of the H[ydro]graphic Office, and by his energy br[ought] the office up to a high standard.

He justified the department's judgm[ent in] the selection by running his ship st[raight] into a dock in New York harbor to [avoid] sinking a packed excursion boat. Thi[s was] a display of quick judgment, nerve[, and] pluck that pleased the department so [much] that the Captain was sent a complime[ntary] letter.

ARMAMENT OF THE MAIN[E.]

A Second-Class Battleship Bui[lt at] the Brooklyn Navy Yard.

The Maine was placed in comm[ission] Aug. 17, 1895. She is a twin-screw[, ar]mored turret ship, of the belted [type,] and is known as a second-class [bat]tleship. Like the Texas, the Maine [was] built at a Government navy yard. [The] Texas was built at Norfolk; the Ma[ine at] the New York Navy Yard. Both ships [were] authorized when Secretary Whitney [began] the work of rehabilitating a then de[cadent] navy.

The Maine is of Navy Departme[nt de]signs throughout. The hull was bu[ilt by] navy yard workmen, and the engines [were] constructed by the Quintard Iron [Works.] That firm obtained the contract on [a bid] of $735,000. There were no other bidd[ers.]

The vitals of the ship are protected [from] gun-fire by an armor belt 180 feet in [length.] This belt has a maximum thickness [of 12] inches. Below the water line the [belt] tapers to a thickness of 6 inches. [To de]flect an end-on or a fore-and-aft fire, [heavily] armored and sharply inclined V-s[haped] bulkheads are placed forward and a[ft, the] ends joining the armor belt. The bul[kheads] are 6 inches thick, and well backed.

In her main battery the ship mount[s four] 10-inch and six 6-inch rifles. A num[ber of] guns of smaller calibre are distribu[ted at] advantageous places. The 10-inch rif[les are] mounted in pairs in two steel turrets. [One] of these is situated aft, the other fo[rward.] The turret armor is 10½ inches thick[. The] protective power of these massive sh[ields is] increased by their circular shape, [which] tends to deflect a missile unless the [blow] is directly given.

The guns are breech-loading rifles[, with] bores 10 inches in diameter. The len[gth of] each gun is 329 inches. The weight i[s lit]tle more than 24 tons. From them [with a] service charge of 250 pounds of [powder is] throws a 500-pound shell a distance [of ...] miles, with an initial velocity of 2,0[00 feet] per second.

The 6-inch rifles are of the breech-[loading] pattern. These weapons measure 190 [inches] in length and weigh five tons each

"All the News That's Fit to Print."

The New York Times.

THE WEATHER.
Fair; wind northeasterly, becoming southerly.

OL. L...NO. 15,926. NEW YORK, WEDNESDAY, JANUARY 23, 1901.—SIXTEEN PAGES. ONE CENT In Greater New York, Jersey City, and Newark. } Elsewhere, TWO CENTS.

EEN VICTORIA DEAD AT OSBORNE

sed Away Quietly at 6:30 o'Clock Last Evening.

NE AT THE BEDSIDE

ily, with Bowed Heads, Listened to Bishop's Prayers.

EN BADE THEM FAREWELL

to Have Spoken Words of Great Moment to Prince of Wales.

ERT EDWARD NOW KING

Council and Parliament Will Meet in London To-day, and the Proclamation of the New Monarch's Succession Will Follow—Grief Over the Queen's Death and Admiration for Her Character Universal in the United Kingdom, the British Colonies, Europe, and America—Arrangements for the Funeral Not Yet Announced.

VES, Isle of Wight, Jan. 23.—Queen ria is dead. The greatest event in memory of this generation, almost most stupendous change in existing tions in England that could be imd, has taken place quietly, almost y, upon the anniversary of the of Queen Victoria's father, the of Kent.

end of this splendid career came in nply furnished room in Osborne e. This most respected of all wo living or dead, lay in a great four-bed. Around her were gathered majority of her descendants. Well n view of her dying eyes there hung trait of the Prince Consort. It was ho designed the room and every of the Castle. In scarcely audible the white-haired Bishop of Winer prayed beside her, as he had before prayed with his sovereign, was her Chaplain at Windsor.

n bowed heads the imperious ruler German Empire, the man who is King of England, the woman who acceeded to the title of Queen, the es and Princesses, and those of than royal designation listened to ishop's ceaseless prayer.

urally, the family, while recognize claim for public information, in hat some details of the events of the deathbed shall be sacred for esent, and have imposed the strict crecy on the whole household. The is, however, said to have bidden ell, in a feeble voice, to her fam- She first recognized the Prince of , to whom she spoke a few words at moment; then Emperor William he others present filed past and a whispered good-bye. All those bedroom were in tears.

o'clock passed. The Bishop continis intercession. One of the younger en asked a question in a shrill, sh treble, and was immediately ed. The women of the royal family faintly and the men shuffled un-

IE END QUITE PEACEFUL.

exactly 6:30 Sir James Reid held up and, and the people in the room that England had lost her Queen. ishop pronounced the benediction.

Queen passed away quite peace- She suffered no pain. Those who now mourners went to their rooms. minutes later the inevitable ele- of materialism stepped into this ic chapter of international history, for the Court ladies went busily to work ordering their mourning from London.

The wheels of the world were jarred when the announcement came; but in this palace at Osborne everything pursued the usual course. Down in the kitchen they were cooking a huge dinner for an assemblage the like of which has seldom been known in England, and the dinner preparations proceeded just as if nothing had happened.

An incident characteristic of the Queen's solicitude for others occurred two days ago, when, in one of the intervals of consciousness, she summoned strength to suggest to her dressers, who had been acting as nurses, that they take the opportunity of getting some fresh air.

QUEEN ASKS FOR HER DOG.

On Monday afternoon the Queen asked that her little Pomeranian be brought to her bedside.

It was feared that the Queen was dying at about 9 o'clock yesterday morning, and carriages were sent to Osborne cottage and the rectory to bring all the Princes and Princesses and the Bishop of Winchester to her bedside. It seemed then very near the end; but, when things looked the worst, the Queen, in one of the rallies due to her wonderful constitution, opened her eyes and recognized the Prince of Wales, the Princess, and Emperor William. She asked to see one of her faithful servants, a member of the household. He hastened to the room, but before he got there the Queen had passed into a fitful sleep.

Four o'clock marked the beginning of the end. Again the family were summoned, and this time the relapse was not followed by recovery.

The Prince of Wales was very much affected when the doctors at length informed him that his mother had breathed her last. Emperor William, himself deeply affected, did his best to minister comfort to his sorrow-stricken uncle, whose new dignity he was the first to acknowledge.

OUTSIDE OSBORNE HOUSE GATES.

No member of the royal family left Osborne House yesterday for the customary drives. A changing group of correspondents and townspeople loitered about the gates all day long, but never reached the proportions of the crowd of Monday.

It was a melancholy day. Occasional drizzles obscured the emerald hills beyond the castle. Greater simplicity or a more entire lack of any of that pomp traditionally attached to royalty could not be found in any country house in the kingdom than here, where the best-beloved monarch of centuries was dying and the ruler of another great nation waited by her bedside as grandson rather than as Emperor.

Two stalwart policemen guarding the gates against intruders were the sole reminders of officialdom. They were compelled in the morning to refuse admission to three dusky visitors from India who drove up arrayed in such gorgeous robes that the bystanders instinctively lifted their hats, mistaking them for potentates. The trio announced themselves as lecturers touring England in behalf of a foreign mission, and insisted upon an audience with the Prince of Wales to tender the sympathies of India.

Many of the country gentry and a few titled personages appeared at the lodge and registered their names in the visitors' book, the thrifty flunky who officiated doing a profitable business by selling the original copies of official bulletins to souvenir enthusiasts. Artists and photographers obtained pictures of the gates and grounds and any prominent persons who appeared.

THE LORD CHAMBERLAIN ARRIVES

Everybody feared that the Queen would never waken from the sleep which the noontime bulletin spoke of, and everybody was watching the flag on the castle tower, expecting it to sink to half mast. Lord Clarendon, the new Lord Chamberlain, with Prince Christian of Schleswig-Holstein and the Duke of Argyll, arrived at Osborne in the afternoon. The arrival of the Lord Chamberlain was an ominous sign, as he announces to a new monarch his accession to the throne.

When the 4 o'clock bulletin announced that the Queen was sinking, all the watchers at the gates of Osborne House made up their minds to remain to the end. The cold was intense, and a few favored ones sought shelter in the royal lodge, just inside, where they waited in absolute silence.

NEWS OF THE EVENT ANNOUNCED.

The telephone bell rang at 7:04 P. M., but before a royal servant had time to take the message the Chief of the Queen's Police emerged from the darkness, and, with bared head, said

"Gentlemen, the Queen passed away at 6:30."

All present reverently uncovered, and then shrill whistles outside and the ringing of the bells of the bicycles in waiting were the signals for messengers to race to Cowes with the news. In a few moments the place was deserted. Simultaneously, mounted messengers, on white horses, dashed from Osborne. What happened within the royal residence is purely surmise.

On their arrival at Cowes the correspondents found the news had been known both at East and West Cowes fifteen minutes before it had been announced to those in waiting at the gates of Osborne House. The streets were already filled with sorrowful crowds discussing her Majesty's death.

Prince and Princess Louis of Battenberg arrived at Osborne just too late to see her Majesty alive.

From all parts of the world there are still pouring into Cowes messages of condolence. They come from crowned heads, millionaires, tradesmen, and paupers, and are variously addressed to the Prince of Wales and the King of England.

RESULT OF ROBERTS'S NEWS?

The record of the last days of the reign of Victoria is not yet fully known. The correspondent of The Associated Press was the only correspondent admitted to Osborne House, and his interview with Sir Arthur John Bigge, private secretary to the late Queen, was the only official statement that was given out.

For several weeks the Queen had been failing. On Monday week she summoned Lord Roberts and asked him some very searching questions regarding the war in South Africa. On Tuesday she went for a drive, but was visibly affected. On Wednesday she suffered a paralytic stroke, accompanied by intense physical weakness. It was her first illness in all her eighty-one years, and she would not admit she was sick. Then her condition grew so serious that, against her wishes, the family were summoned. When they arrived her reason had practically succumbed to paralysis and weakness.

The events of the last few days, described in the bulletins, are too fresh to need repetition.

THE LAST BULLETINS.

OSBORNE HOUSE GATES, Isle of Wight, Jan. 22.—An official bulletin issued at 8 o'clock said:

The Queen this morning shows signs of diminishing strength, and her Majesty's condition again assumes a more serious aspect.
JAMES REID,
R. DOUGLAS POWELL,
THOMAS BARLOW.

The bulletin issued at noon said there had been no change for the worse in the Queen's condition since the morning bulletin.

At 4 P. M. another bulletin was posted. It said the Queen was slowly sinking.

At 6:45 P. M. the end was announced as follows:

Her Majesty the Queen breathed her last at 6:30 P. M., surrounded by her children and grandchildren.
JAMES REID,
R. DOUGLAS POWELL,
THOMAS BARLOW.

THE QUEEN'S FUNERAL.

Will Probably Be at Frogmore—Many Royalties Expected.

COWES, Isle of Wight, Jan. 23.—The body of Queen Victoria is being embalmed to-night, and will probably be taken to Windsor on Saturday.

The coffin arrived last evening from London.

Emperor William's arrangements are not settled, but it is believed that he will not depart until after the funeral, which will probably be a ceremony never before equaled in this country.

LONDON, Jan. 23.—There is little doubt that the funeral of Queen Victoria will take place at Frogmore, Hertfordshire, though nothing in regard to this matter has yet been announced.

Her Majesty was so closely related to the European Courts, big and little, that the gathering of royalties at the obsequies will be unprecedented.

ATHENS, Jan. 22.—King George will start for London to-night.

PARIS, Jan. 23.—The French Government will be represented at the funeral of Queen Victoria by an extraordinary embassy.

The members have not yet been chosen, but the embassy will be headed by Vice Admiral de Lajaille, who on several occasions welcomed Queen Victoria at Cherbourg in the name of France.

TO-DAY'S CEREMONIES.

Privy Council and Parliament to Meet—The Proclamation of the King.

LONDON, Jan. 23.—The Privy Council will meet in London to-day, and the proclamation of the King will take place thereafter at all places required by custom.

The King will come to London to preside over the Council. The Ministers will attend, give up their seals of office, be resworn, receive the proclamation of the King, pass votes of condolence and congratulation, and adjourn.

After giving up their seals the Ministers receive them back from the new ruler. The Privy Councilors will also be sworn afresh.

Shortly before midnight yesterday an official announcement was issued calling Parliament to assemble at 4 o'clock this afternoon to enable members of the House of Lords and House of Commons to take the oath of allegiance to the King. Precedent orders that Parliament shall meet within twenty-four hours of the death of the ruler.

At the offices of the Lord Chamberlain and of the City Remembrancer, at the Guildhall and at the College of Heralds, the officials were busy yesterday preparing for the formalities which for the first time in a generation, are to take place—the proclaiming of a new ruler of the United Kingdom. All the ancient gazettes, Court circulars, and other papers which describe the ceremonial of 1837 were taken from the libraries, that the officials might familiarize themselves with the ancient pageantry whereby a sovereign is proclaimed. The City Remembrancer said yesterday:

"It will depend on the pleasure of the new monarch to decide how far the ancient customs will be modified to suit modern methods; but, in a country where precedents are so firmly adhered to as England, it may be anticipated that we shall follow closely on the acts which prevailed when the Queen ascended the throne. The Privy Council, which is a very large body, will meet at once at St. James's Palace, where the form of proclamation declaring that 'we, etcetera, with one voice and consent of tongue and heart declare and proclaim the high mighty Prince Albert Edward, etcetera, who, by the death of the monarch, has become our only lawful and rightful liege, etcetera.'

"This proclamation will give the new title the King may assume, but this is not yet announced to us. The proclamation will then be sent to Heralds' College, and the following day the Earl Marshal, the Garter King at Arms, the Herald's Pursuivants, and other officials, with the college members and the Household troops, will proceed from the palace, clad in their splendid surcoats, and proceed to Trafalgar Square. There the King at Arms will halt, command silence, and read the proclamation. Proceeding down the Strand to Temple Bar, a halt will again be made, to demand an entrance into the City to proclaim the King. There the Lord Mayor and Sheriffs, in their state carriages, will form a great procession, and when the Earl Marshal's party comes just within the City boundary the proclamation will be read again, and the procession will pass down Ludgate Hill and Cheapside to the Royal Exchange, where similar ceremonies will close the spectacle."

DEEP GLOOM IN LONDON.

Places of Amusement All Closed—How the News Was Received.

LONDON, Jan. 23.—Silence, gloom, and darkness characterize London to-night. From Whitechapel to Mayfair streets usually gay with nightly festivity are dark, deserted, and desolate, and this depression of the public mind is likely to continue for many days to come.

Only a few hours ago the pleasure-seeking populace was hurrying to the theatres and music halls, only to find in every case the doors closed and big, black-bordered bills announcing that the performances had been suspended. The people, thus turned into the streets, gave for a short time an unusually thronged appearance to the West End. Many turned in the direction of Buckingham Palace and Marlborough House, where absolute silence reigned. Small bills, signed "Balfour," were posted outside, announcing the death of the monarch.

Everywhere, in vehicles and on the streets, the one topic of conversation was what would happen under the new reign, rather than the life and death of Victoria. Much interest was evinced in the way in which the enormous fortune of the dead Queen would be distributed, the general notion being that Osborne House would go to Princess Beatrice, and that she and Princess Christian would come into a considerable portion of Queen Victoria's wealth.

The probability that the King will take up a practically permanent residence in Buckingham Palace was much canvassed. This is a question that comes very much home to Londoners. Queen Victoria's preference for Balmoral Castle and Osborne House has been a complaint of long standing in the metropolis, and it is hoped that the new reign will see a change in this respect. The presence of the Court in London would give a brightness and gayety to the city which have long been absent.

Not until Queen Victoria has been laid to rest beside the Prince Consort at Frogmore will the theatres or music halls reopen. Moreover, business will come to a practical standstill. Music in all the hotels and public places ceased last evening. Fashionable resorts were empty, and very few of the nightly habitués were in evidence.

Americans who have passed through great National calamities may recall the crêpe-draped buildings and the National hush; but they can ill-conceive, since the death of Lincoln, any such expression of gloom as has already fallen on the United Kingdom. Marlborough House, so long the home of the new monarch; Buckingham Palace, where Queen Victoria made her last stay in London, and St. James's Palace, the residence of so many former monarchs, are to-night all black and deserted. Sentries in black overcoats keep silent vigil before the closed gates and bolted doors.

Early in the evening from St. Paul's, Westminster Abbey, and other churches bells were solemnly tolling or ringing muffled peals. In some cases the shops were already exhibiting signs of mourning. Beyond these things, however, and the boys crying extra editions in every direction, there was little that would outwardly indicate the passing of the country through an experience novel to almost the whole people.

SORROW IS UNIVERSAL.

Telegrams arriving from all parts of the country and the colonies re-echo the deep feeling of sorrow pervading all classes. These show that everywhere bells have been tolled and public performances and private functions suspended.

In Dublin the expressions of regret were universal. The bells of St. Patrick's Cathedral were tolled. Earl Cadogan, the Lord Lieutenant, was absent from Dublin yesterday, but it is expected that he will return immediately to preside at a meeting of the Irish Privy Council to proclaim the new King.

The news was received with the greatest sorrow at Balmoral, Windsor, and Eton, where Queen Victoria was regarded in an especially personal manner by the inhabitants.

Princess Beatrice telegraphed the tidings to ex-Empress Eugénie at Farnborough.

SCENES YESTERDAY AFTERNOON.

The gloomy faces of the crowds incessantly approaching the bulletin board at the Mansion House indicated yesterday how little the public hoped to receive better news of the condition of the Queen. Men of all ages and conditions, women and even children were content to spend a long time in awaiting their turn to get within reading distance of the board. As the throng moved slowly past the notice board, those who were unable to get there personally sent messenger boys with notebook and pencils to copy the text of everything posted. The grief of all was evident. Never were there so many black ties in the city before the actual arrival of a time of general mourning.

There was a remarkable scene outside the Mansion House early in the afternoon. On receipt of the alarming reports something resembling a groan was uttered by the hundreds of people assembled, and then some one started singing the national anthem. All heads were bared, and in a moment the crowds were singing "God Save the Queen" with a fervor proving how earnestly they wished for her Majesty's recovery. The passengers in passing carriages, cabs, and omnibuses joined in the singing, the drivers reverently doffing their hats.

At 4:35 P. M. the following was posted:

Osborne, 4 P. M.

My painful duty obliges me to inform you that the life of our beloved Queen is in the greatest danger. ALBERT EDWARD.

In reply the Lord Mayor, Frank Green, dispatched the following:

"I have received your Royal Highness's sad intimation with profound grief, which is shared by the citizens of London, who still pray that under Divine Providence the irreparable loss to her Majesty's devoted family and loyal subjects throughout the empire may still be averted. Will your Royal Highness be pleased to accept this heart-felt expression of my deep and sincere sympathy?"

THE FINAL ANNOUNCEMENT.

The latest bulletins previous to the announcement of the Queen's death, especially the message sent by the Prince of Wales, dispelled the last gleam of hope. The crowds silently dispersed from in front of the Mansion House, and only a few groups awaited the appearance of the inevitable announcement. This came at 7 o'clock in the form of a dispatch to the Lord Mayor from the new King as follows:

Osborne, 6:45 P. M.

My beloved mother has just passed away, surrounded by her children and grandchildren. ALBERT EDWARD.

The Lord Mayor immediately sent the following reply:

"Your Royal Highness's telegram announcing the nation's great loss I have received with profound distress and grief, and have communicated this most sad intimation to my fellow-citizens. Her Majesty's name and memory will forever live in the hearts of her people.

"May I respectfully convey to your Royal Highness and to all the members of the royal family the earnest sympathy and condolence of the City of London in your great sorrow?"

The scrap of paper a foot square, posted on the wall of the Mansion House, gave the first notice to London's homeward hurrying thousands of the death of the Queen. Excavations by which the street had been torn up made access to the bulletin difficult, but the bared heads of a silent group under a flickering gas jet told the crowds on the 'bus tops and sidewalks that the Queen was no more.

"BIG BEN" IS TOLLED.

A quarter of an hour later more than a thousand newsboys had invaded the streets with black-ruled newspapers, crying, "Death of the Queen," while through the dark streets boomed the deep-toned notes of "Big Ben," the big bell of St. Paul's Cathedral, the bells of the city re-echoing the news.

The shops closed as soon as the bells began to toll, and the blinds of the Mansion House were drawn down as soon as the message from the Prince of Wales was received by the Lord Mayor.

The bell tolled at St. Paul's Cathedral was the gift of William III., and is used only on occasions of the death of royal personages, Archbishops of Canterbury, Lord Mayors of London, and Bishops of London. The tolling continued for two hours at intervals of a minute and could be heard for miles in the direction of the wind.

Some hundreds of people stood in front of the cathedral around the spot where Queen Victoria prayed on the sixtieth anniversary of her accession to the throne.

LONDON PRESS COMMENTS.

Universal Grief Reflected in Editorials—Labouchere's Warm Eulogy.

LONDON, Jan. 23.—All the morning papers appear in heavy mourning borders, with editorials eulogistic of the dead Queen and recalling the leading events and characteristics of her reign. Very few political references as to the future are made. The Daily Mail says:

"We can but regret that the Queen was not permitted to see the end of the South African struggle. She has been taken from us in a dark hour which, we may hope, is a prelude to the dawn, and when we can ill spare her ripe experience and her vast knowledge of measures and men."

"Let us think of her this morning," says the Daily Chronicle, "by her highest title, not by her crown and sceptre, but by her own magnificent and splendid ideal of womanhood. This it is which touches the heart's core of a proud and imperial race. We have lost mother, wife, and Queen."

The Chronicle remarks that President McKinley was slightly premature in sending a communication to "His Majesty, the King," inasmuch as the Prince of Wales has not yet been proclaimed by the Privy Council.

The Daily Telegraph publishes two editorials under the captions "The Queen" and "The King." In the latter it says:

"Most happily for him, he has, with infinite credit to himself, passed through a period of probation in some ways more difficult and certainly more prolonged than that to which any successor to a throne in modern times has been subjected. He assumes the burden of his imperial task equipped with all the invaluable experience which the most painstaking discharge of great duties could secure him during the lifetime of his august mother. So accustomed have we become to his direct, personal patronage of every charity and every beneficial movement, many of which he initiated himself, that we are apt to forget the exhausting nature of the strain almost daily imposed upon his strength. He has won among the masses of the people a popularity that has been vouchsafed to few of his predecessors."

The Times says:

"The confidence inspired by her personal character enabled Queen Victoria on many occasions to use her intimate knowledge with effect in smoothing the rugged places of international relations or in modifying a policy which, through sheer inadequacy of information, would have led to undesirable friction. We have also to thank the Queen for influence of the most potent kind consistently and vigorously used to enforce high ideals of social and personal virtue, of religious faith and of Christian life."

Referring to the intellectual upheaval and the enormous social and economic progress which characterized the Victorian era, The Times expresses regret that the impetus has to some extent spent itself.

"At the close of Victoria's reign," continues The Times, "we find ourselves somewhat less secure of our position than we could desire, somewhat less abreast of the problems of the age than we ought to be, considering the initial advantages we secured."

"The great English-speaking Republic beyond the Atlantic has not failed to send us officially by the mouth of President McKinley, and unofficially by innumerable newspaper articles and other tokens of popular feeling, proof of how heartily and profoundly it shares in our grief. Need we say for ourselves and our colonies how dear to us in such an hour is the fellowship in woe which our American kinsmen so generously and warmly tender us?"

In another article The Times says:

"If anything can in some measure console the nation for the irreparable loss it has sustained, it is the well-founded conviction that the Queen has left behind her a worthy successor, who may be trusted to walk in her footsteps.

"In the whole range of English social and political life no position is more difficult to fill satisfactorily and without reproach than that of the heir apparent, and it may be justly said that the way this position has been filled has contributed to the remarkable increase in the devotion to the throne and the dynasty which has been one of the most striking characteristics of Victoria's reign.

"As Albert Edward has been a scrupulously constitutional Prince, we may confidently predict that he will be a scrupulously constitutional King. In the fulfillment of this onerous task he will have by his side a Queen who is already enthroned in the hearts of her loving subjects."

Henry Labouchère, M. P., in Truth has a remarkable tribute to Queen Victoria, a tribute all the more remarkable because of his democratic ideas and frank criticisms of royalty.

"Among all her millions of subjects," he says, "there are but few who will not mourn for her loss as for one of their own household. Nor will the mourners be found among her own subjects alone. It is not too much to say that never in the history of the world has a single death caused such universal grief. Alike in happiness and sorrow, she lived a life beyond reproach, without thought of self and unreservedly devoted to the duties of the hour. Although occupying perhaps the proudest position ever filled by a woman, and never wanting in a certain queenly dignity, her tastes, habits, demeanor, and even her dress were marked by the rarest simplicity.

"She has been indeed the mother of her people, and as a mother she will be mourned. In all the affairs of State she manifested the same wisdom that inspired her private life, nor did her own country alone enjoy the fruits of her experience and sagacity. Through her kindred and descendants abroad her influence for many years has been felt in Continental politics, always on the side of peace; and, in at least one crisis, she is known to have rendered service to the whole of Europe.

"Her sudden and lamentable breakdown was due entirely to worry and overwork. She had been greatly distressed by events in South Africa and by domestic griefs."

The Daily News says that Queen Victoria was always a peacemaker. It refers to the incident of her modifying in a pacific sense Lord Russell's dispatch in the Trent case.

The Standard, expressing regret that the Queen was not spared to see peace restored in South Africa, says: "The end for which she strove and prayed has yet to come, and the hope is perhaps visionary that the common grief of Britons and Afrikanders may abate those racial animosities which stand in the way of pacification."

Referring to the conspicuous success of Queen Victoria's reign, The Standard says:

"There was a time when republicanism was a serious phrase on English lips. To-day no whisper of discontent with the monarchical Constitution breaks the mourning of a loyal nation around the bier of the sovereign. It will be said of her in the annals of our land that she strengthened the Throne by loving the people, and that she was a great Queen and the mother of Kings because she was a good, noble, and true-hearted woman."

THE NATIONS' TRIBUTES.

Enmity for Great Britain Hushed and Only Sympathy Expressed.

PARIS, Jan. 23.—The news of the death of Queen Victoria was known in Paris at 8 o'clock last evening through special editions of the evening papers, which newsboys carried throughout the city. Great sympathy was expressed on all sides.

As soon as definite information reached Parliament the Presidents of the chambers announced that the next session would be adjourned as a sign of mourning.

When the news was known at the Ministry of Foreign Affairs, M. Delcassé, the Foreign Minister, went to the British Embassy to express to the Acting Ambassador the condolence of the French Government. President Loubet postponed his visit until the return of Sir Edmund Monson.

Not until then, moreover, will the arrangements relative to mourning be made. The British flag, draped with crape, will be placed over the entrance to the embassy to-day.

Last evening there was a steady stream of callers to inscribe their names in the register at the embassy.

Few and far between, indeed, are the Paris papers this morning which do not sound the note of regret at the passing of Victoria. In addition to long obituaries, special writers publish appreciations, reviewing the Queen's life work, noting in what respects it contributed to the greatness of the British nation, and speculating in some cases upon the reign about to open. Foremost of these special writers is M. Hanotaux, who, in Le Journal, refers to the extent of England's debt to Victoria.

"Her temperament and judgment, thanks to the precious lessons of Lord Melbourne," says M. Hanotaux, "were in complete accord with English Parliamentary institutions. Her success as a sovereign was due to her close attention to the affairs of State, her frequent journeys, her interviews with foreign statesmen, and above all, to the extraordinary position of being allied to several of the reigning sovereigns of Europe."

Le Gaulois says:

"Her action may be summed up in a brief phrase, little authority and much influence. The changes which are about to take place express better than blind and foolish flattery the place she occupied in Europe. That will be her true funeral oration, the final word of which will be that she, the possessor of most ordinary faculties, accomplished more than certain conquerors, and has left a greater gap than Catherine or Elizabeth."

Le Siecle says:

"Doubtless the Prince of Wales will follow the good example of his mother, whose death will mark no change of policy or opinion in Great Britain. He will peaceably enjoy the loyalty of the empire, accorded during the long reign of the Queen."

Le Temps, discussing the outlook, says:

"The sadness, alarm, anxieties, moral sufferings, and pecuniary cares arising out of the Transvaal war have created a new feeling in England. Queen Victoria has been like a mother of a family, a living link with the prosperity of the past, an anchor of security for the British people. With her disappearance will come the unknown, the groping into the dark future."

BERLIN, Jan. 22.—The news of the death of Queen Victoria had been hourly expected in Berlin, and on its arrival special editions of the newspapers sold like wildfire, the announcement being read with silent and respectful sympathy. The fact that Empress Augusta Victoria started to-day for Homburg to be near Dowager Empress Frederick added to the sad circumstances of the occasion.

Immediately after the receipt of the news Count von Eulenburg, the Chief Court Marshal, ordered the flags half masted on all public buildings. Although the hour of the evening was somewhat advanced, a number of the embassies and legations, including the United States Embassy, did the same.

Special mourning orders to the Schloss, the army, the Court, and the public departments were issued this evening. These will be published to-morrow and go immediately into effect.

The German nation fully shares in the feelings of the British people toward the venerable and illustrious sovereign who has just breathed her last.

Semi-official paragraphs in the press this evening rebut the idea, commonly held in Germany, that the new King will be inclined to be hostile toward Germany. On the contrary, they assert that he will act in the interests of Great Britain and the British people alone.

A sense of gratification is felt by all Germans that Emperor William was present at Osborne during the last hours of Queen Victoria's life and that the lofty feelings of filial piety which prompted his action have met with such full and unqualified recognition on the part of the British nation.

THE HAGUE, Jan. 22.—The Dutch press printed the news of the death of Queen Victoria with mourning borders.

The Court will go into mourning; but it is probable that there will be no change in the arrangements for the marriage of Queen Wilhelmina.

ROME, Jan. 22.—A most painful impression was produced by the receipt of the news of Queen Victoria's death.

King Victor Emmanuel, Queen Helena, the Pope, and members of the Government immediately telegraphed condolences.

GRIEF IN CANADA.

Flags at Half Mast Everywhere and Amusement Places Closed.

TORONTO, Ontario, Jan. 22.—To Torontonians no tidings fraught with greater sorrow ever flashed over the wires than those which recorded the death of the Queen. All classes of the community show their heartfelt grief. From early morning till the announcement of her Majesty's death, great crowds gathered and waited around the different newspaper offices, eagerly scanning each bulletin as it was posted up. When at last the dreaded news came, heads were reverently uncovered, and the crowds dispersed silently. For half an hour the bells kept tolling their mournful messages, while national flags, half-masted, swung from every pole.

The children in every school in the city this forenoon sang for the last time "God Save the Queen." The Mayor will proclaim a day of mourning.

MONTREAL, Jan. 22.—The bulletin officially announcing the death of her Majesty turned Montreal into a city of mourning. No sooner was the fact announced than the fire bells began to ring out at minute intervals, and mingled with them came the tolling of the big cathedral bells of both the English and Catholic churches. Flags appeared at half-mast everywhere, and the crowds in the streets and at the bulletin boards of the various papers, their heads in most cases bared, reverently read the announcement.

All entertainments of a social nature have been canceled, and even skating rinks, hockey rinks, and places of public amusement have been closed.

OTTAWA, Jan. 22.—The news of the Queen's death reached Ottawa at 2 P. M. The Secretary of State at once issued a proclamation continuing in office all who held positions under the Crown. This is merely formal.

All public buildings in the Dominion at once placed the union jack at half mast, and it will so remain until sundown on the day of the Queen's funeral.

ST. JOHN'S, N. F., Jan. 22.—The announcement of Queen Victoria's death has called forth expressions of the keenest regret in Newfoundland, the oldest colony of the British Empire. The Colonial Cabinet met this evening and adopted resolutions of condolence, which were cabled to London.

To-morrow will be observed as a day of mourning throughout the colony.

Arrangements are being made for the proclamation of the new sovereign upon receipt of an official intimation of his accession.

HALIFAX, N. S., Jan. 22.—Symbols of mourning for Queen Victoria are everywhere displayed. Flags fly half-mast on ships and from the frowning fortress, and the royal standard, for the first time in many years, is half-mast at the Citadel.

All performances have been canceled, and on the day of the Queen's funeral the tolling of half a hundred bells will mingle with the loud notes of minute guns for the departed sovereign.

A sketch of the life of Queen Victoria will be found on Pages 6 and 7 of this issue.

AMERICAN TRIBUTES TO QUEEN VICTORIA

President McKinley Cables Condolences to the New King.

WASHINGTON FLAGS LOWERED

Such a Mark of Respect Had Never Been Before Paid on the Death of a Monarch—Action by Congress.

WASHINGTON, Jan. 22.—Four days of anxiety, in a large measure, prepared official Washington for the news which was flashed across the cable this afternoon from England. So it happened that all things that could be decently done in anticipation of the death of Queen Victoria had been disposed of, and all was in readiness for the execution of the formalities which are indispensable to such occasions. The President and his advisers were in receipt from time to time of all news which came from Osborne House. When the end came it found appropriate measures of condolence framed, and even orders, ready for execution, looking to the half-masting of the flags over the executive departments and the carrying out of the usual formalities.

The half-masting of the National ensign was an unusual tribute. This has been done once or twice on the occasion of the funeral of some great ruler, but never before in the case of the death of a monarch. The adjournment of the House was also an unusual mark of respect.

THE PRESIDENT'S MESSAGE.

The news announcing the death of Queen Victoria was conveyed to President McKinley simultaneously with its receipt by the newspapers. Soon afterward the President sent the following message of condolence to the new King:

Washington, Jan. 22, 1901.

His Majesty the King, Osborne House, Isle of Wight:

I have received with profound sorrow the lamentable tidings of the death of her Majesty the Queen. Allow me, Sir, to offer my sincere sympathy and that of the American people in your personal bereavement and in the loss Great Britain has suffered in the death of its venerable and illustrious sovereign, whose noble life and beneficent influence have promoted the peace and won the affection of the world.

WILLIAM McKINLEY.

Secretary of State Hay cabled the following message to Ambassador Choate at London:

Department of State, Jan. 22, 1901.

Choate, Ambassador, London:

You will express to Lord Lansdowne the profound sorrow of the Government and people of the United States at the death of the Queen and the deep sympathy we feel with the people of the British Empire in their great affliction. JOHN HAY.

The actual dispatch of the message from the President to the new King of England and from Secretary Hay to Ambassador Choate was delayed only long enough to receive the physicians' statement announcing the demise of the Queen, and then they were sent forward at once and copies were furnished to the press.

The flag on the Executive Mansion was placed at half-mast at 3:30 o'clock.

THE SENATE'S RESOLUTION.

The Senate was in executive session when the news of Queen Victoria's death was announced, but the bulletin announcing her death was passed around by the doorkeepers. Expressions of regret and of admiration for the virtues of the dead sovereign were heard on all hands. Senators Allison and Morgan held a hurried consultation, as the result of which the latter drew up a resolution, which the former presented when the executive session closed. The resolution was as follows:

"That the death of her Royal and Imperial Majesty, Victoria, of noble virtues and great renown, is sincerely deplored by the Senate of the United States of America."

The resolution was adopted unanimously.

Afterward Mr. Allison offered the following resolution:

"That the President pro tem. of the Senate cause to be conveyed to the Prime Minister of Great Britain a suitably engrossed copy of the foregoing resolution."

This was agreed to.

Senator Lodge, evidently voicing the sentiment of most of his colleagues, said later:

"The Queen's death is to the people of the United States a real sorrow. Her reign, the longest in English history, has been a great and memorable one, but it has perhaps nothing greater or more memorable than her own ability and purity of character; her fidelity to her high duties, and her devotion to those ideals of conduct and domestic life which appeal most profoundly to all English-speaking people. The Queen has always been a steadfast friend to the United States, and during her long life has made that friendship traditional in her family. Americans can never forget that England was withheld from active interference in our own civil war largely, if not wholly, by the influence of the Queen and the wise counsels of Prince Albert."

THE HOUSE ADJOURNS.

The House received the news at about 2 o'clock, and for the time being it was the theme of universal discussion among the members. Speaker Henderson had shown deep interest in the Queen's condition, and the first bulletin announcing her death was taken to him in his private office and to Chairman Hitt of the Committee on Foreign Affairs. Mr. Hitt conferred with his colleagues as to the precedents in such cases, and then framed a brief and expressive resolution of sympathy and respect to be introduced in the House later. For a time it was feared that this might give rise to some expressions from Boer sympathizers, but, on the contrary, it was developed that the sentiment of respect for the departed sovereign was shared by all alike.

At the conclusion of the general debate on the District of Columbia Appropriation bill Mr. Hitt offered the resolution, which was as follows:

"Resolved, That the House of Representatives of the United States of America has learned with profound sorrow of the death of her Majesty Queen Victoria and sympathizes with her people in the loss of their beloved sovereign; that the President be requested to communicate this expression of the sentiment of the House to the Government of Great Britain; that, as a further mark of respect to the memory of Queen Victoria, the House do now adjourn."

The reading of the resolution was listened to with impressive silence. Mr. Hitt stated very briefly that this resolution followed the precedents in similar cases. It was, he said, copied almost literally from the resolution adopted upon the occasion of the death of the President of the French Republic, and followed the expression adopted upon the death of the Czar of Russia. He did not, he said, think that the occasion called for any extended remarks, and asked for a vote.

The resolution was unanimously adopted, and the House at 5:05 P. M. stood adjourned until noon to-morrow.

After the adjournment members gathered in knots and discussed the event, the tributes being to the womanly virtues and purity of home life of the Queen, no less than to her national service.

PRAISE FROM CABINET MINISTERS.

Secretary of State Hay, on being informed of the Queen's death, declined to make a statement for publication on the ground that, being under obligation to send an official message to the British Government on the subject, he did not feel called upon to make a further supplementary private statement.

Attorney General Griggs said:

"Hers has been a noble life. Whether she was greater as a Queen or as a woman is hard to say. Her good influence upon

NDEX TO DEPARTMENTS.

"All the News That's Fit to Print."

The New York Times.

THE WEATHER. Fair, with variable winds, mostly east to south.

VOL. L...NO. 16,121. NEW YORK, SATURDAY, SEPTEMBER 7, 1901.—SIXTEEN PAGES. ONE CENT "In Greater New York, Jersey City, and Newark. } Elsewhere TWO CENTS.

PRESIDENT SHOT AT BUFFALO FAIR

Wounded in the Breast and Abdomen.

HE IS RESTING EASILY

One Bullet Extracted, Other Cannot Be Found.

Assassin Is Leon Czolgosz of Cleveland, Who Says He Is an Anarchist and Follower of Emma Goldman.

BUFFALO, Sept. 6.—President McKinley, while holding a reception in the Temple of Music at the Pan-American Exposition at 4 o'clock this afternoon, was shot and twice wounded by Leon Czolgosz, an Anarchist, who lives in Cleveland.

One bullet entered the President's breast, struck the breast bone, glanced and was later easily extracted. The other bullet entered the abdomen, penetrated the stomach, and has not been found, although the wounds have been closed.

The physicians in attendance upon the President at 10:40 o'clock to-night issued the following bulletin:

"The President is rallying satisfactorily and is resting comfortably. 10:15 P. M., temperature, 100.4 degrees; pulse, 124; respiration, 24.

"P. M. RIXEY,
"M. B. MANN,
"R. E. PARKE,
"H. MYNTER,
"EUGENE WANBIN.

Signed by George B. Cortelyou, Secretary to the President."

This condition was maintained until 1 o'clock A. M., when the physicians issued the following bulletin:

"The President is free from pain and resting well. Temperature, 100.2; pulse, 120; respiration, 24."

The assassin was immediately overpowered and taken to a police station on the Exposition grounds, but not before a number of the throng had tried to lynch him. Later he was taken to Police Headquarters.

The exact nature of the President's injuries is described in the following bulletin issued by Secretary Cortelyou for the physicians who were called:

"The President was shot about 4 o'clock. One bullet struck him on the upper portion of the breast bone, glancing and not penetrating; the second bullet penetrated the abdomen five inches below the left nipple and one and one-half inches to the left of the median line. The abdomen was opened through the line of the bullet wound. It was found that the bullet had penetrated the stomach.

"The opening in the front wall of the stomach was carefully closed with silk sutures; after which a search was made for a hole in the back wall of the stomach. This was found and also closed in the same way. The further course of the bullet could not be discovered, although careful search was made. The abdominal wound was closed without drainage. No injury to the intestines or other abdominal organs was discovered.

"The patient stood the operation well, pulse of good quality, rate of 130, and his condition at the conclusion of operation was gratifying. The result cannot be foretold. His condition at present justifies hope of recovery."

Leon Czolgosz, the assassin, has signed a confession, covering six pages of foolscap, in which he states that he is an Anarchist and that he became an enthusiastic member of that body through the influence of Emma Goldman, whose writings he had read and whose lectures he had listened to. He denies having any confederate, and says he decided on the act three days ago and bought the revolver with which the act was committed in Buffalo.

He has seven brothers and sisters in Cleveland, and the Cleveland Directory has the names of about that number living in Hosmer Street and Ackland Avenue, which adjoin. Some of them are butchers and others are in other trades.

Czolgosz is now detained at Police Headquarters, pending the result of the President's injuries. He does not appear in the least degree uneasy or penitent for his action. He says he was induced by his attention to Emma Goldman's lectures and writings to decide that the present form of government in this country was all wrong, and he thought the best way to end it was by the killing of the President. He shows no sign of insanity, but is very reticent about much of his career.

While acknowledging himself an Anarchist, he does not state to what branch of the organization he belongs.

HOW THE DEED WAS DONE.

Assassin Came with the Crowd to Greet the President and Shot When Two Feet from Him.

BUFFALO, Sept. 6.—Czolgosz's attempt on the life of the President was made at about 4 o'clock in the Temple of Music, where Mr. McKinley had gone to hold a reception at that hour. He had spent the day at Niagara with about 100 invited guests, and arrived at the exposition grounds at 3:30. Mrs. McKinley proceeded to the Mission Building and the President went directly to the Temple of Music.

A vast crowd had assembled long before the arrival of Mr. McKinley. The daily organ recital was nearing its end as the President entered and went to the slightly raised dais at one end of the hall.

The President, though well guarded by United States Secret Service detectives, was fully exposed to such an attack as occurred. He stood at the edge of the raised dais, and throngs of people crowded in at the various entrances to see their Chief Executive, perchance to clasp his hand, and then fight their way out in the good-natured mob that every minute swelled and multiplied at the points of ingress and egress to the building.

The President was in a cheerful mood and was enjoying the hearty evidences of good-will which everywhere met his gaze. Upon his right stood John G. Milburn of Buffalo, President of the Pan-American Exposition, chatting with the President, and introducing to him persons of note who approached. Upon the President's left stood Mr. Cortelyou.

THE ASSASSIN APPEARS.

It was shortly after 4 o'clock when one of the throng which surrounded the Presidential party, a medium-sized man of ordinary appearance and plainly dressed in black, approached as if to greet the President. Both Secretary Cortelyou and President Milburn noticed that the man's hand was swathed in a bandage or handkerchief. Reports of bystanders differ as to which hand. He worked his way with the stream of people up to the edge of the dais, until he was within two feet of the President.

President McKinley smiled, bowed, and extended his hand in that spirit of geniality the American people so well know, when suddenly the man raised his hand and two sharp reports of a revolver rang out loud and clear above the hum of voices and the shuffling of myriad feet. The assassin had fired through the handkerchief which concealed the revolver.

There was an instant of almost complete silence, like the hush that follows a clap of thunder. The President stood stock still, a look of hesitancy, almost of bewilderment, on his face. Then he retreated a step while a pallor began to steal over his features. The multitude seemed only partially aware that something serious had happened.

Then came a commotion. With the leap of a tiger three men threw themselves forward as with one impulse and sprang toward the would-be assassin. Two of them were United States Secret Service men, who were on the lookout and whose duty it was to guard against just such a calamity as had here befallen the President and the Nation. The third was a bystander, a negro, who had only an instant before grasped the hand of the President. In a twinkling the assassin was borne to the ground, his weapon was wrested from his grasp, and strong arms pinioned him down.

Then the vast multitude which thronged the edifice began to come to a realising sense of the awfulness of the scene of which they had been witnesses. A murmur arose, spread, and swelled to a hum of confusion, then grew to a babel of sounds, and later to a pandemonium of noises.

The crowds that a moment before had stood mute and motionless in bewildered ignorance of the enormity of the deed, now with a single impulse surged forward, while a hoarse cry welled up from a thousand throats, and a thousand men charged forward to lay hands upon the perpetrator of the dastardly crime.

CONFUSION REIGNS.

For a moment the confusion was terrible. The crowd surged forward regardless of consequences. Men shouted and fought, women screamed and children cried. Some of those nearest the doors fled from the edifice in fear of a stampede, while hundreds of others from the outside struggled blindly forward in the effort to enter the crowded building and solve the mystery of excitement and panic which every moment grew and swelled within the congested interior of the palatial edifice.

Inside on the slightly raised dais was enacted within those few feverish moments a tragedy, so dramatic in character, so thrilling in its intensity, that few who looked on will ever be able to give a succinct account of what really did transpire. Even the actors who were playing the principal rôles came out of it with blanched faces, trembling limbs, and beating hearts, while their brains throbbed with a tumult of conflicting emotions which left behind only a chaotic jumble of impressions which could not be clarified into a lucid narrative of the events as they really transpired.

But of the multitude which witnessed or bore a part in the scene there was but one mind which seemed to retain it's equilibrium, one hand which remained steady, one eye which gazed with unflinching calmness, and one voice which retained its even tenor and faltered not at the most critical juncture.

They were the mind and the hand and the eye and the voice of President McKinley.

After the first shock of the assassin's shots, he retreated a step, then, as the detectives leaped upon his assailant, he turned, walked steadily to a chair and seated himself, at the same time removing his hat and bowing his head in his hands.

In an instant Secretary Cortelyou and President Milburn were at his side. His waistcoat was hurriedly opened, the President meanwhile admonishing those about him to remain calm and telling them not to be alarmed.

"But you are wounded," cried his secretary; "let me examine."

"No, I think not," answered the President. "I am not badly hurt, I assure you."

Nevertheless his outer garments were hastily loosened, and when a trickling stream of crimson was seen to wind its way down his breast spreading its stain over the white surface of the linen their worst fears were confirmed.

A force of Exposition guards were on the scene by this time, and an effort was made to clear the building. The crush was terrific. Spectators crowded down the stairways from the galleries, the crowd on the floor surged forward toward the rostrum, while despite the strenuous efforts of police and guards the throng without struggled madly to obtain admission.

IN THE HOSPITAL.

The President's assailant in the meantime had been hustled to the rear of the building by Exposition Guards McCauley and James, where he was held while the building was cleared, and later turned over to Superintendent Bull of the Buffalo Police Department, who took the prisoner to No. 13 Police Station, and later to Police Headquarters.

As soon as the crowd in the Temple of Music had been dispersed sufficiently the President was removed in the automobile ambulance and taken to the Exposition Hospital, where an examination was made.

The best medical skill was summoned and within a brief period several of Buffalo's best-known practitioners were at the patient's side. The President retained the full exercise of his faculties until placed on the operating table and subjected to an anaesthetic.

Upon the first examination it was ascertained that one bullet had taken effect in the right breast just below the nipple, causing a comparatively harmless wound. The other took effect in the abdomen, about five inches below the left nipple, two inches to the left of the navel, and about on a level with it.

Upon arriving at the Exposition Hospital the second bullet was probed for. The walls of the abdomen were opened, but teh ball was not located. The incision was hastily closed and after a hasty consultation it was decided to the remove the patient to the home of President Milburn. This was done, the automobile-ambulance being used for the purpose.

Arrived at the Milburn residence, all persons outside the medical attendants, nurses, and the officials immediately concerned were excluded and the task of probing for the bullet, which had lodged in the abdomen, was begun by Dr. Roswell Park.

When it was decided to remove the President from the Exposition Hospital to the Milburn residence, the news was broken to Mrs. McKinley as gently as might be, by the members of the Milburn family. She bore the shock remarkably well, and displayed the utmost fortitude.

CROWD READY TO LYNCH.

While the wounded President was being borne from the Exposition to the Milburn residence between rows of onlookers with bared heads, a far different spectacle was being witnessed along the route of his assailant's journey from the scene of his crime to Police Headquarters. The trip was made so quickly that the prisoner was safely landed within the wide portals of the police station and the doors closed before any one was aware of his presence.

The news of the attempted assassination had in the meanwhile been spread broadcast by the newspapers. Like wildfire it spread from mouth to mouth. Then bulletins began to appear on the boards along "Newspaper Row," and when the announcement was made that the prisoner had been taken to Police Headquarters, only two blocks distant from the newspaper section, the crowds surged down toward the terrace, eager for a glimpse of the prisoner. At Police Headquarters they were met by a strong cordon of police, drawn up across the pavement on Pearl Street, who denied admittance to any but officials authorised to take part in the examination of the prisoner.

In a few minutes the crowd had grown from tens to hundreds, and these in turn quickly swelled to thousands, until the street was completely blocked by a surging mass of eager humanity. It was at this juncture that some one raised the cry of "Lynch him!" Like a flash the cry was taken up, and the whole crowd re-echoed the cry, "Lynch him!" "Hang him!" Closer the crowd surged forward.

Denser the throng became as new arrivals each moment swelled the swaying multitude. The situation was becoming critical when suddenly the big doors were flung open and a squad of reserves advanced with solid front, drove the crowd back from the curb, then across the street, and gradually succeeded in dispersing them from about the entrance to the station.

By this time there were probably 30,000 people assembled in the vicinity of Pearl, Seneca, Erie Streets, and the Terrace. The crowd was so great that it became necessary to rope off the entire street in front of Police Headquarters, and at a late hour to-night the police were still patrolling in the streets in the neighborhood, in squads of three or four. Inside the station house were assembled District Attorney Penny, Superintendent of Police Bull, Capt. Reagan of the First Precinct, and other officials.

The prisoner at first proved quite communicative, so much so in fact, that little dependence could be placed on what he said. He first gave his name as Fred Nieman, said his home was in Detroit, and that he had been in Buffalo about a week. He said he had been boarding at a place in Broadway. Later this place was located as John Nowak's saloon, a Raines-law hotel, 1,075 Broadway. Here the prisoner occupied Room 8.

THE PRISONER'S STORY.

Nowak, the proprietor, said he knew very little about his guest. He came there, he declared, last Saturday, saying he had come to see the Pan-American, and that his home was in Toledo. He had been alone at all times about Nowak's place, and had had no visitors. In his room was found a small traveling bag of cheap make. It contained an empty cartridge box and a few articles of clothing.

With these facts in hand the police went at the prisoner with renewed vigor in the effort to obtain either a full confession or a straight account of his identity and movements prior to his arrival in Buffalo. He at first admitted that he was an Anarchist in sympathy at least, but denied strenuously that the attempt on the life of the President was a result of a preconcerted plot on the part of any Anarchist society.

At times he was defiant and again indifferent. But at no time did he betray the remotest sign of remorse. He declared the deed was not premeditated, but in the same breath refused to say why he perpetrated it. When charged by District Attorney Penny with being the instrument of an organised band of conspirators, he protested vehemently that he never even thought of perpetrating the crime until this morning.

After long and persistent questioning it was announced at Police Headquarters that the prisoner had made a confession, which he signed.

MRS. McKINLEY COURAGEOUS.

Bears Up Well When She Hears of the Attempt on Mr. McKinley's Life.

BUFFALO, N. Y., Sept. 6.—After the President was cared for at the Exposition grounds, Director General W. I. Buchanan started for the Milburn residence to forestall any information that might reach Mrs. McKinley there by telephone or otherwise. Very luckily, he was first to arrive with the information. The Niagara Falls trip had tired Mrs. McKinley, and on returning to the Milburn residence she went to her room to rest.

Mr. Buchanan broke the news as gently as possible to the nieces of Mr. and Mrs. McKinley, and consulted with them and Mrs. Milburn as to the best course to pursue in breaking the news to Mrs. McKinley. It was finally decided that on her awaking, or shortly thereafter, Mr. Buchanan should break the news to her, if, in the meantime her physician, Dr. Rixey, had not yet arrived.

Mrs. McKinley awoke from her sleep at about 5:30 o'clock. She was feeling splendidly, she said, and at once took up her crocheting, which, as is well known, is one of her favorite diversions.

Immediately on Mr. Buchanan's arrival at the Milburn home he had telephonic communication therewith cut off, for already there had been several calls, and he decided on this as the wisest course to pursue lest Mrs. McKinley, hearing the continued ringing of the bells, might inquire what it meant.

While the light of day remained, Mrs. McKinley continued with her crocheting, keeping to her room. When the day began to wane and the President had not arrived, she began to feel anxious concerning him. "I wonder why he does not come?" she asked one of her nieces. There was no clock in Mrs. McKinley's room, and when it was 7 o'clock she had no idea it was so late, and this is when she began to feel anxious concerning her husband, for he was due to return to Mr. Milburn's house about 6 o'clock.

At 7 o'clock Dr. Rixey arrived at the Milburn residence. He had been driven hurriedly down Delaware Avenue in an open carriage, and at once entered the house. At 7:20 o'clock Dr. Rixey came out of the house accompanied by Col. Webb Hayes, a son of the late ex-President Hayes, who is a friend of President McKinley. They entered a carriage and returned to the Exposition hospital.

After Dr. Rixey had gone, Mr. Buchanan said that the doctor had broken the news in a most gentle way to Mrs. McKinley. He said she stood it bravely, though considerably affected. If it was possible to bring him to her, she wanted it done. Dr. Rixey assured her that the President could be brought with safety from the Exposition grounds, and when he left the Milburn house it was to complete all arrangements for the removal of the President.

A big force of regular patrolmen were assigned to the Milburn residence.

"CAUGHT THE ASSASSIN."

Capt. Wiser of Coast Artillery Says His Men Did So.

WASHINGTON, Sept. 6.—The War Department to-night received the following telegram from Capt. John B. Wiser, commanding the Seventy-third Company of Coast Artillery at Buffalo:

"BUFFALO, N. Y., Sept. 6, 1901.—Adjutant General, U. S. A., Washington: President shot at reception in Temple of Music about 4 P. M. Corporal Bertschey and detail of men of my company caught the assassin at once and held him down till the secret service men overpowered him and took the prisoner out of their hands, my men being unarmed. Condition of President not known. Revolver in my possession.

"WISER, Commanding."

OPINIONS OF SURGEONS.

Injury to Stomach Serious for a Man of the President's Age—Danger of Peritonitis.

According to well-known surgeons, there are in New York four or five persons each year who, through various causes, suffer from injuries similar to those received yesterday by President McKinley at Buffalo. Operations similar to those performed on the President have been successful and the patients have recovered. The prominent surgeons interviewed last evening said that the chances of recovery would be much greater if President McKinley were a younger man.

Dr. John B. Walker of 33 West Thirty-third Street said:

"Any injury to the stomach similar to that which has been inflicted on President McKinley is serious. There have been cases of stomach perforation where the patients have recovered. The diagnosis of any perforated wound of the stomach in an adult is very serious. The trouble is that inflammation following such an injury is more acute to an older person than to one more youthful. The fear is that the contents of the stomach will ooze into the intestines and peritonitis set in."

"Do you recall any recent cases similar to that of President McKinley," was asked.

"Dr. Bull performed an operation on a young man a short time ago. The intestines were perforated and an operation similar to that performed on President McKinley resulted in complete recovery. If President McKinley were a man between thirty-five and forty years of age the chances would be more in his favor. I cannot recall at this time a case of a man of the age of the President recovering from similar wounds. There is one advantage the President had, and that is the prompt assistance of a surgeon. Dr. Roswell Park is one of the most eminent surgeons in the United States."

"What other cases do you recall?"

"The case of the football player in Princeton who was shot by a negro is one of the latest. In that case the young man was of powerful physique. He did not receive the attention of a surgeon for twelve hours, and the result was that peritonitis set in and death occurred in a few days."

MR. ROOSEVELT EN ROUTE.

One Receipt of News the Vice President Leaves for Buffalo.

BURLINGTON, Vt., Sept. 6.—The first news of the attempted assassination of President McKinley reached Vice President Roosevelt at Isle La Motte at 5:30 o'clock this afternoon, when the Vice President was informed over the telephone that there was a rumor that the President had been shot. It was confirmed by another message a moment later.

The Vice President seemed stunned by the news, and put his hands to his head, then exclaimed, "My God!" Those around him were immediately informed of the tragedy, and it was decided to announce it to the company of a thousand persons who had gathered to hear Col. Roosevelt speak at the annual outing of the Vermont Fish and Game League. Senator Proctor made the announcement, and men, women, and children wept.

A later bulletin was received, stating that the President was resting quietly and that the chances were favorable for his recovery. "Good!" exclaimed the Vice President, and his face lighted up. He showed his pleasure by eagerly announcing the good news to the assembly.

The Vice President then left immediately on the yacht Elfrida, owned by W. Seward Webb, and came to this city as quickly as possible, having directed that all messages should be held for him here. The yacht was to have gone to Arrow Point, where a special train was waiting for the Vice President, but the train was sent on to Burlington, and was there when the yacht came into the harbor, at 8:15.

President Clement of the Rutland Railroad placed the train at the disposal of the Vice President, and made arrangements to take him on it to Buffalo. Col. Roosevelt was asked at the wharf for a statement for publication, and said:

"I am so inexpressibly grieved, shocked, and horrified that I can say nothing."

He boarded the train at once and left for Buffalo.

CABINET WILL ASSEMBLE.

Postmaster General Smith and Secretaries Root and Gage Off for Buffalo.

PHILADELPHIA, Sept. 6.—Postmaster General Charles Emory Smith was greatly affected by the news of the shooting of President McKinley, and expressed himself as shocked beyond measure. He immediately telegraphed to Washington and Buffalo, asking for further particulars than the early news dispatches contained. Mr. Smith said he hoped the President's injuries might not prove so serious as was at first intimated.

Mr. Smith left here on a late train to-night for Buffalo. He expects to be at the President's bedside by 9 o'clock to-morrow morning.

NEWBURY, N. H., Sept. 6.—A message containing information from Buffalo was received here early this evening and forwarded by messenger to the home of Secretary Hay. No reply came to it, and up to a late hour Secretary Hay could not be reached.

BUCKFIELD, Me., Sept. 6.—John D. Long, Secretary of the Navy, who has been passing his vacation at the Long homestead, two miles from this place, learned to-night of the shooting of President McKinley. He was deeply affected, and proceeded to his home at once, declaring that he was undecided about future plans. The Secretary positively refused to say anything for publication.

PITTSBURG, Sept. 6.—When informed of the shooting of President McKinley, Attorney General Knox said: "I cannot imagine how any living creature could harbor such a thought as to take the life of the President. I am so shocked at the awful news that I cannot talk further."

Mr. Knox left at 11 P. M. for Buffalo. Just before leaving he said:

"I can only express the common sentiment of horror at the cruelty of the dastardly blow inflicted upon the lovable and beloved man who has stood for all that is best for the people, who have so implicitly trusted him. His bodily wounds, grievous as they are, will cause him less pain than the thought that any human heart could have harbored against him the malice that inspired the deed."

DUBLIN, N. H., Sept. 6.—Secretary of the Interior Hitchcock, who has been at Mount Monadnock, when informed to-night of the tragic incident at Buffalo, said:

"I am too horrified to make any expression whatever." He immediately prepared to leave for Buffalo.

Secretary of War Elihu Root left the Grand Central Station at 11:10 last night for Buffalo in a special train. He was accompanied by a Dr. Dixon, a specialist, with whom he is hastening to the bedside of the President. The train was made up of a single coach and locomotive, and all possible speed will be made to reach Buffalo on record-breaking time.

When Secretary Root was asked to express an opinion of the President's injury, he said:

"What is there to say? I do not know how seriously injured President McKinley is, but I hope his condition is not so serious as reported. I am almost overcome by the terrible news."

Secretary Root came up from Southampton, L. I., in a special train. With Dr. Dixon and a valet, he rode in a cab to the Grand Central Station. The special train had already been made up, and in less than three minutes after their arrival at the station they were speeding on their way to Buffalo.

Special to The New York Times.

CHICAGO, Sept. 6.—Secretary of the Treasury Gage, who was visiting his son, Eli Gage, in Evanston, seemed dazed by the news, and with bowed head walked slowly into the house. Preparations were made at once for the Secretary to go to Buffalo, accompanied by his son. Before he took the train for Buffalo, an hour later, Secretary Gage said:

"I am too shocked to speak. The news of such a happening is simply overwhelming to me. The President was always confident that no harm would ever come to him. He is a man who is honored by all. I received no official message that he had been assassinated. The first tidings were brought me by friends."

WASHINGTON STUNNED BY THE TRAGEDY

No Member of Cabinet Is at the Capital City.

MILITARY GUARD DETAILED

Under the Law Vice President Roosevelt Will Discharge the Purely Routine Duties of the President.

Special to The New York Times.

WASHINGTON, Sept. 6.—For the third time in thirty-seven years Washington has been stunned by the shooting of a President of the United States. Like lightning out of the fair September sky the report from Buffalo arrested attention here about 5 o'clock, and in a few moments anxious crowds were hurrying from all parts of the city to the offices of the newspapers seeking additional information. People stopped in their hurry to ask of every one met whether the President had been killed, and there was the utmost impatience because of the brevity and indefiniteness of the bulletins and the failure of assurance that the wounds inflicted upon Mr. McKinley were not fatal. To-night the street in front of the newspaper offices is crowded with women and men hungering with anxiety and waiting to catch the announcements that come at long intervals through a megaphone operated by a man in an upper window of a newspaper office.

Grief has not checked a torrent of indignation at the crime committed against humanity and a President who has always trusted himself implicity to the protection of his fellows, venturing from day to day to walk the streets without guard. The rage against the assassin was immediate and outspoken with men of all parties, for Mr. McKinley has no personal enemies here or elsewhere.

The disability of the President occurred at a moment when the Administration was entirely unrepresented at Washington by a Cabinet officer. When the information of the shooting reached the White House by a telephone message from Buffalo, Col. Montgomery and a few clerks were the only members of the President's official family present, Col. Pruden getting the news while he was dining at home. From the moment he heard the news, Col. Montgomery began making efforts to reach the members of the Cabinet, except Secretary of Agriculture Wilson, who is in Buffalo. There was a stream of visitors to the White House from the moment the news of the shooting was received until late to-night, but few of the visitors were persons high in official life.

HOW THE NEWS WAS RECEIVED.

The force at the White House since the President's departure has been in constant communication with him, and while he has conducted most of the business of his office at his home, in Canton, Ohio, the majority of the papers with which he has had to deal have been prepared in Washington and forwarded through the White House clerical force. All reports received from him by officials here were cheerful and high-spirited.

The work of the official day was done when the news of the calamity arrived here and the executive departments had generally emptied themselves of their workmen, and very few of the officials were to be found at their desks.

Mr. Adee, the acting head of the State Department, was met at the station as he was leaving for his country home near Laurel, Md., and returned at once to the State Department. He waited for official confirmation of the news, and it was not until he received a copy of the bulletin issued by the physicians through Secretary Cortelyou that he undertook to acquaint officially the Governments of all the nations of the world with the facts of the shooting. He then drew up a message, which will be sent to every United States Embassy, Legation, and Consulate throughout the civilized world directing them to acquaint the Governments to which they are accredited of the facts. With these he embodied a condensation of the physicians' bulletin with Mr. Cortelyou's statement.

In the Navy Department Mr. Hackett, the acting Secretary, who had also quitted the building, was speedily recalled by Capt. Cowles, the acting head of the Navigation Bureau, and he immediately put himself in readiness to take any official action that might be necessary to meet the emergency. At Buffalo in the Exposition grounds the navy had a splendid representation in the shape of the marine battalion under Capt. Leonard, and this force will be immediately available if it is decided by the persons about the President that a guard is necessary near his person.

At the War Department Gen. Gillespie, Chief Engineer of the army, was acting Secretary in the absence of Secretary Root, and Assistant Secretary Sanger, who is away on leave. He also had quitted the building, but he had not been gone half an hour before word reached him and he hastily returned to his desk. He immediately sent messages to the Secretary of war and to Gen. Brooke, commanding the Department of the East, giving such unofficial information as was available.

Gen. Gillespie finally got into communication with Secretary Root and Assistant Secretary Sanger, and as a result of the telephonic talk he proceeded to use some of the forces at his disposal. He telegraphed an order to Fort Foster, N. H., to have an officer, a physician, and a squad of men proceed immediately to the house where the President is lying to act as a guard.

PROVIDING FOR EMERGENCIES.

Steps were next taken to provide for the future of the Executive branch of the Government. It was realized that even under the most favorable conditions the President's injuries are of such a character as to make it almost certain that he cannot undertake for a long time to discharge the duties of Chief Executive, even in the most formal way. Every member of the Cabinet able to travel is expected to at once go to Buffalo, and there a Cabinet council will be held to decide upon the course to be followed by the Executive branch. Vice President Roosevelt is in readiness to do whatever is necessary and to meet the obligations imposed upon the Vice Presiden[t by] the Constitution of the United S[tates]. These are contained in Paragraph 6, [Sec]tion 1, Article II., in the following wo[rds]:

6. In case of the removal of the Pre[sident] from office, or of his death, resignatio[n, or] inability to discharge the powers and dut[ies of] the said office, the same shall devolve o[n the] Vice President, &c.

Under the terms of this article, as[...] as Mr. Roosevelt is assured by prope[r au]thority, probably in this case by the s[...] member of the Cabinet, Secretary [...] who will doubtless be in Buffalo by [to]morrow evening, he will undertake at [...] in a provisional way to discharge such [du]ties as may devolve on him. Much wi[ll de]pend upon the report of the physician[s on] the character of the President's inj[ury] as to the extent to which Mr. Roos[evelt] will discharge the Presidential duti[es, if] he undertakes them at all, and it is a[...] certain that in the absence of great e[mer]gency in public affairs, even if calle[d to] assume these obligations, the Vice P[resi]dent will confine himself in the exe[rcise] of his powers to the discharge of the [...] routine and indispensable functions.

Such public men as were in the city c[alled] at the White House during the eve[ning]. They included Assistant Secretary Sp[auld]ing of the Treasury Department, Assi[stant] Secretary Hackett of the Navy De[part]ment, ex-United States Senator H. [...] Blair, Controller Dawes, and Reg[ister] Lyons of the Treasury, and Capt. Tow[...] Assistant Commissioner of Indian Af[fairs]. There were also calls from representa[tives] of several foreign legations.

No official confirmation of the sho[oting] came to the White House for three h[ours] after its occurrence, when Col. Mont[gom]ery, the chief operator at the White H[ouse,] was informed at 7:20 o'clock by Secre[tary] Cortelyou at Buffalo that a surgical o[pera]tion upon the President was in pro[gress] and that "so far everything is favora[ble."] Later he gave information of the co[nclu]tion of the operation, and followed [this] statement with other messages giving [pri]vate information as to the President's [con]dition and his removal to Mr. Milb[urn's] residence.

STRONG MILITARY GUARD.

During the early evening a conference [was] held at the War Department of such o[f the] prominent army officers as could be g[ath]ered at short notice by Gen. Gille[spie.] He informed them that he had comm[uni]cated with Gen. Brooke at Governors [Isl]and and that the General had replied [that] he would start immediately for Bu[ffalo,] where he expected in the early mornin[g to] take personal charge of all arrangem[ents] made for the guarding of the President.

Meanwhile he had directed that [the] troops which had been placed as a g[uard] around the hospital in the Expo[sition] grounds be transferred to the Mi[lburn] home, where the President lies, to serv[e as] a guard and keep back the public and [pre]serve quiet. Gen. Brooke has at Bu[ffalo] at his disposal a company of coast a[rtil]lery, stationed in the Exposition grou[nds,] a company of the Fifteenth Infantry, stationed at Fort Porter, within the l[imits] of the Exposition preserves, and [...] troops at Fort Niagara.

The conference decided that there [was] little more that the War Department [could] undertake at this time. Surgeon Ge[n.] Van Reypen of the Navy, who came [...] to the Navy Department, called at [Gen.] Gillespie's office, and, discussing the [case] from a medical point of view, took o[cca]sion to mention Dr. Nicholas Senn of [Chi]cago as an expert of high grade in [such] cases of injury, and the suggestion [was] promptly telegraphed to Buffalo tha[t his] services be secured.

Assistant Secretary Ailes of the Tre[asury] Department received a message to-n[ight] from Secretary Gage at Chicago st[ating] that he was about to leave at once [for] Buffalo, where he will arrive to-m[orrow] morning.

Admiral Dewey arrived in Washi[ngton] early in the afternoon. He proceede[d at] once to his suburban home and was [oc]cupied with the details of the approa[ching] Schley court of inquiry when the [news] reached him by the telephone. He at [once] sought all the particulars and placed [him]self in readiness for any service [that] might be required of him, informing [Act]ing Secretary Hackett of that fact.

The Admiral found himself unable t[o ex]press his feelings at the news, an[d all] that could be extracted from him was [that] he was plunged in grief too deep fo[r ut]terance at this time. He said tha[t he] could not now express an opinion a[s to] the effect that the calamity might [have] on the court of inquiry, or even whe[ther] it would result in the postponement o[f the] approaching sitting.

DIPLOMATS' CONDOLENCES.

Owing to the absence of many of [the] Diplomatic Corps at Buffalo and of [...] others at the various Summer resorts [there] were only two representatives of this [...] of rank in Washington to-day. Mi[nister] Wu was one of these, and when see[n to-] night he was a picture of distress. He [said] he realised keenly the tremendous in[debt]edness of China to President McKi[nley's] kindly impulses in her great trials i[n the] past year, and was shocked at the [...] calamity that had befallen him. He [said] he could not conceive of any sort of m[otive] for such an inexcusable deed as th[at of] Nieman's, and he was severe in his d[enun]ciation of Anarchists. He asked why [they] were permitted to hatch such plots a[s this] in a Republic where the people could [eas]ily change their President if they we[re in] the slightest degree dissatisfied with [his] official conduct or his private person[ality.] In conclusion, he expressed the hope [that] the President would shortly recover.

Another diplomatic representative [in] Washington was Señor Herran, repre[sent]ing the Government of the United Sta[tes of] Colombia. He also was greatly distr[essed,] and he affirmed that his whole co[untry] would sympathise with the Presider[nt in] this moment of pain. He also could no[t un]derstand, he said, why such a benev[olent] character as President McKinley shou[ld be] thus assaulted by one of the people, [and] he declared it is time that the Anarc[hists] should be suppressed.

It was somewhat gratifying to the [offi]cials here that the very first expressi[on of] official sympathy should come from [the] Island of Cuba, in the shape of the fo[llow]ing telegram:

(Received at War Department, [...] Sept. 6, [...]

Adjutant General, Washington:
Mayor and City Council of Havana [...] called, expressing sorrow and solicitude fo[r the] President, and desire that his family be a[dvised] of these expressions.
SCOTT, Adjutant Gen[eral.]

Mr. H. T. Scott of the Union Iron W[orks] at San Francisco, at whose house [the] President staid while visiting that [city,] telegraphed the Navy Department as [fol]lows:

"So shocked with news, words fail t[o ex]press our feelings."

Messages of sympathy and of inqui[ry al]ready have begun to arrive at the [...] Department.

"All the News That's Fit to Print."

The New York Times.

THE WEATHER. Cloudy, probably rain at night; west winds.

VOL. LIV....NO. 17,161. C NEW YORK, TUESDAY, JANUARY 3, 1905.—TWELVE PAGES. ONE CENT In Greater New York, Jersey City and Newark. | Elsewhere, TWO CENTS.

POMP AND DISPLAY AT THE WHITE HOUSE

Uniforms the Rule at President's New Year Reception.

ROOSEVELT'S NEW PHRASE

"This Is Indeed a Happy Occasion," He Said, Discarding "De-light-ed"—Exclusive Reception Party.

Special to The New York Times.

WASHINGTON, Jan. 2.—A more brilliant New Year's reception than that of to-day has seldom taken place in the White House. Uniforms were the rule, and the man who did not have one on was conspicuous. Color was everywhere, and the brilliance of the scene was enhanced by the soft glow from myriads of shaded electric lights.

Rare varieties of palms were disposed effectively about the vestibule and main corridor, while in the great rectangular basins between the vestibule and the corridor palms and ferns formed a striking background for the scarlet uniforms of the Marine Band. In the state dining-room, in the East Room, and in the Red, Blue and Green parlors rare cut flowers were arranged with consummate art and effectiveness, the delicate colors of lilies and orchids being accentuated here and there by a blazing of flaming red or a splash of vivid green.

The receiving party was arranged in the arc of a circle in the South end of the Blue Parlor, facing the party behind the line. Between the two sections was a lane formed by old gold silk velvet cord, through which the guests passed from the Red Parlor to the Green Parlor. Near the entrance to the Red Room the President and Mrs. Roosevelt stood.

But persons who entered the room were liable to meet with an uncomfortable experience if they were so thoughtless as to hold in their hands a handkerchief, a muffler, or any other article of that sort. Neither was any person allowed to enter with a hand in his pocket or behind him.

Standing directly in the doorway was a secret service officer, whose sharp eyes were on the hands of all who passed. Anybody who carried his hand in an unusual way or held anything in it received an admonition and he could not enter unless he conformed to the requirements. The Secret Service leader much when Czolgosz entered the line at Buffalo with a handkerchief wrapped around his hand. An extra detail of police was on duty, as well as several Secret Service officers beside the one in the door.

The beginning of the reception was announced by a flourish sounded by trumpeters of the Marine Band, stationed near the foot of the main stair case. The fan are signalized the approach of the President. Preceded by his military aide, Colonel Charles S. Bromwell, and his naval aide, Commander Cameron McR. Winslow, President Roosevelt, escorting Mrs. Roosevelt, descended the stairs, followed by the members of the cabinet and their ladies, constituting the immediate receiving party.

The President, as usual, wore a turn-down collar. He wore one when he was inaugurated Vice President, and will undoubtedly wear one when he is inaugurated President. No influence strong enough to induce him to discard this article has yet been discovered or invented. He had on his regulation frock suit and wore a dark four-in-hand tie. But he no longer says "de-light-ed." To-day his way was to smile soberly and say "This is indeed a happy occasion."

The whole corps attended the reception, and their gayety was a feature of the occasion. The absence of the German Ambassador, Baron Sternberg, and his wife, who are the guests of the German Emperor in Berlin, was a matter of distinct note. It was also observed that the Minister from Corea, who had gone to Macon, Ga., to be married to Mrs. Dunlap Ford, had made a hurried journey back to Washington so as not to miss the pleasure of greeting the President on New Year's.

Aside from the Cassini-Takahira incident perhaps the most distinctly interesting event of the day was the way that the receiving party with the President and his wife was made up. Official Washington was very little in evidence here. There were only four wives of Representatives asked to the Blue Room. These were Mrs. Sereno E. Payne, Mrs. Dalzell, Mrs. Grosvenor, and Mrs. Joseph Sibley. The Senatorial ladies were Mrs. Fairbanks and her daughter, Mrs. Timmons; Mrs. Cullom, and Miss Fisher, her sister.

Mrs. Alger and her daughter, Mrs. Bailey of Harrisburg, and Mrs. Julius C. Burrows; Miss Helen Cannon, the daughter of the Speaker, and her sister, Mrs. Le Socur, and a guest, Mrs. Loose of Chicago, were among the specially invited guests.

Mrs. Chaffe was the only army woman present. The navy was represented by Mrs. Dewey and Mrs. Elliott, wife of the Commandant of the Washington Navy Yard. This exclusiveness in the make-up of the Blue room party sent a pang to the heart of the official and old residential society of Washington. It is to-night a bitter theme of conversation at many a fireside, where otherwise all would have been joy unrestrained.

The bridegroom and bride of the Diplomatic Corps, Jonkherr R. De Marees van Swinderon, the Netherlands Minister, and his wife, formerly Miss Glover, of this city, received a cordial greeting. Aside from their regard for the Minister, the President and Mrs. Roosevelt are friends of the bride's family, and there was more than mere official heartiness in the greetings they extended to the representatives of Queen Wilhelmina, who had cut short their wedding trip in order that they might attend the reception.

President Roosevelt closed his New Year's day by attending the performance by Mme. Schumann-Heink and her company of the comic opera "Love's Lottery" at the New National Theatre to-night. The President, together with Miss Belle Hagner, Miss Ethel Roosevelt, Miss Cornelia Landon, Mme. Drolet, and Master Philip Roosevelt, occupied the Presidential box, while Masters Theodore Roosevelt, Jr., Kermit Roosevelt, George Russell, Jack Roosevelt, and George Roosevelt were seated in the orchestra chairs just below the Presidential box.

Newark Druggist Dies in Store.

Special to The New York Times.

NEWARK, Jan. 2.—Alexander M Levy, seventy years old, for twenty years druggist at Congress and Lafayette Streets, was found dead in his store here this morning, probably of heart disease.

SHIP BLOWS UP IN MIDSEA.

Seven of Naphtha Laden Marpesia's Crew Picked Up—Eleven Killed.

HAMILTON, Bermuda, Jan. 2.—The Danish steamship Gallia, which sailed from Hamburg Dec. 8 for Savannah, has arrived here with seven survivors of the crew of the iron Norwegian bark Marpesia, Capt. Jensen, from New York Dec. 9, for Cette. The Marpesia was blown up at sea by the explosion of her cargo of naphthia, and eleven of her crew were killed.

The Marpesia took out from this port 4..,000 gallons of naphtha, valued at $44,650. Her agents in New York were Benham & Boyesen.

The Marpesia was an iron three-masted vessel of 1,497 tons gross, and 1,353 tons net. She was built by Reid & Co. at Port Glasgow, Scotland, in 1866, and was owned by C. Hannevig of Christiania, Norway.

RUNAWAY IN FIFTH AVENUE.

With Woman in Hansom, Horse Raced Twelve Blocks Through Crowds.

Dashing up Fifth Avenue at a terrific pace, a runaway horse attached to a hansom which contained a woman, ran from Thirtieth Street to Forty-fourth Street yesterday afternoon before he was stopped. The animal was checked by a mounted policeman, after two men had made unsuccessful attempts to stop him, and had been thrown to the asphalt and cut and bruised.

The runaway several times narrowly missed collision with vehicles. The driver kept the animal in the centre of the avenue and his cries, combined with the screams of the woman, gave the hansom a comparatively free way. At Forty-second street, where traffic regulations are enforced, the runaway just escaped a cross-bound car by a few inches. After running more than half a mile, Mounted Policeman Arthur Werner, by leaping over his horses's neck and grabbing the bridle of the runaway animal, brought it to a stop.

The hansom was owned and driven by Samuel Parker, who has a stand at the Grand Central Station. In the hansom was a woman, richly dressed, who fainted when the horse was brought to a standstill. She refused to state her name and address to the police, and when she was revived, called another hansom and was driven away.

Parker was driving north in Fifth Avenue, and his horse, which is a large gray gelding, took fright when opposite the Holland House, at Thirtieth Street. The animal took the bit in its teeth and Parker was unable to stop him. He, however, managed to swerve the animal into the centre of the avenue and shouted to other drivers who were on either side. Throughout the run Parker retained his presence of mind and did all in his power to prevent accident. When the horse broke into a run the passenger started to jump from the hansom. Parker, however, closed the door and prevented her from leaping out. He then devoted his efforts to keeping his horse free from the traffic.

At Thirty-eighth Street a man who heard the screams of the woman and the cries of Parker ran to the centre of the avenue and attempted to stop the animal. He managed to grab the bridle, but was unable to keep his hold, and was thrown to the asphalt and turned several somersaults. He received cuts and bruises and his clothes were ruined, but he refused to give his name. At Forty-first Street Thomas Ralli of 167 West Sixty-eighth Street tried to stop the runaway. Ralli seized the bridle, but could not hold on. He was thrown to the street after being dragged several yards. He also received several cuts and bruises. It was then that Mounted Policeman Werner, who is stationed at Forty-second Street, made the third and successful attempt to check the frenzied horse. Werner was loudly praised for his act.

SUBMARINE BOATS HELD.

Consignment, Supposed to be for Russia, Delayed at Newport News.

Special to The New York Times.

NEWPORT NEWS, Va., aJn. 2.—The German steamship Adria, with submarine torpedo boats supposed to be destined for Russia lashed to her docks, and a pilot on board, was scheduled to sail at 4 o'clock this afternoon, but is delayed at the ship yards.

Reports of Government interference are current, but cannot be confirmed. Strict secrecy is being observed by all concerned.

RED RIBBON FOR LOOMIS.

French President Decorates Our Assistant Secretary of State.

WASHINGTON, Jan. 2.—Announcement was made to-day by Ambassador Jusserand that President Loubet of France had conferred upon Francis B. Loomis, the First Assistant Secretary of State, the decoration of Grand Officer of the Legion of Honor, which is the highest but one of the decorations within the power of the President of the French Republic to bestow.

One of the reasons which led to the conferring of the decoration upon Mr. Loomis was the interest aroused in France by his speech in behalf of international arbitration, delivered last September before the Interparliamentary Union.

GERMAN DIET VOTE FOR SALE.

Goes with Large Landed Estate in the Duchy of Mecklenburg.

BERLIN, Jan. 2.—A Mecklenburg newspaper prints an advertisement offering for sale a large landed estate carrying the right to "a hereditary seat and a vote in the Diet."

The Vorwaerts (Socialist) says, evidently joking, that the Social Democratic Executive Committee intends to buy the estate so as to put one of the party's followers into the Feudal Diet of that duchy which is the only State of Germany without its own Constitution.

Killed Boy on Dare.

Special to The New York Times.

DALLAS, Texas, Jan. 2.—"I dare you to shoot me," said N. R. Griggs, a twelve-year-old boy, to his companion, an Italian named Pantacosta to-day at Houston. The banter was accepted, and Pantacosta fired a target rifle bullet into Griggs's abdomen, from which death soon ensued. Pantacosta was arrested, charged with murder.

HIGGINS-ODELL DEAL TO MAINTAIN MACHINE

Speaker Nixon in It—Submits Slate to ex-Governor.

BLACK MEN WILL NOT FIGHT

Leaders of Faction Reject Scheme to Oust Odell—Brackett May Continue Opposition Alone.

Special to The New York Times.

ALBANY, Jan. 2.—Probably a quarter of an hour ride in the rain never before had such a tonic effect on any man as the ride which he took with Governor Higgins from the Executive Mansion to the Capitol to-day, had on Benjamin B. Odell, Jr. The ex-Governor and present chairman of the Republican State Committee is a man of moods. When he arrived last night he was plainly in the dumps. After he had talked with Secretary of State Obrien, who was one of the most ardent supporters of Frank S. Black for the senatorship, he "perked up some." His talk with Senator Depew apparently improved his disposition still more, and his ride with Governor Higgins to the Capitol to-day completed the metamorphosis.

The best informed opinion here to-night is that Governor Higgins, while continuing to exercise an independence in big matters which will be convincing as to who is the real Governor, will do all that he can to aid State Chairman Odell in maintaining the efficiency of the State organization.

When the State Chairman came to Albany yesterday he was uncertain what the future had in store for him politically. When he left Albany on the 2:15 train, immediately after the inauguration ceremonies, he was confident from the assurances he had received that any attempt which might be made to unhorse him by the bitter political enemies he made by deciding in favor of Senator Depew in the Senatorial contest was foredoomed to failure.

A substantial evidence of the fact that his leadership is to be recognized was given immediately after his return to the Ten Eyck Hotel from the Capitol, when Speaker Nixon went to his room with him for the purpose of having him pass upon the list of Assembly committees which the Speaker had framed. Senator Platt has said that he has a list to submit to Speaker Nixon, but from the developments to-day it can be said with reasonable assurance that the committees which will be announced by the Speaker will be the list approved to-day by Mr. Odell.

Senator John Raines, who will be the majority leader of the Senate, after a talk with Lieut. Gov. Bruce, to-ady announced that the Senate committees would be made up under the rule of priority. That understanding, if adhered to, will preclude the naming of Senator Elsberg of New York as Chairman of the Cities Committee.

It was learned this evening on excellent authority that certain of ex-Gov. Black's supporters, who desired to be revenged on Odell, made overtures to some of the friends of Senator Platt, looking to the deposing of Odell as State Chairman. Their proposition was the re-election of Col. George W. Dunn.

Nothing is likely to come of it, as several of the leaders who were most conspicuous in the movement to elect Black Senator, and who will be most formidable at Albany this Winter, regarded such a movement as the height of folly.

"Lou" Payne, George W. Aldridge, and Secretary of State O'Brien took breakfast together this morning at the Ten Eyck, and came to the conclusion that they would not look for trouble because of their disappointment over the outcome of the Senatorial contest.

Senator Brackett did not come to the inauguration ceremonies. About the only Black supporter on the ground who was slinging to-day vitriol was Superintendent of Prisons Cornelius V. Collins. He indulged in talk about ex-Gov. Odell's qualities as a quitteer, which were even more stinging than the observations of the Saratoga Senator on the same subject.

It looks very much as if Senator Brackett might have to conduct his insurgent movement single-handed and alone this Winter. He is very likely to be in the position Senator Coggeshall was when he constituted, so far as the Senate was concerned, "The independent part of Oneida County."

While Chairman Odell was in conference with Speaker Nixon about the committees this afternoon Senator Depew was holding a public reception in the Ten Eyck. A crowd went to shake his hand and congratulate him. As they passed in they were given a drink of punch, and as they came out they were handed a cigar, which led a Senatorial wit to remark: "The punch was a bracer to enable us to stand one of Chauncey's stories, and the cigar was to soothe us into the belief that it was one of the best we had ever heard."

NIAGARA TURBINES TESTED.

Largest in the World, and Trial Is a Great Success.

Special to The New York Times.

NIAGARA FALLS, N. Y., Jan. 2.—The Canadian Niagara Falls Power Company, the ally of the Niagara Falls Power Company on the American side of the river, set in motion to-day two of their 10,000 horse power turbines. The officers of the power company, the commissioners of the Niagara Falls Queen Victoria Park, and other guests were witnesses. The trial was a great success.

These are the largest working turbines and dynamos in the world, and their successful operation marks an important era in electrical development. Francis Lynde Stetson of New York and President W. H. Beatty of the Canadian company turned on the power, and each machine under full power developed 12,000 volts and ran without a hitch.

After the test a luncheon was served at the Hospice of Mount Carmel on the high bluff of the Niagara. The guests, including Mr. Stetson, made congratulatory speeches, and the names of King Edward and President Roosevelt were heartily cheered.

Chauffeurs Fined for Speeding.

YONKERS, N. Y., Jan. 2.—Paul Satori, chauffeur for Alfred G. Vanderbilt, and Harry Stienson, who serves Samuel Untermyer in like capacity, were fined $25 each for speeding their automobiles, by City Judge Kellogg to-day, both pleading guilty. Mr. Untermyer was in court when Stienson was arraigned and they left together.

COLORADO ELECTION FRAUDS.

Evidence to Show 18,000 Spurious Votes for Adams.

Special to The New York Times.

DENVER, Col., Jan. 2.—Repeaters and those who hired them last Election Day have made written confessions, and written evidence to prove that there were eighteen thousand fraudulent votes cast for Alva Adams in Denver at the late election has been prepared for presentation to the President of the Senate Wednesday afternoon by Attorneys John M. Wildron and James H. Brown.

Since Election Day Attorney Brown has had a large corps of assistants working on a recanvass of every precinct of the city, and while he asserts that there were 20,000 illegal ballots cast at the election of Nov. 8, the affidavits he will file with the records of the new canvass will make the assertion that fully 18,000 spurious votes were cast for the Democratic candidate for Governor.

Harry C. Riddle, Republican member of the Elections Commission, has prepared a minority report on the vote cast in Denver, in which he asserts that gross frauds were practiced by people working under the pay of the Democrats, and that there were enough fraudulent votes cast to turn the result of the election.

DENIES ARMOR PLATE DEAL.

Official of Midvale Company Says They Want Whole Order.

Special to The New York Times.

PHILADELPHIA, Jan. 2.—If the Government divides the $3,000,000 armor plate order which will be given out on Jan. 12, among the Midvale Steel, the Bethlehem Steel, and the Carnegie Steel Companies, it will not be with the consent of the Midvale Company, according to a statement made to-night by an officer of the company.

He contradicted the story that Charles M. Schwab had got the three companies to combine and submit bids differing little in price. The Midvale Company wants the whole order, and will submit bids with that purpose in view.

James F. Sullivan, Vice-President of the Midvale Company, said he had not seen Mr. Schwab, and that he knew of no such action as had been reported. Whether a combine has been effected will be known, he said, when the bids are opened by the Government officers.

OFFER TO HELP COTTON UP.

Webber Says That Southern Farmers Does Not Need New York Aid.

MEMPHIS, Jan. 2.—E. F. Webber, President of the Memphis Cotton Exchange, said to-day that he had received a telegram from New York regarding a proposition by banking interests to render financial assistance to Southern farmers who desire to hold their cotton for higher prices. Mr. Webber said he would take no notice of the telegram because, so far as he knew, it came from no official source, being signed simply with the letter "B."

Mr. Webber said he believed the farmers in the South to be in a position to hold their cotton without financial aid. The small farmer, he said, had marketed enough cotton to carry him over until the next crop, and in many instances had from five to ten bales on hand awaiting higher prices.

CONNECTICUT'S MURDER ROLL

Nutmeg State Rejoices That There Were Only Twenty Last Year.

HARTFORD, Conn., Jan. 2.—Twenty homicides were committed in Connecticut during the calendar year of 1904, thirteen less than the figure for 1903, and three below the average for the past nine years. Seven of the year's homicides were accidental, of which five were committed by boys.

Of the twenty victims of the homicides all but three were males, and in every case the slaying was done by men. One of the slayers is now in State prison under sentence of death; another was executed in November, two have been sentenced to State prison for life for murder in the second degree, and two are serving terms in State prison for manslaughter. Some have not been tried. In three cases the murderers escaped and have not been apprehended.

MOVE IN CALEB POWERS CASE.

Kentucky's Attorney General Wants Court to Declare Him Guilty.

FRANKFORT, Ky., Jan. 2.—Attorney General Hays filed a petition to-day for a rehearing in the case of Caleb Powers, charged with complicity in the murder of ex-Governor William Goebel.

The Powers case now stands with the last verdict of guilty reversed and a new trial ordered. Attorney General Hays appealed for a rehearing on the decision by the Court of Appeals. In other words the court is asked to reverse itself, and let the death sentence stand.

Up to to-day the court was composed of three Democrats and three Republicans. To-day, however, Judge James Cantrill, a Democrat, was sworn in to succeed a retired Republican. There is doubt as to whether Judge Cantrill will sit in the case, as he presided in three trials of Powers in the lower courts.

WINS NEWSBOYS' HEARTS.

Mrs. Duncan Plays Princess Bountiful with $5 in Gold.

Four city newsboys spied Mrs. Butler Duncan, Jr., as she was alighting from a train in Long Island City yesterday, and followed her to her electric cab. Jimmie Cullen succeeded in asking her first if she wanted a newspaper.

"Certainly," said Mrs. Duncan, who, upon fumbling in her purse, found a five-dollar gold piece. "This is all I have," she continued. "Get it changed and divide with your boy friends."

"Sure," said James, and then gave effusive thanks.

The quartet waited long enough on the Long Island shore to eat a turkey dinner. Then they came to Manhattan, to the theatre, and to peanuts between and during the acts.

CHATTANOOGA'S SPEED, 16.7.

New Cruiser Exceeds Contract Speed of 16.5 Knots an Hour.

NEWPORT, R. I., Jan. 2.—The official record made by the new protected cruiser Chattanooga on her four hours' speed run at sea yesterday was 16.7 knots an hour.

The speed called for by the contract was 16.5. After slight repairs to her machinery are completed the gunboat will be subjected to a twenty-four-hour trial for the purpose of testing her general efficiency.

STOESSEL, AFTER LONG CONFERENCE, SURRENDERS CITY

Articles of Port Arthur's Capitulation Signed at 4:30 o'Clock Yesterday Afternoon.

REMNANTS OF FLEET OUT

860 Wounded Escape on Ship—Sunken Vessels Blown Up.

MIKADO SENDS HUMANE ORDER

Russian Officers Tell of Sore Straits of the Garrison.

TALK OF PEACE IS NOW HEARD

Roosevelt May Be Asked to Act—Baltic Fleet May Be Recalled—News Kept from Russians—Wild Joy at Tokio.

TOKIO, Jan. 2.—Port Arthur capitulated at 4:30 o'clock this afternoon. Gen. Nogi received from Gen. Stoessel at 9 o'clock last night a letter formally offering to surrender. He appointed officers to meet Russian officers in conference at noon to-day.

The text of Gen. Nogi's telegram announcing the capitulation of the Russian forces is as follows:

"The plenipotentiaries of both parties concluded their negotiations to-day at 4:30 o'clock. The Russian Commissioners accepted on the whole the conditions stipulated by us and consented to capitulate. The document has been prepared and signatures are now being affixed. Simultaneously with the conclusion of negotiations both armies suspended hostilities.

"It is expected that the Japanese Army will enter the City of Port Arthur to-morrow."

An earlier report from Gen. Nogi said:

"At 5 in the afternoon Jan. 1 the enemy's bearer of a flag of truce came into the first line of our position south of Shuishiying and handed a letter to our officers. The same reached me at 9 o'clock at night. The letter is as follows:

"'Judging by the general condition of the whole line of hostile positions held by you I find further resistance at Port Arthur useless, and for the purpose of preventing needless sacrifice of lives I propose to hold negotiations with reference to capitulation. Should you consent to the same, you will please appoint Commissioners for discussing the order and conditions regarding capitulation, and also appoint a place for such Commissioners to meet the same appointed by me.

"'I take this opportunity to convey to Your Excellency assurances of my respect. STOESSEL.'

"Shortly after dawn to-day I will dispatch our bearer of a flag of truce with the following reply addressed to Stoessel:

"'I have the honor to reply to your proposal to hold negotiations regarding the conditions and order of capitulation. For this purpose I have appointed as Commissioner Major Gen. Ijichi, Chief of Staff of our army. He will be accompanied by some staff officers and civil officials. They will meet your Commissioners Jan. 2, noon, at Shuishiping. The Commissioners of both parties will be empowered to sign a convention for the capitulation without waiting for ratification and cause the same to take immediate effect. Authorization for such plenary powers shall be signed by the highest officer of both the negotiating parties, and the same shall be exchanged by the respective Commissioners.

"'I avail myself of this opportunity to convey to your Excellency assurances of my respect. 'NOGI.'"

Marshal Yamagata, Chief of General Staff, under orders from the Emperor, dispatched the following cablegram to Gen. Nogi:

"When I respectfully informed his Majesty of Gen. Stoessel's proposal for capitulation, His Majesty was pleased to state that Gen. Stoessel had rendered commendable service toh is country in the midst of difficulties, and it is His Majesty's wish that military honors be shown to him."

It is believed here that the Port Arthur garrison has received liberal terms. There is a general disposition to be magnanimous in view of the garrison's marvelous defense. In military circles the opinion is expressed that the discussion between the Commissioners covered only a few questions, including allowing the garrison to march out carrying their arms, permitting the garrison to return to Russia with or without their officers, and requiring their parole not to take any further part in the war.

A dispatch from the Japanese Army before Port Arthur received at noon to-day says:

"The enemy's forces occupying Keekwan Mountain and 'Q' Fort, following an explosion at 12:30 this morning, opened a sudden and fierce rifle fire, which suddenly stopped.

"Our scouts were dispatched to the scene, and immediately afterward found the enemy evacuating these places. Our forces immediately occupied these two forts, and also the heights known as 'M' and 'N' south of the forts.

"This morning almost all the enemy's ships, large and small, were blown up in the entrance and inside the harbor. Our offensive movements have been suspended pending the negotiations."

Gen. Nogi's telegram announcing that Gen. Stoessel was prepared to discuss terms of capitulation reached Tokio early this morning, but was not made public until 10 o'clock.

The fall of Wan-Tai, popularly known as Signal Hill, following the loss of new Pan-Lung, is regarded here as a clear indication that the Port Arthur garrison had lost its power of serious resistance.

It is probable that the back of the Russian defense was broken when 203-Meter Hill was captured. The Russians desperately sought to retake that eminence, and sent infantry and marines against it in a series of counter-attacks, fruitlessly losing thousands of men.

FORTRESS A VERITABLE HELL.

Bayonet Main Weapon of Defense for a Month—Ammunition Gave Out.

CHE-FOO, Jan. 2.—The Russian officers have a single word for what the fortress has been for the past five days, during which the Japanese have bombarded and assaulted it ceaselessly nightand day—hell. They use that word unprofanely and convincingly, declaring that the horrors witnessed were beyond any description.

There was not a single spot in town that was safe from shrapnel. Many of the hospitals were hit and the wounded refused to stay in them. Some lay in the streets on heaps of débris, exposed to the bitterly cold weather, and some staggered back to the front, hurling stones and defying the Japanese till taken prisoners or death came mercifully to end their sufferings.

The stock of ammunition, which had been carefully husbanded for months, was almost gone, and it was all too evident that Japan was about to grasp the prize which had cost her an army of men and countless treasure.

Commander Kartsow of the Russian torpedo boat destroyer Vlastni said to-night:

"Port Arthur falls of exhaustion—exhaustion not only of ammunition, but of men.

"The remnant of the garrison left had been doing the work of heroes for five days and five nights, but yesterday they reached the limit of human endurance.

"In the casemates of the forts one saw everywhere faces black with starvation, exhaustion, and nerve strain. You spoke to them, but they did not give answer, only staring dumbly.

"The lack of ammunition alone would not have suggested the seeking of terms. Scant ammunition had long been common in the fortress, and during the past month many of the forts had nothing with which to return the fire of the enemy. Golden Hill has had no ammunition for three months.

"The Russians sat in the casemates firing not more than once to the 200 shots sent by the Japanese. When the assault came they repulsed the enemy with bayonets. But the men themselves having existed for three months on reduced rations, were so worn that it is marvelous they stood the final strain so long.

"In fact, for months we held Port Arthur practically by bayonets alone, until flesh and blood could do no more. When a man fell there was none other to replace him. Thus the garrison was gradually worn down. Two Hundred and Three Meter Hill alone cost us 5,000 men. The capture of that hill was the beginning of the end.

"Yesterday Gen. Soessel would still fight. His wound, which was received early in the siege, had been bothering him, but his determination to fight while one man stood had not been diminished.

"'But we cannot fight,' said his Generals. 'Our men cannot move. They sleep standing. They cannot see the bayonets at their breasts. We can order, but the yecannot obey.'

"'Then you Generals fight,' said Stoessel, clinching his fists.

"He seemed fanatical on the subject, but finally he was brought to see reason by the insistence of his subordinates, Admirals Lechinsky and Wiren, Gens. Smyrnoff and Fock, and many others, sometimes with broken voices, urged the step which all dreaded so long.

"I am sure Port Arthur would have sought terms a month ago had it not been for Gen. Stoessel, who with bulldog tenacity steadily refused to permit such action. He had told his Emperor that he would never surrender, and he meant to keep his word.

"The greatest loss suffered by Port Arthur occurred a fortnight ago, when Major Gen. Kondratenko was killed. Officers and men alike regarded him as the brightest star in Port Arthur's firmament. When his death become known the fall in the spirits of the soldiers was plainly visible.

"Gen. Kondratenko was seated in one of the casemates of a certain fort discussing with seven other officers the best way of counter-mining against the Japanese when an eleven-inch shell burst, killing everybody in the casemate.

"Gen. Nogi has taken Port Arthur with his artillery and his tunnels. His rifle bullets were seldom found to be of any use. We constantly endured a bombardment fiercer than any in history. The Japanese periodically assaulted and then, if repulsed, they calmly resumed their bombardments.

"We who came here do not know the terms of surrender suggested by Gen. Stoessel to Gen. Nogi nor the answer to them, having left Port Arthur even before the messenger had been dispatched. The general impression, however, is that Stoessel has proposed that the army shall go free and that he alone be made a prisoner. Even that concession seemed to wrench out the sturdy old man's heart.

SENSATION IN LONDON.

Stoessel's Surrender the One Topic of Discussion—Hayashi's Tribute.

LONDON, Jan. 2.—The capitulation of Port Arthur was the sensation of London to-day. It was the one topic of discussion, from the street corners, where groups were sheltered from the driving snow, to the comfortable service clubs, the legations, and the residences and offices of Cabinet Ministers.

Everywhere the utmost admiration was expressed for the defenders and the attacking army, and the probability that Gen. Nogi has made concessions to the gallant Gen. Stoessel was received with much satisfaction.

The announcement of the fall of the Russian stronghold created little surprise in official and diplomatic circles, where it had been discounted by recent events. It was known as early as last October that, notwithstanding the brave showing in the official dispatches, that Stoessel's resources were nearly at an end.

Nowhere, not even at the Russian Embassy, was there a doubt concerning the generosity of the Japanese in arrangement of the final terms.

In diplomatic circles the main question was that of the effect of the surrender. The consensus of opinion was that it [illegible] tend in the direction of peace, [illegible] none dared venture to say that peace is

At the Foreign Office itwas stated that the British Government's attitude is unchanged; that, while peace is most desirable, affairs have not reached a stage where any foreign power could hope to offer its good offices with the assurance that it would be considered a friendly act by either of the belligerents.

At the Russian Embassy the same spirit of determination to prosecute the war to the bitter end was expressed. In fact, it was confidently stated that Russia would only regard the surrender of Port Arthur in the light of a fresh incentive and would spare no efforts for its recapture. First Secretary Poklewsky-Koziel, in the absence of Ambassador Benkendorff from the embassy, gave voice to this sentiment when he said that he felt satisfied the surrender of the fortress would only serve to unite all Russia in the determination to put forth her whole strength in the Spring with a view to retrieving the situation.

The general tone at the Russian Embassy formed a striking contrast to the cheerfulness and activity prevailing at the Japanese Legation. Minister Hayashi was the recipient during the day of hundreds of telegrams of congratulation from all parts of Great Britain and other countries.

MINISTER HAYASKI'S VIEW.

The Minister declined to discuss the probability of peace negotiations. He said, however:

"The fall of Port Arthur will at any rate end the horrible slaughter in one part of the theatre of war, and I sincerely hope that in some way it will facilitate final peace. This depends upon Russia and not upon us. It may strengthen the determination of Russia to continue the war at all costs. Its effect on Japan, however, cannot be doubted. Our fleet is free, and the release of the besieging army gives us increased forces available for services elsewhere. Our base becomes more secure than ever."

Speaking of Gen. Stoessel, Minister Hayashi said:

"The surrender will in no way affect the glory belonging to him and his men nor our admiration for their splendid defense."

Baron Suyematsu, son-in-law of Marquis Ito and former Japanese Minister of the Interior, said:

"Now that we have again got Port Arthur we will not allow any other power to hold it after we have beaten Russia; and I am now more than ever confident that Japan will be victorious. I do not expect the fall of Port Arthur will make much difference with the progress of the war, though Japan undoubtedly will be in a better position."

FIERCE FIGHT NEAR MUKDEN.

Russians Report Repulse of Japanese with Great Loss.

MUKDEN, Jan. 2.—A heavy cannonade and rifle fire commenced on the Russian centre early this morning and continued during the day.

It is reported here that the Japanese attacked in an effort to break the centre, but were driven back with great loss.

GEN. KUROKI'S HEADQUARTERS, Via Tien-Tsin, Jan. 2.—The positions of the Japanese and the Russian armies south of Mukden have not been materially changed during the last two months. In few places are the lines more than a mile apart, and they are so close before the Japanese left that loud talking in the Russian trenches can be heard.

Though the Russians became very quiet during the first half of December they have renewed the bombardment of the Japanese centre and left in the last fortnight and have selected several points to which they devote most attention. The Japanese usually lie low in their trenches and remain silent. Often several hundred

"All the News That's Fit to Print."

The New York Times.

THE WEATHER.
Fair to-day and to-morrow; rising southerly winds.

VOL. LV...NO. 17,617. ••••• NEW YORK, THURSDAY, APRIL 19, 1906.—TWENTY TWO PAGES. ONE CENT In Greater New York, Jersey City and Newark. | Elsewhere, TWO CENTS.

OVER 500 DEAD, $200,000,000 LOST IN SAN FRANCISCO EARTHQUAKE

Nearly Half the City Is in Ruins and 50,000 Are Homeless.

WATER SUPPLY FAILS AND DYNAMITE IS USED IN VAIN

Great Buildings Consumed Before Helpless Firemen—Federal Troops and Militia Guard the City, With Orders to Shoot Down Thieves—Citizens Roused in Early Morning by Great Convulsion and Hundreds Caught by Falling Walls.

SAN FRANCISCO, April 18.—Earthquake and fire to-day have put nearly half of San Francisco in ruins. About 500 persons have been killed, a thousand injured, and the property loss will exceed $200,000,000.

Fifty thousand people are homeless and destitute, and all day long streams of people have been fleeing from the stricken districts to places of safety.

It was 5:13 this morning when a terrific earthquake shock shook the whole city and surrounding country. One shock apparently lasted two minutes, and there was almost immediate collapse of flimsy structures all over the city.

The water supply was cut off, and when fires started in various sections there was nothing to do but let the buildings burn. Telegraph and telephone communication was cut off for a time.

The Western Union was put completely out of business and the Postal Company was the only one that managed to get a wire out of the city. About 10 o'clock even the Postal was forced to suspend.

Electric power was stopped and street cars did not run, railroads and ferry-boats also ceased operations. The various fires raged all day and the fire department has been powerless to do anything except dynamite buildings threatened. All day long explosions have shaken the city and added to the terror of the inhabitants.

Following the first shock there was another within five minutes, but not nearly so severe. Three hours later there was another slight quake.

First Warning at 5:13 A. M.

Most of the people of San Francisco were asleep at 5:13 o'clock this morning when the terrible earthquake came without warning.

The motion of the disturbance apparently was from east to west. At first the upheaval of the earth was gradual, but in a few seconds it increased in intensity. Chimneys began to fall and buildings to crack, tottering on their foundations.

The people became panic-stricken, and rushed into the streets, most of them in their night attire. They were met by showers of falling bricks, cornices, and walls of buildings.

Many were crushed to death, while others were badly mangled. Those who remained indoors generally escaped with their lives, though scores were hit by detached plaster, pictures, and articles thrown to the floor by the shock. It is believed that more or less loss was sustained by nearly every family in the city.

Steel Frame Buildings Stand.

The tall, steel-frame structures stood the strain better than brick buildings, few of them being badly damaged. The big eleven-story Monadnock office building, in course of construction, adjoining the Palace Hotel, was an exception, however, its rear wall collapsing and many cracks being made across its front.

Some of the docks and freight sheds along the water front slid into the bay. Deep fissures opened in the filled-in ground near the shore, and the Union Ferry Station was badly injured. Its high tower still stands, but will have to be torn down.

A portion of the new City Hall, which cost more than $7,000,000, collapsed, the roof sliding into the courtyard, and the smaller towers tumbling down. The great dome was moved, but did not fall.

The new Post Office, one of the finest in the United States, was badly shattered.

The Valencia Hotel, a four-story wooden building, sank into the basement, a pile of splintered timbers, under which were pinned many dead and dying occupants of the house. The basement was full of water, and some of the helpless victims were drowned.

Fires Start in Many Places.

Scarcely had the earth ceased to shake when fires started simultaneously in many places. The Fire Department promptly responded to the first calls for aid, but it was found that the water mains had been rendered useless by the underground movement.

Fanned by a light breeze, the flames quickly spread, and soon many blocks were seen to be doomed. Then dynamite was resorted to, and the sound of frequent explosions added to the terror of the people. These efforts to stay the progress of the fire, however, proved futile.

The south side of Market Street, from Ninth Street to the bay, was soon ablaze, the fire covering a belt two blocks wide. On this, the main thoroughfare, were many of the finest edifices in the city, including the Grant, Parrott, Flood, Call, Examiner, and Monadnock Buildings, and the Palace and Grand Hotels.

At the same time commercial establishments and banks north of Market Street were burning. The burning district in this section of the city extended from Sansome Street to the water front, and from Market Street to Broadway.

Fires also started in the Mission, and the entire city seemed to be in flames.

Long Detours Around Fires.

The flames, fanned by the rising breeze, swept down the main streets until within a few hundred feet of the ferry station, the high tower of which stood at a dangerous angle.

The big wholesale grocery establishment of Weelman, Peck & Co. was on fire from cellar to roof, and the heat was so oppressive that passengers from the ferry boats were obliged to keep close to the water's edge, in order to get past the burning structure.

It was impossible to reach the centre of the city from the bay without skirting the shore for a long distance so as to get entirely around the burning district.

About 8 o'clock the Southern Pacific officials refused to allow any more passengers from trans-bay points to land, and sent back those already on the boats. The ferry and train service of the Key Route was entirely abandoned owing to damage done to the power house by the earthquake at Emeryville.

Lack of Dynamite Felt.

There was little dynamite available in the city. The Southern Pacific soon brought some in. At 9 o'clock Mayor Schmitz sent a tug to Pinola for several cases of explosives. He sent also a telegram to Mayor Mott of Oakland. At 10:30 he received this reply to his Oakland message:

"Three engines and hose companies leave here immediately. Will forward dynamite as soon as obtainable."

The town of San Rafael, despite its own needs, sent fire fighting apparatus here.

Mayor Schmitz gave orders to use dynamite wherever necessary, and the firemen and United States soldiers, who assisted them, blew down building after building. Their efforts, however, were useless, so far as checking the headway of the flames was concerned.

The shortage of water was due to the breaking of the mains of the Spring Valley Water Company at San Mateo. The water needed so badly in the city ran in a flood over San Mateo.

Burning of the Opera House.

The fire swept down the streets so rapidly that it was practically impossible to save anything in its way. It reached the Grand Opera House on Mission Street, and in a moment had burned through the roof. The Metropolitan Opera Company from New York had just opened its season there, and all the expensive scenery and costumes were soon reduced to ashes.

From the opera house the fire leaped from building to building, leveling them almost to the ground in quick succession.

The Call editorial and mechanical departments, in the handsome building at Third and Market Streets, were totally destroyed in a few minutes, and the flames leaped across Stevenson Street toward the fine fifteen-story stone and iron building of Claus Spreckels, which, with its lofty dome, was the most notable structure in San Francisco. Two small wooden buildings furnished fuel to ignite the splendid pile.

Thousands of people watched the hungry tongues of flames licking the stone walls. At first no impression was made, but suddenly there was a cracking of glass and an entrance was effected. The inner furnishings of the fourth floor were the first to go. Then, as if by magic, smoke issued from the top of the dome.

This was followed by a most spectacular illumination. The round windows of the dome shone like so many full moons; they burst and gave vent to long, waving streamers of flames. The crowd watched the spectacle with bated breath. One woman wrung her hands and burst into a torrent of tears. "It is so terrible," she said.

The tall and slender structure which had withstood the forces of the earth appeared doomed to fall a prey to fire. After a while, however, the light grew less intense, and the flames, finding nothing to consume, gradually went out, leaving the building standing, but completely gutted.

At California and Sansome Streets stood the Mutual Life Building, a modern structure of architectural beauty, to which the flames were soon communicated. An attempt was made to save it, but the fire was irrepressible. The flames gained, and in a few moments the big building was beyond hope. The Anglo California Bank was swept by the flames and came down in a rush.

Time and again attempts were made with dynamite to clear a space which should prevent the flames from spreading to other buildings, but freely as the explosive was used the fire crept and climbed from one structure to another.

An unusually loud report showed that a gas house at Eighteenth and Market Streets had blown up. The fire caused by the explosion quickly communicated in various directions. As the gas house exploded a feeling of despair overcame the men who were performing the rescue work.

Scare at Palace Hotel.

The Palace Hotel, the rear of which was constantly threatened, was the scene of much excitement, the guests leaving in haste, many with only the clothing they wore. Finding that the hotel was surrounded on all sides by streets, and was likely to remain immune, many returned and made arrangements for the removal of their belongings, though little could be taken away owing to the utter absence of transportation facilities.

The Parrott Building, in which was located the chambers of the State Supreme Court, the lower floors being devoted to an immense department store, was ruined, though its massive walls were not all destroyed.

A little further down Market Street, the Academy of Sciences and the Jennie Flood Building and the History Building kindled and burned like so much tinder. Sparks carried across the wide street, ignited the Phelan Building, and the army headquarters of California, Gen. Funston commanding, were burned.

Still nearing the bay, the waters of which did the firemen good service along the docks, the fire took the Rialto Building, a handsome skyscraper, and converted scores of solid business blocks into smoldering piles of bricks.

Thousands Watch the Flames.

Banks and commercial houses, supposed to be fireproof, though not of modern build, burned quickly, and the roar of the flames could be heard even on the hills, which were out of the danger zone. Here many thousands of people congregated and viewed the awful scene.

Great sheets of flame rose high in the heavens, or rushed down some narrow street, joining midway between the sidewalks, making a horizontal chimney of the former passageway.

The dense smoke that arose from the entire business district spread out like an immense funnel and could have been seen miles out at sea. Occasionally as some drug house or place stored with chemicals was reached, most fantastic effects were produced by the centred flames and smoke which rolled out against the darker background.

One of the first orders issued by Chief of Police Dinan this morning was for the closing of every saloon in the city. This step is taken to prevent drink-crazed men from rioting in the streets.

Mayor Schmitz sent out word to the bakeries and milk stations throughout the city that their food supplies must be harbored for the homeless. Provisions were made to place tents in every park in the city, and those who have lost all will be given food and shelter.

Early in the morning the prisoners confined in the city prison on the fifth floor of the Hall of Justice were transferred in irons to the basement of the structure. Later they were removed to the Broadway Jail, and if necessity arises they will be taken to a branch county jail on the Mission Road.

The Mayor also established a base of rescue, and soon had forces out where they could accomplish most. Many men were sent down to the lodging house district near Market Street. There it was found that many frame buildings, packed with people, had collapsed, burying their occupants in the ruins.

The rescuers jumped into the wrecks and pulled out the dead, the dying, and the injured. Practically every physician in the city immediately volunteered his assistance, and soon there was a well-equipped medical corps organized which began ministering to the injured.

For hours bodies were taken out in the lodging house district, and hundreds of men volunteered to go into the ruins to get more.

The pretentious City Hall, bounded by Larkin and McAllister Streets and City Hall Avenue, was badly shattered by the earthquake, and the ruins later were burned. It took twenty years to build the City Hall, the pride of the coast. When the first shock was felt the building rocked and swayed until it cracked. Part of the interior fell and the ruins caught fire. An alarm was turned in and the firemen responded. Chief Sullivan, awakened by the shock at his quarters in a firehouse, hastened to put on his clothes. As he reached for them the tower of the California Hotel dropped upon his building and crushing through the roof killed him.

The firemen arrived at the City Hall, but were helpless. They hitched their hose to the fire plugs, but there was no water supply.

Every possible precaution has been taken to guard property. Immediately after the destructive shocks the police turned out on guard, and the Governor and Gen. Funston, commanding the Pacific Division of the United States Army, were asked to send troops.

A thousand men from the Presidio, sent by Gen. Funston, arrived downtown at 9 o'clock to patrol the streets. The Thirteenth Infantry, 1,000 strong, arrived from Angel Island a little later and went on patrol duty at once.

The soldiers were ordered to shoot down vandals caught robbing the dead and to guard with their lives the millions of dollars' worth of property placed in the streets to escape the flames.

The First California Artillery, 200 strong, two companies, was detailed to patrol duty on Ellis Street. Two more companies patrolled Broadway in the Italian section. The Ellis Street contingent of guardsmen were under the command of Capt. G. A. Grattan. Capt. William A. Miller commanded the forces on Broadway.

The city is under martial law, and all the downtown streets are patroled by cavalry and infantry. Details of troops are also guarding the banks.

Early this morning Mayor Schmitz, who established his office at Police Headquarters, named the following citizens as a Committee of Safety:

James D. Phelan,	Paul Cowles,
Herbert Law,	M. H. De Young,
Thomas Magee,	Claus Spreckles,
Charles Fee,	Rudolph Spreckles,
W. P. Herrin,	C. W. Fay,
Thornwell Mullalley,	John McNaught,
Garret W. Enerney,	Dent Robert,
W. H. Leahy,	Thomas Garrett,
J. Downey Harvey,	Frank Shea,
Jeremiah Dinan,	James Shea,
John J. Mahoney,	Robert Pisis,
Henry T. Scott,	T. P. Woodward,
I. W. Hellman,	Howard Holmes,
George A. Knight,	George Dillman,
I. Steinhart,	J. B. Rogers,
S. G. Murphy,	David Rich,
Homer King,	H. T. Cresswell,
Frank Anderson,	J. A. Howell,
W. J. Bartnett,	Frank Maestretti,
John Martin,	Clem Tobin,
Allan Pollock	George Toumey,
Mark Gerstle,	E. D. Pond,
H. V. Ramsdell,	George A. Newhall,
W. G. Harrison,	William Watson.
R. A. Crothers,	

THE BUILDINGS DESTROYED.

A Partial List of the Structures Torn Down or Injured.

SAN FRANCISCO, April 18.—The following is an incomplete list of the buildings destroyed or injured:

Call Building, entirely destroyed.

Claus Spreckels Building, burned out.

Hearst Building, collapsed.

New Chronicle Building, hardly damaged.

The White House, walls badly cracked; all plate glass windows gone; every piece of stock in building removed before 9:30 A. M.

Winchester Hotel, Third Street, totally destroyed by earthquake shock.

Grand Opera House, entirely destroyed.

Claus Spreckels house and stables, Van Ness Avenue, badly damaged and will have to be largely rebuilt.

St. Luke's Episcopal Church, Van Ness Avenue, will have to be pulled down.

Mechanics' Library Building, Post Street, cornices fell to street; building slightly injured.

Crocker Building, Market and Post Streets, slightly damaged, principally around light shaft.

Lick House, walls and roof largely caved in.

Upham Building, Pine and Battery Streets, totally destroyed; loss, $550,000.

Fire house adjoining California Hotel in Bush Street; Chief Sullivan and wife, sleeping in engine house, severely bruised by bricks crashing through roof from hotel.

California Hotel, Bush Street, upper walls collapsed and upper floors wrecked.

The building in course of construction to be occupied by the Hamman baths will have to be rebuilt. It is in Post Street near the Olympic Club. The walls are badly warped and twisted and the roof has fallen in.

San Francisco Gas and Electric Company's Post Street plant, only slightly injured.

St. Francis Hotel, exterior slightly cracked and seamed, but not seriously injured

Pacific Union Club, Post and Stockton Streets, front injured and fissures in rear wall.

St. Dominic's Church in Pierce Street, total loss. The interior of the church is wrecked and there are fissures in the walls. The structure will have to be pulled down. The parochial house in the same block is nearly a wreck. It is estimated that the loss to the parish is $300,000.

The ornamental top on St. Dunstan's, the apartment house at Sutter Street and Van Ness Avenue, fell into the street.

The Concordia Club building in Van Ness Avenue has several fissures in the side, and rebuilding will be necessary.

The Hotel Grinado, badly damaged; stone coping about roof fell.

ALL SAN FRANCISCO MAY BURN; CLIFF HOUSE RESORT IN SEA

Flames Carried From the Business Quarter to Residences

PALACE HOTEL AND MINT GO; BIG BUILDINGS BLOWN UP.

Other Shocks Felt During the Afternoon—Insane Asylum Is Wrecked and Hundreds of Former Inmates Are Roaming About the Country—Reports of Heavy Loss of Life at San Jose.

SAN FRANCISCO, Thursday, April 19.—12:15 A. M. (3:15 A. M. New York Time.)—At midnight the fire still roars. Fleeing inhabitants can see from miles around the pillars of fire towering skyward. The crash of falling ruins and the muffled reports of the exploding dynamite reach the ear at regular intervals.

A disaster that staggers comprehension and in point of terror and damage is unprecedented on the coast has not yet reached its culmination.

The Merchants' Exchange Building, one of the handsomest and most substantial edifices in the city, is in flames, as is also the Crocker-Woolwarth Building.

The former building is a fourteen-story structure, seven floors of which are occupied by the Southern Pacific Railway Company as offices. The Crocker-Woolworth Building is a twelve-story terra cotta and granite structure and stood directly opposite the Palace Hotel.

The immense D. O. Mills Building is surrounded by fire and probably will burn. The Lick House, the Occidental Hotel, and the Russ House in this immediate vicinity are in immediate danger.

The exact loss of life never will be known. Hundreds have been incinerated. To-night the city resembles one vast shambles with the red glare of the fire throwing shadows across the worn and panic-stricken faces of the homeless.

At the morgue in the Hall of Justice fifty bodies lie. Before the eyes of an Associated Press reporter three thieves were shot dead.

The Japanese quarter has been burned and the people fled in terror, packing on their backs what household effects they could tie together.

At 9 o'clock to-night an Associated Press man who went to a high hill overlooking the city noted that the sky on the east and south sides was illuminated for a distance of four or five miles. The illumination on the southern side was in a duller glow, showing that the flames were not consuming property of such great proportions as was the case on the east side.

In the business district toward the water front the flames were either checked or blocked at about Washington Street, and at the corner of Kearny Street the Hall of Justice could be noted standing, but it was impossible to determine what damage had been done to the interior. From the Hall of Justice to the south the fire cut its way through some of the choicest buildings in the city, the Pacific Mutual and the Italian-American Bank Building being reduced to ashes.

Down Kearny Street on both sides at 10 o'clock the conflagration was still raging with fury, but the direction of the wind prevented its advance up the hills to the west toward the residence quarter.

To the west of Kearny, up to Dupont, most of the buildings were burned as far south as California Street. All around the new fourteen-story Merchants Exchange Building the fire burned fiercely, licking the sides of the steel giant, but it resisted the influence of the heat.

Then came the destruction of the Western Union Building, at the corner of Pick and Montgomery Streets. In this building were the offices of the Associated Press. Earlier in the day the occupants had been ordered out by the authorities on account of danger, and The Associated Press established a temporary station in The Bulletin editorial rooms. Then the latter place was closed, and this dispatch is written on a doorstep near Chinatown, the illumination of the burning buildings furnishing light for the writer.

It appeared that the great Mills Building would block some of the southward sweep of the blaze, as it had already checked an advance northward earlier in the night. If this proves true the limits of the fire will be determined, but predictions on this point are as unreliable as the strong wind, which every five minutes is changing from one direction to another.

The city to-night in face of its appaling disaster, is fairly quiet and orderly. Liquor cannot be had anywhere and the formidable presence of Federal troops, militia and naval reserves has had its effect on the element that might be disposed to be disorderly.

The Mayor's proclamation authorizing the shooting of looters on sight has been scattered broadcast in circulars and few reports of thieving are received.

It is impossible to give anything like an accurate statement concerning the killed. Unquestionably many people were either killed outright, imprisoned or rendered unconscious in collapsed buildings which were afterward burned.

At 10 o'clock the Occidental Hotel began burning and the great Crocker Building containing the Crocker-Woolworth National Bank was ablaze.

On Geary Street the Albert Pike Memorial Temple of the California bodies of the Scottish Rites Masons, containing scenery that cost $20,000 and costumes valued at $15,000, collapsed. The new Jewish synagogue adjoining was cracked to its foundations.

While five dying men were taken from a collapsed building at Second and Jessie Streets Fathers Hogan, Rogers, and Huber of St. Patrick's Church granted them the last rites of the Catholic Church. This ceremony was performed while a mass of coping overhead threatened to crush the priests to death. Three of the men died.

A shoemaker, Joseph Lindsay, was four hours in a demolished building and when dug out it was found that he had not been hurt.

The entire Larkin Street frontage of the City Hall for a distance of several hundred feet was thrown out into the street, and that thoroughfare for two blocks is piled high with boulders of mortared brick and twisted iron.

Latest reports from Leland Stanford University at Palo Alto indicate that the magnificent stone buildings of that institution have suffered severe damage. Many of the buildings were ruined by cracks that split them from cornice to foundation.

The University of California at Berkeley, across the bay, escaped serious injury. The buildings are intact. Only a few structures collapsed in Berkeley, the shock being slight there

Artillerymen from the Presidio with their supply wagons and the army commissary wagons are aiding in getting the fleeing inhabitants and their baggage out of the threatened quarters.

270 Dead in an Asylum.

The insane asylum at Agnews is a total wreck, 270 of the inmates being killed. It is reported that the attachés of the institution who were about at the time of the earthquake were saved. The ruins took fire shortly after the collapse. One hundred and twenty bodies have been removed.

There were about 700 persons in the building. Hundreds of the inmates who escaped death are roaming about the country in a state of panic.

Half San Francisco Gone.

OAKLAND, Cal., April 18, 10 P. M.—It looks now as if the entire City of San Francisco would be burned.

At 10 o'clock to-night the fire

EARTHQUAKE'S AUTOGRAPH AS IT WROTE IT 3,000 MILES AWAY.

Tracing Made by the Seismograph Needle in the Office of State Geologist John M. Clarke, State Museum, Albany, Showing How the Earthquake Traveled Across Continent in 19 Minutes.

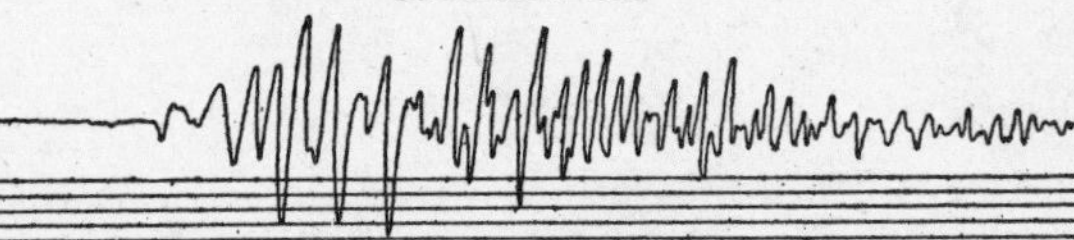

The drawing represents the vibration of the north and south pendulum of the seismograph during the time of the most intense activity, beginning in San Francisco at 5:13 A. M., in Albany at 8:32. In Albany the violent agitation ended at 8:48 A. M. The straight lines at the side of the wavy line indicate the normal condition of the record as the recording drum revolves, and this serves to show the contrast between the ordinary progress of the record and that during a disturbance. The spaces between the dots indicate lapses of one minute each.

The same violent disturbance was noticeable on the seismograph at Washington between 8:32 and 8:35 A. M., thus verifying the time of transit across the continent—19 minutes.

"All the News That's Fit to Print."

The New York Times.

THE WEATHER.
Fair to-day; fair, colder to-morrow; fresh westerly winds.

VOL. LVII...NO. 18,164. NEW YORK, FRIDAY, OCTOBER 18, 1907.—EIGHTEEN PAGES And Part I. of Autumn Review of Books. ONE CENT In Greater New York, Jersey City, and Newark. { Elsewhere, TWO CENTS.

BANK HERE IS SAFE IN HEINZE CRASH

Clearing House Committee Finds the Mercantile National in Sound Condition.

BUTTE BANK CLOSES DOORS

Otto Heinze & Co. Suspended from Stock Exchange—Ridgely Likely to Succeed Heinze in the Mercantile.

At the instance of the New York Clearing House Committee, which met late yesterday afternoon, an examination of the Mercantile National Bank, from the Presidency of which F. Augustus Heinze resigned in the morning, was made last night. For this work the committee selected James G. Cannon, Vice President of the Fourth National Bank; Edward Townsend, President of the Importers and Traders' Bank, and Walter E. Frew, Vice President of the Corn Exchange Bank. Early this morning they made a report, saying that the bank's capital was intact, and that it would open for business as usual this morning.

In addition to this move by the Clearing House, Mr. Heinze's resignation was followed by announcements of the suspension of Otto Heinze & Co. on the Stock Exchange and the closing of Heinze's Butte Savings Bank.

At the meeting at the Clearing House in the afternoon there were present J. Edward Simmons, President of the Fourth National Bank, and Alexander Gilbert, President of the Clearing House and of the Market and Fulton National Bank, besides three members of the official Clearing House Committee—William A. Nash, President of the Corn Exchange Bank; Dumont Clarke, President of the American Exchange National Bank, and Edward Townsend. James T. Woodward, President of the Hanover National Bank and Chairman of the Clearing House Committee, was out of town, as was also A. Barton Hepburn, President of the Chase National Bank and another member of the committee.

During the meeting the affairs of the Mercantile National and the events of the last few days in Wall Street, particularly the sensational incidents connected with the United Copper Company, were carefully gone over, and the resolution reached to make an examination of the Mercantile National at once, that institution being a member of the Clearing House, and therefore subject to examination by it. It was virtually decided that if the examination proved the bank to be in sound condition the Clearing House, which means all the great banks which are members of it, would stand by the Mercantile National and see it through any troubles which might follow the events of the last few days.

The committee, therefore, selected the bankers named to make the examination, and this committee went up to the Western Union Building, where the Mercantile National Bank offices are, and began an examination of its books, which lasted far into the night. Practically all the officers of the bank and the greater part of the clerical staff remained on hand to help the committee in the work.

Upon leaving the bank the committee went immediately to the home of J. Edward Simmons, at 28 West Fifty-second Street. At midnight the following statement was given out by Mr. Simmons:

"Mr. Nash, the Acting Chairman of the Clearing House Committee, states that the committee, with the full co-operation of the officers and Directors of the Mercantile National Bank, made an examination of its condition after the close of business to-day. The examination was very thorough, and was not completed until a late hour. Mr. Nash and his associates were convinced from the result of the examination that the bank was perfectly solvent and able to meet all its indebtedness. The capital of $3,000,000 is intact and with a large surplus."

Mr. Simmons was asked if this meant that the Clearing House had decided to stand by the bank in case there was a run.

"There certainly can be no other meaning to the action the Clearing House has taken," he said.

Mr. Simmons said the bank would open its doors this morning, as though nothing had happened.

"Has it been decided yet who will be the President of the Mercantile National?" Mr. Simmons was asked.

"There is little doubt that Mr. Ridgely will accept the Presidency," he replied. "He has not yet signified his intention of accepting, but I am quite sure he will take the position offered him."

Charles A. Hanna, the National bank examiner in this city, made arrangements to receive a duplicate report from the Clearing House Examination Committee for the purpose of informing Controller of the Currency Ridgely of the status of the bank.

Heinze Out; Offer to Ridgely.

An offer of the Presidency was made to Mr. Ridgely in Washington in the morning by telegraph, following the resignation of F. Augustus Heinze, who withdrew from the office after a protracted meeting of the Board of Directors. The Directors met at 11 o'clock in the morning and were in constant session until after 1 o'clock. It was then announced that Mr. Heinze had resigned the Presidency. In doing so he made the following explanation:

In view of the difficulties in which my brother's firm finds itself, I have determined that it is proper that I should give liberally of my time in assisting them to straighten out their affairs. In aid of this, I have, after consulting with my fellow-Directors of the bank and my personal friends, and consulting as well my own personal interests as a large stockholder of the bank, this day resigned as its President, remaining, however, as a Director, and have joined with by fellow-Directors in a request that Mr. Ridgely accept the place made vacant by my resignation.

The condition of the Mercantile and the effects upon it of the developments of the last few days in the affairs of the copper company of its former President were carefully gone into. The discussion of the situation was vigorous, and there were plainly differences of opinion, but the final result of the meeting was

Continued on Page 4.

AMERICAN HOTEL FOR BERLIN.

It Hears of a Colossal Structure to be Run on Our Lines.

Special Cable to THE NEW YORK TIMES.

BERLIN, Oct. 17.—It is announced here that an American syndicate has acquired a block of choice property in Berlin at the corner of the Unter den Linden and Pariser-Platz, for the purpose of erecting a colossal building containing a palatial hotel, a grand opera house, and a roof garden, the whole establishment to be run upon American lines.

The opera house, it is stated, will have seating capacity for three thousand persons.

It is understood the plans for the colossal edifice will soon be laid before the Kaiser with a request for his approval of them. His assent will have to be given before the building can be erected. It is said the structure will cover more ground than is covered by the Waldorf-Astoria, and that it will exceed in magnificence any building of its kind in Europe.

AGED WOMAN'S BACK BROKEN.

Struck by an Auto While Returning from Father Mayer's Funeral.

Mrs. Amelia Greenblatt of 115 East Eighth Street attended the funeral yesterday of her late pastor, the Rev. John B. Mayer, in the St. Nicholas Roman Catholic Church in Second Street. The service ended at noon and Mrs. Greenblatt started from the church to go to her home.

She crossed the sidewalk and stepped into Second Avenue almost in front of an automobile driven by Rudolph Plain of 379 Gates Avenue, Brooklyn. Plain, who was driving from the Williamsburg Bridge toward Bond Street, sounded his horn loudly as he came down the avenue into which throngs were flocking from the church.

The loud blast of the horn startled Mrs. Greenblatt, who is 54 years old, and she stood still, apparently stupefied by her danger. Plain put on his brakes and tried to swing his machine to one side. Before he could stop the car, however, it had struck the woman and flung her to one side against the curbstone.

Women in the crowd screamed in horror. Policeman Burke of the Fifth Street Station lifted the woman in his arms and put her in the tonneau of the auto which Plain had succeeded in stopping. Then he ordered the chauffeur to drive up Avenue A to Bellevue Hospital at top speed.

The trip to the hospital of more than a mile was made in less than three minutes. Physicians who examined Mrs. Greenblatt said that her spine was broken.

The Rev. Father Mayer, whose funeral Mrs. Greenblatt had attended, died on Monday at the age of 56. He was born in Germany, came here in 1870 and was ordained a priest and assigned to the St. Nicholas Church seven years later. His long pastorate there endeared him to the German population of the parish over which he presided and hundreds visited the church yesterday.

PUMP THEM IN—KIPLING.

Immigration of Whites to Canada Will Keep Out Yellow Men.

TORONTO, Oct. 17.—"Pump in the immigrants from the old country; pump them in."

That is the solution Rudyard Kipling suggests for the Asiatic problem on the Pacific Coast. Mr. Kipling, accompanied by his wife, arrived here last night from a tour of the Canadian Northwest.

"Immigration is what Canada wants in the west," said Mr. Kipling. "You must have laborers there. You want immigration, and the way to keep the yellow man out is to get the white man in. If you keep out the white then you will have the yellow man, for you must have labor. Work must be done and there is certain work a white man won't do so long as he can get a yellow man to do it. Pump in the immigrants from the old country. Pump them in. England has five millions of people to spare."

Mr. Kipling expressed the opinion that both in the mother country and in Canada the labor party is opposed to immigration. "In England," he said, "the party is opposed to immigration because it would remove its great grievance with regard to the unemployed. In Canada there is a feeling in opposition to immigration because labor feels that it will be swamped."

Mr. Kipling, on being asked if the statement which appeared in a local paper that he was in Canada on behalf of the British Government and to formulate a scheme for their consideration as to Asiatic immigration was true, laughed and said: "I have still some sense of humor left." Pressed for an answer in the affirmative or negative, he said, laughing merrily: "Well, say that I am."

GOV. SMITH FREES SLAYER.

Atlanta People Think He Indorses the Unwritten Law.

Special to The New York Times.

ATLANTA, Oct. 17.—By granting a pardon to L. D. Strong of Macon to-day, Gov. Hoke Smith, in the opinion of many here, indorsed the "unwritten law."

Six months ago Strong, who is a prominent business man of Macon, killed Henry Smith, a Macon merchant, alleging, on the girl's confession, that Smith had mistreated Strong's 16-year-old sister. Strong went to Smith's place of business and shot him five times in the presence of many people. Smith lived a few minutes, and as he died, swore that he was innocent. Public sympathy was with Strong, but the jury convicted him and he was sent to the penitentiary. At once a movement for pardon was begun, and it culminated to-day when Gov. Smith, on the recommendation of a prison commission, gave him freedom.

MAGILL ON THE STAND.

Says Nagging of His Mother and Sister Caused Wife's Despondency.

DECATUR, Ill., Oct. 17.—Taking the stand to-day in his own behalf, Fred H. Magill, accused of murdering his first wife in order that he might wed Faye Graham, told in a matter-of-fact way of the events that led up to Mrs. Magill's death and the finding of her body by him the next morning.

Just before he retired that night, the witness said, his wife requested him to get her a bottle of beer. He got a bottle from the ice chest and then retired. In the morning when he awoke he saw his wife was not around. He made search of the house and found her in the spare room, lying with a blanket wrapped tightly around her head. He spoke to her, but got no reply, and upon examination he found she was dead. Witness said he detected the odor of chloroform.

Asked what, in his opinion, caused his wife's despondency he replied:

"Her headaches and the nagging of my mother and sister."

Magill was on the stand four hours. His testimony concluded the case for the defense.

CONRIED AND BOYD AT ODDS IN STOCKS

Opera Director's Brother Handled the Dealings of the Opera House Superintendent.

PROFIT FIGURES WIDE APART

$40,000, Says Boyd, Perhaps $300, Says Conried, and He'll Pay in Due Time.

Feeling that he was not getting rich enough from his salary as Superintendent of the Metropolitan Opera House and having heard of the many opportunities for obtaining money following the antics of the bulls and bears in Wall Street, Andrew Boyd who, besides having been Superintendent of the Opera House for many years is a close personal friend of Heinrich Conried, decided last January that he would take a little flyer in stocks with his savings. To-day he is a sadder, but wiser man. He met the same fate as many other lambs, though, he says, in a different way from many of them.

In his career in the theatrical business Mr. Boyd has always made it a practice to lay aside a little for a rainy day. This little he put in the bank from time to time until it grew to $1,000. Then he bought a bond. This nucleus made him all the more anxious to save, and another bond and yet others were added to the savings until the amount had reached about $10,000, all in interest bearing bonds.

Then, last January, when the stock market was active, Mr. Boyd grew interested in it through Alexander Conried, a stock broker, brother of Heinrich Conried, Director of the Metropolitan Opera Company.

Alexander Conried has no office, and, so far as known, he has no direct connection with any brokerage firm in "the Street." He is what is known as a "wandering broker," taking business from whom he can get it and putting it where he thinks it will be to his best advantage. Mr. Boyd says he gave Mr. Conried $6,000 to be used as margin in stock speculations.

The stocks that Conried bought for Boyd, copper being among the number, began to drop rapidly. The $6,000 in margins soon became $5,000, then $4,000, $3,000, $2,000, and $1,000, and when the $500 mark had been reached, according to Boyd, Conried told him he would have to advance more money if he would save the $6,000 he had already put up.

Then it is said he gave Conried $4,000 in bonds as additional margins. This money Boyd thought had saved the day for him. He watched the quotations in the papers, and each day he noticed, so he says, that his stocks were getting better and better. Finally he figured out for himself a large profit, and asked Mr. Conried for it. He says he didn't get it, and on this point Mr. Conried agrees with him, but adds that there were no such profits as Mr. Boyd had figured out.

Mr. Boyd took his side of the case to a lawyer yesterday. When Mr. Conried heard of this he consented to give his version of the affair, and it is a very different version, to a TIMES reporter.

"My trades for Mr. Boyd were just the same as trades for all other clients," he said.

"Mr. Boyd did put up margins for me to buy stocks for him, but it is absurd to say that I made $40,000 in the market for him and failed to turn it over to him. I bought copper around 118 and it went off. I bought other stocks for him and they went up. I really think that the amount of his winnings in the market would reach only about $300.

"It is quite true that when I closed out his account I owed him several thousand dollars, and could not pay it to him at the time the account was closed because the money was locked up in several other accounts, and I had to wait until they were straightened out. I have paid him a part of the money, and expect to close out the balance within a few days. The whole thing is really very greatly exaggerated."

J. VIPOND DAVIES HURT.

Consulting Engineer Stops Runaway and Saves Children—His Hip Broken.

J. Vipond Davies, chief consulting engineer of the Hudson Tunnel Company, who lives in 24 Bowne Avenue, Flushing, Queens Borough, had one hip broken and received internal injuries yesterday morning while preventing a team of runaway horses from running down a group of school children.

Mr. Davies was on his way through Amity Street, Flushing, to the Main Street railroad station to catch the 8:30 o'clock train for Long Island City, when two teams of horses hitched to moving vans, owned by G. Anderson & Son, which were backed against the sidewalk, took fright at an automobile driven by William Haak of Franklin Place. One of the teams became unmanagable and started off.

The horses were heading direct toward a group of school children when Mr. Davies sprang and caught the nearest horse by the bridle. He was swung from his feet, but managed to change the course of the team from the street toward the sidewalk.

Mr. Davies was clinging to the bridle when the team crashed into a tree. He was thrown against the tree and fell to the ground so that the front wheels of the van passed over his legs. The team was checked by the collision and the horses were quickly caught, while Mr. Davies was picked up and carried into the office of Dr. E. T. Lawrence at 147 Amity Street.

When Mr. Davies learned the extent of his injuries, at his own request he was taken to his home. His condition is said to be serious.

THIS ISSUE OF THE NEW YORK TIMES includes AUTUMN BOOK LIST NUMBER of The New York Times Saturday Review (FIRST SECTION)

Second Section To-morrow.

FIRST WIRELESS PRESS MESSAGE ACROSS THE ATLANTIC

Signalizing the Opening of the Marconi Service to the Public, and Conveying a Message of Congratulation from Privy Councillor Baron Avebury, Formerly Sir John Lubbock.

Form 168

THE WESTERN UNION TELEGRAPH COMPANY.

INCORPORATED

24,000 OFFICES IN AMERICA. CABLE SERVICE TO ALL THE WORLD.

This Company TRANSMITS and DELIVERS messages only on conditions limiting its liability, which have been assented to by the sender of the following message. Errors can be guarded against only by repeating a message back to the sending station for comparison, and the Company will not hold itself liable for errors or delays in transmission or delivery of Unrepeated Messages, beyond the amount of tolls paid thereon, nor in any case where the claim is not presented in writing within sixty days after the message is filed with the Company for transmission.

This is an UNREPEATED MESSAGE, and is delivered by request of the sender, under the conditions named above.

ROBERT C. CLOWRY, President and General Manager.

RECEIVED at 813 Sixth Ave. Corner 46th St.

TELEPHONE: 2907 BRYANT.

1B Lr Sn Dh & 53 Collect D,, P R, Land lines,

London Via Marconi Wireless:Glace Bay N S Oct 17th,

Times, New York.

This message marks opening transatlantic wireless handed

Marconi company for transmission Ireland Breton limited 50 words

only send one many messages received Times signalise event

quote trust introduction wireless more closely unite people states

Great Britian who seem form one Nation though under two Governments

and whose interests are really identical.

Avebury Marshall .... 1210 Am Oct17th

ALWAYS OPEN. MONEY TRANSFERRED BY TELEGRAPH. CABLE OFFICE.

The above message was immediately followed by others which appear in another column of The Times this morning.

MARCONI CONGRATULATES THE NEW YORK TIMES

GLACE BAY, NOVA SCOTIA, Oct. 17.—Mr. Marconi says: "Congratulate New York Times on having received first westward press message."

FROM THE PRIME MINISTER OF FRANCE.

WEST STRAND, London, Oct. 17, via Marconi Wireless Telegraph to Glace Bay, N. S.—THE NEW YORK TIMES's Paris correspondent forwards to me the following message for transmission across the Atlantic by Marconi wireless telegraph:

"Dans l'inauguration du prodigieux mode de communication mis désormais à leur disposition, les deux grandes républiques ne peuvent que trouver une heureuse occasion de se feliciter et de formuler les voeux les plus cordiaux pour le mantien de la paix dans le travail pour le bonheur des peuples dans la solidarité."

"CLEMENCEAU."

[Translation.]

In the inauguration of the marvelous means of communication put at their disposition from this time forward, the two great Republics could not but find it a happy occasion to congratulate themselves and to express the most cordial wishes for the maintenance of peace in the work for the happiness of the people in the joint responsibility.

CLEMENCEAU.

MISS VANDERBILT MUST TAKE CHANCES

By No Means Certain She Will Be Admitted to Austrian Court in Vienna.

A HIGH OFFICIAL SAYS SO

Unless Emperor Dispenses with Proof of Considerable Ancestral Nobility She Will Be Shut Out.

Special Cable to THE NEW YORK TIMES.

VIENNA, Oct. 17.—A Court official of high rank, of whom I inquired what would be Miss Gladys Vanderbilt's status with respect to the Court in the event of her marriage to Count Szechenyi, said:

"The lady in question would be received at Court in Budapest, but not in Vienna, unless the Emperor should dispense with the proof of nobility with respect to sixteen of her ancestors, which otherwise she would be required by Austrian Court etiquette to furnish.

"Such a concession is sometimes made, and very likely it would be made in the case we are speaking of, out of consideration for the social standing of Count Szechenyi and the importance of the Vanderbilt family."

It seems, in view of this authoritative statement, that Miss Vanderbilt, if she marries the Count, may find herself in a rather unpleasant predicament when she comes to live in Vienna.

NEWPORT, Oct. 17.—Miss Gladys Vanderbilt is not spending all the time with her fiancé, Count Szechenyi, although he is a guest at her mother's house. This morning she was at the Casino with a number of young women friends, the Count remaining at The Breakers.

At noon she drove about town in her basket phaeton with her chum, Miss Josephine Pearson. They had a "college ice" together in a Thames Street drug store. Miss Vanderbilt seemed to be thoroughly enjoying the absence of a crowd of curious sightseers, and to fully appreciate the fact that she was being left entirely unnoticed.

This evening Miss Vanderbilt and Count Szechenyi attended a dinner given in their honor by Mrs. Charles H. Baldwin at Snug Harbor, and later accompanied Mrs. Baldwin and her other guests to the Opera House to see William Collier in "Caught in the Rain." This was Miss Vanderbilt's first appearance at the Newport Opera House since her engagement, and she and the Count were naturally the centre of attraction between the acts.

H. P. WHITNEY ARRESTED?

Colorado Authorities Accues Visitors of Slaughtering Deer Wantonly.

Special to The New York Times.

DENVER, Col., Oct. 17.—Two men who say they are Frank Carnegie, nephew of Andrew Carnegie, and Harry Payne Whitney of New York, came to Colorado two weeks ago to hunt bear. They hired guides and started out with a pack of hounds. Reaching the game country, they began to slaughter deer promiscuously, both for the sport and for bait for traps.

Deputy Warden Bush finally arrested the hunters and their guides, took them before a Justice of the Peace, and prosecuted them for wanton destruction of deer. Bush says he had an offer of $300 to drop the case before the trial. After the trial began, he says, the Justice was called out of court by his wife, and when he returned he dismissed the case. The State Game Warden is investigating the case.

ROCKEFELLER TOO SAVING.

Supt. Jones of Forest Hill Resigns Because Expenses Are Cut.

Special to The New York Times.

CLEVELAND, Oct. 17.—Asserting that John D. Rockefeller wants to cut expenses too much, C. C. Jones, for some seven months superintendent of the Forest Hill estate, has resigned, and will leave for New York on Nov. 15. Jones says that Rockefeller insisted on curtailing expenses to such an extent that he could not keep up the place. He allowed some trimming of costs when he took the position, but recently, he says, Mr. Rockefeller wanted to reduce the pay of the men and he demurred. An argument followed and Mr. Jones resigned.

"When I came here I thought I was to run the estate," said Mr. Jones, "but soon found that such was not the case. Mr. Rockefeller insisted on changes and orders that I did not believe were for the best, and I found that I couldn't look after the place as it should be and follow the suggestion that he made, so I quit."

SAVED BY SENATOR SCOTT.

He Stops Runaway and Rescues Two Mexican Women.

Special to The New York Times.

CITY OF MEXICO, Oct. 17.—United States Senator Nathan B. Scott of West Virginia, here on a pleasure trip, made a daring rescue of two prominent Mexican women in a runaway accident in one of the principal streets here last evening.

Senator Scott, who is almost 65 years old, jumped from the sidewalk, seized the reins, and stopped the runaway horses after a desperate struggle.

Latest Shipping News.

Arrived—S. S. Emilia, Trieste, Sept. 4; S. S. Olinda, Nuevitas; S. S. Fagertun, Port Antonio.

DEUTSCHLAND STUCK CLOSE TO HER PIER

Capt. Kaempff Gives Up Attempt to Get Liner Off After Three Hours' Work.

PASSENGERS SENT TO BED

Hundreds of Friends Exchange Greetings with Them as Seven Tugs Strive in Vain.

The Hamburg-American liner Deutschland from Hamburg for this port, stuck in the mud last night in the Hudson River, with her big freeboard actually scraping against the end of her Hoboken pier. After waiting for nearly three hours in the hope that the big ship might be warped into her dock, her 500 cabin passengers and 300 steerage passengers reluctantly went to bed, convinced that it would be morning before they could set foot on American soil.

During the time that a flotilla of tugs struggled to pull the ship off the mud and up to her pier hundreds of persons waiting to welcome home-coming voyagers lined the pier, exchanging greetings with the marooned passengers, for though the boat touched her pier there was no way for the passengers to reach it except by sliding down a forty-foot rope ladder, and this Capt. Kaempff would not permit.

The accident came as a climax to a voyage replete with fog and rough weather. Soon after leaving Hamburg the liner ran into weather that compelled her to slacken speed, and soon after there followed forty-eight hours of dense fog. Delayed by these conditions, the Deutschland did not reach Quarantine until 9 o'clock last night, instead of early yesterday morning, when she was due.

It was an hour later before the big boat slowed down near her pier to let the tugs make their lines fast to her. Usually there are at least fourteen tugs employed to swing the steamship into her dock, but last night only seven answered Capt. Kaempff's call.

Six of these made lines fast to one side to pull the stern around, while the other made fast to her bow, against which it shoved, apparently without effect. The tugs puffed and steamed, but the ship scarcely moved, and in the meantime the tide was rapidly running out.

For half an hour the struggle was kept up, and then the Deutschland's keel touched bottom. Amidships, one side of the boat grated against the pier, while the bow and stern swung far away from the structure.

WIRELESS JOINS TWO WORLDS

Marconi Transatlantic Service Opened with a Dispatch to The New York Times.

MESSAGES FROM EMINENT MEN

Prime Minister Clemenceau, the Duke of Argyll, Lord Avebury and Others Send Greetings.

10,000 WORDS THE FIRST DAY

Marconi in Personal Supervision at Glace Bay and Greatly Pleased with the Results.

SIR HIRAM MAXIM'S TRIBUTE

His Message to Peter Cooper Hewitt in New York, Who Is Trying to Pick Up the Oversea Messages.

By Marconi Transatlantic Wireless Telegraph to The New York Times.

LONDON, Oct. 17.—This message marks the opening of the transatlantic wireless service. It is handed to the Marconi Company here for transmission to Ireland, and thence to Cape Breton, Nova Scotia, and New York. As it is limited to fifty words, I can send at present only one of the many messages received for transmission to The New York Times to signalize the event. This message, from Privy Councillor Lord Avebury, formerly Sir John Lubbock, follows:

"I trust that the introduction of the wireless will more closely unite the people of the United States and Great Britain, who seem to form one nation, though under two Governments, and whose interests are really identical. AVEBURY."

MARCONI'S CONGRATULATIONS.

The above message, received early yesterday morning, was quickly followed by one from The Times's correspondent at Glace Bay, as follows:

"Glace Bay, N. S., Oct. 17.

"Mr. Marconi says: 'Congratulate New York Times on having received first westward press message.'"

Then came in full the original message filed by The Times's correspondent in London, from which the short dispatch above was condensed, to meet the fifty-word limit imposed by the Marconi Company upon the first message transmitted. The full message follows:

MESSAGES FROM EMINENT MEN.

By Marconi Transatlantic Wireless Telegraph to The New York Times.

LONDON, Oct. 17.—This message marks the opening of the transatlantic wireless service. It is now eleven years since William Marconi, in May, 1896, announced in New York that he had discovered the secret by which messages might be flashed through space without the assistance of wires or cables such as were used in the ordinary methods of telegraphy at that time. Mr. Marconi's statements were received with skepticism, and his prediction of the wonders which he felt confident could be worked by means of his application of the Hertzian waves was openly disputed even by electricians, who ought, from their knowledge of the feats achieved by the electric spark, to have recognized that the limits of its potentialities had not been reached.

Mr. Marconi, as this message testifies, has now accomplished all that he expressed his confidence in being able to do. This message, which I have handed in at the Lon-

"All the News That's Fit to Print."

The New York Times.

THE WEATHER.

Fair to-day and probably Friday; wind light to fresh southwest.

VOL. LVII...NO. 18,492. **** NEW YORK, THURSDAY, SEPTEMBER 10, 1908.—SIXTEEN PAGES. ONE CENT In Greater New York, Jersey City, and Newark. { Elsewhere, TWO CENTS.

BOSSES HAVE DECIDED TO ACCEPT HUGHES

Parsons, Whom the "Test" Results in Manhattan Surprised, Admits It.

RENOMINATION NOW SURE

The Governor Will Have 513 Delegates at Least, 8 More Than Are Needed—Woodruff Talks.

Developments in the Republican camp yesterday practically insure the renomination of Gov. Hughes at the Republican State Convention, which will meet in Saratoga next Monday.

While there was at first an effort among the Republican leaders who have opposed the Governor's renomination to magnify the opposition shown in the primary "tests" on Tuesday and to minimize the pro-Hughes sentiment, President Herbert Parsons of the Republican County Committee lost no time in climbing down from the fence and making a dash for the Hughes band wagon.

Republican State Chairman Timothy L. Woodruff gave out a long statement in which he sought to justify the objections of the anti-Hughes leaders to the Governor's renomination. Chairman Woodruff did not deviate yesterday from the position he has maintained for the last few weeks—that "the delegates must decide." It is asserted, though, that Mr. Parsons is not playing a lone game, but merely had the good sense to head a procession that may develop into a foot race of bosses and bosslets into the Governor's camp, and that Mr. Woodruff in all probability will be the second in line.

Test Made It Clear—Parsons.

President Parsons, who has been subjected to a great deal of pressure emanating from Oyster Bay and from the managers of the Taft campaign, made his first open statement on the question of the Governor's renomination yesterday. He said:

"The result of the test votes taken in this county shows that a considerable majority of the enrolled Republicans prefer that Gov. Hughes should be renominated. We took the test to put the question up to them, and, if their desires were explicit, to act accordingly. The test shows that there is some bitter opposition. But in view of the controlling sentiment in favor of the Governor's renomination, which the test has made clear, it is my opinion that a large majority of the delegates from New York County to the State Convention will favor Gov. Hughes's renomination."

Hughes Sure of 513 Delegates.

If President Parsons, who will control the delegation from New York County, makes good his statement, the renomination of Gov. Hughes is assured. New York County has 187 delegates in the State Convention. A simple majority of one from that number will give the Governor 94 of the New York delegates.

The number of delegates from up State either instructed for, committed to, or reliably classed for Gov. Hughes, number 362. Friends of State Chairman Timothy L. Woodruff, who is leader of the Republican organization in Kings County, admit that 57 of the delegates from Kings at least will go to the State Convention either pledged to or instructed for Gov. Hughes.

This will give the Governor a total of 513 delegates, according to the present line-up. Only 505 delegates are needed to nominate. And a dozen counties, with an approximate aggregate of 100 delegates, are in the doubtful column, with a probability that a majority will go to the convention to work for the renomination of Gov. Hughes when they learn that a large majority of the New York delegates will be for the Governor, and that nothing can be gained by opposing his renomination.

Those Pledged to Him Now.

Here is a list of up-State counties where the delegates have either been instructed for Gov. Hughes, stand committed to him, or can be depended upon to be for his renomination at the Saratoga Convention:

County	Delegates	County	Delegates
Broome	12	Monroe	36
Cattaraugus	11	Nassau	9
Cayuga	12	Oneida	22
Chautauqua (2 A.D.)	8	Oswego	12
Chenango	7	Rensselaer	10
Clinton	7	Rockland	5
Cortland	6	Saratoga	11
Delaware	9	Schuyler	4
Dutchess (1 A.D.)	7	Steuben	13
Erie	30	Suffolk (2 A.D.)	3
Franklin	8	Tompkins	6
Greene	6	Westchester	29
Herkimer	9	Wyoming	6
*Jefferson	13	Yates	4
Lewis	5		
Total			362

*All of 1st and part of 2d A. D.

In the Doubtful Column.

Here are the counties placed by the leaders in the doubtful column:

County	Delegates	County	Delegates
Essex	6	Seneca	5
Orange (1 A.D.)	9	Sullivan	8
Otsego	9	Ulster	14
Queens	18	Washington	9
St. Lawrence	15		
Total			93

The Anti-Hughes Force.

Here are the up-State counties which either have elected or will elect anti-Hughes delegates:

County	Delegates	County	Delegates
Albany	28	Orange (1 A.D.)	8
Chemung	3	Putnam	3
Columbia	7	Richmond	8
Dutchess (part 2 A. D.)	7	Schenectady	11
		Schoharie	5
Fulton and Hamilton	5	Suffolk (2 A.D.)	7
		Tioga	6
Jefferson (2 A.D.)	1	Warren	6
Montgomery	5	Wayne	9
Niagara	13		
Ontario	9		
Total			143

These delegates have been instructed for Senator Horace White of Syracuse or Speaker James W. Wadsworth, Jr.:

FOR WADSWORTH.

County	Delegates	County	Delegates
Allegheny	9	Livingston	7
Chautauqua (1 A.D.)	10	Orleans	6
Genesee	7		
Total			39

FOR WHITE.

County	Delegates	County	Delegates
Onondaga	30	Madison	8
Total			38

Both State Chairman Woodruff and County President Herbert Parsons of the Republican County Committee said yesterday that it would be futile to attempt at this time to figure out to a mathematical certainty how many delegates from their respective bailiwicks would be against the Governor at the convention. These delegates, it would seem, constitute about the only element of uncertainty in the situation, but in the aggregate they will not have any effect on the result.

Self-Justification by Woodruff.

The analysis by State Chairman Woodruff of the result of the primary test was strangely in contrast with the statement of President Parsons, based on the returns from the districts in which the primary test was made. While President Parsons insisted that the returns disclosed a decided Hughes sentiment, Mr. Woodruff in his statement asserted that these same returns justified the declaration of the leader that the Governor was unpopular with the Republican voters. Mr. Woodruff said:

"The magnitude of the opposition man-

Continued on Page 2.

NO WATER TO FIGHT A FIRE.

Low Pressure Gives Brooklyn Factory Blaze a Dangerous Start.

Inadequate water pressure permitted a fire which started shortly before midnight last night on the third floor of the six-story factory building at 552 to 556 State Street, Brooklyn, to spread so rapidly that twenty minutes after the fire had been discovered Deputy Fire Chief Lally sent in five alarms.

For ten or fifteen minutes after their arrival the firemen were unable to throw streams of water into the flames, and even after that time the pressure was not up to the standard. The water tower threw a spray of water which might almost have come from an atomizer, so small was it.

By midnight every one of the six floors, which were occupied by the Empire Cork Specialty Company, was in flames, and fire was leaping out of all the windows and threatening momentarily to communicate the blaze to the tenements on either side of the factory or to those in the rear of it in Atlantic Avenue. The tenants in these buildings were ordered out by the police.

It took the reserves from five precincts to handle the crowds, which were record ones for Brooklyn. Deputy Commissioner Baker took charge of the police.

Chief Croker and Deputy Fire Commissioner Wise responded to the fifth alarm, and Chief Croker took command. By 12:30 o'clock he believed that it was under control. The tenements adjoining the burning building on both sides had been somewhat injured by flames.

The damage was estimated at $75,000 to the building and stock of the cork company. The factory is owned by Percy G. Williams, the theatrical manager.

The blaze tied up the trolley cars, which run through Atlantic Avenue or up Flatbush Avenue from Fulton and Livingston Streets. The lines affected included the Flatbush Avenue, Seventh Avenue, St. John's Place, Fifth Avenue, and Third Avenue.

TESTS CHURCH WELCOMES.

Minister, Disguised as Workingman, Cordially Greeted in All But One.

Special to The New York Times.

CHICAGO, Sept. 9.—To disprove the assertion of the Socialists that the churches only welcome the rich and scorn the workingman, the Rev. John Thompson, pastor of the McCabe M. E. Church, spent his August vacation disguised as a workingman and attending services at nine wealthy churches of the city.

In a threadbare and shiny blue serge coat, trousers that were worn at the edges, a cheap cotton shirt and tie, old shoes and a black felt hat, the minister was so well disguised that even his friends might have passed him by. In fact he sat in a street car beside one of the members of his own congregation and was not noticed.

"I made the experiment," he said to-day, "to find what, if any, truth there might be in the charge that the workingman and the poorly dressed visitor are not made welcome in our churches. I found, as I had hoped, that it was just the other way.

"In the nine churches that I visited I found the congregation always attentive, and in eight of the churches the ministers were cordial. In the ninth, I must say, I was surprised to see how crusty the minister was, and I was practically repulsed when I spoke to him at the end of the service."

THINK PRISONER IS MONROE.

Man in Trenton Jail Said to Answer the Desperado's Description.

Special to The New York Times.

TRENTON, Sept. 9.—"Samuel Worthington," who was arrested here for stealing a ride on a train and is now serving thirty days in jail, may prove to be "Bill" Monroe, the Orange County desperado, who is wanted for assault and arson at Middletown, N. Y.

Monroe has been chased in many directions by Sheriffs' posses. Only recently he attended the fair at Middletown, N. Y., disguised as a woman and tacked a notice on a tree stating that he had made such a visit.

"Worthington" gave his address as Middletown, and admitted that he had been arrested once for horse stealing and another time for assault. He said that he served time for these offenses in Pennsylvania.

Squire Manfred Naar, who committed Worthington to jail, communicated with the Sheriff of Orange County asking that some one who knows Monroe be sent to Trenton to see whether Worthington is the much-sought-for outlaw. A Deputy Sheriff of Orange County has started for this city for this purpose.

GLAD HE LED LYNCHERS.

Ex-Senator Sullivan Will Stand Consequences for Directing Shooting.

MEMPHIS, Sept. 9.—A special from Oxford, Miss., quotes former United States Senator W. V. Sullivan as follows with reference to the lynching last night:

"I led the mob which lynched Nelse Patton, and I'm proud of it. I directed every movement of the mob, and I did everything I could to see that he was lynched. Cut a white woman's throat! And a negro! Of course I wanted him lynched. I saw his body dangling from a tree this morning, and I'm glad of it.

"When I heard of the horrible crime I started to work immediately to get a mob. I did all I could to raise one. I was at the jail last night and heard Judge Roane advise against lynching. I got up immediately after and urged the mob to lynch Patton.

"I roused the mob and directed it to storm the jail. I had my revolver, but did not use it. I gave it to a Deputy Sheriff and told him to 'shoot Patton, and to shoot to kill.' He used the revolver and shot. I suppose the bullets from my gun were some of those that killed the negro.

"I don't care what investigation is made, or what are the consequences. I am willing to stand them. I wouldn't mind standing the consequences any time for lynching a man who cut a white woman's throat. I will lead a mob in such a case any time."

Claim of $1,000 Filed Against Thaw.

PITTSBURG, Penn., Sept. 9.—A claim of $1,000 was filed before Referee in Bankruptcy Blair against Harry K. Thaw today by Dr. Jackson R. Campbell of New York.

CROKER IS FOR BRYAN, ALSO FAVORS BETTING

Thinks Republican Anti-Trust Laws Have Not Helped Condition of the Individual Citizen.

GAMBLING IS HUMAN NATURE

America with Hughes Anti-Betting Laws Is a Free Country No Longer—King Edward the Finest Sportsman.

Special Cable to THE NEW YORK TIMES.

DUBLIN, Sept. 9.—"I am out of politics," said Richard Croker to the correspondent of THE NEW YORK TIMES, who saw him to-day in his beautiful Irish home some miles out from this city. "I know nothing of what is going on, and, anyhow, there is too much water between here and America for me to do anything. Moreover, anything I do say is so misrepresented. "Why," exclaimed Mr. Croker, indignantly, "only the other day it was said that I hoped Taft would win!"

"Your sympathies are with Bryan then?" he was asked.

"Certainly, I hope Bryan will win. He would make a fine President."

"What are his chances?"

"That I do not know, but there has been a great change in public feeling in recent years."

"How will the Republican anti-trust laws affect the issue?"

"They look very nice on paper, but how do they affect the individual? Have they lessened the cost of living or increased the wages of the individual? I say they have not. I judge things by their results, and I say the individual is no better off to-day. As a matter of fact, the cost of living has never been higher and wages are no better. That is the result which has been brought about under the Republican régime."

"What do you think the Democrats will do with regard to the New York Governorship?"

"That I don't know," replied Mr. Croker, and for a moment he contemplated the graveled walk upon which we were standing. Then, looking up with a gleam of scorn in his gray eye, he said:

"Look what they've been doing there! Why, they've broken up horse racing!"

Gov. Hughes's Anti-Betting law was, in Mr. Croker's opinion, enough to damn any party.

"They are ruining the country; ruining the race tracks, in which a great deal of money is invested; ruining the breeders of horses, many of whom are breaking up their studs, and that in a free country! It is a free country no longer. You have more freedom over here. I go to race meetings here and I see a fine crowd of people, ladies and gentlemen, enjoying themselves, and King Edward himself at their head.

"King Edward is the finest sportsman in the world. If there was anything wrong in it do you think he would be at the head of all kinds of sport in this country? In London you have a national sporting club. They encourage all kinds of sport and are allowed to make a certain amount of money; the rest goes to hospitals and charities."

Mr. Croker added that he was not against a certain supervision of betting and gambling and would favor the introduction of the Paris mutuel system of betting, but he certainly would not endeavor to stop betting altogether. It was in human nature to gamble and in the spirit of free people.

"That's why it is tolerated over here; because it is the will of the people, and that's why the King is at its head."

Continuing his argument as to the ethics of gambling, Mr. Croker said it was in the very essence of human nature to gamble.

"If I insure this house," he said, indicating the beautiful mansion in which he lives, "I merely bet with the insurance company that it will be burned down, and the company bets it won't; and if I insure my horse, I bet he will break his neck, and the company takes the risk that he won't. It is the same, to a large extent, in business of all kinds."

"But, Mr. Croker, a man may bet with what he cannot afford to lose; he may mortgage his coat."

"That," replied Mr. Croker, "is his own affair. If he didn't put his money on a horse he would probably get rid of it some other way."

Mr. Croker added that there was no reason why gambling laws should not apply equally to the Stock Exchange and the race track.

"Gov. Hughes's policy," he said, "would get us back to the Puritanical days of the Know Nothings."

Mr. Croker hopes to visit New York in the Fall, but his mission there will have nothing to do with politics.

PARKER UNWILLING.

Doesn't Desire to Hold Public Office Again, He Says.

Alton B. Parker, who returned here from Washington yesterday, made it plain that, as THE TIMES indicated, he does not intend to run for Governor.

"I am not willing to run for Governor of New York," said Judge Parker. "I did not feel that the situation and the question presented justified me in saying more yesterday than that it is my desire never again to hold public office. My friends, I felt, would understand that I said precisely what I meant, and my answer was intended to inform them and no one else."

Judge Parker will entertain Mr. Bryan at dinner next Sunday.

OGDEN M. REID A REPORTER.

Starts on the Staff of His Father's Newspaper and Seems to Like It.

Ogden Mills Reid, only son of Whitelaw Reid, Ambassador to St. James's, is now hunting down the elusive political item as a reporter on his father's newspaper, The Tribune. He began yesterday, and last night he was waiting in vain at the Hotel Knickerbocker to form the acquaintance of William James Conners of Buffalo and the Democratic State Committee. Later, at an hour when the seasoned reporter would have called it a day's work, he cheerfully volunteered to go on a still hunt for Republican State Chairman Timothy L. Woodruff, who is a mighty difficult man to find after Republican State Headquarters has closed for the day.

"He takes to the work as a fish takes to water," said one of the veteran workers on The Tribune, in discussing young Mr. Reid's first day as a newspaper reporter.

Young Mr. Reid's appearance as an active worker on The Tribune staff recalls the story printed recently in THE TIMES that Whitelaw Reid had refused several offers to purchase his newspaper on the ground that he desired to leave it as a legacy to his son.

The latter is a Yale graduate of the Class of 1904. Subsequently he took a course at the Yale Law School. At the university he was chiefly noted for his interest in aquatic sports. In appearance he does not greatly resemble his father, the Ambassador.

MRS. LAWSON RESCUED AT SEA

Hangs On to Railing of Steam Yacht Capsized in Collision.

Special to The New York Times.

BOSTON, Mass., Sept. 9.—Mrs. Arnold Lawson's ability to maintain a hold on the railing of the steam yacht My Gypsy saved her from drowning this afternoon.

When the yacht was struck by the outward bound fishing vessel Boyd and Leeds Mrs. Lawson caught the railing as she was going overboard, and held on until rescued by the tug Metropolitan. At times she was immersed in the sweeping seas, but when the yacht had been righted from the effects of the collision she pluckily returned to it and informed the party of friends aboard that her experience was "nothing."

The My Gypsy, which is the yacht that Thomas W. Lawson gave his deceased wife, in charge of Capt. Crockstad, had just cleared for a short sail, and Mrs. Lawson was sitting at the stern of the boat on deck. Capt. Crockstad tried to run the My Gypsy across the bow of the schooner.

The bowsprit of the Boyd and Leeds caught the signal mast of the steam yacht. The yacht was suddenly careened to port.

Mrs. Lawson, when the boat began to capsize, was swept down the deck on her yacht chair. When the chair hit the rail she was thrown overboard, but managed to get a hold on the rail.

The big ocean tug Metropolitan closed in, and the crew reached out and hauled Mrs. Lawson aboard their boat.

THREAT TO BURN WHITEFACE.

Man Arrested for Attempt to Blackmail Mountain Lumber Company.

Special to The New York Times.

LAKE PLACID, N. Y., Sept. 9.—Probably never before has a mountain been made a medium for blackmail, but that is the use to which John St. Clair of Bloomingdale is charged with putting Mount Whiteface in a letter to the T. J. & J. Rogers Company of Ausable Forks, demanding the immediate payment of $200 under penalty of a fire, which, in addition to burning the company's holdings of about 15,000 acres of timber land about the base, would probably have swept the entire mountain, destroying forever the wonderful scenic beauty of Whiteface.

The letter was sent to the company over the name of L. H. Murphy. The company officials decided to set a trap for the man. A check for $100 was mailed to L. H. Murphy, at Bloomingdale. St. Clair, it is charged, called for mail in the name of Murphy, and he was followed to this village by ex-Sheriff S. W. Barnard. After an unsuccessful attempt to cash a check for $100 at the American House, the man succeeded in getting it cashed by a tradesman and was arrested by Deputy Sheriff Allen.

WANAMAKER BUILDING PLANS.

$6,000,000 Raised for Construction of Last Section of Philadelphia Store.

PHILADELPHIA, Sept. 9.—A mortgage for $6,000,000 on the Philadelphia store of John Wanamaker, including the property bounded by Chestnut and Market, Thirteenth and Juniper Streets, and the properties 1224 and 1226 Market Street, was recorded to-day. The mortgage, or trust deed, was to secure $6,000,000 worth of 5 per cent. five-year gold bonds, of which the Land Title and Trust Company is made trustee.

The purpose of Mr. Wanamaker is to borrow $6,000,000 and to issue 6,000 bonds of $1,000 each, secured by these properties. This, it is understood, is to complete financial arrangements by which Mr. Wanamaker will begin at once the construction of the last section of his store on the Chestnut Street side.

By the terms of the mortgage or trust deed Mr. Wanamaker can sell the old plant to replace it with the new one, but he must keep up the insurance on the properties and pay taxes, &c.

Officers of the trust company say all the bonds have been subscribed for at par by financial men of this city and New York.

TO BUY FRANKLIN HOUSE.

Say American Syndicate Has Option on Building in Paris.

PARIS, Sept. 9.—Michael J. Doyle of Philadelphia announced to-day that he had secured an option for an American syndicate upon the house in this city built and occupied by Benjamin Franklin when he was cultivating friendly relations with France during the American Revolution. The receptions given by Mr. Franklin in this house made it famous.

Subsequently Napoleon I. lived there for a time, and after his divorce from Josephine he turned the property over to her. Mr. Doyle declines to give the names of those interested or the purposes for which it is planned to use the property.

Special to The New York Times.

PHILADELPHIA, Sept. 9.—The Michael J. Doyle mentioned in a dispatch from Paris is probably Michael Francis Doyle, a well-known lawyer, who has been abroad for some time and is prominent in civic associations.

Nothing was known here of his intention to purchase the Franklin house, and if he was acting for a syndicate, it is probable that they have kept their plans secret for fear of enhancing the price.

AERONAUT AND TIGER FALL FROM BALLOON

Men, Women, and Children Flee in Terror as Animal Lands in Fair Grounds.

ATHLETE SERIOUSLY HURT

The Tiger, Uninjured by 100-Foot Drop, Takes Refuge in the Balloon Tent.

Nearly 15,000 persons, many of them children, yesterday being Children's Day at the Richmond County Fair, stood in the fair grounds at Dongan Hills, S. I., late in the afternoon looking up into the air, where young William Coby, in spangles and tights, sat smiling and bowing on a trapeze attached to a balloon which slowly rose above the heads of the crowd. The young trapezist had one arm around a pet tiger cub, which he supported on the trapeze, and which with him was soon to drop in a thrilling dive with a parachute.

Children shouted in delight, and men and women waved hats or handkerchiefs at the athlete. Suddenly from somewhere in the crowd there arose a cry. Instantly it was taken up by others, and presently the multitude were shouting to the trapezist:

"Look out! Your balloon's on fire."

Coby, looking downward, had not seen a spiral of flame which caught the eye of some one in the crowd as it ate its way around one of the hempen supports which attached the trapeze to the balloon. He was nearly 100 feet in the air, but perhaps the voices of the crowd reached his ears. At any rate he turned his eyes upward.

Then he leaped into activity. He tried to free his parachute and prepare for the leap which would enable him to float easily to the ground. But he was an instant too late, however. Before he could free the parachute the bar on which he stood working at the ropes with nervous fingers dropped from the supporting balloon.

A cry of horror arose from the crowd as Coby's figure whirled downward, spinning over and over in the air. Beside him in the downward dive shot the tiger cub, its paws and tail thrashing around in the air.

It was only a few seconds before Coby and his tiger cub struck the turf on the inside of the race track course from which they had ascended. Instantly the crowd pressed forward. But suddenly men and women, dragging children by the hands or carrying infants in their arms, turned back in a wild panic, and fled toward the grandstand, opposite which the balloon ascension had been made.

"The tiger! Look out for the tiger!" was the cry that went up.

Apparently uninjured by its fall the tiger cub made for the crowd in long leaps. Although the crowd did not know it, the animal's only object apparently was to gain the shelter of the tent used to house the balloon. Once within the tent it lay whimpering in terror.

Coby was carried to his dressing tent, and there Dr. Mord from the Smith Infirmary looked him over. He found that the man had received internal injuries and a severe concussion of the spine, and advised his immediate removal to the infirmary. He was taken there in an ambulance.

Coby is only 18 years old, and lives at 903 Bremer Street, Milwaukee. He is a professional balloonist and parachute jumper, and had been exhibiting daily at the fair since its opening on Monday. The police arrested his manager, Frank Robinson, later, asserting that he had not used proper precaution in seeing to it that the balloon and its apparatus were in proper shape before permitting the ascent. Robinson was bailed out by the officials of the fair. The balloon dropped near by, and was found to be only slightly damaged. Robinson wanted to reinflate it and make an ascent himself, but this was not allowed.

Samuel Haber of 209 Spring Street, Manhattan, got a fractured kneecap in the excitement following the fall of Coby and the tiger cub. He was running from the animal when he fell. He, also, was taken to the infirmary.

Yesterday was Democratic day at the fair, and among the visitors were Charles F. Murphy, Col. Henry Watterson, J. Hamilton Lewis, and State Chairman Conners.

HUMAN DYNAMO IN TEXAS.

Electrically Charged Boy Furnishes Power for Fan or Lights.

Special to The New York Times.

GALVESTON, Texas, Sept. 9.—A living storage battery is the only thing to which E. G. Atloy, an American born child of Russian parents, living with his widowed mother in Houston, Texas, can be compared. The boy, who is 7 years old, is a human magnet, and possesses all the electric properties of a dynamo engine in addition.

A metal filling had been put in one tooth, and when the boy came home he picked up the knob used to connect an electric fan with an electric light wire in his mother's residence and thrust it into his mouth.

A threaded metal cap was on the end which screws into the cup for the electric bulb. As the metal cap touched the metal tooth filling the boy's head jerked slightly and the fan began to revolve and then to buzz frantically at full speed. This kept up as long as the circuit was completed in the boy's mouth.

The mother was frightened and feared witchcraft, but the boy seemed pleased at the sensation.

A piece of iron held in the boy's hand for a few moments becomes highly magnetized. A hammer with an iron handle held in his hands will attract tacks at a distance of four feet.

The boy says that he feels only an agreeable sensation. He has red hair of the reddest possible hue, large freckles, and blue eyes.

FIREMAN'S SON STARTS A FIRE

Eight-Year-Old Boy Wanted to See the Engines Turn Out.

Acting Capt. Rehahn of the 152d Street Police Station was at a small fire in the cellar of the tenement at 2,803 Eighth Avenue last night, when he heard a boy say to another that he knew who started the fire. Rehahn grabbed the youth, who led him to Colonial Park, where in some bushes the policeman found eight-year-old William Donnelly, Jr., son of a fireman, who lives at 2,811 Eighth Avenue.

According to Rehahn, the boy admitted that he started the blaze to see the engines turn out. Young Donnelly was paroled in the custody of his father, who will take him to the Children's Court today to answer a charge of malicious mischief.

MRS. SAGE 80 YEARS OLD.

She Receives Many Flowers and Telegrams at Long Island Home.

Special to The New York Times.

LAWRENCE, L. I., Sept. 9.—An unusual number of parcels and telegrams came here yesterday for Mrs. Russell Sage. Most of the parcels contained flowers, and the telegrams and letters were for the most part congratulations upon her eightieth birthday.

Mrs. Sage spent the day quietly at her home. It is the cottage in which Mr. Sage died, and is one of the favorite houses maintained by Mrs. Sage.

Several friends called to pay their respects to Mrs. Sage on her birthday, but many did not know she was in town. She was pleased at the receipt of congratulations sent by institutions she had helped. She expects to remain in her Lawrence cottage thoughout September.

HARRIMAN IN FAST RUN.

Line Clear for His Special Train Speeding to Omaha.

OGDEN, Utah, Sept. 9.—E. H. Harriman's special train reached Ogden at 3:15 o'clock this afternoon. The train consists of several private cars and a baggage car. Every district on the Salt Lake Division has been kept clear during the day to give the special right of way for a record run. One of the fastest trips on record was made between these points.

After a stop of twenty minutes at Ogden, the Harriman party pulled out for Omaha, and another record run is scheduled for the thousand-mile journey.

BOSTON PAWNSHOPS BUSY.

Loans Taken Out on $425,000 Worth of Property in Two Days.

BOSTON, Sept. 9.—Personal property valued at $425,000, including more than 700 watches, was pawned in the City of Boston yesterday and to-day. O. W. Farley of the loan division of the Bureau of Criminal Investigation spent the busiest day in the history of the department recording the loans.

No reason for the unusual amount of pawning is known except that yesterday followed a holiday.

WILL BUY CHEYENNE CANYON.

New York Syndicate to Add to Attraction of Famous Scenic Resort.

Special to The New York Times.

COLORADO SPRINGS, Col., Sept. 9.—A syndicate of New York capitalists has secured an option on the famous South Cheyenne Cañon including the seven falls at the head of which Helen Hunt Jackson, the poet, was buried, also the cave of winds and the Manitou cliff dwellers' ruins.

The purchase price is given by Attorney R. S. Ellis, who represents the owners, as $500,000. Although a payment has been made, the names of the purchasers are withheld at present. The buyers plan considerable outlay to add to the attraction of these famous scenic environs, which are visited by thousands of tourists annually.

RETALIATE ON ERIE ROAD.

$2 a Mile Charge for Observation Engine Forces Inquiry by State Board.

Special to The New York Times.

TRENTON, Sept. 9.—The State Railroad Commission is indignant at the proposition of the Erie Railroad to the effect that it will charge $2 a mile for an observation engine for a tour of inspection by the commission over the Erie lines in this State. This would make the trip cost the State $300. The Commissioners aver that there must be something radically wrong with the Erie lines that the officials should seek to put such a price on an observation engine for the use of the three Commissioners to get the best possible view of the tracks, &c.

In retaliation the commission has put all of its force of inspectors on the Erie lines, and will order a thorough report of the Erie system at once.

Under the law the commission is entitled to ride free of expense on all lines in the State, but the law is silent on observation engines.

GUN FIGHT TO CATCH WOMAN.

Alleged Black Hand Agent Opens Fire on Officers Who Try to Capture Her.

BESSEMER, Mich., Sept. 9.—Mrs. Frank Galler, who, it is alleged, as a "Black Hand" agent, has for several weeks been terrorizing business men, was captured here to-day after a gun fight with officers. She is the wife of a miner.

Five officers were lying in wait at Powder Mill Creek, near a box where money was to be deposited. About 4 o'clock the woman cautiously crept along the road, grabbed the box, and ran. Upon being pursued by officers she drew a pistol and began a fusillade. The fire was promptly returned, until officers who were stationed at a turn in the road grabbed the woman and placed her under arrest. The woman's husband, Frank Galler, has also been jailed. The couple, with four children, came from Venice, Italy, five years ago.

POLICEMAN ARRESTS 15 MEN.

Overawes Fighting Striking Lamplighters and Strikebreakers with His Gun.

Alone and unaided Policeman McGrath of the West 152d Street Station arrested fifteen Italians at 185th Street and Broadway last night, thirteen of whom were striking lamplighters and the other two strikebreakers. McGrath, who was on a bicycle and in plain clothes, saw the thirteen attack the two, and threatening to shoot them he managed to make them all stand.

He was pondering over what to do with his prisoners when he saw Sergt. Kennison on the steps of his home near by. He called him and the two men managed to make the fifteen walk to the horse shed of a near-by roadhouse, where they kept them until they summoned the patrol wagon from the station.

All fifteen were taken to the station, where Frank Masietto of 2,515 Amsterdam Avenue and Joseph Maglieri of 570 West 165th Street, the strikebreakers, were held for carrying concealed weapons. The other thirteen, among whom the police said was the leader of the strikers, Joseph Vende of 517 West 168th Street, were all charged with disorderly conduct.

WRIGHT FLIES OVER AN HOUR

Follows 57-Minute Flight at Fort Myer with One of 62 Minutes 15 Seconds.

AMERICA RULES IN AVIATION

Lieut. Lahm Also Makes Trip with Wright and Record for "Doubles" Is Smashed.

PLANES OBEY EVERY TOUCH

In Early Morning Flight Aviator Outdoes Delagrange—Achievements Watched by High Officials.

Special to The New York Times.

WASHINGTON, Sept. 9.—In three successive flights in his aeroplane to-day, Orville Wright broke three world's records and wrested from France for America the laurels of the air.

In his first flight at an early hour this morning he drove his machine in circles over the Fort Myer parade ground for 57 minutes and 31 seconds, beating the previous endurance record made by Delagrange by 25 minutes 46 1-5 seconds.

In his second flight, late in the afternoon, he remained in the air for 62 minutes and 15 seconds, surpassing his own previous record by 4 minutes and 44 seconds.

His last flight was made with Lieut. Lahm of the Signal Corps in the seat beside him. Together they sailed for 6 minutes and 16 seconds, surpassing the record for doubles formerly made in Virginia by Orville Wright and his mechanician by 2 minutes and 36 seconds.

As far as altitudes attained were concerned the most spectacular flight of the day was the first. Then with few people to watch him Wright determined to familiarize himself with the upper air. From his normal course of some forty feet above the parade ground Mr. Wright turned the nose of his skimming craft upward for little runs at a height of 150 feet from the ground.

But as a demonstration of perfect mastery of his planes, and consequent mastery of the air, the long flight in which he broke his own and all other records for endurance was unequaled. When Mr. Wright descended from his morning flight he said that if he had known how near the hour limit he had come he would have stayed up longer, and there is no doubt that he would have done it. But the experience he gained in his 57 minutes of constant attention to the tricks of aviation in his early flight told its own story in the inventor's assurance in the afternoon, and in the perfect response to the slightest touch he made on his three levers.

Leading Officials Watch Flight.

The most representative company that has yet watched the daily experiments gathered this afternoon, following the report of Mr. Wright's early success. Gen. Nelson A. Miles came to Washington for the express purpose of watching the flights, and studied the manœuvres of the inventor. Secretary of War Wright and Secretary of the Navy Metcalf were on the grounds long before the flight took place, and the army was represented by Gens. Oliver and Murray, Col. Hatfield, and many others. The French Military Attaché, Major Fournier, who recently witnessed some of Wilbur Wright's attempts at Le Mans, was also present. The crowd numbered several thousands.

It was 5:17:45 o'clock when the heavy weights dropped from the derrick and gave the forward impetus to the airship, waiting balanced on its monorail. Wright had taken his seat a moment before without the least apparent uneasiness, and in a businesslike way took hold of the controlling levers.

As viewed from behind at close quarters the enormous planes with the large twin propellers whirring with an irregular rattle behind them seemed to flutter off down the parade ground like a wounded bird. As the distance increased, however, the impression of irregular motion conveyed by the propellers was lost, and the machine seemed to be sliding over the grass on its skids like an iceboat over a frozen lake. The aeroplane was fully 100 yards from the starting point before it could be seen that it had left the ground, and was skimming the highest weeds under its own power.

Then like a giant gull, snow white in the sunlight, the tips of the planes tilted to the left, and still on the rise the aeroplane passed over the aerodrome at the other end of the field, missing its gable roof by only a few feet. Mr. Wright held his planes and rudder rigid until a complete half circle had been described, and then brought the ship back to an even keel as he sped up the field along the side of Arlington National Cemetery.

Dips Machine to the Crowd.

The crowd, intent on watching the start had given only a straggling cheer as the falling weights jerked the machine along the starting rail, and the cheer was quite lost in the whir of the propellers and the backward rush of a powerful current of air. But as Wright soared over the spectators crowding around the starting point, a long yell told their spontaneous enthusiasm. The aviator did not move his hands from the levers to wave an acknowledgment, but instead he dipped the nose of the bird-like structure, swooped to within twenty feet of the ground, and returned as a

"All the News That's Fit to Print."

The New York Times.

THE WEATHER.
Fair, warmer to-day; clouding to-morrow; light, variable winds.

VOL. LVIII...NO. 18,854. * * * NEW YORK, TUESDAY, SEPTEMBER 7, 1909.—EIGHTEEN PAGES. ONE CENT In Greater New York, Jersey City, and Newark { Elsewhere, TWO CENTS.

GAYNOR, UNPLEDGED, CONSENTS TO RUN

Writes Business Men He Will Accept Support of Any Party, but Make No Promises.

SAYS TAMMANY IS FOR HIM

Assured by Leaders of the Nomination, He Declares—Is for War on Machine Control and "City Spoliation."

Supreme Court Justice William J. Gaynor of Brooklyn has announced his willingness to become a candidate for Mayor in a letter written to a committee of influential Brooklyn citizens who urged him soon after his return from Europe to enter the fight. The long-awaited declaration of his position was made public last night together with the names of the committee of citizens and their letter to the Brooklyn jurist.

Justic Gaynor reviews the entire Mayoralty situation, assails "mere political control," which has resulted in "spoliation of the city treasury." He declares, however, that he has reason to believe that he will receive the Democratic nomination and Republican support, as well as that of the Independence League.

An interesting part of the letter is that in which Justice Gaynor refers to the printed statements that he would not receive the indorsement of the Republican organization unless he made some definite pledge of his position. While declaring that he does not believe that the majority of the organization demand any such condition of him, he emphatically states that he will pledge himself to no organization.

"I shall not take a nomination from any organization to which is annexed any pledge, promise or condition whatsoever other than to be Mayor in fact, and do my duty if elected," says he.

In referring to his expectation of welcoming all voters to his standard, Justice Gaynor says: "When an organization or party vouches for one and nominates him and wants him elected I have always understood that it welcomes help from any and all quarters to elect him."

Promises from Tammany.

He goes on to make the significant declaration that he has received assurance from influential Democrats that the Tammany City Convention will give him an "unconditional nomination" and that "no one can prevent the election of delegates who will nominate me." He states that he is aware that there is opposition to him in the organization, but that he does not believe "an undivided delegation can be brought into the convention opposed to my nomination."

"As to the Independence League," he continues, "inasmuch as it has always stood for the uplifting of city government, I think I may justly expect its support."

Justice Gaynor concludes with a solemn pledge to discharge his trust with fidelity and honesty, ending with the words, "No party or party machine can drag us down if we stand fast together: on the contrary, we may lift city politics up in all parties, and make the spoliation of the city's treasury, through mere machine political control, a thing impossible in the future."

Here is Justice Gaynor's answer:

Justice Gaynor's Letter.

Sept. 4, 1909.

"Messrs. Abraham Abraham, James McMahon, Archibald R. Watson, Judson G. Wall, Michael H. Drummond, James Creelman, Charles M. Higgins, M. M. Belding, Jr., and Frank J. Price.

Dear Sirs—Your letter added to my very great anxiety, already caused by similar letters and requests and public discussion, but has finally helped to enable me to see my way through it. I put myself in your hands, and consent to be a candidate for nomination for Mayor. No doubt you have observed that several bodies of citizens have nominated me already. I specially note your statement, 'We do not care who, or what party convention, joins in nominating and voting for you if you will give us your consent to run,' etc. It requires me to say something of recent occurrences in order that there may be no misunderstanding, and I trust I may say it without a bit of unkindness to any one.

The Republican City Committee has met since your letter was written and apparently give out a statement that the Republican City Convention will not nominate any one who will not pledge himself in advance not to accept a nomination from the Democratic City Convention also. Although, published in all of the newspapers, and in no way questioned, I have doubted whether it was in fact authorized. I know that many Republicans will not acquiesce in it. As is well enough known, I have long been of those who look upon such extreme partisanship in city or local elections as most unfortunate. Its main result is to play everything year after year into the hands of party machines.

In years gone by I have worked shoulder to shoulder with Republicans and Democrats alike and together in efforts to prevent official wrongdoing and lift the city Government up and make it intelligent and decent. I so worked successfully with those who prevented the fraudulent purchase of the water company, and other even worse things, still in general remembrance, and with those who moved upon and destroyed John Y. McKane and his corrupt control, results and benefits from which were accepted by leaders and the machines of both parties in turn through series of years.

We never paused then to inquire of one another's politics, or to put any ban or bar on one another because of politics, and we shall not do the like now. Must I now in order to run for Mayor first set up and unjustly offend men who so worked with us then, and thousands of others who gave us their good-will and sympathy in such work, by saying that I shall not suffer the city convention of their party to also nominate me? If I should do so I could not expect their votes.

The great bulk of the voters here who are Democrats in National politics are in favor of intelligent and good local government the same as the corresponding bulk of Republican voters are. How much better it would be for the city if they should work together instead of proscribing and ostracizing each other.

Base Men in the Minority.

Base men are in the minority in all parties and everywhere. There are 75,000 or more voters in this great city who now never allow National politics to influence their votes in city elections. What,

Continued on Page 7.

HARRIMAN SUFFERS RELAPSE.

Diagnosed as Acute Indigestion—His Physician Says, 'We Hope for the Best.'

Special to The New York Times.

TURNER'S, N. Y., Sept. 6.—That E. H. Harriman has had a relapse was admitted this afternoon by Dr. W. M. Gordon Lyle, his physician, at the Harriman home here. Acute indigestion is Dr. Lyle's diagnosis of his patient's trouble.

The attack came on yesterday after Mr. Harriman had appeared to be doing nicely for several days. A telephone message was sent from the Harriman home in the early hours of this morning to Miss Taylor, Superintendent of St. Luke's Hospital nurses' registry, at 214 West 108th Street, Manhattan, asking her to send her best nurse here with all speed. The nurse arrived within three hours.

According to Dr. Lyle, Mr. Harriman is resting easily to-night. He said that it was he who sent for the nurse. There is a report that there are four other nurses here, but this could not be confirmed. Certain it is that Mr. Harriman's state of health is such that both day and night nurses are required.

When Dr. Lyle was seen this afternoon he was much perturbed over the presence here again of newspaper men. It was pointed out to him, however, that they were withdrawn on the understanding that the press was to be apprised of any change in Mr. Harriman's condition through his office at 120 Broadway. He was told that nothing could be learned from that source to-day.

"It is true," said Dr. Lyle, "that Mr. Harriman has had a relapse. Yesterday he had a sharp attack of indigestion, but he is better to-day, and is now resting comfortably. We hope for the best."

Mr. Harriman's entire family is at Tower Hill, while Judge Robert S. Lovett, general counsel to most of the important Harriman interests, was summoned to Arden and arrived last night. It is said that two of the physicians who were called into consultation with Dr. George W. Crile, the Cleveland surgeon, shortly after Mr. Harriman's return from Europe, are again at Arden. They are Dr. Walter B. James of 17 West Fifty-fourth Street and Dr. George E. Brewer of 61 West Forty-eighth Street.

Dr. Lyle gave out this bulletin at 4 P. M.: "Mr. Harriman had an attack of acute indigestion at 11 P. M. last night, having partaken of a dinner a little heartier than his strength would allow. His condition is improved to-day, although there are still slight indications of a bad stomach."

At Dr. Brewer's home last night it was said that the doctor was at Cedar Camp in the Adirondacks, so far as any of his household here knew. He may have gone to Arden from there, however. There was no response to the telephone when a Times reporter tried to reach Dr. James's house over the wire.

DYNAMITE HOUSE AND PLANT.

Official Who Had Discharged Men Kicks Explosive to the Ground.

Special to The New York Times.

TYRONE, Penn., Sept. 6.—The handsome residence of Thomas Calderwood, an official of the American Lime and Stone Company, and all of the buildings of the company at the quarry near here, were completely wrecked and one unidentified fire engineer was killed by explosions of dynamite early to-day.

Calderwood some time ago discharged some foreign employes of his company, and it was the general belief here that the explosions were acts of revenge.

Mr. Calderwood arose at 5 o'clock and smelled something burning. Upon investigation he found a large bundle of dynamite securely bound with wire on his kitchen window. He immediately tore the window open, and kicked it to the ground, and shouted for his wife and daughter to run for their lives. They had barely reached the street before the explosion occurred. Every window in the house was smashed to atoms. The doors and walls were badly damaged. Windows for blocks were broken.

At the quarries a ton of dynamite had been stored. The whole amount was exploded, completely destroying the buildings about the works, and blowing a large steel car 100 feet from the tracks.

The home of Harry Houck, near the quarries, was completely destroyed. The scales used for weighing cars were wrecked, and windows were broken in the houses within a radius of five miles.

HUGHES'S DEPUTIES AT RACES

Make No Secret of Their Mission, but Find No Betting at Sheepshead Bay.

Four investigators of race-track conditions from Albany visited the Sheepshead Bay race course yesterday, as the representatives of Gov. Hughes, after presenting themselves, with credentials which were accepted, to Sheriff Hobley of Kings County

The investigators made no secret of their mission, but made no claim to official standing of any kind, except to say that they came to observe what was going on and ascertain the conditions concerning betting at the race track for a report to the Governor.

The visitors watched the proceedings of the holiday crowd through the afternoon, and agreed that they saw nothing fitting the description of race-track betting published in an afternoon newspaper early last week, which report caused Gov. Hughes to request reports from the New York police officials and the officials of Kings County on the matter of race-track bookmaking.

MISS STEWART A PRINCESS.

Emperor Francis Joseph Confers the Rank in Her Own Right.

VIENNA, Sept. 6.—Emperor Francis Joseph has conferred upon Miss Anita Stewart, whose marriage to Prince Miguel of Braganza will take place Sept. 15, the rank of Princess in her own right.

Miss Anita Stewart is the daughter of Mrs. James Henry Smith by her first husband, William Rhinelander Stewart, whom she divorced in South Dakota to marry Mr. Smith. When Mr. Smith died in Kobe, Japan, he left his stepdaughter an income of $40,000 a year, to which her mother will add another $40,000 a year on her marriage to Prince Miguel next month in London.

In order to get the consent of his father, Dom Miguel, the Prince had to renounce all claim to the throne of Portugal in favor of his younger brother, Prince Francis Joseph.

LONDON APPLAUDS PEARY'S EXPLOIT

Instant Acceptance of His Report a Contrast to Skepticism Toward Dr. Cook.

HAD AWAITED HIS VERDICT

Admiral Nares Thinks It Peculiar That the Announcements Should Come So Close Together.

Special Cable to THE NEW YORK TIMES.

LONDON, Sept. 6.—The news that Commander Robert E. Peary had reached the north pole was made known throughout London by late editions of the evening papers, which displayed the brief announcement under headlines which suggested none of the reservations with which the reports of the discovery by Dr. Cook have been received.

In marked contrast with the skepticism with which Dr. Cook's reports were printed is the immediate and whole-hearted acceptance of Peary's dispatch. Nothing could show this better than a comparison of headlines upon the two announcements.

A Difference in Headlines.

"North pole reached by Peary. Official news that the American flag was hoisted April 6, 1909." That is the way in which Commander Peary's dispatch is presented to its readers by a London paper which headed Dr. Cook's report as follows: "The north pole reported discovered. American explorer's statement."

With the general public a similar readiness to accept Commander Peary's statement is strikingly apparent and bears out the saying frequently heard here recently to the effect that had it been Commander Peary instead of Dr. Cook who had come forward with a bare announcement of the discovery of the pole not a single voice would have been raised in question. It is a testimony to Commander Peary's high reputation as a man and an explorer that the world accepts his word without a shadow of hesitation.

Had Awaited Peary's Testimony

Mr. Peary's announcement is hailed with peculiar satisfaction, because, throughout the controversy that has been raging in the last few days, it has been stated again and again that Mr. Peary's testimony would settle the question definitely. "Peary will know the truth," it was said. Thus, Peary is the witness for whom the whole world is waiting. There was a consensus of opinion among the people with whom I talked to-night that if Commander Peary contests the claims put forward by Dr. Cook, the latter will find it an extremely difficult task to establish his pretensions to be the discoverer of the pole, even should the "proofs" which he is now withholding prove to be as good as he says they are.

Cook Expects Confirmation.

Dr. Cook, on being informed in Copenhagen to-night of the news from Mr. Peary, said:

"I hope it is true, for Peary's reports will confirm all my claims."

An arctic explorer to whom to-night I showed Mr. Peary's message to THE NEW YORK TIMES, saying, "I have the pole," made the comment that Mr. Peary, by implication, denied any other claim to the honor of discovering the pole, and that, consequently, it was to be inferred that the confirmation which Dr. Cook expects from Mr. Peary is hardly likely to be forthcoming.

Peculiar Coincidence, Says Nares.

Sir George Nares, who led the arctic expedition of 1875-6, when interviewed to-night with regard to Commander Peary's message announcing the discovery, said:

"It is difficult to avoid the conclusion that Commander Peary's Eskimos at Etah must have known that Dr. Cook had crossed Smith's Sound and passed Etah last Winter to reach Ellsmere Land. Dr. Cook, then," continued the Admiral, "gets down from his Eskimo headquarters at Annotook to Upernavik by a Greenland route never before traversed, passing all the sea glaciers in Baffin Bay just in time to catch a Danish Government vessel which leaves Upernavik early in the year before the whaling vessels are due.

"My first impression was that Dr. Cook had got hold of Commander Peary's Eskimos in some way or other and ought to have communicated either with Commander Peary or with the Eskimos at Etah.

"The question now arises how it comes about that Cook and Peary announce at practically the same time the discovery of the north pole. Is it not a peculiar fact that this coincidence takes place, in view of the possibility of news having reached Etah of the success of one or the other of the men?"

Capt. Scott of the exploring ship Discovery stated to-night that Commander Peary's message put it beyond doubt that the Stars and Stripes was the first flag to fly at the north pole.

The Proper Witness Arrives.

"Just at the very moment when men were saying that only the evidence of an independent witness who had himself visited the north pole could estab-

Continued on Page 2.

In order not to miss The New York Times of to-morrow, in which will be printed exclusively Lieut. Peary's own story of his discovery of the North Pole, order a copy from your newsdealer early to-day.

COOK GLAD PEARY REACHED THE POLE

Unmoved When, Wreathed with Flowers at Banquet, He Hears the News.

HOPE NOW FOR OTHERS

Believes More Expeditions Will Reach the Pole Within the Next Ten Years.

COPENHAGEN, Sept. 6.—Copenhagen was electrified to-night by the report of Commander Peary's announcement that he had reached the north pole. Dr. Cook was immensely interested and said:

"That is good news. I hope Peary did get to the pole. His observations and reports on that region will confirm mine."

Asked if there was any probability of Peary's having found the tube containing his records, Dr. Cook replied:

"I hope so, but that is doubtful on account of the drift. Commander Peary would have reached the pole this year, probably, while I was there last year. His route was several hundred miles east of mine. We are rivals, of course, but the pole is good enough for two.

"The fact of two men having reached the pole along different paths," continued the explorer, "should furnish large additions to scientific knowledge. Probably other parties will reach it in the next ten years, since every explorer is helped by the experience of his predecessors, just as Sverdrup's observations and reports were of immeasurable help to me.

"I can say nothing more concerning Commander Peary's success without knowing further details, than that I am glad of it."

While Dr. Cook was conversing casually this morning with some friends, a possibility of the dénouement which electrified the world to-day was laughingly suggested. Dr. Cook remarked:

"It is quite possible that Peary will turn up now. He is about due to get back if he carries out his plans."

Those who have had the best opportunities to become acquainted with Dr. Cook here believe that he is not likely to enter into a controversy with Commander Peary.

It is doubtful if history furnishes a more dramatic episode than the breaking of the news to Dr. Cook that Peary had realized the goal of his life's ambition and repeated struggles. Dr. Cook was seated at a dinner, surrounded by explorers and correspondents, in the gilded ballroom of the Tivoli Casino. Around his neck was hung a garland of pink roses, according to the Scandinavian method of honoring heroes, which the explorer wore blushingly and with visible embarrassment. Several speeches, acclaiming him, had been given and repeated toasts to him drunk with clamorous cheers.

Amid this scene a whisper went around that Peary had planted the Stars and Stripes at the pole. Cook was perfectly cool and unmoved. He made a striking speech, in which he paid high tribute to the work of Sverdrup, who sat near, to whose discoveries he largely owed his success; to John R. Bradley, who had financed the expedition; to "the intelligence, endurance, and faithfulness" of the Eskimos who had assisted in the preparations, and those who had accompanied him. The whole story of the expedition, he said, has not come out, and will not come out for some time, nor will it come out in installments, but only when it is completed.

Dr. Cook did not permit the whispers which came to his ear of Peary's success to move him in the least, but when he had finished he was surrounded by correspondents who looked for some sign of emotion, but the explorer said smilingly: "I am glad."

Nothing but arctic exploration has been thought of here for the last few days. The people at first refused to believe that such a report as that telling of Peary's success had been received. They thought it must be a canard or a practical joke. The Danish news agency, which received the telegram from London, feared that it had been imposed upon and cabled to London for confirmation before it would circulate the report.

Minister Egan characterized it as one of the most dramatic events of history. The rumor spread that Peary was returning by way of Denmark, and this made an immense sensation. Some questioned the authority of the Peary telegram on the ground that it was improbable that a scientific man would use such dramatic language.

After the dinner to-night Dr. Cook stood about talking with Sverdrup and the other guests in a most unconcerned manner. Later, with the roses still decorating his shoulders, his hosts led him through the Casino grounds to an automobile. A crowd of several hundred, half of the number being women, surrounded and followed him, cheering, but the people were not able to get near enough to shake hands, because of a cordon of police.

PEARY DISCOVERS THE NORTH POLE AFTER EIGHT TRIALS IN 23 YEARS

Notifies The New York Times That He Reached It on April 6, 1909.

HE WIRES FROM LABRADOR

Returning on the Roosevelt, Which He Reports to Bridgman Is Safe.

IS NEARING NEWFOUNDLAND

Expects to Reach Chateau Bay To-day, When He Will Send Full Particulars.

McMILLAN SENDS WORD

Explorer's Companion Telegraphs Sister: "We Have the Pole on Board."

SEVEN VAIN EXPEDITIONS

Many Years Consumed in Learning the Feasible Route—Picked Men Were His Assistants.

Commander Robert E. Peary, U. S. N., has discovered the north pole. Following the report of Dr F. A. Cook that he had reached the top of the world comes the certain announcement from Mr. Peary, the hero of eight polar expeditions, covering a period of twenty-three years, that at last his ambition has been realized, and from all over the world comes full acknowledgment of Peary's feat and congratulations on his success.

The first announcement of Peary's exploit was received in the following message to THE NEW YORK TIMES:

> Indian Harbor, Labrador, via Cape Ray, N. F., Sept. 6.
> THE NEW YORK TIMES, New York:
> I have the pole, April sixth. Expect arrive Chateau Bay, September seventh. Secure control wire for me there and arrange expedite transmission big story. PEARY.

Following the receipt of Commander Peary's message to THE NEW YORK TIMES several other messages were received in this city from the explorer to the same effect.

Soon afterward The Associated Press received the following:

> INDIAN HARBOR, Via Cape Ray, N. F., Sept. 6.—To Associated Press, New York.
> Stars and Stripes nailed to the pole. PEARY.

To Herbert L. Bridgman, Secretary of the Peary Arctic Club, he telegraphed as follows:

> Herbert L. Bridgman, Brooklyn, N. Y.:
> Pole reached. Roosevelt safe. PEARY.

This message was received at the New York Yacht Club in West Forty-fourth Street:

> INDIAN HARBOR, Via Cape Ray, N. F., Sept. 6.—George A. Carmack, Secretary New York Yacht Club:
> Steam yacht Roosevelt, flying club burgee, has enabled me to add north pole to club's other trophies.
> (Signed) PEARY.

Cipher Shows Authenticity.

The telegram to Mr. Bridgman was sent in cipher. The cipher used was a private one and indicated clearly that the dispatch was undoubtedly from Commander Peary.

Commander Peary also sent a message to his wife at South Harpswell, Me., where she has been spending the Summer.

"Have made good at last," said the explorer to his wife. "I have the old pole. Am well. Love. Will wire again from Chateau."

The message was signed simply "Bert," an abbreviation of Robert, Commander Peary's first name. Mrs. Peary sent a wife's characteristic reply, with love and a blessing and a request for him to "hurry home."

By a strange coincidence, Mrs. Frederick A. Cook, too, was in South Harpswell, Me., when she received the first news from her husband.

Peary's Companion Reports.

Two messages were received in this country also from Donald B. McMillan, who accompanied Peary. Mr. McMillan was an instructor in mathematics and physical training at the academy in Worcester, Mass., until the close of school last year, when he obtained a leave of absence of two years to go on the Peary expedition.

In addition to his message to Dr. D. L. Abercrombie, Principal of the academy, Mr. McMillan sent the following to Mrs. W. C. Fogg, his sister, who is Postmistress at Freeport, Me.:

> Indian Harbor, Sept. 6, 1909.
> Mrs. W. C. Fogg, Freeport, Me.:
> Arrived safe. Pole on board. Best year of my life. BEN.

Follows Cook's Report Quickly.

These messages, flashed from the coast of Labrador to New York and thence to the four corners of the globe while Dr. Frederick A. Cook is being acclaimed by the crowned heads of Europe and the world at large as the discoverer of the north pole, added a remarkable chapter to the story of an achievement that has held the civilized world up to the highest pitch of interest since Sept. 1, when Dr. Cook's claim to having reached the "top of the world" was first telegraphed from the Shetland Islands.

The two explorers, Dr. Frederick A. Cook and Commander Robert E. Peary, both Americans, had been in the arctic seeking the goal of centuries, the impossible north pole, whose attainment has at times seemed beyond the reach of man. Both were determined and courageous, and both had started expressing the belief that their efforts would be crowned with success.

Peary the Better Known.

Peary was well known to both scientists and the general public as a persistent striver for the honor of reaching the "farthest north." Dr. Cook, on the other hand, had held the public attention to a lesser degree. He made his departure quietly and his purpose was hardly known except to those keenly interested in polar research.

Then suddenly, and with no word of warning, a steamer touched at Lerwick, in the Shetland Islands, and Dr. Cook's claim to having succeeded where expedition after expedition of the hardiest explorers of the world had failed was made known. Dr. Cook's announcement was that he had reached the pole on April 21, 1908.

Three days later Dr. Cook arrived at Copenhagen and received a welcome such as no explorer had ever received before.

Peary Announces Success.

Five days after the receipt of the Lerwick message, almost to the hour, came the sensational statement from Indian Harbor, Labrador, that Commander Peary also had been successful on his third expedition to the coveted goal, the date being April 6, 1909.

He filed his brief messages and continued on his way to the south, leaving the world to marvel at a dramatic situation such as has seldom been recorded—the double achievement of a purpose that for almost ten centuries had baffled the endeavor of man and had taken many an explorer to his death in the frozen north.

It is almost certain that Commander Peary did not know of Dr. Cook's announcement when he sent his messages from Indian Harbor.

Under ordinary circumstances Commander Peary's announcement would have evoked world-wide interest, but the existing conditions conspired to add many times to the importance of his communication.

According to Dr. Cook's account of his expedition, he buried the American flag at the pole in a metal tube; Peary's words would indicate that the Stars and Stripes were raised by him and left standing.

How the News Came.

The message from Commander Peary to THE NEW YORK TIMES was received in New York at 12:39 yesterday through the Postal Telegraph Company. It was handed in at Indian Harbor, Labrador, and was sent from there by wireless telegraph to Cape Ray, Newfoundland, and from Cape Ray to Port aux Basques by the Newfoundland Government land lines; thence to Canso, Nova Scotia, by cable, and to New York from there over the lines of the Commercial Cable Company.

PEARY REPORTS TO THE TIMES

ANNOUNCES HIS DISCOVERY OF THE POLE AND WILL SEND A FULL AND EXCLUSIVE ACCOUNT TO-DAY.

Indian Harbor, Labrador, via Cape Ray, N. F., Sept. 6.

The New York Times, New York:

I have the pole, April sixth. Expect arrive Chateau Bay September seventh. Secure control wire for me there and arrange expedite transmission big story.

PEARY.

PEARY'S MESSAGE TO HIS WIFE.

SOUTH HARPSWELL, Me., Sept. 6.—Commander Robert E. Peary announced his success in discovering the North Pole to his wife, who is summering at Eagle Island here, as follows:

> INDIAN HARBOR, via Cape Ray, Sept. 6, 1909.
> Mrs. R. E. Peary, South Harpswell, Me.:
> Have made good at last. I have the old Pole. Am well. Love. Will wire again from Chateau.
> (Signed) BERT.

In replying Mrs. Peary sent the following dispatch:

> SOUTH HARPSWELL, Me., Sept. 6, 1909.
> To Commander R. E. Peary, Steamer Roosevelt, Chateau Bay:
> All well. Best love. God bless you. Hurry home.
> (Signed) JO.

CONFIRMED BY FELLOW-VOYAGER.

> INDIAN HARBOR, Labrador, Sept. 6, 1909.
> Dr. D. W. Abercrombie, Worcester Academy, Worcester, Mass.:
> Top of the earth reached at last. Greetings to Faculty and boys.
> (Signed) D. B. McMILLAN.

DR. COOK CABLES THE TIMES.

To the Editor of The New York Times:

COPENHAGEN, Sept. 6.

Glad Peary did it. Two records are better than one, and the work over a more easterly route has added value.

COOK.

WASHINGTON CREDITS PEARY.

Believes Cook, Too, but Has Said That He Must Produce Records.

Special to The New York Times.

WASHINGTON, Sept. 6.—There was instant acceptance among the geographers in Washington of the assertion in Commander Peary's laconic cable message that he had discovered the north pole. And there was just as ready rejoicing for Peary is popular with the scientific men in the National capitol, and they are ready to take his word at its face value without examination or delay.

In the manner of their acceptance of this announcement of a second discovery of the point that has baffled discovery for so many years there is a sharp contrast to the attitude of the same men toward the announcement from Dr. Cook. Most of them, indeed, accept Cook's assertion, and announce their belief that the Brooklyn man actually did reach the north pole in April, 1908. But there

"All the News That's Fit to Print."

The New York Times.

THE WEATHER.
Unsettled Tuesday; Wednesday, fair, cooler; moderate southerly winds, becoming variable.
For full weather report see Page 23.

VOL. LXI...NO. 19,808. NEW YORK, TUESDAY, APRIL 16, 1912.—TWENTY-FOUR PAGES, ONE CENT In Greater New York, Jersey City, and Newark. | Elsewhere, TWO CENTS.

TITANIC SINKS FOUR HOURS AFTER HITTING ICEBERG; 866 RESCUED BY CARPATHIA, PROBABLY 1250 PERISH; ISMAY SAFE, MRS. ASTOR MAYBE, NOTED NAMES MISSING

Col. Astor and Bride, Isidor Straus and Wife, and Maj. Butt Aboard.

"RULE OF SEA" FOLLOWED

Women and Children Put Over in Lifeboats and Are Supposed to be Safe on Carpathia.

PICKED UP AFTER 8 HOURS

Vincent Astor Calls at White Star Office for News of His Father and Leaves Weeping.

FRANKLIN HOPEFUL ALL DAY

Manager of the Line Insisted Titanic Was Unsinkable Even After She Had Gone Down.

HEAD OF THE LINE ABOARD

J. Bruce Ismay Making First Trip on Gigantic Ship That Was to Surpass All Others.

The admission that the Titanic, the biggest steamship in the world, had been sunk by an iceberg and had gone to the bottom of the Atlantic, probably carrying more than 1,400 of her passengers and crew with her, was made at the White Star Line offices, 9 Broadway, at 8:20 o'clock last night. Then P. A. S. Franklin, Vice President and General Manager of the International Mercantile Marine, conceded that probably only those passengers who were picked up by the Cunarder Carpathia had been saved. Advices received early this morning tended to increase the number of survivers by 200.

The admission followed a day in which the White Star Line officials had been optimistic in the extreme. At no time was the admission made that every one aboard the huge steamer was not safe. The ship itself, it was confidently asserted, was unsinkable, and inquirers were informed that she would reach port, under her own steam probably, but surely with the help of the Allan liner Virginian, which was reported to be towing her.

As the day passed, however, with no new authentic reports from the Titanic or any of the ships which were known to have responded to her wireless call for help, it became apparent that authentic news of the disaster probably could come only from the Titanic's sister ship, the Olympic. The wireless range of the Olympic is 500 miles. That of the Carpathia, the Parisian, and the Virginian is much less, and as they neared the position of the Titanic they drew further and further out of shore range. From the Titanic's position at the time of the disaster it is doubtful if any of the ships except the Olympic could establish communication with shore.

Titanic Sank at 2:20 A. M. Monday.

In the White Star offices the hope was held out all day that the Parisian and the Virginian had taken off some of the Titanic's passengers, and efforts were made to get into communication with these liners. Until such communication was established the White Star officials refused to recognize the possibility that there were none of the Titanic's passengers aboard them.

But by nightfall came the message from Capt. Haddock of the Olympic to Cape Race, Newfoundland, telling of the foundering of the Titanic and of the rescue of 655 of her passengers by the Cunarder Carpathia, which, the wireless message said, reached the position of the Titanic at daybreak. All they found there, however, was lifeboats and wreckage. The biggest ship in the world had sunk at 2:20 o'clock yesterday morning.

Mr. Franklin admitted late last night that the Parisian and the Virginian, though they were among the first to answer the Titanic's calls for help, could not have reached the scene before 10 o'clock yesterday morning, seven and a half hours after the big Titanic buried her nose beneath the waves and pitched downward out of sight. The Carpathia, so the wireless dispatch from Capt. Haddock to Cape Race announced, reached the scene of the Titanic's foundering at daybreak, several hours before the expected arrival of the Virginian and the Parisian.

1,465 Lives Lost First Report.

It is unbelievable, so White Star Line officials were compelled to concede finally, that the Carpathia should have failed to pick up every lifeboat which still floated on the waves. If they failed to pick up more than 655 passengers, it was because the others of the ship's complement had gone with her to the bottom.

But it was not until nearly nightfall that the extent of the disaster was realized. Before that the reassuring nature of the bulletins issued by the White Star line was sufficient to quiet the fears of those who had relatives or friends aboard the unfortunate ship and to prevent widespread belief in a serious disaster.

Capt. Haddock's message from the Olympic, which is printed in another column of THE TIMES, strongly indicated that none but the 655 taken from life boats by the Carpathia had been saved. This message was relayed immediately to the White Star offices, but Mr. Franklin positively declined to make the text of the message public. He offered still the hope that passengers were aboard the Parisian and the Virginian, and even when the admission was wrung from him that there seemed little hope of the saving of any others than the 655 aboard the Carpathia, he clung to the hope that in some unexplained way there were other passengers abroad the two Allan liners.

First Reported Titanic in Tow.

Throughout the day there had been reassurances that the Titanic was being towed to port by the Virginian, and when Capt. Haddock's message proved this to be untrue only the admission was made at the White Star offices that the Titanic had sunk. Mr. Franklin said that Capt. Haddock's message was brief and "neglected to say that all the crew had been saved." But the inference was not that all the passengers had been saved. Rather it was that many of them had died, and presently Mr. Franklin admitted the fear that there had been a terrible loss of life on the Titanic.

This version of Capt. Haddock's wireless had been given at the White Star offices:

Capt. Haddock of the Olympic sends a wireless message to the White Star offices here that the steamer Titanic sank at 2:20 A. M., after all the passengers and crew had been lowered to life boats and transferred to the Virginian. The steamship Carpathia, with several hundred passengers of the Titanic, is now en route to New York.

At 9 o'clock, however, he modified this statement, declaring:

As far as we know the situation, there have been rumors from Halifax that three steamers were at the scene of the Titanic's sinking, namely, the Virginian, the Parisian, and the Carpathia. We have heard from Capt. Haddock of the Olympic, who says that the Titanic sank at 2:20 o'clock this morning. Haddock also informs us that the Carpathia has 675 survivors on board. It is very difficult to say whether the Virginian and the Parisian have any survivors on board until we can get a report from those vessels.

Fears Serious Loss of Life.

We have asked for that report from Capt. Haddock, and we are expecting a reply at any time. The Carpathia is proceeding to New York direct. We very much fear that there has been serious loss of life, but it is impossible for us to say definitely concerning this sad part of the situation until we are able to reassure ourselves whether or not any of the Titanic's passengers are aboard the Allan liners.

We are hopeful that the rumors which have reached us by telegraph from Halifax that there are passengers aboard the Virginian and the Parisian will prove to be true, and that these vessels will turn up with some of the passengers. It is the loss of life that makes this thing so awful. We can replace the money loss, but not the lives of those who went down.

Another version of the message from the Olympic was current last night and included the sentence: "Loss likely total 1,800 souls." This sentence was not in the message received by THE TIMES from Cape Race nor in that sent to the White Star line offices.

Continued on Page 2.

THE PROBABLE LOSS.	
Number Aboard.	
First cabin	325
Second cabin	285
Steerage	710
Crew, (estimated)	800
Total	2,120
Saved.	
By the Carpathia	866
Probably drowned	1,254

The Lost Titanic Being Towed Out of Belfast Harbor.

CAPT. E. J. SMITH,
Commander of the Titanic.

PARTIAL LIST OF THE SAVED.

Includes Bruce Ismay, Mrs. Widener, Mrs. H. B. Harris, and an Incomplete name, suggesting Mrs. Astor's.

Special to The New York Times.

CAPE RACE, N. F., Tuesday, April 16.—Following is a partial list of survivors among the first-class passengers of the Titanic, received by the Marconi wireless station this morning from the Carpathia, via the steapship Olympic:

Mrs. JACOB P. ——— and maid.
Mr. HARRY ANDERSON.
Mrs. ED. W. APPLETON.
Mrs. ROSE ABBOTT.
Miss G. M. BURNS.
Miss D. D. CASSERERE.
Mrs. WM. M. CLARKE.
Mrs. B. CHIBINACE.
Miss E. G. CROSSBIE.
Miss H. ROSEBIE.
Miss JEAN HIPACK.
Mrs. HY. B. HARRIS.
Mrs. ALEX. HALVERSON.
Miss MARGARET BAYS.
Mr. BRUCE ISMAY.
Mr. and Mrs. ED. KIMBERLEY.
Mr. F. A. KENNYMAN.
Miss EMILE KENCHEN.
Miss G. F. LONGLEY.
Mrs. A. F. LEADER.
Miss BERTHA LAVORY.
Mrs. ERNEST LIVES.
Miss MARY CLINES.
Mrs. SINGRID LINDSTROM.
Mr. GUSTAVE J. LESNEUR.
Miss GIORGETTA A. MADILL.
Mme. MELICARD.
Mrs. TUCKER and maid.
Mrs. J. B. THAYER.
Mr. J. B. THAYER, Jr.
Mr. HENRY WOOLMER.
Miss ANNA WARD.
Mr. RICHARD M. WILLIAMS.
Mrs. F. M. WARNER.
Miss HELEN A. WILSON.
Miss WILLARD.
Miss MARY WICKS.
Mrs. GEO. D. WIDENER and maid.
Mrs. J. STEWART WHITE.
Miss MARIE YOUNG.
Mrs. THOMAS POTTER, Jr.
Mrs. EDNA S. ROBERTS.
Countess of ROTHES.
Mr. C. ROLMANE.
Mrs. SUSAN P. ROGERSON. (Probably Ryerson).
Miss EMILY B. ROGERSON.
Mrs. ARTHUR ROGERSON.
Master ALLISON and nurse.
Miss K. T. ANDREWS.
Miss NINETTE PANHART.
Miss E. W. ALLEN.
Mr. and Mrs. D. BISHOP.
Mr. H. BLANK.
Miss A. BASSINA.
Mrs. JAMES BAXTER.
Mr. GEORGE A. BAYTON
Miss C. BONNELL.
Mrs. J. M. BROWN.
Miss G. C. BOWEN.
Mr. and Mrs. R. L. BECKWITH
Miss RUTH TAUSSIG.
Miss ELLA THOR.
Mr. and Mrs. E. Z. TAYLOR.
GILBERT M. TUCKER.
Mr. J. B. THAYER.
Mr. JOHN B. ROGERSON.
Mrs. M. ROTHSCHILD.
Miss MADELEINE NEWELL.
Mrs. MARJORIE NEWELL.
HELEN W. NEWSOM.
Mr. FIENNAD OMOND.
Mr. E. C. OSTBY.
Miss HELEN R. OSTBY.
Mrs. MAMAM J. RENAGO.
Mlle. OLIVIA.
Mrs. D. W. MERVIN.
Mr. PHILIP EMOCK.
Mr. JAMES GOOGHT.
Miss RUBERTA MAIMY.
Mr. PIERRE MARECHAL.
Mrs. W. E. MINEHAN.
Miss APPIE RANELT.
Major ARTUR PEUCHEN.
Mrs. KARL H. BEHR.
Miss DESSETTE.
Mrs. WILLIAM BUCKNELL.
Mrs. O. H. BARKWORTH.
Mrs. H. B. STEFFASON.
Mrs. ELSIE BOWERMAN.

The Marconi station reports that it missed the word after "Mrs. Jacob P." In a list received by the Associated Press this morning this name appeared well down, but in THE TIMES list it is first, suggesting that the name of Mrs. John Jacob Astor is intended. This supposition is strengthened by the fact that, except for Mrs. H. J. Allison, Mrs. Astor is the only lady in the "A" column of the ship's pasenger list attended by a maid.

NAMES PICKED UP AT BOSTON.

BOSTON, April 15.—Among the names of survivors of the Titanic picked up by wireless from the steamer Carpathia here to-night were the following:

Mr. and Mrs. L. HENRY.
Mrs. W. A. HOOPER.
Mr. MILE.
Mr. J. FLYNN.
Miss ALICE FORTUNE.
Mrs. ROBERT DOUGLAS.
Miss HILDA SLAYTER.
Mrs. P. SMITH.
Mrs. BRAHAM.
Miss LUCILLE CARTER.
Mr. WILLIAM CARTER.
Miss CUMMINGS.
Mrs. FLORENCE MARE.
Miss ALICE PHILLIPS.
Mrs. PAULA MUNGE.
Mrs. JANE ———
Miss PHYLLIS O. ———
HOWARD B. CASE.
Miss MINEHAN.
Miss BERTHA ———

Biggest Liner Plunges to the Bottom at 2:20 A. M.

RESCUERS THERE TOO LATE

Except to Pick Up the Few Hundreds Who Took to the Lifeboats.

WOMEN AND CHILDREN FIRST

Cunarder Carpathia Rushing to New York with the Survivors.

SEA SEARCH FOR OTHERS

The California Stands By on Chance of Picking Up Other Boats or Rafts.

OLYMPIC SENDS THE NEWS

Only Ship to Flash Wireless Messages to Shore After the Disaster.

LATER REPORT SAVES 866.

BOSTON, April 15.—A wireless message picked up late to-night, relayed from the Olympic, says that the Carpathia is on her way to New York with 866 passengers from the steamer Titanic aboard. They are mostly women and children, the message said, and it concluded: "Grave fears are felt for the safety of the balance of the passengers and crew."

Special to The New York Times.

CAPE RACE, N. F., April 15.—The White Star liner Olympic reports by wireless this evening that the Cunarder Carpathia reached, at daybreak this morning, the position from which wireless calls for help were sent out last night by the Titanic after her collision with an iceberg. The Carpathia found only the lifeboats and the wreckage of what had been the biggest steamship afloat.

The Titanic had foundered at about 2:20 A. M., in latitude 41:16 north and longitude 50:14 west. This is about 30 minutes of latitude, or about 34 miles, due south of the position at which she struck the iceberg. All her boats are accounted for and about 655 souls have been saved of the crew and passengers, most of the latter presumably women and children.

There were about 2,100 persons aboard the Titanic.

The Leyland liner California is remaining and searching the position of the disaster, while the Carpathia is returning to New York with the survivors.

It can be positively stated that up to 11 o'clock to-night nothing whatever had been received at or heard by the Marconi station here to the effect that the Parisian, Virginian or any other ships had picked up any survivors, other than those picked up by the Carpathia.

First News of the Disaster.

The first news of the disaster to the Titanic was received by the Marconi wireless station here at 10:25 o'clock last night [as told in yesterday's New York Times.] The Titanic was first heard giving the distress signal "C. Q. D.," which was answered by a number of ships, including the Carpathia,

"All the News That's Fit to Print."

The New York Times.

THE WEATHER
Local showers today; Tuesday, fair; fresh, shifting winds, becoming northwest.
For full weather report see Page 17.

VOL. LXIII...NO. 20,610. NEW YORK, MONDAY, JUNE 29, 1914.—EIGHTEEN PAGES. ONE CENT In Greater New York, Jersey City and Newark. | Elsewhere TWO CENTS.

HEIR TO AUSTRIA'S THRONE IS SLAIN WITH HIS WIFE BY A BOSNIAN YOUTH TO AVENGE SEIZURE OF HIS COUNTRY

CALIFORNIA GOES ON ROCKS IN FOG

Tory Island, Off Northwest Irish Coast, Scene of Mishap to Anchor Liner.

IN NO IMMEDIATE DANGER

Bows Badly Stove In and Ship Taking Water Through Two Holes in Hold.

PASSENGERS STILL ABOARD

Ship Carries 1,000 Persons—Rescue Vessels, Called by Wireless, Standing By Throughout Night.

Special Cable to THE NEW YORK TIMES.

LONDON, June 28.—The Anchor liner California, with more than 1,000 persons aboard, has gone ashore on Tory Island, off the northern coast of Ireland. The destroyer Swift, the fastest and largest vessel of her class in the world, and other vessels have gone to her assistance in response to wireless calls for aid.

The ship is said to be in no immediate danger.

LONDONDERRY, June 28.—In a thick fog and rain which rendered Tory Island invisible from the mainland, the Anchor Line steamer California, bound from New York for Glasgow, went ashore tonight on the rocks off that island. Wireless calls for help brought speedy assistance from a number of small gunboats and torpedo boats which were patrolling the Northwest Irish Coast for gun runners in connection with the Ulster movement.

The latest news received here is that the California is stuck fast on the rocks, but is in no immediate danger. She struck with such force that the lower part of her bows was badly stove in, and she is making water through two holes in her forehold and second hold.

The steamer, which has on board 121 saloon and more than 300 second cabin passengers, lies in five fathoms of water forward and seven fathoms aft.

The passengers and crew are still on board. There was no panic when she struck the rocks.

Several steamers, including one liner, and the gunboats are standing by, and other vessels are expected to arrive at the scene during the night.

LONDON, June 28.—Capt. Coverley of the California late tonight sent out this wireless dispatch:

"Ran ashore in fog about half mile from the lighthouse. Di dnot hear foghorn. Sea quiet. Three men-of-war and steamer Cassandra standing by to transfer passengers."

CARRIED 841 PASSENGERS.

Place Where California Struck Ten Miles Out of Her Course.

The California sailed from New York at noon on Saturday, June 20, for Glasgow via Moville with 116 first-class, 350 second-class, and 375 third-class passengers. She signaled Malin Head yesterday afternoon, and should have been off Moville about 8 o'clock. Tory Island is more than ten miles out of her course.

The California carried a crew of 240 officers and men, and was commanded by J. A. Coverley, one of the most experienced Captains in the Anchor Line service. This was his second voyage on the California after having been twelve years on the Calabria in the New York-Mediterranean service, and more recently in command of the liner Elysia in the Indian service of the Anchor Line.

The California is the second largest vessel of the Anchor Line in the New York trade, and was built at Glasgow by D. & W. Henderson Bros. in 1907. She is 470 feet long, with a beam of 58 feet 2 inches and a depth of hold of 23 feet 6 inches. She is a twin-screw steamer, with an average speed of 15 knots.

The Captains and other officers of the Anchor Line are accustomed to fog around the coasts of Scotland and Ireland and always keep a man on the lookout on the foc'sle head, as well as in the crow's nest, and the officers are on double watches nearing the land, which means that there are three on the bridge all the time in addition to the commander, who comes up and stays while the fog lasts.

The stormy, rocky coast of the North of Ireland is looked upon by mariners as the most dangerous part of the British Isles, and steamers proceed very cautiously when entering or leaving Lough Foyle, where the small calling port of Moville is situated.

This is the third steamship within two weeks that has gone ashore during a fog in those waters. The hospital ship Maine was wrecked on the west coast of Scotland. Her patients and crew were taken off in small boats. She became a total wreck. The liner Buelow of the North German Lloyd on her way up the English Channel to Bremen from China went ashore near Portland. She landed passengers and cargo.

The fog was also responsible for three collisions, beginning with the one between the Empress of Ireland and the Storstad in the St. Lawrence River, in which 1,019 lives were lost. Another took place in the English Channel off Portsmouth between the North German Lloyd liner Kaiser Wilhelm II. and the Johnston Line steamer Incemore, and 100 miles east of Sandy Hook on June 3 a collision occurred between the American liner New York and the Hamburg-American steamer Pretoria.

Capt. Kinnard of the Cameronia, a sister ship of the California in the Anchor Line service, was found last night on board his ship, which is laid up for overhauling at Robbins's Dry Dock in the Erie Basin.

"The California was a good, strong ship," he said, "and unless she is badly on the reef there will be hope of getting her off safely. At Tory Island

Continued on Page 2.

STAYS IN AIR 21 HOURS.

Berlin Aviator's Feat Held to be a World's Record.

BERLIN, June 28.—Herr Landmann, an aviator, today concluded a non-stop flight of 21 hours 49 minutes.

It is asserted that this flight constitutes a world record.

DEWEY IN CANAL PARADE.

Will Be Invited to Make Trip Aboard His Old Flagship Olympia.

Special to The New York Times.

WASHINGTON, June 28.—Admiral George Dewey may take his old flagship, the Olympia, through the Panama Canal next March in the naval parade. Rear Admiral Clark, retired, has been ordered to take command of his old ship, the Oregon, for the occasion, and Secretary Daniels said this afternoon that he had decided to invite Admiral Dewey to take part. If the Admiral does not feel like making the journey via the canal, he may go overland to San Francisco and go aboard the Olympia upon the arrival of the pageant fleet there.

The President and Secretary Daniels will make addresses upon the arrival of the fleet at the exposition city. It is likely that Admiral Dewey and Admiral Clark also will speak. The entire brigade of midshipmen will be taken to San Francisco for the occasion. This will probably take the place of their annual cruise.

The Oregon and the Olympia will be moored at a specially constructed wharf and will be on exhibition throughout the entire exposition. Behind them will be anchored seven typical modern naval ships—a dreadnought of the New York or Oklahoma type, a battleship of the Connecticut or Minnesota type, an armored cruiser of the Tennessee or Montana type, one of the three scout cruisers, a destroyer, a submarine, and a collier, each of the latest build. In addition, the entire Atlantic Fleet will remain throughout nearly the whole of the exposition.

Neither Admiral Dewey nor Rear Admiral Clark has been aboard his ship since relinquishing their commands shortly after the close of the Spanish-American war.

A NEW GAME FOR BROADWAY.

But Auto Owners Hope Trundling Stolen Tires Won't Become Popular.

Harry E. Sullivan with his brother and two women rode up to Shanley's Restaurant, in West Forty-third Street, last evening in a limousine auto with a new white tire strapped like a life preserver to the back. Two men who had the appearance of chauffeurs came down the street after the owners of the auto entered the restaurant. With businesslike briskness they unbuckled the new white tire and trundled it down the street. The taxicab starter at Shanley's scratched his head. Then he spoke to Patrolman Louis Fick.

"They did it so natural," he explained, "that I didn't think to bother them."

The patrolman jumped into an auto and started in pursuit of the tire. By its tread-prints on the damp pavement he followed it down to Ninth Avenue, up to Forty-fourth Street, around the corner, and there the artful dodgers foiled him by rolling it into the street where its trail was lost in a maze of tire tracks. The tire was worth $75.

"If it's as easy as that," said Mr. Sullivan when he heard of his loss, "rolling rubber hoops in Broadway is apt to become a popular pastime. The first rule of the game is: 'A rolling tire must gather no moss.'"

SCORES BRYAN AND TREATY.

Francis B. Loomis Calls Colombian Agreement "Stupendous Blunder."

Special to The New York Times.

SAN FRANCISCO, June 28.—Bryan's proposed treaty between the United States and Colombia is vicious as to motives and purpose, says Francis B. Loomis, former Assistant Secretary of State. In a statement here tonight Mr. Loomis said:

"Bryan's Colombian treaty is a covert attempt to loot the United States Treasury by lobbyists and political brigands, into whose hands the Secretary of State is playing.

"Bryan and the President are trying to besmirch and discredit the achievement of the previous Administration, which made the canal a reality.

"The treaty is one of the most stupendous blunders made by Bryan, who is running wild with his 'world peace' theories. The United States owes Colombia nothing, either by treaty or otherwise.

"Mr. Bryan's contention that the people of Latin America feel aggrieved because we refuse to permit the Colombian troops to cross the Isthmus for the purpose of engaging in bloody encounters, and closing the lines of transit is not supported by ascertainable facts. The truth is the important Governments of South America such as Argentina, Brazil, and Chile care nothing about Colombia, and they deplore her misdeeds as much as we do."

STATE'S TOLL OF ACCIDENTS

Automobiles Killed Nearly Half as Many as Railroads in April.

Special to The New York Times.

ALBANY, June 28.—There were nearly half as many deaths in New York State from automobile accidents during April as there were from railroad accidents. This is shown in the vital statistics issued by the State Department of Health for April. The deaths resulting from railroad accidents numbered 58, from automobiles 25, from street cars 15, and other vehicles 20. Landslides killed 12 individuals, and 3 others died from injuries inflicted by animals. There were 128 suicides during the month and 35 homicides.

The other external causes of death ran the total up to 735 for the month.

$120,000 FOR SHACKLETON.

Sir James Caird's Gift for His Antarctic Expedition.

Special Cable to THE NEW YORK TIMES.

LONDON, June 28.—Sir James Key Caird, the millionaire jute manufacturer of Dundee, has given $120,000 toward the expenses of the Shackleton antarctic expedition.

Sir James made the gift after Sir Ernest Shackleton had personally explained to him the programme which he hoped to carry out.

Sir Ernest says the gift puts the expedition on a sound basis, and there is now no fear that it will not start well equipped.

FEDERALS DESERT AGUASCALIENTES

Next Big Town South of Zacatecas Is Evacuated by Huerta's Forces.

CARRANZA-HUERTA DEAL?

American, Reaching Vera Cruz, Reports Parleys Are On in Mexican Capital.

ENVOYS TOLD OF REBEL NOTE

Says He Must Consult His Associates—Answer Is Regarded as Favorable.

ZACATECAS, June 27, via EL PASO, June 28.—Aguascalientes, capital of the States of the same name, has been evacuated by the Federals, according to information reaching Gen. Villa's headquarters today.

Owing to this, his plan of campaign has been changed, and the troops of the division are returning to Torreon.

Part of the division left last night. The rest will leave for the north today. Gen. Villa will follow his troops during the day. Last Wednesday it was announced that the Villa troops would be taken toward Aguas Calientes overland.

Late reports show that the losses of the Federals here were much greater than at first supposed. The number of prisoners taken by Villa's troops exceed 4,300. The number of killed was close to that figure.

The latest casualty report of the Constitutionalists was over 700 dead and 1,100 wounded, but these figures are not complete.

Special to The New York Times.

EL PASO, June 28.—A message was received today stating that 2,000 Federals, fleeing from Zacatecas toward San Luis Potosi, had been overtaken by Gen. Benavide, head of the Zaragoza brigade, and had been decisively defeated at Salinas, a point about midway between Zacatecas and San Luis Potosi. Four hundred Federals were killed or wounded, according to the message.

CARRANZA-HUERTA DEAL?

Report of Peace Negotiations Comes from Mexico City.

VERA CRUZ, June 28.—Secret peace negotiations between Gen. Carranza and President Huerta have been in progress in the capital, according to Antonio Magnon, an American who arrived from Mexico City today. Mr. Magnon said it was positively known that representatives from Carranza had been in the capital for several days in conference with President Huerta, but that the details of the discussions had been kept secret.

It was thought in the capital that a peace agreement between Huerta and Carranza based upon Huerta resignation, was certain to come soon, Carranza having been forced to make some concessions because of his disagreements with Gen. Villa and Gen. Angeles.

It is reported in Mexico City that supporters of Villa and Carranza have been fighting near Monterey.

Mr. Magnon said also that President Huerta's volunteer forces at San Luis Potosi, including all the noted chieftains, such as Gen. Pasquale Orozco and Gen. Antonio Rojas, had refused to cooperate further with the regular army or to withdraw toward the capital, but would fight the Constitutionalists in that region. The volunteer leaders, most of whom are veterans of the three years' border warfare, and all frontiersmen, and, according to Mr. Magnon, say that the Federal recruits are hopeless as soldiers and only hamper the actions of the veteran volunteers.

Gen. Joaquin Maass, Federal commander at San Lois Potosi, went to the capital last Friday to confer with President Huerta, Mr. Magnon said, and was still there when Magnon left Saturday. Mr. Magnon said Gen. Maass, whom he had known for years, confirmed the reported action of the volunteers.

The Federals are fortifying Aguascalientes against a Constitutionalist advance, but it is understood in the capital that Gen. Villa plans to direct his next blow against Queretaro, cutting both the National and Central Railways and compelling the abandonment by the Federal forces of much territory in order to prevent themselves from being cut off from the capital.

Mr. Magnon said that he learned at Soledad that the Federals were gathering railway equipment for the narrow gauge Inter-Oceanic Railroad and preparing for the withdrawal of Gen. Rubio Navarrete and his entire force, now stationed at the San Francisco railroad bridge, guarding it against a possible American advance.

Gen. Garcia Pena, according to Mr. Magnon, is still at Soledad, but there are many indications that the Federal forces before Vera Cruz are being rapidly reduced, and that only a thin fringe of rural guards will be left to maintain the outposts. Mr. Magnon said it was generally believed in the capital that the refusal of the volunteers to take orders from the regular officers would be a severe blow to President Huerta, as they were his most trustworthy troops.

MEDIATING POWERS VEXED?

Rumor That They Resent Mexico's Delay in Thanking Them.

Special Cable to THE NEW YORK TIMES.

MEXICO CITY, June 28.—It is rumored here that the mediating powers are somewhat offended by Mexico's delay in thanking them for their good offices, and also that they consider Gen. Huerta's recent statement to THE NEW YORK TIMES rather impolitic. It is pointed out that, whatever the fate of the peace arrangements may be, the

Continued on Page 5.

Propose Pan-American Memorial to Columbus

A splendid tomb topped by a great light is proposed to be erected in Santo Domingo, in the Caribbean Sea, by subscriptions from peoples of all lands. See NEXT SUNDAY'S TIMES.

OUR GUNS FIRE ON SANTO DOMINGO

Few Shots from the Machias Stop Bombardment of Puerto Plata by President Bordas.

WARNED BY CAPT. RUSSELL

Told Not to Endanger Foreigners in Attack on Rebels There—Refugees Taken Off by Our Boats.

Special to The New York Times.

WASHINGTON, June 28.—Following general instructions from the Navy Department to protect the lives and property of Americans and foreigners in Santo Domingo, the little American gunboat Machias on Friday afternoon entered the inner harbor of Puerto Plata, and with a few shots from her main battery silenced a battery of President Bordas's forces that was bombarding the town.

The bombardment was in violation of emphatic orders from Capt. Russell, commanding the American squadron, that the attack on the city, which is in the hands of rebels, be conducted in such a way as not to imperil the lives of foreigners.

Capt. Russell is in personal command of the first line battleship South Carolina, that was detached from service at Vera Cruz when conditions in Santo Domingo became threatening. His dispatch to the department, which, like all dispatches from Santo Domingo, took two days to come, makes no mention of casualties. His dispatch follows:

PUERTO PLATA, June 26, 1914.

This afternoon, about 5:30, when the Bordas artillery ashore fired shells into the city of Puerto Plata, the Machias anchored in the inner harbor and with some shots from her main battery stopped the artillery fire into the city, after which there was no further firing. We have the situation well in hand, and no additional vessels, either United States or foreign, will be needed to prevent the bombardment of Puerto Plata. The prompt stopping of the artillery fire into the city this afternoon will have a very reassuring effect upon the Americans and other foreigners in the city, who have recently displayed great anxiety about their protection and safety.

At 8:30 P. M. Friday the revenue cutter Algonquin took on board forty-two persons for passage to San Juan, thirty-three being Porto Ricans and nine Americans, ten men, thirteen women, and nineteen children, and then steamed for San Juan. The Clyde Line steamer Seminole, from Norfolk en route to Santo Domingo City, arrived at 3 P. M. Friday, and after delivering mail took away from Puerto Plata four persons—one French, two Spanish, and one Chinaman. The Clyde Line steamer Algonquin, en route to New York, arrived at 7 P. M. Friday and took away from Puerto Plata twenty-four persons—five Americans, thirteen British, three French, and three Cubans. These passengers were put on board the three vessels named by the South Carolina boats. RUSSELL.

The Navy Department today was emphatic that Capt. Russell's summary enforcement of his orders indicated no change in policy, and that the silencing of President Bordas's battery did not mean that American intervention on a wider scale would be undertaken. The orders had been emphatic, and the attacking forces seemed to think they could be disregarded with impunity. The United States has never indicated its sympathies as to the contending forces, though as under the treaty it was responsible for the Custom House at Puerto Plata, its obligation in this instance was clearly not to encourage attack by the Government's troops.

The Machias is a gunboat of 1,177 tons, 204 feet in length, and with 32 feet beam. Her main battery consists of eight guns of about 4-inch calibre and four smaller guns. She was formerly used by the Naval Militia of Connecticut.

Secretary of the Navy Daniels said the other day that there was no intention to send more ships to the island, and Friday's incident is not thought to have changed his mind on that score.

$500,000 FIRE AT DOVER, N. J.

Incendiaries Destroy Richardson & Boynton Stove Plant.

DOVER, N. J., June 28.—All of the plant of the Richardson & Boynton Company, except the shipping department building, was destroyed by fire today. The firm manufactured stoves and ranges, and its plant, which was Dover's largest industry, covered thirty acres of ground. The loss is $500,000, partly covered by insurance. The works, which ordinarily employ 1,100 men, were shut down three weeks ago for repairs.

Charles Helfer, a night watchman, says he made the rounds of the works at 6:30 A. M. and found everything all right. At 7:30 o'clock he saw smoke coming from the trimming shop. Men who were in the street say they saw flames in three or four different places at the same time.

Dover's two steamers and an auto chemical engine and truck manned by the Volunteer Fire Department responded to the general alarm. All the buildings were frame except the shipping building, which is built of concrete. The water pressure was inadequate, and the flames spread rapidly to the casting and cleaning shop, the mounting, boiler, patent filing, drill and patternmakers' shops, each in a separate building. Three Lackawanna Railroad box cars in the yard near the shipping building were burned. All the finished stock on hand was in the shipping building. The firemen concentrated their efforts to save that building.

For an hour or two there was fear the flames might spread to the town. The firemen successfully defended the nearest buildings.

Incendiarism is suspected. Secretary and Treasurer W. L. R. Lynd, who is also Mayor of Dover, said he couldn't account for the fire. There was no fire in any building of the plant, and the engines had been cold since the shutdown. It is recalled that a threatening letter was sent to Mayor Lynd demanding he should prevent the delivery of the Slattery anti-Catholic lectures. He declined to interfere, and the lectures were delivered on May 15 and 16 last.

The plant will be rebuilt at once. At noon a gang of laborers was put to removing the débris. The company has offices in New York.

Francis Ferdinand Shot During State Visit to Sarajevo.

TWO ATTACKS IN A DAY

Archduke Saves His Life First Time by Knocking Aside a Bomb Hurled at Auto.

SLAIN IN SECOND ATTEMPT

Lad Dashes at Car as the Royal Couple Return from Town Hall and Kills Both of Them.

LAID TO A SERVIAN PLOT

Heir Warned Not to Go to Bosnia, Where Populace Met Him with Servian Flags.

AGED EMPEROR IS STRICKEN

Shock of Tragedy Prostrates Francis Joseph—Young Assassin Proud of His Crime.

Archduke Francis Ferdinand and his Consort the Duchess of Hohenberg Slain by Assassin's Bullets.

Special Cable to THE NEW YORK TIMES.

SARAJEVO, Bosnia, June 28, (By courtesy of the Vienna Neue Freie Presse.)—Archduke Francis Ferdinand, heir to the throne of Austria-Hungary, and his wife, the Duchess of Hohenberg, were shot and killed by a Bosnian student here today. The fatal shooting was the second attempt upon the lives of the couple during the day, and is believed to have been the result of a political conspiracy.

This morning, as Archduke Francis Ferdinand and the Duchess were driving to a reception at the Town Hall a bomb was thrown at their motor car. The Archduke pushed it off with his arm.

The bomb did not explode until after the Archduke's car had passed on, and the occupants of the next car, Count von Boos-Waldeck and Col. Morizzi, the Archduke's aide de camp, were slightly injured. Among the spectators, six persons were more or less seriously hurt.

The author of the attempt at assassination was a compositor named Gabrinovics, who comes from Trebinje.

After the attempt upon his life the Archduke ordered his car to halt, and after he found out what had happened he drove to the Town Hall, where the Town Councillors, with the Mayor at their head, awaited him. The Mayor was about to begin his address of welcome, when the Archduke interrupted him angrily, saying:

"Herr Burgermeister, it is perfectly outrageous! We have come to Sarajevo on a visit and have had a bomb thrown at us."

The Archduke paused a moment, and then said: "Now you may go on."

Thereupon the Mayor delivered his address and the Archduke made a suitable reply.

The public by this time had heard of the bomb attempt, and burst into the hall with loud cries of "Zivio!" the Slav word for "hurrah."

After going around the Town Hall, which took half an hour, the Archduke started for the Garrison Hospital to visit Col. Morizzi, who had been taken there after the outrage.

As the Archduke reached the corner of Rudolf Street two pistol shots were fired in quick succession by an individual who called himself Gavrio Princip. The first shot struck the Duchess in the abdomen, while the second hit the Archduke in the neck and pierced the jugular vein. The Duchess became unconscious immediately and fell across the knees of her husband. The Archduke also lost consciousness in a few seconds.

The motor car in which they were seated drove straight to the Konak, where an army Surgeon rendered first aid, but in vain. Neither the Archduke nor the Duchess gave any sign of life, and the head of the hospital could only certify they were both dead.

The authors of both attacks upon the Archduke are born Bosnians. Gabrinovics is a compositor, and worked for a few weeks in the Government printing works at Belgrade. He returned to Sarajevo a Servian chauvinist, and made no concealment of his sympathies with the King of Servia. Both he and the actual murderer of the Archduke and the Duchess expressed themselves to the police in the most cynical fashion about their crimes.

ARCHDUKE IGNORED WARNING.

Servian Minister Feared Trouble if Heir Went to Bosnia.

Special Cable to THE NEW YORK TIMES. [Dispatch to The London Daily Mail.]

VIENNA, June 28.—When the news of the assassination of the Archduke Francis Ferdinand and the Duchess was broken to the aged Emperor Francis Joseph he said: "Horrible, horrible! No sorrow is spared me."

The Emperor, who yesterday left here for Ischl, his favorite Summer resort, amid acclamations of the people, will return to Vienna at once, in spite of the hardships of the journey in the terrible heat.

The Archduke, who was created head of the army, went to Bosnia to represent the Emperor at the grand manoeuvres there. This was the first time the Archduke had paid an official visit to Bosnia. The Emperor visited the provinces immediately after their annexation, in 1908, and the manner in which he mixed freely with the people was much criticised at the time, as those in his party were always afraid lest some Slav or Mohammedan fanatic might attempt the monarch's life. The Emperor's popularity, however, saved him from all danger of this kind.

Before the Archduke went to Bosnia last Wednesday the Servian Minister here expressed doubt as to the wisdom of the journey, saying the country was in a very turbulent condition and the Servian part of the population might organize a demonstration against the Archduke. The Minister said if the Archduke went himself he certainly ought to leave his wife at home, because Bosnia was no place for a woman in its present disturbed state.

The Minister's word proved correct. The people of Sarajevo welcomed the Archduke with a display of Servian flags, and the authorities had some difficulty in removing them before the Archduke made his state entry into the city yesterday, after the conclusion of the manoeuvres. In these manoeuvres were the famous Fifteenth and Sixteenth Army Corps, which were stationed on the frontier throughout the recent Balkan war, and they carried out the evolutions before the Archduke.

Greeted with Cheers.

The details of the tragedy, as received in Vienna, were as follows: The Archduke was driving in a motor car toward the Town Hall in Sarajevo, with the Duchess of Hohenberg by his side. A large crowd assembled to watch them go by. The Archduke, raising his hand to his military cap, acknowledged the cheers, while the Duchess was smiling and bowing, her pretty face framed by her blonde hair.

Suddenly the Archduke's sharp eye caught sight of a bomb hurling through the air. His first thought was for his wife, and he threw up his arm in time to catch the bomb, which thus was turned aside from its course and fell on the pavement and exploded. The Archduke's motor car hastened on its way, its occupants unharmed, but the two Adjutants who were seated in the next motor car were injured by splinters from the bomb. Several persons on the pavement were very seriously hurt by the explosion of the bomb, which was thrown by a young man named Tabrinovitch, (Gabrinovics,) who is a typist from Trebenje, in Herzegovina, and is of Servian nationality. He was arrested some twenty minutes later.

The Archduke and his wife left the Town Hall, intending to visit those who had been injured by the bomb, when a schoolboy 19 years old, named Prinzip, who came from Grahovo, fired a shot at the Archduke's head. The boy fired from the shelter of a projecting house.

Wore Bullet-Proof Coat.

The boy must have been carefully instructed in his part, for it was a well-guarded secret that the Archduke always wore a coat of silk strands which were woven obliquely, so that no weapon or bullet could pierce it. I once saw a strip of this fabric used for a motor-car tire, and it was puncture-proof. This new invention enabled the Archduke to brave attempts on his life, but his head naturally was uncovered.

The Duchess was shot in the body. The boy fired several times, but only two shots took effect. The Archduke and his wife were carried to the Konak, or palace, in a dying condition.

Later details show that the assassin darted forth from his hiding place behind a house and actually got on the motor car in which the Archduke and his wife were sitting. He took close aim first at the Archduke, and then at the Duchess. The fact that no one stopped him, and that he was allowed to perpetrate the dastardly act indicate that the conspiracy was carefully planned and that the Archduke fell a victim to a political plot. The aspiration of the Servian population in Bosnia to join with Servia and form a great Servian kingdom is well known. No doubt today's assassination was regarded as a means of forwarding this plan.

Break News to Children.

The Archduke's children are at Glumex, in Bohemia, and relatives already have left Vienna to break the news to them. The Duke of Cumberland motored to Ischl immediately upon receipt of the news and was received by the Emperor, who will arrive in Vienna at 6 o'clock tomorrow. The bodies of the Archduke and his wife will not be brought to Vienna until tomorrow a week.

The Archduke Charles Francis Joseph, the new heir to the throne, is at Reichenau, near Vienna, with his wife, Princess Zita of Parma, and their little son and daughter. He is expected in Vienna tonight.

When the first news of the assassination became known in Vienna, early this afternoon, crowds collected in solemn silence and discussed the report, which was not credited at first. Every one connected with the press was stormed by crowds asking whether confirmation had been received, and on hearing the truth they said, "How awful!" and then dispersed, to go about their ordinary business or pleasure. The newspapers are getting out extra editions, and the whole city talks of nothing else.

New Heir Popular.

The Archduke Charles Francis Joseph, who is now heir to the throne, always has enjoyed great popularity. He was trained for the throne from the first, although he was kept somewhat in the background, being sent to country garrisons. He was not allowed to undertake to act as the representative of the Duchy of Vienna to as great an extent as the Viennese would have wished. This, however, did not detract from his popularity, while the Princess Zita, his wife, won all hearts before she married the heir to the throne, and the birth of a son two years ago completed her popularity, if, indeed, anything was lacking.

General opinion here connects the assassins with the Servian faction, and it is feared that it will lead to serious complications with that unruly kingdom, and may have far-reaching results. The future of the empire is a subject of general discussion. It is felt that the Servians have been treated too leniently, and some hard words are being said about the present foreign policy.

All the public buildings are draped in long black streamers and the flags are all at half-mast.

BRAVERY OF ARCHDUKE.

Gave First Aid to Those Wounded by the Bomb.

SARAJEVO, Bosnia, June 28.—Archduke Francis Ferdinand, heir to the Austro-Hungarian throne, and the Duchess of Hohenberg, his morganatic wife, were shot dead in the main street of the Bosnian capital by a student today while they were making an apparently triumphant progress through the city on their annual visit to the annexed provinces of Bosnia and Herzegovina.

The Archduke was hit full in the face and the Duchess was shot through the abdomen and throat. Their wounds proved fatal within a few minutes after they reached the palace, whence they were hurried with all speed.

Those responsible for the assassination took care that it would prove effective, as there were two assailants, the first armed with a bomb and the other with a revolver. The bomb was thrown at the royal automobile as it was proceeding to the Town Hall, where a reception was to be held, but the Archduke saw the deadly missile coming and warded it off with his arm. It fell outside the car and exploded, slightly wounding two aids de camp in a second car, and half a dozen spectators.

It was on the return of the procession that the tragedy was added to the long list of those that have darkened the pages of the recent history of the Hapsburgs.

As the royal automobile reached a prominent point in the route to the palace, an eighth grade student, Gavrio Prinzip, sprang out of the crowd and poured a fusillade of bullets from an automatic pistol at the Archduke and the Duchess. Both fell mortally wounded.

Prinzip and a fellow-conspirator, a compositor from Trebinje, Nedeljo Gabrinovics, barely escaped lynching by the infuriated spectators and were finally seized by the police, who afforded them protection. Both men are natives of the annexed province of Herzegovina.

Wards Off the Bomb.

The first attempt against the Archduke occurred just outside the Girls' High School. The Archduke's car had restarted after a brief pause for an inspection of the building, when Gabrinovics hurled the bomb. This was so successfully warded off by the Archduke that it fell directly beneath the following car, the occupants of which, Count von Boos-Waldeck and Col. Merizzo, were struck by splinters of iron.

Archduke Francis Ferdinand stopped his car, and after making inquiries as to the injuries of his aids and lending what aid he could, continued his journey to the Town Hall. There the Mayor began the customary address, but the Archduke sharply interrupted and snapped out, "Herr Burgomeister, we have come here to pay you a visit and bombs have been thrown at us. This is altogether an amazing indignity."

After a pause, the Archduke said: "Now you may speak."

On leaving the hall the Archduke and his wife announced their intention of visiting the wounded members of their suite at the hospital on their way back to the palace. They were actually bound on their mission of mercy when, at the corner of Rudolf Street and Franz Josef Street, Prinzip opened his deadly fusillade.

A bullet struck the Archduke in the face. The Duchess was wounded in the abdomen and another bullet struck her in the throat, severing an artery. She fell unconscious across her husband's knees. At the same moment the Archduke sank to the floor of the car.

Plunges Into River.

After his unsuccessful attempt to blow up the imperial visitors Gabrinovics sprang into the River Miljachka in an effort to escape, but witnesses plunged after him and seized him.

A few yards from the scene of the shooting an unexploded bomb was found.

"All the News That's Fit to Print."

The New York Times.

THE WEATHER
Partly cloudy, showers this morning; Tuesday, fair; moderate west to northwest winds.
For full weather report see Page 15.

VOL. LXIII...NO. 20,645. NEW YORK, MONDAY, AUGUST 3, 1914.—SIXTEEN PAGES. ONE CENT In Greater New York, Jersey City and Newark. | Elsewhere TWO CENTS.

RUSSIA INVADES GERMANY; GERMANY INVADES FRANCE, BUT DOES NOT DECLARE WAR; ENGLAND'S DECISION TODAY; BELGIUM MENACED, LUXEMBURG AND SWITZERLAND INVADED; GERMAN MARKSMEN SHOOT DOWN A FRENCH AEROPLANE

England Is Holding Back Though Germany Is Seizing Her Ships.

CABINET IN NIGHT SESSION

Believed to Have Reached Final Decision, Which Will Be Announced Today.

SEEK $250,000,000 WAR LOAN

Demand for Funds Likely to be Laid Before Parliament at Once.

CALL OUT NAVAL RESERVES

Britain's Territorial Troops Hurrying to Camps—Kitchener Gives Up Trip Abroad.

TRAP THREE GERMAN SPIES

Kaiser's High Sea Fleet Rushes Through Kiel Canal and Begins Holding Up English Vessels.

Special Cable to THE NEW YORK TIMES.

LONDON, Monday, Aug. 3.—A fateful Cabinet council wherein England's part in the Armageddon was to have been decided began at 6:30 o'clock last night and finished at 8:15. An earlier one had met at 11 A. M. and sat until 1:55 P. M. At the second meeting, though no official statement was issued, it was indicated that Great Britain was still not involved.

The Cabinet will meet again, it was announced, this, Monday, morning, and Premier Asquith will make an announcement of England's position in the House of Commons.

Toward midnight a report was issued that the Government would apply to Parliament for a war loan of $250,000,000.

The swiftness and apparent success of the German plans have created surprise even in quarters where the efficiency and thoroughness of the German General Staff's preparations are most clearly realized.

All local trains have been held up for many hours by Government operations on the railroads.

The British Government has established a censorship on all dispatches going out of the country, even cablegrams.

Belgium an Issue.

The question of the neutrality of Luxemburg and Belgium will be found to have played a most important part in shaping the policy of the British Government in the present crisis. Only last Friday the British Ambassadors in Paris and Berlin were instructed to ask the French and German Governments, respectively, whether they would respect Belgian neutrality in the event of war.

The French Government immediately declared that it would respect Belgian neutrality, and the French Minister in Brussels was instructed to give assurances to that effect to the Belgian Government.

In behalf of the German Government Dr. von Jagow, the Foreign Secretary, replied to Edward Goschen, British Ambassador to Berlin, that he was unable to say whether Germany would respect Belgian neutrality, adding that assurances on this point would prejudice Germany from a military standpoint.

Lord Kitchener, who was to have started for Egypt tomorrow, has postponed his departure. Events have moved so rapidly that his journey across France and thence by a British cruiser to Egypt is no longer considered practicable. A different route may be taken later in the week, unless, indeed, Lord Kitchener's services are required in the meantime for purposes other than those originally intended.

Die Cast, Says London Times.

The London Times says today in an editorial:

"The die is cast. The great European struggle, which the nations have so long struggled to avert, is begun.

"Germany declared war upon Russia on Saturday evening, and yesterday her troops entered Luxemburg, crossed the French frontier from Lorraine without any declaration at all. It is idle to dwell upon events such as these. They speak for themselves in a fashion which all understand.

"They mean that Europe will be the scene of the most terrible war she has witnessed since the fall of the Roman Empire. The losses of human life and the accumulated wealth of generations which such a contest must involve are frightful to think of.

"That it should come about despite the zealous efforts of diplomacy and against the wishes of almost all the nations whom it is destined to affect is a grim satire upon the professions of peace yet fresh upon the lips of those who have plunged the Continent into its miseries and calamities.

"The blame must fall mainly upon Germany. She could have stayed the plague had she chosen to speak to Vienna as she speaks when she is in earnest.

"She has not chosen to do so. She preferred to make demands upon St. Petersburg and Paris which no Government could entertain and defeat the last efforts of this country and others for mediation. By irrevocable acts she has lived up to the worst principles of the Frederican tradition, which disregards all obligations of right or wrong at the bidding of immediate self-interest.

Violation of Traditions.

"She believes her admirable military organization has enabled her to steal a march upon her rivals. She has been mobilizing in all but the name while their mobilization was retarded by conversations. She continued until her moment had come, then she flung the mask aside while her Ambassador was still in Paris. While by customs traditional among all civilized peoples she was still at peace with France she sent soldiers into Luxemburg and invaded the territory of the republic.

It is hard to say which of these acts was the grosser. In the infringement of public right with Luxemburg she makes no pretense of a quarrel. She herself was party to the guarantee of its neutrality contained in the treaty of 1867. The other guarantors are Great Britain, France, Russia, Italy, Austria-Hungary, Belgium, and Netherlands. She solemnly pledged herself with some of them, including France and ourselves, to respect this neutrality.

How Germany Keeps Her Word.

"The world sees how Germany keeps her word. She has been weak enough, or cynical en. ugh, to issue an explanation of her breach of faith. Let Englishmen who have been disposed to trust her judge it for themesvles. She has not, she says, committed a hostile act by crossing the frontiers, by forcibly seizing Government offices, and by forcibly interrupting telephonic communication. These are merely measures to protect the railways from possible attack by the French. For her sudden invasion of France no excuse has as yet been

Continued on Page 2.

Switzerland Now Invaded by Germans, Basle Seized

Special Cable to THE NEW YORK TIMES.

LONDON, Monday, Aug. 3.—A Daily Telegraph dispatch from Paris says:

"Simultaneously with the invasion of Luxemburg the German Army has invaded Switzerland and occupied the Swiss station of Basle.

"Basle contains two stations, one German and one Swiss. Basle is now entirely in the hands of the Germany Army."

Basle is the great railway centre of Switzerland. Important railways run northward from it through the western edge of Germany, some diverging into France. The Germans have seized it, probably because as the terminus of these railways it is important to their control and management.

Ultimatum to Belgium, Must Aid German Troops

LONDON, Aug. 3.—Germany has sent an ultimatum to Belgium in which she offers an entente provided Belgium facilitates the movements of German troops.

TREASURE SHIP HEADS FOR A GERMAN PORT

Kronprinzessin Cecilie, With $10,600,000 Gold for London and Paris, Headed for Home.

Special Cable to THE NEW YORK TIMES.

LONDON, Aug. 2.—The Kronprinzessin Cecilie signaled by wireless off Malin head at 4:15 o'clock this morning. At first it was supposed that she might have turned back to New York. A message, however, shows that she is taking the northern route.

LONDON, Aug. 2.—The North German Lloyd steamship Kronprinzessin Cecilie signaled by wireless to Malin Head at 4:15 o'clock this morning. The position of the vessel was not ascertained.

Malin Head is the northernmost point of Ireland. The Kronprinzessin Cecilie left New York last week for Bremen by way of Plymouth and Cherbourg. She has on board a large amount of gold. In ordinary circumstances she would have communicated first with the Fastnet station, off the southern coast of Ireland.

It is believed, therefore, that the vessel is skirting the north of the British Isles with the intention of entering the North Sea and making her way direct to some German port.

There was a rumor afloat last night of the Kronprinzessin Cecilie being captured by British men-of-war. Nothing of this nature had been heard at the agent's office.

When told the Kronprinzessin Cecilie had been reported going around the north coast of Ireland, though she was to have gone to Plymouth and Cherbourg, Mr. Von Helmuth simply said the situation may have changed in international relations since she left this country.

The Kronprinzessin Cecilie sailed from New York at one A. M. last Tuesday for Plymouth, Cherbourg and Bremen, with 332 first, 131 second and 704 steerage passengers. In her specie room she had $10,600,000 in gold consigned to London and Paris and about 3,500 sacks of mail.

On this voyage the Kronprinzessin Cecilie, which is under the command of Capt. Charles Polack, commodore of the fleet, was to go fifty miles further north than she did on her last trip, and her course could be made still further north to cut off corners at the captain's discretion, as the ice has disappeared from the Atlantic tracks and the ice patrol ships have been withdrawn.

On her last eastward voyage the liner, which can average 23½ knots, reached Plymouth at 10 P. M. on Sunday night, and on this voyage she should have been fully two hours earlier, according to the reckoning of the line's officials here.

Under normal conditions the Kronprinzessin Cecilie, after landing passengers and mails at Plymouth, crosses to Cherbourg to land the Paris mails and passengers and then proceeds up Channel to Bremen, where she usually arrives at daybreak on Tuesday. As Plymouth and Cherbourg are both naval stations and strongly fortified, it is probable that the liner has taken the Anchor Line route, passing to the north of Ireland and will then go around the north of Scotland into the North Sea to Bremen direct.

She had only 300 tons of express freight abroad, the agent said yesterday.

ON THE FRENCH FLANKS.

Two German Armies Massing—Troops Pouring Into Luxemburg.

Special Cable to THE NEW YORK TIMES.

BRUSSELS, Monday, Aug. 3, 3:30 A. M.—The Germans are still pouring troops into Luxemburg. A force of 100,000 is already massed along the Belgian frontier opposite Dinant. Artillery and stores in trainloads are filling every railway station.

An unconfirmed report has been received that the Germans are massing another army on the French frontier at Limburg.

Should this be true, the Germans would have two armies acting on the flank of the French advance.

FRANCE AT DISADVANTAGE.

Germans May Be Numerically Superior at First, Expert Says.

Special Cable to THE NEW YORK TIMES.

LONDON, Monday, Aug. 3.—France is likely to have to bear the brunt of a superior German attack for some time, according to Col. Repington, The London Times's military expert, who considers that Russia will be unable to make herself felt for perhaps a considerable period.

Austria has not committed herself to serious operations against Servia, and may now abandon them and adopt a defensive attitude in regard to Servia and transfer the bulk of her forces to Galicia to co-operate with Germany against Russia, hampered by slow mobilization.

"In this situation," says Col. Repington, "France runs the risk for a certain period of finding herself faced by superior numbers, possibly by a superiority of 200,000 men."

Russian Forces Cross German Border at Many Points.

SEIZE RAILROAD STATION

Now Hold Eydtkuhnen, German Town on the Main Line Into Russia.

FRENCH INVASION REPORTED

Berlin Hears That Attacks from the West Have Also Been Started.

COSSACKS MAKING A DASH

Two Squadrons Are Reported Marching on Johannesburg, 15 Miles from the Border.

AVIATOR DROPPING BOMBS

Assaults on Nuremburg by French Airman Denounced in Berlin's Official Report.

Special Cable to THE NEW YORK TIMES.

BERLIN, Aug. 2.—The most memorable day in the history of modern Germany has passed. The Fatherland is engaged in war against the empire of the Czar and all but engaged in war with France. Russia began hostilities in the very first hours of yesterday morning by an attack on German soldiers going along the frontier. No formal declaration of war by Russia preceded this event.

At the very moment when THE NEW YORK TIMES correspondent is writing this dispatch, apparently official information has arrived that the French have crossed the frontier into German territory.

So if this news is confirmed there is also war with France.

Earlier in the course of the day French aviators, according to report from military sources, hurled bombs on to Bavarian railways in the vicinity of Nuremberg. Apparently they caused no damage.

In the meantime events are following upon each other with bewildering rapidity. The Russians have occupied the well-known German railway station of Eydtkuhnen, which all Americans going to Russia are acquainted with. At many other points Cossacks and other Russian troops have crossed the frontier. A Russian who tried to throw bombs from a railway train was arrested.

Mobilization Goes On.

While extra editions of the newspapers are keeping Berlin informed of these epoch-making pieces of news from hour to hour, the first day of mobilizatiton proceeds according to orders. The most indelible impression which one received was the incredible calm with which the faithful sons of the supreme War Lord rallied to the colors.

Nowhere does chauvinistic rejoicing or wild howling for war reign. Iron earnestness rules the hour.

During the entire day I have scarcely seen more soldiers than usual. The only difference was that those seen wore the new gray field uniforms, which look in the highest degree businesslike.

Germany's famous sense of military duty is showing its noblest side. Everybody went joyfully to the place long ago assigned to him. Everywhere in Berlin one finds friends and acquaintances who tomorrow, Tuesday, Wednesday, or Thursday must report to their regiments.

Crowds Out, Day and Night.

Unter den Linden and the square before the Imperial Palace is packed full of tens of thousands of people from early morning until late at night. Everybody is waiting for the Kaiser.

The most imposing of all the patriotic demonstrations was that in front of the statue of Bismarck in the Reichstag Square, where a religious service was held. The Emperor and Empress were present at the service in the Garnisonkirche (Garrison Church), and were acclaimed with wild enthusiasm.

"In the afternoon the imperial couple went out in an automobile several times along the Unter den Linden and into the Tiergarten. The enthusiasm of the people knew no bounds. The Kaiser wore an expression of the greatest gravity.

Yesterday's address by the Emperor to the people from the window of the imperial palace is looked upon primarily as an appeal to the Social Democrats. The latter seem to be ready to do their full duty as German citizens.

The Russian Advance.

BERLIN, Aug. 2.—A Russian column, with artillery, has crossed the German frontier at Schwinden, southeast of Bialla.

Two squadrons of Russian Cossacks are riding in the direction of Johannesburg, in East Prussia, fifteen miles from the frontier.

A Russian patrol last night crossed the German frontier near Eichenreid, in Posen, and attacked the German guard at the railroad bridge over the Warthe. Two Germans were slightly wounded.

This information was issued today by the imperial staff.

The staff also announced the crossing of the frontier by the Russian column near Schwinden. The above information, the staff adds, shows that Russia has invaded German territory and that war has actually begun.

A French aviator has been dropping bombs from an aeroplane in the neighborhood of Naumburg, Bavaria, according to an announcement made by the military authorities today.

In announcing the dispatch, the authorities add that this action was a crime against the rights of man, as there had been no declaration of war.

Last night a hotelkeeper in Kochem and his son tried to blow up the Prussian State railroad tunnel at Kochem. Their attempt failed and the men were shot and killed.

While a train was crossing a bridge at Thorn today a passenger tried to throw a bomb from the window of a coach, probably with the hope of destroying the bridge. He was arrested.

An official statement issued today says:

"In consequence of a Russian attack on German territory, Germany is in a state of war with Russia. The French reply to the German representation is of an unsatisfactory character.

"Moreover, France has mobilized, and an outbreak of war with France must therefore be reckoned with any day or any moment."

Another statement declares that Russia has invaded Germany in a time of peace "in flagrant contradiction of Russia's peaceful assurances."

BERLIN, via Brussels, Aug. 2.—The Russian Ambassador at Berlin has received his passports.

TOKIO, Monday, Aug. 3.—Russia has seized a German steamer at Vladivostok.

DANISH FRONTIER COVERED.

Half a German Army Corps There—Transports, Torpedo Boats Swarm.

Special Cable to THE NEW YORK TIMES.

COPENHAGEN, Monday, Aug. 3, 4 A. M.—A private telegram to The Burlingske Tidende from Kolding states that Germany is stationing half an army corps in the north of Schleswig.

A division has been detailed to occupy the neighborhood, which traps 8,000 men quartered in Hadersleben. This concentration near the Danish frontier is confirmed by another private telegram, which states also that a large fleet of German transports passed through Femern Belt this afternoon. German torpedo boats are constantly passing through the belt.

HURL MILLION MEN AT FRANCE.

Kaiser Actually Began Mobilizing Friday, Two Days Ahead of Foe.

Special Cable to THE NEW YORK TIMES.

LONDON, Aug. 3.—The German Emperor officially ordered the mobilization of the entire forces of Germany at 5:15 o'clock Sunday afternoon. Actually the mobilization began on July 31 (Friday).

The French mobilization, which was ordered at midnight Saturday, will take seven or eight days to complete, when a million men will be in the field.

The German plan of campaign is believed to be to fling almost the entire strength of the German Army, twenty-two army corps, or 1,000,000 men, upon France.

Three army corps, 125,000 men, with reserves will be left to face Russia.

First Naval Battle Opens; Cruisers Fight Off Libau

Special Cable to THE NEW YORK TIMES.

AMSTERDAM, Monday, Aug. 3.—The news has just been received here that the German cruiser Augsburg is bombarding the Russian naval port, Libau, in the Baltic.

A Russian cruiser is attacking the Augsburg.

Part of the town of Libau is said to be in flames.

This news is confirmed by a wireless report from the German cruiser to Berlin.

Two Armies of Kaiser Enter France and Begin Hostilities.

ONE SEIZES LUXEMBURG

Hundred Thousand Men Enter Duchy, Violating the Guarantee of Neutrality.

CAPITAL IN THEIR HANDS

Protests of Authorities Ignored—March Then Begun on the French Town of Longwy.

22 GERMANS SLAIN IN FIGHT

Attack of Patrol Is Beaten Off, But Cannon Firing Is Reported.

SECOND INVASION TO SOUTH

Force Said to Number 20,000—Heavy Fighting Reported and a German Repulse.

Special Cable to THE NEW YORK TIMES.

LONDON, Monday, Aug. 3.—German troops have invaded French territory at two points without issuing a declaration of war.

One of the invading forces is moving southwest from the neutral Duchy of Luxemburg, into which a large force was flung early yesterday morning.

The other movement, nearly ninety miles to the southeast, is directed almost from the heart of the provinces of Alsace-Lorraine, which Germany wrested from France in 1870.

By invading and occupying the Duchy of Luxemburg Germany struck the first serious blow of the war.

This operation opens up the famous Trou de Treves gap in the French fortified lines, which is approached by the Luxemburg Railway. About this place apprehensions were expressed by military men in France a year ago.

The German troops are now marching on the fortified French town of Longwy, which is close to the Luxemburg frontier.

Almost at the same time with the news of this aggressive movement by Germany word came of an actual violation of French territory in the vicinity of Cirey, near Nancy.

An early report said German cavalry were reconnoitring there.

Later reports said that the invading force numbered 20,000 men, and that there had already been heavy fighting on the Franco-German frontier at that point, resulting in the repulse of the Kaiser's forces.

While the story of heavy fighting was not confirmed, the French Ambassador received official word that German troops had crossed the frontier. It is believed that the advance is in force.

Twenty-two Germans Killed.

A Daily Mail dispatch from Paris, filed at 8 o'clock last night, gives these facts of various hostile encounters:

"Two officers and twenty men of a German patrol, which crossed the frontier near Longwy, were killed, and the attack was repelled.

"Germans crossed the frontier at Cirey, twenty-five miles from Nancy, last night.

"Germans fired on a customs post at Petit Croix last night.

"Zeppelins manoeuvred over French territory near Epinal.

"A German spy was shot dead by a guard at the Soissons railway bridge last night.

"M. Eyschen, Minister of State of Luxemburg, in a message to M. Viviani, the French Premier, states that thirty-five German motor cars, carrying officers, and followed by numerous detachments of cavalry, crossed the Moselle by the bridges of Wasserbillig and Remich, on the eastern border of Luxemburg. The Minister adds that he had addressed a protest to the German Emperor and the German Foreign Minister."

How Germans Seized Luxemburg.

A Daily Mail dispatch from Brussels says:

"German troops are concentrating in Lorraine near the French town of Belfort.

"It is believed that German troops are moving toward the French frontier by way of Luxemburg and Metz.

"The newspaper Patriote has received the following telegram from its correspondent at Arlon, Belgium:

"'At 3 o'clock this morning the Luxemburg Government was informed that German troops on motor cycles were approaching from Treves. The German motor cyclists raced up to the gates of the Town of Luxemburg. They dismounted and inspected the viaducts and bridges, making sure that these were intact, and examined the railway to see that the rails had not been tampered with. The Germans then rode off.

"'A fresh detachment of German officers and of men in uniform arrived shortly afterward, but departed after surveying the town through glasses.

"'The authorities immediately drew up a proclamation urging the inhabitants to remain in the railway stations, and all the public services in the capital and the Grand Duchy were taken over by the Germans.

"'At 9 A. M. five motor cars containing German officers arrived from Treves and disappeared in the direction of Longwy over the French frontier.

"'Three German military trains passed through Luxemburg today. Thirty thousand Germans are said to be between the Moselle River and the City of Luxemburg.

"'German soldiers also occupied Trois Vierges and other Grand Ducal stations.

"'Telegraphic and telephonic communication between Brussels and Luxemburg are cut.'"

Protested Vainly to Germans.

Another version of the Luxemburg invasion reached London from William Maxwell in a despatch to The Daily Telegraph from Arlon. He says: "At 7 o'clock this morning an armored train from Treves steamed into the city with 200 soldiers and officers. The engine was in the middle of the train, which consisting of three wagons. The soldiers belonged to the Twenty-ninth Regiment. The officer demanded an interview with Major Van Dyck, who commands the defensive force of the Duchy, which consists of 200 men. The Major protested verbally and in writing against the breach of neutrality. The German commander signed the protest and returned it. His men then detrained and occupied the railway.

"Other trains followed in quick succession until 40,000 troops were in the city.

"Armored trains went north toward Trois Vierges, southeast toward Thionville, and southwest toward Longwy, in order to assure communications in all directions.

"Rumor declares that the troops are already in contact, but I have reason to doubt the truth of this.

"I am just returning from the nearest German post at Steinfort. Cavalry patrols occupy the roads. As I left the Germans were sending a pigeon post.

"The Belgian troops are not yet on the frontier, but are expected tonight. There is nothing to prevent the Germans from walking through. It seems, however, that they intend to observe the neutrality of Belgium for the present."

The abstention of both Germany and France from issuing a declaration of war is probably due to the anxiety of both over Italy. If France declared war first, Italy would necessarily be forced to participate in the conflict by the terms of the Triple Alliance. If Germany declared war first, Italy could maintain that she was not bound by the treaty to support her allies.

German Challenge to England.

The occupation of Luxemburg is regarded as a direct challenge to Great Britain, which was the chief power outside of France in guaranteeing the neutrality of the Duchy by the treaty of London of 1867.

England asked Germany for a pledge that she would not violate the neutrality of Belgium, which is similarly guaranteed, but Germany refused.

Germany yesterday declared in a message to the Luxemburg authorities that the seizure of the Duchy's railways, which are part of the Prussian State system, was not a hostile act but merely a measure of precaution.

An invasion of Belgium south of Liege is expected.

A dispatch from Arlon, Belgium, says:

"According to advices received here, 100,000 German troops are crossing the Grand Duchy of Luxemburg and concentrating on the French frontier near Liege.

"Frontier engagements are reported, in which the Germans are said to have lost.

"More than 25,000 men are engaged in digging trenches in front of the German and French positions.

"The strategical line from Malmedy, in Rhenish Prussia, to Liege, is guarded by military on both the German and the Belgian sides."

Report of German Repulse.

Details of a reported second invasion of French territory are very scanty.

According to an evening newspaper published at Liege, 20,000 German troops crossed the French frontier yesterday morning near Cirey, between Nancy and Strasburg.

They encountered French forces, the report says, and were repulsed with heavy losses. This news lacks confirmation.

A dispatch from Belfort, France, says:

"A collision between French and German border patrols occurred yesterday near Belfort and at Jencheral, to the southeast. A body of German cavalry advanced to Suaree, also southeast of Belfort, and seized horses which had been requisitioned by the Mayor of the community."

Military men point out that the German Army is apparently duplicating the first movement of the Franco-Prussian war. It was on Aug. 2, 1870, forty-four years ago today, that the French and Germans clashed in the first battle of that war at Saarbrucken, where the Prince Imperial, under the orders of the Emperor, received his famous "Baptism of Fire."

France Denounces Germany.

The French Embassy here issued this statement:

"French territory has been invaded

German Troops Shoot Down French Aeroplane; Report of a German Airship Destroyed

BERLIN, Aug. 2.—German troops today fired upon and brought to earth a French aeroplane near Wesel, 140 miles from the northeastern frontier of France.

Several other hostile air craft were seen in the Rhine provinces Saturday night. One was observed flying from Keprich in the direction of Andernach, ten miles northwest of Coblenz. Others were sighted near Duere flying in the direction of Cologne.

Two aviators were killed in battle in the recent Balkan war. Both were officers of the Bulgarian Army. Capt. Popoff was killed by a shrapnel shell while flying over Adrianople in November, 1912, and a month later Dr. Jules Constantine was killed by rifle fire at Tchataldja. In February of the same year Capt. Monte of the Italian Army was wounded by the rifle fire of Arabs in Tripoli.

Aeroplanist Said to Have Wrecked an Airship

Special Cable to THE NEW YORK TIMES.

LONDON, Aug. 3.—The Standard publishes a report that the French aviator Roland Garros met and engaged a German airship in midair and destroyed it. It says the results to himself and his machine are unknown. The Standard fails to give the source of its story, and there is no foundation that in any way confirms it in responsible quarters.

The Standard reports that German and French aviators met in the air at Longwy and that the Frenchman shot the German, who fell 300 feet and was killed.

French Air Fleet Moved Up to the Border

BRUSSELS, Aug. 2.—All the French aeroplanes at Sedan are reported to have been dispatched toward Nancy, a short distance from the German border.

Persons arriving here from Cologne say that the Germans have placed rapid-fire guns on the terrace of the Hotel Hansa in that city. The travelers believe the guns are intended for use against hostile aeroplanes.

The New York Times

"All the News That's Fit to Print."

PUBLISHED EVERY DAY IN THE YEAR BY THE NEW YORK TIMES COMPANY.

ADOLPH S. OCHS, Publisher and President.
B. C. FRANCK, Secretary.

Address all communications
THE NEW YORK TIMES.
TELEPHONE 1000 BRYANT.

Publication Office............Times Square
Times Annex.......43d St., west of Broadway
Downtown..............15 Beekman Street
Wall Street...............2 Rector Street
Harlem..........263 West 125th Street
Bronx........149th St. and Bergen Av.
Brooklyn..........304 Washington Street
Staten Island.....Ferry House, St. George
Jersey City..............836 Jersey Avenue
Long Island City.......863 Jackson Avenue
Hoboken...................61 Second Street
Paterson....................13 Park Avenue
Elizabeth.................90 Broad Street
Washington.......................Post Building
Philadelphia..........Public Ledger Building
Chicago..............1,202 Tribune Building
St. Louis.........400 Globe-Democrat Building
San Francisco..................613 Call Building
Detroit......................826 Ford Building
London.................3 Pall Mall East, S. W.
Paris.................32 Rue Louis le Grand
Berlin....................60 Friedrichstrasse

ONE CENT Greater New York, Jersey City, Newark. Elsewhere Two Cents. Five Cents Sunday.

Subscription Rates—by mail, Postage Paid.
DAILY AND SUNDAY, per Week......$0.17
DAILY AND SUNDAY, per Month........0.75
DAILY AND SUNDAY, per Year..........8.50
DAILY, per Week.......................0.12
DAILY, per Month......................0.50
DAILY, per Year.......................6.00
To Foreign Addresses—Daily and Sunday, $2.00 per month; Daily, $1.50 per month.
SUNDAY, with Picture Section and Review of Books, per Year..............2.50
To Canada, per Year...................3.50
To Foreign Addresses, per Year........5.20
THE ANNALIST, per Year................4.00
THE NEW YORK TIMES BOOK REVIEW, per Year, (to Canada $1.50)....1.00
THE NEW YORK TIMES INDEX. Quarterly—Paper Cover, per Copy, $1.50; per Year, $6.00; Full Cloth, per Copy, $2.00; per Year, $8.00.

Entered as second-class mail matter.

Readers of The New York Times may have the Daily and Sunday Editions mailed to any part of the Country at the rate of 75c. per month. Daily Edition, 50c. per month. Orders may be sent through newsdealers, directly to the Publication Office, or telephone Bryant 1000.

NEW YORK, SUNDAY, AUG. 16, 1914.

THE CONTRAST.

By a coincidence so strange in history as almost to justify the superstitious, two ideals present their fruits to the judgment of the day and of posterity in the same month, the same week, the same day. The European ideal bears its full fruit of ruin and savagery just at the moment when the American ideal lays before the world a great work of peace, good-will, and fair play. The infernal blaze of destruction there lights up the fulfillment of a great work of construction here. While the madmen of Europe tug at the pillars of the temple of civilization, the Panama Canal is thrown open to the world.

Scandal did not stain it, though previous experience had led to a cynical disbelief in the possibility of a Panama Canal being created without scandal. Not a dollar of taxation was taken from a toiler's pocket to build it. Not one of the agencies of the Government employed on it was dilatory or inefficient. It is not only a triumph of engineering, but a triumph of administration. It is a triumph of statesmanship, not in the usual sense of that phrase—a victory over a crafty opponent — but the statesmanship which rose sagaciously and honorably over selfish considerations. In the face of large temptations, the great work was presented to all the nations of the earth on even terms, the nation that built it taking its place in line among the rest. That nation sought no advantage at the expense of others.

The contrast is made complete by the opening of the canal at the moment when the ideal of self-aggrandizement has wrought its inevitable disaster. It is while the military nations are doing their utmost to destroy twentieth-century civilization and throw the world into the past that the great democratic nation opens a door looking upon the future. As one ideal fulfills itself in hurling the world backward the other beckons it forward. While the European madness is tearing nations apart America completes a labor of peace designed to bring them together; and which will, when the delirium of today is over, bring them together.

A comment is heard to the effect that there is a sad irony in opening the canal to the world's trade at a moment when there is no trade to go through it. No, there is a felicity in the contrast which makes this seem the time of all others that we should have chosen, if we had had a choice, to offer our work to the world. The difference between the foundations on which the American system was built and those on which the European system rests could never otherwise have been so impressively illustrated. The skeptics who watched so cynically for the downfall of the fanciful and quixotic experiment launched on this side of the Atlantic, who knew that nothing could endure that was so different from the practical and common-sense system of royalty and militarism, should be here today to watch the flowering of one ideal in destruction and the other in creation.

If 1914 is to be remembered as Europe's terrible year, it will be remembered as a year glorious for America. It began with the firm refusal of the United States to take advantage of the distracted state of Mexico, a refusal which no European nation would have given and which no European nation could understand. The system under which Poland was partitioned and Hungary absorbed was the same as that which devoured Bosnia, seeks to devour Servia, and violates its treaties to crush Belgium. The system which, having broken Spanish rule in Cuba, handed Cuba over to her people instead of devouring her, is the same which plays in Mexico a helpful and creative part instead of a selfish and greedy part. It is the same which, completing a work for which the world has waited for four centuries, hands it over to the world. It is fortunate that twice in the same year the United States has been able to demonstrate the value of her own ideal, and doubly fortunate that that year happened to be the one in which Europe was demonstrating the terrible hopelessness of hers.

A sympathetic student of the American experiment, DE TOCQUEVILLE, wrote that the time had not yet come to judge how that experiment would work in the field of foreign relations and that judgment must be suspended. But he added:

> As for myself, I have no hesitation in avowing my conviction that it is most especially in the conduct of foreign relations that democratic Governments appear to me to be decidedly inferior to Governments carried on upon different principles.

Eighty years after these words were written the European theory of foreign relations was that each nation must gain only at the expense of others; that each must regard the others with fear and suspicion and must acquire from the others the utmost that could be gained without danger to itself; that for this purpose unsleeping vigilance was necessary, that the attitude of each to the others must be of hostile watchfulness, and that immense standing armies were the only guarantee of what they called peace, but what in reality was only truce. That theory culminated on Aug. 1, 1914, in conflagration. On Aug. 15, 1914, the American democracy opened the Panama Canal.

THE DAVIS CUP SERIES.

Court generalship on the part of BROOKES and WILDING's wonderful command of the ball, together with greater experience in championship battles which put the physical powers of the players to severe strains, account sufficiently for the victory of the Australasian players in the Davis Cup matches at Forest Hills. Though MCLOUGHLIN is the fastest server in the world and one of the most snapping of volleyers, it was manifest on the second day of his playing that his nerves and muscles were not seasoned enough to outlast the sound, careful, steady campaign waged by his older and cooler opponents. BUNDY, while justifying his selection as MCLOUGHLIN's partner, could not retrieve the breaks of the American champion forced by the terrific character of the playing.

But tennis is a game in which players develop by the experience of many seasons. MCLOUGHLIN at thirty, or at thirty-five, or at forty and even older, will display the qualities which in these matches proved the deciding factors, and much is to be hoped from a player of the skill and steadiness of BUNDY. With the development of its champions the game of tennis has itself displayed a remarkable development away from its former garden-party character. Success in it taxes the utmost powers of the contestants, and the popular interest it stirs is shown by the attendance and by the triumphant way in which this series managed to withstand the submerging influence in the news columns of a great European war.

Though the Australasians were victors in the series, the matches have placed MCLOUGHLIN at the head of the tennis players of the world, since he has defeated its champions in two successive singles. His skill, power, and judgment have never been surpassed and were a revelation to the spectators and to his opponents.

THE GERMAN PLEA.

The Chancellor of the German Empire has issued a statement especially addressed to the American people. He expresses confidence in our "sense of justice," asks us to "examine the "point of view of the German Gov-"ernment in an unprejudiced way," and declares that "the sympathy of "the American Nation will then lie "with German culture and civiliza-"tion, fighting against a half Asiatic "and slightly cultured barbarism."

Such an examination discloses two facts of particular interest. One is that the Chancellor seeks to limit the issue apparently to one raised by the action of Russia, and describes that issue as "a life and death struggle "between Germany and the Muscovite "races of Russia," with whom "highly "civilized France, bound by her un-"natural alliance," is co-operating. We are forced to say, in all candor, that this presentation of the case does not accord with the facts as they are known to the world. It is only a few years since Germany was on the best terms with Russia, and engaged in the Bund of the Three Emperors, with the object of maintaining the prestige and influence Germany had acquired in the war on France. Then the "Muscovite races of Russia" were not feared, and Germany was ready to add her strength to theirs to accomplish common ends and advance common interests. In the present conflict it certainly was not Russia that first demanded the "humiliation" of a friendly power, but Austria. It has never been explained why the action of Austria was not prevented, and the Chancellor omits all mention of it. On the face of the facts, the description of this war as a struggle for life by Germany "against a half Asiatic barbarism" seems singularly like an afterthought.

The second fact revealed by an unprejudiced examination of the Chancellor's statement is his charge that England is "availing itself of the long-"awaited opportunity to commence "war for the destruction of commer-"cially prosperous Germany." For this assertion we know of no conclusive evidence. In the first place, Germany commenced the war by a violation of the neutrality of Belgium, which England, and Germany as well, was bound by the most solemn agreement to observe and to protect. In the second place, England alone of all the great commercial nations has long granted to Germany and to all others entire freedom of trade for every port for which Parliament legislates. And the present Government, with the full assent of the majority of the English people, has steadily refused to place any obstacle to the entry of Germany upon all her markets. It was a policy as wise as it was magnanimous, and was utterly inconsistent with any desire for the destruction of prosperous Germany. We are bound to say that the assumption that Germany was forced into this war by fear of destruction by England, like the assumption that she is fighting for life against Pan-Slavism, seems like an afterthought.

It is not to be inferred from these suggestions that we think that, in the beginning of this war and in the action of the two Governments and the two peoples that has contributed to causing the war, the blame lies wholly on one side. There has been much jealousy, suspicion, animosity on both sides, unreasonable, unmanly, and provocative. The efforts of humane and far-sighted men in each country to check the tendency to a rupture—and those of the Kaiser have at times been vigorous and sincere—have been patient and honest. They have come to nought and the dread conflict has broken on the world. Certainly we in this land, equally friendly to the peoples of both England and Germany, must view it with the deepest regret and do all in our power to mitigate its horrors. We are bound, while exercising our best judgment as to its merits, to abstain from partisanship of any sort and to preserve an attitude consistent with mediation should that happily at any time become practicable. There are indications in the statement of the Chancellor—his designation of France as a "highly civilized" nation and his reference to the "heavy heart" with which the Germans see England ranged among their opponents—of a temper that, perhaps, when the awful futility of the war is disclosed by losses on all sides, will lend itself to the consideration of possible adjustment. For such a contingency the United States should be prepared.

GOVERNMENT AND BUSINESS.

The conference between the President and Treasury officials and leading men of business is full of promise of whatever may be expected from co-operation instead of antagonism. It would have been impossible before the President signed the Currency bill with his memorable declaration that it was the organization of the new peace as the basis of a new prosperity. In that spirit, and still in the President's words, the present situation should be worked out "along lines of accommodation." The men of different ideas should get together, and consider what is good for the country, rather than what is good for any special interest.

They were men of substance who advised with the country's administrators, and they gave sober advice to the men who had been prosecuting instead of consulting with some of them. Their counsel also differs from that obtainable with some degree of superabundance at the political end of the avenue opposite the White House. The contrast between the two lines of thought is striking, for the legislative department is thinking of almost nothing of what occupied the attention of the Treasury conference. The Treasury conference also has ideas exclusively its own, for which it may become necessary to seek aid by enactments. The contrast, therefore, should not be pursued with any spirit of antagonizing either line of relief against the other, but for the sake of promoting agreement between them.

Still using the President's line of thought, repeated now several times, the conference shows that the antagonism between Government and business has disappeared, and there has come upon business the spirit of co-operation which is the essence of statesmanship. On the part of Government there has appeared a recognition that "men of big business are honest, incorruptible, and patriotic." With Government and business in this mutual mood much may be accomplished.

The results of the conference had no bearing upon any one interest or section. No subsidy was asked, nor means of profit for any class through taxes upon any other class. It was suggested that the Treasury's surplus should be so disposed that it would promote exports which might be made by anybody, and which it would be for the benefit of everybody to have promoted. And, since the present times are exceptionally disturbed, it was suggested that the Government should assist insurance against war risks for everybody's shipments. The recommendation that our navigation laws should be amended was general, and must be approved by all who favor the creation of a mercantile marine.

It would be borrowing trouble to hint that the consideration of details may be less harmonious. At present it suffices to applaud all that was done or said in principle, and to suggest to both Government and business the words of the Psalmist, "Be-"hold how good and how pleasant it "is for brethren to dwell together in "unity." As Mayor GAYNOR said, "there are no dividends in quarrels." At last it is seen that there is no profit in hunting business men when they are not misbehaving, and that the country may profit by letting them profit, or even by helping them to profit.

THE WORLD'S GOLD PROBLEM.

The proposal of the Bank of England to regard gold paid to its account in Ottawa as paid to it in London is only one of the similar incidents of the present unprecedented deadlock in international trade. Argentina passed a law enabling its Minister at Washington to receive gold in trust to pay it to those entitled to receive it. This bears generally upon our South American trade. It has been financed through London, and stopped short with the war. What England could not accomplish for itself it was still less able to do for others, and the South American trade is thrown at our bankers' heads, with Argentina substituting Washington for London.

The Ottawa expedient is but one of England's similar measures. On Saturday it was announced that England is proposing similar arrangements for South Africa and Australia. In all these cases the motive is the danger and difficulty of ocean transit, when shipping and insurance are scarce and difficult. As measures for breaking the intolerable deadlock they are useful makeshifts, but they are not otherwise admirable. They are proofs of international distrust, springing from disorders which are a reproach to civilization and Christendom alike. If all men were honest, and nations never broke the peace, there would be no need of gold. All commerce could be cleared by book credits and debits, as it was in the days of the old Venetian bankers. Coins then were so debased that their value was unreliable, and merchants' accounts were kept in an ideal coin of the bankers. It never passed from hand to hand at all, but was transferred from one to another by book entries.

The world is larger now, and its commerce is perhaps too complex to allow of any hope of restoration of that ancient ideal. Yet there was a hint of reversion in the proposal of the National City Bank to match the debits and credits of those who could not otherwise get together, and could not transport the gold which one wished to pay as much as the other wished to receive it. This meritorious proposal was much broadened by the suggestion, at the conference of the President with business men at the Treasury, that the Federal Reserve Board take up the question of establishing an international clearing house for the selling of debits and credits of the nations.

Nothing like that would be possible so long as we remained a country of 27,000 banks, and no one of them entitled to international recognition. In 1907 there was no bank which could deal with any foreign central bank as representative of the country. The Federal Reserve Bank has not yet been organized, but already it is perceived of what great assistance to the country and to other nations our central bank may be. Not to move gold at all is even better than having one great central store in some convenient country which might serve the world under a universal guarantee of security. One thing is sure, out of the present disorganization there will grow a better organization of international payments than the one which has so lamentably broken down.

ROCKLAND COUNTY FARMERS

Threatened with Expulsion by the Palisade Park Commission.

To the Editor of The New York Times:

A condition of things exists today in Rockland County of this State which appears to me to call for the intervention of one having authority. Between Haverstraw and Tuxedo there is a scattered population of several hundred people. In nearly every case they own the land on which they live. They have in many instances inherited it from Revolutionary times. Their properties comprise from a few acres to a hundred or even several hundred. Their land furnishes them the source of their living.

I have been the rector of the church among them (which is maintained, together with a school for their children, by a wealthy lady of New York) for about ten years. In all that time I do not think I have given away $30 in charity. Only in case of serious sickness or accident have I ever been asked for a penny piece. They are with very few exceptions an industrious and contented people.

They are now threatened with expulsion from the homes in which they were born and which were in many cases the homes of their fathers and forefathers. The agents of the Palisade Park Commission are asking them to set a price upon their land or offering them a price and telling them that if they do not accept what is offered they will get less and be obliged to give up their homes after all. To illustrate, there are two aged women who have a comfortable home and two acres of land. They sell butter for groceries and live in entire comfort. The agent of the commission offered them the other day $350. Of course it was refused. The next day or so the offer was reduced to $300.

Some of the finest characters on the mountain said to me yesterday: "If they drive us out of our homes they take from us our means of living." And that is the plain and terrible truth. Driven from their little properties, they will be driven to poverty or even starvation. What are men 70 to 80 years old to do for a living if you expel them from their homes and their little farms? Where are women of 60 to 80 to find new homes? The price per acre which the commission is said to offer is $15. Where can homes be bought for such a price?

MYTTON MAURY,
Rector St. John's Church.
Hastings-on-Hudson, N. Y., Aug. 15, 1914.

A Polish View of Prussia.

To the Editor of The New York Times:

When we were telling the world about the inhuman treatment of our peasants in Prussia, where by the law of 1904 they are not allowed to build houses on their own land and compelled to live in carts with their families, and about the children who because they pray in Polish are flogged cruelly and in some instances butchered to death by Prussian schoolmasters, the world looked aghast and wondered whether such acts could be committed by a civilized Government.

Our contention that the Prussian is just as much a barbarian at heart as a Russian and an irresponsible danger to peace and civilization was doubted in some quarters. The developments of the last week and the unnecessary and wanton Hunlike destruction of ancient architectural treasures of Belgium and the brutal treatment of the stranded and helpless Americans in Germany show a bit of the true nature of the Prussian, who, by virtue of the treatment which he accords to his own wife, has long ago forfeited all rights to being recognized as a cultured man.

Z. N.
Lake Placid, N. Y., Aug. 15, 1914.

ANTI-GERMAN SENTIMENT.

Two Reasons Why the Kaiser Is to Blame for the War.

To the Editor of The New York Times:

Prof. Münsterberg has recently tried to enlighten what he considers our ignorance of German motives in the great war. He asserts that the Kaiser was forced into war against his will, and that the German cause is just and German methods in general righteous and honorable. Permit me to point out in reply that anti-German sentiment is not altogether prejudice, for it is based on two sufficient reasons.

The first reason is the arrogant note from Austria to Servia. Such a note, as any one might have known, would rouse the indignation of Russia. But Austria can hardly have made her demands without the consent of Germany. What wonder, then, that Italy should refuse to be the cat to pull from the fire the chestnuts of the Austrian monkey, or that the neutral world should regard the German Government as the prime mover of the war!

For such aggression, however, the rulers of Germany might plead her racial and national necessities. That is a debatable question. But there is no room for debate as to the conduct of the war. The Kaiser and his Ministers may perhaps have been unable to stop the fighting, but it lay in their power to conduct the campaign as they chose—honorably or dishonorably. In violating the neutrality of Luxemburg and of Belgium they have violated the written word of Germany. They stand before the world, perjured and forsworn, and their sniveling excuses can only make their conduct the more contemptible.

American public opinion is not so insane as Prof. Münsterberg thinks. We may not know much about experimental psychology, but we can see plainly enough that Germany is the aggressor in the greatest war the world has ever known. And it does not take a theologian to perceive that the blame for the conduct of that war falls fairly and squarely on the shoulders of the Kaiser and his military satellites.

HENRY HARMON CHAMBERLIN.
Nantucket, Mass., Aug. 14, 1914.

NAMES FOR THE WAR.

Several Are Suggested to Describe the Present Conflict.

To the Editor of The New York Times:

Your recent comment as to a name for the great European struggle now going on prompts the following suggestions: "The War of Alliances" or "The Alliance War" or "The War of the Allies."

Of course there have been many European wars in which alliances figured, but I think this feature has not figured in the historical nomenclature. The suggested names embody the salient fact of this European war and seize its unique characteristic.

Seriousness aside, if something "snappy" and designed for the comic supplement rather than the gilded page of history is wanted, let our German-American friends import the term "der Wilhelmskrieg," which the rest of us might translate as "willy-waw," defined in the dictionaries as a "sudden and violent squall." H. C. F.

Danville, Va., Aug. 14, 1914.

To the Editor of The New York Times:

From the rapidly extending scope of the war beyond the sea I think the historians may soon be able to agree upon "The Pan-European War" as a suitable name.

GENEVA LANE.
New York, Aug. 14, 1914.

To the Editor of The New York Times:

As some newspaper correspondents are taking time by the forelock and seeking a name for the present war—the number of nations involved rendering it inappropriate to term it Russo-German or Franco-German—I beg to contribute to the discussion the suggestion that it be called "The War of the German Aggression." This, aside from its harmony with the language of the historical writer, seems a proper title not only according to their critics, but from the admissions of the German authorities themselves, that it is the inevitable result of Germany's desire for expansion, even at the expense of other nations and races. JOHN S. ALEXANDER.

New York, Aug. 14, 1914.

To the Editor of The New York Times:

I have read your editorial calling attention to the fact that the war in Europe had not yet received a name. Until the war is concluded and some phenomenal event occurs to mark the combat I believe the name "Continental War" will meet all the requirements. If you will note, the peninsular nations have thus far held aloof from the contest—Italy, Greece, Spain, Denmark, Norway, and Sweden. FREDERIC W. CARY.

Norwich, Conn., Aug. 14, 1914.

Not a Slav-Teuton Struggle.

To the Editor of The New York Times:

The present hostilities are the sequence of the war of 1870 and the annexation of Alsace and Lorraine. When in that year the forces of Napoleon III. had been overwhelmed at Sedan, France was eager for peace. The proclamation issued by William I. had solemnly assured the French that the war was directed against the French Emperor, not against the French nation. On that basis an honorable and lasting peace between France and Germany would have been possible. Bismarck willed it otherwise. He wanted to weaken and to humble France by dismemberment. He took Alsace and Lorraine in total disregard of the wishes and sentiments of the inhabitants. Thereby he created a sore on the body politic that has remained bleeding through all the decades past. It was this sore that played so ominous a part in the growth of European militarism. It was this sore that made inevitable the Franco-Russian alliance. German officialdom did not altogether overlook the dangers provoked. Through the mouth of von Moltke it declared coolly: "What we have gained by the sword we must be ready to defend with the sword for the next half century."

At present we are treated to a lot of talk about the conflict between Slav and Teuton. The issue is not clearly stated, as far as any armed clash is concerned. For many years Europe has looked with anxious concern at the Russian colossus, semi-barbarian, menacing Western civilization. The natural barrier to the advance of Czarism would have been a close combination of the nations representing Western progress—Germany, France, and Great Britain. Such a combination was made impossible, in part through the Alsace-Lorraine question, in part through the survival of feudalistic ideas in the Hohenzollern realm. M. U.

New York, Aug. 14, 1914.

Lovers of "the Fatherland."

To the Editor of The New York Times:

I have read the recently published sheet, "The Fatherland, devoted to Fair Play for Germany and Austria," and aimed at the enlightenment of the American public as to the European situation, and the bias of the American press. "The Fatherland" needs no comments. The question which arises at the conclusion of the reading is: Why do gentlemen who have such unbounded admiration for the Fatherland, its ruler, its form of Government, its institutions, find it so convenient and agreeable to settle themselves so far from home? M. F.

New York, Aug. 14, 1914.

An Egocentric View.

To the Editor of The New York Times:

Hans Krieger, thinking that some other huskies with whom he and his pal had just picked a quarrel were going to attack him, grabbed hold of two children as his quickest means of defense. "Oh, Hans!" they cried, "you know you promised not to draw us into your scrapping!"

"It cuts me to the heart to have to do this," replied Hans with an air of innate nobility, "but it is necessary for the preservation of my idealism." HENRY RAFEL.

Long Branch, Aug. 14, 1914.

CHRISTIAN PROGRESS.

Admiral Mahan Points to the Civilization It Has Produced.

To the Editor of The New York Times:

In your issue of Aug. 7 a correspondent, "A. H. W.," asks that some intelligent, sincere Christian answer the question, "What has Christianity done toward civilizing the world?"

I would reply that if "A. H. W." will compare the conditions of the countries in which Christianity has existed with those where it has only begun to touch, in such matters as the status of women, the administration of justice, the conditions of settled government, he (or she) will find an answer. Such inquiry must be made by one capable of distinguishing substantial general results amid numerous perplexing details.

There is no such thing as "Christian Europe" or a Christian State. There is a Europe, and there are States, in which exists a large body of persons who hold the Christian faith and earnestly, if imperfectly, try to practice it in their lives. The presence of these through the centuries has been the leaven which has effected what is called Christian civilization. The result, Christian civilization, is found only where the Christian leaven is found; from which may certainly be inferred that to this cause it is due.

If "A. H. W." wishes further development, he can find it in an article in the April North American, "Twentieth Century Christianity." A. T. MAHAN.

Quogue, L. I., Aug. 14, 1914.

"Americans Abroad."

To the Editor of The New York Times:

While conditions among stranded Americans in European ports and trying to reach them have improved somewhat though leaving much to be desired, the following lines, exemplifying a great truth, given to the world by a great American General, may find some response among the few thousand of our own people still in foreign parts and the several hundred who have managed to get back to base. It is an iambic measure entitled "Americans Abroad."

Beyond a shipless sea today
Americans are forced to stay
Because they cannot get away,
Though some have got the price to pay.
Grim-visaged War has laid its hands
Upon all European lands,
And those Americans who went
Abroad to get their money spent
And have a lovely time and see
The Old World sights they knew to be
All over Europe, now are stuck
And playing in most painful luck.
The warring nations tell them to
Pack up and get out p. d. q.,
Then stop all means of travel and
Bring every movement to a stand.
The pie supply is short, and they
Have no desire to feed on hay.
And though they want to get away
They cannot leave, nor can they stay,
And all the stranded tourists yell
In one wild chorus: "WAR IS HELL!!!!"

One American who has got back said to me that if Gen. Sherman had lived to get caught with the others stranded on the Continent just what he would have said about war would have made his famous remark sound like the evening prayer of a child at its mother's knee. W. J. LAMPTON.

New York, Aug. 14, 1914.

German Military Arrogance.

To the Editor of The New York Times:

Who has visited Germany even for a day without being amazed by the insolent bearing of the soldiers and the insulting buccaneering of the officers? This attitude has not been assumed toward alien peoples, but to their fellow countrymen and even to the women of their native land—those women whom the Kaiser has so frequently urged to keep up a supply for cannon to mow down.

It seems to be the personality of this same Kaiser which pervades the whole of German militancy. Much as I have always admired him, I can but feel that his is the responsibility.

Is it amiss that a nation that could mother "watchful waiting" should fervently hope the day will soon come when self-respect, as we know it in private life, will replace the bullying tactics which have so long held absolute sway in the so-called diplomacy of monarchial countries? UBIQUE.

New York, Aug. 14, 1914.

The German "Defeats."

To the Editor of The New York Times:

Could you help me out a little and explain what the good old English word "defeat" means? Is Webster's definition wrong? The reason I ask is that every time I look at one of those "Extras" with their six-inch headlines I notice "another defeat" of the German Army or "German Army Cut to Pieces," or "Germans Routed," &c., and with all those "defeats" they are getting further and further into their enemies' countries. Does "defeat" mean "unwillingness of the Germans to fight on their own soil" or something like it? H. KASTOR.

New York, Aug. 14, 1914.

"B" Is Right.

To the Editor of The New York Times:

The newspaper report of a battle states that 30,000 Germans and 10,000 Belgians were lost. A argues that "lost" means killed; B, that "lost" means those killed, captured, disabled, and missing. Will you kindly put us right through the columns of your paper? HARRY W. CAYGILL.

New York, Aug. 14, 1914.

Why German-Americans Protest.

To the Editor of The New York Times:

We Americans of German nativity do not protest because you receive no news from Germany. We protest because the American press prints everything it receives from London or Paris, no matter how absurd the information is. GEORGE v. S.

New York, Aug. 14, 1914.

THE LEADER.

(Quantum lenta solent inter viburna cupressi.)

He towers among his critics. They are still,
And silent, too, the clamorous jingo band
Who into conflict would have plunged the land.
All pause, in deference to his wiser will.

Though grief tug at his heart-strings, there's no trace
Of tremor or of weakness in his mien.
His tearless eye far-seeing is, and keen.
Men note but courage, firmness, in his face.

He deals with world-wide issues in such poise
Beholders marvel at restraint so rare.
Yet no detail of weight escapes his care,
The while his statesmanship lacks blatant noise.

At home, his brief commands are sage and clear;
To those abroad he lends his helpful aid.
As prompt his heartening of commerce, trade.
Hopes turn toward him, and the land forgets its fear.

Not an autocracy to plunge in blood
A helpless continent, his temperate rule.
No vain ambition mars his judgment cool.
His faith's a rock, unswerved by stress or flood.

As cypresses 'mid lesser shrubs do tower,
Towers our Chief Magistrate 'mid rulers all.
God Lincoln sent, to stay the nation's fall.
So God sends Wilson for this crisis-hour.

ELLA A. F[illegible]NNING.

"FIATISM RUN MAD."

Glass So Terms Vanderlip's Suggestion of Bank Note Reserve.

WASHINGTON, Aug. 15.—The suggestion attributed to Frank A. Vanderlip of New York, that Congress should authorize national banknotes to be used as reserves in the place of gold, was characterized as "fiatism run mad" by Representative Carter Glass of Virginia, Chairman of the Banking and Currency Committee, tonight. Mr. Glass said:

"A telegram I received today states that many of the New York bankers are violently opposed to such a scheme and that national banknotes are a liability of the banks issuing the same, and not an asset. A liability is not a good reserve against another liability. I have replied that I fully concur in this view, and am opposed to the proposition to put the banking business of the country on a paper basis.

"The suggestion to use national banknotes as reserve comes from a prominent banker in New York who was engaged some months ago in denouncing as 'fiat money' the notes authorized to be issued under the Federal Reserve act. These Federal reserve notes will have 40 per cent. gold reserve behind them, and 100 per cent. of short-time commercial paper, besides all the assets of the reserve banks. They have not one element of fiatism about them.

"If Mr. Vanderbilt really thinks that notes authorized by the Federal Reserve act constitute 'fiat money,' what, in the name of Heaven, must he think of the proposition which he now makes to Congress to open wide the throttle and permit currency and credit issues to be based on the liabilities rather than the assets of the banks, without one dollar of gold reserve as security?

"It seems to me that this is fiatism run mad. Furthermore, it suggests that we should temporarily repudiate our gold obligations at home to help certain banks to meet their gold obligations abroad, and I do not think the proposition will be entertained for a minute."

WANTS DATA ON INCOMES.

Murdock Aiming at Inheritance Tax as Federal Revenue Producer.

Special to The New York Times.

WASHINGTON, Aug. 15.—Victor Murdock, the Progressive leader in the House, who declares that certain Americans, fewer than 2,000 in number, have incomes which are greater than the total income of the Government, offered a resolution today asking the Treasury Department for information as to big incomes with a view to certain legislation. Mr. Murdock seeks data upon which to base a Federal inheritance tax law.

"It is desirable for Congress to inquire into the social and economic importance of a graduated inheritance tax as corrective of the evils attendant upon the possession of swollen private fortunes through which a relatively few men dominate businesses which should not be related one to another in menace to the Nation's economic life," says the resolution, which continues:

"Be it resolved, that the Secretary of the Treasury be and he is hereby requested to furnish the House of Representatives the number of persons paying taxes upon incomes of $250,000 a year and less than $500,000 a year; the number of persons paying taxes upon incomes of more than $500,000 and less than $750,000; the number of persons paying taxes upon incomes of more than $750,000 a year and less than $1,000,000 a year, and the number of persons paying taxes upon incomes of $1,000,000 a year or more, with the amount of each income which amounts to $1,000,000 or more."

Mr. Murdock thinks this information should be in the possession of Congress before additional taxes are levied on account of the European conflict. The resolution was referred to the Ways and Means Committee.

INCOME TAX COMPROMISE.

Government Names Minimum Penalties in Non-Fraud Cases.

WASHINGTON, Aug. 15.—The Treasury Department has determined to accept offers in compromise of the specific penalty for failure on the part of individuals or corporations to make returns within the period prescribed of their annual net incomes for the income tax in cases where such failure was due to misunderstanding of the law or ignorance as to its requirements. The minimum offers that will be received are $5 from individuals and $10 from corporations organized for profit.

This statement was made in announcements sent today to Collectors of Internal Revenue by Acting Commissioner Williams. It was stated that in cases of corporations not organized for profit the specific penalty would not be asserted this year, provided the required return had been filed by Dec. 31, 1914. The foregoing, it was added, applied only to cases in which there was no intention of evading the law or escaping taxation.

In all instances, however, wherein returns are not made until the liability to make returns are discovered by investigation of Collectors or Revenue Agents the above schedule will not necessarily apply, but each individual case will be decided on its merits and the amount of the offer in compromise which may be favorably received will be determined accordingly.

SENATE PASSES OPIUM BILL.

Provides for Federal Registration by Dealers in Drugs.

Special to The New York Times.

WASHINGTON, Aug. 15.—The Senate this afternoon passed a bill that would regulate closely the manufacture of and trade in opiates. The bill would require the registration at the office of the nearest Collector of Internal Revenue of every dealer in or manufacturer of opium or opiates. An exception is made, however, in favor of the persons handling preparations containing not more than two grains of opium, or one-fourth of a grain of morphine, or a grain of heroin, or one grain of cocaine.

Senator Lane of Oregon, one of the two physicians in the Senate, bitterly denounced these exceptions. He said they would permit the continued manufacture and sale of dangerous soothing syrups for babies. Already, he said, the deaths of 10,000 babies a year could be ascribed to opiates in patent remedies for infantile troubles.

"Not only that," said Mr. Lane, "but the little nerves of the babies never forget the delightful tingling the opiates gave them. Later, when they grow up, should any trouble require the use of opiates, they then recall their childish sensations and become addicted to the drug."

1,000 FIGHT FOREST FIRES.

Fierce Blazes Raging in the Northwestern States and California.

WASHINGTON, Aug. 15.—With 1,000 forest fire fighters battling in the national forests of Montana and Northern Idaho, fifty uncontrolled fires burning and weather conditions more threatening than at any time since the great fires of 1910, the forest officials here today said that the situation was grave.

The one hope left of escaping widespread losses of life and property they said was moderate winds. More than 2,000 fires have been fought this season, of which about 100 have been in Montana and Idaho, 200 or more in California and 350 in Oregon and Washington. These are the regions of greatest exposure though conditions reported growing serious in the Black Hills of South Dakota, and parts of Wyoming. Near Glacier Park a fire is burning which, though now believed to be under control, with a fire line forty-four miles long, menaced the destruction of 1,000,000,000 feet of green timber.

In Northern California one very bad fire was recently fought for days by a force gathered from far and near by the Forest Service until 1,000 men were fighting the flames. In Oregon fire is threatening the national forest watershed upon which the City of Portland depends for its water supply.

Loss of lives has been reported from several points.

THE PANAMA CANAL OFFICIALLY OPENED

Government Steamship Ancon, with Col. Goethals Aboard, Traverses the Route.

SHE MAKES A RECORD TRIP

Nine Hours from Ocean to Ocean—Many Local Dignitaries Guests of the Government.

PANAMA, Aug. 15.—The Panama Canal is open to the commerce of the world. Henceforth ships may pass to and fro through that great waterway, a new ocean highway for trade thus being established.

The steamship Ancon, owned by the United States War Department and leased to the Panama Railroad for service between New York and Colon, with many notable people on board, today made the official passage which signalized the opening of the canal. She left Cristobal at 7 o'clock this morning and reached Balboa, at the Pacific end, at 4 o'clock this afternoon, having navigated the waterway in nine hours.

The Ancon did not anchor at Balboa, but proceeded into deep water in the Pacific, beyond the fortified islands, where she lie in the channel of the canal until her return to Balboa to land her passengers. She will remain at the Balboa docks for some time, discharging her cargo, hers being the first commercial voyage made through the canal.

The canal having been officially opened, it will be used tomorrow for the transfer of four cargo ships, which will thus shorten their routes. The private yacht Lasata, owned in Los Angeles, also will be transferred to the Pacific, homeward bound.

The trip of the Ancon was the fastest yet made by a large ocean steamer, the locking operations having been quicker, owing to longer experience. The steamer went through the Gatun locks in seventy minutes, a speed never before reached. The others lockages were equally rapid.

Col. George W. Goethals, builder of the canal and Governor of the Zone, watched the operations closely, and was manifestly pleased at the improved handling of the locks. He said that even this would be made much better with time. Capt. Hugh Rodman, Superintendent of Transportation, who directed the trip, voiced similar sentiments.

In conformity with a promise made by Col. Goethals, the flag of the American Peace Society fluttered from the foremast of the Ancon. Beneath her decks, however, were two huge pieces of artillery which are destined to form an important part of the defenses of the waterway.

All of the seventy-four regular officers and men aboard the Ancon appeared in spotlessly white uniforms, and the ship itself glistened with new paint, over which fluttered signal flags and the ensigns of all nations. At the fore truck was the ensign of the Republic of Panama, while at the mainmasthead fluttered the house pennant of the Panama Steamship fleet. On the jackstaff was the flag of the United States.

Local Dignitaries on Board.

Invitations to be guests on this first trip had been much coveted, and the rails were lined with local canal officials and those of the Republic of Panama, together with the members of their families, as the big steamer backed away from her berth. Col. Goethals and Capt. Rodman were on the bridge beside Capt. Sukeforth, commanding the steamer. President Porras of the Republic of Panama and his staff were also on board.

The Panama National Band and the regimental band of the Tenth United States Infantry played "The Star-Spangled Banner" as the ship pulled away, but the music was almost drowned by the whistles of the steamers in the harbor.

To assure unimpeded passage for the Ancon, all of the traffic, including that of the working boats in Culebra Cut, was brought to a standstill from early this morning on. The several thousand canal workers enjoyed a holiday, and they, together with villagers of all types from the surrounding territory, lined the banks at various vantage points.

The Ancon was fully loaded, the cargo that she had brought from New York having been purposely left on board to give the canal a test with the ship drawing its full depth of water.

Garrison Congratulates Goethals.

Special to The New York Times.

WASHINGTON, Aug. 15.—Secretary Garrison of the War Department, which had direct jurisdiction over the construction of the Panama Canal, today sent a congratulatory telegram to Col. Goethals and to his co-laborers in the construction of the canal, in recognition of their work and in honor of the opening of the canal today. In his message Mr. Garrison said:

"On behalf of the Government and the people of the United States I express to you, and through you to all concerned in the achievement, the intense gratification and pride experienced today. By the successful passage of vessels through the canal the dream of the centuries has become a reality. A stupendous undertaking has been finely accomplished, and a perpetual memorial to the genius and enterprise of our people has been created. The fully earned and deserved congratulations of a grateful people go out to you and your co-laborers."

WHAT SOUTH AMERICA NEEDS

List of Supplies Which America Can Provide.

Information as to the supplies, of which there is a shortage in various Central and South American countries, was given out yesterday by the Bureau of Foreign and Domestic Commerce. Santos reports a large demand for coal, wheat, papers, leather, flour, soaps, drugs, cement, general provisions, codfish, wine, and olive oil; Corinto wants cotton goods and hardware; Callao wants coal, wheat, and newspaper paper; Asuncion wants sawmill supplies, cotton fabrics, canned goods, electrical supplies, wire, paints, printing paper, iron, windmills, tin and glass goods; Ceiba wants dry goods, cutlery, and wines; Bahia wants coal, flour, petroleum, codfish, cement, and provisions; La Paz wants flour, sugar, rice, kerosene, canned goods, cotton and woolen goods, hardware, and electrical supplies; Guatemala requires hardware, agricultural implements and machines, and Rio de Janeiro flour, coal, and oil.

THE MINNESOTA IS HERE.

Battleship, Which Was at Vera Cruz, Anchors in North River.

The Minnesota of the Second Division of the Atlantic fleet, the only American battleship that was anchored in the inner harbor of Vera Cruz when that port was captured by the marines and sailors under Rear Admiral Fletcher, arrived in New York from Mexican waters yesterday. She had been away from home waters more than seven months.

The battleship anchored off West Eighty-second Street, where she will remain several weeks. When the big fighter was boarded by the reporters every officer hurried to greet the newspapermen, and the question all asked was, "How about the war in Europe?"

"All the News That's Fit to Print."

The New York Times.

EXTRA
5:30 A. M.

Weather Today and Sunday: Fair.

VOL. LXIV...NO. 20,923. ..... NEW YORK, SATURDAY, MAY 8, 1915.—TWENTY-FOUR PAGES. ONE CENT In Greater New York, Jersey City and Newark. | Elsew TWO C

LUSITANIA SUNK BY A SUBMARINE, PROBABLY 1,260 DEAD; TWICE TORPEDOED OFF IRISH COAST; SINKS IN 15 MINUTES; CAPT. TURNER SAVED, FROHMAN AND VANDERBILT MISSING; WASHINGTON BELIEVES THAT A GRAVE CRISIS IS AT HAN

SHOCKS THE PRESIDENT

Washington Deeply Stirred by the Loss of American Lives.

BULLETINS AT WHITE HOUSE

Wilson Reads Them Closely, but Is Silent on the Nation's Course.

HINTS OF CONGRESS CALL

Loss of Lusitania Recalls Firm Tone of Our First Warning to Germany.

CAPITAL FULL OF RUMORS

Reports That Liner Was to be Sunk Were Heard Before Actual News Came.

Special to The New York Times.

WASHINGTON, May 7. — Never since that April day, three years ago, when word came that the Titanic had gone down, has Washington been so stirred as it is tonight over the sinking of the Lusitania. The early reports told that there had been no loss of life, but the relief that these advices caused gave way to the greatest concern late this evening when it became known that there had been many deaths. Although they are profoundly reticent, officials realize that this tragedy, involving the loss of American citizens, is likely to bring about a crisis in the international relations of the United States.

It is pointed out that the sinking of the Lusitania is the outcome of a series of incidents that have been the cause of concern to this Government in its endeavor to maintain a strictly neutral position in the great European war.

Nation's Course in Doubt.

It is impossible to say tonight what effect the loss of American lives on the Lusitania will have on the Government. Judged from the little that can be learned it is a safe prediction that President Wilson will endeavor to ascertain all the facts, including evidence as to whether a German submarine was responsible for the sinking of the vessel, before proceeding to determine the course to be pursued. The news that many lives had been sacrificed, probably as many as a thousand, was given to him at the White House about 10 o'clock this morning, but no word came from him as to what effect this intelligence had on him.

The State Department tonight sent instructions to the American Embassy in London to send the names of any Americans who might have been killed or injured in the disaster. A bulletin from THE TIMES, saying probably 1,000 lives had been lost, was sent to the White House as soon as received and laid before President Wilson. The news that two torpedoes had been fired into the Lusitania by a submarine and that the Lusitania sank fifteen minutes afterward was also sent to the White House, but reached there after the President had gone to bed. The President retired about 11 o'clock.

On account of the many inquiries it had received from friends and relatives of passengers on the Lusitania and the intense public interest in the tragedy, orders were given tonight to the telegraphers and cipher clerks in charge of the telegraph office in the State Department to remain at their posts all night. They also had instructions to make public any messages bringing official details regarding the Lusitania's passengers. Usually the telegraph office closes at midnight.

Rumors of Congress Session.

There were reports this evening that Congress would be called in extra session, but these were not justified and the most that can be said is that while the Government is greatly concerned over the situation, it has shown no inclination toward excitement or taking hasty action.

Senator W. J. Stone, Chairman of the Committee on Foreign Relations, said tonight:

"I cannot comment on a supposed

Continued on Page 4.

The Lost Cunard Steamship Lusitania
X Where the First Torpedo Struck. XX Where the Second Torpedo Struck.

Cunard Office Here Besieged for News; Fate of 1,918 on Lusitania Long in Doubt

Nothing Heard from the Well-Known Passengers on Board—Story of Disaster Long Unconfirmed While Anxious Crowds Seek Details.

Official news of the sinking of the Lusitania yesterday reached New York in fragmentary reports, and several hours elapsed between the first unverified rumor of the disaster and the cable messages that told at night of the saving of some of the passengers and gave meagre details of the most sensational incident of its kind in the war.

The early accounts that indicated all on board had been saved reassured hundreds of friends and relatives of passengers. Later, it was made known that lives had been lost and probably many persons had been injured

Among the prominent passengers rescued was George A. Kessler. The list of those of whom no word was received included A. G. Vanderbilt, Charles Frohman, Charles Klein, Justus Miles Forman, and Elbert Hubbard, besides persons widely known in society.

A cablegram sent to Farley Hopkins of The Yale News staff at New Haven, by his father, who was aboard the Lusitania, stated that the vessel was sunk, not beached, that three hundred persons had been already landed, and that the rest in small boats were making for shore. The message reached New York at 8:15 o'clock and was signed "Lee Higginson & Co., London."

Word of the safety of Charles E. Lauriat, Jr., of Boston, Mass., a member of the firm of Charles E. Lauriat & Co., booksellers, who was a first-cabin passenger, reached relatives there in a cablegram early this morning. The message, dated at Queenstown, 2:40 A. M. Read simply:

> Charles E. Lauriat, Jr., safe and well.

For more than half a century it was the boast of the Cunard Line that it never had lost a life. The regon was sunk in collision near Fire Island in 1886, but no lives were lost until five passengers were swept off the Campania's forward deck by a wave on Oct. 5, 1905. The sinking of the Lusitania is the first big disaster the Cunard Line has had.

Message to Cunard Office.

The first word of the sinking of the Lusitania received here reached the local offices of the Cunard Line, 21 State Street, at 11:41 o'clock yesterday morning, but was not made public until late in the afternoon. The message, which was sent from the head office in Liverpool, read:

> The Lusitania, we regret to advise, an unconfirmed report states to have been torpedoed by a submarine at 2 P. M., Friday, ten miles from Kinsale, and sunk at 2:30. There is no news as to the safety of passengers or crew.

Following this dispatch there was a message which had been picked up by the wireless station at Land's End, evidently a distress call from the liner, which said:

> Come at once. Big list. Position ten miles west Kinsale.

A third dispatch from Queenstown stated:

> All available craft in harbor dispatched to assist. Weather here beautifully fine. Wind southeast, light.

By 3 o'clock in the afternoon the news of the sinking of the Lusitania had been spread in the city and the Cunard offices were besieged by relatives and friends of the passengers on board. Owing to the alterations in and additions to the passenger list on sailing day, last Saturday, it took some time to get the correct figures, which were finally given out as 290 first, 601 second, and 362 third class passengers. Of the cabin passengers thirty-six had been transferred fro mthe Cameronia on Saturday morning. This delayed the Lusitania's departure from 10 o'clock to 12:28.

1,918 Persons on Board.

The officers and crew numbered 665 men instead of the usual complement of 960, on account of fewer men being carried in the engineers' and stewards' departments. Thus there were in all 1,918 persons on board.

The Cunard agents told all inquirers that they would give out the messages as fast as they were received and had no intention of keeping back the news from the public. Several bulletins were received from the Liverpool office, but few of them contained any definite statements and they were cancelled, in some instances, within an hour. One received at 4 P. M. read:

> Motor fishing boats towing two boats filled with passengers, probably fifty. Tug Stormcock making Kinsale. Some passengers on board. Many rescue vessels are now apparently making Queenstown.

The first dispatch stating positively that the Lusitania had sunk reached the Cunard office at 5 P. M. It read:

> Old Head Kinsale Station reports about twenty boats, all belonging to Lusitania, are in vicinity where sunk. About fifteen boats are making for the spot to resume.

An unconfirmed report was received late in the afternoon that all the passengers and crew had been saved in small boats and rafts. This information was given out to the people waiting in the Cunard office, and many of them went home. It was estimated that fully 500 inquiries were received by telephone and telegraph in the afternoon from relatives and friends of passengers on board. Long-distance calls were received from St. Louis, Atlanta, Montreal, and Toronto.

The next bulletin made public at the Cunard office was the following:

> Liverpool, May 7,
> 1:51 P. M., (New York Time.)
> Following received by Admiralty, Galley Head, 4:25 P. M.: Several boats, apparently survivors, southeast nine miles. Greek steamer proceeding to assist.

The next bulletin was:

> Liverpool, May 7,
> 2:33 P. M., (New York Time.)
> Queenstown wires Old Head: Large steamer just arrived in vicinity, apparently sending assistance. Tugs, patrols, &c.,

Continued on Page 3.

List of Saved Includes Capt. Turner; Vanderbilt and Frohman Reported Lost

LONDON, Saturday, May 8,—5:30 A. M.—The Press Bureau has received from the British Admiralty at Queenstown a report that all the torpedo boats and tugs and armed trawlers, except the Heron, which went out from Queenstown to the relief of the Lusitania have returned.

These vessels have landed 595 survivors and forty dead. Fifty-two more survivors are reported aboard a steamer, while eleven others and five bodies have been landed at Kinsale, making the total number of survivors 658, besides forty-five dead. The numbers will be verified later, and it is considered possible Kinsale fishing boats may have rescued a few more.

Among the survivors is the Captain of the Lusitania, William T. Turner. Some of the survivors at Queenstown say that Alfred Gwynne Vanderbilt was drowned. Every effort to find Mr. Vanderbilt and Charles Frohman, the theatrical manager, among the survivors has failed.

The Central News says that the number of the Lusitania's passengers who died of injuries while being taken to Queenstown will reach 100.

QUEENSTOWN Saturday, May 8, 4:45 A. M.—The list of the Lusitania's survivors, as far as compiled, follows:

TURNER, Captain.
MATHEWS, A. T., Montreal.
ABRAMOWITZ, S.
LANE, G. B.
MEYERS, W. G. E.
TRIMMINS, J. T.
WITHERBEE, Mrs. A. F.
MACKWORTH, Lady.
ADAMS, Mrs. HENRY, Boston.
RANKIN, ROBERT, New York.
SHARP, SAMUEL.
BYRNE, M. B., New York.
DAVIS, EMILY.
WALKER, ANNIE.
HOUSNELL, E.
CROSS, A. B.
YOUNG, PHILIP, Montreal.
VASSAR, W. A. F., London.
STEELE, GEORGE.
CROSLEY, CYRUS.
PARKER, JAMES.
COLEBROOK, the Rev. R.
MORRIS, H. C. S.
FISH, Mrs., and two children.
MARTIN, Miss R.
GAUTLETT, F. J., New York.
MAYCOCK, Miss MAY.
HENDERSON, VIOLET.
MARDERUD, UNO.
LEVIN, THOMAS D.
THOMAS, D. A., Cardiff, Wales.
EVANS, T. J. M.
CLARKE, A. R.
BURGESS, W. G.
CHARLES, J. H., and daughter, Toronto.
LONEY, Miss, New York.
HERRIS, JOHN.
HOLLAND, Miss.
BRANDELL, Miss JOSEPHINE, New York.
PERRY, F. K. A.
GRAB, O. H.
MOSLEY, G. G., New York.
BROOKS, J H., New York.
JEFFRY, A. M.
CAIRNS, M.
HAMMOND, O. H., New York.
MANLEY, A.
NEATH, H.
NORTH, Miss.
WINTER, Miss.
WINTER, Miss.
DUGUID, GEORGE.
MOORE, DANIEL.
McCONNELL, JOHN W., Memphis, Tenn.
SHARPE, Miss.
CONNER, Miss.
DALY, H. M.
CLIFFE, PATRICK.
BOHAN, JAMES, Toronto.
CROSLEY, Mrs. CYRUS.
BRETHERTON, Mrs. CYRIL H., and two children, Los Angeles, Cal.
HOPKINS, A. L., New York.
LASSETTER, Mrs. H. B., of Sydney, Australia, wife of General Lassetter.
LASSETTER, Master P.
LAURIAT, CHARLES E., Jr., Boston, Mass.
PAYNTER, Miss IRENE, Liverpool, England.

KINSALE, Ireland, May 8.—Eleven survivors of the Lusitania have been landed here, together with the bodies of five persons who were dead. Among the survivors are:

SMITH, J. RESTON, New York.
BOTTOMLEY, FREDERICK
BOYLE, N. L.
HOTCHKISS, CHARLES.
HARRIMAN, CORNELIUS.
LIVERMORE, VERNAR.
SULLIVAN, Mrs. F.

Consul's List of Saved.

WASHINGTON, May 8.—Consul Lauriat at Queenstown sends this report:

"Total saved of all nationalities, 700. The following are American survivors of Lusitania. Other names will follow

CRAB, O. S.
PEARL, Major and Mrs., and two children.
SMITH, Mrs. JESSIE TAFT.
HARDWICK, CHARLES C.
EARL, STUART D.
PEARL, AMY.
STANLEY, Mrs.
LINES, L. B.
HILL, C. T.
RANKIN, ROBERT.
LONEY, Miss.
DOHERTY, Mrs. WILLIAM and infant.
PHILLIPS, THOMAS.
McADAMS, WILLIAM.
HOUGHTON, J. H.
SWEENEY, JOHN M.
HAMMOND, OADEN H.
BROOKS, J. H.
JEFFRY, CHARLES T.
LUND, Mrs. C. H.
SHEPPERDSON, ARTHUR.
MOORE, Dr. D. V.
BERNARD, CLINTON.
LIGHT, HERBERT.
LINNSON, J., Jr.
WILLIAMS, EDITH.
LEARY, JAMES J.
SLIDELL, THOMAS.
WOLFENDEN, Mrs. JOHN.
HOLLAND, Mrs. NINA.
MESH, Mrs. THOMAS.
KESSLER, GEORGE A.
McMURRAY, L.
KAY, ROBERT.
LOCKHART, R. R.
CANNON, OWEN.
HARRIS, DURIGHT C.
JUDSON, FRED S.
COLLIS, ED M.
WRIGHT, R. C.
GAUNTLET, F. J.
KNOX, S. N.
O'DONNELL, PATRICK.

Saw the Submarine 100 Yards Off and Watched Torpedo as It Struck Ship

Ernest Cowper, a Toronto Newspaper Man, Describes Attack, Seen from Ship's Rail—Poison Gas Used in Torpedoes, Say Other Passengers.

Queenstown, Saturday,
May 8, 3:18 A. M.

A sharp lookout for submarines was kept aboard the Lusitania as she approached the Irish coast, according to Ernest Cowper, a Toronto newspaper man, who was among the survivors landed at Queenstown.

He said that after the ship was torpedoed there was no panic among the crew, but that they went about the work of getting passengers into the boats in a prompt and efficient manner.

"As we neared the coast of Ireland," said Mr. Cowper, "we all joined in the lookout, for a possible attack by a submarine was the sole topic of conversation.

"I was chatting with a friend at the rail about 2 o'clock when suddenly I caught a glimpse of the conning tower of a submarine about a thousand yards distant. I immediately called my friend's attention to it. Immediately we both saw the track of a torpedo followed almost instantly by an explosion. Portions of splintered hull were sent flying into the air, and then another torpedo struck. The ship began to list to starboard.

"The crew at once proceeded to get the passengers into boats in an orderly, prompt, and efficient manner. Miss Helen Smith appealed to me to save her. I placed her in a boat and saw her safely away. I got into one of the last boats to leave.

"Some of the boats could not be launched as the vessel was sinking. There was a large number of women and children in the second cabin. Forty of the children were less than a year old."

Poison Fumes from Torpedoes.

From interviews with passengers it appears that when the torpedoes burst they sent forth suffocating fumes which had their effect on the passengers, causing some of them to lose consciousness.

Two stokers, Byrne and Hussey of Liverpool, gave a few details. They said the submarine gave no notice and fired two torpedoes, one hitting No. 1 stoke hole and the second the engine room. The first torpedo was discharged at 2 o'clock. In twenty-five minutes the great liner disappeared.

Signals have been received at Queenstown that an armed trawler, believed to be the Heron, and two fishing trawlers are bringing in 100 more bodies.

The Cunard Line agent states that the total number of persons aboard the Lusitania was 2,160.

Loss of the Lusitania Fills London With Horror and Utter Amazement

Special Cable to THE NEW YORK TIMES.

LONDON, Saturday, May 8.—Stupefaction is the word which best describes the first impression created by the news of the sinking of the Lusitania. People seemed unable to realize that at this stage of the world's progress such a deed could be committed as an act of war.

"I have no words for it," said Lord Rosebery, and everywhere one found the same sentiment repeated.

It was some hours between the time

Continued on Page 3.

SOME DEAD TAKEN ASHO

Several Hundred Sur ors at Queenstown and Kinsale.

STEWARDTELLS OF DISAS

One Torpedo Crashes Into Doomed Liner's Bow, Anot Into the Engine Room.

SHIP LISTS OVER TO P

Makes It Impossible to Lo Many Boats, So Hundre Must Have Gone Down.

ATTACKED IN BROAD

Passengers at Luncheon—War Had Been Given by Germans fore the Ship Left New York

Only 650 Were Saved, Few Cabin Passenge

QUEENSTOWN, Satu day, May 8, 4:28 A. M. Survivors of the Lusitar who have arrived here es mate that only about 650 those aboard the steam were saved, and say only small proportion of the rescued were saloon passe gers.

Official Confirmation

WASHINGTON, May —A dispatch to the St Department early tod from American Cons Lauriet at Queenstov stated that the total nu ber of survivors of t Lusitania was about 700.

LONDON, Saturday, May —The Cunard liner Lusita which sailed out of New Y last Saturday with 1,918 so aboard, lies at the bottom the ocean off the Irish coast

She was sunk by a Gern submarine, which sent two t pedoes crashing into her side 2:30 o'clock yesterday aft noon while the passeng seemingly confident that great, swift vessel could el the German underwater cr were having luncheon.

The great inrush of wa caused the liner to list heav to port, so that she could launch many of her lifeboats

About 1,260 of those board the great ship, includ many Americans, apparen went down with her, as a sta ment issued late this morn by the Admiralty says the to number of survivors is o 658.

There were 1,253 passeng on board the steamship, cluding 200 who were tra ferred to her from the stean Cameronia. The Americ totaled 188. The crew nu bered 665.

It is believed that only a f first class passengers we saved as they thought the sh would remain afloat, and ma little effort to escape.

There appears to be a lar proportion of the ship's cr among the survivors landed Queenstown. Only a few of

"All the News That's Fit to Print."

The New York Times.

THE WEATHER
Fair, colder today; tomorrow warmer, probably rain; wind northwest.
For full weather report see Page 23.

VOL. LXVI...NO. 21,619. NEW YORK, TUESDAY, APRIL 3, 1917.—TWENTY-FOUR PAGES. ONE CENT In New York City. | TWO CENTS New England and Middle States. | THREE CENTS Elsewhere.

PRESIDENT CALLS FOR WAR DECLARATION, STRONGER NAVY, NEW ARMY OF 500,000 MEN, FULL CO-OPERATION WITH GERMANY'S FOES

ARMED AMERICAN STEAMSHIP SUNK; 11 MEN MISSING

The Aztec Is First Gun-Bearing Vessel Under Our Flag to be Torpedoed.

SURPRISE ATTACK AT NIGHT

12 Navy Men and Their Chief Among 17 Survivors Picked Up by a Patrol.

11 IN A LIFEBOAT THAT SANK

Liner St. Paul, with Cannon, Reaches British Port in Safety—Had 61 Passengers.

PARIS, April 2.—The American steamer Aztec has been sunk by a submarine near an island off Brest. Some of the crew were rescued and are being brought into Brest. A number of the men are missing, and little hope is held that they can be saved, as the steamer was torpedoed at night while a heavy sea was running.

A French patrol picked up nineteen of the crew of the Aztec. Twenty-eight men are reported missing.

William Graves Sharp, the American Ambassador, was informed this afternoon by the French Government of the torpedoing of the Aztec and immediately cabled the State Department at Washington.

Representatives of the American Government will proceed to Brest to take the depositions of survivors of the disaster.

Bluejackets and Officer Saved.

WASHINGTON, April 2.—French Admiralty dispatches to the French Embassy here tonight announcing the sinking without warning of the first armed American merchantman, the freighter Aztec, by a German submarine, said apparently Lieutenant W. F. Gresham and twelve American bluejackets, constituting the armed guard of the vessel, had been saved, but that eleven of the crew were reported missing.

The Admiralty report said the Aztec, bound from New York to Havre, was torpedoed without warning yesterday off Ouessant. The torpedo struck squarely amidships, emitting a powerful gas and putting the wireless out of commission.

The guard with the Captain and three other members of the crew in the second boat to put off apparently were picked up by the French patrol boat Sirrius after three hours. Eleven men are thought to have been drowned when the first boat to put off was smashed.

The third boat, containing the second officer and eighteen men, is not directly accounted for, but the fact that only eleven are reported missing leads to the belief that it must have been picked up.

The Navy Department tonight gave outt he names of the navy members on the Aztec as follows:

Officer in charge—Lieutenant William F. Gresham of Tennessee.

Crew—John I. Eopolucci, boatswain's mate; mother, Annie M. Eopolucci, 649 I Street, Southeast, Washington.

Jacob J. Hilfiker, electrician; father, Jake Hilfiker, 2,206 Preston Street, Baltimore, Md.

Thomas E. Dillon, Quartermaster; father, Thomas I. Dillon, 78 Boyd Avenue, Jersey City, N. J.

William H. Douglas, coxswain; mother, Sarah D. Douglas, 1,459 South Second Street, Terre Haute, Ind.

Adolph Hendrickson, coxswain; father, Charles Hendrickson, 3,034 Eleventh Avenue, Minneapolis, Minn.

Samuel Earl Israel, seaman; mother, Annie Israel, Kellerman, Ala.

Clarence H. Kelley, Quartermaster; mother, Margaret Kelley, 454 South Broad Street, Trenton, N. J.

Joseph Kiewinsky, seaman; father, John Kiewinsky, Rural Free Delivery, Route 3, Box 40, Newburg, W. Va.

William F. Zominger, gunner's mate; brother, Donnie Rominger, Elizabethton, Tenn.

Joseph A. Rucker, seaman; guardian, Joseph W. Rucker, Roanoke, Ala.

Clarence W. Whitney, Quartermaster; father, James H. Whitney, Front and Broadway, Cincinnati, Ohio.

All the naval crew were taken from the United States dispatch boat Dolphin at Washington to be placed on the Aztec.

Officials tonight said the disaster would not affect the policy of arming ships, which would be continued in the most efficient manner possible.

First Armed American Ship Sunk.

The American steamship Aztec, the third armed merchant vessel to sail from

Continued on Page 24.

Text of the President's Address

Gentlemen of the Congress:

I have called the Congress into extraordinary session because there are serious, very serious, choices of policy to be made, and made immediately, which it was neither right nor constitutionally permissible that I should assume the responsibility of making.

On the 3d of February last I officially laid before you the extraordinary announcement of the Imperial German Government that on and after the first day of February it was its purpose to put aside all restraints of law or of humanity and use its submarines to sink every vessel that sought to approach either the ports of Great Britain and Ireland or the western coasts of Europe or any of the ports controlled by the enemies of Germany within the Mediterranean. That had seemed to be the object of the German submarine warfare earlier in the war, but since April of last year the Imperial Government had somewhat restrained the commanders of its undersea craft, in conformity with its promise, then given to us, that passenger boats should not be sunk and that due warning would be given to all other vessels which its submarines might seek to destroy, when no resistance was offered or escape attempted, and care taken that their crews were given at least a fair chance to save their lives in their open boats. The precautions taken were meagre and haphazard enough, as was proved in distressing instance after instance in the progress of the cruel and unmanly business, but a certain degree of restraint was observed.

The new policy has swept every restriction aside. Vessels of every kind, whatever their flag, their character, their cargo, their destination, their errand, have been ruthlessly sent to the bottom without warning and without thought of help or mercy for those on board, the vessels of friendly neutrals along with those of belligerents. Even hospital ships and ships carrying relief to the sorely bereaved and stricken people of Belgium, though the latter were provided with safe conduct through the proscribed areas by the German Government itself and were distinguished by unmistakable marks of identity, have been sunk with the same reckless lack of compassion or of principle.

I was for a little while unable to believe that such things would in fact be done by any Government that had hitherto subscribed to humane practices of civilized nations. International law had its origin in the attempt to set up some law which would be respected and observed upon the seas, where no nation has right of dominion and where lay the free highways of the world. By painful stage after stage has that law been built up, with meagre enough results, indeed, after all was accomplished that could be accomplished, but always with a clear view, at least, of what the heart and conscience of mankind demanded.

This minimum of right the German Government has swept aside, under the plea of retaliation and necessity and because it had no weapons which it could use at sea except these, which it is impossible to employ, as it is employing them, without throwing to the wind all scruples of humanity or of respect for the understandings that were supposed to underlie the intercourse of the world.

I am not now thinking of the loss of property involved, immense and serious as that is, but only of the wanton and wholesale destruction of the lives of noncombatants, men, women, and children, engaged in pursuits which have always, even in the darkest periods of modern history, been deemed innocent and legitimate. Property can be paid for; the lives of peaceful and innocent people cannot be. The present German submarine warfare against commerce is a warfare against mankind.

It is a war against all nations. American ships have been sunk, American lives taken, in ways which it has stirred us very deeply to learn of, but the ships and people of other neutral and friendly nations have been sunk and overwhelmed in the waters in the same way. There has been no discrimination.

The challenge is to all mankind. Each nation must decide for itself how it will meet it. The choice we make for ourselves must be made with a moderation of counsel and a temperateness of judgment befitting our character and our motives as a nation. We must put excited feeling away. Our motive will not be revenge or the victorious assertion of the physical might of the nation, but only the vindication of right, of human right, of which we are only a single champion.

When I addressed the Congress on the 26th of February last I thought that it would suffice to assert our neutral rights with arms, our right to use the seas against unlawful interference, our right to keep our people safe against unlawful violence. But armed neutrality, it now appears, is impracticable. Because submarines are in effect outlaws, when used as the German submarines have been used against merchant shipping, it is impossible to defend ships against their attacks as the law of nations has assumed that merchantmen would defend themselves against privateers or cruisers, visible craft giving chase upon the open sea. It is common prudence in such circumstances, grim necessity indeed, to endeavor to destroy them before they have shown their own intention. They must be dealt with upon sight, if dealt with at all.

The German Government denies the right of neutrals to use arms at all within the areas of the sea which it has proscribed, even in the defense of rights which no modern publicist has ever before questioned their right to defend. The intimation is conveyed that the armed guards which we have placed on our merchant ships will be treated as beyond the pale of law and subject to be dealt with as pirates would be. Armed neutrality is ineffectual enough at best; in such circumstances and in the face of such pretensions it is worse than ineffectual; it is likely only to produce what it was meant to prevent; it is practically certain to draw us into the war without either the rights or the effectiveness of belligerents. There is one choice we cannot make, we are incapable of making; we will not choose the path of submission and suffer the most sacred rights of our nation and our people to be ignored or violated. The wrongs against which we now array ourselves are no common wrongs; they cut to the very roots of human life.

With a profound sense of the solemn and even tragical character of the step I am taking and of the grave responsibilities which it involves, but in unhesitating obedience to what I deem my constitutional duty, I advise that the Congress declare the recent course of the Imperial German Government to be in fact nothing less than war against the Government and people of the United States; that it formally accept the status of belligerent which has thus been thrust upon it; and that it take immediate steps not only to put the country in a more thorough state of defense, but also to exert all its power and employ all its resources to bring the Government of the German Empire to terms and end the war.

What this will involve is clear. It will involve the utmost practicable co-operation in counsel and action with the Governments now at war with Germany, and, as incident to that, the extension to those Governments of the most liberal financial credits, in order that our resources may so far as possible be added to theirs.

It will involve the organization and mobilization of all the material resources of the country to supply the materials of war and serve the incidental needs of the nation in the most abundant and yet the most economical and efficient way possible.

It will involve the immediate full equipment of the navy in all respects, but particularly in supplying it with the best means of dealing with the enemy's submarines.

It will involve the immediate addition to the armed forces of the United States, already provided for by law in case of war, of at least 500,000 men, who should, in my opinion, be chosen upon the principle of universal liability to service, and also the authorization of subsequent additional increments of equal force so soon as they may be needed and can be handled in training.

It will involve also, of course, the granting of adequate credits to the Government, sustained, I hope, so far as they can equitably be sustained by the present generation, by well conceived taxation.

I say sustained so far as may be equitable by taxation, because it seems to me that it would be most unwise to base the credits, which will now be necessary, entirely on money borrowed. It is our duty, I most respectfully urge, to protect our people, so far as we may, against the very serious hardships and evils which would be likely to arise out of the inflation which would be produced by vast loans.

In carrying out the measures by which these things are to be accomplished we should keep constantly in mind the wisdom of interfering as little as possible in our own preparation and in the equipment of our own military forces with the duty—for it will be a very practical duty—of supplying the nations already at war with Germany with the materials which they can obtain only from us or by our assistance. They are in the field and we should help them in every way to be effective there.

I shall take the liberty of suggesting, through the several executive departments of the Government, for the consideration of your committees, measures for the accomplishment of the several objects I have mentioned. I hope that it will be your pleasure to deal with them as having been framed after very careful thought by the branch of the Government upon whom the responsibility of conducting the war and safeguarding the nation will most directly fall.

While we do these things, these deeply momentous things, let us be very clear, and make very clear to all the world, what our motives and our objects are. My own thought has not been driven from its habitual and normal course by the unhappy events of the last two months, and I do not believe that the thought of the nation had been altered or clouded by them. I have exactly the same things in mind now that I had in mind when I addressed the Senate on the 22d of January last; the same that I had in mind when I addressed the Congress on the 3d of February and on the 26th of February. Our object now, as then, is to vindicate the principles of peace and justice in the life of the world as against selfish and autocratic power, and to set up among the really free and self-governed peoples of the world such a concert of purpose and of action as will henceforth insure the observance of those principles.

Neutrality is no longer feasible or desirable where the peace of the world is involved and the freedom of its peoples, and the menace to that peace and freedom lies in the existence of autocratic Governments, backed by organized force which is controlled wholly by their will, not by the will of their people. We have seen the last of neutrality in such circumstances. We are at the beginning of an age in which it will be insisted that the same standards of conduct and of responsibility for wrong done shall be observed among nations and their Governments that are observed among the individual citizens of civilized States.

We have no quarrel with the German people. We have no feeling toward them but one of sympathy and friendship. It was not upon their impulse that their Government acted in entering this war. It was not with their previous knowledge or approval. It was a war determined upon as wars used to be determined upon in the old, unhappy days, when peoples were nowhere consulted by their rulers and wars were provoked and waged in the interest of dynasties or of little groups of ambitious men who were accustomed to use their fellow men as pawns and tools.

Self-governed nations do not fill their neighbor States with spies or set the course of intrigue to bring about some critical posture of affairs which will give them an opportunity to strike and make conquest. Such designs can be successfully worked out only under cover and where no one has the right to ask questions. Cunningly contrived plans of deception or aggression, carried, it may be, from generation to generation, can be worked out and kept from the light only within the privacy of courts or behind the carefully guarded confidences of a narrow and privileged class. They are happily impossible where public opinion commands and insists upon full information concerning all the nation's affairs.

A steadfast concert for peace can never be maintained except by a partnership of democratic nations. No autocratic Government could be trusted to keep faith within it or observe its covenants. It must be a league of honor, a partnership of opinion. Intrigue would eat its vitals away; the plottings of inner circles who could plan what they would and render account to no one would be a corruption seated at its very heart. Only free peoples can hold their purpose and their honor steady to a common end and prefer the interests of mankind to any narrow interest of their own.

Does not every American feel that assurance has been added to our hope for the future peace of the world by the wonderful and heartening things that have been happening within the last few weeks in Russia? Russia was known by those who knew her best to have been always in fact democratic at heart in all the vital habits of her thought, in all the intimate relationships of her people that spoke their natural instinct, their habitual attitude toward life. The autocracy that crowned the summit of her political structure, long as it had stood and terrible as was the reality of its power, was not in fact Russian in origin, character, or purpose; and now it has been shaken off and the great, generous Russian people have been added, in all their naive majesty and might, to the forces that are fighting for freedom in the world, for justice, and for peace. Here is a fit partner for a League of Honor.

One of the things that has served to convince us that the Prussian autocracy was not and could never be our friend is that from the very outset of the present war it has filled our unsuspecting communities, and even our offices of government, with spies and set criminal intrigues everywhere afoot against our national unity of counsel, our peace within and without, our industries and our commerce. Indeed, it is now evident that its spies were here even before the war began; and it is unhappily not a matter of conjecture, but a fact proved in our courts of justice, that the intrigues which have more than once come perilously near to disturbing the peace and dislocating the industries of the country, have been carried on at the instigation, with the support, and even under the personal direction of official agents of the Imperial Government, accredited to the Government of the United States.

Even in checking these things and trying to extirpate them we have sought to put the most generous interpretation possible upon them because we knew that their source lay, not in any hostile feeling or purpose of the German people toward us, (who were, no doubt, as ignorant of them as we ourselves were,) but only in the selfish designs of a Government that did what it pleased and told its people nothing. But they have played their part in serving to convince us at last that that Government entertains no real friendship for us, and means to act against our peace and security at its convenience. That it means to stir up enemies against us at our very doors the intercepted note to the German Minister at Mexico City is eloquent evidence.

We are accepting this challenge of hostile purpose because we know that in such a Government, following such methods, we can never have a friend; and that in the presence of its organized power, always lying in wait to accomplish we know not what purpose, can be no assured security for the democratic Governments of the world. We are now about to accept the gauge of battle with this natural foe to liberty and shall, if necessary, spend the whole force of the nation to check and nullify its pretensions and its power. We are glad, now that we see the facts with no veil of false pretense about them, to fight thus for the ultimate peace of the world and for the liberation of its peoples, the German peoples included; for the rights of nations, great and small, and the privilege of men everywhere to choose their way of life and of obedience.

The world must be made safe for democracy. Its peace must be planted upon the tested foundations of political liberty. We have no selfish ends to serve. We desire no conquest, no dominion. We seek no indemnities for ourselves, no material compensation for the sacrifices we shall freely make. We are but one of the champions of the rights of mankind. We shall be satisfied when those rights have been made as secure as the faith and the freedom of nations can make them.

Just because we fight without rancor and without selfish object, seeking nothing for ourselves but what we shall wish to share with all free peoples, we shall, I feel confident, conduct our operations as belligerents without passion and ourselves observe with proud punctilio the principles of right and of fair play we profess to be fighting for.

I have said nothing of the Governments allied with the Imperial Government of Germany because they have not made war upon us or challenged us to defend our right and our honor. The Austro-Hungarian Government has, indeed, avowed its unqualified indorsement and acceptance of the reckless and lawless submarine warfare, adopted now without disguise by the Imperial German Government, and it has therefore not been possible for this Government to receive Count Tarnowski, the Ambassador recently accredited to this Government by the Imperial and Royal Government of Austria-Hungary; but that Government has not actually engaged in warfare against citizens of the United States on the seas, and I take the liberty, for the present at least, of postponing a discussion of our relations with the authorities at Vienna. We enter this war only where we are clearly forced into it because there are no other means of defending our right.

It will be all the easier for us to conduct ourselves as belligerents in a high spirit of right and fairness because we act without animus, not with enmity toward a people or with the desire to bring any injury or disadvantage upon them, but only in armed opposition to an irresponsible Government which has thrown aside all considerations of humanity and of right and is running amuck.

We are, let me say again, the sincere friends of the German people, and shall desire nothing so much as the early re-establishment of intimate relations of mutual advantage between us, however hard it may be for them for the time being to believe that this is spoken from our hearts. We have borne with their present Government through all these bitter months because of that friendship, exercising a patience and forbearance which would otherwise have been impossible.

We shall happily still have an opportunity to prove that friendship in our daily attitude and actions toward the millions of men and women of German birth and native sympathy who live among us and share our life, and we shall be proud to prove it toward all, who are in fact loyal to their neighbors and to the Government in the hour of test. They are most of them as true and loyal Americans as if they had never known any other fealty or allegiance. They will be prompt to stand with us in rebuking and restraining the few who may be of a different mind and purpose. If there should be disloyalty, it will be dealt with with a firm hand of stern repression; but, if it lifts its head at all, it will lift it only here and there and without countenance except from a lawless and malignant few.

It is a distressing and oppressive duty, gentlemen of the Congress, which I have performed in thus addressing you. There are, it may be, many months of fiery trial and sacrifice ahead of us. It is a fearful thing to lead this great, peaceful people into war, into the most terrible and disastrous of all wars, civilization itself seeming to be in the balance.

But the right is more precious than peace, and we shall fight for the things which we have always carried nearest our hearts—for democracy, for the right of those who submit to authority to have a voice in their own Governments, for the rights and liberties of small nations, for a universal dominion of right by such a concert of free peoples as shall bring peace and safety to all nations and make the world itself at last free.

To such a task we can dedicate our lives and our fortunes, everything that we are and everything that we have, with the pride of those who know that the day has come when America is privileged to spend her blood and her might for the principles that gave her birth and happiness and the peace which she has treasured.

God helping her, she can do no other.

The War Resolution Now Before Congress

This resolution was introduced in the House of Representatives last night by Representative Flood, Chairman of the Foreign Affairs Committee, immediately after the President's address:

JOINT RESOLUTION, Declaring that a State of War Exists Between the Imperial German Government and the Government and People of the United States and Making Provision to Prosecute the Same.

Whereas, The recent acts of the Imperial German Government are acts of war against the Government and people of the United States:

Resolved, By the Senate and House of Representatives of the United States of America in Congress assembled, that the state of war between the United States and the Imperial German Government which has thus been thrust upon the United States is hereby formally declared; and

That the President be, and he is hereby, authorized and directed to take immediate steps not only to put the country in a thorough state of defense but also to exert all of its power and employ all of its resources to carry on war against the Imperial German Government and to bring the conflict to a successful termination.

MUST EXERT ALL OUR POWER

To Bring a "Government That Is Running Amuck to Terms."

WANTS LIBERAL CREDITS

And Universal Service, for "the World Must Be Made Safe for Democracy."

A TUMULTUOUS GREETING

Congress Adjourns After "State of War" Resolution Is Introduced—Acts Today.

Special to The New York Times.

WASHINGTON, April 2.—At 8:35 o'clock tonight the United States virtually made its entrance into the war. At that hour President Wilson appeared before a joint session of the Senate and House and invited it to consider the fact that Germany had been making war upon us and to take action in recognition of that fact in accordance with his recommendations, which included universal military service, the raising of an army of 500,000 men, and co-operation with the Allies in all ways that will help most effectively to defeat Germany.

Resolutions recognizing and declaring the state of war were immediately introduced in the House and Senate by Representative Flood and Senator Martin, both of the President's birth-State, Virginia, and they are the strongest declarations of war that the United States has ever made in any war in which it has been engaged since it became a nation. They are the Administration resolutions drawn up after conference with the President, and in language approved and probably dictated by him, and they will come before the two Foreign Affairs Committees at meetings which will be held tomorrow morning and will be reported at the earliest practical moment.

Unreservedly With the Allies.

Before an audience that cheered him as he has never been cheered in the Capitol in his life the President cast in the lot of America unreservedly with the Allies and declared for a war that must not end until the issue between autocracy and democracy has been fought out. He recited our injuries at Germany's hands, but he did not rest our cause on those; he went on from that point to range us with the Allies as a factor in an irrepressible conflict between the autocrat and the people. He showed that peace was impossible for the democracies of the world while this power remained on earth. "The world," he said, "must be made safe for democracy."

We had learned that the German autocracy could never be a friend of this country; she had been our enemy while nominally our friend, and even before the war of 1914 broke out. He called on us to take our stand with the democracies in this irrepressible conflict, with before our eyes "the wonderful and heartening events that have been happening in the last few weeks in Russia." He reaffirmed his hope for peace and for freedom, and looked to the war now forced upon us to bring these about; for, he said, a world compact for peace "can never be maintained except by a concert of the democracies of the world."

The objects for which we fight, he said, are democracy, the right of those who submit to authority to have a voice in their own government, the right and liberties of small nations, the universal dominion of right, the concert of free peoples to bring peace and safety to all nations, and to make the world free. These have always been our ideals, and to accomplish them, we accept the war Germany has made upon us. In fighting it we must not only raise an army and increase the navy, but must aid the Allies in all ways, financial and other, and so order our own preparations as not to interfere with the supply of munitions they are getting from us.

Trouble-making Pacifists Barred.

The President delivered this speech before an audience that had been carefully sifted. All day Washington had been in the hands of belligerent pacifists, truculent in manner, and determined to break into the Capitol. They tried to take possession of the Capitol steps, up which the President must go when he entered, and met the same fate that Coxey's rioters fell in with twenty-three years ago at the hands of the police, who dispersed them.

A handful of them fell upon Senator Lodge and assaulted him. Others en-

"All the News That's Fit to Print."

The New York Times.

THE WEATHER
Fair today and tomorrow; moderate northwest to north winds.
For full weather report see Page 21.

VOL. LXVII...NO. 21,839. NEW YORK, FRIDAY, NOVEMBER 9, 1917.—TWENTY-TWO PAGES. ONE CENT In Greater New York. | TWO CENTS Within Commuting Distance. | THREE CENT[S] Elsewhere.

REVOLUTIONISTS SEIZE PETROGRAD; KERENSKY FLEES; PLEDGE IS GIVEN TO SEEK "AN IMMEDIATE PEACE"; ITALIANS AGAIN DRIVEN BACK; LOSE 17,000 MORE MEN

WOODS MUST GO AS POLICE HEAD, HYLAN DECIDES

Mayor-Elect Will Ask Him to Retire if He Fails to Resign.

SUCCESSOR NOT YET FOUND

Murphy Will Refrain from Interference, Congressman Smith Declares.

HYLAN SHOCKS JOBHUNTERS

Announces Delay in Considering Appointments—Craig Against Pay-as-You-Go Plan.

Mayor-elect John F. Hylan, it was said yesterday, has no intention of retaining Arthur Woods at the head of the Police Department. Friends of the Mayor-elect said that he expected to find a man after his own liking, who, measured up to the job, to succeed the Police Commissioner before Jan. 1, when the Mayor-elect assumes office. Unless Judge Hylan had received the resignation of Commissioner Woods by the time he was ready to appoint his successor, the Police Commissioner, it was said, would be asked to retire.

At the headquarters of Judge Hylan persons who enjoy the confidence of the Mayor-elect said last night that he regarded the administration of the Police Department under Commissioner Woods as having been one of the vital issues in the campaign, even though less attention was paid to it by Judge Hylan in his speeches than to some other branches of the Mitchel Administration. The wire-tapping episode, which aroused such a storm of protest in certain quarters at the time of the charities investigation, and in which the Police Department under Commissioner Woods was directly concerned, was condemned both by Tammany Hall and its organized allies, the Democratic Fusion Committee and the Business Men's Association, in their platforms. Judge Hylan, it was said, felt that he was bound by the terms of the platform on which he was elected.

Expect Woods to Resign.

It is the belief of Judge Hylan's friends that Commissioner Woods will follow the usual practice and submit his resignation when the change of administration occurs, even though a provision in the New York City Charter provides for a five-year term, which in the case of the present incumbent does not expire until April, 1919. But even should this belief not prove justified, the Charter provisions relating to the Police Commissionership are regarded by Judge Hylan's friends as sufficiently plastic to provide the Mayor-elect with the means of creating a vacancy at the head of the Police Department whenever he desires to do so.

It was said at Hylan headquarters last night that the Mayor-elect as yet had not given serious consideration to the task of finding a successor for Commissioner Woods. Reports indicating that the Police Commissionership would go to a "good Tammany man," of whom some have been named in the speculation over patronage, and that Charles F. Murphy, leader of Tammany Hall, was particularly anxious to have his wishes consulted in the filling of this office, it was said both at the headquarters of Judge Hylan and at Tammany Hall, might be discarded as without justification.

Judge Hylan, it was said last night by his friends, was keenly alive to the fact that Mayors stood or fell by the public verdict on the administration of the Police Department. Leader Murphy also, it was asserted, was not oblivious of the fact that, while Judge Hylan was Mayor, Tammany would be on trial, and that any attempt on the part of Tammany Hall to lay violent hands on the Police Department would arouse a storm of resentment at the very beginning of the new administration. Among the friends of Judge Hylan the prediction was made freely yesterday that the Mayor-elect would make clear to the political leaders that he did not need any help in picking a new Police Commissioner.

A statement made yesterday by County Clerk William F. Schneider, Chairman of the Democratic Fusion Committee, which body was largely instrumental in making Judge Hylan the nominee for Mayor, was regarded as not altogether void of significance.

Wants Hylan to be Foot Free.

"The appointment of a Police Commissioner should be left entirely to the Mayor," said Mr. Schneider. "The political organizations which were behind Judge Hylan's candidacy should scrupulously avoid any divided responsibility in the administration of the Police Department. Tammany's political foes have always made the Police Department an issue in city elections, and the course of Tammany in relation to police administration has been disastrous to that organization. The selection of a Police Commissioner should be undertaken by Judge Hylan solely on his own responsibility and without any interference or advice by politicians."

Leader Murphy did not appear at Tammany Hall yesterday. It was learned that the Tammany chief was preparing to go away for a rest, as is his practice after a hard-fought campaign. In his absence Congressman Thomas F. Smith, Secretary of Tammany Hall, did the talking.

"Mr. Murphy has been leader of Tammany Hall for sixteen years," said Congressman Smith. "In all that time he has neither recommended nor had anything to do with the selection of a Police Commissioner. There is every

Continued on Page 3.

Insists Emperor Charles Will Be Polish Ruler

Special Cable to THE NEW YORK TIMES.

THE HAGUE, Nov. 8.—In spite of recent denials, the Lokal-Anzeiger repeats that the Austrian Emperor is to be named King of Poland. It says this was decided on at a Crown Council on Monday.

Poland is to be joined to Austria, and Galicia is to belong to the future Kingdom of Poland. Lithuania and Courland will be separate States, such as Prussia, and be represented by Grand Dukes. The paper points out that in Austria even the Germanic parties appear to approve this, but that special emphasis is laid on and guarantees demanded for "the strengthening of Germanic-Austria."

The paper seems to question whether German interests have been sufficiently considered in this settlement.

THREAT OF DICTATOR IN GERMAN SNARL

Government Attempts to Force Dropping of Demand for Radical Vice Chancellor.

HERTLING DENIES PROMISES

Opposition to Attack Chancellor as Soon as Reichstag Meets Unless He Yields.

COPENHAGEN, Nov. 8.—The threat that a military dictatorship is inevitable unless insistence upon a radical Vice Chancellor is dropped and the Government of Count von Hertling as it now stands is accepted is held out over the progressive democratic elements in Germany.

Count von Hertling, through a semi-official note in the Norddeutsche Allgemeine Zeitung, announces that no promises whatever were made to give the radicals the two posts they desired. Representatives of the Reichstag majority have issued an equally authoritative announcement that they adhere to their old position.

The radical press indicates that the Chancellor's compromise proposal to appoint a radical Deputy to the newly created Ministry for occupied territories with a seat in the Prussian Cabinet is not acceptable because such a post would be merely temporary, and the occupant would be powerless in the face of the military authorities.

The situation is drifting rapidly toward the goal desired by the reactionaries, that is, a split in the present alignment in the Reichstag and the formation of a new coalition embracing the Conservatives and the National Lib[erals] ... which would have a bare majority in the Reichstag, is by no means impossible, despite the apparent unity proclaimed by the majority caucus.

The Catholic Centrum is by no means adverse to following the Chancellor along a road marked with party advantages. The National Liberals, who for the most part are Conservatives and annexationists and whose hearts never were in the present majority bloc, intimate strongly in their formal announcement of Herr Friedberg's withdrawal of his acceptance of the Vice Presidency of the Prussian Cabinet their dissatisfaction with the attitude of the Radicals and the Socialists.

The Socialists apparently have abandoned the dictum expressed by Philipp Scheidemann on Sunday that the new von Hertling Government, which differs from that of Dr. Michaelis only in the person of its chief, provided all necessary guarantees of responsible popular Government as a pre-condition to peace.

The Tageblatt and other Radical newspapers say that if Chancellor von Hertling bows to the "hidden powers" and the influence of the Court clique, the opposition will introduce on Nov. 22, when the Reichstag reconvenes, a resolution of lack of confidence in the Government. Count von Hertling's position is much like that of Dr. Michaelis after his "as I interpret it" speech.

LONDON, Nov. 8.—The German political crisis is represented as being as acute as ever in special dispatches from Amsterdam. Some say that Count von Hertling's Chancellorship is in danger of immediate shipwreck.

The refusal of Herr Friedberg, leader of the National Liberty Party, to accept the Vice Presidency of the Prussian Ministry and the prospect that Dr. Helfferich is to be retained as Vice Chancellor are regarded as matters impossible of settlement. Count von Hertling is reported to have succumbed to military and junker influence.

The Cologne Gazette blames the Progressives and the Socialists for the reawakening of the crisis, and says that the prospect for a political truce has disappeared.

OTTO H. KAHN TALKS FINANCE WITH WILSON

New Yorker at the White House Discusses Economic Condition of the Country.

WASHINGTON, Nov. 8.—Otto H. Kahn, head of Kuhn, Loeb & Co., called today on President Wilson. He would not discuss his visit except to say that it was for the purpose of talking over the economic condition of the country.

Otto H. Kahn has given considerable attention to the question of war taxation, and has advocated methods that would lay as little strain as possible on business in general while taking heavy levies from profits or incomes which could afford it without danger of drying up the sources of revenue. In May, when the question of taxing profits was beginning to receive much consideration, he pointed out that a very heavy tax on excess profits would be more desirable than a moderate tax on general profits.

"It appears," he said at that time, "that a 40 per cent. tax on excess profits over and above the average earnings for the last three years would yield for the present year the amazing total of at least $800,000,000 in addition to the yield from the corporate income tax at the rate of 4 per cent."

In August he urged that undue burdens on incomes and business profits should be avoided, while the taxes should be laid as widely as possible in order not to lay so much burden on any one as to be crushing.

"All I am advocating," he said at that time, "is in effect that in the public interest not too much be exacted at once, but that by dividing the burden over a reasonable number of years, capital in no one year, and especially not during the first year of the war, should be so excessively taxed as to produce an unscientific and dangerous strain. If the great fund of capital is suddenly and too greatly reduced the effect upon commerce and industry is apt to be sudden and withering."

CADORNA IS OUTFLANKED

A General Among the Troops Cut Off on the Middle Tagliamento.

INVADERS CAPTURE 80 GUNS

Berlin Reckons Total at More Than 2,300; That of Prisoners Over 250,000.

ROME ADMITS WITHDRAWAL

Official Report Shows That Rearguard Actions Are Proceeding West of the Livenza.

BERLIN, Nov. 8, (via London.)—Austro-German forces in Northern Italy have crossed the Livenza River, and in outflanking operations on the middle Tagliamento have captured 17,000 Italian troops, among them a General. Eighty guns have been added to the booty, which now includes more than 2,300 guns. The total number of prisoners taken since the drive began now exceeds 250,000.

These developments of the campaign are announced in the afternoon report from Army Headquarters, the text of which follows:

Our detachments, advancing on the mountain roads, have broken the resistance of the enemy rear guard. By an outflanking movement our attacking columns cut off the retreat of the enemy troops still holding out on the middle Tagliamento between Tolmezzo and Gemona and on the permanent fortified works of Monte San Simeone.

Up to the present 17,000 Italians, among them a General, with 80 guns, have had to surrender.

In the plain, fighting has developed along the Livenza River. By a vigorous advance German and Austro-Hungarian divisions, in spite of destroyed bridges, have forced the crossing and have thrown the enemy back westward.

The total number of prisoners captured has now been increased to more than 250,000 and the booty in guns to more than 2,300.

Tonight's report says:

In Italy we are fighting our way forward in the mountains and on the plains.

Retreat Continues, Rome Reports.

ROME, Nov. 8.—The withdrawal of the Italian line was continued yesterday, the War Office announced today. The larger units retired unmolested.

Italian troops fought numerous rearguard actions, in the course of which they succeeded in holding up the Austro-German advance temporarily. Italian airplanes continued bombarding hostile forces along the Tagliamento and brought down five enemy machines.

The text of the statement follows:

During yesterday we continued the withdrawal of our line. The larger units have retired without being molested by the enemy.

Numerous engagements took place between the hills of Vittorio and the confluence of the Monticano and the Livenza, in the course of which our brave troops succeeded in detaining the enemy's advance.

In spite of strong resistance on the part of hostile machines, our aviators renewed their bombardments of enemy troops along the Tagliamento. Five enemy airplanes were brought down.

As the Vittorio hills and the Monticano River lie to the west of the Livenza, the statement of the Italian War Office is equivalent to an admission that the Austro-Germans have crossed the latter stream.

Final Stand Beyond the Livenza?

By The Associated Press.

ITALIAN ARMY HEADQUARTERS, Nov. 8.—The bulk of the Austro-German invading forces today presents a main frontage of about thirty-five miles along the Tagliamento River, with reconnoissance parties thrust forward eight or ten miles west of the river, for the purpose of feeling for the points of least resistance. This is producing detached engagements, but no battle in force has yet occurred.

The Livenza River, to which the Italian withdrawal is now in progress, is only one of a series of successive defense parallels. The Italian Army still has in reserve large bodies of troops, which, however, naturally feel the effects produced by the recent retirement of their main body. Heavy reinforcements at this moment, therefore, would render invaluable assistance, in the opinion of the military authorities.

The enemy territorial occupation in Eastern Friuli presents a sinister aspect far beyond its military purport. The Alps heretofore have been the traditional boundary between the Northern Teutonic and the Southern Latin races. The Austro-Germans recognize the Alpine boundary, except for Trent and Trieste.

Now for the first time the Teutonic forces are occupying territory in the Friuli plains, which are the easternmost part of Venetia and age-long possessions of the Latins. Such an invasion strikes at the very heart of the principle of nationality, and also thrusts a Teutonic wedge southward along the Adriatic. This brings up the grave question of whether Germany will finally secure territorial lodgment with ports and naval bases on the Adriatic, thus realizing her aim to

Continued on Page 4.

British Government Denies Lack of Concern for Italy

LONDON, Nov. 8.—The following official announcement was issued tonight:

"A statement from a correspondent of The Associated Press at Italian Headquarters appeared in the British press today. This statement sets out to remind the Allies that something more than assurances were needed for getting reinforcements in men and munitions to the threatened Italian lines, and purported to reflect the feeling of Italians, who were represented as distrusting the allied efforts to help them. It was also stated that the enemy masses were so overwhelming that nothing but effective reinforcements would turn the tide.

"This alarmist statement is absolutely uncalled for and is calculated to do grave harm by suggesting that the seriousness of the military situation in Italy is not appreciated by her allies, and that the latter are not giving her the support she requires. There is no truth whatever in these assertions. The statement that the enemy masses are overwhelming is an absurd exaggeration."

The Associated Press issued this statement last night:

"The dispatch to which the foregoing British official statement refers was sent by The Associated Press correspondent at Italian Headquarters on Nov. 7. This correspondent is an American Staff man, who was present at the beginning of the Italian retreat and accompanied the Italian Army back to its present position.

"The dispatch in question was passed by the Italian military censors at General Cadorna's headquarters, and, as it was sent through France, also passed the French censorship."

LONDON HAILS OUR WAR MISSION

Comes at Critical Period of the War with New Assurance of Victory.

ENVOYS MAKE BRISK START

Begin Conferences on First Day —Benson Visits Jellicoe— Trip Was Uneventful.

Special Cable to THE NEW YORK TIMES.

LONDON, Nov. 8.—The American mission, headed by Colonel E. M. House, arrived in Europe at a crucial period of the world war. With Russia in the throes of a fresh revolution that may lead to anything, and with Italy engaged in a desperate struggle against both a foreign enemy and internal difficulties the landing of the American mission at a British port is an encouragement to the stalwart and a rebuke to the faint hearted.

To England in particular it possesses special significance. It is a concrete expression of the union of Anglo-Saxon races in the greatest war for liberty the world has ever seen, and also an augury of the victorious overthrow of despotic forces which make the world unsafe for democracy.

The statement which Colonel House gave to the British press tonight supplemented the announcement issued in America by the President. In all quarters it is hailed as a plain definition of the objects aimed at by America and a pledge of America's intention to fight on till those ends are attained.

Great Britain's confidence in the issue of the struggle has never been seriously undermined. There have been times of depression when the end seemed far distant but the country as a whole has set itself resolutely to travel the long and weary road. England never for one moment doubted its ability to win through itself.

There were those who questioned the possibility of a final decision being reached in this war. There still are a few of these, chiefly to be found among that clique which believes that a negotiated peace with an unregenerate and unrepentant Germany is an acceptable solution.

America's clear perception of the issue at stake and America's undivided purpose to fight, as Colonel House put it, until it becomes certain that no group of selfish men can again bring about disaster to the world, more than counterbalances all that history has written, or may yet write, on the wrong side of the allied ledger.

Colonel House explained today to the English newspaper representatives the circumstances under which the American mission had come to participate in the Allied War Council shortly to be held in Paris. He was asked if the United States was going to sign the pact of London and he quietly, but clearly, made it patent that the question did not arise.

Various phrases in President Wilson's announcement drew a query as to whether any criticism of the past conduct of the war by allied Governments was implied.

Colonel House decisively negatived any such suggestion. In this respect it may be stated emphatically that the American participation in the war council of the Allies is most heartily welcomed by those who most clearly see

Continued on Page 11.

AWAITS LIGHT FROM RUSSIA

Washington Reserves Judgment, Hoping Revolt Is Only Local.

EXPECTS A COUNTER-MOVE

Kerensky, with Conservatives and Perhaps the Army Behind Him, May Save the Country.

DARK DAYS SEEN AHEAD

And Allied War Conference Faces Another Huge Problem —Bigger Burden for Us.

Special to The New York Times.

WASHINGTON, Nov. 8.—Until accurate official reports are received, official and diplomatic Washington are reserving judgment on the new Russian crisis and all that it involves, including possibly civil war, and a still further weakening of Russia's position in the war against Germany.

Dark as the news dispatches make the situation in Petrograd appear, there is a strong hope among officials and diplomats that there may be a silver lining to the cloud. On every hand keen sympathy was expressed for Premier Kerensky and those who have been standing with him against terrific odds in opposing the extremist elements who, by their activities, have threatened to disorganize the Russian military machine, and have worked for separate peace, regardless of its effect on the future of Russia and her pledges to her allies.

The State Department has received no official confirmation of the Maximalist successes in Petrograd. In the last six days Secretary Lansing has received only two messages from Ambassador Francis, and neither dealt with the political situation. One bore date of Friday last and the other of Tuesday.

The Russian Embassy officials said they had no advices from Petrograd on the basis of which comment could be made. Jean Soukine, First Secretary, after a telephone conversation this afternoon with Ambassador Bakhmeteff, who is in Memphis, stated that in the absence of official intelligence the Embassy held that the action of the Maximalists in Petrograd, as told in the news dispatches, was local to the capital and by no means representative of the will or of the Russian nation.

This point was emphasized here today that the dispatches from Petrograd stated that the Maximalists had taken control of the telegraph offices and that this put them in a position to exaggerate reports of the situation in their own favor.

First Secretary Soukine stated that the Embassy was unable to present the views of the Government, being without instructions, but he pointed out that Petrograd was the centre of Bolsheviki activity. To this fact, he said, was due the present situation in Petrograd, which did not represent the conditions throughout Russia. Mr. Soukine stated that the local character of the disturbance was proved by the fact that the Central Executive Committee of the Petrograd Council of Soldiers' and Workmen's Delegates did not express the will of the Pan Russian Council's Executive Committee, which only a few days ago refused to approve the creation by the Petrograd Council's Executive Committee of a military revolutionary committee, and at the same time urged that measures be taken to prevent the consummation of the designs of the Bolsheviki.

The embassy officials suggested that "Petrograd is likely to be isolated." No interpretation of this statement was given, but it was believed to indicate a belief that the Bolsheviki would find themselves without national support and that the army might decline to accept orders from their Military Revolutionary Committee, which now, according to the announcement in Petrograd, is the sole Governmental authority.

Expect a New Government.

In many quarters it was thought that another Government will be formed for Russia, now that some members of the Provisional Government had been arrested. The new Government would probably be formed at Moscow, it was said, and be dominated by the conservative Socialist elements, although it might be a coalition, including members of the Constitutional Democratic Party as well as Socialists and Laborites, of which last-named party Premier Kerensky is a member.

No doubt was expressed in diplomatic circles that the Allied Powers would recognize any Government formed to oppose the Bolsheviki, even if the latter maintained their hold upon Petrograd. Moscow was regarded as the probable choice for the provisional capital, because all the elements there have been in sympathy with the Government as against the extremist Socialists. Moscow also is held to be a more purely Russian city, and, as compared with Petrograd, practically free from the elements that have made the life of the Government precarious.

It is believed that unless the army goes over en masse to the Bolsheviki, the temporary ascendency of the rad-

Continued on Page 2.

Reverses Cited as Showing Greater Need Than Ever For Unified Direction of Allied War Policy

By CHARLES H. GRASTY.

Special Cable to THE NEW YORK TIMES.

ROME, Nov. 8.—My observations here confirm previous insistence upon the urgent need of centralized methods of managing the war. At bottom this war is the biggest business enterprise ever undertaken, and, while the Kaiser handles his end of it as such, each of the Allies is more or less playing its own separate game. With an infinity of resources, they have discussed and postponed critical decisions until the advantage has been lost.

To mention one recent instance: If the Korniloff movement had been handled by the Allies as the Kaiser would have handled such an opportunity, the Russian situation might have been stabilized and the Italian drive rendered impossible.

There has not been a single allied action, with the exception of the battle of the Marne, ranking as a great aggressive stroke. The Allies are not organized to initiate and execute big policies. Instead of looking ahead and planning on a big scale, they yield where pressure is applied, with the result that usually they trail along a few days or weeks behind Germany. Purely local and political matters divide and divert attention in the allied Chancelleries.

Coming on top of many previous heartbreaking lost opportunities, the present menace in Italy is quite serious enough to rally the Entente Powers at last into substituting for the town meeting some plan under which they can see the war situation as a whole and concentrate with foresight, originality, and driving power, as we understand those things in America.

In a word, after three years, it is time to quit playing amateur against professional. If America gives the lead, all the rest will follow, as there are directed against us none of the petty jealousies peculiar to Europe, and all the allied countries have complete confidence in our disinterestedness and sound leadership.

Plans for the conduct of the war on the basis of a unified western front extending from the North Sea to the Adriatic are now under consideration by Premiers Lloyd George and Painlevé and other high civil and military officials in conference in Rome.

STOCKS TUMBLE ON RUSSIAN NEWS

Flood of Liquidation Hits Exchange, Heightened by Action of Short Sellers.

NEWS CHECKS BROAD RISE

No Action Considered Yet in Regard to Publishing Proportion of Short Sales.

The stock market suffered one of the most drastic declines of the year yesterday, following the receipt of dispatches which told of the Kerensky Government's downfall. Owners of securities considered the Russian news more disturbing than developments on the Italian front, although in banking circles the new republic's reversion to a condition of political chaos did not seem to increase pessimism over the war outlook greatly. In a wild hour of trading the active speculative stocks dropped 4 to 11 points from their previous levels, thereafter recovering part of the distance under active bidding from investors and traders who covered short contracts and what looked like banking support.

The decline was made all the more emphatic because it occurred suddenly in the midst of a rather broad rise of prices. Starting slightly higher than Wednesday's closing quotations, the prominent railroad and industrial shares advanced in many cases more than a point before 11 o'clock, and were moving along normally when the first reports came from London of the changed conditions in Russia. There was a quick drop of a couple of points in the next quarter hour, and then a short period of steadiness, a lull before the storm.

Big Sales of Steel Common.

When brokerage houses with wire connections began to get in their orders after flashing out the Russian news, a flood of selling struck the Exchange, which was heightened by the operations of short sellers in the Street and out. Steel common was poured forth in blocks running as high as 5,000 shares, and International Mercantile Marine preferred dropped under heavy selling from 98 to 91½, frequently by quarters and half points, and without a period of recovery. Reading, Southern Pacific, New York Central, and Union Pacific were pressed for sale, and numerous high-grade railroad bonds lost more ground than in any preceding day since Jan. 1.

The movements of some of the more active stocks from their best to their lowest prices, with their net declines, are in the following table:

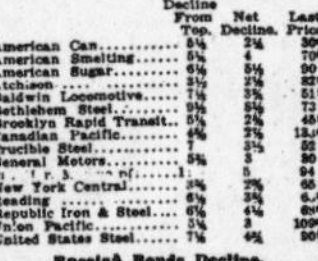

	Decline From Top.	Net Decline.	Last Price.
American Can	5¼	2¼	30⅝
American Smelting	5⅛	4	70⅝
American Sugar	6⅛	5½	90
Atchison	3½	2⅜	87⅝
Baldwin Locomotive	7⅛	3⅝	51¼
Bethlehem Steel	9½	8½	73
Brooklyn Rapid Transit	5⅛	2⅜	45¼
Canadian Pacific	4⅝	2⅝	[illegible]
Crucible Steel	7	3½	52
General Motors	5⅜	3	80
[illegible]	[illegible]	5	94
New York Central	3⅜	2⅝	65
Reading	6½	3⅝	[illegible]
Republic Iron & Steel	6⅝	4¼	[illegible]
Union Pacific	3⅛	3	109⅝
United States Steel	7⅛	4⅝	90⅝

Russian Bonds Decline.

The Russian situation had a naturally adverse effect on the Russian bonds dealt in on the Curb. From Wednesday's last price of 56 the 5½s declined to 48, with sales of $30,000, and the 6½s dropped from 64 to 58 with transactions involving $25,000. Russian exchange fell away from 13.35 cents per ruble to 11.75 cents for transfers by check, approaching the previous minimum record of 11½ cents. At times the market was report-

Continued on Page 3.

HOPE STRONG MAN WILL RULE RUSSIA

Zemstvos' Agent Here and Herman Bernstein Agree That Kerensky Must Go.

GREAT REACTION EXPECTED

Salchnovsky Thinks Revolt May Lead to Constitutional Monarchy.

The elimination of Kerensky from the affairs of the Russian Government was declared to be the most probable as well as the most desirable result of the present Maximalist revolt by persons familiar with Russian affairs and in sympathy with the moderate parties there.

Alexander Sakhnovsky, head of the American offices of the Union of Zemstvos, predicted that the reaction toward a stronger form of government might go as far as the setting up of a constitutional monarchy under the Grand Duke Michael, who was named as the successor of Nicholas in the first announcements of the revolution last March, but was immediately pushed out of the way by the tide of radical sentiment.

"Russians who have landed in New York within the last few days," said Mr. Sakhnovsky, "bring reports that the whole nation outside of the radicals of Petrograd is disgusted with the violence, disorder, and uncertainty which have prevailed for months past. There is a strong tide setting toward a more compact and powerful government, and Moscow would undoubtedly be the natural centre of such a movement.

"In Moscow the Bolsheviki are not 1 per cent. of the total population, and all Russia outside of Petrograd would stand together, I believe, against the extreme policy of the Maximalists. This will be particularly true if, as is possible, Lenine and Trotzsky call in the German fleet to their aid.

"In any event, it will take a stronger Government than that of Kerensky to bring about order. The excellence of Kerensky's motives and ideals is recognized, but he is too gentle a man for his position at the present time. It has been shown that the policy of mildness with the Bolsheviki does not pay. Moreover, he lacks the executive experience which is necessary to the head of the Government. A man like Prince Lvoff would be considerably more useful, and I believe, from the reports I receive, that sentiment in Russia is setting in that direction.

"As for the Grand Duke Michael, he has always been very popular, and the fact that he has married a woman not of royal blood, the divorced wife of a Moscow lawyer, has increased his popularity. I am confident that Russia as a whole will not yield to a faction of Petrograd."

Herman Bernstein, who was in Petrograd during the Maximalist riots of last July, said that he was confident that Trotzsky was only the agent of Lenine, who from his hiding had been directing this revolt, as he had done the rising of that period.

"It can't win," he said, "for Lenine and Trotzsky are both extremely unpopular. They had a better chance last July, when, if they had only had well-laid plans, they would have been able to dominate Petrograd. As it was, they failed at the time, and the popular execration directed against Lenine after the bloodshed of July was such as to convince me that he will never be able to dominate the Russian people.

"But undoubtedly Kerensky cannot

Continued on Page 2.

MINISTERS UNDER ARRES[T]

Winter Palace Is Take[n] After Fierce Defense by Women Soldiers.

FORT'S GUNS TURNED ON [...]

Cruiser and Armored Cars Als[o] Brought Into Battle Waged by Searchlight.

TROTZSKY HEADS REVOL[T]

Giving Land to the Peasant[s] and Calling of Constituent Assembly Promised.

PETROGRAD, Nov. 8.—With the ai[d] of the capital's garrison complete co[n]trol of Petrograd has been seized by th[e] Maximalists, or Bolsheviki, headed b[y] Nikolai Lenine, the Radical Sociali[st] leader, and Leon Trotzsky, President [of] the Central Executive Committee of th[e] Petrograd Council of Workmen's an[d] Soldiers' Delegates. Their action ha[s] been indorsed by the All-Russia Con[gress] of Workmen's Councils.

A proclamation has been issued de[claring] that the Revolutionary Govern[ment] purposes to negotiate an "imme[diate] democratic peace," to turn th[e] land over to the peasantry, and to con[voke] the Constituent Assembly.

Premier Kerensky has fled. He [is] variously said to be headed for Mosco[w] and the northern front of the army, an[d] orders for his arrest have been issue[d]. Last night he was reported to be a[t] Luga, eighty-five miles southwest [of] Petrograd. Several members of his Cab[i]net have been taken into custody.

The Preliminary Parliament is de[clared] dissolved.

Little serious fighting has attended th[e] revolt so far. The Provisional Govern[ment] troops holding the bridges over th[e] Neva and various other points yeste[r]day were quickly overpowered, save a[t] the Winter Palace, the chief guardia[ns] of which were the Women's Battalio[n]. Here last night a battle royal too[k] place for four hours, during which th[e] Bolsheviki brought up armored cars an[d] the cruiser Aurora and turned the gu[ns] of the Fort of St. Peter and St. Pa[ul] upon the palace before its defender[s] would surrender.

Prior to the attack the Workmen's an[d] soldiers' leaders sent the Provision[al] Government an ultimatum demandin[g] their surrender and allowing twen[ty] minutes' grace. The Government replie[d] indirectly, refusing to recognize th[e] Military Committee.

Vice President Kameneff of the Work[men]'s and Soldiers' Delegates told Th[e] Associated Press today that the obje[ct] of taking possession of the posts an[d] telegraphs was to thwart any effo[rt] the Government might make to ca[ll] troops to the capital. The Russkia Vol[ia] and the Bourse Gazette have been com[mandeered].

The city today presented a normal as[pect]. Even the noonday band accom[panying] the guard of relief under th[e] previous administration continued i[ts] function. There were the customar[y] lines in front of the provision stores an[d] children played in the parks and ga[r]dens. There was even a notable lessen[ing] of the patrols, only a few arme[d] soldiers and sailors moving about th[e] streets.

How the Revolt Developed.

The Maximalist movement towa[rd] seizing authority, rumors of which ha[ve] been agitating the public mind eve[r] since the formation of the last Coal[i]tion Cabinet, culminated Tuesday nigh[t] when, without disorder, Maximali[st] forces took possession of the Telegrap[h] office and the Petrograd Telegrap[h] Agency.

Orders issued by the Government fo[r] the opening of the spans of the bridge[s] across the Neva later were overridde[n] by the Military Committee of the Coun[cil] of Workmen's and Soldiers' Dele[gates]. Communication was restore[d] after several hours of interruption. No[where] did the Maximalists meet wi[th] serious opposition.

An effort by militiamen to dispers[e] crowds gathered in the Nevski and L[i]tainy Prospekts during the evening pro[voked] a fight in which one man is re[ported] to have been killed. Minor dis[turbances], some of them accompanied by shooting, occurred in various quar[ters] of the city. A number of perso[ns] are reported to have been killed [or] wounded.

Yesterday morning found patrols [of] soldiers, sailors, and civilians in th[e] streets maintaining order. Further tha[n] a continuation of suppressed excitemen[t] the streets of the city presented no un[usual] aspects. The shops and bank[s] which had opened for business bega[n] closing up about noon.

Shortly after noon a Soviet force occu[pied] the telephone exchange, where [a] small guard had been stationed f[or] weeks. An effort by Government force[s] to retake the exchange led to a bri[ef] fusillade, by which it is believed a num[ber] of casualties was caused. The Max[i]malists remained in possession of th[e] building.

Toward 5 o'clock in the afternoon th[e] Military Revolutionary Committee issue[d] its proclamation stating that "progre[ss]" was in its hands. It read:

To the Army Committees of the Active Army and to all Councils of Workmen's and Soldiers' Delegates and to the Garrison and Proletariat of Petrograd:

We have deposed the Government of Kerensky, which rose against the revolution and the people. The changes which resulted in the deposition of the

"All the News That's Fit to Print."

The New York Times.

THE WEATHER
Fair today; Thursday snow; diminishing northwest to north winds.
For full weather report see Page 23.

VOL. LXVII...NO. 21,900. NEW YORK, WEDNESDAY, JANUARY 9, 1918.—TWENTY-FOUR PAGES. ONE CENT In Greater New York. | TWO CENTS Within Commuting Distance. | THREE CENTS Elsewhere.

PRESIDENT SPECIFIES TERMS AS BASIS FOR WORLD PEACE; ASKS JUSTICE FOR ALSACE-LORRAINE, APPLAUDS RUSSIA, TELLS GERMANY SHE MAY BE AN EQUAL BUT NOT A MASTER

OTZKY DISTRUSTS ALLIES

inks They Want Him to Give In to Berlin and Make Peace.

US HELPING THEIR ENDS

sheviki Will Fight, He Asserts, Unless Terms Desired Are Accepted by Teutons.

YS THEIR TROOPS REBEL

mp from Trains When Sent West—Confirms Report of 25,000 Intrenched.

By ARTHUR RANSOME.
cial Cable to THE NEW YORK TIMES.
Dispatch to The London Daily News.

ETROGRAD, Jan. 6.—I had a hur- t talk with Leon Trotzky, the Bol- viki Foreign Minister, at the Smolny stitute just as, after a final consulta- with the Russian members of the ce delegation, he was starting for st-Litovsk.

e was leaving with the mistaken viction that the Entente Govern- nts wanted Germany to succeed in king an advantageous separate peace h Russia so that guarding herself the east she might agree more will- ly to surrender what the Allies want the west. The Allies would then me the Bolsheviki for the lost free- m of Poland, Lithuania, and Cour- d. He was under the impression t Lloyd George had made a state- nt that allowed such an interpreta-

assured him that he was mistaken, he was difficult to convince. He d: "That is the allied policy."

asked his opinion of a possible inter- ional labor conference to decide the ditions of peace. He said: "It would no harm."

asked whether the Bolsheviki would ht in case the Central Powers re- ed to accept the decisions of that ference. He replied:

The question is not fairly put, for does not guarantee that the Entente vernments would accept the confer- e's rulings. In any case the Bol- viki will fight independently of the nge of such a conference unless they ncide with the democratic peace de- ed by Russia. The attitude of the sheviki would not be influenced by attitude of the allied Governments, only by the attitude of the allied ples."

asked him what his own hopes re for a general and acceptable peace d whether he thought the Germans ired such a peace. He said:

'It is difficult to say, because Ger- ny has not yet been offered a chance a general acceptable peace. But y must need it. Today four Ger- n deserters came to me, a Lieuten- t and three soldiers, and told me the difficulty the Germans have ving troops from this front. They ve given up trying to move large its. They take the men one at a e and the men, knowing where they going to be sent, jump out of the in and escape. At this minute in Kovno district, behind the German nt, there are 25,000 German deserters ncentrated together and armed with chine guns. The Germans have sur- unded them, and being unable to get ir own men to attack they are try- to reduce them by starvation."

asked him what terms he actually ped to get. He refused to be drawn d said laughing:

'If we were really logical we would clare war on England now for the ke of India, Egypt and Ireland. You ve read our peace declaration."

protested that Great Britain made thing out of India. He replied:

"Then give up being so altruistic. u English are the most chauvinist na- n on earth without knowing it."

He laughed, again shook hands, and as off.

USSIA SEEN ON VERGE OF UTTER COLLAPSE

etrograd Faces Famine and Pa- ralysis; While Anarchy Reigns in Provinces.

By HAROLD WILLIAMS.
pyright, 1918, by The New York Times Company.
pecial Cable to THE NEW YORK TIMES.

PETROGRAD, Jan. 6.—The Russian ace delegation, accompanied by Leon otzky, left last night for Brest- itovsk to resume negotiations with the legations of the Central Powers, who ready have arrived there. Trotsky pes to induce the Austro-Germans to ansfer the conference to neutral terri- ry—if not to Stockholm, then to Berne. The negotiations with the German and ustrian commissions here in Petro- ad have reached a deadlock. The Bol- eviki flatly refuse to agree to the rman proposals for the resumption of ade or an exchange of prisoners until ter peace is actually signed. At the

Continued on Page Three.

Germans Starve by Hundreds; Vorwaerts Sees Catastrophe

Special Cable to THE NEW YORK TIMES.

AMSTERDAM, Jan. 8. (Dispatch to The London Daily Express.)—"What was uncertain last year has now become a bitter reality. It can no longer be denied that people are starving by the hundreds in Germany."

This statement was made today by a Dutchman who has just spent five weeks traveling through Germany.

Leaflets are in circulation all over Germany, containing the following extract from a recently suppressed number of Vorwärts:

"Many people are dying of sheer hunger. Sixty million people are suffering. They will not always remain silent. Germany is on the verge of a catastrophe worse than Russia's, namely, a German defeat and loss of the whole war."

Any person found posessing a copy of the leaflet is liable to arrest and a heavy sentence of imprisonment.

HAIG SEES VICTORY VISIBLY NEARER

Says the Allies Have Discounted the Enemy's Gains Through Russia's Collapse.

WEATHER HIS CHIEF FOE

Only That Prevented Complete Victory in Flanders—Warm Welcome to Our Troops.

LONDON, Jan. 8.—"The additional strength which the enemy can obtain from the events in Russia and Italy already has been largely discounted, and the ultimate destruction of the enemy's field forces has been brought appreciably nearer," is the confident summing up by Field Marshal Haig, the British Commander in Chief in France and Belgium, of last year's work by the British Army on the western front. The statement is contained in an official report of General Haig's Spring and Summer campaigns, which occupies twenty-six pages in today's Official Gazette.

The report covers the period from the opening of the Arras offensive on April 9 to the conclusion of the Flanders defensive in November. Subsequent events of the year, including the battle of Cambrai, will be treated in a separate report, which is to be published soon.

Field Marshal Haig closes today's report with a brief tribute to the American troops.

"During the year," he says, "the United States has entered the war, and taken up their part with all the well-known energy and ability of that great nation. Already many thousands of American soldiers are in France. Warm as is the welcome they received from the French people, nowhere will they find a more genuine or friendlier greeting than among the ranks of the other great English-speaking armies."

At the outset of his report Sir Douglas explains how the general allied plan of campaign had to be modified on a wholesale scale from the very start, owing to a variety of unexpected developments, such as the Russian situation, the requirements of the Allies, and, particularly in later months, to adverse weather conditions.

He says that in the Flanders offensive the Germans "used up no less than seventy-eight divisions, of which eighteen were engaged a second or third time after being withdrawn to rest and refit," and that, "given a normally fine August, the capture of the whole ridge in a few weeks was well within the power of our men."

"Our captures in Flanders since the end of July," he continues, "amount to 24,000 prisoners, 74 guns, and 941 machine guns. It is certain that the enemy losses exceeded ours.

"The most important of all is that our new and hastily trained armies again have shown that they are capable of meeting and beating the enemy's best troops under conditions which favored his defense."

The report emphasizes "the supreme importance" of training of troops "under officers who are to command them in the task which they are to be called upon to perform."

Among the causes for the miscarriage of the Allies' plans for 1917 Field Marshal Haig gives Russia's failure to "prevent the enemy from transferring forty fresh divisions from her front in exchange for tired ones, used up in the west, or from replacing his losses on the west by drafts of fresh men from the east."

Remarking that the British Spring offensive was launched before Italy was ready, and deploring the weakening of allied forces by the disaster to the arms of the latter, the Field Marshal continues:

"That under such circumstances we won the victories of Arras, Vimy, and Messines, and the French those at Moronvillers, Verdun, and Malmaison constitutes a record of which the Allies have a right to be proud.

"In the operations at Arras, Messines, Lens, and Ypres, 131 German divisions were engaged and defeated by less than half that number of British.

"Without reckoning the possibilities opened up by our territorial gains in Flanders and without considering the effect which a less vigorous prosecution of the war by us might have had in the other theatres, we have every reason to be satisfied with the results achieved in the past year's fighting."

LONDON SEES NO PEACE

Fierce Fighting Ahead Despite the Lloyd George Statement.

NECESSITY PROMPTED IT

Solidification of Public Opinion by Removing Doubt Was Imperative.

TEUTON PRESS HOSTILE

Derisive Comment by German and Austrian Papers, Which Say Sword Will Force Peace.

Germany Announces Extension of the Submarine Barred Zone

LONDON, Jan. 8.—Further extension of the submarine barred zone is announced in a wireless statement sent out by the German Government. It becomes operative on Jan. 11.

The extensions which are particularized in the message affect the region around "enemy supporting points" on the Cape Verde Islands and the point of support of Dakar, French Senegal, with the adjoining coastal district.

The barred zone around the Azores is extended easterly over the Island of Madeira, which "serves our adversaries as a point of support."

Special Cable to THE NEW YORK TIMES.

LONDON, Jan. 8.—Dispatches from America indicate the existence of some measure of disquiet over Lloyd George's statement, based on an idea that its moderation implied belief in the possibility of approaches to peace being made now. Here in London this view finds acceptance only in circles where it may be said that the wish is father to the thought. Generally speaking, the pacifists and that other small section of opinion which believes in the miraculous regeneration of Germany are the only persons who think peace has been brought near at hand by the Prime Minister's statement.

The overwhelming preponderance of informed opinion is that the coming Spring and Summer will witness some of the bloodiest fighting of the war, and that Germany will exhaust every effort to inflict a crushing defeat on the European Allies before America can get fully in. Lloyd George's speech, though it has been described as a hold out to Germany of the olive branch in one hand and the sword in the other, was not determined upon by any considerations of the question whether the moment had arrived for extending the olive branch. The one great reason for the statement was domestic necessity. Solidification of British opinion by removing certain elements of doubt and suspicion was paramount.

Lloyd George, as already has been indicated in these dispatches, fully recognized that necessity. There were two questions in his mind. One was whether the present moment was the most opportune; the other was whether a statement should be made at once by the British Government alone, or should be issued as a joint declaration by the Allies, with America subscribing to it, or giving it a sort of imprimatur.

Upon these questions Lloyd George first of all consulted Asquith. Asquith gave it as his view that the moment was most opportune and that valuable time would be lost were the exchanges of views necessary to obtain a concerted statement by all the Allies entered upon. Also it was believed that clarity of statement might be more easily achieved were the British Government to issue a declaration on its own initiative. There was no likelihood of the British statement failing to meet with full approval of the Allies, seeing that there was a general agreement between the British and allied Governments on their war aims.

Lord Grey concurred, and it was arranged that the statement should be drafted and considered. The draft was drawn up and the document was then studied by the War Cabinet. It was next referred to Asquith and Lord Grey, whose full approval was given just half an hour before Lloyd George read it at the trades union meeting in Central Hall, Westminster.

Its results upon British opinion came up to the highest expectations, and its approval by the Allies was equally satisfactory. "The statement solidified British opinion," said one authority today. "It will equally solidify German opinion. Alsace-Lorraine is the keystone of German patriotism."

Even if on all other points it were possible for the Entente Powers and Central Powers to arrive at a common ground admitting of compromise and negotiations, German acceptance of reconsideration of the Alsace-Lorraine question is only to be obtained from a militarily defeated Germany. This is the view taken by the best informed British opinion, and it is evident as a corollary that it is here believed that much fighting has yet to be done to obtain a satisfactory peace.

In other words there is little or no hope that Germany will come to terms until bowed down by the weight of America's millions, or at least till the tramp of America's armies sounds like a death knell in the ears of her helpless militarists.

Text of President Wilson's Speech

WASHINGTON, Jan. 8.—The President in his address to Congress today spoke as follows:

Gentlemen of the Congress:

Once more, as repeatedly before, the spokesmen of the Central Empires have indicated their desire to discuss the objects of the war and the possible basis of a general peace! Parleys have been in progress at Brest-Litovsk between Russian representatives and representatives of the Central Powers, to which the attention of all the belligerents has been invited, for the purpose of ascertaining whether it may be possible to extend these parleys into a general conference with regard to terms of peace and settlement. The Russian representatives presented not only a perfectly definite statement of the principles upon which they would be willing to conclude peace, but also an equally definite program for the concrete application of those principles. The representatives of the Central Powers, on their part, presented an outline of settlement which, if much less definite, seemed susceptible of liberal interpretation until their specific program of practical terms was added. That program proposed no concessions at all, either to the sovereignty of Russia or to the preferences of the population with whose fortunes it dealt, but meant, in a word, that the Central Empires were to keep every foot of territory their armed forces had occupied—every province, every city, every point of vantage—as a permanent addition to their territories and their power. It is a reasonable conjecture that the general principles of settlement which they at first suggested originated with the more liberal statesmen of Germany and Austria, the men who have begun to feel the force of their own peoples' thought and purpose, while the concrete terms of actual settlement came from the military leaders who have no thought but to keep what they have got. The negotiations have been broken off. The Russian representatives were sincere and in earnest. They cannot entertain such proposals of conquest and domination.

The whole incident is full of significance. It is also full of perplexity. With whom are the Russian representatives dealing? For whom are the representatives of the Central Empires speaking? Are they speaking for the majorities of their respective Parliaments or for the minority parties, that military and imperialistic minority which has so far dominated their whole policy and controlled the affairs of Turkey and of the Balkan States, which have felt obliged to become their associates in this war? The Russian representatives have insisted, very justly, very wisely, and in the true spirit of modern democracy, that the conferences they have been holding with the Teutonic and Turkish statesmen should be held with open, not closed, doors, and all the world has been audience, as was desired. To whom have we been listening, then? To those who speak the spirit and intention of the resolutions of the German Reichstag of the 9th of July last, the spirit and intention of the liberal leaders and parties of Germany, or to those who resist and defy that spirit and intention and insist upon conquest and subjugation? Or are we listening, in fact, to both, unreconciled and in open and hopeless contradiction? These are very serious and pregnant questions. Upon the answer to them depends the peace of the world.

But whatever the results of the parleys at Brest-Litovsk, whatever the confusions of counsel and of purpose in the utterances of the spokesmen of the Central Empires, they have again attempted to acquaint the world with their objects in the war and have again challenged their adversaries to say what their objects are and what sort of settlement they would deem just and satisfactory. There is no good reason why that challenge should not be responded to, and responded to with the utmost candor. We did not wait for it. Not once, but again and again we have laid our whole thought and purpose before the world, not in general terms only, but each time with sufficient definition to make it clear what sort of definite terms of settlement must necessarily spring out of them. Within the last week Mr. Lloyd George has spoken with admirable candor and in admirable spirit for the people and Government of Great Britain. There is no confusion of counsel among the adversaries of the Central Powers, no uncertainty of principle, no vagueness of detail. The only secrecy of counsel, the only lack of fearless frankness, the only failure to make definite statement of the objects of the war, lies with Germany and her allies. The issues of life and death hang upon these definitions. No statesman who has the least conception of his responsibility ought for a moment to permit himself to continue this tragical and appalling outpouring of blood and treasure unless he is sure beyond a peradventure that the objects of the vital sacrifice are part and parcel of the very life of society and that the people for whom he speaks think them right and imperative as he does.

There is, moreover, a voice calling for these definitions of principle and of purpose which is, it seems to me, more thrilling and more compelling than any of the many moving voices with which the troubled air of the world is filled. It is the voice of the Russian people. They are prostrate and all but helpless, it would seem, before the grim power of Germany, which has hitherto known no relenting and no pity. Their power apparently is shattered. And yet their soul is not subservient. They will not yield either in principle or in action. Their conception of what is right, of what is humane and honorable for them to accept, has been stated with a frankness, a largeness of view, a generosity of spirit, and a universal human sympathy which must challenge the admiration of every friend of mankind; and they have refused to compound their ideals or desert others that they themselves may be safe. They call to us to say what it is that we desire, in what, if in anything, our purpose and our spirit differ from theirs; and I believe that the people of the United States would wish me to respond with utter simplicity and frankness. Whether their present leaders believe it or not, it is our heartfelt desire and hope that some way may be opened whereby we may be privileged to assist the people of Russia to attain their utmost hope of liberty and ordered peace.

It will be our wish and purpose that the processes of peace, when they are begun, shall be absolutely open, and that they shall involve and permit henceforth no secret understandings of any kind. The day of conquest and aggrandizement is gone by; so is also the day of secret covenants entered into in the interest of particular Governments and likely at some unlooked-for moment to upset the peace of the world. It is this happy fact, now clear to the view of every public man whose thoughts do not still linger in an age that is dead and gone, which makes it possible for every nation whose purposes are consistent with justice and the peace of the world to avow now or at any other time the objects it has in view.

We entered this war because violations of right had occurred which touched us to the quick and made the life of our own people impossible unless they were corrected and the world secured once for all against their recurrence. What we demand in this war, therefore, is nothing peculiar to ourselves. It is that the world be made fit and safe to live in; and particularly that it be made safe for every peace-loving nation which, like our own, wishes to live its own life, determine its own institutions, be assured of justice and fair dealings by the other peoples of the world, as against force and selfish aggression. All the peoples of the world are in effect partners in this interest and for our own part we see very clearly that unless justice be done to others it will not be done to us.

The program of the world's peace, therefore, is our program, and that program, the only possible program, as we see it, is this:

I.—Open covenants of peace, openly arrived at, after which there shall be no private international understandings of any kind, but diplomacy shall proceed always frankly and in the public view.

II.—Absolute freedom of navigation upon the seas, outside territorial waters, alike in peace and in war, except as the seas may be closed in whole or in part by international action for the enforcement of international covenants.

III.—The removal, so far as possible, of all economic barriers and the establishment of an equality of trade conditions among all the nations consenting to the peace and associating themselves for its maintenance.

IV.—Adequate guarantees given and taken that national armaments will reduce to the lowest point consistent with domestic safety.

V.—Free, open-minded, and absolutely impartial adjustment of all colonial claims, based upon a strict observance of the principle that in determining all such questions of sovereignty the interests of the population concerned must have equal weight with the equitable claims of the Government whose title is to be determined.

VI.—The evacuation of all Russian territory and such a settlement of all questions affecting Russia as will secure the best and freest co-operation of the other nations of the world in obtaining for her an unhampered and unembarrassed opportunity for the independent determination of her own political development and national policy, and assure her of a sincere welcome into the society of free nations under institutions of her own choosing; and, more than a welcome, assistance also of every kind that she may need and may herself desire. The treatment accorded Russia by her sister nations in the months to come will be the acid test of their good-will, of their comprehension of her needs as distinguished from their own interests, and of their intelligent and unselfish sympathy.

VII.—Belgium, the whole world will agree, must be evacuated and restored, without any attempt to limit the sovereignty which she enjoys in common with all other free nations. No other single act will serve as this will serve to restore confidence among the nations in the laws which they have themselves set and determined for the government of their relations with one another. Without this healing act the whole structure and validity of international law is forever impaired.

VIII.—All French territory should be freed and the invaded portions restored, and the wrong done to France by Prussia in 1871 in the matter of Alsace-Lorraine, which has unsettled the peace of the world for nearly fifty years, should be righted, in order that peace may once more be made secure in the interest of all.

IX.—A readjustment of the frontiers of Italy should be effected along clearly recognizable lines of nationality.

X.—The peoples of Austria-Hungary, whose place among the nations we wish to see safeguarded and assured, should be accorded the freest opportunity of autonomous development.

XI.—Rumania, Serbia, and Montenegro should be evacuated; occupied territories restored; Serbia accorded free and secure access to the sea; and the relations of the several Balkan States to one another determined by friendly counsel along historically established lines of allegiance and nationality; and international guarantees of the political and economic independence and territorial integrity of the several Balkan States should be entered into.

XII.—The Turkish portions of the present Ottoman Empire should be assured a secure sovereignty, but the other nationalities which are now under Turkish rule should be assured an undoubted security of life and an absolutely unmolested opportunity of autonomous development, and the Dardanelles should be permanently opened as a free passage to the ships and commerce of all nations under international guarantees.

XIII.—An independent Polish State should be erected which should include the territories inhabited by indisputably Polish populations, which should be assured a free and secure access to the sea, and whose political and economic independence and territorial integrity should be guaranteed by international covenant.

XIV.—A general association of nations must be formed under specific covenants for the purpose of affording mutual guarantees of political independence and territorial integrity to great and small States alike.

In regard to these essential rectifications of wrong and assertions of right, we feel ourselves to be intimate partners of all the Governments and peoples associated together against the imperialists. We cannot be separated in interest or divided in purpose. We stand together until the end.

For such arrangements and covenants we are willing to fight and to continue to fight until they are achieved; but only because we wish the right to prevail and desire a just and stable peace, such as can be secured only be removing the chief provocations to war, which this program does remove. We have no jealousy of German greatness, and there is nothing in this program that impairs it. We grudge her no achievement or distinction of learning or of pacific enterprise such as have made her record very bright and very enviable. We do not wish to injure her or to block in any way her legitimate influence or power. We do not wish to fight her either with arms or with hostile arrangements of trade, if she is willing to associate herself with us and the other peace-loving nations of the world in covenants of justice and law and fair dealing. We wish her only to accept a place of equality among the peoples of the world—the new world in which we now live—instead of a place of mastery.

Neither do we presume to suggest to her any alteration or modification of her institutions. But it is necessary, we must frankly say, and necessary as a preliminary to any intelligent dealings with her on our part, that we should know whom her spokesmen speak for when they speak to us, whether for the Reichstag majority or for the military party and the men whose creed is imperial domination.

We have spoken now, surely in terms too concrete to admit of any further doubt or question. An evident principle runs through the whole program I have outlined. It is the principle of justice to all peoples and nationalities, and their right to live on equal terms of liberty and safety with one another, whether they be strong or weak. Unless this principle be made its foundation, no part of the structure of international justice can stand. The people of the United States could act upon no other principle, and to the vindication of this principle they are ready to devote their lives, their honor, and everything that they possess. The moral climax of this, the culminating and final war for human liberty, has come, and they are ready to put their own strength, their own highest purpose, their own integrity and devotion to the test.

GERMAN PRESS SAY 'NO' TO LLOYD GEORGE

Talks Like a Conqueror, They Say—Refuse to Take Speech as Peace Offer.

By GEORGE RENWICK.
Copyright, 1918, by The New York Times Company.
Special Cable to THE NEW YORK TIMES.

AMSTERDAM, Jan. 8.—The views in the German press regarding Lloyd George's speech are just what might have been expected from Germany in her present frame of mind.

The Düsseldorfer Nachrichten, which is the new name of the Düsseldorfer General Anzeiger now that it has passed into the Krupp sphere of influence, says England posing as the innocent victim of a German created war is now merely ridiculous. It continues:

"The main point is that England now has bound herself to fight to the last for Alsace-Lorraine. We do not believe the British people will carry the war to the uttermost for this aim. As far as we are concerned there is no Alsace-Lorraine question, and Kühlmann's 'No, never!' has been heard both in London and Paris. Lloyd George's speech, therefore, cannot serve the interests of peace. It is merely intended to bring the Brest-Litovsk negotiations into disrepute and whip up the failing spirits of the western powers. Let there be no more peace offers. Only swords can bring this enemy to reason."

The militarist Post says Lloyd George speaks like a conqueror, but "we will show him we are the victors, not the vanquished."

The Boersen Courier cannot see how the speech can be regarded as a peace offer.

The Boersen Zeitung looks upon it as an indication that the whole political and military situation has been changed and sees a complete forced alteration in England's war aims.

The Pan German Deutsche Zeitung believes that Lloyd George is endeavoring to drive a wedge between Germany and her allies by making a peace offer to the latter. Only victory over England can bring real peace, it adds.

The Cologne Volkszeitung wonders if a new Lloyd George is coming on the scene and it says that it will await with interest and see if he realy intends to improve his manners and follow in Lansdowne's footsteps. It lays no real importance, it says, on his statement regarding reconsideration of the great crime of 1871, with reference to Alsace-Lorraine, for the matter is one in which the main consideration is what France desires. On that point Germany harbors no illusions.

The Norddeutsche Allgemeine Zeitung, semi-official organ, says:
when he made his first war speech, that
"Mr. Lloyd George knows today, as the territorial integrity of the Austro-Hungarian monarchy, as well as that of the other allies of Germany, must form the cornerstone in the building of a new peace. Nevertheless, he adheres to his imperialistic war aims, with their unmeasured demands, and only by a change in tone tries to give the impression that he takes into account the alteration of the military and political situation. It is characteristic of him and his allies."

A Vienna dispatch to the Pester Lloyd (Budapest) says that in political circles the peace conditions offered by the British Prime Minister are considered impossible of acceptance.

LONDON, Jan. 8.—A reply from the Central Powers to the statement of British war aims made by Premier Lloyd George Saturday is awaited here with the greatest interest. It is believed that Germany and her allies cannot decline to reply in some form.

While no German official or semi-official reply has yet been issued, much newspaper comment, however, has reached here by way of Amsterdam. Some of the German newspapers recognize the moderation of the speech, but, with the exception of the Socialist Vor-

Continued on Page Two.

APPEALS TO GERMAN PEOPLE

Wilson Declares We Must Know for Whom Their Rulers Speak.

READY TO FIGHT TO END

Insists That Principle of Justice to All Nations Is Only Basis for Peace.

DEMANDS FREEDOM OF SEAS

Congress Cheers Utterance as Momentous Declaration of Entente War Aims.

Special to The New York Times.

WASHINGTON, Jan. 8.—The terms upon which Germany may obtain peace were given to the American Congress for the benefit of the whole world by President Wilson today. With scant notice of his coming, notice barely sufficient to enable the Senate and the House to make the necessary arrangements for a joint session, the President appeared at the Capitol, and in an address, brief by comparison to the momentous issues discussed, enumerated the conditions for a cessation of hostilities, the rejection of which will place upon Germany the responsibility for the further bloodshed that must precede the final victory of the allied nations.

President Wilson's address bore striking resemblance to the speech made last Saturday by Mr. Lloyd George, the British Prime Minister, before the Trade Union Conference on Man Power, in which he specified the war aims and peace conditions of the British Government. The diversions in the President's address from statements of the Prime Minister were for the most part more in the form than in the substance.

But in the opinion of many of those who compared Mr. Wilson's address with the utterances of Mr. Lloyd George the President was more definite in declaring that the wrong done to France through the annexation of Alsace-Lorraine must be righted and he differed from Mr. Lloyd George with regard to the Russian situation in that he held out to the Russian people an offer of assistance from America, and tendered sympathy for the aims that those now in control of the affairs of that perturbed country are seeking to achieve.

Leaves No Doubt of Unity.

By the President's official utterance he has pledged this Government to the achievement of ends that affect Europe more intimately and deeply than the United States. No doubt was left in the minds of those who listened to the President's words that this Government has entered heart and soul into the cause of the Entente Allies, to fight for the objects for which they are fighting, to free Europe from the menace of Prussianism, to take Alsace-Lorraine from German domination, to prevent Russia from becoming part of the German Empire, to see that Italy has restored to her those portions of the Austro-Hungarian Empire that are inhabited by a people who are Italian in heart and blood, to bring all the Polish peoples into a common Government, to restore Belgium, Serbia, and the small nations that have been devastated by Teuton hordes, to their own, to give the separate nationalities of Austria-Hungary, Turkey and the Balkan States the right to govern themselves as separate entities, to have Northern France restored to French control.

And, in addition to these aims, the allied nations, in order to find a peace acceptable to them, must be assured of freedom of the seas, the establishment of an equality of trade conditions among the nations of the world, the reduction of armaments, and an association of nations in a league to enforce peace. There must also be no secret agreements among nations that would threaten again the peace of the world.

Immediately following the delivery of the President's address, there was a disposition manifest to refer to his outline of the conditions which Germany must accept before the war could end as a definition of peace terms. But in the official quarters best qualified to interpret the meaning of the President, it was declared that his statement must be taken as a definition of war aims. The President left no doubt that, unless Germany consented to enter into peace exchanges on the basis of the conditions set forth in his address, the United States and the Allies would fight on until the Central Powers realized that there could be no peace in any other way. "It was an outline of war aims, not a peace address," declared one official.

Terms Clear and Definite.

Never before has President Wilson or any other spokesman for a nation at war with Germany made such a clear

"All the News That's Fit to Print."

The New York Times.

THE WEATHER
Fair today and Tuesday; diminishing northwest winds.
For weather report see next to last page.

VOL. LXVIII...NO. 22,206. NEW YORK, MONDAY, NOVEMBER 11, 1918. TWENTY-FOUR PAGES. TWO CENTS Metropolitan District | THREE CENTS Within 200 Miles | FOUR CENTS Elsewhere

ARMISTICE SIGNED, END OF THE WAR! BERLIN SEIZED BY REVOLUTIONISTS; NEW CHANCELLOR BEGS FOR ORDER; OUSTED KAISER FLEES TO HOLLAND

SON FLEES WITH EX-KAISER

Hindenburg Also Believed to be Among Those in His Party.

ALL ARE HEAVILY ARMED

Automobiles Bristle with Rifles as Fugitives Arrive at Dutch Frontier.

ON THEIR WAY TO DE STEEG

Belgians Yell to Them, "Are You On Your Way to Paris?"

LONDON, Nov. 10.—Both the former German Emperor and his eldest son, Frederick William, crossed the Dutch frontier Sunday morning, according to advices from The Hague. His reported destination is De Steeg, near Utrecht.

The former German Emperor's party, which is believed to include Field Marshal von Hindenburg, arrived at Eysden, [midway between Liége and Maastricht,] on the Dutch frontier, at 7:30 o'clock Sunday morning, according to Daily Mail advices.

Practically the whole German General Staff accompanied the former Emperor, and ten automobiles carried the party. The automobiles were bristling with rifles, and all the fugitives were armed.

The ex-Kaiser was in uniform. He alighted at the Eysden station and paced the platform, smoking a cigarette.

Many photographs were taken by [of?] the members of the Imperial party. On the whole the people were very quiet, but Belgians among them yelled out "En voyage a Paris." (Are you on your way to Paris?)

Chatting with the members of the staff, the former Emperor, the correspondent says, did not look in the least distressed. A few minutes later an imperial train, including restaurant and sleeping cars, ran into the station. Only servants were aboard.

The engine returned to Visé, Belgium, and brought back a second train, in which were a large number of staff officers and others, and also stores of food.

The preparations began for the departure at 10 o'clock this morning, but at 10:40 o'clock the train was still at Eysden. The blinds of the train were all drawn.

The Daily Mail remarks that, if the party arrived in Holland armed, all of them must be interned.

While other dispatches con-

Continued on Page Three.

Kaiser Fought Hindenburg's Call for Abdication; Failed to Get Army's Support in Keeping Throne

By GEORGE RENWICK.

Special Cable to The New York Times.

AMSTERDAM, Nov. 10.—I learn on very good authority that the Kaiser made a determined effort to stave off abdication. He went to headquarters with the deliberate intention of bringing the army around to his side. In this he failed miserably.

His main support consisted of a number of officers, nearly all of Prussian regiments, who formed themselves into two regiments and placed themselves at his Majesty's disposal. To do anything with such support was seen, of course, to be Gilbertian.

During the night the Kaiser called the Crown Prince, Hindenburg, and General Gröner to him, and the consultation lasted a couple of hours. Both officers strongly pressed the Kaiser to bow to the inevitable, and Hindenburg informed him that any more delay in coming to a decision to abdicate would certainly have the most terrible consequences and lead to serious events in the army. For those consequences Hindenburg said he must refuse responsibility.

The Crown Prince, it is said, was the first to give way. General Gröner fully supported Hindenburg's view, but when the conference broke up the Kaiser remained unconvinced of the advisability of abdication. He is said to have come to his final decision an hour or so later, after several communications had reached him from Berlin and after another short and stormy talk with Hindenburg.

Meanwhile, his son-in-law, the Duke of Brunswick, for himself and his heir, had abdicated. "Brunswick's Fated Chieftain" was forced without fighting to abdicate. Reports have it that the republican movement in Brunswick, which long before the war was chafing under autocratic conditions, began to be noticed even before it was set in motion at Kiel.

Kaiser Shivered as He Signed Abdication

LONDON, Nov. 10.—Emperor William signed his letter of abdication on Saturday morning at the German Grand Headquarters in the presence of Crown Prince Frederick William and Field Marshal Hindenburg, according to a dispatch from Amsterdam to the Exchange Telegraph Company.

The Crown Prince signed his renunciation of the throne shortly afterward.

Before placing his signature to the document, an urgent message from Philipp Scheidemann, who was a Socialist member without portfolio in the Imperial Cabinet, was handed to the Emperor. He read it with a shiver. Then he signed the paper, saying:

"It may be for the good of Germany."

The Emperor was deeply moved. He consented to sign the document only when he got the news of the latest events in the empire.

The ex-Kaiser and former Crown Prince were expected to take leave of their troops on Saturday, but nothing had then been settled regarding their future movements.

GERMAN DYNASTIES BEING WIPED OUT

King of Wuerttemberg Abdicates — Sovereign of Saxony to Follow Suit.

PRINCES MAY BE EXILED

Socialists Are Demanding That Every Sovereign in the Empire Shall be Dethroned.

LONDON, Nov. 10.—A Havas dispatch from Basle says:

"Wilhelm II., the reigning King of the monarchy of Württemberg, abdicated on Friday night."

A Wolff Bureau dispatch from Stuttgart, by way of Amsterdam, says that the King has issued a proclamation saying that his person would never serve to hinder the development of the wishes of the people.

According to a report received from Berne, the German Socialists are demanding that every dynasty in Germany be suppressed and all the Princes exiled. It is reported that the Kings of Bavaria and Saxony intend to abdicate soon.

Here is a list of the rules, until several days ago, of the various parts of the German Empire. Those who have abdicated and those reported to be on the point of abdication are marked by an asterisk:

ANHALT—Duke Edward, son of the late Duke Friedrich of Anhalt and of Princess Antoinette of Saxe-Altenberg. Succeeded his brother April 13, 1861.

BADEN—Friedrich II., succeeded to

Continued on Page Two.

MORE WARSHIPS JOIN THE REDS

Four Dreadnoughts in Kiel Harbor Espouse the Revolutionary Cause.

GUARDSHIPS ALSO GO OVER

Those Protecting Mines in the Great Belt and the Baltic Abandon Their Posts.

LONDON, Nov. 10.—The crews of the German dreadnoughts Posen, Ostfriesland, Nassau, and Oldenburg, in Kiel Harbor, have joined the revolution, says a Copenhagen dispatch. Marines occupied the lock gates at Ostmoor and fought down a coast artillery division which offered resistance.

According to the British Wireless Service three German destroyers have anchored outside of Stockholm. All the guardships in the Baltic, it is said, have joined the revolutionary movement.

Six more cruisers flying the red flag arrived at Hamburg last night, says a Wolff News Agency dispatch received in Copenhagen.

An Amsterdam dispatch states that the Berlin Vossische Zeitung and Vorwärts confirm the fact that the inception of the revolution at Kiel was mistaken for the idea that a cruise had been ordered and that it was intended to give battle to the British fleet.

Up to Friday night the number of persons killed at Kiel was twenty-eight, according to information re-

Continued on Page Three.

BERLIN TROOPS JOIN REVOLT

Reds Shell Building in Which Officers Vainly Resist.

THRONGS DEMAND REPUBLIC

Revolutionary Flag on Royal Palace — Crown Prince's Palace Also Seized.

GENERAL STRIKE IS BEGUN

Burgomaster and Police Submit—War Office Now Under Socialist Control.

LONDON, Nov. 10.—The greater part of Berlin is in control of revolutionists, the former Kaiser has fled to Holland, and Friedrich Ebert, the new Socialist Chancellor, has taken command of the situation. The revolt is spreading throughout Germany with great rapidity.

Dispatches received in London today announce these startling developments. The Workmen's and Soldiers' Council is now administering the municipal government of the German capital.

The War Ministry has submitted, and its acts are valid only when countersigned by a Socialist representative. The official Wolff telegraphic agency has been taken over by the Reds.

The red flag has been hoisted over the royal palace and the Brandenburg Gate. The former Crown Prince's palace is also in possession of the revolutionists.

There was severe fighting in Berlin between 8 and 10 o'clock last night and a violent cannonade was heard from the heart of the city.

Burgomaster and Police Join.

A Copenhagen dispatch states that Dr. Liebknecht, the famous Socialist, who spent many months in prison for antagonizing the German Imperial Government and who was recently released, has issued the following announcement in Berlin in behalf of the Workmen's and Soldiers' Council:

"The Presidency of the police, as well as the Chief Command, is in our hands. Our comrades will be released."

A dispatch from Berne states that the Burgomaster of Berlin has placed himself and his staff at the disposal of the new Government.

Some German newspapers describe the movement as Bolshevism. The people are shouting "Long live the Republic!" and singing the "Marseillaise."

Officers Shelled by Reds.

When revolutionary soldiers attempted to enter a building in Berlin in which they supposed that a number of officers were concealed shots were fired from the windows. The Reds then began shelling the building. Many persons were killed and wounded before the officers surrendered.

When the cannonade began the people thought the Reichsbank was being bombarded, and thousands rushed to the square in front of the Crown Prince's palace. It was later determined that other buildings were under fire. Among those killed in the fighting at the "Cockchafer" Barracks was one of the workmen's leaders known as "Comrade" Habersroth.

The Reds, at last reports, were maintaining order.

Berlin was occupied by forces of the Soldiers' and Workmen's Councils on Saturday afternoon, according to a Wolff Bureau report received in Copenhagen. News of Emperor William's abdication was received in the city on that afternoon with general rejoicing, which was tempered by the fear that it had come too late.

Russians Aid in Outbreak.

How far the example of the Russian Bolsheviki influenced the German upheaval is an interesting question. Red flags figured frequently in the various risings and Chancellor Ebert's motor car floats the international emblem.

The shoulder straps were torn from the uniforms of officers in a number of German cities and even the soldiers' insignia were stripped from them. Russian prisoners played a part in the demonstrations in two or three towns.

Delegates of the revolutionary German navy arrived in Berlin on Friday, according to a dispatch from Copenhagen. They conferred for several hours with the Minister of Marine and with members of the Reichstag majority parties.

It is stated that Hugo Haase, a Socialist leader in the Reichstag, has the situation at Hamburg in hand.

It is officially announced from Berlin, according to a Copenhagen dispatch, that the War Ministry has placed itself at the disposal of Chancellor Ebert. This action was for the purpose of assuring the provisioning of the army and assisting in the solution of demobilization problems.

Serious food difficulties are expected in Germany, owing to the stoppage of trains. The Council of the Regency will take the most drastic steps to re-establish order.

In the new German Government there will be only three representatives of the majority parties, namely, Erzberger, Gothein, and Richthofen, says a dispatch from Copenhagen. The other posts will be occupied by Socialists and independents.

Reds Announce Success.

BERLIN, Nov. 9, (German Wireless to London, Nov. 10)—(Associated Press.)—The German People's Government has been instituted in the greater part of Berlin. The garrison has gone over to the Government.

The Workmen's and Soldiers' Council has declared a general strike. Troops and machine guns have been placed at the disposal of the Council. Guards which had been stationed at the public offices and other buildings have been withdrawn.

Friedrich Ebert (Vice President of the Social Democratic Party) is carrying on the Chancellorship.

The text of a statement issued by the People's Government reads:

In the course of the forenoon of Saturday the formation of a new German People's Government was initiated. The greater part of the Berlin garrison, and other troops stationed there temporarily, went over to the new Government.

The leaders of the deputations of the Social Democratic Party declared that they would not shoot against the people. They said they would, in accordance with the People's Government, intercede in favor of the maintenance of order. Thereupon in the offices and public buildings the guards which had been stationed there were withdrawn.

The business of the Imperial Chancellor is being carried on by the Social Democratic Deputy, Herr Ebert.

It is presumed that, apart from the representatives of the recent majority group, three independent Social Democrats will enter the future Government.

Scheidemann Exhorts Calm.

Deputy Scheidemann, (leader of the majority Socialists in the Reichstag,) in a speech today, said:

"The Kaiser and the Crown Prince have abdicated. The dynasty

Continued on Page Four.

Socialist Chancellor Appeals to All Germans To Help Him Save Fatherland from Anarchy

BERNE, Nov. 10, (Associated Press.)—In an address to the people, the new German Chancellor, Friedrich Ebert, says:

Citizens: The ex-Chancellor, Prince Max of Baden, in agreement with all the Secretaries of State, has handed over to me the task of liquidating his affairs as Chancellor. I am on the point of forming a new Government in accord with the various parties, and will keep public opinion freely informed of the course of events.

The new Government will be a Government of the people. It must make every effort to secure in the quickest possible time peace for the German people and consolidate the liberty which they have won.

The new Government has taken charge of the administration, to preserve the German people from civil war and famine and to accomplish their legitimate claim to autonomy. The Government can solve this problem only if all the officials in town and country will help.

I know it will be difficult for some to work with the new men who have taken charge of the empire, but I appeal to their love of the people. Lack of organization would in this heavy time mean anarchy in Germany and the surrender of the country to tremendous misery. Therefore, help your native country with fearless, indefatigable work for the future, every one at his post.

I demand every one's support in the hard task awaiting us. You know how seriously the war has menaced the provisioning of the people, which is the first condition of the people's existence. The political transformation should not trouble the people. The food supply is the first duty of all, whether in town or country, and they should not embarrass, but rather aid, the production of food supplies and their transport to the towns.

Food shortage signifies pillage and robbery, with great misery. The poorest will suffer the most, and the industrial worker will be affected hardest. All who illicitly lay hands on food supplies or other supplies of prime necessity or the means of transport necessary for their distribution will be guilty in the highest degree toward the community.

I ask you immediately to leave the streets and remain orderly and calm.

COPENHAGEN, Nov. 10.—The new Berlin Government, according to a Wolff Bureau dispatch, has issued the following proclamation:

Fellow-Citizens: This day the people's deliverance has been fulfilled. The Social Democratic Party has undertaken to form a Government. It has invited the Independent Socialist Party to enter the Government with equal rights.

WAR ENDS AT 6 O'CLOCK THIS MORNING

The State Department in Washington Made the Announcement at 2:45 o'Clock.

ARMISTICE WAS SIGNED IN FRANCE AT MIDNIGHT

Terms Include Withdrawal from Alsace-Lorraine, Disarming and Demobilization of Army and Navy, and Occupation of Strategic Naval and Military Points.

By The Associated Press.

WASHINGTON, Monday, Nov. 11, 2:48 A. M.—The armistice between Germany, on the one hand, and the allied Governments and the United States, on the other, has been signed.

The State Department announced at 2:45 o'clock this morning that Germany had signed.

The department's announcement simply said: "The armistice has been signed."

The world war will end this morning at 6 o'clock, Washington time, 11 o'clock Paris time.

The armistice was signed by the German representatives at midnight.

This announcement was made by the State Department at 2:50 o'clock this morning.

The announcement was made verbally by an officila of the State Department in this form:

"The armistice has been signed. It was signed at 5 o'clock A. M., Paris time, [midnight, New York time,] and hostilities will cease at 11 o'clock this morning, Paris time. [6 o'clock, New York time.]

The terms of the armistice, it was announced, will not be made public until later. Military men here, however, regard it as certain that they include:

Immediate retirement of the German military forces from France. Belgium, and Alsace-Lorraine.

Disarming and demobilization of the German armies.

Occupation by the allied and American forces of such strategic points in Germany as will make impossible a renewal of hostilities.

Delivery of part of the German High Seas Fleet and a certain number of submarines to the allied and American naval forces.

Disarmament of all other German warships

"All the News That's Fit to Print."

The New York Times.

THE WEATHER
Showers today; Tuesday probably fair; fresh north winds.
☞ For weather report see next to last page.

VOL. LXVIII...NO. 22,423. NEW YORK, MONDAY, JUNE 16, 1919. TWENTY-EIGHT PAGES. TWO CENTS Metropolitan District 50 Mile Radius | THREE CENTS Within 100 Miles | FOUR CENTS Elsewhere

ALCOCK AND BROWN FLY ACROSS ATLANTIC; MAKE 1,980 MILES IN 16 HOURS, 12 MINUTES; SOMETIMES UPSIDE DOWN IN DENSE, ICY FOG

UR TROOPS CROSS BORDER TO STOP JUAREZ FIGHTING

antry, Cavalry, and Artillery nter Mexico and Are Rounding Up Villistas.

NS ALREADY IN ACTION

neral Erwin States That He urposes Only to Protect City and Plans No Intervention.

IOTS HIT AMERICANS

Killed, Several Wounded, When Villa Renewed Attack on Juarez.

L PASO, Texas, Monday, June 16.— 24th Infantry, Fourth Battalion, ssed the international border at Juarez 11 o'clock last night.

he 5th and 7th Cavalry Regiments ssed at three fords east of El Paso. battalion of the 82d Artillery ssed east of the stock yard.

here were approximately 3,600 Ameri- troops on Mexican soil ten minutes er they were ordered to make the ssing.

Colonel Selah R. H. Tompkins of the Cavalry was in command of the valry brigade which crossed at the ds and Colonel Hadsell was in com- nd of the infantry. Two armored tor cars crossed the international dge at 10:55.

The first shrapnel shot from United ates Army guns was fired over Juarez 12:30 in the morning in the direction the Juarez race track to dislodge llistas. A second shot followed in five nutes, which struck near the race ack, followed at two-minute intervals m two guns placed near the interna- nal bridge on the Mexican side.

Following a signal rocket, the Ameri- n cavalry near San Lorenze started enveloping movement to the east d southeast of Juarez to surround the bels, then in the vicinity of the race ack. It was not known whether Villa s with his men or not.

A second green signal rocket indi- ed that the cavalry were advancing a charge.

Heavy firing by the American artil- y is going on.

Following the killing of one artillery- n of the 82d Artillery and the serious unding of another by Mexican snipers neral Erwin ordered twenty-five ex- rt riflemen to that point to return the ipers' fire. The shots which killed artilleryman were fired before merican artillery began the bombard- ent of the race track.

The reason given at military head- arters for ordering the troops to cross s "to prevent firing from the Mex- n side on El Paso."

Brig.-Gen. James G. Erwin told the ssociated Press immediately after is- ing the order for the crossing that it s not to be an invasion of Mexico, at the situation was fully understood General Francisco Gonzales and the rranza officials and that no resistance s anticipated from the Carranza rces which have been fighting in arez. No strong resistance was ex- cted from the Villa forces, General win added.

A statement issued by General Erwin ads:

"Upon the affidavits of three repu- ble citizens of El Paso that the Vill- tas fired into El Paso and upon the vestigation of the wounding of the exican girl (in El Paso) showing she s wounded by a shot fired by Villistas d upon investigation by the district spector of these headquarters and two ficers of the police force of El Paso, was shown that shots, undoubtedly ming from the direction of the Villista rces, had been fired into El Paso.

"Further, because of the wounding of veral innocent and law abiding per- ns residing in El Paso and the wound- g of two United States soldiers, who, the discharge of their duty, all of ese on June 14 and 15 therefore, un- r the authority given me in telegrams om the headquarters of the Southern epartment, June 12, 1918, I ordered oops of my command to cross the order and disperse the Villistas. But, pon no account, were they to under- ke an invasion into Mexico.

"As soon as I have accomplished this d have assured the safety of the citi- ns of El Paso, then the troops of my mmand will be withdrawn to the merican side of the border."

Earlier in the day General Erwin d ordered the port closed and the ternational bridges taken over by e military, after Corporal Edward eilly, Motor Transport Company, and

Continued on Page Five.

President Wilson to Sail for Home About June 24

PARIS, June 15.—President Wilson probably will remain in Paris only three or four days after his return from Belgium next Friday. He will then embark at a French port for the United States.

President Wilson expects to visit Belgium Wednesday or Thursday, accompanied by Mrs. Wilson and Rear Admiral Grayson. They will leave Paris Tuesday night by special train returning to Paris Friday morning.

Elaborate plans for the entertainment of President Wilson and his party in Brussels have been made by King Albert and Queen Elizabeth.

GERMANS OBJECTED STRONGLY TO TERMS

Reply to Allies Showed They Thought Themselves Equal Negotiators.

PROTESTS AVAILED LITTLE

Final Answer from Council Gives Relief on Only a Few Points.

By RICHARD V. OULAHAN.

Copyright, 1919, by The New York Times Company.
Special Cable to THE NEW YORK TIMES.

PARIS, June 15.—The memorandum of the German peace plenipotentiaries, which is now made public, shows that the Germans attempted to pose as negotiators with equal rights in the Peace Conference, instead of as defeated foes, come to learn the character of the punishment they should undergo.

Read in light of the knowledge of the modifications in the treaty made by the Council of the great Powers, its complaint and argument regarding many of the severest features of the treaty failed to move the allied statesmen. Yet the German representations were successful in some important particulars.

The German plenipotentiaries laid great stress on President Wilson's Fourteen Points, but sought to persuade the allied peacemakers that these were intended in every instance to apply to the treatment of Germany in making peace instead of being intended to have application mainly to the smaller nations which Germany had conquered or sought to conquer.

In this connection the German delegates advanced the contention that the treaty was inconsistent with the President's declaration that the Allies were making war on the German people, entirely overlooking that in imposing punishment on the German Government its subjects were obliged to bear their share of the burden in expiation of the wrongs they had approved.

Naive contentions of this sort appear throughout the voluminous document. Sequestration of German territory, such as the Sarre Basin, and the cession of German territory to France and the smaller nationalities cause the German plenipotentiaries to indulge in disquisitions on how wrong it is for the Allies not to live up to their assertion of the rights of peoples to self-determination.

In the response now being completed to the German complaints and counter-proposals the Council of the Great Powers adopts a moderated tone which is apparently intended to give a light coating of sweetness to the nasty dose they told Germany to swallow. Of the many German contentions, designed to prove the great wrong being committed, the allied peace answer will reject practically all except that concerning Upper Silesia, which is to have a plebiscite to determine whether it shall go to Poland, as the draft of the treaty stipulates, or remain under German control.

This part of the German memorandum makes interesting reading, if for no other reason than in showing the character of the argument advanced to prove that non-German peoples who are released from German citizenship through territorial transfers really would be happier if they remained German subjects.

The German contentions for more lenient terms with respect to payment of reparation are to be treated in the allied response in a manner somewhat conciliatory. The proposal in the enemy memorandum that the total reparation be fixed at a hundred billion marks without interest and to include the cost of material delivered during the armistice is rejected by the Allies who, however, agree to have the Allied Reparations Commission fix the amount of reparation within a few months instead of taking advantage of the period of two years for so doing as provided in the treaty.

The German memorandum also proposed that a German commission work in

Continued on Page Six.

Captain John Alcock

Lieutenant Arthur W. Brown

Airmen Who Accomplished the First Non-Stop Transatlantic Flight

FOCH OFF TO RHINE; PERSHING TO GO, TOO

Departures Emphasize Allies' Serious Plans to Meet Eventualities.

SIGNATURE SEEMS LIKELY

Conference Officials Who Doubted Now Inclined to Share Wilson's Optimism.

By RICHARD V. OULAHAN.

Copyright, 1919, by The New York Times Company.
By Wireless and Cable to THE NEW YORK TIMES.

PARIS, June 15.—Speculative comment as to whether the German Government will accept the allied peace conditions appears to have little value in the face of the belief of President Wilson and others who have the advantage of obtaining reports from intelligence agents in Germany that the enemy plenipotentiaries will be instructed to sign the treaty.

The statements coming from various places in Germany that officials have begun to remove supplies and documents to points remote from the western frontier do not have with the President and others who are well informed the effect which the German authors evidently intended them to have.

It would not be surprising, if one may judge from information received by the allied chiefs, if the Scheidemann Cabinet resigned when called upon to say, as it will be this week, whether the German Government will accept the peace conditions. That a new ministry would be speedily formed, probably with Erzberger at its head, is the belief in the best informed circles in Paris.

No doubt is felt that the new Ministry would respond to the apparently widespread demand among the German people that peace—even the most severe sort of peace dictated by the victorious Allies—be brought about without delay.

The Allied Governments, however, are taking no chances. They have completed practically all their preparations for meeting possible eventualities. Purely military measures and plans for renewing the blockade have been made.

One matter under consideration is the best means of taking care of the Allied ships now in German ports, including the ships which carried food for the German population. Should Germany determine to resist, these ships could all be seized by the German authorities. Most of them are in strongly fortified ports.

The actual state of war will be revived automatically on the expiration of the armistice, which becomes inoperative at the end of the five-day period allowed the German Government to determine whether it will accept the peace conditions. If Germany accepts, as is generally believed, the armistice will be re-

Continued on Page Eight.

Northcliffe, Congratulating Capt. Alcock, Says That Airplane is Faster Than Cables

Special Cable to THE NEW YORK TIMES.

LONDON, June 15.—Lord Northcliffe has sent the following letter to Captain Alcock:

"My Dear Alcock—A very hearty welcome to the pioneer of direct Atlantic flight. Your journey with your brave companion, Whitton Brown, is a typical exhibition of British courage and organizing efficiency.

"Just as in 1913 when I offered the prize, I felt that it would soon be won, so do I surely believe your wonderful journey is the warning to the cable monopolists and others to realize that within the next few years we shall be less dependent upon them unless they increase their wires and speed up. Your voyage was made more quickly than the average press message of 1919.

"Moreover, I look forward with certainty to the time when London morning newspapers will be selling in New York in the evening, allowing for the difference between British and American time, and vice versa in regard to New York evening journals reaching London the next day.

"Then we shall no longer suffer from the danger of garbled quotations due to telegraphic compression. Then, too, the American and British peoples will understand each other better as they are brought into closer daily touch.

"Illness prevents me shaking you by the hand and personally presenting the prize, but I can assure you that your welcome will be equal to that of Hawker and his gallant American compeer, Read, whose great accomplishment has given us such valuable data for future Atlantic work.

"I rejoice at the good augury that you departed from and arrived at those two portions of the British Commonwealth, the happy and prosperous Dominion of Newfoundland and the future equally happy and prosperous Dominion of Ireland.

"Yours sincerely, "NORTHCLIFFE."

Labor Fails to Move Congress to Repeal of War-Time Dry Law

Lawmakers Are Unresponsive to Big "Wet" Demonstration and Inclined to Put Responsibility Up to President—Enforcement Act Unlikely Before July 1.

Special to The New York Times.

WASHINGTON, June 15.—Republican leaders remain unimpressed by the protest of labor yesterday against the enforcement of wartime prohibition, and no action will be taken by Congress looking to the repeal of prohibition, which becomes operative July 1. This opinion was expressed tonight by a member of the House Steering Committee, who, while opposed to prohibition, said the responsibility for lifting the ban rests with the President and that no action to carry out the President's recommendation for lifting the ban on beer and light wines will be taken by the House.

Judged by informal canvasses made by Anti-Saloon League leaders, any move to break down wartime prohibition, even as to light wines and beer, would not succeed in Congress. Wartime prohibition passed by a good majority, and national prohibition passed the House by the necessary two-thirds vote. Men who voted for both measures say they would place themselves in an inconsistent position before their constituents if they should support a resolution to repeal the wartime prohibition law, even though the act was passed solely as a food conservation measure.

The position of most members of Congress is that the nation must go on a dry basis early in January through the operation of the National Prohibition Amendment, and that there is no compelling reason why the conservation law should be repealed to permit the "wets" another six months of freedom. The only thing which is influencing some members to look upon repeal with favor is the cutting off of returns from internal revenue six months earlier than had been estimated by the fiscal agents. They admit it would be wise for the Government to have this money now when direct taxes are so heavy and the present returns from the revenue law are insufficient.

Politics is involved in the attitude of the Republican leaders. They do not want to put themselves in a position of bowing to the demands of labor or catering to the liberal sentiment. They say the Democratic Administration insisted upon wartime prohibition, and the South forced through the national amendment, and it would be dangerous for the Republican Party to go against an apparent sentiment for a dry nation.

Furthermore, Republican members of the House Judiciary Committee have received an opinion from a lawyer of national repute that the President has power to repeal the wartime prohibition proclamation and that no act of Congress is necessary.

It seems now that there will be no legislation to enforce wartime prohibition, as less than two weeks remain before July 1. Indications are that the House Judiciary Committee in the next week will report a bill to enforce wartime prohibition and the national amendment, but with both branches of Congress busy considering supply measures which must be passed by July 1, there is not much chance the enforcement bills will be passed. The Department of Justice can enforce the wartime prohibition law without additional legislation, but will be hampered by lack of funds and special agents.

ZURICH REDS RIOT; 2 DEAD, 17 HURT

Prefecture Stormed and Its Archives Burned by a Mob.

POLICEMAN MORTALLY HURT

Mob Returns Fire of the Guards—Rumor of Leader's Arrest Started the Rioting.

PARIS, June 14.—Serious anarchist and Bolshevist disorders broke out in Zurich, Switzerland, last night at 8 o'clock. Firing was still going on at 9 o'clock, according to a dispatch received from Geneva.

Reports received this morning state that the local workmen's union of Zurich, which has some extremist members, was holding a meeting in memory of Rosa Luxemburg, the German radical leader, who was killed following her arrest in Berlin early in the year, when the news was circulated that the Secretary of the union, Conrad Wyss, had been arrested on Wednesday.

A furious crowd marched upon the Prefecture, stoned the windows, broke down solid doors, and, after a half hour of battering, looted the Hall of Justice and burned the archives in the principal corridor of the building.

One of the guards fired on the crowd, his shots being answered. A number of casualties are reported, but details are lacking, as telephone and telegraph lines appear to have been tampered with.

There are large foreign colonies of anarchists, Bolsheviki, and revolutionaries in Zurich.

BERNE, June 14.—The casualties in the disturbance at Zurich are given officially as two persons killed and seventeen wounded. One policeman was mortally hurt.

Among the rioters were many German anarchists and communists.

POPE TO DISCUSS WORLD SITUATION

Will Deal with Post-War Conditions in Allocution at Consistory on June 26.

ROME, June 15.—Pope Benedict will hold a Consistory June 26. The function will be for the appointment of Bishops and the confirmation of the Patriarch of Antioch of the Greek Melchite Rite.

The only importance of the Consistory to the outside ecclesiastical world will be a papal allocution, which it is asserted will deal with the situation of the world after the war.

LAND AT CLIFDEN, IRELAND, IN A BOG

Airmen Moving at an 120-Mile Speed Were Unable to See Sun, Moon, or Stars for Hours Owing to Fog.

THEY LOOPED THE LOOP UNINTENTIONALLY AT TIMES

Fliers Temporarily Dazed and Deafened by Landing—Alcock Expects to Continue Journey to England—London Unprepared for Quick Flight.

Captain Alcock's Own Narrative Of His Flight From Newfoundland to Ireland

By Captain J. Alcock, D. S. C.

Special Cable to THE NEW YORK TIMES.
(By Courtesy of The London Daily Mail.)

LONDON, June 15, (By telegraph from Clifden, Ireland.)—We have had a terrible journey. The wonder is that we are here at all. We scarcely saw the sun or the moon or the stars. For hours we saw none of them.

The fog was very dense and at times we had to descend to within 300 feet of the sea. For four hours the machine was covered in a sheet of ice, caused by frozen sleet. At another time the fog was so dense that my speed indicator did not work, and for a few seconds it was very alarming.

We looped the loop, I do believe, and did a very steep spiral. We did some very comic stunts, for I had no sense of the horizon.

Winds were favorable all the way, northwest, and at times southwest. We said in Newfoundland we would do the trip in sixteen hours, but we never thought we should. An hour and a half before we saw land we had no certain idea where we were, but we believed we were at Galway or thereabouts.

Our delight in seeing Eastal Island and Turbot Island, five miles west of Clifden, was great. People did not know who we were when we landed and thought we were scouts on the lookout for the Vimy.

We encountered no unforeseen conditions. We did not suffer from cold or exhaustion, except when looking over the side. Then the sleet chewed bits out of our faces. We drank coffee and ale and ate sandwiches and chocolate.

The flight has shown that the Atlantic flight is practicable. It should be done not with an aeroplane or a seaplane but with a flying boat.

We had plenty of reserve fuel, using only two-thirds of our supply. The only thing that upset me was to see the machine at the end get damaged. From above, the bog looked like a lovely field, but the machine sank into it up to the axle and fell over on to her nose.

[Alcock's message to the Daily Mail, by whose courtesy the NEW YORK TIMES is enabled to print it, did not reach London until after 10 o'clock to-night, although filed in Ireland shortly after 5 o'clock in the afternoon.]

LONDON, June 15, (Associated Press.)—The final goal of all the ambitions which flying men have held since the Wright brothers first rose from the earth in a heavier than air machine was realized this morning when the young British officer, Captain John Alcock, and his American navigator, Lieutenant Arthur W. Brown, landed on the Irish coast after the first non-stop flight across the Atlantic Ocean.

Their voyage was without accident and without unforeseen incident, so far as can be learned. It was a straightaway, cleancut flight, achieved in 16 hours and 12 minutes, from Newfoundland to Clifden, Ireland, a distance of more than 1,900 miles.

The report of Alcock and Brown to the Aero Club was as follows:

Landed at Clifden at 8:40 A. M., Greenwich mean time, 15th of June, Vickers-Vimy Atlantic machine leaving Newfoundland coast at 4:28 P. M., Greenwich mean time, 14th of June. Total time, 16 hours 12 minutes. ALCOCK AND BROWN.

But the brief and modest description which comes from the airmen at Clifden tells of an adventurous and amazingly hazardous enterprise. Fog and mists hung over the North Atlantic and the Vickers-Vimy biplane climbed and dived, struggling to extricate herself from the folds of the airplane's worst enemies. She rose to 11,000 feet and swooped down almost to the surface of the sea, and at times the two voyagers found themselves flying upside down, only ten feet above the water.

Mists robbed the night of the advantage of the full moon and the wireless apparatus was torn away by the wind soon after the start. So the two young pioneers of the Atlantic flight without a stop were thrown upon their own resources. The skilful navigation which brought the machine near to the centre of the Irish coast line was one of the finest features of the flight.

Before coming to earth near the Clifden wireless station Alcock circled the wireless aerials, seeking the best spot to reach the earth, but no suitable ground was found, so he chanced it in a bog.

The wireless staff rushed to the aid of the aviators. They found Brown dazed and Alcock temporarily deafened by the force of the impact. As soon as they were able to be escorted to the wireless station they telegraphed the news to their friends, then had breakfast.

"That is the best way to cross the Atlantic," said Lieutenant Brown after he had eaten.

Wireless Out of Action.

The Daily Mail's correspondent found Alcock and Brown at Clifden, packing their gear into a huge sack. Alcock's face lit up with a smile

Section 1

"All the News That's Fit to Print."

The New York Times.

THE WEATHER
Fair and continued cool Sunday; fair Monday; moderate winds.
For full weather report see Page 26.

Section 1

VOL. LXVIII...NO. 22,436. NEW YORK, SUNDAY, JUNE 29, 1919. 122 PAGES. In Nine Parts, Including Picture and Magazine Sections (Rotogravure) and Book Section. FIVE CENTS

PEACE SIGNED, ENDS THE GREAT WAR; GERMANS DEPART STILL PROTESTING; PROHIBITION TILL TROOPS DISBANL

WILSON PROMISES TO ACT

Must Wait Until Complete Demobilization, His Word from Paris.

THIS WILL TAKE 7 WEEKS

President Calls Attention of Congress to His Request for Repeal.

LIQUOR MEN UNPREPARED

Had Hoped Until Announcement That Executive Would Intervene at the Eleventh Hour.

Special to The New York Times.

WASHINGTON, June 28.—President Wilson will not lift the ban which provides for war-time prohibition until the demobilization of the army has been terminated.

But when demobilization has been completed, the President will lift the ban. Formal announcement to this effect was made at the White House tonight. The President is in agreement with A. Mitchell Palmer, his Attorney General, that he cannot at this time lift the ban on wartime prohibition. He agrees with the Attorney General that the language of the law is such that he will be free to act on his own initiative, without Congressional action, not immediately after the signing of the treaty of peace, but when the army has been demobilized. As the army has not yet been demobilized, and there are yet a million men in the army, called into service under the emergency of war, the President, in the failure of Congress to vest him with power to call off wartime prohibition, takes the position that he cannot interfere with the putting of wartime prohibition into effect.

The responsibility for putting wartime prohibition into effect is put squarely up to Congress by the President. He takes the position that the law calling for wartime prohibition was an act of Congress, that its terms are clear, and that he had asked Congress to provide for the repeal of the legislation. Congress, having failed to act so far, has left the President's hands tied with legal strings so far as lifting the ban is concerned, and he makes this situation very plain in a cablegram sent to the White House just before he left Paris today.

President Wilson's cablegram was made public at the White House at 8 o'clock tonight by Joseph P. Tumulty, the Private Secretary to the President.

In his message the President said that he could not act until the army had been completely demobilized, and since there were still a million men in the service there was no chance of his taking immediate action. He called attention to the fact that the present difficulty could have been obviated if Congress had heeded his recommendation of several months ago.

The President in his message left no doubt as to what action he will take when demobilization is terminated.

"When demobilization is terminated," says the final sentence of his cablegram, "my power to act without Congressional action will be exercised."

When demobilization has been terminated will be determined by the President upon information to be supplied to him by Secretary Baker and by Attorney General Palmer. The prospects are that six, or perhaps seven, weeks will elapse before demobilization is terminated, which means that the President will probably not be in position, under his construction of the law, to act before the middle or latter part of August in lifting the ban.

It means that wartime prohibition will go into effect on July 1, even though there is no adequate provision legally made for its real enforcement, and that it will remain in effect until the termination of demobilization unless Congress meanwhile adopts the President's request for a repeal of the legislation which provided for the institution of wartime prohibition.

Congress is free at any time to enact the necessary legislation. So far all attempts to bring about repeal have failed on Capitol Hill and there is no present indication that Congress intends to change.

Not only has the President asked Congress to repeal the legislation standing in the way of lifting the ban, but in his cabled statement of today the President declares without equivocation that he will exercise his power to act when demobilization is terminated, and makes it clear he will then lift the ban unless Congress by repealing the act of Nov. 21, 1918, does away with wartime pro-

Continued on Page Eleven.

President Sends A Prohibition Message; Says He Will Act When Demobilization Ends

WASHINGTON, July 28.—The following message from President Wilson, stating his stand on the prohibition question, was made public at the White House tonight by Secretary Tumulty:

I am convinced that the Attorney General is right in advising me that I have no legal power at this time in the matter of the ban on liquor. Under the act of November, 1918, my power to take action is restricted. The act provides that after June 30, 1919, "until the conclusion of the present war and thereafter until the termination of demobilization, the date of which shall be determined and proclaimed by the President, it shall be unlawful, &c." This law does not specify that the ban shall be lifted with the signing of peace, but with the termination of the demobilization of the troops, and I cannot say that this has been accomplished. My information from the War Department is that there are still a million men in the army under the emergency call. It is clear, therefore, that the failure of Congress to act upon the suggestion contained in my message of the twentieth of May, 1919, asking for a repeal of the act of Nov. 21, 1918, so far as it applies to wines and beers, makes it impossible to act in this matter at this time. When demobilization is terminated, my power to act without Congressional action will be exercised.

WOODROW WILSON.

VIOLENCE GROWS IN BERLIN FERMENT

Bomb Hurled at Building in Which Officials Were Conferring on Strike.

SHOTS FIRED AT MINISTERS

Railway Strikers Ignore Orders from Noske and Union Chiefs to Resume Work.

Special Cable to THE NEW YORK TIMES.

BERLIN, June 28, (via Copenhagen.)—Vorwärts, even Die Freiheit and also Ledebour, in his first speech after his release from prison, earnestly warn the people against riots and political revolt which, in view of the enormous military strength gathered in Berlin, can only lead to awful bloodshed.

Doubtless the big leaders of the Independent Socialists do not wish any outbreaks at present. Nevertheless the air is charged with the spirit of rebellion, and nobody here would be surprised if tomorrow there were a repetition of the events of January and March on a much larger scale.

The minor leaders of the Independents, Communists and Sparticides desire to inflame this unrest, communicating it to ever-growing circles of the workers, and inciting the lawless elements to the most audacious and wholesale crimes. Unknown parties shortly after 2 o'clock this morning threw a bomb against the façade of the building of the Public Works Department. It exploded with a terrific noise, shattering about 200 windows. Nobody was hurt. Later, when the ministers and the railway employes' delegates left the building, after trying vainly all night to reach an agreement, unknown persons fired revolvers at the government members, without hitting any one.

Incite Lawlessness in Berlin.

Though ten or more members of the Executive Committee of the Berlin Soldiers and Workers' Councils, after being arrested yesterday on suspicion of conniving with the Hamburg revolutionists for the overthrow of the Federal Government, have been released for lack of evidence nobody doubts for one moment that telephone congratulations were exchanged between them and the Hamburg revolutionists, as overheard by officials, but the identity of the man who answered the Hamburg announcement of the successful revolt with "Bravo!" and promised the Executive Committee's aid in starting a revolt against the Government in Berlin could not be established.

Members of that Executive Committee have never made any secret of their intention to overthrow the Government at the first opportunity, and doubtless the weaker heads among them yesterday believed that the time had come. The lawless element believe this, and it cannot be denied that they are quite right, if the absence of any effective policing of the capital is any justification.

Insecurity has reached an incredible degree. Lately men disguised as officers have been ascending street cars and, with pointed revolvers, collecting pocketbooks and jewels from the passengers in true Wild West fashion. This

Continued on Page Three.

DUTCH UNWILLING TO GIVE UP KAISER

Majority of the People Firmly Opposed to Yielding to Allies' Demand.

HOPEFUL AT AMERONGEN

Troelstra Says Chamber Would Surrender Ex-Ruler to Germany Only.

Special Cable to THE NEW YORK TIMES.

THE HAGUE, June 27.—The question of the delivery of the ex-Kaiser is again on the tapis here. There is no doubt that a majority of Netherlanders are already forgetting Germany's and the ex-monarch's record and violently oppose his surrender.

Appeals such as the recent one from the German Officers League and echoes from the German press only serve to strengthen these feelings. The officers' appeal stated that the German officers would be dishonored forever if Holland delivered the ex-Kaiser to the Allies, and ended with the statement: "It is even yet not certain whether a German can be found to sign the peace treaty."

The NEW YORK TIMES correspondent questioned Pieter Troelstra, the Socialist leader, the report emanating from Germany that the Dutch Social Democrats opposed the surrender of the ex-Kaiser. Troelstra replied:

"Our party has taken no official attitude. As we have not yet considered the question officially no resolution has been taken and no official correspondence carried on.

"It is true that we are against his surender on principle and would oppose it. I consider that we must wait until we receive the allied demand, so that the matter is not urgent.

"I can certainly say that as Socialists we believe in the right of asylum. English Socialists defend the right of asylum and London has always been a city for political refugees. Switzerland and the Netherlands have been free for centuries and it is a matter of tradition."

When asked if the question were put to a vote in the Dutch Chamber other parties would oppose the delivery of the ex-monarch, Troelstra replied in the affirmative.

"It is impossible," he said, "to deliver a refugee to an enemy. It is against all rights. If Germany should demand the Kaiser it would be another question. We should be in favor of that. I feel nothing but antipathy for his personality, but only his own Government has a right to demand him. I believe that all parties would vote in favor of a demand from the German Government."

Plead Ties with Dutch Queen.

Special Cable to THE NEW YORK TIMES.

BERLIN, June 28.—The League of Officers of the Former Prussian Army and German Navy has addressed a message to the Dutch Queen pleading that she had refused to extradite the "all highest war lord, our beloved unforgettable King, his Majesty Kaiser Wilhelm, who because of high treason in his own country, and not forced by the enemy's arms,

Continued on Page Three.

LEAGUE OPPONENTS UNITING

Republican Senators Now Seem Agreed on Policy of Reservations.

McCUMBER IS WON OVER

But North Dakota Senator Opposes Any Action Nullifying the Covenant.

SHANTUNG ACTION ASSAILED

Borah Calls It Indefensible—Norris Demands a Reservation Regarding It.

Special to The New York Times.

WASHINGTON, June 28.—With unexpected swiftness the Republican opposition in the Senate to the League of Nations covenant, as embraced in the Treaty of Peace, began to crystallize today, after the cables had brought word that Germany had signed the treaty, and that the President, in his message to the American people, had expressed the hope that the treaty would be "ratified and acted upon in full and sincere execution of its terms."

The President's message, coupled with his statement in interviews at Paris that he hoped the Senate woud ratify the treaty with the League of Nations covenant in it, without amendment, had the effect, it appeared, of bringing closer the elements of opposition among the opponents of the League. Instead of influencing wavering Senators toward an attitude favoring the ratification of the League of Nations covenant, the President's appeal appeared to have exactly the opposite effect.

While the opponents of the covenants, before Germany signed, were admittedly divided as to a policy to pursue in fighting the covenant when the treaty should come before the Senate, they seemed, for the first time since the League fight started, to have come to some general agreement.

Every Republican Senator to whom THE NEW YORK TIMES correspondent talked said decisively that he believed that, if the League covenant was to be accepted by the Senate some character of qualifying resolution would have to be passed, along with the treaty ratification, to express dissent from features objected to.

Even Senator McCumber of North Dakota, the one Republican member of the Foreign Relations Committee who has all along advocated adoption of the covenant, after the President's message had been read in the Senate, said that he believed it would be necessary for that body to adopt "explanatory reservations" in the ratification of the treaty, respecting features involved in the covenant. Mr. McCumber spoke of such reservations being necessary as to the Monroe Doctrine and the right of the United States to determine its purely domestic questions, like immigration, racial equality, and the tariff.

The North Dakota Senator made it clear that he would not favor any resolution of reservation that would have the effect of nullifying the covenant. He wanted the treaty of peace ratified, with the League of Nations included. But he insisted that the Senate should not hesitate to express its dissent from features that affected purely American affairs. If this were not done, he said, there might come some development in the future that might impel the Senate to take action which, in effect, would take America out of the League.

McNary for Interpretation.

Senator McNary, Republican, Oregon, who only a few days ago announced himself as favoring the League of Nations, declared today that he would not oppose a resolution that would enable opponents of the covenant to make clear their dissent from matters to which they objected. This, he said, might be done through a resolution of "interpretation," which was another way of saying one of "qualification."

At the same time Senator McNary agreed with Senator McCumber that no resolution ought to be adopted that would have the effect of rejecting the League of Nations covenant.

Talk of direct amendment of the covenant was not so insistent today among the more radical Senators. They appeared to be willing now to stand behind qualifying resolutions that would amply set forth the features subject to objection. They maintained, however, that Article X., guaranteeing the territorial integrity of members of the League, should come out. On this point

Continued on Page Five.

Wilson Says Treaty Will Furnish the Charter for a New Order of Affairs in the World

WASHINGTON, June 28.—The following address by President Wilson to the American people on the occasion of the signing of the Peace Treaty was given out here today by Secretary Tumulty:

My Fellow Countrymen: The treaty of peace has been signed. If it is ratified and acted upon in full and sincere execution of its terms it will furnish the charter for a new order of affairs in the world. It is a severe treaty in the duties and penalties it imposes upon Germany; but it is severe only because great wrongs done by Germany are to be righted and repaired; it imposes nothing that Germany cannot do; and she can regain her rightful standing in the world by the prompt and honorable fulfillment of its terms.

And it is much more than a treaty of peace with Germany. It liberates great peoples who have never before been able to find the way to liberty. It ends, once for all, an old and intolerable order under which small groups of selfish men could use the peoples of great empires to serve their ambition for power and dominion. It associates the free Governments of the world in a permanent League in which they are pledged to use their united power to maintain peace by maintaining right and justice.

It makes international law a reality supported by imperative sanctions. It does away with the right of conquest and rejects the policy of annexation and substitutes a new order under which backward nations—populations which have not yet come to political consciousness and peoples who are ready for independence but not yet quite prepared to dispense with protection and guidance—shall no more be subjected to the domination and exploitation of a stronger nation, but shall be put under the friendly direction and afforded the helpful assistance of governments which undertake to be responsible to the opinion of mankind in the execution of their task by accepting the direction of the League of Nations.

It recognizes the inalienable rights of nationality, the rights of minorities and the sanctity of religious belief and practice. It lays the basis for conventions which shall free the commercial intercourse of the world from unjust and vexatious restrictions and for every sort of international co-operation that will serve to cleanse the life of the world and facilitate its common action in beneficent service of every kind. It furnishes guarantees such as were never given or even contemplated for the fair treatment of all who labor at the daily tasks of the world.

It is for this reason that I have spoken of it as a great charter for a new order of affairs. There is ground here for deep satisfaction, universal reassurance, and confident hope.

WOODROW WILSON.

DEPORT THIRTY 'RED' AGITATORS

Fifteen Have Been Shipped Away in a Week—18 More Waiting at Ellis Island.

MOST OF THEM ANARCHISTS

Number Includes Some Suspected of Having a Hand in Plot Against Officials.

The deportation of alien agitators and conspirators who have abused their sojourn in America by preaching the overthrow of the United States Government, some of them coming under suspicion of the Secret Service for plots against President Wilson and other high public officials, has begun. Within the last seven days, fifteen of these disturbers, among them the editors of two anarchist newspapers, have been deported from New York, and eighteen others are now on Ellis Island awaiting the sailing of ships that will return them to the lands of their nativity.

The Secret Service agencies of the Government have been quietly, but thoroughly, at work for weeks, and every day or two a new batch of aliens who have urged the destruction of American institutions are rounded up and their records submitted to the proper authorities with a view to immediate deportation.

In the last four weeks thirty anarchist, I. W. W., and Bolshevist agitators have been deported by way of Ellis Island. This number does not include the Seattle and Spokane I. W. W. disturbers and other radicals who were sent East for deportation as a result of Bolshevist strikes in the Pacific Northwest several months ago. Some of those agitators also have been deported, and the cases of several others, recommended for the "homeward voyage," are soon to be decided by the courts.

Most of the deportations have taken place since bombs were set off at the homes of Attorney General Palmer and

Continued on Page Nine.

AMERICA GREETED BY KING GEORGE

"Brothers in Arms Will Continue Forever to be Brothers in Peace."

SENDS MESSAGE TO WILSON

"We Lay Down Our Arms in Proud Consciousness of Valiant Deeds Nobly Done."

LONDON, June 28, (Associated Press.)—King George has sent the following message to President Wilson:

"In this glorious hour when the long struggle of nations for right, justice and freedom is at last crowned by a triumphant peace, I greet you, Mr. President, and the great American people in the name of the British nation.

"At a time when fortune seemed to frown, and the issues of the war trembled in the balance, the American people stretched out the hand of fellowship to those, who on this side of the ocean were battling for a righteous cause. Light and hope at once shone brighter in our hearts, and a new day dawned.

Together we have fought to a happy end; together we lay down our arms in proud consciousness of valiant deeds nobly done.

Mr. President, it is on this day one of our happiest thoughts that the American and British people, brothers in arms, will continue forever to be brothers in peace. United before by language, traditions, kinship, and ideals, there has been set upon our fellowship the sacred seal of common sacrifice.

GEORGE, R. I.

After news of the signing of peace had been received here the following was issued over King George's signature:

The signing of the treaty of peace will be received with deep thankfulness throughout the British Empire. This formal act brings to its concluding stages the terrible war which has

Continued on Page Three.

ENEMY ENVOYS IN TRUCULENT SPIRI

Say Afterward They Would Not Hav Signed Had They Known They Were to Leave First by Different Way.

CHINA REFUSES TO SIGN, SMUTS MAKES PROTES

These Events Somewhat Cloud the Great Occasion at Versailles—Wilson, Clemenceau, and Lloyd George Receive a Tremendous Ovation.

President Wilson Starts for Home

PARIS, June 28, (Associated Press.)—President Wilson left Paris on his homeward journey tonight. His train started from the Gare des Invalides for Brest at 9:45 P. M.

Mr. Wilson's party was accompanied to Brest by General Leorat and Colonel Lobez, the President's French aids, and also by Stephen Pichon, French Foreign Minister; Georges Leygues, French Minister of Marine, and Captain André Tardieu, a member of the French peace delegation. Ambassador Wallace, General Pershing, Premier Clemenceau, and Colonel House were at the station to say good-bye.

The crowd in the station, numbering upward of a thousand, wildly cheered the departure of the President, who raised his hat to cries of "Vive Wilson." Mrs. Wilson threw kisses to the crowd as the train departed.

The superdreadnought Oklahoma will accompany the George Washington to the United States.

VERSAILLES, June 28, (Associated Press.)—Germany and the alli and associated powers signed the peace terms here today in the same im perial hall where the Germans humbled the French so ignominiously fort eight years ago.

This formally ended the world war, which lasted just thirty-sev days less than five years. Today, the day of peace, was the fifth annive sary of the murder of Archduke Francis Ferdinand by a Serbian student Serajevo.

The peace was signed under circumstances which somewhat dimm the expectations of those who had worked and fought during long yea of war and months of negotiations for its achievement.

Absence of the Chinese delegates, who at the last moment we unable to reconcile themselves to the Shantung settlement, struck the fir discordant note. A written protest which General Smuts lodged wi his signature was another disappointment.

But bulking larger than these was the attitude of Germany and th German plenipotentiaries, which left them, as evident from the expressi of M. Clemenceau, still outside of formal reconciliation and made th actual restoration to regular relations and intercourse with the alli nations dependent, not upon the signature of the "preliminaries of peace today, but upon ratification by the National Assembly.

To M. Clemenceau's warning in his opening remarks that they wou be expected, and held, to observe the treaty provisions loyally and com pletely the German delegates, through Dr. Haniel von Haimhausen, replie after returning to the hotel that had they known that they would treated on a different status after signing than the allied representative as shown by their separate exit before the general body of the con ference, they never would have signed.

Under the circumstances the general tone of sentiment in the histori sitting was one rather of relief at the uncontrovertible end of hostiliti than of complete satisfaction.

The ceremony had been planned deliberately to be austere, befittin the sufferings of almost five years, and the lack of impressiveness an picturesque color, of which many spectators, who had expected a magnif cent State pageant, complained, was a matter of design, not mere omission.

The actual ceremony was far shorter than had been expected, in vie of the number of signatures which were to be appended to the treaty an the two accompanying conventions, ending a bare forty-nine minut after the hour set for the opening.

Premier Clemenceau called the session to order in the Hall of Mirro at 3:10 P. M.

The signing began when Dr. Hermann Müller and Johannes Bell, th German signatories, affixed their names. Herr Müller signed at 3:1 o'clock and Herr Bell 3:13 o'clock.

President Wilson, the first of the allied delegates, signed a minut later. At 3:49 o'clock the momentous session was over.

The most dramatic moment connected with the signing came unex pectedly and spontaneously at the conclusion of the ceremony, when Pre mier Clemenceau, President Wilson and Premier Lloyd George descende from the Hall of Mirrors to the terrace at the rear of the palace, whe thousands of spectators were massed.

GREAT DEMONSTRATION FOR ALLIED LEADERS.

With the appearance of the three who had dominated the councils o the Allies there began a most remarkable demonstration. With cries o "Vive Clemenceau!" "Vive Wilson!" "Vive Lloyd George!" dense crowd swept forward from all parts of the spacious terrace. In an instant th three were surrounded by struggling, cheering masses of people, fightin among themselves for a chance to get near the statesmen.

It had been planned that all the allied delegates would walk across the terrace after signing, to see the great fountains play, but none of the othe plenipotentiaries got further than the door.

President Wilson, M. Clemenceau and Mr. Lloyd George were caugh in the living stream which flowed across the great space and became par of the crowd themselves. Soldiers and bodyguards struggled vainly t

The New York Times.

EDITORIAL SECTION Section 2

E SUNDAY, OCTOBER 8, 1922. E

ERUM PROVES BOON FIGHTING DIABETES

avages of Disease Checked by Insulin Discovered by Canadian Doctors.

OUND IN PANCREAS TISSUE

eatment Developed With Rare Success at California Metabolic Clinic.

ELIEF ALMOST CERTAIN

esident of Carnegie Corporation, Aiding Research, Reports on Value of New Method.

Experiments in the treatment of abetes, hitherto regarded as practically incurable, have met with remarkable success, according to reports officials of the Carnegie Corporation, which has made an appropriation research work at the Potter Metabolic Laboratory and Clinic in California. The treatment that is being administered has given relief in practically the cases under observation.

The ravages of the disease have been checked by application of a serum discovered by Canadian physicians working under Dr. J. J. R. Macleod of the University of Toronto. This serum has been used at the Potter laboratory. Thus far relief has been dependent upon constant application of the serum. It too early, physicians say, to describe treatment as a "sure cure" for abetes, for the experiments at the otter laboratory have been going on for ly about eighteen months.

Dr. Henry S. Pritchett, President of e Carnegie Corporation, who recently sited the Potter clinic and observed e experiments there, has made a report on the study and treatment there diabetes, for incorporation in the nual report of the corporation.

Dr. Potter First Started Work.

Dr. Potter's metabolic research began the French Hospital here. He removed to Santa Barbara, Cal., where a etabolic clinic and laboratory was ilt by public-spirited Californians. e Carnegie Corporation has aided the ork by an annual appropriation. Dr. otter died in 1919, and since then the ork has been carried on under the direction of W. D. Sansum.

Intensive studies on the internal secretion of the pancreas had been carried on in the meantime under Dr. acleod in Canada. It has long been own that some pathology of the ncreas is responsible for diabetes. . F. G. Banting, working under Dr. acleod, carried on intensive experiments to extract a substance from pancreatic tissues. This substance was t injected into dogs suffering with abetes. The diabetic symptoms disappeared with the application of the rum, which is known as insulin. onvincing results of the efficacy of e serum were obtained by Dr. Banting in the cases of humans suffering th the disease.

"On account of the admirable facilities in the Potter Metabolic Clinic in nta Barbara and the opportunity afforded by the close association of laboratory and hospital," Dr. Pritchett's port says, "Dr. Macleod and his associates most generously and kindly communicated to Dr. Sansum and his staff Santa Barbara such full information they had and because of the urgent eed for such an extract of the pancreas urged their immediate co-operation. With the information thus generously given through Dr. Macleod, the aff of the Potter Metabolic Clinic began strenuous efforts in the insolation the internal secretion of the pancreas now known as insulin. They ere immediately successful and within o months had been able to secure a fficient amount of insulin to use on e severe cases of diabetes.

Success of Treatment Established.

"The results have been so convincing at there can be no doubt of the great alue of this substance in the treatment diabetes and it is quite within the ssibilities that the discovery may result in the relief and cure of great numbers of people from this scourge. The llowing cases will illustrate the extraordinary sort of results which have en obtained:

"A patient of 53 years of age was sent the clinic on the verge of diabetic oma, apparently death within a few ays awaited him. Following the administration of insulin he became immediately free from sugar, his diet could increased to normal and he is rapidly aining in strength and weight.

"A boy of 12 in extreme illness rough diabetes became free from sugar fter twenty-four hours of treatment ith insulin has remained free although his diet has been increased to ractically normal. This boy is gaining eight at the rate of half a pound a ay and is leading the type of life that ny normal active child would lead. y the older dietary methods partial tarvation would have been necessary ven to prolong life, to say nothing of estoration to health. The results in the ther cases have been equally astonishing.

Expense of Serum Is Very Great.

"The problem is of course still in its fancy. Insulin is prepared at present t very great expense. Cheaper methods f production must be devised. A study f the intricate chemistry of the product ill undoubtedly add materially to our nowledge of the oxidative processes oing on in the body about which practically nothing is known at present. But he great gains seem to be that patients with the use of this new agent will ot only be able to be sugar free, but will be able to have normal diets with the strength and health which can ome alone from the use of such food.

"The brilliant success which has come rom this study and the still more brilliant prospects of the future which it olds out form a source of the greatest ncouragement to the trustees of the orporation that their gifts may, if iven with discretion, advance the cause f medical knowledge and thereby increase human happiness and usefulness n the most desirable fashion. Mr. Carnegie had always in mind the desire to "find the efficient man and enable him o do his work." Not every research can show the brilliant results which ave come out of these investigations, but all patient, long-continued study adds, little by little, to the sum of knowledge, enriches life, and helps to orn away misfortune.

"Not the least pleasing feature of this investigation lies in the generous and admirable attitude in which two sets of nvestigators, each of whom has received modest help from the Carnegie Corporation, have co-operated toward heir common end. It was a graceful and generous act on the part of Dr. Macleod and his colleagues to put at he service of the Potter Metabolic Clinic the full results of their important researches, but this action is in entire consonance with the spirit and the purpose of true scientific research."

Ohio's Pig-Stealing 'Lions' Now Declared Wild Wolves

MOUNT VICTORY, Ohio, Oct. 7.—The "lions" claimed by Mount Victory persons to be roving over this vicinity for the last fortnight have been identified as wild wolves, according to Michael Phelps, Hardin County farmer, who says he caught them in his pigpen last night stealing a pig.

Phelps's report was confirmed today by half a dozen other farmers whose pigpens had been visited by the animals during the night. Phelps declared he was within five feet of the animals when they fled.

Phelps says he met the wolves when he went out to feed his swine. As he opened the gate two animals rushed out, one holding a squealing pig in its mouth. When the animals saw Phelps they dropped the pig and escaped.

Among those who say they actually saw the wolves on their pig-theft raid last night were Mrs. Phelps, Mrs. Al Carrothers and her fifteen-year-old son William, Frank Gebert, Riley Copeland and Tom Longberry.

HEBREW AID SOCIETY IN NEED OF $500,000

Jewish Labor Unions Here Open Drive With a Pledge of $100,000.

20 YEARS OF RELIEF WORK

Appeal Calls Attention to Extent of Activities and Necessity for Prompt Aid.

A campaign to raise $500,000 in this country for the European relief work of the Hebrew Sheltering and Immigrant Aid Society started last week with a meeting of New York's Jewish labor unions at which $100,000 was pledged.

The society, housed in the old Astor Library on Lafayette Street, is an institution of twenty years' standing, and in the last two years has transmitted to its fourteen branches in Europe $13,000,000. In the same period the society has helped more than 100,000 Jewish immigrants arriving in this country with advice, the finding of homes and of occupations. A program of Americanization is carried out among those newly arrived in this country.

In 1920, when every Jewish agency in Europe had broken down as a result of the war, the Hias, as it is popularly known, placed its entire machinery at the disposal of European Jewry. The first commission went across in February, 1920. Since that time it has, through its fourteen branches and fifty co-operating communities, given information regarding immigration regulations, filled out applications for passports and visas, prepared legal documents, located relatives, traced lost baggage, transmitted $12,990,255 from American residents to their relatives in Europe and sent 113,990 cables to residents in America in behalf of their relatives abroad.

Service was given to 55 per cent. of the 190,000 Jewish immigrants who arrived in the United States from January, 1920, to June 30, 1922. The society maintains a bureau at Ellis Island, an office in Washington, and branches in Baltimore, Boston, Chicago, Philadelphia, San Francisco and Seattle.

The appeal issued to the Jews of America by the society says:

"The earnest situation that confronts our people in Europe is that the Hebrew Sheltering and Immigrant Aid Society of America—which they know, love, respect and bless, under the name of 'Hias'—will be forced to close its aid to them and abandon them to the mercy of fate. It may be that not all of you have a clear idea of the extent and importance of the rescue work and aid that Hias brought, and is still bringing, to the unfortunate Jewish wanderer in Poland, Galicia, Rumania, Ukrainia, Bukovina, Bessarabia, Littau, Latvia, and other countries and districts where it has bureaus and officers, but the immigrants, your flesh and blood, know that Hias is the only human guardian, the only friend in need, the only light and guide.

"Hias is the first door upon which they knock, where they hear the first friendly word, where they receive the desired information: Hias takes care that no injustice is done them, that they receive all rights and privileges to which they are entitled under local as well as American laws.

"The financial condition of Hias has reached its most critical state. Hias has no reserve fund and relies for its expenses upon its daily income. Because of the increase in expenses which the work in Europe entails and because our income did not increase proportionately, our society has a deficit.

"We desire to bring to your kind attention the grave danger that threatens the unprotected and helpless Jewish emigrants waiting impatiently in Europe for the supreme moment when they may be reunited with their beloved husbands, fathers and children in this country. These sufferers have as yet had no warning of the impending calamity that awaits them."

OLD FRANKLIN HOME TO GO.

Philosopher's First Dwelling in Philadelphia Will Be Razed.

PHILADELPHIA, Oct. 7.—Benjamin Franklin's first Philadelphia home is to be wiped out of existence. The house at 111 Spring Street, where the philosopher took up his residence upon his arrival from Boston, is to be torn down, along with numerous others, to provide for the approach to the new Delaware River bridge.

The house is a ramshackle, tottering shanty, and the street on which it is situated is only an alley. Wilfred Jordan, Curator of Independence Hall, plans to preserve the windows and panels of the old structure, all being splendid examples of Colonial workmanship.

SOLDIERS QUIT GERMANY.

Their Departure Will Leave Only 1,209 American Troops There.

COBLENZ, Oct. 7.—Departure of Casual Detachment No. 49, comprising two officers and fifty men, who are to sail from Hamburg on the steamship Reliance about the middle of the present month, will leave the American forces in Germany at a strength of 113 officers and 1,096 men.

Maj. Gen. Henry T. Allen, commanding the American forces, also has charge of the French occupational troops, numbering 244 officers and 8,606 men.

AUTOMATIC PHONES START SATURDAY

After Two Years Installation Is Complete for 1,700 in Pennsylvania Exchange.

TO BE EXTENDED RAPIDLY

Intricate Mechanism Will Soon Do the Work Now Performed by Many Girls.

The first of the automatic telephone central offices, where connections are made by machinery instead of by girls, will be opened in the Pennsylvania central district next Saturday at midnight. At that time a switch will be thrown and 1,700 telephone subscribers will begin using the instruments wherewith, instead of calling the operator, they start automatic switching by using the dial.

At first the system will be used in only a part of the Pennsylvania central district, but it will be rapidly extended. The Academy central district will be opened as a dial area in December, the Walker district in January and the Hillcrest exchange in Mount Vernon will become automatic in March. The difficult and intricate installations in the telephone buildings are being made as rapidly as possible, and it is expected that within ten years every telephone in the metropolitan district will be used without a word being spoken to an operator, because the operator will be made of brass or steel. It will make possible faster extension of service and eliminate the problem of getting girls enough to operate the great telephone system of the future.

The Operating Dial.

When the new apparatus is in service Pennsylvania subscribers will use a telephone instrument which has a three-inch movable dial mounted on the base. Around the edge of the dial are ten finger holes, in which are numbers from one to nine, and letters of the alphabet, and in the tenth hole zero and the word "operator."

To make a local call the first three letters of the exchange wanted are dialed and then the four figures of the number. When the receiver is removed from the hook a low humming sound, equivalent of the operator's "number, please," will be heard. Then the user will place a finger in the hole where the first letter shows, and turn the dial until a stop prevents further rotation. Then the other two letters and each figure of the number will be manipulated in the same way.

If the call line is busy the operator will send back a busy signal. Otherwise it will ring the number wanted, and the ringing signal will be heard. When the receiver is placed upon the hook the apparatus automatically disconnects and is ready to receive a new call. For long distance calls information or some other special call code numbers have been arranged. For toll calls the dial users will indicate "operator." For, although the instrument is almost human in its working, it can't write toll tickets or check time.

Engineers Busy Two Years.

Engineers have been two years building the intricate machines in the Pennsylvania Terminal, testing them, solving new problems that came up every day, and making apparatus as nearly foolproof as possible. There are 100 central offices, with 4,500,000 daily telephone calls, and the task is a huge one. For not only has the Pennsylvania office to be constructed, but in every other office in the city special apparatus has been built to receive the dial calls, and switch them to the manual boards. The task of wiring the Pennsylvania central office was in itself staggering, for more than 7,000,000 soldered connections had to be made by hand.

The Pennsylvania automatic switchboard rooms are places of fascination and mystery to the novice, where lights shift and flash in red and green, where delicate bits of mechanism move, picking out connections with such precision and flexibility that it seems as if they could almost think. The apparatus necessary to establish a connection between two machine switching telephones may be divided into six classifications.

Steps in the Connection.

The first is the line switch, which connects the subscriber's telephone with the central office apparatus; the second is the sender, which does the work of the manual operator; the third is the district selector, which helps to find a trunk line to the desired central office; the fourth is the office selector, which picks out an idle trunk line to that office; the fifth is the incoming selector in the distant office where the lines in that office are divided into groups of 500, and the sixth piece of apparatus is the final selector, where the lines are subdivided into groups of 100, where the last connection is made with ease and dispatch.

Each Pennsylvania subscriber's line is permanently connected to a line switch which, when the receiver is removed from the hook, resolves until it finds an idle line to the first piece of mechanism, known as the "district selector frame." This little rotator jumps on an idle wire the moment it reaches it, and as it has twenty wires to choose from there is almost no need for a subscriber to ever wait more than a few seconds.

The calling line is permanently connected to what is known as a sender selector, which in turn picks out an idle sender. In calling "Pennsylvania 1750" the letters "P E N" are dialed, followed by the numerals 1750. When the dialing is completed the sender, governed by the impulses recorded when "P E N" was dialed, trips a switch which carried the connection to that particular section on the "district selector frame" on which the "P E N" trunks are located, where an idle trunk line to the incoming selector frame in the Pennsylvania office is picked out.

The impulses resulting from dialing the digits 1-7 cause another piece of apparatus on the incoming selector frame to locate that particular bank of terminals in which are the "1700" lines. Then the electrical impulses resulting from dial 5-0 carry the connection to the final selector frame where another piece of apparatus effects the last step and completes the connection. The bell begins ringing automatically or the busy signal is returned.

When a subscriber dials a call to a telephone served by a central office other than Pennsylvania, a signal lamp lights in front of an operator at the switchboard in that other office. By depressing a key the number which has been dialed is displayed before the operator in the manner of a carriage call indicator. She then completes the connection by plugging in a cord on the subscriber's line just as though the number had come to her verbally.

Dr. Lyman Heads W. Va. College.

MORGANTOWN, W. Va., Oct. 7.—Dr. George H. Lyman, chief inspector of plant pathology in the Department of Agriculture at Washington, was elected today Dean of the West Virginia University College of Agriculture. Dr. Lyman will come here on Jan. 1 and will succeed Dr. J. L. Coulter, resigned.

Paradise Feathers Valued at $15,000 Seized at Nine Millinery Shops

Bird of paradise wings and plumes valued at $15,000 were taken to the Federal Building yesterday by Customs Agents Pike, Barron, Norke, Brown and Fitzpatrick, who, under the direction of Assistant United States Attorney Herman L. Falk, removed them from nine millinery stores in various parts of the city.

As the importation of bird of paradise wings and plumes is forbidden by law, the Federal authorities lately have been curious as to the origin of so many of the prohibited plumes on hats worn in the city.

Procuring search warrants from United States Commissioner S. N. Hitchcock, Assistant United States Attorney Falk and the customs agents visited nine establishments and the bird of paradise feathers found were seized under the "wild bird feather exclusion act."

"To recover the feathers," said Mr. Falk, "it is incumbent on the storekeepers to establish that the feathers taken were legally in their possession before the passage of the wild bird feather exclusion law in October, 1913. If the storekeepers are unable to do so, the feathers will be condemned by the Federal District Court and ordered destroyed."

It is unlikely that prosecutions will follow the seizure, because the Government is not in possession of evidence to prove that the feathers in litigation were smuggled into this country since 1913, it was said, although the law presumes that the feathers were imported after the law became effective.

LAST 2 YEARS BREAK HEAT RECORDS HERE

Daily Average Temperature Has Been Two to Three Degrees Above the Normal.

DROUGHT AIDS BEER SALES

Pennsylvania Reservoirs Fail—Freak Weather Laid to the Absence of Sun Spots.

With the revival of unseasonably hot weather in September and the present month, New York City has passed through twenty-four months of abnormally high temperature, every day averaging between two and three degrees higher than normal.

Temperatures in July and August of this year were slightly below normal, but eighteen of the twenty-four months of the last two years have had abnormally high temperatures. At the present rate, October will run up the greatest excess in any of the twenty-four months. The mercury recorded 87 on Thursday, the highest mark ever known on an Oct. 5. The second highest was 83 degrees on the same day of the year 1891. On Oct. 3 a new record was set at 84 degrees, against a previous high record of 80 degrees on Oct. 2, 1879.

The average temperature for September was 67.4, nearly a full degree above the average. July and August were less than one degree below normal, while June was more than two degrees above normal. The total excess for the two years for New York City is calculated at about 1,500 degrees.

Moreover, unusual heat has not been peculiar to this city. The weather has been a little hotter than usual during this period over most of the world. This is due, according to some scientists, to the condition of the sun, which is at present in that period of the eleven-year sun spot cycle when spots are fewest. The earth is said to be a little hotter at this period, although records are not clear on the subject, leaving the point in dispute.

Dry Spell Near Record.

There has been only one more prolonged dry spell than the present, according to the New York City records. That occurred in the year 1884, when there were fifty-one consecutive days in September and October during which the total rainfall was less than one-hundredth part of an inch. Another record year was 1872, when for twenty-four consecutive days in February and March there was no precipitation.

Considerable rain in August and early in September this year has so far prevented serious damage from the drought. Some of the worst suffering has occurred in mountain towns in Pennsylvania, where the reservoirs supplying drinking water have gone nearly dry. At Johnstown, for example, the Mayor urged the population to take to beer. In many other parts of Pennsylvania and in some up-State sections of New York, it is asserted, real beer has almost entirely supplanted drinking water.

While evidences that the dry spell was breaking up and that a good deal of rain was in sight have been reported from Washington, the late vegetable crops in New Jersey and other sections have been severely threatened, while the drought has caused numerous forest fires. Thousands of square miles of timber land have been burned over in the United States and Canada.

The greatest revolution in weather experience so far this month occurred at Middletown, N. Y., where on Oct. 1 the thermometer reached 92 degrees in the shade. Pastures were reported drying up, with consequent reduction in the milk supply. Such heat has never been known in this region at this time of year.

Recent rainfall has relieved conditions in some parts of Northern New York and New England. In general, the drought came so late and after such comparatively plentiful rains that the damage to crops has been slight.

Weather Here Capricious.

Heat late in the Fall is nothing extraordinary in New York. A warm spell is likely to appear unexpectedly even in the dead of Winter. Few parts of the world have a more capricious climate. All records were shattered last Nov. 17 when the temperature suddenly ran up to 73. Nature was fooled. Leaves sprouted and streaks of green appeared in the tanned grass.

The temperature has soared into the seventies on three other November days. These sudden freaks of temperature are attributed to the fact that the city lies on the weather path between the hot Southern States and the St. Lawrence River Valley, which is one of the great weather factories of the world.

Conditions on the St. Lawrence are always either drawing hot air northward over New York City and through the flue created by the Hudson River Valley or hustling cold air down from the North across New York City, owing to opposite conditions in the South.

Reports of oldest inhabitants, trappers and nature fakers on the kind of Winter we are going to have have not yet been received. November is their day.

All signs went wrong last Winter. Because of the thick fur found on skunks, trappers of the Middletown section warned the world of the approach of terrific cold. Adirondack and Canadian guides alleged that squirrels and other small quadrupeds were storing up huger hoards than ever before. Migratory birds were said to be flying South at a swifter pace than in former years. Fishermen reported the sagacious deep sea fish seeking lower oceanic levels to escape a Winter of unparalleled fierceness. In spite of these veteran forecasters the Winter was generally mild.

Harding Greets the Portuguese.

WASHINGTON, Oct. 7.—President Harding cabled to Lisbon today his felicitations on the national anniversary of the Portuguese republic. His message, addressed to President José d'Almeida, said: "I beg Your Excellency to accept my cordial felicitations on this national anniversary of the republic, and best wishes for the continued prosperity and happiness of the Portuguese people."

FURS WORTH $100,000 STOLEN IN 3 MONTHS

Thieves Invade Lofts While Employes Are at Luncheon.

ONE HELD FOR GRAND JURY

Furriers' Security Alliance Issues Warning to Its Members.

John C. Stott, General Manager of the Furriers' Security Alliance, 303 Fifth Avenue, issued the following bulletin yesterday:

"Sneak thieving to the amount of $100,000 has occurred in the fur industry in the City of New York during the past three months. The alliance has to date succeeding in having whom we believe to be the leader of the gang operating held for the action of the Grand Jury. The popular method of operating is to enter the furrier's place at lunch time, cut the wires to the bell on the show room door, or removing, as happened in one case, a section of the partition to the stock room and removing the garments. The value of each loss is from $2,000 to $5,000.

"Please be careful in the future and when leaving your office or show room have an employe present during this period. If any suspicious character is seen in your show room or building please report same immediately to the alliance."

The arrest was that of Louis Hasenfield, 25 years old, of 104 Second Street, who on Friday was held in $3,000 bail in Jefferson Market Court. He is described as clean shaven, blond, and a wearer of "snappy" clothes. The alliance is attempting to learn if Hasenfield, who is also known as Louis Hess, is the man who identifies himself to furriers as a "Holmes man." Mr. Stott believes the "Holmes man" was the thief.

Hasenfield was arrested at noon, Sept. 29, opposite 134 West Twenty-sixth Street, where Greenberg & Co., have a loft on the fifth floor. Greenberg said that all his employes were out for lunch leaving the show room empty. Returning after a short visit to the factory, he saw a man, laden with coats, making his departure. Greenberg demanded to know what the stranger was doing and the visitor bolted, dropping seven Hudson Seal coats on the landing. Attracted by Greenberg's shouts, the colored elevator boy ran after the man and caught him on the other side of the street.

Two days before Greenberg's place was entered, another thief, working the same way and at the same time, made off with $4,000 worth of fur garments. About three weeks ago, Mr. Stott said yesterday, the store of William Jackman's Sons, Inc., of 35 West Thirty-fifth Street was entered and $1,800 worth of mink was stolen. Another robbery was that of Hochstim & Bossack of 115 West Twenty-seventh Street, who suffered an $11,000 loss.

TO TRAIN GIRL SCOUT HEADS

New York University Will Give Courses in Leadership.

Courses in Girl Scout leadership will in the future be included in the regular curriculum of the Extramural Division of New York University, according to Dr. James E. Lough, dean of the division.

"New York University is interested in the development of Scout leaders," said Dean Lough, "in view of the fact that scouting for girls has become well established as a social service. Part of the program of the Extramural Division is to offer educational work and to conduct training courses along all lines of social service. We realize that girls, especially in metropolitan districts, need just such training as these Scouts offer. It makes them self-reliant and fills the 'growing-up' period with wholesome work and fun."

Classes will be organized as troops and visits to Scout troops throughout the city will be arranged in order to combine practice with theory.

'DON'T GET HURT' IS SAFETY WEEK CRY

Accident Prevention Will Be Taught Everywhere in City During Next Seven Days.

BOY SCOUTS TO AID TRAFFIC

Three Thousand Speakers Enlisted and Warnings Shown to Cut Down Fatalities.

The permanent accident prevention program inaugurated by the Safety Institute of America, with Judge Elbert H. Gary at the head of its Public Safety Committee, opens today. This is "Safety Week," and, according to the plans of the Gary committee, during the next seven days the residents of New York will hear and at every turn read the slogan, "Don't Get Hurt."

The child at school will be taught a safety lesson each day of the week, the worker in the factories will attend noonday rallies with safety as the theme, the theatregoer at night will receive safety literature with his program, the movie patron will see safety films, the housewife will be asked to give special attention during the week and thereafter to a list of "household safety suggestions," while the man in the street will see safety posters, banners, tags, buttons and other devices, all pleading with him for his own life and that of his fellow.

Many clergymen this morning will discuss public safety in their sermons, and there will be safety lessons in the Sunday schools. Tonight there will be a safety radio program. The program for the remainder of the week follows:

MONDAY.

Children's Day.

9 A. M.—Safety exercises in schools.

12 M.—Parade of 15,000 children from Forty-second Street north in Fifth Avenue to Seventy-second Street and Central Park.

Dedication of monument erected to the memory of 1,504 children killed by accidents in 1921. Central Park.

Address by the Mayor.

Presentation of Safety Institute hero medals to boys and girls for saving the lives of children. At the monument.

Life-saving demonstration by Boy Scouts and Girl Scouts.

Evening—Radio program.

TUESDAY.

Transportation Day.

Steam and electric railways, ferries, steamboats and docks will engage in a continuous demonstration. Literature will be displayed and distributed. Floats and bands will be featured.

Evening—Radio program.

WEDNESDAY.

Police Day.

Morning—Special demonstrations of traffic management at points of importance throughout the city.

12 M.—Police parade to the monument on Park Avenue. Presentation of the Police Safety Medal offered by Arthur Williams, President of the Safety Institute of America, to the policeman who during the year has done the most notable act in saving the life of a child.

Address by the Police Commissioner. At the monument.

Evening—Radio program.

THURSDAY.

Automobile Day.

Morning—Boy Scouts, under the direction of traffic officers, will manage traffic for a short period at hundreds of points throughout the city.

Automobile floats will tour each borough.

12 M.—Automobile parade in Fifth Avenue to Central Park. Crippled children will be the guests and will be given an afternoon of entertainment.

Evening—Radio program.

FRIDAY.

The State Commissioner of Labor has requested every industrial plant in the city to conduct a safety drive among its employes and to hold a mass meeting.

Evening—Radio program.

SATURDAY.

Merchants will conduct safety drives among their employes. Special window displays will be arranged.

Use War Campaign Methods.

All day yesterday and far into the night thousands of Boy Scouts, policemen, representatives of trade associations and of women's clubs were busy in every section of the five boroughs posting Safety Week warning signs and appeals. The campaign, managed throughout by business men, has been organized after the fashion of the Liberty Loan and food conservation campaigns during the war. Arthur Williams, former Food Administrator for New York, is President of the Safety Institute and Judge Gary's Committee of One Hundred includes many of the men who planned and directed the various war campaigns. The four-minute men of war days have re-enlisted. More than 2,000 men speakers and 1,000 women speakers are being assigned to the schools, clubs, business organizations and motion picture theatres which have requested safety speakers.

The headquarters of the Safety Institute in East Twenty-ninth Street during the last few days has resembled a political headquarters on the eve of election day. Volunteer workers from the United States Steel Corporation, the New York Edison Company, the various insurance companies, the State Labor Commissioner's office, railroad offices and the numerous other agencies co-operating in the drive were busy mailing literature, scheduling safety rallies and parades, filling last-minute orders for posters, buttons and tags and answering such queries as "How many of the pedestrians killed by automobiles last year were pedestrians?" "How many children are killed near their homes and how many on the way to and from school?" "How many motorists have been convicted of manslaughter?" "What are the principal causes of household accidents?"

Hope to Cut Down Usual 70 Deaths.

The immediate goal of Safety Week is to save the lives of the seventy persons who would be killed by accident during this week in the ordinary course of events. During the corresponding week of 1921, Oct. 8 to 14, exactly seventy persons lost their lives through accident within the city limits of New York. During the year 1921, accidents took 3,485 lives, an average of sixty-seven per week. In the first nine months of 1922 the weekly average has been seventy deaths a week.

Throughout the week fatal accidents will be reported to the Safety Institute of America by telephone from the office of Dr. Charles Norris, Chief Medical Examiner, who has arranged for the immediate reporting of all fatal accidents from the various borough branches of his department.

The accident score will in turn be reported to the Safety Institute, to each borough organization and to the press daily. The Borough of Manhattan has the largest score to shoot at. During the corresponding week of the previous year accidents took thirty lives in Manhattan, twenty-one in Brooklyn, twelve in the Bronx, five in Queens and two in Richmond. The comparison of scores of the various boroughs will be on the basis of percentage of reduction.

Evangelist Flanks Bible With Two Loaded Pistols

McALESTER, Okla., Oct. 7.—The Rev. W. E. Smith, itinerant evangelist, opened his services in Latimer County last night by removing a loaded gun from his hip pocket and placing it beside the open Bible. After the convocation, a second gun was placed on the left of the Scriptures.

The meeting was carried to a normal conclusion without incident notwithstanding previous threats, anonymously communicated to the preacher, that he would not be permitted to speak.

Mr. Smith told his audience that "a certain element" did not wish him to hold his meetings and intimated that tonight he might appear with sidearms.

Soon after services were under way two automobiles loaded with men attired in the regalia of the Ku Klux Klan arrived.

TAKING THOUGHT IS KEYNOTE OF SAFETY

Aim of Accident Prevention Society Is to Make People Think, Says Dr. Lawson.

HOW TO MINIMIZE LOSSES

Deaths and Injuries in War Are Dwarfed by Those Following Accidents, Founder Declares.

In connection with "Safety Week," which begins today, Dr. Franklin D. Lawson of this city, founder and President of the Society for the Prevention of Accidents, Inc., says that the keynote of safety from accidents consists in devising a method of keeping in the minds of all a constant prevision of the proximity of danger—in other words, a means of making people think.

"By making people think," said Dr. Lawson, "the S. P. A. is affording them the maximum of protection, and for that reason I want everybody to join our organization. The very sight of the S. P. A.'s emblem of caution, whether worn by members of the organization, attached to automobiles, or in print, will accomplish our great and fixed purpose—to make the public think.

"The society is making a study, both physical and psychological, of the causes of all kinds of accidents and the various ways and means of preventing and avoiding them," continued Dr. Lawson. "Articles, stories, statistics, pictures and advice resulting from the researches of competent specialists and the personal experience of thousands of persons will be so worded, arranged and circulated that they will sink deeply with lasting impression into the minds and memories of millions. And the S. P. A. is dedicated to humanity for the safety and protection of everybody, everywhere, without regard to age, race, creed, occupation or condition.

"In my New York hospital experience I found that about 95 per cent. of all accidents were due to a disregard of certain simple, fixed principles. It is my belief that the S. P. A. will stop needless suffering, deaths and loss of property caused by accidents. Preventable accidents, in my opinion, cause more misery and destruction today than anything else in the world.

"In order to prove such an assertion it is only necessary to make some comparisons with the loss of life and maiming of individuals in the World War. In their nineteen months of fighting, 50,300 men of the United States forces were killed and 206,000 injured; here in this country, during the same period, 126,000 persons were killed and more than 2,000,000 were injured by accidents. In addition, fires in the United States last year resulted in the loss of property valued at $483,000,000. Investigation showed that 80 per cent. of these fires resulted from carelessness and should have been prevented by the exercise of a little forethought and caution.

"In the last five years 52,185 persons have been killed and a much larger number injured in automobile accidents alone.

"Think, then, of the unnecessary anguish, lives lost, property destroyed, time wasted and billions of dollars involved in the insurance companies as a result of accidents that might have been prevented. It is for this reason that I say an ounce of prevention is worth a ton of cure. None of us are immune from accidents, and without caution we do not know when or how we may become victims of them.

"Warnings, signals, rules, laws, &c., for safety amount to nothing unless observed and obeyed. The S. P. A. will interest its members in the importance of these things and of using intelligent care and caution at all times. The society will insist upon the enforcement of all laws intended for public safety, and the effective and impartial punishment of all evaders and breakers of such laws. It will also reward acts of bravery in the saving of life and in extraordinary, timely prevention of great disaster, and will help ameliorate suffering resulting from accidents.

"It is my belief that as a member of the S. P. A., an organization having a great humanitarian purpose, the individual will deem it both a privilege and pleasure to further that purpose. By joining it the individual will not only become interested in its objects, but will either consciously or subconsciously exercise more care and caution himself.

"Yearly membership in the Society for the Prevention of Accidents costs $1; five-year membership, $3; life membership, $25; and charter membership, $100. All membership subscriptions should be made payable to the Society for the Prevention of Accidents and sent to Kenneth Patterson, Assistant Treasurer of the National City Bank of New York, Madison Avenue and Forty-second Street, New York City. The National City Bank is the depository of all funds of the society, and a regular accounting of all receipts and expenditures is made."

The office of the society is at 7 East Forty-second Street, New York.

WANT LOOSE-LEAF REPORTS.

Foreign Trade Men Make Suggestion to Government.

A suggestion has been made to the Department of Commerce by the National Automobile Chamber of Commerce to adopt the loose-leaf manual form in the publication of commerce reports. The suggestion was made to the department at Washington by J. Walter Drake and G. F. Bauer, Chairman and Secretary, respectively, of the Foreign Trade Committee, and Gordon Lee, chief of the United States Automotive Division.

"The change, if made," said Mr. Drake, "will be of great advantage to business men. Valuable information, now perishable in many instances, could readily be stored for future use in devising foreign sales campaigns that, based on facts, would be directly reflected in domestic prosper"

REGISTRATION HERE BEGINS TOMORROW

Republican and Democratic Leaders Plan Drives to Get Voters Out.

TAMMANY WILL WORK HARD

"Al" Smith's Candidacy a Spur to the Voters of New York City.

LITERACY TEST A FEATURE

Provision Is Made to Examine All the New Voters Not Provided With Certificates.

The registration of voters will begin in this city tomorrow and continue throughout the week. It will be a busy time for political leaders of all parties who this year will strive harder than ever to get out as nearly as possible 100 per cent. of the vote qualified to participate in the contest at the polls on election day.

Registration is a necessary preliminary both to voting on election day and enrolment with a party which entitles a voter to take part in primary elections and, generally speaking, makes him a full-fledged member of the party of his choice with a voice and a vote in its affairs.

All the Republican county leaders in this city met on Friday and talked over ways and means of getting the voters of their party to register. So important do the Republican leaders regard the matter that George K. Morris, Chairman of the Republican State Committee, is making a special trip up-State to enjoin all the leaders there to see that nothing is permitted to stand in the way of getting the Republicans to the last man and woman to their respective registration places.

"If we can get all the enrolled Republicans in the State to register and vote it will be enough to put our ticket over with many thousands of votes to spare," said one of the leaders yesterday.

Tammany Leaders Busy.

With "Al" Smith's candidacy as an incentive, Tammany and Democratic leaders in other boroughs feel that there will be a rush of Democrats to the registration places everywhere in this city. They are making preparations, too, for a house-to-house canvass during registration week by their election district workers to make sure that every Democratic voter comes out and registers.

The fusion of the Socialists and Farmer-Laborites on a common ticket, sponsored by the American Labor Party, will, it is believed certain, insure a pretty full registration of the radical and semi-radical vote.

Under normal conditions the registration this year should equal, or almost equal, the figures for last year, when there was a Mayoralty election. Those figures, however, fell more than 100,000 behind the figures of the preceding year—1920—when a President of the United States and a Governor both were elected.

Here are the registration figures for the five boroughs for last year and the year preceding:

	1921.	1920.
Manhattan	453,681	503,830
Brooklyn	452,262	494,926
Bronx	185,753	109,423
Queens	130,480	145,339
Richmond	34,339	30,356
Total	1,265,518	1,373,[illegible]

A new feature incidental to this year's registration is the first application of the literacy test act under a law which went into force on Jan. 1. Under this law new voters are required to establish their ability to read fifty words in English and to write ten words legibly before they can qualify for the right to vote. Under the terms of the election law a "new voter" is a person who either through naturalization or by attaining his majority has become eligible to vote in this State, "if so entitled."

Text of the Law.

Here follows the full text of Section 166 of the election law which contains the provisions governing the literacy test and its application:

"1. There shall be in the place of registration, where registration is required to be personal, one hundred extracts from the Constitution of this State, of approximately fifty words each, which extracts shall be selected by the Secretary of State. Such extracts shall be printed in English on uniform pasteboard slips in double small pica type, and the slips shall be kept by the inspectors in a box so constructed as to conceal the slips from view. The new voter, if required to prove his ability to read and write English, shall draw out at random one of such slips and read aloud intelligibly all of the matter printed thereon and shall then write legibly in English ten words of the matter on such slip, to be selected by the inspector. Each slip shall be returned to the box immediately after each test, and the contents of the box shall be shaken up by an inspector before another drawing.

"A new voter may present to the Board of Inspectors a certificate of literacy signed by the principal or other head of a public school in the city or town in which the voter applies to be registered, or of any school in such city or town whose course of instruction has been or shall be recognized by the State Department of Education as being of required standard, to the effect that such principal or head has examined the voter, or his educational credentials, and certifies that the voter is able to read and write English, and that the signature of the voter appended to such certificate was made in the presence of such principal or other head, to which certificate of literacy shall be appended the affidavit of the person signing such certificate that at the time of such examination and the signing of such certificate he was the principal or head, as the case may be, of such school. There-

"All the News That's Fit to Print."

The New York Times.

THE WEATHER
Fair and mild today and Wednesday; fresh northwest winds.
Temperature yesterday—Max. 56, min. 38.
For full weather report see Page 17.

VOL. LXXII...No. 23,656. NEW YORK, TUESDAY, OCTOBER 31, 1922. TWO CENTS In Greater New York | THREE CENTS Within 200 Miles | FOUR C Elsewh

HUGHES DEFENDS FOREIGN POLICIES IN PLEA FOR LODGE

Declares in Boston Speech That Aim Is Helpfulness but Not Entanglement.

NO DICTATION TO EUROPE

Troubles Abroad Are Called Political—Arms Conference a Proof of Our Friendship.

'HOLY WAR' NOT AUTHORIZED

But Pressure Was Used on Turks for Moderation—Lodge's Services Are Eulogized.

Special to The New York Times.

BOSTON, Oct. 30.—"Friendship for all nations, alliances with none," is the policy of the Harding Administration in foreign affairs as declared by Secretary Hughes and an audience of more than 3,000 men and women cheered in Symphony Hall tonight when the Secretary of State expounded it in an appeal for the re-election of Senator Lodge.

The meeting was a part of the Republican campaign in this State, and Mr. Hughes's address was an answer to criticisms directed at the Administration by Democrats and pro-Leaguers.

"If we had sought to reform the world," he said, "we would have reformed nothing."

Several times during his speech, the Secretary paid tribute to the services of Senator Lodge as Chairman of the Committee on Foreign Relations. Each mention of the Senator evoked cheers, and there was a particularly loud outburst when he declared that for Massachusetts to refuse Mr. Lodge another term would be a loss not only to this State, but an "irreparable loss" to the country and the world.

Says Conference Rescued World.

The Secretary discussed at length the results of the Conference for Limitation of Armament where he and Senator Lodge sat as American delegates. That conference, he said, rescued the world from despair. He was presented to the audience by former Governor John L. Bates.

Mr. Bates caused a ripple when he took sharp issue with recent remarks attributed to George Harvey, Ambassador to the Court of St. James's.

"I want to say just a word to the women who are here," said ex-Governor Bates. "I want to refer to the man across the seas who recently lost his bearings and discussed the question whether women have souls. If he came here tonight he would find out that the women of Massachusetts had souls."

TEXT OF MR. HUGHES'S SPEECH.

Mr. Hughes's speech was as follows:

I come to Massachusetts with a special sense of privilege. In the agreeable task of reviewing with you some of the achievements of the Administration, I could not fail at once to recognize the large part—indeed, the disproportionate share to which you have happily been accustomed—which has been taken by this Commonwealth.

You have given us the Vice President, Calvin Coolidge, whose sagacious counsel we are permitted to have at the Cabinet table; the Speaker of the House of Representatives, Frederick H. Gillett, whose qualities command an esteem which knows no partisan division; the Secretary of War, John W. Weeks, whose forthright character and keen practical judgment have been of inestimable value in solving the difficult problems left for his department by the Great War; and the veteran leader, the Chairman of the Committee on Foreign Relations of the Senate, the accomplished scholar and statesman, whose exceptional gifts and disinterested devotion to public duty displayed through his long career have given his leadership that special quality which we associate with the Massachusetts tradition.

It was Theodore Roosevelt who said of Henry Cabot Lodge that throughout his long service in the Senate and House he had "ever stood foremost among those who upheld with far-sighted fearlessness and strict justice to others our national honor and honesty."

"One-Man Rule" Not Attempted.

This contribution of the Commonwealth of Massachusetts—and I have mentioned only a part of it—is but one phase of a generous co-operation which has been the distinctive feature of this Administration. Of course, there have been differences of view, freely expressed. That is a wholesome sign; there have been no attempts to establish a one-man rule.

The Executive has fully appreciated the great powers confided to him by the Constitution and he is exercising them. They have been respected; he has not usurped others. The Executive has not sought to dominate Congress; he has worked with Congress, each according to the assigned authority. The Executive has not attempted to coerce the Senate. Reserving and exercising his full authority of initiative and negotiation, he has co-operated with the Senate. The result is that we have had the discussions and debates which testify to political health, but we have not had the unnecessarily provoked and injurious clashes which defeat achievement.

In the sphere of administration, the Executive maintains his control and assumes his responsibility. But he selects his advisers and department heads to perform each in his place their proper duties, looking to them for the competent discharge of the public business under his constant and adequate supervision.

The American Government is being conducted without usurpation and with the proper influence and power of effective and constitutional leadership. That is the reason wasteful expenditures have been cut, necessary economies enforced, efficiency vastly increased, and our great national concerns safeguarded.

Tribute to Harding Leadership.

This method and result are due to the spirit and purpose which have dominated the Administration. They are due to the sagacity, the steadiness, the inexhaustible energy, the

Continued on Page Four.

Lloyd George Gets an Offer Of Lecture Tour in America

Copyright, 1922, by The New York Times Co. By Wireless to THE NEW YORK TIMES.

LONDON, Oct. 30.—Ex-Premier Lloyd George, says The Pall Mall Gazette, has had this week a most definite and attractive offer to undertake a lecture tour in America.

In the prevailing circumstances the offer was declined, but not finally so. If the result of the election goes heavily against him he may follow his French friend, Georges Clemenceau, to the United States.

PHILADELPHIA, Oct. 30.—Georges Clemenceau will address the Philadelphia Forum early in December, that organization announces. Senator Pepper will preside at the meeting. M. Clemenceau's topic will be "The Case of France."

DROPS OUR CONTROL OF CHINESE RAILWAY

Washington Takes Similar Action to Allies as Last Troops Leave Siberia.

CHINA FORMALLY NOTIFIED

Control Was First Established With the Sending of Troops in 1918—Our Rights Reserved.

Special to The New York Times.

WASHINGTON, Oct. 30.—Following the withdrawal of all allied troops from Siberia, the United States Government has followed the action of Great Britain, France, Italy and Japan in relinquishing control of the Chinese Eastern Railway. Tomorrow Minister Schurman at Peking will deliver to the Chinese Government a note from Secretary Hughes serving formal notice of this action.

The control of the Chinese Eastern Railway was established in an agreement framed in connection with the dispatch of American and allied troops into Siberia in the Summer and Fall of 1918, and provided that the operation of the Chinese Eastern and Trans-Siberian Railways within the zone of activities of the allied forces should be placed under the supervision of a special inter-allied commission, comprising, under Russian chairmanship, a representative of each power having military forces in Siberia. The agreement also provided for a technical board of railway experts of the Allies to administer the technical and economic management.

It was stipulated that these arrangements should end upon the withdrawal of the foreign military forces from Siberia, and that all the foreign railway experts appointed under the terms of the agreement should then be recalled.

Text of the Note.

The text of the American note follows:

"I have the honor to inform you, by direction of my Government, that, in view of the final withdrawal from the Siberian mainland of allied troops, the representatives of the United States on the inter-allied committee at Vladivostok and the technical board at Harbin have been instructed to proceed, in concert with their colleagues on those bodies, to the winding up of the affairs of each organization and the termination today of further activity.

"In conveying this information to the Government of China I am directed to say that the United States confirms the resolution with respect to the Chinese Eastern Railway adopted by the nine powers of the Washington conference and the further resolution on the same subject adopted by the powers other than China.

"The first resolution reads: 'Resolved, That the preservation of the Chinese Eastern Railway for those in interest requires that better protection be given to the railway and the persons engaged in its operation and use, a more careful selection of personnel to secure efficiency of service, and a more economical use of funds to prevent waste of property; that the subject should immediately be dealt with through the proper diplomatic channels.

"The second resolution reads: 'The powers other than China agreeing to the resolution regarding the Chinese Eastern Railway reserve the right to insist hereafter upon the responsibility of China for performance or non-performance of the obligations toward the foreign stockholders, bondholders and creditors of the Chinese Eastern Railway Company, which the powers deem to result from the contracts under which the railway was built and the action of China thereunder and the obligations which they deem to be in the nature of a trust resulting from the exercise of

Continued on Page Six.

MUSSOLINI FORMS CABINET FOR ITALY WITH FASCISTI AIDS

New Premier Gives Seven Ministries to His Group—Other Parties Represented.

ROME IN FEVER OF DELIGHT

Fascisti, Many Thousands Strong, Enter the City Today in Triumph.

AMITY TO AMERICA PLEDGED

Public Order Enjoined and Strong Government Promised—Communists Disband.

Copyright, 1922, by The New York Times Company. Special Cable to THE NEW YORK TIMES.

ROME, Oct. 30.—With Benito Mussolini's coming to Rome today and his formation of a new ministry the so-called "Fascisti revolution" is at an end. All is over except the shouting. Nothing remains to be done but have a triumphal march of the Fascisti militia through Rome to give the population a chance to vent its pent-up enthusiasm, then have them demobilize and return to normalcy.

Nowhere is the fact that Fascisti action is over more clearly shown than in a manifesto issued by the Fascisti leaders today saying:

"From this moment Mussolini is the Government of Italy. He is now responsible for the safety of the State, of the Ministers and of Parliament. Any act against the Government institutions would be rebellion against Mussolini."

Mussolini entered Rome in the morning. He traveled as far as Civitavecchia on a special train put at his disposal by the Government, but there he was obliged to descend because the rails had been torn up by the military to prevent a Fascisti advance on Rome. He was met, however, by one of the King's private motor cars, in which he proceeded to Rome.

His progress was very slow because all [illegible] were filled with thousands of Fascisti marching to the city who insisted on Mussolini stopping every few minutes to receive their acclamations.

Visits Quirinal in Soiled Uniform.

Mussolini proceeded to the Quirinal Palace on his arrival and was immediately ushered into the King's presence, wearing a soiled black shirt and bearing obvious traces of his long journey in an open motor car along muddy roads.

His arrival brought a huge crowd under the windows of the palace. So insistent were they that the King was obliged to appear three times on a balcony, sending the people into a frenzy of enthusiasm.

After a half hour's conversation with the King, Mussolini drove to his hotel, where Fascisti sentinels at the door presented arms. In the square in front of the hotel the Fascisti helped the Government police keep the multitude of several thousand in order. Mussolini appeared at a window and said in a booming voice:

"Today Italy has not only got a Cabinet but (here he pronounced his words very slowly with great emphasis and distinctness), she has also got a Government, a strong Government, such as she has needed for many years past, but never obtained."

These words were greeted with delirious enthusiasm, which caused Mussolini to appear three more times, waving his hand to the crowd.

Seven Fascisti in Cabinet.

Immediately afterward a list of the new Ministers was published. Mussolini has not formed a Cabinet composed entirely of Fascisti. In fact, not only are they not all Fascisti, but the Cabinet includes some who hitherto have been most strenuous enemies of Fascismo. The Ministry, as announced, includes seven Fascisti, five Nationalists, one Democrat and one member of the Catholic Party.

Mussolini's intention has obviously been to form a Cabinet representing all groups in the Chamber with the Fascisti in control. He has reserved for himself the arduous task of shaping both the internal and foreign Italian policies, as he will himself keep the portfolios of the interior and foreign affairs.

Only one minister in the present Cabinet retains office, namely, Senator Count Theofile Rossi. The most notable figures in the Cabinet are General Diaz, "Duke of Victory," who led the Italian army in its last victorious offensive against the Austrians, and Admiral Count Thaon di Revel, who has been a

Continued on Page Five.

Two Army Aviators Are Killed, Two Hurt, In Collision of Airplanes at Honolulu

Copyright, 1922, by The Chicago Tribune Co.

HONOLULU, Oct. 30.—Two army aviators were killed and two others seriously injured this morning when their planes met in a head-on collision 200 feet above Luke Field. The dead are Lieutenant Thomas V. Hynes of the Sixth Pursuit Squadron, stationed at Luke Field, and Sergeant Ross L. Owens of the same detachment. The injured are Captain T. W. Allen and Lieutenant A. F. Hebbard of the Schofield Barracks, Air Detachment.

Both planes were making practice flights just above a derrick on a ferry slip at Luke Field when they met in collision. Lieutenant Hynes was piloting a De Haviland-4 with Sergeant Owens as an observer. Captain Allen was piloting a Curtiss with Lieutenant Hebbard as passenger.

The force of the collision severed the fuselage of the Curtiss plane just behind the cockpit, causing it to dive nose first. The plane struck a barge tied up in the ferry slip. The wooden floor of the barge acted as a cushion which saved the occupants of the plane from being hurled beneath the engine.

Lieutenant Hynes's plane also took a nose dive, but it cleared the barge and fell into the water. Hynes and Owens were buried beneath the wreckage and drowned. Hynes's body was recovered and a diver from the navy yard is seeking the body of Sergeant Owens.

The Curtiss plane is believed to have been at a "blind angle" with the other plane, the result being that neither of the pilots was able to see the other in time to avoid the accident. Both were attempting to make a landing.

Lieutenant Hynes's home was in New York City. He was not married. Sergeant Owens's home was at Wyoming, N. Y. Captain Allen is a native of Pittsfield, Ill. He has a wife and child here. Lieutenant Hebbard comes from Elizabeth, N. J.

Hynes took part in the transcontinental air race two years ago and he was considered one of the best aviators here.

BRIBERY CHARGED BY WESTERN UNION

Printing Company Official, Accused of Paying Illegal Gratuity to Employe, Is Arrested.

BID OF RIVAL INVOLVED

Wire Concern Alleges That a Scheme to Overcharge on Printing Bills Was Discovered.

Charged with paying an employe of the Western Union Company to pilfer a letter from the Western Union files, Walter L. Hopkins, Secretary of Wynkoop-Hallenbeck-Crawford Company, was held in $200 bail by Magistrate Earl Smith in the Tombs Court yesterday. The charge was technically that of giving an illegal gratuity. It was alleged that Hopkins was detected handing $25 to a Western Union employe who had furnished the letter. Hopkins denied the charge.

A trap was arranged by the District Attorney's office and Joseph L. Fagan, a lawyer of the Western Union Company, after the Western Union had received reports that another employe had been bribed to put his "O.K." on excessive printing bills.

"The Western Union Company," said Mr. Fagan, "had a contract with the Wynkoop-Hallenbeck-Crawford Company to do all the printing of telegraph blanks and other forms on a cost plus 5 per cent. basis. This contract called for about a million dollars' worth of printing annually.

"It was provided by this agreement that the Western Union should have the privilege of auditing the books of the printing house in order to verify the fact that the charges were not more than cost plus 5 per cent.

"From certain information we came to the conclusion that we were being overcharged, and we later learned that one of our employes had been bribed to conceal this fact. We made a further investigation and established apparently that bills of $808,000 rendered from April 1 to Dec. 31, 1921, contained overcharges amounting to $100,000.

"The matter was taken up with the District Attorney, who obtained a full statement from our auditor, who had gone over the books of the printing firm. Then, through another of our employes and Detective John Cunniffe of the District Attorney's office, a trap was set and the defendant was caught in the act of passing $25. This amount is insignificant as against earlier payments, but, of course, it is necessary to proceed on a specific transaction."

The auditor who made a statement to the District Attorney is alleged to have told other employes that fat gratuities were to be obtained by treachery to the Western Union. He is alleged to have asserted that another Western Union auditor was receiving $100 a month for covering up overcharges against the Western Union.

John J. Ward, another Western Union accountant, reported to his superiors that he had heard these boasts and rumors. Ward was then assigned to work on the books of the Wynkoop-Hallenbeck-Crawford Company.

The contract of this firm had until the end of the present year to run. The contract was not renewed but was turned over to a rival printing house. Ward reported that a bribe was offered him to obtain the letter of the rival printing house containing its bid. It was arranged by the District Attorney, it was asserted, that Detective John Cunniffe should be present at this interview.

A general denial was made yesterday by the printing company.

MASKED KIDNAPPERS ROUTED IN OKLAHOMA

Two Men Killed When Four Try to Seize Head of Anti-Klan Organization.

HENRIETTA, Okla., Oct. 30.—Murder charges were filed late today here against George Frew and Homer Pennequine, Dewar coal miners, as the result of the death this afternoon of Tom Bogus, of Spelter City, from gunshot wounds received in a battle with four masked men, one of whom was killed, on the streets of Spelter City Sunday night.

Frew and Pennequine have not yet been arrested. L. D. Williams, Assistant County Attorney, in charge of the investigation says he has has information that both men are wounded, one in the head, only a scalp wound, and the other in the knee.

The battle followed an attempt of the masked men, clothed in blue jumpers and overalls, with black face masks, to seize Bogus. They called him from a motion picture theatre and tried to kidnap him in a motor car.

Bogus, who is President of an anti-Ku Klux Klan organization called the "True Blue Americans," is said to have opened fire. The masked men returned the fire, and a constable joined in the shooting and fired at the masked party. Reese Adkins, one of the masked men, was killed.

It was reported today that one of the masked men wounded was taken to a Muskogee hospital for treatment, but officials of all hospitals there denied that he had been received.

BUS OPERATOR TELLS OF $25,000 DEMAND

Says He Lost Permit and $8,000 After Refusing Fee for "Big Chief."

BANTON TO GET EVIDENCE

Witness Swears He Was Asked to Form Company in Which the "Boys" Were to Share.

Louis Riedl, after being asked by Mayor Hylan to undertake bus operation for the City Administration in September, 1919, and receiving a temporary permit from the Board of Estimate, was subjected to a demand for $25,000 from Daniel O'Connor, described as a Brooklyn Democratic politician and a friend of Joseph Fennelly, Assistant Commissioner of Public Works and Democratic leader of the Second Brooklyn Assembly District, according to testimony before the Transit Commission yesterday.

Riedl testified that he refused to pay the $25,000 demanded, which he said O'Connor told him was not for "Red Mike," meaning Mayor Hylan, but for the "Big Chief," with the result that he was prevented from operating his buses, his permit was rescinded, he lost between $7,000 and $8,000 and supervision over the city bus lines was transferred from John A. McCullom, Chief of the Division of Franchises of the Board of Estimate, named in the board's first resolution, to Grover A. Whalen, Commissioner of Plant and Structures, with whom the supervision has remained.

Former Justice Clarence J. Shearn, special counsel of the commission, said after the hearing that the testimony would be brought to the attention of District Attorney Joab H. Banton for possible criminal investigation. The identity of the "Big Chief" was not disclosed, but it was said that the term as used by a Brooklyn Democrat did not have the same significance as if used by a Manhattan Tammany man. Judge Shearn attempted to ascertain from Mr. Riedl if the reference to the "Big Chief" might not have been to some city official, but the witness replied that he did not know.

Supplied Buses in Strike.

Mr. Riedl's story, supplemented by records of the Board of Estimate and the old Public Service Commission, threw considerable light on the hitherto unexplained mystery as to how he came to lose his permit at the very beginning of city bus operation, and showed an apparent change of plan on the part of Mayor Hylan and his associates on the Board of Estimate to put the bus operation entirely under the control of Mr. Whalen, and to eliminate any supervision by the old Public Service Commission.

Mr. Riedl had previously supplied more than 200 buses for service in Brooklyn during the B. R. T. strikes, at the request of the City Administration, and had received the thanks of Mayor Hylan, conveyed in a letter from Joseph A. Guider, the Brooklyn Commissioner of Public Works. In September, 1919, because of the bankruptcy of some of the Manhattan surface lines, the Madison Street, Spring and Delancey Street, Avenue C and Broadway-Sixth Avenue lines were ordered discontinued on Sept. 20 by a court order, and Mr. Riedl was asked by the Mayor to provide buses and drivers to be placed on these routes.

O'Connor was the man who first induced him to operate buses in Brooklyn, Mr. Riedl testified, but it was Commissioner Guider who took him to Mayor Hylan regarding the Manhattan operation. Mr. Riedl said he told the Mayor that he was not interested in the proposal unless the operation was for a considerable period. He said that the Mayor promised to have the Board of Estimate grant him a permit, and added "Leave that to me."

Threatened, He Says.

Mr. Riedl said that O'Connor's demands for the $25,000 payment were made at a series of meetings in Manhattan. After his refusal to meet this attempt at extortion, Mr. Riedl said, eleven of the bus drivers and buses he had collected were directed by city officials to return to New Jersey, and that he was informed by a city detective that he would not be permitted to operate buses, although he had thirty ready in the neighborhood of Delancey Street. He added that he had been threatened with violence if he persisted, and that finally the city officials took the bus drivers he had engaged away from him by telling them they could only operate under Mr. Whalen's supervision. Mr. Riedl declared that the city began bus operation with the very buses and men he had hired to work under his supervision, and that he was out the money, between $7,000 and $8,000, he had spent to build up his organization.

Judge Shearn begun the day's hearing by introducing in evidence certain rec-

Continued on Page Two.

MRS. GIBSON'S TALE OF HALL MURDER UNDER CRITICISM

Story News to Her Son—Is She Mrs. Gibson or Mrs. William Easton?

SAID SHE WAS A WIDOW

Prosecutor Mott Declines to Comment on Attacks on Veracity of Mrs. Gibson.

CHARLOTTE MILLS APPEALS

Again Asks Governor's Help—Mrs. Hall Willing to Confront Mrs. Gibson, Her Counsel Says.

The credibility of Mrs. Jane Gibson, who says she was an eye-witness of the murder of the Rev. Edward Wheeler Hall and Mrs. Elenor R. Mills at the Phillips farm, outside New Brunswick, on the night of Sept. 14 last, was subjected to criticism yesterday. Mrs. Gibson's son William was quoted by two persons as professing ignorance of his mother's going out on her mule on the murder night, although she had said he could corroborate her story.

It was also learned that Mrs. Gibson, who had represented herself as the widow of a clergyman who had died 17 years ago, is now known to many in New Brunswick as the wife of William H. Easton, a tool maker, who told reporters yesterday that he considered her story "amazing." William H. Easton's address is the same as Mrs. Gibson's in the New Brunswick city directory, and her 21-year-old son is known as William Easton as well as William Gibson.

Deputy Attorney General Wilbur A. Mott, who on previous occasions had expressed complete confidence in Mrs. Gibson's veracity, yesterday appeared to be weakening in his faith in his star witness. When asked by a reporter last night what he thought of the conflicting statements she had made Mr. Mott refused to answer. The State prosecutor did not present the case to the Grand Jury, and did not give any indication that he intends to do so in the near future. On the contrary, it was learned last night that the authorities are now working on lines not covered by Mrs. Gibson's statement.

Mrs. Frances Noel Hall announced yesterday through her attorney, Timothy Newal Pfeiffer, that she was willing to confront Mrs. Gibson if the prosecution asked her to do so, and to deny that she witnessed the murder of Hall, and Mrs. Mills. It was also announced on Mrs. Hall's behalf that Frances Voorness, Mr. Hall's 10-year-old niece, gives partial corroboration to Mrs. Hall's statement that she was at home on the night of the murder. The little girl says Mrs. Hall put her to bed and heard her say her prayers about 9 o'clock.

Charlotte Mills, the 16-year-old daughter of the murdered choir singer, appealed to Governor Edwards and the people of New Jersey yesterday to force some action in bringing the murderers to justice. She said Deputy Attorney General Wilbur A. Mott, who superseded the county authorities a week ago, had promised action, but had taken none.

The suggestion that Mrs. Gibson was Mrs. Easton caused reporters to talk with Easton when he finished his day's work at the factory yesterday. Easton is an undersized man of middle age, with gray hair, parted in the middle, and an embarrassed manner, especially evident when he is asked about Mrs. Gibson. He goes to and from his work in a small automobile, which has been observed in Mrs. Gibson's barn.

Neighbors of Mrs. Gibson told reporters that Easton lived at the Gibson house off and on, and that when he had got his job at the automobile factory, where Mack trucks are made, he had given his address as Rural Free Delivery, Route 6, Box 15, which is Mrs. Gibson's address, and had given as his next of kin his wife, J. M. Easton, same address. The New Brunswick City Directory also lists Arthur, Mary, William and Mary H. Easton and Jane Gibson living on Rural Free Delivery Route 6. Mrs. Gibson is said to have a daughter living with friends of relatives in Newark.

When Easton was asked if Mrs. Gib-

Continued on Page Three.

Hylan Is Rebuked for 'Sincerely Yours' In Campaign Letter to Lawyer's Wife

Herbert C. Drescher, attorney, of 2 Rector Street, living at 2,023 Avenue Q, Brooklyn, last night made public a letter sent to Mayor Hylan, voicing strong objection to the Mayor sending his wife a campaign letter ending with "Sincerely yours." He also asked the Mayor who was paying for the thousands of these letters on the official stationery of the Mayor's office advocating the candidacy of William B. Carswell for the Supreme Court justiceship.

In his letter to the Mayor Mr. Drescher said:

"Your form letter dated Oct. 17, 1922, in which you advocated the election of Mr. Carswell to the Supreme Court bench, has been received by my wife, to whom it was addressed, and has been referred to me for my attention.

"Replying to your letter to my wife, allow me to record my strongest objections to your 'sincerely yours' closing. Such objections are made because of the fact that my wife is a married woman who, I am informed, has never been introduced formally or otherwise to Your Honor. Hence, a letter written even by the Mayor of this city to a lady who is not even an acquaintance should not be closed, in my humble opinion, along that 'sincerely yours' line preceding your signature.

"The unquestionable purpose of your letter is to boost the candidacy of William B. Carswell. I believe that the letter will fail in such object, but to the contrary will tend to impair Mr. Carswell's chances of election, for the simple reason that your Brooklyn 'neighbors,' in spite of your plurality last year, now appreciate the real characteristics of their present Mayor.

"My wife did not vote for you last year or at any time previous. I have never voted for you. I dare say you will never receive our future votes for public office.

"You write that 'it was through Mr. Carswell's legal skill that I was able to accomplish a great deal for the people.' Merely as a point of information, may I ask for more particulars as to anything that you ever accomplished for the people?

"Relative to your letter, may I ask as a voting citizen and taxpayer why same is written on the Mayor's letterhead. I presume that I as well as other taxpayers must pay for such stationery.

"I should appreciate further light on the question of who pays for the printed stamped envelopes and the printing bill for the many thousands of these letters which I understand you have sent to all your 'fellow citizens' in Brooklyn town. Likewise, who pays the labor expense involved in folding, sealing and mailing these thousands of 'sincerely yours' letters."

A New Art, Geometrism, Startles Paris; More Advanced Than Cubism and Dadaism

PARIS, Oct. 30 (Associated Press).—"Geometric art," a new movement in painting which seeks to express life and soul in geometrical lines instead of in the soft strokes of the conventional school of painting, strikes a startling note in the fifteen Autumn Salon, which holds its "varnishing day" tomorrow.

Artists of ten nationalities, including Americans, have hung in the exhibition more than fifty "line pictures," which make the followers of Cubism seem hopelessly conventional. The contributors to the new idea are enthusiastic over its possibilities, believing their movement will eventually contribute a new school of art.

Geometrism treats of conventional subjects, such as nudes, landscapes and interiors, but employs carefully worked out lines according to the rules of geometry. The pictures are said to have a keen appeal for mathematicians.

Francis Picabia, the Spanish artist who invented Dadaism, is the leader of the new method of expression. He contributes two of the most amazing pictures in the Salon, entitled "Leaf of Vine" and "Spanish Night." Naturally, the titles have nothing to do with the appearance of the pictures, the motif of which several hundred artists cannot agree upon.

There are between fifty and sixty Americans out of the 1,300 artists exhibiting. With but few exceptions, the Americans do much to contribute to the saner, more beautiful part of the Salon, the dominant impression of which is not beauty but frankness.

The nudes, which this year far outnumber all other kinds of pictures, are in some cases startling, and surprise is expressed that the jury of the Salon, even in the face of its traditional liberality, approved some of them.

"The Virgin of Alsace," the figure of a woman with a baby, the canvas standing fifty feet high, is the most commanding single contribution. It was executed by Antoine Bourdelle, and is to be placed at the highest point of the Vosges Mountains.

Hot in Chicago, Yukon Ice-Free, Wyoming Buried Under Snow

CHICAGO, Oct. 30.—Indian Summer weather continues here today, with high temperature about equal to yesterday's, which was 75.

DAWSON, Y. T., Oct. 30.—The present is the latest open season known on the Yukon River. The river has only slush ice in it, and the tributaries are practically free of ice. Boats could run to White Horse at this time. Three large dredges working on the Yukon expect to continue operations until Christmas.

CHEYENNE, Wyo., Oct. 30.—Wyoming was digging itself out of four inches of snow today, with more still coming down. The storm throughout the State, it was said, was highly beneficial to the farmers and ranchers, as in many places the range was so dry that the grass was brittle enough to break off and blow away.

SWIFT FACTORY FIRE KILLS 1; OTHERS DYING

One Victim, Leaping Five Stories to Death, Cracks Flagstone Sidewalk.

WORKERS CAUGHT IN TRAP

Men and Women Battle Desperately to Escape in Spectacular Brooklyn Blaze.

One man lost his life, two other men and a girl may die, and many were hurt in a factory fire in Brooklyn early last night that might have been one of the worst in the history of the city had it started a few minutes earlier, before hundreds of workers went home. Reports of many girls trapped on upper floors and lost persisted for many hours afterward. The police were unable to substantiate these reports, but scores of firemen still were flooding the stark shell of the building early this morning, hoping by daylight to be able to begin a search in the mass of glowing débris that filled the basement and piled above the level of the first floor.

In face of eye-witness stories of girls who had leaped back from flame-filled windows to perish in the cauldron behind them the police, lacking a single name of a person definitely missing, were inclined to believe that horror at what they had witnessed had led to exaggerated impressions of the casualties.

Nearly all those who got out jumped from the top story of the building—a five-story structure at 126-142 Thirteenth Street, between Second and Third Avenues. Not one person who was on that top floor, occupied by Louis Weinstein, clothing manufacturer, escaped unscathed.

Ruston Begins Investigation.

District Attorney John E. Ruston of Brooklyn cancelled a series of campaign speaking engagements to hurry to the fire. A preliminary investigation, which he will continue today, led him to believe that in many respects the building did not conform to the fire laws. He said he learned that there were two stairways in the big building, but that one of them stopped at the third floor. Only a single, flimsy wooden stair led from the fifth floor to the ground, and workers in the spreading upper lofts had to cross the entire floors to reach it.

There was only one narrow exit on the ground floor at the front. Front and rear fire escapes, it was said, were far from adequate and were reported to have been weak and rickety. There was an abandoned elevator shaft which was not always closed off by fire doors, and another elevator which, though used, ran only as far as the third floor. In one corner was a bricked-in fire tower which no one appeared to have been able to reach.

Nearly all the victims were caught on the top floor where they fought desperately for life, despairing at times, only to take new hope as the crowd below shouted and gesticulated while the clang of approaching apparatus rose above the roar of the flames.

The fire was one of the hottest with which the department has had to cope in some time. All the apparatus in Brooklyn was summoned for a fight

Continued on Page Three.

MILLER ARRAIGNS SMITH'S BEER PLA AS 'FALSE PROMIS

No State Act Could Ove National Prohibition, He Declares.

OPENS TRANSIT CAMPA

Governor Pledges Himself Universal Five-Cent Fare.

TAUNTS SMITH ON N

Also Asks the Former Gove Where He Stands on Port Authority.

Governor Miller, starting last the week's speaking tour of the with which he winds up his camp struck out vigorously at his oppo former Governor Smith, on three —light wine and beer, transit and Port Authority.

Referring to the prohibition que for the first time in the campaign Governor declared that in appealin votes by holding out the hope of wine and beer in this State Mr. was making "false promises," in a tempt to deceive the people. "N an act of the Legislature, an am ment of our State Constitution nor referendum to the people of this could affect the situation in the slig or amount to as much as a gest he said, "and the man who is see votes on the pretense that it w merely insults the intelligence of people to whom that appeal is m

After a detailed discussion of th sit problem and a comparative ana of his record and the record of hi ponent on that question, the Gove made a definite promise that not would a five-cent fare be continu single lines in the city, but that a " versal five-cent fare," meaning a cent fare with transfers to any would be re-established.

The Governor opened his campai Public School 115, 177th Street, Audubon Avenue. He had arrived Albany early in the afternoon. O arrival he expressed himself as "h pleased" with the results of his paign, and when pressed for an ex sion of opinion as to the result said am not running to lose."

The meeting was one of the mos thusiastic of the campaign. The ernor's attacks on Mayor Hylan's sit record repeatedly produced app by an audience of 3,000. His ana of the transit record of Smith as ernor also got a hearty response. lice lines had to be drawn to mak approach to the hall possible.

He Discusses Prohibition.

Turning to the light wine and question at the outset of his sp Governor Miller said:

"You will recall, as I well recall, two years ago this town was plas with posters telling people what my decessor had done for them, with peals to every group and to every terest, and that there were whispe of dire results to happen if I s be elected; you were not going t able to even play baseball; all of innocent pleasures of the people to be taken away from them; we to have a return to the blue Those appeals had a powerful influ

"Two years have gone by and people know whether those app were honest or dishonest. They whether any legitimate enterprise any legitimate amusement of the pe has been interfered with.

"A similar appeal, equally disho is now being made in somewhat ferent fashion. The alluring hop held by the Democratic platform by the Democratic candidate for Go nor that if he is elected the people have light wines and beer. He kn you know, every intelligent cit knows, that whether he is elected whether I am elected, it can have no fluence whatever upon that ques that the Governor of this State and Legislature of this State cannot, if would, give the people of this S light wines and beer.

"They might, it is true, violate t oath of office, but every one kn that the Constitution of the Un States and the act of Congress of United States is supreme over anyt which the State of New York migh could do. If anyone has any doub that subject, he merely has to look our sister state across the river, w a campaign was waged two years precisely upon the same kind of pro that the Democratic candidate of State is now making the people. they know, too, that the State of Jersey, like every other State in Union, is precisely in the same posi with respect to light wines and bee when that false promise was made

"I refuse to deceive the people. my opponent wishes to do so, he is come to take that course."

Referring to a statement attrib to Mr. Smith that he was going to cuss transit in New York for the six days, the Governor said: "C ously enough that is precisely wh propose to do. As Governor," he "Mr. Smith made a distinct recor the transit problem and one which people of this town can hardly forgotten."

Promise Universal 5-Cent Fare.

"The five-cent fare," continued G ernor Miller, "has been saved and plan of reorganization of the Tra Commission proposes to reinforce by putting back of it an additional gu antee of $25,000,000 in the elimination two items alone; namely, a reduction interest charges amounting to nea thirteen millions by the reduced val tions and the elimination of taxes, say nothing or other charges.

"The five-cent fare has been saved is now in order, first, to restore five-cent fare as it was, not to what we now have, a double and treble five-cent fare, but first to rest the five-cent fare as it was before system of disintegration and destruc began, and finally to establish a u versal five-cent fare.

"I think that, without boasting

"All the News That's Fit to Print."

The New York Times.

THE WEATHER
Increasing Cloudiness today; rain with rising temperature tomorrow.
Temperatures yesterday—Max., 50; min., 38.
For weather report see Page 30.

VOL. LXXVI....No. 25,276. NEW YORK, FRIDAY, APRIL 8, 1927. TWO CENTS In Greater New York | THREE CENTS Within 200 Miles | FOUR CENTS Elsewhere in the U. S.

AR-OFF SPEAKERS SEEN AS WELL AS HEARD HERE IN A TEST OF TELEVISION

E A PHOTO COME TO LIFE

oover's Face Plainly Imaged as He Speaks in Washington.

HE FIRST TIME IN HISTORY

ctures Are Flashed by Wire and Radio Synchronizing With Speaker's Voice.

OMMERCIAL USE IN DOUBT

t A. T. & T. Head Sees a New Step in Conquest of Nature After Years of Research.

erbert Hoover made a speech in ashington yesterday afternoon. An dience in New York heard him and w him.

lore, than 200 miles of space inter- ning between the speaker and his dience was annihilated by the tele- sion apparatus developed by the Bell boratories of the American Tele- one and Telegraph Company and monstrated publicly for the first time sterday.

The apparatus shot images of Mr. oover by wire from Washington to w York at the rate of eighteen a cond. These were thrown on a screen motion pictures, while the loud- eaker reproduced the speech. As ch syllable was heard, the motion the speaker's lips and his changes expression were flashed on the reen in the demonstration room of Bell Telephone Laboratories at 55 thune Street.

When the television pictures were rown on a screen two by three ches, the likeness was excellent. It as as if a photograph had suddenly me to life and begun to talk, smile, d its head and look this way and at. When the screen was enlarged two by three feet, the results were t so good.

Phone Hides His Face.

At times the face of the Secretary uld not be clearly distinguished. He oked down, as he read his speech. d held the telephone receiver up, so at it covered most of the lower part his countenance. There was too ch illumination also in the back- ound of the screen. When he moved face, his features became clearly stinguishable. Near the close of his lk he turned his head to one side, d in profile his features became ear and full of detail.

On the smaller screen the face and tion were reproduced with perfect delity.

After Mr. Hoover had spoken, Vice resident J. J. Carty of the American elephone and Telegraph Company and hers in the demonstration room at ashington took his place and con- rsed one at a time with men in New ork. The speaker on the New York d looked the Washington man in the e, as he talked to him. On the small reen before him appeared the living ce of the man to whom he was lking.

Time as well as space was eliminated. ecretary Hoover's New York hearers d spectators were something like a ousandth part of a second later than e persons at his side in hearing him d in seeing changes of countenance. The faces and voices were projected om Washington by wire. It was own a few minutes later, however, at radio does just as well.

Similar Test by Wireless.

In the second part of the program e group in New York saw and heard rformances in the Whippany studio the American Telephone and Tele- aph Company by wireless. The first ce flashed on the screen from Whip- ny, N. J., was that of E. L. Nelson, engineer, who gave a technical de- ription of what was taking place. r. Nelson had a good television face. screened well as he talked.

Next came a vaudeville act by radio om Whippany. A. Dolan, a come- an, first appeared before the audi- nce as a stage Irishman, with side hiskers and a broken pipe, and did monologue in brogue. Then he made quick change and came back in ackface with a new line of quips in gro dialect. The loudspeaker part ent over very well. It was the first audeville act that ever went on the ir as a talking picture and in its pos- bilities it may be compared with the red Ott sneeze of more than thirty ears ago, the first piece of comedy ver recorded in motion pictures. For he commercial future of television, if has one, is thought to be largely in ublic entertainment—super-news reels ashed before audiences at the mo- ent of occurrence, together with dra- atic and musical acts shot on the ther waves in sound and picture at e instant they are taking place at e studio.

The next number from the studio at hippany was a regular radio pro- ram piece—a short humorous dialect lk by Mrs. H. A. Frederick of Moun- in Lakes.

Before and between the acts the an- ouncer of the Whippany studio made

Continued on Page Twenty.

Voorhis Hopes When He Is 100 To Visit Smith in White House

Hope that he might celebrate his one hundredth birthday with Governor Smith in the White House was expressed yesterday by John R. Voorhis, veteran Grand Sachem of the Tammany Society and President of the Board of Elections. Mr. Voorhis will be ninety-eight years old next July and, if Governor Smith should be nominated for and elected President, his one hundredth birthday would occur in July, 1929, a few months after the inauguration.

"As near as I can determine, it looks as though Governor Smith would be nominated," Mr. Voorhis said. "The opposition to him is diminishing and the general sentiment for him is increasing. So far as his election is concerned, it is too far ahead to tell much about it."

Mr. Voorhis, who is still remarkably active, was seen at Tammany Hall. He stopped there on his return from a trip to Brownsville, where he went to inspect quarters sought by the Board of Elections for the storage of voting machines.

$840,000 FUR STRIKE AUDIT WAS HOPELESS

Accountants at Bribe Inquiry Testify Meagre Data Failed to Show Where Money Went.

REIGN OF TERROR KEEPS UP

Pickets Still Make Trouble, Says Frayne, Although There Is No Strike Now.

Accountants engaged by the American Federation of Labor's special committee to check up the expenditure of $840,000 by the Communist-led Joint Board of Furriers during last year's strike testified yesterday at the John Doe inquiry into allegations of police bribery that they could not find a single original voucher which specifically stated the use to which the money was put. Instead of original vouchers they said a forged cash book was furnished to them and not the book of original entry, as well as a large number of checks made out to "bearer," endorsed by the late Abraham Goodman, the Joint Board's counsel, and others.

The General Strike Committee handling the funds of the union checked out the money to counsel and to chairmen of various committees such as hall and picket committees, and the furthest the accountants were able to penetrate into the tangle of checks was to obtain some of the "receipts" for the money signed by subcommittee officers who received it from the Strike Committee, they asserted. They told Magistrate Joseph E. Corrigan, presiding at the inquiry, that they were never able to learn to whom the committee chairmen paid the money or whether some of it went for relief and court fines and how much was expended in this way.

Says Audit Was Hindered.

Every obstacle was placed in the way of the accountants by the Joint Board officers, according to the witnesses, until finally the union demanded individual receipts for every scrap of paper supplied for examination, with the understanding that

Continued on Page Nine.

THEFT OF 300 PAPERS ON MEXICO REVEALED BY FORGERY INQUIRY

Secret Military Reports Among Documents Stolen in Wholesale Diplomatic Robberies.

SOME WERE "DOCTORED"

Calles Turned Them Over to Us When It Became Known That We Knew He Had Them.

SUBJECT OF MYSTERY NOTE

Many Papers Believed Stolen From Our Embassy in Skillful Plot—Washington Disclaims "Leak."

By RICHARD V. OULAHAN.
Special to The New York Times.

WASHINGTON, April 7.—Pilfering of the United States Government's confidential correspondence relating to Mexico has been established through investigation which dovetails with the subject matter of the "mystery note" delivered to the Mexican Foreign Office recently by James R. Sheffield, the American Ambassador in Mexico City.

This pilfering was conducted on a wholesale scale, as nearly or quite 300 documents belonging to the United States Government were stolen. These documents were turned over to President Calles of Mexico, who, when the fact that he had them became known to the United States Government, delivered them to the State Department.

Included in this large batch of confidential papers was a considerable number of reports of a military nature, most of them supposed to have been taken from the office of the military attaché of the embassy in Mexico City.

Some time ago rumors were circulated in Washington that a "leak" in the State Department had been discovered and that an employe of the department had been dropped from the rolls in connection with the alleged "leak."

No "Leak," Officials Believe.

It is now being asserted that the alleged "leak" was associated with the established fact that confidential documents of the United States Government relating to Mexico had come into the possession of the Mexican Government.

While Government officials today maintained their attitude of silence concerning the pilfering of confidential diplomatic and military papers, it was indicated that there had not been any leak in the State Department. The denial took the form of a statement, in answer to inquiries, that it was not believed that any such leak had existed.

Officials showed a disinclination to discuss the matter and would not go further than to express that belief, with the additional information that they had not heard of any leak.

Other reports are that confidential military papers of the United States relating to Mexico had been offered for sale for $50,000. Another report is that official documents, presumably belonging to the Mexican Government, had been offered for sale to the American Embassy in Mexico City.

Signs of Skillful Plotting.

From what is known of the matter it is evident that a skillfully arranged effort to obtain confidential documents pertaining to the relations of the United States and Mexico has been in progress for some time. There are features of it as intriguing as elements of a fantastic novel having to do with international plotting.

It has been established, according to information obtained, that some of the stolen documents were "doctored" by having forged words and phrases inserted in them with the suspected intention of making it appear that the Coolidge Administration had hostile in-

Continued on Page Four.

2 Boys Killed, 5 Hurt, When Truck Hits Auto On Which 10 Were Riding Home From School

Two school boys were killed and five others were injured yesterday when a truck crashed into a coupe on which they were riding at Beverly and Rugby Roads, Brooklyn.

The boys killed were Lawrence Moen, 11 years old, of 360 East Seventh Street, and Caesar Salya, 10 years old, of 698 Coney Island Avenue. Attilio Salya, 14, brother of Caesar, received internal injuries and was sent to the Kings County Hospital, with Nicholas Demarinio, 13, of 239 East Ninth Street, whose right leg was fractured, and Timothy Barlow, 11, of 240 East Ninth Street, who was badly cut and bruised. John Ledischi, 13, of 260 East Ninth Street, was cut and bruised. After being treated at the hospital he was sent home. Columbus Salya, another brother of the dead boy, received similar injuries, but ran home before a doctor reached the scene. He was treated at home last night.

The boys, with three others, were leaving Holy Innocents Parochial School, at Beverly Road and East Seventeenth Street shortly after 4 o'clock, when one of them hailed a friend driving past in a coupe. The boys had attended a confirmation class for confirmation next Sunday.

In the coupe were Stephen J. Collins of 1,042 Flatbush Avenue, and his wife. Asked if he could give them a ride home Mr. Collins told the boys to climb on. Those who could not find places on the running board clambered on the back of the car.

When the coupe reached Rugby Road, a short distance away, the boys' shouts of pleasure changed suddenly to screams of fright. As the coupe started across Rugby Road a truck driven by Frank Whalen of 646 Seventy-fourth Street, bore down on it and before Collins could get the coupe out of the way the truck crashed into it, striking Moen and Caesar Salya, who were standing on the running board. Moen was instantly killed. The coupe was whirled around and hurled across the street. As it slammed against the curb five of the boys were thrown off. Collins, his wife and the other boys were only slightly injured.

The Salya boy was hurried to the hospital, but was dead when he got there. Collins and Whalen were questioned by Assistant District Attorney Bernard Becker, who directed that both men be held for the action of the Brooklyn homicide court this morning. Collins said he did not see the truck coming because his vision was obscured by the boys standing on the running board of his car.

Caruso Convicted of First Degree Murder; Killed Doctor After Death of Little Son

A jury in the Kings County Court late last night brought in a verdict of guilty of murder in the first degree against Frank Caruso for the killing of Dr. Casper S. Pendola of Maspeth in February.

Caruso, 36 years old and the father of five children, killed the physician when he found his 9-year-old son, Joseph, who was being treated by Dr. Pendola for diphtheria, had died.

The jury returned to the court room at 11:51 o'clock, after most of those who had listened all day to the trial had left the room. The defendant heard the foreman's announcement with little visible concern. He arose at the call of the clerk, walked a few steps forward and gave his pedigree in an even tone.

Caruso said he had been sixteen years in this country. He was a native of Italy. He lived at 36 Third Street, Brooklyn, and had been convicted and fined $100 eight years ago for having a pistol.

The case went to the jury at 6 P. M. Twice the jury returned to the court room, once to inquire about the different degrees of murder, and again to have a part of Judge McLaughlin's charge read. In the first hour of its deliberation a report reached the Court that it stood 7 to 5 for first degree murder.

After the verdict was announced Judge McLaughlin, turning to the jury, said: "I thank you for the careful consideration you have given to this case. The verdict will make for law and order. Any other finding would have been a miscarriage of justice."

In summing up George Voss, attorney for Caruso, declared that the defendant was moved to the frenzy that resulted in the killing because Dr. Pendola laughed when he heard that Caruso's son had died following treatment for diphtheria. He told the jurors that under the same circumstances they would have felt the urge to kill. He asked them not to class Caruso with the cold-blooded gangsters who murder with deliberation. He raised the technicality that the doctor had been killed by strangulation instead of stabbing, as charged in the indictment.

In his summing up Chief Assistant District Attorney Joseph V. Gallagher said that the testimony of a Holy Family Hospital ambulance surgeon and the autopsy report of Assistant Medical Examiner Gregory Robillard showed that Dr. Pendola had been stabbed to death. He said that the two knife wounds indicated that the murder was premeditated.

County Judge McLaughlin, in his charge to the jury, said the murder was neither legally justifiable nor excusable. After explaining the distinction between first and second degree murder he cautioned the jury to abandon all sympathy and sentiment in deciding the case.

Caruso will be sentenced on April 18.

HUGE POTASH 'TRUST' UNDER FEDERAL FIRE

Tuttle Sues French and German Groups, Alleging Scheme to Monopolize Markets Here.

$50,000,000 ANNUAL TRADE

American Concern Also Named in Complaint—Case Second Under Wilson Tariff Act.

Acting under instructions from the Department of Justice, United States Attorney Charles H. Tuttle began yesterday an injunction suit against a German syndicate called the Deutsche Kalisyndikat Gesellschaft, to restrain it from carrying out an alleged plan to create in the United States a monopoly in the sale of potash. It is charged that the plan violates the Sherman Anti-Trust law and the Wilson Tariff act and that a group of German and French producers of potash are now in this city to complete arrangements with certain American distributing agencies to make the monopoly complete and effective.

It is charged that the German companies have an exclusive selling agency in this city which operates under the name of the Potash Importing Corporation of America, that the French companies have a similar agency, and that these two groups have agreed to divide the business in this country and to handle the product with a single agency at prices to be agreed upon between them.

Danger to Our Interests Seen.

The danger of such a monopoly, to the interests of the people in this country is indicated by Alexander B. Royce, a special assistant to the United States Attorney, in charge of trust cases, who said:

"The Government petition charges that beginning May 1, 1927, the French and German companies have agreed to continue the division of the United States business. It is also charged that these two groups have been dividing the sales of potash in this country since August, 1924. The complaint alleges that because the mines of the French and German companies constitute the only source of a large supply of potash, users in the United States are almost wholly dependent upon them."

It is explained that the syndicate is a combination of the owners of all the potash mines in Germany, that their headquarters and principal office is in Berlin, and that associated with them are the French companies which own potash mines in Alsace, the greater part of the product being shipped to the United States. From the close of the war until 1924 the French companies, it is asserted, sold potash to importers in this country independently of each other and free from agreements on prices, quantities, or conditions.

The Defendants Named.

The corporate defendants are the German syndicate, the Société Commerciale de Potasses d'Alsace, Mines Domaniales de Potasse d'Alsace, the Société Anonyme des Mines de Kali Sainte-Thérèse and the Potash Importing Corporation of America. The individual defendants are Dr. Maximilien Kempner, Dr. Oskar Eckstein, A. Diehn, Robert Kunze, Dr. Ernst Frohnknecht, all of whom are officers and employes of the syndicate; le Cornee, whose Christian name is not known, and René Gide, who are described as active in the control of the French potash industry; E. K. Howe, H. A. Forbes, Walker B. Howe and René Gide, a resident of this city, especially interested in the product of the Société Commerciale des Potasses d'Alsace. The latter is evidently a son or other relative of the René Gide first mentioned.

That the Government has been aware of the alleged negotiations by the defendants to monopolize the potash trade in the United States is indicated by the fact that it has been known that all the German defendants are guests at the Hotel Plaza, and all of the French defendants have quarters at 25 West Forty-third Street, and because certain movements of representatives of the two factions are known.

Mr. Royce said 1,000,000 tons of pot-

Continued on Page Three.

WARNS NIGHT CLUBS OF COMING CLEAN-UP

Banton Declares New Theatre Padlock Measure Also Applies to Them.

SURE OF PUBLIC SUPPORT

He Will Act on Complaints, He Says—Playhouse Owners Are Perturbed Over New Bill.

Governor Smith's approval of the Wales Theatre Padlock bill caused District Attorney Banton to announce yesterday that the bill was as directly applicable to night clubs and cabarets as to theatres, and to declare that "women in night clubs had better put on clothes, too." Mr. Banton, who drew the bill and enlisted the support necessary for its passage, said it was backed by the public, which would make convictions easy.

The District Attorney, while denying that he would spy on either the theatres or the night clubs, intimated strongly that the public as well as the police would report violations, said he would act promptly upon complaints of private citizens or policemen, and that clean entertainments would soon result. He added that, "as in all cases where a moral principle is involved, the Governor was found on the side of right-thinking people."

Theatrical producers and managers, for the most part, expressed disappointment over Governor Smith's action in signing the bill. Arch Selwyn, declaring that it had been a "very, very foolish thing for the Governor to do" expressed the opinion that the bill would mean "new graft in various departments of the city." An exception was A. L. Erlanger, who expressed approval of the Governor's action.

Banton Issues Statement.

In a statement issued soon after he had learned that Governor Smith had signed the bill, District Attorney Banton said:

"The producers and managers of plays now before the public had better go through them (the plays) and cut out their dirty lines and scenes. Authors of plays yet to be produced had better keep in mind this new law.

"We now have the right kind of law and the law is backed by the public. Public sentiment, when aroused, makes it easy for us to get convictions against indecent shows. Without it we find it hard to get convictions. Under this new law we shall find that theatre owners will be the best kind of censors of plays produced in their theatres—and that, after all, is what is effective in keeping the stage clean.

"This new law increases efficiency in the administration of the statute against obscenity in the theatres in the following particulars:

"First—Heretofore it has been necessary to proceed against the play as a whole. The amendment permits the arrest of those who interject into the play an obscene act.

"Second—All plays, or parts thereof, which depict or in any way deal with the subject of degeneracy are prohibited.

"Third—Therefore the owner of the theatre, like the ostrich, could hide his head in the sand and pretend not to know what was going on about him, and conviction of the owner or lessee of a theatre has been next to impossible, as in the case of John Cort, who for eleven months was one of the principal owners of the theatre in which 'Sex' was produced. From now on the owner or lessee of the property will be held responsible for a violation on his property, and on conviction of the actors or producers, the licensing authority may revoke the license and refuse to issue a new license for a period not exceeding one year."

Law Called Unconstitutional.

Commenting on a statement by William H. Klein, attorney for the Shuberts, that the new law was unconstitutional, Mr. Banton said:

"The license granted by a public official is only a privilege and the power to grant such license implies the power to revoke it. It is within the legislative power to define just what that official power is. This new law places the licensing power, in the case of the theatrical performance, on a par with any other licensing power in ex-

Continued on Page Eight.

SMITH APPROVES THEATRE PADLOCKS; VETOES GAS CUT-OFF

Governor Declares Majority of the People and Producers Desire a Clean Stage.

APPLIANCE BILL A PUZZLE

Tempted to Sign It Because of Graft Talk, He Finally Rejects It as Too Broad.

30-DAY BILLS CLEANED UP

Port Authority, Sewage Plant and Salary Measures Approved—One Baumes Proposal Vetoed.

By W. A. WARN.
Special to The New York Times.

ALBANY, April 7.—Although less than two weeks have elapsed since the Legislature adjourned sine die, Governor Smith today finished work on the huge mass of legislative measures the lawmakers sent to his desk for veto or approval, for the consideration of which the Governor is allotted thirty days under the law. The speed with which the thirty-day bills were disposed of is thought to establish a State record.

The Governor left this evening for New York City, where he will remain until Monday, when he will go to the Sea View Golf Club at Absecon, N. J. for an indefinite stay, accompanied by Mrs. Smith and other members of his family. He is badly in need of rest, having worked under high pressure for weeks.

Among the bills approved by the Governor today were the Theatrical Padlock bill, on which a hearing was held yesterday; the bill giving the Governor veto power over New York State members of the Port Authority Commission; the bill authorizing the State to surrender the northern end of Ward's Island to the New York City authorities as a site for a modern sewage disposal plant; a bill approving the New York-New Jersey-Pennsylvania compact for developing new water supply facilities on the Delaware River and a number of bills providing salary increases to be paid out of the New York City treasury to judges and some other county officials within the city.

Important Bills Vetoed.

Governor Smith vetoed the Thayer bill, which would have repealed the aldermanic ordinance under which a certain patented gas cut-off appliance must be installed in all buildings above a certain height and which was denounced by spokesmen for New York City realty interests at a hearing yesterday as prolific in graft to the promoters. The Governor said this measure had been so loosely drawn and would have such far-reaching disastrous effects that he felt compelled to withhold his approval.

Among other measures vetoed were a bill that would have enabled the Montauk Riding and Driving Club in Brooklyn to disregard vital provisions of the Tenement House law in the erection of a "club apartment" structure in Brooklyn, designed to have on the ground floor a huge arena for horse shows and driving meets; a bill which would have permitted osteopaths to perform minor operations and one which would have conferred the title of doctor on optometrists.

In all 3,401 bills were introduced at the recent session of the Legislature. Of these 861 reached the Governor's desk. Out of this number he approved 731, which now will take their place on the statute books. He vetoed 130. Approximately 400 bills were among the thirty-day lot.

Of forty-six bills permitting claim suits to be brought against the State in the Court of Claims, Governor Smith vetoed twenty-four and approved twenty-two. Some pension and retirement bills affecting New York City were among the measures which the Governor failed to give his approval. In a so-called omnibus veto were included forty bills rejected by the Governor as unnecessary or faultily drawn.

About the most important measure in this batch was one of the Baumes Crime Commission measures, providing for the establishment of bureaus of criminal identification in all cities with

Continued on Page Twelve.

SOVIET OFFICES IN TIENTSIN RAIDED BY CHINESE POLICE; NOW CUT OFF IN SHANGHAI

MORE DOCUMENTS SEIZED

Permission for Tientsin Search Is Given by French Consul.

THREAT TO MOVE EMBASSY

Soviet Consul General, Before Isolation at Shanghai, Says It May Go to Hankow.

PEKING EXPECTS RUPTURE

Wellington Koo Resigns as Premier in North—American Missionary Is Missing.

Special Cable to THE NEW YORK TIMES.

TIENTSIN, China, April 7.—The Chinese police, with the sanction of the French Consul, raided today the Soviet bank [the Dahl Bank] and also the offices of the Chinese-Eastern Railway and other Soviet offices, all in the French concession, and seized documents.

The raid was prompted by the discoveries in the Soviet buildings at Peking yesterday.

TIENTSIN, April 7 (AP).—Chinese police this afternoon entered the French concession, with permission of the Consul, and searched the Dahl Bank and various Soviet trade missions. The Chinese detained all persons pending the search and removed documents for examination.

French police took no direct part in the raid, but maintained order outside.

Shanghai Consulate Under Guard.

SHANGHAI, April 7 (AP).—Police, assisted by White Russian volunteers, late today surrounded the Soviet Consulate in the international settlement with orders to prevent any one from entering or leaving the premises.

No reason for this action was given, but it was stated that there was no present intention to raid the Consulate.

Among the visitors whom the police held up was the Chinese Commissioner of Foreign Affairs, who was informed that he would not be allowed to enter unless he consented to be searched. The Commissioner refused to permit this and left.

The possibility of the removal of the Soviet Embassy at Peking to Hankow, the seat of the Cantonese or Nationalist Government, was suggested today by Wilhelm F. Linde, Soviet Consul here, as a result of yesterday's raid by Northern soldiers on buildings attached to the Russian Embassy.

Mr. Linde said that such a removal was not impossible in discussing the incident with newspaper men after he had called upon the Norwegian Consul General, Dean of the consular corps in Shanghai, to announce that he would hold the consular body responsible if the Soviet Consulate here were raided also.

The Soviet Consul General also declared that if the Peking raid was carried out with the approval of the diplomatic corps, it would set a precedent that would endanger the foundation of diplomatic prerogatives. In this connection he said that he understood that permission for the entry of the Chinese troops and police into the legation grounds at Peking had been granted solely by the Dean of the diplomatic corps and not from all the members.

Yangtse Evacuation Goes On.

While interest continued to centre here on the international possibilities of the Peking raid in so far as it may cause serious repercussions in Moscow, foreigners in various sections of China are steadily evacuating the areas where anti-foreign agitation has been spreading.

Hankow, scene of a growing tenseness, was the centre of riotous anti-foreign outbreaks over last week-end, resulting in further plans for a rapid departure of the comparatively few remaining foreigners.

"Situation growing worse steadily" was a wireless message received from there today.

With lawlessness in the city apparently increasing, the commander of the United States Yangtse River patrol is urging Americans still in the city to leave as soon as possible. Japanese are leaving the city in increasing numbers, while German and Russian nationals are preparing to leave soon.

Dr. C. P. Triberg of St. Peter, Minn., a member of the Augustana Synod Mission of the American Lutheran Church, was reported missing today and it is feared he has been captured by bandits. All the members of the mission, which was centred in the Province of Honan, are leaving China, fifty-four of the ninety-four members leaving tomorrow on the President Pierce.

In line with the decision to bring all British gunboats out of the upper Yangtse area, the British consuls and the remainder of the British communities at Chung-king, I-chang,

Court Banishes Man for Life From State of North Carolina

Special to The New York Times.

DANVILLE, Va., April 7.—J. H. Anderson of this city was banished from the State of North Carolina for life today by Judge W. E. Haring, sitting at Yanceyville. Anderson also was told by the Court that if he was found within 200 miles of Danville henceforth he would be arrested and required to serve two years on the roads.

A jury had convicted him after twenty-four hours' deliberation of an assault on a young woman. Anderson was permitted to choose between sentence or exile, and he chose the latter.

DAWES CONTINUES REED COMMITTEE

Declares It Has Legal Authority to Function During the Recess of Congress.

FESS TAKES GOFF'S PLACE

Naming of Ohio Senator Instead of Shortridge of California Surprises Washington.

CHICAGO, April 7 (AP).—Vice President Dawes, guided by a Supreme Court decision, today held that the Senate Campaign Fund Investigating Committee retains its powers although Congress has adjourned, and appointed Senator Simeon Fess, Republican, Ohio, to succeed Senator Guy D. Goff, Republican, West Virginia, who resigned as a member of the committee.

The Vice President followed the opinion of the high court in the recent case against Mal Daugherty, whose testimony was wanted by a Senate committee.

The filibuster in the expiring hours of the Senate of the Sixty-ninth Congress and the failure of the resolution of Senator James A. Reed of Missouri, the Chairman, to continue the committee, and the resignation of Senator Goff, left the decision to the Vice President.

Senators Goff, Borah, Republican, Idaho, and Walsh, Democrat, Montana, all expressed opinions that the committee continued legally to exist. Senator Keyes, Republican, New Hampshire, Chairman of the Committee on Audit and Control of the Contingent Fund of the Senate, held that the committee was dead and that he should not approve further expenditures from the fund by the committee.

Gives Reasons for Decision.

Vice President Dawes returned here yesterday from a vacation trip to Panama and late today advised Senator Fess of his selection to the Goff vacancy on the committee. At the same time the Vice President made public his action and basis for it in a statement in part as follows:

"In my judgment the Supreme Court of the United States in the case of John J. McGrain, Deputy Sergeant-at-Arms of the United States Senate, appellant, v. Mal S. Daugherty, rendered Jan. 17, 1927, conclusively disposes of the question in the affirmative. The Supreme Court was passing on the question of the powers of a Senatorial committee authorized by a resolution 'to sit and perform its duties at such times and places as may be deemed advisable or necessary by said committee.'

"It held that this language of the resolution extended the powers of the committee beyond the Congress which passed the creating resolution. Senate resolution 195, Sixty-ninth Congress, creating the present Senatorial Investigating Committee, contains the following language:

"'Said committee is hereby empowered to sit and act at such time or times and at such place or places as it may deem necessary.'

"The holding of the Supreme Court,

Continued on Page Two.

Earl Carroll's Friends Will Seek a Parole; No Pardon Is Asked; Term Starts Tuesday

Special to The New York Times.

WASHINGTON, April 7.—Inquiries at the Department of Justice today indicated that friends of Earl Carroll, New York theatrical producer, who was sentenced to a term of a year and a day at Atlanta for perjury in connection with the famous bath tub case, will attempt to obtain a parole for Mr. Carroll at the appropriate time if executive clemency is refused before the sentence begins, as now seems assured.

Up to date no application for the exercise of executive clemency in behalf of Mr. Carroll has been received at the Department of Justice, which handles such matters before they are sent to the President for consideration. It was explained to friends of Mr. Carroll that executive clemency is rarely extended before the execution of a sentence, and then only in cases where precarious health or facts tending to throw doubt on the guilt of persons accused are cited.

In most instances the Attorney General will not consider recommending a pardon until at least one-third of the sentence of a person convicted has been served. A prisoner likewise is not eligible for parole until he has served one-third of the time for which he has been sentenced.

Under the mandate of the New York Court Mr. Carroll's sentence will begin on April 12, and as things now stand he will have to surrender himself to the custody of the authorities on that date.

Section 1

"All the News That's Fit to Print."

The New York Times.

THE WEATHER
Generally fair today and tomorrow; moderate to fresh southerly winds.
Temperature yesterday—Max., 80; Min., 53.
For weather report see Page 31.

Section 1

VOL. LXXVI....No. 25,320. NEW YORK, SUNDAY, MAY 22, 1927. Including Rotogravure Picture Section in three parts—Magazine and Book Sections in Rotogravure. FIVE CENTS In Manhattan, Bronx and Brooklyn | Elsewhere TEN CENTS

LINDBERGH DOES IT! TO PARIS IN 33½ HOURS; FLIES 1,000 MILES THROUGH SNOW AND SLEET; CHEERING FRENCH CARRY HIM OFF FIEL[D]

COULD HAVE GONE 500 MILES FARTHER

Gasoline for at Least That Much More—Flew at Times From 10 Feet to 10,000 Feet Above Water

ATE ONLY ONE AND A HALF OF HIS FIVE SANDWICHES

Fell Asleep at Times but Quickly Awoke—Glimpses of His Adventure in Brief Interview at the Embassy.

LINDBERGH'S OWN STORY TOMORROW.

Captain Charles A. Lindbergh was too exhausted after his arrival in Paris late last night to do more than indicate, as told below, his experiences during his flight. After he awakes today, he will narrate the full story of his remarkable exploit for readers of Monday's New York Times.

By CARLYLE MACDONALD.

Special Cable to THE NEW YORK TIMES.

PARIS, Sunday, May 22.—Captain Lindbergh was discovered at the American Embassy at 2:30 o'clock this morning. Attired in a pair of Ambassador Herrick's pajamas, he sat on the edge of a bed and talked of his flight. At the last moment Ambassador Herrick had canceled the plans of the reception committee and, by unanimous consent, took the flier to the embassy in the Place d'Iena.

A staff of American doctors who had arrived at Le Bourget Field early to minister to an "exhausted" aviator found instead a bright-eyed, smiling youth who refused to be examined.

"Oh, don't bother; I am all right," he said.

"I'd like to have a bath and a glass of milk. I would feel better," Lindbergh replied when the Ambassador asked him what he would like to have.

A bath was drawn immediately and in less than five minutes the youth had disrobed in one of the embassy guest rooms, taken his bath and was out again drinking a bottle of milk and eating a roll.

"No Use Worrying," He Tells Envoy.

"There is no use worrying about me, Mr. Ambassador," Lindbergh insisted when Mr. Herrick and members of the embassy staff wanted him to be examined by doctors and then go to bed immediately.

It was apparent that the young man was too full of his experiences to want sleep and he sat on the bed and chatted with the Ambassador, his son and daughter-in-law.

By this time a corps of frantic newspaper men who had been madly chasing the airman, following one false scent after another, had finally tracked him to the embassy. In a body they descended upon the Ambassador, who received them in the salon and informed them that he had just left Lindbergh with strict instructions to go to sleep.

As Mr. Herrick was talking with the reporters his son-in-law came downstairs and said that Lindbergh had rung and announced that he did not care to go to sleep just yet and that he would be glad to see the newspaper men for a few minutes. A cheer went up from the group who dashed by Mr. Herrick and rushed upstairs.

Expected Trouble Over Newfoundland.

In the blue and gold room, with a soft light glowing, sat the conqueror of the Atlantic. He immediately stood up and held out his hands to greet his callers. THE NEW YORK TIMES correspondent being first to greet him.

"Sit down, please," urged every one with one voice, but Lindbergh only smiled again his famous boyish smile and said:

"It's almost as easy to stand up as it is to sit down."

Questions were fired at him from all sides about his trip across the ocean, but Lindbergh seemed to dismiss them all with brief, nonchalant answers.

"I expected trouble over Newfoundland because I had been warned that the situation there was unfavorable. But I got over that hazard with no trouble whatsoever."

Sleet and Snow for 1,000 Miles.

"However, it wasn't easy going. I had sleet and snow for over 1,000 miles. Sometimes it was too high to fly over and sometimes too low to fly under, so I just had to go through it as best I could.

"I flew as low as 10 feet in some places and as high as 10,000 in others. I passed no ships in the daytime, but at night I saw the lights of several ships, the night being bright and clear."

Everyone then wanted to know if the flier had been sleepy on the voyage.

"I didn't really get what you might call downright sleepy," he said, "but I think I sort of nodded several times. In fact, I could have flown half that distance again. I had enough fuel

Continued on Page Two.

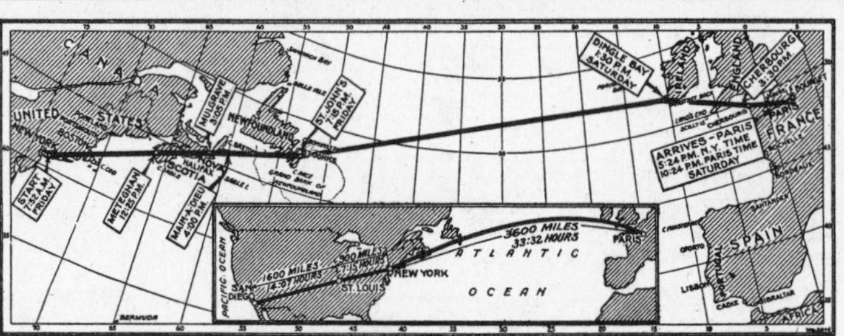

MAP OF LINDBERGH'S TRANSATLANTIC ROUTE, SHOWING THE SPEED OF HIS TRIP.

LEVINE ABANDONS BELLANCA FLIGHT

Venture Given Up as Designer Splits With Him—Plane Narrowly Escapes Burning.

BYRD'S CRAFT IS NAMED

Lindbergh Cheered at Ceremony—Commander, Now Last in Field, Waits on Weather.

Through no fault of his own, Clarence D. Chamberlin, who with Bert Acosta established a world's non-stop flying record a few weeks ago, will not fly the record-breaking monoplane in an attempt to establish a second New York-Paris non-stop flight.

G. M. Bellanca, designer of the plane, and Charles S. Levine of the Columbia Aircraft Company, owner of the ship, came to the parting of the ways last night and the designer finally severed his connection with the promoter. Then Levine issued a statement that the proposed flight, which has been talked of for weeks, was off.

The statement said:

"Due to the crowning blow of Mr. Bellanca's resignation, the plane will be placed in the hangar. Mr. Bellanca's resignation causes us to abandon plans for the New York-Paris flight for the present."

At the very moment that the statement was issued the plane was near the runway at Roosevelt Field with gas tanks filled and oil and equipment aboard ready for the start for Paris.

Plane Threatened by Fire.

A few minutes later, as it was being wheeled off, preparatory to being housed for the night, it narrowly escaped being destroyed by fire. When the word came to the field that the flight was definitely off mechanics were ordered to empty one gasoline tank to lighten the machine. The gasoline spilled on the ground and while the ship was being towed away a careless spectator threw the stub of a lighted cigarette down.

In an instant there was a terrific flare and a dense burst of smoke as the gasoline blazed up.

"The Bellanca's gone," was the cry that rose from thousands of spectators who had gathered at the field.

Word was flashed to the army air station at Mitchel Field that there had been an accident and ambulances and fire-fighting apparatus were sent across the road. An ambulance from the Nassau County Hospital at Mineola was also sent to Roosevelt Field, as well as fire apparatus from Mineola.

The plane, however, was beyond the danger line and was not injured.

It had been announced that the Columbia would take off at 8 o'clock and Chamberlin was in his flying clothes ready to climb into the cockpit with the unnamed pilot who was to have accompanied him on the trip.

With the elimination of the Bellanca monoplane, only Lieut.

Continued on Page Four.

Times Wide World Photo

CAPTAIN CHARLES A. LINDBERGH,
Who Flew Alone Across the Atlantic, New York to Paris, in Thirty-three and One-half Hours.

New York Stages Big Celebration After Hours of Anxious Waiting

Harbor Craft, Factories, Fire Sirens and Radio Carry Message of the Flier's Victory Throughout the City—Theatres Halt While Audiences Cheer.

New York bubbled all day yesterday with excitement and expectancy, first yearning for word of Captain Lindbergh, then half-doubting, gaining confidence as the afternoon progressed and finally acclaiming the victory of the young aviator with street demonstrations where the crowds were thickest, in which the ancient phrase, "I told you so," was often repeated. It was evident during the day that New York had confidence in the lad from the West.

On the streets and elsewhere Lindbergh was the one topic of conversation the whole day long. In the subway, on the elevated, in trains and cars, motion-picture houses, theatres, wherever a few had gathered, or even where one man could find another to talk to, one heard "Lindbergh — Lindbergh — Lindbergh."

And such expressions as this:

"He'll make it, all right."

"Some baby!"

"Well, if he's hit Ireland, he's safe anyway."

"He's away ahead of his time."

"What's the difference in time between here and there, anyway?"

Confused On Difference in Time.

To this latter question there were some amazing answers. One woman who had the aviator's running time mixed with the difference in time between New York and Paris solemnly informed her companion that there was thirty-six hours difference in time between the cities. She said it with an air which signified: "I don't mean maybe." A surprising number of persons insisted that the difference in time was three hours.

Early in the day, even before there was any good reason why there should be definite news, the interest of the people was demonstrated in two ways. At every news stand there were little groups scanning the headlines and buying newspapers. In every newspaper office the switchboards were literally swamped with inquiries. It was not sufficient that the operator said there was no word, or, later, that Lindbergh's plane had been seen over Ireland. The inquirers wanted specific information:

"Well, when will you get the first news?" they asked. And later:

"If he's over Ireland how long will it be before he gets to Paris?"

"Is he all right?"

The questions that were asked, considering that no news could possibly come direct from Captain Lindbergh before he landed, were as surprising as the guesses at the difference in time.

The Times Gets 10,000 Phone Calls.

The telephone inquiries came from all sorts of people and all directions. Not a few rang up THE TIMES office and apologetically explained that they were on golf links or elsewhere at a distance, and hence could not

Continued on Page Three.

LINDBERGH TRIUMPH THRILLS COOLIDGE

President Cables Praise to "Heroic Flier" and Concern for Nungesser and Coli.

CAPITAL THROBS WITH JOY

Kellogg, New, MacNider, Patrick and Many More Join in Paying Tribute to Daring Youth.

Special to The New York Times.

WASHINGTON, May 21.—The triumph of Captain Charles A. Lindbergh in flying from New York to Paris without a stop created a tremendous sensation in the national capital and found immediate response in a host of official messages and statements congratulating the daring aviator upon his achievement.

President Coolidge expressed his admiration in a message transmitted through Ambassador Herrick in Paris for delivery to the young flier in person.

With a single possible exception, this city has never been more thrilled since the armistice, when Woodrow Wilson mingled with noisy thousands in celebrating the end of the war. The exception was when Walter Johnson arose from apparent defeat and won the deciding world series baseball game in 1924.

"The American people," the President said, "rejoice with me at the brilliant termination of your heroic flight. The first non-stop flight of a lone aviator across the Atlantic crowns the record of American aviation, and in bringing the greetings of the American people to France you likewise carry the assurance of our admiration of those intrepid Frenchmen, Nungesser and Coli, whose bold spirits first ventured on your exploit, and likewise a message of our continued anxiety concerning their fate."

Secretary Kellogg, in a message similarly transmitted, said:

"I heartily congratulate you on the success of your great adventure in accomplishing a non-stop flight from New York to Paris. It is a great step in the advancement of aviation. Every one in the United States is proud of your accomplishment."

Knew Lindbergh as a Boy.

In a statement issued here Mr. Kellogg referred to his personal friendship for Lindbergh, whom he has known for years through the young man's late father, a Representative in Congress from the Secretary's home State of Minnesota.

"News has just reached me," Mr. Kellogg said, "of the success of Lindbergh in completing his flight from New York to Paris. It is an achievement of which every American can justly be proud. I have known Lindbergh since he was a boy and rejoice at this culmination of his ambitions, which could only have been gained by scientific knowledge, superb courage and physique and sterling character. Our rejoicing in Lindbergh's success, however, is tempered by our continued ignorance of the fate of Nungesser and Coli, whose courage and valor have now been equaled, but cannot be surpassed."

Hanford MacNider, Acting Secre-

Continued on Page Four.

CROWD ROARS THUNDEROUS WELCOM[E]

Breaks Through Lines of Soldiers an[d] Police and Surging to Plane Lifts Weary Flier from His Cockpit

AVIATORS SAVE HIM FROM FRENZIED MOB OF 100,0[00]

Paris Boulevards Ring With Celebration After Da[y] and Night Watch—American Flag Is Called For and Wildly Acclaimed.

By EDWIN L. JAMES.

Special Cable to THE NEW YORK TIMES.

PARIS, May 21.—Lindbergh did it. Twenty minutes aft[er] 10 o'clock tonight suddenly and softly there slipped out of t[he] darkness a gray-white airplane as 25,000 pairs of eyes strain[ed] toward it. At 10:24 the Spirit of St. Louis landed and lines [of] soldiers, ranks of policemen and stout steel fences went dow[n] before a mad rush as irresistible as the tides of the ocean.

"Well, I made it," smiled Lindbergh, as the little whi[te] monoplane came to a halt in the middle of the field and the fi[rst] vanguard reached the plane. Lindbergh made a move to jum[p] out. Twenty hands reached for him and lifted him out as if [he] were a baby. Several thousands in a minute were around t[he] plane. Thousands more broke the barriers of iron rails rou[nd] the field, cheering wildly.

Lifted From His Cockpit.

As he was lifted to the ground Lindbergh was pale, an[d] with his hair unkempt, he looked completely worn out. He h[ad] strength enough, however, to smile, and waved his hand to t[he] crowd. Soldiers with fixed bayonets were unable to keep ba[ck] the crowd.

United States Ambassador Herrick was among the first [to] welcome and congratulate the hero.

A NEW YORK TIMES man was one of the first to reach t[he] machine after its graceful descent to the field. Those fi[rst] to arrive at the plane had a picture that will live in the[ir] minds for the rest of their lives. His cap off, his famous loc[ks] falling in disarray around his eyes, "Lucky Lindy" sat peeri[ng] out over over the rim of the little cockpit of his machine.

Dramatic Scene at the Field.

It was high drama. Picture the scene. Almost if not qu[ite] 100,000 people were massed on the east side of Le Bourg[et] air field. Some of them had been there six and seven hou[rs].

Off to the left the giant phare lighthouse of Mount Va[lé]rien flashed its guiding light 300 miles into the air. Clos[e] on the left Le Bourget Lighthouse twinkled, and off to t[he] right another giant revolving phare sent its beams high in[to] the heavens.

Big arc lights on all sides with enormous electric gla[re] were flooding the landing field. From time to time rock[ets] rose and burst in varied lights over the field.

Seven thirty, the hour anounced for the arrival, had co[me] and gone. Then 8 o'clock came, and no Lindbergh; at 9 o'clo[ck] the sun had set but then came reports that Lindbergh had be[en] seen over Cork. Then he had been seen over Valentia in I[re]land and then over Plymouth.

Suddenly a message spread like lightning, the aviator h[ad] been seen over Cherbourg. However, remembering the me[s]sages telling of Captain Nungesser's flight, the crowd w[as] skeptical.

"One chance in a thousand!" "Oh, he cannot do it witho[ut] navigating instruments!" "It's a pity, because he was a bra[ve] boy." Pessimism had spread over the great throng by [10] o'clock.

The stars came out and a chill wind blew.

Watchers Are Twice Disappointed.

Suddenly the field lights flooded their glares onto the lan[d]ing ground and there came the roar of an airplane's motor. T[he] crowd was still, then began a cheer, but two minutes later t[he] landing glares went dark for the searchlight had identified t[he] plane and it was not Captain Lindbergh's.

Stamping their feet in the cold, the crowd waited patient[ly]. It seemed quite apparent that nearly every one was willing [to] wait all night, hoping against hope.

Suddenly—it was 10:16 exactly—another motor roar[ed] over the heads of the crowd. In the sky one caught a glimp[se] of a white gray plane, and for an instant heard the sound [of] one. Then it dimmed, and the idea spread that it was y[et] another disappointment.

Again landing lights glared and almost by the time th[ey] had flooded the field the gray-white plane had lighted on t[he] far side nearly half a mile from the crowd. It seemed to st[op] almost as it hit the ground, so gently did it land.

And then occurred a scene which almost passed descr[ip]tion. Two companies of soldiers with fixed bayonets and t[he] Le Bourget field police, reinforced by Paris agents, had h[eld] the crowd in good order. But as the lights showed the pla[ne]

Home Run Record Falls as Ruth Hits 60th; Pirates Lose; Giants Out of Race

[RU]TH CRASHES 60TH [TO] SET NEW RECORD

[Babe] Makes It a Real Field Day [B]y Accounting for All Runs in 4-2 Victory.

[OLD] MARK OF 59 BEATEN

[Fans] Go Wild as Ruth Pounds [B]all Into Stands With One On, Breaking 2-2 Tie.

[CON]NECTS LAST TIME UP

[Zach]ary's Offering Converted Into [Histori]chal Smash, Which Old Fan [Wat]ches—Senators Then Subside.

[Bab]e Ruth scaled the hitherto un[scal]ed heights yesterday. Home [run] 60, a terrific smash off the [south]paw pitching of Zachary, nes[tled] in the Babe's favorite spot in [the ri]ght field bleachers, and before [the ro]ar had ceased it was found that [the] drive not only had made home [run r]ecord history but also was the [winni]ng margin in a 4 to 2 victory [over] the Senators. This also was the [Yank]s' 109th triumph of the season. [Thei]r last league game of the year [will] be played today.

[Wh]en the Babe stepped to the plate [in th]at momentous eighth inning the [score] was deadlocked, Koenig was on [third] base, the result of a triple, one [man] was out and all was tense. It [was] the Babe's fourth trip to the [plate] during the afternoon, a base on [balls] and two singles resulting on [his o]ther visits plateward.

[The] first Zachary offering was a [ball] one, which sailed over for a [calle]d strike. The next was high. [The B]abe took a vicious swing at the [third] pitched ball and the bat con[necte]d with a crash that was audible [in all] parts of the stand. It was not [neces]sary to follow the course of the [ball.] The boys in the bleachers in[dicat]ed the route of the record [home]r. It dropped about half way [to th]e top. Boys. No. 60 was some [home]r, a fitting wallop to top the [Babe']s record of 59 in 1921.

[Wh]ile the crowd cheered and the [Yank]ee players roared their greet[ings] the Babe made his triumphant, [almo]st regal tour of the paths. He [jogge]d around slowly, touched each [bag] firmly and carefully and when [he i]mbedded his spikes in the rubber [of the plate] to record officially Homer [60 h]ats were tossed into the air, [paper]s were torn up and tossed lib[erall]y and the spirit of celebration [perme]ated the place.

[The] Babe's stroll out to his position [was] the signal for a handkerchief [wav]e in which all the bleacherites, [to th]e last man, participated. Jovial [Babe] entered into the carnival spirit [and] punctuated his Ringly strides [with] a succession of snappy military [salut]es.

Ruth 4, Senators 2.

[Ru]th's homer was a fitting climax [to a] game which will go down as [the] Babe's personal triumph. The [Yan]ks scored four runs, the Babe [perso]nally crossing the plate three [times] and bringing in Koenig for [the f]ourth. So this is one time where [it w]ould be fair, although not orig[inal,] to record Yankee victory [a]s Ruth, 4, Senators 2.

[Th]ere was not much else to the [game]. The 10,000 persons who came [to th]e Stadium were there for no [othe]r purpose than to see the Babe [mak]e home run history. After each [of B]abe's visits to the plate the ex[pecta]nt crowd would relax and wait [for h]is next effort. They saw him [walk] with a base on balls, follow [with] two singles and then clout the [recor]d-making circuit smash.

[Th]e only unhappy individual within [the] Stadium was Zachary. He real[ized] he was going down in the rec[ords] as the historical home run vic[tim,] in other words the goat. Zach[ary] was one of the most interested [spec]tators of the home run flight. [He t]ossed his glove to the ground, [mutt]ered to himself, turned to his [mate]s for consolation and got every[thin]g but that. There is no deny[ing t]hat Zachary was putting every[thin]g he had on the ball. No pitcher [likes t]o have recorded after his name [the f]act that he was Ruth's victim [on h]is sixtieth homer.

[The] ball that the Babe drove, ac[cordi]ng to word from official sources, [was] a pitch that was fast, low and [on] the inside. The Babe pulled [away] from the plate, then stepped [into] the ball, and wham! According [to U]mpire Bill Dinneen at the plate [and] Catcher Muddy Ruel the ball [trav]eled on a line and landed a foot [insid]e fair territory about half way [to th]e top of the bleachers. But [when] the ball reached the bleacher [barri]er it was about ten feet fair [and] curving rapidly to the right.

[F]an Rushes to Babe With Ball.

[Th]e ball which became Homer [60 w]as caught by Joe Forner of 1,937 [First] Avenue, Manhattan. He is [abou]t 40 years old and has been fol[lowin]g baseball for thirty-five, ac[cord]ing to his own admission. He [is] far from modest and as soon [as th]e game was over rushed to the [dres]sing room to let the Babe know [he] had the ball.

[Fo]r three innings both sides were [bloc]ked. The Senators broke through [in th]e fourth for two runs.

[Th]e Yanks came back with one [run] in their half of the fourth. Ruth [open]ed with a long single to right [and] moved to third on Gehrig's sin[gle t]o centre. Gehrig took second on [the] throw to third. Meusel drove [a fly] to Goslin, Ruth scoring and [Gehr]ig taking third after the catch. [Wi]th two out in the sixth Ruth [singl]ed to right. Gehrig's hit was [so f]ast that it went right through [Ruel']s for a single, Ruth holding sec[ond]. The Babe tied the score on [Meu]sel's single to centre. Lazzeri [was] an easy third out.

[Th]e box score:

[WA]SHINGTON (A.)	ab.	r.	h.	po.	a.	e.
[...] rf	3	0	1	2	0	0
[...] 2b	3	0	0	3	4	0
[...] cf	4	0	1	1	0	0
[...] lf	4	1	1	5	0	0
[...] 1b	4	0	0	9	0	0
[...] c	2	1	1	2	0	0
[...] 3b	3	0	1	1	4	0
[...] ss	4	0	0	2	1	0
[...]y, p	3	0	0	0	1	0
[...]son	1	0	0	0	0	0
Total	30	2	5	24	10	0

NEW YORK (A.)	ab.	r.	h.	po.	a.	e.
Combs, cf	4	0	0	3	0	0
Koenig, ss	4	1	1	3	5	0
Ruth, rf	3	3	3	4	0	0
Gehrig, 1b	4	0	2	10	0	1
Meusel, lf	3	0	1	3	0	0
Lazzeri, 2b	3	0	0	2	2	0
Dugan, 3b	3	0	1	1	1	0
Bengough, c	3	0	1	1	2	0
Pipgras, p	2	0	0	0	2	0
Pennock, p	1	0	0	0	1	0
Total	30	4	9	27	12	1

[a B]atted for Zachary in ninth.

[Wash]ington ....0 0 0 2 0 0 0 0 0—2
[New] York ....0 0 0 1 0 1 0 2 .—4

[Two]-base hit—Rice. Three-base hit—Koe[nig]. Home run—Ruth. Stolen bases—Ruel, [...]e, Rice. Sacrifices—Meusel. Double [play]—Harris and Bluege; Gillis, Harris and [...]e. Left on bases—New York 4, Wash[ingto]n 7. Bases on balls—Off Pipgras 4, [Braxt]ock 1, Zachary 1. Struck out—By [Zach]ary 1. Hits—Off Pipgras 4 in 6 innings, [Braxt]ock 1 in 3. Hit by pitcher—By Pipgras [...]). Winning pitcher—Pennock. Umpires [Din]neen, Connolly and Owens. Time of [game]—1:38.

> **Cards Still Can Tie in Race; Pirates Need Only One Victory**
>
> With the definite elimination of the Giants from the National League pennant race interest is centred in the West, where the Cardinals still have a forlorn chance. By winning two from the Cubs, with whom they open a final two-game stand today, the Cards can tie the Pirates, providing the latter lose their two remaining games in Cincinnati. A single victory for Pittsburgh or one defeat for the Cards will settle the race in the Pirates' favor. The following table shows the pennant chances of the two clubs:

If Win.	Won.	Lost.	P.C.
Pittsburgh.			
2	95	59	.617
1	94	60	.610
0	93	61	.604
St. Louis.			
2	93	61	.604
1	92	62	.597
0	91	63	.591

REDS HALT PIRATES IN PENNANT CHASE

Triumph by 2-1 Score and Cut Pittsburgh's Lead Over Cards to Two Games.

CRITZ AND LUCAS STAR

Former's Spectacular Fielding and Latter's Fine Pitching Win as Buccaneer Bats Fail.

By The Associated Press.

CINCINNATI, Sept. 30.—Checked in all but one inning by the brilliant twirling of Red Lucas and the sensational defensive work of Hughie Critz around second base, the league-leading Pirates lost to the Reds, 2-1, today, thereby prolonging the settlement of the National League pennant race, with only two days to go.

Lucas held the Buccaneers to six hits, two of which were bunched in an eighth-inning rally that fell one run short of knotting the score after the Cincinnati clan had pounced upon Vic Aldridge in the sixth and seventh frames for the tallies that turned out to be the deciding margin.

The setback left the Pirates dormie two, to borrow a golfing phrase, on the Cardinals. Pittsburgh holds a two-game lead, and each club has two more to play. One victory for the Pirates will clinch the pennant tomorrow or Sunday in the closing games with the Reds here, while a defeat for St. Louis in either remaining game with the Cubs would put the Cards out of the battle.

The box score:

PITTSBURGH (N.)	ab.	r.	h.	po.	a.	e.
L. Waner, rf	4	0	1	2	0	0
Barnhart, lf	4	0	2	2	0	0
P. Waner, rf	4	0	0	5	0	0
Wright, ss	4	0	0	1	3	0
Traynor, 3b	4	0	2	1	2	0
Gr'tham, 2b	4	0	0	0	3	0
Harris, 1b	2	0	0	10	0	0
Gooch, c	2	0	0	2	0	0
aBrickell	1	1	0	0	0	0
Spencer, c	0	0	0	1	0	0
Aldridge, p	2	0	0	0	2	0
bE. Smith	1	0	1	0	0	0
cCom'sky	0	0	0	0	0	0
Miljus, p	0	0	0	0	0	0
Total	32	1	6	24	9	0

CINCINNATI (N.)	ab.	r.	h.	po.	a.	e.
Dressen, 3b	3	1	2	1	1	0
Walker, rf	3	0	0	3	0	0
Pipp, 1b	3	0	0	11	2	0
Bressler, lf	4	0	0	3	0	0
Allen, cf	4	1	1	4	0	0
Ford, ss	4	0	2	2	6	1
Critz, 2b	4	0	3	3	5	0
Picinich, c	1	0	0	0	0	0
Hargrave, c	0	0	0	0	0	0
Lucas, p	3	0	0	1	3	0
Total	29	2	8	27	17	1

a Batted for Gooch in eighth.
b Batted for Aldridge in eighth.
c Ran for E. Smith in eighth.

Pittsburgh ....0 0 0 0 0 0 0 1 0—1
Cincinnati ....0 0 0 0 0 1 1 0 .—2

Two-base hits—Critz, Dressen. Three-base hit—L. Waner. Sacrifices—Picinich, Walker, Pipp. Double play—Ford, Critz and Pipp. Left on bases—Pittsburgh 5, Cincinnati 8. Base on balls—Off Aldridge 1, Lucas 1. Struck out—By Aldridge 1, Miljus 1. Hits—Off Aldridge 8 in 7 innings; Miljus none in one. Hit by pitcher—By Aldridge (Dressen). Losing pitcher—Aldridge.

BAN JOHNSON ASSAILS LANDIS AND WHITE SOX

Says Commissioner and the Chicago Club Attempted to Embarrass League.

CHICAGO, Sept. 30 (AP).—President Ban Johnson of the American League assailed the White Sox and Commissioner Landis today, berating them for lack of cooperation and accusing them of deliberately attempting to embarrass the league.

Johnson, who refused to say when his resignation as head of the league would become effective, praised the seven other members of the American League for "their common sense and business judgment in maintaining their ordinary relations with their Presidential office."

"The childish spite and rebellion on the part of the Chicago club has been matched, even outdone, by petty action of the office of the Commissioner of Baseball," he said.

"Nothing to say. Nothing at all," said Landis. "I have a copy of his statement."

The American League head's complaint of lack of cooperation was for the period since he offered his resignation as President last July. He said he would not quit the office until he had the business of the league in good shape.

BRAVES CRUSH PHILLIES.

Make 18 Safeties and Triumph, 12-2—Brown Leads Attack.

BOSTON, Sept. 30 (AP).—The Braves fell upon the offerings of Tabor and Scott for eighteen hits today, and took the second game of the series from the Phillies, 12 to 2. Brown's three doubles featured the Braves' attack. Neither team made an error.

The box score:

PHILADELPHIA (N.)	ab.	r.	h.	po.	a.	e.
Sand, 3b	3	1	0	1	3	0
Th'pson, 2b	4	0	2	4	4	0
Williams, rf	4	0	2	1	0	0
W'tstone, 1b	3	0	0	8	0	0
Leach, cf	4	0	0	5	0	0
Mokan, lf	1	0	0	1	0	0
Holman, lf	2	0	1	0	0	0
Jonnard, c	2	0	0	0	1	0
O'Donnell, c	2	0	0	2	0	0
Cooney, ss	3	1	1	0	2	0
Dietrich, ss	1	0	0	0	1	0
Tabor, p	1	0	0	1	1	0
Scott, p	2	0	0	1	0	0
Total	31	2	6	24	12	0

BOSTON (N.)	ab.	r.	h.	po.	a.	e.
Rich'rg, rf	4	2	2	1	0	0
Gautreau, 2b	3	3	1	1	5	0
J. Smith, cf	4	3	3	3	0	0
Brown, lf	4	2	3	2	0	0
Fournier, 1b	3	0	1	13	1	0
Farrell, ss	4	1	2	3	2	0
Moore, 3b	5	1	2	0	3	0
Hogan, c	5	1	3	3	0	0
Genewich, p	4	0	1	1	2	0
Total	35	12	18	27	13	0

Philadelphia ....1 0 0 0 1 0 0 0 0— 2
Boston ....3 4 0 1 0 3 1 0 .—12

Two-base hits—Cooney, Brown 3, J. Smith, Hogan, Genewich. Stolen bases—J. Smith, Brown, Fournier. Sacrifices—Wrightstone, J. Smith, Brown, Farrell, Genewich. Double plays—Thompson and Wrightstone; Dietrich, Thompson and Wrightstone; Genewich, Farrell and Fournier. Left on bases—Philadelphia 5, Boston 9. Bases on balls—Off Tabor 2, Scott 3, Genewich 2. Struck out—By Scott 2, Genewich 3. Hits—Off Tabor 6 in 1 1-3, Scott 12 in 6 2-3. Hit by pitcher—By Tabor (Fournier).

GIANT DEFEAT ENDS THEIR GALLANT RACE

Last Pennant Hope Snuffed as Robins Win by 10-5 at Ebbets Field.

VANCE PROVES BAFFLING

Holds McGrawmen Safely While His Mates Pound Three New York Hurlers.

By JAMES R. HARRISON.

According to every known system of mathematics, including logarithms, the Giants are out of the 1927 pennant race. Their last chance evaporated yesterday afternoon at Ebbets Field when Dazzy Vance and the artful Dodgers plastered a 10-5 defeat on the McGrawmen. Now the Giants haven't got a chance to win the pennant.

For more than two months now the Giants have been in the throes of a nerveracking struggle. At one time they were only half a game out of first place. From a distant point some eight games in the rear they battled forward until they were so close to the Pirates' coat tails that Barney Dreyfuss turned a quaint shade of purple and could not sleep at night.

But it all ended yesterday when Vance baffled our lads while the Messrs. Henry, Barnes and Fitzsimmons were doing no baffling to speak of. In fact, they were not even mildly mysterious. Going into the seventh the score was 4 to 4, but Barnes was knocked out with nobody down, and before Fitzsimmons could apply the brakes the Dodgers were in possession of six runs.

Giants Take the Lead.

The Giants still have a chance to tie the Cardinals for second place, but this is considered most unlikely.

The Dodgers scored four of their runs in the fifth and the six others in the seventh. The efforts of the Giants were more scattered. They rapped Vance for two in the first. Mueller was hit, Reese singled off Vance's glove, and when the Dazzler hurled the ball over Herman's head Mueller scored and Reese went to second, scoring on Roush's single to right.

In the second Harper doubled to centre, took third on Statz's bad return and counted on Cummings's sacrifice fly.

The score was 3-0 for the Giants when the Dodgers suffered a rush of blood to the head and scored four runs in the fifth. Singles by Flowers and Butler and DeBerry's walk filled the bags, with one out. Vance's fly scored Flowers and Statz's double admitted two. The Jigger romped in on Carey's two-bagger.

By dint of much effort the Giants tied the score in their half of the seventh, and this was the exact situation when the Robins went into another trance and scored six runs in their section of the frame.

Barnes, who had relieved Henry at the start of the inning, walked Butler. Reese fumbled DeBerry's bunt and Vance strolled, filling the bases with none out. Whereupon Barnes was given an indefinite sick leave and the good Fitzsimmons wheeled in to take his place. Statz greeted Freddy with a short single to right, scoring Butler.

Harper's Triple Wasted.

With the bases still thickly populated the ancient Carey paddled a double down the left-field foul line and three Robins winged swiftly home. The other details don't matter much. Felix bunted Carey to third and Max scored on Herman's two-bagger. Partridge's base hit sent the Babe home.

The box score:

NEW YORK (N.)	ab.	r.	h.	po.	a.	e.
Mueller, lf	4	1	0	2	0	0
Reese, 3b	3	1	1	1	1	1
Roush, cf	4	0	1	2	0	0
Hornsby, 2b	2	0	0	1	2	0
Terry, 1b	4	0	1	9	1	0
Jackson, ss	4	0	0	2	3	0
Harper, rf	2	1	2	3	0	0
Cummings, c	3	0	1	2	0	0
aMann	0	0	0	0	0	0
Taylor, c	1	0	0	2	0	0
Henry, p	2	0	0	0	0	0
bOtt	1	0	0	0	0	0
Barnes, p	0	0	0	0	0	0
Fitzsim'ns, p	0	0	0	0	1	0
cDevormer	1	0	0	0	0	0
Total	31	5	6	24	8	1

BROOKLYN (N.)	ab.	r.	h.	po.	a.	e.
Statz, cf	4	2	2	3	0	1
Carey, rf	5	1	2	1	0	0
Felix, lf	3	0	0	3	0	0
Herman, 1b	3	1	1	10	0	0
Flowers, ss	4	1	2	0	2	1
Part'dge, 2b	4	0	1	5	2	1
Butler, 3b	2	2	1	1	2	1
DeBerry, c	2	2	0	4	1	0
Vance, p	3	1	0	0	1	1
Total	29	10	9	27	8	5

a Ran for Cummings in seventh.
b Batted for Henry in seventh.
c Batted for Fitzsimmons in ninth.

New York ....2 1 0 0 0 0 1 0 1— 5
Brooklyn ....0 0 0 0 4 0 6 0 .—10

Two-base hits—Statz, Carey (2), Herman. Three-base hit—Harper. Sacrifices—Hornsby, Cummings, Vance, Felix, De Berry. Double plays—Terry, Jackson and Terry; Hornsby and Terry; Flowers, Partridge and Herman. Left on bases—New York 5, Brooklyn, 4. Bases on balls—Off Vance, 3; Henry, 3; Barnes, 2. Struck out—By Vance, 4; Henry, 1; Fitzsimmons, 2. Hit by pitcher—By Vance (Mueller); by Fitzsimmons (Butler). Hits—Off Henry, 5 in 6 innings; Barnes, 0 in 0, (none out in seventh); Fitzsimmons, 4 in 2. Losing pitcher—Barnes. Umpires—Moran, Rigler and Wilson. Time of game—1:45.

INDIANS DIVIDE 2 GAMES.

Win First From Browns, 5-4; Then Lose by 9 to 4.

ST. LOUIS, Sept. 30 (AP).—The Browns and Indians divided a double-header here today, the Indians winning the first, 5 to 4, and the Browns taking the second, 9 to 4.

J. Sewell's homer in the sixth with two on was the feature of the first game. In the second game, Wright held the visitors to five hits while his teammates were garnering 13.

FIRST GAME.

CLEVELAND (A.)	ab.	r.	h.	po.	a.	e.
Gill, lf	5	0	1	0	0	0
Ussatti, 2b	3	0	0	0	2	0
Summa, rf	4	1	1	2	0	0
Hodapp, 1b	4	1	2	12	0	1
J. Sewell, ss	4	1	1	5	2	0
L. Sewell, c	4	0	1	4	1	0
Langford, cf	3	2	2	1	0	0
Lind, 2b	1	0	0	1	3	0
Hudlin, p	3	0	0	0	4	0
Total	31	5	8	27	13	1

ST. LOUIS (A.)	ab.	r.	h.	po.	a.	e.
Adams, 3b	4	1	1	1	0	0
Rice, rf	4	2	2	4	0	0
Sturdy, 1b	4	0	3	9	1	0
Williams, lf	4	0	1	0	1	0
E. Miller, cf	4	0	1	3	0	0
Schang, c	4	0	0	3	1	0
Melillo, 2b	3	0	0	4	3	0
Kress, ss	4	1	1	2	4	0
Blaeh'der, p	3	0	1	1	3	0
aBennett	1	0	0	0	0	0
Total	35	4	10	27	13	0

a Batted for Blaeholder in ninth.

Cleveland ....0 0 0 0 0 3 1 0 1—5
St. Louis ....1 0 0 1 0 0 2 0 0—4

Two-base hits—E. Miller, Kress, Langford (2), Blaeholder. Home run—J. Sewell. Sacrifices—Hudlin, Melillo. Stolen base—Sturdy. Double plays—Schang, Kress and Sturdy; Melillo and Sturdy. Passed ball—Schang. Hit by pitcher—By Blaeholder (Lind). Bases on balls—Off Hudlin 2, Blaeholder 4. Struck out—By Hudlin 3, Blaeholder 2.

SECOND GAME.

CLEVELAND (A.)	ab.	r.	h.	po.	a.	e.
Gill, lf	3	1	0	3	0	0
Ussatti, 3b	4	1	1	1	1	0
Summa, rf	3	1	0	0	0	0
Hodapp, 1b	3	0	1	9	0	1
J. Sewell, ss	4	1	1	1	1	1
Myatt, c	4	0	1	7	0	0
Langford, cf	4	0	0	2	1	0
Lind, 2b	4	0	1	2	6	0
Underhill, p	1	0	0	0	0	0
McKain, p	2	0	0	0	2	0
aBurnett	1	0	0	0	0	0
Total	33	4	5	24	12	2

ST. LOUIS (A.)	ab.	r.	h.	po.	a.	e.
Allen, 2b	3	3	1	3	2	1
Rice, 3b	4	2	2	0	1	0
Sturdy, 1b	5	2	3	8	1	1
Williams, lf	4	1	2	5	0	0
E. Miller, cf	3	0	1	1	0	0
Bennett, rf	4	0	2	4	0	0
Kress, ss	3	0	2	2	6	0
Dixon, c	3	0	0	3	0	0
Wright, p	3	1	0	1	0	0
Total	34	9	13	27	10	2

a Batted for Underhill in fifth.

Cleveland ....4 0 0 0 0 0 0 0 0—4
St. Louis ....2 2 0 4 0 0 1 0 .—9

Two-base hits—J. Sewell, Myatt, Allen, Kress, Rice. Sacrifices—E. Miller, Bennett. Double play—Lessatti, Lind and Hodapp. Left on bases—St. Louis 1, Cleveland 5. Bases on balls—Off Wright 3, Underhill 6, McKain 1. Struck out—By Wright 3, McKain 3, Underhill 2. Hits—Off Underhill 8 in 4 innings, McKain 5 in 4. Wild pitch—McKain.

MAJOR LEAGUE BASEBALL

AMERICAN LEAGUE.

YESTERDAY'S RESULTS.
New York 4, Washington 2.
Chicago 5, Detroit 4 (1st game). (13 innings.)
Chicago 4, Detroit 1 (2d). (6 innings; darkness.)
Cleveland 5, St. Louis 4 (1st).
St. Louis 9, Cleveland 4 (2d).
Boston at Philadelphia. (Postponed by agreement.)

STANDING OF THE CLUBS.

	Won.	Lost.	P.C.
New York	109	44	.712
Philadelphia	89	62	.589
Washington	84	68	.553
Detroit	80	71	.530
Chicago	68	82	.453
Cleveland	66	85	.437
St. Louis	58	92	.387
Boston	51	101	.336

WHERE THEY PLAY TODAY.
Washington at New York (3 P. M.).
Boston at Philadelphia (2).
St. Louis at Chicago.
Cleveland at Detroit.

NATIONAL LEAGUE.

YESTERDAY'S RESULTS.
Brooklyn 10, New York 5.
Boston 12, Philadelphia 2.
Cincinnati 2, Pittsburgh 1.
Other clubs not scheduled.

STANDING OF THE CLUBS.

	Won.	Lost.	P.C.
Pittsburgh	93	59	.612
St. Louis	91	61	.599
New York	90	62	.592
Chicago	85	67	.559
Cincinnati	74	77	.490
Brooklyn	64	87	.424
Boston	58	93	.384
Philadelphia	51	100	.338

WHERE THEY PLAY TODAY.
New York at Brooklyn (3 P. M.).
Philadelphia at Boston.
Pittsburgh at Cincinnati.
Chicago at St. Louis.

VEACH'S HOME RUN WINS FOR TOLEDO

Blow Nets 3 Tallies and Beats Buffalo, 5-2, in Little World Series Opener.

JESS BARNES ALSO A HERO

Former Giant Holds Bisons to Five Hits Before 9,890 Fans—Teams Off for East.

By The Associated Press.

TOLEDO, Ohio, Sept. 30.—The Toledo club, champions of the American Association, upholding the honor of their circuit in the junior world's series for the first time, defeated the Buffalo Internationals, 5 to 2, today in the twice postponed inaugural of the series.

It was almost a personal victory for Bobby Veach, who drove in three Toledo runs with a fence-clearing homer, and Jess Barnes, the Toledo twirler and former Giant, who held the Bisons to five scattered hits.

The official attendance was 9,890. At midnight tonight the two teams and about 500 Toledo rooters left on special trains for Saturday and Sunday games at Buffalo. They return here Tuesday to resume the series, until one team has won five games.

The box score:

BUFFALO (I.)	ab.	r.	h.	po.	a.	e.
Tyson, cf	4	0	2	1	0	0
Carter, lf	3	0	0	0	0	1
Fisher, rf	4	1	1	1	0	0
Bissonett, 1b	4	0	1	11	1	0
Cohen, ss	4	0	0	1	4	1
Huber, 3b	4	0	0	2	4	0
Malone, 2b	3	0	0	5	4	1
Devine, c	3	1	1	3	1	0
Mangum, p	1	0	0	0	0	0
Stryker, p	1	0	0	0	2	0
aFalk	0	0	0	0	0	0
Leverens, p	0	0	0	0	0	0
Total	31	2	5	24	16	3

TOLEDO (AA.)	ab.	r.	h.	po.	a.	e.
Leb'veau, rf	3	1	1	1	0	0
Maguire, 2b	3	0	0	3	4	1
Marriott, 3b	4	1	0	0	4	0
Veach, lf	4	2	3	1	0	0
Grimes, 1b	3	1	0	12	2	0
Koehler, cf	3	0	1	4	0	0
O'Neil, c	3	0	0	3	0	0
Cote, ss	3	0	2	2	7	0
Barnes, p	3	0	0	1	1	0
Total	29	5	7	27	18	1

a Batted for Stryker in eighth.

Buffalo ....0 0 0 1 0 0 0 1 0—2
Toledo ....0 2 3 0 0 0 0 0 .—5

Three-base hit—Veach. Home run—Veach. Left on bases—Toledo 2, Buffalo 4. Sacrifices—Carter, Maguire. Double play—Huber, Malone and Bissonette. Struck out—By Barnes 2, Mangum 1, Stryker 1. Hits—Off Mangum 5 in 1-1-3 innings, Stryker 1 in 5 2-3. Base on balls—Off Barnes 1, Leverens 1. Umpires—Guthrie and Finneran. Time of game—1:36.

WHITE SOX WIN TWICE.

Beat Tigers, 5-4, in 13 Innings; Then Score, 4-1—Falk Stars.

CHICAGO, Sept. 30 (AP).—Chicago took both games of a double-header from Detroit here today, by scores of 5 to 4 and 4 to 1, respectively. Bib Falk's batting was the winning factor for the White Sox. He broke up the first game with a single in the thirteenth inning, which enabled Tommy Thomas to register his eighteenth victory of the season.

The box scores:

FIRST GAME.

DETROIT (A.)	ab.	r.	h.	po.	a.	e.
Blue, 1b	5	1	2	17	0	2
Gehringer, 2b	6	1	1	3	6	1
Manush, cf	5	1	0	6	0	0
Heilmann, rf	5	0	3	4	0	0
Ruble, lf	3	0	0	2	0	0
aNeun	1	0	0	0	0	0
Fothergill, lf	1	0	1	0	0	0
McManus, 3b	5	1	3	0	0	0
Tavener, ss	4	0	0	0	4	1
Bassler, c	5	0	0	5	2	0
Gibson, p	5	0	0	0	6	0
Total	44	4	9	*38	18	2

CHICAGO (A.)	ab.	r.	h.	po.	a.	e.
Hunnef'ld, ss	6	1	2	5	0	0
Kamm, 3b	4	1	2	2	4	0
Barrett, rf	5	0	1	1	0	0
Falk, lf	6	0	2	4	0	0
Neis, cf	5	0	0	6	1	0
Clancy, 1b	5	1	1	11	1	0
Ward, 2b	4	0	1	2	4	0
McCurdy, c	5	1	1	7	2	0
Thomas, p	5	0	0	1	3	0
Total	45	5	9	39	14	0

a Batted for Ruble in eighth.
* Two out when winning run was scored.

Detroit ....0 0 0 0 1 2 0 1 0 0 0 0 0—4
Chicago ....0 0 0 0 3 1 0 0 0 0 0 0 1—5

Two-base hits—Heilmann (2), Blue, McManus. Three-base hits—Hunnefield, Clancy. Home run—McManus. Stolen base—Gehringer. Sacrifices—Kamm, Ruble, Tavener, Barrett. Double plays—Neis, McCurdy, Kamm and McCurdy. Left on bases—Detroit, 5; Chicago, 6. Bases on balls—Off Thomas, 2; Gibson, 2. Struck out—By Thomas, 3; Gibson, 2. Struck out—By Thomas, 3; Gibson, 4. Umpires—McGowan, Evans and Hilderbrand. Time of game—2:14.

SECOND GAME.

DETROIT (A.)	ab.	r.	h.	po.	a.	e.
Blue, 1b	3	0	1	7	0	0
Gehr'g'r, 2b	3	0	0	1	3	0
Manush, cf	3	1	2	2	0	0
Heilmann, rf	2	0	1	1	0	0
Ruble, lf	2	0	1	0	0	0
McManus, 3b	2	0	0	0	0	0
Tavener, ss	3	0	1	3	1	0
Woodall, c	3	0	1	0	1	0
Stoner, p	3	0	0	0	2	0
Total	21	1	6	15	7	0

CHICAGO (A.)	ab.	r.	h.	po.	a.	e.
Hun'f'ld, ss	3	0	1	0	2	0
Kamm, 3b	1	2	1	4	1	0
Barrett, rf	2	1	0	1	0	0
Falk, lf	3	0	1	0	0	0
Neis, cf	3	0	0	1	0	0
Clancy, 1b	3	0	0	4	1	0
Ward, 2b	2	0	2	1	0	0
Crouse, c	3	0	0	6	2	0
Faber, p	1	1	1	1	3	0
Total	19	4	6	18	9	0

Detroit ....0 0 0 1 0 0—1
Chicago ....0 0 3 0 1 .—4

Sacrifices—Kamm, Ruble, Faber. Double plays—Gehringer, Tavener and Blue. Left on bases—Detroit 5, Chicago 5. Bases on balls—Off Faber 2, Stoner 3. Struck out—By Faber 4. Wild pitch—Stoner. Umpires—Hildebrand, Evans and McGowan. Time of game—1:03.

PACIFIC COAST LEAGUE.

AT SAN FRANCISCO.

		R.	H.	E.
Portland	3 0 0 0 2 0 0 0 3	8	15	3
Missions	0 0 1 0 0 0 0 0 0	1	7	2

Batteries—Hughes and Yelle; Pillette and Baldwin.

AT OAKLAND.

		R.	H.	E.
San Francisco	0 0 2 0 0 0 0 0 0	2	6	3
Oakland	1 0 2 0 3 5 0 0 .	11	15	1

Batteries—Ferguson and Jolley; Delaney and Read.

AT SACRAMENTO.

		R.	H.	E.
Los Angeles	0 1 0 2 0 0 1 0 0	4	10	2
Sacramento	0 0 0 7 0 0 0 3 .	10	14	2

Batteries—Cunningham and Hannah; Keefe and Severeid.

AT LOS ANGELES.

		R.	H.	E.
Seattle	1 0 2 0 1 0 0 2 1	7	10	4
Hollywood	4 0 0 1 0 0 0 2 1	8	9	3

Batteries—Nance and Borreani; McCabe and Cook.

STANDING OF THE CLUBS.

	W.	L.	P.C.		W.	L.	P.C.
Oakland	118	74	.614	Portland	93	94	.497
S. Frisco	103	88	.544	Hollywood	90	103	.466
Seattle	97	90	.518	Missions	85	108	.440
S'cramento	98	94	.510	L. Angeles	79	114	.400

DI VODI WINS BOUT; GROVE FOULS HIM

After Two Warnings the Loser Is Disqualified in Third Round at Dexter Park.

SANSTOL GETS SEMI-FINAL

Batters Ferrentino Hard to Get Verdict in Six Rounds—Harry Wallach Is Victor.

Andy DiVodi of Bay Ridge triumphed over Izzy Grove of the east side at Dexter Park last night when Grove fouled him after 2 minutes and 49 seconds of the third round. Up to this point neither man had a decided advantage.

After two warnings by Referee Denny on blows which were fairly low, Grove sunk a very low punch and DiVodi dropped to the floor. The referee promptly awarded the bout to DiVodi. A sizable crowd witnessed the bouts.

DiVodi and Grove met smartly in the centre of the ring at the start of the fight. DiVodi jarred his opponent with a left hook and successive right crosses. Grove came back with left jabs which were generally effective.

The second round started at an even faster pace. The fighters swung away and Grove's body punching brought an admonition from the referee. Near the end of the round they both slugged, but the bell saved one of them from dropping under the others' fire.

Grove pressed his advantage in the third, but DiVodi stood up under his attack and action continued at an accelerated pace. After Grove received a second warning from the referee he sunk a low blow and the bout was over.

Sanstol Batters Rival.

Joey Ferrentino of South Brooklyn and Pete Sanstol met in the semi-final bout. It started slowly, but in the second round Sanstol opened fire and gave Ferrentino a good battering. Ferrentino bled from the mouth and was nearly knocked out in this session. He came back strongly in the third, however, and held his opponet fairly even.

In the fourth they both slugged and Sanstol finally pinned his opponent to the ropes and let fly with both hands. Ferrentino partially evened the score in the fifth, when one of his wild swings caught Sanstol on the eye, opening a cut and nearly knocking him out. Sanstol kept to his feet and came bck strongly in the next session to give Ferretino another pummeling and won the decision.

In the bout before the semi-final, Harry Wallach, Brownsville southpaw, 144½ pounds, easily outclassed Bobby Robadou of Philadelphia, 139 pounds. Wallach pounded his rival all over the ring but failed to rock Robadou with a single blow.

Smith Wins Close Bout.

In the third six-round bout Willie Smith of Ridgewood, 153 pounds, gained a verdict over Ernest Sarjeis, Chile, 157½ pounds. The fight was close, with Smith just earning the decision.

Al Parenti of South Brooklyn, 142½ pounds, won the second six-rounder by vanquishing Al Snyder of Williamsburg, 139½ pounds. Parenti gave his opponent an unmerciful beating, rolling up a big margin on points.

In the opening six-rounder Charley Raymond of Wallabout Section, 116½ pounds, outpointed Dick Welch of Mulberry Bend, 115½ pounds in a fast encounter.

Johnny Krieger of Yorkville, 161½ pounds, knocked out Ruby Cohen of the Brooklyn Navy Yard, 163 pounds, after 57 seconds of the fifth round of their bout. Krieger pummeled Cohen from the opening bell of the first round.

WALKER-BERLENBACH SIGN FOR COAST BOUT

Kearns Hopes to Have Fight in Los Angeles Billed as for the Light-Heavyweight Title.

Mickey Walker, world's middleweight champion, and Paul Berlenbach, former light-heavyweight titleholder, yesterday were signed to contracts for a ten-round bout in Los Angeles on Nov. 21, 22 or 23, which will be billed as for the world's light-heavyweight title. The contest was signed by Promoter Dick Donald, the man who made California ring history with the Ace Hudkins-Sammy Baker welterweight battle and its gate of $92,000 in Los Angeles last Summer, at the Park Central Hotel, where Jack Kearns, manager of Walker, is making his headquarters.

Attending the signing were Walker and Berlenbach, Kearns, Ben Stern, who is looking after Berlenbach's ring business since the break between the Astoria Assassin and his old manager, Dan Hickey; Billy McCarney, who acted as agent for Donald in the preliminary negotiations, and Teddy Hayes, trainer of Walker.

MALONEY STOPPED BY HEENEY IN FIRST

Is Put Away in 1 Minute 17 Seconds Before 13,000 in Garden Bout.

QUICK FINISH SURPRISES

Right to Jaw Knocks Out the Boston Boxer—Dempsey Acclaimed at Ringside.

By JAMES P. DAWSON.

Jack Dempsey came back to a New York ring last night at Madison Square Garden to a reception which dinned into his ears and must have warmed his heart, and then sat back in his first-row seat to see Tom Heeney, chunky New Zealand heavyweight, knock out Jim Maloney, Boston Irishman, in the first round of what was to have been a ten-round bout featuring a card which attracted 13,000 people to Tex Rickard's arena of sport.

A solid right-hand smash to the jaw sent Maloney nose-diving into the canvas from an exchange at the ropes near a neutral corner and the Hub lad was counted out on his knees after exactly 1 minute 17 seconds of action.

The knockout came as a shock, not in the sense that it was unexpected, but in that it came so suddenly. The men had hardly warmed to their task —were doing little more than sizing each other up, as a matter of fact, and the fans were settling back to enjoy a battle which promised to go a few rounds anyway, when Heeney's finishing right curled over to Maloney's unprotected jaw, and Maloney pitched headforemost to the canvas.

Dempsey was among the most surprised of the big throng. With his wife he entered the arena just as Maloney and Heeney were clambering up to the platform. Mrs. Dempsey went to Promoter Rickard's private box to watch the mêlée, while the former champion, acknowledging the greetings of countless friends clustered in the glare of the powerful ring lights, sat near the ring.

Dempsey Receives Ovation.

The reception Dempsey received was one of the greatest ever accorded anybody in a Garden ring. The man who was making his first public appearance in fight surroundings since the night a little more than a week ago when he failed to wrest the title from Gene Tunney in Chicago was affected by it, too.

James J. Jeffries, world's champion of another generation, was led to the ring by Boxing Commissioner William Muldoon. Jeffries climbed through the ropes to greet the former champion of the present generation and, as these two ring heroes greeted each other, the din of the crowd was terrific.

It would have been a grand climax to have the distinguished guests of the night and the throng which paid $35,930 witness a thrilling, heart-stirring spectacle. But that was not to be. Somehow or other the feeling overtook you as you sat at the ringside that this fight was to be short. It was. And it was the battle which probably means an end to the career of a man who only a year ago was being seriously considered for a fight with Champion Gene Tunney. The knockout by Heeney, coming as it did on top of the one-round knockout scored recently by George Godfrey, and the knockout by Jack Sharkey, of which he also was the victim, just about put finis to the career of Maloney.

Touchstone Turns Tables.

Benny Touchstone, Florida heavyweight, turned the tables on Harold Mays, Bayonne heavyweight, in the ten-round semi-final, carrying off the decision after a bitter battle which started with the first bell and didn't end until the final gong clanged. The triumph enabled Touchstone to square accounts with Mays for a decision the New Jersey lad won in their previous meeting.

Touchstone squared this account and more. He won by the margin of seven rounds to three, losing only the first, fifth and eighth sessions.

Napoleon Jack Dorval, picked by Jack Kearns after his break with Jack Dempsey as the most likely successor to the heavyweight throne, knocked out Farmer Joe Smith, Stamford gladiator, in the first round of their scheduled six-round battle. A long left to the body and a right to the jaw finished the farmer for the night after 2 minutes 46 seconds of the first round.

In the other bout scheduled for six rounds Andre Castano, Spanish heavyweight, knocked out Larry Bello of Brooklyn in the fourth round. A right to the jaw ended an exciting struggle.

Lew Warshaw, Brooklynite, carried off the decision over Frankie Goodman, Missourian, in their four-round encounter, which was the second bout on the card. In the opening skirmish, slated for four rounds, Rosey Boutot, former amateur boxer, making his first professional effort, knocked out Tony Clifford of Brooklyn in two rounds.

FLOWERS DEFEATS LATZO.

Former Middleweight Champion Gets Judges' Decision in Wilkes-Barre.

WILKES-BARRE, Pa., Sept. 30 (AP)—Tiger Flowers, former middleweight champion, tonight battled his way to a ten-round judges' decision over Pete Latzo of Scranton, former welterweight titleholder. Latzo made his middleweight début after he lost his welterweight crown to Joe Dundee of Baltimore a few months ago.

Newspaper men at the ringside gave Latzo an even break in two rounds—the second and the fifth—but aside from that the fight was all Flowers. Short, choppy blows by the Georgia warrior puzzled Latzo throughout the contest.

Flowers weighed 168 and Latzo 164 pounds.

Athletics Play Two Games Today.

PHILADELPHIA, Sept. 30 (AP).—Today's scheduled game between the Red Sox and Athletics has been called off to permit a double header to be played tomorrow, winding up the baseball season in Philadelphia.

BOXING BOUTS TONIGHT.

Ridgewood Grove S. C.—Tony Vaccarelli vs. Joey Kaufman; Arthur De Champlian vs Joe Barbara; Willie Seigel vs. Joey Goodman; Canada Lee vs. Jimmy La Ducca; Guy Mastrione vs. Harry Meyer. Five six-round bouts. Jimmy Rappaport vs. Frankie Minerva; Sammy Farber vs. Mike Gatt. Two four-round bouts.

Fourteenth Regiment Armory, Brooklyn—Nick Palmer vs. Joe La Salle; Johnny Ciccarelli vs. Pete Martin; Tommy Aboba vs. Billy Flood. Three eight-round bouts. Joey (Kid) Mack vs. Johnny Long, six rounds. Jimmy Dunne vs. Henry Stark; Carl Anderson vs. Nick Santis. Two four-round bouts.

Ninth Coast Artillery—Irish Mickey Whalen vs. Al Matera, ten rounds. Four other matches.

> **Five Leading Batsmen In Each Major League**

AMERICAN LEAGUE.

Player and Club.	G.	AB.	R.	H.	PC.
Heilmann, Detroit	139	493	104	192	.389
Simmons, Phila.	103	394	82	152	.386
Gehrig, New York	154	581	148	218	.375
Fothergill, Detroit	140	519	91	187	.360
Ruth, New York	150	537	157	192	.358

Leader a year ago today, Manush, Detroit, .378.

NATIONAL LEAGUE.

Player and Club.	G.	AB.	R.	H.	PC.
P. Waner, Pitts.	154	617	113	234	.379
Hornsby, N. Y.	153	562	132	202	.359
L. Waner, Pitts.	148	619	132	217	.350
Stephenson, Chi.	151	576	99	197	.342
Traynor, Pitts.	148	568	92	193	.340

Leader a year ago today, Hargrave, Cincinnati, .334.

FUGAZY RESTORED TO GOOD STANDING

Commission Acts After Promoter Reimburses Chapman —Clubs Get Their Dates.

The difficulties in which Promoter Humbert Fugazy recently found himself with the State Athletic Commission were adjusted yesterday at the board's meeting and his name was stricken from the list of ineligibles. Fugazy, suspended last Tuesday until he paid to Charlie Cardio, manager of Red Chapman, that part of Chapman's forfeit of $2,000 which had not been drawn against, yesterday paid the money to the commission.

The scramble for dates for the 1927-28 indoor season was settled, the commission feels, to the satisfaction of the rival clubs which filed applications for weekly dates. Monday was awarded to the Lenox S. C. in Harlem; New Broadway Arena, Brooklyn, and the Brighton Boxing Club in Staten Island. The St. Nicholas Arena received Tuesday and the Pioneer A. C. Wednesday. On Thursdays the Columbus S. C. of Yonkers is licensed to run, and Madison Square Garden received its long established date, Friday of every week through the season without opposition. The only club getting Saturday was the New Ridgewood Grove S. C. in Brooklyn.

Matchmaker Jess McMahon applied to the commission for three Monday dates and two Thursday dates as he needed them, giving the den disclosed that other attractions there will deprive the arena of five Friday night shows. He was advised, however, to apply for the individual rates as he needed them, giving the commission two weeks to consider each application as it developed.

HAGENLACHER RUNS LEAD TO 1,000-708

Challenger Wins Second Block of World's 18.2 Play From Cochran, 500 to 376.

HIS AVERAGE IS 35 10-14

While Cochran's Is 28 12-13 and 23 18-30 for Match Against Rival's 33 10-30.

By The Associated Press.

CHICAGO, Sept. 30.—Eric Hagenlacher of Germany tonight strengthened his grip on Welker Cochran's world 18.2 balkline billiard crown by winning the second block of their world's championship 1,500-point match to gain a lead of 1,000 to 708.

Hagenlacher won the second 500-point block, 500 to 376. He also won the first, played last night, 500 to 332.

Starting from his unfinished run of last night, Hagenlacher scored only four before he missed an easy left-handed draw shot. Thus at the end of the seventeenth inning the total score was: Hagenlacher, 504; Cochran, 332.

Gathering the ivories by a remarkable three-cushion shot in the nineteenth inning, Hagenlacher scored a run of 135 for a match total of 642. Time and again the challenger nursed the balls, and, when apparently about to miss, used massé and bank shots to group the balls. He missed his 136th try with a two-cushioned draw.

Cochran was in poor form, and in the nineteenth and twentieth innings scored only ten points for a total score of 396.

Hagenlacher made only ten in the twentieth inning for a total of 652.

Hagenlacher scored 84 in the twenty-first and 2 in the twenty-second for a grand match total of 738. A long two-cushion draw shot the length of the table by Cochran in the twenty-second inning drew the loudest applause of both nights. He ran 45 and missed.

The grand total score at the end of the twenty-fifth inning was: Hagenlacher, 907; Cochran, 527. The champion scored 26 in the twenty-third, 22 in the twenty-fourth and 38 in the next, while Hagenlacher picked up 113, 17 and 39 in the same inning.

Tonight's score by innings:

Hagenlacher—*4 3 135 10 84 2 113 17 39 38 11 2 1 59—Total 500. Average 35 10-14. High run 135.

Cochran—54 6 4 0 45 26 22 38 85 94 2 0 0—Total 376. Average 28 2-13. High run 94.

Grand average—Hagenlacher 33 10-30. Cochran 23 18-30

High match run—Lagenlacher 154, Cochran 94.

*Unfinished from last night.

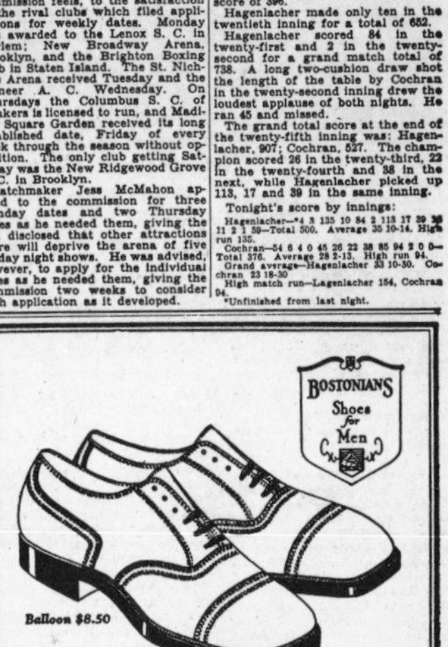

Horses and Equipment.

"All the News That's Fit to Print."

The New York Times.

Copyright, 1929, by The New York Times Company.

THE WEATHER
Rain today and probably tomorrow; somewhat colder tomorrow.
Temperatures Yesterday—Max. 54, Min. 43.
U. S. Weather Forecast—For details see Page 63.

VOL. LXXIX....No. 26,211. NEW YORK, TUESDAY, OCTOBER 29, 1929. TWO CENTS in Greater New York | THREE CENTS Within 200 Miles | FOUR CENTS Elsewhere Except 7th and 8th Postal

STOCK PRICES SLUMP $14,000,000,000 IN NATION-WIDE STAMPEDE TO UNLOAD; BANKERS TO SUPPORT MARKET TOD

BINGHAM ACCUSES SENATORS OF PLOT TO BESMIRCH HIM; NORRIS TO ASK FOR CENSURE

BINGHAM'S ATTACK BITTER

Charges Lobby Inquiry With Throwing at Him 'Political Slime.'

CALLS ITS METHODS UNFAIR

Caraway Asking Those to Stand Who Approve Eyanson Episode, Gets No Response.

OTHER MEMBERS HIT BACK

Norris Will Draw Up Resolution Against Connecticut Senator for Presentation Today.

Special to The New York Times.

WASHINGTON, Oct. 28.—Senator Hiram Bingham of Connecticut bitterly attacked in the Senate today the lobby investigating committee which had shown that he had employed an official of the Connecticut Manufacturers' Association as his tariff adviser, and drew, in turn, from the four members active in the committee's work, a series of vigorous assaults on his course.

Senator Bingham charged that the Senators who examined him as a witness had treated him unfairly, and by "twisting and torturing his testimony" had indicated that the committee's whole effort was to cover him with as much "political slime" as possible. "This modern Spanish Inquisition" was one way in which he characterized the inquiry.

Senator Norris, chairman of the Judiciary Committee of which the lobby committee is a subcommittee, said he would offer a resolution tomorrow. His resolution, it is said, will be one of censure for the Connecticut Senator. The Nebraskan did not hear all the accusations made against the subcommittee, and explained that he would read Senator Bingham's speech before acting.

"In the beginning," Senator Norris said, "I was disposed to sympathize with Senator Bingham, but if he said what he is reported to have said, I think the Senate should take some action."

Charges Committee Was 'Packed.'

Senator Bingham, whose speech was a surprise to his Republican colleagues, contended that the composition of the Lobby Committee, consisting of two Democrats, Senators Caraway of Arkansas and Walsh of Montana, two Western insurgent Republicans, Senators Blaine of Wisconsin and Borah of Idaho, and one Administration Republican, Senator Robinson of Indiana, showed plainly that the committee had been politically "packed" against him.

His speech, he declared, was inspired by the attitude the committee had shown in its examination of himself and Charles L. Eyanson, assistant to the president of the Connecticut Manufacturers' Association, who had come to Washington, was placed temporarily on the Senate payroll, and sat with Mr. Bingham in the finance committee hearings on the tariff bill. By attaching so much importance to his action, he intimated, the committee had sought to influence action against the industrial schedules in the pending bill.

Charging the committee had used "police court methods," Senator Bingham said:

"The testimony has been twisted and turned by innuendo, by implication and by every unfair means in the power of these attorneys to damage my reputation, and Mr. President, I resent and shall resent it to the end of time."

Senators Caraway, Walsh, Blaine and Robinson replied to Senator Bingham as he proceeded with his accusations of unfair treatment.

Although he believed in the "noble principle of protection," Senator Robinson stated, he could not approve Senator Bingham's actions.

"I have no animus whatever against the senior Senator from Connecticut," the Indiana Republican said, "and I am sure that at this moment the other members of the committee have none. But in view of the evidence, and the Senator's own statement, I am forced to be opposed to the methods he used and forced to condemn the devious tactics employed when he hired Mr. Eyanson. I stand for protection, but I stand for it openly, and I am opposed to this sort of proceeding."

Bingham Addresses the Senate.

Rising to a question of personal privilege, Senator Bingham declared:

"On Friday afternoon last I received from the Senator from Ar-

Continued on Page Twenty-six.

Robot to Guide Airplane, Relieving Strain on Pilot

Special to The New York Times.

WASHINGTON, Oct. 28.—A robot airplane pilot which, it is claimed, will automatically stabilize a plane on the lateral, longitudinal and vertical axes, has been patented in Germany by a Berlin company, according to information received by the Department of Commerce.

Its action is said to be comparable to the stabilization of one axis carried out on steamers by means of the robot known as "Iron Mike."

This automatic control, manipulated by a push button, is intended to relieve the strain on the pilot's nerves and body during the flight and leave him free for navigation. In case of emergency, however, the pilot can take control, it is said.

KAROLYIS GET RIGHT TO ENTER COUNTRY

Stimson Raises Ban Against Hungarian Count and Countess Placed by Hughes in 1925.

LIBERAL POLICY IS SEEN

Secretary, Granting Visa, Says Department in Past Acted on Different Set of Rules

Special to The New York Times.

WASHINGTON, Oct. 28.—The ban against admitting Count and Countess Michael Karolyi of Hungary into the United States was lifted by Secretary Stimson today with announcement that upon applications filed by them in ordinary course on Sept. 30 unconditional temporary visas of the kind given non-immigrant foreigners would be granted, permitting them to come to this country for six months.

The application was filed with the American Consulate at Paris and reported favorably upon by H. Merle Cochran, the Consul in charge, who has been stationed at the Paris post since March 3, 1927.

The announcement of Secretary Stimson came as a complete surprise, but he denied that it was any refutation of the policy followed by his two immediate predecessors in office, Charles E. Hughes and Frank B. Kellogg, who had held that the Count could not be admitted into the United States to conduct political activities.

Indicates More Liberal Policy.

Nevertheless, it was looked upon as an abandonment of that policy, in so far as Count Karolyi and his wife were concerned, and in general pointed to a more liberal attitude in individual cases under the political clauses of the immigration act. It means, one official said, that the world is getting away from the World War and its immediate aftermath, and that it is now felt that American institutions are not being considered in danger from the efforts of individual agitators.

Secretary Stimson declared that in the past the State Department has acted in the Karolyi case on one set of facts while he was acting on an-

Continued on Page Twenty.

SENATORS RENEW DEMAND ON HOOVER FOR TARIFF STAND

Johnson and Harrison Call for His Guidance as Chamber Clashes Over Bill's Fate.

CONFERENCE DEMISE SEEN

Accusing Republicans of This Aim, Simmons Holds President Responsible With Party.

SMOOT ISSUES CHALLENGE

He Denies "Killing Plan" and Pleads for Passage—Robinson Pledges Democratic Aid in Speeding It.

Special to The New York Times.

WASHINGTON, Oct. 28.—During a debate amply illustrating the nervousness of the Senate over the ultimate fate of the Smoot-Hawley tariff bill today, President Hoover was again called upon to solve the situation by declaring his position on the duties on agricultural and industrial products.

This demand, made by Senators Johnson, Republican, of California, and Harrison, Democrat, of Mississippi, was injected when Senator Johnson sought definite information on Senator Reed's Saturday night statement in Philadelphia that the bill was "dead."

Spokesmen of all Senate factions entered into the discussion, which ended with a consensus that if something were not done to limit the debate, there would be no chance of even sending the bill into conference before the special session automatically ends on Dec. 2.

Chairman Smoot of the Finance Committee summarized the situation when he said it was "up to the Senate" to decide whether it wanted a bill or not. He promised that he would do all he could to obtain progress in the Senate and in conference and repudiated a suggestion by Senator Simmons that Republicans would try to "kill" the measure in conference.

Hope for Reaching Conference.

Senator Reed reiterated his conviction that the House never would consent to any bill which the Senate, dominated by the Democratic-Progressive coalition, would pass. He assured the Senate that, as a conferee, he would stand by all of its amendments, even the debenture, to which he is strongly opposed personally.

About the only ray of hope in the day was the statement of Senator Robinson, the Democratic leader, that the bill could still reach conference if every one would get together and try to take it there.

Several amendments to the bill were disposed of late today. The most important was when the Senate refused an amendment by Senator Wagner of New York to cut the duty on olive oil from 7½ to 6 cents per pound and then adopted an amendment by Senator Goldsborough of Maryland to increase the duty to 9½ cents.

Johnson Asks Bill's Chances.

Senator Johnson precipitated the debate on the bill as a whole by asking, in the language of Mr. Dooley, "Where are we at?" and inquiring "whether we are going to have a tariff bill or whether, as has been decreed, as the Senator from Pennsylvania is quoted in saying, no tariff bill will be passed at all."

"If we are not to have a tariff bill, let us not go through the motions in regard to a bill," interposed Senator Simmons. "I hope the Senator will inquire of the other side whether it proposes that the Senate shall not be

Continued on Page Eighteen

City Traffic Lights Now Blink 20 Hours a Day; Whalen Also Cuts Intervals to Speed Vehicles

Traffic in all the five boroughs of New York now is controlled by lights for twenty consecutive hours each day as the result of an order issued, without previous notice yesterday by Police Commissioner Whalen and effective last night. At the same time he increased the frequency of light changes in one more effort to relieve congestion.

The new order, which increases the span of time in which the lights are in use by four hours daily, was expected to necessitate considerable expansion of the details of handling them, but no word was given out as to how this would be arranged.

Heretofore the lights have been operated between 8 A. M. and midnight. Now they blink their "stop" and "go" signals from 7 A. M. to 3 A. M., covering of all the time during which traffic in any sizable amount is on the streets.

Commissioner Whalen said the change was to cut down accidents resulting from speeding in the hours immediately after midnight. He added that the same condition needed to be corrected between 7 and 8 A. M.

The order affecting the entire city, except Broadway south of Fulton Street, resulted in cutting in less than half the intervals in which crosstown traffic is permitted to move, reduced the alternate periods slightly and retained the five-second intervals of darkness between lights.

Under the old schedule three minutes was allowed for a complete cycle of lights, divided as follows: Fifty-five seconds for east-west traffic, five seconds of darkness, 115 seconds for north-south movement and five seconds of darkness, a total of 180 seconds.

One-third has been cut from this total under the new schedule, which operates thus: Twenty-five seconds for east-west traffic, five seconds of darkness, eighty-five seconds for north-south traffic and five seconds of darkness, a total of 120 seconds.

The commissioner said he believed that the shortening of the periods automatically would act to make traffic move faster on the signals.

Philip D. Hoyt, First Deputy Police Commissioner, in charge of traffic, made an automobile tour of the entire theatrical district last night to observe the new system at work. He said that he was well satisfied with the new schedule and thought it would prove successful. He encountered no traffic tie-up in his tour.

Roosevelt's Memory Honored In Navy Day Fete on Ships

Ships at sea and in port officially celebrated Navy Day yesterday. Although major land celebrations were held on Sunday, the anniversary of the birth of Theodore Roosevelt, similar ceremonies aboard ships were reserved for yesterday.

Open house was kept by ships in port and the public was invited to visit them. Flags appropriate for the day were broken out on all government ships, and even some commercial craft in the harbor here, flew pennants in honor of the navy.

The Los Angeles and the new all-metal dirigible and other lighter-than-air craft at Lakehurst, N. J., were ordered out and cruised north along the Atlantic coast, passing over this city and Long Island.

SENATOR T. E. BURTON, LONG ILL, DIES AT 77

Ohio Statesman Had Served in Congress for 41 Years—First Elected to the House.

STRONG ADVOCATE OF PEACE

Was Among Early Hoover Supporters—President Visited Him in Last Illness at Capital.

Special to The New York Times.

WASHINGTON, Oct. 28.—Senator Theodore E. Burton of Ohio died tonight at 9:50. He did not emerge from the coma in which he had lain since 2 P. M. yesterday. At 9:45 his night nurse noted that Senator Burton's temperature was rising and his pulse, until then strong and regular, had become irregular.

William Nelson, the Senator's chauffeur and faithful friend, was sent from the seventh-floor apartment to the lobby to summon by telephone Dr. Robert W. Baker, the Senator's physician.

Nelson telephoned to Dr. Baker and rushed back upstairs. When he arrived in the Senator's bedroom Miss Grace Burton was at the bedside with the night nurse. Senator Burton's heart beats were then barely distinguishable and in a few moments the end came.

MacDonald Sent Message.

Earlier in the day Senator Burton's physician said Mr. Burton might live for another twenty-four hours, although he had not once emerged from the unconsciousness into which he lapsed at 2 P. M. yesterday after a sinking spell from which it was feared he might not rally.

Opiates had been administered periodically during the day to relieve possible suffering and afford the exhausted body of the Senator as much rest as possible.

Prime Minister MacDonald wirelessed a message of sympathy from aboard the liner upon which he is returning to England.

Body to Lie in Senate.

The body of Senator Burton will lie before the rostrum of the United States Senate chamber Wednesday morning during a brief service to be presided over by the chaplains of the House and Senate, according to tentative arrangements made at a late hour tonight. The Rev. Z. B. Phillips, chaplain of the Senate; the Rev. James Shera Montgomery, chaplain of the House, and Dr. Jason N. Pierce, pastor of the First Congregational Church, where President Coolidge worshipped and which Mr. Burton attended, will conduct the services in the Senate chamber.

One Senator and one member of the House will deliver brief eulogies. Senator Simeon D. Fess of Ohio, who talked over funeral arrangements with Miss Grace Burton, niece of the Senator, late tonight, probably will speak for the Senate. Speaker Nicholas Longworth of Ohio may speak for the House.

Preceding the service in the Senate chamber, a short ceremony at Senator Burton's apartment at 2,101 Connecticut Avenue, to be attended only by relatives and close friends, is expected.

Burial to Be in Cleveland.

The body will be taken to Cleveland for the principal service on Thursday at the First Congregational Church, where the body probably will lie in state. City Manager W. R. Hopkins will be asked to take charge of the Cleveland arrangements.

Vice President Curtis is expected to name sixteen Senators who will escort the body to Cleveland, leaving here Wednesday night. Senator James E. Watson of Indiana, Republican floor leader, and Senator Joseph T. Robinson of Arkansas, the Democratic leader, probably will head the escort.

Elected to House in 1888.

For forty-one years Theodore Elijah Burton served in Congress with distinction as a Representative or Senator from his native State of Ohio. His reputation was founded upon integrity, his work was marked by energy and his ability was recognized by friend and foe alike.

Senator Burton was a man of caution, who did not take a stand

Continued on Page Twenty-four.

EUROPE IS DISTURBED BY AMERICAN ACTION ON OCCUPATION DEBT

London Urges an Explanation of Move for Direct Payments by Germany.

BANK'S PRESTIGE INVOLVED

Britain and Continent Feel That We Do Not Have Faith in Young Plan Institution.

SCHEME IS LAID TO HOOVER

President Is Said to Wish to Avoid Clash in Congress Over Linking of Reparations and War Debts.

By EDWIN L. JAMES.

Special Cable to THE NEW YORK TIMES.

LONDON, Oct. 28.—There appears to exist in London a certain absence of understanding as to the significance of the conversations between Washington and Berlin which now are about to ripen into diplomatic negotiations in the German capital for the preparation of a treaty dealing with the future payments by the Reich to the United States to cover costs of the army of occupation. It seems the French capital shares with London the lack of information on which to base exact appreciation of the move.

Germany's debt to the United States for occupation costs has been figured as part of the German reparations debt. This was true in drafting the Dawes plan and also in writing the Young plan. Under the Dawes plan America received about 100,000,000 marks (about $24,000,000) annually and during the Young committee negotiations the Washington Government agreed to join with Germany's other creditors in making the concessions involved in reducing the normal Dawes plan payments.

Thus, instead of 100,000,000 marks yearly, America would receive annual sums varying from 40,000,000 marks (about $9,600,000) to 76,000,000 marks (about $18,240,000), but these smaller sums would be paid over fifty-seven instead of twenty years, thus reducing in effect the size of the sacrifices America made.

Would Pass Through Bank.

These payments to the United States were included in the Young plan. Annex VII, laying down the annual payments to be made by Germany, include for each year an item to go to the United States. This would mean, of course, that together with other sums paid on the reparations account the amounts to liquidate the American claim would pass through the Bank for International Settlements.

It appears from what can be learned here regarding the negotiations scheduled to begin this week that Washington seeks to have this part of the German payments pass directly from Germany to the United States and not go through the International bank. It is reported the motive of the American Government is to keep absolutely clear of the international bank and be independent of the Young plan.

Bearing in mind that the Young plan has an American stamp and that the International Bank is largely of American origin and will be headed by an American, it can be seen that there arises the danger of a new American move which may be interpreted in a manner to cause some irritation. Although the American Government has refused an invitation to have the Federal Reserve Bank name a director of the new bank, it remains true that the Young plan and the bank loom in the minds of Europeans as American things.

It can only be unfortunate for Eu-

Continued on Page Seven.

Architects Picked to Plan Rockefeller Centre, Which May Have Opera House as a Nucleus

The first definite step toward the erection by John D. Rockefeller Jr. of an ideal city unit in the midst of New York was taken yesterday with the announcement of the names of the architects who are to design the improvements.

The actual designing will be in the hands of the firm of Reinhard & Hofmeister of 420 Lexington Avenue. This firm, composed of L. Andrew Reinhard and Henry Hofmeister, will have the cooperation of three architects of international reputation as consultants. The consultants are Harvey W. Corbett, Raymond M. Hood and Benjamin W. Morris.

The property to be transformed into a unified area of modern and beautiful structures, and probably to contain also the new home of the Metropolitan Opera Company, looking out upon a "Place de l'Opera" of New York's own, comprises three city blocks between Fifth and Sixth Avenues, Forty-eighth and Fifty-first Streets.

The announcement of the appointment of the architects was made by John R. Todd, president of the Todd, Robertson, Todd Engineering Corporation. The announcement was made in behalf of the Metropolitan Square Corporation, Todd, Brown, Inc., and the Todd, Robertson, Todd Engineering Corporation, the last two of which will develop the property, negotiate leases and supervise improvements.

The property was leased from Columbia University last January at $90,000,000 for twenty-four years, or a yearly rental of $3,750,000, with the privilege of three renewals for twenty-four years each. Mr. Rockefeller at that time expressed the hope that the new opera house would be part of the new development.

Mr. Todd's announcement last night was as follows:

His announcement last night was:

"Reinhard & Hoffmeister have been chosen architects to prepare plans for the development of the three city blocks leased by John D. Rockefeller Jr. from Columbia University, at Forty-eighth to Fifty-first Street and Fifth to Sixth Avenue, New York City.

"In their work they will have the cooperation of Harvey W. Corbett, of Corbett, Harrison & MacMurray; Raymond M. Hood, of Hood, Godley & Fouilhoux, and Benjamin W. Morris, consultants.

"The work of all of these men, particularly of the consultants, is very well known and requires no comment. It is, however, of interest that Mr. Morris is the architect of the new opera house. Also that he was the first architect to propose the placing of the opera house, with the plaza in front of it, in the centre of the three blocks."

Sixteen Leading Issues Down $2,893,520,108; Tel. & Tel. and Steel Among Heaviest Losers

A shrinkage of $2,893,520,108 in the open market value of the shares of sixteen representative companies resulted from yesterday's sweeping decline on the New York Stock Exchange.

American Telephone and Telegraph was the heaviest loser, $448,905,162 having been lopped off of its total value. United States Steel common, traditional bellwether of the stock market, made its greatest nose-dive in recent years by falling from a high of 202½ to a low of 185. In a feeble last-minute rally it snapped back to 186, at which it closed, showing a net loss of 17⅛ points. This represented for the 8,131,055 shares of common stock outstanding a total loss in value of $142,293,446.

In the following table are shown the day's net depreciation in the outstanding shares of the sixteen companies referred to:

Issues.	Shares Listed.	Losses in Points.	Depreciation.
American Radiator	10,096,289	10⅜	$104,748,997
American Tel. & Tel.	13,203,093	34	448,905,162
Commonwealth & Southern	30,764,468	3⅛	96,138,962
Columbia Gas & Electric	8,477,307	22	186,500,754
Consolidated Gas	11,451,188	20	229,023,760
DuPont E. I.	10,322,481	16⅜	169,030,625
Eastman Kodak	2,229,703	41⅞	93,368,813
General Electric	7,211,484	47½	342,545,490
General Motors	43,500,000	6⅝	288,625,000
International Nickel	13,777,408	7⅞	108,497,088
New York Central	4,637,086	22⅝	104,914,071
Standard Oil of New Jersey	24,843,643	8	198,749,144
Union Carbide & Carbon	8,730,173	20	174,615,460
United States Steel	8,131,055	17½	142,293,446
United Gas Improvement	18,646,835	6	111,881,010
Westinghouse Elec. & Mfg.	2,589,265	34½	88,682,326
			$2,893,520,108

The stocks included in the foregoing table are typical, but include only a few of the "blue chips" that fell widely. Some of the medium-priced stocks were swept down almost as sharply as the "big stocks." The loss in open market value by General Motors, for instance, was greater than that of some of the higher priced issues such as Steel, Consolidated Gas and New York Central.

For some of the market's trading favorites yesterday was the most disastrous day since they were admitted to trading.

AIRLINER IS LOST WITH 5 IN STORM

Last Reported Heading for New Mexico Region Where the T. A. T. Plane Crashed.

SEEN NEAR MOUNT TAYLOR

One of Passengers on Craft Bound East Is W. E. Merz of Mount Vernon.

By The Associated Press.

ALBUQUERQUE, N. M., Oct. 28.—An eastbound Western Air Mail passenger liner with two passengers, two pilots and a steward aboard bound from its western terminus at Alhambra, Cal., to Kansas City, is lost somewhere in Eastern Arizona or Western New Mexico, officials of the line announced tonight.

The passengers were Dr. A. W. Ward, dental authority of San Francisco, and W. E. Merz of Mount Vernon, N. Y. Dr. Ward was en route to Fort Worth, Texas. He had expected to leave the plane at Amarillo. Mr. Merz had been registered at a Los Angeles hotel, and was believed en route to his home.

The plane was last reported headed for the Mount Taylor region in Western New Mexico, where only a few weeks ago a T. A. T. liner was wrecked with the loss of eight lives.

Some parts of the Mount Taylor region are next to inaccessible. Foot parties only are able to traverse some sections because of deep can-

Continued on Page Twenty-eight.

BANKERS MOBILIZE FOR BUYING TODAY

Wall St. Is Certain Coalition Has Decided to Throw Funds Into Market for Support.

INVESTMENT TRUSTS TO AID

Financiers at Meeting Agree Prices Are Now Attractive and Money Is Plentiful.

That heavy banking support would come into the market today was the consensus of leading bankers last night. Prominent financiers asserted that many stocks had reached, at yesterday's close, extremely attractive levels, gauged by any yardstick. Pointing out that there was plenty of money in the country and that funds in the hands of investment trusts had in many cases not yet been utilized to purchase securities, these financiers said that they expected a heavy flow of money to the Stock Exchange today, attracted by the high yield basis upon which several sound issues are selling.

One prominent banker definitely asserted that he knew of buying on a large scale planned for today and among informed members of the financial district the opinion prevailed last night that the banking group which came to the rescue of the market last Thursday had made definite plans to support stocks today.

A meeting of the bankers was held last night at the offices of J. P. Morgan & Co. It was attended by:

CHARLES E. MITCHELL, chairman of the National City Bank.
ALBERT H. WIGGIN, chairman of the Chase National Bank.
WILLIAM C. POTTER, president of the Guaranty Trust Company.
SEWARD PROSSER, chairman of the Bankers Trust Company.
GEORGE F. BAKER JR. of the First National Bank.
THOMAS W. LAMONT of the Morgan firm.

Several other Morgan partners also attended. The meeting lasted until after 6 o'clock and upon its conclusion Mr. Lamont and George Whitney, also a partner in the Morgan firm, spoke to waiting reporters.

Orderly Market Is Aim.

In an informal discussion of the situation on the stock market they said that the banking group was adhering to its original purpose of preventing a recurrence of demoralized trading conditions on the floor of the Stock Exchange. The group does not intend to attempt to prevent a decline in security prices, but to maintain an orderly market. The trading on the Stock Exchange yesterday, it was said, while involving a wide decline, was orderly throughout the day. In every case there were bids present. Stocks could at all times be sold at a price, in contrast to the condition which prevailed last Thursday when in many cases offers of stock on the floor found no takers.

It was made clear that because the

Continued on Page Two.

PREMIER ISSUES HARD

Unexpected Torrent Liquidation Agai Rocks Markets.

DAY'S SALES 9,21

Nearly 3,000,000 Shares Traded In Final Hour— Tickers Lag 167 Minute

NEW RALLY SOON BRO

Selling by Europeans and " Psychology" Big Facto in Second Big Break.

The second hurricane of li tion within four days hit the market yesterday. It came sude and violently, after holders of had been lulled into a sense of rity by the rallies of Friday an urday. It was a country-wide lapse of open-market security in which the declines establishe the actual losses taken in d and cents were probably the disastrous and far-reaching i history of the Stock Exchange.

That the storm has now blo self out, that there will be orga support to put an end to a re which has ripped billions of d from market values, appeared tain last night from statemen leading bankers.

Although total estimates o losses on securities are difficu make, because of the large nu of them not listed on any exch it was calculated last night tha total shrinkage in American s ties on all exchanges yesterday aggregated some $14,000,000,000, a decline of about $10,000,000, New York Stock Exchange s ties. The figure is necessar rough one, but nevertheless giv idea of the dollars and cents sions in one of the most extr nary declines in the history of ican markets.

It was not so much the little t or speculator who was struc yesterday's cyclone; it was the men of the country, the in tions which have purchased co stocks, the investment trusts a vestors of all kinds. The little ulators were mostly blown o their accounts by the long d from early September. Thou of them went headlong out o market on Thursday. It was big man, however, whose hol were endangered yesterday and threw his holdings into the Exchange for just what they bring, when hysteria finally him.

Market Leaders Hard Hit.

Shares of the best known Ame industrial and railroad corpora smashed through their old lo Thursday, and most of them t lowest level for many years, as after wave of liquidation swept market during its day of utter fusion and rout. As bid after was filled for stocks and more more offered, stocks of the grade dropped almost perpe ularly, with 2, 3, 5 and even 10 between sales under probably most demoralized conditions of ing in the history of the Stock change and the Curb. United S Steel declined 17½, General El lost 47½, United States Indu Alcohol, 39½; Standard Gas, 40½ lumbia Gas, 22; Air Reduction, Allied Chemical & Dye, 36; more & Ohio, 13⅛; A. M. Byers pany, 30½; Chesapeake & Ohio, New York Central, 22⅝; Peoples 40½; Westinghouse Electric, Western Union, 39½, and Wort ton Pump, 29.

These are the blue chips of market, seasoned stocks based o country's leading industries, which have lead the way up ladder of fluctuations over months of the now thoroughly funct bull market. They, and others, are the issues in which ulation has been most rampant. stocks of all kinds were affecte the market's second debacle. good went down with the bad levels undreamed of in Wall S a month or so ago were cra through before the resistless as of a headlong and in many senseless wave of liquidation.

Causes of Crash Varied.

Yesterday's far-reaching decli stocks may be ascribed mainly general loss of confidence in market and the inability of any or group to stem such a torre selling, which came from all of the world. European selling f

"All the News That's Fit to Print."

The New York Times.

THE WEATHER
Fair and continued cold today; tomorrow cloudy and warmer.
Temperatures yesterday—Max. 30, min. 20.
U. S. Weather Forecast—For details See Page 38.

OL. LXXIX....No. 26,243. + * * * * NEW YORK, SATURDAY, NOVEMBER 30, 1929. TWO CENTS In Greater New York | THREE CENTS Within 200 Miles | FOUR CENTS Elsewhere Except 7th and 8th Postal Zones

BYRD SAFELY FLIES TO SOUTH POLE AND BACK, LOOKING OVER 'ALMOST LIMITLESS PLATEAU'; DROPS FOOD, LIGHTENS SHIP ON PERILOUS TRIP

MAN HEARD CRASH OTEL AT THE TIME HSTEIN WAS SHOT

She Saw Man With Angry Agonized Look Near McManus's Room.

ERTAIN ON HIS IDENTITY

M. A. Putnam, "Surprise" ness for State, Attacked by the Defense.

MOND TELLS OF BIG BET

ies He Won $40,000 From hstein on One Card—Admits hat They Had a Quarrel.

agile woman with gray hair, schoolgirl complexion, took the yesterday in the Criminal Building to aid the State in ort to convict George A. Mc- of the murder of Arnold Roth- In clear tones she identified as Mrs. Marian A. Putnam of ille, N. C., chief of the sur- witnesses for the prosecution. ening the gray squirrel collar roadtail fur coat, she said that ad been a guest at the Park al Hotel on the night of Nov. 8, when Rothstein received a wound which caused his death ays later. She added that she gistered at the hotel on Oct. 30. stant District Attorney George others, urbane in manner and ng of voice, asked her to tell she had heard and seen that

Mrs. Putnam turned her thin oward the jurymen and folded ands, asparkle with four dia- rings. Quietly she told how ad heard a "crash" and had man walking down a corridor e third floor, leading from 349, part of a suite hired by nus.

w Agony or Anger in Face.

had looked at the man's face. e the imprint of agony or an- He had his hands clasped over domen as he followed her down rpeted passageway. Mrs. Put- aid she locked the door of her and said nothing about the even the following morning she learned of the shooting.

hrough the events of the eve- Mr. Brothers led the witness. ld a straightforward story un- e prosecutor's questioning and nd then a faint smile curved ght lips. Mrs. Putnam settled comfortably in the witness and slipped out of the heavy at. As she replied to the ques- she smoothed the lace ruffles wristbands of her black vel- ess and adjusted the cream-col- lace fichu at her neck.

completed her story and then D. C. Murray, attorney for the e, began his cross-examination. ow-moving lawyer, his grizzled omewhat rumpled, favored the s with a prolonged stare be- e started his questions. Suave- t searchingly he delved into Putnam's past. His questions blunt, but were met with com- by the witness.

ymond Tells of Winnings.

made impeaching admissions a detached calm that almost d the perfect poise which had displayed shortly before by er witness, Nathan (Nigger Raymond. Raymond, who told e had won $40,000 from Roth- when the slain man drew the at high card, admitted that obably had been guilty of a pas—the expression was his when he asked Rothstein to him I. O. U.'s for $200,000 he on.

ng the cross-examination of ond the defense developed that d quarrelled with Rothstein in icab subsequent to the poker Raymond said that he had no ection of any blows having been .

n Raymond left the stand the se sought to have stricken from ecord all testimony regarding oker game. Mr. Murray told ourt that the prosecution had to carry out its promise to that the game gave McManus otive for the murder. Judge efused to grant the motion. Putnam admitted that she been registered at the Park

ontinued on Page Fourteen.

Byrd Lauds Radio Amateurs For Help in Message Relays

LOS ANGELES, Nov. 29 (AP).—A congratulatory message sent by Commander Richard E. Byrd just before the start of his flight over the South Pole, was read today at the convention of the Pacific division of the American Radio Relay League.

The message, received by B. E. Sandham, Los Angeles amateur short wave radio operator, read:

"Greetings from Little America to the radio amateurs of the Pacific division. Am glad for this opportunity to acknowledge the big debt our North and South Pole expeditions owe to the amateur radio operators.

"I wish to thank them for their helpfulness and to express my admiration of the high sense of honor they show in handling messages.

"It is radio that has made this expedition possible.

"Cordial good wishes in which all of Little America join.

"RICHARD BYRD."

WINTER GRIPS NATION; MERCURY AT 20 HERE

Icy Blast Sweeping Out of the Northwest Kills 9, Spreads Damage, Blocks Shipping.

BLIZZARDS RAGE IN WEST

One Frozen to Death in New York and No Let-Up in the Frigid Wave Is Seen.

Winter came howling out of the northwest and the Arctic wastes yesterday, bringing blizzards to the Western States and Canada, hampering shipping on the Great Lakes, and holding the West, the Middle West, the East and many Southern States in the grip of sub-freezing temperatures.

It was the frigid season's first general offensive, and it scattered death, suffering and property damage widely. White River, Ontario, which usually claims the distinction of recording low temperatures, shared with Thief River Falls, Minn., first place on the icy list yesterday, both communities recording 26 below zero. At least eight persons died in the North Central States as a result of the sudden zero snap, according to the Associated Press. New York City added one death to the list. ears were felt for the safety of hunters caught unprepared for the severe cold in the Minnesota woods. Near the cradle of Winter, where a 30-mile gale was driving a blizzard over the Saskatchewan Lakes, the fate of fifty fishermen, pushing northward on a 50-mile trip, was in doubt. The fishermen had been gone for three days.

Cold to Continue Here Today.

New York had an uncomfortable sample of Winter, and last night the local Weather Bureau gave practically no hope of a let-up today in the cold temperatures.

This city felt its lowest temperature of the season at 10 o'clock last night when the thermometer registered 20 degrees above zero, 12 below freezing. Even the maximum temperature at 9:30 A. M. was only 30 degrees, or 2 below freezing. The average temperature for the day was 26 degrees, compared with a normal Nov. 29 reading of 39. The coldest Nov. 29 on record occurred in 1872 when the thermometer registered 15 degrees.

The cold here was aggravated by a biting northwest wind, blowing at thirty-eight miles an hour. The city's firemen were put to their first severe test of the season in what was a busy "fire" day in Manhattan, the Bronx and Brooklyn. Up to 9 o'clock last night the number of fires for the day totaled thirty in Manhattan, ten in the Bronx and forty-three in Brooklyn.

Fair Weather Forecast.

Although the barometer in the New York Weather Bureau was rising last night, indicating fair weather for today, the cold snap will continue, according to the official forecaster, and the thousands of football spectators who will swarm into the Yankee Stadium for the Army-Notre Dame game this afternoon will have to wear their warmest clothes and wraps.

"Fresh northeast winds and continued cold" was the prediction for today. At the Weather Bureau it was even considered possible that today might be a little colder than yesterday.

A woman on Staten Island was New York's addition to the list of victims of the cold. She was Mrs. Gladys Todd, 53 years old, who was foun ddead in the back yard of her home, at 4 Schrenkheisen Place, Mar-

Continued on Page Twelve.

FIRST MESSAGE EVER SENT FROM THE SOUTH POLE

By Commander Richard E. Byrd

WIRELESS TO THE NEW YORK TIMES.

ABOARD AIRPLANE FLOYD BENNETT, in flight, 1:55 P. M. Greenwich mean time [8:55 A. M. New York time], Friday, Nov. 29.—My calculations indicate that we have reached the vicinity of the South Pole, flying high for a survey. The airplane is in good shape, crew all well. Will soon turn north. We can see an almost limitless polar plateau. Our departure from the Pole was at 1:25 P. M.

BYRD

The difference in the times mentioned in this dispatch, that is between 1:55 P. M. in the date line and 1:25 P. M., given by the Commander as that of his departure from the South Pole, is probably accounted for by the lapse between the writing of the dispatch by the Commander and its coding and sending by the wireless operator, Harold I. June. Greenwich time is five hours ahead of New York time and twelve hours ahead of time at Little America.

The Commander's last sentence was evidently added after he began to fly away from the Pole; the first part written before he left there.

CAPITAL DISPLAYS KEENEST INTEREST

President, Waiting News, Is the First in Washington to Hear of Byrd's Success.

OFFICIALS LAUD FLIGHT

Admiral Hughes Says the Commander Is a Worthy Successor to Admiral Wilkes.

Special to The New York Times.

WASHINGTON, Nov. 29.—President Hoover, who had waited anxiously all day for word of the progress of the daring flight to the South Pole, was the first person in Washington, outside of the staff of THE NEW YORK TIMES bureau, to learn of the successful flight of Commander Byrd to the South Pole and back to the base at Little America.

The word was flashed to the White House tonight from the Washington Bureau of THE NEW YORK TIMES. It was transmitted to the President before dinner by Secretary Walter H. Newton.

All day the President had asked for word of the progress of the flight and late in the afternoon had indicated his deep interest. When the news was taken to him, the President expressed his delight over the successful outcome.

Official Washington expressed the most intense relief and the greatest delight at the successful termination of the flight.

Admiral Charles F. Hughes, the Acting Secretary of the Navy, was among the first to be informed.

"We are greatly pleased at the success of Commander Byrd's flight," he said. "He is a worthy successor to Admiral Wilkes, the American naval officer who first discovered the Antarctic Continent."

Earlier in the day Admiral Hughes had said:

"The Navy Department is intensely interested and, knowing Commander Byrd, we are thoroughly confident that he will return successfully."

Davison Congratulates Expedition.

F. Trubee Davison, Assistant Secretary of War for Aeronautics, declared the success of the flight demonstrated again the value of aircraft.

"The flight of Commander Byrd and his brave companions to the South Pole," he said, "is another epic in the annals of the achievements of heavier-than-air craft and proves once again the value of the airplane in exploration of unknown areas where distances can be traveled in hours which under ordinary forms of transportation would require weeks and months. On behalf of the War Department and the Army Air Corps, I wish to congratulate the Byrd Antarctic Expedition. Their achievement will be lauded by Americans the world over."

Major Clarence M. Young, the Assistant Secretary of Commerce for Aeronautics, declared the Byrd flight was simply another demonstration of the "limitless purposes which aviation can serve."

"The flight to the South Pole and back was surely a major accomplish-

Continued on Page Three.

President Sends His Congratulations to Byrd, Saying Spirit of Great Adventure Still Lives

Special to The New York Times.

WASHINGTON, Nov. 29.—After being informed tonight of Commander Byrd's successful flight to the South Pole and back to the base at Little America, President Hoover gave to THE NEW YORK TIMES the following message of congratulations on behalf of himself, and the American people, to be transmitted by radio to Commander Byrd:

Commander Richard E. Byrd, Little America:

I know that I speak for the American people when I express their universal pleasure at your successful flight over the South Pole. We are proud of your courage and your leadership. We are glad of proof that the spirit of great adventure still lives.

Our thoughts of appreciation include also your companions in the flight and your colleagues, whose careful and devoted preparation have contributed to your great success.

HERBERT HOOVER.

BYRD'S FEAT STIRS ENTHUSIASM HERE

Victorious Flight Hailed With Tributes to Commander's Daring and Foresight.

With the reception of news from Little America of the return of Commander Byrd and his companions from their flight over the South Pole, explorers, aviators, aeronautical designers and builders whose names are known throughout the world of aviation and scores of others offered their congratulations to the Commander and expressed their enthusiasm over the success of his efforts. Some of these comments follow:

Anthony H. G. Fokker, designer of the plane in which Commander Byrd crossed the Atlantic—I didn't expect anything but success from Byrd and Balchen. The Commander is an excellent organizer and Balchen is a fine pilot. With all the qualities fliers need for such an expedition, they have proved the unquestioned value and possibility of the airplane.

Mayor Walker—That's marvelous news. I can sum up the way I feel about it in a single sentence. I knew Dick Byrd would do it. He has made another great contribution to scientific advancement and world knowledge. The American flag will certainly look great down there. I know I speak for the people of this city when I say that we rejoice with him and his intrepid companions in this epoch-making exploit. We will await his return to New York with impatience, so that the city can give him the welcome he so richly deserves. New York City has honored Commander Byrd before. It is glad to honor him again, for it feels that in a very real sense he is one of us.

Lieutenant Governor Herbert H. Lehman—It is glorious news. Commander Byrd's successful flight to the South Pole will go down in history as one of the greatest of human exploits. Its success is all the more noteworthy because achieved in the face of great obstacles after the most painstaking preparation. The nation whose flag he has now carried to the uttermost ends of the globe rejoices with him and his gallant crew for the success they have

Continued on Page Four.

BYRD'S FAMILY GETS NEWS OF FLIGHT

Virginia Governor at Capitol Gets News and Mother Hears It at Winchester.

Special to The New York Times.

RICHMOND, Va., Nov. 29.—Although he knew that his brother, Commander Richard Evelyn Byrd, intended to hop to the South Pole "about this time of the year," Governor Harry F. Byrd said in his office tonight that no one in the family or any one else had known exactly what day the plane Floyd Bennett would leave the base.

Commander Byrd's mother, Mrs. Richard E. Byrd Sr., and Thomas Byrd, his brother, received news of the successful flight at their home in Winchester.

Governor Byrd flew to Richmond late today from Norfolk to get news of his brother. He had been at Chapel Hill for the Virginia-Carolina football game on Thanksgiving Day and stopped in the capital to be the guest of Governor O. Max Gardner of North Carolina. Accompanying Governor Byrd in another plane was Colonel Willard D. Newbill of his staff.

From the Executive Mansion the Governor relayed news of the flight to his mother at Winchester.

When Commander Byrd duplicated his top of the world feat by flying over the South Pole at the very bottom of the world his mother, thought it "glorious" and was "thrilled to death," she said tonight.

"I was in Washington when we heard Dick had hopped off," she said. "My son Tom drove up there to get me when I phoned him and we went back to Winchester to wait for news. THE NEW YORK TIMES called me about 6 o'clock but said they would not release the news generally until later.

"Dick had sent me a Thanksgiving radio message a few hours before they hopped off, 'We are off.' We were very uneasy, but I was never so happy in my life as when we heard he had landed safely back at Little America. We really were quite uneasy because this flight seemed more hazardous than anything he ever tried. Nobody knew anything much about Antarctica.

"When Tom heard Dick had gone over safely he said he was 'tremen-

Continued on Page Two.

BRITISH APPLAUD FLIGHT AS TRIUMPH

Thrill Over Byrd's Feat Puts Polar Land Dispute in the Background.

NEWS EAGERLY AWAITED

German Press and People Followed Commander's Course With Keen Interest.

Special Cable to THE NEW YORK TIMES.

LONDON, Saturday, Nov. 30.—Great Britain watched Commander Byrd's progress over the Antarctic wastes to the South Pole and his return as a magnificent adventure, and what claims he may make to any rich coal or mineral deposits over which he has flown or staked with the American flag is an issue that is exciting no comment here.

Even the publication by New York newspapers of a summary of the State Department's answer to the British Government's year-old note concerning sovereignty over the Antarctic lands, which was read here as clearly indicating that the United States does not intend to abandon its claims based on earlier discoveries by American explorers, was not allowed to distract attention from Commander Byrd's performance or to cause a controversy almost on the eve of the five-power naval parley in London.

Hailed as Byrd Triumph.

The Daily Chronicle outstripped its London rivals this morning by alone printing a full account of Commander Byrd's South Pole flight, as transmitted to it by THE NEW YORK TIMES and associated newspapers. The remainder of the London newspapers were able in their final editions to announce only the bare fact of the aviator's epoch-making flight, with full acknowledgment of the source of their information.

The feat, therefore, was hailed here not only as a personal triumph for Commander Byrd and his three companions, Balchen, June and McKinley, but as an outstanding feat in newspaper organization.

Stupendous as is the accomplishment of a flight of 1,560 miles over the frozen wastes to the South Pole and back in 18 hours and 55 minutes in itself, it has been brought home more vividly to the public mind here by the fact that within a few hours of Commander Byrd's return to his base on the Ross ice shelf, at 10:10 o'clock London time last night, the leading newspapers of the world were able to reproduce the story of the exploit.

It has not escaped notice that scientific development, from the short-wave radio to the finer details of aircraft construction, have been pressed into use on this occasion.

Scientists, aviators and public men on every hand are expressing admiration for Commander Byrd's initiative and courage in carrying out successfully a flight which for scientific results may stand alone.

Commander Byrd had been flying over twelve hours before the British

Continued on Page Four.

CROSSES GLACIER PASS AT 11,500 FEET

Commander Takes Chance and Plane Roars Upward Amid Swirling Drift Out Through Gorge to Tableland

FLYING TIME FOR THE WHOLE CIRCUIT ABOUT 18 HOURS

With Two New Ranges Discovered, the Four Air Argonauts, Guided by Chief, Turn Back to Wild Welcome at Base Camp.

By RUSSELL OWEN.

Wireless to THE NEW YORK TIMES.

LITTLE AMERICA, Antarctica, Nov. 29.—Conqueror of two Poles by air, Commander Richard E. Byrd flew into camp at 10:10 o'clock this morning, having been gone eighteen hours and fifty-nine minutes. An hour of this time was spent at the mountain base refueling.

The first man to fly over the North and South Poles and the only man to fly over the South Pole stepped from his plane and was swept up on the arms of the men in camp who for more than an hour had been anxiously watching the southern horizon for a sight of the plane.

Deaf from the roar of the motors, tired from the continual strain of the flight and the long period of navigation under difficulties, Commander Byrd was still smiling and happy. He had reached the South Pole after as hazardous and as difficult a flight as has ever been made in an airplane, tossed by gusts of wind, climbing desperately up the slopes of glaciers a few hundred feet above the surface.

Radiant Airmen Borne in Triumph.

His companions on the flight tumbled out stiff and weary also, but so happy that they forgot their cramped muscles. They were also tossed aloft, pounded on the back and carried to the entrance of the mess hall.

Bernt Balchen, the calm-eyed pilot who first met Commander Byrd in Spitzbergen and who was with him on the transatlantic flight, came out first. There was a little smudge of soot under the nose, but the infectious smile which has endeared him to those who know him, was radiant.

He was carried away and then came Harold June who, between intervals of helping Balchen and attending to fuel tanks and lines and taking pictures, found time to send the radio bulletins which told of the plane's progress.

And after him Captain Ashley McKinley was lifted from the doorway, beaming like the Cheshire cat because his surveying camera had done its work all the way.

Dumped Food of Forty-five Days, But Not Fuel.

Men crowded about them eager for the story of what they had been through, catching fragments of sentences. It had evidently been a terrific battle to get up through the mountains to the Plateau.

"We had to dump a month and a half of food to do it," said Commander Byrd. "I am glad it wasn't gas. It was nip and tuck all the way."

"Yes," chuckled Balchen. "Do you remember when we were sliding around those knolls picking the wind currents to help us and there wasn't more than 300 feet under us at times? We were just staggering along, with drift and clouds and all sorts of things around us."

When the plane approached the mountains on the way south, Commander Byrd picked out the Livingston Glacier, a large glacier somewhat to the west of the Axel Heiberg Glacier, as the best passageway.

Swooping Upward Through Swirling Drift.

The high mountains shut them in all around as they forced their way upward, Balchen, conserving his fuel to the utmost, coaxing his engines, picking the up-currents of air as best he could to help the plane ride upward.

Clouds swirled about them at times, puff-balls of mist driven down the glacier; drift scurried beneath them; it was a wicked place for an airplane to be, hemmed in by the wall of the towering peaks on either side.

This was the time when they had to lighten ship and Byrd, looking around for what could best be spared, decided to dump some food. There was a dump valve in the fuselage tank, but he had determined to go through and did not know what winds he might face at the top of the glacier. So food was thrown overboard, scattered over the ridged and broken surface of the Livingston Glacier.

"It is an awful looking place," Commander Byrd said.

Over the "Hump" and Vast Panorama Unfolds.

They finally reached the hump at an elevation of 11,500 feet, as indicated by the barograph, although it might have been a little more, because of the difference in pressure inland.

But there was little space under the staggering plane, buffeted by the winds that eddied through the gigantic gorge. Once at the top, Balchen could level off for a time and then gain altitude.

Then there came into view slowly the long sweep of mountains of the Queen Maud Range, stretching to the southeast, and the magnificent panorama of the entire bulwark of mountains along the edge of the Polar Plateau.

Beheld Tinted Slopes of Myriad Mountains.

"It was the most magnificent sight I have ever seen," Commander Byrd said. "I never dreamed there were so many mountains in the world. They shone under the sun, wonderfully tinted with color, and in the southeast a bank of clouds hung over the mountains, making a scene that I shall never forget."

Over the plateau the Commander set his course for the pole. They had had a beam wind all the way in to the mountains which

"All the News That's Fit to Print."

The New York Times.

LATE CITY EDITION
POSTSCRIPT
THE WEATHER—Fair with moderate temperature today and tomorrow.
U. S. Weather Forecast—See next to last page.

VOL. LXXXI....No. 26,901. NEW YORK, SATURDAY, SEPTEMBER 19, 1931. TWO CENTS In New York City | THREE CENTS Within 200 Miles | FOUR CENTS Elsewhere Except 7th and 8th Postal Zones

JAPANESE SEIZE MUKDEN IN BATTLE WITH CHINESE; RUSH MORE TROOPS TO CITY

TOKYO ALLEGES ATTACK

But Chinese Say Assault Was Unprovoked and Unanswered.

MANCHURIANS LIST 70 DEAD

Japanese Demand Surrender of Chinese Troops and Police—Foreigners Protected.

NAVY ORDERED ON ALERT

Warships Will Be Held Ready for Call to Ports—Some Japanese Suspect Army in Move.

By HUGH BYAS.

Wireless to THE NEW YORK TIMES.

TOKYO, Saturday, Sept. 19.—A violent clash between Chinese and Japanese soldiers in the vicinity of Mukden was followed by all-night fighting which culminated in the capture of the Mukden inner walled city by Japanese troops at 4:30 A. M. today. The fighting is still proceeding in the streets and suburbs.

Japanese reinforcements are being speeded to Mukden by special trains from Port Arthur and other points.

The affair began, according to reports available, at 10:30 o'clock last night, when three companies of Chinese troops began destroying the South Mancuhuria Railway line at Hokutaiei, a village three miles from Mukden, on the main line. A smaller number of Japanese troops posted there as guards drove the Chinese away and occupied the village.

Chinese Said to Have Reattacked.

The Chinese re-attacked with machine-guns and even field guns, it is said, and surrounded the Japanese. At midnight Japanese troops at Mukden, numbering three battalions, began an attack on the inner walled city, which they captured after four and a half hours of fighting. The Japanese demand the surrender of the Chinese garrison and the Chinese police of Mukden.

By 6:30 A. M. the Japanese had completely occupied the walled city. Military police were detailed to preserve order, while the troops began an attack on the military airdrome and arsenal.

Telegrams from Seoul say that part of the Korean garrison has been ordered to Manchuria.

Officials do not try to conceal the extreme gravity of the affair, but there are still hopes it may prove a local incident capable of settlement as such. The atmosphere of Manchuria for weeks past has been of the kind in which guns go off of themselves.

Frontier incidents were to be expected and both governments must have expected some such affair. The agitation the army here has been conducting over the Nakamura murder has created widespread anxiety and the question all Japanese are asking is whether the affair was premeditated or is an isolated incident such as is likely to occur in a bellicose atmosphere.

Officials Express Surprise.

Hurried inquiries here tend to show it was not foreseen and, as far as the Japanese Government is concerned, unpreventable.

The official theory is that the Mukden commander imagined an attack on the bridge at Hokutaiei, otherwise Peitayeng, was the commencement of a concerted attack on Japanese troops. Anticipating that the cutting of the bridge was the prelude to a general assault, he determined to get his blow in first, and immediately attacked Chinese Army headquarters.

The Chinese did not offer serious resistance and the casualties, it is hoped, were few.

A Mukden dispatch to the Tokyo Asahi reports that on the night of Sept. 15, when General Honjo, the new commander of the Japanese garrison in Manchuria, arrived, orders were issued to all Japanese troops in Manchuria. The test was carried out satisfactorily and the next morning troops began their march.

General Honjo, who has been touring Manchuria, addressed the troops in several places on the great increase in banditry and ordered them to take drastic measures against

Continued on Page Eight.

Stimson, Mellon and Lamont Meet Hoover in Night Session

Special to The New York Times.

WASHINGTON, Sept. 18.—A three-hour conference was held at the White House tonight with President Hoover and Secretaries Stimson, Mellon and Lamont attending.

No information as to its nature could be obtained, but it was assumed that it dealt with international political, financial and economic conditions.

The secretaries arrived separately at the White House about 8 o'clock. It was just after 11 o'clock when they departed.

LINDBERGHS ARRIVE IN CHINA FROM JAPAN

Land Safely in Nanking After 800-Mile Oversea Flight From Fukuoka.

CROSS THE YELLOW SEA

They Will Be the Guests of the American Consul on Visit to the Capital of China.

By The Associated Press.

NANKING, Saturday, Sept. 19.—Colonel and Mrs. Charles A. Lindbergh arrived here at 2:36 P. M., today 1:36 A. M. (Eastern Daylight Time) after a flight of 800 miles from Fukuoka, Japan.

Take Off from Fukuoka.

FUKUOKA, Japan, Saturday, Sept. 19 (AP).—Colonel and Mrs. Charles A. Lindbergh took off at 8:35 A. M. today (7:35 P. M. Friday, Eastern Daylight Time) on a flight of nearly 800 miles across the Yellow Sea to Nanking, China.

The colonel estimated the flight would require about seven hours. He said if unfavorable weather was encountered, he and Mrs. Lindbergh would return to Fukuoka.

Flight Delayed From Yesterday.

By HALLETT ABEND.

Wireless to THE NEW YORK TIMES.

NANKING, China, Sept. 18.—Colonel and Mrs. Charles A. Lindbergh are expected here between 2 and 3 o'clock tomorrow afternoon, but the American Consul had expected them today and it was not until 3 P. M. that he learned they had postponed their departure from Japan for a day.

Hence the Consul, who will entertain the American and his wife, hastily set about revising the four-day entertainment program for them.

The only high Chinese official who will be in this capital to greet the Lindberghs will probably be Foreign Minister C. T. Wang.

Effects of the recent disastrous flood on the Yangtse River will be seen by the Lindberghs when they arrive here. There is no water within the old walled city, but Nanking's business section is badly flooded, with water knee deep in many shops and streets.

The only approach to the city's leading hotel is by rickshaw, and even then the coolies pulling such conveyances must plow through water up to their thighs. The lobby stands eight inches under water.

Yangtse Still Dangerous.

NANKING, Sept. 18 (AP).—Although the flooded Yangtse River swept away one wharf especially constructed for the Lindbergh monoplane, preparations for the reception of the flier and his wife are complete.

As the Yangtse here still is running a terrific current, the Nanking Aviation Bureau has advised Colonel Lindbergh to exercise great care in landing. Chinese Navy launches and Aviation Bureau motor boats will sweep the river clear of all craft. The United States gunboat McCormick will be standing by, ready to render assistance.

When the Lindberghs arrive their plane will be moored to a new and especially constructed wharf. They will board a boat and then proceed through flooded streets to the South gate of the Nanking City Hall, where motor cars will be waiting.

The Lindberghs landed at Fukuoka

Continued on Page Nine.

MRS. COLLINGS' STORY ATTACKED AT INQUEST AS SHE STAYS AWAY

Prosecutor Stresses Details Omitted in First Recital of Raid on Cruiser.

POLICEMAN CHIEF WITNESS

Quotes Widow as Saying Two Boats Passed During Tragedy but She Made No Outcry.

SHE IS TOO ILL TO ATTEND

Lawyer, Defending Her Story Again, Says It Has Been Proved True—Silent on Private Inquiry.

Mrs. Lillian Collings absented herself yesterday from the inquest at Huntington, L. I., into the strange death of her husband, Benjamin, but her story of a murderous attack by pirates in Long Island Sound was related from the witness stand by the young policeman who first questioned her.

Alexander G. Blue, Suffolk County District Attorney, did his best to emphasize what he considered omissions and inconsistencies in the widow's account of her husband's murder, but when he had finished it was not clear whether the omissions signified anything more important than the failure of a policeman to ask the proper questions.

Much stress was laid upon Mrs. Collings's smiling, stoical calmness after she was rescued from the motor boat Bo Peep in which the supposed pirates left her after pitching her husband overboard and casting the yacht Penguin adrift with her 5-year-old daughter, Barbara, aboard. How much of it was due to the restraint of breeding or hysteria even the observant young officer, Sergeant Robert Forrest of the Cove Neck police force, confessed himself powerless to say.

Forrest, a bronzed young policeman with a manner as sharp as the crease in his uniform trousers, indicated clearly by his manner that his skepticism of the story he was telling at second hand matched if it did not exceed that of Mr. Blue, who has said frankly that he does not believe it.

Widow's Story Defended.

While Mrs. Collings's story was being subjected to indirect attack in Huntington it was being vigorously defended in Stamford by her attorneys, who said that she was prevented from attending the proceedings on Long Island only by physical inability. Homer S. Cummings, prominent Stamford attorney, said the widow who bore up so strongly until her husband's body was found under circumstances that tended to bear out her fantastic story, had collapsed and was under the care of two doctors.

To Mr. Cummings, Mrs. Collings's failure to cry out or resist was "God-given wisdom," while her slain husband's failure to make use of a revolver was "an error of judgment" as the whole tragedy resulted from his "temporizing" with the invaders of his yacht. The lawyer refused to affirm or deny that members of the dead man's family had retained private detectives to conduct an investigation, but he hinted that if the Long Island authorities "are getting nowhere" the family might feel called upon to take action on their own account.

"Too much stress is being laid on the inconsistencies in Mrs. Collings's statement," he said. "Knowing as we do now that the story in its essence is true, the main thing to do is to find the assailants."

Two Witnesses Heard.

Forrest and Amza Biggs Jr., the constable who found Collings's body, with skull fractured and arms and legs trussed up with stout rope on the beach at Lloyd's Bend, near the spot where Mrs. Collings said the attack occurred, were the only witnesses of the eight subpoenaed who had a chance to tell their stories in the little courtroom of the Huntington Town Hall under the eye of Coroner William B. Gibson, who presided.

Toward midafternoon a sudden adjournment until next Friday was taken at the request of Mr. Blue, who soon afterward told reporters that he had received important information which might lead to immediate arrests. Investigation of the information which was given him by his brother-in-law, Fred Meyer, a lifeguard at Crab Beach in Northport, proved it to be valueless, and Mr. Blue commented somewhat ruefully that he was "right back where I started."

Today, Mr. Blue said, he would go away for a yachting trip on the Sound, leaving the investigation in the hands of his young assistant, Fred Munder. He did not explain

Continued on Page Four.

White House Inquiry for Brewery Data Stirs Wets; For Outsider, Says Secretary

By RICHARD V. OULAHAN.

Special to The New York Times.

WASHINGTON, Sept. 18.—When it became known today that "the White House" had asked the Census Bureau for information as to how many people had been employed in the beer-brewing business in the United States prior to national prohibition, trusting anti-prohibitionists saw in this move that after all it was true, as had been reported, that President Hoover had decided, as a means of ameliorating the unemployment situation, to recommend to Congress that the manufacture and sale of beer, and perhaps of light wines, should be authorized.

But inquiry at the White House did not stimulate the hope engendered in the hearts of the trusting ones. Walter H. Newton, of the President's secretariat, said that he had made the inquiry, but not at the instance of President Hoover. A request "from some one outside the White House" had been received by him and not by the President, Mr. Newton explained, and he had asked the Department of Commerce to obtain the information desired from the Census Bureau, one of its branches.

Mr. Newton declined to say whether the request came from anybody in the government or whether he had given the brewery employment information to the President. He took the position that he was not called upon to furnish such details to newspapers, but left the impression that the request was in line with a myriad of inquiries on a variety of subjects which he was receiving constantly from people in the Minnesota Congressional district which he had represented for twelve years, and from many personal and political friends throughout the country.

Anybody who wanted this information could get it, said Mr. Newton, by applying to the Census Bureau. This was true, as figures on those employed in breweries before prohibition and in near-beer manufacturies after prohibition were readily obtained by newspaper men who went to the bureau after it had become known that "the White House" had asked for the data.

What seemingly gave substance to the wet hope arising from the inquiry made by "the White House" was

Continued on Page Fifteen.

NERVOUSNESS STILL IN BRITISH MARKETS

Stock Liquidation Continues, Holland Withdraws Gold and Foreign Exchanges Drop.

STERLING MAINTAINS RATE

But Pressure From New York Indicates Inroads on Recent Credits—Stocks Fall Here.

Special Cable to THE NEW YORK TIMES.

LONDON, Sept. 18.—Financial nervousness, which it was hoped had been dispelled by the creation of the National Government, which completes its fourth week in office Monday, has returned to London, and all the markets today passed through an uncomfortable time.

The stock-selling movement of the past few days was continued; British funds fell 2 to 3 points, there was a large withdrawal of gold for Holland, foreign exchanges took an unfavorable trend and tenders had to be revised for treasury bills, not all which were allotted, adversely for the government, at an average rate of 4 5-16 per cent.

The dollar sterling rate was maintained at a pegged figure, and finished at 4.85 11/16, but was subjected to heavy pressure in the afternoon from New York, which presumably means further inroads on the government's French and American credits specially granted to maintain it. Leading foreign exchanges which were not pegged moved sharply against sterling, the Belgian rate falling to 34.86 Belgas and the Swiss to 24.88½ francs.

Dutch Exchange Still Low.

Despite the further withdrawal from the Bank of England of £1,781,000 in bar gold, the Dutch exchange remained below the gold export point at 12.04 florins. French exchange, however, was quiet again and closed at 123.97 francs. The foreign market was acutely weak, and sales were effected only with difficulty, although German bonds again showed marked resistance.

Declines were general in the miscellaneous market and even gold shares failed to stand against the prevailing tendency. Financiers ascribe all this partly to the uncertainty regarding the coming general election and the "unnecessary alarm" some foreign investors have taken over the naval unrest, although some say developments within the borders of the selling countries account for at least a

Continued on Page Nine.

WORLD COURT ENTRY IS URGED BY THE BAR

Meeting Asks Senate to Ratify Protocol as Step to Peace and Trade Recovery.

NEW TRUST LAW SOUGHT

Advance Rulings on Mergers by Trade Commission Endorsed, Also Federal Bus Control.

From a Staff Correspondent of The New York Times.

ATLANTIC CITY, N. J., Sept. 18.—Entry of the United States into the World Court as a step for the promotion of world peace and for restoration of confidence requisite to business recovery was urged today by the convention of the American Bar Association in session here. It adopted the report of its committee on international law calling upon the Senate to ratify the Root protocol of adherence at the session of Congress in December.

Amendment of the anti-trust laws in a manner designed to promote efficiency of business and to enable it to overcome some of the difficulties under which it is struggling to emerge from the depression, and Federal regulation of motor vehicles acting as common carriers in interstate trade, were two other measures approved by the convention. Both of these measures will be pressed by the association before Congress.

The convention also instructed its special committee on Federal taxation, headed by Hugh Satterlee of New York, to represent the association before the Congressional Joint Committee on Internal Revenue Taxation when it considers the proposal to confer jurisdiction on the United States Board of Tax Appeals over proceedings for the recovery of overpayments on taxes, a proposal endorsed by the association.

The convention's action on this matter followed a report presented by Mr. Satterlee in which it was frankly stated that "in view of the existing treasury deficit, tax revision and, quite likely, material changes in the system of taxation, seem bound to come as soon as political exigencies permit." This was regarded as a polite statement that a general increase in the tax rate may be expected after the coming Presidential election.

Dispute on Air Property.

A clash between real estate interests, represented by Nathan W. MacChesney of Chicago, counsel for the

Continued on Page Six.

Catholic Leaders Take Refuge at Vatican; Italians Reported Waiting to Arrest Five

By The Associated Press.

VATICAN CITY, Sept. 18.—Five leaders of the Catholic Action organization are voluntary prisoners in the Vatican, fearing to leave Vatican City because of their participation in the recent Italo-Vatican controversy, it was learned today.

One of them is Count dalla Torre, editor of Osservatore Romano, who has not left the Vatican since the dispute started almost four months ago. An Italian detective stands outside the gate leading to his editorial offices night and day, presumably to arrest him as soon as he sets foot beyond the papal confines.

Count dalla Torre, and the Jesuit Father Rosa are slated for dismissal by the Pope as a concession to the Italian Government in recognition of the settlement of the controversy.

The other voluntary prisoners are an officer of the Palatine Guards, who is said to have furnished the Pope with information for his speech against the head of the Fascist university group, and former heads of Catholic Action connected with the defunct Popular party.

Count dalla Torre has been editor of Osservatore Romano for several years, and chairman of the Executive Committee of Azione Cattolica Italiana since the inception of this federation of lay Catholic organizations, in 1922.

Osservatore Romano is the lay Catholic official daily; the official organ of the Holy See is the Acta Apostolicae Sedis.

Continued on Page Four.

RELIEF COMPROMISE REACHED AT ALBANY AFTER CONFERENCE LASTING TILL 2 A. M. ROOSEVELT'S COMMISSION PLAN ADOPTE[D]

UP-STATE INQUIRY KILLED

Scathing Attack by Democrats Fails to Swerve Assembly Majority.

SAY MACY BROKE PROMISE

Minority Speakers Charge the Republicans Bar Light on Own "Corruption."

MAJORITY SCORES A COUP

Quotes Tremaine as Opposing Inquiry—McNaboe Stirs Senate Fight on Seabury.

From a Staff Correspondent of The New York Times.

ALBANY, Sept. 18.—Disregarding a fierce attack by the Democrats, the Republican majority in the Assembly voted down the rival measure for a legislative investigation of twelve up-State Republican counties.

With the Democrats directing a heavy fire of assault on the contrast between the opposing party's stand on an inquiry of their own territory and their fervid insistence on a New York City investigation, the Republicans held to their position and by a vote of 76 to 70 defeated the proposal.

The vote came on a move by Assemblyman Irwin Steingut to discharge the Ways and Means Committee from consideration of his bill and although two Erie Republicans joined the Democrats in urging discharge, the majority was able to block the bill.

The procedure followed in the Assembly had been planned for duplication in the Senate but since the adjournment until tomorrow was taken hastily because of the conference on unemployment relief, the Senate failed to take any action. Tomorrow, however, the Republican majority in the Senate is also expected to vote down the proposal.

The action of the Assembly Republicans appeared to satisfy the Democrats regardless of the refusal to let the bill come out of committee. What the Democrats really wanted was to compare their opponent's position on up-State investigation with their stand on New York City affairs and to get a record vote. They succeeded in doing this in a lengthy and sometimes acrimonious debate.

Democrats Accuse Macy.

The Democratic drive succeeded in getting the three Republican members of the Hofstadter committee, Potter, Moffat and Lamont, on the tally sheet as opposed to an investigation of Republican areas.

The Democrats, headed by Assemblyman Steingut, aimed a good portion of their cannonade at W. Kingsland Macy, Republican State Chairman. Recalling his efforts to force a New York City inquiry, they asserted he had failed to fulfill a promise to erase corruption wherever found by not bringing his forces into line for an up-State investigation.

The Republicans scored one hit when Eberly Hutchinson, chairman of the Ways and Means Committee, disclosed an interview with State Controller Morris S. Tremaine in which he was quoted as saying that he did not see the necessity for a legislative inquiry up-State. The Democrats had based their demand on reports of corruption made by the Controller's audit.

"The Republican majority has decided to kill an investigation of their own up-State communities," said Mr. Steingut. "Why? Are they afraid? What a difference politics makes. They shouted for reforms, for inquiries, for investigations, for honesty in office, &c.

"Their State Chairman, King Macy, declared that he was in favor of punishing corrupt public officials whether Republican or Democrat. So they went to New York on a fishing expedition. They're still fishing; but do they want to go fishing up-State? Oh, no. That's different. They might find something wrong with the Grand Old Party.

Deception Is Charged.

"Thousands, possibly millions of dollars, have been stolen from various public funds, and in Republican strongholds. But that's okay. Seventy-six votes tells the story. Mr. Macy's Assembly agent, Potter, carries the deception through, but the

Continued on Page Two.

Three Unemployment Measures Passed by One or Both Houses

By The Associated Press.

ALBANY, Sept. 18.—Three bills were passed by one or both houses of the Legislature today embodying ideas contained in the Governor's unemployment relief program.

Both houses approved a bill increasing the State income tax 50 per cent to provide the $20,000,000 fund proposed for relief work.

Two unemployment bills were passed in the upper house.

One provided for a five-day week on all public works construction, the other eliminated from the labor law a section exempting contractors from paying the prevailing rate of wages outside of cities and villages.

YOUNG IS CONFIDENT OF ADEQUATE RELIEF

Relying on Local Funds Largely, He Predicts There Will Be No Winter Suffering.

NATIONAL SUPPORT READY

No "Drive" by Gifford Committee, He Says at Capital—Chairman Also Confident.

Special to The New York Times.

WASHINGTON, Sept. 18.—Owen D. Young, chairman of the Committee of Mobilization of Relief Resources of the President's Organization for Unemployment Relief, expressed confidence today that State, municipal and private resources would be able to cope with unemployment distress the coming Winter, but at the same time left the door open for consideration of the expenditure of Federal funds in relief programs.

Mr. Young gave his views in an interview following meeting of his committee, where plans for aiding local relief drives were discussed. The chief function of this committee, he said, will be to assist local relief agencies through publicity and other means which these agencies could not command. The Young committee itself will not conduct drives for funds.

"I don't think we will let anybody suffer in the United States during the the coming Winter," Mr. Young said. "What that implies I don't know," but I have every reason to believe that the States and municipalities and private agencies will provide sufficient funds. There will be no suffering."

"Then relief will be carried forward even if a Federal appropriation is necessary?" Mr. Young was asked.

"You may interpret that as you please," he replied after a second's thought.

Members Report on Districts.

At the committee meeting, Mr. Young described briefly the scope of the committee's work and Walter S. Gifford, chairman of the President's organization, told how this and other national committees will cooperate. Committee members exchanged reports on conditions in their own sections and outlined relief needs as they now appear, with the reservation that conditions may change radically within several weeks before cold weather sets in.

The meeting was held after Mr. Young paid a brief call on the President during which he was photographed on the White House lawn.

"The reports varied, according to localities," Mr. Young said. "You can't compare conditions in highly industrialized districts, such as Detroit, and rural areas like Oklahoma. But in every locality there was clear recognition of the situation and a determination to meet it. We are much better prepared than we were at this time last year."

Mr. Young termed the committee which he heads "basically a promotional clearing house."

"Communities throughout the country already are perfecting their plans for funds," he said, "whether public or private, to meet their own needs. These funds will be administered and distributed where they are raised.

Not Soliciting Private Funds.

"In these individual campaigns for funds this committee does not engage. Its purpose is solely to provide aid of a national character, which local communities could not enlist themselves. The great majority of these local campaigns will occur during the five weeks beginning Oct. 19.

Continued on Page Two.

ALL DIFFERENCES SETT[LED]

Concessions Made Both Sides in Gainin[g] Agreement.

WICKS BILL IS AMEN[DED]

Measure Will Be Ru[shed] Through Legislature Today Aid of Emergency Messag[e]

THEN SESSION WILL [END]

Threat of Veto Halted Rep[ub]lican Plan to Adjourn [and] Brought About Negotiatio[ns]

By W. A. WARN.

Special to The New York Times.

ALBANY, Saturday, Sept. [19.—] All outstanding differences bet[ween] Governor Roosevelt and the R[epub]lican majority in the Legisla[ture] over unemployment relief [legis]lation were removed at a confe[rence] which ended at 2 o'clock this m[orn]ing after going on for five hou[rs.]

The Wicks bill, amended so [as to] be acceptable to both sides, wi[ll be] passed by the Senate and Asse[mbly] under an emergency message [from] the Governor when the Legisla[ture] meets later today.

The extraordinary session will [come] to an end late this afternoo[n in] accordance with the present [pro]gram.

Mutual concessions were ma[de to] arrive at the harmonious unders[tand]ing. The Republicans yielded on [two] points and Governor Roosevel[t on] one.

The Republicans receded from [their] contention that the administ[ration] commission to be appointed by [the] Governor should be connected [with] the State Department of Social [Wel]fare and agreed that it shall fun[ction] as a wholly free and indepen[dent] temporary agency of the State [whose] life is to be terminated when [the] emergency is ended through p[rocla]mation by the Governor.

Agree on Local Relief.

The other concession made by [the] Republicans consisted in agreei[ng to] place in the amended Wicks bi[ll an] absolute limitation of $20,000,00[0 on] expenditures to be made by the [State] in connection with unemploy[ment] relief.

This was to meet objections [raised] by the Governor on the ground [that] in its present form the bill vir[tually] would give to localities a "[blank] check" and possibly obligate [the] State far beyond the huge sum [con]templated.

Governor Roosevelt withdrew [his] objections to the machinery se[t up] in the Wicks bill for local relie[f dis]tribution.

The Republican leaders were [abso]lutely determined that bodies ap[point]ed by the cities and Boards o[f Su]pervisors in county territory ou[tside] of the cities should handle the [dis]tribution of the funds for home [and] work relief.

The conference, which began [at ...] o'clock last night in Lieut. [Gov]ernor Herbert H. Lehman's sui[te at] the De Witt Clinton Hotel, we[re at]tended by the Governor and the [Lieu]tenant Governor, Samuel I. R[osen]man, counsel to the Governor; [Sen]ator Fearon, president of the Se[nate;] Speaker McGinnies of the Asse[mbly,] and Senator Dunnigan and Asse[mbly]man Steingut, leaders of the D[emo]cratic minority.

At an earlier conference last[ing] ning the chief Republican legis[lative] leaders had agreed that the Gov[ernor] should have his way in appoint[ing a] commission for administering [relief] which should have no conne[ction] with the State Welfare Commi[ssion.]

All day long warlike gesture followed warlike gesture at the [Cap]itol, coming both from the [first] floor where the lawmakers si[t and] the second floor where Gov[ernor] Roosevelt had been at his desk [with] a "happy warrior" expression o[n his] face, receiving bulletins from [the] third floor front."

While the Governor was sm[iling] frowning brows were displaye[d on] the Republican sides of the S[enate] and Assembly, though yesterday [was] to have been the closing day o[f the] session.

The Assembly, as a matter of [fact] had already adopted and sent t[o the] Senate a concurrent resolution [pro]viding for final adjournment [at ...] o'clock, Eastern Standard [Time,] when the prospect for a

"All the News That's Fit to Print."

The New York Times.

5 A. M. EDITION
WEATHER—Rain today; tomorrow fair and colder.
Temperatures Yesterday—Max., 56; Min., 50.

VOL. LXXXII....No. 27,318. Entered as Second-Class Matter, Postoffice, New York, N. Y. NEW YORK, WEDNESDAY, NOVEMBER 9, 1932. ***** TWO CENTS In New York City | THREE CENTS Within 200 Miles | FOUR CENTS Elsewhere Except in 7th and 8th Postal Zones

ROOSEVELT WINNER IN LANDSLIDE! DEMOCRATS CONTROL WET CONGRESS; LEHMAN GOVERNOR, O'BRIEN MAYOR

VOTE FOR M'KEE

Brien Is 245,464 Behind Ticket as Protests Rise

FINAL LEAD IS 616,736

nds Concedes Defeat rly, Saying 'Day of Miracles Is Past.'

EE TOTAL IS 137,538

usands of "Write-In" Votes Wasted as Backers Fail Record Choice Properly.

LQUIT POLLS 248,425

Greatest Vote in History of ty for a Socialist—Runs Far Ahead of Party.

rogate John P. O'Brien, Tam-'s candidate, was elected Mayor ew York yesterday, but over-wing his victory, which was a one conclusion, was the tremen- "write-in" vote cast for Acting r Joseph V. McKee.

al returns from the city showed O'Brien to have received a lity of 616,736 over his nearest nent, Lewis H. Pounds, Repub-

Judge O'Brien's vote was 768, Mr. Pounds polled 439,032; Morris Hillquit, Socialist, polled ighest vote ever given a candi- of his party in the city by re- g 248,425 votes.

Vote Listed by Boroughs.

boroughs, the totals were as vs:

	O'Brien.	Pounds.	Hillquit.
ttan	309,236	113,278	39,398
....	181,349	48,284	67,949
yn	388,605	155,478	112,740
....	176,237	105,451	25,821
ond	30,321	16,511	2,517
tal........	1,055,768	439,032	248,425

vote for Mr. McKee, put early morning at 137,538, actually was more than that, if ballots in the voters had abbreviated his , or used initials, or spelled it gly, were counted.

vote was unprecedented, par- rly as the use of voting ma- s made it much more difficult name to be writen in than on old paper ballots.

ge O'Brien had a clear majority 5,000 votes over the combined of Pounds, Hillquit and McKee, he McKee ballots cast aside as would have reduced this, it was ed out last night.

vote for Mr. McKee by ghs was as follows:

hattan, 26,334, with ten election dis- missing.
x, 24,453, complete.
klyn, 43,328, complete.
ns, 36,303, complete.
mond, 6,790, complete.
total, 137,538.

vote for Mr. McKee, made out any campaign on his part, n the face of his own disavowal e movement, kept him in the cal picture as a candidate to be oned with for the full four-year to be voted on in 1933.

term for which Judge O'Brien elected starts on Jan. 1, 1933, ends on Jan. 1, 1934.

vote for Mr. O'Brien indicated an 381,263 votes behind Gover- Roosevelt in the city, in actual cast, though his plurality was 245,464 smaller than that given e Presidential candidate.

Pounds conceded Mr. O'Brien's ry as early as 9:30 in the eve- and he sent the latter a tele- of congratulation.

said later he could have been d only by a miracle, and that days of miracles were past. Mr. ee, receiving election returns at Park Lane, also sent a short

Continued on Page Seven.

THE GOVERNOR-ELECT.

© New York Times Studio.
Colonel Herbert H. Lehman.

JUDGES IN 'DEAL' WIN; PROTEST VOTE HEAVY

Steuer and Hofstadter Elected With Lydon and Leary to Supreme Court Bench.

290.000 FOR INDEPENDENTS

Bar Leaders Elated by Big Count for Deutsch and Alger—Call It 'Warning to Bosses.'

City Court Justice Aron Steuer and State Senator Samuel H. Hofstadter were elected yesterday over their independent opponents, Bernard S. Deutsch and George W. Alger, by a vote of about 2 to 1.

The protest vote against the so-called deal by which Senator Hofstadter and Justice Steuer received bipatrisan nominations for two of four vacancies on the Supreme Court bench in the first judicial district exceeded all expectations, but it was not enough to upset the combined strength of the Republican and Democratic organizations.

Justice Richard P. Lydon, who was nominated by both major parties for re-election, and Municipal Court Justice Timothy A. Leary, who had the Democratic nomination for the fourth vacancy on the bench, were elected with comfortable margins. Municipal Court Justice George L. Genung, who had the Republican nomination, trailed far behind the independent candidates.

Since Justice Lydon's re-election was virtually uncontested, his totals were not computed in the early returns. Of the other, Justice Steuer and Judge Leary were running slightly ahead of Senator Hofstadter, whose lead was large enough, however, to preclude the possibility of his being overtaken by Mr. Deutsch, his nearest rival.

The Complete Returns.

The complete returns for the entire first judicial district, comprising the boroughs of Manhattan and the Bronx, follow:

Steuer	565,405
Leary	547,112
Hofstadter	544,032
Deutsch	293,125
Alger	287,167
Genung	203,222

The totals recorded for the judiciary candidates in Manhattan follow:

Steuer	367,295
Hofstadter	357,430
Leary	331,442
Deutsch	147,886
Alger	145,346
Genung	138,304

Final returns from the Bronx, where the independent candidates ran strongest, showed the following totals:

Leary	215,670
Steuer	193,110
Hofstadter	186,602
Deutsch	145,239
Alger	141,821
Genung	66,918

The independent candidates did not

Continued on Page Twelve.

STATE VICTORY SOLID

Lehman Gets Record Party Plurality of 887,000.

WAGNER CLOSE TO HIM

National Ticket Has Margin of 615,000—Full Slate Is Elected.

RELIEF BONDS ARE VOTED

Republicans Have Narrow Edge Up-State—Hill Admits 'Protest' Defeated Them.

By JAMES A. HAGERTY.

Lieut. Gov. Herbert H. Lehman, Democratic nominee for Governor, defeated Colonel William J. Donovan, Republican, yesterday, in the Democratic whirlwind that swept New York State, by a plurality of about 887,000, a record for a Democratic candidate in this State.

Governor Franklin D. Roosevelt and Speaker John N. Garner, the Democratic candidates for President and Vice President, carried the State by a plurality of about 615,000, as against Governor Roosevelt's heretofore record Democratic plurality of 725,000, which he received as candidate for re-election to the Governorship two years ago.

With Governor Roosevelt and Colonel Lehman were swept into office the other Democratic candidates on the State-wide ticket, United States Senator Robert F. Wagner, candidate for re-election; M. William Bray, for Lieutenant Governor; State Controller Morris S. Tremaine, Attorney General John J. Bennett Jr. and the two candidates for Representatives-at-Large, Elmer E. Studley and John Fitzgibbons.

Colonel Lehman led Governor Roosevelt by 88,279 in actual votes cast in New York City and also led the Governor in many cities and counties up-State. His indicated plurality exceeded that of Governor Roosevelt by more than 250,000, but exceeded the indicated plurality for Senator Wagner by only about 35,000.

Returns on the proposition and proposed constitutional amendment were slow in coming in, but a large majority for the proposal to issue $30,000,000 in bonds for unemployment relief was indicated, and scattering returns indicated that the constitutional amendment to throw open the forest reserve to the development of recreational facilities had been beaten.

The vote for President and State-wide candidates follows:

FOR PRESIDENT.

New York City, complete—Roosevelt, Democrat, 1,437,231; Hoover, Republican, 575,031; Thomas, Socialist, 120,486; actual plurality for Roosevelt, 862,200.

Up-State, 431 election districts missing—Roosevelt, 1,022,121; Hoover, 1,254,032; actual plurality for Hoover, 231,911; indicated plurality for Hoover, 247,107; indicated plurality for Roosevelt in the entire State, 615,093.

FOR GOVERNOR.

New York City, complete—Lehman, Democrat, 1,525,510; Donovan, Republican, 542,492; plurality for Lehman, 983,018.

Up-State, 561 election districts missing—Lehman, 1,056,088; Donovan, 1,141,735; actual plurality for Donovan, 85,647; indicated plurality for Donovan, 95,817.

Indicated plurality for Lehman in the entire State, 887,201.

FOR UNITED STATES SENATOR.

New York City, complete—Wagner, Dem., 1,433,343; Medalie, Rep., 517,733; plurality for Wagner, 920,610.

Up-State, 1,301 districts missing—Wagner, 915,699; Medalie, 964,418;

Continued on Page Sixteen.

The President's Message To the President-Elect

From a Staff Correspondent.

PALO ALTO, Cal., Nov. 8.—President Hoover conceded his defeat for re-election at 9:17 o'clock tonight, Pacific Time, and dispatched this telegram of congratulations to Governor Roosevelt:

Palo Alto, Cal., Nov. 8, 1932.

The Hon. Franklin D. Roosevelt,
Biltmore Hotel,
New York, N. Y.

I congratulate you on the opportunity that has come to you to be of service to the country and I wish for you a most successful administration. In the common purpose of all of us I shall dedicate myself to every possible helpful effort.

HERBERT HOOVER.

Governor Roosevelt had not received President Hoover's message when he left for his home shortly before 2 o'clock this morning. Pending its receipt he said he preferred not to make reply or comment on the message.

DEMOCRATS CONTROL STATE SENATE, 26-25

Republican Margin in Assembly of 6 Votes Is Reduced to 2—Lose by 4 Up-State.

ALSO TWO SENATE SEATS

Moffatt Is Re-elected, While Hastings and Dr. Love Are Defeated in City Race.

The slender working majority of two votes by which the Republicans control the present State Senate was swept away in yesterday's Democratic landslide. The next Senate will be made up of 25 Republicans and 26 Democrats, giving the Democrats a majority of one. The present Senate has 27 Republican and 25 Democratic members. Twenty-six votes are required to pass a bill in that branch of the Legislature.

In the Assembly, where 76 votes are required to control legislation, the Republican majority of six is cut down to two in the 1933 Legislature. The Republicans won 77 seats and the Democrats 73 at yesterday's elections for the Assembly.

The Democrats won four Assembly districts north of the Bronx away from the Republicans, one district in Monroe County, one district in Oneida and two in Sullivan and Schoharie counties. The Republicans, however, reduced the up-State Democratic gains by recapturing from them Schuyler county in the southern tier, where last year they succeeded in electing their candidate for the Lower House.

Post Is Defeated.

The Republicans also managed to strengthen their New York City representation by electing Herbert Brownell Jr. in the Tenth (Manhattan) District. This was the district where Langdon W. Post, Democratic incumbent was turned down by Tammany for supporting legislation to broaden the powers and continue the Hofstadter Committee and ran as an independent, polling 5,053 votes. Mr. Brownell defeated his Tammany opponent by a scant plurality of 307 votes. He received 8,907 votes, Sylva La Chappelle, the Democrat, 8,600.

The Democrats gained two Senate districts up-State, the Thirty-first, made up of Rensselaer County, and the Thirty-sixth, made up of Oneida. In the Thirty-fourth, composed of St. Lawrence and Franklin Counties, Warren T. Thayer, the present Republican incumbent, managed to win again after a hard fight.

The New York City Republicans will have three representatives in the Legislature, Senator-elect George Blumberg, who won by a plurality of approximately 500 over Senator John A. Hastings, Democratic incumbent in the Seventh Senatorial

Continued on Page Five.

OVERTURN IN SENATE

Bingham, Watson, Moses and Smoot Are Defeated.

DEMOCRATIC MAJORITY 12

Party Adds to Control in House—May Rule Both Branches This Winter.

LA GUARDIA LOSES SEAT

Mrs. Pratt Defeated, Wadsworth Wins—Texas Sends Garner Back to the House.

The Democratic wave of victory yesterday gave that party complete control of Congress and in its onrush carried down to defeat the four Republican leaders of the Senate.

Senator Smoot of Utah, Republican dean of the Senate and chairman of the powerful Finance Committee; Senator Watson of Indiana, floor leader; Senator Moses, president pro tempore and Senator Jones of Washington, chairman of the Appropriations Committee, all were relegated to the ranks of "lame ducks." No such upset has occurred in recent history.

While returns early this morning showed the new Senate will be Democratic by a majority of twelve and the House overwhelmingly Democratic, there was a possibility that in the session of the old Congress convening on Dec. 5, the Democrats will achieve a slender control of the whole body.

Changes in Coming Session.

They now have a majority of one in the House, in the old Congress that still is to hold a "lame-duck" session; in the Senate the numbers were evened with the defeat of Senator Barbour of New Jersey for the short term beginning next month, and there was, early this morning, an even chance that Colorado would elect Walter Walker, a Democrat, also for the short term. In that event the Senate in December would be: Democrats 49, Republicans 46, Farmer-Labor 1.

On the basis of incomplete returns, the new Senate stood at Democrats 54, Republicans 34, Farmer-Labor 1, and seven States still in doubt.

The next Congress not only will be Democratic; it will be wet.

New York Republicans fared especially ill in the election, which saw Representative La Guardia, fiery "liberal" Republican who led a bloc that controlled the House temporarily in the last session, defeated by J. J. Lanzetta, Democrat. Representative Ruth Pratt also failed of re-election.

Moses Loses in Close Race.

Of the most prominent Republicans who were unseated, Senator Watson went down first, conceding his defeat by Frederick Van Nuys, Democrat.

Senator Moses ran nip and tuck with Fred H. Brown, Democrat, until after midnight in the poll of ballots, when returns from Manchester, N. H., spelled his certain defeat.

Senator Smoot was defeated by Professor E. D. Thomas and Mr. Jones by Homer T. Bone. Both of the victors were Democrats. Senator Jones, who is better known as the author of the "five-and-ten" law than for his important committee chairmanship, was defeated coincident with adoption of a State referendum in Washington repealing that State's prohibition law.

An important Republican defeat in the House was that of Representative Haugen of Iowa, co-author of the McNary-Haugen bill, who went down before F. Bierman, Democrat.

McAdoo Wins Seat.

William Gibbs McAdoo, former Democratic Secretary of the Treasury, who was credited with switching the Democratic National Convention to Franklin D. Roosevelt through

Continued on Page Six.

THE PRESIDENT-ELECT.

© New York Times Studio.
Franklin D. Roosevelt.

The Electoral Vote

ROOSEVELT 448.

State	Votes	State	Votes
Alabama	11	Nebraska	7
Arizona	3	Nevada	3
Arkansas	9	New Jersey	16
California	22	New Mexico	3
Colorado	6	New York	47
Florida	7	North Carolina	13
Georgia	12	North Dakota	4
Idaho	4	Ohio	26
Illinois	29	Oklahoma	11
Indiana	14	Rhode Island	4
Iowa	11	South Carolina	8
Kansas	9	South Dakota	4
Kentucky	11	Tennessee	11
Louisiana	10	Texas	23
Maryland	8	Utah	4
Massachusetts	17	Virginia	11
Minnesota	11	Washington	8
Mississippi	9	West Virginia	8
Missouri	15	Wisconsin	12
Montana	4	Wyoming	3
HOOVER 59.			
Connecticut	8	New Hampshire	4
Delaware	3	Pennsylvania	36
Maine	5	Vermont	3
DOUBTFUL 24.			
Michigan	19	Oregon	5

Votes in Electoral College, 531; needed to elect, 266.

Wets in Control in Both Houses, But Short of Two-Thirds in Senate

Modification of Volstead Act Appears Certain, and House Has Easy Majority for Repeal, but Upper Chamber Support Is Uncertain on Basis of Returns.

Complete control of the next Congress by forces opposed to Federal prohibition was one of the results which came with the political upheaval that took place with yesterday's election.

With full returns from the major portion of the country and definite trends established in the remainder, it appeared certain that those demanding a change in the dry laws would hold between fifty and fifty-five seats in the Senate and 300 or more in the House of Representatives.

Up until an early hour this morning, only nineteen outspoken drys had been returned definitely to the House, while twenty-four Senators, most of whom did not come up for re-election this year, remained among the prohibitionists. Around 100 House seats still were in doubt, and several Senators and re-elected Representatives were yet undecided how to align themselves on the question.

The aggregation chosen yesterday represented a veritable checker-board of views on prohibition reform, but the extent of the majorities indicated a good chance for immediate modification of the Volstead act to allow light wines and beer. The gains in both Houses were chiefly among Democrats, whose party has been pledged to that course.

Modification in the next Congress appeared much more probable on the basis of yesterday's election than outright repeal of the Eighteenth Amendment. Sixty-four Senate seats and 290 in the House will be required for the latter, whereas only a bare majority of 49 in the Senate and 218 in the House would be needed to change the national prohibition (Volstead) law.

The House was sure of the necessary two-thirds for repeal, as early this morning the anti-prohibitionists had already captured 292 seats; the

Continued on Page Eight.

SWEEP IS NATIONAL

Democrats Carry 40 States, Electoral Votes 448.

SIX STATES FOR HOOVER

He Loses New York, New Jersey, Bay State, Indiana and Ohio.

DEMOCRATS WIN SENATE

Necessary Majority for Repeal of the Volstead Act in Prospect.

RECORD NATIONAL VOTE

Hoover Felicitates Rival and Promises 'Every Helpful Effort for Common Purpose.'

Roosevelt Statement.

President-elect Roosevelt gave the following statement to THE NEW YORK TIMES early this morning:

"While I am grateful with all my heart for this expression of the confidence of my fellow-Americans, I realize keenly the responsibility I shall assume and I mean to serve with my utmost capacity the interest of the nation.

"The people could not have arrived at this result if they had not been informed properly of my views by an independent press, and I value particularly the high service of THE NEW YORK TIMES in its reporting of my speeches and in its enlightened comment."

By ARTHUR KROCK.

A political cataclysm, unprecedented in the nation's history and produced by three years of depression, thrust President Herbert Hoover and the Republican power from control of the government yesterday, elected Governor Franklin Delano Roosevelt President of the United States, provided the Democrats with a large majority in Congress and gave them administration of the affairs of many States of the Union.

Fifteen minutes after midnight, Eastern Standard Time, The Associated Press flashed from Palo Alto this line: "Hoover concedes defeat."

It was then fifteen minutes after nine in California, and the President had been in his residence on the Leland Stanford campus only a few hours, arriving with expressed confidence of victory.

A few minutes after the flash from Palo Alto the text of Mr. Hoover's message of congratulation to his successful opponent was received by THE NEW YORK TIMES, though it was delayed in direct transmission to the President-elect. After offering his felicitations to Governor Roosevelt on his "opportunity to be of service to the country," and extending wishes for success, the President "dedicated" himself to "every possible helpful effort * * * in the common purpose of us all."

This language strengthened the belief of those who expect that the relations between the victor and the vanquished, in view of the exigent condition of the country, will be more than perfunctory, and that they may soon confer in an effort to arrive at a mutual program of stabilization during the period between now

"All the News That's Fit to Print."

The New York Times.

LATE CITY EDITION
WEATHER—Fair and slightly warmer today and tomorrow.
Temperatures Yesterday—Max., 40; min., 27.

VOL. LXXXII....No. 27,401. Entered as Second-Class Matter, Postoffice, New York, N. Y. NEW YORK, TUESDAY, JANUARY 31, 1933. **** TWO CENTS In New York City | THREE CENTS Within 200 Miles | FOUR CENTS Elsewhere Except in 7th and 8th Postal Zones.

HITLER MADE CHANCELLOR OF GERMANY BUT COALITION CABINET LIMITS POWER; CENTRISTS HOLD BALANCE IN REICHSTAG

GROUP FORMED BY PAPEN

Nationalists to Dominate in Government Led by National Socialist.

DR. HUGENBERG GETS POST

Frick in Interior Ministry to Control Police, but Army Has Non-Partisan Chief.

REDS URGE STRIKE TODAY

Cabinet Stresses That It Will Not Attempt Monetary or Economic Experiments.

By GUIDO ENDERIS.
Special Cable to THE NEW YORK TIMES.

BERLIN, Jan. 30.—Adolf Hitler, leader of the National Socialist party, today was appointed Chancellor of Germany after being twice rejected last year for that office.

Herr Hitler was manoeuvred into heading a coalition government of National Socialists and Nationalists by Lieut. Col. Franz von Papen, former Chancellor. The new Cabinet is a compromise between a Presidential and a Parliamentary government.

The composition of the Cabinet leaves Herr Hitler no scope for gratification of any dictatorial ambition. He accepted the Chancellorship on less sweeping terms than he laid down in his audiences with the President in August and November of last year. He swore obedience to the republican Constitution today after the President had accepted Colonel von Papen's Cabinet slate.

The New Cabinet.

The new Cabinet is composed as follows:

Chancellor—Adolf Hitler.
Vice Chancellor and Reich Commissioner for Prussia—Lieut. Col. Franz von Papen.
Foreign Minister—Baron Constantin von Neurath.
Interior Minister—Dr. Wilhelm F. Frick.
Defense Minister—General Werner von Blomberg.
Finance Minister—Count Lutz Schwerin von Krosigk.
Economy and Food Minister—Dr. Alfred Hugenberg.
Labor Minister—Franz Seldte.
Transportation Minister—Baron Paul Eltz von Ruebenach.
Aviation Minister—Hermann Wilhelm Goering.
Employment Commissioner—Guenther Gereke.

Dr. Frick, former Interior Minister of Thuringia, and Herr Goering are Hitler's leading aides. Baron von Neurath, Count Schwerin von Krosigk and Baron von Ruebenach are holdovers from the Cabinet of Lieut. Gen. Kurt von Schleicher, which fell Saturday. Herr Goering also will be Acting Minister of Interior of Prussia. Herr Seldte is a leader of the Stahlhelm (Steel Helmet veterans' society) and stands far to the Right politically.

Ultimatum From Hindenburg.

President von Hindenburg had no personal contact with Herr Hitler during the negotiations leading to formation of the Cabinet, but informed quarters say the President threatened to precipitate a Presidential crisis unless Herr Hitler and Dr. Hugenberg made peace and got down to business. This ultimatum enabled Colonel von Papen to round up his new Cabinet without further parleys and march it before President von Hindenburg shortly after noon. It was immediately sworn in.

The speed with which it was projected into office is said to have bewildered Herr Hitler even more than its other members and left him cogitating on whether he had been stampeded into taking the Chancellorship on anything but his own terms.

Colonel von Papen kept his plans so secret that most of the afternoon papers, including Herr Hitler's official organ, were compelled to make over their regular evening editions to tell of the formation of the new Cabinet.

The National Socialists are in a minority in the Cabinet. The Chancellor's activities are severely limited through the presence in his Cabinet of Colonel von Papen, Baron von Neurath, Count Schwerin von Krosigk, Dr. Hugenberg and Herr Seldte. The preponderance of Conservatives is believed to have de-

Continued on Page Three.

Hitler Pledges Fight in Cabinet

By the Associated Press.

BERLIN, Jan. 30.—A proclamation emphasizing that the present Cabinet is not truly representative of Hitlerism and the nation was issued today by the new Chancellor, Adolf Hitler. In it the Nazi leader announced a determination to "carry on the fight within the government as tenaciously as we fought outside."

"After a thirteen-year struggle the National Socialist movement has succeeded in breaking through to the government; the struggle to win the German nation, however, is only beginning," the proclamation said.

"The National Socialist party knows that the new government is no National Socialist Government, but it is conscious that it bears the name of its leader, Adolf Hitler. He has advanced with his shock troops and has placed himself at the head of the government to lead the German people to liberty.

"Not only is the entire authority of State ready to be wielded, but in the background, prepared for action, is the National Socialist movement of millions of followers united unto death with its leaders. Our historic mission is now in the field of political economy."

Calling Herr Hitler's appointment "historic," the document lauded President von Hindenburg with these words:

"In this hour we wish to thank President von Hindenburg, whose immortal fame as a Field Marshal in the battlefields of the World War binds his name perpetually to that of young Germany, which is striving with burning heart to gain its liberty."

MODERATE CABINET PLANNED IN FRANCE

Daladier Is Unable to Get Socialist Support and Turns to Centre.

HITLER IS MADE AN ISSUE

Premier-Designate Rejects Left Demands for Cut in Military Budget on Berlin News.

By P. J. PHILIP.
Wireless to THE NEW YORK TIMES.

PARIS, Tuesday, Jan. 31.—France this morning was moving rapidly toward a new governmental alignment. Balked by the demands of the Socialists in forming a Cabinet with a Left orientation, Edouard Daladier, the Radical Premier-designate, turned with greater success to the Centre parties for collaboration.

M. Daladier announced at 1 A. M. that he expected to complete his Cabinet during the morning and to submit the list to President Lebrun this afternoon. In addition to the Premiership, he expects to take the portfolio of War, which he held in the fallen Cabinet of Joseph Paul-Boncour. M. Paul-Boncour, in the new line-up, would be Foreign Minister.

Other selections announced by M. Daladier are Georges Bonnet as Finance Minister, Lucien Lamoureux as Minister of the Budget, Camille Chautemps as Minister of the Interior, Henri Queuille as Minister of Agriculture, Georges Leygues as Minister of Marine, Anatole de Monize as Minister of Education and Laurent Eynac as Minister of Posts and Telegraphs.

Hitler's Rise a Factor.

The shift in party alignment is undoubtedly due in part to the selection of Adolf Hitler as Chancellor of Germany, but there are two other big factors. The first is the discontent which has been growing strongly in this country during the past two months against Parliamentary government and the second is the definite split which occurred today between the Radicals and the Socialists.

Twice within six weeks the Socialists, by withdrawing their support, have overthrown radical Cabinets. Today they imposed unacceptable conditions for their collaboration or support.

Whether M. Daladier can form a Cabinet independent of the Socialists and whether, if he succeeds, he will be able to get sufficient support on the Right in Parliament remain uncertain. Even within his own party there is a strong faction opposed to association with the Right. Furthermore, there is no certainty the Centre will accept a Cabinet under such a strongly Radical leader. But M. Daladier has strong support in the Senate, which is controlled by the Radical party.

Yesterday was spent in negotiations between M. Daladier and the Socialist leaders and among the Socialists themselves. M. Daladier first, however, took the precaution to discuss the budget situation with the finance leaders of his own party, Georges Bonnet, Lucien Lamoureux and Louis Malvy. Then, on sure ground as to the extent to which his party would go in meet-

Continued on Page Six.

HOOVER SKEPTICAL OF SUCCESS ON DEBT

Sees Roosevelt Making Wrong Approach—Holds Economic Topics Should Come First.

QUICK ACTION HIS AIM

He Favored Joint Stand With Britain at World Parley—London Discusses Debts.

By ARTHUR KROCK.
Special to THE NEW YORK TIMES.

WASHINGTON, Jan. 30.—Since the visit of Sir Ronald Lindsay, British Ambassador, to President-elect Roosevelt at Warm Springs, President Hoover has necessarily taken a back seat in the making of arrangements for the coming of the representatives of Great Britain to Washington after Mr. Roosevelt takes office. The fact that the journey was undertaken on the suggestion of the President-elect, who wished to make his position clear to the British Cabinet through the Ambassador instead of through Mr. Hoover's State Department, virtually eliminated the President and Secretary Stimson as active factors.

Mr. Hoover and those who have worked with him closely on the war debts problem have scrupulously kept the pledge of silence made at the White House conferences, so far as the press is concerned. No amount of questioning has induced them to discuss the fundamental difference in method between the administration and Mr. Roosevelt. They have declined even to talk about it in confidence with their newspaper friends.

But, in a situation like this one, certain facts become known to under-officials, and they slowly emerge. It was in this way that THE NEW YORK TIMES correspondent learned that Norman H. Davis had been responsible for adding the clause in the joint communiqué from the White House that extended the invitation to British "representatives" to come here for a concurrent discussion of economic problems of mutual interest to the two nations at the same time the debt "representative" was asked to appear in Washington.

More Facts Transpire.

By the same route other facts about the Roosevelt-Hoover debt situation have now become known, although Mr. Hoover and Secretaries Mills and Stimson continue to refuse to confirm, deny or privately converse about what has passed between "the two Presidents" and Mr. Stimson. Among these facts are:

The President feels that his successor has been going about the debt-discussion business in the wrong way and that he has got himself into a "hole." From the first it has been Mr. Hoover's position that economic topics of common Anglo-American interest should be discussed first between British and American representatives. Tentative agreement having been reached, it was the President's plan that the two nations should then move promptly into the World Economic Conference

Continued on Page Four.

NEW BRITISH RATES AFFECT U. S. GOODS FINISHED IN CANADA

After April 1, 50 Per Cent 'Empire Content' Is Required for Preferential Duty.

1,000 PLANTS INVOLVED

Many Expected to Be Moved to England or Withdrawn to United States.

HUGE CAPITAL AT STAKE

$1,500,000,000 Invested in Factories in Dominion—Political Struggle There Foreseen.

Special Cable to THE NEW YORK TIMES.

LONDON, Jan. 30.—United States manufacturers who apply minor finishing touches on their goods in Canada and then send them to Great Britain under imperial tariff preferences as "empire goods" will lose that privilege under an order issued by the Board of Trade tonight.

"Certain classes of empire goods imported into Britain," the order says, "in order to qualify for the imperial preferences agreed upon at Ottawa, must contain in the future a minimum of 50 per cent of empire material and labor instead of 25 per cent as at present."

The regulation will go into effect April 1. The list of goods affected is being withheld.

The Board of Trade regulations are being published as "Import Duties [Imperial Preferences] No. 1 Regulations, 1933." Copies, including a schedule of the goods on which the increased percentage applies, will soon be issued by the government printer.

William Watson, chairman of the industries committee of the Scottish National Development Council, recently said he had heard Canadian manufacturers refer to the British tariffs as a "huge joke." One hundred and fifty American companies, he added, had established branch plants in Canada in the last fifteen months, and, since the empire labor content required only 25 per cent, the activities of these factories in the majority of cases were purely nominal. The Laborite Daily Herald says the new regulation is aimed primarily at the United States.

1,000 Plants Involved.

The order of the British Board of Trade raising the empire content on goods exported from Canada to the United Kingdom from 25 to 50 per cent strikes a blow at the more than 1,000 American branch plants in Canada which have been established across the border in order to enjoy the advantages of preferences granted on exports from Canada to Britain. These branch plants, owned by the greatest industrial organizations in the United States, represent an investment estimated by some at $1,500,000,000.

The raising of the quota of empire content on goods to enjoy imperial preference was a heatedly debated question at the Imperial Economic Conference at Ottawa last August. While the Canadians demanded that the British requirement be raised to meet the Canadian, which ranges between 50 and 60 per cent, the British were not inclined to meet this demand, regarding it as excessive.

The conference finally agreed to take no official action on the matter but to leave it to the discre-

Continued on Page Four.

MORTGAGEES STAY $200,000,000 DEBT OF IOWA'S FARMERS

Insurance Companies Here Act to Suspend Foreclosures Pending Legal Relief.

GOVERNOR'S PLEA HEEDED

Policy Announced by New York Life Followed by Other Eastern Organizations.

NEBRASKA NAMES BOARD

Bryan Appoints Seven Conciliators as Debtors' Resistance Drive Spreads Through West.

In the most extensive private effort to cooperate with the owners of mortgaged farms ever made, a number of the leading Eastern life insurance companies, with nearly $200,000,000 invested in Iowa farms, have decided to suspend foreclosure activities throughout that State until the Legislature can enact its program to improve the position of the debtors.

This decision became known yesterday after the publication of an announcement of such a policy in behalf of his own company only, by Thomas A. Buckner, president of the New York Life Insurance Company. This company has been the object of stormy criticism in Iowa.

Although the other companies are not planning any formal statement, it was revealed that Mr. Buckner's announcement substantially outlined the general procedure for the present.

Yesterday's action came partly as a result of the recent proclamation by Governor Clyde Herring of Iowa, asking all holders of realty mortgages to refrain from foreclosing until the Legislature has had time to act, and partly as a gesture on the part of the Eastern underwriters to overcome some of the bad feeling toward them that has been engendered in the last month.

No Action on Other States.

As far as could be determined, the insurance companies are not at present planning similar action with respect to mortgages in other States. They regard the Iowa situation as peculiar to that State, because of certain laws now on the statute books there which make it possible for holders of chattel mortgages and other liens, which are in reality secondary to the first mortgages, to foreclose.

In defense of the forced sales of Iowa farms in the last month, insurance officials said many of these had been brought about, not through any effort on their part or any desire to foreclose, but because of the demands of the holders of secondary claims.

It is contended that with public sentiment in Iowa running as strongly against the Eastern insurance companies as it is, it has become extremely difficult to obtain the cooperation with individual mortgagors which is necessary for effecting renewals, and that, of course, such renewals are impossible where local holders of second mortgages and other liens insist on pressing their claims.

The attention of the East was first drawn to the situation generally when a group of 800 farmers forced the New York Life Insurance Company to raise its bid from $3,000 to $33,000 on a farm being sold at

Continued on Page Eight.

Roosevelt, at 51, Celebrates His Birthday; Cuts 80-Pound Cake for Georgia Children

Special to THE NEW YORK TIMES.

WARM SPRINGS, Ga., Jan. 30.—Franklin D. Roosevelt today celebrated his fifty-first birthday anniversary by cutting an eighty-pound birthday cake in the presence of 150 patients and staff members of the Warm Springs Foundation and by a dinner at his cottage, which was attended by members of his family and James A. Farley, Frank C. Walker, Edward J. Flynn and Henry Morgenthau Jr.

The ceremony of cutting the birthday cake brought much pleasure to nearly ninety crippled patients, who regard Mr. Roosevelt with great affection. The cake, the gift of the four sons of the President-elect, was placed in the centre of a long table in the dining room of Meriwether Inn, around which were crowded some of the older patients in wheeled chairs and all the children.

As Mr. Roosevelt entered and took his seat the patients began to chant, "A happy birthday, Mr. Roosevelt." The shrill voices of children rose high.

After photographers had taken pictures of Mr. Roosevelt, Mrs. Roosevelt and the group, the President-elect, addressing the children particularly, said:

"Now let's all blow together, and blow out the candles."

This was accomplished with the expenditure of much childish breath and much laughter.

"You may think that there is only one surgeon here, but I am going to show you that there are two," said the President-elect, wielding a large knife on the cake.

The first slice went to Mrs. Roosevelt, and he continued cutting until the waiters had served every person in the room.

Mr. Roosevelt, as cheers resounded, announced the gift of a check of $1,000 from an anonymous donor for the patients' aid fund. He remained at the hotel for more than an hour, chatting with the patients. The dinner at his cottage was private.

LEHMAN ASKS $84,000,000 IN NEW TAXES, 1% ON '33 GROSS INCOMES, ¾% ON SALES; STATE BUDGET CUT 23% TO $234,998,53

Gov. Lehman's Revenue Proposals

Special to THE NEW YORK TIMES.

ALBANY, Jan. 30.—Governor Lehman's chief proposals on the budget included the following:

INCOME TAXES—Lowering of exemptions for a single person from $2,500 to $1,000 and a married person from $4,000 to $2,500, the $400 exemption for dependents to remain unchanged. Emergency rate to be continued. Establishment of a 1 per cent gross income tax, no personal exemption allowed, on every single person whose income is $1,000 or more and every married person whose income is $2,500 or more. Capital gains and losses excluded, and interest, bad debts, contributions and other actual losses subtracted. This tax, an emergency levy for one year, to be in addition to the regular State income tax. Both the lowered exemption and the emergency tax to be applicable on 1933 incomes, payable in April, 1934.

SALES TAX—Enactment of a three-quarter of 1 per cent levy on retail sales of all tangible personal property, exclusive of food products and motor fuel, effective from April 1, 1933, to June 30, 1934.

MOTOR FUEL TAX—An increase of 1 per cent per gallon, as an emergency levy effective from April 1, 1933, to June 30, 1934, making the tax per gallon 4 cents.

SALARIES—Reductions for State employes receiving more than $2,000 a year of from 6 per cent on the first $2,000 to 33.9 per cent on that portion of a salary exceeding $15,000.

FEES FOR PAMPHLETS—Reports and other documents of departments to be charged for on a basis to cover the cost of preparation and publication.

PUBLIC SERVICE FEE—Authorization for the commission to charge against a company investigated a part of the cost of such inquiry.

MACHADO SAYS FOES STIR CUBAN UNREST

President Accuses Them of Killing Innocent Persons in Terror Campaign.

DENIES HE IS A DICTATOR

Opposition Is Open, Courts Are Free and Curbs Are Bar to Anarchy, He Asserts.

By RUSSELL PORTER.
Special Cable to THE NEW YORK TIMES.

HAVANA, Jan. 30.—President Machado, in an interview at the Presidential Palace today, denied that his government is a dictatorship and insisted that a majority of the Cuban people are supporting him. He promised to hold an honest Presidential election next year, at which, he said, he would not be a candidate for a third term.

Replying to charges of the Opposition that he is trying to perpetuate his own régime by illegal, unconstitutional and repressive methods, General Machado asserted he would resign his office "tomorrow" if he could do so without endangering peace and order. To charges that hundreds of political prisoners have been killed after arrest by his secret police, that hundreds have been kept in prison incommunicado for months and other hundreds exiled, he replied that those killed were members of a radical terroristic group who had attacked police, that only ten or fifteen political prisoners are now in prison and that those in exile had left the country voluntarily.

Opposed to Intervention.

President Machado declared himself unequivocably opposed to any intervention by the United States to straighten out the tangled situation here.

The above is a summary of written answers which the President returned through a government press attaché to a questionnaire which this reporter was required to submit in order to obtain an interview. The President granted a brief personal interview, which was attended by Dr. Orestes Ferrara, the Secretary of State, and an interpreter, as General Machado speaks only a few words of English.

In an informal oral interview before the questionnaire was answered, President Machado conceded that he had committed some unjust acts. Every head of a State sometimes had to do unjust things as well as just ones, he argued. But he had received many injustices as well as given them, he continued, and he thought the things he had done for the good of Cuba more than balanced the injustices. In everything he had done, he said, he had done his duty to Cuba as he saw it, in the same spirit and on the same ground as his service for Cuba in the Army of Liberation in the rebellion against Spain.

Machado Mild in Appearance.

President Machado is an inscrutable, enigmatic person, who is the

Continued on Page Six.

NEW POLICE FEES TO BRING IN $791,404

O'Brien Approves Mulrooney's Proposal to Raise Present Charges and Add Others.

TAXI LICENSES DOUBLED

Mayor and Tremaine Confer on Water and Finance—Justices Take 10% Cut.

Mayor O'Brien took the first definite step yesterday toward building up new revenues for the city when he approved suggestions for increasing old fees charged by the Police Department and for adding new charges. The changes will provide altogether an increased revenue of $791,404.

Police Commissioner Mulrooney listed his suggestions in response to a letter from the Mayor last December in which all city department heads were asked to submit proposals to increase the city's revenues this year. Mayor O'Brien said the Police Commissioner's proposals were covered in a general way in the findings of the Mayor's committee on new sources of revenue, but he emphasized that the credit for them went to Mr. Mulrooney.

Present fees will be increased in accordance with Mr. Mulrooney's schedule, to provide an added return amounting to $502,704 a year, while the new charges will bring in $288,700. Mr. O'Brien said that ordinances would be prepared where necessary to put the charges into effect. The Police Department can increase some of the fees without such action.

$50,000 From One Levy.

Among the new fees is a $5 charge for testing low-pressure boilers in hotels and apartment houses. No charge is now made by the Police Department. The levy is expected to bring in $50,000 a year. The department also proposed a fee of $1 for qualifying examinations for various classes of stationary and portable engineers and firemen, estimating the yield at $2,500 a year from this source.

Certificates for the successful candidates approved by the Police Department for these positions are to be charged for at the rate of $5 each, producing new income estimated at $10,000 a year. Renewal certificates issued each year would be subject to a new charge of $1 each, bringing the city $10,900.

The department makes about 60,000 searches of its records every year for private corporations. Mr. Mulrooney suggested a fee of $1 for the first five years on this service and 25 cents for each succeeding year. He estimated the income at $60,000.

Suburban real estate buses, which pay no fees to the Police Department, will be charged $10 each for the privilege of using the city streets. The estimated receipts are $2,000 a year.

Law firms desiring transcripts of police arrest records, previously fur-

Continued on Page Eleven.

CENT ADDED ON GASOLIN

Sales Impost Propose on All Retail Items Except Food.

FOR LOWER EXEMPTION

Governor Suggests Drop $1,500—Pay Cut for State Employes Urged.

BUDGET SMALLEST SINCE '2

Deficit of $105,900,000 ar Relief Measures Partly Offse Big Cuts in Appropriations.

Text of Governor Lehman's Budget Message, Pages 12 and 13

By W. A. WARN.
Special to THE NEW YORK TIMES.

ALBANY, Jan. 30.—New or add tional taxes, of an aggregate $84,000,000, were recommended Governor Lehman in his annu budget message, which was tran mitted to the Legislature this ev ning with his constitutional budg bill, calling for total appropriatio for the next fiscal year from funds and for all purposes of $23 998,531, a decrease of 23.7 per cen

The principal new revenues wou be derived from drastic increases the personal income taxes, es mated at $46,000,000; from a ret sales tax, with an estimated yie of $23,000,000, and an increase 1 cent per gallon in the State t on motor fuel, calculated to pr duce $15,000,000.

The increase in personal incom tax consists of a lowering of e emptions to the Federal levels a establishment of a new 1 per ce emergency tax on gross incom without exemptions, but with so deductions. These changes wou affect incomes of the calendar ye 1933 on which tax would be paid April, 1934.

The budget message contained figures on a prospective beer ta Upon consideration, the Govern said, he had decided not to inclu any estimate of revenues from th source, inasmuch as Congress h not yet acted favorably on the pr posal to legalize beer.

"I reserve the right to subr amendments to this revenue pr gram if and when Congress leg izes the sale of beer," the Govern said.

"In the event that Congress mo ifies the Volstead act so as to ma possible the sale of beer, a cons erable amount of revenue—althou probably not so much as ma assume—can be realized on the sa of that beverage."

To Meet $105,000,000 Deficit.

The Governor pointed out in h message that, although this yea budget total would be lower th any since 1925, new revenues wou be necessary to dispose of an a cumulated net deficit on June the end of the current fiscal ye estimated at $105,900,000, and lea something like an adequate ca surplus on June 30, 1934, the end the fiscal year for which the pr ent budget is made will expire.

This is necessary even though t estimated intake from taxes ready in force during the interve ing period should leave abo $24,000,000 in excess of the amoun appropriated which could be a plied toward wiping out the defic

The amount of additional tax asked is considerably below for casts made which in some instanc have run well in excess of $100,00 000. Governor Lehman himself cently estimated the latter figu would be necessary.

The comparatively low budg was made possible by material ductions in appropriations ma for the administrative departmen including graduated cuts in salaries above $2,000, received State officials and employes n protected by the Constitution their salary rights, together wi reductions in amount of State to the common schools and county and town highway purpos

The Governor himself, whose s ary is fixed by the Constitutio largely as an example to oth State officials, has ordered a volu

Continued on Page Thirteen.

"All the News That's Fit to Print."

The New York Times.

LATE CITY EDITION
WEATHER—Fair today; tomorrow cloudy, warmer, rain following
Temperatures Yesterday—Max., 40; min., 28.

Copyright, 1933, by The New York Times Company.

OL. LXXXII....No. 27,435. Entered as Second-Class Matter. Postoffice, New York, N. Y. NEW YORK, MONDAY, MARCH 6, 1933. P TWO CENTS In New York City. | THREE CENTS Within 200 Miles | FOUR CENTS Elsewhere Except in 7th and 8th Postal Zones

ROOSEVELT ORDERS 4-DAY BANK HOLIDAY, PUTS EMBARGO ON GOLD, CALLS CONGRESS

TLER BLOC WINS REICH MAJORITY; RULES IN PRUSSIA

-at-Homes Turn Out and ve Government 52% of 39,000,000 Record Vote.

IS ROLL UP 17,300,000

44% of Total Poll and en Wrest the Control of Bavaria From Catholics.

ECTION IS PEACEFUL

In Is Closely Guarded—The Stahlhelm Holds Parade Under Sunny Skies.

FREDERICK T. BIRCHALL.

cial Cable to THE NEW YORK TIMES.

ERLIN, Monday, March 6.—n almost mathematical precision the results in yesterday's man elections for the Reichstag the Prussian Diet bear out the ictions based on the pre-election campaign. Just as two and make four, so suppression and midation have produced a Nazionalist triumph. The rest of world may now accept the fact ltra-Nationalist domination of Reich and Prussia for a pro-d period with whatever results may entail.

2 o'clock this morning, when 00,000 out of the Reich's eligible of 44,000,000 counted and every indication of a probtotal vote of 90 per cent, exing all precedents Nazi-Naalist control of the Reichstag assured. The Nazis will have leat 288 seats and the Nationa 53 more, giving them toer 341 seats, or a clear 52 per in a total of 648.

e tabulated vote follows:

	Vote.	Seats.
onal Socialists	17,300,000	288
onalists	3,100,000	53
alists	7,000,000	118
munists	4,800,000	81
rists and Bavari-People's Party	5,500,000	91
ple's Party and ed Groups	1,014,000	12
(Democratic)	333,000	5
tal	39,047,000	648

e Nazis have increased their to 44 per cent of the adult ulation, or 11 per cent over that ast November and 6½ per cent their previous high-water total ast July. The Nationalist ine is barely 1 per cent over vote of last November. This, efore, is a Nazi rather than a ionalist triumph.

Nazis Control Bavaria.

art from the size of the vote—90 per cent of the eligible voters g as nearly unanimous as any ion in any large country has shown—the sensation of the ion is that the Nazis have ated control of Bavaria from Catholics. They have wiped out deficit in their November vote pared with that of July and e beaten the Bavarian People's y by approximately 600,000. is likely to dispose of any m of restoring the Wittelsbach archy in Bavaria, as it will of idea of a possible secession of aria from the Reich.

re than this, in the city of gne, the Catholic capital of many, under the influence of unexpected 25 per cent increase he total vote—three-fourths of new vote has gone into the Nazi col—Herr Hitler's party has come in an ace of seizing control e.

e so-called stay-at-home vote e out with a vengeance and al- t the whole of it went to the s; while, in addition, the Hit- s gained a full 10 per cent the other parties.

Gain 4,000,000 Votes.

e Nazis have increased their vote by more than 4,000,000, most 30 per cent over the November total. The Centrists and alists throughout the country e almost held their own. The munists lost more than 20 per of their lost votes did not go the Socialists, as had been exed. While a few may have gone

Continued on Page Eight.

Mob Attacked Stalin's Home In Wide Revolt, Tokyo Hears

Wireless to THE NEW YORK TIMES.

TOKYO, Monday, March 6.—Private information reaching Tokyo states that discontent due to famine conditions is so acute in Soviet Russia that a mob attacked Joseph Stalin's house in Moscow on Jan. 20 and was driven off by troops after 400 persons had been killed. Other reports from Siberia, partly corroborated by information reaching military circles here, indicate the farmers are in widespread revolt. Serious disturbances occurred at Irkutsk, and 80,000 men are said to have joined the revolt, including Communists and Red soldiers.

The Japanese discount a good part of these rumors, but they come from too many sources to be entirely ignored. It is believed these disturbances are much more serious than the Soviet Government has admitted.

CERMAK NEAR END; LAPSES INTO COMA

Death Is Imminent From Shot Aimed by Zangara at Roosevelt.

FAMILY AT HIS BEDSIDE

Third Transfusion Futile in 19-Day Fight to Save Chicago Mayor in Miami Hospital.

By The Associated Press.

MIAMI, Fla., Monday, March 6.—Physicians of Mayor Anton Cermak early this morning relinquished hope for his life.

In a bulletin issued at 12:30 A. M., the physicians said that Mayor Cermak was in a condition of coma and that he probably would live only a few hours. The bulletin said Mr. Cermak was "failing rapidly."

It was issued after a third blood transfusion had been administered yesterday in an attempt to save his life.

The Mayor's right lung, punctured on the night of Feb. 15 by a bullet from the pistol of the assassin, Joseph Zangara, in an attempt to kill Franklin D. Roosevelt, was aspirated yesterday and physicians found a gangrenous condition.

Father Morrison of St. Bartholomew's Church in Chicago entered the sun parlor room at 1:15 A. M. Mayor Cermak's wife was a Roman Catholic and his children are of that faith.

Dr. Frederick Tice of Chicago told newspaper men at 1:25 A. M. that the Mayor probably would live an hour. He said Cermak's breathing was very labored. He called members of the family and said Mr. Cermak's life was "a matter of an-other hour."

Members of Family Weep.

Members of the family, summoned to the bedside, emerged weeping.

Joseph Cermak, a brother, his wife and Mrs. John Kallal, a sister, came from the sun porch at 12:35 A. M. Mrs. Cermak and Mrs. Kallal took their seats on the lawn before the sun porch door and wept.

Vivian Graham, a granddaughter, emerged soon and joined the group. Daughters of the Mayor had been at his side a short time before.

At midnight newspapermen were allowed to go into the sun porch where the Mayor lies in an oxygen room and see the patient through the glass window of the oxygen apparatus.

The Mayor lay back on his pillow, hands folded over his chest, breathing heavily. Dr. Frank Jirka and Dr. E. S. Nichol were attending him.

Dr. Jirka, who is Mr. Cermak's son-in-law, said the Mayor recognized members of the family. "My wife asked him if he knew her. He told her, 'Yes, kiss me.'"

The greatest air of concern prevailed in the little sun porch, where a heavy guard of police and detectives was maintained.

"Reaction" After Transfusion.

After the blood transfusion yesterday afternoon Mr. Cermak suffered a "slight reaction," causing a weakening of the pulse and irregular respiration, the doctors said.

Reports immediately upon conclusion of the transfusion were that the operation apparently was successful. One pint of blood given by Thomas Pendray Jr. of Miami was

Continued on Page Fourteen.

JAPANESE PUSH ON IN FIERCE FIGHTING; CHINA CLOSES WALL

Jehol Forces Offer Stoutest Resistance of Campaign as They Are Cornered.

BUT LOSE ANOTHER PASS

Chang's Troops at Kupei Bar Retreat Southward to the Peiping Area.

NANKING ADMITS DEFEAT

Asserts 'What Will Happen Next Depends on Military'—Tientsin Fears Clashes.

By The Associated Press.

TOKYO, March 5.—Rengo (Japanese) news agency dispatches from Chengteh (Jehol City) today said the final phase of the Japanese campaign in Jehol Province, a move to seize passes in the Great Wall north and northeast of Peiping, was producing some of the most bitter fighting of the whole drive. Cornered Chinese units were resisting desperately.

The Sixteenth Infantry Brigade of Major Gen. Tadashi Kawahara, en route to Koupei Pass through the wall, fought fiercely with remnants of the troops of Tang Yu-lin, Governor of Jehol Province, ten miles west of the provincial capital, Chengteh. Thereafter the detachment advanced to Changshanku, which is sixteen miles northeast of the pass.

Marshal Chang Hsiao-liang, military commander of North China, was reported to have sealed the pass against Governor Tang and his followers. Governor Tang himself was reported to have fled to Fengning, which is about forty miles northwest of Chengteh.

Pass in Wall Taken.

Fighting in the shadow of the Great Wall preceded the occupation by the Fourteenth Infantry Brigade of Major Gen. Heijiro Hattori of Fanchia Pass, which is one of three important Great Wall passes south of Chengteh. General Hattori faced a large Chinese force south of the wall.

Major Gen. Kaoru Nakamura, commanding the Thirty-third Infantry Brigade, en route from Lingyau to Culehliing Pass, summoned an air squadron to aid him before he succeeded in routing remnants of Marshal Chang's Sixteenth Brigade.

The Fourth Cavalry Brigade of Major Gen. Kennosuke Mogi, pushing on from Chihfeng, 100 miles northeast of Chengteh, captured Weichang, fifty-five miles to the southwest, the centre of the Jehol opium-producing region, after stiff fighting.

Thousands of Chinese Dead.

Special Cable to THE NEW YORK TIMES.

SHANGHAI, Monday, March 6.—While members of the Nanking Government are expected to discuss a unified policy at Peiping this week, Jehol reports today tell of indescribable confusion among the Chinese forces there, with thousands killed, wounded and missing among the troops in Marshal Chang Hsiao-liang's best brigades, which originally totaled 20,000.

War Minister Ho Yin-ching arrived by airplane at Peiping at noon, and Acting Premier T. V. Soong and others are expected to follow him there for a belated stocktaking of the present situation. The Chinese troops in Jehol appear to be scrambling for the passes out through the Great Wall, with the Japanese bombing Chinese concentrations near Kupei and Hsifeng passes and at Dolonnor, in Northern Jehol.

The Japanese artillery is in action at Sanshihchiatze, between Pingchuan and Lingyuan.

The Japanese brigade led by General Hattori is expected to attack the main Chinese force tomorrow at Paishihlatzushan Hill, twenty miles south of Pingchuan and thirty-three miles from Hsifeng Pass.

The Chahar Provincial Government is reported to be negotiating with the Japanese for inclusion of that province in Manchukuo, but the Chinese military deny this.

The Nanking Foreign Office yesterday made this terse and incisive statement:

"Jehol is lost. What will happen

Continued on Page Eight.

Relief Wages Will Be Paid Despite Holiday, Gibson Says

Harvey D. Gibson, chairman of the Emergency Unemployment Relief Committee, declared yesterday that the bank holiday would not interfere with the payment of wages to unemployed men and women holding emergency jobs through the committee's work and relief bureau.

"Emergency wages must be paid and some way must be found to pay them," Mr. Gibson said. "I have no doubt that we will find a way to do it. We are not worried about it at all. Arrangements can certainly be made to meet the emergency relief payroll."

The weekly payroll of the committee exceeds $1,000,000.

BEWILDERED CITY STILL PAYS IN CASH

Faces Use of Scrip Calmly and Continues to Patronize the Theatres and Stores.

HOPEFUL MOOD PREVAILS

Merchants and Travel Lines Uncertain on Use of Tender—Many Extending Credit.

Bewildered but still cheerful, the city followed its usual routine yesterday, talked of the possibility of using scrip instead of cash, but still patronized the movie theatres, restaurants and concert halls.

Railroads reported, generally, that there had been no appreciable decrease in week-end travel, that there had been "no embarrassment" and that they were carrying on as usual, on an all-cash basis.

A spokesman for the Pennsylvania Railroad reported that the outward movement yesterday was good and an official of the New York Central reported everything going smoothly with enough cash on hand to meet all the road's needs for the present, including payrolls.

One form of nuisance cropped up at Pennsylvania Station. It started Saturday night, when persons with banknotes of large denominations demanded change. There was a tremendous number of $100 notes, quite a few $500 notes and even a few $1,000 notes were presented for change. One or two of the more timid persons tried to cover up their real purpose by buying Newark tickets.

Railroads Accept Only Cash.

None of the railroads is accepting anything but cash for transportation. This is in accord with general practice, an official pointed out, and up to yesterday no change in that plan had been proposed. Officers of the New York Central Railroad held a special meeting yesterday apparently to arrange for eventualities that might arise from the banking situation, but no decision was reached so far as could be learned.

Airplane lines and steamship lines, on the other hand, were accepting checks from old clients and were following a policy of being "reasonable" about accepting checks from other customers.

"We will maintain a sensible and reasonable attitude during this crisis," said John Gammie, assistant manager of the Cunard Line. "We will try to carry on much as we did in ordinary times. We haven't taken up the matter of scrip, but it is likely that a meeting of steamship line officials may be called to decide on a policy with regard to it."

Rise in Grocery Store Sales.

Increased sales were reported in most of the chain grocery stores in the poorer districts on Saturday, owners reported yesterday. They believed it might have been caused by a desire to stock up before an inflation policy might be decided upon by the government.

The Grand Union Grocery Stores, an official said last night, are planning to issue coupon books redeemable for food at their stores. The books would be sold to industrial and commercial concerns that would use them as part payment to employes. The same official considered it likely that guaranteed Clearing House scrip might be acceptable at the Grand Union stores.

A spokesman for the Great Atlantic and Pacific Tea Company, which maintains chains of grocery stores in several States, said his concern had not yet formulated any

Continued on Page Three.

BANKS HERE ACT AT ONCE

City Scrip to Be Ready Today or Tomorrow to Replace Currency.

EMERGENCY STEP PRAISED

Financiers Look for Little Interruption in Business Under Federal Program.

'TRUST DEPOSITS' TO AID

Cash Now Can Be Placed in New Accounts and Drawn Upon Without Limitation.

Clearing House certificates will be issued in New York, if needed, just as soon as they are printed, possibly today and probably not later than tomorrow, as a result of President Roosevelt's proclamation of last night.

The President's emergency decree not only made the banking holiday national and extended it through Thursday when Congress meets in special session, but it also gave the banks permission to issue scrip in the form of Clearing House certificates to take the place of regular currency.

Thus there will be little or no interruption in the ordinary routine of New York's business affairs, which can be carried on with scrip as a substitute medium of exchange just as well as with other currency. Paychecks, for instance, would be converted into scrip by the banks, which would be open for that purpose and for receiving new deposits.

Leading bankers indicated their approval of the President's proclamation last night and signified their belief that the use of scrip would be just as successful in New York as it was in the 1907 panic.

May Pay in Currency.

There is a possibility, some bankers said, that the New York banks might pay out currency when they reopen in place of, or in addition to, clearing house certificates. Such action would be possible only with the express permission of the Secretary of the Treasury under the President's order. These bankers said that the local banks have large amounts of till money on hand and that they could, if permitted, meet substantial demands from their depositors out of these cash holdings. From the standpoint of the central banking system the paying out of this till money to the public would have no effect upon the position of the national currency, since it is already a part of total money in circulation.

Subject always to the sanction of the Secretary of the Treasury, the banks will be able, under the President's proclamation, to operate along nearly normal lines. Under the provision for creation of special trust accounts, business men, merchants and wage earners will be able to find a safe depository for any cash they receive instead of having to face the dangers of carrying large amounts of currency. Those who withdrew money from the banks just before the shutdown and who have since been worrying about its safety will be able to redeposit the funds in special trust accounts and be assured of getting it back again without limitation.

Lehman Defers State Action.

When informed of the President's proclamation late last night, Governor Lehman withheld comment for the present as to whether he would issue a new decree extending the New York State holiday. Although such an action probably would be regarded as a mere formality, it was thought likely that the Governor would take it. Before President Roosevelt's proclamation was made public, Governor A. Harry Moore of New Jersey issued a decree last night extending the banking holiday in New Jersey indefinitely.

In both New York and New Jersey the banking holiday was proclaimed first for two days—Saturday and today—and was to have ended with the close of business this afternoon. Under the original proclamations by Governors Lehman and Moore the New York and New Jersey banks were to have been reopened tomorrow morning.

All security and commodity exchanges will remain closed, barring unexpected changes in present

Continued on Page Three.

The President's Bank Proclamation

Special to THE NEW YORK TIMES.

WASHINGTON, March 5.—The text of President Roosevelt's proclamation on the banking situation, issued at the White House at 11 o'clock tonight, was as follows:

BY THE PRESIDENT OF THE UNITED STATES OF AMERICA.

A Proclamation

WHEREAS there have been heavy and unwarranted withdrawals of gold and currency from our banking institutions for the purpose of hoarding; and

WHEREAS continuous and increasingly extensive speculative activity abroad in foreign exchange has resulted in severe drains on the nation's stocks of gold; and

WHEREAS these conditions have created a national emergency; and

WHEREAS it is in the best interests of all bank depositors that a period of respite be provided with a view to preventing further hoarding of coin, bullion or currency or speculation in foreign exchange and permitting the application of appropriate measures to protect the interests of our people; and

WHEREAS it is provided in Section 5 (b) of the act of October 6, 1917 (40 stat. L. 411) as amended, "that the President may investigate, regulate or prohibit, under such rules and regulations as he may prescribe, by means of licenses or otherwise, any transactions in foreign exchange and the export, hoarding, melting or earmarkings of gold or silver coin or bullion or currency * * *";

WHEREAS it is provided in Section 16 of the said act "that whoever shall wilfully violate any of the provisions of this act or of any license, rule or regulation issued thereunder, and whoever shall wilfully violate, neglect or refuse to comply with any order of the President issued in compliance with the provisions of this act, shall, upon conviction, be fined not more than $10,000 or, if a natural person, imprisoned for not more than ten years or both * * *";

NOW, THEREFORE, I, FRANKLIN D. ROOSEVELT, PRESIDENT OF THE UNITED STATES OF AMERICA, IN VIEW OF SUCH NATIONAL EMERGENCY AND BY VIRTUE of the authority vested in me by said act and in order to prevent the export, hoarding or earmarking of gold or silver coin or bullion or currency, do hereby proclaim, order, direct and declare that from Monday, the sixth day of March, to Thursday, the ninth day of March, nineteen hundred and thirty-three, both dates inclusive, there shall be maintained and observed by all banking institutions and all branches thereof located in the United States of America, including the Territories and Insular Possessions, a bank holiday, and that during said period all banking transactions shall be suspended.

During such holiday, excepting as hereinafter provided, no such banking institution or branch shall pay out, export, earmark or permit the withdrawal or transfer in any manner or by any device whatsoever of any gold or silver coin or bullion or currency or take any other action which might facilitate the hoarding thereof; nor shall any such banking institution or branch pay out deposits, make loans or discounts, deal in foreign exchange, transfer credits from the United States to any place abroad, or transact any other banking business whatsoever.

During such holiday, the Secretary of the Treasury, with the approval of the President and under such regulations as he may prescribe, is authorized and empowered (a) to permit any or all of such banking institutions to perform any or all of the usual banking functions, (b) to direct, require or permit the issuance of clearing house certificates, or other evidences of claims of assets of banking institutions, and (c) to authorize and direct the creation in such banking institutions of special trust accounts for the receipt of new deposits which shall be subject to withdrawal on demand without any restriction or limitation and shall be kept separately in cash or on deposit in Federal Reserve Banks or invested in obligations of the United States.

As used in this order the term "banking institutions" shall include all Federal Reserve Banks, national banking associations, banks, trust companies, savings banks, building and loan associations, credit unions, or other corporations, partnerships, associations or persons, engaged in the business of receiving deposits, making loans, discounting business paper, or transacting any other form of banking business.

IN WITNESS WHEREOF I have hereunto set my hand and caused the seal of the United States to be affixed.

Done in the City of Washington this 6th day of March, 1 A.M., in the year of Our Lord One Thousand Nine Hundred and Thirty-three, and of the Independence of the United States the one hundred and fifty-seventh.

(SEAL) FRANKLIN D. ROOSEVELT.

By the President:
CORDELL HULL,
Secretary of State.

ROOSEVELT MEETS GOVERNORS TODAY

Conference Will Centre on Bank Problem—Confidence in President Apparent.

Special to THE NEW YORK TIMES.

WASHINGTON, March 5.—The Governors conference which, President Roosevelt called nearly a month ago to discuss with him interlocking governmental problems will meet with him tomorrow morning in the White House at 11 o'clock. But its discussion will be largely directed toward the more immediate issue of banking moratoriums, with the possibility that what is done may indicate the eventual Federal action to be suggested by President Roosevelt.

The present situation so far overshadows the issues which Mr. Roosevelt stressed in originally calling the conference that they have become entirely secondary. It was his first intention to confine the discussion to a limitation on overlapping Federal and State

Continued on Page Two.

ON GOLD STANDARD, WOODIN DECLARES

Other High Officials Concur in His View of Suspending Payments for Period.

Special to THE NEW YORK TIMES.

WASHINGTON, March 5.—Secretary of the Treasury William H. Woodin declared tonight emphatically that the United States had not gone off the gold standard on account of the proclamation of the President. He was supported in this view by other high officials of the administration, both in the executive and legislative branches, among them Senator Key Pittman, chairman of the Committee on Foreign Relations.

Secretary Woodin said:

"It is ridiculous and misleading to say that we have gone off the gold standard, any more than we have gone off the currency standard.

"We are definitely on the gold standard. Gold merely cannot be obtained for several days. In other

Continued on Page Six.

USE OF SCRIP AUTHORIZED

President Takes Steps Under Sweeping Law of War Time.

PRISON FOR GOLD HOARDER

The Proclamation Provides for Withdrawals From Banks Against New Deposits.

CONGRESS SITS THURSDAY

Day of Conference With the Cabinet and Financial Men Precedes the Decree.

Special to THE NEW YORK TIMES.

WASHINGTON, March 5.—To prevent the export, hoarding or earmarking of gold or silver, coin or bullion or currency, President Roosevelt issued a proclamation at 11 o'clock tonight, in which he ordered a bank holiday from tomorrow through Thursday, March 9. Earlier in the day he had summoned a special session of Congress to meet on Thursday.

This sweeping action was taken after a day of conferences, among officials and bankers, the President taking recourse to war powers granted under the trading-with-the-enemy act.

As a result of the proclamation all banking activities will be suspended during the holiday, except as permitted by regulations of the Secretary of the Treasury, thus taking this country technically off the gold standard until the four-day period expires.

In order that there may not be a complete suspension of all banking and exchange operations, the proclamation authorizes the issuance of Clearing House certificates, which may be used as currency until the banks return to more normal functioning.

Points of the Proclamation.

The main points in the proclamation are:

1. A national banking holiday from March 6 to March 9 inclusive.

An embargo on the withdrawal of gold and silver for export or domestic use during that period, except with permission of the Secretary of the Treasury.

3. The issuance of Clearing House certificates or other evidence of claims against the assets of banking institutions to permit business to carry on.

4. Authorization to banking institutions under regulations of the Secretary of the Treasury to receive new deposits and make them subject to withdrawal on demand without any restrictions or limitations.

Friends of the President said he had a definite three-point program for the solution of the banking problem and that tonight's action included two of them. The first, they said, was a protection of the currency against unreasonable withdrawal. The second was to furnish a temporary currency. The third is permanent reorganization of the whole banking system, which, they predicted would be proposed to the special session of Congress meeting here Thursday.

Officials Act Quickly.

The Federal Reserve Board and Secretary Woodin, with the advice of former Secretary Ogden L. Mills acted immediately after the issuance of the proclamation to make it effective.

The proclamation was issued at 11 o'clock, bringing to an end a series of conferences held by Treasury officials and the new Cabinet throughout the day.

The proclamation affects all Federal Reserve Banks and national banks, trust companies, savings banks, building and loan associations, credit unions or other institutions engaged in any form of banking business.

The proclamation provides for a fine of $10,000 or imprisonment of not more than ten years or both for any violation of its provisions by gold hoarding or otherwise.

The President acted under Section 5 (b) and Section 16 of the trading with the enemy act to place these extraordinary restrictions on the nation's banking structure. The courts have interpreted the act as giving the President authority to bring about a complete suspension of gold and silver payments as well as an embargo on gold.

Section 5 (b) of the trading-with-

"All the News That's Fit to Print."

The New York Times.

LATE CITY EDITION
WEATHER—Possibly showers today, tomorrow; temperature same.
Temperatures Yesterday—Max., 68; Min., 55

VOL. LXXXII....No. 27,538. Entered as Second-Class Matter, Postoffice, New York, N. Y. NEW YORK, SATURDAY, JUNE 17, 1933. TWO CENTS In New York City. | THREE CENTS Within 200 Miles | FOUR CENTS Elsewhere Ex In 7th and 8th Postal

PRESIDENT STARTS RECOVERY PROGRAM, SIGNS BANK, RAIL AND INDUSTRY BILLS; WHEAT GROWERS WILL GET $150,000,00

CITY TO SELL BONDS DIRECT TO PUBLIC; $50,000 FOR STAFF

Interest Up to 5½% Provided in Scheme to Get Money and Reduce Bank Loans.

CANVASSERS TO BE HIRED

All Kinds of Securities Will Be Offered—Outstanding Issues Drop Sharply.

BERRY PROGRAM ADOPTED

He Foresees Wide Market for Offerings—Long-Term Issue Is Likely—No Action on Taxes.

Direct sale of city securities to the public at interest rates not exceeding 5½ per cent was authorized by the Board of Estimate yesterday. The action was taken upon the recommendation of Controller Charles W. Berry.

The Board appropriated $50,000 for a corps of trained bond salesmen to sell the securities. At the same time it raised the interest rate on baby bonds sold recently from 4¾ per cent to 5½ per cent. The baby bonds were issued in multiples of $10. Their use was restricted solely to payment of taxes. The plan adopted yesterday extends this sale to other forms of city securities without restrictions.

City Securities Decline.

Prices of New York City bonds dropped 1 to 3 points in the over-the-counter market yesterday. The movement was held to reflect the uncertainty regarding the city's ability to raise new revenues rather than its move to sell its obligations direct to the public. The ground lost canceled only part of the gains built up earlier in the week. The long-term 4½s closed at 82 bid, 84 asked, and the 6s due 1935 to 1937, at 93½ bid, 95 asked.

New York City banks are already large holders of the city's short-term securities and current market conditions do not permit the sale to investors. Thus, bankers who have been identified with the city's financing in the past appeared to be pleased that the city was about to make an effort to place the new short-term securities direct with the public instead of calling on them to underwrite the new issues.

As far as the city's plan to sell fifty-year bonds to the public is concerned, it was pointed out in banking circles that the current yield on long-term bonds of the city was 5.60 per cent and that new bonds would necessarily have to meet the competition of outstanding issues. It was further stated that new long-term financing was out of the question at present, in so far as the bankers were concerned, because of the heavy discounts ruling on old issues.

Controller Berry declared his belief that a wide market existed for city securities. In addition he announced a plan to float a fifty-year issue of corporate stock or serial bonds by selling them directly to the public. He said frankly that direct selling was undertaken to cut down the 5¾ interest rate charged by the city's bankers on loans.

Bids to Be Asked First.

Corporate stock, under the City Charter, may be offered for sale only upon public letting when sealed bids are received. The charter also provides, however, that the Controller may sell at private sale the unsold portion of stock remaining after public sale. Taking advantage of this provision, the Controller said he would first advertise the public sale, with notice that any portion not bid in would be sold over the counter at par.

By authorizing an interest rate of not more than 5½ per cent, the Board of Estimate eliminated one large difficulty in the public sale of city securities. It had been pointed out that if the securities bore a 4½ per cent rate, they would be in disadvantageous competition with other issues bearing 5¾ per cent. Securities sold only a quarter-point below the current rate will be readily absorbed, the Controller believes.

Without any salesmanship, Mr. Berry said, the Finance Department had marketed more than $24,000,000 of the baby bonds carrying a 4¾ per cent rate. Of that total he said $15,000,000 was bought by taxpayers in liquidation of their taxes for the first half of this year. Raising the interest rate to 5½ per cent, in Mr. Berry's opinion, will bring substantial sums into the city treasury now in prepayment of the second half year's taxes. Purchasers will have the advantage of the interest between now and Nov. 30.

Many property owners, the Controller reported, were not aware of the opportunity for profitable investment presented to them in the city's securities. The city's

Continued on Page Seven.

Harvard Defeats Yale Crew For Third Successive Year

For the third successive year Harvard won its annual crew race with Yale on the Thames River at New London, Conn., last evening. The Crimson captured the seventy-first varsity four-mile contest by a length and three-quarters, coming from behind in the last mile to triumph before a crowd of 35,000.

Harvard started the race in front, but at the half-mile mark Yale had gained the lead. The Eli oarsmen maintained their advantage until the three and a half-mile mark was reached when the Crimson went ahead by an eighth of a length. Harvard gained steadily to the finish line.

Harvard also took the junior varsity race, after trailing the Eli boat up to the last quarter-mile. Its late spurt gave the Crimson the victory by the scant margin of half a length. Yale won by a wide margin in the freshman race, also at two miles, scoring by five lengths. The two minor contests were held yesterday morning.

Complete Details on Page 9.

COMMON COLD LAID TO 2 AGENTS UNITED

Vaccination Against Virus Instead of Bacteria Is Urged at Doctors' Meeting.

NERVES CUT TO EASE PAIN

Whooping Cough Vaccine Is Upheld—Type 1 Pneumonia Serum Found Effective.

By WILLIAM L. LAURENCE.
Special to THE NEW YORK TIMES.

MILWAUKEE, June 16.—Evidence leading to a new theory on the origin and prevention of the common cold and epidemic influenza was presented here today before the closing sessions of the convention of the American Medical Association.

The findings on the two ailments, which so far have baffled all the efforts of medical science to combat them, were reported before the section on pharmacology and therapeutics by Dr. Alphonse R. Dochez, Dr. Yale Kneeland Jr. and Katharyne C. Mills of the College of Physicians and Surgeons, Columbia University.

There are two schools of thought on the origin of colds and influenza. One contends the diseases are due to the type of micro-organisms known as filterable viruses, which are invisible under the most powerful microscope and pass through any porcelain filter employed by bacteriologists.

The other school holds the two ailments are due to the various kinds of bacteria generally present in the upper respiratory tracts.

Studies of Dr. Dochez and his coworkers lead them to conclude that colds and influenza are due neither to a virus alone nor solely to the action of the bacteria, but rather to a combination of the two agents.

The virus, according to this hypothesis, acts as the "preparer of the soil," the "initiating agent" for the bacteria.

The investigators said they believed the way for prevention of colds and influenza lay in vaccination against the virus and not against the bacteria.

Dog Distemper Is Cited.

"From observations," the paper states, "the inference has been drawn that there may exist in respiratory disease a complex etiology (causality), comprising an initiating agent which can give rise to a mild disturbance like the common cold, and in certain instances one or another pathogenic bacteria which are by it empowered to invade the host and give rise to more severe secondary manifestations.

"There are two diseases in animals which immediately come to mind in this connection—in dog distemper and particularly in swine influenza it has been shown that more than one etiological agent is required to produce the typical disease.

"It has been demonstrated that in swine influenza there exists a filterable virus which by itself produces only the mildest of diseases; if administered together with a culture of certain bacterium it gives rise to typical, highly contagious swine influenza.

"But the culture of the organism alone, even if given in large doses, produces absolutely no effect at all.

"Here we have what might possibly be an analogue to human pandemic influenza, reconciling the divided views as to the rôle of a filterable virus on the one hand and of the influenza bacterium on the other.

"There is evidence that both colds and influenza are due to a complex etiology—a filterable virus acting in

Continued on Page Seven.

REICH ASKS RETURN OF AFRICAN LANDS AT LONDON PARLEY

Also Seeks Other Territory, Presumably in Europe, for 'Works of Peace.'

LINKS PLAN AND DEBTS

Hugenberg Statement Is Held to Confirm Nazi Hints of Eastward Expansion Aim.

MONEY RATIO PACT READY

Stabilization Plan Is Likely to Go to Conference Next Week—Two Boards Start Work.

By FREDERICK T. BIRCHALL.
Special Cable to THE NEW YORK TIMES.

LONDON, June 16.—The World Economic Conference went to work in two sections today—monetary and economic, respectively. The monetary commission, as it is called, made the most progress.

It divided itself into two committees, one to consider temporary, the other permanent, remedies for the distressful monetary conditions. Each of these quickly laid out a program of work. One of the subcommittees, under the chairmanship of Senator Key Pittman of the United States, will consider the advisability of remonetizing and extending the use of silver.

The chief feat of the economic commission was to draw out the Germans. Through the medium of Dr. Alfred Hugenberg, German Minister of Economy and Agriculture, it is now determined what Germany wants at the conference. She wants to recover her colonies in Africa. Also, apparently, she wants some further territory, presumably in Europe, for the "settlement of her active race and for the construction of great works of peace."

Revelation to Conference.

This was somewhat of a revelation to a conference called to deal with economic questions, not to apportion territory. This did not, however, cause much of a sensation, Germany being what she is under her present control and Dr. Hugenberg being hardly a person whom Chancellor Hitler would select as his chosen mouthpiece.

Nevertheless, there it is on record in plain words, at the close of a long statement by the head of the German delegation, dealing with the economic hardships of a "noncolonial" country and the responsibility of Germany's "international indebtedness" for the present parlous state of national economies.

The latter is taken as rather an expression of Dr. Hugenberg's personal fear—shared by few others—of a future demand for the issuance of that 3,000,000,000 marks' worth of "if and when" bonds to which Germany agreed in lieu of reparations at the Lausanne conference. The statement is also believed to be due to the German Minister's personal dislike, which he has frequently expressed, of the interest rates and the capital extent of Germany's private debt.

The official English translation of his actual declaration of Germany's colonial and territorial aspirations follows:

"From the German viewpoint wise and peaceful cooperation between debtor and creditor countries might include two large-minded measures whereby Germany's

Continued on Page Four.

Wiley Requested Sea Duty; Policy on Air Officers to Go On

By The Associated Press.

WASHINGTON, June 16.—The navy disclosed today that Lieut. Commander Herbert V. Wiley, sole surviving officer of the airship Akron, was ordered to sea "at his own request."

Rear Admiral Ernest King, Chief of Naval Aeronautics, made the explanation in relation to orders for the officer to report to the cruiser Cincinnati as navigating officer.

Secretary Swanson has said he foresaw no change in the navy's policy of ordering fliers to sea duty.

"Lieut. Commander Wiley testified before the joint Congressional committee that he believed in the navy's system of occasional sea duty for airship officers," Admiral King said.

This system was termed a "mistaken policy" by the Congressional committee in reporting on its investigation of the Akron disaster. Since then Lieut. Commander Wiley has been serving on the trial board of the new airship Macon, which has successfully passed trial flights.

KIDNAPPERS SEIZE ST. PAUL BREWER

Hold William Hamm, 39, for $100,000 Ransom—Death Threat Made in Note.

SANKEY LINKED TO GANG

Fugitive in Bohn and Boettcher Abductions Is Identified as Sender of Missive.

By The Associated Press.

ST. PAUL, June 16.—William Hamm, aged 39, St. Paul millionaire, was kidnapped yesterday and is being held for $100,000 ransom, it was announced tonight.

News of the kidnapping was withheld by the police in an effort to discover the identity of the abductors and bring about their arrest. When officials became convinced this was impossible immediately they decided to make the abduction known and enlist the aid of the public in apprehending the kidnappers.

Mr. Hamm is president and treasurer of the Hamm Brewing Company of St. Paul and son of the late William Hamm, a local capitalist.

The first news of the kidnapping was received yesterday by William W. Dunn, manager of the company, through a telephone call.

"We have kidnapped Mr. Hamm," said a voice. "You will hear from us later."

Cabman Names Verne Sankey.

Today Mr. Dunn received a note which stated Mr. Hamm was being held for $100,000 ransom and that unless the money was paid Mr. Hamm would be killed. Attached to the bottom of the note was postscript signed by Mr. Hamm, in which he urged immediate payment of the money.

The note was delivered by a taxi driver who told the police that he was approached by a man Thursday night.

"This man told me," the driver stated, "that he would give me $2 if I would take a note to Mr. Dunn. He said that his name was Gordon and that he lived in the Lowry Hotel. I took the note and delivered it."

Police said that the taxi driver later identified a picture of Verne Sankey, sought for two kidnappings already, as the man who gave him

Continued on Page Three.

Roosevelt Takes Special Train for Boston To Embark on Vacation Voyage 'Down East'

Special to THE NEW YORK TIMES.

WASHINGTON, June 16.—President Roosevelt left on his vacation tonight after working hard all day and signing all the important bills passed in the final days of Congress. Following a driving four months, filled with great responsibilities, the President boarded his train soon after 8:30, saying that he felt "tired but happy that Congress has ended its important legislative program so successfully."

The last visitor appeared at the Executive Offices just before 7. Then, closing his desk, the President took a plunge in his swimming pool. He had his secretaries and office staff with him at dinner and gave final instructions for work to be done during his vacation, which will last until the first week in July.

Hundreds of friends were at the station to say good-bye. The special train on the Pennsylvania Railroad, which followed the Federal Express to Boston, carried the President's party, including Stephen Early, his assistant secretary, and Miss Marguerite Le Hand, his personal stenographer, in addition to correspondents and photographers.

From Boston the President will go to Groton to see his sons Franklin Jr. and John. The former was graduated there yesterday. After luncheon with his family, the President will motor to Marion, on Cape Cod, where he will set sail on the Amberjack II with his son James and several of the latter's companions. The President will navigate the schooner to Portland, Me., stopping at convenient places for watering and revictualing.

Franklin Jr. and John will join him at Portland and continue the trip by water to Campobello Island, N. B., arriving about June 28. Joined there by Mrs. Roosevelt, the President will return on the cruiser Indianapolis on its speed trial from Eastport to the mouth of the Potomac.

On this trip he will not be accompanied by newspaper men or photographers.

AIDS FARMERS THIS YEAR

Wheat Processing Tax, 30 Cents, to Take Effect Soon After July 1.

ACREAGE CUTS IN 1934-35

Payments to Growers on Production Allotments Will Also Include This Year's Crop.

WILL PROTECT CONSUMERS

Wallace Promises No Undue Price Rises—Will Give Decision on Cotton Today.

Special to THE NEW YORK TIMES.

WASHINGTON, June 16.—Soon after July 1, Secretary Wallace announced today, the farm relief plan under which wheat growers agreeing to curtail their crops will receive approximately $150,000,000 will become operative.

The acreage reduction and allotment provisions of the Farm Relief Act will be applied to the wheat crops of 1934 and 1935, and the fund of $150,000,000 will be raised by a processing tax of around 30 cents a bushel levied against milling. By Sept. 15 two-thirds of the $150,000,000 will have been distributed among wheat growers who have complied with the government's terms.

Eligibility to share in this distribution requires that growers agree to reduce planting up to a maximum of 20 per cent next year. The exact reduction called for will depend on the outcome of the negotiations at the economic and monetary conference for joint international action to reduce world wheat production. It is possible that no reduction actually will be required.

No attempt will be made to reduce the already planted and growing 1933 crop, although the bonuses embrace this year.

Decision on Cotton Today.

Secretary Wallace will announce, probably tomorrow, the decision on what course will be followed with respect to cotton. The belief is that a 25 per cent destruction of the present cotton crop by leasing agreements, to be paid for out of a fund built up by a processing tax of 4 cents a pound, will be required. Cotton growers probably will have the opportunity to rent their land to the government for around $10 an acre and acquire the right to take options on cheap government-owned cotton.

The government reserved the right to establish the amount of reduction of the domestic wheat crop of 1934 at a later date so that the United States might retain a free hand in negotiating for world reduction at the London conference.

The Adjustment Administration will not know until actual operations are begun what the exact amount of the processing tax will be. On the basis of prices paid for wheat on farms for the first half of June, the tax would be about 30 cents because that amount represents the difference between the current farm price and the established average price of 1909-14, which is the base period on which the parity plan is based.

Basis for Payment.

The amounts to be paid to each individual wheat grower will be determined on the basis of his average production for the past three years and the percentage of that production which went into domestic consumption.

The average annual output for the country as a whole in that period was about 800,000,000 bushels, and of this amount about 500,000,000 bushels went into domestic consumption. With these totals the administration has produced a formula under which the individual grower will receive 30 cents on five-eighths of his production for the last three years.

If a grower's average production from 1930 to 1933 was 1,000 bushels, he would be entitled to benefit payments this year aggregating $187.50.

Secretary Wallace, in announcing the decision, stated that, contrary to the popular impression, the processing tax was not to be superimposed on the current market price for wheat. The farmer would continue to sell his wheat for what-

Continued on Page Two.

Powers Granted to the President

Special to THE NEW YORK TIMES.

WASHINGTON, June 16.—Extraordinary powers granted in the first session of the Seventy-third Congress to President Roosevelt are:

To establish control over all industry with the view to fixing minimum wages and maximum hours of work, regulating production and otherwise to promote, encourage and require fair competition.

To set up a system of government licenses for business if necessary to require conformance to the above.

To initiate and direct, through a Federal director of public works, a $3,300,000,000 public works program as a further government contribution to re-employment.

To direct, through a Federal director of relief, expenditure of $500,000,000, supplied by the Reconstruction Finance Corporation, for relief of destitution.

To invoke the Presidential powers of the World War to regulate transactions in credit, currency, gold and silver, even to embargo gold or foreign exchange; to fix restrictions on the banking business of the Federal Reserve System irrespective of the Federal Reserve Board.

To eliminate the old system for compensation and allowances for veterans and set up an entirely new pension system, with himself at the head.

To reduce by executive order the salaries of government employes by an amount not to exceed 15 per cent upon the finding of commensurate reduction in cost of living.

To transfer, eliminate, consolidate or rearrange bureaus in the executive branch of the government in the interest of public economy.

To repeal by executive proclamation certain new taxes voted in Industrial Recovery Act upon showing of restoration of business or in event of repeal of the Eighteenth Amendment.

To publish heretofore secret income tax returns to the extent he may deem in the public interest, and under such rules and regulations as he may prescribe.

To inflate the currency either by requiring open market operations in Federal securities, devaluing the gold dollar by not more than 50 per cent, issuing United States notes up to $3,000,000,000 or accepting up to $200,000,000 in silver in payment of the allied war debts.

To employ more than 250,000 unemployed young men in reforestation operations as still further government contribution to re-employment.

To appoint a coordinator of railroads to effect economies among the carriers and increase service to the public.

To appoint a Tennessee Valley Authority to develop natural resources of Tennessee River basin, including completion of Muscle Shoals project

WIDE WORK SPREAD ASKED BY JOHNSON

Recovery Chairman Urges Industry to Unite for Shorter Week, More Employes,

AND PAY TO MEET PRICES

Forced Down in Plane at Pittsburgh, He Addresses Coal Men by Radio.

Special to THE NEW YORK TIMES.

CHICAGO, June 16.—General Hugh S. Johnson, chairman of the Industrial Administrative Board, warned industry tonight that a critical economic stage had been reached at which there was danger of relapse from recent improvement because prices had risen faster and further than wages.

Such a relapse will be prevented, he told delegates to the annual convention of the National Coal Association in an address over the National Broadcasting Company's network from Pittsburgh, where he was forced down while flying here, by an immediate movement on a broad front for spreading work on a living-wage basis.

"The President has pointed out the way to start our business on a strong, sound, upward spiral," General Johnson said in his first public utterance as administrator.

"'The idea,' said he today, 'is simply for employers to hire more men to do the existing work by reducing the work hours of each man's week and at the same time paying a living wage for the shorter week.'"

Such a program cannot be undertaken unless all competing companies and industries adopt it at about the same time, he pointed out, hailing the approval of a simple, basic code in line with the President's policy at the convention here as an expression of industry's willingness to cooperate.

Suggests Industry's Course.

"The simplest and most direct course for each industry," he said, "is now to submit as an industry entirely what it would like to do, first, to carry out our primary purpose, which is to put men back to work at decent living wages in the shortest possible time, and second, those provisions which you find it absolutely necessary to include to protect the willing and forward-

Continued on Page Three.

TREASURY TO ORDER $25,000,000 WORK

Roberts and Farley Decide to Ask Bids at Once on More Federal Buildings.

PROJECTS HERE INCLUDED

Vesey Street Plans Already Prepared—22 Sites Have Been Selected in This State.

Special to THE NEW YORK TIMES.

WASHINGTON, June 16.—Bids will be asked at once by the Treasury Department on Federal buildings to cost $25,000,000, it was announced today after a conference between Postmaster General Farley and L. W. Robert, Assistant Secretary of the Treasury.

Already bids have been asked on twenty-two projects to cost about the same and bids will be sought within the next ninety days on sixty-two additional projects calling for expenditures of $50,000,000.

This will put $100,000,000 of the $3,300,000,000 construction appropriation under the National Industrial Recovery Act to work by Oct. 1 through Treasury-Postoffice building alone.

It is the hope of General Hugh S. Johnson, Federal Industrial Control Administrator, to get $1,000,000,000 turning over in construction of various kinds by Oct. 1. He estimates that for every $1,000,000,000 in construction awarded, 1,000,000 men can be put to work.

Mr. Robert has been in conference with Mr. Johnson relative to the general program. Both wish to get the money at work quickly, rather than to spread it out over a long period and the Treasury's policy will be directed to that end.

$494,604,187 Authorized.

Treasury figures showed that, under the regular $700,000,000 building program, projects with a limit of cost of $494,604,187 have been authorized, while under the so-called relief program, $85,865,900 was authorized.

The government, under the $700,000,000 regular Treasury-Postoffice program has completed 355 projects with a limit cost of $121,387,119. There are 280 projects with a limit of cost of $321,254,310 under contract, while eighty-one projects are

Continued on Page Two.

ROOSEVELT HAILS GO

He Calls Recovery A Most Sweeping La in Nation's History.

JOHNSON ADMINISTRAT

Col. Sawyer Is Named to Di Public Works, Eastman a Railway Coordinator.

'MILLION JOBS BY OCT.

Employers Urged to Hire M Men With Government Sto ping Unfair Competition

Text of President's statem on recovery policies, Page 2.

Special to THE NEW YORK TIMES.

WASHINGTON, June 16.—Ass ing unprecedented peacetime trol over the nation's economic President Roosevelt placed in ation today his sweeping prog for recovery from the depressi

Within two hours he signed of Congress giving him co over industry, power to coordi the railroads, and authority to work on a $3,300,000,000 pu works program, and then began active administration of these other major measures.

In signing the National Indus Recovery Act the President dec that it was "the most impo and far-reaching legislation enacted by the American Congr and said that it "represents a preme effort to stabilize for all the many factors which make the prosperity of the nation the preservation of American s ards."

The Glass-Steagall Banking form Act, which the President scribed as "the second most portant banking legislation e ed in the history of the count the long-disputed Independent fices Act, including the vete legislation; the Deficiency Act, Taxation Act, and the Farm C its Act received the Presid signature during the day.

Administrators Are Named

Turning to the administr side of the industrial recovery gram, the President appo General Hugh S. Johnson, fo soldier and manufacturer, as ministrator of industry; available $400,000,000 under public works title for State r and allotted $238,000,000 to Navy Department for laying thirty-two new war vessels u the terms of the London trea

A special recovery board named by Mr. Roosevelt to with General Johnson. It con of Secretary of Commerce R chairman; Attorney General mings, Secretaries Wallace, kins and Ickes, Budget Dir Douglas and Chairman Marc the Federal Trade Commissio

General Johnson also will hav advisory council of business labor leaders, the personne which has not yet been annou Among those reported under sideration, however, are Myro Taylor, Alfred P. Sloan, Walt Teagle, Gerard Swope and Vereen.

Colonel Donald H. Sawyer named temporary administrat public works and was directed, a special Cabinet board cons of Secretary Ickes, chairman; retaries Wallace, Roper and kins, Assistant Secretary of Treasury Robert, Colonel Geor Spaulding, and Budget Dir Douglas, to submit to the dent without delay the work which construction can be taken promptly and to outl program for future work.

Eastman Rail Coordinator

Joseph B. Eastman, a memb the Interstate Commerce Com sion, was appointed coordinat railroads and was directed to his work at once. His most i tant immediate concern will b railway wage scale negotia following which, savings by th duction of duplicating facilitie be undertaken.

General Johnson conferred the President late today and left by airplane for Chicag meet with leaders of the bi nous coal industry. He said th would return late tomorrow and that he hoped to name a group of men to aid him in pe

"All the News That's Fit to Print."

The New York Times.

LATE CITY EDITION
With Added News
Of Brooklyn, Queens, Long Island
On Pages B 1-2-3-4 Following Page 17

Copyright, 1933, by The New York Times Company.

THE WEATHER—Cloudy, warmer and rain today; tomorrow colder.
Temperatures Yesterday—Max., 49; min., 38.

OL. LXXXIII....No. 27,709. Entered as Second-Class Matter, Postoffice, New York, N. Y. NEW YORK, TUESDAY, DECEMBER 5, 1933. PP TWO CENTS In New York City. | THREE CENTS Within 200 Miles | FOUR CENTS Elsewhere Except in 7th and 8th Postal Zones

LEGAL LIQUOR DUE TONIGHT; CITY READY TO CELEBRATE; STORES TO OPEN TOMORROW

DERMEN REDUCE ITY'S 1934 BUDGET Y ONLY $3,604,264

nmany Men Ignore Pleas or Economy and Adopt Total of $551,004,248.

0,934,248 FUNDS NEEDED

Aneny Committee Offers rogram of New Revenue to Meet This Deficit.

0,547,000 SAVING ASKED

dwin's Minority Report Urging Job and Pay Cuts Is Rejected.

noring all last-minute pleas for stic economies to fit the city's im- red financial position, the Board Aldermen adopted, at 1 o'clock morning, a 1934 budget aggre- ng $551,004,248, after cutting a nt $3,604,264.74 from the tenta- figure of $554,608,512 set by the rd of Estimate on Oct. 31.

y its action, which followed hfully the recommendations of joint Board of Estimate and rd of Aldermen budget commit- headed by Controller George Aneny, the Tammany board be- athed to the incoming Fusion ninistration of Mayor-elect F. H. Guardia the almost inevitable den of overcoming a minimum icit of $20,934,248 in order to put city's financial house in order.

he only departure by the board n the path laid down for it by joint report was to abolish the t of Deputy Clerk of the City rt in Kings County, held by a porter of Joseph V. McKee in recent election. The spirited ate over this additional saving 4,640 caused a split in the ranks the board, so that the final vote adoption of the budget was 51 , with Aldermen Joseph Tinsley the Bronx and Walter Hart of oklyn supporting the negative ot cast by Alderman Joseph rk Baldwin 3d, the sole Repub- n member.

Act to Wipe Out Deficit.

o close the gap between the defi- of $24,608,512 handed to it by Board of Estimate, the lower rd adopted resolutions which roved a program estimated by McAneny committee to increase 1934 general fund by $8,930,000 new revenues from various li- se, inspection and service fees, 1,500,000 from tax arrears funds to the 10 per cent penalty effec- on Jan. 1, and by some $10,- 000 by way of restoration of ey spent by the city out of tax enues to meet interest and rtization on city subway bonds.

he last-mentioned item was in- led on the assumption that the rt of Appeals would affirm the ent decision of the Appellate Di- on holding that the city had no t to make such expenditures. ore the money thus spent can estored, however, the Board of nsportation will have to market ew form of city security in the oe of certificates of indebted- .

he McAneny report summarized ollows the means by which the cit gap was to be closed:

her reductions in the budget	$3.669.624
ased revenue from tax pen- es	1,500,000
oration to general fund of nsit carrying charges paid m the budget during the rent year	10.543.500
sources of revenue	8.930.000
al	$24.643.124

Final Approval Likely.

he Board of Estimate has until . 31 to put the seal of its ap- val upon the lower board's ac- , but there is little doubt that ill do so. It received the joint mittee's report in executive ses- before the Board of Aldermen and later approved it in open ting and sent it along with the mmendation that it be ap- ved by the other branch of the many Legislature.

fore the Board of Aldermen put ugh the program of the Mc- ny committee it rode down out ceremony a minority report e finance committee, submitted Alderman Baldwin. He urged tic reductions in the number of in virtually every city de- ment, as well as substantial cuts in the higher brackets, aring that his program would a total saving of $40,547,200, h would be augments by new nues to bring the total saving 48,475,998.

outstanding feature of his ram was the suggestion that 00,000 be saved in 1934 by giv- all city and county employes salaries of more than $2,000 a th's leave without pay.

a single elimination of jobs

Continued on Page Four.

Republicans Assert Nation Rebels At Roosevelt 'Top Sergeant' Rule

'We Are Not in War,' Declares Statement by National Committee, Which Charges 'Dictatorship' Tactics—Excerpts From Smith's Editorials and Speech Are Quoted.

Special to THE NEW YORK TIMES.

WASHINGTON, Dec. 4.—Under the caption "Tories, Chiselers, Dead Cats, Witch Doctors, Bank Wreckers, Traitors" the Republican National Committee resumed its campaign against the Roosevelt recovery program tonight.

The second major onslaught by the committee was issued from headquarters of the committee in the form of a printed document of thirty-five pages in which it is proclaimed that "the Forgotten Man of 1932" is still forgotten, that the radio is being censored and that private initiative is in the "guardhouse." The statement asserts that "the American people object to the attempt upon the part of this administration to conduct itself along the lines of a dictatorship."

Whether or not the attack on the President's program was the unanimous voice of the membership of the Republican National Committee went unanswered.

The statement was issued as the expression of the committee. No word as to its actual authorship or the identity of those who suggested it came from the committee office. It was just handed out without comment.

The foreword to the document declared that no administration since that of George Washington has been more protected from partisan criticism than has that of President Roosevelt. No other administration in history, it is declared, has had its requests for legislation granted 100 per cent; granted, it says, with little or no partisan opposition. Congress, it continued, gave President Roosevelt more power than it gave Lincoln to save the Union or Wilson to wage the World War.

"A month or six weeks ago," the committee statement continued, "there began to be criticism of the policies of the administration. It was pointed out in the columns of the public press that the President's recovery program was not working, because it was not workable, that many of the policies ran contrary to fundamental economic laws, sound business practices, plain common sense and particularly to the spirit of American institutions and the convictions and traditions of the American people."

This criticism, it is asserted, did not originate with the partisan opponents of President Roosevelt, but came "from outstanding members of the Democratic party," found "virile expression" in the editorial columns of stanch Democratic

Continued on Page Two.

DAWES BANK LOAN DUE RFC ON DEMAND

Status Shifted When $62,157,596 Balance of $90,000,000 Was Unpaid a Year Ago.

$2,283,958 INTEREST PAID

More Time Asked of Senators to Itemize $91,633,679 Face Value Collateral.

Special to THE NEW YORK TIMES.

WASHINGTON, Dec. 4.—The remainder of the $90,000,000 loan from the Reconstruction Finance Corporation to the Central Republic Bank and Trust Company of Chicago, of which former Vice President Dawes became chairman of the board several weeks before the advance was made, has been overdue almost a year and never renewed, Chairman Jones of the RFC has reported to the Senate Banking Committee.

Of the principal there was still due $62,157,596.85 on Nov. 5, Mr. Jones informed Chairman Fletcher. On that date the repayments on the loan amounted to $27,842,403.15.

The bank also has paid $2,283,958.95 in interest to the RFC, bringing total payments to $30,126,362.10. The bank owed the RFC $1,839,192.14 in accrued, overdue and unpaid interest.

The $90,000,000 loan was made several weeks after General Dawes resigned as chairman of the RFC to become chairman of the board of the Central Republic Bank and Trust Company. He said at the time that the bank negotiated the loan to put itself in an "impregnable position" and that it was "for current requirements and not for the purpose of liquidation."

Three Disbursements on Loan.

The report of Chairman Jones to the Senate committee, submitted at the request of Chairman Fletcher, disclosed that the loan was granted in two authorizations, one of $16,000,000 on June 25, 1932, and another of $74,000,000 two days later. The RFC disbursed the loan to the bank in three instalments, one of $10,000,000 on June 27, 1932; another of $30,000,000 on June 29, 1932, and a third of $50,000,000 on Oct. 6, 1932.

The loan became due on Dec. 23, 1932. The committee was informed that the loan has never been renewed, and is now regarded by RFC officials as having the status of a demand note. It is not being considered by them as in default, although long overdue.

Under its status of a demand note the loan may be called at any time. Officials pointed out, however, that the RFC has not yet called any overdue loans.

Chairman Fletcher, acting for the banking committee, requested Mr. Jones, in reporting on the status of the loan to submit an itemized report of the collateral and its present market value. As the collateral consists of some 7,000 items, it was explained that the RFC was not able to complete the itemized list in time to be submitted with the report.

The collateral is on deposit at the Federal Reserve Bank of Chicago. The Senate committee was informed that it has a face value of

Continued on Page Two.

BRITAIN WILL AVOID HARDSHIP TO IRISH

Thomas, Dominions Secretary, Is Conciliatory on Eve of Reply to de Valera.

LOSS ON ANNUITIES CITED

Plebiscite Is Considered on Plan for Declaration of an Irish Republic.

Wireless to THE NEW YORK TIMES.

LONDON, Dec. 4.—On the eve of making his anxiously awaited pronouncement on Anglo-Irish relations tomorrow, J. H. Thomas, Dominions Secretary, told the House of Commons today that Britain had "no intention of imposing any hardship on the Free State."

Taxes on Irish goods entering Britain, he said, had yielded about £2,000,000 ($10,240,000) less to date than the amount of the Free State's default on annuity payments. The default so far had totaled £7,353,000.

Rejecting the suggestion by a Conservative member that the duties be increased, Mr. Thomas explained:

"We are more concerned at getting the money due to this country than over imposing new duties."

The Cabinet met two hours today to discuss the government's reply to President de Valera of the Free State, which Mr. Thomas will read in Parliament tomorrow. Mr. de Valera is said to have asked what Britain's attitude would be toward a declaration of an Irish republic.

No hint as to its contents has been given but it is felt it may prove more conciliatory than was once expected.

It is understood the Admiralty is taking steps to repurchase certain wharves and docks at Milford Haven, Wales, which about a year ago were handed over to the government disposals board.

These docking facilities were constructed during the World War as a submarine base and a depot for units engaged in fighting German submarines. One of the reasons suggested for this new activity on the part of the Admiralty is that the government is preparing to surrender its right to dock naval vessels in certain ports in Southern Ireland under the terms of the Free State treaty.

Plebiscite Proposed.

By The Associated Press.

DUBLIN, Dec. 4.—A clear-cut plebiscite on the establishment of an Irish republic, similar to the national balloting invoked by Chancellor Hitler in Germany last month, was the plan advanced today to decide whether President de Valera is backed by the Irish people.

The Irish Cabinet meets tomorrow to consider Britain's answer to President de Valera's inquiry regarding Britain's attitude toward Irish secession.

McEntee Conciliatory.

Special Cable to THE NEW YORK TIMES.

DUBLIN, Dec. 4.—President de Valera's government is simply "sitting tight" until J. H. Thomas makes his statement in the Commons tomorrow.

A significant reference to the developing crisis was made by a mem-

Continued on Page Ten.

MONTEVIDEO PLANS AMERICAN PARLEY TO REVIVE TRADE

Steering Committee Adopts Argentina's Suggestion to Speed Recovery.

EUROPE TO GET BID LATER

Revival of London Conference Will Be Urged to Formulate World Economic Program.

By JOHN W. WHITE.

Special Cable to THE NEW YORK TIMES.

MONTEVIDEO, Dec. 4.—The steering committee of the Pan American Conference today unanimously approved a resolution presented by Foreign Minister Carlos Saavedra Lamas of Argentina, proposing the creation of a preparatory committee for a Pan American economic and commercial conference.

Señor Saavedra Lamas, in a long speech supporting his suggestion, proposed that the United States Secretary of State, Cordell Hull, in the name of all Pan American republics, undertake to persuade the European nations to reconvene the London Economic Conference with a prearranged program designed to coordinate the recovery plans of European and American States.

Broader Outlook Is Taken.

Two developments at the Pan American conference today marked a trend toward broader international cooperation. First, the steering committee voted to admit observers of Spain and Portugal to the conference, and second, the Secretary-General of the conference published a memorandum from the League of Nations which sought to concentrate in the League peace efforts in this hemisphere, as well as elsewhere.

Members of the United States delegation here denied tonight that Secretary Hull had committed himself to preparations for a Pan American economic conference or to the reconvening of the London conference, as was first reported.

Señor Saavedra Lamas, it was stated, had suggested to Mr. Hull the appointment of an economic committee within the present conference to study several subjects which the Argentine Foreign Minister proposed to submit. The chief of the American delegation, it was stated, agreed this would be a good idea and expressed special interest in facilitating the economic work of the present conference.

Mr. Hull, according to the American spokesmen, had no knowledge of the nature of the subject Señor Saavedra Lamas proposed to introduce. Therefore, it is argued, his attitude could scarcely be interpreted as approval of a list of topics not yet given out.

"Economic Content" Is Urged.

"After a half-century of existence we must suppose that Pan Americanism has acquired sufficient experience to enable it to assume a definite rôle," said Señor Saavedra Lamas. "That rôle must not be reduced to a mere expression of sentiments or to mere spiritual communion. It must have content, and this content, under the force of present circumstances, cannot be purely moral or exclusively judicial. In the historical hour in which we are living, Pan Americanism must have an economic content.

"The Treaty of Versailles said:

Continued on Page Three.

"Problems of Recovery"

The third of the series of ten articles on sound money and recovery by Dr. O. M. W. Sprague appears today on the Editorial Page of The Times.

The fourth article will be printed on Friday.

CARDINAL ATTACKS NAZI CHURCH PLAN

Faulhaber Asks Protestants to Join Catholics in Defense Against Paganism.

REICH BISHOP RETREATS

Mueller Quits Hitlerite Group and Bars Political Links by His Cabinet Members.

By GUIDO ENDERIS.

Wireless to THE NEW YORK TIMES.

BERLIN, Dec. 4.—A call to German Protestants to make common cause with Catholics in defense of Christianity against pagan and racial teachings by Nazis was issued from the pulpit of St. Michael's Church in Munich by Cardinal Faulhaber yesterday. He warned that efforts were being made to repudiate the Old Testament and even Christ for the sake of racial ideology.

"In such a situation," he continued, "a bishop cannot keep silence. Not blood but faith is the foundation of religion.

"There is a big difference between the children of Israel before and after the death of Christ. After Christ's death Israel was relieved of being the medium of revelations."

Demands Old Testament.

Therefore, he explained, it is necessary to distinguish between the Holy Writ of the Old Testament and the Talmud writings of a later period. The latter, in his view, were not inspired by the Holy Ghost, while from the Old Testament "comes the message of the only and almighty God."

"The Holy Writ of the Old Testament must, therefore, be kept in high honor," the Cardinal said, "and must not be eliminated from schools or textbooks. German classicists obtained inspiration from the Bible through the centuries and many expressions would have to be rooted out of the German language if the Old Testament is to be banned."

In appealing to Protestants for concerted defense against all attacks on the Old Testament the Cardinal said that for Protestantism the Old Testament was more important as the basis of faith than for Catholicism.

Mueller Quits Nazi Group.

The conflict in German Protestantism took a sensational turn today when the Rev. Dr. Ludwig Mueller, Reich Bishop of the Evangelical Church, resigned his protectorate of the Nazi German Christians' Society, the political organization which elevated him to office. Simultaneously, in a pastoral letter to members of his ecclesiastical cabinet and all officials in the administration of the Reich Church he forbade membership "in

Continued on Page Twelve.

Rare Stone Stolen From Barnard Arch; Theft May Delay Sculptor's Work a Year

A sample specimen of labradorite, which is to be the base of George Grey Barnard's rainbow arch war memorial, was taken by vandals from the front of the full-sized model of the arch, now on public exhibition in the former power house at 216th Street and the Harlem River.

The theft was disclosed yesterday through a public notice written by the noted sculptor, in which he appealed to the person or persons who removed the mineral to bring it back. He began work on the war memorial on Armistice Day fifteen years ago, and the loss of the labradorite sample, he said, would delay his work another year.

In his appeal, posted in the exhibition hall, Mr. Barnard pleaded for the return of the sample specimen, which he said was the particular piece he required to continue his work on the arch. He suggested it be placed near the arch or mailed to him at his studio and home, 700 Fort Washington Avenue, promising that no questions would be asked.

"To me it adds endless search and delay in the matching of my materials," he wrote. "I trusted those to whom I dedicated the rainbow arch, so I left it unsecured, valuable to me as it is. Please respect my faith in you."

The sculptor and his friends search every day at the foot of the massive war memorial in the hope that whoever removed the mineral may have brought it back.

More than ten days have elapsed since the sample disappeared, but so far there has not been the slightest clue as to the manner in which it disappeared or its probable whereabouts. The belief has been voiced that a visitor may have taken it as a souvenir, never realizing its intrinsic value to the sculptor and his life work, which symbolizes the hope for peace.

The sample measures 9 by 5 inches and is described as a very rare kind of labradorite. It was brought to New York from Dr. Grenfell's island in Labrador, from which come the finest specimens. Beautifully iridescent, it attracted much attention during the short period it was on display. Labradorite is a triclinic feldspar, showing a gorgeous play of blue, green and other colors. Against it, when the memorial is completed, the heroic figures of marble will stand out in bold relief.

The arch, the full-sized model of which was placed on view on Nov. 16, is to be Mr. Barnard's tribute to the American young men who lost their lives in the World War. He plans to build it at his own expense. Eight years will be required for construction.

SUPPLIES TIED UP HERE

Toasts to End of Dry Era May Have to Be Drunk in Contraband.

AMPLE STOCKS IN STORAGE

But Dealers Will Be Unable to Sell Today—Applicants Besiege State Board.

1,000 CAFES ARE LICENSED

Extra Police to Curb Revelry in Midtown Area—Liquor Ships Race for Port.

Although the sale of alcoholic beverages becomes legal tonight, wines and whiskies will be available only in the 1,000 restaurants, clubs and hotels that have licenses.

Dinners, dances and other formal fêtes that are to be held tonight at licensed places to mark the end of prohibition, will go on as scheduled, but there will be no legal liquor for parties at home.

In deciding to wait until 9 P. M. to ratify the repeal amendment, Utah made it impossible for New Yorkers to obtain legal bottled goods for consumption off the premises. Retail liquor stores must close here by 8 P. M. Restaurants and cabarets that expected an influx of individual celebrants may reap the benefit.

Hotel Guests Excepted.

In hotels, bottled goods may be sold to guests, if they have rooms. The action also limits celebrations to six hours, unless the police curfew at 3 A. M. is extended today. Previously it had been announced the curfew might be deferred until 4 A. M. if that was desired by the public, but no requests had been received.

Up to late yesterday only about a dozen licenses had been issued for retail liquor stores. Clerks in the offices of the New York State and City Alcoholic Beverage Control Boards worked late last night to get more out in time.

The boards had devoted their activities earlier in an effort to get out the store licenses. Then they changed their plans and issued permits for restaurants and clubs. With a whole day in which to do so, they may be able to issue more neighborhood restaurant licenses.

Whether enough legal wines and whisky would be available in view of the confusion and delay attending issuance of licenses, and the inability of the liquor stores to open, was regarded as highly doubtful last night. Thus New York faced the anomalous situation of heralding the return of legal drinking with bootleg drinks.

Jersey May Be Officially Dry.

In New Jersey there was confusion also because of the failure of Governor A. Harry Moore to act on a State control bill passed by the Legislature last week and which the New Jersey Attorney General contends is unconstitutional. If Governor Moore vetoes the bill, and if the Legislature fails to repass it the State would be bone-dry even to 3.2 beer because of a law passed in 1898, which prohibits the sale of any alcoholic beverage without a license. The 3.2 beer law is operative only until the expiration of national prohibition. Meanwhile, authorities in various communities were going ahead with plans for local licensing and other control.

Whether the 300 or more trucks set for the dash from licensed warehouses to restaurants, hotels and clubs that have licenses will be able to fill orders in a ratio to their receipt could not be ascertained.

Edward P. Mulrooney, chairman of the State control board, predicted that "the rush for liquor will be somewhat dampened because the public is short of money, and there will be a shortage of liquor for some time."

Informed last night that Utah had decided to delay ratification, Mr. Mulrooney made the following comment:

"That will not alter our plans in any way. It will merely mean that the liquor licenses will not be effective until several hours later than was expected."

Preparations by those who intend to engage in the industry gave little indication that there was a fear of lack of demand. And the liquor shortage was said by other officials

Continued on Page Sixteen.

Utah Decides to Vote After 9 P. M. Our Time

By The Associated Press.

SALT LAKE CITY, Utah, Dec. 4.—Delegates to Utah's convention to ratify prohibition repeal, which will meet here tomorrow amid much ceremony to cast for their State the deciding vote in the nation, agreed tonight to recess after the appointment of credentials and resolutions committees tomorrow afternoon and reassemble at 7 P. M. (9 P. M. Eastern Standard Time) for final action.

"We are determined no other State shall take this glory away from Utah," said Franklin Riter, president of the Utah League for Prohibition Repeal and a delegate to the convention, in commenting upon Utah's apparent determination to await ratification by Pennsylvania and Ohio before acting, in order to be the thirty-sixth State to ratify.

REPEAL CUTS PRICE OF DRINKS IN HALF

Cocktails Will Be 25 Cents in Some Places Celebrating End of Prohibition.

WHISKY AT $3 A QUART

Imported Champagne Offered at $5 to Take Home, or $8 at Hotel Table.

The price of drinks will be brought down today by repeal to almost half the recent bootleg and speakeasy level.

Although there were differences of five or ten cents among the lists tentatively issued by the various licensed establishments yesterday, the cost of a cocktail seemed generally about thirty cents and a highball about forty-five, while a bottle of imported still wine would be served for about $2.50 and champagne $8.

Retailers said blended whisky would be about $3 a quart.

Cover charges seemed generally to have been repealed with prohibition. While many establishments raised their dinner dance and supper dance prices about a dollar for repeal night celebrations, the public may dance and eat thereafter in first-class hotels and restaurants where wine and liquor is served for about $2 a person.

A survey of representative speakeasies that have ministered to the dry years revealed yesterday that they would reduce their prices to the repeal level.

A controlling influence seems to have been exercised on the cost of repeal drinking by the schedule of prices published by the Society of Restaurateurs. It has been adopted in licensed Childs Restaurants and has been raised five or ten cents in hotels, restaurants and speakeasies where the maintenance of a more expensive establishment seems to warrant.

Restaurateurs' List.

As republished today by the Society of Restaurateurs for the guidance of repeal drinkers, the prices of liquors for consumption on the premises should be:

	Cents.
Gin and whisky cocktails	30
Rum cocktails	35
Old fashioned	40
*Rye whisky	30
*Scotch whisky	45-60
Dubonnet	35
Gin fizz	35
Sherry flip	35
Cordials	50
Pousse cafe	50
Golden fizz	40
Silver fizz	40
Sherry	30

*Ginger ale and seltzer for highballs charged extra at 5 to 10 cents.

A few places offer cocktails even below the society's schedule. At the Vanderbilt Hotel, for instance, a cocktail is promised for 25 cents; as also in the Childs restaurants, whose president, G. D. Strohmeyer, said yesterday that the proposed "Childs Special" was unlike anything he had ever seen, but that he found it very palatable. He said it was a clear drink, midway between green and yellow. He believed it was made with a gin base.

In all discussion of prices for consumption in public the reservation was made yesterday that the schedules proclaimed in effect today would be temporary, pending a determination of the public taste

Continued on Page Sixteen.

FINAL ACTION BY UTAH

Pennsylvania, Ohio Will Precede Western State in Ending Dry Law.

WASHINGTON IS PREPARED

Proclamations on Ratification and Taxes Await Last State's Action.

DRYS MAKE A LAST STAND

Capital Holds Fight for Writ Futile—Doran Resigns to Head Distillers.

Special to THE NEW YORK TIMES.

WASHINGTON, Dec. 4.—National prohibition will pass into history as an unsuccessful experiment late tomorrow afternoon or evening—thirteen years, ten months, eighteen days and a few hours after it was declared in effect.

By that time the States of Pennsylvania, Ohio and Utah, by duly authorized conventions, will have ratified the Twenty-first Amendment to the Constitution, which also will establish in history the first repeal of an amendment—the Eighteenth.

Actual repeal of the Eighteenth Amendment, which will carry with it a collapse of the Volstead Act except as it applies to strictly Federal territory, will come when the last of the three State conventions has voted. However, an official proclamation is to be issued by Acting Secretary of State Phillips the minute that telephonic or telegraphic advice reaches Washington that ratification is an accomplished fact.

Four Tax Levies Will Pass.

A similar proclamation is also expected to be made by President Roosevelt. By that proclamation, provided in the National Industrial Recovery Act, four "recovery" taxes, levied to supply $220,000,000 a year to finance the huge public works program, will be automatically repealed—three as of Jan. 1 and one as of July 1—to be supplanted by the pre-prohibition levies on alcoholic beverages.

While preparations were going forward today for the formalities of repeal, the Federal Government also was perfecting its plans for assuming control of the liquor traffic until Congress meets and determines a policy of its own.

The new Federal Alcohol Control Administration, provided for in fair competition codes for various branches of the liquor trade, was officially set up in Washington today.

Headed by Joseph H. Choate Jr. of New York, the new administration took offices in the Transportation Building and settled quietly to its immediate two-fold task—to regulate the industry to the best social and commercial advantage possible, and to supply at the same time every legitimate demand for alcoholic beverages that might be made by a people so long athirst.

Dr. Doran Resigns His Post.

The last stage of prohibition witnessed the passing from government service of the individual who has been closest to enforcement from the time of the birth of the "noble experiment" at midnight Jan. 16, 1920, until the day it finally passed away.

Dr. James H. Doran, lately Commissioner of Industrial Alcohol but at one time Commissioner of Prohibition, resigned the former position today to become head of the new code authority of the distilling industry.

In his new capacity Dr. Doran will be the chief contact between the liquor-making industry and whatever Federal body may now or hereafter regulate the traffic. Dr. Doran entered the government service as a chemist twenty-six years ago. He is generally acknowledged as probably the leading authority in the United States on all phases of the liquor problem.

Commenting on Dr. Doran's resignation, Mr. Choate said:

"The FACA is very much pleased with the spirit of cooperation shown by the distilled spirits industry and feels that Dr. Doran's connection with the industry will insure an effective operation of the newly constituted association. Throughout his twenty-six years of government service he has earned

Continued on Page Sixteen.

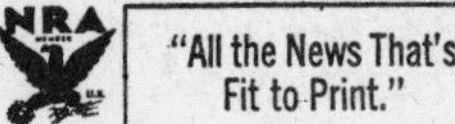

The New York Times.

Copyright, 1934, by The New York Times Company.

5:30 A. M. EXTRA

WEATHER—Cloudy, warmer today; local showers tomorrow.
Temperatures Yesterday—Max., 81; Min., 67

VOL. LXXXIII....No. 27,949. Entered as Second-Class Matter, Postoffice, New York, N. Y. NEW YORK, THURSDAY, AUGUST 2, 1934. P TWO CENTS In New York City. | THREE CENTS Within 200 Miles | FOUR CENTS Elsewhere Except in 7th and 8th Postal Zones

VON HINDENBURG DIES AT 86 AFTER A DAY UNCONSCIOUS; HITLER TAKES PRESIDENCY

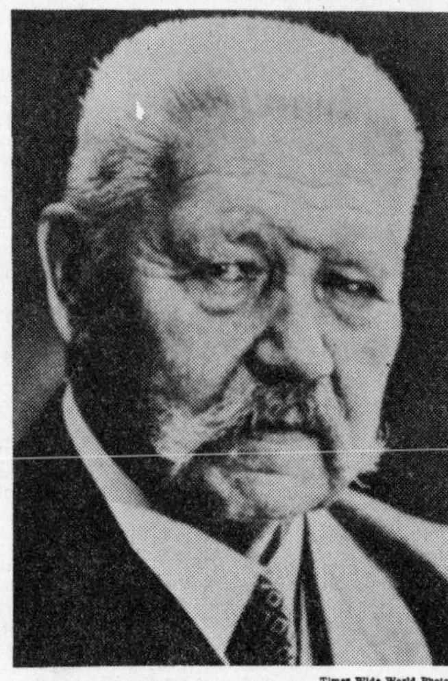

Times Wide World Photos.

PRESIDENT PAUL von HINDENBURG

END COMES AT 9 A.

Reich President Dies His Home in East Prussia.

MADE A VALIANT FIG

Disappearance of House F at Neudeck Announces News to World.

THERE HAD BEEN NO H

He Lapsed Into Coma A Hitler Reached Bedside for Last Meeting.

By The Associated Press.

NEUDECK, Germany, Thurs Aug. 2.—President von Hindenb died at 9 A. M. today.

The President's death was cated to correspondents by the appearance of the house flag f the flagstaff.

Death came to the 86-year leader of the German people former war marshal after a val fight against a complication of ments.

Chancellor Hitler has assu the Presidency.

Unconscious For Hours

By GUIDO ENDERIS.

Wireless to THE NEW YORK TIMES.

BERLIN, Thursday, Aug. 2 physician's bulletin at 6 o'clock morning stated that President von Hindenburg remained in state of unconsciousness into w he lapsed last evening. His d was believed to be a matter on hours.

The President had consist lost strength since early morn All hope that his once rugged stitution would carry him along a time was definitely dissipate bedside bulletins that reached lin from Neudeck during the

At midnight the Propag Ministry announced that no ther bulletin would be forthco during the night. This secre ness served only to heighten mystery surrounding Chanc Hitler's convocation of his Cab

Neither foreign corresponden Berlin nor those besieging President's estate at Neudeck been able to break the news bargo which hedged the Marshal's deathbed. Only seeped through official qua was placed at the disposal of German and foreign press.

Hitler Advances Time of Vis

Chancellor Hitler advanced time of his flight to Neudeck more than an hour yesterday m ing because of an urgent summ from Professor Ferdinand Sa bruck, the President's chief p cian. It was reported Dr. Sa bruck notified Herr Hitler tha patient was rapidly sinking.

The last meeting between President and the man whom elevated to the Chancellorship rebuffs which have now be historic, received only brief tion in the day's official bulle Herr Hitler found the Pres momentarily conscious and ass him of the prayerful thought the saddened nation. The P dent shook the Chancellor's and thanked him cordially fo visit; then he dropped into a sleep.

Herr Hitler flew back to B late in the afternoon. Among who accompanied him to Neu was Ernst F. S. Hanfstaengl, of his Anglo-American publicit partment, but only Herr Hitler admitted to the sick chamber.

Hope that the President w linger on vanished early last ning when Dr. Sauerbruck, or half of the attending physic announced that the patient lapsing into unconsciousness that his heart action was fast ing. A bulletin issued at 2:30 P stated that the President was steadily losing ground, despi restful night. He was cons most of the forenoon and was to converse with those around during part of the afternoon.

Up to two months ago Pres von Hindenburg's rugged f and his soldierly bearing gav evidence of physical decline. collapse began to set in a m ago when it was discovered atrophied prostate gland preci recourse to a major operation

Continued on Page B [Preceding Page 4].

TWO REFORM BILLS ARE SIDETRACKED; LEHMAN FIGHTS ON

Quorum Lacking for Report on County Plans as Republicans Walk Out of Committee.

BATTLE ON FLOOR IS DUE

Governor, Assailing 'Despicable' Action, Is Expected to Spur Democrats in Assembly.

SMITH TARGET IN SESSION

Republicans Deny Entering Agreement—Say He Is Trying to 'Bedevil' Situation.

By W. A. WARN.

Special to THE NEW YORK TIMES.

ALBANY, Aug. 1.—The Assembly Judiciary Committee met this afternoon and voted to report eleven minor bills, but failed to take any action on the proposed constitutional amendments, sponsored by Senator Dunnigan and Senator Mastick, to prepare the way for county government reforms.

The Republican majority in the Assembly contrived to block these yesterday after their adoption in the Senate, sending them back to committee.

Governor Lehman pronounced as "despicable" the failure of the committee to act on the measures, the adoption of which he and ex-Governor Smith, as head of the New York City Charter Revision Commission, have so much at heart.

The Governor said he was firmly backing the position taken by Mr. Smith in a telegram transmitted on behalf of the entire Charter Commission to Speaker McGinnies yesterday protesting against the action of the Republican majority in "repudiating" its agreement to pass the County Reform Bills.

Governor Is Silent on Plans.

Governor Lehman has not indicated what further steps he may be contemplating to force favorable action on the two side-tracked measures.

They have both been adopted by the Senate, together with another proposed amendment to the Constitution, in which both the Mastick and Dunnigan proposals are joined and which the Assembly yesterday concurred in by unanimous vote.

While the Judiciary Committee, like the Assembly itself, has a Republican majority, it has become apparent through developments of the last few days that the Democrats in the Legislature are no more eager to pass these constitutional amendments than are a majority of the Republicans.

While engaging on the floor of the Assembly today in an apparent effort to make political capital out of the Republican blockade established yesterday against the Dunnigan and Mastick measures, the Democrats did not bestir themselves to rescue the amendments.

Chance for Steingut to Act.

Assemblyman Steingut, minority leader, has not filed the necessary three days' notice of a motion to take the two resolutions from the Judiciary Committee, possibly on the assumption that the committee had not had an opportunity to act when the Assembly met today.

Now that the committee has met and failed to act the way is open for Mr. Steingut to proceed, but unless action is taken by the Assembly before the end of the week the adoption of the two resolutions would be to no purpose.

Under the Election Law, Monday is the deadline for publication of notice that the amendments are to be submitted to the 1935 Legislature for concurrent action.

Governor Lehman was aroused when he learned of developments at the committee meeting.

"The action in refusing to report or act on the bills is despicable," he said. "I am back of the position taken by Governor Smith 100 per cent.

"Until I learned of the action of the Judiciary Committee in refusing to report the bills, I was convinced that in accordance with the agreement reported by former Governor Smith, the bills would be reported out and passed.

"There is still time to pass these bills, and they should be passed. I am amazed that any condition like this could exist."

Lehman Action Is Expected.

Hence, with the Governor so stirred by the situation, observers at the capital believe he will move to compel more vigorous intervention by the Assembly Democrats to save the measures.

Most of the Democrats, and Republicans also, have already quit their legislative labors for the week and returned to their homes or gone to the Saratoga races or elsewhere. In order to get anything

Continued on Page Four.

Giant Seaplane Tops All Records; Lindbergh Hails Test of Clipper

Sikorsky Machine, Under Transport Conditions With a Full Load, Averages 157.5 Miles an Hour Over a 1,242-Mile Course —Range Would Cover Ocean Trade Routes.

By REGINALD M. CLEVELAND.

Special to THE NEW YORK TIMES.

BRIDGEPORT, Conn., Aug. 1.—All existing world's records for transport seaplane flight (previously held abroad) were toppled like ninepins here today as the giant Sikorsky S-42, the Brazilian Clipper, carrying a full transport load and with Colonel Lindbergh in charge for Pan American Airways, flew 1,242.8 miles at an average speed of 157.5 miles an hour. Eight long-standing and recent world marks were shattered by impressive margins. The two other official ones had already been won by the plane in previous test flights.

As Edwin C. Musick, chief pilot of the airlines, sent the four-engined flying boat four times over a course of 311 miles which included Manhattan's river front, Long Island Sound and the Atlantic Ocean, it was evident that history was being written for American aviation.

Starting at the Stratford Lighthouse, the course ran through five control points, George Washington Bridge, Staten Island Lighthouse, Fire Island Lighthouse, Block Island, Point Judith Lighthouse and back to the place of beginning.

The elapsed time for the flight was 7 hours, 53 minutes, 58 seconds, for a distance equal to that from Newfoundland to the Azores. Yet Pilot Musick used only 69 per cent of the 3,000 horsepower of the four Pratt & Whitney Hornet engines streamlined into the wide silver wing. He had fuel enough for another lap when he landed. The margin of range, with a mail load, for any of the ocean trade routes, Atlantic or Pacific, by way of the islands, had been amply proved.

Cruising speed only was used and less than full horsepower because the flight was an acceptance test for the airline of this craft, which will cut two days' time from the run between Miami and Buenos Aires and put that South American capital within five and one-half days of New York.

Strictly transport conditions prevailed during the flight.

When the plane crossed the starting line against the blue of a morning sky at 9:24:38, Eastern daylight time, she had only six persons aboard. They were Colonel Lindbergh, as official representative of Pan American Airways' technical

Continued on Page Seven.

SMITH ACTS TO OUIT IN CHARTER DISPUTE

Reported Ready to Resign if Board Does Not Agree to Reconsider City Rule Vote.

LETTER ALREADY DRAFTED

Seabury Said to Be Weighing Similar Action—Crucial Meeting Tonight.

Alfred E. Smith will resign from the New York City Charter Revision Commission unless the commission at tonight's meeting changes its decision to retain the city legislature in substantially its present form, according to reports last night in Albany from a source close to the former Governor.

Mr. Smith was said to have long been disgusted with the opposition to thoroughgoing reform of the city charter among members of the commission. According to the report from Albany, Mr. Smith was quoted as saying in private conversation that he was "sick and tired of the bickering and opposition in the commission" and that he "would like a vacation."

The fact that the former Governor has for some time been considering resignation or taking some other drastic action to bring sharply to public attention the failure of the commission to make real progress was confirmed by persons in the city close to Mr. Smith.

Letter Already Drafted.

It was felt that Mr. Smith might be led to resign at tonight's meeting if the commission voted to restore to the Borough Presidents their administrative and patronage powers, as some members of the commission fear will be done. According to a report by The Associated Press, Mr. Smith has already drafted his letter of resignation.

Samuel Seabury, vice chairman of the commission, declined last night to deny or to comment on a report that he also intended to resign. Earlier in the day Mr. Seabury had stated that he would make no comment until after the outcome of tonight's meeting on what he plans to do in case the opposition on the commission succeeds in restoring borough government.

These reports came as fear was expressed by members of the commission and civic organizations favoring drastic charter revision that a successful drive would be made at tonight's meeting to restore to the Borough Presidents their present administrative and patronage powers. Such a result, it was said, would largely nullify all the progress made by the commission. Both Mr. Smith and Mr. Seabury have fought for stripping Borough Presidents of their powers and for a single chamber legislature.

Confusion existed yesterday among members of the commission, as well as among civic organizations, over the effect of the action taken Tuesday night by the commission to retain the Board of Estimate and to revamp the Board of Aldermen into a smaller but much stronger Council.

Many condemned it as merely retaining the present form of city legislature, while others saw in it

Continued on Page Four.

BUSINESS TAX YIELD IS UNDER $3,000,000

$2,092,681 Total, With Mail Returns Still Due, Far Short of $8,000,000 Expected.

BUDGET NOW UNBALANCED

Mayor Denies City Plans to Restore Half of Pay Cut—Chides Levy on Figures.

The city's hope of realizing $8,000,000 from its new business tax received a severe blow last night when Controller Joseph D. McGoldrick announced that the total collected up to 6 P. M. on the final day for payment was only $2,092,681.47.

It was pointed out, however, that a last-minute ruling permitting payment of taxes by mail without penalty, provided the letters containing tax checks or money orders were postmarked before midnight, would probably bring in additional payments today.

Nevertheless it was predicted that the total return, even with the last-minute checks, could not possibly come to much more than $3,000,000—only three-eighths of the sum the city had hoped to garner from the new tax.

McGoldrick Withholds Comment.

Mr. McGoldrick withheld comment on the tax payments pending the final compilation today. It was indicated, however, that he was convinced that the total returns would be materially less than the sum expected when the tax was imposed.

Failure of the revenues from the business tax to come up to expectations will have the effect of unbalancing the city budget, it was said. The budget was balanced after the passage of the City Economy Bill by salary reductions and furloughs and by imposition of new taxes, of which the business tax was one.

A total of $1,094,800.27 was received yesterday in payment of the tax in the City Collector's office in the five boroughs. During the day 16,748 returns were filed.

Several times recently administration spokesmen have expressed the fear that the business tax revenue would be materially below the original estimates. None, however, believed that the revenue would be as small as last night's figures indicated it would be.

In view of the fact that failure to pay the tax on time brings with it a 10 per cent penalty plus payment of 5 per cent interest a month on the whole tax sum due, it was felt in the Finance Department that few concerns would withhold their payments. It was not disclosed how many payments were made under protest and threat of court action to test the constitutionality of the tax measure.

Cut in Reserve Is Hailed.

The revision of the bankers' agreement to provide reduction in the tax delinquency reserve fund in the budgets of 1935, 1936 and 1937 from the original $50,000,000 to $25,000,000 was praised yesterday by Peter Grimm, chairman of the Citizens Budget Commission. Mr. Grimm telegraphed Controller McGoldrick and Governor Lehman, who were mainly responsible for

Continued on Page Nine.

NEW ORLEANS TENSE AS POLICE AWAIT A MOVE BY TROOPS

300 More Patrolmen Sworn In as the Militia Removes Machine Guns From View.

GUARD FORCE IS REDUCED

Gov. Allen Orders Guardsmen to Investigate Alleged Gambling and Vice Graft.

Special to THE NEW YORK TIMES.

NEW ORLEANS, Aug. 1.—New Orleans anxiously watched the growing tension tonight as armed State and city forces faced each other in a political crisis precipitated by the tactics of Senator Huey Long.

George Reyer, Superintendent of Police, completed tonight the swearing in of 500 supernumerary policemen for emergency use. The machine guns manned by National Guardsmen, which have been protruding from the windows of the registration office, were removed.

The 500 emergency policemen, called for service by order of Mayor Walmsley, were armed with automatic shotguns and pistols. They were divided into two platoons, 300 on the day shift and 200 on night duty.

Of the former, 200 will be held at police headquarters, and 100 stationed at the City Hall and the First Precinct station. All of the men on night duty are stationed at police headquarters, with police automobiles and patrol wagons held in readiness to transport them wherever they might be needed.

Policemen now ready for duty number 1,300. All regular members of the department have been instructed to be ready for duty at all times, day or night.

Explains Machine Guns.

The appearance of machine guns in the registration office was explained by Adjt. Gen. Fleming at a conference with Mayor Walmsley this afternoon.

"The members of the artillery unit guarding the registration office," Adjutant General Fleming said, "were relieved Tuesday night by members of the machine gun unit. The machine gun unit always carries its machine guns along wherever it is sent."

He denied the machine guns were intended for intimidation.

Mayor Walmsley and the Finance Commissioner, A. Miles Pratt, in statements issued today, denied there was any intention on the part of the city government to seize any records in the registration office.

The presidents of the chief organizations of business men met today and debated the situation. They adopted a resolution which censured no one and asked the world to understand that "the business of this city is being conducted along the usual, efficient lines with no interruptions whatsoever."

Three members of the new police commission created by the Long-controlled Legislature to take supervision of the police force out of the hands of the Mayor and Council filed their credentials. No attempt was made to call a meeting of the board.

Prosecution of the 500 odd men charged with miscounting ballots in the last election, being regarded as impossible under a law taking effect today, District Attorney Stanley nolle prossed the cases. The charges were brought after a

Continued on Page Fourteen.

Overnight Air Service To West Coast Starts

Starting overnight service between the nation's coasts on the "Lindbergh Line," a fourteen-passenger Douglas plane of the Transcontinental & Western Air Line took off from Newark Airport yesterday afternoon at 5:25 Eastern daylight time. It is due in Los Angeles at 7 this morning.

Elliott Roosevelt, second son of the President; Lieut. Commander Frank M. Hawks, noted speed pilot; two paying passengers, newspapermen and airline officials were aboard as passengers.

The plane also carried two copies of THE NEW YORK TIMES addressed respectively to Frank L. Shaw, Mayor of Los Angeles, and Harry Chandler, publisher of The Los Angeles Times.

20% CUT IN NAVIES URGED BY SWANSON

But Secretary, in Rejoinder to Tokyo Premier, Says 5-5-3 Ratio Should Continue.

OUR PLANE PROGRAM CUT

Navy Now Thinks Equipping of All Ships Will Require 274 Fewer Than 1st Estimate.

Special to THE NEW YORK TIMES.

WASHINGTON, Aug. 1.—A general reduction of 20 per cent in naval armaments by all the powers signatory to the London Naval Treaty was advocated today by Secretary Claude A. Swanson, but he insisted that the 5-5-3 ratio of naval strength fixed by the Washington Treaty of 1922 should stand intact. If agreed to by the powers, the 20 per cent reduction should be a real and not a "blue print" one, he declared.

Meanwhile, Admiral William H. Standley, chief of naval operations, made known that the navy had revised its estimates, but had reached no final decision on the number of planes necessary under the Vinson Naval Building Bill to outfit old and new ships in the next five years. High navy officials now figure that only 910 new planes would be needed, or 274 fewer than previously had been estimated. The navy now has 1,000 planes.

No comprehensive reason was given by naval officials for this reduced estimate, but it was partly explained by the fact that when the earlier estimates were made no decision had been reached to abandon the building of flying-deck cruisers.

Secretary Swanson's statement came as a rejoinder to yesterday's declaration by Premier Keisuke Okada that, while Japan did not expect to attain parity with the United States and Britain at the 1935 naval conference, she could not favor continuation of the present ratio system, which "hurts the self-respect of nations."

Asked to comment on the Japanese Premier's speech, Mr. Swanson said:

"I adhere to the same position I always have. The naval powers met in London and distributed to the naval powers the naval strength they thought was just and right. Naval strength is relative. Both naval and military armaments are relative.

"I represented the navy at the Geneva conference and we offered there the proposition to have any reductions up to 33 1-3 per cent in the different categories of ships,

Continued on Page Three.

Wagner and Prall Hurt in Auto Plunge; Senator Drives Into Brook to Avoid Crash

Special to THE NEW YORK TIMES.

WESTPORT, N. Y., Aug. 1.—Trapped on a curve of a narrow Adirondack highway, Senator Robert F. Wagner drove his automobile over a twenty-foot embankment into a mountain brook rather than have a collision with an oncoming car near here this morning. Senator Wagner and Representative Anning S. Prall, his only companion, were both seriously but not critically injured.

Senator Wagner suffered two fractured ribs on the right side, severe lacerations of the face and knees and numerous body bruises. He may also have concussion of the brain.

Representative Prall suffered a compound fracture of both bones of his lower right leg and lacerations of the hands and forehead.

Witnesses of the crash carried the injured men three miles to the offices of Dr. Harold J. Harris here, where both remained tonight. Dr. Harris said that both were resting comfortably and in no great pain, but that because of the severe shock he did not consider it advisable to move them to a hospital.

Dr. Harris said that he thought it might be best for Senator Wagner to remain in the recovery room in his offices for several days, but that Mr. Prall might be taken to a New York City hospital tomorrow. He said there was "no evidence of skull fractures or concussions, but we never are sure until after twenty-four hours."

The legislators were on their way north on a fishing expedition when the accident occurred. They were bound for the Seigneur Club at Lucerne, Que. Senator Wagner had only recently returned from Portland, Ore., where he attempted to adjust the marine workers' strike and was fired on by mistake.

The highway through the mountains between Wadhams and this village, which is on Lake Champlain, is narrow and winding. Senator Wagner attempted to pass a truck on a curve, only to find another truck approaching from the opposite direction.

Rather than hit either truck he turned his machine off the road. It tumbled down the embankment into the brook but did not overturn. Both occupants were thrown against the windshield and dashboard, but were conscious when they were extricated from the wreckage, and remained so while they were being brought to the office of Dr. Harris here.

SOCIALIST SUPPORT SOUGHT BY AUSTRIA

Neutrality of the Party in Fight With Nazis to Be Rewarded by Release of Leaders.

FOE HANGED IN INNSBRUCK

Minor Rebels to Be Held and Put at Hard Labor—Officials Linked to Putsch.

By G. E. R. GEDYE.

Wireless to THE NEW YORK TIMES.

VIENNA, Aug. 1.—There are signs that the Austrian Government is preparing for radical changes in policy and is contemplating steps calculated to obtain from the Social Democrats assurance of at least neutrality toward the government's fight to the finish with the Nazis.

For eighteen months the Nazis have carried on terroristic activities in Austria, involving a considerable loss of life and enormous property damage. But until yesterday the death penalty had been reserved exclusively for Socialists.

Even the stern ordinance directed against Nazi terrorists, which Chancellor Dollfuss introduced fourteen days before he was slain, proclaiming death as the only admissible penalty for those possessing explosives, had a Socialist for its first victim. He was hanged the night before Dr. Dollfuss was assassinated.

Three Nazis Now Hanged.

Yesterday, however, two Nazis at last were hanged. Today another Nazi was hanged in Innsbruck, Friedrich Wurnig who shot and killed Police Commandant Franz Hickel of Innsbruck on the day of the Dollfuss slaying.

Still more important from the viewpoint of the government, having been committed to a final struggle, is the fact that it has arrested men like Dr. Anton Apold, director of the Alpine Mining Company, and General Karl Bardolf, former adjutant to Archduke Franz Ferdinand, who were always behind the scenes in negotiations between Germany and Austria. Governor Kernmaier of Carinthia, another prominent protector of Nazis, also has been arrested.

The first move to conciliate the Socialists will be the release of prominent leaders who have been imprisoned without trial since February. It is likely they will be free in a day or so. The leaders to be released are Burgomaster Karl Seitz, head of the party, and Herr Danneberg, Herr Helmer, Frau Proft and Frau Postranetzky, members of the central executive committee of the party, and more officers of the Republican Defense Corps, General Koerner, Major Eiffler and Captain Loew.

Whether such release will have

Continued on Page Three.

HITLER CONSULTS CABINET IN SECRET

Ministry Meets Two Hours in Emergency Session—Von Papen in Attendance.

NEW ELECTION POSSIBLE

Friend Says Chancellor Intends to Occupy the Presidency—Army an Unknown Factor.

Wireless to THE NEW YORK TIMES.

BERLIN, Aug. 1.—Chancellor Hitler convoked the German Cabinet for an emergency session at 9:30 o'clock tonight.

The Ministers, among them Vice Chancellor Franz von Papen, had been hastily summoned. They remained with the Chancellor about two hours.

Beyond a more-than-laconic bulletin announcing that the Cabinet had been called, nothing was divulged. There was no indication as to the purpose of the session, and this quickly gave rise to rumors that President von Hindenburg had already died, but that the announcement was being withheld until tomorrow.

The reading public has received only official communiqués concerning the Reich President. The controlled press appears to have been instructed to abstain from any speculative comment on the implications involved in a vacancy in the Presidency.

Hitler Is Seen Taking Power.

Copyright, 1934, by The Associated Press.

BERLIN, Aug. 1.—Adolf Hitler intends to be both President and Chancellor of Germany, one of his close friends told The Associated Press today.

This would give to Herr Hitler a dictatorship as absolute as any in the world.

Despair gripped many Conservatives who had looked upon President von Hindenburg as an anchor against extreme Nazism.

Herr Hitler's plan, The Associated Press informant said, is to call the Cabinet together to read a brief law assigning the dual power to himself.

"The whole thing will take but a few minutes," he said, "for the Cabinet will, of course, endorse the proposal. It will simplify the Führer's [Hitler's] whole work immensely if he need not first ask somebody whether he may do this or that."

An indication of the reliability of this source is that Sunday he revealed the President's turn for the worse and was the first to tip off the fact that Herr Hitler was going to Venice to meet Premier Mussolini.

Under the German Constitution Dr. Erwin Bumke, President of the Supreme Court, would become Act-

Continued on Page Two.

"All the News That's Fit to Print."

The New York Times.

LATE CITY EDITION
Cloudy and warmer today, possibly occasional rain; tomorrow partly cloudy and colder.
Temperatures Yesterday—Max., 69; Min., 56

Copyright, 1935, by The New York Times Company.

VOL. LXXXV....No. 28,376. Entered as Second-Class Matter, Postoffice, New York, N. Y. NEW YORK, THURSDAY, OCTOBER 3, 1935. P TWO CENTS In New York City. | THREE CENTS Within 200 Miles | FOUR CENTS Elsewhere Except in 7th and 8th Postal Zones.

BIG ITALIAN FORCE INVADES ETHIOPIA; MUSSOLINI RALLIES 20,000,000 FASCISTI; ROOSEVELT TO KEEP US 'UNENTANGLED'

ARNEKE OF CUBS OWNS TIGERS, 3-0, IN SERIES OPENER

cago Ace Yields Only Four Hits to Beat Rowe Before 48,000 at Detroit.

CORD FOR CLASSIC TIED

ning Pitcher Makes Eight ssists—An Early Fielding Lapse Costly to Losers.

TORS SCORE IN FIRST

nt Twice on Galan's Double, ror and Hartnett's Single—Demaree Gets Homer in 9th.

By JOHN DREBINGER.
Special to THE NEW YORK TIMES.

ETROIT, Oct. 2.—The Tigers, mpions of the American League last two years and encircled by largest crowd ever to witness all game in this city, felt certain ay their hour had arrived. They e launching the 1935 world se-, they had the mighty Schoolboy we on the pitching mound, and athering of 48,000 was on hand ee the towering Arkansan come his own.

stead, another Arkansan stole the thunder of the show as the g, lean and broad-shouldered Warneke, ace right-handed her of the Cubs, spun a mas-ul four-hit shut-out, tied a ld series fielding record and Mickey Cochrane and his Ti-s into all sorts of knots to win first struggle for the world's eball championship by 3 to 0.

was an amazing performance in amazing setting and left the wd even more confounded than year, when the flamboyant ans and the Cards struck these ers amidships. For there is ing particularly awe-inspiring ut this Chicago team, bossed by jolly Charlie Grimm, which last week had catapulted itself a pennant on the wings of a nty-one-game winning streak.

Last Year's Fall Re-Enacted.

ut something did bewilder those ers. Stumbling exactly as they done in the opening rounds of first game a year ago, the erican Leaguers saw the Cubs h off with two runs before the inning had been completed, from the shock of this unex-ted development they never re-ered.

the ninth inning Frank Dema-arched a home run into the sely packed left-field bleachers, that fell like a blow upon a ater already counted out.

a period of twenty-nine rs Detroit has played host to five these baseball classics. It has to come home a winner, and as crowd filed silently out of the k it doubtless wondered if the ers will ever win one.

ertainly the Tigers, who spread-ed the field in the American gue flag race this year, never n came close to getting started ard their objective today. In th, they hardly got off their goal

Submerged by Kindness.

heir collapse last year was attrib-d to the swashbuckling Cards , there is nothing swashbuckling ut the Cubs. They are a quiet, l-behaved lot and seemed to other the Tigers with kindness attention.

nce, when Cochrane, who a year was buffeted all about the e by those rampaging Cardi-, was guilty of a short passed , the Chicago batter politely pped aside while Mickey scram-d for the ball and then handed Tiger catcher his mask, offer-soothing words of condolence.

t while that Tiger panic was those alert, swift-moving Cubs assume a commanding lead. er Demaree drove his home run o the densely packed temporary achers in left, where some 20,000 rooters had waited in vain all ernoon for Hank Greenberg or nebody else in a Tiger uniform nd one.

nd that was about all there was it—that and an amazingly cool crafty piece of pitching by the ular Warneke, who was engag-in his first mound struggle with huge fellow Arkansan, Rowe.

Rowe Finds His Master.

oday Rowe was still the school-, learning perhaps quite a bit n the right-handed ace of the cago hurling staff in the art flinging a baseball when the sure is on at its height.

fact there were times when rneke seemed to be playing the re game himself. For not only the blank the Tigers but, by king eight assists, he equaled the ld series record set by the fa-Nick Altrock of the White in 1906.

arneke might even have sur-

Continued on Page Thirty-one.

'Tour of Sky' Opens Planetarium; 800 Get a New Vision of Universe

Enthralled New Yorkers See Stars, Sun and Moon Enact Cosmic Drama in Make-Believe World Shorn of Space and Time—Museum Spectacle Ready for the Public Today.

By WILLIAM L. LAURENCE.

A cosmic ray from interstellar space lighted the stars last night at the official opening of the Hayden Planetarium of the American Museum of Natural History and presented before 800 enthralled New Yorkers a new vision of the universe they live in.

It was a fitting prelude to an awe-inspiring spectacle of artificial stars in a man-made heaven going through their celestial paces at the bidding of man.

A first-night audience of invited guests was transported for an enchanted hour into a make-believe world where, like the Olympians of old, they were masters of space and time.

To every one present, particularly to those who never had visited any of the three other planetaria in the United States or the eighteen in Europe, it was like seeing the splendors of the universe for the first time. It was a new, bright and shiny world—resplendent and magnificent, fresh and mysterious—turning the mind's eye to Genesis and Creation's first day. No dweller in cities has ever seen the stars in such splendor.

But the "Olympians-for-an-hour" saw more than a bright new universe with its seeming myriads—actually only 4,500—of stars and constellations. Not only did they receive an insight into the inner workings of the cosmos; they were taken behind the scenes and shown how it works.

From the moment the cosmic ray entered the cunning trap devised for it, filling the primeval-like darkness with the unearthly shriek of what might have been some prehistoric monster, the circular wall of the planetarium chamber, with its strange, "man-from-Mars" contraption standing in its centre, vanished not only from view but from consciousness as well.

There were no longer 800 men and women sitting in a dark theatre with a huge dome overhead. Instead each felt suddenly alone in the vastness of space, making a journey among the stars at a speed so inconceivably great that time

Continued on Page Twenty-one.

LEHMAN BACKS LAW TO FINGERPRINT ALL

He Favors Campaign to End Public Prejudice and Aid Fight on Crime.

SHARP TILT OVER PAROLE

Valentine Says System Fails—Dr. Moore Hits Back in Crime Conference Session.

From a Staff Correspondent.

ALBANY, Oct. 2.—A movement for universal fingerprinting as an important weapon against crime gained strength today at Governor Lehman's conference on crime, and drew support from Mr. Lehman, who expressed certainty that some extension of the present identification system would be recommended to the next Legislature and approved.

The Governor gave his viewpoint during a tour of the round table discussions, which were marked during the day by numerous sharp debates. There was a stiff exchange on the topic of parole between Lewis J. Valentine, Police Commissioner of New York City, and Dr. Joseph W. Moore, chairman of the State Parole Board.

Commissioner Valentine struck sharply at the present parole system, and his talk touched off fireworks, bringing the reply from Dr. Moore that the Valentine address "for concentrated misinformation transcends anything I have listened to for some time."

Parole has been a leading subject throughout the conference, with police officials openly hostile to the current system and penologists taking the view that improvements must be made but that parole must be acknowledged as a vital principle.

Sanford Bates, director of the Federal Bureau of Prisons, told a general meeting tonight that despite abuses, parole must be recognized as an integral part of any penal system.

Public Prejudice Expected.

Mr. Lehman acknowledged in his remarks before the Detection and Apprehension Round Table that there was a public prejudice against fingerprinting, but he saw no bona fide reason "why fingerprinting should not be made universal."

"I have been fingerprinted," he said. "I think the last four Governors of this State have been glad to be fingerprinted and I cannot see any reason whatsoever why any law-abiding citizen of this State should object to being fingerprinted and I think it would be a very great service, not only to the police, but to many other agencies of government."

He felt that because of the force of opposition, through public opinion, which could be expected a campaign of education would have to precede the day of universal fingerprinting. But he was convinced that the people of New York joined in a "determined desire to bring to the law enforcement agencies of the State every means of carrying out their work and every means of protecting them in that work."

He had no doubt that "any reasonable extension of fingerprinting in connection with law enforcement and detection and apprehension will meet with ready response from

Continued on Page Eighteen.

BULGARS FOIL PLOT TO OVERTURN BORIS

Martial Law Declared as 60 Are Arrested in Attempt to Set Up a Republic.

COLONEL VELTCHEFF HELD

Ex-Premier Gueorguieff Also Seized—Plan to Kill King at Review Today Reported.

Wireless to THE NEW YORK TIMES.

SOFIA, Bulgaria, Oct. 2.—Martial law was declared this morning throughout Bulgaria following the discovery of a conspiracy by Colonel Damian Veltcheff and his friends of the Zveno group of alleged revolutionaries. The aim of the conspiracy is said to have been the overthrow of the Royalist régime and the substitution of a republic for King Boris.

Order was nowhere disturbed in the country. Up to the present time sixty persons have been arrested.

Rumors concerning forthcoming troubles had been circulating in Sofia for the last few days. This morning the Cabinet council decided to arrest thirty politicians and thirty officers on a charge of high treason. Among those arrested was Colonel Kimon Gueorguieff, former Premier.

The leader of the conspiracy, Colonel Veltcheff, was arrested when he attempted to cross the Bulgarian-Yugoslav frontier at Slivnica. He has lived for the last few months in exile in Yugoslavia, where he fled to escape persecution by his political adversaries.

Assassination Plot Reported.

Official circles are reluctant to give full information about the aims of the conspiracy. Under these conditions the wildest rumors are circulating in Sofia, among them a story passed about by Macedonians that Colonel Veltcheff and his friends attempted to assassinate King Boris.

The celebration of Bulgaria's national holiday tomorrow has been postponed as a result of the situation. Public meetings are being closely watched by troops and patrols are guarding the streets of the capital. Those arrested are to be court-martialed within the next few days and the government is expected to take the severest measures against them.

Behind the scenes there is evidently going on a desperate struggle between Colonel Veltcheff and his friends, who are pro-Yugoslav and pro-French, and the present government of Premier Andrew Toscheff and King Boris, who are advocating a pro-Italian policy. The defeat of Colonel Veltcheff is regarded as a victory for the government's foreign policy.

King Boris actively participated in today's decision. It is believed in neutral circles that the government's report about the alleged conspiracy was largely exaggerated in order to enable it to take drastic measures against its adversaries.

The Plan to Kill the King.

By The Associated Press.

SOFIA, Oct. 2.—Conspirators in the revolt that the government claimed, today it had nipped, planned to assassinate King Boris, it was learned upon good authority.

There were no official revelations

Continued on Page Six.

$545,356,833 BUDGET OFFERED BY MAYOR, A CUT OF $36,937,709

Tax Levy Estimate $8,075,766 Under 1935—Total Requests Had Been $582,294,543.

$203,944 SURPLUS IS SEEN

La Guardia Also Forecasts a Lowered Tax Rate Next Year—Assails Mandatory Rises.

Mayor's budget message and budget tables, Page 16.

Mayor La Guardia's executive tax levy budget for 1936 aggregating $545,356,833.11 was presented to the Board of Estimate in City Hall at 6 o'clock last night, with a statement showing that the city's estimated income next year exceeds the budget by $203,944.43.

The new budget is $8,075,766.79 below the current budget total of $553,432,599.90. For the last five days the Mayor had devoted himself almost entirely to the task of cutting 1936 departmental estimates, which amounted to $582,294,543.04. He cut these requests by $36,937,709.93. This was accomplished although he had to allow increased amounts for certain departments.

"We have submitted a balanced budget, and there is no question about that," said Budget Director Rufus E. McGahen. "It was not an easy thing to achieve. The reason for its accomplishment was the intensive concentration on it for the last five days by the greatest little budget director in captivity—and that's His Honor the Mayor."

Gross Total $613,183,150.

With his budget the Mayor submitted a budget message, explaining appropriations in detail and informing the Board of Estimate of some of the underlying principles of the budget. The tax levy budget is considered apart from the city's gross annual expenditures. Departmental expenditures from other than tax levy funds are estimated at $67,826,317.06 next year, a cut of $1,627,726.37 under the 1935 estimate. The gross total of the 1936 budget is $613,183,150.17 against the gross of $622,886,643.33 for 1935.

The Board of Estimate will begin public hearings on the tax levy budget next Monday at 11 A. M., having considered the budget in executive session meanwhile. Following those hearings the budget goes to the Board of Aldermen, where it may be reduced, but not increased. Thereafter, it passes into the form of the budget "as proposed for adoption," and becomes effective upon the votes of both branches of the Municipal Assembly.

James J. Lyons, Borough President of the Bronx, thanked the Mayor yesterday for submitting a "real, honest-to-goodness budget that is not a sham." The Mayor assured him that the budget was not too realistic. In his budget message the Mayor explained that the 1936 total was assembled with an eye on 1937. Describing budget-making as both difficult and delicate, he asked his colleagues "not

Continued on Page Seventeen.

Dr. K. F. Mather Defies Teacher's Oath Law; Its Author Denounces Him as Red Aide

Special to THE NEW YORK TIMES.

BOSTON, Oct. 2.—Dr. Kirtley F. Mather, Harvard Professor of Geology, became the first member of the Harvard faculty tonight to publicly declare that he would refuse to take the teacher's oath as required by a new State law.

He made this declaration at the opening convocation of the Boston Centre for Adult Education. He later expressed his belief that several hundred Harvard professors would join him in his stand.

At the conclusion of Dr. Mather's remarks, Representative Thomas Dorgan of Dorchester announced himself as author of the Teacher's Oath Bill and denounced the geologist as a Communist sympathizer and the Twentieth Century Club, in whose building the meeting was held, as a hotbed of Russian revolutionism.

"I admire your courage," Mr. Dorgan shouted at Dr. Mather. "But I am the author of the Teacher's Oath Bill. I am Representative Dorgan. I want to ask you a question. Do you mean to say that the Teacher's Oath Bill is repugnant to our sacred Constitution?"

"That," replied Dr. Mather, "is a question for the Supreme Court to decide. But if you want my personal opinion, I certainly think it is."

"Well, then, I want to ask you one other question," Mr. Dorgan cried. "Are you a member of the Cultural Relations Something-or-Other, that plays ball with Soviet Russia? Anyhow, I've got your name down on a list here."

Dr. Mather admitted he was a member of the society which Mr. Dorgan probably had in mind, and asked why the question was put.

"That's all I want to know," Mr. Dorgan replied. Whereat Dr. Mather countered:

"And I am also a member of the Civil Liberties League, the Newton School Committee and the Y. M. C. A."

At that, the meeting broke up in a demonstration by about 200 men and women who cheered and shouted approval of Dr. Mather's stand on the teacher's oath, as well as his answers to Mr. Dorgan.

Dr. Mather declared that the Teachers' Oath Bill is representative of undemocratic tactics such as "constitute the entering wedge in America for additional legislation that ultimately would regiment all schools, churches and cultural institutions in obedience to whatever State officials happen to be in power." He said:

"I don't see how I can possibly conform to a law which I believe violates my constitutional rights as a citizen and a teacher. I do not know what the consequences will be, but at the present moment it is my intention to refuse to take the teacher's oath."

Dr. Mather later said he did not know what Harvard's action on the Oath Bill would be, but that he understood there was no penalty attached, enforcement and discipline resting with school principals and local school committees.

PRESIDENT WARNS NATION

Foreign War a Potent Peril, He Tells 45,000 at San Diego Fair.

CONQUEST IS DEPLORED

But Our Feelings Must Not Drag Us Into Conflict, He Declares.

SEES BIG NAVAL 'BATTLE'

Executive, as 'Enemy' on the Houston, Watches 130 Ships in Great Manoeuvres.

The President's address at San Diego appears on Page 14.

By CHARLES W. HURD.
Special to THE NEW YORK TIMES.

SAN DIEGO, Calif., Oct. 2.—A policy of keeping the United States "unentangled and free" was enunciated today by President Roosevelt in his first public utterance recognizing the gravity of the threat of war abroad.

In the last speech of a series which he has delivered since leaving Washington Thursday, the President espoused the "good neighbor" policy, but expressed in plain words the determination that, while the American people oppose policies of conquest by foreign countries and deplore restrictions on conscience and conduct imposed by other governments, such feelings will not be permitted to drag this country into war.

Loud and prolonged applause and cheers followed the statement that the country would remain "unentangled and free." The whole speech was well received.

Mr. Roosevelt spoke before a crowd of 45,000 in the high school stadium, standing on an open platform at one end.

He was introduced by Governor Merriam of California, a Republican, who termed him "a statesman whose influence is felt around the world."

Washington's Views Cited.

Mr. Roosevelt reviewed in some detail the accomplishments of the past two and one-half years which, he said, have brought the United States to a point where "we stand once more upon an economic plateau."

He then stepped from statistical and social description into a discussion of foreign policy.

Mr. Roosevelt declared that "centuries ago the greatest writer in

Continued on Page Fourteen.

Moves in the War Crisis

ADDIS ABABA—The Ethiopian Government confirmed yesterday reports that the Italians had violated the Ethiopian frontier in the northeast near French Somaliland. A protest was sent to the League, which was again asked to dispatch observers. Emperor Haile Selassie is to proclaim a general mobilization today.

ROME—Mussolini said in a speech broadcast to 20,000,000 Italians "mobilized" in town squares that war against Ethiopia was about to begin. As to sanctions, he asserted Italy would meet "war with war."

PARIS—Germany was reported to have assured France that she would not try to profit from the present situation and Italy was said to have given assurance that economic and financial sanctions alone would not lead to war.

LONDON.—The British received the news of the Italian invasion calmly as the Cabinet heard and approved a report from Anthony Eden on his activities at Geneva. The Cabinet took no action on the latest developments in the African crisis. The King called in the Foreign and War Secretaries.

SAN DIEGO.—President Roosevelt, addressing 45,000 persons, again pledged the nation to remain "unentangled" in its international relations, holding that foreign war was a "potent danger."

WASHINGTON.—Secretary of State Hull appealed to the world for economic and political peace and declared that the United States would adhere to its program of lowering trade barriers as the best means of attaining it. At a gathering of members of various faiths he urged the churches to engage in a "flaming crusade" to turn men from war.

NEW YORK.—The widest break in the stock market since July, 1934, was recorded after Mussolini's speech. Leading issues were off 1 to 4 points. Cotton and wheat prices soared sharply, and the influx of foreign capital continued unabated.

BRITAIN'S CABINET GETS EDEN REPORT

It Approves Minister's Firm Stand at Geneva, but Takes No Other Action in Crisis.

KING CALLS IN OFFICIALS

Confers With Foreign and War Chiefs—Public Calm, Firmly United for Aid to League.

By FREDERICK T. BIRCHALL.
Wireless to THE NEW YORK TIMES.

LONDON, Oct. 2.—While Italy was going through its spectacular mobilization of millions, and the Ethiopian Emperor was proclaiming an advance of Italian forces beyond an undemarcated frontier of Eritrea into a "No Man's Land" he has created by the withdrawal of his troops, the British Cabinet met today and listened to a report from Anthony Eden, Minister for League of Nations Affairs, regarding the League Council's intentions. There is comparative calm and coolness here. The hour for Britain's intervention has not yet struck. The universal prayer is that its striking may be long delayed. For Britain desires peace.

News of the Italian test mobilization was received with interest but not alarm. It was expected to be spectacular and striking, and it is. News of the Italian advance similarly was greeted as something that had been looked for. A few more evening newspapers, which naturally sensationalized the news, were sold, but that is all.

Eden Wins Approval.

The Cabinet heard Mr. Eden and, it is officially asserted, approved his actions at Geneva, but did nothing more. He looked disappointed when he left the meeting after two hours' discussion, but he has come from an atmosphere different from that which prevails here in London.

There is nothing bellicose in official or public sentiment here, but there is a growing stern determination to stick by the League in the strictest sense, though that does not necessarily imply telling the League what it should do in given circumstances—in other words, giving it "a lead."

Before the Cabinet meeting the King received successively Sir Samuel Hoare, the Foreign Secretary, and Viscount Halifax, Secretary for War. This, too, could be readily sensationalized, but to do so would give a wrong impression. The King returned last week-end from a prolonged stay at Balmoral Castle. He leaves next week-end for a stay at Sandringham. It is the custom of British rulers to keep in touch during critical times with the Ministers most affected. King George is following this custom during the short period of his stay in London, for he meticulously abides by all the traditions of British sovereignty.

That is a superficial aspect of today's happenings here, but to go a little deeper: The Cabinet met with

Continued on Page Two.

ITALY WILL FIGHT, MUSSOLINI ASSERTS

Premier Tells the 'Mobilized' Throngs He Will Do All He Can to Localize Conflict.

HE WARNS ON SANCTIONS

Says 'War' Will Be Met With War—People Cheer Him for Stand on Ethiopia.

Premier Mussolini's message to the mobilized nation, Page 3.

By ARNALDO CORTESI.
Wireless to THE NEW YORK TIMES.

ROME, Oct. 2.—Premier Benito Mussolini threw down the gauntlet to the world this evening.

While an enormous crowd of Black Shirts, filling the Piazza Venezia and all adjacent streets as far as the eye could see, shouted themselves hoarse with frantic applause, and while their shouts were echoed by 20,000,000 other Black Shirts standing in front of loud-speakers in the principal square of every city, town and village in Italy, the Premier let it be clearly understood—but did not actually say so—that hostilities against Ethiopia are about to begin.

"We have been patient with Ethiopia for forty years—it is enough now," he cried.

Italians Support War Move.

The unfeigned satisfaction with which this announcement was received by all social strata of Italy removes any doubt, if any ever existed, that the Italian people are now behind him in his African venture. Indeed, the best commentary on the present temper of the Italians is that the only criticisms of Mussolini's speech that were heard were expressions of regret that he did not seize the occasion offered by today's manifestations to declare war.

Mussolini made it plain he did not believe sanctions would ever be applied against Italy but said that in any case they would be powerless to make him change his course. He said:

"To economic sanctions we shall answer with our discipline, our spirit of sacrifice, our obedience. To military sanctions we shall answer with militarism. To acts of war we shall answer with acts of war."

But, he said, he was reluctant to think that either France or Great Britain would actually assume responsibility for bringing Europe to the verge of war.

"Until there is proof to the contrary," he said, "I refuse to believe the authentic people of France will join in supporting sanctions against Italy. And until there is proof to the contrary, I refuse to believe the authentic people of Britain will want to spill their blood and send Europe to its catastrophe for the sake of a barbarian country unworthy of ranking among civilized nations."

But though willing to face any sanctions the League of Nations

Continued on Page Three.

ETHIOPIA WILL ARM TODAY

Emperor Tells League 50,000 Foes Have Crossed Border.

ITALIAN AIR BASE READY

Addis Ababa Fears Casualties Among Journalists in Hotels if Radio Is Bombed.

EMPRESS TO AID DEFENSE

250,000 Men Are Marching to the Border in Advance of General Mobilization.

By G. L. STEER.
Special Cable to THE NEW YORK TIMES.

ADDIS ABABA, Ethiopia, Oct. 2.—The Ethiopian frontier has been invaded by Italian forces in the neighborhood of Assab, the Ethiopian Government announced today on the receipt of a telegram from the Jibuti Consul, Lij Andergé Masai.

[General mobilization will be ordered in Ethiopia today, according to The Associated Press. The Emperor decided on this step after protesting to Geneva that 50,000 Italians had crossed the frontier.]

French sources reported that the frontier, which is east of lonely Mount Mussa Ali, was crossed last week when the Italians hurriedly pushed forward from the terminus of one of their six roads leading inland from Assab. The Italians, with the aid of armored cars and trucks and without encountering any opposition, were said to have occupied a good advance base for airplanes in the western foothills more than fifty-six miles from the sea.

French Control Their Border.

French authorities, on hearing the report, sent a detachment of native troops to the northern frontier of French Somaliland. Between their line and the southern slope of the mountain there is space only for a track for sixty-three miles. The Italians are said to have already run a track for supplies to the new base, where there is a large number of native troops with a few white officers. This base has armored cars and airplanes of the latest colonial type, including some new Savoia-81 planes ordered from Rome early this year.

Between this post and Assab there are reported to be 60,000 troops, but in view of the shortage of water in this country, which was mapped only recently by friends of the late Baron Franchetti, it is improbable that more than 15,000 can be accommodated at the new base. As there is no concentration of Ethiopian troops nearer than the Aussa Sultanate these troops can soon threaten the Diredawa-Harrar railway without danger to themselves.

Fears are felt here for the Hulhul Bridge between Diredawa and French Somaliland, which thus far has been only lightly defended by Lij Worku, former chief of the railway police and now Governor of Aisha, and a few men with automatics, all that can be sustained in this dry, volcanic region.

Frontier Fixed in 1908.

According to the latest Italian military maps, which were issued in Rome last June or July, there is no frontier between Eritrea and Ethiopia anywhere south of a point west of the potash mines at Kululli near the River Endeli. This, however, is not an accurate geographical statement because under Article I of the Eritrean delimitation treaty signed by Ethiopia and Italy on May 16, 1908, the frontier was delimited as running southwest parallel to the coast for sixty kilometers till it reaches French Somaliland.

Demarcation upon the ground did not follow, but, as the next article said, the demarcation was to adapt the frontier "to accidents of the terrain" and there is no article defining the frontier in relation to the tribes, which gave some initial plausibility to the Italian claim at Ualual.

It is almost certain now that Empress Menen will go to Dessye when the fighting starts with an extremely strong contingent of the Imperial Guard. Mules for the journey are being purchased. Dessye is the capital of her old province of Wallo

Continued on Page Two.

"All the News That's Fit to Print."

The New York Times.

LATE CITY EDITION
Fair and somewhat warmer today. Tomorrow rain and warmer.
Temperatures Yesterday—Max., 39; min., 17.

Section 1

VOL. LXXXV....No. 28,533. Entered as Second-Class Matter, Postoffice, New York, N. Y. NEW YORK, SUNDAY, MARCH 8, 1936. P Including Rotogravure Picture, Magazine and Book Review. TEN CENTS | TWELVE CENTS Beyond 200 Miles Except in 7th and 8th Postal Zones.

HITLER SENDS GERMAN TROOPS INTO RHINELAND; OFFERS PARIS 25-YEAR NON-AGGRESSION PACT; FRANCE MANS HER FORTS, BRITAIN STUDIES MOVE

STRIKE PEACE HOPE REVIVED AS MAYOR OFFERS A NEW PLAN

OWNERS ARE RECEPTIVE

Realty Board Acts Today on Move to Submit to Arbitration.

UNION ASSENT IS HINTED

Resumption of Negotiations Is Held Likely After La Guardia and Strikers Confer.

300 AT TUDOR CITY QUIT

More Park Av. Buildings Also Affected—Closed-Shop Issue No Longer a Factor.

Hope for settlement of the strike of elevator operators and other building service employes was revived last night after another appeal to both sides by Mayor La Guardia to submit the dispute to arbitration.

The Mayor made his proposal in identical telegrams addressed to the Building Service Employes Union, the strike organization, and the Realty Advisory Board, which has played the rôle of spokesman for large realty interests in the strike. Accompanying the Mayor's proposal was a detailed plan of settlement minus the closed shop.

The fact that the Mayor dispatched his peace plan after he had conferred at City Hall with strike leaders was taken as a clear indication that it was acceptable to the union, which had previously indicated its readiness to abandon the closed-shop demand.

William D. Rawlins, executive secretary of the Realty Advisory Board, declared after receipt of the Mayor's telegram that the peace plan might be looked upon with favor in the form in which it was submitted.

He announced that the directors of the Realty Advisory Board would consider the Mayor's proposal at a meeting this afternoon at the board's offices, 12 East Forty-first Street. The proposal will be analyzed by Walter Gordon Merritt, counsel for the board, after which a reply to the Mayor will be drafted.

New Negotiations Hoped For.

It was hoped last night that today's meeting of the Realty Advisory Board's directors would lead to a resumption of negotiations at City Hall tomorrow morning and to a settlement of the strike.

The Mayor's appeal for peace came after another day in which there were no important strike developments.

Although the union called out some 300 employes in Tudor City, preliminary to extending the walkout in the Grand Central area tomorrow, and appeared to be holding its lines in other parts of the city, there was no marked extension of the strike during the day.

Upon the intervention of the Mayor the union called off the strike in some 170 buildings controlled by the New York State Mortgage Commission after the commission had agreed to abide by any settlement ultimately reached with the realty interests of the city. The commission controls about 140 buildings in Manhattan and thirty in the Bronx.

In making known the dispatch of telegrams to the contending groups, pleading with them to bring the strike to a termination, Mayor La Guardia said:

"I am convinced that the strike can be settled if both sides are willing to do so. Resistance on one side and provocation on the other will get nowhere. Misrepresentations from either side are not helpful. The real issue now is wages and working conditions, and surely arbitration should be accepted by both sides.

"The Mayor will maintain law and order, protect life and property, and that goes for both sides. He will continue his efforts to end this controversy regardless of abuse from either side."

Closed-Shop Demand Eased.

The Mayor's plea was made public after he had conferred again with James J. Bambrick, strike leader, and other union spokesmen. His statement that "the real issue now is wages and working conditions" was taken as another indication that the union was will-

Continued on Page Thirty-seven.

Butler and Shaw Swap Retorts Not 'Courteous'

By The Associated Press.

SAN PEDRO, Calif., March 7.—Nicholas Murray Butler and George Bernard Shaw let go with both barrels of caustic sarcasm today at each other through the medium of interviews.

Said Dr. Butler, president of Columbia University, with regard to the gibes of G. B. S. at the American Constitution and the President:

"Anything George Bernard Shaw may say about politics is too ludicrous to comment upon. This won't surprise Mr. Shaw because it represents an opinion I have had about him for a long time. And he knows it."

Said G. B. S.:

"I suppose if Dr. Butler had an automobile that had been running for thirty years and was still running he would insist that it shouldn't be exchanged for a new motor car. That is the way with your Constitution. Dr. Butler's antiquated automobile wouldn't bring much of a 'trade-in.'

"Anyway, I'm 'G. B. S.' and Dr. Butler isn't 'N. M. B.'"

LEHMAN CRIME PLEA POLITICS, SAYS IVES

Speaker Ascribes Attack on Assembly Members to Quest for Re-election Issue.

DEFENDS ALL COLLEAGUES

He Calls on the Governor for 'Appropriate Action' on Dodge and Geoghan.

The text of Mr. Ives's address is printed on Page 38.

Special to THE NEW YORK TIMES.

ALBANY, March 7.—Governor Lehman is making a "political football" of his crime program and picking a fight with the Legislature merely to develop an issue on which to run for re-election, Speaker Irving M. Ives of the Assembly asserted tonight in a State-wide radio broadcast.

The Speaker went on the air over WOKO and a chain of stations to reply to the radio attack of two weeks ago in which the Governor charged that "powerful groups of lawyer legislators" were banding together to hamstring his program in the Assembly.

Mr. Ives offered a detailed statement of his position on the crime bills, saying that his attitude was that of many Democrats and Republicans, and demanded that Governor Lehman "take appropriate action" in the cases of District Attorney William C. Dodge of New York and District Attorney William F. X. Geoghan of Kings. He said:

"Two glaring examples of the failure of law enforcement are to be found in New York City. The first is the case of District Attorney William F. X. Geoghan of Brooklyn, who, unable to secure convictions in the notorious Drukman case, was superseded by Special Prosecutor Hiram C. Todd, who obtained these convictions with admirable promptness.

Demands Governor Act.

"The second example is that pertaining to District Attorney William C. Dodge of New York County, who, after having shown himself unable to break up racketeering gangs which for years have been preying upon the public of New York, was finally superseded in this assignment by Attorney Thomas Dewey as special prosecutor. Where Mr. Dodge failed, Mr. Dewey has not failed and instead has obtained a number of convictions.

"Obviously, there must be some laxity of law enforcement somewhere in these cases, and I recommend that the Governor, in view of the facts, take appropriate action."

The Speaker enumerated "certain basic truths that have emerged from the confusion and misunderstanding which this anti-crime controversy has provoked."

He declared that "the intemperate charges directed at the Assembly by the Governor are utterly false and ridiculous."

He asserted that "the Governor has sought to claim credit for inaugurating all anti-crime programs offered in this State since the 1935 session of the Legislature, to the

Continued on Page Thirty-eight.

HOOVER DECLARES FREEDOM IN PERIL, LIFE 'MORTGAGED'

He Tells Colorado Republicans We Face Enslaving Taxes, Repudiation or Inflation.

'COMMON MAN' MUST PAY

Future 'Fireside Talks' Will Be With Collector, He Says—Hits 'Planned Economy.

The text of Mr. Hoover's speech is printed on Page 36.

Special to THE NEW YORK TIMES.

COLORADO SPRINGS, March 7.—Crushing taxes, repudiation of debts or inflation are certain sequels to the New Deal, Herbert Hoover declared tonight before the Young Republican League of Colorado in a speech which was broadcast nationally.

The administration's spending and what he regarded as its steps toward dictatorship have failed to solve the problems of the depression or end unemployment, he said.

The former President asserted that the youth of the nation faced a choice between the old American system, with its political liberty and equality of economic opportunity, and a "planned economy" involving regimentation and bureaucracy.

The freedom and opportunities of youth "are being mortgaged," Mr. Hooover asserted, adding that "taxation enslaves as well as dictatorship."

More Taxes "Inevitable."

He warned that the nation's "future fireside talks" would be with the tax collector, and some believed that present taxes on wealth, designed to complete the cycle of "shirtsleeves to shirtsleeves in three generations," take the shirt also.

"Do not mistake," he went on. "The new taxes of today are but part of them. More of them are as inevitable as the first of the month. The only alternatives are repudiation or inflation. No matter what nonsense you are told about corporations and the rich paying the bill, there will be two-thirds of it for the common man to pay after the corporations and the rich are sucked dry."

He said, further:

"And where do we get to after all this attempt to supplant the American system? At the time of the election in 1932 the American Federation of Labor reported 11,600,000 unemployed. Today, after three years of the New Deal, they report 11,600,000 unemployed.

"To get these people back to their jobs was the outstanding job of our government. It was the excuse given for all these doings. But the grim fact remains that it has failed in its primary purpose. And $15,000,000,000 will be added to the national debt before the New Deal is over."

The Record on Platform Pledges.

Mr. Hoover contrasted the administration's actions and party platform promises of 1932, and said that when he was President all but two of the thirty-seven Republican platform promises were carried out, despite depression difficulties. Two secondary promises, he said, "broke against the obstinacy of a Democratic Congress."

The trend of events in this country since 1932, he said, followed the pattern of European nations that succumbed to dictatorship, and he added that the New Deal had "imitated the intellectual and vocal technique of typical European revolution."

The great contributions to civili-

Continued on Page Thirty-six.

Rumania's War Council Called to Special Session

By The Associated Press.

BUCHAREST, March 7.—The Rumanian Defense Council tonight was called to a special session Monday, to devise means for improving and rapidly increasing the nation's armaments. The council consists of King Carol, former Premiers and the general staff of the army.

The semi-official newspaper, Dimineata, predicted that the League of Nations would apply economic sanctions against Germany as a result of remilitarizing the Rhineland.

Commenting on Chancellor Adolf Hitler's speech before the Reichstag, the newspaper said, "Germany is laughing today, but France and England will be laughing tomorrow."

MUSSOLINI ACCEPTS PEACE PARLEY BID

League Invitation Satisfactory in Principle as Basis for Talks, He Tells Cabinet.

ITALY WILL NOT AID PARIS

Imposition of Sanctions Said to Have Freed Nation of Locarno Obligations.

By ARNALDO CORTESI.
Wireless to THE NEW YORK TIMES.

ROME, March 7.—At almost the minute when Chancellor Adolf Hitler, in Berlin, was announcing the reoccupation of the Rhineland, Premier Benito Mussolini, in Rome, was informing the Italian Cabinet Council that he had decided to accept "in principle" the invitation of the League of Nations to negotiate peace with Ethiopia.

These two facts, though seemingly unrelated, are likely to have some important repercussions on each other. The turmoil created in Europe by Hitler's move, which has directed attention from East Africa and pushed sanctions into the background, is expected to help Mussolini to drive a hard bargain with the Negus and to settle the Italo-Ethiopian conflict with all possible speed.

Italy, as soon as her best energies are no longer fettered in Africa, will be able to make her weight felt in the European balance of power and participate in the process of readjustment in the next few years.

The text of Mussolini's reply to the League's peace appeal is not yet known and will not be made public until it has arrived at Geneva. Therefore, it is still uncertain whether he has agreed unreservedly to negotiate or whether he has pledged his acceptance with important reservations.

Newspapers, usually regarded as the government's mouthpieces, are at variance on this point. The Giornale d'Italia thinks, as the invitation of the League contained no limitations, there are no conditions in Mussolini's reply. The Tribuna on the contrary says that Mussolini's acceptance does not tie him down to anything and implies the widest reservations. It also

Continued on Page Thirty-nine.

PARIS APPEALS TO LEAGUE

Rejects Reich Proposal of a Substitute for Locarno Treaty.

ALLIES SUPPORT PROGRAM

Russia and Czechoslovakia to Aid to 'Limit' in Effort to Clear Rhineland.

BELGIUM ACTS AT BORDER

French Officials Say Military Moves to Drive Back Germans Await Geneva Decisions.

By P. J. PHILIP.
Wireless to THE NEW YORK TIMES.

PARIS, March 7.—France has laid Germany's latest treaty violation before the Council of the League of Nations. That is the procedure called for in the situation.

At the same time the French Government today made it quite clear that there could be no negotiation with Germany of any substitute for the Treaty of Locarno or anything else as long as a single German soldier remained in the Rhineland in contravention of Germany's signed undertakings.

While no public mention of French troop movements is being made here, it is obvious that the necessary precautions will be taken, probably on the same scale as last March, when the Reich government denounced the military clauses of the Treaty of Versailles and reorganized her army.

[France ordered all northeastern border fortifications garrisoned at full strength, The Associated Press reports, and Belgium canceled leaves for troops garrisoning her eastern frontier.]

Withdrawal Held Essential.

What is essential, in the French view, is that the German Government must be compelled, by diplomatic pressure first and by stronger pressure if need be, to withdraw from the Rhineland. For what is found most intolerable in all today's happenings is this renewed appearance of the mailed fist in diplomacy—not, in French opinion, in the service of common peace and order, but as a menace and provocation.

Everything that can be done to avoid war will be done. But there should be no mistaking this fact in Germany or elsewhere: that rather than submit to this last crashing piece of Teutonism, France will fight.

Meanwhile, as always, the French have presented their case. The Cabinet met twice today, once in reduced numbers at the Elysée Palace with President Albert Lebrun and later at the Quai d'Orsay. Between the two meetings Foreign Minister Pierre-Etienne Flandin called in the Ambassadors of all signatory powers of the Locarno agreements for consultation and to acquaint them with his government's views.

General Marie Gustave Gamelin, chief of the General Staff, took part in the Elysée Palace meeting.

The Cabinet has been summoned for tomorrow morning to be kept fully apprised of the situation and to learn the attitude of other governments whose opinions have been sought by French diplomatic representatives.

After the second Cabinet meeting, Mr. Flandin in the famous clock room at the Quai d'Orsay, read to the biggest assembly of newspaper men there had been there since the days of the Versailles treaty a long declaration setting forth his government's views and decisions. It was a direct indictment of German veracity and an exposure of all treaty infractions involved in today's actions.

Invokes Mediation Clause.

One of his most damning declarations was the invocation of that section of the Locarno Pact by which France and Germany agreed that if any difference should arise between them which could not be dealt with by ordinary diplomatic means, they would submit it to conciliation and arbitration.

That procedure, it is argued here,

Continued on Page Thirty.

HOLLAND
MUENSTER
DORTMUND
ESSEN
Krefeld
DUESSELDORF
CASSEL
COLOGNE
RHINE
Aachen
EUPEN
MALMEDY
BELGIUM
RHINELAND
Coblenz
GERMANY
FRANKFURT-AM-MAIN
MAINZ
LUXEMBURG
TRIER
Mannheim
Saarbruecken
Metz
LORRAINE
KARLSRUHE
Nancy
STUTTGART
STRASBOURG
ALSACE
FRANCE
FREIBURG
MULHAUSEN
Belfort
0 25 50 miles
SWITZERLAND

GERMAN ARMY AGAIN ON THE RHINE.

The shaded portion of the map shows the district demilitarized under the Treaty of Versailles. It included all German territory on the west of the Rhine and a zone fifty kilometers wide along the east bank. The stars show where the principal garrisons were established.

GERMANY'S ACTION ASSAILED BY EDEN

He Uses Severe Tone Toward Reich Envoy, but Attitude of Cabinet Is Deemed Milder.

By AUGUR.
Special Cable to THE NEW YORK TIMES.

LONDON, March 7.—Foreign Secretary Anthony Eden used strong words to condemn the German Government's action when Ambassador Leopold von Hoesch of Germany presented to him this morning Chancellor Adolf Hitler's memorandum concerning the Rhineland.

Mr. Eden said the British Government must consider the entry of German regular troops into the forbidden zone to be in defiance of treaty obligations and a flagrant breach of a territorial frontier. The terms of the Treaty of Locarno impose definite duties on the British Government. The implications of the situation now created will therefore be carefully gone into.

But to Charles Corbin, the French Ambassador, Mr. Eden said that the government, while determined to comply with treaty obligations, was equally desirous of avoiding hasty action and it advised the French Government to study the points of the German offer, for they appear to be not without value.

Action Had Been Expected.

The fact is that at the bottom of their hearts Cabinet Ministers here are not so displeased with Hitler's proposals as it officially must be said they are. For sometime past the demilitarized zone has been written off as lost. A chance to obtain a solid counter-value for a hopeless item on the balance sheet appears attractive for practical politicians in London.

The real question awaiting reply is whether Hitler offers advantages that upon closer inspection may be found ephemeral once the fact of the illegal military occupation of the Rhineland is accepted without demur.

Officials in Berlin, it is known here, were alarmed when Foreign Minister Pierre-Etienne Flandin of France put a direct question to Mr. Eden concerning British aid in case of an infraction by Ger-

Continued on Page Thirty-three.

ARMY MARCHES IN AS HITLER SPEAKS

In Full War Equipment It Goes to Rhineland, Ending Its Advance Near Frontier.

By OTTO D. TOLISCHUS.
Wireless to THE NEW YORK TIMES.

BERLIN, March 7.—Germany today resumed her "watch on the Rhine" when, with an astonishing bravado that dared challenge Europe to war or to peace and left the world breathless for the moment, the new German Army crossed the military frontier, which hitherto has separated it from France, and occupied the demilitarized Rhineland zone created by the Versailles treaty and reaffirmed at Locarno.

The move was carried through with that German efficiency which drew from foreign military experts tribute to the German Army command and amid manifestations of both popular enthusiasm and grave apprehension. It brought back echoes of the last German westward march nearly twenty-two years ago, but also it was made to look like a dress rehearsal for more serious business.

Even while Chancellor Adolf Hitler was serving notice of the contemplated move to diplomats of the Locarno powers assembled in the chancellery at 11 A. M. field-gray masses of the troops of occupation were already on the march.

Planes Circle Cologne.

A few minutes before Hitler began to announce this move to the world in his speech before the Reichstag the first military flying squadrons already were circling Cologne's cathedral spires. As he began to talk infantry, artillery, motorized cavalry, tanks, machine-gun units, anti-aircraft artillery and all other paraphernalia of modern warfare already were closing the Rhine bridges, and two hours after he had finished, his advance guards already had reached Saarbruecken, their westernmost point for the present, only three kilometers from the French frontier.

According to an official announcement, troop movements will continue all day tomorrow. Occupation of the zone, which comprises

Continued on Page Thirty-one.

VERSAILLES CURB BROKEN

Hitler Smashes Locarno, Citing Franco-Soviet Treaty as Reason.

READY TO REJOIN LEAGUE

Battle for Equality Ended, He Tells Joyous Reichstag—Sets Vote for March 29.

URGES AIR PACT IN WEST

Bilateral Neutralization of Rhine Proposed—Hand Is Extended to Lithuania.

Hitler's Reichstag speech and other texts on Pages 31, 32, 33.

By GUIDO ENDERIS.
Wireless to THE NEW YORK TIMES.

BERLIN, March 7.—Germany to-day cast off the last shackles fas-tened upon her by the Treaty of Versailles when Adolf Hitler, a[s] commander-in-chief of the Reic[h] defense forces, sent his new bat-talions into the Rhineland demili-tarized zone.

The Chancellor's marching order[s] were timed to synchronize wit[h] Germany's notification to the pow-ers concerned and to a listenin[g] Reich that she no longer consid-ered herself bound by the Locarn[o] terms because the fundament[al] basis and inherent purpose of th[e] pact had been destroyed throug[h] the conclusion of the mutual as-sistance treaty between France an[d] the Soviet Union.

Hitler related to the Reichsta[g] all he had done. After he had pr[o]posed a daring peace program [he] was greeted with a burst of en-thusiasm when he announced tha[t] with complete sovereignty over a[ll] German territory restored, th[e] Reich was prepared not only to re-turn to the League of Nations, bu[t] also to cooperate in any system [of] collective security that gave prom-ise of success.

Sees Struggle Closed.

"After three years of ceasele[ss] battle," Hitler concluded, "I loo[k] upon this day as marking the clo[se] of the struggle for German equali[ty of] status and with that re-won equali[ty] the path is now also clear for Ge[r]many's return to European colle[c]tive cooperation."

To give the German people [an] opportunity to pass judgment [on] his leadership, Hitler said, he d[e]cided to dissolve the Reichstag an[d] order a plebiscite on Sunda[y], March 29, in which German vote[rs] will be able to record their con[fi]dence or lack of it in the gover[n]ment's home and foreign policies.

The announcement of Germany['s] denunciation of the Locarno pa[ct] which she voluntarily negotiat[ed] with France and Belgium in 19[25] and for which Great Britain a[nd] Italy stood sponsors, provoked le[ss] jubilation in the Reichstag than d[id] the news that German troops [at] that very hour were again marc[h]ing to their peace garrisons in t[he] Rhineland. That news unloosed [a] cyclone of rejoicing as the 660 De[p]uties rose to greet it.

But the Chancellor's speech as [a] whole must be counted an o[ut]standing political pronounceme[nt] and oratorical achievement with [re]spect to both its contents and for[ce]ful delivery and also the inter[nal] sincerity that marked the recital [of] the reasons that had determin[ed] him to abrogate Locarno.

Offers Non-Aggression Pacts.

The speech was easily Hitle[r's] boldest utterance on German f[or]eign policy. While it was not fr[ee] from recriminations and indictme[nt] of France's refusal to grasp G[er]many's outstretched hand, th[e] hand was once more revealed [in] offering France and Belgium [a] twenty-five-year non-aggressi[on] pact at the very moment when t[he] roll of German regimental dru[ms] was being heard along the Rhi[ne] for the first time since 1919.

The proposed non-aggression pa[ct] which Hitler said was open also [to] the Netherlands, constituted [the] only part of his seven-point pe[ace] scheme that he offered as a s[ub]stitute for the discarded Loca[rno] accord.

Germany is also prepared, he c[on]tinued, to negotiate immediat[ely] for the creation of a demilitariz[ed]

Continued on Page Thirty.

Brief Attack of Cold Is Repelled by Sun; Rising Temperatures Forecast for Today

Winter tried to take possession of the city again yesterday, just two weeks before the official arrival of Spring. But a bright sun in a clear sky turned Winter back with a jump of 7 degrees in temperature within little more than an hour in the afternoon.

A forecast for continuing rising temperatures and fair skies is expected to bring a moderate day of above-freezing weather today and warmer weather and rain tomorrow.

From midnight Friday until 3 o'clock yesterday afternoon the mercury remained below freezing and brought a renewed touch of Winter to the city. At 8 A. M. the temperature dropped to a low of 17—the coldest since the days of snow and ice on Fifth Avenue and Broadway.

Within the next hour the mercury rose ten degrees and then dropped back for several hours before renewing an upward course at noon. At 3 P. M., when the mercury stood at 32, a shift in light winds from the north to the southwest sent it up quickly to a high of 39 at 4:15, after which it fell slightly.

The average temperature for the day was 28, which is seven degrees below the normal. The coldest March 7 in the records of the Weather Bureau was in 1890, when the mercury dropped to 6, and the warmest was in 1921, when it rose to 69.

Since Jan. 1, when the day was 9 hours and 17 minutes long, the length of the day has increased gradually and will be 11 hours and 32 minutes long today. On March 18 the vernal equinox will begin with the day and night each 12 hours long. Two days later, on March 20, at 1:58 P. M., Spring will begin.

"All the News That's Fit to Print."

The New York Times.

LATE CITY EDITION
Cloudy, mild, with occasional rain today; clearing, colder tonight. Tomorrow colder.
Temperatures Yesterday—Max., 52; Min., 38.

VOL. LXXXVI....No. 28,811. Entered as Second-Class Matter, Postoffice, New York, N. Y. NEW YORK, FRIDAY, DECEMBER 11, 1936. P TWO CENTS In New York City. | THREE CENTS Within 200 Miles. | FOUR CENTS Elsewhere Except in 7th and 8th Postal Zones.

EDWARD VIII RENOUNCES BRITISH CROWN; YORK WILL SUCCEED HIM AS GEORGE VI; PARLIAMENT IS SPEEDING ABDICATION ACT

CODE FOR INDUSTRY VOTED HERE TO BACK AIMS OF NEW DEAL

Association of Manufacturers Pledges Cooperation for 'Era of Good Feeling.'

ASKS FOR CENSUS OF IDLE

Moley Urges Business Join in Federal Planning—McCarl for Industrial Board.

LABOR GIVES 30-HOUR PLAN

Industrial Progress Council in Washington Hears Program for a Shorter Week.

Industry and New Deal

The National Manufacturers Association meeting here adopted a code for industry pledging "era of good feeling" and cooperation with social aims of New Deal. The text of the code is on Page 30.

The Council for Industrial Progress in Washington heard labor's plan to promote employment by a thirty-hour week and Federal regulation of working conditions. Employers did not oppose new labor laws, but spokesmen insisted that they should conform to the Constitution. Page 33.

Code Is Adopted Here

A declaration of principles for American industry, calling for an era of good feeling both at home and abroad, pledging cooperation with the government in the national interest and embracing, at least in principle, some of the most important social reforms of the New Deal, was adopted yesterday afternoon at the final session of the forty-first annual convention of the National Association of Manufacturers, held in the Waldorf-Astoria Hotel.

The declaration was in harmony with the keynote speech delivered at Wednesday's session by Colby M. Chester, chairman of the General Foods Corporation and president of the association, and in striking contrast to the bitter criticisms of the New Deal uttered by industrialists at previous meetings.

In closing the convention Mr. Chester asserted his belief that it had "written a new, sound and progressive note in the industrial life of the nation in its declaration of principles," and predicted that it would have the support of "a united industry" within the year.

Census of Idle Is Urged

Resolutions were adopted urging a government census of unemployed and opposing governmental ownership of the railroads or any transportation system.

Addresses were made by Raymond Moley, editor of the magazine Today; John R. McCarl, former Controller General; George H. Mead, president of the Mead Corporation and chairman of the business advisory council to the Department of Commerce, and James A. Emery, general counsel of the association.

Mr. Moley urged joint economic planning by the government and business. He warned industry that it must recognize the meaning of the election returns—that the people voted for security of wages and living standards—and offer them a rational plan to attain these ends if it does not wish to be compelled to submit to impractical and drastic legislation.

A balanced budget through the reduction of relief expenditures and other government spending was advocated by Mr. McCarl. He urged industry to accept the responsibility for reducing the need for relief by giving more jobs. He also suggested that business organize a National Industrial Board to cooperate with the government in the "collective" solution of social and economic problems.

According to Mr. Mead, business wants "constructive regulation," contrary to a general public impression, although it is opposed to "government ownership or control." Business also believes in economic security, he said, adding that "practical" economic security and

Continued on Page Thirty-one

4,336,000,000 Francs Set As French Budget Deficit

Wireless to THE NEW YORK TIMES.

PARIS, Dec. 10.—There will be a deficit of 4,336,000,000 francs in the French budget during the coming year, according to figures put before the Chamber of Deputies this morning by the finance commission.

The ordinary expenditure under the budget is estimated at slightly more than 48,000,000,000 francs and the income at 43,685,000,000 francs. With these figures before them, the Deputies began to vote in rapid succession for most of the 140 articles in the law having to do with the collection of revenue despite the protest of one Right Deputy who argued that to vote revenues before expenditures was contrary to all good sense and logic.

JAPAN WITHDRAWS DEMANDS ON CHINA

Indicates Dropping of Moves for Anti-Red Cooperation and Autonomy of North China.

ARMY IS UNDER CRITICISM

Foreign Office Wants Public to Know the Military Interfere With Major Policies.

By HUGH BYAS

Wireless to THE NEW YORK TIMES.

TOKYO, Dec. 10.—Withdrawal of all the Japanese demands regarding North China autonomy and of that for cooperation against communism was implied in a statement issued to the press today by Eiji Amau, Foreign Office spokesman.

Japan asks Nanking to fulfill the agreements already reached on lesser points, but the request is not accompanied by a threat or warning except that if Japanese lives or property are endangered or Japanese rights violated the government will take "adequate measures."

Ambassador Shigeru Kawagoe's failure to obtain satisfaction from China, even in minor matters, is explained as due to Chinese indignation over the invasion of Suiyuan Province by Mongols and Manchukuoans.

Mr. Amau said nothing to connect the Japanese Kwantung Army with these events, but the public was already aware that Manchukuo's Premier had proclaimed sympathy with the Mongolian rising and knew he would not have taken such a step without being prompted.

Mr. Amau's statement, read in conjunction with Foreign Minister Hachiro Arita's report to the Privy Council yesterday, suggested that the Foreign Office wants the public to know how the Kwantung army interferes with major policies on which all branches of the Tokyo government have agreed.

The statement claims that a definite agreement was reached with China regarding suppression of anti-Japanese movements—including revision of the control of the press, of Kuomintang (Nationalist party) branches—engagement of Japanese advisers, control of Korean exiles and reduction of tariffs.

Consulate Involved

China further agreed to reopening of the Chengtu Japanese Consulate and accepted most of Japan's demands for settlement of recent incidents.

A hitch occurred over air services. No agreement was reached regarding joint defense against communism though both sides concurred on several items.

Economic cooperation in North China was agreed on in principle. This stage having been reached, the Chinese, "taking advantage of the Suiyuan affair," broke off negotiations, threatened to repudiate all the concessions already made and evaded Ambassador Kawagoe's repeated requests for a further interview with Foreign Minister Chang Chun. Mr. Kawagoe was said to have handed Mr. Chang a note embodying the agreed points, requesting that they be put into effect.

"Japan is now watchfully waiting for China's response and is prepared to take adequate measures if China fails to control anti-Japanese movements or if Japanese life and property interests are jeopardized," said the statement.

It is pertinent to recall that Mr.

Continued on Page Twelve

CROWDS IN LONDON CALM

News Is Received With British Reserve as Thousands Gather.

QUEEN MARY IS CHEERED

Many Break Through Police Lines When She Calls at Home of Duke of York.

TENSION OF WEEK ENDED

People Sad at Losing Edward but Relieved the Suspense at Last Is Over.

Wireless to THE NEW YORK TIMES.

LONDON, Dec. 10.—As the news of King Edward's abdication sped to the far corners of the empire this afternoon Britain received confirmation of her worst fear with mixed emotions, sadness at losing so popular and beloved a sovereign and relief that the gnawing suspense of the last week at last had drawn to an end.

Massed thousands stood silently outside the towering iron gates of Parliament while the terse, restrained statement of the first monarch in England's history ever to renounce the throne voluntarily was read to the House of Commons. Presently, as the twilight shadows of Westminster Abbey lengthened over Parliament Square, word sped from mouth to mouth that the reign of Edward was coming to an end.

Although the atmosphere a few minutes before had been highly charged with tension and anxiety the news was received calmly and with typical British reserve. There was no demonstration and no show of feeling save for the serious, strained faces in the crowd and the flutter of women's handkerchiefs here and there.

Crowds Gather Throughout Day

Throughout the day, from dawn until after midnight, crowds of varying proportions gathered outside all the buildings associated with the historic happenings of the day. People clustered about No. 10 Downing Street, the Houses of Parliament and all the royal residences, standing stolidly and silently by when allowed or moving along without protest if required. If any emotion was perceptible that could be described as a corporate reaction, it was one of bewilderment and incredulity that such a thing ever could actually happen.

A throng composed mostly of women, which at times reached 10,000 or more, stood on the pavement before Buckingham Palace forming

Continued on Page Twenty

Edward Plans Radio Talk To British Empire Tonight

Special Cable to THE NEW YORK TIMES.

LONDON, Dec. 10.—King Edward will broadcast to the empire tomorrow night at 10 o'clock, immediately after he has signed the Abdication Act and ceased to be King, in the character of a private person. It is expected Parliament will have disposed of its business by then.

[American networks will broadcast the message at 5 P. M., Eastern Standard Time.]

The British Broadcasting Corporation has arranged for a worldwide hook-up.

Many persons feel the King's decision to broadcast is not wise. He has already sent a message to Parliament with a penciled note to the Prime Minister, commending the Duke of York to the support of the whole empire. These will be broadcast four times tonight and printed in every British newspaper.

MRS. SIMPSON CRIES LISTENING AT RADIO

Shaken and Exhausted by the Climax in Career of King Who Forsook Throne for Her.

WILL REMAIN AT CANNES

Edward Will Not Visit Her Now—Britons in France Question Her Course.

Wireless to THE NEW YORK TIMES.

CANNES, France, Dec. 10.—With tears streaming down her face, Mrs. Wallis Warfield Simpson, for whose sake Edward VIII has abdicated as King and Emperor of the greatest empire the world has ever known, listened today as did all the rest of the world to the news over the radio from the scene in the British Parliament.

She heard the words announcing that the King Emperor of whom so much had been expected had laid down his scepter and crown so as to be free to marry her some months hence and live the life of an ordinary mortal.

Says King Won't Go to Riviera

At 1 o'clock this afternoon the following statement was made by Herman L. Rogers, at whose villa Mrs. Simpson is staying:

"There is definitely no change so far as Mrs. Simpson's plans are concerned. She will stay here until after Christmas. She is now at the villa and in the best of health. There has been no change in the household.

"It cannot be stated if she has

Continued on Page Twenty

Soviet Orders Militia Punished for Arrests Without Warrants in Spite of New Charter

Special Cable to THE NEW YORK TIMES.

MOSCOW, Dec. 10.—The first charges of violating the new Constitution were brought at Kazan today in connection with the arrests of eleven persons there by the militia on its own initiative.

According to the new Constitution, "no one may be subjected to arrest except upon the decision of a court or with the sanction of the prosecutor." Apparently no such authorization was obtained, and Moscow authorities have called the Kazan militia's action an "outrageous violation" of the Constitution and ordered that the guilty be suitably punished.

According to an investigation in Kazan, a doorman at a restaurant was arrested this week purely on suspicion. When he failed to arrive home his father made inquiries, and on finding his son in jail complained to the public prosecutor. The latter showed little interest. A correspondent of the Moscow newspaper Izvestia then took up the matter and spurred the prosecutor to visit the jail, where he found eleven persons arrested without warrants.

Today also the first Soviet death sentence for the infringement of private ownership and personal property and the murder of a private individual was imposed in a Moscow court.

Two employes of a State antique shop had been selling valuable old books to two highly paid ballet dancers. Thus the employes had learned their clients had money and valuables. They invaded the young dancers' home in their absence, killed their mother and cook with a brass pestle and looted the apartment. The criminals were traced, arrested, convicted and tonight they will be shot.

Hitherto the death penalty has been imposed in murder cases only where the safety or welfare of the State was involved, the normal penalty for an ordinary murder being not more than ten years.

Nikolai V. Krylenko has assumed his duties as head of the All-Union Commissariat for Justice, newly created under the Constitution. Today he began reorganizing the whole legal profession of the country into voluntary associations, which will give legal aid to any accused persons demanding their services. Any accused person is entitled to free legal counsel if he desires. Legal aid offices are also being established by trade unions.

Because of the new legal guarantees many more lawyers than hitherto will be needed. Accordingly steps are being taken to enroll thousands more students in the law schools already established, and plans are being formed for the creation of many more schools in the various republics.

BALDWIN TELLS OF EVENTS

Relates to the Commons How He Warned King Against Marriage.

DENIES ANY BITTERNESS

Says Ruler, Far From Feeling Resentment, Had Become a Firmer Friend to Him.

LEGAL ISSUE IS REFUTED

Churchill Declares It Is Now Clear That There Was Never a Constitutional Crisis.

By CHARLES A. SELDEN

Special Cable to THE NEW YORK TIMES.

LONDON, Dec. 10.—The momentous session of Parliament that received today King Edward's message of abdication was best described by Prime Minister Stanley Baldwin himself when he said near the close of his narrative of the crisis:

"This House of Commons today is a theatre which is being watched by the whole world."

Never since the first British Parliament was called by Simon de Montfort 672 years ago had it been the theatre for such an impressive tragedy as that enacted today.

There have been greater political issues, perhaps, and more fateful struggles between Crown and Commons. There have been long Parliaments, short Parliaments and rump Parliaments. But there has been no precedent for today's enactment of the tragedy in which a monarch signed away his sovereignty over an empire of 500,000,000 people for his love of a woman.

And while the play was on, the wars of one hemisphere and the efforts in the other hemisphere to prevent wars were merely side shows.

Extra Police on Hand

Standing room only was the situation in the legislative chamber itself, while there was not even standing room left in the acres of lobbies and for many blocks outside on the streets that lead to the Houses of Parliament.

So many extra companies of police were assigned to duty around the buildings that it was feared serious disorder was anticipated by the authorities, but nothing could have been further from the fact. There was as much decorum in witnessing this self-effacement of Edward VIII as there was last January when the multitudes gathered to mourn for his father and to proclaim him.

Needless to say, the House itself was filled as it had not been since the session at which war was declared in 1914. In the diplomatic gallery, every seat was taken by Ambassadors and Ministers from nearly all nations.

What little daylight sometimes seeps into the Commons chamber on a Winter afternoon was completely shut out by a dense fog, so there was nothing but mellow illumination from the lights above the stained glass ceiling.

House Is Ill at Ease

The House was ill at ease during the hour's interval prior to the great moment when Prime Minister Baldwin entered with the King's message of abdication. The familiar cry, "Prayers are over," after the customary, brief devotional exercise with which every session opens, was followed by many involuntary, at least unusual, "Amens," suggestive of a devout wish that for this once they might be answered quickly.

There was no "King's man" in this House. But it was equally true there were no anti-King men.

The King's own message was received with sorrow and sympathy. When Mr. Baldwin made his long statement of the events that preceded the decision to abandon the throne, there vanished the last trace of the bitterness that had developed in the last week from fear that the Crown might try to override the Commons.

"We are not judges," said Mr. Baldwin, and it was one of his utterances to which members gave their warmest assent.

"While there is not a soul among us who will not regret this from the bottom of his heart," said the

Continued on Page Sixteen

Associated Press Photo.

SUCCESSOR TO THE BRITISH THRONE
The Duke of York

YORK GETS OVATION AT HOME IN LONDON

Cheering and Singing Theatre Crowds Surge About His Car While Auto Horns Salute.

HE DOFFS HAT TO THRONG

New Monarch Expected to Use Name 'George' as Symbol of Strength and Steadiness.

Special Cable to THE NEW YORK TIMES.

LONDON, Dec. 10.—Thousands of Londoners shouted a welcome tonight to a shy and awkward young man who was ready to step into the dazzling light of the greatest throne on earth.

With the abdication of King Edward VIII, the 41-year-old Duke of York was about to take his place on the world wide stage as the latest in the long line of English sovereigns. And tonight, in front of his town house at 145 Piccadilly, the crowds had their first chance to show him that they were glad.

A surging throng of theatre-goers on the way home surrounded his car as he returned after having dinner with Edward at Fort Belvedere. Cheering and waving hats, they filled the wide roadway in front of the house and blocked traffic so completely police were powerless to keep it moving.

Before the Duke entered the house he turned to the crowd and raised his hat several times. That was the signal for a great demonstration. Hundreds of motorists set up a deafening salute with their horns, while the crowd began singing the national anthem and "For He's a Jolly Good Fellow."

Popular Reign Indicated

It was a demonstration of some importance in the story of the British throne, for it showed that the Duke may be a popular King even without any of the brilliant qualities of his elder brother.

Tomorrow night he will become King, and Saturday morning his accession will be proclaimed with the stately pageantry that has come down unchanged from medieval times. For individual kings may come and go, but the British monarchy that has survived many shocks before this will keep its place as the keystone of the vast and loosely jointed empire.

Heralds in uniforms of gold will

Continued on Page Eighteen

EDWARD CHEERFUL AFTER TAKING STEP

Reported Like Man Who Has Had Crushing Load of Worry Lifted From Shoulders.

PACKS FOR HIS DEPARTURE

Knowledge That He Will Not Be Barred From Returning to England Relieves Him.

By FERDINAND KUHN Jr.

Wireless to THE NEW YORK TIMES.

LONDON, Dec. 10.—The blue and white flag of the Duchy of Cornwall fluttered slowly to the foot of its mast at 10 o'clock this morning on the high turret over Fort Belvedere.

It was a signal that made history, for at that moment King Edward was renouncing the greatest throne on earth so that he could marry the woman he loved. With his three brothers as his only witnesses, he signed the instrument of abdication as his "final and irrevocable decision" to retire into private life.

He will remain King until tomorrow afternoon, when the Abdication Bill is expected to reach him from Parliament. As soon as he signs it, however, his unhappy days as King will come to an end after the shortest reign in 453 years. The Duke of York will come to the throne as George VI and Edward will leave England as the first man in all the 1,000 years of the British monarchy to have left the throne of his own accord.

Edward Again Cheerful

Although he has not shown himself to the public for almost a week, it was reported on good authority tonight that he was like a man who had had a crushing load of worry lifted from his shoulders.

The depression and jumpiness of the last few days had vanished and the King was said to be cheerful and purposeful, superintending the packing of his belongings, dealing with State papers, which arrived incessantly from London, and looking forward to more happiness than he has known in a long time.

Workmen and tractors were busy all day on Edward's private flying field at Smith's Lawn in Windsor Great Park, apparently preparing it for the take-off of an important airplane. Four police cars were on duty and a cordon of police and

Continued on Page Sixteen

KING MAKES HIS DECISION

Chooses Woman Over Throne After 'Long and Anxious' Thought.

FINALE LIKELY TOMORROW

New Reign, Expected to Bring Back Calm of George V's, Is to Be Proclaimed Then.

CROWNING PLAN MAY HOLD

Edward Can Use Either of Two Titles, Earl of Rothesay or Baron of Renfrew.

Edward's letter, the Abdication Bill, Baldwin's speech, Page 17.

By FREDERICK T. BIRCHALL

Special Cable to THE NEW YORK TIMES.

LONDON, Dec. 10.—Some time Saturday morning, perhaps even as soon as tomorrow night, Edward VIII will cease to be a King and Emperor. He has made his choice between a woman and a throne and the woman has won.

Today at Fort Belvedere, his country home near Windsor Castle, and in the presence of his three brothers, the Dukes of York, Gloucester and Kent, the King signed a message to his Ministers announcing his determination "after long and anxious consideration" to renounce the throne to which he had succeeded on the death of his father. This, said the message, is "my final and irrevocable decision."

The message was carried by Prime Minister Stanley Baldwin this afternoon to a crowded session of the House of Commons and there read, not without emotion, by the Speaker.

Bill Introduced in House

There is no question of whether the House should accept it. Under the British Constitution there can be none, for it was an expression of the King's will and the King rules, though he does not govern, Britain and the empire. But immediately afterward, as soon as the Prime Minister in a speech that will be memorable for the restrained feeling it expressed and the leaders of the Opposition each after his fashion had voiced their regret, a bill was introduced that will implement the monarch's decision.

Tomorrow this formal bill of abdication will be rushed through all its stages in both houses, Commons and Lords. It will then be carried to the King for his royal assent. The moment he signs it he ceases to be King and his brother, the Duke of York, who is nearest to him, will reign in his stead.

The new King will take the throne, according to the best information available tonight, as George VI and for that choice there is a reason. It is desired, now that this storm is over and the skies are clearing, to get back to the ordered peace and quiet stability of the monarchy under the last King George, to leave behind this brief era of conflict between will and duty and to concentrate anew on the empire and its common destiny.

Proclamation Likely Tomorrow

Another era will begin probably at noon on Saturday when the accession of the new King is proclaimed from the balcony of St. James's Palace, again at old gray Charing Cross and finally from the steps of the Royal Exchange in the City of London, each time with all the pomp and ceremony that the monarchy has upheld here throughout a thousand years. Kings may change but the old order remaineth; that is to be Britain's watchword still.

And thus, in circumstances that will arouse wonder and pity as long as history continues to be written, ends the brief reign of King Edward VIII. It has lasted ten months and twenty-two days before this strange storm that love of woman created has brought it to a close, and the empire still endures. Even a newcomer can

Continued on Page Sixteen

"All the News That's Fit to Print."

The New York Times.

LATE CITY EDITION

Generally fair, continued warm today. Tomorrow partly cloudy and warm. scattered thunder showers.

Temperatures Yesterday—Max., 91; Min., 71

'Copyright, 1937, by The New York Times Company.

VOL. LXXXVI.....No. 29,020. Entered as Second-Class Matter, Postoffice, New York, N. Y. NEW YORK, THURSDAY, JULY 8, 1937. PP TWO CENTS In New York City. | THREE CENTS Within 200 Miles. | FOUR CENTS Elsewhere Except in 7th and 8th Postal Zones.

BRITAIN APPROVES DIVISION OF PALESTINE INTO 3 PARTS; WILL PUSH PLAN AT ONCE

REPORT ENDORSED

Free Jewish and Arab States and British-Ruled Area Fixed

PROTECTORATES ARE SEEN

London Will Exert All Its Energies to Win Consent of League and U. S. to Scheme

IRON HAND WILL BAR RIOTS

Jews and Arabs in Palestine Voice Skepticism Regarding Success of Partition

Official summary of Palestine report, Pages 16 and 17.

By FERDINAND KUHN Jr.

Special Cable to THE NEW YORK TIMES.

LONDON, July 7.—Admitting that Arab and Zionist aspirations are "irreconcilable" and that the present mandate has been unworkable, the British Government tonight proposed a threefold partition of Palestine, including the creation there of the first independent Jewish State since the days of Emperor Titus.

The partition was recommended in a monumental 404-page report by the Royal Commission under Earl Peel, which last November began a searching inquiry into the causes of Arab-Jewish bloodshed.

The report was published tonight, together with a statement by the Cabinet accepting the proposals in their entirety and pledging immediate action to bring them into effect.

The new plan is not only intended as a remedy but as a surgical operation. It will require a speedy ending by the League of Nations of the present mandate and the complete metamorphosis of Palestine as it has existed since the end of the World War.

Independent Nations Planned

In place of a single State under British control, with Jews and Arabs trying to live side by side, there will be two independent nations—a Jewish State, mostly in the plains along the seacoast, and an Arab State in the hills, to include the whole of Trans-Jordan, with a port at Jaffa.

In addition, Britain hopes to receive a permanent mandate for the holy cities of Jerusalem and Bethlehem and a corridor to the sea, while the towns of Tiberias and Acre and the vital naval base at Haifa in the Jewish area will be kept "temporarily" under British control.

The hopes and dreams of twenty years will be shattered by some of these proposals, which are more drastic than any in the realm of Empire affairs since the creation of the Irish Free State and the partition of Ireland in 1921.

The present Jewish National Home, stretching from Lebanon to Egypt, will be shrunken to an area no larger than that of the State of Delaware. It will include only one-quarter of the present area of Palestine and one-half of its populated area, but it will give the Jews by far the most productive parts of the country and will include virtually the entire area of present Jewish colonization.

Capacity for Immigration

Yet even this tiny State—smaller than any in the world today except the little principalities of Europe—should be able to absorb 60,000 immigrants every year in the opinion of well-informed authorities here.

And it will be for the Jewish State itself and not for officials of the British Colonial Service to determine in the future how many immigrants the new nation can receive from the persecution areas of Central and Eastern Europe.

Naturally, there will be a transitional period, during which the minorities in the Jewish and Arab States can choose their future homes. At least 225,000 Arabs now live in the Jewish area and will have to be moved with the help of British funds and a grant from the Jewish State.

In addition, there will have to be a reorganization of the civil services throughout Palestine and settlement of a host of problems arising from the division of the country.

While all these decisions are being worked out Britain will rule Palestine with an iron hand to prevent

Continued on Page Eighteen

Dog Again Escapes Death For Biting Yonkers Child

Special to THE NEW YORK TIMES.

YONKERS, N. Y., July 7.—Bismark, a German shepherd dog, once again has escaped the death penalty for biting children and is under parole, pending good behavior, in the custody of his master, Robert E. Cook of 239 New Main Street, Yonkers.

Last Spring, City Judge Charles Boote ordered the dog destroyed for nipping a youngster, but he revoked the order after many "character witnesses," children and adults living in the neighborhood, had appealed in behalf of the animal.

However, Bismark got in trouble again June 19, when he bit Joseph Buchieri, 15 years old, of 164 Montague Street, as the youngster was walking past Mr. Cook's parked automobile, where the dog was on duty as inner guard. But the child's parents would not make a complaint, and today Bismark was freed again after the S. P. C. A. had determined he did not have rabies.

JAPANESE BATTLE CHINESE AT PEIPING

Troops Use Machine Guns and Artillery Before 5-Hour Conflict Is Halted

MANY REPORTED KILLED

Tokyo Says Nanking Forces Opened Attack While Night Manoeuvres Were Staged

By HALLETT ABEND

Wireless to THE NEW YORK TIMES.

SHANGHAI, Thursday, July 8.—A threat to "wipe out" Chinese troops unless they agreed to disarm immediately terminated at 10 o'clock this morning a sanguinary five-hour clash between the Chinese and a Japanese force on the outskirts of Peiping. The Chinese retreated across the Yingting River under machine-gun and rifle fire, suffering heavy losses. Scores of bodies were reported floating downstream.

Unless the Peiping-Fengtai situation is entirely adjusted, meeting all Japanese requirements, within a few hours, there is every probability that the Japanese Army will launch a determined effort at military occupation of Peiping. This information was given out by the Japanese Embassy in Shanghai at 12:30 this afternoon after receiving detailed reports from Japanese Army headquarters in Tientsin.

Cessation of the fighting, which occurred at 10 A. M., was under a one-hour armistice with the understanding that the Japanese Army would renew the attack upon the Chinese forces unless by 11 o'clock the Chinese had entirely withdrawn beyond the west bank of the river.

The fighting started last night and

Continued on Page Fifteen

WAGNER INDICATES HE IS OUT OF RACE; LEVY IS CANDIDATE

Friends Hear Senator Will Not Be Drafted for Mayor—He Calls on President

WIDE OPEN FIGHT IS LIKELY

Borough Head Invites Prial to Be Running Mate—Battle Among Republicans Seen

Senator Robert F. Wagner indicated definitely to friends in Washington yesterday that he had made up his mind to stay in the United States Senate, and not yield to the movement to draft him for the Democratic nomination for Mayor.

Those who talked to him felt that there was little likelihood of his changing his mind. Democratic leaders in the city, prominent in the draft-Wagner movement, said last night, however, that they felt that there still was a chance he might be persuaded to make the race.

Immediately following the indicated withdrawal of Senator Wagner, Borough President Samuel Levy in a formal statement announced his candidacy for Mayor, and his willingness to fight for the nomination in the primaries with Frank J. Prial as a running mate. Mr. Prial already has announced his candidacy for Controller.

The Wagner withdrawal had insured an open race for the organization designation, but President Levy's statement indicated that the party might be on the road to a wide-open primary fight, regardless of the action of the leaders. Mr. Levy is assured of considerable support within the Tammany organization. An alliance with Mr. Prial, if consummated, would be a strong combination in the primaries.

Appealed to by Civic Bodies

Mr. Levy, in his statement, said that many representatives of civic organizations and other bodies had told him that there was a real demand that he become a candidate on the basis of his record as Borough President for the past seven years.

"I have decided to respond to the requests made and will enter the Democratic primaries as a candidate for that office (Mayor)," Mr. Levy said.

"I have noted the announcement by the Hon. Frank J. Prial that he intends to enter the Democratic primaries seeking the nomination at the hands of the people for the office of Controller of the City of New York. It has been urged upon me that he would make a most fitting running mate and in recognition of services that he has rendered to the people of the City of New York I would be glad to have him as such. My petitions will be issued to all the citizenry of the five counties within a short time. I will welcome any determination that is made by the voters of the city as to their indication of whom they really desire as the Democratic candidate for that high office.

"All that I offer is my willingness to serve and my assurance that, if elected, I will give to the people the very best that there is in me."

Mr. Prial, reached for comment last night, said that he had not discussed the matter with Mr. Levy, but that he regarded the latter's statement as very complimentary.

Continued on Page Nineteen

Mae West Admits Marriage to Wallace; Fights His Suit for Access to Property

Special to THE NEW YORK TIMES.

LOS ANGELES, July 7.—Mae West, screen actress, admitted for the first time today that on April 11, 1911, she was married to Frank Wallace, former New York vaudeville performer.

The admission was contained in an answer filed in Superior Court to a suit brought by Mr. Wallace May 3 to confirm the fact of his marriage to her and to establish a community property interest in Miss West's holdings.

He asked the court to decree the marriage valid and to allow him access to such property.

Miss West, while fully admitting that she went through the ceremony with Mr. Wallace in Milwaukee, denied that she had lived as his wife and asked the court to allow no decree in his favor.

Her answer attempted to break down the validity of her marriage by making the observation that on Feb. 3, 1916, Mr. Wallace obtained a license in New York to wed one Ray Blakesly and that his wedding to Miss Blakesly took place three days later.

The actress asserted that at the time Mr. Wallace applied for this license he asserted that he had never been married before.

Ray Blakesly, according to Miss West's answer, obtained a divorce from Mr. Wallace in New Jersey May 1, 1935.

Miss West had previously refused to comment on the marriage, although confronted several times with copies of the certificate which gave not only her own name but that of her parents.

Wisconsin relief workers assigned to reindex public records in Milwaukee accidentally in April, 1935, turned up a marriage certificate issued on April 11, 1911, to one Mae West and Frank Wallace, then showing at the Gaiety Theatre in a vaudeville act-and-dance piece called "A Florida Enchantment."

Miss West's comment, when told of the certificate, was, "I never heard of the guy." After a moment's consideration, she added that in 1911 she was not old enough to marry.

Frank Wallace in May, 1935, stated that they were married in 1911, later in the year returning to New York as a vaudeville team. He said that, to keep the marriage secret, Miss West lived with her parents in Brooklyn and he with his in Queens.

Frequently since 1935 Mr. Wallace has been in court attempting to have an order signed directing the service of papers on Miss West.

One Dead, Many Felled in 91° Heat; Warm Weather Due to Continue

Humidity Adds to Discomfort of Year's Highest Temperature—Two Boys Drowned, Scores Rescued as Throngs Rush to Beaches—Midwest in Grip of Torrid Wave

One death was attributed to the heat and several persons were prostrated yesterday as the mercury climbed to a new high for the year, 91.4 degrees, one degree less than the record for the date.

Two boys were drowned and more than 130 others were rescued from drowning at various resorts in the metropolitan area. Most of the rescues occurred in the Rockaways. First-aid cases—for cuts, bruises, sunburn—soared past the 300 mark.

The weather, made oppressive by an unusually high humidity for the temperature, sent perspiring throngs to the beaches in every mode of conveyance. Traffic on the roads leading to the resorts was heavy and at many points snarled. Coney Island and the Rockaways reported the largest weekday crowds of the season. Both had estimated crowds of 300,000 persons.

The Weather Bureau predicted fair and continued warm weather today.

The high temperature of 91 was recorded at 4 P. M. The previous high for the year was 89 degrees, established on June 1, and the record high for the date 92, established in 1934. The low was 71 degrees, at 6:15 A. M. The average was 81 and the normal 73.

The humidity ranged between 70 and 80 per cent of saturation between 8 and 10 A. M., then dropped steadily until, at 4 P. M., it reached 40. It started rising again after that and was 42 at 6 P. M.

At no time during those hours, however, was the humidity low in relation to the temperature, not even when the moisture content of the atmosphere was 40. Usually when the temperature is high the humidity is low.

The Weather Bureau pointed out that at 6 P. M., when the humidity was 42 with a temperature of 90 degrees, a more normal humidity would have been between 30 and 35 per cent.

Benjamin Stern, 72 years old, of the Hotel Bretton Hall, Broadway and Eighty-sixth Street, was stricken on the beach at Twenty-ninth and the Ocean, Edgemere. He was dead when an ambulance arrived from St. Joseph's Hospital. The police listed the cause of death as a heart attack, "apparently induced by the heat."

Amador Morales, 47, of 119 East

Continued on Page Twenty-three

TAYLOR ASKS HALT IN CITY'S SPENDING

Warns Board Unencumbered Debt Margin Has Fallen to $62,284,087

WOULD REVIEW PROJECTS

Questions $165,000,000 Plans—Unreserved Financing Is Lowest Since 1926

A sharp warning that the city's unencumbered debt margin with pending commitments has dwindled to $62,284,087 as of April 1 was issued yesterday by Controller Frank J. Taylor in a report to the members of the Board of Estimate. Since Jan. 1, when the unencumbered debt margin was $235,886,532, there has been a net decrease of $173,602,445, he reported.

Declaring it was "time to call a halt" on new projects, the Controller, who is a candidate for renomination, urged the board members to "clean house" by thoroughly reviewing various projects on which $165,000,000 in authorized appropriations and reservations are pending against the debt limit.

He excluded about $75,000,000 marked for schools, colleges and hospitals. The major items in the $165,000,000 are $105,672,000 for the Independent Subway System, $17,822,863 for PWA projects other than for water and rapid-transit purposes and $11,326,900 for Corrections, Docks, Health, Parks, Sanitation and other departments.

Mr. Taylor declared that by counting an additional amount of $13,987,000, estimated to be the increased costs for the Fulton Street and the Concourse subway lines over the estimates in the Mayor's capital outlay budget of April 1, the unencumbered debt margin would be reduced further to $48,297,087.37.

Figure Lowest Since 1926

Mr. Taylor made no comparisons with the preceding years of Mayor La Guardia's administration, but other records showed the unencumbered debt margin as of Jan. 1, 1934, was $462,570,435; in 1935 it was $366,883,295, and in 1936, $256,547,728. It had not fallen below $100,000,000 since the last two years of Mayor John F. Hylan's administration and Mayor James J. Walker's first year, in 1926. In the latter year it reached the low of $42,174,670.

Mr. Taylor said that although the constitutional debt limit on Jan. 1, 1937, based upon the assessed valuation of taxable realty for 1936, was $333,347,902.63, a comparable figure as of April 1, based on lower 1937 assessed valuations, was $301,744,490.27, a net decrease of $31,603,412.36.

At the end of his long report, which was accompanied by elaborate tables of figures and schedules, Mr. Taylor said $301,744,490 was the city's actual debt-incurring power, but that the unencumbered authorizations by which he whittled it down to $62,284,087 were first steps toward contracts that could not be ignored.

Asks Care in Commitments

"It may at once be freely admitted," he said, "that the reservations in the form of unencumbered authorizations for improvements against which no contracts have yet been authorized by the board or registered by the Controller, or 'appropriations authorized' within

Continued on Page Three

TELEGRAPH 'TRUST' SCORED IN INQUIRY

Monopoly Complaint Against Western Union, Postal, to Be Urged on Cummings

OFFICE OPTIONS INVOLVED

Bar to Competition in Local Areas Seen—New Deal's '33 Merger Policy Contrasted

By FELIX BELAIR Jr.

Special to THE NEW YORK TIMES.

WASHINGTON, July 7.—The anti-trust division of the Department of Justice has decided to recommend to Attorney General Cummings that the Western Union and Postal Telegraph companies be prosecuted for alleged violation of the anti-trust laws by practices tending to lessen competition between the companies.

The decision to propose court action to the Attorney General resulted, it was learned, from a preliminary but intensive investigation of the two companies, which disclosed to the satisfaction of the anti-trust division that both had negotiated exclusive contracts with property owners in New York and elsewhere to the mutual detriment of both agencies, from the public point of view.

According to some officials familiar with the results of the investigation, both Western Union and Postal have made a practice of taking options on properties with the stipulation that the competitor company not be permitted to rent or lease space within the same buildings or vicinity. This practice is in violation of the anti-trust statutes, according to officials.

Decision on whether court action should be brought rests with the Attorney General, it was stated, and the matter has not yet been presented officially to him for action.

"Public Interest" Studied

One of the primary considerations that has confronted the anti-trust division in connection with its investigation of the Western Union and Postal activities has been the question whether the public interest, as well as that of the companies themselves, would be served by the suggested prosecution.

Long consideration of the question led to the conclusion that all interests would be benefited if the outcome of such litigation were favorable to the government's case. It was concluded that some of the practices of the companies necessarily involved preventable expense to the two agencies and that such expense probably was reflected in rates charged the public.

It was further concluded that if a court decision could be obtained directing both Postal and Western Union to cease and desist from the practices complained of, competition between the two companies would be placed on a sounder basis. This was thought to be particularly true of Postal, which was represented to the government investigators as contemplating a refinancing program.

This latter consideration was given at the Department of Justice as the reason why the anti-trust division had delayed recommending prosecution of the two companies to the Attorney General. With refinancing negotiations pending, of-

Continued on Page Twenty-two

TWO DEAD, 19 SHOT, IN ALUMINUM RIOT; TROOPS CALLED OUT

Police and Strikers Battle at Gates of the Alcoa Plant, Opening for Work

CASUALTIES ON BOTH SIDES

Tennessee Governor Rushes Infantry, Riot Gun and Gas Forces to the Scene

Day's Strike Developments

Two men were killed, nineteen shot, and many injured at Alcoa (Tenn.) aluminum plant before troops were called out. Page 1.

S. W. O. C. counsel accused the Youngstown Sheet and Tube Company of collusion with police and National Guard to break the strike. Page 7.

Five Ford employes were identified at Detroit NLRB hearing as assailants of union leaders on May 26. Trial examiner barred Company attempts to show C. I. O. terroristic tactics. Page 5.

John L. Lewis ordered nation-wide organization of maritime workers by the C. I. O. and approved New York shipyard strikes. Page 6.

The Newspaper Guild in Seattle rejected a compromise offer made by the management of The Seattle Star, closed since Saturday. Page 9.

Three shipyards here planned to reopen today as test of C. I. O.'s power to force closed shop. Page 6.

Transport Workers Union, C. I. O. affiliate, reopened its fight for a referendum of city subway system employes. Page 8.

35,000 cloakmakers in 1,500 shops here will halt work today, efforts to prevent stoppage having failed. Page 8.

Machine Guns Guard Plant

Special to THE NEW YORK TIMES.

ALCOA, Tenn., July 7.—A club and gun fight between strikers and the police in which twenty-one men were wounded, two fatally, caused National Guardsmen to mount guard today with machine guns, riot guns and tear gas over the plant here of the Aluminum Company of America.

Three companies of the Guardsmen, totaling 210 men and officers, took charge of the situation after they had been ordered from Athens and Elizabethton, and a special riot gun and gas squad from Nashville by Adj. Gen. R. O. Smith. He acted upon the report of an observer at the scene, after the police and the strikers had each blamed the other for starting the shooting as the plant reopened after a strike that had lasted seven weeks.

Witnesses agreed that the mêlée at the gate of the plant, which fabricates aluminum, began about 1 P. M., when pickets surrounded a truck that was about to enter. Both sides used clubs at first. Then firing started, with observers estimating that from 100 to 500 shots were discharged before the pickets gave way.

Henson Klick, 30, a striker, and W. M. Hunt, 42, a special policeman, died in the crowded local hospital.

Klick had been shot through the

Continued on Page Four

WARSHIP'S PLANES START SEARCH FOR MISS EARHART; NO DEFINITE SIGNAL HEARD

COLORADO IN ACTION

Director of Hunt Says Fliers' Fate Should Be Known Monday

104,000 SQ. MILES COVERED

Itasca, Swan Have Scanned Area North of Howland—Lexington Speeds West

PUTNAM STILL HOPEFUL

Husband of Lost Flier Believes She May Be Found in Area Below Howland Islands

By The Associated Press.

ABOARD U. S. S. COLORADO, July 7.—Three planes catapulted from the battleship Colorado launched the navy's aerial search for Amelia Earhart's round-the-world plane tonight but returned after two hours to report no trace sighted of the missing flier and her navigator, Frederick J. Noonan.

The Colorado, cruising off Howland Island, tiny atoll that was the goal of the Earhart plane after it took off from Lae, New Guinea, catapulted its planes at 2:05 P. M., mid-Pacific time (10:05 P. M., Eastern daylight time). The planes returned at 4:25 P. M. (12:25 A. M. Thursday, Eastern daylight time).

Mysterious Signals Continue

By The Associated Press.

HONOLULU, July 7.—Weak carrier wave signals, possibly from the radio of Amelia Earhart's missing monoplane, were reported heard again today by the Coast Guard just as hope for the safety of the foremost woman flier sank to its lowest point since she disappeared with her navigator in mid-Pacific last Friday.

Authorities agreed that if the signals came from the plane Miss Earhart and her navigator, Frederick J. Noonan, must have reached land because the radio would not operate if the plane alighted on the water.

Expects to Know by Monday

Admiral Orin G. Murfin, directing the search, said today it should be known by mid-afternoon Monday whether the round-the-world flier and her navigator are still alive.

The admiral, commandant of the Fourteenth Naval District, with headquarters here, said the aircraft carrier Lexington should reach the search area Monday morning. If it used all its planes, it would be able to scout thoroughly 36,000 square miles about the Phoenix Islands in six hours.

Disclosure that the Lexington carried ninety-eight planes instead of fifty-seven as previously reported came from Lieut. Commander J. L. Reynolds, Admiral Murfin's aide. He said in the absence of advices to the contrary, naval headquarters was taking it for granted the huge fighting ship carried a full complement of ninety-eight aircraft.

If first results proved fruitless, Admiral Murfin said, the Lexington would continue the hunt as long as she had gasoline and fuel oil. He said the supply probably would last three days.

The rescue director said naval calculations indicated prevailing winds would have blown the fliers off their course toward tthe Southeast as they approached Howland Island last Friday in their unsuccessful attempt to fly 2,556 miles from New Guinea to the little American outpost in the Pacific.

Coast Guardsmen again reported hearing the unidentified "carrier waves" which had been reported nightly since Saturday, but said they were weaker than before.

The minesweeper Swan, which helped the Itasca search a great area north of Howland without success, was ordered to accompany the Colorado and Itasca.

Lexington's Speed a Factor

When the Lexington's 98 planes would get into action remained problematical. At her 33-knot speed, which exceeds the pace of the At-

Continued on Page Twelve

$160,000,000 Mortgage Canceled for 50 Cents

Special to THE NEW YORK TIMES.

TRENTON, July 7.—Mercer County will receive only the regular fee of 50 cents although two clerks spent a day canceling a $160,000,000 mortgage.

The mortgage was issued by the Philadelphia & Reading Railway Company and the Philadelphia & Reading Coal and Iron Company in 1882 to the Pennsylvania Company for the Insuring of Lives and Granting Annuities of Philadelphia.

In canceling the mortgage the clerks were required to compare the hand-written copy on file at the court house with the original produced by the railroad. The copy on file covered 126 pages of extra size paper, bound in leather.

Twenty-eight counties in New Jersey, New York, Pennsylvania, Delaware and Virginia in which the railroad company owns property will receive copies of the cancellation.

ASK COURT BILL AID AS ACT OF LOYALTY

President's Friends Say He Must Be Supported, That 'New Party' Looms

GUFFEY ATTACKS HUGHES

Declares He Leads Foes—Pennsylvanian Yields Floor After Sharp Questioning

By TURNER CATLEDGE

Special to THE NEW YORK TIMES.

WASHINGTON, July 7.—Administration spokesmen in the Senate moved today to put support of the compromise Judiciary Reorganization Bill on the basis of loyalty to President Roosevelt, warning Democratic opponents that the blame for any split in the party, which resulted in the defeat of the bill would rest on their shoulders.

During three hours of debate on the court issue, Senators Guffey and Logan told the opposing Democrats repeatedly that the country would judge their votes as evidence of their support or lack of support of the President.

Asserting that Chief Justice Hughes was "the real master of tactics behind the scenes" for the opposition, Senator Guffey said that the whole issue had boiled down to a question of whether the overwhelmingly Democratic Senate was going to follow the leadership of Mr. Roosevelt and Senator Robinson or the leadership of Chief Justice Hughes and Senator McNary, the Republican leader.

"I must commend the astute and able leadership of my friend, the senior Senator from Oregon, who has managed to get the maximum of political advantage for his own party by the somewhat novel process of maintaining silence as deep

Continued on Page Two

Piece of Kingsford-Smith's Landing Gear, Found Off Burma, Identified by Builders

By The Associated Press.

LOS ANGELES, July 7.—The Lockheed Aircraft Company's vice president, C. B. Squier, identified tonight a rubber tire and landing gear found in the Andaman Sea off the coast of Burma as part of the airplane equipment of Air Commander Sir Charles Kingsford-Smith, who was lost on a flight from London to Australia on Nov. 8, 1935.

"The identification is positive," said Mr. Squier. "The landing gear was found by N. M. Andrews, an English resident of Moulmein, Burma, on a fishing trip several weeks ago.

"Inspection of the equipment indicates Sir Charles landed on land, for if he had landed on water the wheels would have been folded into the wing, the normal flight position in the type of our plane he was flying."

Mr. Squier said the strut supporting the gear itself was in good condition, although one shaft was twisted, indicating Sir Charles might have "pancaked" his plane.

Conqueror of the Pacific and Atlantic Oceans, around-the-world flier and aviation's "knight of the air," Air Commodore Sir Charles Kingsford-Smith has been missing since Nov. 8, 1935, when he and his co-pilot, Tom Pethybridge, were flying from England to Australia. They were last sighted over the Bay of Bengal.

A widespread search, spurred by reports of faint radio signals, was made for Sir Charles and his companion. No trace of them or of their plane was found, however.

The search went on for almost a month. Finally, on Dec. 6, 1935, the Prime Minister of Australia, J. A. Lyons, told a sorrowing Parliament that Sir Charles, one of the world's greatest air pilots, and Mr. Pethybridge, must be regarded as dead. The mystery of their disappearance was never solved.

In the World War Sir Charles was credited with bringing down six German planes but was finally shot down in a "dog fight."

In June, 1927, he made a record flight around the Australian Continent, covering 7,539 miles in ten days. On May 31, 1928, he and Charles T. P. Ulm, Lieut. Harry W. Lyon and James Warner took off the Oakland (Calif.) Airport for Australia. By June 9, after 7,800 miles of wonderful flying, he landed in Australia, the first flight over the South Pacific.

"All the News That's Fit to Print."

The New York Times.

THE WEATHER
Generally fair and warmer today. Tomorrow mostly cloudy, mild temperatures, colder at night.
Temperatures Yesterday—Max., 46; Min., 26

Copyright, 1938, by The New York Times Company.

VOL. LXXXVII....No. 29,267. Entered as Second-Class Matter, Postoffice, New York, N. Y. NEW YORK, SATURDAY, MARCH 12, 1938. TWO CENTS In New York City. | THREE CENTS Within 200 Miles. | FOUR CENTS Elsewhere Except in 7th and 8th Postal Zones.

NAZIS SEIZE AUSTRIA AFTER HITLER ULTIMATUM; GERMAN TROOPS ENTER, INVITED BY VIENNA; SEYSS-INQUART CHANCELLOR; LONDON PROTESTS

A. E. MORGAN DEFIES PRESIDENT'S AIRING OF TVA BOARD ROW

Again and Again He Declines at Hearing in Roosevelt's Office to Give Facts'

SAYS IT IS UP TO CONGRESS

He Is Told He Should Resign if Not Willing to Support Accusations He Made

TWO COLLEAGUES HEARD

Lilienthal and H. A. Morgan Put Before Chief Executive Data Defending Their Course

A summary of Mr. Roosevelt's inquiry in TVA on Page 8.

By TURNER CATLEDGE
Special to THE NEW YORK TIMES.

WASHINGTON, March 11.—President Roosevelt met open defiance today in his efforts to investigate dissension in the Tennessee Valley Authority when Arthur E. Morgan, chairman of the board, refused to submit evidence in support of his charges against his fellow directors and reiterated, instead, his demand for a Congressional investigation.

Chairman Morgan sat with the other board members, Dr. Harcourt A. Morgan and David E. Lilienthal, for six hours in the President's office, the most unusual meeting of its kind ever held in Washington.

Time and time again the TVA chairman heard the President repeat demands for him to bring forth evidence to back his charges. He heard the other directors spread before the President the grounds on which they had countercharged that the chairman was undermining the TVA and that they could work with him no longer.

Dr. Morgan even heard the suggestion from the President's lips that he should resign if he were unwilling to support with facts his accusations that "fairness" and "decency" were impossible in the TVA administration with the other two members on the board.

Says He Is an "Observer"

Except for rare intervals when he defended himself with a sentence or two against the charges of his associate directors, Chairman Morgan remained openly defiant of the proceedings. Throughout, he maintained the position he had stated shortly after 11 A. M. when he marched into the President's office behind the others:

"I am an observer and not a participant in this alleged process of fact finding."

As the conference temporarily ended early tonight, President Roosevelt told the three TVA board members that it was their duty to the country not to continue their "personal" row any longer. He told them that if they could not reach a settlement among themselves, it was the duty of those who could not see their way to do so, to resign. He gave them until 11 A. M. next Friday to submit any other statements or evidence to prove their charges, and, furthermore, to determine whether they would be able to compose their differences without a resignation.

This statement from the President was widely interpreted in Washington as an ultimatum to Chairman Morgan either to drop or substantiate his statement by next Friday or quit.

Expect Morgan to Resist

Simultaneously the Presidential statements aroused wide speculation as to whether Mr. Roosevelt had the power to remove Chairman Morgan or any of the other two TVA directors. From Dr. Morgan's attitude, observers concluded that he would resist any effort at ouster until his case was heard before a Congressional committee.

Various data concerning the dispute were brought into the open at the Presidential hearing and the two groups made it plainer than ever that they are separated by a chasm of professional and personal feeling which will require little short of a political miracle if it is to be patched up.

Opening the meeting with a statement of the necessity, in the public interest, of disclosing the facts upon which Chairman Morgan had based his charges against the other directors, the President turned to Dr. Morgan for a reply, but received, instead, a refusal to answer.

The President read the accusations made in recent statements by Chairman Morgan and at the end of each asked for specifications. As often as Mr. Roosevelt demanded "facts," Dr. Morgan stood on his previous statement, in which he had said in effect that he would have nothing to do with the President's personal inquiry.

The questioning revealed that Dr.

Continued on Page Eight

Flower Peddler Freed By Defiant Magistrate

In defiance of a letter from Chief Magistrate Jacob Gould Schurman urging city magistrates to impose heavier fines on flower vendors, Magistrate Sabbatino suspended sentence yesterday on a peddler in Coney Island Court, declaring that "nobody can tell me what to do except my Creator, through my conscience."

After releasing Thomas Hyden, 23-year-old peddler, of 337 Eighty-seventh Street, Brooklyn, Judge Sabbatino made public the letter from his chief. Terming the instructions "insulting," he said:

"In the letter I received, I was told that I should sentence floral peddlers to pay fines of $5 or to serve two-day jail terms, and should be even stricter with second offenders. The people of this city should heed the many robberies that are committed instead of worrying about floral peddlers."

WHITNEY ARRESTED ON SECOND CHARGE

Accused by the State of Using $109,384 Yacht Club Fund to Get a Loan

BAIL PLACED AT $25,000

Prompt Indictment Will Be Sought—Bennett-Dewey Feud Is Revealed

For the second time in two days Richard Whitney, senior partner of the brokerage film which bears his name and former president of the New York Stock Exchange, was arrested, fingerprinted, photographed, haled into court and held in bail yesterday on a charge of grand larceny in the first degree.

This time he was accused of the theft of bonds with a face value of $153,200 and present market value of $109,384 belonging to the New York Yacht Club, of which he had custody as treasurer of the club, and their use as collateral for a personal loan of $450,000 from the Public National Bank and Trust Company without the permission or knowledge of the club. He was released in $25,000 bail on this charge after arraignment in the Felony Court before City Magistrate Thomas A. Aurelio, who held him for the grand jury.

Total Bail $35,000

He now has his liberty on $35,000 bail, as he was freed in $10,000 on Thursday by Judge William Allen in the Court of General Sessions on the charge of stealing $105,000 in securities from the estate of his father-in-law, George R. Sheldon, of which he was an executor and trustee, and of which his wife, his sister-in-law, the widow of Judge Daniel F. Murphy of the Court of Special Sessions; Harvard University and St. Paul's School at Concord, N. H., were the beneficiaries.

Ambrose V. McCall, Assistant State Attorney General, who has been conducting daily hearings on behalf of Attorney General John J. Bennett Jr. since the Whitney firm was suspended by the Stock Exchange on Tuesday, informed Magistrate Aurelio that his investigation had already shown shortages of nearly $1,000,000 in the Whitney accounts. He said that in view of this and other circumstances Attorney General Bennett regarded the $10,000 bail asked by District Attorney Thomas E. Dewey of New York County in the Sheldon estate case as entirely insufficient.

Feud Is Revealed

Mr. McCall's statements brought into the open a feud that has been developing behind the scenes since District Attorney Dewey called a witness from the Attorney General's inquiry before the grand jury and obtained the indictment in the Sheldon case by a surprise move.

Hurrying here from Albany yesterday morning, Attorney General Bennett made no secret of his resentment at Mr. Dewey's action. He said that a district attorney had never before stepped into a case while it was under investigation by the Attorney General, and that he saw no necessity of Mr. Dewey acting as he had done. In the ordinary course of events, Mr. Bennett explained, his office would have presented the Sheldon case to the grand jury and prosecuted it just as it intends to do with the yacht club case, under Article 23-A of the General Business Law. He said his office has concurrent jurisdiction with the county prosecutor.

In view of the indictment obtained by Mr. Dewey, the Attorney General said he did not intend to accept Mr. Whitney's offer to testify at the State investigation. If it had not been for Thursday's indictment, he added, the broker would have been questioned at yesterday afternoon's hearing. In fact, Mr. Bennett said, Mr. Whitney would have been questioned Thursday except for an engagement his attorney,

Continued on Page Eighteen

TAX BILL IS PASSED BY HOUSE, 294 TO 97, WITH 5 ROLL-CALLS

Three Hours of Continuous Voting on Amendments Precede Final Test

'THIRD BASKET' IS OUT

Liquor, Pork Import Levies Replace It—Profits, Gains Imposts Are Retained

By CHARLES W. HURD
Special to THE NEW YORK TIMES.

WASHINGTON, March 11.—The House passed the new Tax Bill today after three hours of continuous voting, in which there were five roll-calls, one of which confirmed its former informal action eliminating a special levy of 20 per cent on the income of large closely held corporations and adopting in its place new taxes on liquor and imported pork products. Final passage was voted 294 to 97.

The bill, which is expected to yield between $5,000,000,000 and $5,300,000,000 annually was ordered sent to the Senate immediately. There the Finance Committee will begin studies of it on Monday in expectation of a quick report.

Final House action on the bill occurred in the presence of almost all members on the floor, that being in itself a rare occurrence.

These members, permitted by the leadership only to vote and not to debate, carried on loud conversation among themselves, laughed and occasionally applauded as some member shouted "Aye" or "Nay" in response to his name through the dreary succession of roll-calls, one teller count and one standing division.

New Corporation Clause Voted

The most important change in the bill, as compared with current tax laws, consists of readjusted rates and schedules for corporation taxes, reported in detail previously, which are expected to make their burden more equitable.

However, the House refused again today, by an overwhelming vote on a roll-call, to reconsider its action continuing in effect the much criticized undistributed profits tax and the capital gains tax.

The results of the roll calls, in the order in which they were taken, follow:

The House adopted, 233 to 153, the McCormack Amendment which eliminated the "third basket" contained in Section 1B.

It adopted, 201 to 182, an amendment by Representative Thompson of Illinois placing a new excise of six cents a pound on imported pork and three cents a pound on imported pork.

It approved, 290 to 96, an additional tax of 25 cents a gallon on spirits, proposed by Representative Robertson, to be added to the $2 rate now in effect.

It defeated, 292 to 94, a motion by Representative Treadway of Massachusetts, to recommit the bill to the Ways and Means Committee with instructions to eliminate the undistributed profits tax and to modify the corporate gains.

The final roll call was an adoption of the bill.

A teller vote resulted in approval, by 135 to 96, of an amendment by Representative Boileau to include Engleman spruce among woods ex-

Continued on Page Seven

Netherlands Likens Crisis To Invasion of Belgium

Wireless to THE NEW YORK TIMES.

THE HAGUE, The Netherlands, March 11.—The news of the dramatic events in Austria has seriously impressed The Netherlands, where it is considered the most alarming intelligence for smaller European countries since August, 1914, when German troops invaded Belgium.

Although German relations with The Netherlands are quite different from those with Austria, it is felt that some pretext or other might serve the Reich some day to intervene in The Netherlands' internal affairs as well.

The attitude of the British Government in the face of the new situation is impatiently awaited. In any case the lesson of Austria will not be lost on The Netherlands.

ROME CHECKS PARIS ON AID FOR VIENNA

Refuses to Cooperate With France and Britain for Support in Crisis

FAILURE FOR BLUM IS SEEN

Premier Designate Is Unable to Form Government—Radicals May Be Called

By P. J. PHILIP
Wireless to THE NEW YORK TIMES.

PARIS, March 11.—It was learned here tonight that yesterday the French and British Governments jointly sounded out Italy as to whether cooperation could be expected in maintaining Austrian independence and that they received a firm negative reply.

However, Nazi Germany's annexation of Austria this evening has profoundly affected the French political situation and, in the opinion of every political party, made the immediate constitution of a government essential. That being so, Premier-designate Léon Blum tonight, after a day of continuous negotiation and argument with one party and another, informed the press that toward noon tomorrow he will announce his decision and intentions.

It is believed that he hopes to be able to announce the formation of a national government including most, if not all, of the parties. Before then, however, he will meet the National Council of the Socialist party, which last January ran counter to his wishes and by a small majority opposed every Socialist Minister in the Chautemps Cabinet.

What course events will take depends on M. Blum's ability to persuade his own party that the time has come for them to take the lead in the formation of a government which will represent France and not

Continued on Page Two

ITALY GETS SHOCK

Visit of Hitler Probably Will Be Canceled as Result of the Coup

ROME-BERLIN AXIS SHAKEN

Parleys With Britain Likely to Be Speeded and Accord Is Now Thought Probable

By ARNALDO CORTESI
Wireless to THE NEW YORK TIMES.

ROME, March 11.—The news from Austria struck Italy with the impact of an exploding bomb and left the official world here aghast. An official spokesman told an unusually large audience of newspaper men this evening that the Italian Government considered the situation so grave that it did not feel it could make any statement at present.

The general impression is, however, that whatever Italy may decide to do she will not make any attempt to intervene in Austria militarily and will not concentrate divisions at Brenner Pass as in July, 1934, after the assassination of Chancellor Engelbert Dollfuss. No troop movements certainly have been reported.

The greatest uncertainty and confusion reigned in Italian quarters, where the day's developments apparently were entirely unexpected. But it seems clear that Chancellor Hitler's action in forcing Chancellor Kurt Schuschnigg to resign has shaken the Rome-Berlin axis to its very foundations. Whether the axis will be able to survive depends on the turn of events in the next few days and the explanations Berlin furnishes in reply to Rome's inquiries. Worth recording in any case are the widespread rumors that Hitler's visit to Italy in May will be canceled. Such a cancellation would be an unmistakable symptom that the axis was doomed.

No Hint to Rome

The very surprise and shock caused by Dr. Schuschnigg's resignation prove that Hitler acted without giving the Rome end of the axis the slightest inkling of his intentions. As late as last night Italian circles close to the government were still saying that the Austrian plebiscite would lead to a clarification, which Rome heartily favored. Now the latest developments have brought the Italo-German situation to a climax.

It is declared here that Hitler could not have chosen a better moment for a coup in Austria. The Anglo-Italian negotiations are not yet properly under way and therefore Italy cannot definitely count on British support in any action she might meditate in Central Europe. France is in the throes of a Cabinet crisis, while Russia also is going through a far from happy period internally. If Italy therefore had thought of intervening in Austria in any way she would scarcely be likely to be followed by any other powers.

The events in Austria are also likely to have deep repercussions on the Anglo-Italian negotiations. Italy obviously will now enter them in a much weaker position since her principal strength in relation to Britain hitherto was that in the field of foreign politics she and Germany acted as a unit. The wobbling of the axis cannot but increase for Italy the necessity of reaching an understanding with Britain and thus deprive her of a considerable part of her bargaining points.

Agreement Facilitated

On the other hand, the events in Austria cannot but make both Italy and Britain more determined to reach an agreement as soon as possible.

Even if the Rome-Berlin axis survives this blow, it is doubtful whether it will ever again regain the strength it had hitherto. Public opinion is convinced Germany has betrayed Italy; therefore it is difficult to imagine that the atmosphere of perfect cordiality and mutual confidence existing hitherto can ever be restored. Perhaps an open break will be avoided so as to gloss over the fact that a pillar that has upheld the whole of Italian foreign policy in the last two years has fallen to the ground, but it seems that the process of a breaking up of the axis has begun.

No course appears open to Italy but to save what she can of her position in Central Europe by di-

Continued on Page Two

Mechanic on New Army Planes Held as Spy; Trapped by Counter-Espionage in Plant

Following several days of intensified counter-espionage activities around Long Island air fields, Federal authorities yesterday arraigned Otto Hermann Voss, a naturalized German mechanic employed in the Seversky aircraft plant, for espionage. Waiving examination, Voss was held in $10,000 bail.

The government invoked the same severe World War statute under which two renegade soldiers and a German woman were held as German spies on Feb. 26. Voss was charged with delivering and inducing others to deliver "to agents of a foreign power certain documents, writings, code books, signal books, photographs, instruments and information relating to the defense of the United States." The maximum punishment for conviction is imprisonment for twenty years.

The Seversky Aircraft Corporation at Farmingdale, L. I., is now building pursuit planes for the army that have broken several world records at speeds over 300 miles an hour and are recognized as one of the best types of fighting ships.

The background of the case was not revealed beyond what appeared in the complaint and the few words spoken by Lester C. Dunigan at the arraignment before United States Commissioner Isaac Platt. Mr. Dunigan said that after a conference with John F. Dailey, Acting United States Attorney, it had been decided that any statement at this time "would be out of order."

It was reported, however, that four men who were poor mechanics worked near Voss for three weeks until two Department of Justice agents arrested him Wednesday. Then they disappeared. Voss worked in the "day-dreaming" or experimental, section of the plant's assembly division, where Major de Seversky tests new ideas and materials.

Voss, it was learned, visited Germany for about a month last Summer. His wife at their home at 225 Jericho Turnpike, Floral Park, was on the verge of collapse after two long sessions of questioning by Federal agents. They were at her home on Wednesday and Thursday. Mrs. Voss asserted her husband was innocent and believed he came under suspicion when his name was found in a paper on the person of a friend arrested as a spy suspect recently.

The defendant, 39 years old, was silent at his arraignment. He is 6 feet tall with old scars on both cheeks. Mr. Dunigan said Voss worked at the plant at intervals for several years. His alleged illegal activities were dated from Jan. 2, 1936.

The Austrian Situation

Following an ultimatum from Berlin, the Schuschnigg government in Austria retired yesterday afternoon and was succeeded by one headed by the Nazi leader, Arthur Seyss-Inquart, as Chancellor. He immediately asked the Reich to send troops to help in preserving order, and some 50,000 highly armed and mechanized forces crossed the border. Nazi mobs took possession of Vienna and raided the Jewish quarter. The swastika was flown over public buildings, and Fatherland Front forces were disarmed. There were similar demonstrations in other cities.

Europe was aghast at the coup of Hitler. His action struck Italy with the force of an exploding bomb. The impression was that Italy would not retort with force, but it was believed the Rome-Berlin axis had been shaken and that Hitler's visit to Rome might be canceled. No advance notice of Germany's intention is believed to have been given to Mussolini.

In Paris it was understood Italy had been asked if she would join in a united effort to save Austria, but had refused. Parties tried to get together to form a new Cabinet to deal with the situation, but the parties were still too deeply divided to make that accomplishment possible. It was believed Léon Blum would not be able to gain sufficient support to head a government.

Britain delivered a sharp protest to Berlin, saying Germany's action was bound to produce "the gravest reactions, of which it is impossible to foretell the issue." Other warnings were delivered earlier, but Foreign Minister von Ribbentrop retorted that Germany saw no reasons to confer with Britain until her purposes had been achieved elsewhere. [All the above dispatches on Page 1.]

Premier Negrin of Spain announced that Italy and Germany had made unofficial proposals for some agreement with the Loyalists, but they were determined not to enter on negotiations. [Page 2.]

BRITISH APPALLED BY REICH METHODS

Government Sends to Berlin a Sharp Rebuke Assailing the Tactics Employed

LONDON NOT TO INTERVENE

German Troops Start Across Border While Ribbentrop Is Guest of Chamberlain

By FERDINAND KUHN Jr.
Special Cable to THE NEW YORK TIMES.

LONDON, March 11.—At the very moment which German troops were cross the Austrian frontier the British Government, tonight delivered to Berlin one of the sharpest protests it has yet made in its post-war relations with Germany.

The strength of the protest showed how strongly the British Government felt over the day's events and particularly over the methods by which Germany had finally attained her ends in Austria.

Referring especially to the second German ultimatum that had preceded the actual invasion, the British described it as "coercion backed by the force of an independent State in order to create a situation incompatible with its national independence."

Such action, it was pointed out, was bound to produce the "gravest reactions of which it is impossible to foretell the issue."

The protest was delivered at the Wilhelmstrasse by Sir Nevile Henderson, the British Ambassador.

British Warning Disregarded

In invading Austria tonight Germany flatly disregarded the warnings of the British Government earlier in the day that threat or use of force would damage the prospects of the Anglo-German talks and threaten future chances for reconciliation in Europe.

The warning was delivered personally to Joachim von Ribbentrop, German Foreign Minister, by Prime Minister Neville Chamberlain and Foreign Minister Viscount Halifax after luncheon at 10 Downing Street.

But the British Minister's words produced no effect upon Herr von Ribbentrop or upon his master in Berlin. Herr von Ribbentrop is said to have told Mr. Chamberlain, indeed, that the Fuehrer saw no reason for starting negotiations for reconciliation with Britain until German purposes "elsewhere" had been achieved.

While these words were being spoken the German Army was rolling along the express highways leading to the Austrian border and Berlin was preparing the ultimatums that forced the Austrian Government from power.

Britain will, of course, do nothing in the way of intervention. At this late stage in the absorption of Austria there was little left for Britain to do except to protest. Yet today's shattering events in Vienna have already had repercussions that may affect British policy profoundly.

Tonight the government is appalled—there is no other word to describe it—at the recklessness of

Continued on Page Three

REICH ARMY MOVES; 50,000 AT FRONTIER

Force of Infantry, Artillery and Engineers Begin March Into Austria as Planes Fly

BAVARIAN ROADS CHOKED

Vehicles Are Commandeered in Munich—Border Villages Fired by Excitement

Wireless to THE NEW YORK TIMES.

MUNICH, Germany, Saturday, March 12.—With a dramatic suddenness that stunned the world the German Army embarked yesterday on its first campaign beyond the Reich's borders and without firing a shot achieved a victory that lay Austria prostrate at its feet, transformed the European equilibrium and set the borders fixed by the peace treaties into motion for a readjustment, of which the end is not in sight.

All day yesterday German forces, some 50,000 strong, made up of infantry, cavalry, artillery, motorized divisions, air force units and engineers with bridge building materials were moving to the Austrian frontier. Their mission was to avenge what is termed in Germany "the betrayal of Berchtesgaden"—Chancellor Kurt Schuschnigg's recent proclamation of a plebiscite on Austrian independence.

Last night, following Dr. Schuschnigg's overthrow and a telegram from the new Chancellor, Dr. Arthur Seyss-Inquart, to Chancellor Hitler requesting German military aid in preventing bloodshed, German troops marched into Austria in close formation at three points—Salzburg, Kufstein and Mittenwalde.

[According to an Associated Press dispatch from Vienna troops crossed also at Passau, on the way to Linz, Austria.]

Orders No Resistance

According to information given out at Munich army headquarters, the troops began to cross the border shortly after 10 o'clock, although their coming had been heralded by Dr. Seyss-Inquart in semi-hourly broadcasts beginning soon after 7 o'clock. The broadcasts included instructions to the Austrian military and civil authorities and the population not to resist the troops.

All the points where the troops crossed are on the southern border of Bavaria; Mittenwalde in particular is the starting point toward Scharnitz and the Fern-Alpine passes leading to Innsbruck and beyond that city to the Brenner Pass, where, in 1934, Premier Mussolini lined up his troops to prevent just such a development as occurred yesterday.

The troops involved are in the main the Seventh Army Corps stationed at Munich under the command of General Ritter von Schobert. But it also was noted that General Walter von Reichenau, known as the army's most National Socialist general, who had been Munich commander until the Feb. 4 shift, broke off his trip to the meeting of the International Olym-

Continued on Page Two

SCHUSCHNIGG GOES

Resigns After Threat of Invasion as Powers Fail to Back Him

PLEBISCITE IS CALLED OFF

Goering and Hess Expected in Vienna Today—Catholic Mayor Reported Arrested

Censorship Is Started

By The Associated Press.

VIENNA, March 11.—Censorship has started.

An order posted in the correspondents' room in the Central Telegraph Office tonight said all telephone conversations from the room must be in German.

Correspondents for the International News Service, an American organization, were detained against their will, without charges, at the office.

By G. E. R. GEDYE
Wireless to THE NEW YORK TIMES.

VIENNA, Saturday, March 12.—Under threats of force from Berlin, Chancellor Kurt Schuschnigg of Austria yielded this evening and resigned in dramatic circumstances. The Nazis, with Dr. Arthur Seyss-Inquart, former Interior Minister, as Chancellor, are in power.

[Fifty thousand German troops from all arms of the service and many planes began crossing the Austrian border at 10 o'clock last night at Salzburg, Kufstein and Mittenwalde, according to a dispatch from Munich.]

To an unprepared public listening over the radio to a typical program of pleasant Viennese melodies the voice of the man who may have been the last Chancellor of an independent Austria announced at 7:45 P. M. that, in his own words, he had "yielded only to force" to avoid bloodshed and that under the threat of a German invasion that was to start at the very moment he spoke he had resigned office.

Plebiscite Is Postponed

Apart from the statement in a broadcast at 6 o'clock that "the Chancellor and Fatherland Front Leader, in consultation with President Miklas, has decided to postpone the plebiscite, there was no warning for the public when the program was interrupted for the announcer to say, "an important declaration is just coming." Then, without even mention of Dr. Schuschnigg's name, his voice was heard at the microphone.

When Dr. Schuschnigg had finished, thousands of Nazis began swarming into Vienna's streets to take over control unopposed. An hour afterward Dr. Seyss-Inquart also addressed the nation over the radio, calling on every one to maintain order and declaring that there was no question of resistance if the German army should march in.

Up to noon Dr. Schuschnigg had remained firm in the face of all threats. Then came the first ultimatum from Germany, conveyed by Dr. Edmund Glaise-Horstenau, Austrian Minister Without Portfolio, on his return from Berlin. Austria was to postpone the plebiscite or she would be invaded.

Final Ultimatum Delivered

At 4 P. M. an airplane landed in Vienna. It brought Dr. Schuschnigg a final and this time an official ultimatum. The man who delivered it was believed to have been Josef Buercke, Nazi leader in the Saar.

At first it was rumored that Field Marshal Hermann Goering and Rudolf Hess, deputy leader of the German Nazi party, had arrived and were going to speak to the crowds in the Karlsplatz at 10 P. M., but this proved untrue. It was stated later, however, that Marshal Goering and Herr Hess would arrive today.

In any event, this ultimatum was quite different from that Dr. Glaise-Horstenau delivered. It was an official statement from the German Government that unless Dr. Schuschnigg resigned by 7:30, 300,000 Germans would cross the frontier, headed by two motorized divisions.

Even so, up to the last moment Dr. Schuschnigg held out, pondering whether he should put up or offer formal resistance. The hesitation in Dr. Schuschnigg's farewell speech when he said first that the Austrian troops had been or-

Continued on Page Three

"All the News That's Fit to Print."

The New York Times.

LATE CITY EDITION
Rain and cooler today. Tomorrow generally fair with little change in temperature.
Temperatures Yesterday—Max., 72; Min., 58

Copyright, 1938, by The New York Times Company.

VOL. LXXXVIII...No. 29,469. Entered as Second-Class Matter, Postoffice, New York, N. Y. NEW YORK, FRIDAY, SEPTEMBER 30, 1938. PP THREE CENTS NEW YORK CITY and Vicinity | FOUR CENTS Elsewhere Except in 7th and 8th Postal Zones.

FOUR POWERS REACH A PEACEABLE AGREEMENT; GERMANS TO ENTER SUDETEN AREA TOMORROW AND WILL COMPLETE OCCUPATION IN TEN DAYS

DEWEY NOMINATED BY REPUBLICANS; ATTACKS TAMMANY

HAILED IN OVATION

Prosecutor Promises to Rid State of 'Corruption' in 'Bigger Job'

CHOICE BY ACCLAMATION

O'Brian and Corsi Nominated for Senate—A. V. McDermott for Attorney General

Mr. Dewey's acceptance, Page 14; Republican platform Page 13

By JAMES A. HAGERTY
Special to THE NEW YORK TIMES.

SARATOGA SPRINGS, Friday, Sept. 30.—Asserting that the time had come to remove the influence of the "corrupt" Tammany machine from the State government, District Attorney Thomas E. Dewey of New York County last night accepted the Republican nomination for Governor.

Received with wild enthusiasm by the delegates and alternates to the Republican State Convention, Mr. Dewey promised that the fight against organized crime would continue on a wider front than ever before if he were elected Governor. He declared that it was the duty of the State to protect its citizens from economic catastrophe, see that every worker had a job and provide necessary relief and adequate housing. He promised to discuss these and other issues in detail during the campaign.

Mr. Dewey was nominated by acclamation at the morning session yesterday, and the choice was genuinely unanimous.

At an early hour this morning the convention nominated John Lord O'Brian of Buffalo for United States Senator for the full six-year term.

The nomination of Mr. O'Brian, after a three days' search for a candidate, completed the ticket headed by Mr. Dewey. Edward Corsi of Manhattan was chosen as candidate for United States Senator for the two-year balance of the term of the late Senator Royal S. Copeland.

Other nominations were:

Lieutenant Governor—State Senator Frederic H. Bontecou of Dutchess County.

Attorney General—Colonel Arthur V. McDermott of Brooklyn.

Controller — Julius Rothstein of Utica.

Representatives at Large — Mrs. Helen Rogers of Buffalo and Richard B. Scandrett Jr. of Orange County.

Dewey Defends Decision to Run

Mr. Dewey's first words, after he had been cheered intermittently for a quarter of an hour after his entrance into the hall last evening, were:

"I accept your nomination."

This brought another storm of applause, the delegates and alternates seeing in him a candidate who had a chance to end the long series of Republican defeats in State elections and win the first Republican State campaign since the election of Nathan L. Miller.

Mr. Dewey first met the argument, advanced even by some of his friends, that he should not leave the office of District Attorney with his work unfinished. He had been told, he said, that it was too risky to venture into a State campaign and urged to play safe.

"Had I taken that advice, I should have been shirking the bigger job, the harder fight," he said. "I shall not shirk that fight."

The audience seemed to feel that in Mr. Dewey they had a fighting candidate and roared its approval.

Friends also urged him to stay as District Attorney on the assumption that he was the only man in New York City who could run a large law office, investigate rackets and prosecute crime.

"Well, the trouble with that is: It just is not true," he declared.

Points to Prosecuting Staff

Mr. Dewey added that as a candidate for District Attorney he had made a single promise, that the people would be represented by an office of competent, hard-working lawyers.

"And I specifically promised that my assistants would not be chosen by Al Marinelli, Charlie Schneider or any other of the Tammany district leaders who are now selecting my opponent at the Democratic State Convention," he continued, bringing laughter and cheers.

Mr. Dewey said that he had a staff of seventy-two energetic, high-principled lawyers who knew how

Continued on Page Fifteen

Rainstorm and Winds Due to Hit City Today

A rainstorm accompanied by fresh to strong winds, possibly reaching gale force, will strike New York some time today but there is virtually no possibility of tornado conditions similar to those which yesterday damaged Charleston, S. C., it was said at the Weather Bureau here last night.

Bureau officials said the tornado that struck Charleston was probably of "purely local origin." It resulted, however, from a low pressure area that was moving northeastward and was expected to be centered around New York today. Clearing weather is forecast for New York tomorrow.

The following additional advisory report from Washington was received last night at the local office of the Weather Bureau:

"Northeast storm warnings ordered at 9 P. M. from the Virginia Capes to Eastport, Me.; disturbance of moderate but increasing intensity central over Eastern North Carolina, moving northeastward in conjunction with area of high pressure over New England and Eastern Canada, will be attended by increasing northeast or east winds becoming strong and probably reaching gale force from Virgina Capes to the New Jersey coast tonight and north from New Jersey to Eastport on Friday."

DEMOCRATS AWAIT LEHMAN'S REPLY

Draft of Governor Dominates Convention Opening—Labor Party Alignment Sought

The Democratic keynote and Mr. Farley's speech, Page 16.

By WARREN MOSCOW
Special to THE NEW YORK TIMES.

ROCHESTER, N. Y., Sept. 29.—Governor Herbert H. Lehman, faced all day today with a relentless draft movement from the leaders of the Democratic party, failed at a conference tonight to announce his willingness to run again. Despite this, the party leaders indicated that they expected he would be nominated tomorrow to oppose Thomas E. Dewey.

Whatever hints came from the closed-mouthed group of leaders who filed from the Governor's suite at the Hotel Seneca just before midnight were to the effect that it was a question of ironing out the rest of the places on the ticket which was holding up a formal announcement, rather than a declination by the Governor.

They named State Chairman James A. Farley as the spokesman, and his only comment was that there would be another conference at 9 A. M., just five hours before the nominations are to be made on the second day of the party's State convention.

The leaders went into the night conference fully prepared to let the Governor name the rest of the ticket, revise the platform and arrange with the American Labor party for united support of the Democratic nominees.

Tactics of Persuasion

During the day they sent to him a long list of personal friends and social welfare advocates who argued that he owed it to the State to accept the nomination. They contended that Mr. Dewey would have to take a social point of view differing from that held by Mr. Lehman.

Another group concentrated on Mrs. Lehman to overcome her objections to spending four years more in Albany. She has spent ten years there, four as the wife of the Lieutenant Governor and six as the wife of the Governor, and her husband accepted a third nomination in 1936 over her protest.

The Democrats built their entire case against Mr. Dewey around Governor Lehman and the New Deal, despite the fact that the Governor and the New Deal recently have not been so closely associated as in the past.

The Governor went over the platform this afternoon with David F. Lee of Binghamton, the chairman of the resolutions committee, and made changes in a text that had already been approved by high party leaders.

Later he listened over the radio as Robert F. Wagner and James A. Farley went the limit for the New

Continued on Page Seventeen

TORNADOES KILL 26 IN CHARLESTON; HUNDREDS INJURED

Storms Strike City Without Warning, Causing Loss Estimated Up to $5,000,000

OLD LANDMARKS DAMAGED

City in Darkness, With Troops Guarding Streets—Roosevelt, Red Cross Rush Help

From a Staff Correspondent

CHARLESTON, S. C., Sept. 29.—Two tornadoes dipped down into this city at about 8:05 o'clock this morning and brought death to at least twenty-six persons, injuries to hundreds and damage to property estimated at between $2,000,000 and $5,000,000.

Before the storm passed on, the freak winds, which reached a velocity of 72 mines an hour, raged over the old parts of Charleston, damaging many of the landmarks which make this historic city one of the most colorful in the South. Dwellings were razed by the twisters which left their occupants among the dead and injured.

Power and telephone lines were cut by falling walls, trees and poles in the affected areas. Tonight, however, although the city was in darkness and with only meager communications, the residents were taking the situation without panic, cleaning up the debris and putting the streets in order.

Major Gen. Charles P. Summerall, U. S. A., retired, now president of Citadel College and head of the local chapter of the American Red Cross, announced that the Red Cross had provided cots for 1,100 persons tonight. This afforded the first official information about the number rendered homeless by the collapse of their dwellings or by damage to their homes which made them uninhabitable.

Cots Are Set Up for Homeless

Cots were placed in the Y.M.C.A., the Y.W.C.A., the Murray Vocational School, Sumter Guard Armory and the County Agricultural Building. Additional buildings were held in reserve and were being put in order for possible use by the homeless.

In arriving in Charleston by one of the Eastern Air Lines planes, this correspondent and a Times Wide World photographer were afforded a survey of the debris-laden streets in the affected areas by the pilot, J. W. Williams, who circled the city three times.

Flying southward and coming over the northwest section of the city along the Ashley River, observers first noticed a clump of dwellings which had been razed. In these lived several Negroes, who were numbered among the dead or missing. This mass of debris seemingly was separated by at least two miles from any other visible evidence of destruction.

As the plane flew south along the Battery, observers could see the damaged roof of St. Michael's Episcopal Church at Broad and Meeting Streets, the debris about St. Philip's Church, near by, both of which are pre-Revolutionary structures, and the Huguenot church.

The worst destruction was observed as the plane flew up the Cooper River. Gone was most of the roof of the City Market, a row

Continued on Page Three

4 Conferees Said to Plan A Non-Aggression Pact

By The Associated Press.

LONDON, Friday, Sept. 30.—Informed sources said today they understood Prime Minister Neville Chamberlain had obtained from Chancellor Adolf Hitler and Premier Benito Mussolini an agreement to negotiate a four-power non-aggression pact as soon as the Czechoslovak problem was solved.

He was said to have obtained the agreement, envisaging a pact with Great Britain, Italy, France and Germany as its signers, at the Munich four-power conference.

Responsible political circles said that Mr. Chamberlain, through his insistence on negotiations in the Czechoslovak crisis, had brought the three other nations to the stage where negotiation of a four-power pact was possible.

Such a settlement, it was believed, would not only lead to a non-aggression pact but might bring about withdrawal of Italian soldiers from Spain.

LITVINOFF URGES RIGHTS FOR SPAIN

Condemns Roles of Italy and Reich and Asks League to Speed Troop Withdrawals

By CLARENCE K. STREIT
Wireless to THE NEW YORK TIMES.

GENEVA, Sept. 29.—While the four statesmen talked in private at Munich today of Czechoslovakia, and perhaps Spain, Maxim M. Litvinoff of Russia, representing Europe's great outsider, talked in public to the League Assembly's political commission about the Spanish and Czechoslovak situations.

Supporting the request of Premier Juan Negrin of Loyalist Spain for a League commission to guarantee to the world that its voluntary withdrawal of non-Spanish combatants was loyally executed, the Soviet Foreign Commissar said it "cannot even bring down upon us the wrath of the present dictators of Europe, before whom some members of the League have now become accustomed to tremble."

Mr. Litvinoff, in a scathing attack on German and Italian intervention in Spain, found Spain too entitled to the benefit of the principle of self-determination.

"It is a democratic principle," he said, "if I may so, from among the watchwords of the Russian revolution of 1917 but by no means despised (when it serves their purpose) by (those who at this very moment perhaps are imposing their will upon Europe's democracies.

"The Spanish people too is fighting for its right to self-determination. For its right to set up the internal regime it pleases and dispose of its natural resources and foreign trade."

He reminded the committee then

Continued on Page Ten

CZECHS DEPRESSED

Expected Any Agreement to Be at the Expense of Their Nation

RUNCIMAN VIEW ASSAILED

Prague Fears Difficulties in Withdrawing Army From Its Present Border Positions

By EMIL VADNAY
Wireless to THE NEW YORK TIMES.

PRAGUE, Czechoslovakia, Sept. 29.—The Czech Government contributed its share today toward the success of the Munich conference. A communique issued this afternoon reads:

"A conference of the government Wednesday was devoted to the examination of the British note containing proposals for the step-by-step realization of the Franco-British plan, which was accepted Sept. 21 as the basis for the settlement of the Sudeten German question.

"The answer to the note takes a positive stand—with certain reservations concerning the British proposals, the gradual execution of the various transfers and the drawing of new frontiers. The answer was transmitted to the British Government before the opening of the four power conference at Munich."

The Czech Minister in Berlin, Dr. V. Mastny, left Prague by airplane this afternoon after a conference with President Eduard Benes to act as an observer in Munich. In the event Czechoslovakia should officially be invited to participate, former Premier Milan Hodza would join him as chief representative.

[In Munich early this morning it was said there was no word of Czechoslovak action on the four-power agreement, according to The Associated Press.]

Public Opinion Depressed

Public opinion here is deeply depressed. Every one complains that the agreement that will probably be reached at Munich will be almost entirely at Czechoslovakia's expense. The relief throughout the world that apparently at the last moment Prime Minister Neville Chamberlain's endeavors succeeded in saving the peace of Europe is shared by the Czechs, but the fact that they must foot the bill causes much discontent.

Viscount Runciman's letter to Mr. Chamberlain, published in the British White Paper, advocating the cession of the Sudetenland, caused indignation here and was the subject of sharp criticism. It was recalled that Lord Runciman consulted with Sudeten politicians only when he tried to test the feelings of Sudeten Germans. Whenever he visited the border zone, it was said, he seemed mostly impressed by the Henleinist demonstrations. He never paid a visit to the regions where, according to Czech contentions, he would have had the opportunity of examining the ordinary life of the population and hear the other side of the story.

President Benes and the government are complete masters of the domestic situation. It will not be easy, however, to withdraw a mobilized army from the present frontier and order them to abandon various lines of fortifications built by them at tremendous sacrifice and demobilize men who a week ago went out singing with enthusiasm to the defense of the border. Tens of thousands of anti-Nazis would have to quit their homes in the defense of which they volunteered to fight after having sent their wives and children into the interior.

These grave problems can only be solved if the people are fully convinced that there is no other possibility.

Troops March to Border

In the meantime troops are marching along roads toward the borders, streets in the cities are pitch dark and telegraph traffic remains cut as well as the long distance telephone service. Interurban telephone service has been restored today for urgent calls. Railroad travel is under the control of the army as well as is practically the whole industry of the country. The population endures various inconveniences with good humor. German propaganda is making attempts to sap morale. Rumors about the flight of Cabinet Ministers and their arrests for embezzlement of public funds have been printed and the Germans even succeeded in printing editions of faked Czech news-

Continued on Page Four

Economic Collapse of Czechoslovakia Seen; Reich Gets the Basic Industrial Resources

By ROBERT CROZIER LONG
Wireless to THE NEW YORK TIMES.

BERLIN, Sept. 29.—Pending the definitive fixing of Czechoslovakia's new frontiers it is impossible to assess precisely Germany's gain in raw materials and manufacturing resources.

But even assuming a conservative delimitation, Germany will acquire valuable material assets and will, indeed, leave to the shrunken republic little but the munitions works of Pilsen and Bruenn, for which, as if in irony, a State with indefensible frontiers will have no use.

Czechoslovakia is primarily an industrial country. Of nearly 15,000,000 inhabitants returned by the last occupation census eight years back, more than 5,000,000 were engaged in industry and a little fewer in agriculture. But as inner Bohemia and Moravia are largely flatlands suitable for farming, it is in the peripheral districts claimed by Germany and, it seems, by Poland that most of the industries and their raw materials are located. All this frontier district with, perhaps, the exception of a few small areas the Czechoslovak population will lose.

Czechoslovakia's industry is largely based on lignite, or brown coal. Germany will acquire this main thermic resource, which occurs in two large fields, one in the Western Egerland salient and the other some distance northeast between Komotau and Aussig. The republic's bituminous coal mines, with associated smelting and engineering plants, lie in the neighborhood of Teschen, Bohumin and Karvina, just west of the Slovak frontier, to which Polish irredentists lay claim.

Between Teschen in the extreme east and Asch in the extreme west of the Bohemian-Moravian complex lies much of the greatest part of Czechoslovakia's manufacturing industry, nearly all in German-speaking territory. The big Germanic identation south of Freiwaldau, on the Silesian frontier, contains textile and glass works, with some chemical plants.

Farther west, after a break in the German frontier population, stretches the Trautenau-Gablonz district with some bituminous coal and important textiles and paper concerns, and still farther west is the Reichenberg center with textile mills, important mechanical and light industries and automotive works.

Farther to the west are the sugar mills of Boemisch Leipa, which draw raw material from the agricultural south, and next comes Aussig, center of the republic's most important chemical concern. Far-

Continued on Page Eight

Text of 4-Power Accord

By The Associated Press.

MUNICH, Germany, Friday, Sept. 30.—The official communiqué issued at the end of the four-power conference here this morning follows:

Germany, the United Kingdom, France and Italy, taking into consideration the agreement which has already been reached in principle for cession to Germany of the Sudeten German territory, have agreed on the following terms and conditions governing the said cession and the measures consequent thereon and by this agreement they each hold themselves responsible for the steps necessary to secure its fulfillment:

I

The evacuation will begin on Oct. 1.

II

The United Kingdom, France and Italy agree that the evacuation of the territory shall be completed by Oct. 10 without any existing installations having been destroyed and that the Czechoslovak Government will be held responsible for carrying out the evacuation without damage to the said installations.

III

The conditions governing the evacuation will be laid down in detail by an international commission composed of representatives of Germany, the United Kingdom, France, Italy and Czechoslovakia.

Occupation by stages of the predominantly German territories by German troops will begin on Oct. 1. The four territories marked on the attached map will be occupied by German troops in the following order:

Territory marked No. 1 on the 1st and 2d of October; territory marked No. 2 on the 2d and 3d of October; territory marked No. 3 on the 3d, 4th and 5th of October; territory marked No. 4 on the 6th and 7th of October.

The remaining territory of preponderantly German character will be ascertained by the aforesaid international commission forthwith and be occupied by German troops by the 10th of October.

The international commission referred to in Paragraph III will determine the territories in which a plebiscite is to be held. These

Continued on Page Five

ITALIANS SHOUT JOY ON NEWS OF ACCORD

Rome's Streets Echo as People Greet Solution—Victory for Dictatorships Is Seen

By ARNALDO CORTESI
Wireless to THE NEW YORK TIMES.

ROME, Friday, Sept. 30.—The news that an agreement had been reached in Munich caused an explosion of joy in Rome and everywhere in Italy.

Italy had remained calm throughout the crisis, having always been sustained by a secret hope that the Czechoslovak question would not be made a pretext for a general conflagration, but the knowledge that the danger of war had been definitely removed was learned with intense relief and caused every one to exult.

Many streets in Rome echoed with cheers when special editions of newspapers gave the announcement for which every Italian had been waiting anxiously, that the conference in Munich had reached an understanding.

See Victory for Dictatorships

Italians believe that the solution represents a victory for the dictatorships as against the democracies. Chancellor Adolf Hitler, they point out, obtained without war what he wanted—namely, the dismemberment of Czechoslovakia and annexation to Germany of the Sudeten territories—whereas the democracies, which were bound by treaties to protect Czechoslovakia, were unable or unwilling to take the steps necessary to safeguard the territorial integrity of their ward. Italians, therefore, feel that the balance leans in Herr Hitler's favor.

Great curiosity exists on how the questions of Hungarian and Polish minorities have been dealt with. All Italians feel sure that, owing to the presence of Premier Benito Mussolini, this problem also came up for discussion, and they will be very disappointed if he did not succeed in doing something for his protégés.

All Italians feel equally sure that Signor Mussolini would not overlook the opportunity offered by his contacts with Prime Minister Neville Chamberlain of Great Britain and Premier Edouard Daladier of France to broach other subjects that, although not connected directly with the Czechoslovak problem, are of great importance to Italy.

The Spanish civil war, Italo-French and Italo-British relations and an understanding on the lines of the four-power pact of 1933 are among the subjects included under this head. It is generally conceded, however, that the success or failure of Signor Mussolini's efforts in these fields will be visible only in the subsequent development of the European situation.

Yesterday was a day of alternate

Continued on Page Five

CHAMBERLAIN HERO OF MUNICH CROWDS

People Stand Outside Hotel for Hours to Get Glimpse of Him and Cheer Him

By The Associated Press.

MUNICH, Germany, Sept. 29.—Men and women of Munich stood cheerfully for hours today for a glimpse of the 69-year-old man who started this business of man-to-man talks for peace.

That man was Britain's Prime Minister, Neville Chamberlain, a strange figure in black amid the patriotic panorama of this cradle of Nazism.

Every second man who stood and waited and cheered wore a swastika lapel button. Every second woman was of the handsome, well-turned-out sort of which Munich is proud.

They packed lawns in front of the old-fashioned Regina Palace Hotel, headquarters of the British delegation to the four-power conference. The crowd was packed eight and ten feet deep around a square formed by brown-shirted Storm Troopers before the hotel entrance.

Inside additional dozens were camped on the hotel's twin stairways and in every conceivable spot in the tiny red, white and gold lobby.

Little to See Most of Time

Most of the time there wasn't anything to see.

Every half-hour two steel-helmeted, black-coated honor guards with bayonets on shoulders snapped through the manual of arms on a hasty signal. Every now and then new black-shirted guards stamped to posts in front of the hotel's baroque marble pillars and the preceding guard goose-stepped away.

There were exciting intervals when Brownshirts filed in and out and the crowd held its breath in anticipation.

There were real cheers, like the kind one hears in an American football stadium, when the slim, black-coated Chamberlain, with a smile and a careful walk, came out. There were Hitler salutes, it is true, but many of the throng kept their hands at their sides and there was lots of noise of the kind one might hear anywhere where people are glad.

After Mr. Chamberlain had driven away in the sticky Munich afternoon for the conference of the statesmen beneath the gorgeous pagan panels of the Fuehrerhaus, the palace Herr Hitler built to glorify the birth here of the Nazi movement, the same people stood into the night, joking and waiting.

They were still waiting when the British Prime Minister came downstairs again for the third meeting with Chancellor Adolf Hitler, Premier Benito Mussolini of Italy and Premier Edouard Daladier of France. Then there was a thunder

Continued on Page Five

NAZI DEMANDS MET

Hitler Gets Almost All He Asked as Munich Conferees Agree

GUARANTEE FOR PRAGUE

Polish and Hungarian Claims Are to Be Satisfied—Vote in Doubtful Areas Provided

The war for which Europe had been feverishly preparing was averted early this morning when the leading statesmen of Britain, France, Germany and Italy, meeting in Munich, reached an agreement to allow Reich troops to occupy predominantly German portions of Czechoslovakia's Sudetenland progressively over a ten-day period beginning tomorrow. Most of Chancellor Hitler's demands were met. Prime Minister Chamberlain, whose peace efforts were finally crowned with success, received the loudest applause of Munich's crowds.

Before the start of the conference the Czech Government sent to the British Government a memorandum on its position with regard to the Anglo-French proposals. The Czechs felt that whatever agreement was reached would be at their expense and public opinion was deeply depressed.

Italians shouted their joy in Rome and elsewhere at the announcement of the Munich agreement. They regarded the solution as a victory for the dictatorships over the democracies.

Meanwhile, in Geneva, Foreign Commissar Litvinoff denounced Italian and German intervention in Spain and demanded that the principle of self-determination be recognized for the Loyalist government.

[All the above dispatches are on Page 1.]

Paris was relieved at the Munich agreement, but continued its war preparations. [Page 4.] Likewise in London, where the tension was relaxed, precautions went forward. [Page 5.]

Pope Pius broke down and sobbed as he appealed in a world radio broadcast for prayers for peace. [Page 6.] President Roosevelt urged the people of this country to offer such prayers. [Page 6.]

Powers Make Accord

By FREDERICK T. BIRCHALL
Wireless to THE NEW YORK TIMES.

MUNICH, Germany, Friday, Sept. 30.—The four-power conference to decide the fate of Czechoslovakia and avert a general European war by bringing pressure to bear on her to accept its decisions has met here, reached an agreement and adjourned.

In something less than nine hours of actual conversation time it has settled everything to the satisfaction—more or less—of the conferees.

It may be said at once that the decisions give Germany just about all she has demanded except the total extinction of Czechoslovakia as an independent State, which has never in fact been among her formulated demands, although that has been implied.

The decisions indicate, moreover, that the Poles and Hungarians will receive their shares of the spoils of Czechoslovakia dismemberment. The only change discernible from Chancellor Adolf Hitler's Godesberg memorandum is in the period allowed for the fulfillment of the demand. That has been slightly extended and beginning tomorrow the predominantly German territories are to be evacuated and occupied progressively until Oct. 10.

Property Must Be Left

The four governments—Britain, France, Germany and Italy—agree that the evacuation must be completed "without any existing installations being destroyed." This covers the German demand, previously objected to by the British, that Czech farmers in Sudeten territory must leave their farms, stock and crops intact behind them when they evacuate, without compensation for them.

The territories to be evacuated are divided into four categories designated on maps appended to the agreement. The first category will be occupied on Oct. 1 and 2 and the second category on Oct. 2 and 3.

Continued on Page Five

"All the News That's Fit to Print."

The New York Times.

LATE CITY EDITION
Partly cloudy and warm with scattered showers today and tomorrow.
Temperatures Yesterday—Max., 88; Min., 70

Copyright, 1939, by The New York Times Company.

VOL. LXXXVIII...No. 29,797. Entered as Second-Class Matter, Postoffice, New York, N. Y. NEW YORK, THURSDAY, AUGUST 24, 1939. PP THREE CENTS NEW YORK CITY and Vicinity | FOUR CENTS Elsewhere Except in 7th and 8th Postal Zones.

GERMANY AND RUSSIA SIGN 10-YEAR NON-AGGRESSION PACT; BIND EACH OTHER NOT TO AID OPPONENTS IN WAR ACTS; HITLER REBUFFS LONDON; BRITAIN AND FRANCE MOBILIZE

U.S. AND ARGENTINA PLAN TRADE PACT, WELLES DISCLOSES

Our Commerce Will Get Full Equality With That of All Foreigners, He Asserts

BEEF NOT TO BE INCLUDED

Long Preliminary Talks Ease Difficulties, With Offset Seen to Our Recent Losses

Special to THE NEW YORK TIMES.

WASHINGTON, Aug. 23.—The United States intends to negotiate a reciprocal trade treaty with Argentina as a move to put American commerce with that republic on a footing of equality with that of European competitors, Sumner Welles, Acting Secretary of State, stated today. There have been more than four years of preliminary discussion.

The State Department, making public a list of products upon which this country would make tariff concessions, set Oct. 4 as the closing date for submission of briefs by interested Americans and Oct. 16 for the opening of public hearings.

It was emphasized that fresh, chilled or frozen Argentine meats, the entry of which into this country is banned by the Tariff Act of 1930, and fine wools would not be a subject of discussion in the negotiations. This was expected by officials to remove the most serious objections which might have been advanced to conclusion of a reciprocal agreement. Barring of the entry of Argentine fresh beef here has long been a subject of some friction between the two countries in their commercial relations.

"It may be noted that during the fifteen-year period 1924-38 our exports to Argentina have exceeded our imports from that country by $486,900,000," Mr. Welles said in a statement.

Trade Cut by Foreign Pacts

"Our trade with Argentina has suffered in recent years for lack of a trade agreement. The trade of certain European countries with Argentina has been developing at our expense under the influence of their commercial agreements with Argentina. The placing of American commerce in Argentina on a footing of full equality with that of our European competitors was a subject which was gone into fully in preliminary discussions leading up to the present announcement.

"The agreement will enable us to maintain our competitive position in a market of great present and prospective importance.

"On our side we must, of course, offer reciprocal benefits. The products of interest to Argentina with respect to which consideration will be given in the course of the negotiations, with a view to seeing what concessions could be granted, are listed in connection with the announcement of the proposed negotiations. The concessions, which will in due course be formulated, should, of course, permit an increase in Argentina's exports to this country, but will not have injurious effect upon American production.

"The types of wool included in the list are the coarser types, of which there is only a very small production in this country."

Barter Agreement With Germany

It was presumed that in referring to European competitors Mr. Welles was speaking principally of Germany, which concluded a barter agreement with Argentina after the Pan-American Conference in Lima last December. England has long been a large trader with Argentina, however, and is a heavy buyer of Argentine beef.

Among the products upon which the United States will consider lowering duties in favor of Argentina are:

Tallow, oleo oil and oleo stearin, extract of meat, including fluid, pickled or cured beef packed or not packed in air-tight containers; dead turkeys, dead birds, chicken eggs, corn or maize, including cracked corn; asparagus in its natural state, and some wools.

With the possible exception of that made with Brazil, a reciprocal trade treaty with the Argentine would be the most important yet consummated with a Latin-American country, officials indicated. Be-

Continued on Page Thirty-five

BRITAIN ACTS FAST

Air Force Is Ready for Hostilities—Warships Mass in Skagerrak

EXPORT EMBARGO IS FIXED

Parliament Meets Today in an Emergency Session—King to Convene Privy Council

By FERDINAND KUHN Jr.
Special Cable to THE NEW YORK TIMES.

LONDON, Aug. 23.—The British Government prepared for action today with every indication that it was ready to go to war with Germany whenever a call for help from Poland should come.

Warning notices went out to reservists in all departments of the armed and civilian services; the King was returning to London to hold a meeting of the Privy Council tomorrow; Londoners were ordered to darken their windows until further notice; the air force was poised for instant action, and a concentration of an undisclosed number of British warships was reported in the Skagerrak, between the Norwegian and Danish coasts, as if to remind Germany of the blockade that she had to endure during the World War.

The emergency was underlined by a Board of Trade announcement placing an immediate embargo on unlicensed exports of essential war materials "in order to conserve the stocks in this country." The list included copper, nickel and rubber, which the Germans have been buying in large quantities in the past week or two, and also aluminum, lead, iron and steel scrap and raw cotton.

Parliament Session Today

Tomorrow both houses of Parliament will meet in emergency sesison to give the government sweeping powers of a sort unknown in democratic England since World War days. The new law will be something like the old Defense of the Realm Act, enabling the government to issue Orders in Council, without prior or subsequent Parliamentary sanction, for any purpose that the national interest may require.

Trade-union leaders were invited to examine the bill today and they came away satisfied that all possible safeguards of individual liberty would be included.

The real business of the Parliamentary session, however, will be to hear a complete review of the international situation by Prime Minister Chamberlain in the House of Commons and by Viscount Halifax, the Foreign Secretary, in the House of Lords. All indications are that the Prime Minister's words and the subsequent debate will be more sombre in tone than anything heard in the Commons chamber since Aug. 3, 1914, when Sir Edward Grey made his famous speech on the eve of the World War.

Everywhere it was agreed that a crisis of the utmost gravity now confronts Britain, a crisis far more serious than that of last Autumn, when this country was not committed as it is now. The British determination to carry out all the pledges to Poland was reaffirmed in the government message handed to Chancellor Hitler today by Sir

Continued on Page Five

The Developments in Europe

The signing of the Russo-German non-aggression pact, which many world capitals feared might be Chancellor Hitler's "go-ahead signal," took place in Moscow early this morning, half a day after German Foreign Minister von Ribbentrop had arrived in the Russian capital. The pact, which runs for ten years, in addition to prohibiting attack by either party against the other, forbids either to join any association of powers aimed at the other. Moreover, it provides that if one party is an "object of warlike acts" the other will not support such acts. [Page 1; text of the treaty, also Page 1.]

Signature of the pact followed a day that seemed to bring Europe closer to the brink. When the British Ambassador to Germany conveyed to Chancellor Hitler a warning that Britain would fight for Poland he was bluntly rebuffed. In Berlin word freely circulated that the German Army would march at 6 P. M. today (noon in New York). [Page 1.]

In the face of Herr Hitler's rebuff Britain went ahead with war preparations, including the sending of notices to reservists, poising of the air force and concentration of warships in the Skagerrak, north of Denmark. Parliament prepared to meet today to grant the government sweeping emergency powers. [Page 1.] Reinforcements were reported being sent to the Mediterranean, where the bases at Gibraltar and Malta were on the alert. [Page 3.] The dominions, led by Canada and Australia, were beginning to swing into line behind Britain. [Page 6.]

France, convinced that Germany intends to invade Poland within a few days, called up further reservists after a meeting of the Permanent Committee on National Defense. [Page 1.]

Poland remained outwardly calm, still doubting that Herr Hitler would risk precipitating a general war. [Page 2.]

In Turkey allegiance to the coalition powers was affirmed, although German Ambassador von Papen was flying to Angora from Germany, presumably to try to break that allegiance. [Page 1.] But in Rumania, another State guaranteed by France and Britain, informed circles said that country would strive to remain neutral [Page 7.]

Only in Rome were signs of war lacking. Although the press continued to attack Poland, no unusual defense preparations were evident. [Page 1.]

In an attempt to head off disaster King Leopold of the Belgians, speaking for the seven Oslo powers, appealed for peace. [With the text of the appeal, Page 5.]

President Roosevelt, disturbed by the outlook, was speeding back to Washington [Page 1], where officials were clearing the decks for action if it became necessary to safeguard United States neutrality and help Americans to escape from danger zones. [Page 3.] The State Department advised citizens not to go to Europe [Page 3] and those who were trying to return home found ships still running normally from foreign ports. [Page 3.]

In the Far East the army and navy leaders in Japan were understood to have shaped a policy to be followed in view of the new situation arising from the Russo-German treaty. [Page 4.] In China some observers believed the treaty would mean increased Soviet aid in resisting Japan. [Page 4.]

FRANCE MOBILIZES; NOW EXPECTS WAR

People Confident of Strength to Meet Aggressor as Hopes of Peace Diminish

By P. J. PHILIP
Wireless to THE NEW YORK TIMES.

PARIS, Thursday, Aug. 24.—Convinced by a report from French Ambassador Robert Coulondre at Berlin and by a reply that Chancellor Adolf Hitler gave yesterday to Prime Minister Neville Chamberlain's message through British Ambassador Sir Nevile Henderson at Berchtesgaden that an invasion of Poland is intended by the German Government within the next few days, the French Government last night decided to call up a further contingent of reservists today.

This decision was communicated to the press in an official statement from Premier Edouard Daladier's office as follows:

"On account of the international situation the French Government has decided to complete military measures already taken by calling up an additional contingent of reserve soldiers."

During last night notices were

Continued on Page Two

TURKEY REAFFIRMS PLEDGES TO ALLIES

Will Honor Pact With France and Britain—German Envoy Flies to Woo Her

Special Cable to THE NEW YORK TIMES.

ISTANBUL, Turkey, Aug. 23.—No official pronouncement has yet been made about the Russo-German non-aggression pact. In official quarters the position of Turkey is said to be unchanged; she has made agreements for mutual assistance against aggression with France and Britain and stands by them.

The Turkish people are still bewildered over yesterday's news, but less alarm about its possibilities is noticeable since last night's official British communiqué was published.

Until the Turkish Government has authentic information about the terms of the pact Turkish newspapers will be reticent. Cumhuriet, only Turkish newspaper with an editorial on the subject today, assumed the Soviet Union would stipulate that if Germany was guilty of aggression against any of her Western neighbors, the pact would become null and void.

In this case, the newspaper said, it should act as a deterrent against war in Europe, for the newspaper could not believe the Soviet Government will remain indifferent to the fate of its neighbors on the Baltic and Black Seas simply because it signed a pact of non-aggression with Germany.

Cumhuriet added that although a pact of non-aggresison was not an alliance, it implied friendly feelings, and it believed, therefore, that the anti-Comintern pact was political, not ideological, and that the Russo-German pact may be regarded as a truce.

Von Papen Flies to Turkey

BUDAPEST, Hungary, Aug. 23 (AP).—Franz von Papen, Germany's Ambassador to Turkey, passed by plane through Budapest today, en route from Salzburg to Angora.

Diplomatic circles conjectured his mission now was to renew attempts to draw Turkey out of the British-French bloc. They recalled German and Italian claims that Turkey's alliance with Britain and France was dependent upon Russia's not joining the opposition camp.

Wireless to THE NEW YORK TIMES.

BUDAPEST, Hungary, Aug. 23.—The international situation was dis-

Continued on Page Five

Sidney Howard Killed by Tractor on Estate; Playwright Is Crushed in Berkshire Garage

Special to THE NEW YORK TIMES.

TYRINGHAM, Mass., Aug. 23.—Sidney Coe Howard, playwright, was crushed to death today by a two and a half ton tractor in his garage on his 700-acre estate here.

Mr. Howard had put in a morning of hard work on a new play based on Carl Van Doren's "Benjamin Franklin" and, as was his custom, was going to seek relaxation in physical work on his estate, which included one of the most modern dairy farms in this part of the State. The chore he had set for himself was harrowing a twenty-eight-acre field which he had recently bought to extend his property.

Driving alone to the garage a quarter of a mile from his studio in the fields, Mr. Howard entered, turned on the ignition switch of the tractor and cranked it. The machine lurched forward, pinning the playwright against the wall of the structure. The tractor, put in the garage the night before by an employe, was believed to have been left in high gear.

Fred L. Fairbanks, superintendent of the estate, discovered Mr. Howard while on an inspection trip. The garage, a former Shaker schoolroom, is set off by itself on the estate and is seldom visited by any one except by those on business.

Mr. Fairbanks found his employer in an upright position, his head bent over his chest. He was pinned at the chest by the hood of the tractor, which had stalled after crushing him against the wall.

After starting the tractor and moving Mr. Howard's body, Mr. Faifbanks ran to the nearest telephone on the estate to notify Mrs. Howard and summon aid. Mrs. Howard was shopping in Lee, five miles away. When she returned

Continued on Page Nineteen

QUICK ACTION SEEN

Berlin Talks of 6 P. M. Deadline for Move Against Poland

DICTATOR WARNS BRITISH

Henderson So Wrought Up on Leaving Parley With Hitler That He Is Speechless

By OTTO D. TOLISCHUS
Wireless to THE NEW YORK TIMES.

BERLIN, Thursday, Aug. 24.—While Foreign Minister Joachim von Ribbentrop was in Moscow discussing, in the view of some German quarters, not so much a new non-aggression pact as "Poland's fourth and final partition," Chancellor Hitler yesterday received Sir Nevile Henderson, the British Ambassador, for a fifteen-minute conference.

According to reliable information, the conference ended on a rather blunt note that is interpreted in diplomatic quarters as possibly Herr Hitler's last word. The communiqué, issued last night, reads:

"Complying with the wish of the British Government, the Fuehrer received Sir Nevile Henderson at the Berghof today. The Ambassador delivered a letter from the British Prime Minister addressed to the Fuehrer, which was drawn up in the same sense as yesterday's British communication regarding the Cabinet session.

"The Fuehrer left no doubt in the mind of the British Ambassador that the obligations assumed by the British Government could not induce Germany to renounce the defense of her vital national interest."

Hitler's Tone Reported Blunt

Actually Herr Hitler's tone to Sir Nevile was reported to have been even more blunt than the communiqué indicates. In effect, Herr Hitler told the Ambassador that Britain had no business in Eastern Europe and that her guarantee of Poland merely encouraged Polish resistance to German demands, therefore it was up to Britain to persuade the Poles to yield or face the consequences.

Sir Nevile left the conference so wrought up he was speechless. Not trusting his memory to repeat the exact shadings of Herr Hitler's answer, he asked that it be put in writing and he returned for it a half hour later. He got it couched in the same strong terms that Herr Hitler used to him before.

At the same time there are also well-authenticated reports that, in addition to Prime Minister Chamberlain's letter, Sir Nevile also delivered to Herr Hitler an oral message that if Herr Hitler would give the Poles time Britain would try to induce Poland to come forth with new proposals. In that connection some circles launched—perhaps not unintentionally—the suggestion that Foreign Minister Josef Beck of Poland might after all ask to see Herr von Ribbentrop and even Herr Hitler. A preliminary meeting with the former might be arranged at Riga, Latvia, on Herr von Ribbentrop's return from Moscow. But Polish circles declare the suggestion was "extremely unlikely" because it spelled surrender.

As during the last few days the word in Berlin is that the zero hour, which will set the German Army on the march, will come today, and these rumors are supplemented with the additional detail that the exact hour is 6 P. M. [noon, New York time], which might mean "contact with the enemy" some time tomorrow. Furthermore, orders to postpone action, issued after Herr von Ribbentrop's departure for Moscow, have been canceled again.

Germans Elated by News

How much all that is merely a part of the "war of nerves" and how much is bitter reality remains to be seen. In fact the tension developing in Germany, at least in an atmosphere of fantastic unreality, is made no more real by the delayed Summer heat that lures the populace to the woods and beaches, and, together with the elation over the Russian pact and renewed confidence in Herr Hitler's diplomatic superiority over the democratic statesmen, helps to hide the war clouds.

However, the rebuff to Britain yesterday, which in some quarters is compared with the rebuff administered to the French Ambassador by King William of Prussia just preceding the Franco-Prussian War

Continued on Page Two

Text of the Berlin-Moscow Treaty

By The Associated Press.

MOSCOW, Thursday, Aug. 24.—The text of the German-Russian non-aggression pact announced here today follows:

The German Reich Government and the Union of Soviet Socialist Republics, moved by a desire to strengthen the state of peace between Germany and the U.S.S.R. and in the spirit of the provisions of the neutrality treaty of April, 1926, between Germany and the U.S.S.R., decided the following:

Article I

The two contracting parties obligate themselves to refrain from every act of force, every aggressive action and every attack against one another, including any single action or that taken in conjunction with other powers.

Article II

In case one of the parties of this treaty should become the object of warlike acts by a third power, the other party will in no way support this third power.

Article III

The governments of the two contracting parties in the future will constantly remain in consultation with one another in order to inform each other regarding questions of common interest.

Article IV

Neither of the high contracting parties will associate itself with any other grouping of powers which directly or indirectly is aimed at the other party.

Article V

In the event of a conflict between the contracting parties concerning any question, the two parties will adjust this difference or conflict exclusively by friendly exchange of opinions or, if necessary, by an arbitration commission.

Article VI

The present treaty will extend for a period of ten years with the condition that if neither of the contracting parties announces its abrogation within one year of expiration of this period, it will continue in force automatically for another period of five years.

Article VII

The present treaty shall be ratified within the shortest possible time. The exchange of ratification documents shall take place in Berlin. The treaty becomes effective immediately upon signature.

Drawn up in two languages, German and Russian.

MOSCOW, 23d *of August*, 1939.

For the German Government:
RIBBENTROP.

In the name of the Government of the U.S.S.R.:
MOLOTOFF.

NO MILITARY MOVES APPARENT IN ITALY

Country Remains Tranquil as Regime Fails to Whip Up Any War Fervor Among People

By HERBERT L. MATTHEWS
Wireless to THE NEW YORK TIMES.

ROME, Aug. 23.—The Italian ship of state sailed tranquilly on the edge of the European tornado today. There have been no conferences, communiqués, evacuation orders, special mobilization or troop movements.

There have been only some diplomatic visits to Count Ciano, the Foreign Minister, including those of the British and French Ambassadors. This is the fourth time since last Thursday that Sir Percy Loraine saw Count Ciano, which shows the degree of pressure the British are bringing to bear as well as their anxiety to make the Italian leaders realize Britain's determination to support Poland. Presumably, Sir Percy delivered a copy of the same note that was presented to Chancellor Hitler, although that has not been admitted.

André François-Poncet's visit was his first since returning to Rome last Friday. He has tried steadily to see the Foreign Minister but hitherto without success. It is believed he also impressed on Count Ciano France's intention to abide by her pledges.

The Hungarian Minister, Baron Frederick Villani, also saw Count Ciano today, reviving reports about Germany's demands on Budapest.

Italian People Are Calm

The Italian people are not being whipped up to the fervor that would be required to enter a war in the next few days. Nowhere do you see air shelters being hastily dug or gas masks being distributed.

Only in the newspapers do the commentators warn their readers that a conflict seems near, while relatively full accounts of the developments in various capitals are given. The British Cabinet's statement last night is published fully in all newspapers here, whereas the German press ignored it. If readers trusted their Italian newspapers this evening they would have a biased but reasonably correct appreciation of the dangers of the present situation.

On the other hand, so far as they know their country is making no last-minute efforts to meet the

Continued on Page Four

PRESIDENT SPEEDS TO ACT ON CRISIS

Disturbed by War Threat, He Will End Cruise Today and Board Train at Red Bank

By FELIX BELAIR Jr.
Special to THE NEW YORK TIMES.

RED BANK, N. J., Aug. 23.—Admittedly disturbed by the European war crisis, President Roosevelt is hurrying here aboard the navy cruiser Tuscaloosa after scrapping plans for a more ceremonious landing at Annapolis in order to be back at the White House in the event of an outbreak of hostilities.

A small White House secretarial staff is awaiting the arrival of the President off Sandy Hook early tomorrow to give him a bundle of official diplomatic reports on the latest developments abroad. Mr. Roosevelt plans to study the reports aboard his special train en route to Washington.

After debarking from the Tuscaloosa about 8 A. M. tomorrow the President will motor here with Brig. Gen. Edwin M. Watson, his secretary, and Rear Admiral Ross T. McIntire, White House physician. He is expected to stop long enough before entraining for the capital to telephone Secretary of State Cordell Hull, as well as to the embassies in London and Paris about overnight developments.

To Get War Supplies Report

Back at the White House in the early afternoon the President will have before him a report of the War Industries Committee on the status of the nation's munitions and other heavy industries. The committee has been canvassing the aviation and other industries in the past few days with a view to American preparedness.

Prior to the departure of the White House staff late today it was understood the War Industries Committee had drafted a report informing the President that the aviation and several other industries were prepared for any emergency that might arise and that aircraft manufacturers were ahead of schedule on orders of military planes from France and Great Britain.

Among Presidential intimates as well as the capital's political observers interest centered during the day on the question of whether Mr. Roosevelt considered the situation abroad sufficiently grave to call a

Continued on Page Three

BARS HOSTILE UNION

Treaty Forbids Either to Join Any Group Aimed at Other

ESCAPE CLAUSE OMITTED

Von Ribbentrop's Car, Flying Swastika, Passes Beneath Red Flag at Kremlin

By The Associated Press.

MOSCOW, Thursday, Aug. 24.—Germany and Soviet Russia early today signed a non-aggression pact binding each of them for ten years not to "associate itself with any other grouping of powers which directly or indirectly is aimed at the other party."

By the pact they also agreed to "constantly remain in consultation with one another" on their common interests and to adjust differences by arbitration.

The non-aggression clauses bound each power to refrain from any act of force against the other and if either party is "the object of warlike acts by a third power" to refrain from supporting that third power.

The pact did not include the usual escape clause providing for its denunciation in case one of the contracting parties attacked a third power. This provision has been written into most non-aggression agreements signed in the past by Moscow.

Arrives by Plane

By G. E. R. GEDYE
Special Cable to THE NEW YORK TIMES.

MOSCOW, Thursday, Aug. 24.—With the meticulous punctuality of a perfectly staged arrival, two huge Focke-Wulf Condor planes conveying Joachim von Ribbentrop, the German Foreign Minister, and his thirty-two assistants, landed at the Moscow airdrome on the stroke of 1 P. M. yesterday.

Adequate but not excessive police precautions were taken at the airdrome. For the first time the Soviet authorities displayed the swastika banner, five of which flew from the front of the airdrome building, but were placed so as not to be visible from the outside.

Vyacheslaff M. Molotoff was not present to welcome Herr von Ribbentrop, probably because he is not only Commissar of Foreign Affairs but also Premier, and therefore higher in rank than Herr von Ribbentrop. Instead the visitor was received by Vladimir P. Potemkin, Vice Commissar of Foreign Affairs; Mr. Barkoff, protocol chief; Mr. Merkuloff, Vice Commissar of Internal Affairs, under whom falls the NKVD, formerly the GPU; Mr. Alexandroff, chief of the Central European Department of the Foreign Office, and General Suvoroff, commander of the Moscow garrison.

Almost the entire staff of the huge German Embassy, headed by the Ambassador, Count Friedrich Werner von der Schulenburg, with the military, naval and air attachés in uniform, was present. The German civilians mostly wore top hats and cutaway coats.

The Italian Ambassador, Augusto Russo, with his military attaché in uniform, also was present. The feature of the reception most commented upon was the absence of any Japanese representative.

The German Embassy staff stood lined up like troops on parade. As each was presented to Herr von Ribbentrop he sprang to attention, clicked his heels, gave the Hitler salute and shook hands, again saluting and heel-clicking.

In Old Austrian Embassy

From the airdrome the party drove to the city through streets where police in their white Summer jackets stood every ten paces. For Herr von Ribbentrop the Soviet Government provided a large American car from the Kremlin car park, flying the swastika flag.

The party drove directly to the former Austrian Embassy, where they are being housed. Subsequently Herr von Ribbentrop and leading members of his mission had luncheon at the embassy with Count von der Schulenburg.

At about 3:30 P. M. Herr von Ribbentrop, accompanied by Count von der Schulenburg and an expert translator whom the Germans brought from Berlin, drove through the gates of the Kremlin with its

Continued on Page Six

"All the News That's Fit to Print."

The New York Times.

EXTRA

Partly cloudy and somewhat warmer today. Tomorrow generally fair with moderate temperatures.

Temperatures Yesterday—Max., 67; Min., 61

VOL. LXXXVIII...No. 29,805. Entered as Second-Class Matter, Postoffice, New York, N. Y. NEW YORK, FRIDAY, SEPTEMBER 1, 1939. THREE CENTS NEW YORK CITY and Vicinity | FOUR CENTS Elsewhere Except in 7th and 8th Postal Zones.

GERMAN ARMY ATTACKS POLAND; CITIES BOMBED, PORT BLOCKADED; DANZIG IS ACCEPTED INTO REICH

BRITISH MOBILIZING

Navy Raised to Its Full Strength, Army and Air Reserves Called Up

PARLIAMENT IS CONVOKED

Midnight Meeting Is Held by Ministers—Negotiations Admitted Failure

By The Associated Press.

LONDON, Friday, Sept. 1.—The British Parliament was summoned to meet today at 5 P. M. [12 noon in New York].

British Call Up Forces

By FERDINAND KUHN Jr.

Special Cable to THE NEW YORK TIMES.

LONDON, Friday, Sept. 1.—All attempts to bring about direct negotiations between Germany and Poland appeared to have broken down tonight as Great Britain mobilized her fleet to full strength, stretched her other defensive preparations close to the limit and began moving 3,000,000 school children and invalids from the crowded cities into the safety of the countryside.

Censorship was established over cables after London had been cut off for hours from communication with the Continent.

It was the peak of the crisis, but a day of rumors had not shifted the fundamental issue nor given a conclusive answer to the question of peace or war.

At midnight the British Government was not yet convinced that Germany really intended to attack Poland and provoke a world war.

Terms Called Smoke Screen

All that had happened during yesterday, including the sudden broadcasting of Chancellor Hitler's sixteen-point demands, was interpreted here as a smoke screen rather than as the flash of guns.

After hearing Herr Hitler's "terms" officials here quietly announced tonight that "the government primarily interested in the proposals is, of course, the Polish Government."

Until the Polish Government has had time to consider them, it was said in Whitehall that "it would be highly undesirable for any comment to be made."

It was fully expected that Poland would reject them later today; indeed, Polish circles here were describing them tonight as "utterly unacceptable," for they would involve dismemberment of Poland and loss of Poland's capacity to defend her independence. In any event, there was no sign of any intention here to put pressure on Warsaw to accept.

Much might have been said about the German "proposals" here tonight if the government had not been so anxious to leave the first decision to Warsaw without any prompting. That the British regarded them as artful went without saying, since they conveyed a first impression of reasonableness that was not borne out by the terms themselves.

Until the announcement on the German wireless tonight, the British Government had not been told about them officially, and the Polish Government was not informed until Josef Lipski, Polish Ambassador to Berlin, visited Foreign Minister Joachim von Ribbentrop a few minutes before the broadcast took place.

Shortly after midnight last night, Sir Nevile Henderson, the British Ambassador in Berlin, had heard the "points" read to him by Herr von Ribbentrop, but the reading was so fast that the Ambassador could not even take notes of them in detail. In any event, he was told Herr Hitler's "points" were not being given to him or his government officially, on the ground that it was already too late.

Time Limit Expired

On Tuesday Herr Hitler had asked that a Polish negotiator should arrive in Berlin within twenty-four hours; and as nobody had arrived from Warsaw when the time limit expired, Sir Nevile was told that the "points" could not even be communicated officially to London.

The German time table with the

Continued on Page Four

Bulletins on Europe's Conflict

London Hears of Warsaw Bombing

LONDON, Friday, Sept. 1 (AP).—Reuters British news agency said it had learned from Polish sources in Paris that Warsaw was bombed today.

French Confirm Beginning of War

PARIS, Friday, Sept. 1 (AP).—The Havas news agency said today that official French dispatches from Germany indicated that "the Reich began hostilities on Poland this morning."

The agency also reported that the Polish Embassy here had announced that "Germany violated the Polish frontier at four points."

"German reports of pretended violation of German territory by Poland are pure invention, as is the fable of 'attack' by Polish insurgents on Gleiwitz," the embassy announcement said.

Attack on Entire Front Reported

LONDON, Friday, Sept. 1 (AP).—A Reuters dispatch from Paris said:

"The following is given with all reserve: According to unconfirmed reports received here, the Germans have begun an offensive with extreme violence on the whole Polish front."

First Wounded Brought Into Gleiwitz

GLEIWITZ, Germany, Friday, Sept. 1 (AP).—An army ambulance carrying wounded soldiers arrived at the emergency hospital here today at 9:10 A. M.

The men, carried in a wagon, were on stretchers. One had on a first-aid field bandage. It could not be ascertained where the ambulance came from.

At about 9:30 a half-mile long truck train manned by the engineering corps drove through the heart of the city with pontoon bridge building material. In the train were caterpillar tread, twenty-passenger motor vans.

Obviously the train had been on the road for a considerable time. All equipment was thickly covered with gray mud.

A scouting plane of the air force was patrolling an area over Gleiwitz.

Early today Gleiwitz residents reported that artillery fire

Continued on Page Four

DALADIER SUMMONS CABINET TO CONFER

News of Attack on Poland Spurs Prompt Action—Military Move Thought Likely

By The Associated Press.

PARIS, Friday, Sept. 1.—Edouard Daladier, Premier and War Minister of France, informed that German troops crossed the Polish frontier today, summoned an urgent meeting of his Cabinet for 10:30 A. M.

It was probable that Parliament would be called tomorrow.

Reports of the German invasion came from Berlin and from the Polish Embassy here. The Ministers were called to the Elysee Palace to meet with President Albert Lebrun.

Upon receipt of word of the German operations M. Daladier rushed to the War Ministry and called General Marie Gustave Gamelin, supreme commander of land, sea and air forces, into consultation.

A little later Daladier summoned Foreign Minister Georges Bonnet.

The Polish Embassy said that Germans violated the Polish frontier at four points and at the same time it characterized German charges that Poles had crossed into Germany as "pure invention."

Havas, Frnch news agency, announced that "a German declaration of war against Poland probably will lead France and Great Britain to take new military measures."

Britain and France are committed to aid Poland in any fight to save her independence.

Ministers Stand Firm

By P. J. PHILIP

Wireless to THE NEW YORK TIMES.

PARIS, Aug. 31.—The Cabinet met with President Albert Lebrun for more than two hours this evening at the Elysée Palace. At the close of the meeting Minister of the Interior Albert Sarraut handed the press the following communiqué:

"MM. Edouard Daladier, President of the Council, and Georges Bonnet, Minister of Foreign Affairs, laid before the Cabinet a detailed account of the international situation as a whole.

"The Cabinet was unanimous in formally maintaining the engagements taken by France."

Later M. Daladier had further conversations with M. Bonnet, Fi-

Continued on Page Four

BRITISH CHILDREN TAKEN FROM CITIES

3,000,000 Persons Are in First Evacuation Group, Which Is to Be Moved Today

By FREDERICK T. BIRCHALL

Special Cable to THE NEW YORK TIMES.

LONDON, Friday, Sept. 1.—The greatest mass movement of population at short notice in the history of Great Britain is under way. It is an evacuation, under government order, of little children, invalids, women and old men from congested areas.

From London, Birmingham, Manchester, Liverpool, Edinburgh, Glasgow and twenty-three other cities the great exodus is going on as this dispatch is being written. The numbers are stupendous. More than 3,000,000 of these helpless human beings are being taken out of danger of German bombs.

Nothing like it has ever been attempted anywhere; yet it is going on without mishap—so far, indeed, without serious confusion.

Scenes everywhere were much the same whether in the aristocratic West End or the proletarian East Side, but one that this correspon-

Continued on Page Three

HOSTILITIES BEGUN

Warsaw Reports German Offensive Moving on Three Objectives

ROOSEVELT WARNS NAVY

Also Notifies Army Leaders of Warfare—Envoys Tell of Bombing of 4 Cities

By JERZY SZAPIRO

Wireless to THE NEW YORK TIMES.

WARSAW, Poland, Friday, Sept. 1.—War began at 5 o'clock this morning with German planes attacking Gdynia, Cracow and Katowice.

At Gdynia three bombs exploded in the sea.

The regular German Army started an offensive in the direction of Dzialdowka—in Upper Silesia and Czestochowa. The German plan apparently is to cut off Western Poland along the line of Dzialdowka-Lodz-Czestochowa.

The offensive is developing, from East Prussia, toward Silesia and northwards from Slovakia.

At 9 o'clock an attempt was made to bombard Warsaw. The planes, however, did not reach even the suburbs.

A military attack on the garrison at Westerplatte in the Danzig area was repulsed.

The Foreign Office at 8:45 A. M. issued a communiqué saying that military action had begun in Westerplatte in the Danzig area as well as in Buschkowa near Gdynia, and in Dzialowka, Chojnice and Lowa.

Hostilities have begun and Poland has been attacked, said the communiqué.

Three cities in Upper Silesia suffered artillery bombardment, particulars of which are lacking, it was said.

While this dispatch was being telephoned, the air-raid sirens sounded in Warsaw.

Danzig Fighting Reported

WARSAW, Poland, Friday, Sept. 1 (AP).—It was reported today that Tczew and Czestochowa were bombed by German airplanes early this morning.

There was no official confirmation of the bombing.

Fighting was reported at Danzig.

It was reported officially that German troops had attacked Polish defenses near Mlawa, bordering the southern part of East Prussia. There was no announcement of the damage resulting from the bombing.

Mist and clouds were overhanging the city. A light drizzle apparently afforded momentary protection against air raids. Warsaw went to work as usual.

Roosevelt Warns Navy

WASHINGTON, Friday, Sept. 1 (AP).—President Roosevelt directed today that all naval ships and army commands be notified at once by radio of German-Polish hostilities.

The White House issued the following announcement:

"The President received word at 2:50 A. M. Eastern standard time

Continued on Page Five

Soviet Ratifies Reich Non-Aggression Pact; Gibes at British and French Amuse Deputies

By G. E. R. GEDYE

Special Cable to THE NEW YORK TIMES.

MOSCOW, Aug. 31.—With Premier and Foreign Commissar Vyacheslaff M. Molotoff, working under high pressure—so suddenly applied without any previous indication and contrasting so sharply with earlier delaying tactics this week as to suggest German insistence that the matter be finally settled—the Supreme Soviet [Parliament] tonight unanimously ratified the Russo-German non-aggression pact.

Ratification, which was first foreshadowed at midday, was preceded by a speech by Mr. Molotoff so precise in its definition of Soviet obligations to refrain from participating on the side of Great Britain and France in any war against Germany, so voluble in its defense against charges of inconsistency against Communist Russia for embracing Fascist Germany, and so insistent on the inevitability of friendship between "not merely the governments but also the peoples" of Germany and Russia as to extinguish the last faint hopes of the western democracies that Moscow might yet find loopholes or excuses for joining them at some subsequent date in resisting German aggression against Poland.

Mr. Molotoff's speech contained nothing to justify constantly repeated suspicions of the existence of a secret German-Soviet pact entitling the latter to participate in a partition of Poland.

The Premier's speech contained much trenchant and seemingly irrefutable evidence of blunders by the British and French Governments in handling the question of Soviet cooperation. It was not diffi-

Continued on Page Eight

FREE CITY IS SEIZED

Forster Notifies Hitler of Order Putting Danzig Into the Reich

ACCEPTED BY CHANCELLOR

Poles Ready, Made Their Preparations After Hostilities Appeared Inevitable

Special Cable to THE NEW YORK TIMES.

DANZIG, Friday, Sept. 1.—By a decree issued early this morning Albert Forster, Nazi Chief of State, proclaimed the annexation of the Free City to the Reich, thus settling by a fell stroke the original point of contention in the international crisis.

In a telegram to Chancellor Hitler Herr Forster explained his action as necessary to remove "the pressing necessity of our people and State." Herr Forster also issued a proclamation to the people of Danzig saying the hour awaited for twenty years had arrived because "our Fuehrer, Adolf Hitler, has freed us."

[A NEW YORK TIMES dispatch from Berlin this morning said Herr Hitler telegraphed Herr Forster today thanking him and all Danzigers, and stating:

"The law for reannexation is in effect immediately."

The Chancellor stated, furthermore, that Herr Forster was appointed head of the civil administration of the Danzig area.]

In a four-article decree Herr Forster declared the Constitution of Danzig no longer valid. He declared himself sole administrator of the Danzig part of the German Reich, and he declared that until the Reich's legal system had been introduced by command of Herr Hitler all laws except the Constitution remained in effect. Then Herr Forster immediately wired Herr Hitler of his action, begged the Chancellor to give his approval of the move and through Reich law complete the annexation.

The German flag is now flying everywhere over Danzig, Herr Forster said, and all church bells resound to the event. "We thank God," he declared, "that He gave the Fuehrer the strength and the possibility to free also us from the evil Versailles treaty."

Hitler Accepts Danzig

By The Associated Press.

BERLIN, Friday, Sept. 1.—The German official news agency, D. N. B., announced today that Albert Forster, Nazi Chief of State in Danzig, had proclaimed the reunion of the Free City with the Reich.

Herr Hitler today accepted the Free City of Danzig into the Reich.

"I acknowledge your proclamation of the return of the Free City of Danzig to the Reich," Herr Hitler's telegram said. "I thank you, Gauleiter Forster, and all Danzig men and women, for your loyalty which you have displayed for so many years.

"Greater Germany welcomes you with joy in her heart.

"The law of reunion will be enacted forthwith. I appoint you, Herr Forster, chief of the civil administration in the Danzig territory."

Forster's telegram to Herr Hitler read:

My Fuehrer.

I have just signed and then put into effect the following basic law, concerning the reunion of Danzig with the German Reich.

The basic State law of the Free State of Danzig and the reunion of Danzig with the German Reich is effective Sept. 1, 1939.

To lift the immediate distress of the people and State of the Free City of Danzig, I decree the following basic State law:

ARTICLE I

The Constitution of the Free City of Danzig has been suspended effective immediately.

ARTICLE II

All legal and administrative power will be executed exclusively by the head of State.

ARTICLE III

The Free City of Danzig with its territory and its peoples forms

Continued on Page Five

Hitler Acts Against Poland

The port of Gdynia, north of Danzig (toward top of map), was blockaded this morning. At Gleiwitz (shown by cross) artillery fire was heard after a Polish-German skirmish had been reported there. Cracow, to the east, was among Polish cities said to have been bombed.

Hitler Tells the Reichstag 'Bomb Will Be Met by Bomb'

Chancellor Vows 'Fight Until Resolution' Against Poland—Gives Order of Succession As Goering, Hess, Then Senate to Choose

Chancellor Adolf Hitler of Germany, in a world broadcast this morning, opened "a fight until the resolution of the situation" against Poland, announcing that "from now on bomb will be met by bomb."

At the same time he announced, to face any eventuality, that if anything "happened" to him, Field Marshal Hermann Goering was to be in charge; if to Marshal Goering, Rudolph Hess; if to Herr Hess, the Senate, which he proposes to appoint, will select a successor.

The Chancellor, after attempting to narrow the conflict with Poland by assuring the Western powers that he had no designs on their frontiers, by assuring the neutrality of the sideline powers and by acknowledging the friendliness of Italy and the new relations with Russia, issued a defy to Poland's allies.

Says He Will Carry on

"I shall carry on this fight regardless of against whom I may come," he declared.

At the same time he held the door open for Poland to capitulate to his demands, declaring that he did not intend to make war against women and children. He said that if a solution did not come from the present Polish Government, it would come from a future Polish Government.

The Chancellor expressed confidence, toward the close of his address, that his decision, which was being broadcast over amplifiers hastily erected by electricians at the last moment in the streets of Berlin and the provincial capitals, would be accepted by the German people.

The scene enacted in the Kroll Opera House in Berlin was carried over sound waves to most of the nations of the world. From Berlin hook-ups had been arranged with the three major networks of the United States, and, according to the announcer for the German broadcasting system, over the Italian, Hungarian, Spanish, Norwegian, Swedish, Danish, Yugoslav, British and French national networks.

The summons to the Reichstag, ordered by Herr Hitler himself, had been sent out only a few hours before the meeting. Most of the members had been awaiting the signal, and when the opera house opened shortly before 10 o'clock [5 o'clock, New York time] this morning, they were dressed in the uniforms of their military formations.

After Herr Hitler finished speaking the deputies enacted a law incorporating Danzig into the Reich, declaring Danzig citizens were now Germans, voiding the Constitution of the Free City and extending to its territory the jurisdiction of German law.

At 5:10 A. M., Marshal Goering opened the meeting and turned the floor over to the Chancellor.

In the early part of his address, Herr Hitler electrified his audience with this declaration:

"We have all been suffering under the tortures that the Versailles treaty has been inflicting upon us."

Then, speaking with measured deliberateness of Germany's claims to the pre-war German areas, he announced, as he had on a previous occasion:

"The Treaty of Versailles is, for us Germans, and has been, for us Germans, not a law."

Anticipating what the announcement's reiteration would lead to, the Deputies roared applause. Then Herr Hitler, his indignation rising as he proceeded, set about building up the German case, asserting that his proposals for a peaceful solution of the problem of Danzig and the Polish Corridor had been rejected, and charging that the Poles had visited atrocities on Germans, especially women and children, "killing many of them."

SUMMARY OF SPEECH

A summary of Herr Hitler's speech was translated as follows:

"For months we have been suffering under the burdens of the Treaty of Versailles. Danzig was and is a German city. All these regions have only Germany to thank for their cultural development.

"Minorities in the Polish Corridor have been shamefully mistreated. Here, as in other respects, I have tried to solve the problems by peaceful means. In the fifteen years of National Socialism we have been

Continued on Page Three

HITLER GIVES WORD

In a Proclamation He Accuses Warsaw of Appeal to Arms

FOREIGNERS ARE WARNED

They Remain in Poland at Own Risk—Nazis to Shoot at Any Planes Flying Over Reich

By OTTO D. TOLISCHUS

Special Cable to THE NEW YORK TIMES.

BERLIN, Friday, Sept. 1.—Charging that Germany had been attacked, Chancellor Hitler at 5:11 o'clock this morning issued a proclamation to the army declaring that from now on force will be met with force and calling on the armed forces "to fulfill their duty to the end."

The text of the proclamation reads:

To the defense forces:

The Polish nation refused my efforts for a peaceful regulation of neighborly relations; instead it has appealed to weapons.

Germans in Poland are persecuted with a bloody terror and are driven from their homes. The series of border violations, which are unbearable to a great power, prove that the Poles no longer are willing to respect the German frontier. In order to put an end to this frantic activity no other means is left to me now than to meet force with force.

"Battle for Honor"

German defense forces will carry on the battle for the honor of the living rights of the reawakened German people with firm determination.

I expect every German soldier, in view of the great tradition of eternal German soldiery, to do his duty until the end.

Remember always in all situations you are the representatives of National Socialist Greater Germany!

Long live our people and our Reich!

Berlin, Sept. 1, 1939.

ADOLF HITLER.

The commander-in-chief of the air force issued a decree effective immediately prohibiting the passage of any airplanes over German territory excepting those of the Reich air force or the government.

This morning the naval authorities ordered all German mercantile ships in the Baltic Sea not to run to Danzig or Polish ports.

Anti-air raid defenses were mobilized throughout the country early this morning.

A formal declaration of war against Poland had not yet been declared up to 8 o'clock [3 A. M. New York time] this morning and the question of whether the two countries are in a state of active belligerency is still open.

Reichstag Will Meet Today

Foreign correspondents at an official conference at the Reich Press Ministry at 8:30 o'clock [3:30 A. M. New York time] were told that they would receive every opportunity to facilitate the transmission of dispatches. Wireless stations have been instructed to speed up communications and the Ministry is installing additional batteries of telephones.

The Reichstag has been summoned to meet at 10 o'clock [5 A. M. New York time] to receive a more formal declaration from Herr Hitler.

The Hitler army order is interpreted as providing, for the time being, armed defense of the German frontiers against aggression. The action is also suspected of forcing international ,diplomatic action.

The Germans announced that foreigners remain in Polish territory at their own risk.

Flying over Polish territory as well as the maritime areas is forbidden by the German authorities and any violators will be shot down.

When Herr Hitler made his an-

Continued on Page Three

"All the News That's Fit to Print."

The New York Times.

LATE CITY EDITION
Partly cloudy today, showers tonight, little change in temperature. Tomorrow showers.
Temperatures Yesterday—Max., 64; Min., 53

VOL. LXXXIX...No. 30,077. Entered as Second-Class Matter, Postoffice, New York, N. Y. NEW YORK, THURSDAY, MAY 30, 1940. THREE CENTS NEW YORK CITY and Vicinity | FOUR CENTS Elsewhere Except in 7th and 8th Postal Zones.

ALLIES ABANDONING FLANDERS, FLOOD YSER AREA; A RESCUE FLEET AT DUNKERQUE; FOE POUNDS PORT; ONE FORCE CUT OFF FROM THE SEA AS LILLE FALLS

PRESIDENT TO ASK $750,000,000 MORE FOR ARMY PROGRAM

Nazi Blitzkrieg Held to Show the $3,300,000,000 Allotted Fails to Meet Needs

FOR TANKS, GUNS, PLANES

Tax Bill to Be Offered in House Today—D. M. Nelson Named Procurement Director

By FELIX BELAIR Jr.
Special to THE NEW YORK TIMES.

WASHINGTON, May 29—On the eve of his first meeting with the reconstituted Council of National Defense, President Roosevelt was putting finishing touches today on a new request for $750,000,000 as a supplemental appropriation for further expansion and mechanization of the military establishment to take account of European war developments since he sent his preparedness message to Congress two weeks ago.

The projected increase in funds for the Army, over and above the omnibus $3,300,000,000 defense program already pending, was mapped by the President in a White House conference with Treasury and War Department officials.

It was the President's plan to send up the supplemental request in a few days. Subject to additions, the new program contemplates placing orders immediately for the following:

About 3,000 new pursuit and bombing planes.

Between 1,500 and 2,000 tanks.

About 500 heavy howitzers.

A supply of aerial bombs of various sizes, to cost between $20,000,000 and $30,000,000.

Other modern weapons of war which have been developed in Army laboratories, but not yet put into actual production.

German Drive Appraised

There was no official announcement on the results of the meeting, and Secretary Woodring, who acted as spokesman for the group, said only that they had reviewed "the whole military situation."

From others present, however, it was learned that the nation's military establishment had been reappraised in the light of Germany's advances in Western Europe since the President's preparedness message was first submitted to Congress.

Other developments in the national defense program were:

1. The Senate Naval Affairs Committee brought out a measure increasing the air force limit of the Navy to 10,000 planes and 16,000 pilots, with a report warning that the "country at this time is facing the possibility that the Allies may be defeated and that we may have to defend ourselves in both oceans at the same time."

2. Senate leaders were planning to take up tomorrow the $1,500,000,000 bill providing an 11 per cent increase in under-age surface tonnage, with indications that the measure would be disposed of without delay.

Procurement Officer Named

3. Secretary Morgenthau named Donald M. Nelson, executive vice president of Sears, Roebuck & Co., as director of the Treasury's Procurement Division, thereby adding another business executive to the list of those on whom the administration is relying for the success of the defense program.

4. Administration - Congressional plans for placing emergency rearmament financing on a "pay-as-you-go" basis gathered momentum, with an announcement by Representative Doughton, chairman of the House Ways and Means Committee, that he would introduce tomorrow a measure raising the statutory debt limit by $3,000,000,000 and imposing upward of $656,000,000 in new defense taxes.

5. Secretary Hull modified aviation restrictions under the Neutrality Act to permit the delivery of American planes by American pilots to Halifax, N. S., thereby removing the ban on through deliveries over the Maritime Provinces.

6. White House sources explained that there would be the closest possible relations between Presi-

Continued on Page Eight

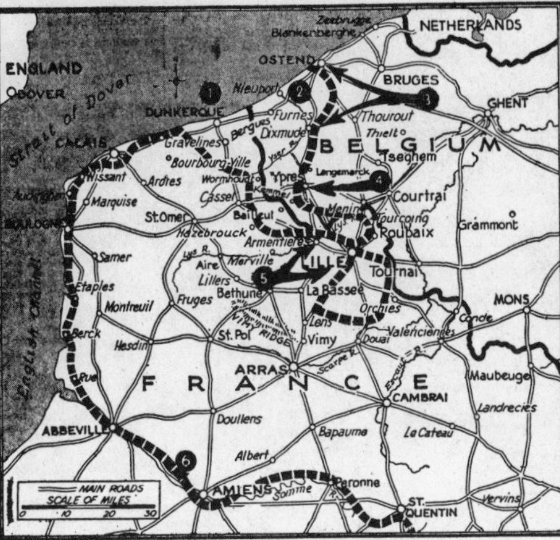

ALLIES STRIKE FOR COAST IN EVER-TIGHTENING POCKET

To keep the exit at Dunkerque (1) open French and British sea, land and air forces were waging a furious struggle yesterday; to retard the German advance the Allies were understood to have opened sluice gates on the Yser to flood the region below Nieuport (2). In the sector that had been held by the Belgians the Nazis pushed to Ostend and Dixmude (3). Farther south they were reported to have taken Ypres (4). Their most important operation of the day, however, was the bisecting of the pocket by the capture of Lille and Armentieres (5), thus cutting off from the sea the Allied forces in the lower section. Along the Somme the French eliminated a German bridgehead west of Amiens (6). The broken lines show the approximate battlefronts.

HULL ORDER SPEEDS PLANES TO ALLIES

Allows Our Pilots to Fly Craft Over Three Canadian Maritime Provinces

Special to THE NEW YORK TIMES.

WASHINGTON, May 29—The way was opened today for expediting deliveries of American airplanes to the Allied fighting lines when Secretary Hull modified regulations of the Neutrality Act to permit the delivery of such aircraft by American pilots to ports in the three eastern Canadian Provinces.

The step was designed to facilitate deliveries to the Allies because of the urgency of their military situation. It was taken at the request of the French Government.

Mr. Hull ruled that "American nationals may travel in belligerent aircraft over the Canadian Provinces of New Brunswick, Nova Scotia and Prince Edward Island." This means that pilots from the United States may fly new planes to Halifax, whence they will be flown across the Atlantic by pilots of the Allies or sent across by ship.

American pilots have been delivering planes in Ottawa and other Canadian cities. As before, they must still conform under the new order to regulations by pushing planes over the Canadian border from the United States.

Previously, while American pilots could fly planes over Canadian territory, once they were pushed over the border the fliers could not enter the three eastern maritime Provinces because American ships are barred from them and aircraft regulations conform to shipping rules. Newfoundland was excluded from the modification today because there was no actual need for including it.

The Department of Commerce announced that April shipments of aircraft and equipment to the Allies included 196 planes and 285 engines.

Of the planes, France received seventy completely powered craft and ninety-eight in a knock-down condition. The United Kingdom obtained twenty-three assembled and powered and Canada four.

Of the engines, 230 went to France, forty-three to Canada and twelve to the United Kingdom. The French plane acquisitions were valued at $9,176,538, those of the United Kingdom at $2,139,000 and those of Canada at $288,296.

With a variety of other equipment included, French purchases for the month totaled $14,443,071; those of the United Kingdom $2,908,621 and those of Canada $728,929.

The Department of Commerce announced that total exports of aero-

Continued on Page Ten

Berlin Exchange Slumps As Optimism Is Decried

Wireless to THE NEW YORK TIMES.

BERLIN, May 29—In what was apparently a strong reaction to warnings against over-optimism, which have been circulated generally among the population following the German victories in the West, the Berlin Boerse today took a sudden nose dive.

Most issues dropped between 1 and 4 per cent. In shipping, Hapag dropped 5 per cent and North German Lloyd dropped 3 per cent. Fixed interest securities were quiet and generally unchanged. The close was irregular, with call money at 1⅞-2⅛.

Utilities, motor works and other heavy industries led the recession, while metal works in the Rhineland were among those that showed the maximum decline.

URUGUAY ON GUARD FOR FIFTH COLUMN

Check on Assembly, Increase in Army Urged—Nazis Take Bold Tone in Ecuador

Special Cable to THE NEW YORK TIMES.

MONTEVIDEO, Uruguay, May 29—The Uruguayan Government is frankly alarmed over Nazi fifth column activities.

After several Cabinet meetings at which the problem was closely studied, President Alfredo Baldomir has sent to Congress, with a request for urgent action, two bills. One provides for general rearmament and the other modifies Article 38 of the Constitution, which guarantees the right of assembly.

It has been rumored in well-informed diplomatic circles in more than one South American capital yesterday and today that Uruguay fears an invasion of Nazi fifth columnists from Southern Brazil. Official circles tonight emphatically denied any such fear and also denied that Uruguay had requested assistance from any other government.

The President's office earlier in the day, however, had published the details of the plans for rearmament and for modifying the constitutional guarantees.

Article 38 of the Constitution says that "all persons have a right to form themselves into associations," whatever may be the object sought, except they do not constitute an association declared by law to be illicit.

Since the law doesn't define what constitutes an illicit association, the bill that President Baldomir sent to Congress yesterday defines such il-

Continued on Page Six

ITALY BARS IMPORTS EXCEPT BY BARTER

Cancels Permits to Bring In Goods or to Buy Exchange for Payments Abroad

By HERBERT L. MATTHEWS
By Telephone to THE NEW YORK TIMES.

ROME, May 29—The Ministry of Foreign Exchange issued an order today to all banks and industrial firms canceling permits for importation and permission to acquire foreign currency to pay for imports. Thus Italy cuts herself off commercially from the world, except for barter agreements, and even there Italian ships coming in are not departing to bring back further imports.

This is the most serious indication yet given of the expectation of war, certainly as serious as the postponement of the sailing of Italian vessels announced last Friday.

The Conte di Savoia is due back from New York Sunday. No one expects her to depart, even on June 23, when she is scheduled to go. That will leave only the Conte Grande out of the Mediterranean among the large Italian ships. She sailed for South America a week ago.

[The steamship Roma arrived yesterday at Naples, according to The Associated Press, and is now expected to remain there instead of proceeding to Genoa, as scheduled. The Roma was to have left Genoa for New York June 29.]

Trade with the United States will suffer most heavily by the decision taken today. It has been possible for importers to acquire dollars at

Continued on Page Four

11,000 Times Speedier Way Found To Obtain Atomic Power Element

By WILLIAM L. LAURENCE

Development of a process that speeds up by 11,000 times the extraction of U-235, the element recently discovered to possess 5,000,000 times the power output of coal, promising to make it possible to utilize atomic energy as a new source of enormous power for all purposes, and to place in the hands of the nations at war, especially Germany, the most powerful fuel ever to be discovered, is to be announced in the forthcoming issue of Nature, leading British scientific weekly, advance proofs of which have reached THE NEW YORK TIMES. Germany, more than any other European nation, has been concentrating on developing this power. If the tests succeed the Allied blockade could be materially offset.

The new process for extracting U-235 that promises to revolutionize methods of power production and to usher in a new civilization based on the utilization of atomic power, was developed by Professor Wilhelm Krasny-Ergen of the Wenner-Grens Institute, Stockholm, Sweden, one of the leading scientific research institutions in Europe.

On May 5 it was announced that a tiny amount of U-235, a relative of uranium, had been isolated at the University of Minnesota and at the General Electric Company, and that pioneer experiments at the physics laboratories at Columbia University, under the direction of Professor

Continued on Page Eighteen

NAZIS TIGHTEN TRAP

They Drive a Line Across Pocket, Encircling Foes in South

SAY YPRES IS TAKEN

Zeebrugge and Ostend Fall—Large Stores Are Reported Seized

By GEORGE AXELSSON
Wireless to THE NEW YORK TIMES.

BERLIN, May 29—Remnants of the Allied Armies cut off in Flanders came a step nearer to being wiped out today when the Germans, simultaneously pressing from east and west toward the middle, managed to drive a wedge right across the pocket, thus separating the French and British divisions north of Lille from those in the south, who now are surrounded on all sides, no longer having access to the sea.

The Germans tonight claim to be in the city of Lille, in Ypres and Armentières and to have burned Dunkerque under heavy artillery bombardment. The Belgian capitulation permitted the Germans to take Bruges, Zeebrugge, Ostend and Thourout without a struggle.

Piercing the Allied lines at Lille, where, however, fortifications still seem to hold out, permitted the Germans to make two pockets out of the big one. The smaller of these, south of Lille, is square with the sides between nine and twelve miles long, and inside this narrow space are compressed the French divisions that only a few days ago tried to break the strong German hold at Valenciennes, as well as British contingents that figured in desperate resistance in the sector between Arras and Cambrai.

Refugees Also in Trap

Hemmed in with these troops is an incalculable number of refugees and other civilians, who are exposed to bombs and shell fire on the same terms as the soldiers fighting one another in this area.

The larger northern pocket reaches from Lille to the sea, and although it is some thirty miles wide the situation of the troops enclosed in it appears to be hardly more enviable than that of their comrades surrounded to the south. They are being hard pressed on three sides by withering German fire as well as from the air.

Their only chance of retreat, should they choose this way out, seems to be the narrow strip of coast between Dunkerque and Nieuport, but the Germans are said to be continuously shelling and bombing this district, making an exit, even if protected by Allied warships, seem most difficult.

Crowded together in an area bounded by Dixmude, Ypres—which the Germans claim to have taken by storm tonight — Armentières, Bailleul and Bergues, remnants of the British Expeditionary Force and whatever French and Belgians remain thereabout appear to have a choice only between death or surrender.

The situation up there, according to latest reports received in Berlin, indicates that the Allies have chosen to fight to the last. The Germans stand before Dixmude, where the British are holding them, and a similarly bitter struggle is raging at

Continued on Page Four

The International Situation

On the Battle Fronts

The Battle of Flanders became yesterday a wholly rear-guard action, with the Allies trying to evacuate as many as possible of the troops caught in the German pocket. The trapped men fought on "desperately but not despairingly," Paris reported. [Page 1.]

The port of Dunkerque was still in Allied hands (although the Germans reported its embarkation area in ruins), as was Nieuport, just above the Belgian border. Ships were said to be waiting at the coast to take off the men who could get to them, although how they stayed afloat in the torrent of German bombing seemed a mystery. The British and French fleets were furiously bombarding German forces on the Channel, hoping to cover the withdrawal. The task of evacuation was made doubly difficult by a German force that, Paris reported, had straddled the Franco-Belgian border near Cassel and Mount Kemmel. The French said that defense floodgates had been opened, inundating part of the area west of the Yser. On other fronts the French asserted that they had eliminated a German bridgehead on the Somme west of Amiens, and had repulsed a German thrust near Rethel, on the left flank of the invaders. [Included in the foregoing.]

The desperate situation of the Allied army of the north was made evident by Berlin dispatches telling of the success of the German effort to cut the opposing forces in two. The invaders drove a wedge between the two Allied wings to the north of Lille. Thus there are now two pockets; the forces south of Lille are completely surrounded, in a square-shaped area whose sides measure only nine to twelve miles. The pocket above Lille was greatly reduced by German advances pressing down from the north and up from the south. [Page 1.]

Early this morning shattered remnants of the British Expeditionary Force began arriving at British ports. Most of them were wounded. To the survivors still in Flanders King George sent a message saying they had displayed "gallantry that has never been surpassed in the annals of the British Army." [Page 1.]

The Allies recorded a victory in Norway. They took Narvik, and the Germans admitted its loss. The British said their warships had sunk seven German troop transports in the Narvik area in the last three days. [Page 1.]

Repercussions Elsewhere

Britain took drastic measures to guard against possible fifth column activities on the part of aliens. Beginning June 3, all aliens must be in their "ordinary place of residence" from 10:30 P. M. to 6 A. M.; they are forbidden to own bicycles, boats or aircraft without special permission. [Page 3.]

Italy, by decreeing an end to import and foreign currency permits, cut herself off from the world commercially, except for her barter arrangements. And even they have ceased to mean anything, as Italian vessels no longer are being sent abroad for cargoes. The new regulations gave the strongest indication yet of Italy's intention to join Germany in the field soon. [Page 1.]

Because Russia had refused to accept Sir Stafford Cripps, Left-Wing Labor member of the British Parliament, as a "special trade envoy," London conferred Ambassadorial status on him. Sir Stafford is in Athens, en route to Moscow. With offers of improved trade with Britain, he will seek to woo Russia away from Germany. [Page 4.]

The Nazi fifth-column technique stirred fears in South America. Uruguay's Congress received from President Baldomir two bills, one of which would provide for rearmament, the other modifying the Constitution to deny the right of assembly to anti-democratic organizations with foreign connections. [Page 1.]

What has happened in Flanders impelled a reappraisal in Washington of American defense plans, with the result that President Roosevelt decided to ask Congress for $750,000,000 (in addition to the $3,300,000,000 already projected) to be used to buy 3,000 pursuit and bombing planes, 1,500 tanks, 500 heavy howitzers and at least $20,000,000 in aerial bombs. [Page 1.] The Senate Naval Affairs Committee, recommending House-adopted bills to speed air and naval preparedness, said the country's defense plans must be based on the possibility of defeat for the Allies. [Page 9.]

ALLIES GET NARVIK IN LAND-SEA FIGHT

Warships Support Troops in Final Thrust From Beis and Rombaks Fjords

By JAMES MacDONALD
Special Cable to THE NEW YORK TIMES.

LONDON, May 29—Narvik, Norway's important iron ore port, the prize of an unrelenting struggle ever since Germany invaded Norway on April 9, has been captured by Allied forces, the War Office and Admiralty announced in a joint communiqué today. The communiqué also announced the capture of Fagernaes, on the shore of Narvik Harbor, and Forsneset, five miles east of Narvik on the railway line over which Swedish iron ore reaches Narvik for shipment to Germany.

Fierce fighting by Norwegian, French, British and Polish forces continues in the district. An unofficial report received here today said British naval forces had sunk seven German troop transports in Narvik waters since Sunday.

British warships are reported high up in Rombaks Fjord, shelling German positions on the Ofoten railway. In a narrow part of the fjord the Germans have sunk four ships in an attempt to block off the British naval vessels.

Other reports reaching London today said German planes had raided Bodoe, at the entrance to Vest Fjord, about ninety miles south of Narvik, last evening, dropping 200 bombs and machine-gunning the town. Of the population of 6,000, it is said at least 5,000 are now

Continued on Page Five

HARRIED B. E. F. MEN ARRIVING IN BRITAIN

Many of Wounded Had to Wade Out to Boats Under Constant Fire of German Forces

By The United Press.

LONDON, Thursday, May 30—Shattered remnants of the British Expeditionary Force—blood-stained, muddy and walking like men asleep—began arriving in British ports early today.

Most of the first arrivals were wounded. They described a constant, pitiless German bombing and strafing bombardment of the French ports from which Viscount Gort is attempting to save his trapped divisions.

They said the shattered British forces were "sliding off a stretch of coast thirty miles long."

German bombs rained down continually, even on hospital ships, they said. Quays and harbor works of the French ports were under terrific German air attack, which went on all through last night.

Allied warships and the Royal Air Force worked and fought like beavers to aid the rescue of the battered armies of Flanders whose fate was teetered on the Channel's brink. Under a screen of intense curtain fire from long-range naval guns, the B. E. F. was backing out through the Dunkerque area,

Continued on Page Five

Dispatches from Europe and the Far East are subject to censorship at the source.

COAST FIGHT RAGES

Communications Lines and Bases Bombarded Constantly by Nazis

DUNKERQUE SHELLED

Allies Inflicting Heavy Losses as They Battle in Rear-Guard Actions

By G. H. ARCHAMBAULT
Wireless to THE NEW YORK TIMES.

PARIS, May 29—The full import of the Belgian defection during the course of the battle in Flanders may be gathered from the indication given tonight by a spokesman for the General Staff that King Leopold's army represented about half the Allied forces engaged on that front.

French and British in that area continue to fight desperately, though not despairingly yet, with the knowledge that at present at least little help can be given them. Their valor is described as very comforting in the circumstances, and it is added that whatever happens their honor will be safe.

Breaking the anonymity rule that has prevailed hitherto, it is announced this evening that, under General Georges Maurice Jean Blanchard's direction, General René-Jacques-Adolf Prioux is striving to fight his way to the coast in the general direction of Dunkerque, where Vice Admiral Jean Marie Abrial of the French Navy is cooperating and is holding that base, where he has organized a service of supplies with vessels of all kinds of tonnage.

Prioux a Cavalry Man

General Prioux was a corps commander at the beginning of the war; he is sixty-one years of age and comes from the cavalry arm.

No one has yet come from that inferno in Flanders to describe the scene; doubtless it baffles the imagination. For the battle is being waged on land, in the air, on the sea and under the sea. Every engine of death yet devised by man is in action and the fight never ceases day or night. Nor is it confined to the actual battlefield. All bases, all lines of communication are bombed continually on both sides, with the Germans concentrating a great effort on Dunkerque.

The communiqué issued from French General Headquarters this morning said that "information from accurate sources warrants the affirmation that the losses suffered by the Germans in the engagements yesterday and last night were particularly high."

The French and British are fighting mostly rear-guard actions against very superior numbers, but whenever any unit finds itself in approximately equal strength it counter-attacks "to progress over the enemy dead."

Position Very Critical

Nevertheless despite heroic deeds it cannot be gainsaid that the position of the Allied division is very critical.

The exact position of General Blanchard's forces is not known; his front in any case must be very fluid. Doubtless he has shortened his lines in order to constitute a sort of mobile fortress moving toward the sea and fighting every inch of the way. The tragic aspect of his situation lies in the fact that the prime task of Leopold's army was to cover the coast.

It is revealed today in this connection that it was at the Belgian King's repeated insistence that the Allies took up positions on the Scheldt to protect Antwerp and also that the order to retreat was deferred until May 15, although the Allied High Command had urged withdrawal on the eleventh or twelfth.

There is confirmation today of the indication given yesterday in these dispatches that before the capitulation there were French detachments between the Belgians and the sea. It is hoped that though relatively small they may have acted effectively along the coast. It is believed, moreover, that it has been possible to flood part of the country west of the Yser River. Water lines of this sort proved of great value in the last war in this very region.

On the coast the Allies have lost Ostend. They hold Nieuport and

Continued on Page Two

"All the News That's Fit to Print."

The New York Times.

LATE CITY EDITION
Fair, with little change in temperature today and tomorrow.
Temperatures Yesterday—Max., 80; Min., 63

Copyright, 1940, by The New York Times Company.

VOL. LXXXIX..No. 30,174. Entered as Second-Class Matter, Postoffice, New York, N. Y. NEW YORK, WEDNESDAY, SEPTEMBER 4, 1940. THREE CENTS NEW YORK CITY and Vicinity | FOUR CENTS Elsewhere Except in 7th and 8th Postal Zones.

ROOSEVELT TRADES DESTROYERS FOR SEA BASES; TELLS CONGRESS HE ACTED ON OWN AUTHORITY; BRITAIN PLEDGES NEVER TO YIELD OR SINK FLEET

R.A.F. REPELS RAIDS

Fliers Turn Back Three Drives on London—Reich Perfecting Technique

PLANES REACH BERLIN

2½-Hour Alarm in City —British Hit Hard at French Coast

By JAMES B. RESTON
Special Cable to THE NEW YORK TIMES.

LONDON, Wednesday, Sept. 4—German bombers started ringing that big London doorbell early yesterday morning. They rang it again in the afternoon while Prime Minister Winston Churchill and his Ministers were commemorating the first anniversary of the war, and they kept ringing it right up till last midnight, when the third "all clear" of the day was sounded over the capital.

It was a day of fierce air battles, fought at great height in blue and silver sky all over Southeast England, and at the end, though Reich Marshal Hermann Goering's night shift was still operating all over the island, the British Air Ministry announced that twenty-five Nazi planes had been shot down to fifteen of Britain's planes. Eight British pilots were said to be safe, though it is not known whether they are in condition to fly.

[British bombing planes flew high over Berlin shortly after last midnight. Berlin spokesmen were quoted as saying that most of the Royal Air Force planes were turned back by severe anti-aircraft fire between Wittenberg and Magdeburg, but several planes escaped through the anti-aircraft barrage and reached Berlin, where they were again met with anti-aircraft fire.]

These German bombers, which have already overwhelmed five countries in the past twelve months, have now perfected a technique in attacking this vast, sprawling city, and they tried to work it again yesterday morning in the first raid.

Two Formations Meet

Just at 10 o'clock, timed to perfection, one wave of bombers approached the Thames Estuary from their bases in Belgium. Simultaneously, another formation, flying high through a light haze, came up from bases in France and met them over the Kentish coast. Altogether they were about 250 of them, and defying anti-aircraft batteries at first they started along the banks of the Thames toward London.

As they came inland, however, they met first one, then a second squadron of British fighters, who dived through Nazi fighter patrols into the bombers, broke up the formation and then attacked them singly and drove them back over the coast.

Some German bombers dropped their dynamite in Kent and Essex, but all that is said about the effect of these bombs is that they caused few casualties and little damage.

What can be said is that, if these bombers were trying to get into the heart of London to attack objectives here, they certainly failed, for while sirens were sounded everywhere in Greater London nobody in the heart of the city saw any fighting.

There was an interesting sidelight to the second mass raid of the day. At 2:45 P. M. Mr. Churchill, who somehow contrives to look more confident every day, walked into Westminster Abbey to attend the special service in commemoration of the day a year ago when Britain declared war on Germany. Alongside him walked tall, gaunt Viscount Halifax, Foreign Secretary; dapper Arthur Greenwood, Minister without portfolio; Sir Kingsley Wood, Chancellor of the Exchequer; Anthony Eden, War Secretary, and Joseph P. Kennedy, United States Ambassador to Great Britain.

They took their places in the cool church beside a great audience. At 2:50 P. M., as they were sitting there waiting for the service to start, air-raid sirens started echoing through the great cathedral.

Mr. Churchill got up, walked over to the cloisters and had a long talk with the Dean. In a few minutes he returned and took his place beside his Ministers in the chancel. It was announced that the service would proceed.

Around the city the British fight-

Continued on Page Three

The International Situation

Destroyer-War Base Deal

Completion of a deal by which the United States will transfer to Britain fifty over-age destroyers and obtain ninety-nine-year leases on eight shore and island bases stretching from Newfoundland to British Guiana was announced by President Roosevelt yesterday in a message to Congress. Coincidentally, the British Government pledged not to scuttle or surrender its fleet under any conditions. [Page 1, Column 8.]

The objective of the arrangement with Britain is to build a 4,500-mile iron fence in the Atlantic to assure this country's safety for a century, an authoritative State Department source said. To attain this, any interpretations of international law and parts of treaties in conflict must be subordinated, he said. Since this country's purpose is its defense, no well-intentioned nation can call the move a hostile act, he declared. [Page 1, Column 7.]

President Roosevelt, en route to Washington, disclosed that he looked upon the agreement as a means of keeping an enemy from the country's front door. Listing it as in some ways more important for defense than Jefferson's Louisiana purchase, he hinted there might be other similar arrangements. [Page 1, Column 6.]

The President had acted on an opinion from Attorney General Jackson, who held that the Executive had the right to negotiate the transfer without Senate consent and the constitutional power to dispose of the vessels. [Page 1, Column 5.]

Wendell L. Willkie, Republican Presidential nominee, said the country would undoubtedly approve the arrangement, but criticized Mr. Roosevelt's failure to obtain Congress's approval. [Page 1, Column 3.]

London rejoiced. A Foreign Office spokesman described the agreement as a practical method for each nation to contribute to the other's defense requirements. [Page 1, Column 4.]

Axis spokesmen did not challenge the deal's legality under neutrality laws. In Berlin it was belittled as unlikely to affect the war's outcome. It was said to be a bargain for the United States and evidence that Britain was "cracking up." In Rome it was expected the Italians would be embittered. [Page 15, Column 1.]

Developments in Congress

The House opened debate on the Selective Service Training Bill, the discussion following the lines of the Senate's deliberation. Indications were that the bill would pass by a good margin, the principal controversy centering on the question of industrial conscription. Leaders planned for final action Friday. [Page 17, Column 1.]

The Senate Finance Committee opened hearings on the excess profits tax and defense expansion amortization bill. The probability of changes in the measure increased as witnesses hit at its effects on business. [Page 10, Column 1.]

The War in Europe, Asia and Africa

German bombers hammered at Britain's airfields, harbors and naval bases, engaging the Royal Air Force in battles all over Southern England. Three raids on London were repelled. [Page 1, Column 1.]

Several R. A. F. bombers reached Berlin early today to provoke violent anti-aircraft fire after the British had loosed a powerful aerial counter-offensive in which their planes had bombed German industrial centers, the French coast and Italian power stations. [Page 3, Column 1.]

In the central Mediterranean, new type Italian bombers scored a victory, damaging a British battleship, an aircraft carrier, a cruiser and a destroyer, the Rome High Command announced. The R. A. F. again pounded Assab, port in Italian Eritrea. [Page 4, Column 6.]

Led by Tahiti, France's most important colony in Oceania, the French-protected Society Islands have voted to throw in their lot with Britain, repudiating Vichy, it was reported. [Page 6, Column 1.]

A virtual Japanese ultimatum demanding a military base and passage for troops was reported to have been rejected by French Indo-China and conflict there was believed inevitable. [Page 6, Column 3.]

In an attempted Iron Guard coup three gunmen broke through King Carol's palace guard and fired several shots into the air. Others equally vainly besieged a radio station, fought with troops. [Page 1, Column 2.]

A clash between Hungarian and Rumanian troops over the occupation of Transylvania was reported at Bucharest. [Page 4, Column 1.]

BUCHAREST CHECKS IRON GUARDS' COUP

Shots Fired in Front of Royal Palace—Handbills Call On Carol to Abdicate

By EUGEN KOVACS
Wireless to THE NEW YORK TIMES.

BUCHAREST, Rumania, Sept. 3—A group of the Iron Guards, dissatisfied with the conduct and policy of other Iron Guards who are Ministers and who participated in the Crown Council, organized and carried out several attempts tonight against different public buildings in Bucharest. All these attacks failed.

A small group consisting of three persons appeared in an automobile this evening at 8:30 before the Royal Palace and one of them fired two shots in the air. A policeman on duty in front of the gates of the palace fired at the car but failed. The man who fired the shots tried to escape, however, but was arrested, while the car disappeared.

The regular news bulletin broadcast at 10 o'clock was canceled.

A second group, consisting of young men wearing military uniforms and disguised as Iron Guards, attacked the Bucharest radio station. The guard fired and succeeded in repelling the attacking group.

At the cabin of transmission of the Central Telephone Exchange a man was found who cut off some lines so that the telephone connection with abroad was cut off for a while. At the State Railway repair works in the suburb of Grivitza an-

Continued on Page Four

WILLKIE FOR PACT, BUT HITS SECRECY

Regrets President Did Not Put Deal With Britain Before Congress and People

By JAMES A. HAGERTY
Special to THE NEW YORK TIMES.

RUSHVILLE, Ind., Sept. 3—Asked today to comment on President Roosevelt's announcement of the agreement to turn over to Great Britain fifty over-age destroyers in return for air and naval bases in British Western Hemisphere areas, Wendell L. Willkie, Republican nominee for President, declared that the country undoubtedly would approve the program, but criticized the President's failure to obtain prior approval of Congress as smacking of totalitarianism.

In a statement prepared with care and with realization that it might have important foreign repercussions, Mr. Willkie said:

"The country will undoubtedly approve of the program to add to our naval and air bases and assistance given to Great Britain. It is regrettable, however, that the President did not deem it necessary in connection with this proposal to secure the approval of Congress or permit public discussion prior to adoption.

"The people have a right to know of such important commitments prior to and not after being made. We must be extremely careful in these times when the struggle in the world is between democracy and to-

Continued on Page Fourteen

BRITISH JUBILANT

Destroyers Strengthen Their Fleet at Point of Greatest Strain

MORAL EFFECT GREAT

But Press Warns People Gesture Does Not Mean U. S. Will Enter War

By RAYMOND DANIELL
Special Cable to THE NEW YORK TIMES.

LONDON, Sept. 3—It would be impossible to overstate the jubilation in official and unofficial circles caused today by President Roosevelt's announcement that fifty United States destroyers were coming to help Great Britain in her hour of peril. They will be manned by British crews and will fly the white ensign of the Royal Navy, it is true, but they are coming, nevertheless.

It was tangible proof that American talk of giving "all aid short of war" was more than idle chatter and that this country's friends across the Atlantic, despite German propaganda and the heavy bombardment of British cities and towns, had decided there was still lots of fight left in the British lion and that it was not too late to help turn the tide against totalitarian domination of Europe.

Destroyer Losses Offset

Under the arrangement, it was pointed out by authoritative sources, the United States gained security against future aggression, while the British fleet at one stroke acquired fifty 1,200-ton destroyers as an offset to the thirty lost since the beginning of hostilities.

These destroyers are badly needed at this stage of the war with British seapower engaged in a death grapple with the German Empire. Since the French were knocked out as an ally, the whole job of protecting convoys and maintaining the lifelines of the Empire against the new enemy in the Mediterranean has fallen upon the British fleet, while the air force has concentrated chiefly on destroying the enemy's supplies and defending the homes of the people of this island, which is under repeated bombardment from the air throughout its length and breadth.

Added to this multiplication of the navy's duties has been the necessity of blockading the whole Continent of Europe while standing by to resist the very real threat of a German invasion which, as War Secretary Anthony Eden warned today, still hangs over this country.

As great as was Britain's need the material gain by today's transaction was matched in British minds by the intangible implications of most open indication yet of Anglo-American cooperation for defense against the Nazi threats.

The Times, London, will point out editorially tomorrow that such cooperation between a belligerent and a neutral is "a new departure" but one that is dictated by the necessities of modern war. The editorial goes on to say:

"The tragic fate of some of the smaller peoples of Europe might have been averted if they had not been restrained from planning for

Continued on Page Fifteen

RULING BY JACKSON

Opinion Holds Transfer by President Needs No Senate Action

AN 'EXECUTIVE' DEAL

Opponents in Congress Seek to Find Means of Obstructing It

Attorney General Jackson's opinion is printed on Page 16.

By LEWIS WOOD
Special to THE NEW YORK TIMES.

WASHINGTON, Sept. 3—President Roosevelt has unqualified power to exchange fifty over-age destroyers for British naval and air bases in the Western Hemisphere without Senate consent, in the opinion of Attorney General Jackson, made public today, but, while Mr. Jackson asserted the Executive's right to dispose of naval vessels, he again refused to sanction the legality of delivery of "mosquito boats" now under construction.

Under a World War law the Attorney General ruled that it would be entirely proper to transfer the destroyers, since these were not built "with the intent that they should enter the service of a belligerent," but turning over the uncompleted mosquito boats, he argued, would be impossible, as this would legally mean that they were intended for a belligerent.

Opponents of the British-American deal sought tonight to find means of obstruction and delay, but this seemed to hinge upon the extent to which the direct interest of a taxpayer could be proved and the general opinion here was that the adversaries were blocked from court action and could depend only upon sufficient massing of public opinion. Apparently the Administration felt legally secure.

Writing his opinion to President Roosevelt last Tuesday, Mr. Jackson went into detail as to constitutional power and especially stressed the responsibility of the Executive to use every authority for national defense at a time when "present world conditions forbid him to risk" any constitutionally avoidable delay.

"No Future Commitments"

The Attorney General conceded that the wide Presidential power over foreign relations was not unlimited, but in this case, Mr. Jackson contended, there were no promises or future commitments by the United States which would require Senate consent or, indeed, any Congressional action. The agreement provided an opportunity to establish naval and air bases for coastline defense, he maintained, but needed no appropriation of money. Thus it was unnecessary for the Senate to ratify "an opportunity that entails no obligation," he declared.

Alluding to precedents, Mr. Jackson remarked that the "proposition falls far short" of the acquisition of the Louisiana Territory by President Jefferson from a belligerent during a European war. Outside of constitutional power, he went on,

Continued on Page Sixteen

Writer on British Destroyer Sees U-Boats in Raids and One Sunk

By BRYDON TAVES

ABOARD A BRITISH DESTROYER, in the North Atlantic, Sept. 3 (UP)—Germany is shooting the works to make good the threat of total blockade of the British Isles, but after eight days aboard a little British flotilla leader I can say that hundreds of ships are entering and leaving British ports each week.

German submarine and air attacks marked my voyage. Not one day passed without action. The British crew was either manning gun and depth-charge stations to fight off a U-boat or manning anti-aircraft stations to fight attacking planes.

I saw one British merchantman take a long-range torpedo squarely amidships and sink within a half hour. The next day our destroyer evened the score.

A "tin fish," meant for us, missed by a scant thirty feet as we whipped around. Then we rocked from the concussion of our own depth charges and I saw an oil patch spread slowly over the surface, marking that U-boat's end.

The destroyer was engaged in a typical convoy job, and its duties were something between those of a conscientious sheep dog and a sister of charity leading a bunch of orphans across Times Square.

We were one destroyer and one smaller warship escorting a thirty-ship convoy spread over fifteen square miles of ocean. Watching the line of hulls stretching out behind us, I remembered what a naval officer in a convoy control room in a West coast port told me just before I sailed.

"Give me fifty over-age American destroyers," he said, "and I will

Continued on Page Four

UNITED STATES ACQUIRES DEFENSE BASTIONS

Bases at the places indicated by circled dots are being leased by Great Britain to this country for ninety-nine years. The leases for those in Newfoundland and Bermuda are in effect outright gifts; the leases for the others are in exchange for fifty over-age United States destroyers. The bases in the Caribbean area will supplement present American defense centers (black diamonds) in guarding approaches to the Panama Canal.

ROOSEVELT HAILS GAIN OF NEW BASES

Exchange of Over-Age Ships for British Leases Offers Outer Defense Line, He Says

By CHARLES HURD
Special to THE NEW YORK TIMES.

ON BOARD ROOSEVELT TRAIN, Sept. 3—President Roosevelt indicated that the chief value of the trade with Great Britain of fifty over-age destroyers for naval and air base sites in British crown colonies in the Western Hemisphere lay in the fact that this outer line of defenses would keep any enemy away from this country's front door.

For that reason, he said, his agreement with the British Government was more important for the defense of this country than anything since the Louisiana Purchase in 1803, which assured American military control over the Mississippi River.

There may be other similar negotiations, he added, but he cautioned newspaper reporters not to try to guess where they would be, listing the odds at 10 to 1 that such guesses would be wrong.

The President did not deny a suggestion made by a reporter that perhaps Greenland might be the site for another base. He merely renewed his caution against speculation.

The President's view of the agreement, which has been known to be in progress for several weeks, was given at a special press conference on his private train at the same hour that his offices in Washington sent to Congress a message that the exchange was accomplished.

A dozen newspaper reporters heard Mr. Roosevelt read the text of the message to Congress, which he completed during a trip from Hyde Park, N. Y., to Tennessee, North Carolina and West Virginia. He read the message, after laughingly telling them that there was no story. While the document, with supporting papers, was being made public in Washington at noon, he began his press conference at 11:50 A. M. Eastern time.

Mr. Roosevelt called the press conference to meet in the tiny vestibule of his private car forty-five minutes after he departed from South Charleston, W. Va., where he inspected work being done to restore to high productivity a long abandoned Navy ordnance plant built in 1917-18 to construct armor plate and shells.

Among the statements he made

Continued on Page Ten

SHIP TRADE IS HELD NOT HOSTILE ACTION

State Department Stresses Defense Phase of Exchange of Vessels for Bases

Special to THE NEW YORK TIMES.

WASHINGTON, Sept. 3—No country could consider the transfer of fifty United States destroyers to Great Britain and the obtaining by this country of naval and air bases in British New World territory as a hostile act, an informed State Department source said today.

Only a nation seeking world conquest could use this as a pretext for belligerent action, the source asserted.

The intention of this government in completing the agreement was merely to strengthen its own defenses and no other considerations were entertained, State Department officials said, in insisting that the United States had the opportunity to obtain a 4,000 or 5,000 mile ring of steel around the eastern part of the hemisphere on terms unequaled since the Louisiana Purchase. They added that the protection would last for 100 years.

It was made clear that it was no time to consider any technical provisions which might be sought in international law by opponents of the agreement but that in these dangerous days, when the world is almost literally on fire, defense considerations must come first.

This view was expressed in answer to questions of correspondents about the Second Hague Convention of 1907, of which the United States and Germany are signatories, but Great Britain is not.

Hague 1907 Convention Is Quoted

Article VI of this convention asserts:

"The support in any manner, directly or indirectly, by a neutral power of a belligerent power, by warships, ammunition or war materials of any kind whatever, is forbidden."

Article VIII says:

"A neutral government is also bound to display the same vigilance to prevent the departure from its jurisdiction of any vessel intended to cruise, or menace in hostile operations, which had been adapted entirely or partly within the said jurisdiction for use in war."

Article XXVIII, however, states: "The provisions of this present convention do not apply except to the contracting powers and then only if all the belligerents are parties to the convention."

One could accurately visualize a

Continued on Page Sixteen

LINE OF 4,500 MILES

Two Defense Outposts Are Gifts, Congress Is Told—No Rent on Rest

FOR 50 OLD VESSELS

President Holds Move Solely Protective, 'No Threat to Any Nation'

Texts of messages on leasing of naval bases, Page 10.

By FRANK L. KLUCKHOHN
Special to THE NEW YORK TIMES.

WASHINGTON, Sept. 3—President Roosevelt informed Congress today that he had completed an arrangement by which the United States will transfer to Great Britain fifty over-age destroyers and obtain from Britain ninety-nine-year leases for sea and air bases at eight strategic continental and island points in the Western Hemisphere.

The new American defense line thus established will stretch 4,500 miles from Newfoundland to British Guiana and include other bases on the islands of Bermuda, the Bahamas, Jamaica, St. Lucia, Trinidad and Antigua.

It is intended to make difficult, if not impossible, naval and air attacks upon the United States and much of the New World. The exact sites of the bases will be determined later by the two governments.

A solemn pledge by the British Government to the United States not to scuttle or surrender the British fleet under any conditions was revealed coincidentally by the State Department's publication of correspondence between Secretary Hull and the British Ambassador, the Marquess of Lothian.

Secretary Hull was informed that it represented the "settled policy" of His Majesty's Government not to "surrender or sink" the British fleet.

Reshaping of Naval Defense

The deal, carrying with it far-flung international as well as domestic defense implications, was hailed by President Roosevelt as the most important since the Jefferson Administration completed the Louisiana Purchase in 1803.

Informed official circles contended that it assured the British Fleet as an Atlantic sea-screen for the United States and made it possible for the American Fleet to remain in the Pacific.

Some thought it might lead to an informal defensive alliance between this country and Australia similar to the arrangement recently completed administratively with Canada, although others disagreed on this point.

President Roosevelt informed Congress that he had given the right to bases in Newfoundland and Bermuda as an outright gift, "generously given and gladly received," but that "the other bases mentioned have been acquired in exchange for fifty of our over-age destroyers."

Previously, the President had insisted that the destroyer and base deals were separate.

Legal Basis for Procedure

Mr. Roosevelt explained in his message that he had acted upon a legal opinion by Attorney General Jackson which held that the Chief Executive had the right to dispose of the destroyers and complete the deal without consultation with the Senate and without its approval.

The President made clear that he would not seek the Senate's endorsement by remarking that he sent his statement merely "for the information of Congress."

Chairman Walsh of the Senate Naval Affairs Committee and several other Senators publicly condemned the proposed deal as illegal under domestic and international law when it was reported in the press some weeks ago that President Roosevelt had agreed to give Britain fifty destroyers after pleas from Prime Minister Winston Churchill.

In view of Senator Walsh's stand, some Senators privately expressed the opinion that there might be an attempt to have the Naval Affairs Committee open an investigation of the whole transaction.

After the President's message was

Continued on Page Twelve

"All the News That's Fit to Print."

The New York Times.

Copyright, 1940, by The New York Times Company.

LATE CITY EDITION
Partly cloudy and colder today. Tomorrow fair and slightly warmer.
Temperatures Yesterday—Max., 49; Min., 40

VOL. XC...No. 30,247. Entered as Second-Class Matter, Postoffice, New York, N. Y. NEW YORK, SATURDAY, NOVEMBER 16, 1940. THREE CENTS NEW YORK CITY and Vicinity | FOUR CENTS Elsewhere Except in 7th and 8th Postal Zones.

COVENTRY WRECKED IN WORST RAID ON ENGLAND, WITH 1,000 CASUALTIES; BRITISH SMASH BERLIN RAIL DEPOTS

ROOSEVELT NAMES DR. MILLIS TO NLRB, REPLACING MADDEN

Witt, Board Secretary, and 2 Others Quit as Shake-Up Looms in 'Leftist' Group

LEISERSON HAILS CHOICE

End of Deadlock Between Him and Smith Forecast—Madden Nominated for Claims Bench

By CHARLES HURD
Special to THE NEW YORK TIMES.

WASHINGTON, Nov. 15—President Roosevelt today appointed Dr. Harry A. Millis of Chicago to succeed J. Warren Madden, former chairman of the National Labor Relations Board. Dr. Millis, who is 67, served on the old NRA Labor Board in 1934 and 1935, prior to its reconstitution under the Wagner act.

This appointment of a man whose nomination was expected to result in considerable shuffling in the board personnel, especially its "left wing" element, was followed within a few hours by the resignation of three important aides of the board, including Nathan Witt, the secretary.

The appointment broke an impasse which has existed since Aug. 27, when Mr. Madden's term expired and his necessary retirement left the board consisting only of Dr. William Leiserson and Edwin S. Smith, whose opposing views made it impossible for them to reach agreements on many controversies before them.

Mr. Smith had voted much of the time with Chairman Madden, just as Dr. Leiserson is expected hereafter to vote generally with Dr. Millis. Dr. Leiserson called selection of Dr. Millis a "splendid appointment."

Madden Named for Court Post

Coincident with appointment of Dr. Millis, Mr. Roosevelt sent to the Senate a nomination of Mr. Madden to fill a vacancy on the United States Court of Claims, where he would receive $12,500 a year as contrasted with his former $10,000 NLRB post. Mr. Smith immediately wrote to Mr. Madden expressing regret that he had not been reappointed to the NLRB.

The appointment of Dr. Millis was expected to receive quick confirmation by the Senate.

The President, in nominating Dr. Millis, did not indicate whether he would be designated as chairman of the board, but this was the assumption in well-informed circles.

Dr. Millis is a Professor of Economics at the University of Chicago and has been acting as labor relations conciliator for the General Motors Corporation and the C. I. O. United Automobile Workers. Prior to his call to the University of Chicago he was on the faculties of Stanford University and the Universities of Arkansas and Kansas. His long experience in labor affairs includes various temporary appointments by the Federal Government. Recently he has made studies on collective bargaining for the Twentieth Century Fund.

Activities in the offices of the NLRB as a result of the appointment gave graphic indication of the changes anticipated there, as well as the division of feeling within the board.

Mr. Witt submitted his letter of resignation addressed to the board and made it public together with a somewhat longer letter to Mr. Madden, complimenting the latter's work.

Pay Tribute to Ex-Chairman

Soon after Mr. Witt took this step, Alexander B. Hawes, chief administrative examiner, and Thomas I. Emerson, associate general counsel, filed their own resignations. Both also paid tribute to Mr. Madden.

Mr. Emerson's principal work, in his five-year association with the NLRB, has been to direct the work of lawyers in the Review Section who passed upon examiners' reports. This Review Section was sharply criticized for its alleged collective lack of experience by the special House committee that studied the NLRB a year ago, and Dr. Millis was expected to overhaul its organization.

All three officials asked that their resignations be effective immediately. Mr. Hawes wrote to the board that he had served for three years under the "fearless and able chairmanship" of Mr. Madden and "I do not wish to remain with the board, now that he has not been reappointed."

Mr. Emerson publicly announced that, concerning Mr. Madden, "I have supported his policies throughout," and that it was difficult for him to see "how the members of the board could have performed a more courageous, competent and worth-while public service."

Mr. Witt's letter to the board based his resignation on failure to reappoint Mr. Madden. His person-

Continued on Page Twenty

Hull Decides to Remain In Cabinet, Friends State

Special to THE NEW YORK TIMES.

WASHINGTON, Nov. 15—Cordell Hull has reached a decision to continue as Secretary of State in the third Roosevelt administration, according to officials who said today that he has so informed friends. Mr. Hull is in Augusta, Ga., on a vacation and President Roosevelt is cruising on the Presidential yacht Potomac, consequently no comment was available from either official.

The decision turned upon the international situation, it was said. It was understood that Secretary Hull would have preferred to retire to private life. The war emergency and his familiarity with United States foreign policy for eight years induced him to remain in office, it was explained.

Mr. Hull will be the first Secretary of State to serve more than eight years. Only four have served that long, the last being Hamilton Fish, sixty-four years ago.

C. I. O. STRIKE SHUTS WAR PLANES PLANT

5,200 Vultee Workers Idle—Hillman Voices Hope for Quick Wage Accord

Special to THE NEW YORK TIMES.

LOS ANGELES, Nov. 15—Work on $80,000,000 worth of military aircraft production, described in Washington as "vital to our national defense," came to a halt today as members of the C. I. O. United Automobile Workers went on strike at the Downey plant of Vultee Aircraft, Inc., fourth largest plane producer on the West Coast.

Early this morning hundreds of pickets drew up across the huge plant's entrances. The last outgoing night shift came out with tool kits in hands. The first ingoing day shift stopped short before such picket line banners as "They Shall Not Pass!" and "Keep Out! This Means You!"

The plant, where top-speed wheels had long hummed twenty-four hours a day, was hushed and 5,200 workers found themselves idle.

Agents of the War Department, National Defense Commission and Labor Department were at work on a remedy for a situation causing the greatest interruption to date in defense production.

Secretary Perkins assigned Edward H. Fitzgerald, one of the department's veteran labor conciliators, to help Lyman Sisley, first department conciliator in the situation. Mr. Sisley has spent night and day working toward a solution since the matter was put up to him by the disputants Wednesday night.

Seek New Conversations

Upon Captain Fitzgerald's arrival from San Francisco, he and Mr. Sisley, who long have teamed together in West Coast conciliation endeavors, outlined a new peace plan which, they said, they were seeking to lay before the union leaders. The aim, it was understood, was to bring company and union negotiators around one table. Company officials said they would attend.

Company representatives charged that Vultee was being used by the union as a guinea pig for a nationwide drive to bring all airplane manufacture under the C. I. O. banner.

The union has control only in one other West Coast airplane plant, that of North American Aviation, Inc., a much smaller establishment.

Union representatives assert that all they are after is an increase to 75 cents an hour from the present 50 cents an hour minimum wage at the Vultee plant, where they claim a large majority of the 3,800 production workers among the 5,200 total employes.

They want the rate to be retroactive to Oct. 11. They point out that they have a 75-cent minimum in local automobile manufacturing plants.

The company has offered to increase the minimum to 55 cents after three months of employment and 60 cents after six months, asserting that it takes six months to train a beginner.

Agreement on Other Points

All other points in a proposed contract between the company and the union, both sides state, have been agreed on.

Vultee is producing military planes exclusively, basic trainers for the United States Army, Vanguard pursuit planes for foreign account and a new secret type combat plane.

Highways to and from the plant were choked today with automobiles of idle workers, many bearing out-of-State license plates. Two cars, one with an Ohio license plate, were rigged up with loudspeakers to address union messages. A field kitchen with soup kettles was set up for picketers.

Police reported no disorder, but disruption of traffic. Union agents questioned persons who approached

Continued on Page Twenty

$58,000,000 TUNNEL TO QUEENS OPENED; 3,000 AT CEREMONY

Officials Praise New Unit of City's Interborough Arteries—Mrs. Harvey Cuts Tape

DRIVERS QUICK TO USE IT

Long Line Waits at Manhattan End, but a 'First' Has to Be Drafted at the Other

The $58,000,000 Queens Midtown Tunnel under the East River was opened to the public at 1:20 P. M. yesterday, nearly an hour after the close of dedicatory exercises held under lowering skies in the presence of 3,000 guests of the New York City Tunnel Authority, assembled in the traffic plaza at the Queens end of the new tube.

It was 12:36 P. M. when Council President Newbold Morris, acting in the absence of Mayor La Guardia, formally accepted the new traffic artery for the city. The acceptance came at the end of a speaking program in which city and Federal officials took part. Afterward there was a motor parade of guests through the tunnel to Manhattan and return, followed by a motorcade along the new Midtown Highway in Queens to its intersection with the Connecting Highway between Queens and Brooklyn.

At the start of the trip along the Midtown Highway that traffic artery, reached by a ramp from the Queens portal of the new tunnel, was opened to public use by Borough President George U. Harvey after Mrs. Harvey had cut a ribbon stretched across the highway.

"First" Has to Be Hunted

Not until the motor parades were over was the new tunnel ready for public use, and even then it was necessary for a police motorcyclist to scurry out into the streets of Long Island City to find a "first car" to make the crossing to Manhattan.

Harry E. Sochovit, gasoline station operator, of 585 East Sixteenth Street, Brooklyn, was the first motorist to pay a toll for use of the tunnel. It was just 1:20 P. M. when he drove his tan coupé up to a toll booth, handed over his quarter, posed for photographers and sped on toward Manhattan.

At 1:30 P. M., with a crowd of 4,000 persons watching, John Topf, a chauffeur of 26-13 Jackson Avenue, Long Island City, entered the Manhattan end of the tunnel bound for Queens, where he paid his quarter on leaving the traffic plaza. There was a long line of cars waiting to enter the Manhattan portal of the tunnel, some having arrived as early as 9 A. M. The absence of a waiting line at the Queens portal was explained by the fact that the available space was pre-empted by guests' cars taking part in the opening ceremonies and the parades that followed.

Head of Authority Presides

Alfred B. Jones, chairman of the Tunnel Authority, presided at the dedicatory exercises and introduced a group of speakers that included Senator Robert F. Wagner, Mr. Morris, Borough President Stanley M. Isaacs of Manhattan, Borough President Harvey, Maurice E. Gilmore, Regional PWA Director, and George McAneny, president of the Regional Plan Association. Jesse H. Jones, Secretary of Commerce and chairman of the Reconstruction Finance Corporation, was unable to be present but sent a telegram. John J. Carmody, PWA Administrator, was also unable to attend and sent a telegram.

Deputy Mayor Rufus E. McGahen read a letter from Mayor La Guardia voicing his regret at not being able to be present. Regret at the Mayor's absence was also expressed by Chairman Jones, who added that

Continued on Page Nineteen

Helgoland, German Ship, Reported Caught, Sunk

Shipping circles received reports yesterday that the 2,927-ton German freighter Helgoland, which fled from Barranquilla, Colombia, Oct. 28, had been cornered and sunk in the Caribbean by British warships, according to The Associated Press.

The Hamburg-American line freighter, built in 1939, was reported to be carrying pilots of Scadta, German air line in South America, when she slipped out of port at night. She was reported to have put to sea to refuel a raider attacking South Atlantic shipping.

SPAIN IMPOSES GAG ON U. S. REPORTERS

Forbids Them to Send News, Charging We Refuse to Admit Spanish Writer

By T. J. HAMILTON
Special Cable to THE NEW YORK TIMES.

MADRID, Nov. 15—The Spanish Government today forbade all representatives of American newspapers and news agencies in Spain to send out any dispatches after a time to be fixed within a day or two.

It was stated that the action was taken in reprisal for the alleged refusal of the United States to grant a visa to the recently appointed Washington correspondent of E. F. E. [the foreign service of the official Spanish news agency, E. F. E.-Cifra.] Unofficially, however, it was understood that the United States had not refused a visa to the E. F. E. correspondent, but that it was merely a matter of Spain's expecting the wheels of the State Department in Washington to grind faster than usual.

The following communiqué was issued by the Press Bureau tonight:

"It is authorized to file stories to America declaring that, since the American authorities have not permitted the entry into the United States of a representative of the E. F. E. agency and the setting up of an office of said agency in said country, The United Press and The Associated Press agencies in this country will be abandoned."

Later an official spokesman said this order would apply also to The International News Service and to the Madrid correspondents of The Chicago Tribune and THE NEW YORK TIMES.

A spokesman for the director general of the Press Bureau at first stated that American correspondents would not be permitted to file dispatches after midnight Sunday night. Later, however, the correspondents were informed that they would be notified either directly by the Press Bureau or through their embassy when the prohibition would take effect.

Weddell to Ask Information

Special to THE NEW YORK TIMES.

WASHINGTON, Nov. 15—The State Department today cabled Alexander W. Weddell, the United States Ambassador in Madrid, requesting information concerning the suspension by the Spanish Government of American newspaper and news agency correspondents and their services.

The department denied, as alleged in Madrid, that it had refused visas for correspondents of E. F. E., the official Spanish news agency, or

Continued on Page Five

Hoover Urges Aid to 5 Little Democracies; Says Famine and Disease Peril War Victims

Special to THE NEW YORK TIMES.

POUGHKEEPSIE, N. Y., Nov. 15—Former President Herbert Hoover in an address at Vassar College tonight renewed his plea for international assistance to the conquered nations of Europe, with a warning that famine and its accompanying epidemic diseases would reach an acute stage there this Winter or next Spring.

Mr. Hoover named specifically "the five little democracies" of Finland, Norway, Holland, Belgium and Central Poland, and asserted that the United States had a moral responsibility toward these nations, all of which, he said, "sacrificed and fought against overwhelming odds to maintain freedom and their democratic ideals."

"I am not making any proposals as to the French, although they are indeed suffering, because of the present obscurity of their food and political situation," he added.

Reiterating his proposal for a lifting of the British blockade to permit the passage of shiploads of food to be distributed under German guarantees and neutral control, Mr. Hoover emphasized the increased urgency of the situation since he first advanced the program three months ago.

"The people of Brussels are already on a ration of seven ounces of bread a day," he pointed out. "Typhus already rages in Warsaw. Holland is killing its animals for lack of feed."

Though lives and "infinite suffering" still could be saved, Mr. Hoover asserted, no time should be lost in the effort, for three months would be required to set up the necessary organization.

At the same time he discussed arguments that Germany would ben-

Continued on Page Seven

R.A.F. STRIKES AGAIN

Returns to Berlin After Losing Ten Planes in Raids on Reich

HAMBURG ALSO BATTERED

Bremen Attacked and 26 Nazi Airports From Norway to Brittany Bombed

By JAMES MacDONALD
Special Cable to THE NEW YORK TIMES.

LONDON, Saturday, Nov. 16—The heavy Royal Air Force bombers that battered Berlin railroad stations and freight yards for several hours yesterday morning and Thursday night carried out only one phase of widespread raids that had for their objectives twenty-six Nazi air bases and harbors and shipping all the way from Stavanger, Norway, to Lorient, Brittany, according to an Air Ministry announcement.

[Another British raid on Berlin last night was announced by the German radio in a broadcast heard here by the National Broadcasting Company. Six raiders were reported downed as soon as they crossed the Channel, and only twelve penetrated to the Berlin area, three of them being shot down in the city and three in the outskirts, according to The United Press, however, Berlin enjoyed a raidless night.]

London officials would not disclose the size of their fleet of night raiders, but it was believed to have been large because the attack embraced so many points and was declared to have entailed heavy bombardments, particularly of Berlin.

The Air Ministry announced the loss of ten of the British raiders, which is a greater number than usual.

Cross-Channel Gun Duel

Meanwhile freakish weather entered the war picture again. After a spell of brilliant sunshine over the Strait of Dover in the forenoon, when British and German long-range gunners had a hot argument, a southwesterly gale, which is unwelcome news for German strategists who may still be clinging to plans for the invasion of Great Britain, sprang up last night. Heavy rain clouds scudded across the sky, while the wind churned up a rough sea.

The cross-Channel shelling began just before daybreak yesterday and lasted several hours. Big shells screeched angrily in both directions, but as far as the English side of the strait is concerned there was comparatively small damage and no casualties whatever, it was said, despite the fierceness of the barrage.

The British raiders who flew to Berlin during the night had the advantage of a full moon and perfect weather, according to the Air Ministry. The first wave is said to have reached the Nazi capital two hours after dark and was followed by other waves for several hours thereafter.

The reason for bombing Berlin's various large railroad terminals and extensive freight yards, it was pointed out here, is that Berlin is the most important focal point for the railroads of Central Europe. Whatever damage is done to them would affect not only Germany herself but also her transport to the adjacent countries she has conquered.

Power Plants Bombed

Targets in Berlin included the Stettiner Station, the Schlesischer Station and Anhalter Station, the Tempelhof railroad yards and freight yards between the Potsdamer and Anhalter Stations. Other Berlin objectives were the power station in the Charlottenburg district and the Wilmersdorf power station in the heart of the German capital.

One pilot who took part in the Berlin raid said he witnessed a terrific explosion which momentarily drowned out the city's guns. He told of seeing a big building go "sky high" and several fires breaking out all around.

Hamburg suffered a British bombardment that was said to have lasted nearly an hour. The principal goal there was the Rhenania Ossag Mineral Oil Works where fifteen bomb bursts were seen, according to R. A. F. reports.

Shipping and docks at Ostend, Havre and Lorient also were raided during the early hours of the morning as well as late Thursday night, it was added. Heavy attacks

Continued on Page Two

The International Situation

The compact industrial city of Coventry, lying northwest of London in the geographical heart of England, was devastated Thursday night by an estimated 500 German planes raining incendiary and demolition bombs on it for ten and a half hours. Casualties totaled at least 1,000 persons, many of them firemen, policemen and air-raid precaution workers who went about their jobs regardless of the storm of death from the skies. The bombing was done from a high altitude, the British said, the German planes dumping their loads indiscriminately over the city, and vital manufacturing plants suffered less than churches, schools, hospitals and the homes of the workers. [Page 1, Column 8.]

The Nazis boasted that it was the "greatest attack in the history of aerial warfare" and said it had crippled British aviation production. They said the raid was in retaliation for the British attack on Munich Nov. 8 while the Brown Shirts were celebrating the seventeenth anniversary of their beer hall revolt. [Page 3, Column 2.]

They were back over England again last night, subjecting some London areas to what was described as one of the heaviest raids of the war. Many fires were started. During the day the Royal Air Force took a measure of revenge for Coventry by shooting down eighteen planes with the loss of only one of their own, the Air Ministry said. [Page 1, Column 6.]

While the Germans were over Coventry, the Royal Air Force was giving Berlin what apparently was its heaviest attack, the Air Ministry reporting that the German capital's railway yards and stations—nerve center of the transportation system of Central Europe—were heavily and effectively attacked under perfect weather conditions. Power stations also were reported hit. Berlin said the raid was the heaviest of the war. Another attack was in progress last night. Hamburg, the German base at Stavanger, in Norway, and twenty-six Nazi airdromes were other objectives of the British pilots. [Page 1, Column 5.]

The Greeks continued to drive the Italian invaders before them all along the front, reports from Athens said, shock troops advancing to within a few miles of Koritza, and the defenders of Yanina, in the southwest, driving toward the border to threaten the Albanian port of Porto Edda. The Italians were reported in disorderly retreat in the latter area, where they previously had made their greatest advance into Greece. The land actions were supported by British and Greek bomber and fighter planes, harassing the Italian rear and attacking the ports through which reinforcements and supplies from Italy must come. [Page 1, Column 7.]

The Yugoslav border city of Bitolj was bombed again by three unidentified planes, the fourth time its neutrality had been invaded since the start of the Grecian campaign. The first bombing was Nov. 5, when three planes, unofficially identified as Italian, dropped bombs on the city, killing nineteen persons and wounding many others. Belgrade already was tense with reports of German troop concentrations along the Yugoslav-Rumanian border and the continued evacuation of German nationals from Greece. [Page 4, Column 5.]

That some new Axis military move was imminent seemed apparent with the announcement in Berlin and Rome of a conference at Innsbruck, Austria, of General Field Marshal Wilhelm Keitel, Chief of the German High Command, and Marshal Pietro Badoglio of Italy. The official Germany agency said it was a natural development, military action always following political action. The probability that what they discussed was a German-Italian attack on Gibraltar was seen in some quarters, who read that significance into the trip to Paris and Berlin of Spain's Foreign Minister, Ramon Serrano Suner. [Page 4, Col. 1.]

A Spanish ban on United States reporters was interpreted by some observers as another indication of impending military action against Gibraltar. The Spanish explanation of the order was that it was in retaliation for the refusal of Washington to grant a visa to a correspondent for the official Spanish news agency, EFE, or to allow it to operate in this country. State Department officials in Washington denied that any such refusal had been made. Not even an application has been made, they said. [Page 1, Column 4.]

The United States, however, did follow Britain in protesting to Spain against seizure of the former international zone of Tangier in Africa, which is on the Atlantic side of the Strait of Gibraltar and control of which would aid any attack on that British fortress. [Page 5, Column 1.]

BOMBING OF LONDON HEAVIEST IN MONTH

200 Planes Raid Capital, 80 in One Formation—Damage Is Reported Widespread

By The United Press.

LONDON, Saturday, Nov. 16—More than 200 German raiders, taking advantage of a full moon, a cloudless sky and a slight haze, last night and early today gave London its heaviest and most protracted pounding in a month.

Large formations of as many as eighty Nazi planes swept the capital and maintained a Blitzkreig intensity for several hours after midnight and then dwindled to the customary parade of nuisance raiders until dawn. [The "all clear" sounded shortly before 7 A. M., according to The Associated Press.]

Two of the night raiders were reported to have been shot down.

Bombs damaged two hospitals. Incendiaries penetrated the dispensary of one hospital but were doused quickly by the staff before the flames reached medical supplies, some of an explosive nature. At the second hospital, two explosives landed on the grounds but did not cause any casualties.

Scores of Fires Started

LONDON, Saturday, Nov. 16 (AP)—German raiders during the night have started scores of fires, leveled apartment houses and buried civilians in the wreckage.

One whole block of apartments caved in, and the casualties were believed to be heavy. Sweating rescuers toiled in the ruins amid falling anti-aircraft shrapnel and bomb explosions. Firemen working their

Continued on Page Three

700 ITALIANS TAKEN AS GREEKS PUSH ON

Drive Is Aimed at Cutting Off Fascisti in South Albania—Koritza Again Bombed

By C. L. SULZBERGER
By Telephone to THE NEW YORK TIMES.

ATHENS, Greece, Nov. 15—Slashing its way further into Albania, the Greek Army completed its second day of full-fledged offensive action tonight by capturing 700 more Italian soldiers and forcing enemy units to retreat on at least two sectors.

Major encounters are obviously occurring, and once again the military communiqué refers to intensive infantry, artillery and aerial action. Three Italian planes were shot down and two Greek aircraft failed to return to their bases, it was said.

The Greek drive is aimed in two directions. The forces on the Epirus and the Pindus fronts are seeking to cut off Italian troops in Southern Albania. These units were heavily concentrated between Porto Edda and Konispolis when the war started. They launched the original attack, the impetus of which carried them considerably south of the Kalamas River.

Having cleaned up the Pindus sector and eliminated the remaining Italian outposts around Mount Smolika, the Greek Army is pushing down the Albanian side of Mount Grammos, north of Konitsa, and fighting through Albania westward in the direction of Porto Edda.

This action is supported by another push from the region of Kalpaki and the march north by the units stationed near the Kalamas

Continued on Page Four

'REVENGE' BY NAZIS

Industrial City Bombed All Night in 'Reply' to R.A.F. Raid on Munich

CATHEDRAL IS DESTROYED

Homes and Shops Bear Brunt of Mass Assault—Military Damage Is Minimized

By RAYMOND DANIELL
Special Cable to THE NEW YORK TIMES.

LONDON, Nov. 15—Daybreak today unveiled scenes of devastation wrought in another night of widespread air raids, but there was nothing to match the bruised and battered face of Coventry, a little Midlands city that was the victim of one of the worst bombardments from the air since the Wright brothers presented wings to mankind.

There the Nazi bombers accomplished what they tried to do to this capital in the early days of the Battle of London, by using as big a force of sky marauders against that compact city of 250,000 as they used against London with its 8,000,000 inhabitants. The tons of bombs they dropped caused at least 1,000 casualties, wrecked countless homes and destroyed the lovely fourteenth-century St. Michael's Cathedral, one of the finest examples of perpendicular architecture left in these islands.

To accomplish the full purpose of the assault, which the Germans said was intended as revenge for the Royal Air Force bombing of Munich while Reichsfuehrer Hitler was speaking there last Friday, Nazi raiders made repeated feints against London to keep the defenders busy while the main body of attackers roared over Midlands industrial centers and concentrated the fury of their bombings on Coventry.

Debris Marks Cathedral Site

Visitors to Coventry today found a scene of devastation where the cathedral once stood. The blackened arches and window faces of fretted stone, for all their disfigurement, still retained traces of their stately grace. But blocks of masonry, heavy pieces of church furniture and plaques commemorating the lives of famous men merged in the common dust heaped up between the teetering walls.

Elsewhere in the city other buildings had been severely damaged. Throughout the day business men and shopkeepers salvaged what remained of their possessions by grubbing among shattered timber and piled-up bricks. Some shopkeepers were doing business on the sidewalks. On roads leading away from the city could be seen a pitiful parade of refugees who were trying to reach billets in the countryside before black-out time.

Coventry lies in the very heart of England, almost equidistant, about ninety miles, from four great ports—Liverpool, Bristol, London and Hull. An industrial center specializing in the manufacture of motor cars and cycles, Coventry is an important cog in Britain's war machine.

But it was not Coventry's factories that took the worst punishment from the raiders, but human life, little homes, churches and hospitals—as it has been everywhere in Britain since the Nazis, forced to fly high above barrage balloons and anti-aircraft guns, began their concentrated bombings.

Scenes of Damage Everywhere

It was impossible today to stroll through many of the streets of the ancient city, where Lady Godiva is said to have made her famous ride, without seeing tragic evidence of the hell loosed from the skies through the night, when bombs crashed at intervals of one or two minutes.

Coventry is now like a city that has been wrecked by an earthquake and swept by fire. Its people looked dazed today as they poked about the ruins of their homes and surveyed the wreckage of the downtown business section, and they laughed bitterly at the chalked mottoes of defiance to Hitler scrawled on pavements and buildings.

The local authorities lost no time in starting to repair the damage and in caring for the injured, homeless and hungry. Herbert Morrison, the Minister of Home Security, was on the scene directing relief operations. Orders were issued for the release of stores of emergency food if necessary, and shopkeepers and wholesalers who normally compete against one another cooperated to assure the distribution of essential supplies.

There was much to be done. Tele-

Continued on Page Three

"All the News That's Fit to Print."

NEWS INDEX, PAGE 35, THIS SECTION

The New York Times.

LATE CITY EDITION
Partly cloudy and continued warm today and tomorrow.
Temperatures Yesterday—Max., 91; Min., 75

Section 1

Copyright, 1941, by The New York Times Company.

VOL. XC..No. 30,465. Entered as Second-Class Matter, Postoffice, New York, N. Y.

NEW YORK, SUNDAY, JUNE 22, 1941.

Including Rotogravure Picture, Magazine and Book Sections. TEN CENTS New York City and Vicinity

HITLER BEGINS WAR ON RUSSIA, WITH ARMIES ON MARCH FROM ARCTIC TO THE BLACK SEA; DAMASCUS FALLS; U.S. OUSTS ROME CONSULS

MUST GO BY JULY 15

Ban on Italians Like Order to German Representatives

U. S. DENIES SPYING

Envoys Told to Protest Axis Charges—Nazis Get 'Moor' Text

By BERTRAM D. HULEN

Special to THE NEW YORK TIMES.

WASHINGTON, June 21—The Italian Embassy was directed by the State Department in a note published today to close all its consular offices and other agencies in this country having connections with the Italian Government by July 15. This was the reply to the Italian demand for the closing of all American Consulates in Italy.

At the same time Sumner Welles, Under-Secretary of State, announced that he had sent to Dr. Hans Thomsen, the German Chargé d'Affaires, the text of President Roosevelt's message to Congress yesterday denouncing the sinking of the American freighter Robin Moor in the South Atlantic on May 21.

This message, which accused Germany of being an international outlaw, engaging in piracy and attempting to intimidate the United States by the sinking and to drive American commerce from the seas, contained notice that this country would not yield before such measures and stated that compensation would be sought for the sinking.

It was transmitted "for the information" of the German Government, but constituted in effect a note of protest. A further communication will be sent asking damages when a final determination has been reached of the extent of damages that should be sought.

Will Deny Improper Acts

In addition, the State Department instructed the American Embassies in Berlin and Rome to inform the respective governments that the United States objects to all allegations of improper acts by American consular officials in those countries and to complete arrangements for the withdrawal of the consular officials and their staffs by July 15, the limit set by the German and Italian Governments.

The Axis governments had charged that the American Consuls had spied for the British. No reply has been made by the State Department to the German protests against the order closing Nazi consulates in this country, but the protest will be rejected. The United States alleged subversive activities as the reason for the demand for them to be closed by July 10.

The notes to the German and Italian Embassies were sent by messenger last night. However, no direct charge of improper activities was made against the Italian consuls in the note Mr. Welles sent to Don Ascanio dei principi Colonna, the Italian Ambassador. He merely stated that the continued functioning of Italian consular establishments within United States territory "would serve no desirable purpose."

In addition, the closing of Italian agencies having connections with the Rome government was requested. The Italian Embassy, as in the earlier case of the German Embassy, was exempted, but the closing of the office of the Italian Commercial Counselor in New York was demanded, along with the consulates.

Welles Note to Colonna

The note from Mr. Welles to Prince Colonna follows:

June 20, 1941

His Excellency
Don Ascanio dei principi Colonna
Royal Italian Ambassador
Excellency:

I have the honor to inform Your Excellency that the President has directed me to request that the Italian Government promptly close all Italian consular establishments within United States territory and remove therefrom all Italian consular of-

Continued on Page Two

Hope Dims for Submarine; Diver Balked at 370 Feet

Knox Believes All 33 Are Dead on the O-9 and Expects Rites at Scene for Navy 'Heroes'—Pressure Halts Descent

By RUSSELL PORTER

Special to THE NEW YORK TIMES.

PORTSMOUTH, N. H., June 21—As hope faded rapidly for the crew of the Submarine O-9, which failed to rise after submerging yesterday morning twenty-four miles east of this city, it became known tonight that the Navy might be unable to complete its salvage operations, and might be compelled to leave the bodies entombed where they lie—440 feet below the surface of the Atlantic.

This theory was based upon the assumption that the two officers and thirty-one men must already be given up as lost, but that assumption has become stronger with every new development since the submarine was reported missing.

Last night cork insulation from the interior of the hull was picked up, showing that at least part of the submarine had collapsed, and early today, after fourteen hours of dragging, grapnels located an object believed to be the sunken craft. Since then no signals from the O-9 have been received on the sensitive sound-detection devices on the salvage ships in response to their repeated messages.

The view that the O-9's fate was sealed was strengthened this afternoon when reporters and photographers, visiting the scene in a Navy press boat, saw one of the Navy's most experienced divers fail in an attempt to reach the O-9 after descending 370 feet, or within seventy feet of where the Navy believes it has located the submarine with grapnel lines.

The diver, George Crocker, 30 years old, of Seattle, asked to be hauled up when he became convinced that he was not getting enough air pressure from his life lines of helium-oxygen mixture to overcome the increasing sea pressure as he went lower and lower.

A message from the Falcon said: "Diver descended 370 feet. Had difficulty in breathing. Brought to surface. Will continue attempts by varying diving techniques."

On the salvage ship the dive was called "the most dangerous in submarine history." It was pointed out that no one had ever made a successful "working" dive at 440 feet and that any diver who went down so far, where he would have to grope his way in complete darkness under terrific sea pressure, 195.8 pounds to the square inch, could do so only at extreme risk to his life.

Colonel Frank Knox, Secretary of the Navy, returning tonight on

Continued on Page Thirty

ARMY ASKS GUARD BE KEPT IN SERVICE

Recommends Congress Act to Hold State Troops, Reserve Officers Indefinitely

By HALLETT ABEND

Special to THE NEW YORK TIMES.

WASHINGTON, June 21—Members of the National Guard and Reserve Officers Corps will be kept in active service beyond the single year planned when they were called, if a recommendation made today by the War Department is approved by President Roosevelt and Congress.

Instead of a return to civilian life, starting Sept. 15, their terms of service in uniform may be extended indefinitely, or at least until the Army selectees have been sufficiently trained in ample numbers to permit the Guardsmen to be demobilized. The recommendation to the President does not specify any limit to the proposed extension of service.

At present there are 289,800 National Guardsmen, including their 21,800 officers, on active duty with the Federal Army. They were inducted into service in increments beginning Sept. 15 of last year. Some went into uniform as late as March of this year. Their terms of service, at time of induction, were limited to twelve months, which may not be extended except by act of Congress.

In addition to the National Guardsmen, who comprise eighteen divisions and one cavalry brigade now on active service, the government has called up 51,500 Reserve officers under the same terms, making collectively 341,300 officers and men who would be affected.

Today's War Department recommendation to the President that steps be taken to retain in the service these Guardsmen and Reserve officers was taken, according to the official announcement, because "the War Department has been flooded with queries from the field" as to whether or not the specified one-year limit of sefvice would hold good or be changed.

"These queries are to be expected," continues the announcement, "because whatever the decision, there are many adjustments which the citizen-soldier must make in his affairs."

Selectees May Be Retained

As yet no decision has been reached in the War Department whether or not to seek authority to retain selectees in the Army beyond the one-year training period specified in the Selective Service Act, but presumably such a step

Continued on Page Nineteen

NAVY MAY REPLACE SHIPYARD STRIKERS

Weighs Putting Own Machinists to Work to End Long Tie-Up in San Francisco

By The Associated Press.

SAN FRANCISCO, June 21—Striking A. F. L. machinists in a $300,000,000 defense program have come to a showdown with the United States Navy and their own international officers.

Reliable reports, not officially denied, indicated that the Navy might install its own machinists in the huge Bethlehem shipyards Monday if the local union did not heed the order of its international president to call off the strike by that time.

The same reports indicated that the Army also might be on hand

Continued on Page Twenty-eight

The International Situation

SUNDAY, JUNE 22, 1941

At 5:30 o'clock this morning, Berlin time, two statements were read over the German radio that constituted a declaration of war upon the Soviet Union by Germany. A proclamation of Adolf Hitler, read by Propaganda Minister Goebbels, said that Russia, with Britain and the United States, had sought to "throttle" Germany and that he had therefore decided to put the fate of the German people in the hands of the army. A statement by Foreign Minister von Ribbentrop contained the actual declaration of war. The Finns and the Rumanians were mentioned as allies. Berlin reported subsequently that troops were on the march in East Prussia. [Page 1, Column 8; with map.]

Yesterday was a good day for British arms.

In the Syrian campaign Damascus was occupied. The British announced its capture and Vichy reported its evacuation to avoid street fighting and destruction of the city. Another British force was pushing nearer Beirut, supported by the fleet and the air arm, while a third column was moving toward Tadmur. [Page 1, Column 5; Map on Page 12.]

No less encouraging to the British was a victory much closer to home in the largest British daylight air attack of the war. In a sweep two waves of 150 planes each pounded the French Channel coast, going particularly for airdromes, and engaged German air defenses. The British reported downing twenty-six Nazi planes in these attacks for a loss of five of their own. Late last night the British were continuing their attacks across the Channel. [Page 1, Column 4; Map, Page 18.]

The Libyan theatre was quiet, but British pressure in East Africa was indicated by a protest from Vichy against what was declared to be a virtual ultimatum from General Wavell to French Somaliland to join the Free French or suffer an intensified blockade. London confirmed the representations of General Wavell. [Page 14, Column 1.]

Washington continued the accelerated pace of its anti-Axis diplomatic offensive. The Italian Embassy was instructed to close the forty-nine Italian consulates and seven agencies in this country before July 15. President Roosevelt's message to Congress on the Robin Moor was handed to the German Embassy while the State Department instructed the United States embassies in Berlin and Rome to inform those governments that the United States objected categorically to any allegations of improper acts by United States consuls. [Page 1, Column 1.]

Italian consular circles here were silent concerning the Washington order, but Italian anti-Fascist quarters expressed jubilation. [Page 3, Column 1.]

R. A. F. BLASTS FOE

Bags 26 Nazi Planes in Record Day Raids on Invasion Coast

GERMANY IS BOMBED

British on 11th Straight Night Offensive Into Western Reich

Special Cable to THE NEW YORK TIMES.

LONDON, Sunday, June 22—Twenty-six Nazi fighter planes were destroyed in daylight yesterday by Royal Air Force fliers on their fifth straight day of raiding the Germans' invasion coast and air bases in Northern France.

Twice before dark, waves of R. A. F. warcraft—reportedly numbering at least 150 planes each—swept over the Channel in offensive operations.

Bombers attacked the Nazi's airdromes on each occasion while strong forces of fighters blasted the way for the big planes through formations of German defense fighters. While the major raids were going on, other strong R. A. F. units patrolled over the French coast and battled Messerschmitts.

Attack Goes On; Big Bombs Used

Last night and early this morning the R. A. F. was still attacking the invasion coast, using some of the latest type of high-powered bombs.

Explosions rolled across the Channel like peals of thunder, shaking the ground and rocking buildings for miles along the Kentish coast, observers there reported.

A night curtain of fog hung over the Strait of Dover and little could be seen of the raids. The latest British attacks were apparently being made in the Boulogne area, where some of the heaviest daylight bombing was carried out.

Meanwhile R. A. F. bomber forces were again attacking Western Germany, officials here said briefly early today. The attacks marked the eleventh consecutive night in which the British have bombed industrial centers and war bases in the Reich.

Two Nazi bombers were shot down during the night in small scattered enemy raids on the east and southeast coasts of England. A few German bombs were reported dropped there; there were no accounts of casualties or damage.

The R. A. F. coastal patrol squadrons reported destroying at least two enemy planes and one Nazi

Continued on Page Eighteen

SYRIAN CITY TAKEN

French Withdraw After a Hard Fight—British Closer to Beirut

TADMUR PUSH IS ON

Allied Planes Harassing Vichy Troops, Whose Defense Falters

By C. L. SULZBERGER

By Telephone to THE NEW YORK TIMES.

ANKARA, Turkey, June 21—French troops evacuated the city of Damascus today after a persistent bombardment by British artillery and withdrew to new positions outside the Syrian capital, according to official advices from Beirut. Early in the afternoon it was learned that the Allied vanguard was already beginning to enter the city. This evening the British reported complete occupation.

The Damascus airport at Mezze has been taken by Indian detachments of the Allied forces and one of the key points east of Damascus has been surrounded by Druz tribesmen fighting on the side of the British.

The Beirut radio announced tonight that a British motorized column pushing westward from Iraq was now heading toward Tadmur. The British column, it was said, has been bombed constantly by the French Air Force, which has just been reorganized and reinforced by French squadrons coming from North Africa. Some German planes also were said to have arrived in Syria.

Advance in High Gear

It is clear that the Allied advance is beginning to move into high gear. Unconfirmed reports that the British forces have reached Beirut indicate that it may also fall soon. Beirut's fate depends largely on whether the British will call in their superior naval forces to shell the city proper. So far this has been avoided in order to keep damage and casualties at a minimum.

[A dispatch from Cairo said that Australian forces had been progressing toward Beirut for two days and had passed Ras Damour.]

The Allies, convinced of the seriousness of the French resistance, evidently have begun to fight this undeclared war in earnest and intend to get it over with fast at any cost. The main center of French resistance in the east has been Damascus, and the capture of the city is of great importance.

The Allied counter-move to the French attack in the south, which developed earlier in the week, is now proceeding with dispatch in the Merdjayoun district. The fortress of Merdjayoun is in Allied hands and it is obvious that the region is being rapidly cleared, since the coastal advance is dependent to a large degree on a corollary advance in the center.

Considerable concentrations of French artillery had been brought up around Damascus. The French dug in and placed batteries in many of the villas and gardens in the outer sections of the city. These batteries were slowly picked off by British gunners with Royal Air Force support, but the principal British effort was artillery shelling. The British sought to avoid excess damage by aerial bombardment, which is less accurate than artillery fire.

Tadmur Believed Periled

The French admission that a British column is pressing toward Tadmur would seem to indicate that perhaps the town is endangered. Several days ago reliable sources here reported the existence of the column, but this was steadfastly denied by Beirut.

While there have been new reports that the trouble for the British in Iraq is far from over, the fact that they are able to spare considerable forces from there would indicate that everything is under control. It is known that British forces also are working westward along the North Syrian frontier toward Aleppo, but the exact strength of these units is not known here.

British military circles admit that the Syrian adventure can no longer

Continued on Page Twelve

WHERE GERMAN ARMIES MARCH ON RUSSIA

The German declaration of hostilities against Russia, made this morning, indicated that the attack would be made from Narvik in the north of Norway, to the Carpathian Mts. in the Balkans.

The Hitler Proclamation

The text of Adolf Hitler's proclamation, as recorded here by Columbia Broadcasting System, follows:

It was a difficult step for me to send my Minister to Moscow in order to attend to work against the policy of encirclement of Britain.

I hoped that at last it would be possible to put away tension.

Germany never intended to occupy Lithuania. The defeat of Poland induced me to again address a peace offer to the Allies. This was declined because Britain was still hoping to bring about European coalition.

That is why Cripps [Sir Stafford Cripps, British Ambassador] was sent to Moscow. He was commissioned under all circumstances to come to an agreement with Moscow. Russia always put out the lying statement that she was protecting these countries [evidently Lithuania, Estonia and Latvia, the Baltic States].

The penetration of Russia into Rumania and the Greek liaison with England threatened to place new, large areas into the war. Rumania, however, believed she was able to accede to Russia only if she received guarantees from Germany and Italy for the remainder of the country. With a heavy heart, I did this, for if Germany gives guarantees, she will fulfill them. We are neither Englishmen nor Jews.

I asked Molotoff [Soviet Foreign Commissar V. M. Molotoff] to come to Berlin, and he asked for a clarification of the situation. He asked, "Is the guarantee for Rumania directed also against Russia?"

I replied, "Against every one."

And Russia never informed us that she had even more far-reaching intentions against Rumania.

Molotoff asked further, "Is Germany prepared not to assist Finland, who was again threatening Russia?"

My reply was that Germany has no political interests in Finland, but another attack on Finland could not be tolerated, especially as we do not believe that Finland is threatening Russia.

Molotoff's third question was, "Is Germany agreeable that Russia give guarantees to Bulgaria?"

My reply was that Bulgaria is a sovereign State and I did not know that Bulgaria needed guarantees. Molotoff said Russia needed a passage through the Dardanelles and demanded bases in the Bosporus.

A few days later she [Russia] concluded the well known friendship agreement which was to incite the Serbs against Germany. Moscow demanded the mobilization of the Serbian Army.

When I still was silent, the men in the Kremlin went one step further. Russia offered to deliver war material against Germany. This was at the same time that I advised Matsuoka [Japanese Foreign Minister Yosuke Matsuoka] to bring about a lessening of the tension with Russia.

Serbian officers flew to Russia, where they were received as allies. Victory of the Axis in the Balkans at first foiled the plan to involve Germany in a long war and then, together with England and with the hope of American supplies, to throttle Germany.

Now the moment has come when I can no longer look at this development. Waiting would be a crime against Germany.

For weeks the Russians have been committing frontier violations. Russian planes have been crossing the frontier again and again to prove that they are the masters. On the night of June 17 and again on June 18 there was large patrol activity.

The march of the German Armies has no precedent. Together with the Finns we stand from Narvik to the Carparthians. At the Danube and on the shores of the Black Sea under Antonescu [Rumanian Dictator Ion Antonescu], German and Rumanian soldiers are united.

The task is to safeguard Europe and thus save all.

I have therefore today decided to give the fate of the German people and the Reich and of Europe again into the hands of our soldiers.

BAD FAITH CHARGED

Goebbels Reads Attack on Soviet—Ribbentrop Announces War

BALTIC MADE ISSUE

Finns and Rumanians Are Called Allies in Plan of Assault

Statement by von Ribbentrop is printed on Page 6.

By C. BROOKS PETERS

By Telephone to THE NEW YORK TIMES.

BERLIN, Sunday, June 22—As dawn broke over Europe today the legions of the National Socialist Germany began their long-rumored invasion of Communist Soviet Russia. The non-aggression and amity pact between the two countries, signed in August, 1939, forgotten, the German attack began along a tremendous front, extending from the Arctic regions to the Black Sea. Marching with the forces of Germany are also the troops of Finland and Rumania.

Adolf Hitler, in a proclamation to the German people read over a national hook-up by Propaganda Minister Dr. Joseph Goebbels at 5:30 this morning, termed the military action begun this morning the largest in the history of the world. It was necessary, he added, because in spite of his unceasing efforts to preserve peace in this area it had definitely been proved that Russia was in a coalition with England to ruin Germany by prolonging the war.

[The German radio announced early today that documentary proof would shortly be given of a secret British-Russian alliance, made behind Germany's back.]

Designed "to Save Reich"

The German action, Herr Hitler explained to his fellow-National Socialists, is designed to save the Reich and with it all Europe from the machinations of the Jewish-Anglo-Saxon warmongers.

The German Foreign Minister, Joachim von Ribbentrop, followed Dr. Goebbels on the air with a declaration of the Reich Government read before the foreign correspondents in the Foreign Office. Herr von Ribbentrop said he received V. G. Dekanosoff, the Russian Ambassador, this morning and informed him that in spite of the Russian-German non-aggression pact of Aug. 23, 1939, an amity pact of Sept. 28, 1939, Russia had betrayed the trust that the Reich had placed in her.

Proclamation Heard Here

The announcements made in Berlin were heard here by short wave listening stations of both the Columbia and National Broadcasting Systems.

Adolf Hitler's proclamation was followed by a statement containing a formal declaration of war by the Nazi Foreign Minister, Joachim von Ribbentrop.

Berlin announced that the German Army was on the march, and that "German troops all along the Russian border from the Baltic to the Balkans are moving into their last-minute positions."

A London broadcast by the British Broadcasting Corporation, however, formally denied that report.

"It can be definitely stated," said the BBC, "that no actual troop movements on the part of either Germany or Russia have as yet taken place."

Moscow Reports Accord

The only word from Moscow, received several hours after the German announcement, was a London report of a statement issued in the Russian capital declaring that the Soviet and Great Britain were now "in full accord" on the international situation.

Herr Hitler's proclamation, read by Dr. Goebbels at 5:30 A. M., Berlin time, include a vicious attack on the Reich's former associate in European policy, and a charge that Russia had acted in

Continued on Page Seven

"All the News That's Fit to Print."

The New York Times.

LATE CITY EDITION
Cloudy and somewhat warmer today with occasional showers. Tomorrow showers, moderately warm.
Temperatures Yesterday—Max., 76; Min., 54

VOL. XC....No. 30,519. Entered as Second-Class Matter, Postoffice, New York, N. Y. NEW YORK, FRIDAY, AUGUST 15, 1941. THREE CENTS NEW YORK CITY and Vicinity

ROOSEVELT, CHURCHILL DRAFT 8 PEACE AIMS, PLEDGING DESTRUCTION OF NAZI TYRANNY; JOINT STEPS BELIEVED CHARTED AT PARLEY

TREASURY WEIGHS INCREASED RATE OF SECURITY TAX

Doubled Levy and Broader Base Are Considered as Curb on Inflation, Says Morgenthau

DISMISSAL PLAN IS URGED

It Would 'Cushion' Workers in Defense After Arming Ends —House to Get Projects

By JOHN MacCORMAC
Special to THE NEW YORK TIMES.

WASHINGTON, Aug. 14—Secretary Morgenthau stated today that the Treasury was studying the question of higher social security taxes on a broader basis and the supplementing of them by a "dismissal" wage with a view to preventing inflation now and providing a cushion against post-war dislocation.

He said that he had intended to suggest such a plan to the House Banking and Currency Committee if that body had not postponed his appearance from today to Sept. 15.

Mr. Morgenthau explained that the Treasury had considered various means of controlling inflation, including the restriction of installment buying and fixing of prices which already have been decided on, the diminution of consumer purchasing power by the sale of defense bonds and higher taxes, and lastly an increase in social security contributions.

Bank Reserves Under Scrutiny

He hinted that still another method of restricting credit might ultimately be tried, admitting that excess bank reserves required "careful watching." This was the first intimation from Treasury circles that the proposals of the Federal Reserve Board in January for increased powers to increase bank reserve requirements might have merit.

What the Treasury contemplates, it was explained, is an increase not in unemployment contributions but in the Social Security old-age benefit tax of 1 per cent on employer and employe. In the last fiscal year this realized $690,000,000.

According to the original act it was to have been increased to 1½ per cent in 1940-41-42, to 2 per cent in 1943, to 2½ per cent in 1946-47-48 and to 3 per cent after 1949. Because of the recession in 1938, however, Secretary Morgenthau and Marriner S. Eccles, Governor of the Federal Reserve Board, recommended that it be kept at 1 per cent to prevent deflation.

Effect of Tax Rise Is Told

If the tax were increased to 2 per cent it would mean, as a result of the increase in payrolls brought about by defense activity, that at least $1,500,000,000 would be withdrawn this year from purchasing power.

Since the Treasury contemplates broadening the scope of the act to bring in agricultural, domestic and other workers not now covered, the amount would be greater. An increase to 3 per cent would be a $2,500,000,000 bulwark against inflation.

Addition of a "dismissal tax" equivalent to three months' pay for every worker when the war ends would increase still more substantially the amount to be levied and thus to be withdrawn from consumer purchasing power, it was said.

Mr. Morgenthau said that th. Treasury was studying the whole question of Social Security rather than enforced savings.

"I also think," he said, "we should move in the direction of what some people call 'a separation wage.' A certain percentage can be set toward which employer and employe contribute and build up

Continued on Page Nine

Defense Plant Cost Is $3,549,770,000

By The Associated Press.

WASHINGTON, Aug. 14—New industrial plants and expansions to existing ones authorized since the beginning of the defense program number 2,082, government statisticians estimated today, and their cost will aggregate $3,549,770,000.

The government is committed to plant financing totaling $2,720,936,000, and private financing will amount to $828,834,000. For the most part the financing by private sources has been limited to the smaller projects.

U. A. W. BARS REDS FROM UNION POSTS

Ban on Nazis, Fascists and Communists Is Voted After Bitter Debate in Buffalo

By LOUIS STARK
Special to THE NEW YORK TIMES.

BUFFALO, Aug. 14—After two and a half hours of turbulent debate, the United Automobile Workers-C. I. O. convention tonight adopted a strong declaration amending the constitution to bar from office members of Communist, Fascist or Nazi organizations.

Opponents of the proposal who insisted on a roll call vote found that they had been beaten by 1950 to 920, according to an unofficial tabulation.

The report which was adopted, referred to as a "super-minority" report, offered by Harvey Kitzman of Racine, Wis., went farther than the majority report, which would have banned from office supporters "of any organization whose loyalty is to a foreign government." The latter report did not mention Communists, Nazis or Fascists by name.

Opponents of the resolution which was adopted urged its defeat because it would be a sign of support for Philip Murray and John L. Lewis, respectively president and ex-president of the C. I. O., and would show that the delegates were

Continued on Page Thirty-six

NAZIS GAIN IN SOUTH

Seize Iron Ore Center—See Ukraine Army in Hopeless Trap

SOVIET ADMITS LOSS

Yields 2 Defense Bases, but Says Germans Pay 'Terrible Price'

By C. BROOKS PETERS
By Telephone to THE NEW YORK TIMES.

BERLIN, Aug. 14—In a special communiqué issued from Reichsfuehrer Hitler's field headquarters somewhere on the Eastern Front the Germans declared this evening that the defense of the Western Ukraine by the Russian armed forces was facing complete collapse.

German, Rumanian, Hungarian and Italian troops were said to be in relentless pursuit of the Soviet armies, pushing them southward between the Dniester and Dnieper Rivers toward the Black Sea. Odessa was reported to be encircled by Rumanian troops and Nikolaev, after Odessa the most important Ukrainian port, beleaguered from east and west by German and Hungarian units.

[The Russians acknowledged that they had abandoned Pervomaisk and Kirovograd, important towns in the defense of Odessa. It appeared that the Ukraine army's escape across the Dnieper had become doubtful. Moscow, however, denied that Odessa was encircled and reported the drives toward Leningrad checked. The Soviet press listed more than thirty Nazi divisions as having been wiped out or badly smashed.]

In the drive toward the lower regions of the Dnieper German motorized forces were officially reported to have occupied the Krivoy Rog iron ore area, which supplies the important Donets basic industrial sector east of the Dnieper.

Continued on Page Eight

International Situation

FRIDAY, AUGUST 15, 1941

Out of an unprecedented series of secret conferences between the President of the United States and the Prime Minister of Britain somewhere on the Atlantic, with American naval planes circling overhead, there emerged yesterday a joint declaration of peace aims, indications of new steps to speed up material aid to Britain and Russia and the probability that an understanding had been reached for fuller Anglo-American cooperation in dealing with the Far East, France and other storm centers throughout the world.

The joint declaration evolved at the dramatic meeting, which was attended by the Army, Navy and Air chiefs of both nations, consisted of an eight-point program founded on "the final destruction of the Nazi tyranny." One of the points stated that aggressor and potential aggressor nations must be completely disarmed pending the establishment of a "permanent system of general security." [All the foregoing, Page 1, Column 8.]

London quarters saw greater significance in the fact that the meeting was held and in its undisclosed decisions than in the eight-point program, which, however, won approval. It was assumed that the discussions centered on matters more pressing than peace aims. [Page 1, Column 4.]

One of the participants in the conferences, Lord Beaverbrook, Britain's Minister of Supply, arrived in Washington by plane to arrange for shipment of tanks, planes and foodstuffs in "the largest possible" quantities. [Page 4, Column 1.] His arrival heightened expectations in the capital that the Administration would move quickly to increase aid to all the nations resisting aggression. Predictions were made that the President would seek from $7,000,000,000 to $10,000,000,000 more for the lease-lend program. Congressional reaction to the conferences was overwhelmingly favorable. [Page 1, Column 7.]

In Berlin an official spokesman pooh-poohed the meeting as a "propaganda bluff," and official circles described the eight-point program as an "unhappy" reminder of President Wilson's fourteen points. [Page 5, Column 1.] The Italian reaction was largely one of relief that the conferences had not produced a more drastic move. [Page 5, Column 6.] Vichy circles followed the German line by likening the peace aims disparagingly to those of the World War President. [Page 5, Column 2.]

In the Russo-German war a special Berlin communiqué reported that the complete collapse of Russian forces in the Western Ukraine had been sealed by deep thrusts behind their lines. The communiqué declared that Odessa and Nikolaev, another port near by, were encircled. The capture of the Krivoy Rog iron ore area, which was said to produce 61 per cent of Russia's ore output, also was announced. [Page 1, Column 3; Map, Page 2.]

A Soviet communiqué admitted that Russian troops had been forced to abandon two key points in the area guarding Odessa and Nikolaev, about 100 miles above the Black Sea coast. [Page 8, Column 2.]

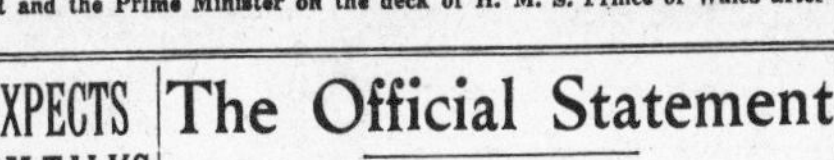

HISTORIC MEETING AT SEA BETWEEN MR. ROOSEVELT AND MR. CHURCHILL
The President and the Prime Minister on the deck of H. M. S. Prince of Wales after church services last Sunday
Associated Press Wirephoto

TALKS HELD AT SEA

Closer War Cooperation to Doom Aggressors Pledged by Leaders

SOVIET AID INCLUDED

Disarmament of Axis Is Envisaged in a World Freed From Want

By FRANK L. KLUCKHOHN
Special to THE NEW YORK TIMES.

WASHINGTON, Aug. 14—A joint declaration of eight bases for world peace to follow "final destruction of the Nazi tyranny" was made public through Washington and London today in the names of President Roosevelt and Prime Minister Winston Churchill after a series of historic and dramatic conferences between the two leaders somewhere on the Atlantic.

The chiefs of the United States and British Governments insisted that aggressor and potential aggressor nations must be completely disarmed and they made clear that there would be closer Anglo-American cooperation in the war effort, at least as far as the production and distribution of modern sinews of war, including those to be provided to the Soviet Union, were concerned.

Mr. Roosevelt and Mr. Churchill held out for all peoples, including those of the nations that are now aggressors, an equal part in a better world after the elimination or defeat of Reichsfuehrer Hitler. This would have its base in opportunity to work in peace and justice and in the right of all peoples to have access to raw materials through lowering of trade barriers. The declaration indicated that there was to be no harsh retribution for the common people in Axis countries.

Further Statements Expected

This statement was expected by official Washington to be followed by further declarations and actions setting forth definitive Anglo-American policies concerning the Far East, France and other key regions and making clearer the exact extent and form of Anglo-American collaboration.

The President and the Prime Minister were assisted at their conferences, presumably held with due ceremony, by "high-ranking" army, navy and air officers of both countries. It would cause surprise in official circles if military situations and problems in all parts of the world had not been canvassed and decisions taken.

The Roosevelt-Churchill statement was silent regarding such matters, however, and Secretary of State Cordell Hull refrained in his press conference today from direct answers to questions on what decisions, if any, had been taken on the prosecution of the war and whether the United States would play a more belligerent part.

Hitlerite Peril Studied

The only hint on this subject was an assertion in the declaration that the President and the Prime Minister "in several" meetings had "considered the dangers to world civilization arising from the policies of military domination by conquest upon which the Hitlerite government of Germany and other governments associated therewith have embarked, and have made clear the steps which their countries are respectively taking for their safety in the face of these dangers."

That the conferences, from which the veil of secrecy was only partly torn, would result in action was indicated by the arrival in Washington today of Lord Beaverbrook, British Minister of Supply, who took part in the Roosevelt-Churchill talks and who, the joint statement said, will confer with United States officials on the "whole problem of the supply of munitions of war."

President Roosevelt is expected

Continued on Page Two

LONDON EXPECTS MORE FROM TALKS

Britons Believe Discussion of War Aid, Still Secret, Will Prove Important

By ROBERT P. POST
Wireless to THE NEW YORK TIMES.

LONDON, Aug. 14—The fact that Prime Minister Winston Churchill and President Roosevelt have met is regarded in Great Britain as far more important than anything that was announced as the outcome of their meeting.

The British took full note of the eight-point peace program the two statesmen released after their three-day meeting at sea, but it would have pleased most Britons far more if a little less had been said in the vaguest terms.

In fact, some quarters felt a sort of shiver when they compared the eight-point Roosevelt-Churchill program with President Wilson's fourteen points. At least, some persons said, Mr. Wilson had fourteen points instead of eight and some of them suggested specific changes.

But the measure of disappointment apparent in London tonight can perhaps be best judged in the light of what the statement left unsaid rather than what it said. Leaving out the entire question of statement as to the future it would appear obvious that the important fact is that Mr. Roosevelt and his chief military and diplomatic advisers conferred with Mr. Churchill and his heads of staff.

There are few persons in these islands who think that Mr. Churchill at great personal risk and inconvenience crossed the Atlantic to consult with Mr. Roosevelt on such statement as "their countries seek no aggrandizement, territorial or other." Mr. Churchill made the trip at President Roosevelt's personal request. But even at that request he would hardly have made the trip just to produce a set of war aims such as Lord Privy Seal Clement R. Attlee announced today.

Therefore, it is generally agreed here that the real purpose of the conference was how and where the United States and Britain could best work together to defeat Germany.

That statement implies that the two men discussed military plans, including not only the future of Iceland but the possible seizure of other bases by the United States.

It implies also that the whole question of United States supplies to Britain. If any proof of this is

Continued on Page Four

The Official Statement

By The United Press.

WASHINGTON, Aug. 14—The text of the official statement on the Roosevelt-Churchill meeting follows:

The President of the United States and the Prime Minister, Mr. Churchill, representing His Majesty's Government in the United Kingdom, have met at sea.

They have been accompanied by officials of their two governments, including high ranking officers of their military, naval and air services.

The whole problem of the supply of munitions of war, as provided by the Lease-Lend Act, for the armed forces of the United States and for those countries actively engaged in resisting aggression has been further examined.

Lord Beaverbrook, the Minister of Supply of the British Government, has joined in these conferences. He is going to proceed to Washington to discuss further details with appropriate officials of the United States Government. These conferences will also cover the supply problems of the Soviet Union.

The President and the Prime Minister have had several conferences. They have considered the dangers to world civilization arising from the policies of military domination by conquest upon which the Hitlerite government of Germany and other governments associated therewith have embarked, and have made clear the steps which their countries are respectively taking for their safety in the face of these dangers.

They have agreed upon the following joint declaration:

The President of the United States of America and the Prime Minister, Mr. Churchill, representing His Majesty's Government in the United Kingdom, being met together, deem it right to make known certain common principles in the national policies of their respective countries on which they base their hopes for a better future for the world.

FIRST, their countries seek no aggrandizement, territorial or other;

SECOND, they desire to see no territorial changes that do not accord with the freely expressed wishes of the peoples concerned;

THIRD, they respect the right of all peoples to choose the form of government under which they will live; and they wish to see sovereign rights and self-government restored to those who have been forcibly deprived of them;

FOURTH, they will endeavor, with due respect for their existing obligations, to further the enjoyment by all States, great or small, victor or vanquished, of access, on equal terms, to the trade and to the raw materials of the world which are needed for their economic prosperity;

FIFTH, they desire to bring about the fullest collaboration between all nations in the economic field with the object of securing, for all, improved labor standards, economic adjustment and social security;

SIXTH, after the final destruction of the Nazi tyranny, they hope to see established a peace which will afford to all nations the means of dwelling in safety within their own boundaries, and which will afford assurance that all the men in all the lands may live out their lives in freedom from fear and want;

SEVENTH, such a peace should enable all men to traverse the high seas and oceans without hindrance;

EIGHTH, they believe that all of the nations of the world, for realistic as well as spiritual reasons, must come to the abandonment of the use of force. Since no future peace can be maintained if land, sea or air armaments continue to be employed by nations which threaten, or may threaten, aggression outside of their frontiers, they believe, pending the establishment of a wider and permanent system of general security, that the disarmament of such nations is essential. They will likewise aid and encourage all other practicable measures which will lighten for peace-loving peoples the crushing burden of armaments.

FRANKLIN D. ROOSEVELT.
WINSTON S. CHURCHILL.

ANOTHER AID BILL IS SEEN IN CAPITAL

Reaction to Roosevelt-Churchill Parley Is Largely Favorable —Some Criticism Sharp

By TURNER CATLEDGE
Special to THE NEW YORK TIMES.

WASHINGTON, Aug. 14—Expectations of new moves by the United States Government to enlarge and accelerate material aid to Great Britain, Russia and China and other countries that may later resist the aggressions of the Axis powers sprang high in Washington today following disclosure of the Roosevelt-Churchill meeting at sea.

They were heightened even further by the arrival early this afternoon of Lord Beaverbrook, the British Minister of Supply, who flew here directly from the Roosevelt-Churchill conference with a view to discussing expansion of material aid with American officials. He announced at a press conference that he had come to the United States to get tanks, airplanes and foods in quantities as large as the United States could supply, adding that Britain was able now to use all the equipment she could get.

Predictions that the Administration would soon request a new lease-lend appropriation of $7,000,000,000 to $10,000,000,000 were heard immediately at the Capitol, where the Roosevelt-Churchill statement caused practical legislators to look more to what it forecast for the immediate future than to the post-war aims outlined therein.

Reaction to the statement was overwhelmingly favorable among those who expressed themselves despite the expected criticism from opponents of the President's foreign policy. Among these, however, there was a question whether to accept the discussions of President Roosevelt and Prime Minister Winston Churchill as in reality a "peace offensive" on the part of the democracies br to brand them as another step toward active participation by the United States in the war.

There was considerable reluctance among members of Congress to discuss the sea meeting at all until more details concerning its setting and purpose had been disclosed; also there was an undertone of disappointment, which spread through various groups, that the President had not taken Congress and the people more into his confidence in this latest stroke of diplomacy.

One of the most outspoken critics

Continued on Page Three

"All the News That's Fit to Print."

The New York Times.

Copyright, 1941, by The New York Times Company.

LATE CITY EDITION
Increasing cloudiness with rising temperature today. Tomorrow cloudy, somewhat colder.
Temperatures Yesterday—Max., 34; Min., 25

VOL. XCI No. 30,634. Entered as Second-Class Matter, Postoffice, New York, N. Y. NEW YORK, MONDAY, DECEMBER 8, 1941. THREE CENTS NEW YORK CITY and Vicinity

JAPAN WARS ON U. S. AND BRITAIN; MAKES SUDDEN ATTACK ON HAWAII; HEAVY FIGHTING AT SEA REPORTED

CONGRESS DECIDED

Roosevelt Will Address It Today and Find It Ready to Vote War

CONFERENCE IS HELD

Legislative Leaders and Cabinet in Sober White House Talk

By C. P. TRUSSELL

Special to THE NEW YORK TIMES.

WASHINGTON, Dec. 7—President Roosevelt will address a joint session of Congress tomorrow and will find the membership in a mood to vote any steps he asks in connection with the developments in the Pacific.

The President will appear personally at 12:30 P. M. Whether he would call for a flat declaration of war again Japan was left unannounced tonight. But leaders of Congress, shocked and angered by the Japanese attacks, were talking of a declaration of war on not only Japan but on the entire Axis.

The plans for action tomorrow were made tonight in a White House conference at which the President, surrounded by his Cabinet and by Congressional leaders of both parties, went through reports, some official, some unconfirmed, of the continued assaults of the Japanese upon American Pacific outposts.

Meet Far Into Night

The conference lasted until after 11 o'clock and at its close an official statement was issued. This said that the President had reviewed for his conferees the latest advices from the Pacific and declared:

"It should be emphasized that the message to Congress has not yet been written and its tenor will, of course, depend on further information received between 11 o'clock tonight and noon tomorrow. Further news is coming in all the time."

Congressional leaders asserted as they left the White House that they did not know what the President would say tomorrow.

"Will the President ask for a declaration of war?" Speaker Rayburn was asked.

"He didn't say," answered the Speaker.

Asked whether Congress would support a declaration of war, Mr. Rayburn observed:

"I think that is one thing on which there would be unity."

Politics Declared Dropped

"There is no politics here," said Representative Joseph W. Martin Jr., Minority House Leader. "There is only one party when it comes to the integrity and honor of the country."

"The Republicans," said Senator Charles L. McNary of Oregon, the Senate minority leader, "will all go along, in my opinion, with whatever is done."

Unless international developments and plans changed overnight, it was indicated, the Presidential recommendations would be directed for the present, at least, at Japan only. This was asserted authoritatively in the face of widespread expectation that any

Continued on Page Six

TOKYO ACTS FIRST

Declaration Follows Air and Sea Attacks on U. S. and Britain

TOGO CALLS ENVOYS

After Fighting Is On, Grew Gets Japan's Reply to Hull Note of Nov. 26

By The Associated Press.

TOKYO, Monday, Dec. 8—Japan went to war against the United States and Britain today with air and sea attacks against Hawaii, followed by a formal declaration of hostilities.

Japanese Imperial headquarters announced at 6 A. M. [4 P. M. Sunday, Eastern standard time] that a state of war existed among these nations in the Western Pacific, as of dawn.

Soon afterward, Domei, the Japanese official news agency, announced that "naval operations are progressing off Hawaii, with at least one Japanese aircraft carrier in action against Pearl Harbor," the American naval base in the islands.

Japanese bombers were declared to have raided Honolulu at 7:35 A. M. Hawaii time [1:05 Sunday, Eastern standard time].

Premier-War Minister General Hideki Tojo held a twenty-minute Cabinet session at his official residence at 7 A. M.

Soon afterward it was announced that both the United States Ambassador, Joseph C. Grew, and the British Ambassador, Sir Robert Leslie Craigie, had been summoned by Foreign Minister Shigenori Togo.

The Foreign Minister, Domei said, handed to Mr. Grew the Japanese Government's formal reply to the note sent to Japan by United States Secretary of State Cordell Hull on Nov. 26.

[In the course of the diplomatic negotiations leading up to yesterday's events, the Domei agency had stated that Japan could not accept the premises of Mr. Hull's note.]

Sir Robert was summoned by

Continued on Page Five

PACIFIC OCEAN: THEATRE OF WAR INVOLVING UNITED STATES AND ITS ALLIES

Shortly after the outbreak of hostilities an American ship sent a distress call from (1) and a United States Army transport carrying lumber was torpedoed at (2). The most important action was at Hawaii (3), where Japanese planes bombed the great Pearl Harbor base. Also attacked was Guam (4). From Manila (6) United States bombers roared northward, while some parts of the Philippines were raided, as was Hong Kong, to the northwest. At Shanghai (5) a British gunboat was sunk and an American gunboat seized. To the south, in the Malaya area (7), the British bombed Japanese ships, Tokyo forces attempted landings on British territory and Singapore underwent an air raid. Distances between key Pacific points are shown on the map in statute miles.

GUAM BOMBED; ARMY SHIP IS SUNK

U. S. Fliers Head North From Manila—Battleship Oklahoma Set Afire by Torpedo Planes at Honolulu

104 SOLDIERS KILLED AT FIELD IN HAWAII

President Fears 'Very Heavy Losses' on Oahu—Churchill Notifies Japan That a State of War Exists

By FRANK L. KLUCKHOHN

Special to THE NEW YORK TIMES.

WASHINGTON, Monday, Dec. 8—Sudden and unexpected attacks on Pearl Harbor, Honolulu, and other United States possessions in the Pacific early yesterday by the Japanese air force and navy plunged the United States and Japan into active war.

The initial attack in Hawaii, apparently launched by torpedo-carrying bombers and submarines, caused widespread damage and death. It was quickly followed by others. There were unconfirmed reports that German raiders participated in the attacks.

Guam also was assaulted from the air, as were Davao, on the island of Mindanao, and Camp John Hay, in Northern Luzon, both in the Philippines. Lieut. Gen. Douglas MacArthur, commanding the United States Army of the Far East, reported there was little damage, however.

[Japanese parachute troops had been landed in the Philippines and native Japanese had seized some communities, Royal Arch Gunnison said in a broadcast from Manila today to WOR-Mutual. He reported without detail that "in the naval war the ABCD fleets under American command appeared to be successful" against Japanese invasions.]

Japanese submarines, ranging out over the Pacific, sank an American transport carrying lumber 1,300 miles from San Francisco, and distress signals were heard from a freighter 700 miles from that city.

The War Department reported that 104 soldiers died and 300 were wounded as a result of the attack on Hickam Field, Hawaii. The National Broadcasting Company reported from Honolulu that the battleship Oklahoma was afire. [Domei, Japanese news-agency, reported the Oklahoma sunk.]

Nation Placed on Full War Basis

The news of these surprise attacks fell like a bombshell on Washington. President Roosevelt immediately ordered the country and the Army and Navy onto a full war footing. He arranged at a White House conference last night to address a joint session of Congress at noon today, presumably to ask for declaration of a formal state of war.

This was disclosed after a long special Cabinet meeting, which was joined later by Congressional leaders. These leaders predicted "action" within a day.

After leaving the White House conference Attorney General Francis Biddle said that "a resolution" would be introduced in Congress tomorrow. He would not amplify or affirm that it would be for a declaration of war.

Congress probably will "act" within the day, and he will call the Senate Foreign Relations Committee for this purpose, Chairman Tom Connally announced.

[A United Press dispatch from London this morning said that Prime Minister Churchill had notified Japan that a state of war existed.]

As the reports of heavy fighting flashed into the White House, London reported semi-officially that the British Empire would carry out Prime Minister Winston Churchill's pledge to give the United States full support in case of hostilities with Japan. The President and Mr. Churchill talked by transatlantic telephone.

This was followed by a statement in London from the Netherland Government in Exile that it considered a state of war to exist between the Netherlands and Japan. Canada, Australia and Costa Rica took similar action.

Landing Made in Malaya

A Singapore communiqué disclosed that Japanese troops had landed in Northern Malaya and that Singapore had been bombed.

The President told those at last night's White House meeting that "doubtless very heavy losses" were sustained by the Navy and also by the Army on the island of Oahu [Honolulu]. It was impossible to obtain confirmation or denial of reports that the battleships Oklahoma and West Virginia had been damaged or sunk at Pearl Harbor, together with six or seven destroyers, and that 350 United States airplanes had been caught on the ground.

The White House took over control of the bulletins, and the Navy Department, therefore, said it could not discuss the matter or answer any questions how the Japanese were able to penetrate the Hawaiian defenses or appear without previous knowledge of their presence in those waters.

Administration circles forecast that the United States soon might be involved in a world-wide war, with Germany supporting Japan, an Axis partner. The German official radio tonight attacked the United States and supported Japan.

Axis diplomats here expressed complete surprise that the Japanese had attacked. But the impression gained from their attitude was that they believed it represented a victory for the Nazi attempt to divert lease-lend aid from Britain, which has bee

Continued on Page Four

JAPANESE FORCE LANDS IN MALAYA

First Attempt Is Repulsed—Singapore Is Bombed and Thailand Invaded

By The Associated Press.

SINGAPORE, Monday, Dec. 8—The Japanese landed in Northern Malaya, 300 miles north of Singapore, today and bombed this great British naval stronghold, causing small loss of life among civilians and property damage.

About 300 Japanese troops landed on the east coast of Malaya and began filtering through jungle-fringed swamps and rice fields toward Kota Bahru airdrome, which is ten miles from the northern terminus of a railroad leading to Singapore.

An official report from the

Continued on Page Two

Tokyo Bombers Strike Hard At Our Main Bases on Oahu

By The United Press.

HONOLULU, Dec. 7—War broke with lightning suddenness in the Pacific today when waves of Japanese bombers attacked Hawaii this morning and the United States Fleet struck back with a thunder of big naval rifles. Japanese bombers, including four-engined dive bombers and torpedo-carrying planes, blasted at Pearl Harbor, the great United States naval base, the city of Honolulu and several outlying American military bases on the Island of Oahu. There were casualties of unstated number.

[The United States battleship Oklahoma was set afire by the Japanese attackers, according to a National Broadcasting Company observer, who also reported in a broadcast yesterday that two other ships in Pearl Harbor were attacked.

[The Japanese news agency, Domei, reported that the battleship Oklahoma had been sunk at Pearl Harbor, according to a United Press dispatch from Shanghai.

[Governor Joseph B. Poindexter of Hawaii had talked with President Roosevelt late yesterday afternoon, saying that a second wave of Japanese bombers was just coming over, and the Gov-

Continued on Page Thirteen

ENTIRE CITY PUT ON WAR FOOTING

Japanese Rounded Up by FBI, Sent to Ellis Island—Vital Services Are Guarded

The metropolitan district reacted swiftly yesterday to the Japanese attack in the Pacific. All large communities in the area, including New York City, Newark, Jersey City, Bayonne and Paterson, went on immediate war footing.

One of the first steps taken here last night was a round-up of Japanese nationals by special agents of the Federal Bureau of Investigation, reinforced by squads of city detectives acting under FBI supervision. More than 100 FBI men, fully armed, were assigned to the detail.

The prisoners were sent to Ellis Island, where they will be held pending action at Washington. It was indicated hundreds would be detained.

Earlier Mayor La Guardia had convened his Emergency Board and directed that Japanese nationals be confined to their homes pending decision as to their status and had their clubs and other meeting places closed and put under police guard.

A police sergeant and five policemen immediately went to the Japanese Consulate at 630 Fifth Avenue in Rockefeller Center where the Consul General, Morito Morishima, and his staff were preparing to leave, and posted a guard there. The Consul General and his staff were escorted to their homes when they left. They were not to move about the city without police in attendance.

Rear Admiral Adolphus Andrews, commander of the North Atlantic Squadron, told reporters at a conference in the Federal

Continued on Page Three

HULL DENOUNCES TOKYO 'INFAMY'

Brands Japan 'Fraudulent' in Preparing Attack While Carrying On Parleys

Texts of Secretary Hull's note and Japan's reply, Page 10.

By BERTRAM D. HULEN

Special to THE NEW YORK TIMES.

WASHINGTON, Dec. 7—Japan was accused by Secretary of State Cordell Hull today of making a "treacherous and utterly unprovoked attack" upon the United States and of having been "infamously false and fraudulent" by preparing for the attack while conducting diplomatic negotiations with the professed desire of maintaining peace.

But even before he knew of the attack, Mr. Hull had vehemently brought the diplomatic negotiations to a virtual end with an outburst against Admiral Kichisaburo Nomura, the Japanese Ambassador, and Saburo Kurusu, special envoy, because of the insulting character of the reply they deliv-

Continued on Page Eleven

Lewis Wins Captive Mine Fight; Arbitrators Grant Union Shop

The three-man arbitration board appointed by President Roosevelt to arbitrate the union shop dispute in the captive coal mines last night reversed the decision of the National Defense Mediation Board and ruled that all workers in the captive mines should be required to join John L. Lewis's United Mine Workers as a condition of employment.

The decision was made by a two to one vote, with Benjamin F. Fairless, president of the United States Steel Corporation, dissenting. Dr. John R. Steelman, who took a leave of absence from his post as director of the United States Conciliation Service to serve as chairman of the arbitration panel, and Mr. Lewis voted in favor of extension to the captive mines of the union shop provision of the standard Appalachian agreement.

Despite his dissent, Mr. Fairless promised that the coal mining subsidiaries of United States Steel would put the ruling into effect. All eight steel companies operating captive mines had given formal assurances before the decision was reached that they would accept it as binding.

The arbitration award ended a dispute in which Mr. Lewis had repeatedly defied the President by calling strikes that menaced the production of steel and that had had its repercussions in the enactment by the House of the Smith anti-strike bill.

In explaining his vote for the union shop, Dr. Steelman pointed out that 95 per cent of the 53,000 captive miners had voluntarily assumed membership in Mr. Lewis's C. I. O. union and that 99.5 per cent of all the miners in the nation were now members of the union.

Since the bulk of the industry, including many owners of captive mines, was already operating under the union shop, it could not be argued that the United Mine Workers was endeavoring to take

Continued on Page Forty-three

The International Situation

MONDAY, DEC. 8, 1941

Yesterday morning Japan attacked the United States at several points in the Pacific. President Roosevelt ordered the United States forces into action and a declaration of war is expected this morning. [Page 1, Columns 7 and 8.] Tokyo made its declaration as of this morning against both the United States and Britain. [Page 1, Column 2.] The first Japanese assault was directed at Pearl Harbor Naval base in Hawaii. Many casualties and severe damage resulted. [Page 1, Columns 4 and 5; Map, Page 13.] United States Army aircraft took off from the Philippines this morning and some points in the Archipelago were bombed. [Page 8, Column 2.] Singapore and Hong Kong were bombed and a Japanese landing in Northern Malaya and a move on Thailand were reported. [Page 1, Column 3.] In Shanghai, Japanese marines occupied the waterfront; a British gunboat was sunk, a United States gunboat seized. [Page 9, Column 1.]

Factional lines dissolved as an angered Congress prepared to meet this morning. [Page 1, Column 1.] Secretary of State Hull accused Japan of having made a "treacherous and utterly unprovoked attack" after having been "infamously false and fraudulent." [Page 1, Column 6.] He released the text of his diplomatic exchanges with Japan [Page 10], while the President gave out the text of his fruitless appeal to the Japanese Emperor. [Page 12.] The White House was the hub of Washington activity and news bulletins were released there. [Page 12, Column 3.]

The Federal Bureau of Investigation was ordered to begin a round-up of some Japanese in this country. [Page 6, Column 8.] As New York City went on a war footing and public precautions were taken, the FBI began the detention of Japanese nationals. [Page 1, Column 4.]

The unification of the country under the impact of the attack was swift. [Page 6, Column 6.] Formerly conspicuous isolationists indicated full support for the war effort. [Page 6, Column 4.]

Prime Minister Churchill notified Tokyo that a state of war existed. [Page 4, Column 1.] Declarations were made last night or early today by Australia, Canada [Page 14 Column 1], the Netherlands Indies [Page 7, Column 2] and Costa Rica. [Page 15, Column 1.]

Libya was the scene of a renewed tank battle and the Tobruk corridor was reported again clear of Axis forces. [Page 20, Column 2, with map.] On the Moscow front the German line was broken at two places, said Soviet sources. [Page 37, Column 2.]

NEWS BULLETINS

are broadcast by The New York Times every hour on the hour over Station WMCA—570 on the dial.

WEEKDAYS
8 a. m. through 11 p. m.

SUNDAYS
9 a.m., 1 p.m., 5 p.m., 11 p.m.

"All the News That's Fit to Print."

NEWS INDEX, PAGE 55, THIS SECTION

The New York Times.

LATE CITY EDITION
Continued cool today with light winds.
Temperatures Yesterday—Max., 57; Min., 45
Sunrise, 7:34 A. M.; Sunset, 5:45 P. M.

Section 1

VOL. XCII. No. 30,969. Entered as Second-Class Matter, Postoffice, New York, N. Y. NEW YORK, SUNDAY, NOVEMBER 8, 1942. Including Magazine and Book Sections. TEN CENTS New York City and Vicinity

AMERICAN FORCES LAND IN FRENCH AFRICA; BRITISH NAVAL, AIR UNITS ASSISTING THEM; EFFECTIVE SECOND FRONT, ROOSEVELT SAYS

U.S. DRIVES ON BUNA

American Troops Flown to Area Closing In on Big Japanese Base

PAPUA IS OVERRUN

All Except Beachhead of Buna-Gona Seized in New Guinea Push

By The Associated Press.

AT UNITED NATIONS HEADQUARTERS, Australia, Sunday, Nov. 8—American combat troops are in action near Buna, vital Japanese base on the north New Guinea coast, General Douglas MacArthur disclosed today.

Simultaneously, General MacArthur disclosed that the Allies have occupied Goodenough Island to the northeast of New Guinea, off Collingwood Bay, in an obvious flanking movement.

[American Army troops on Guadalcanal advanced on Friday (Solomons time) in the area to the west of Henderson airfield, the Navy reported yesterday. They crossed the Malimbui River a few miles south of Koli Point, where the Japanese recently landed reinforcements, but met little opposition.]

It was from Buna, in midsummer, that the Japanese began a drive across tortuous trails of the Owen Stanley Mountains which carried to within thirty-two miles of Port Moresby, Allied base on the south coast, before it was stalled. Late in September the Allies began encircling and infiltration movements which rolled the Japanese back and yesterday's communiqué had mentioned bitter fighting at Oivi, which is fifty-five miles south of Buna.

Japanese Resist at Oisi

"American ground troops in force, transported by air from Australia during the last month, have penetrated Central and Northern Papua to the vicinity of Buna," a communiqué stated.

"The Allied forces now control all of Papua except the beach head in the Buna-Gona area."

The surprising development came as a thrust around the eastern end of New Guinea from Milne Bay where Japanese troops landed in July only to be pinned against the sea and slain or forced to their ships.

"Units from Milne Bay," the communiqué said, "have now completed clearing remnants of hostile forces from the islands to the north and have occupied adjacent strategic points."

While this disclosure was being made, Australian ground forces still were meeting fierce resistance at Oivi where the retreating Japanese are making a stand. Today's communiqué said the Australians maintained constant pressure and were resorting to their hitherto successful tactics of local encircling movements in efforts to dislodge the defenders.

The Allied air force continued to support the overland drive with strafing attacks on the Japanese troops.

Island Attacked Oct. 22

AT UNITED NATIONS HEADQUARTERS, Australia, Sunday, Nov. 8 (U.P.)—The announcement of sweeping Allied gains in New Guinea came as a surprise to observers here, although an Australian offensive through mountainous central New Guinea had been making steady progress toward the north coast for the past five weeks.

[Delayed dispatches from Harold Guard, United Press staff correspondent in New Guinea, revealed that the Americans had

Continued on Page Forty-five

LEADS IN AFRICA

Lieut. Gen. Dwight Eisenhower
Associated Press

R. A. F. ROCKS GENOA; U. S. RAID ON BREST

Bombers From Britain Pound North Italy 2 Nights in Row —Hit Nazis on Coast

Special Cable to THE NEW YORK TIMES.

LONDON, Sunday, Nov. 8—Bombers from Britain struck a heavy blow at Northern Italy over Friday night, blasting the port of Genoa again in support of the Eighth Army's battling of the Nazis and Italians in the African desert.

Again last night the Royal Air Force sent its big bombers over Northern Italy, British officials reported briefly early today. The announcement meant that the R.A.F. from here was seeing to it that the Axis forces in Africa got no help from home.

American heavy bombers, both Flying Fortresses and Liberators, escorted by Allied fighters, carried out a smashing attack on the docks and U-boat pens at Brest in occupied France yesterday afternoon, United States Army headquarters here announced.

Bombs were seen to strike the targets at Brest. The communiqué str ssed that sharp Nazi anti-aircraft fire and enemy fighter opposition were encountered over the coast of Brittany.

The Brest raiders shot down four Nazi fighters. All the United States bombers returned, but one Allied fighter was lost.

The R. A. F.'s fighter squadrons

Continued on Page Twenty-one

NAZIS NEAR LIBYA

British Drive Out to Bar New Stand by Enemy or Reinforcements

FOE BOMBED ALL NIGHT

Pursuers Reported to Be Within 40 Miles of Halfaya Pass

By The United Press.

CAIRO, Egypt, Nov. 7—The British Eighth Army under Lieut. Gen. Bernard L. Montgomery hurled armored forces, motorized infantry and swarms of planes tonight at the remnants of German General Field Marshal Erwin Rommel's once-proud Afrika Korps—possibly only 25,000 out of an original 140,000—now trying to brace for a stand at Halfaya [Hellfire] Pass on the Libyan frontier, 240 miles west of the Alamein battleground.

The main body of the British forces was reported to be well west of Matruh, 110 miles west of El Alamein, and advance striking forces were believed to be as far as 200 miles west of El Alamein, or close to the Egyptian-Libyan frontier, 240 miles west of El Alamein.

How many men Marshal Rommel had left in the Halfaya area could not be established. Already 20,000 prisoners have been counted in British hands. Marshal Rommel's desert casualties were estimated at approximately 20,000 more. In addition, 75,000 Italian troops had been left far behind the swirling battleground, ready to surrender when the British could find time and men to round them up.

Marshal Rommel entered the battle with a maximum of 140,000 troops in the forward area. It was doubted whether he had more than one or two divisions left to attempt another stand at Halfaya unless he had been able to rush large reinforcements from the rear.

It appeared possible tonight that the Axis forces might not even attempt to stand at Halfaya, but would, instead, continue their headlong flight as deeply as possible into Libya in an effort to open a gap between themselves and the Eighth Army.

Such a manoeuvre, however, may already be doomed to failure. General Montgomery has ordered that every attempt be made to cut off Marshal Rommel's retreat. It was believed that he might have sent a hard-hitting, fast-moving

Continued on Page Four

SHOCK TROOPS LEAD

Simultaneous Landings Made Before Dawn at Numerous Points

PLANES GUARD SKIES

An Armada Pours Men on the Beaches—Early Actions Satisfactory

By WES GALLAGHER
Associated Press Correspondent

ALLIED HEADQUARTERS IN NORTH AFRICA, Sunday, Nov. 8—American soldiers, marines and sailors from one of the greatest armadas ever put into a single military operation swarmed ashore today on the Vichy-controlled North Africa shore before dawn, striking to break Hitler's hold on the Mediterranean.

[Reports reaching Allied headquarters in North Africa today disclosed that successful landings had been made by American assault parties on beaches of North Africa near two main objectives outlined in operational plans, an Associated Press dispatch stated.

Headquarters stressed the need, however, of caution in evaluating the first reports.]

Tall, decisive Lieut. Gen. Dwight D. (Ike) Eisenhower, supreme commander of the huge forces involved in the operation, worked throughout the night directing the first great American blow at the Axis.

Included in the forces were crack combat troops, Rangers (airborne units) and the cream of America's airmen.

British naval and air force units supported the American landing forces, who were preceded by a snowstorm of leaflets and a radio barrage promising the French that the United States had no intention of seizing French possessions and only sought to prevent Axis infiltration.

Ships Crowded to Funnels

It undoubtedly was the longest over-water military operation ever attempted, with hundreds of ships in great convoys coming thousands of miles under the protection of British and American sea and air might.

I came on one of these big convoys.

Fighting-fit American soldiers

Continued on Page Five

WHERE THE UNITED STATES PREPARES FOR NEW FRONT

As the survivors of Marshal Rommel's beaten German legions fled westward toward the Libyan border (1), powerful American land, sea and air forces landed behind them at various places in Vichy France's colonies along the Mediterranean (2) and on the shores of the Atlantic, apparently in Morocco (3). British naval and aerial units are assisting them. There was no indication of military action against Vichy's possessions on the western bulge of the Atlantic (4). A large and comprehensive map of the African and Mediterranean theatre of war will be found on Page 1 of Section 4 of this issue of THE TIMES. However, Section 4 had gone to press before the announcement last night of the landing of American troops.

LANDING PLAN KEPT SECRET BY WRITERS

Americans Selected for Duty, Bureaus Sworn to Silence—Eisenhower Slipt Away

By RAYMOND DANIELL
Special Cable to THE NEW YORK TIMES.

LONDON, Sunday, Nov. 8—For weeks American newspaper men have been the custodians of one of war's biggest secrets. It was not an easy secret to keep because through all that time they had to improvise excuses for the absence of a large number of the members of their London staffs to conceal the fact that they had gone with the expeditionary forces.

Most London offices of Amer-

Continued on Page Fourteen

President's Statement

Special to THE NEW YORK TIMES.

WASHINGTON, Nov. 7—President Roosevelt's statement announcing the opening of a second front in French North and West Africa follows:

In order to forestall an invasion of Africa by Germany and Italy, which, if successful, would constitute a direct threat to America across the comparatively narrow sea from Western Africa, a powerful American force equipped with adequate weapons of modern warfare and under American command is today landing on the Mediterranean and Atlantic coasts of the French colonies in Africa.

The landing of this American Army is being assisted by the British Navy and air forces, and it will, in the immediate future, be reinforced by a considerable number of divisions of the British Army.

This combined Allied force, under American command, in conjunction with the British campaign in Egypt is designed to prevent an occupation by the Axis armies of any part of Northern or Western Africa and to deny to the aggressor nations a starting point from which to launch an attack against the Atlantic coast of the Americas.

In addition, it provides an effective second-front assistance to our heroic allies in Russia.

The French Government and the French people have been informed of the purpose of this expedition and have been assured that the Allies seek no territory and have no intention of interfering with friendly French authorities in Africa.

The government of France and the people of France and the French possessions have been requested to cooperate with and assist the American expedition in its effort to repel the German and Italian international criminals, and by so doing to liberate France and the French Empire from the Axis yoke.

This expedition will develop into a major effort by the Allied Nations and there is every expectation that it will be successful in repelling the planned German and Italian invasion of Africa and prove the first historic step to the liberation and restoration of France.

Blow to Knock Italy Out of the War Called Goal of American Invasion

Special Cable to THE NEW YORK TIMES.

LONDON, Sunday, Nov. 8—Allied Army, Navy and air forces commanded by Lieut. Gen. Dwight D. Eisenhower, commander of all American forces in the European theatre, have struck a powerful blow to free the Mediterranean from Axis control and knock Italy out of the war. That, in the opinion of military observers here, is the meaning of the movement of United States forces that now become part of the gigantic pincers with which it is expected that the last vestiges of the German and Italian forces in North Africa will be annihilated.

The movement now under way called for the finest timing. It was essential that, before that huge armada of whose presence at Gibraltar the Nazis were aware got under way, Britain's Eighth Army in Egypt should break through Marshal Erwin Rommel's defenses and start the westward push that is fast becoming a rout. Now United States soldiers swarming ashore at many points in French North Africa are closing Marshal Rommel's back door.

The first stage of the battle just beginning will be a struggle for the control of roads, railways and airfields in Algeria and the neighboring colony of Tunisia. Once the control of these has been won, Allied reinforcements and supplies will be able to dispense with the long journey around the Cape of Good Hope that has been one of

Continued on Page Thirteen

U.S. MEETS 'THREAT'

Big Expeditions Invade North and West Africa to Forestall Axis

EISENHOWER AT HEAD

President Urges French to Help, Calls Move Aid to Russia

Texts of President's appeal to French people and Eisenhower's message to North Africans, Page 8.

By C. P. TRUSSELL
Special to THE NEW YORK TIMES.

WASHINGTON, Nov. 7—Powerful American forces, supported by British naval and air forces, landed simultaneously tonight at numerous points on the Mediterranean and Atlantic coasts of French North Africa, forestalling an anticipated invasion of Africa by Germany and Italy and launching effective second front assistance to Russia, President Roosevelt announced tonight.

Lieut. Gen. Dwight D. Eisenhower is in command.

The President made the announcement even as the American forces, equipped with adequate weapons of modern warfare, he emphasized, were making the landings.

President Speaks to France

Soon he was speaking direct to the French Government and the French people by short-wave radio and in their own tongue, giving assurances that the Allies seek no territory and have no intention of interfering with friendly French, official or civilian. He called upon them to cooperate in repelling "the German and Italian international criminals."

By doing so, he said, they could help liberate France and the French Empire.

[United States and British planes dropped leaflets in France and French Africa containing messages to the people from President Roosevelt and General Eisenhower, London reported.]

General Eisenhower himself, the White House let it be known, also spoke by radio to the French people, explaining the purposes of the invasions.

His proclamation, delivered while the American troops were making their landings, gave specific directions to French land, sea and air forces in North Africa as to how they could avoid misunderstanding and prevent action against them by a system of signals. This is a military operation, General Eisenhower explained, that is directed against the Italian-German military forces there, and the only objective is to defeat the enemy and free France.

"We count on your friendship and we ask your aid," he said. "I have given formal orders that no offensive action shall be undertaken against you on condition that for your part you take the same attitude."

British Forces to Follow

In telling the American people of the surprise action of large American forces under American command in this vital Vichy French region, apparently beginning, in effect, a pincer movement against the fleeing armies of General Field Marshal Erwin Rommel before the British Eighth Army at the western edge of Egypt, the President also gave assurances that "a considerable number of divisions" of the British Army would soon be

Continued on Page Three

Major Sports Yesterday

FOOTBALL

Making both touchdowns in the second half, Notre Dame defeated Army before 75,142 spectators at the Yankee Stadium. With a scoring pass in the first period and several goal-line stands, Navy thrilled 74,000 fans at Philadelphia by upsetting Penn. Both Fordham and Columbia lost free-scoring contests here and the Big Three—Princeton, Yale and Harvard—all went down to defeat. Iowa toppled hitherto unbeaten Wisconsin. Scores of leading games:

Alabama	29	So. Carolina	0	Miss. State	7	Tulane	0
Amherst	35	Trinity	6	Missouri	26	Nebraska	6
Boston Coll.	28	Temple	0	Moravian	32	C. C. N. Y.	0
Brown	20	Holy Cross	14	Navy	7	Penn.	0
Colgate	35	Columbia	26	Notre Dame	13	Army	0
Cornell	13	Yale	7	Ohio State	59	Pittsburgh	19
Dartmouth	19	Princeton	7	Oklahoma	76	Kan. State	0
Duke	42	Maryland	0	Oregon	14	U. C. L. A.	7
Duquesne	7	St. Mary's	7	Penn State	18	Syracuse	13
Georgia	75	Florida	0	Rice	40	Arkansas	9
Ga. Pre-Fl.	41	Auburn	14	So. Calif.	21	California	7
Ga. Tech	47	Kentucky	7	Stanford	20	Washington	7
Great Lakes	42	Purdue	0	Texas	20	Baylor	0
Illinois	14	Northwestern	7	Tex. A. & M.	27	S. M. U.	20
Indiana	7	Minnesota	0	Texas Tech	13	T. C. U.	6
Iowa	6	Wisconsin	0	Vanderbilt	19	Mississippi	0
La. State	26	Fordham	13	Wash. State	25	Mich. State	13
Michigan	35	Harvard	7	Williams	31	Wesleyan	6

HORSE RACING

Good Morning won the Florence Nightingale Purse by half a length from Too Timely on the war-relief program before 22,099 racegoers who bet $1,550,089 at Belmont Park. Aonbarr defeated Riverland by a neck in the Grayson Handicap at Pimlico.

HOCKEY

The New York Rangers downed the Montreal Canadiens, 4—3, in the overtime opening game at Madison Square Garden.

(Complete Details of These and Other Sports Events in Section 5.)

War News Summarized

SUNDAY, NOVEMBER 8, 1942

The White House announced last night that powerful American forces were landing on the Atlantic and Mediterranean coasts of French North Africa to forestall a German invasion. The announcement stated that the landing was to prevent the creation of an Axis threat to the Atlantic coast of the Americas across the narrow sea in Western Africa. France has been assured that the Allies seek no territory. [1:8.]

American correspondents with the African expeditionary force told of simultaneous landings by the United States troops at many points hundreds of miles apart. [1:4.]

Britain's Eighth Army continued its pursuit in North Africa of Marshal Rommel's shattered army. Twenty thousand prisoners had been taken, according to Cairo. British columns were said to be 200 miles west of El Alamein, close to the Libyan border. [1:3; map, P. 4.]

London announced that British heavy bombers had launched a "concentrated and effective" attack on Genoa Friday night and again raided Northern Italy last night. United States bombers attacked the U-boat base at Brest, France, and other planes from Britain pounded Nazi targets from the Netherlands to the Bay of Biscay. [1:2; map, P. 21.]

Moscow reported that the Soviet armies held on all fronts and killed some 1,800 of the enemy on the Stalingrad and Caucasus fronts. The German advances in the Nalchik region had apparently been halted. [38:4-5.]

General Douglas MacArthur's headquarters announced that American troops in force had been transported by air to New Guinea and had penetrated to the vicinity of Buna, Japanese base on the north coast. [1:1; map, P. 45.]

The United States Navy announced that Army forces on Guadalcanal Island in the Solomons had attacked Japanese troops to the east of the airfield Nov. 6 and had encountered little opposition. Announcement was also made that at least 5,188 Japanese had been killed in land fighting on Tulagi and Guadalcanal since the United States occupation Aug. 7. [46:1 with map.]

United States bombers attacked successfully the docks at Rangoon, Burma, and returned to their bases in India. [46:8.]

"All the News That's Fit to Print."

The New York Times.

LATE CITY EDITION
Continued moderately cool today; moderate winds.
Temperatures Yesterday—Max., 74; Min., 67
Sunrise, 6:39 A. M.; Sunset, 7:17 P. M.

VOL. XCII..No. 31,274. Entered as Second-Class Matter, Postoffice, New York, N. Y. NEW YORK, THURSDAY, SEPTEMBER 9, 1943. THREE CENTS IN NEW YORK CITY

ITALY SURRENDERS, WILL RESIST GERMANS; ALLIED FORCES LAND IN THE NAPLES AREA; RUSSIANS IN STALINO, CLEAR DONETS BASIN

SOVIET TIDE RISES

Swift Red Army Blows Capture Key City, Free Rich Region

DRIVE NEARS DNIEPER

More Rail Hubs Fall—Thrust Toward Kiev Also Extended

By The United Press.

LONDON, Thursday, Sept. 9—The Red Army recaptured Stalino, Russia's twelfth city, yesterday and freed the Donets Basin, which before the war produced more steel than Japan and Italy combined, in a great surge that took it to Grishino, ninety miles east of Dniepropetrovsk on the lower Dnieper River.

While the armies of Gen. Rodion Y. Malinovsky and Gen. Fedor Tolbukhin drove the enemy from the rich Donets Basin, crowded with coal mines and factories, the army of Gen. Konstantin Rokossovsky drove to a point ninety-six miles northeast of Kiev by capturing Borzna, twenty-three miles west of Bakhmach.

Bakhmach and Romni, forty-two miles to the southeast, were surrounded on three sides, a Moscow radio bulletin reported, and thus the Bakhmach-Kremenchug railroad was cut. The roads leading from Bakhmach to Kursk and Gomel had been cut previously and only the lines to Kiev and Odessa remained open.

Picked Troops Take Stalino

Red Army shock troops, picked from the sixteen infantry divisions that had driven the Germans through city after city in six days of tireless fighting, took Stalino by storm.

The Russian communiqué said the Red Army troops drove in on Stalino throughout Tuesday night and yesterday morning. They fought through the suburbs and then stormed the city from north and south, routing the enemy in a street-by-street fight and capturing a great store of spoils.

Twenty-five miles northwest of Stalino the Russians took Krasnoarmeiskoye, a big railroad junction controlling two of four rail roads leading west from the basin.

In all the Russians took, in addition to Stalino, a city of 462,000 persons, more than 150 towns in the Donbas alone, twenty of them important, in gains of up to twelve and a half miles. During their Donbas offensive the Russians took twelve towns of more than 50,000 persons each.

The Germans at Krasnoarmeiskoye were so swiftly beaten that the Russians took nineteen planes and several loaded railroad trains.

March on Kiev Gains

On the Kiev front, the Russians took more than sixty towns in advances of up to twelve and a half miles. Their capture of Borzna in that area meant that the battle for the Dnieper River line had started. An advance of twenty-three miles to Nezhin would cut the only remaining German supply line east of the river. The Russians had already advanced 101 miles in nine days from Rylsk, half the distance to Kiev.

More than 1,000 Germans were killed at Borzna, and 1,000 were killed in another sector.

South of Bryansk the Russians advanced up to six miles to take several villages. They were reported only twenty miles south of Bryansk. The Soviet communiqué, recorded from the Moscow radio, reported that the Russians were advancing west of the Naviya railroad junction in this area, driving the Germans through dense forests.

West and southwest of Kharkov nearly four miles were gained in some sectors and about 1,200 Germans were killed.

The Germans were first to ad-

Continued on Page Twenty-two

New Fascist Regime Set Up, Nazis Report

By Cable to THE NEW YORK TIMES.

LONDON, Thursday, Sept. 9—The German radio announced early today that a "National Fascist government has been set up in Italy and functions in the name of Benito Mussolini."

The announcement, called a "proclamation by the National Fascist Government of Italy," said "this Badoglio betrayal will not be perpetrated. The National Fascist Government will punish traitors pitilessly."

The broadcast, in Italian, said nothing about the whereabouts of Mussolini, who has been reported under arrest. It was preceded by the playing of "Giovinezza," the Fascist anthem.

FOE'S MARCUS LOSS 80%, NIMITZ SAYS

U. S. Carrier Planes Alone Hit at Japanese Isle—Hell Cat Fighter Excels in Test

By ROBERT TRUMBULL
By Telephone to THE NEW YORK TIMES.

PEARL HARBOR, Sept. 8—Admiral Chester W. Nimitz, Commander in Chief of the Pacific Fleet, issued today a communiqué that gave the first details of the raid on Marcus Island Sept. 1. Coincidentally three naval air officers who participated in the action gave an interview covering all phases of the raid, which they said destroyed a surprisingly well-fortified Japanese air base.

Action Consisted of Bombing

Admiral Nimitz's communiqué said that a United States Pacific Fleet task force under command of Rear Admiral Charles A. Pownall attacked the little island, 1,185 miles southeast of Tokyo, at dawn Sept. 1. The air officers revealed that the action consisted entirely of bombing and strafing by carrier-borne aircraft.

They said that the new Grumman F6F Hellcat fighter was employed in combat for the first time in the

Continued on Page Twenty-two

IN HEART OF ITALY

American 7th Army Is Reported in Van of Naples Operation

MORE POINTS NAMED

Landings Rumored at Genoa, Pizzo, Gaeta and Leghorn

By Wireless to THE NEW YORK TIMES.

ALLIED HEADQUARTERS IN NORTH AFRICA, Thursday, Sept. 9—The Allies have carried the land campaign against the Nazis in Italy to the vicinity of Naples in new operations announced within twelve hours of the disclosure by Gen. Dwight D. Eisenhower that the Italian armed forces had unconditionally surrendered.

The news was announced here a few minutes past 6:30 A. M. in the following thirteen words:

"Further operations have started on the Italian mainland in the vicinity of Naples."

In the absence of the slightest expansion of the communiqué, no details are available as to the forces participating. The single fact remained that the attack had been pressed near Italy's southern metropolis and port, second only to Genoa, in what obviously was a major amphibious thrust.

Naples is a city of more than 700,000 population—nearer 1,000,000 if the suburbs are included. The assault was launched eighty-three years and two days after Garibaldi entered the city alone in a dramatic liberation gesture, which culminated in the unification of the country ten years later.

Although there is no indication just how near the city itself the landing or landings were carried out, it is plain that Naples is the objective of the sea-borne invaders.

[This dispatch did not indicate the make-up of the landing parties. A Tunis radio broadcast

Continued on Page Four

War News Summarized

THURSDAY, SEPTEMBER 9, 1943

Italy has surrendered unconditionally, and all hostilities between that country and the United Nations ceased yesterday. An armistice was signed last Friday, the same day that Italy was invaded, but the victors reserved the right to withhold announcement until the most favorable moment for the Allies. The armistice terms had been approved by the United States, Britain and Russia.

General Eisenhower, announcing the surrender, promised support to all Italians who helped fight the Germans. Marshal Badoglio issued a proclamation ordering all fighting against the "Anglo-American forces" to cease and commanding resistance to "attacks from any other quarter."

Allied radios and planes carried messages urging the Italians to take vengeance on their "German oppressors" and to prevent trains, ships and trucks from carrying German troops or supplies. [All the foregoing, 1:8; map, P.3.]

Landings in the Naples area followed only a few hours after the surrender announcement and it was believed the Allies were attempting to cut off German troops in southern Italy. The American Seventh Army was reported among the invading forces. [1:3; map, P. 4.] Earlier, the Italian Navy and merchant marine had been urged to take their ships to designated points and to scuttle the vessels as a last resort to keep them from the Germans. [7:4.]

Wild demonstrations of joy were reported from all over Italy, but in the north they gave way to sober realization of continued danger when the Germans occupied Milan and other cities and imposed martial law. [3:1.] No official comment came from Berlin, but the German radio, after withholding the news for hours, was furious at the "treachery." [1:5-6.]

Germany's Balkan satellites were so shaken by the Italian surrender that Bulgaria, Rumania and Hungary were reported ready to follow Italy out of the war. [10:3.]

President Roosevelt, in a radio address last night, termed the surrender a great victory for the Italian people as well as for the United Nations. But he warned: "The time for celebration is not yet. Our ultimate objectives in this war continue to be Berlin and Tokyo." [1:5-6.]

The actual fighting in Italy was of a minor nature. Land forces advanced on both coasts. [3:6.] Airfields were hit by Allied bombers and the Rome radio reported heavy raids on suburbs of the city. [4:1.]

With one Axis partner out of the war, the two others continued to be hit hard. The Red Army captured Stalino and cleared the Germans out of the Donets Basin. [1:1; map, P. 22.] Allied bombers from Britain struck enemy airfields in France and Belgium [23:2], while down in New Guinea Japanese troops were providing weak opposition as the Allies closed in on Lae. [22:1.]

The naval task force that raided Marcus Island Sept. 1 destroyed 80 per cent of the Japanese military installations. We lost three planes. [1:2.]

U. S. SOLDIERS IN LONDON CHEER THE NEWS

Americans in front of the Red Cross Washington Club in the British capital when the news of Italy's surrender was announced.

Associated Press Radiophoto, passed yesterday by censor

Announcements of the Surrender

By Broadcast to THE NEW YORK TIMES.

ALLIED HEADQUARTERS IN NORTH AFRICA, Sept. 8—The texts of the proclamations by Gen. Dwight D. Eisenhower and Premier Pietro Badoglio follow:

By GENERAL EISENHOWER

This is Gen. Dwight D. Eisenhower, Commander in Chief of the Allied Forces.

The Italian Government has surrendered its armed forces unconditionally. As Allied Commander in Chief, I have granted a military armistice, the terms of which have been approved by the Governments of the United Kingdom, the United States and the Union of Soviet Socialist Republics. Thus I am acting in the interest of the United Nations.

The Italian Government has bound itself to abide by these terms without reservation. The armistice was signed by my representative and the representative of Marshal Badoglio and it becomes effective this instant.

Hostilities between the armed forces of the United Nations and those of Italy terminate at once. All Italians who now act to help eject the German aggressor from Italian soil will have the assistance and the support of the United Nations.

By PREMIER BADOGLIO

The Italian Government, recognizing the impossibility of continuing the unequal struggle against the overwhelming power of the enemy, with the object of avoiding further and more grievous harm to the nation, has requested an armistice from General Eisenhower, Commander in Chief of the Anglo-American Allied forces. This request has been granted. The Italian forces will therefore cease all acts of hostility against the Anglo-American forces wherever they may be met. They will, however, oppose attack from any other quarter.

CITY 'JUMPS GUN' IN WAR BOND DRIVE

Rallies, Sales Begin on Vast Scale—State Savings Banks Will Invest $600,000,000

As President Roosevelt and Secretary of the Treasury Henry J. Morgenthau Jr. opened the Third War Loan Drive for $15,000,000,000 last night over the radio, it was announced here that in the campaign to raise the State's quota of $4,709,000,000 the mutual savings banks in the State would buy $600,000,000 in Government bonds. The United States Steel Corporation and its subsidiaries will buy $100,000,000 in Government securities, with parts of the total allocated to districts where the corporation operates.

Restive to get its drive under way, New York City held preliminary rallies yesterday as Army convoys took into the five boroughs Navy gunners who had been rescued at sea. The largest meetings were held in Times Square and on the steps of the Sub-Treasury Building at Wall and Broad Streets.

Burgess Hails Italy's Surrender

The thousands assembled in the streets for these two gatherings cheered wildly as speakers announced the capitulation of Italy. Ticker tape, confetti and torn paper were thrown from the windows of buildings where workers in the financial community were listening to the rally.

The unconditional surrender of Italy is "bullish news" and will be a great help in the bond drive, W. Randolph Burgess, chairman of the War Finance Committee for New York State, said later in the

Continued on Page Sixteen

President Hails Victory But Warns of Real Foes

By JOHN H. CRIDER
Special to THE NEW YORK TIMES.

WASHINGTON, Sept. 8—President Roosevelt hailed the surrender of Italy tonight as "a great victory for the United Nations" and also "a great victory for the Italian people" against "their real enemies, the Nazis," but cautioned against over-optimism. Addressing the nation on the opening of the Third War Bond drive, the President said "the time for celebration is not yet" and added that "our ultimate objectives in this war continue to be Berlin and Tokyo."

Toward the middle of his speech the President interpolated three words which gave basis to reports that Allied armies already were on the move again in the Mediterranean when he spoke of troops in landing barges moving up to enemy coasts "at this moment."

"This war does not and must not stop for one single instant," he declared. "Your fighting men know that. Those of them who are moving forward through jungles against lurking Japs—those who are landing at this moment in barges moving through the dawn up the strange enemy coasts—those who are diving their bombs down on the target at roof-top level at this moment—every one of these men knows that this war is a full-time job and that it will

Continued on Page Seventeen

Germans Charge Betrayal by Italy In Plot With Russian Government

By GEORGE AXELSSON
By Wireless to THE NEW YORK TIMES.

STOCKHOLM, Sweden, Sept. 8—Berlin's newspapers branded Italy's capitulation as cowardly treachery last night. The German press abounds in scatching denunciation of Premier Pietro Badoglio and King Victor Emmanuel, as well as the Italian people.

"Mussolini was too great a person for a nation like that," a German official said. This is the second time that Victor Emmanuel has broken his word, the newspapers say, because the King "left Germany in the lurch" in 1915 when he joined the Allies.

Forgetting its praise of the Italians during the heyday of their pact, Berlin now condemns the Italians as third-rate individuals. "The cowardly perfidy of Badoglio caps the crime," one paper said, "by being committed in collusion with the Soviet Government, which is treason not only against Italy and Germany but also against all Europe."

Berlin added that the Germans had no intention of giving up their entrenchments in Italy, where they hoped to offer efficient resistance. Italy, since last night, is German-occupied territory to the extent that the Germans have been able to gain a firm footing there. In the Italian provinces occupied by the Germans, Berlin boasts fascism will be revived even if "we leave it to the Italians in those provinces to organize themselves along fascist lines.

Official circles are reviving accusations of broken words of honor

Continued on Page Nine

GEN. EISENHOWER ANNOUNCES ARMISTICE

Capitulation Acceptable to U. S., Britain and Russia Is Confirmed in Speech by Badoglio

TERMS SIGNED ON DAY OF INVASION

Disclosure Withheld by Both Sides Until Moment Most Favorable for the Allies—Italians Exhorted to Aid United Nations

By MILTON BRACKER
By Wireless to THE NEW YORK TIMES.

ALLIED HEADQUARTERS IN NORTH AFRICA, Sept. 8—Italy has surrendered her armed forces unconditionally and all hostilities between the soldiers of the United Nations and those of the weakest of the three Axis partners ceased as of 16:30 Greenwich Mean Time today [12:30 P. M., Eastern War Time].

At that time, Gen. Dwight D. Eisenhower announced here over the United Nations radio that a secret military armistice had been signed in Sicily on the afternoon of Friday, Sept. 3, by his representative and one sent by Premier Pietro Badoglio. That was the day when, at 4:50 A. M., British and Canadian troops crossed the Strait of Messina and landed on the Italian mainland to open a campaign in which, up to yesterday, they had occupied about sixty miles of the Calabrian coast from the Petrace River in the north to Bova Marina in the south.

The complete collapse of Italian military resistance in no way suggested that the Germans would not defend Italy with all the strength at their command. But the capitulation, in undisclosed terms that were acceptable to the United States, the United Kingdom and the Union of Soviet Socialist Republics, came exactly forty days after the downfall of Benito Mussolini, the dictator who, by playing jackal to Adolf Hitler, led his country to the catastrophic mistake of declaring war on France three years and three months ago this Friday.

Negotiations Begun Several Weeks Ago

The negotiations leading to the armistice were opened by the war-weary and bomb-battered nation a few weeks ago, it was revealed today, and a preliminary meeting was arranged and held in an unnamed neutral country.

The Italians who had approached the British and American authorities were bluntly told that the terms remained what they had been: unconditional surrender. They agreed, and the document was signed five days ago. But it was agreed to hold back the announcement and its effective date until the moment most favorable to the Allies.

That moment came today, when the Allied Commander in Chief, in a historic broadcast, announced the armistice. He concluded with the reminder that all Italians who aided in the ejection of the Germans from Italy would have the support and assistance of the United Nations.

One hour and fifteen minutes after the General's voice had gone out over the air, Marshal Badoglio faced a microphone in Rome and confirmed the armistice. He concluded with the promise that the Italian forces would oppose attacks "from any other quarter," although they were laying down the arms that they had taken up against the Anglo-American armies.

Military Aspect Emphasized

Although it was emphasized that the armistice was a strictly military instrument, "signed by soldiers," it was disclosed that it contained a clause binding Italy to comply with political, economic and financial conditions to be imposed at the Allies' discretion.

[It was believed that the armistice conditions were substantially the same as those imposed on France in 1940, which allowed the Germans to use all strategic French ports and military bases to wage war against Britain, The United Press reported.]

Immediately after the announcement of the armistice, the Allies made two appeals—one to the Italian people and one to the Italian Fleet—urging them to rally to a cause that was, in effect, the liberation of their own country. The appeal to the people was disseminated by radio and air-borne leaflet, while that to the Navy was broadcast by Admiral Sir Andrew Browne Cunningham, the Allies' Mediterranean naval commander.

The Italian people, particularly transport, railroad and dock workers, were asked not to give the slightest aid to the Germans. The men who man Italian ships received specific instructions how to bring their vessels into the protection of the United Nations.

Although the fear was proved unjustified by Marshal Badoglio's broadcast, the Allies had taken no chances of a German move to forestall his giving the news to the people. As a safeguard, they had obtained from the Italians an agreement to leave one senior military representative behind when the others returned to Rome. This man is now in Sicily and presumably, had Marshal Badoglio not gone on the air, his representative would have broadcast the decision to the Italian public.

As a further earnest of good faith, Marshal Badoglio had arranged to send the text of the proclamation that he made this evening to Allied Headquarters here. He kept his word.

1,181 Days at War and Losses

Italy quit the war after 1,181 days, during which she steadily lost territory and prestige. Last May 7, with the fall of Tunis and Bizerte, the last Italian soldier in North Africa was doomed. Since then, Sicily, part of Metropolitan Italy, was occupied in thirty-eight days.

The Italians endured two raids on military targets in Rome

Continued on Page Three

"All the News That's Fit to Print"

The New York Times.

6 A. M. EXTRA

Partly cloudy and warmer today; moderate to fresh winds.
Temperatures Yesterday—Max., 67; Min., 51
Sunrise, 5:25 A. M.; Sunset, 8:24 P. M.

VOL. XCIII..No. 31,545. Entered as Second-Class Matter, Postoffice, New York, N. Y. NEW YORK, TUESDAY, JUNE 6, 1944.† THREE CENTS NEW YORK CITY

ALLIED ARMIES LAND IN FRANCE IN THE HAVRE-CHERBOURG AREA; GREAT INVASION IS UNDER WAY

ROOSEVELT SPEAKS

Says Rome's Fall Marks 'One Up and Two to Go' Among Axis Capitals

WARNS WAY IS HARD

Asks World to Give the Italians a Chance for Recovery

The text of President Roosevelt's address is on Page 5.

By CHARLES HURD

Special to THE NEW YORK TIMES.

WASHINGTON, June 5—President Roosevelt hailed tonight the capture of Rome, first of the three major Axis capitals to fall, as a great achievement on the road toward total conquest of the Axis. Rome, he said, marked "one up and two to go."

The President spoke for a quarter-hour on the radio, as had been announced yesterday, but his speech was notable for its lack of heroics. It was in no sense a speech of triumph, but rather a tribute to the United Nations forces and leadership that drove the Germans from Rome.

With this tribute he combined a solemn warning that much greater fighting lies ahead before the Axis is defeated, as well as high tributes to the Italian people, whom he again welcomed as a people into the family of nations opposed to the Axis.

"Italy should go on," Mr. Roosevelt said, "as a great mother nation, contributing to the culture and the progress and the good-will of mankind, developing her special talents in the arts, crafts, and sciences, and preserving her historic and cultural heritage for the benefit of all peoples.

"We want and expect the help of the future Italy toward lasting peace. All the other nations opposed to fascism and nazism ought to help to give Italy a chance."

Shrines Should Live, He Says

President Roosevelt saw considerable significance in the fact that Rome should be the first Axis capital to fall. He remarked its shrines, "visible symbols of the faith and determination of the early saints and martyrs that Christianity should live and become universal," and added that "it will be a source of deep satisfaction that the freedom of the Pope and of Vatican City is assured by the armies of the United Nations."

There is significance, too, he added, in the fact that Rome was liberated by a composite force of soldiers from many nations.

Reviewing the military picture, the President pointed out that "it would be unwise to inflate in our own minds the military importance of the capture of Rome." He cautioned his auditors that the Germans have retreated "thousands of miles" across Africa and back through Italy "they have suffered heavy losses, but not great enough yet to cause collapse."

"Therefore," he added, "the victory still lies some distance ahead. That distance will be covered in due time—have no fear of that. But it will be tough and it will be costly."

Turning to the relief problem in the newly liberated portion of Italy, Mr. Roosevelt noted that some persons thought of the financial cost, but he maintained that the work would pay dividends "by eliminating fascism" and any future desire by Italians to "start another war of aggression." Relief has been planned, he added, but transport demands are so great that "improvement must be gradual."

He warned Italy that it "cannot grow in stature by seeking to build up a great militaristic empire,"

Continued on Page 5

Conferees Accept Cabaret Tax Cut

By The Associated Press

WASHINGTON, June 5—A House-Senate conference committee agreed today to cut back the cabaret tax from 30 to 20 per cent, but eliminated a provision exempting service men and women from the levy.

The group decided to put the national debt limit at $260,000,000,000 as originally requested by the Administration.

The action is subject to House and Senate votes. The conferees met informally today, but members said that the decisions probably would stand as their final recommendation.

The House, at the insistence of a group of Republicans, passed a bill raising the debt ceiling only from $210,000,000,000 to $240,000,000,000. The Senate then put the figure at $260,000,000,000 and attached a rider reducing the cabaret tax from 30 to 20 per cent and exempting men and women in uniform from paying the tax on their checks.

Some tax experts argued that this exemption would make administration of the excise on night clubs impossible.

FEDERAL LAW HELD RULING INSURANCE

Supreme Court, 4-3, Decides Business Is Interstate and Subject to Trust Act

Special to THE NEW YORK TIMES.

WASHINGTON, June 5—The Supreme Court, by a four-to-three decision today, held that the insurance companies of the country, with assets of $37,000,000,000 and annual premium collections in excess of $6,000,000,000, are in interstate commerce and thus subject to the Sherman Anti-Trust Law.

The decision upset precedents which began with a contrary decision by the court more than seventy-five years ago and have been reaffirmed repeatedly since the adoption of the anti-trust law in 1890.

The majority decision, written

Continued on Page 13

PURSUIT ON IN ITALY

Allies Pass Rome, Cross Tiber as Foe Quits Bank Below City

PLANES JOIN IN CHASE

1,200 Vehicles Wrecked —Eighth Army Battles Into More Towns

By The Associated Press.

ROME, June 5—The Allies' armor and motorized infantry roared through Rome today without pausing, crossed the Tiber River and proceeded with the grim task of destroying two battered German armies fleeing to the north.

Fighter-bombers spearheaded the pursuit, jamming the escape highways with burning enemy transport and littering the fields with dead and wounded Germans. The enemy was tired, disorganized and bewildered by the slashing assault, which in twenty-five days had inflicted a major catastrophe on the Germans and liberated Rome almost without damage.

Railway Yards Bombed

Five hundred American heavy bombers blasted railway yards at five points in northern Italy between Venice and Rimini along which the Germans might attempt to move reinforcements and equipment to bolster their beaten armies. Hour after hour, the Allies' planes swept down on highways leading northward and tore the fleeing enemy apart. Twelve hundred combat vehicles were destroyed from dawn to dark yesterday, and hundreds more today. Farther north, medium bombers smashed bridges and rail facilities.

[The Germans have abandoned the entire left bank of the Tiber from Ostia, at its mouth, to Rome, according to a Vichy broadcast quoted by The Associated Press.

[The Germans are already entrenched in mountain positions

Continued on Page 2

FIRST ALLIED LANDING MADE ON SHORES OF WESTERN EUROPE

June 6, 1944

General Eisenhower's armies invaded northern France this morning. While the landing points were not specified, the Germans said that troops had gone ashore near Havre and that fighting raged at Caen (1). The enemy also said that parachutists had descended at the northern tip of the Normandy Peninsula (2) and heavy bombing had been visited on Calais and Dunkerque (3).

POPE GIVES THANKS ROME WAS SPARED

Voices Appreciation to Both Belligerents in Message to Throng at St. Peter's

By Wireless to THE NEW YORK TIMES.

VATICAN CITY, June 5—Pope Pius XII appeared on the balcony of St. Peter's at 6 P. M. today to thank God that Rome had been spared from the ravages of war while before him in the densely packed square of St. Peter's and the new broad Via Della Conciliazione tens of thousands of Romans cheered themselves hoarse.

It was the third time today that the Pontiff had showed himself to cheering crowds, as he had appeared twice at a window of his office this morning. But this was a solemn, sacred occasion and no one knowing anything about Pius XII can doubt the fervor of his thankfulness that Rome had been saved.

The Pontiff seemed strong and well and his voice carried far, though it was difficult to hear every word he said because of the crowd.

"We must give thanks to God for the favors we have received," said the Pope. "Rome has been spared. This day will go down in the annals of Rome."

He went on to say he hoped that Italians would be worthy of the grace shown them and put aside hatred and all personal vendettas. He then thanked both belligerents—the Allies and Germany—for having left Rome intact.

After a prayer of thankfulness to the Blessed Virgin and Saints Peter and Paul, guardians of Rome, the Pontiff gave his blessing, "urbe et orbis," as the immense crowd knelt before him.

[The Associated Press estimated the crowd was between 250,000 and 500,000.]

The world has changed for Rome but the Vatican goes on imperturbably as it has through so many other conquests in centuries gone by. It is neutral in fact and spirit. The Pope and all high officials went about their daily routine today as in the past. Except for the tanks and armored cars running along the street in front of St. Peter's one could never know what had happened today.

Continued on Page 5

Italy's Monarch Yields Rule To Son, but Retains Throne

By The Associated Press.

NAPLES, June 5—Victor Emmanuel III stepped aside as King of Italy today, as he previously had said he would do upon the liberation of Rome, and handed to his 39-year-old son, Crown Prince Humbert, all "royal prerogatives." Italian political pressure had been brought to bear against him since the occupation of Naples.

In a decree signed by himself and countersigned by Premier Pietro Badoglio, head of the Italian Liberation Government, the King named his son Lieutenant General of the Realm. The monarch, however, retained his title as head of the House of Savoy and remains as King without power.

[The first act of the Council of Ministers after the transfer of royal powers was a formal denunciation of the 1940 armistice treaty inflicted on France, The United Press said.]

Victor Emmanuel, who became King July 29, 1900, had announced last April 12 his "irrevocable" decision to withdraw from public life "on the day on which Allied troops enter Rome."

Little more than a figurehead since Benito Mussolini assumed the dictatorship of Italy, Victor Emmanuel had won a reputation in the first years of his reign as a sympathetic monarch, interested in his people and their problems.

Prince Humbert, tall and erect, opposed fascism in Italy at the start, but later made a truce with Mussolini. In effect, Humbert becomes the King's regent.

TEXT OF ROYAL DECREE

The King's withdrawal decree:

I, Victor Emmanuel III, by the grace of God and by the will of the nation King of Italy, in collaboration with the President of the Council of Ministers and with the agreement of the Council, have ordered and order as follows:

My beloved son, Humbert of Savoy, Prince of Piedmont, is nominated our Lieutenant General. In collaboration with responsible Ministers he will in our name superintend all matters of administration and exercise all royal prerogatives without exception, signing royal decrees which will be countersigned and authenticated in the usual way.

We order all concerned to observe this decree and to see that it is observed as the law of the State.

Given at Ravello June 5, 1944.
VICTOR EMMANUEL.
(Countersigned) PIETRO BADOGLIO.

The withdrawal was presented to

Continued on Page 4

ALLIED WARNING FLASHED TO COAST

People Told to Clear Area 22 Miles Inland as Soon as Instructions Are Given

By Cable to THE NEW YORK TIMES.

LONDON, Tuesday, June 6—The British Broadcasting Corporation began its 8 A. M. news bulletin this morning with quotations from a Supreme Headquarters' "urgent warning" to inhabitants of the enemy-occupied countries living near the coast.

Gen. Dwight D. Eisenhower has directed that whenever possible in France a warning shall be given to towns in which certain targets will be intensively bombed.

This warning, the broadcast said,

Continued on Page B

PARADE OF PLANES CARRIES INVADERS

Witness Says First 'Chutists Met Only Light Fire When They Landed in France

The first eyewitness account of the Allies' invasion of Europe was given in a pool broadcast from London this morning by Wright Bryan of the National Broadcasting Company, who accompanied the airborne troops in their landings.

His account said the first spearhead of Allied forces landed by parachute in northern France in the first hour of D-day.

"In the navigator's dome in the flight deck of a C-47, I rode across the English Channel with the first group of planes from the United States Ninth Air Force Troop Carrier Command to take our fighting men into Europe," Mr. Bryan said.

He added that just before he left French soil for the return trip he saw seventeen American paratroopers, led by a lieutenant colonel, jump with their arms, ammunition and equipment into German-occupied France."

He declared that his group at the head of the leading wing was met with "only scattering small

Continued on Page B

Eisenhower Instructs Europeans; Gives Battle Order to His Armies

Following are the texts of a statement by Gen. Dwight D. Eisenhower broadcast to the people of western Europe and his Order of the Day to the Allied Expeditionary Force as recorded by The New York Times and the Columbia Broadcasting System:

People of western Europe! A landing was made this morning on the coast of France by troops of the Allied Expeditionary Force. This landing is part of the concerted United Nations plan for the liberation of Europe, made in conjunction with our great Russian Allies. I have this message for all of you. Although the initial assault may not have been made in your own country, the hour of your liberation is approaching.

All patriots, men and women, young and old, have a part to play in the achievement of final victory. To members of resistance movements, whether led by national or outside leaders, I say: "Follow the instructions you have received." To patriots who are not members of organized resistance groups I say, "continue your passive resistance, but do not needlessly endanger your lives until I give you the signal to rise and strike the enemy. The day will come when I shall need your united strength. Until that day, I call on you for the hard task of discipline and restraint."

Citizens of France! I am proud to have again under my command the gallant forces of France. Fighting beside their Allies, they will play a worthy part in the liberation of their

Continued on Page 3

War News Summarized

TUESDAY, JUNE 6, 1944

The invasion of western Europe began this morning.

General Eisenhower, in his first communiqué from Supreme Headquarters, Allied Expeditionary Force, issued at 3:30 A. M., said that "Allied naval forces supported by strong air forces began landing Allied armies this morning on the northern coast of France."

The assault was made by British, American and Canadian troops who, under command of Gen. Sir Bernard L. Montgomery, landed in Normandy. London earlier Berlin had broadcast that parachute troops had landed on the Normandy Peninsula near Cherbourg and that invasion forces were pouring from landing craft under cover of warships near Havre. Dunkerque and Calais were being heavily bombed, the Germans said.

Later announcements from Berlin said that there was fighting between Caen and Trouville and that shock troops had swung into action to halt the invasion. [All the foregoing, 1:8.]

General Eisenhower, in an order of the day to each member of the "great crusade," told his men the enemy would fight savagely and added: "We will accept nothing less than full victory. Good luck." In a broadcast to the "Peoples of Western Europe," he said the day would come when he would need their full help. A special word to France added that Frenchmen would rule the country. [1:6-7.] Almost simultaneously it was announced that General de Gaulle had arrived in London. [6:2.]

The liberation of Rome in no way slowed the Allied pursuit of the tired and disorganized German armies in Italy yesterday. Armored and motorized units sped across the Tiber River to press hard upon the retreating enemy's heels. Five hundred heavy bombers joined with lighter aircraft to smash rail and road routes leading to northern Italy and to add to the foe's demoralization. The Eighth Army, despite heavy opposition, especially northeast of Valmontone, captured a number of strategic towns. [1:3; map P. 2.]

General Clark said that parts of the two German armies had been smashed. He doubted the ability of the German Fourteenth to put up effective opposition and declared that the Tenth had taken a bad beating. [3:1.]

King Victor Emmanuel fulfilled his promise and turned over all authority to his son, Crown Prince Humbert. [1:5-6.]

President Roosevelt warned the people of the United States in a radio talk last night not to over-emphasize the military significance of the liberation of Rome. "Germany has not yet been driven to surrender," he said. "Victory still lies some distance ahead. * * * It will be tough and it will be costly." The President appealed to the world to give Italy a chance to contribute her share to a lasting peace. [1:1.]

In the Pacific theatre Americans were converging on the Biak airfields. Allied planes sank one and damaged two Japanese destroyers and shot down at least eighteen aircraft. [8:1.]

EISENHOWER ACTS

U. S., British, Canadian Troops Backed by Sea, Air Forces

MONTGOMERY LEADS

Nazis Say Their Shock Units Are Battling Our Parachutists

Communique No. 1 On Allied Invasion

By Broadcast to THE NEW YORK TIMES

LONDON, Tuesday, June 6—The Supreme Headquarters of the Allied Expeditionary Force issued this communiqué this morning:

"Under the command of General Eisenhower, Allied naval forces, supported by strong air forces, began landing Allied armies this morning on the northern coast of France."

By RAYMOND DANIELL

By Cable to THE NEW YORK TIMES.

SUPREME HEADQUARTERS ALLIED EXPEDITIONARY FORCES, Tuesday, June 6—The invasion of Europe from the west has begun.

In the gray light of a summer dawn Gen. Dwight D. Eisenhower threw his great Anglo-American forc.. into action today for the liberation of the Continent. The spearhead of attack was an Army group commanded by Gen. Sir Bernard L. Montgomery and comprising troops of the United States, Britain and Canada.

General Eisenhower's first communiqué was terse and calculated to give little information to the enemy. It said merely that "Allied naval forces supported by strong air forces began landing Allied armies this morning on the northern coast of France."

After the first communiqué was released it was announced that the Allied landing was in Normandy.

Caen Battle Reported

German broadcasts, beginning at 6:30 A. M., London time, [12:30 A. M. Eastern war time] gave first word of the assault. [The Associated Press said General Eisenhower, for the sake of surprise, deliberately let the Germans have the "first word."]

The German DNB agency said the Allied invasion operations began with the landing of airborne troops in the area of the mouth of the Seine River.

[Berlin said the "center of gravity" of the fierce fighting was at Caen, thirty miles southwest of Havre and sixty-five miles southeast of Cherbourg, The Associated Press reported. Caen is ten miles inland from the sea, at the base of the seventy-five-mile-wide Normandy Peninsula, and fighting there might indicate the Allies' seizing of a beachhead.

[DNB said in a broadcast just before 10 A. M. (4 A. M. Eastern war time) that the Anglo-American troops had been reinforced at dawn at the mouth of the Seine River in the Havre area.]

[An Allied correspondent broadcasting from Supreme Headquarters, according to the Columbia Broadcasting System, said this morning that "German tanks are moving up

Continued on Page A
Following Page 3

"All the News That's Fit to Print"

The New York Times.

LATE CITY EDITION
Increasing cloudiness with moderate winds today.
Temperatures Yesterday—Max., 46; Min., 29
Sunrise today, 7:13 A. M.; Sunset, 6:36 P. M.

VOL. XCIV...No. 31,797. Entered as Second-Class Matter, Postoffice, New York, N. Y. NEW YORK, TUESDAY, FEBRUARY 13, 1945. THREE CENTS NEW YORK CITY

BIG 3 DOOM NAZISM AND REICH MILITARISM; AGREE ON FREED LANDS AND OAKS VOTING; CONVOKE UNITED NATIONS IN U. S. APRIL 25

IVES ASSAILS FOES OF ANTI-RACE BILLS AS DISFAVOR RISES

But Demand for Immediate Vote by CIO Head Is Unlikely to Head Off Opposition

PRESS FOR PUBLIC HEARING

Legislators Confident of Aid From Minorities—Chamber Attack Called 'Degrading'

The text of the statement by Assemblyman Ives, Page 18.

Special to THE NEW YORK TIMES.

ALBANY, Feb. 12—Irving M. Ives, Republican leader of the Assembly, and Louis Hollander, president of the State Congress of Industrial Organizations, struck back tonight at critics of the Ives-Quinn anti-discrimination bills.

In a statement defending the proposal to set up a five-man commission with power to eradicate discrimination in employment on racial or religious grounds, Mr. Ives sought to set at rest a strong feeling that it would have the effect of increasing rather than eliminating interracial frictions.

Meanwhile, opposition to the measure continued to grow. It was believed that neither Mr. Ives' statement nor Mr. Hollander's appeal to pass the Ives-Quinn proposals "at once and without any crippling amendments" appear likely to head off that opposition.

Pressure for Public Hearing

In the Senate, where the bill remains in the Finance Committee, there is very strong pressure for a public hearing. Senator Elmer F. Quinn, Democratic leader of the Senate and co-sponsor with Mr. Ives of the legislation, described the pressure for a hearing as "terrific."

Mr. Quinn said that he had been besieged in New York over the week-end by representatives of employment agencies who want an opportunity to present amendments to the bill. But supporters of the measure are opposed to granting further hearings.

Advocates of the legislation also believe that only a few legislators will dare to vote against the measure in view of the strong demand for its passage from CIO unions, Negro and other minority groups.

Some Republican strategists are viewing the proposal as an opportunity to regain the favor of minority groups. Democratic leaders in turn are cracking the whip to obtain a solid Democratic vote in favor of the legislation in both Senate and Assembly.

Governor Dewey has avoided taking any stand on the measure, but he has gone on record in his annual message in favor of the enactment of bills along the lines of the Ives-Quinn proposal to put "our State in the forefront of the nation in the handling of that vital issue."

Mr. Hollander in his appeal for strong CIO pressure in favor of immediate enactment of the legislation characterized the attack on the bill made in New York by the State Chamber of Commerce as "degrading and un-American."

Calls Statement Outrageous

"In this outrageous statement," Mr. Hollander continued, "the Chamber of Commerce, representing the most reactionary forces in our State, has the gall to threaten us with possible race riots, pogroms and other evils. This sinister attempt at blackmailing the Legislature into throwing out the Ives-Quinn bill must be repudiated in the sharpest fashion possible."

Assemblyman Wilson C. van Duzer, Republican, of Orange County, joined Senator Frederic Bontecou, Republican, of Dutchess County, and Assemblyman William Stuart, Republican, of Steuben County, in demanding further hearings before the Ives-Quinn bills are put to a vote.

Opposition forces were receiving some encouragement from the

Continued on Page 18, Column 2

WPB Takes Charge Of Match Output

By The Associated Press.

WASHINGTON, Feb. 12—The War Production Board took control today over production and distribution of matches, to assure, it said, the meeting of military requirements and preventing maldistribution of civilian supplies.

The allocation of matches will be controlled at the producer level.

Production of matches this year is expected to total 460,000,000,000 as compared with an average pre-war level of 480,000,000,000. The reduced production is attributed to the labor shortage.

Military requirements will take about a third of the 1945 output, including the entire production of strike-on-box matches and about 35 per cent of the book matches.

Civilians will find it more difficult to obtain strike-on-box and book matches, but the WPB said that the supply of strike-anywhere, or kitchen, matches would be adequate if there were no hoarding.

BIG 3 AGREEMENT LAUDED BY HOOVER

'Strong Foundation' for New World, He Says—Austin Asks Bipartisan Planning

Before 1,000 persons high in the leadership of the Republican party, former President Herbert Hoover, long a spokesman for an important section of his party, gave an enthusiastic endorsement last night to the agreement reached by President Roosevelt, Marshal Joseph Stalin and Prime Minister Winston Churchill at the Big Three conference in the Crimea.

Called upon for an impromptu speech at the fifty-ninth annual Lincoln Day dinner of the National Republican Club at the Hotel Waldorf-Astoria, Mr. Hoover said he believed the agreement provided "a strong foundation" for the reconstruction of the post-war world. He said:

"On the radio this evening there was announced news of tremendous importance to the whole world. That is the agreement reached in the Black Sea area.

"I believe it comprises a strong foundation on which to rebuild the world.

"If the agreement's promises and ideals which are expressed shall be carried out, it will open a great hope to the world.

"It is fitting that it should have been issued to the world on the birthday of Abraham Lincoln."

As Mr. Hoover resumed his seat after his brief remarks, there was applause from every section of the audience.

Senator Warren R. Austin of Vermont, another speaker at the gathering, joined Mr. Hoover in hailing the Crimea agreement as a constructive step toward peace.

Continued on Page 2, Column 3

CLEVE, PRUEM FALL

Allies Capture Two Key Westwall Positions in North and Center

OPPOSITION IS LIGHT

Germans Draft Women for Volkssturm—New Clashes Reported

By CLIFTON DANIEL
By Wireless to THE NEW YORK TIMES.

SUPREME HEADQUARTERS, Allied Expeditionary Force, Feb. 12—With surprising dispatch, Allied troops broke the Germans' hold on key centers of two sectors of the Western Front today, evicting all except a few snipers from Cleve, at the northern end of the line, and from Pruem, in the center.

British and Canadian forces quickly mopped up the Siegfried fortress town of Cleve and also pressed through the full length of the Reichswald (Reich Forest) to its eastern edge.

Gen. H. D. G. Crerar's forces also were converging on Goch, a German position southeast of the Reichswald comparable to that of Cleve in the north. One force had captured Hau, seven miles north of Goch, while another unit was at Kessel, four miles northwest.

[Due west of Goch, General Crerar's forces also cleared Gennep, another fortified town in that area, press services reported.]

Patton Sets Up New Threat

At the same time Lieut. Gen. George S. Patton's American Third Army fought to merge two of its bridgeheads across the Sauer River, twenty-five miles south of Pruem, into a solid six-mile front that would present a new threat to the road and rail network west of Bonn and Coblenz, of which Pruem was one important hub.

[As the two important Westwall strong points of Cleve and Pruem fell, Germany conscripted all women from 16 to 60 years of age for service in the Volkssturm, while reports from Sweden, Switzerland and Moscow told of mounting unrest and new clashes inside Germany, press services said.]

While the slow but ominous encroachments of the Allies' pent-up strength continued, the Germans were apparently hoping to flood out the Allies' armies, which they repeatedly have reported were ready to attack. A German communiqué today said the flooding of the Roer River Valley had forced the Allies to abandon positions in many sectors and to abandon preparations for an attack.

A natural flooding already made operations extremely difficult on the northern flank of the Canadian First Army's advance around Cleve and there were further reports today of explosions along the

Continued on Page 12, Column 5

THE BIG THREE MEETING AGAIN TO MAKE PLANS FOR THE WORLD

Prime Minister Churchill, President Roosevelt and Marshal Stalin on the grounds of Livadia Palace

The New York Times (British Official Radiophoto)

YALTA PARLEY ENDS

Unified Blows at Reich, Policing Spheres and Reparations Shaped

FRANCE TO GET ROLE

Broader Polish, Yugoslav Regimes Guaranteed—Curzon Line Adopted

The text of the report on the Big Three Conference, Page 4.

By LANSING WARREN
Special to THE NEW YORK TIMES.

WASHINGTON, Feb. 12—Allied decisions sealing the doom of Nazi Germany and German militarism, coordinating military plans for Germany's occupation and control and maintaining order and establishing popular Governments in liberated countries were signed yesterday by President Roosevelt, Marshal Stalin and Prime Minister Churchill near Yalta in the Crimea, the White House announced today.

The conference, held in the summer palace of former Czar Nicholas II on the Black Sea shore, also called for a United Nations security conference in San Francisco on April 25.

The parleys, hitherto shrouded in secrecy except for a brief outline of the agenda issued Feb. 7, were held day and night from Feb. 4 until the final signatures were affixed. The announcement did not refer to President Roosevelt's future movements except that he had left the Crimea.

Main Points of Accord

Major decisions of the conference include:

(1) Plans for new blows at the heart of Germany from the east, west, north and south.

(2) Agreement for occupation by the three Allies, each of a separate zone, as Germany is invaded, and an invitation to France to take over a zone and participate as a fourth member of the Control Commission.

(3) Reparations in kind to be paid by Germany for damages, to be set by an Allied commission. The reparations commission, which will establish the type and amount of payments by Germany, will have its headquarters in Moscow. [Secretary of State Stettinius and Ambassador Harriman arrived in Moscow Monday.]

(4) Settlement of questions left undecided at the conference at Dumbarton Oaks and decision to call a United Nations conference at San Francisco April 25 to prepare the charter for a general international organization to maintain peace and security.

(5) Specific agreements to widen the scope of the present Governments in Poland and Yugoslavia and an understanding to keep order and establish Governments in liberated countries conforming to the popular will and the principles of the Atlantic Charter.

(6) A general declaration of determination to maintain Allied unity for peace.

German People Apart

The statement announced common policies for enforcing unconditional surrender and imposing Nazi Germany's doom. The document draws a distinction between the Nazi system, laws and institutions, the German General Staff and its militarism, which will be relentlessly wiped out, and the German people.

"It is not our purpose," it declared, "to destroy the people of Germany, but only when nazism and militarism have been extirpated will there be hope for a decent life for Germans, and a place for them in the comity of nations."

Until this conference the Allies had laid down no iron-clad program for the control and complete reorganization of Germany. Military plans will be made known only

Continued on Page 4, Column 1

MANILA TRAP SHUT; LUZON IS CROSSED

U. S. Forces Unite to Squeeze Capital as Armored Push East Reaches Coast

By GEORGE E. JONES
By Wireless to THE NEW YORK TIMES.

MANILA, Tuesday, Feb. 13—A broad front of American troops embracing three divisions now confronts the stubbornly resisting Japanese garrison in Manila, and there is reason to believe that the drive to complete seizure of the Orient's fourth largest city has now been accelerated.

The First Cavalry Division vet-

Continued on Page 16, Column 3

Red Army Is at Bober River After 16-Mile Gain in Silesia

By The United Press.

LONDON, Tuesday, Feb. 13—Red Army forces, opening the second month of their Winter offensive, pushed sixteen miles across Silesia yesterday in an outflanking drive southeast of Berlin that carried to within seventy-four miles of Dresden. Marshal Ivan S. Koneff's First Ukrainian Army seized 100 Silesian communities as it advanced westward from its bridgehead on the west bank of the Oder and reached the Bober River on a fifteen-mile front. Berlin said the Russians already had forced the Bober at two points.

Far behind the main fighting front, the Russians all but crushed the last organized resistance in long-besieged Budapest, having

Continued on Page 10, Column 5

PACIFIC WAR ROLE FOR SOVIET HINTED

Date of United Nations Parley Follows 'Denouncing' Time of Russo-Japanese Treaty

By JAMES B. RESTON
Special to THE NEW YORK TIMES.

WASHINGTON, Feb. 12—The positive announcements in the Crimean communiqué produced general satisfaction in Washington tonight, but what really interested the capital were the things the Big Three statement did not even mention.

The first of these was Japan. The word does not appear in the longest communiqué ever issued after a meeting of the heads of state, but the date set for the opening of the United Nations Security Conference in San Francisco, April 25, is the day after the date on which Russia must denounce her five-year neutrality pact with Japan unless she wishes it to run for another five years.

There is naturally some reticence here about any hasty conclusions in regard to so decisive a factor in the Far Eastern war. But there has been a growing confidence

Continued on Page 6, Column 6

ROOSEVELT PRESSES WORLD MONEY PLAN

He Asks Congress for Action on Monetary Fund and on Bank of Reconstruction

The President's message on world monetary unity, Page 17.

Special to THE NEW YORK TIMES.

WASHINGTON, Feb. 12—President Roosevelt urged Congress today to take immediate action on the Bretton Woods proposals for an international monetary fund and an international bank for reconstruction and development.

In a special message, the President said that the two projects, involving legislation for American participation in the $8,800,000,000 stabilization fund and the $9,100,000,000 bank, were essential "in our plans for a peaceful and prosperous world," which, he said, could be attained "only if solutions are found to the difficult economic problems we face today."

Mr. Roosevelt recognized the criticisms directed against the stabilization fund proposal, mostly by United States banking groups, by conceding that it was not perfect, but suggested that experience would permit necessary improvements to be made.

Wagner Plans Bill

He asked Congress to act with special promptness on the plan for the international bank, which would guarantee loans for important development and reconstruction projects in the member countries. But he added that "the monetary fund and the bank together comprise a

Continued on Page 17, Column 1

War News Summarized

TUESDAY, FEBRUARY 13, 1945

"Nazi Germany is doomed . . . Only when nazism and militarism have been extirpated will there be hope for a decent life for Germans, and a place for them in the comity of nations."

That was the message for the "common enemy" emanating from Yalta, in the Crimea, where President Roosevelt, Prime Minister Churchill and Premier Stalin, completing their historic conference, made clear the meaning of "unconditional surrender."

The combined military plans call for even more powerful blows from all directions, said their report made public yesterday. Germany will be divided into three separate occupation zones, coordinated through a commission of the three Supreme Army Commanders sitting in Berlin. France will be invited to take over a zone and join the commission.

Germany will be under strict control until all her armed forces have been disbanded, her General Staff broken up "for all time," her war industries eliminated, every vestige of the Nazi party and its doctrines eradicated and other measures taken "to insure that Germany will never again be able to disturb the peace of the world."

The Germans will have to pay in kind for all war damages, and a reparations commission will sit in Moscow to determine the extent and methods of payment.

The principles of the Atlantic Charter will govern the treatment of liberated Europe, it was agreed. A new Polish Government will be formed on a broad basis and universal secret elections will be held. The conference decided that the Curzon Line should be Poland's eastern boundary, with compensations from Germany in the west to be settled at the peace conference.

Yugoslavia was urged to put the Tito-Subasitch agreement into immediate effect and create a broad, provisional Parliament.

The Foreign Secretaries of the three nations will meet three or four times a year. The first time will be after a United Nations Conference to open in San Francisco April 25, which will prepare a charter along the lines of Dumbarton Oaks for the new international organization to maintain peace and security. [All the foregoing 1:8.]

While no mention was made of the Pacific war, it was pointed out that the period for denunciation of the Soviet-Japanese pact of neutrality would expire a day before the San Francisco meeting. [1:6.]

The Subasitch Cabinet will leave London shortly for Belgrade to set up a new Yugoslav Government. [3:4.] With Elas' agreement to disarm within two weeks and the Greek understanding that a plebiscite would be held within a year, difficulties in that country seemed about over. [6:1.]

On the fighting fronts Canadian and British troops captured Cleve, while Americans seized Pruem in two more important breaches of Germany's western defenses. [1:3; maps, P. 12.] The Red Army resumed its drive toward Danzig and also captured Bunzlau, seventy-four miles from Dresden. [1:5-6; map, P. 10.] Himmler ordered all German girls and women conscripted into the Volkssturm to meet the rising Allied threats. [9:1.]

American troops in south Manila joined forces when the First Cavalry made contact with the Thirty-seventh Infantry and also with the Eleventh Airborne Division. Bitter fighting was going on. The Sixth Division cut across Luzon by driving to Dingalan Bay. [1:4; map P. 16.]

Monday Meat Ban Flouted Again; Cafes Exhibit and Serve Steaks

By CHARLES GRUTZNER Jr.

Conservation Monday, which had got off to a false start last week when many restaurants served steaks, roasts and chops, tried the other foot yesterday and stumbled even more badly.

A restaurant opposite Radio City filled one show window with red, juicy steaks—and sold them, nicely broiled, at its dining tables. Less flaunting, perhaps, but equally open was the non-observance by eating places in all parts of the city of Mayor La Guardia's "little brother" to meatless Tuesday and meatless Friday.

More restaurants advertised major meat dishes among their daily specials yesterday than on last Monday. The non-observers included flashy Broadway dining places, chain restaurants, neighborhood eating rooms and lunch wagons.

The special at one of the food chains, with stool-and-counter shops scattered about the city, was sirloin steak with French fried potatoes for 50 cents. Some of the better-known Chinese restaurants in midtown made a feature of roast beef, lamb and pork chops, and roast ham. Even the five-and-dime stores played up veal cutlets (35 cents, with peas and potato) in their window displays.

A recheck of several scattered restaurants that had sold major meat dishes openly the previous Monday showed all selling them again yesterday. One place that had offered sirloin steak at 65 cents a week earlier, had as its special a hot roast beef sandwich at

Continued on Page 24, Column 3

Elliott Roosevelt Made Brigadier By Senate, 53 to 11, on War Record

By JAY WALZ
Special to THE NEW YORK TIMES.

WASHINGTON, Feb. 12—The Senate voted 53 to 11 today to confirm the promotion of Col. Elliott Roosevelt to be brigadier general and then by voice vote confirmed seventy-seven other colonels for the higher rank.

Action was taken on the President's son after he was described both as "an amateur" and as an outstanding leader who had "proved his worth in combat."

Those voting against confirmation, all Republicans, were Senators Owen Brewster of Maine, Harlan J. Bushfield of South Dakota, Hugh Butler of Nebraska, Arthur Capper and Clyde M. Reed of Kansas, Bourke B. Hickenlooper of Iowa, Hiram W. Johnson of California, William Langer of North Dakota, E. H. Moore of Oklahoma, Charles W. Tobey of New Hampshire and Kenneth S. Wherry of Nebraska.

Following a request by Senator Alben W. Barkley, majority leader, that the Roosevelt nomination be considered separately, the two-hour debate centered on the 34-year-old Air Corps officer.

The only other name mentioned was that of Col. William H. Eaton, who was killed in a plane crash in France on Feb. 6. Chairman Elbert D. Thomas of the Military Affairs Committee read a letter from Secretary Stimson asking that the promotion be granted posthumously.

Senator Bushfield raised the question of Colonel Roosevelt's rise from a captaincy since 1940.

Continued on Page 18, Column 4

"All the News That's Fit to Print"

The New York Times.

LATE CITY EDITION
Clear and continued cold with moderate winds today.
Temperatures Yesterday—Max., 33; Min., 23
Sunrise today, 7:46 A. M.; Sunset, 6:36 P. M.

VOL. XCIV No. 31,803. Entered as Second-Class Matter, Postoffice, New York, N. Y. NEW YORK, MONDAY, FEBRUARY 19, 1945. THREE CENTS NEW YORK CITY

U. S. MARINES STORM ASHORE ON IWO ISLAND; 509 PLANES, 36 SHIPS SMASHED IN TOKYO BLOW; BRITISH AT EDGE OF GOCH; PATTON STRIKES AGAIN

STIMSON ASSAILS DELAY ON JOB BILL AS COSTLY IN LIVES

Using 'Plain' Words as 'Duty,' He Says Senate Committee Listens to 'Trivial' Pleas

'DEADLY SHORTAGES' LOOM

Secretary Calls It 'Failure' of Our Democracy Not to Compel Full War Output

Secretary Stimson's address is printed in full on Page 11.

Special to THE NEW YORK TIMES.

WASHINGTON, Feb. 18—Secretary of War Stimson denounced tonight Senate delay in acting on the National Service Bill and called absence of legislation to keep men at their wartime jobs a "failure of American democracy."

In a speech over the Blue Network, he addressed himself "to all Americans, but primarily to those who have sons or husbands or other dear ones at the front" and declared that it was his "duty to speak plainly."

He asserted that we had "reached a crisis in this war" and that "we dare not delay longer" in providing the legislation to give to our fighting men the full support of "our strength." Delay, he warned, meant prolonging of the war and waste of American lives.

He praised the House for having "risen to the occasion" and passed the National Service Bill, and said that the Senate Military Affairs Committee, listening to voices speaking for "special interests" and, by comparison with the national interest, "trivial interests," had kept the bill suffocated for nearly three weeks until "enemies of the measure are beginning to boast today in the streets of Washington that they have killed it."

Roosevelt Plea Possible

It was reported in Senate circles tonight that one of the first acts of President Roosevelt on his return from the Crimea Conference would be to call again for action on the bill.

Some Senators predicted tonight that "some sort of a bill" would be reported by the committee during the week. A group of conservative Republicans and several Democrats were reported to favor a substitute which would give statutory authority to the War Manpower Commission and order a survey of war plants to root out any hoarded labor. Other compromises were also being discussed.

Secretary Stimson was emphatic in his speech about the gravity of the situation. He declared that "ever since the beginning of the war" there had been "an alarming turnover of workers in war industries."

"Every responsible leader of the military and naval forces" from the President down, he said, agreed on the need for adoption of national service legislation to keep workers at their wartime tasks.

"The inevitable result of this failure of American democracy," he went on, "is now becoming apparent at this crisis of the war.

Warns of "Deadly Shortages"

"Shortages, deadly shortages, are now looming up before us at a moment when every ounce of power should be thrown into the combat. I mean both shortages of weapons and shortages of manpower caused by the misplacement of our men."

He pointed out that the United States alone among the Allies had no service law and that Britain and Russia had been working under such laws "since the very beginning of the war."

Our enemies, of course, he added, have been so organized from the start.

"We alone," he proceeded, "are depending upon voluntary and therefore ineffective methods of organization among the workers who

Continued on Page 11, Column 4

Battle in Skagerrak Reported by Swedes

By The United Press.

LONDON, Feb. 18—The Swedish radio said today that a "very large-scale" battle involving a southbound German convoy had been fought yesterday off the Swedish Skagerrak coast.

The battle was reported to have lasted four hours. The broadcast said that Allied naval and air units had probably participated. "Observers say they have never before heard anything like it and are of the opinion that direct hits must have been made on ships," the broadcast asserted.

ORDERS PRICE TAGS ON COTTON CLOTHES

OPA Demands Exact Ceiling Be Shown on Most Such Apparel to Avert Rises

Special to THE NEW YORK TIMES.

WASHINGTON, Feb. 18—Consumers, beginning on March 5, will find most cotton garments, from infants' rompers to women's dresses, tagged with a manufacturer's ticket showing the exact OPA ceiling price permitted on each separate article, Chester Bowles, OPA Administrator, said today in outlining the first step in a broad program to check clothing prices.

The action, the administrator said, would also have the effect of bringing back more of the essential articles of apparel to the low and medium price range. However, the benefits of this part of the program might not be noticeable before early summer, he warned.

Practically all infants' and children's cotton apparel and "a very large part" of the output of men's and women's cotton garments will carry the tags, according to Mr. Bowles.

Eventually from 65 to 90 per cent of all civilian woven cotton apparel will be subject to the program's controls, which, it was explained, would tie in with a recent War Production Board order channeling most of the cotton fabrics available for civilian use into popular and medium priced garments.

The Ticket for Each Garment

The plan, which Mr. Bowles described as one "easy" for both retailers and the buying public to understand, begins with the manufacturer pinning to each piece of clothing given by the order a ticket which will read as follows:

"OPA Ceiling Price $0.00.

"Lot Number —— (or brand name).

"WPB 385 or WPB 328-B."

The WPB figures refer to War Production Orders through which the maker obtained the material in a piece of clothing.

The prices fixed by the manufacturer would be based on OPA regulations, which provided, Mr. Bowles said, for slight variations that had always been allowed in ceiling prices for similar garments in different retail stores. Such variations take into account differences in cost to the retailer, depending on whether he buys di-

Continued on Page 30, Column 5

NAZI BASE DOOMED

British Artillery Pounds Goch to Aid Infantry 1,000 Yards Away

CALCAR FIGHT RAGES

3d Army Enters Reich Above Vianden—7th Also Crosses Line

By CLIFTON DANIEL

By Wireless to THE NEW YORK TIMES.

SUPREME HEADQUARTERS, Allied Expeditionary Force, Feb. 18—From low hills overlooking Goch British gunners picked off targets inside the town today and under a canopy of artillery fire Gen. H. D. G. Crerar's infantrymen assaulted the anti-tank ditches on the eastern defense perimeter of the town, which now looks as if it were doomed.

At the same time the American Third Army again expanded its bridgehead over the Our and Sauer Rivers north of Echternach, spreading it out today to a width of almost five miles. [The United Press said that a new division, not yet identified, had invaded Germany at a new point north of Vianden, Luxembourg.]

[Press services also reported that the American Seventh Army had re-entered Germany in the Saarbruecken area.]

The Canadian First Army, with its Canadian and United Kingdom troops, still carried the burden of the Western Front fighting today, however. Goch, with its reinforced and fortified houses, was one of two strong bastions of the line that the Germans held when the Canadian First Army attacked the northern end of the Westwall ten days ago, but patrols prodding its outskirts today found that opposition was light, the town having been outflanked and all but surrounded.

German Defense Loose

The Germans began to lose coordination in their defense yesterday and it now looks as if they would give up another important stretch of ground, but meanwhile they are fighting fiercely to hold flanks of General Crerar's advance along the Meuse (Maas) on one side and the Rhine on the other. Having lost their firm grip on Goch, the Germans are struggling to retain Calcar, the second most important front-line supply center left to them in the battle area. On the opposite side of the front they are likewise trying to halt the United Kingdom forces creeping down along the Meuse beyond Afferden toward Venlo.

The suddenness of the break in the coordination of German defense was illustrated by the fact that in driving across the road from Goch to Calcar the British made a surprise move and captured more than 900 prisoners in one day. The total number of Germans now captured since the beginning of General Crerar's offensive is more than 8,000. In an effort to minimize the reinforcement and supply of the remnants

Continued on Page 6, Column 2

AMERICAN TANK RUNNING A GANTLET OF STEEL IN MANILA

An amphibious vehicle crossing the Pasig River under Japanese machine gun fire while shells from a protecting barrage laid down by our artillery burst on the far shore. Associated Press (U. S. Signal Corps)

FINAL ROUND IS ON, MONTGOMERY SAYS

Marshal Calls on His Soldiers to Help Strike Knockout Blow at German Army

By The Associated Press.

THE TWENTY-FIRST ARMY GROUP HEADQUARTERS, in Europe, Feb. 18—Field Marshal Sir Bernard L. Montgomery in a personal message to troops under his command declared today: "We now have come to the last and final round, and we want and will go for the knockout blow."

The text of his order follows:

The operations of the Allies on all fronts have now brought the German war to its final stage. There was a time some years ago when it did not seem possible that we could win this war. The present situation is that we can-

Continued on Page 6, Column 5

Americans Seize Hospital In Manila and Free 7,000

By LINDESAY PARROTT

By Wireless to THE NEW YORK TIMES.

ADVANCED HEADQUARTERS, on Luzon, Monday, Feb. 19—Seven thousand persons, including patients, internees and civilians, both American and Filipino, were freed as American troops seized the Philippine General Hospital on Taft Avenue in the Ermita section of Manila, where fanatically resisting Japanese fought back against an ever-tightening ring that was steadily pushing them into Manila Bay.

The hospital was captured after advancing Americans shelled the walls and north and east gates of the hospital grounds, adjoining the campus of the University of Philippines. Gen. Douglas MacArthur's communiqué stated that those released, including 100 Americans, had been evacuated to safety.

Last night the grounds of the hospital, extending to within four blocks of Dewey Boulevard and the

Continued on Page 3, Column 1

RED ARMY NEARING BORDER OF SAXONY

German Resistance Stiffens—Russians Capture Sagan and Break Into Grudziadz

By The United Press.

LONDON, Monday, Feb. 19—Red Army forces in German Silesia yesterday fought through stiff enemy resistance to within nineteen miles of the Saxon border and sixteen miles east of Goerlitz, key industrial city guarding the road to Dresden.

In its tenth major encirclement of the winter offensive the Red Army also surrounded and broke into the outskirts of the Vistula River fortress of Grudziadz in Poland, fifty-seven miles south of Danzig. Two additional pockets of enemy troops were wiped out in Pomerania and in Brandenburg.

In three other actions Russian troops hammered deeper into the streets of the Silesian capital of Breslau, virtually completed the mop-up of the Polish city of Posen, and tightened the ring around enemy troops in East Prussia, where Gen. Ivan D. Chernyakhovsky, 37, commander of the Third White Russian Army, was killed in action.

The new Soviet successes were carried out as six great battles

Continued on Page 5, Column 3

AIR BLOW AT TOKYO 'DECISIVE VICTORY'

Nimitz Says Fifth Fleet Scored 'Complete Tactical Surprise' in Two-Day Attack

By The Associated Press.

ADVANCED HEADQUARTERS, Guam, Monday, Feb. 19—American carrier planes scored a "decisive" victory over the Japanese in the mighty 1,500-plane attacks on the Tokyo-Yokohama area of the Japanese homeland Friday and Saturday, Admiral Chester W. Nimitz announced today.

Admiral Nimitz announced the Americans, scoring a "complete tactical surprise," destroyed 332 Japanese aircraft in the air and 177 on the ground. At least 150 more Japanese planes were probably destroyed or damaged on the first day and an unknown number were damaged on the second day.

He said one Japanese escort carrier was bombed and set afire, nine coastal vessels were sunk, one destroyer was sunk, two escort destroyers sunk, one cargo ship sunk and twenty two enemy coastal ships damaged, besides various Japanese picket vessels destroyed.

Forty-nine American planes were lost in the two days of destructive raids, Admiral Nimitz said. Thirty to forty Yank fliers were lost.

"None of our ships suffered damage from enemy action," the special communiqué reported.

The Fifth Fleet force under Admiral R. A. Spruance, one of the greatest ever assembled, "achieved a decisive victory over the enemy in attacks on Tokyo, Feb. 16 and 17 (east longitude date)," Admiral Nimitz announced.

He said a "complete tactical surprise" was accomplished under a cover of weather so adverse it also hampered enemy operations.

Admiral Nimitz congratulated

Continued on Page 4, Column 6

War News Summarized

MONDAY, FEBRUARY 19, 1945

United States Marines of the Fifth Amphibious Corps went ashore on Iwo Island in the Volcano group, establishing two beachheads. Tokyo reported bitter fighting on the island, 750 miles from the Japanese capital. The landings followed a fierce bombardment by naval craft, including battleships, and land-based planes. Other bombers hit Truk and targets in the Palaus, while carrier aircraft struck Chichi Island in the Bonins, nearer Japan than Iwo. [1:8; map P. 3.]

Five hundred and nine Japanese planes were destroyed, an escort carrier, three other warships and ten more ships were sunk, and heavy damage was done to airfields and factories in last week's 1,500-plane carrier attack on the Tokyo-Yokohama area, Admiral Nimitz announced today. An additional 150 enemy planes were probably destroyed. We lost forty-nine aircraft. [1:7.]

The blows now being struck at Japan were made possible by the heroic stand of the "Dead Army" of Bataan in 1942, General MacArthur said. He reported further gains on Corregidor and Bataan and in the Manila mop-up. [1:5-6.]

British troops in Burma crossed the Irrawaddy in captured Japanese boats thirty miles west of Mandalay, threatening to outflank that city. Another landing was made on the west coast at Ru-ywa, sixty-five miles southeast of Akyab, cutting the enemy's coastal escape road. [5:1.] In China the Japanese recaptured Pingshek and moved on Ichang in an effort to regain twenty-five miles of the Canton-Hankow railway. [3:1.]

Patrols of the Canadian First Army fought their way into the outskirts of Goch amid mounting signs of disintegration in the German defense. The United States Third Army crossed into the Reich near Vianden, and the Seventh reinvaded the Saar Basin southwest of Saarbruecken. [1:3; maps, P. 6.]

Field Marshal Montgomery told his troops they were in the "last and final round." It "may be long and difficult," he said, but a somewhat different "knockout blow" will be "delivered from more than one direction." [1:4.]

RAF planes hit Berlin and Mannheim last night after Wesel, sixteen miles from the Canadian First Army front, had been attacked. Allied bombers were reported over Germany later in the night. Americans from Italy blasted rail targets at Linz, Austria. [7:2.]

The Red Army advanced in most sectors, encircling and fighting into the outskirts of Grudziadz in the "Polish Corridor" and capturing the river strongholds of Sagan and Naumburg in Silesia. [1:6; map P 8.]

It was said in Paris that General de Gaulle had coupled his refusal to meet President Roosevelt in Algiers with an invitation to visit Paris. [9:2.]

Senator Bridges received from Geneva alleged Allied armistice terms to Italy that stripped that country of all military power and considerable territory and placed her economy under Anglo-Saxon control. Some 2,000,000 Italians would help reconstruct ravaged Europe. [7:5.]

Diplomats reaching Mexico City for the Inter-American Conference favored greater power for small nations in post-war plans and, while doubtful of Argentina's intentions, hoped for friendly relations. [1:6-7.]

City-Wide Produce Tie-Up Looms As Drivers Halt Bronx Deliveries

A strike of truckmen affiliated with Local 202, International Brotherhood of Teamsters, was called early today at the Bronx Terminal Market, tying up all produce deliveries in that borough and was threatening to spread city-wide.

However, the full effects will not be felt in the other boroughs until the end of the week, as the contracts in Manhattan and Brooklyn do not expire until Friday.

Meanwhile, carloads of produce were piling up at piers and freight terminals, and Washington wholesale market was crowded with fruits and vegetables as union delegates warned their men not to handle any foodstuffs for sale or delivery to Bronx dealers. Then they added, "tonight the Bronx, next week Brooklyn and Manhattan."

At 1 A. M. when 300 trucks normally would start toward Washington Market to pick up produce for the Bronx Terminal for ultimate distribution through jobbers to retail outlets "not a wheel was turning." Two hundred platform men and 300 chauffeurs, meanwhile, were idling about with instructions from union delegates not to work as a contract that expired Friday had not been signed.

The proposed contract, union representatives said, called for a

Continued on Page 18, Column 3

Mexico Talks Designed to Link Hemisphere to Dumbarton Oaks

By JAMES B. RESTON

Special to THE NEW YORK TIMES

MEXICO CITY, Feb. 18—The Inter-American Conference on Problems of War and Peace will not open until Wednesday but most of the delegates are here and many of the decisions that will be announced in the next few days are now being taken in a series of conferences in the capital.

In this respect the forthcoming conference is not unlike a political convention at home. Preparation is at least two-thirds of the battle and what important decisions have not already been made are likely to be made within the next few days.

The two main political questions before the conference, for example, are what policy the American nations are to take regarding the proposed Dumbarton Oaks international security organization and what they are to do about the Argentine Government whose undemocratic actions at home and defiance of the United States abroad have virtually isolated her from the American community of nations.

There will be many different opinions expressed here about these two questions in the next fortnight and Ezequiel Padilla, Mexican Foreign Secretary, will undoubtedly seize the opportunity to champion greater rights for the small na-

Continued on Page 4, Column 3

LANDING EFFECTED

Nimitz Reports Invasion of Volcano Isle 750 Miles From Tokyo

FIERCE FIGHTING IS ON

Japanese Report Battle at Futatsune Beach on Southwest Coast

By The Associated Press.

ADVANCED HEADQUARTERS Guam, Monday, Feb. 19—American Marines, their path cleared by the most intensive neutralization campaign of the Pacific war, have landed on strategic little Iwo Island, one of the Volcano group, 750 statute miles south of Tokyo.

The landing was made this (Monday) morning. The Fourth and Fifth Marine Divisions made this first Marine operation since the Palaus were invaded last September. [Lieut. Gen. Holland M. Smith, victor over the Japanese on Saipan, was in command of the Marines, The United Press said.]

Admiral Chester W. Nimitz announced in a special communiqué today the momentous development in the fast-moving Pacific war which put American troops on the logical ocean stepping-stone to Tokyo.

Iwo is so close to Tokyo that it is administered by Tokyo prefecture.

American fighters and medium bombers based on Iwo's large airdrome would be within land-based striking range of Tokyo for the first time.

Japanese Tell of Invasion

American troops going ashore in 100 landing boats made a successful landing on Iwo at 8 A. M. Monday (Japanese time), the Tokyo radio announced late last night.

A broadcast, recorded by The United Press in San Francisco, said "part of the enemy forces have landed."

It was the first indication from the enemy radio that a successful landing had been made. Previously Tokyo had reported four "attempted landings" were made on the island Saturday but had been "repulsed."

The text of the enemy broadcast:

"Following a series of abortive landing attempts a part of the enemy forces have finally started landings on Iwo Jima since 1 o'clock this Monday morning.

Heavy Fighting Reported

"The landing is being made on the southeast coast of the island. The Japanese garrison immediately pushing the enemy invaders back to the shore is now engaged in fierce counter-attack against the enemy.

"The landing was preceded by persistent naval and air attacks since early last Wednesday morning."

The Japanese Domei agency reported that "heavy fighting" was in progress between the Japanese garrison and American forces that landed on the island with "about 100 landing vessels."

The Japanese Domei agency declared that the landing forces had hit Futatsune beach, on the southwestern sector of the island.

In an English-language dispatch recorded by the Federal Communications Commission, Domei

Continued on Page 3, Column 5

Fleet in Manila Bay, U. S. Radio Reports

The American Broadcasting Station in Europe declared last night that United States-Seventh Fleet warships "have steamed into Manila Harbor without incident."

Quoting "a dispatch from Luzon," the broadcast said: "Manila Bay is described as now open to American naval vessels." The broadcast was recorded by the Columbia Broadcasting System.

"All the News That's Fit to Print"

The New York Times.

LATE CITY EDITION
Clearing and warm today.
Fair, continued warm tomorrow.
Temperatures Yesterday—Max., 74; Min., 54
Sunrise today, 6:31 A. M.; Sunset, 7:33 P. M.

VOL. XCIV...No. 31,856. Entered as Second-Class Matter, Postoffice, New York, N. Y. NEW YORK, FRIDAY, APRIL 13, 1945. THREE CENTS IN NEW YORK CITY

PRESIDENT ROOSEVELT IS DEAD; TRUMAN TO CONTINUE POLICIES; 9TH CROSSES ELBE, NEARS BERLIN

U. S. AND RED ARMIES DRIVE TO MEET

Americans Across the Elbe in Strength Race Toward Russians Who Have Opened Offensive From Oder

WEIMAR TAKEN, RUHR POCKET SLASHED

Third Army Reported 19 Miles From Czechoslovak Border—British Drive Deeper in the North, Seizing Celle—Canadians Freeing Holland

By DREW MIDDLETON
By Wireless to THE NEW YORK TIMES.

PARIS, April 12—Thousands of tanks and a half million doughboys of the United States First, Third and Ninth Armies are racing through the heart of the Reich on a front of 150 miles, threatening Berlin, Leipzig and the last citadels of the Nazi power.

The Second Armored Division of the Ninth Army has crossed the Elbe River in force and is striking eastward toward Berlin, whose outskirts lie less than sixty miles to the east, according to reports from the front. [A report quoted by The United Press placed the Americans less than fifty miles from the capital.] Beyond Berlin the First White Russian Army has crossed the Oder on a wide front and a junction between the western and eastern Allies is not far off.

[The Moscow radio reported that heavy battles were raging west of the Oder before Berlin, indicating that Marshal Gregory K. Zhukoff had launched his drive toward the Reich's capital. The Soviet communiqué announced further progress by the Red Army forces in and around Vienna.]

Paris is wild with excitement tonight. A special edition of the newspaper France-Soir carries a report by the radio station "Voice of America" that places American forces fifteen and five-eighths miles from Berlin after an airborne landing that had linked up with Lieut. Gen. William H. Simpson's forces advancing eastward from the Elbe. This would put American forces only seventy-five miles from the Red Army vanguard.

No Confirmation at Headquarters

There was no confirmation of this report at Allied Supreme Headquarters, which by its own admission was thirty-six hours behind developments on some sectors of the front.

Resistance was continuing only on the northern and southern flanks. The center had burst wide open. Weimar fell to Lieut. Gen. George S. Patton's infantry, and reports from the front said Erfurt also had been cleared. Schweinfurt and Heilbronn, two German bastions on the south, had fallen to United States Seventh Army forces, who were driving on Bamberg, while farther north Third Army forces were about thirty-five miles from the Czechoslovak frontier in the area east of Coburg.

[The German radio reported American Third Army forces at Lichtenberg, nineteen miles from the Czechoslovak border, The United Press said.]

The offensives to liberate the Netherlands and reduce the Ruhr

Continued on Page 12, Column 2

OUR OKINAWA GUNS DOWN 118 PLANES

Japanese Fliers Start 'Suicide' Attacks on Fleet, Sink a Destroyer, Hit Other Ships

By W. H. LAWRENCE
By Wireless to THE NEW YORK TIMES.

GUAM, Friday, April 13—Japanese attempting to halt the American march to Tokyo, have started "desperate, suicidal" aerial attacks upon our ships and men in the Okinawa area, losing 118 planes on Thursday alone, Fleet Admiral Chester W. Nimitz announced today.

The Japanese succeeded in sinking a destroyer and damaging several other surface units, the communiqué said. All of the damaged vessels remained in action.

It was the first time that the Navy had revealed the suicidal nature of the Japanese air missions against our ships and men. The Japanese radio has been saying that this type of assault was being carried on by a "special attack corps" known in Japanese as "kamakazi," which, translated literally, means "divine wind."

Attack at Low Levels

The Japanese fliers launched their attacks upon our ships and men at a high speed and from low levels, diving directly into a ship or troop concentration to explode their bombs as they crashed.

There was no official estimate of the total number of enemy aircraft engaged in the Okinawa area attack other than the report of the 118 enemy planes destroyed.

Admiral Nimitz reported that the attacks began early on April 12 (Eastern Longitude time) with seven enemy planes shot down during the morning in the vicinity of the Hagushi beaches.

The tempo of the attack was stepped up in the afternoon as the Japanese bore in on our ships in wave after wave. Admiral Nimitz said that ships' guns, carrier aircraft and shore-based anti-aircraft shot down 111 of the attackers.

The revelation of the suicidal Japanese air attacks was the highlight of Admiral Nimitz' regular morning communiqué, which also disclosed the identity of two Marine and two Army divisions that have gone into action on Okinawa. These included the Twenty-seventh Army Division, formed from New York National Guard units, which are seeing action for the first time since the Saipan campaign and previously had engaged in the Gilbert Islands assault. It is com-

Continued on Page 18, Column 3

Army Leaders See Reich End at Hand

By The Associated Press.

WASHINGTON, April 12—High Army officials told Senators today that the end of organized fighting in Germany probably would come within a few days.

Describing the pell-mell dash of American Armies across Germany, General Staff officers expressed the opinion to members of the Senate Military Committee that a collapse of German arms was imminent.

Those who attended said the army chiefs declared that they were so sure of the results that orders had been drawn for a drastic reduction in shipments of durable equipment to Europe.

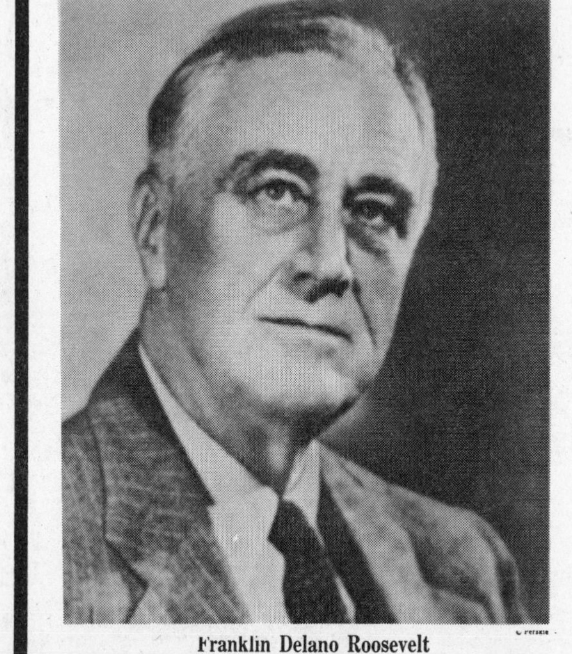

Franklin Delano Roosevelt
1882-1945

SECURITY PARLEY WON'T BE DELAYED

State Department Urges That World Be Shown We Plan No Changes in Policy

By JAMES B. RESTON
Special to THE NEW YORK TIMES.

WASHINGTON, April 12—The United Nations Security Conference will open in San Francisco on April 25, despite the death of President Roosevelt, Secretary of State Edward R. Stettinius Jr. announced tonight.

Mr. Stettinius said that he had been authorized by President Harry Truman to make this announcement after a meeting of the Cabinet at the White House.

Most of the overseas delegations to the San Francisco conference have either arrived in this country or are now on their way, but while this was said to have been a factor in the decision to proceed with the conference, State Department officials urged that every attempt be made to give immediate evidence to the world that President Roosevelt's foreign policy would be sustained by the new Administration.

President Roosevelt had planned to address the San Francisco conference. His interest in an international organization of nations to maintain peace and security had gone back to his service in the Wilson Administration, when he sat in the gallery of the Senate and listened to the debate that resulted in the rejection of the League of Nations Covenant. He had expressed to friends his desire to participate in the San Francisco conference and to see the United States enter the new league during his term in office.

The sudden elevation of Presi-

Continued on Page 2, Column 1

War News Summarized

FRIDAY, APRIL 13, 1945

President Roosevelt died yesterday afternoon, suddenly and unexpectedly. He was stricken with a massive cerebral hemorrhage at Warm Springs, Ga., on the eve of his greatest military and diplomatic successes—the impending fall of Berlin and the opening of the San Francisco Conference to set up a World Security Organization that would make the world free from martial and economic strife [1:7-8.]

Mr. Roosevelt had been sitting in front of the fireplace of his Little White House, having gone to Warm Springs on March 30 for a three-week rest. About 2:15 Eastern war time he said, "I have a terrific headache," lost consciousness in a few moments and died at 4:35. He was 63 years old. [1:6.]

The tragic word spread quickly around the world. Expressions of sorrow poured in from all sections. [4:5.] American soldiers and sailors refused to believe the reports until there was no longer doubt that their Commander in Chief had gone. [4:2-3.]

Harry S. Truman was sworn in as President at 7:09 o'clock last night, and a few minutes later Mrs. Roosevelt left for Warm Springs. [1:7.] The new President immediately called a Cabinet meeting and declared that Mr. Roosevelt's policies would be continued, that the war would be carried on until Germany and Japan surrendered unconditionally and that the San Francisco Conference would open April 25 as scheduled. [1:3.]

Some 500,000 American soldiers of the Third and Ninth Armies, and thousands of tanks, sped along a 150-mile front toward Berlin and Leipzig. The Ninth, surging across the Elbe, according to delayed reports was less than fifty miles from the German capital and 115 from the Russians along the Oder. The Third Army captured Weimar, home of the late German Republic, and was twenty-three miles below Leipzig, with the First closing a pincers from the north. [1:1-2; map P. 2.]

The Moscow radio reported that the Red Army was waging fierce battles east of Berlin, indicating resumption of the drive on that city. Elsewhere Russian troops scored wide gains and cut the last escape railroad from Vienna. [13:1.]

Open cities were ruled out and every German was ordered by Himmler to fight to the death, although Goebbels said "the war cannot last much longer." [12:6-7.]

The Ninth Air Force destroyed at least 117 more German planes yesterday. [11:8.]

In Italy the Eighth Army advanced along a thirty-mile front toward Bologna and the Po Valley; the Fifth Army also made good gains and was eleven miles from La Spezia. [13:8, with map.]

Japanese planes resumed their suicide attacks on American ships off Okinawa, sinking a destroyer and damaging several other vessels. One hundred and eighteen enemy planes were shot down. [1:2.] The Americal Division invaded Bohol, last of the enemy-held central Philippines. [18:6.] The B-29 attack on Koriyama, 110 miles north of Tokyo, set a new Superfortress distance record. [18:2.]

Secretary of State Stettinius and Secretary of War Stimson, denouncing Germany's "steadily increasing" mistreatment of American prisoners, said those responsible would be brought to justice. [13:6-7.]

Clashes between Right and Left wing elements in Iran were reported from Moscow. [13:2.]

LAST WORDS: 'I HAVE TERRIFIC HEADACHE'

Roosevelt Was Posing for Artist When Hemorrhage Struck —He Died in Bedroom

By The Associated Press.

WARM SPRINGS, Ga., April 12—President Franklin D. Roosevelt's last words were:

"I have a terrific headache."

He spoke them to Comdr. Howard G. Bruenn, naval physician.

Mr. Roosevelt was sitting in front of a fireplace in the Little White House here atop Pine Mountain when what was described as a massive cerebral hemorrhage struck him.

The President's Negro valet, Arthur Prettyman, and a Filipino messboy carried him to his bedroom. He was unconscious at the end. It came without pain.

Dr. Bruenn said that he saw the President this morning and he was in excellent spirits at 9:30 A. M.

"At 1 o'clock," Dr. Bruenn added, "he was sitting in a chair while sketches were being made of him by an artist. He suddenly complained of a very severe occipital headache (back of the head).

"Within a very few minutes he lost consciousness. He was seen by me at 1:30 P. M., fifteen minutes after the episode had started.

"He did not regain consciousness, and he died at 3:35 P. M. (Georgia time)."

The artist sketching Mr. Roosevelt was N. Robbins of 520 West 139th Street, New York.

Only others present in the cottage were Comdr. George Fox, White House pharmacist and long an attendant on the President; William D. Hassett, Presidential secretary; Miss Grace Tully, con-

Continued on Page 4, Column 2

END COMES SUDDENLY AT WARM SPRINGS

Even His Family Unaware of Condition as Cerebral Stroke Brings Death to Nation's Leader at 63

ALL CABINET MEMBERS TO KEEP POSTS

Funeral to Be at White House Tomorrow, With Burial at Hyde Park Home—Impact of News Tremendous

By ARTHUR KROCK
Special to THE NEW YORK TIMES.

WASHINGTON, April 12—Franklin Delano Roosevelt, War President of the United States and the only Chief Executive in history who was chosen for more than two terms, died suddenly and unexpectedly at 4:35 P. M. today at Warm Springs, Ga., and the White House announced his death at 5:48 o'clock. He was 63.

The President, stricken by a cerebral hemorrhage, passed from unconsciousness to death on the eighty-third day of his fourth term and in an hour of high triumph. The armies and fleets under his direction as Commander in Chief were at the gates of Berlin and the shores of Japan's home islands as Mr. Roosevelt died, and the cause he represented and led was nearing the conclusive phase of success.

Less than two hours after the official announcement, Harry S. Truman of Missouri, the Vice President, took the oath as the thirty-second President. The oath was administered by the Chief Justice of the United States, Harlan F. Stone, in a one-minute ceremony at the White House. Mr. Truman immediately let it be known that Mr. Roosevelt's Cabinet is remaining in office at his request, and that he had authorized Secretary of State Edward R. Stettinius Jr. to proceed with plans for the United Nations Conference on international organization at San Francisco, scheduled to begin April 25. A report was circulated that he leans somewhat to the idea of a coalition Cabinet, but this is unsubstantiated.

Funeral Tomorrow Afternoon

It was disclosed by the White House that funeral services for Mr. Roosevelt would take place at 4 P. M. (E. W. T.) Saturday in the East Room of the Executive Mansion. The Rev. Angus Dun, Episcopal Bishop of Washington; the Rev. Howard S. Wilkinson of St. Thomas's Church in Washington and the Rev. John G. McGee of St. John's in Washington will conduct the services.

The body will be interred at Hyde Park, N. Y., Sunday, with the Rev. George W. Anthony of St. James Church officiating. The time has not yet been fixed.

Jonathan Daniels, White House secretary, said Mr. Roosevelt's body would not lie in state. He added that, in view of the limited size of the East Room, which holds only about 200 persons, the list of those attending the funeral services would be limited to high Government officials, representatives of the membership of both

Continued on Page 3, Column 3

TRUMAN IS SWORN IN THE WHITE HOUSE

Members of Cabinet on Hand as Chief Justice Stone Administers the Oath

By C. P. TRUSSELL
Special to THE NEW YORK TIMES.

WASHINGTON, April 12—Vice President Harry S. Truman of Missouri, standing erect, with his sharp features taut and looking straight ahead through his large, round glasses, became the thirty-second President of the United States in a ceremony lasting not more than a minute in the Cabinet Room of the White House at 7:09 o'clock tonight.

The oath was administered by Chief Justice Harlan F. Stone two hours and thirty-four minutes after the sudden death of President Roosevelt at Warm Springs. Mr. Truman had picked up a Bible from the end of the big Cabinet conference table, held it with his left hand and placed his right hand upon the upper cover. After repeating the oath, he bowed his head, lifted the Bible to his lips and kissed it.

Even before he had taken the oath Mr. Truman had asked President Roosevelt's Cabinet to continue in service. He also authorized Edward R. Stettinius Jr., Secretary of State, to announce that the United Nations Conference for International Organization would go on as scheduled.

To the newsmen at the White House he sent this word, through Stephen Early, press secretary:

"For the time being I prefer not to hold a press conference. It will be my effort to carry on as I believe the President would have done, and to that end I have asked the Cabinet to stay on with me."

Soon after he became President, Mr. Truman left the White House for the five-room Connecticut Avenue apartment where he has resided with Mrs. Truman and their 20-year-old daughter, Mary Margaret, for four years. He said he was "going home, to bed."

It was shortly after he had finished presiding over the Senate debate on the United States-Mexican Water Treaty late this afternoon that Mr. Truman received word from the White House of President Roosevelt's death. This was at about 5:15 P. M., a half hour before the news was made public. Reaching for his hat, he dashed out of the office, calling back to his staff that he was going to the White House.

Arriving at the White House, the

Continued on Page 3, Column 6

Byrnes May Take Post With Truman

Special to THE NEW YORK TIMES.

WASHINGTON, April 12—James F. Byrnes, recently resigned as Director of War Mobilization and Reconversion, known to be one of President Truman's warmest friends in official Washington, is expected to be called to the White House for consultation, and possibly to take an important post in the Cabinet, in the immediate future.

President Truman's admiration of former Justice Byrnes is well known here. He undoubtedly would have been Mr. Truman's choice as a successor to Cordell Hull as Secretary of State.

"All the News That's Fit to Print"

The New York Times.

LATE CITY EDITION
Rain this afternoon and tonight. Clearing and cool tomorrow.
Temperatures Yesterday—Max., 57; Min., 50
Sunrise today, 6:03 A. M.; Sunset, 7:46 P. M.

VOL. XCIV..No. 31,869. Entered as Second-Class Matter, Postoffice, New York, N. Y. NEW YORK, THURSDAY, APRIL 26, 1945. THREE CENTS IN NEW YORK CITY

TRUMAN OPENS WORLD SECURITY PARLEY; RUSSIANS ENCIRCLE BERLIN, CROSS ELBE; 3D NEAR AUSTRIA; BERCHTESGADEN BOMBED

NEW SLAUGHTERERS NAMED AS SOURCE OF BLACK MARKET

Illegal Meat Sales Traced by Congress Group to Concerns Established Within Year

HEARING ON PRICES HERE

Witnesses Say Wholesalers Get $100 Plus OPA Ceiling for a Beef Carcass

The origin of black market meat in New York City was traced yesterday by a Special House Committee Investigating Food Shortages to the doors of newly established slaughterers who entered this branch of the meat industry during the last year when it has been theoretically unprofitable to produce beef.

These individuals, it was asserted before the committee, are responsible principally for the abnormal rise in meat prices, which were said to be 100 per cent over the Office of Price Administration ceilings on both the wholesale and retail levels.

So brazen have black market activities become, witnesses testified, that wholesalers are obtaining $100 plus the ceiling price for a choice carcass of beef from butchers who are passing the increase, and frequently a slight advantage to themselves, along to their customers.

Long Session Held Here

This was the picture that emerged from a hearing presided over by Representative Clinton P. Anderson, chairman of the committee, which started at 9:30 A. M. in the Hotel Roosevelt and did not terminate until 7:15 P. M., giving thirty witnesses, including Mayor La Guardia, an opportunity to testify on what appeared to be a chaotic price situation in meat.

At one point in the hearing, when Mr. La Guardia took the witness chair, Mr. Anderson indicated that his committee was considering the possibility of recommending a food czar who would have complete authority over production and price functions now divided between the War Food Administration and the OPA.

The Mayor and various consumer representatives, while praising the OPA's ability to do a good job with its meager resources, expressed sympathy for this idea.

The issue of the new slaughterers was raised by Mr. Anderson, who said it seemed strange that at a time when the "big four" packers had cut their beef production because it was unprofitable, new slaughterers, without equal skills, had obtained WFA slaughtering permits and started production.

Agreeing that circumstantial evidence pointed to these new slaughterers as the probable source of most black market meat, Daniel P. Woolley, regional director of OPA, testified that 224 companies were now licensed to slaughter meat in this area, whereas a year ago there were only thirty-eight.

He also disclosed that as a result of OPA investigations, twenty-eight of the newly licensed concerns had accepted permanent injunctions against any further violation of wholesale meat prices; that actions were pending against sixty more and that investigations were being made of all the others except forty-eight that had obtained licenses but decided against operating.

T. C. Wagner, division manager for Safeway Stores, said he had been informed that 122 of 143 slaughterers he knew had not operated before Pearl Harbor. When asked by Mr. Anderson what interpretation he placed on this development, he replied: "I think it means they are operating illegitimately."

Should the OPA find the slaugh-

Continued on Page 20, Column 6

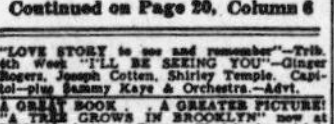

Herriot Liberated By Russian Forces

By The Associated Press.

LONDON, April 25—Edouard Herriot, three times Premier of France who was thrown into a German concentration camp in 1942 after criticizing Marshal Henri-Philippe Pétain's collaboration policies, has been liberated by the Russians, the Soviet communiqué announced tonight.

There were no details of the liberation of the 72-year-old Frenchman who was serving as President of the Chamber of Deputies in the Vichy Government when his blunt protest at a decree by Pierre Laval was followed by announcement of his arrest.

Three times he was reported dead—once by the German news agency DNB—and each time back came other reports that the sturdy head of the French Radical-Socialists survived.

The exact location of the camp from which he was liberated was not mentioned. The Russian communiqué said only that "west of Berlin troops of the First Ukrainian front freed from German captivity the former Prime Minister of the French Republic Herriot."

REPUBLICANS SEEN REJECTING MAYOR

State Chairman Puts Choice Up to City Leaders, Who Are Said to Favor McGoldrick

It became increasingly evident yesterday that Mayor La Guardia has no hope of support for renomination from the Republican leaders addressed by forty-five members of that party in a letter made public by Samuel Seabury, and that without that support the Mayor cannot obtain the Republican nomination.

Glen R. Bedenkapp, Republican State Chairman, one of those to whom the letter was addressed and who came to the city during the day, said the nomination of a Republican candidate for Mayor was entirely up to the five local county leaders. This is the same position taken by Paul E. Fitzpatrick, Democratic State Chairman.

Bedenkapp Sees Two Leaders

Mr. Bedenkapp conferred with John R. Crews, Brooklyn leader, and Edward A. Ruppell, Richmond leader, but said his talks were on purely organizational matters, and that the Mayoralty situation was not discussed.

"I expect to see the other county leaders and Herbert Brownell Jr., Republican National Chairman, before I leave town," Mr. Bedenkapp said. "But La Guardia is not on the agenda."

The Republican county leaders are known to be willing to accept Controller Joseph D. McGoldrick, an independent Democrat, as the Republican nominee for Mayor, but there is doubt that Mr. McGoldrick would accept the Repub-

Continued on Page 24, Column 2

GERMANS TRAPPED

2 Soviet Armies Merge West of Capital After By-Passing Potsdam

RIESA ON ELBE WON

Pillau Falls, Ending Nazi Grip on East Prussia —Bruenn Menaced

By C. L. SULZBERGER
By Wireless to THE NEW YORK TIMES.

MOSCOW, Thursday, April 26—Two powerful Russian armies linked up northwest of Potsdam yesterday, completing the encirclement of devastated Berlin, and plunged deeper into the smoking city to occupy four more city districts and additional groups of suburbs.

The fate of Hitler's capital is now entirely sealed, and the battle for its ruins—described here as "a jungle of stone"—became one vast mopping-up operation, with a huge bag of prisoners, including many infamous war criminals, as the ultimate prize.

While the First White Russian Army and the First Ukrainian Army welded together the arms of their pincers into a ring of steel other combat teams ground on westward beyond Nauen and toward the Elbe.

Treptow District Seized

The Soviet communiqué announced that Marshal Gregory K. Zhukoff had taken three towns northwest of the city as well as four suburbs, bringing the number of the latter in Russian hands well over two dozen. Street-fighting assault groups seized the districts of Treptow and Britz, while well in the rear they cleaned up the hold-out points of Muellrose and Friedland near Frankfort.

Marshal Ivan S. Koneff, as he moved toward Marshal Zhukoff near Potsdam, took the southwestern city districts of Lichterfelde and Zehlendorf. North of Cottbus his forces captured forty more towns.

In the Dresden sector in the south, where the world still awaits confirmation of the Allied link-up with the Russians, Marshal Koneff crossed the Elbe River and captured Riesa, while the Germans made desperate counter-attacks near Bautzen, northeast of the Saxon capital, all of which were beaten off.

On top of these victories on the central front, Marshal Alexander Vasilevsky's Third White Russian Army captured the East Prussian port of Pillau and cleared the East Prussian mainland of the last German hold-out troops.

Far to the south, Marshal Rodion Y. Malinovsky's Second Ukrainian Army was fighting in the outskirts of the Czechoslovak arsenal city of Bruenn [Brno], one of Hitler's last war production centers, after having captured the suburbs of

Continued on Page 9, Column 1

SECRETARY OF STATE ADDRESSING THE SECURITY CONFERENCE

Edward R. Stettinius Jr. speaking to the delegates as an introduction to President Truman's radio speech

Associated Press Wirephoto

SUBWAYS OF BERLIN ARE BATTLEFIELDS

Nazis Use Tubes to Get Behind Russian Lines—City Turned Into a Stone Jungle

By Wireless to THE NEW YORK TIMES.

MOSCOW, April 25—Fanatical German defenders of Berlin launched a series of unavailing counter-attacks today against the relentless Soviet advance. Desperate infantry patrols, armed with tommyguns, were sent by way of the capital's subway tunnels to emerge behind the Russian lines, but the Red Army wiped these units out almost as they appeared.

Surging forward again, the Red

Continued on Page 8, Column 2

RAF 6-Ton Bombs Score Hits On Hitler's Mountain Chalet

By SYDNEY GRUSON
By Wireless to THE NEW YORK TIMES.

LONDON, April 25—The Royal Air Force carried the war right to Adolf Hitler's doorstep today, blasting his Berchtesgaden chalet and near-by mountain-top retreat with six-ton bombs, while the United States Eighth Air Force attacked the vast Skoda arms works at Pilsen in Czechoslovakia and four rail targets near Berchtesgaden, capital of the Nazis Alpine retreat.

First reconnaissance photographs of the attack on Hitler's home showed a large number of bombs bursting on the chalet and on the SS [Elite Guard] barracks in the grounds on the slopes of the Obersalzburg.

Whether Hitler was at Berchtesgaden was the subject of much speculation tonight. He has been

Continued on Page 7, Column 1

War News Summarized

THURSDAY, APRIL 26, 1945

Allied troops from the west and the east were about to meet in Germany for the final overthrow of Hitler's Reich at the moment delegates from forty-six United Nations met in San Francisco to build the basis for a lasting world peace.

Two Russian armies joined northwest of Potsdam to encircle Berlin and cut off all roads from the west. Tempelhof airdrome was partly overrun and the Russians were fighting a series of mopping-up struggles within the city. Other elements, crossing the Elbe near Dresden, captured Riesa. To the north, Pillau was taken, eliminating the East Prussian pocket, and in Czechoslovakia the outskirts of Bruenn were reached. [1:3; map, P. 9.]

Berlin's defenders launched numerous counter-attacks, some fighting through the subways to the Russian rear, where they were wiped out. [1:4; map, P. 8.]

Three Allied armies gained up to fifteen miles in their drive on Hitler's southern redoubt. The United States Third Army cut two more highways leading to the area, was within fifteen miles of the Austrian border, captured Regen and closed in on by-passed Regensburg. The Seventh was fourteen miles from Augsburg and fifty-three from Munich, while the French First Army entered Singen, spread along the Swiss border and crossed into Italy in the Maritime Alps area. The British Second Army was fighting through the streets of Bremen. [1:7; map P. 11.]

The redoubt in which Hitler is expected to make his last stand with SS troops is a fortified area 280 miles wide and eighty deep with an inner citadel around Berchtesgaden. [14:2-3.]

That citadel was blasted by 350 RAF Lancasters, escorted by British and American fighters. Six-ton bombs were dropped on Hitler's chalet and the barracks at Berchtesgaden; the Fuehrer's mountain retreat near the Kehlstein also was hit. American bombers struck the Skoda works and airfield at Pilsen, Czechoslovakia, and targets near Berchtesgaden. [1:5-6.]

The Allied bridgehead over the Po in Italy was rapidly expanded and troops fanned out toward the Brenner Pass. The Fifth Army neared Mantua. On the west, the drive above La Spezia made good headway toward Parma. [11:1, with map.]

In the first general advance since the offensive began, American infantry on Okinawa captured Kakuzu and an important strongpoint on the left. [1:6.] Vigan, on Luzon, fell to Filipino guerrillas; United States troops on Mindanao gained sixteen miles. [17:1.] The Burma oil centers of Yenangyaung and Magwe were taken by British and Indian forces. [17:5, with map.]

President Truman told the United Nations Conference at its opening session it must "rise above all personal interests" and be guided by justice if it is to succeed. "Lip service" to lofty ideals is not enough to achieve a peace worthy of the great sacrifices already made, he said, adding: "If we do not want to die together in war, we must learn to live together in peace." [1:8.]

GENERAL ADVANCE MADE ON OKINAWA

Army Troops Retake Kakuzu —Japanese Opposition Is Lightest in Weeks

By WARREN MOSCOW
By Wireless to THE NEW YORK TIMES.

TWENTY-FOURTH ARMY CORPS HEADQUARTERS, Okinawa, Thursday, April 26—Our troops made their most substantial advances in a week today all along the virtually straight-line front from the east coast of Okinawa to the west. They made gains of 300 to 900 yards and captured a series of points that previously had defied their best efforts.

[Fleet Admiral Chester W. Nimitz announced from Guam that the Twenty-fourth Army Corps had regained Kakuzu, in the center of the island, from which the Americans previously had been driven.]

In each case, Japanese opposition

Continued on Page 17, Column 2

3D ARMY 15 MILES FROM AUSTRIAN LINE

Regen Seized—Battle Rages for Regensburg—3 Forces Drive on Nazi Redoubt

By DREW MIDDLETON
By Wireless to THE NEW YORK TIMES.

PARIS, April 25—Three Allied armies and three Allied air forces intensified Gen. Dwight D. Eisenhower's offensive against Adolf Hitler's Alpine redoubt today.

Armored infantry divisions, biting into the shrinking triangle of German soil held by the Nazis north of Switzerland, east of Lake Constance and west of the Austrian frontier, plunged through the battered German First Army for gains up to fifteen miles. Tanks of Gen. George S. Patton's Eleventh Armored Division, racing southeastward on the left flank of the advance toward the redoubt, have swept to within fifteen miles of the Austrian frontier at Passau, cutting two more highways leading into the redoubt and capturing the communications center of Regen.

Tanks and doughboys of Lieut. Gen. Alexander M. Patch's United States Seventh Army now are across or within five miles of the northern bank of the Danube along their eighty-mile front, and tonight our troops are only fourteen miles from Augsburg and fifty-three miles from Munich, key to the German defenses in the Bavarian foreland.

The center of the front, where

Continued on Page 10, Column 1

Grim War Mood Pervades Opening Of Conference That Seeks Peace

By ANNE O'HARE McCORMICK
Special to THE NEW YORK TIMES.

SAN FRANCISCO, April 25—All the elements of historic drama were present in the opening act of the conference called by the four great powers of the world to draft a charter designed to insure all nations against war.

The visible stage was simply set with the flags of the United Nations, a silhouette-like line of representatives of the American armed services and the four Americans representing the United States, the State of California, the City of San Francisco and the temporary secretariat of the conference.

The setting was an opera house built as a memorial to the dead of the first World War in an American city which is not a capital either of a country or a State but which calls itself for the occasion "the provisional capital of tomorrow."

The visible dramatis personae were the delegates of forty-six nations who filled the body of the theatre. From the press balcony these representatives of countries in all parts of the earth looked oddly alike. They looked like any ordinary audience. Less than a dozen women's hats, the turbans of the Indian delegates and the white kafiyehs of the sons of Ibn Saud were the only notes of color. There was no buzz of talk or hum of excitement.

The crowd outside was as quiet

Continued on Page 5, Column 2

JUSTICE PUT FIRST

We Will Bow Only to That 'Power,' the President Tells Delegates

ASKS A TRUE PEACE

Above Personal Interest —Stettinius, Warren Welcome Visitors

Texts of President Truman's and other addresses, Page 4.

By JAMES B. RESTON
Special to THE NEW YORK TIMES.

SAN FRANCISCO, April 25—The United Nations Conference on International Organization opened here today in a mood of solemn deliberation. There was no great excitement, no ritual, and very little celebration.

The alliance started making peace as it has made war, with efficient determination but with full admission that difficulties lie ahead.

President Harry S. Truman set the tone of the meeting. In a short address by telephone from the White House to the delegates in the Opera House here, which was rebroadcast to the world, he appealed to the world representatives to "rise above personal interests" and create a world security organization which would enforce justice and redeem the terrible sacrifices of the war.

The President charged the diplomats from forty-six United Nations with the task of creating an international organization that would make another world war impossible.

Emphasizing repeatedly that justice must be the criterion of the new organization the delegates had gathered here to establish, President Truman said that all states, large and small, must obligate themselves to use force only in defense of the law.

"Greatest Power on Earth"

"Justice remains the greatest power on earth," he said. "To that tremendous power alone will we submit."

The President's remarks to the delegates were followed by speeches of welcome by Edward R. Stettinius Jr., Secretary of State and president of the conference; Gov. Earl Warren of California and Mayor Roger D. Lapham of San Francisco.

These formal addresses were the only official business of the day, but the Foreign Secretaries of the United States, Russia, Britain and China met for more than an hour this morning in order to discuss some of the problems facing the conference.

First among these problems were the questions of seating the representatives of Poland and Argentina, but although these questions were understood to have been discussed privately among the Foreign Ministers of the four countries sponsoring the conference, no announcement was made about them and officials said privately that no formula had been found for solving either question.

Voting Question to the Fore

So far, the conference preliminaries have been conducted behind the scenes by the Foreign Secretaries of the sponsor powers, the United States, Britain, Russia and China. Tomorrow morning, for the first time, the other countries will have an opportunity to speak when the heads of delegations meet in executive session.

At that time it is expected that each delegation will be permitted to raise any question of procedure, and there were indications tonight that several delegations would raise the question of permitting Poland, Argentina, White Russia and the Ukraine to be represented at the conference.

The Russians have already raised

Continued on Page 3, Column 2

House Likely to Vote Draft Curb On Combat Use of 18-Year-Olds

By C. P. TRUSSELL
Special to THE NEW YORK TIMES.

WASHINGTON, April 25—Signs were apparent today that the House would follow the Senate's lead of yesterday and provide that 18-year-old draft inductees be withheld from combat until after receiving at least six months of military training.

The Senate's action, taken in the face of a direct appeal from General Marshall and indirectly expressed wishes of President Truman that no such restrictions be attached to the pending draft act extension bill, was received with widespread approval on the House side.

A movement was begun to carry the extension measure, as amended by the Senate, to a prompt House vote, rather than send it to conference for a compromise or deletion of the ban which General Marshall had said might lead to military disaster.

Key members of the House predicted that if such a vote were taken enactment of the bill would be completed with the amendment intact, and the measure sent to President Truman.

The amended bill was returned to the House today with a request from the Senate for a conference. Action was deferred but scheduled for tomorrow. Meanwhile, a canvass was begun of the Military Affairs Committee to determine whether a majority of that body preferred a conference or a vote

Continued on Page 6, Column 1

"All the News That's Fit to Print"

The New York Times.

LATE CITY EDITION
Cloudy with showers today. Partly cloudy and cooler tomorrow.
Temperatures Yesterday—Max., 64; Min., 47
Sunrise today, 5:46 A. M.; Sunset, 7:59 P. M.

VOL. XCIV..No. 31,881. Entered as Second-Class Matter, Postoffice, New York, N. Y. NEW YORK, TUESDAY, MAY 8, 1945. THREE CENTS IN NEW YORK CITY

THE WAR IN EUROPE IS ENDED!
SURRENDER IS UNCONDITIONAL;
V-E WILL BE PROCLAIMED TODAY;
OUR TROOPS ON OKINAWA GAIN

ISLAND-WIDE DRIVE

Marines Reach Village a Mile From Naha and Army Lines Advance

7 MORE SHIPS SUNK

Search Planes Again Hit Japan's Life Line—Kyushu Bombed

By WARREN MOSCOW
By Wireless to THE NEW YORK TIMES.

GUAM, Tuesday, May 8—In an island-wide American advance on Okinawa yesterday the First Marine Division drove south to the edge of Dakeshi Village, about a mile from Naha, the capital, straightening out the line on our right flank. In the center the Seventy-seventh Army Division used flame-throwing tanks for considerable advances, while the Seventh Army Division moved forward on the left flank.

[Airfields on Kyushu, southern Japan, were bombed Monday and Tuesday by Superfortresses, two of which were lost in heavy air opposition.

[Allied fliers started operating from the Tarakan airfield although fighting continued on that island off Borneo, and in the Philippines American troops made advances on Mindanao and Luzon.]

Japanese Dead at 36,535

As the United States forces on Okinawa resumed their drive, Fleet Admiral Chester W. Nimitz revealed that Japanese killed on the island had mounted to 36,535 on Monday, showing that the Americans were maintaining their rate of 1,000 a day.

The Americans have not yet taken the main Japanese artillery emplacements on Okinawa, which were the principal targets of the fleet off the island. The fleet's guns continued yesterday, along with carrier aircraft, to support the ground movements.

Meanwhile search bombers of Fleet Air Wing 1 continued to give an impressive demonstration of what the tightening air blockade of Japan will mean. Attacking at mast-head height with bombs and machine guns, these long-range aircraft, based in the Okinawa area, sank four more ships in waters off Korea and damaged five others.

The ships sunk were a large cargo ship, a medium cargo ship, a medium oiler and a large fleet tanker. Two small freighters were

Continued on Page 12, Column 2

Leopold Rescued By 7th Army Troops

By The Associated Press.

WITH THE UNITED STATES SEVENTH ARMY, Tuesday, May 8—Léopold III, King of Belgium, and his wife, Princess Rethy, have been liberated by the Seventh Army, it was announced today.

They were found near Strobl, eight miles east of Salzburg. The Americans had been told of their whereabouts by civilians.

With the King and his wife were eighteen members of their staff and four children. All were in good health.

Elements of the American 106th Cavalry Group had to overpower German Elite Guards to make the rescue. Seventh Army troops are now closely guarding the royal party.

The Pulitzer Awards For 1944 Announced

The Pulitzer Prize awards announced yesterday by the trustees of Columbia University included: For a distinguished novel, to "A Bell for Adano," by John Hersey; for an original American play of the current season, to "Harvey," by Mary Chase.

Among the newspaper awards were those to Hal Boyle, Associated Press war reporter, for distinguished correspondence; to James B. Reston of THE NEW YORK TIMES for his reporting of the Dumbarton Oaks Security Conference; to Joe Rosenthal, Associated Press photographer, for his photograph of marines raising the American flag at Iwo and to The Detroit Free Press for "distinguished and meritorious public service" in its investigation of legislative corruption at Lansing, Mich.

Further details of the awards will be found on Page 16.

MOLOTOFF HAILS BASIC 'UNANIMITY'

He Stresses Five Points In World Charter, but His View on One Is Questioned

By JAMES B. RESTON
Special to THE NEW YORK TIMES.

SAN FRANCISCO, May 7—The major allies who forced Germany's unconditional surrender have reached "unanimity" on the kind of world security organization which should be created at the United Nations conference to protect their newly won victory, Vyacheslaff M. Molotoff, Russian Foreign Commissar, said today.

While the delegates at the conference celebrated the end of the European war, and three Foreign Ministers, T. V. Soong of China, Paul Henri Spaak of Belgium and Trygve Lie of Norway left the conference to deal with urgent official business elsewhere, Mr. Molotoff told the press that the Soviet Union attached the "greatest importance" to five agreements reached by the heads of the Big Four delegations.

First, he said, these leaders agreed to support the principles of justice, international law, human rights and fundamental freedom for all.

Second, he added, the Big Four agreed not to make provision in the security charter for the revision of treaties.

His statement on this point was ambiguous and led to some speculation as to the unanimity of all four on the question.

Revision Power Called Danger

A reference in the United Nations charter to the necessity of revising treaties, Mr. Molotoff stated, "would play into the hands of enemy countries, which would certainly like to undermine and emasculate these treaties." Furthermore, he declared, to give the new League of Nations authority to consider revision of treaties would be a violation of national sovereign rights, which are guaranteed in the Dumbarton Oaks Charter.

For these reasons, he concluded, "the idea of revising treaties was rejected as untenable."

Third, Mr. Molotoff said, it was agreed among the Big Four that treaties directed against Germany, such as Russia's twenty-year alliances with Britain, France, Czechoslovakia, Yugoslavia and the Warsaw Poles, "should remain in force until such time as the Government concerned felt that the international security organization was really in a position to undertake the accomplishment of the tasks of

Continued on Page 15, Column 2

GERMANY SURRENDERS: NEW YORKERS MASSED UNDER SYMBOL OF LIBERTY

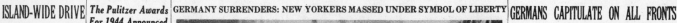

Thousands filling Times Square in spontaneous celebration yesterday. The New York Times

PRAGUE SAYS FOES ACCEPT SURRENDER

Czechoslovak Radio Reports All Fighting in Bohemia Will Be Ended Today

By The Associated Press.

LONDON, Tuesday, May 8—The Czechoslovak-controlled Prague radio announced today that the Germans in Prague and throughout Bohemia, a last major holdout pocket of German resistance, had accepted unconditional surrender.

The announcement came as the United States Third Army was reported to have advanced to the outskirts of the Czechoslovak capital, and three Russian armies hammered toward the same goal from the east and north.

"The German military plenipotentiary is negotiating with the Czechoslovak National Council on the modalities of unconditional surrender," said the broadcast, detailing what purported to be the

Continued on Page 11, Column 2

Wild Crowds Greet News In City While Others Pray

By FRANK S. ADAMS

New York City's millions reacted in two sharply contrasting ways yesterday to the news of the unconditional surrender of the German armies. A large and noisy minority greeted it with the turbulent enthusiasm of New Year's Eve and Election Night rolled into one. However, the great bulk of the city's population responded with quiet thanksgiving that the war in Europe was won, tempered by the realization that a grim and bitter struggle still was ahead in the Pacific and the fact that the nation is still in mourning for its fallen President and Commander in Chief.

Times Square, the financial section and the garment district were thronged from mid-morning on with wildly jubilant celebrators who tooted horns, staged impromptu parades and filled the canyons between the skyscrapers with fluttering scraps of paper. Elsewhere in the metropolitan area, however, war plants continued to hum, schools, offices and factories carried on their normal activities, and residential areas were calmly joyful.

One factor that helped to dampen the celebration was the bewilderment of large segments of the population at the absence of an official proclamation to back up the news contained in flaring headlines and radio bulletins. With the premature rumor of ten days ago fresh in everyone's mind, and millions still mindful of the false armistice of 1918, there was widespread skepticism over the authenticity of the news.

By mid-afternoon loudspeakers were blaring into the ears of the exulting thousands in the amusement district the news that President Truman's proclamation was being held up by the necessity of coordinating it with the announcements from London and Moscow, and that the formal celebration of the long-awaited V-E Day would be delayed until today.

This sobering note gradually

Continued on Page 7, Column 6

SHAEF BAN ON AP LIFTED IN 6 HOURS

Action Comes After Protests From Newspapers and Public —Writer Still Barred

Suspension of filing facilities of The Associated Press in the European theatre was clamped on by Supreme Headquarters, Allied Expeditionary Forces (SHAEF), yesterday in an unprecedented action and was lifted six hours and twenty minutes later.

The ban was continued, however, on all copy submitted for clearance by Edward Kennedy, chief of the press association's staff on the Western Front, who sent the momentous story announcing Germany's final surrender in a dispatch from Reims, France, which was received in New York over the AP wires at 9:35 A. M. (EWT).

It was not until seven hours and fifty-five minutes had elapsed aft-

Continued on Page 4, Column 2

Summary of News of the War and German Surrender

TUESDAY, MAY 8, 1945

The war ended in Europe yesterday after five years, eight months and six days of the bloodiest conflict in history. Grand Admiral Karl Doenitz surrendered unconditonally to the Allies in a little red schoolhouse at Reims, France. At 8:41 P. M. Sunday, New York time, Col. Gen. Gustav Jodl signed for the enemy and Lieut. Gen. Walter Bedell Smith, General Eisenhower's Chief of Staff, for the Allies. In the absence of any official announcement there was some confusion as to the compliance with the surrender. Fighting had been going on in Czechoslovakia and nothing had been heard from German pockets along the French coast. [1:7-8.]

President Truman planned a broadcast from the White House at 9 o'clock this morning. Washington, gratified that the war in Europe was over, was confused by lack of confirmation. [2:2.]

Prime Minister Churchill will also broadcast at 9 A. M. from London and Premier Stalin is expected to make a simultaneous announcement in Moscow. King George will talk over the radio six hours later. [2:8.] London will celebrate V-E Day today, but, unable to restrain its joy, staged many impromptu celebrations yesterday. [2:7.]

Most New Yorkers took the news calmly and thankfully, sobered by realization that the war in the Pacific was far from over. There were, however, noisy outbursts in such centers as Times Square and Wall Street. Scrap paper showers fluttered from roofs and windows. [1:4-5.]

German Foreign Minister Lutz Schwerin von Krosigk broke the news to his people. The future will be difficult, he warned, and then added: "We must make right the basis of our nation. In our nation justice shall be the supreme law and the guiding principle. We must also recognize law as the basis of all relations between the nations." This sudden, complete reversal in German policy was received with skepticism by the Allies. [3:1.]

Perhaps one reason for this was the announcement from Moscow that 4,000,000 men, women and children had been done to death by gas, shooting, famine, poisoning and torture in the German extermination camp at Oswiecim, Poland. [12:5.]

The actual situation in Czechoslovakia was obscure. Late last night a Patriot broadcast said the Germans were negotiating with the Czechoslovak National Council details of surrender in Prague and Bohemia. Fighting had continued throughout yesterday and German planes had bombed public buildings and hospitals. [1:3; map P. 11.].

The United States Third Army continued its general advance into Czechoslovakia and the Fifth and Seventh Armies joined again in the Alps. The British Second Army moved to Denmark and Poles entered the shattered port of Wilhelmshaven. [11:1.] Breslau fell to the Red Army after an eighty-four-day siege; 40,000 Germans were captured. [11:5.]

Japan accepted the surrender of her Axis partner with a statement that she never had expected German aid and would go on to victory without the Reich. [13:1.]

Infantry and marines on Okinawa scored another general advance after naval bombardment had pulverized Japanese strong points. Pacific Fleet planes sank or damaged thirteen more ships off Korea and Japan. [1:1; map, P. 12.] B-29's maintained their assault on Kyushu airfields. Two of the big planes were shot down. [14:3-4.]

On Tarakan Allied troops were within a mile and a half of the eastern shore. Americans gained on Mindanao and Luzon in the Philippines. [12:3-4.]

Foreign Commissar Molotoff said in San Francisco that unanimity on amendments to Dumbarton Oaks assured success of the conference. He declared that the Big Four consultations had ended. [1:2.]

GERMANS CAPITULATE ON ALL FRONTS

American, Russian and French Generals Accept Surrender in Eisenhower Headquarters, a Reims School

REICH CHIEF OF STAFF ASKS FOR MERCY

Doenitz Orders All Military Forces of Germany To Drop Arms—Troops in Norway Give Up —Churchill and Truman on Radio Today

By EDWARD KENNEDY
Associated Press Correspondent

REIMS, France, May 7—Germany surrendered unconditionally to the Western Allies and the Soviet Union at 2:41 A. M. French time today. [This was at 8:41 P. M., Eastern Wartime Sunday.]

The surrender took place at a little red schoolhouse that is the headquarters of Gen. Dwight D. Eisenhower.

The surrender, which brought the war in Europe to a formal end after five years, eight months and six days of bloodshed and destruction, was signed for Germany by Col. Gen. Gustav Jodl. General Jodl is the new Chief of Staff of the German Army.

The surrender was signed for the Supreme Allied Command by Lieut. Gen. Walter Bedell Smith, Chief of Staff for General Eisenhower.

It was also signed by Gen. Ivan Susloparoff for the Soviet Union and by Gen. Francois Sevez for France.

[The official Allied announcement will be made at 9 o'clock Tuesday morning when President Truman will broadcast a statement and Prime Minister Churchill will issue a V-E Day proclamation. Gen. Charles de Gaulle also will address the French at the same time.]

General Eisenhower was not present at the signing, but immediately afterward General Jodl and his fellow delegate, Gen. Admiral Hans Georg Friedeburg, were received by the Supreme Commander.

Germans Say They Understand Terms

They were asked sternly if they understood the surrender terms imposed upon Germany and if they would be carried out by Germany.

They answered Yes.

Germany, which began the war with a ruthless attack upon Poland, followed by successive aggressions and brutality in internment camps, surrendered with an appeal to the victors for mercy toward the German people and armed forces.

After having signed the full surrender, General Jodl said he wanted to speak and received leave to do so.

"With this signature," he said in soft-spoken German, "the German people and armed forces are for better or worse delivered into the victors' hands.

"In this war, which has lasted more than five years, both have achieved and suffered more than perhaps any other people in the world."

LONDON, May 7 (AP)—Complete victory in

Continued on Page 3, Columns 2 and 3

"All the News That's Fit to Print"

The New York Times.

LATE CITY EDITION
Partly cloudy, less humid today.
Cloudy and warm tomorrow.
Temperatures Yesterday—Max., 72; Min., 66
Sunrise today, 5:57 A. M.; Sunset, 8:06 P. M.

VOL. XCIV..No. 31,972. Entered as Second-Class Matter, Postoffice, New York, N. Y. NEW YORK, TUESDAY, AUGUST 7, 1945. THREE CENTS IN NEW YORK CITY

FIRST ATOMIC BOMB DROPPED ON JAPAN; MISSILE IS EQUAL TO 20,000 TONS OF TNT; TRUMAN WARNS FOE OF A 'RAIN OF RUIN'

IRAM W. JOHNSON, EPUBLICAN DEAN N THE SENATE, DIES

olationist Helped Prevent . S. Entry Into League— Opposed World Charter

ALIFORNIA EX-GOVERNOR

an for Vice President With Theodore Roosevelt in '12 —In Washington Since '17

Special to THE NEW YORK TIMES.

WASHINGTON, Aug. 6—Sena- Hiram Warren Johnson of alifornia lifelong isolationist ho helped prevent this country's try into the League of Nations d fought all "foreign entangle- ents" through a second World ar, died in his sleep this morn- g at Bethesda Naval Hospital, ne days after, ill but consistent, had paired his vote against rati- cation of the United Nations harter. Death was caused by a rombosis of a cerebral artery. rs. Johnson was with him when e end came.

When word reached the Capitol the passing of the oldest mem- er of the Senate in point of serv- e, save Senator Kenneth McKel- r, the President pro tempore, the ourning was deep. With great ersonal affection colleagues paid mble tribute to his integrity of haracter, his liberalism and his eadfastness to his ideals and con- ctions. They joined in declaring at the country had lost a great atesman.

Senator Johnson, who was serv- g the fourth year of his fifth erm in the Senate, would have een 79 years old on Sept. 2. Al- ough his health had been failing uring the last two years and ough the thundering voice hich had conveyed his eloquence rough innumerable stirring de- ates had become little more than whisper, friends believed he anned to seek a sixth term in 947.

He went to the hospital July 18. ive days before that he had cast e lone vote in the Foreign Rela- ons Committee, of which he was e ranking minority member, gainst reporting the new World harter to the Senate without hange. He did not participate in he floor debate on this document, which won Senate approval by a ote of 82—2. However, he lashed spiritedly with colleagues while the hearings were in prog- ess.

Funeral arrangements awaited he arrival of the Senator's son, ieut. Col. Hiram W. Johnson Jr., who was flying here from Cali- fornia.

Capper Becomes the Dean

The death of Senator Johnson made Senator Arthur Capper of Kansas, who last month marked his eightieth birthday, the Repub- lican dean of the Senate. It also elevated him to the ranking minor- ity membership on the Foreign Relations Committee, with which Senator Johnson had been so conspicuously identified through the many years of his unshaken position on foreign policy. Mr. Capper, too, with Senators McKellar, Carter Glass of Virginia, David I. Walsh of Massachusetts and Peter G. Gerry, was in the League fight of 1919 and 1920. He supported it, with reservations.

The career of Senator Johnson, from his entrance into the Senate from the Governorship of California in March of 1917, was one distinctly lacking in compromise or reservation. In 1912 he had bolted his party with Theodore Roosevelt and had become his running mate on the Bull Moose ticket. In 1932 he again bolted to support Franklin D. Roosevelt for the Presidency but broke bitterly with the President when he ran for his third term.

In 1919 Mr. Johnson joined with Senators Lodge, Borah, Reed,

Continued on Page 23, Column 4

Jet Plane Explosion Kills Major Bong, Top U. S. Ace

Flier Who Downed 40 Japanese Craft, Sent Home to Be 'Safe,' Was Flying New 'Shooting Star' as a Test Pilot

By The United Press.

BURBANK, Calif., Aug. 6—Maj. Richard Bong, America's greatest air ace, died today in the flaming wreckage of a jet propelled fighter plane which crashed while he was testing it.

Only 24 years old, he wore twenty-six decorations including the nation's highest award, the Congressional Medal of Honor. He had survived countless air battles and shot down forty Japanese planes without a scratch.

The knowledge he gained in those battles was too valuable to risk, so he was brought home to "safe" duty. He was on that "safe" duty today when his P-80, the Shooting Star, hurtled over a clump of trees and burst like a bomb in a field.

Witnesses did not agree on the cause of the crash. One Army flier said that Major Bong overshot the Lockheed airport. Another witness, John McKinney of North Hollywood reported that he saw something fall out of the plane's tail.

"The plane started to wobble up and down, then went into a left bank and hit the ground," he stated. "It exploded and burned and scattered wreckage over about a block square."

Major Bong was trying to get out of the ship when it crashed. He had released the escape hatch and was partly clear. He had pulled the ripcord to his parachute, and the silken folds lay about the body as the flames swept over it.

With a roaring sigh, the plane, like a giant blowtorch, shot over the airport just before 3 P. M. and then lurched over the trees and nosed down into the field, a mile away.

Smoke and flame surged up and crowds rushed from the airport. By the time anyone could reach the scene the ship had been almost consumed.

The crash scene was near the intersection of Cahuenga and Oxnard Boulevards and barely out-

Continued on page 15, Column 2

KYUSHU CITY RAZED

Kenney's Planes Blast Tarumizu in Record Blow From Okinawa

ROCKET SITE IS SEEN

125 B-29's Hit Japan's Toyokawa Naval Arsenal in Demolition Strike

By FRANK L. KLUCKHOHN

By Wireless to THE NEW YORK TIMES.

MANILA, Tuesday, Aug. 7—More than 400 fighters and bombers, speeding at chimney-top level for two hours Sunday over Tarumizu in southern Kyushu in the largest single attack launched by Gen. George C. Kenney's Far East Air Forces to date, leveled that city's munitions factories and aircraft and munitions storage depots and waterfront installations.

Rockets and demolition bombs were poured by waves of B-26 Invaders, B-25 Mitchells and Mustangs and Thunderbolts of the Fifth and Seventh Air Forces from Okinawa, supported by a few B-24 Liberators carrying big bombs.

[Tarumizu, about 350 miles from Okinawa, appeared to be a site at which the Japanese might be preparing a rocket campaign against the American base, said a United Press dispatch. FEAF pilots reported seeing in the area, which has extensive cave construction, what seemed to be Japanese robot planes and also a huge catapult-like machine, extending over the water, that might be a rocket launcher.

[About 125 B-29's hit the Toyokawa naval arsenal of Japan in a demolition bombing Tuesday noon, Strategic Air Forces headquarters at Guam reported.]

The planes over Tarumizu met scant resistance, as our fliers took their time to assure the highest

Continued on Page 11, Column 2

REPORT BY BRITAIN

'By God's Mercy' We Beat Nazis to Bomb, Churchill Says

ROOSEVELT AID CITED

Raiders Wrecked Norse Laboratory in Race for Key to Victory

The text of Mr. Churchill's statement is on Page 8.

By CLIFTON DANIEL

By Wireless to THE NEW YORK TIMES.

LONDON, Aug. 6—The hitherto secret details of the grisly race between Germany and the Allies to find a weapon so destructive that it would insure absolute victory—a race not only between scientists but also between under-cover agents—were recounted in London tonight after it had been disclosed that the first atomic bomb had been dropped on Japan.

"By God's mercy British and American science outpaced all German efforts," said a statement by former Prime Minister Churchill written before he left office and issued from 10 Downing Street by his successor, Clement R. Attlee.

"The possession of these powers by the Germans at any time might have altered the result of the war," Mr. Churchill said, "and profound anxiety was felt by those who were informed."

The British Isles, which endured the terrors of flying bombs and rockets, did hear repeated rumors that Adolf Hitler's V-3 weapon was to be an atomic bomb, but they never knew until tonight how close they came to being the first victims of its destructive power. Much less did they suspect what

Continued on Page 9, Column 1

Steel Tower 'Vaporized' In Trial of Mighty Bomb

Scientists Awe-Struck as Blinding Flash Lighted New Mexico Desert and Great Cloud Bore 40,000 Feet Into Sky

By LEWIS WOOD

Special to THE NEW YORK TIMES.

WASHINGTON, Aug. 6—A blinding flash many times as brilliant as the midday sun and a massive, multi-colored cloud boiling up 40,000 feet into the air accompanied the first test firing of an atomic bomb on July 16, three weeks ago today. Set in the remote desertlands of New Mexico, the experiment was seen against a wild background where rain poured in torrents, and lightning pierced the sky up to the zero hour of the explosion at 5:30 A. M.

A steel tower from which the atomic weapon hung was vaporized. In its place was only a huge, sloping crater. At the moment of the explosion a mountain range three miles distant stood out sharply in brilliant light.

"Then," said the War Department in a description, "came a tremendous, sustained roar and a heavy pressure wave which knocked down two men outside the control tower (10,000 yards, or more than five miles, away.)"

Before the detonation scientists waited in tense expectancy. Minutes lengthened seemingly to hours. Lying face downward, with their feet toward the steel tower, the watchers waited, nearly breathless. They were "reaching into the unknown" and did not know what would happen.

On the instant that all was over these men leaped to their feet. The terrible tension ended, they shook hands, embraced each other and shouted in glee. Behind their triumph was sober consciousness of possessing the means to "insure the speedy conclusion of the war and save thousands of American lives."

The scene of the great drama was the Alamogordo Air Base, 120 miles southeast of Albuquerque. Here the scientists strove to unlock the secret upon which $2,000,000,000 had been spent.

Graphic word pictures of the

Continued on Page 5, Column 1

NEW AGE USHERED

Day of Atomic Energy Hailed by President, Revealing Weapon

HIROSHIMA IS TARGET

'Impenetrable' Cloud of Dust Hides City After Single Bomb Strikes

Truman, Stimson statements on atomic bomb, Page 4.

By SIDNEY SHALETT

Special to THE NEW YORK TIMES.

WASHINGTON, Aug. 6—The White House and War Department announced today that an atomic bomb, possessing more power than 20,000 tons of TNT, a destructive force equal to the load of 2,000 B-29's and more than 2,000 times the blast power of what previously was the world's most devastating bomb, had been dropped on Japan.

The announcement, first given to the world in utmost solemnity by President Truman, made it plain that one of the scientific landmarks of the century had been passed, and that the "age of atomic energy," which can be a tremendous force for the advancement of civilization as well as for destruction, was at hand.

At 10:45 o'clock this morning, a statement by the President was issued at the White House that sixteen hours earlier—about the time that citizens on the Eastern seaboard were sitting down to their Sunday suppers—an American plane had dropped the single atomic bomb on the Japanese city of Hiroshima, an important army center.

Japanese Solemnly Warned

What happened at Hiroshima is not yet known. The War Department said it "as yet was unable to make an accurate report" because "an impenetrable cloud of dust and smoke" masked the target area from reconnaissance planes. The Secretary of War will release the story "as soon as accurate details of the results of the bombing become available."

But in a statement vividly describing the results of the first test of the atomic bomb in New Mexico, the War Department told how an immense steel tower had been "vaporized" by the tremendous explosion, how a 40,000-foot cloud rushed into the sky, and two observers were knocked down at a point 10,000 yards away. And President Truman solemnly warned:

"It was to spare the Japanese people from utter destruction that the ultimatum of July 26 was issued at Postdam. Their leaders promptly rejected that ultimatum. If they do not now accept our terms, they may expect a rain of ruin from the air the like of which has never been seen on this earth."

Most Closely Guarded Secret

The President referred to the joint statement issued by the heads of the American, British and Chinese Governments, in which terms of surrender were outlined to the Japanese and warning given that rejection would mean complete destruction of Japan's power to make war.

[The atomic bomb weighs about 400 pounds and is capable of utterly destroying a town, a representative of the British Ministry of Aircraft Production said in London, the United Press reported.]

What is this terrible new weapon, which the War Department also calls the "Cosmic Bomb"? It is the harnessing of the energy of the atom, which is the basic power of the universe. As President Truman said, "The force from which the sun draws its power has been loosed against those who brought war to the Far East."

"Atomic fission"—in other

Continued on Page 2, Column 3

MORRIS IS ACCUSED OF 'TAKING A WALK'

Fusion Official 'Sad to Part Company'—McGoldrick Sees Only Tammany Aided

The No Deal ticket, headed by Council President Newbold Morris, "can only serve the interests of Tammany Hall," Controller Joseph D. McGoldrick, candidate for reelection on the Republican-Liberal-Fusion party slate, declared yesterday in a fresh attack on the third-party ticket injected over the week-end into the city Mayoralty campaign.

A short while later Gabriel A. Wechsler, general secretary of the City Fusion party, which supported Mayor La Guardia and Mr. Morris in previous city campaigns, accused Mr. Morris of "taking a walk away from the good government forces."

To both charges Mr. Morris declared he would stand on his statement of Sunday that he was not interested in "just taking votes" away from Judge Jonah J. Goldstein, Republican-Liberal-Fusion candidate for Mayor, or from William O'Dwyer, his Democratic-American Labor party opponent.

"I have no comment," he said, "since I stand on my statement of Sunday. We are waging an affirmative campaign."

Informed that Hyman Blumberg,

Continued on Page 19, Column 6

CHINESE WIN MORE OF 'INVASION COAST'

Smash Into Port 121 Miles Southwest of Canton—Big Area Open for Landing

By The Associated Press.

CHUNGKING, China, Aug. 6—Chinese troops have broken into the South China port of Yeungkong and cleared a fifty-mile stretch of the Chinese "invasion coast," west of Hong Kong, Generalissimo Chiang Kai-shek's headquarters said today.

Swaying block-by-block street fighting is raging in the strategic coastal highway town, 121 miles southwest of Canton, a communiqué said.

By breaking into Yeungkong Chinese forces won control of a fifty-mile coastal stretch leading west to Tinpak, which lies east of Luichow Peninsula on the South China Sea. The coastal area now is open to a virtually unopposed landing should American forces choose it for a staging point for supplies to the armies of South China.

West of Luichow Peninsula another 145-mile coastal stretch extending to the Indo-China frontier is under Chinese control and observers believe the Chinese soon may launch a concerted drive from the west and east that would seal off the Japanese on the Luichow

Continued on Page 2, Column 7

Turks Talk War if Russia Presses; Prefer Vain Battle to Surrender

By SAM POPE BREWER

By Wireless to THE NEW YORK TIMES.

ANKARA, Turkey, Aug. 6—Russo-Turkish relations weigh heavy on Turkish minds these days. All leading editors commented today on various aspects of the Russian claims against Turkey.

The Potsdam conference leaves the situation virtually unchanged so far as the Turks can see, but they seem to agree that they would go to war, however hopeless such a war might be, rather than yield before the threat of force. Suggestions from London and Washington that the Russians have been asked to moderate their demands give little reassurance here.

The Potsdam communiqué created more confusion than confidence and the Turks are still trying to decide whether the fact that the conference did not deal with certain specific questions means that it was a failure.

Many point out that all the really thorny questions still are unsettled. The Turks probably do not see a relative importance among world problems of Russian demands on Turkey, but point out that the important question of principle is involved. The general and apparently official argument is that the status of the Straits cannot be modified by a bilateral agreement but must be discussed at a conference of the signatories of the Montreux Convention, with America replacing Japan. The signatories were Great Britain, France, Russia, Japan, Turkey, Greece, Rumania, Yugoslavia and Bulgaria.

The grounds for the Russian claims to Kars and Ardahan are not clear, but throughout the Near and Mideast in recent months

Continued on Page 13, Column 1

War News Summarized

TUESDAY, AUGUST 7, 1945

One bomb hit Japan on Sunday night, but it struck with the force of 20,000 tons of TNT. Where it landed had been the city of Hiroshima; what is there now has not yet been learned.

The attack, dramatically announced by President Truman sixteen hours after the missile had struck, was with an atomic bomb, a "harnessing of the basic power of the universe," he said. "The force from which the sun draws its power has been loosed against those who brought war to the Far East. And the end is not yet."

Details of the missile are closely guarded, but the 125,000 workers who saw materials pour into their factories never saw anything go out. The bomb is the result of pooling British-American scientific knowledge begun in 1940. "We have spent two billion dollars on the greatest scientific gamble in history—and won," Mr. Truman said, and warned:

"We are now prepared to obliterate more rapidly and completely every productive enterprise the Japanese have above ground in any city. It was to spare the Japanese public from utter destruction that the ultimatum of July 26 was issued at Potsdam. If they do not now accept our terms they may expect a rain of ruin from the air."

Secretary of War Stimson detailed the story of research and production and forecast improvements to increase the effectiveness of the "atomic bomb" several times. Congress will be asked to establish a committee to control peacetime use.

Hiroshima was a major military target, a city of 318,000 persons thickly settled around a quartermaster's depot, an embarkation port, armament and airplane parts plants. [All the foregoing 1:3.]

All production was in the United States at two plants at Oak Ridge, near Knoxville, Tenn., and one at Richland, Wash. A scientific laboratory was maintained in Sante Fe, N. M. [1:6.]

Former Prime Minister Churchill told of Britain's part, including costly attacks on German "heavy water" plants and the race to outstrip the Nazis. He praised American scientific achievement and gave full credit to President Roosevelt and his advisers. [1:5.]

Tokyo made no mention of what had happened to Hiroshima but rail service in that area was canceled. [1:7.]

Okinawa sent out 400 planes that left Tarumizu, on Kyushu's Kagoshima Bay, in flaming wreckage. About 125 "Superforts" bombed Toyokawa naval arsenal by daylight. [1:4; map p. 11.]

Chinese troops have broken into the port of Yeungkong and have cleared a large stretch of the south China coast west of Hong Kong and east of the Luichow Peninsula. [1:3; map P. 2.]

Moscow, moving to implement Potsdam decisions, has resumed diplomatic relations with Finland and Rumania. [11:4.]

The Germans received an opportunity to develop democratic talents when the United States and Great Britain authorized local trade unions and political parties in their zones of occupation. [12:2.]

France is expected to ratify the United Nations Charter and then the Bretton Woods monetary plan in the near future. [13:6.] Marshal Pétain was accused of having asked Hitler for help in regaining France's colonies. [13:1.]

Argentina has lifted the state of siege in effect since Pearl Harbor. [14:6.]

ATOM BOMBS MADE IN 3 HIDDEN 'CITIES'

Secrecy on Weapon So Great That Not Even Workers Knew of Their Product

By JAY WALZ

Special to THE NEW YORK TIMES.

WASHINGTON, Aug. 6—The War Department revealed today how three "hidden cities" with a total population of 100,000 inhabitants sprang into being as a result of the $2,000,000,000 atomic bomb project, how they did their work without knowing what it was all about, and how they kept the biggest secret of the war.

One of these, Oak Ridge, situated where only oak and pine trees had dotted small farms before, is today the fifth largest city in Tennessee. Its population of 75,000 persons has thirteen supermarkets, nine drug stores and seven theatres.

A second town of 7,000 was built for reasons of isolation and security on a New Mexico mesa. The third, named Richland Village, houses 17,000 men, women and children on remote banks of the Columbia River in the State of Washington.

None of the people, who came to these developments from homes all the way from Maine to California, had the slightest idea of what they were making in the gigantic Gov-

Continued on Page 3, Column 2

TRAINS CANCELED IN STRICKEN AREA

Traffic Around Hiroshima Is Disrupted — Japanese Still Sift Havoc by Split Atoms

By The United Press.

WASHINGTON, Aug. 6—The Osaka radio, without referring to the atomic bomb dropped on Hiroshima, hinted tonight at the terrific damage it must have caused by announcing that train service in the Hiroshima and other areas had been canceled.

First mention of the bomb came in a Japanese Domei agency dispatch announcing that President Truman and Prime Minister Attlee had disclosed that the new missile had been dropped on Hiroshima.

The Office of War Information began telling the Japanese today what hit them. OWI branch transmitters in San Francisco, Hawaii and Saipan beamed President Truman's statement on the atomic bomb to Japan.

Edward Barrett, director of the OWI's overseas branch, said that the President's announcement and related information on the atomic bomb will dominate the OWI's normal Japanese transmissions for the next several days.

LONDON, Tuesday, Aug. 7 (U.P.)—The Japanese Domei news agency, in a dispatch recorded by the British radio, said today that

Continued on Page 7, Column 3

Reich Exile Emerges as Heroine In Denial to Nazis of Atom's Secret

Special to THE NEW YORK TIMES.

WASHINGTON, Aug. 6—How Germany twice narrowly missed the secret of harnessing atomic energy by splitting uranium atoms and releasing the most powerful destructive force on earth was recalled today in War Department reports on the atomic bomb.

Development of the bomb after more than ten years of experimentation and research marks the first time that Prof. Albert Einstein's theory of relativity has been put to practical use outside the laboratory: the equation by which he showed the existence of a definite relationship of matter, energy and the velocity of light.

That the new bomb may be far from its maximum devastating potential was indicated by the War Department's statement that said:

"The energy we are now able to utilize in the atomic bombs, at 100 per cent efficiency, constitutes only one-tenth of 1 per cent of the total energy present in the material. But even one-hundredth of 1 per cent is still the most destructive force by far on this earth."

The principal character in the dramatic story of the long search for a method of releasing atomic energy is Dr. Lise Meitner, a woman physicist whom the Nazis expelled from Germany as a "non-Aryan." With her associates, Dr. Otto Hahn and Dr. F. Strassmann, both chemists, she had been working in the Kaiser Wilhelm Institute in Berlin, bombarding uranium atoms with neutrons and then submitting the uranium to chemical analysis.

As the War Department tells the story:

To their amazement, they found the element barium in the debris of the smashed uranium atoms.

Continued on Page 7, Column 1

"All the News That's Fit to Print"

The New York Times.

LATE CITY EDITION
Thunderstorms, warm, humid; clear and cooler tonight. Fair tomorrow.
Temperatures Yesterday—Max., 84; Min., 71
Sunrise today, 6:06 A. M.; Sunset, 7:55 P. M.

VOL. XCIV..No. 31,980. Entered as Second-Class Matter, Postoffice, New York, N. Y. NEW YORK, WEDNESDAY, AUGUST 15, 1945. THREE CENTS IN NEW YORK CITY

JAPAN SURRENDERS, END OF WAR! EMPEROR ACCEPTS ALLIED RULE; M'ARTHUR SUPREME COMMANDER; OUR MANPOWER CURBS VOIDED

HIRING MADE LOCAL

Communities, Labor and Management Will Unite Efforts

6,000,000 AFFECTED

Draft Quotas Cut, Services to Drop 5,500,000 in 18 Months

By LEWIS WOOD
Special to THE NEW YORK TIMES.

WASHINGTON, Aug. 14—All manpower controls over employers and workers were abolished tonight, the War Manpower Commission announced, enabling employers to hire men where and when they pleased.

The end of the war threw on the Government the difficult task of trying to readjust perhaps 5,000,000 war workers into new employment. Nevertheless, the WMC said, all its facilities would be used to help workers find new places, with preference going to veterans, displaced migratory war workers and other preferentials.

At the same time President Truman announced that monthly inductions into the Army would be immediately slashed from 80,000 to 50,000, and said 5,000,00 to 5,500,000 men probably would be released from the service within the next year or eighteen months.

The induction rate of 50,000 monthly, the President said, would be sufficient to maintain the occupation forces and allow men of long service overseas to return to their homes.

Under the WMC program, the manpower controls are to be lifted at once and voluntary community action to hurry reconversion will be substituted. In every community, the number of displaced workers and returning veterans will be ascertained in cooperation with local management-labor groups. Full facilities of the United States Employment Service offices will be made available to all employers. Service for veterans will be enlarged.

The WMC program embraced these seven points:

1. All manpower controls are to be lifted at once and in their place voluntary community action to

Continued on Page 12, Column 3

Hirohito on Radio; Minister Ends Life

The Japanese Domei agency said at 11 o'clock last night that Emperor Hirohito had been "graciously pleased to personally read an imperial rescript accepting the Potsdam declaration."

The Domei English-language wireless dispatch, directed to the United States and recorded by the Federal Communications Commission, said that the Emperor had read the rescript over a nation-wide broadcast at noon Wednesday, Tokyo time.

Previously Domei had reported that weeping people had gathered before the Imperial Palace and "bowed to the very ground" in shame.

Japanese War Minister Korechika Anami committed suicide, Domei reported this morning. The wireless dispatch, directed to the American zone, said Anami had taken his life at his "official residence" to "atone for his failure in accomplishing his duties as His Majesty's Minister."

A complete story appears on Page 3.

Third Fleet Fells 5 Planes Since End

By The Associated Press.

GUAM, Wednesday, Aug. 15—Japanese aircraft are approaching the Pacific Fleet off Tokyo and are being shot down, Admiral Chester W. Nimitz announced today.

Five enemy planes have been destroyed since noon today, Japanese time, or 11 P. M. EWT.

Gen. Douglas MacArthur has been requested to tell the Japanese that American defense measures require the Third Fleet to destroy any Japanese planes approaching United States' warships.

GUAM, Wednesday, Aug. 15 (U.P.)—When Admiral Halsey received word of Japan's capitulation today, he sent this message to his fliers:

"It looks like the war is over, but if any enemy planes appear shoot them down in friendly fashion."

SECRETS OF RADAR GIVEN TO WORLD

Its Role in War and Uses for Peacetime Revealed in Washington and London

By WILLIAM S. WHITE
Special to THE NEW YORK TIMES.

WASHINGTON, Aug. 14—The great drama of radar, the war's most powerful "secret weapon" until the atomic bomb was devised, was displayed before a world audience today.

The Joint Board on Scientific Information Policy permitted the Office of Scientific Research and Development, the War Department and the Navy Department to tell the story of a device of which millions had known vaguely for two years, a device which at least three times stood between survival or defeat by the Axis powers for the United States and Great Britain.

It was radar, short for "radio detection and range," that helped the small surviving British air squadrons to beat the German blitz of 1940, thus not only saving the home islands but preserving them as the essential Anglo-American base from which the continental invasion went forward on June 6, 1944.

It was radar, which "sees through the heaviest fog and the blackest night," that more than any other factor broke in 1942 the German submarine attack in the Atlantic which was threatening to starve and strangle the British homeland.

And it was radar that permitted the remnants of the blasted United States Pacific Fleet to stay alive

Continued on Page 14, Column 3

ALL CITY 'LETS GO'

Hundreds of Thousands Roar Joy After Victory Flash Is Received

TIMES SQ. IS JAMMED

Police Estimate Crowd in Area at 2,000,000—Din Overwhelming

By ALEXANDER FEINBERG

Five days of waiting, of rumor, intimation, fact, distortion—five agonizing days following the first indication of a Japanese surrender, days of alternately rising hopes and fears—came to an end for New York, as for the nation and the world, a moment or two after seven o'clock last night. And the metropolis exploded its emotions, harnessed for the most part during the day, with atomic force.

"Official — Truman announces Japanese surrender."

These were the magic words, flashed on the moving electric sign of the Times Tower, at 7:03 P. M. that touched off an unparalleled demonstration in Times Square, packed with half a million persons.

The victory roar that greeted the announcement beat upon the eardrums until it numbed the senses. For twenty minutes wave after wave of that joyous roar surged forth.

Restraint was thrown to the winds. Those in the crowds in the streets tossed hats, boxes and flags into the air. From those leaning perilously out of the windows of office buildings and hotels came a shower of paper, confetti, streamers. Men and women embraced—there were no strangers in New York yesterday. Some were hilarious, others cried softly.

By 7:30 P. M. the crowd in the Square had risen to 750,000 persons; by 8:45 it had swelled to 800,000 and the number continued to rise. People were packed solidly between Forty-third Street and Forty-fifth Street. Individual movement was virtually impossible; one moved not in the crowd but with it.

At 10 P. M. Chief Inspector John J. O'Connell estimated that 2,000,000 persons were in the Times Square area from Fortieth to Fifty-second Street, between Sixth and Eighth Avenues. This constitutes an all-time record, police officials said. At that hour people were still pouring into the Square from subways, buses and on foot.

Those at the north end of the

Continued on Page 5, Column 1

Two-Day Holiday Is Proclaimed; Stores, Banks Close Here Today

By The Associated Press.

WASHINGTON, Aug. 14—Tomorrow and Thursday are days off for Government workers and holidays for pay purposes for workers in general.

And V-J Day, when it comes, will be a premium pay day, too.

President Truman announced both rulings tonight.

He directed agency heads throughout the Government to cut their forces down to a bare skeleton staff Aug. 15 and 16 and not to charge the two days against the employes' annual leave. He said it was in "inadequate" recognition of the four-year efforts on "one of the hardest working groups of war workers."

For other workers under wage control, Wednesday and Thursday count like Christmas and the few other accepted holidays for purposes of overtime pay and in figuring the number of days worked in a week. Many employers already have obtained approval for regular time pay to workers who take the day off.

Postal service for the next two days will "approximate holiday service," the Postoffice Department said.

Local postmasters will have wide discretion in carrying out the President's wishes, it was indicated, and those postal employes required to work tomorrow and next day will have compensating time off at a later date.

It was presumed, but not specifically stated, that Government workers generally will be off on V-J Day, too.

The White House said that the next two days are to be regarded as legal holidays.

Preston Delano, Controller of the

Continued on Page 6, Column 7

PRESIDENT ANNOUNCING SURRENDER OF JAPAN

Mr. Truman reading the message in the White House. Seated are Admiral William D. Leahy, Secretary of State James F. Byrnes and former Secretary of State Cordell Hull. Standing (left to right) are Maj. Gen. Philip Fleming, head of the Federal Works Administration; William H. Davis, Economic Stabilizer; John W. Snyder, Reconversion Director; James Forrestal, Secretary of the Navy; Fred Vinson, Secretary of the Treasury; Tom Clark, Attorney General, and Lewis Schwellenbach, Secretary of Labor. Associated Press Wirephoto

PETAIN CONVICTED, SENTENCED TO DIE

Jurors Recommend Clemency Because of His Age—Long Indictment Upheld

By C. H. ARCHAMBAULT
By Wireless to THE NEW YORK TIMES.

PARIS, Wednesday, Aug. 15—Marshal Henri-Philippe Pétain was convicted at 4:15 A. M. today of intelligence with the enemy and sentenced to death. Because of his age—the former head of the Vichy regime is 89—the jury expressed the hope that the death sentence might not be carried out.

Guards had to arouse Pétain in

Continued on Page 15, Column 5

Terms Will Reduce Japan To Kingdom Perry Visited

By JAMES B. RESTON
Special to THE NEW YORK TIMES.

WASHINGTON, Aug. 14—The Allied terms of surrender will not only demobilize and demilitarize Japan but also deprive her of 80 per cent of the territory and nearly one-third of the population she held when she attacked Pearl Harbor. Thus these terms, already approved by President Truman and our major Allies, will not only destroy the vast empire she conquered in the first eighteen months of this war but also reduce her to little more than the territory she occupied when Commodore Perry introduced her to the western world in 1853.

The main terms of surrender, as

Continued on Page 11, Column 2

World News Summarized

WEDNESDAY, AUGUST 15, 1945

World War II became a page in history last night.

President Truman announced at 7 P. M. that he had received the Japanese reply to the Allied note of last Saturday and that he deemed it full acceptance of the Potsdam declaration of July 26. The Chief Executive said that the Japanese surrender would be made to Gen. Douglas MacArthur in his capacity as Supreme Allied Commander in Chief. Allied military commanders were ordered to stop fighting, but the proclamation of V-J Day will await the signing of the peace treaties. [1:7-8.]

Simultaneously with the President's announcement, Admiral Nimitz flashed "cease fire" orders to all units under his command. [8:3-4.]

The official announcement that the Japanese sneak attack on Pearl Harbor had resulted three years and 250 days later in the inglorious end of the Japanese Empire touched off unrestrained celebrations throughout the Allied world. Here in New York the flash on the moving electric sign on the Times Tower, "Official—Truman announces Japanese surrender," signaled a wild demonstration. [1:3.]

Emperor Hirohito announced the Japanese surrender to his people in his first broadcast to the nation. Weeping Japanese gathered outside the Emperor's palace to bow to the ground in their shame because their "efforts were not enough." [3:2.]

The fury of Allied military might continued to strike the Japanese up to the very last. Even as the Tokyo radio announced that the Japanese reply to the Allied note of Saturday was on its way, our Superfortresses were winging from the Marianas to the Japanese homeland. More than 1,000 planes struck Honshu with 6,000 tons of bombs in a fourteen-hour assault ending early yesterday. [8:1.]

In the midst of rejoicing it was disclosed that the heavy cruiser Indianapolis had been sunk, presumably by an enemy submarine, shortly after she had delivered an atomic bomb cargo to Guam. All men aboard were casualties. [1:6-7.]

The Red Army unleashed fierce new attacks. Russian armored forces raced ninety-three miles unchecked across western Manchuria toward Harbin and other Soviet columns scored new gains all along the 2,300-mile front. [8:6; Pacific area map P. 8.]

The Soviet Union signed "a treaty of friendship and alliance" with China after an agreement had been reached between the two nations on all questions of common interest. [1:6.]

Chinese Communists informed the Generalissimo that they refused to accept his command to remain at their posts. [6:1.]

A French jury sentenced Marshal Pétain to death. [1:4.]

TREATY WITH CHINA SIGNED IN MOSCOW

Complete Agreement Reached With Chungking on All Points at Issue, Russians Say

By Cable to THE NEW YORK TIMES.

LONDON, Aug. 14—The Soviet Union and China have signed a treaty of friendship and alliance, the Moscow radio announced tonight, and have reached "full agreement on all other questions of common interest."

The broadcast said the treaty and "other agreements" would be published shortly after they had been ratified by the two countries.

These are the first fruits of the talks that have been proceeding in

Continued on Page 6, Column 3

Cruiser Sunk, 1,196 Casualties; Took Atom Bomb Cargo to Guam

Special to THE NEW YORK TIMES.

WASHINGTON, Aug. 14—The American heavy cruiser Indianapolis was sunk by enemy action in the Philippine Sea with 1,196 casualties, every man aboard, the Navy announced today.

The 9,950-ton ship left San Francisco on July 16 on a special, high-speed run to deliver essential atomic bomb materials to Guam. The cargo was delivered. The cruiser was lost after having left Guam.

The sinking, which took one of the Navy's heaviest tolls of lives since Pearl Harbor, was disclosed a few minutes before President Truman announced Japan's surrender.

Casualties included five Navy dead, including one officer; 845 Navy missing, including sixty-three officers; 307 Navy wounded, including fifteen officers; thirty Marine missing, including two officers, and nine enlisted Marine wounded. Next of kin have been notified.

The skipper, Capt. Charles B. McVay 3d, 47, of Washington, was wounded.

The Navy Department also reported for the first time that in a previous action on March 31 the Indianapolis, flagship of the Fifth Fleet, was damaged by a suicide plane off Okinawa. She had been at the Mare Island, Calif., Navy

Continued on Page 10, Column 6

YIELDING UNQUALIFIED, TRUMAN SAYS

Japan Is Told to Order End of Hostilities, Notify Allied Supreme Commander and Send Emissaries to Him

MACARTHUR TO RECEIVE SURRENDER

Formal Proclamation of V-J Day Awaits Signing of Those Articles—Cease-Fire Order Given to the Allied Forces

By ARTHUR KROCK
Special to THE NEW YORK TIMES.

WASHINGTON, Aug. 14—Japan today unconditionally surrendered the hemispheric empire taken by force and held almost intact for more than two years against the rising power of the United States and its Allies in the Pacific war.

The bloody dream of the Japanese military caste vanished in the text of a note to the Four Powers accepting the terms of the Potsdam Declaration of July 26, 1945, which amplified the Cairo Declaration of 1943.

Like the previous items in the surrender correspondence, today's Japanese document was forwarded through the Swiss Foreign Office at Berne and the Swiss Legation in Washington. The note of total capitulation was delivered to the State Department by the Legation Charge d'Affaires at 6:10 P. M., after the third and most anxious day of waiting on Tokyo, the anxiety intensified by several premature or false reports of the finale of World War II.

Orders Given to the Japanese

The Department responded with a note to Tokyo through the same channel, ordering the immediate end of hostilities by the Japanese, requiring that the Supreme Allied Commander—who, the President announced, will be Gen. Douglas MacArthur—be notified of the date and hour of the order, and instructing that emissaries of Japan be sent to him at once—at the time and place selected by him—"with full information of the disposition of the Japanese forces and commanders."

President Truman summoned a special press conference in the Executive offices at 7 P. M. He handed to the reporters three texts.

The first—the only one he read aloud—was that he had received the Japanese note and deemed it full acceptance of the Potsdam Declaration, containing no qualification whatsoever; that arrangements for the formal signing of the peace would be made for the "earliest possible moment;" that the Japanese surrender would be made to General MacArthur in his capacity as Supreme Allied Commander in Chief; that Allied military commanders had been instructed to cease hostilities, but that the formal proclamation of V-J Day must await the formal signing.

The text ended with the Japanese note, in which the Four Powers (the United States, Great Britain, China and Russia) were officially informed that the Emperor of Japan had issued an imperial rescript of surrender, was prepared to guarantee the necessary signatures to the terms as prescribed by the Allies, and had instructed all his commanders to cease active operations, to surrender a

Continued on Page 2, Column 3

MacArthur Begins Orders to Hirohito

By Wireless to THE NEW YORK TIMES.

MANILA, Wednesday, Aug. 15—Gen. Douglas MacArthur in his first action as Allied Supreme Commander today directed Emperor Hirohito and the Japanese Government to furnish a radio station in the Tokyo area for "continuous use in handling radio communications between this headquarters and your headquarters." The message, sent in the clear, called for "the earliest practicable" arrangements to end hostilities.

"All the News That's Fit to Print"

The New York Times.

LATE CITY EDITION
Sunny with moderate temperatures today. Tomorrow cloudy.
Temperatures Yesterday—Max., 52; Min., 42
Sunrise today, 7:20 A. M.; Sunset, 4:46 P. M.
Full U. S. Weather Bureau Report Page 37.

VOL. XCV....No. 32,129. Entered as Second-Class Matter, Postoffice, New York, N. Y. NEW YORK, FRIDAY, JANUARY 11, 1946. THREE CENTS IN NEW YORK CITY

17.5% GM PAY RISE URGED BY BOARD; PHONE TIE-UP OFF UNTIL MONDAY; STEEL AND UNION PACT INDICATED

UNO OPENED; ATTLEE ASKS WORLD UNITY

SPAAK IS ELECTED

Belgian Is President of the General Assembly After Floor Fight

SOVIET LEADS OPPOSITION

U.S. Votes on Russian Side for Norwegian—Session Contrasts With League Meeting in 1920

Addresses at the opening of the UNO in London, Page 3.

By JAMES B. RESTON
By Cable to The New York Times.

LONDON, Jan. 10—The fifty-one nations of the greatest war-time coalition in history, representing four-fifths of the people in the world, started today another chapter in man's melancholy search for peace and security.

One hundred and forty-seven days after the close of the war that cost more than 20,000,000 casualties and left countless millions homeless and on the twenty-sixth anniversary of the ratification of the ill-fated League of Nations Covenant, the nations met this afternoon in the blue and gold auditorium of the Central Hall of Westminster for the first meeting of the United Nations General Assembly.

Greeting them on behalf of Britain, which served as the springboard for the final conquest of Germany, Prime Minister Attlee told them frankly that they would succeed in their new venture only if they brought "the same sense of urgency, the same self-sacrifice and the same willingness to subordinate sectional interests" with which they fought the war.

Spaak Elected President

Then, with a little less dignity than marks the balloting at a political convention at home, they proceeded to elect Paul-Henri Spaak, Belgian Foreign Minister, as President of the first General Assembly, despite a determined effort by the Soviet Union to replace him with the Norwegian Foreign Minister, Trygve Lie.

This election produced the only extraordinary incident of the day. When Dr. Eduardo Zuleta Angel of Colombia, chairman of the UNO Preparatory Commission and temporary president of the General Assembly, announced the balloting for the Presidency, the deputy chairman of the Soviet delegation, Andrei Gromyko, Russian Ambassador to Washington, asked to be recognized and strode to the microphone on the improvised modernistic blue and gold stage.

It was known at this point that the candidacy of M. Spaak would win, but Mr. Gromyko, assured that he was supported by the United States, told the General Assembly that his delegation attached great importance to the election and favored the Norwegian Foreign Minister because of his personal capacities and the active movements of his country in the war.

Pole and Ukrainian Back Lie

As soon as Mr. Gromyko had left the rostrum, Foreign Minister Wincenty Rzymowski of Poland asked to be recognized and he then seconded the Russian nomination. When he had finished, D. Z. Manuilsky, the Ukrainian People's Commissar for Foreign Affairs, a striking, white-maned figure with a booming voice, moved that Dr. Lie be elected by acclamation despite the fact that the rules of the Assembly call for elections by secret ballot.

After another short speech for Dr. Lie by Gustav Rasmussen, Danish Foreign Minister, the temporary president called for a vote on whether to decide the issue by secret ballot, but immediately Mr. Gromyko rose again and asked for a vote on the motion to elect Dr. Lie by acclamation.

Some confusion attended those motions during which Mr. Manuilsky voted both for the secret ballot and for the election of Dr. Lie by acclamation, but finally fifteen delegations voted for a secret ballot and only nine voted in favor of putting Dr. Lie in by acclaim. The

Continued on Page 3, Column 2

Delegates Welcome Copies of The Times

By Wireless to The New York Times.

LONDON, Jan. 10—Copies of yesterday morning's issue of THE NEW YORK TIMES were distributed to delegates to the United Nations Organization's General Assembly this evening and they received an enthusiastic reception from all, particularly the American representatives.

"This is about as useful, informative and happy a thing as has happened to an exiled American in a long time," Adlai Stevenson said. He has been here for four months working on the establishment of the UNO.

King George will be among the recipients. Buckingham Palace officials said that he was very happy to have the paper.

Copies are being sent to prominent Britons, including former Foreign Secretary Anthony Eden, Prime Minister Attlee and leading members of the Cabinet, and to the heads of each of the fifty-one delegations to the Assembly. The papers are being flown across the Atlantic.

PRESS STILL BESET IN 'FREE' RUMANIA

Russian and Union Censors Bar Liberal Chief's Effort to Use Grant Given by Moscow

By SAM POPE BREWER
By Wireless to The New York Times.

BUCHAREST, Rumania, Jan. 10—Even before United States Ambassador W. Averell Harriman took off for London at dawn today to report to Secretary of State James F. Byrnes at the United Nations Organization meeting on the Allied commission's work here, the great difficulty of getting a loyal execution of the Moscow communiqué's terms in this test case of Allied cooperation showed itself.

Though press freedom was promised and Rumanian censorship of the domestic press was officially dropped yesterday, first a Russian censor and then an unofficial typographical union censorship clamped down last night on an apparently inoffensive statement by Liberal Party Chief Constantin (Dinu) Bratianu on his party's conception of a "free press."

Mr. Harriman and Sir Archibald Clark Kerr, British Ambassador to Moscow, had a three-hour conversation last night with Premier Petru Groza in which the question of restoring the great liberties to the government discussed, among other things, but if the Premier's ideas on freedom are still the same as those expressed in the previous night's communiqué there is little likelihood that his "assurances" will be acceptable to the United States Government.

The outstanding flaw in M. Groza's statement was the assertion that the present Ministers of Justice, the Interior and Propaganda could be expected to protect such freedom, when it was under their aegis that flagrant abuses

Continued on Page 6, Column 2

CHIANG PROCLAIMS TRUCE AND REFORM AS COUNCIL BEGINS

Marshall Ends Deadlock With Early Meeting, Sends Word to Delegates' Session

TROOP MOVEMENT FROZEN

Civil Liberties, End of Police Abuses, Amnesty, New Voting Basis Promised China

Chiang's announcement of the truce appears on Page 10.

By TILLMAN DURDIN
By Wireless to The New York Times.

CHUNGKING, Jan. 10—Only a few moments before President Chiang Kai-shek proclaimed a sweeping series of political and democratic reforms in China, a formal truce order, hammered out by Gen. George C. Marshall and representatives of the Chinese Government and the Chinese Communist party, brought a cease-fire order to the civil war fronts.

The agreement provided for an immediate halt to hostilities, full restoration of all war-blocked communications and the establishment of a control organization, with American participation, to supervise the carrying out of the armistice compact. The continued movement of Government forces in Manchuria and south of the Yangtze River is not prejudiced under the terms of the agreement.

This agreement highlighted a day of historic happenings in Chungking, all tied together, with dramatic timing and with close political relationship.

Conference Assembles

The Political Consultation Conference, an assemblage of party leaders and non-party persons, dedicated to working out a program of political unity and democratization for China, met in its first session. The truce accord was reached after an emergency early morning meeting of the three negotiators just in time for President Chiang to reveal the agreement in his opening address to the conference.

In his speech President Chiang announced these far-reaching Government measures in the field of civil rights:

Steps to insure freedom of person, of conscience, of publication and of assembly.

Abrogation of secret police activity assuring that rulings were being made under which only proper judicial and police authorities would be permitted to arrest, try or punish individuals.

Equality of "all legal parties before the law" and their right to open activity "within the law."

Release of all political prisoners "except traitors and those found to have committed definite acts injurious to the Republic."

Promotion of local self-government everywhere, with popular election to be held "according to law" and from "the lowest strata upward."

The supreme achievement of bringing at least an armistice and perhaps permanent peace to China came to fruition after a hitch in the discussion yesterday threatened to prolong if not seriously to endanger the negotiations. It is clear that the masterly mediation of General Marshall was a major factor in producing the final success.

Last night the three-man conference brought up a disagreement

Continued on Page 10, Column 2

Japanese Cabinet Has Resigned; Interest of Emperor Is Indicated

By Reuter.

TOKYO, Friday, Jan. 11—The Japanese Cabinet has resigned.

Japan's seven-day political crisis broke when ailing Prime Minister Baron Kijuro Shidehara, who is still confined to bed, informed the Cabinet through Foreign Minister Shigeru Yoshida that he had decided that the Cabinet should resign en masse as a result of General MacArthur's "political purge" directives of Jan. 4.

Mr. Yoshida, who earlier this morning called on the Emperor at the Royal Palace to inform him of the Premier's decision, is expected to make another call this afternoon, when it is believed that Hirohito will again give the resigning Baron Premier an imperial command to form a new Government.

The Premier's personal secretary explained that it would be several days yet before the Premier would be able to attend to state duties, but that the Cabinet would carry on in the meantime to give the Baron time to select a list of names of proposed new members to submit to General MacArthur's headquarters for approval.

By LINDESAY PARROTT
By Wireless to The New York Times.

TOKYO, Jan. 10—Emperor Hirohito will take a hand to break the Cabinet deadlock that has paralyzed Japan since General MacArthur's directive of Jan. 4 outlawed from public office all but two members of the Government of Baron Kijuro Shidehara, it was said in informed circles tonight.

Although the bulk of the Cabinet members have been ordered ejected as members of former ultranationalist societies, it continues to cling tenaciously to its position. Faced with this situation, the Emperor, it is stated, will summon his personal advisers to ask them to find a solution, since the Japanese Government during the past week has, in effect, continued to func-

Continued on Page 10, Column 6

Appeal to Strikers By Union Leaders

Following is the text of the statement issued last night by the Association of Communication Equipment Workers asking its members to delay picketing until Monday:

"This is a special message to the members and officers of the Association of Communications Equipment Workers in all locals throughout the United States.

"Ernest Weaver, national president, and the bargaining committee composed of Messrs. Thornton, Massey and Barry request the officers to comply with a special request made by Secretary of Labor Schwellenbach not to establish picket lines at any location until Monday morning, Jan. 14.

"The Secretary of Labor has arranged a conference of the union and the company at 4 P. M., Friday, Jan. 11, in Washington, D. C. The members and officers of the ACEW are urged to comply with the request of the Secretary of Labor in consideration of the public, the long lines and other telephone workers. ACEW members will remain on strike."

GOVERNMENT TO USE ALUMINUM PATENTS

Alcoa Cedes Rights to RFC for Licensing to Reynolds Metals, Leasing Federal Plants

By WALTER H. WAGGONER
Special to The New York Times.

WASHINGTON, Jan. 10—The Aluminum Company of America agreed today to grant the Government free use of its patents for the production of aluminum together with the right to license them to its competitors acquiring Government-owned plants.

The decision by the country's

Continued on page 15, Column 5

PICKETING DELAYED

Union Calls on Locals to Change Plans After Schwellenbach Plea

PARLEY IN CAPITAL TODAY

Negotiations With Western Electric End Here After Rejection of Offer

By LAWRENCE RESNER

A postponement until Monday of picket lines that had threatened the disruption this morning of the nation's telephone service was ordered last night by leaders of striking telephone installation workers after a last minute appeal by Secretary of Labor Lewis B. Schwellenbach.

Despite this decision, which was announced at 11:20 P. M. by Ernest Weaver, president of the Association of Communications Equipment Workers, a certain amount of difficulty was anticipated in reaching all locals of the union to prevent all picketing.

To expedite a widespread announcement of the order, Mr. Weaver enlisted the aid of the nation's press and radio to publish and broadcast a message to the members of his union to delay action pending results of conferences with Secretary Schwellenbach scheduled to start at 4 P. M. today in Washington.

Leaders Urged to Comply

This message urged the members and officers of the ACEW "to comply with the request of the Secretary of Labor in consideration of the public, the long lines and other telephone workers."

Officials of Western Electric, against whom the installation workers' strike is directed, also agreed to join in the discussions

Continued on Page 13, Column 2

World News Summarized

FRIDAY, JANUARY 11, 1946

Fifty-one nations met in the first General Assembly of the UNO in London, yesterday, and heard Dr. Eduardo Zuleta Angel of Colombia, temporary president, and Prime Minister Attlee plead for international harmony. Paul-Henri Spaak, Belgian Foreign Minister, was elected President of the Assembly. The only incident arose when Soviet delegate Gromyko unexpectedly sought the election by acclamation of Norway's Foreign Minister Lie, but M. Spaak, backed by Britain, won on a secret ballot, 28 to 23. [1:1.]

Canada, Brazil and Poland are slated for two-year terms as non-permanent members of the Security Council, and the Netherlands, Mexico and Egypt for one-year terms. [3:1.]

The UNO Site Committee listened to a broadcast of the London proceedings in the library of the home of President Roosevelt. The members were impressed with Hyde Park. [2:6.]

Despite the Moscow parley's free press demand the Russian censors in Rumania emasculated a statement by Liberal leader Bratianu and the local typographical union, on some papers refused to print what was left undeleted. [1:2.]

Fighting between Iranian patriots and "autonomy" partisans broke out in the Russian-occupied zone between Azerbaijan and Teheran. Five persons were killed. [11:2-3, with map.]

A verbal tilt between Rabbi Stephen S. Wise and Chairman Hutcheson enlivened the Anglo-American Committee hearing. Non-Zionists said Palestine could not absorb all Jews seeking refuge. [2:2.]

The Cabinet in Japan resigned after getting word from Premier Shidehara. [1:2-3.]

In China following upon the Chungking - Communist truce, Generalissimo Chiang Kai-shek guaranteed equality for all political parties, freedom of speech and person, local elections, political amnesty and end of one-party government. [1:3.]

Korea, too, moved toward unity when the five major parties issued a joint statement praising the Moscow decision for self-government. [10:1.]

"We want to go home" demonstrations continued throughout the Pacific area. [4:1.] In Germany a soldier committee seemed satisfied with explanations offered at a conference with officers, but their comrades continued loud protests. [4:2-3.]

The Senate Military Affairs Committee appointed a subgroup to investigate demobilization. Hearings will start Monday and General Eisenhower may be called. [1:6-7.]

A general wage increase of 19½ cents an hour was recommended by the General Motors fact-finding board. This is six cents more than the company offered and 13½ less than the union demanded, but union acceptance is anticipated. The board said the increase was not inflationary. [1:8.]

Leaders of the United Automobile Workers were hastily summoned to a meeting in Detroit tomorrow. General Motors is expected to resume negotiations. Dealings with the other motor companies seemed to be making progress. [1:6-7.]

The General Motors decision added optimism to the resumed negotiations in this city between United States Steel and the union, the first time both sides had met since October. There was great hope that a strike might be averted. [1:6-7.]

What happens in the steel deliberations will largely determine whether 200,000 electrical workers walk out Tuesday. [12:2.]

The threatened disruption of the nation's telephone service scheduled for this morning was delayed until Monday on Labor Secretary Schwellenbach's plea to the Western Electric strikers. [1:5.] Cable operators refused to handle messages and money for soldiers reaching them through Western Union. [1:7.]

Meat packers rejected a Government offer to pay more for its meat without raising retail prices. There seemed little hope of halting a strike. [13:1.]

UAW to Consider Report During Week-End in Detroit

Executive Board and GM Union Committee Are Expected to Accept Federal Findings —General Motors Officials Silent

By WALTER W. RUCH
Special to The New York Times.

DETROIT, Jan. 10—Leaders of the United Automobile Workers, CIO, were summoned hastily today to come to Detroit for two week-end meetings to consider the report of President Truman's General Motors fact-finding board.

As soon as it became known that the report would be released today, R. J. Thomas, international president, requested members of the international executive board of the UAW to come here for a special meeting on Saturday morning.

Almost simultaneously, Walter P. Reuther, vice president of the UAW, and director of its General Motors division, sent out telegrams to the national General Motors committee of the union, scheduling a meeting for Sunday afternoon.

Recommendations were expected to flow from the Saturday meeting into that set for Sunday, with the ultimate outcome likely to constitute a new overture on the part of the UAW toward settlement of the fifty-one-day-old General Motors strike. The UAW, it was learned, was almost certain to take the report of the fact-finding commission as an acceptable compromise of its wage differences with General Motors.

The corporation, however, remained silent on the Washington report. This was not as disquieting as it might have been had the company not withdrawn from the proceedings rather than argue with the UAW over the "ability to pay" issue. One company official explained that the concern could hardly be expected to comment upon the result of a proceeding from which it had withdrawn as a party.

According to the best available sources here, the company now will proceed to sit down with the UAW, as in the past, to negotiate private-

Continued on Page 15, Column 7

Averting of Steel Strike Expected in Parley Here

By RUSSELL PORTER

Possibility of a settlement of the wage dispute in the steel industry without a strike increased yesterday afternoon when representatives of the United States Steel Corporation and the United Steel Workers of America, an affiliate of the Congress of Industrial Organizations, resumed collective bargaining negotiations in a three-hour conference, apparently held in a friendly atmosphere, and adjourned until 2 P. M. today for further discussion.

The conference is being held at the headquarters of the corporation at 71 Broadway.

The negotiations were interrupted last October, when the company refused any concessions to the union's demand for a $2-a-day wage increase unless a compensatory price increase was allowed by the Government. They were resumed after a price increase of about $4 a ton was authorized. The company had asked for $7.

Effect on Other Strikes Seen

Both sides refused comment on the progress of the negotiations after yesterday's meeting, but it was evident they were hopeful of an agreement that would avert the strike, scheduled to begin Monday, which would call out 700,000 workers throughout the industry.

Observers, meanwhile, felt a peaceful settlement of the steel dispute also would head off threatened CIO strikes in the electrical and packing-house industries and might influence compromise solutions of existing strikes in the automobile and other industries.

The recommendations of President Truman's fact-finding board for an increase of 19½ cents an

Continued on Page 12, Column 3

WIRE STRIKE STOPS MESSAGES TO GI'S

Funds Also Held Up Here as Pressure Becomes Severe—No Moves for Settlement

By A. H. RASKIN

Messages and money orders intended for soldiers and sailors overseas were piling up in cable offices here yesterday as the strike of 7,000 Western Union telegraph workers in New York, Long Island and northern New Jersey went into its third day.

With no moves for settlement of the strike in prospect, the pressure of the telegraph tie-up on business activity became increasingly severe. Many large companies, already handicapped by the virtual suspension of normal telegraphic service, reported that mechanical failures were interfering with the operation of inter-office communications between the home offices here and branches in other cities.

The Western Union management and the strikers differed as to the volume of traffic that was being kept up in the face of the

Continued on Page 12, Column 6

Senators to Inquire Into All Phases Of Demobilization of Armed Forces

By C. P. TRUSSELL
Special to The New York Times.

WASHINGTON, Jan. 10—Under pressure from Senators and the War Department, a special Senate Military Affairs subcommittee was created today to investigate the entire question of demobilization of the armed forces. It will begin work as soon as witnesses are available.

Public hearings, said Senator Edwin C. Johnson of Colorado, chairman of the subcommittee, would start Monday if either Kenneth C. Royall, Acting Secretary of War, or General Eisenhower, the first scheduled witnesses, was able to appear then.

Appointed to the subcommittee by Senator Elbert D. Thomas, chairman of the Military Affairs Committee, were, besides Mr. Johnson, Senators Frank P. Briggs, Democrat, of Missouri, and Chapman Revercomb, Republican, of West Virginia.

Senator Johnson, in a letter to Senator Thomas, urged the entire Military Affairs Committee to call General Eisenhower before it for public discussion and interrogation.

"It is distressing and humiliating to all Americans to read in every newspaper in the land accounts of near mutiny in the Army," Senator Johnson said. "The causes for this deplorable situation must be brought out in the open. No American Army must ever be permitted by the Congress to degenerate into a mob."

Senator Revercomb is the author of a resolution which would effect the immediate discharge, on application, of any of an estimated 1,000,000 fathers who are still in the services here and overseas. He said today that he believed Congress should take over the demobilization program.

As plans for the investigation

Continued on Page 4, Column 4

REPORT TO TRUMAN

Fact-Finders Proposing Increase 12½% Short of Union Demand

FIRM OFFERED 13½ CENTS

President Lauds Board, Asks Adoption of Recommendation and End to Walk-Out

The text of the Fact Finding Board's report, Pages 14, 15.

By LOUIS STARK
Special to The New York Times.

WASHINGTON, Jan. 10—President Truman's fact-finding board in the General Motors dispute recommended today a general wage increase of 19½ cents an hour, or 6 cents more than the company offered.

The increase is about 17.5 per cent above present hourly rates as compared with the union demand for a 30 per cent rise.

The average wage in General Motors was estimated as $1.119 an hour. The proposed increase would bring this up to $1.314. The union requested $1.45 an hour.

Last November the Commerce Department estimated that the corporation was able to pay a wage increase of 15 per cent now and a further 10 per cent next year.

The President received the 12,000-word document from the board, headed by Lloyd K. Garrison, at noon and later issued a summary of the findings.

President Lauds Report

Praising the report as "a thorough and reasoned document," Mr. Truman said that he believed "it will commend itself to the good judgment of the American public." He added:

"I sincerely hope that the parties will follow the recommendations and bring about a speedy end to this most costly conflict. I am satisfied that if such a settlement is made the industrial skies will rapidly clear and American industry and labor will go forward to new heights of achievement in the interests of the whole country."

Outstanding in the report is the statement that the proposed wage increase is non-inflationary; that it will not require a price increase, and that it is well within the national stabilization policy.

R. J. Thomas and Walter P. Reuther, president and vice president of the CIO United Automobile Workers, hurried to New York to lay the board's findings before Philip Murray, CIO president, who resumed wage negotiations with the United States Steel Corporation today.

They issued no statement here, but it was said unofficially that the auto workers would accept the recommendations, which were also signed by the other board members, Milton E. Eisenhower, president of Kansas State Agricultural College, and Judge Walter P. Stacy of the Supreme Court of North Carolina.

There was no comment here from General Motors officials.

Report Tied to Steel Dispute

The report, coming as it did with renewal of the steel wage negotiations, caused speculation here to continue to be optimistic on the early settlement of the steel dispute, which threatens a strike of 700,000 workers Monday.

This union requested a wage increase of $2 a day, or 25 cents an hour. Steel union sources have indicated that the organization was prepared to accept $1.60, or 20 cents an hour, which would be slightly in excess of the General Motors recommendation.

Besides the wage recommendation, the Garrison Board proposed that "in line with the customary practice of American industry in similar situations," the status quo prevailing before the strike be restored by reinstatement of the 1945 contract which the company has canceled ("as it had a right to do").

After the contract is reinstated, the board suggested, the parties

Continued on Page 15, Column 1

"All the News That's Fit to Print"

The New York Times.

LATE CITY EDITION
Hot and humid with scattered showers today. Cooler tomorrow.
Temperature Range Today—Max., 90; Min., 73
Temperature Yesterday—Max., 91.6; Min., 73
Full U. S. Weather Bureau Report, Page 35

VOL. XCVI..No. 32,710. Entered as Second-Class Matter. Postoffice, New York, N. Y. NEW YORK, FRIDAY, AUGUST 15, 1947. THREE CENTS IN NEW YORK CITY

LAWS ON GAMBLING BREED CORRUPTION, O'DWYER DECLARES

Mayor Says, However, He Will Enforce Them and Keep the Police Department Clean

ASKS INQUIRIES BY JURIES

Praises Wallander for the Job He Is Doing—Inspector Kennedy Raids Dice Game

By MEYER BERGER

Existing gambling laws, Mayor O'Dwyer said at City Hall yesterday, tend to breed corruption. He said he would, as long as his administration lasts, like to see a grand jury in each county in the city inquire into gambling and its attendant evils.

"The Police Department," the Mayor said, "has a responsibility for enforcing a law which applies outside the fence of a racetrack, but not inside—a law for which a considerable portion of the public has shown very little respect.

"There is a danger of corruption in this picture. One investigation after another during my thirty-seven years in this city has publicly charged corruption in the enforcement of these laws. It is something with which every honest administration of the city's business is deeply concerned. This administration is no exception. We need and will need all the help we can get from law agencies to prevent corruption."

Praises Queens Jury

Mr. O'Dwyer praised the Queens County grand jury inquiring into alleged police grafting on bookmakers, which on Wednesday advocated that the state legalize off-the-track betting because existing laws are unenforceable and breed rackets.

Mr. O'Dwyer was asked what he intends to do about the current situation.

"I am going to enforce the law as best I can and keep the Police Department as clean as I can," he said. "That is why I am so happy to have the aid of grand juries—to do both, enforce the law and prevent corruption."

Someone wanted to know if Police Commissioner Arthur W. Wallander, who has shaken up his force in an anti-gambling crusade, is "fighting for his job."

"The city," the Mayor said warmly, "could stand 100 Wallanders. That's based not only on his record since he became Commissioner but on the thirty-one years I have known him intimately. He can be Commissioner as long as I am Mayor, if he wants it. A man who works as long and as intelligently as he does deserves the job."

Inspector James R. Kennedy, in charge of the Eighth Uniformed Division, Manhattan East, led a raid last night on a four-story vacant building at 203 East 101st Street. The police arrested nineteen men, whom they said were playing dice in a room on the ground floor.

Seventeen of the men were booked at the East 104th Street station for disorderly conduct and two for violation of Section 970 of the Penal Code. The two were Ralph M. Osca, 37 years old, of 1954 Second Avenue, accused of being the "cutter" in the game, and Joseph Benfari, 22, of 219 East 101st Street, charged with being the "steerer."

Inspector Kennedy, who was accompanied by Lieut. George Oest and six plainclothes men, was the only one of twenty-three inspectors who was not transferred in the recent shake-up.

3 Booked for Perjury

Three witnesses who had appeared before the Queens grand jury and who were named by that body on Wednesday in perjury informations, surrendered yesterday in District Attorney Charles P. Sullivan's office in Long Island City. Each was booked on a perjury charge and held for hearing on Nov. 10.

The three are Eugene Conklin, 43 years old, of 41-28 Seventy-seventh Street in Jackson Heights; William (Willie The Ice) Perillo, 42, of 21-12 Twenty-eighth Street, Astoria, and William (Willie Shephard) Mosca, 44, of 32-42 Thirty-third Street, Astoria, all of Queens. They were accused, among other alleged perjurious statements before the grand jury, of denying they are, or were, bookmakers.

The charges against Perillo said he testified that he had quit bookmaking ten months before he appeared as witness and had returned to the ice business, "when

Continued on Page 36, Column 6

Truman Backs Price Inquiry As Possibly Showing Gouge

He Says Clark's Investigation May Reveal Who Is Causing High Cost Levels—Plea for Labor-Farm-Industry Talk Is Rejected

By LOUIS STARK
Special to THE NEW YORK TIMES.

WASHINGTON, Aug. 14—President Truman expressed approval today of Attorney General Tom C. Clark's investigation to determine who might be responsible for conspiring to increase prices of food, clothing and housing.

Reporters, asked whether the President felt that the Federal inquiry would check the rise in prices or indicate those who had profited beyond normal margins.

While Mr. Truman believed that the latter result would be the outcome of Mr. Clark's efforts, he said that as to a possible check on prices the newsmen would have to wait and see.

In giving his endorsement to the Attorney General's investigation, the President indicated that he held high hopes for the inquiry.

The President was asked about the corn crop which has been affected by great flood damage. He said that a Cabinet food committee was looking into the entire food picture, including corn as well as other crops.

The Chief Executive indicated that he had no plan for calling together spokesmen for labor, industry and agriculture to consider the problem of prices, as suggested several days ago by Emil Rieve, administrative chairman of the Full Employment Committee of the Congress of Industrial Organizations.

Recalling that he had convened a labor-management conference in November, 1945, and that it had not been successful, the President turned down Mr. Rieve's proposal.

The question on crops addressed to the President was intended to ascertain if he had been considering some possible limitation on exports in view of the reduced crop outlook in some commodities. He felt, he said, that the Cabinet committee would determine whatever steps might be necessary on the

Continued on Page 14, Column 7

U. S. CANCELS DEBTS OF BILLION BY ITALY IN FINANCIAL PACTS

Frees $60,000,000 in Blocked Properties—Will Return 28 Freight Ships to Rome

WOULD RELIEVE BURDENS

Lovett Expresses Hope Accords Will Reduce the Weight of Peace Treaty Clauses

By WALTER H. WAGGONER
Special to THE NEW YORK TIMES.

WASHINGTON, Aug. 14—The United States today crossed off about $1,000,000,000 in debts owed by Italy and, in addition, liberalized its interpretation of the terms of the financial section of the Italian peace treaty to aid that country's frail economy.

The State Department, in making the agreement public, said the action would relieve Italy of many "burdensome" financial and economic clauses in the peace pact and aid "substantially" in her recovery.

Terms of the debt relief were contained in one of three "memoranda of understanding" with which the two Governments concluded three months of negotiations. The other documents provided for protection of private American property in Italy and the disposal of German assets there. France and Great Britain joined in the negotiations on the last point.

Hopes It Will Help Italy

Robert A. Lovett, Acting Secretary of State, said upon signing the documents relating to American claims that he hoped the agreement would ease Italy's "difficult financial situation."

"These understandings, furthermore," he went on, "reflect the recognition given to the fact that the Italians themselves overthrew the Fascist Government, and beginning September, 1943, your people joined the Allies as a co-belligerent against the Nazis.

"The questions which have been settled in these negotiations constitute an additional substantial step in the establishment of good economic and political relations between our two countries."

On behalf of his government, Ivan Matteo Lombardo, chief of the Italian economic and financial delegation and signer of the agreement, declared that the prosperity of Italy "is highly beneficial to the greater prosperity of this country, which in turn reverberates upon

Continued on Page 4, Column 1

TWO INDIAN NATIONS EMERGE ON WORLD SCENE

The New York Times Aug. 15, 1947

Princely states that have not yet adhered to either India or Pakistan are shown without shading. Pakistan has recognized the independence of Kalat, on the Arabian Sea. The boundaries running through Bengal (A) and the Punjab (B) are to be announced by a commission.

INDIA AND PAKISTAN BECOME NATIONS; CLASHES CONTINUE

Ceremonies at New Delhi and Karachi Mark Independence for 400,000,000 Persons

NEHRU ACCLAIMS GANDHI

But He Warns of Trials Ahead—Death Toll in Communal Fighting Reaches 153

By ROBERT TRUMBULL
Special to THE NEW YORK TIMES.

NEW DELHI, Friday, Aug. 15—India achieved her long-sought independence today through the transfer of British power to the two dominions into which that land of 400,000,000 persons has been divided, India and Pakistan.

While the ceremonies marking this major historic event were taking place communal strife continued to cast a grim shadow over the future.

[Communal clashes, fires and looting continued in Lahore, Punjab, with the rising death toll estimated at 153, The Associated Press reported. In London King George conferred an earldom on Viscount Mountbatten for his role in solving the Indian problem and the Government made available to the Indian Government £35,000,000 of India's sterling balance.]

The Dominion of India reached the goal of freedom here at midnight with minimum celebration and a few speeches that stressed the gravity of the tasks ahead of the new nation.

In Karachi, capital of Pakistan, Mohammed Ali Jinnah will take the oath this morning as Governor General of the Moslem dominion which he was the primary figure in creating against the demand for a united India.

Viceroy at Both Ceremonies

This ceremony at the Sind Provincial Government House, which is now Mr. Jinnah's official residence, will be the only event marking the transfer of power from British to Indian hands in that dominion.

The Viceroy, Viscount Mountbatten, addressed the Pakistan Constituent Assembly yesterday—his last official act as Viceroy—and then flew back to New Delhi to attend the formal transfer here. No special events were scheduled in Karachi, as they were in New Delhi, to mark the actual moment when the rule of the King-Emperor came to an end at midnight except in so far as both dominions continued to owe formal allegiance to the British crown.

Mohandas K. Gandhi, the real hero of the New Delhi ceremony, was absent from the capital of his country in its triumphant hour. At the moment his great dream came true—though not precisely in the form he wished—Mr. Gandhi was in humble surroundings of his own choosing among the Moslems of Calcutta, where he felt he was needed more. But his name was publicly praised by others who remained here to carry on the work to which he has devoted his life.

Climax at Midnight

The Constituent Assembly of the Government of India assumed its sovereign power solemnly in a special session that began at 11 P. M. last night and reached its climax at twelve o'clock. As the hands of the clock in the stately assembly hall of the State Council building met at midnight India's Cabinet Ministers and Members of the Assembly listened in silence to the chimes of the hour.

As the last note died an unidentified member blew a conch shell of the kind used in Hindu temples to summon the gods to witness a great event. Instantly a great cheer arose. India at that moment had become a free member of the British Commonwealth of Nations — free even to leave the commonwealth if she chooses.

The members then stood and repeated after the Assembly President, Dr. Rajendra Prasad, this oath in Hindi and then in English:

"At this solemn moment when the people of India, through suffering and sacrifice, have secured freedom, I, a member of the Constituent Assembly of India, do dedicate myself in all humility to the service of India and her people to the end that this ancient land attain her rightful place in the world and make her full and willing contribution to the promotion of world peace and the welfare of mankind."

Then in accordance with a formal motion made by President

Continued on Page 2, Column 2

RELIEF FROM HEAT LIKELY TOMORROW

Continued High Temperatures Today Expected to Be Ended by Thunder Showers

Relief from the heat wave here was forecast for tomorrow by the Weather Bureau last night. The forecast followed a high temperature of 91.6 degrees at 4:15 P. M. yesterday, the second successive day when the mercury touched 91.

Collars, shirts and dresses are expected to wilt again today as a spokesman for the bureau said it would be hot and humid with the highest thermometer reading near 90. Afternoon or evening thunder showers probably will precede the cool air mass pushing in from the West that, it is hoped, will end the hot spell on the Eastern seaboard.

Meanwhile, in the Midwest, according to The Associated Press, scattered showers cooled that area after a two-week heat wave had reduced harvest prospects, especially for corn.

Locally, the lowest temperature for the twenty-four-hour period yesterday was 73, registered at 6 A. M. The mercury mounted steadily during the early morning, generally recording a point or two higher each hour than for a corresponding hour Wednesday.

By noon the thermometer registered 85, two degrees below the listing at noon Wednesday, but the humidity stood at 72 per cent, 5 higher than at the same time the preceding day.

After that hour the mercury rose and the humidity decreased, the humidity standing at 60 per cent when the high temperature for the day was reached. The highest humidity of the day was 95 per cent at 8 A. M.

[A table of yesterday's temperatures will be found on Page 35.]

Although many persons felt as if they were perspiring more because of accumulated heat, the temperature dropped steadily during the early evening. Thermometer readings for 5, 6 and 7

Continued on Page 34, Column 6

U. S. RENT CURB HERE IS BADLY SNARLED

Many Tenants Tell of Futile Attempts to Get Relief—ORC Soon to Cut Staff

By CHARLES GRUTZNER

A bad snarl in the administration of Federal rent controls in New York came to light yesterday, with the backlog of tenant complaints increasing in area rent offices.

At the same time, the Office of Rent Control announced it would drop "about 150" employes in this city on Sept. 15 in line with a 20 per cent nation-wide reduction in staff. The Federal agency will also close its area offices at St. George, S. I., and Mineola, L. I. The Brooklyn office will take over Staten Island cases, and the Queens office is to absorb the Nassau and Suffolk work loads.

Tenants, attorneys and representatives of veterans and civic organizations told yesterday of repeated and futile attempts to obtain action on cases where excess rents allegedly have been charged for several months and in a few cases for a full year. Their descriptions of local rent offices ranged from "overloaded with work" to "completely demoralized."

Not Covered By City Law

Tenants have been coming to the City Rent Commission at 500 Park Avenue with cases involving apartment house rentals and evictions, although the city law covers only hotels and rooming houses. The apartment dwellers have said they went first to the Federal rent offices and were advised to seek advice from the municipal agency.

The expected passage by the City Council of three bills sponsored by Vice Chairman Joseph T. Sharkey will give the City Rent Commission power to prosecute violations of Federal and City rent laws covering apartments and small houses as well as hotels and rooming houses. Although this will take some of the local burden from

Continued on Page 15, Column 2

Actors Win an Anti-Bias Contract In Fight on Negro Ban in Capital

The League of New York Theatres, an organization of theatre owners, operators and producers, agreed yesterday to sign a new contract with Actors' Equity Association embodying a clause whereby actors shall not be required to play in Washington unless Negroes are admitted to the audiences.

James F. Reilly, executive director of the league, said the disputed clause would be in the next agreement, becoming effective on Aug. 1, 1948, at which time the nation's capital would face a virtual ban that would keep all actors and stage attractions out of its theatres unless the rule against Negroes was revoked. The present two-year contract between Equity and the League expires on Aug. 31.

Mr. Reilly asserted that the time element in the controversial clause was included to permit theatres in Washington to effect a change in policy. He said other factors remained to be cleared up before the agreement is accepted by both sides, but that it was his belief that a complete agreement may be reached "by early next week."

The league's action was taken at a closed meeting yesterday afternoon at the Astor Hotel. While the league made no detailed statement on its capitulation to Equity's contractual demand, it was reported that forty-six members attended, with twenty-nine voting in favor of the Equity condition, seven against and ten abstaining. Attendance by forty-two members constitutes a quorum.

Even as the league acceded to Equity's demand, Marcus Heiman, president of the operating company for the National Theatre in Washington, declared last night that he would not lift the ban on Negroes as patrons.

When informed of the league's vote, Mr. Heiman referred to an announcement he made on Tuesday regarding the situation. He reiterated that the National would drop its whites-only rule only if: 1. The

Continued on Page 10, Column 4

WORLD PEACE TIED TO AMERICAS TALKS

Marshall, at Rio de Janeiro, Says Hemisphere Defense Aim Is Within Framework of U.N.

By C. P. TRUSSELL
Special to THE NEW YORK TIMES.

RIO DE JANEIRO, Aug. 14—Secretary of State George C. Marshall, landing amid applauding crowds of Brazilians at this city's Santos Dumont Airport today, said the United States delegation to the inter-American defense conference had come "for the purpose of helping to consolidate the peace of the world."

In thus going beyond the strictly hemispheric implications of the twenty-nation conference that is to open in the summer capital of Petropolis tomorrow, Secretary Marshall put upon the American republics the obligation of setting an example for all nations.

To the Brazilian and other diplo-

Continued on Page 7, Column 2

'Crudest' U. S. Interference In Greece Charged by Soviet

By THOMAS J. HAMILTON
Special to THE NEW YORK TIMES.

LAKE SUCCESS, N. Y., Aug. 14—Andrei A. Gromyko, Soviet Deputy Foreign Minister, launched a determined attack today on the new United States resolution under which the United Nations Security Council would order Yugoslavia, Albania and Bulgaria to "cease and desist from rendering any further assistance or support in any form to the guerrillas fighting against the Greek Government."

Mr. Gromyko's statement was interpreted as giving unmistakable notice that he would veto both the United States resolution and an Australian proposal, which, without attributing responsibility to either side, orders all four nations to stop the fighting. Both resolutions invoke Chapter VII of the Charter, applying to threats to the peace, breaches of the peace, or acts of aggression, under which the Council can order enforcement measures, going as far as a collective declaration of war by the fifty-five member nations.

The Soviet representative said that the United States resolution constituted "the crudest interference" in the internal affairs of Greece. He added that the Australian resolution was worse than an earlier and milder United States resolution, which he vetoed two weeks ago, and "competes successfully with the second American resolution."

"One cannot solve the Greek question as proposed in the American and in the Australian resolutions," said Mr. Gromyko. "They are missing their mark. They may correspond to the interests of one or two countries but not to the interests of the development of good neighborly relations between states and, consequently not to the interests of the United Nations as a whole."

Mr. Gromyko was silent, how-

Continued on Page 4, Column 4

TASS SAYS GREEKS MOLEST RUSSIANS

Charges Workers in Embassy Are Seized and 'Tortured'—Sees Threat to Relations

By The Associated Press.

LONDON, Friday, Aug. 15—The Soviet news agency Tass said today in a dispatch from Athens that Greek authorities had "been arresting and even subjecting to torture persons at work in the Soviet Embassy" in the Greek capital.

The dispatch said the Soviet Chargé d'Affaires in Athens had protested to the Greek Government that such actions were "incompatible with the maintenance of diplomatic relations between Greece and the Soviet Union."

A summarized version of the dispatch was distributed in London by the Soviet Monitor.

The arrests and torture, the dispatch said, extended to members of "other Soviet institutions in Greece" besides the Embassy.

"Persons who have commercial ties with the trade delegation of the U.S.S.R. are subjected to repressions," it added.

The dispatch failed to make clear, however, whether the persons affected by the alleged maltreatment were Soviet citizens, Greeks working for the Moscow

Continued on Page 3, Column 7

World News Summarized

FRIDAY, AUGUST 15, 1947

Today is Independence Day in India. British rule over the vast land, with its population of 400,000,000, ended at midnight and the territory was divided into two independent nations, the dominions of Pakistan and India. Viscount Mountbatten gave up his role of Viceroy and became Governor General of India. [1:8.] Earlier, he addressed the Pakistan Constituent Assembly and rode to the Government House in a state procession with Mohammed Ali Jinnah, who is the new Governor General of Pakistan. [2:2.]

Britain abolished the India office and named Arthur Henderson as Minister of State for Commonwealth Relations. Lord Mountbatten was rewarded with an Earldom. [3:6-7.]

India's new chapter opened amid more outbreaks of violence. In Lahore, capital of Punjab Province, which is to be divided between Pakistan and India, 153 persons had been reported killed in two days. [2:6.]

In Palestine, fighting between Arabs and Jews in the Tel Aviv region continued for the fifth day. Jewish underground forces went to the rescue of areas attacked by Arab mobs. [1:6-7.]

In Java, fires swept the Netherlands Indies Petroleum Board's main dump at the port of Tandjungpriok. Saboteurs were believed to have set the blaze. [3:1.]

The Indonesian Republic, appearing for the first time before the United Nations Security Council, urged the Council to order the Netherlands to evacuate all of her troops from Java, Sumatra and Madura. [3:5.]

Andrei A. Gromyko declared that a United States resolution before the Security Council, asking it to order Yugoslavia, Albania and Bulgaria to stop aiding Greek guerrillas, was "the crudest interference" in the internal affairs of Greece. His attack was taken to foreshadow a Soviet veto. [1:6-7.]

Moscow may sever relations with Athens, it was feared, following charges that Russians had been tortured by Greeks in Athens. [1:7.]

About $1,000,000,000 of debts owed by Italy were canceled by the United States in an effort to help Italy's difficult economic position. Rome also was relieved of several other "burdensome" clauses of the peace treaty in recognition of Italian help to the Allied cause in the latter part of the war. [1:4.]

The United States has offered to rehabilitate the Ruhr coal mines with 600,000 tons of American steel ingots. [4:4.]

In Nuremberg, twenty-one former officials of the I. G. Farben chemical trust pleaded not guilty when arraigned before the war crimes court on charges of having plotted the war for profit. [5:4.]

President Truman marked the second anniversary of V-J Day by expressing disappointment that world peace, whose attainment had seemed so certain two years ago, had yet to be achieved. [8:6-7.] He said he could see no justification for calling a special session of Congress before January. [4:1.]

Secretary of State Marshall and his party of delegates arrived in Rio de Janeiro for the Inter-American Conference, which opens today. He told a cheering crowd of Brazilians at the airport that the United States delegation would work "to consolidate the peace of the world." [1:5.]

The inquiry undertaken by Attorney General Clark into the high prices of food, clothing and housing was approved by President Truman. He said the investigation might show who was profiteering. [1:2-3.]

Jews, Arabs Battle Amid Fires; Armed Zionist Troops Aid Police

Special to THE NEW YORK TIMES.

JERUSALEM, Aug. 14—For the first time Jewish underground defense forces came today to the rescue of Jewish districts menaced by Arab mobs in the embattled borderland between Tel Aviv and Jaffa.

Three more Jews and one Arab were slain. A fourth Jew died of stab wounds received yesterday. More than fifty Arabs and Jews were wounded.

The three murdered Jews were all truck men whose vehicles were stoned and shot at by Arab gangs. One of them, Aharon Hanovici, 27, was an American. He was discharged last year from the United States Army, in which he served as a truck driver in North Africa with the 404th Quartermaster Company.

The fourth day of the rioting, which appeared to be intensifying rather than diminishing despite appeals from Arab and Jewish leaders, brought wholesale destruction of property. Three great fires lighted the sky tonight over the silent and deserted no man's land between the twin Arab and Jewish cities, whose border areas have been placed under a dawn-to-dusk house curfew. The curfew area was extended eastward today after clashes between Arabs and Jews began to spread.

While counseling Jews to avoid provocation, Haganah, the Zionist secret militia, came into the open with its arms today to reinforce the Palestine police in repelling depredations of roving Arab crowds.

When a small band of Arabs invaded the highly inflammable Maccabi slum quarter of Tel Aviv, Haganah units formed to defend the district. Meantime Arab constables on the roof of a police building opened fire. Someone threw a grenade at the invaders who fled.

Arab gangs were dispersed in

Continued on Page 3, Column 2

"All the News That's Fit to Print"

The New York Times.

LATE CITY EDITION
Sunny with pleasant temperatures today. Fair tomorrow.
Temperature Range Today-Max.,80; Min.,60
Temperatures Yesterday-Max.,90.3; Min.,69
Full U. S. Weather Bureau Report, Page 55

VOL. XCIX..No. 33,758. Entered as Second-Class Matter, Post Office, New York, N. Y. NEW YORK, WEDNESDAY, JUNE 28, 1950. Times Square, New York 18, N. Y. Telephone LAckawanna 4-1000 FIVE CENTS

TRUMAN ORDERS U. S. AIR, NAVY UNITS TO FIGHT IN AID OF KOREA; U. N. COUNCIL SUPPORTS HIM; OUR FLIERS IN ACTION; FLEET GUARDS FORMOSA

114 RESCUED HERE AS LINER GROUNDS AFTER COLLISION

Excalibur, With Hole 15 Feet Wide in Side, Settles on Mud Flat Off Brooklyn

FIRES START ON FREIGHTER

One Person Slightly Injured—Responsibility for the Crash Still to Be Decided

By WILLIAM R. CONKLIN

Thirty-five minutes after a gay departure for a Mediterranean cruise, the American Export Line's Excalibur was disabled in a collision yesterday with a Danish freighter in the Narrows, but all her 114 passengers were taken off safely.

The confetti-speckled cruise ship left Pier 4, Jersey City, at noon for a forty-three-day voyage. At 12:35 P. M. the collision with the inbound Colombia occurred off Sixty-ninth Street, Brooklyn.

The impact crushed the bow of the freighter and tore a hole fifteen feet wide in the port side of the Excalibur forward of the bridge. Fire broke out in the Colombia's forepeak in a paint storeroom.

While passengers and both crews remained calm, water quickly flooded the forward holds of the cruise ship. The Excalibur settled with her bow on a midstream mud bank, with her screw lifted in the air.

Passengers Taken Off by Tugs

Passengers on the sinking ship donned bright orange life preservers and were taken off by two tugs of the Moran Towing Company. Except for one woman who bruised three fingers of her left hand, all passengers were uninjured. They were returned to Pier 4, and the ship line arranged for hotel accommodations for them.

No official on the scene would assess responsibility for the collision. The Coast Guard required both captains to file written reports on the crash today. Under usual procedure, a Coast Guard board of inquiry hears evidence and fixes blame. Unofficially, it was said that a misunderstanding of whistle signals was the probable cause of the accident.

Capt. S. N. Groves of Brooklyn, a veteran of twenty-five years at sea, commanded the Excalibur, a ship of 9,644 gross tons with a top speed of seventeen knots. The Colombia, owned by the United Steamship Lines of Denmark, was commanded by Capt. Christian Mikkelsen of Copenhagen. The freighter was operated by the Scandinavian-American Steamship Company of 25 Broadway. Carrying cotton, wool and lubricating oils, she was bound from Philadelphia to Pier 24 at Congress Street, Brooklyn.

When the collision occurred there was good visibility despite a light haze over the lower bay. Persons in Shore Road Park saw the collision clearly, half a mile off the Brooklyn waterfront.

As the Excalibur's forward holds filled, her nose dropped into a mudbank and she swung to face upstream on the incoming tide.

2 Fireboats Help Freighter

The fireboats William J. Gaynor and Firefighter put lines on the 5,146-ton freighter to fight the fire on board. With the help of the ship's forty-two crewmen they subdued a fire in the forward hold. A collision bulkhead between that point and the forecastle prevented them from tackling another fire in the peak.

With Army, Navy, Coast Guard and Moran tugs helping, the burning vessel was moved into the north side of the Sixty-ninth Street ferry pier. John L. Holian, Deputy Fire Chief commanding the Marine Division, summoned a hook and ladder company to pour streams into the burning peak from the pier. Within an hour, the fire was extinguished.

Joseph H. Boggs, senior assistant purser of the Excalibur, said it was fortunate that the collision had occurred in shoal water.

"Immediately after the crash we

Continued on Page 29, Column 3

SANCTIONS VOTED

Council Adopts Plan of U. S. for Armed Force in Korea, 7 to 1

THE SOVIET IS ABSENT

Yugoslavia Casts Lone Dissent—Egypt and India Abstain

Mr. Austin's statement to the United Nations is on Page 6.

By THOMAS J. HAMILTON
Special to THE NEW YORK TIMES.

LAKE SUCCESS, June 27—The Security Council adopted tonight a United States resolution recommending that members of the United Nations use armed force in repelling the invasion of southern Korea and restoring international peace and security.

The vote on the resolution, which amounted to Security Council authorization for President Truman's decision to send United States naval and air units to the defense of the Republic of Korea, was 7 to 1, with Yugoslavia voting against.

The representatives of India and Egypt did not vote because they had not received instructions from their Governments. The Soviet Union was absent.

Representatives of Britain, France, Nationalist China, Cuba, Ecuador and Norway announced this afternoon that they would vote for the United States resolution without change. However, the Council recessed at 5:12 P. M. to permit Sir Benegal Rau and Mahmoud Bey Fawzi, the representatives of India and Egypt, to try to reach their Governments by telephone.

The vote was finally taken at 10:45 P. M. after both said they had been unable to establish communication with responsible authorities. With Egypt and India again not participating, the Council then rejected, seven to one, a Yugoslav resolution proposing that the Council renew its appeal for compliance with the cease-fire resolution it adopted Sunday, and request the two sides to agree to United Nations mediation.

The Council then recessed again while Sir Benegal and Fawzi Bey again attempted to obtain instructions. Apparently Fawzi Bey did so, but neither he nor Sir Benegal made any further statement, and the Council adjourned at 11 P. M.

Both Security Council members and other delegates who crowded around their table showed their realization that a historic decision for the United Nations and the world was being taken tonight. Warren R. Austin, the United States representative, was determined to avoid postponing a decision until tomorrow, and the Indian and Egyptian representatives cooperated by not requesting a postponement because of their failure to receive instructions.

Mr. Austin said after the meeting that the immediate effect of the resolution "should be to stop

Continued on Page 7, Column 1

President Takes Chief Role In Determining U. S. Course

Truman's Leadership for Forceful Policy to Meet Threat to World Peace Draws Together Advisers on Vital Move

By ARTHUR KROCK
Special to THE NEW YORK TIMES.

WASHINGTON, June 27—Some of those who participated in the meetings Sunday and Monday nights, at which the momentous decisions were taken to resist further Communist aggressions, beginning in the Far East, with the combat air and naval power of the United States, described the President to associates today as determined from the outset to adopt the forceful policy which was announced this morning.

As soon as the first meeting assembled, they said, Mr. Truman made it plain that these were to be the bases of his decision:

1. The situation created by Communist tactics at various points of the world, culminating in the attack of North Korea on South Korea, had been allowed to drift too long.
2. The entire Far East was deteriorating in a manner to threaten the peace of the world, a line had to be drawn at once, and the United States had to draw it.
3. National security was the primary interest, but embedded in this were world peace and the prestige and future effectiveness of the United Nations, which was the architect of the South Korean Government.
4. It was a time for courage, even boldness, and calculated risk, which other members of the United Nations would be invited to share as they saw fit.
5. It was not a time to give the slightest consideration to previous policies or to individuals associated with those policies. If, for example, the fundamental change in the Far Eastern sit-

Continued on Page 4, Column 3

MAINLAND ATTACKS ENDED BY FORMOSA

Chinese Nationalists Halt Air, Navy Forays in Accordance With Request by Truman

By The Associated Press

TAPEI, Formosa, Wednesday, June 28—The Chinese Nationalists today ordered their Air Force and Navy to cease attacks on the Communist mainland in accordance with a United States request.

President Truman had ordered United States warships to protect Formosa against Communist attack and at the same time asked the Nationalists to cease offensive operations.

Nationalist Foreign Minister George Yeh hailed the President's order for warship protection as "a most welcome sign of comradeship in the fight against communism."

Generalissimo Chiang Kai-shek and his Cabinet had met after the United States note was delivered to the United States Embassy. It was understood the note carried with it instructions to see that it was brought personally to Generalissimo Chiang's attention.

Mr. Yeh translated the text to the Generalissimo last night in the presence of United States Charge d'Affaires Robert Strong.

Mr. Strong was with Generalissimo Chiang for about twenty minutes. After his departure the latter consulted with Mr. Yeh, Premier Chen Cheng and other officials.

The decision was announced after Generalissimo Chiang conferred with Gen. Chou Chih-jou, Chief of the Joint General Staff, and other top Nationalist commanders.

The Nationalists were believed to have agreed to Washington's re-

Continued on Page 8, Column 4

HOUSE VOTES 315-4 TO PROLONG DRAFT

Korea Crisis Breaks Deadlock—Bill Expected to Be Sent to White House Tonight

Special to THE NEW YORK TIMES.

WASHINGTON, June 27—The House of Representatives today passed, by a vote of 315 to 4, an extension of the draft for another year.

The bill added authority for President Truman to call to active duty members of the National Guard and the reserve forces for periods not exceeding twenty-one months.

The Senate agreed to vote on the bill tomorrow afternoon. Swift passage is expected there so that the bill may reach President Truman for his signature tomorrow night.

As recently as yesterday the Senate and the House appeared to be in a hopeless deadlock over the manner in which the selective service system could be kept alive without much leeway for the President to put it to use. Today when

Continued on Page 16, Column 5

U. S. FORCE FIGHTING

MacArthur Installs an Advanced Echelon in Southern Korea

FOE LOSES 4 PLANES

American Craft in Battle to Protect Evacuation —Seoul Is Quiet

By LINDESAY PARROTT
Special to THE NEW YORK TIMES.

TOKYO, Wednesday, June 28—The United States is now actively intervening in the Korean civil war, an announcement from Gen. Douglas MacArthur's headquarters here made clear this morning.

[Gen. Douglas MacArthur announced Wednesday that the forces of South Korea now were holding the Communist Korean invaders, a United Press dispatch from Tokyo said. At the same time he reported that United States fliers had begun bombing and strafing missions against North Korean forces. Seoul was reported quiet.]

General MacArthur revealed that a "small advanced echelon" from his headquarters had been established in Korea, presumably cooperating with the United States Military Advisory Group, which has been in Korea since the republic was established there under President Syngman Rhee two years ago.

The MacArthur announcement stated that Far East air forces and elements of the naval forces under the general's command were "conducting" combat missions south of the Thirty-eighth Parallel—the dividing line between Communist North Korea and the United States-recognized Korean Republic. These operations, it was officially stated, are "in support of the Korean Republic," whose Government has now been reinstalled in the capital, Seoul, after isolation of the Northern armored spearheads that had penetrated to the outskirts of the city yesterday.

The announcement said that United States planes, which were providing air cover for the evacuation of women and children dependents of various United States missions, had shot down four North Korean fighters that were interfering with the operation of

Continued on Page 17, Column 3

Statement on Korea

By The Associated Press.

WASHINGTON, June 27—The text of President Truman's statement today on Korea:

In Korea the Government forces, which were armed to prevent border raids and to preserve internal security, were attacked by invading forces from North Korea. The Security Council of the United Nations called upon the invading troops to cease hostilities and to withdraw to the Thirty-eighth Parallel. This they have not done, but on the contrary have pressed the attack. The Security Council called upon all members of the United Nations to render every assistance to the United Nations in the execution of this resolution.

In these circumstances I have ordered United States air and sea forces to give the Korean Government troops cover and support.

The attack upon Korea makes it plain beyond all doubt that communism has passed beyond the use of subversion to conquer independent nations and will now use armed invasion and war.

It has defied the orders of the Security Council of the United Nations issued to preserve international peace and security. In these circumstances the occupation of Formosa by Communist forces would be a direct threat to the security of the Pacific area and to United States forces performing their lawful and necessary functions in that area.

Accordingly I have ordered the Seventh Fleet to prevent any attack on Formosa. As a corollary of this action I am calling upon the Chinese Government on Formosa to cease all air and sea operations against the mainland. The Seventh Fleet will see that this is done. The determination of the future status of Formosa must await the restoration of security in the Pacific, a peace settlement with Japan, or consideration by the United Nations.

I have also directed that United States forces in the Philippines be strengthened and that military assistance to the Philippine Government be accelerated.

I have similarly directed acceleration in the furnishing of military assistance to the forces of France and the associated states in Indo-China and the dispatch of a military mission to provide close working relations with those forces.

I know that all members of the United Nations will consider carefully the consequences of this latest aggression in Korea in defiance of the Charter of the United Nations. A return to the rule of force in international affairs would have far-reaching effects. The United States will continue to uphold the rule of law.

I have instructed Ambassador Austin, as the representative of the United States to the Security Council, to report these steps to the Council.

NORTH KOREA CALLS U. N. ORDER ILLEGAL

Declares Security Council's 'Cease Fire' Invalid Without Assent of China and Russia

Special to THE NEW YORK TIMES

HONG KONG, June 27—The North Korean Government issued a statement today saying that it regarded the cease fire order of the United Nations Security Council illegal for two reasons. It said these were, one, because the Democratic Peoples Republic of North Korea was not represented when its affairs were discussed and, two, because the Soviet Union and (Communist) China did not participate.

On the latter point it cited the United Nations Charter, which requires unanimity of five permanent members of the Security Council on questions of substance. China and Russia are both permanent members. [But the Communist rulers of China have not been recognized by the United Nations as representing that country.]

Drastic measures were taken in North Korea yesterday to organize

Continued on Page 18, Column 5

LEGISLATORS HAIL ACTION BY TRUMAN

Almost Unanimous Approval Is Voiced in Congress by Both Sides—House Cheers

By HAROLD B. HINTON.
Special to THE NEW YORK TIMES.

WASHINGTON, June 27—President Truman's announcement today that United States air and sea power would be employed to expel the Communist invaders from South Korea evoked almost unanimous support in Congress. His statement was read by the majority floor leaders in both houses.

In the House of Representatives, the members rose to their feet and cheered as the reading was completed by Representative John W. McCormack, of Massachusetts. In the Senate, the reading by Senator Scott W. Lucas, of Illinois, brought immediate declarations of support from several Republican Senators.

Showing the same spirit of solidarity in the face of crisis, as the present situation was frequently described, Senate and House conferees agreed on legislation to ex-

Continued on Page 5, Column 1

BID MADE TO RUSSIA

President Asks Moscow to Act to Terminate Fighting in Korea

CHIANG TOLD TO HALT

U.S. Directs Him to Stop Blows at Reds—Will Reinforce Manila

By ANTHONY LEVIERO
Special to THE NEW YORK TIMES.

WASHINGTON, June 27—President Truman announced today that he had ordered United States air and naval forces to fight with South Korea's Army. He said this country took the action, as a member of the United Nations, to enforce the cease-fire order issued by the Security Council Sunday night.

Then acting independently of the United Nations, in a move to assure this country's security, the Chief Executive ordered Vice Admiral Arthur D. Struble to form a protective cordon around Formosa to prevent its invasion by Communist Chinese forces.

Along with these fateful decisions, Mr. Truman also ordered an increase of our forces based in the Philippine Republic, as well as more speedy military assistance to that country and to the French and Vietnam forces that are fighting Communist armies in Indo-China.

After he had started these moves that might mean a decided turn toward peace or a general war, the President sent Ambassador Alan G. Kirk to the Russian Foreign Office in Moscow to request the Soviet Union to use its good offices to end the hostilities. This was an obvious proffer of an opportunity for Russia to end the crisis before her own forces might get involved.

Door Opened for Russia

In the capital this was regarded as being at once a possible face-saving device for Russia in a showdown crisis and a feeler to determine her intentions.

The decisions amounted to a showdown in the "cold war" with Russia, in which this country had at last decided to begin shooting in a limited area. Yet all the decisions followed a carefully worked out formula of action within the framework of the United Nations, as well as unilateral moves that avoided any direct provocation of the Soviet Union.

Mr. Truman based the decision to fight for the South Koreans entirely on the Security Council resolution which called upon all members of the United Nations to help carry it out. And at the Pentagon it was explained that our air and naval forces would fight only below the Thirty-eighth Parallel line that divides South Korea from the Russian-sponsored North Korea.

"The Security Council called upon all members of the United Nations to render every assistance to the United Nations in the execution of this resolution," Mr. Truman stated. "In these circumstances I have ordered United States air and sea forces to give the Korean Government troops cover and support."

Russia Is Not Mentioned

Mr. Truman carefully avoided mentioning Russia in his statement. He pivoted today's great shift in United States foreign policy on a conclusion that the "cold war" had passed from an uneasy passive stage to "armed invasion and war." He blamed "communism."

"The attack upon Korea makes it plain beyond all doubt that communism has passed beyond the use of subversion to conquer independent nations and will now use armed invasion and war," he said. "It has defied the orders of the Security Council of the United Nations issued to preserve international peace and security. In these circumstances the occupation of Formosa by Communist forces would be a direct threat to the security of the Pacific area and to United States forces performing

Continued on Page 2, Column 2

City, T.W.U. in 2-Year Peace Pact; Mayor Signs Fare Rise Resolution

Officials of the Transport Workers Union, C. I. O., the members of the Board of Transportation and Mayor O'Dwyer signed at City Hall yesterday a memorandum of understanding seeking to guarantee two years of peace in the city-owned rapid transit system.

The accord closely followed recommendations made on May 31 by the Mayor's Transit Fact-Finding Board, granting an 11-cent-an-hour increase to 35,929 operating employes, a third week of vacation after ten years and an additional holiday each year. The cost of the changes recommended by the fact-finders amounts to $13,188,515 a year.

The union bound itself not to engage in any strike or other interference with transit operations and not to seek any basic changes in the accord before July 1, 1952. It agreed to resolve all disputes in accordance with the grievance machinery set up in the pact. The union obligated itself also to recognize the board's managerial authority and to "cooperate in the attainment of efficient operations."

The Board of Transportation agreed to retain competent industrial engineers to report on a program for achieving a five-day, forty-hour week for all employes now having a scheduled work-week in excess of forty hours.

Mayor O'Dwyer also signed yesterday afternoon a resolution of the Board of Transportation, effective Saturday, increasing fares on the city-owned surface lines

Continued on Page 28, Column 4

World News Summarized

WEDNESDAY, JUNE 28, 1950

United States air and sea forces were ordered by President Truman yesterday to give Korean troops "cover and support." Moving directly to meet Communist "armed invasion and war" in Asia, the President instructed the Seventh Fleet to "prevent any attack on Formosa," called on the Chinese Nationalists to halt all attacks on the mainland, ordered United States forces in the Philippines strengthened and moved to speed military assistance to those islands and to Indo-China. He instructed Ambassador Kirk in Moscow to urge the Soviet Union to help end hostilities. [1:8; map P. 2.]

Naval and air elements are "conducting combat missions south of the Thirty-eighth Parallel of Korea in support" of the Seoul Government, General MacArthur announced. An advance echelon of his General Headquarters has been set up in Korea, he added. Conflicting reports of the fighting showed positions little changed during the day. [1:5; maps P. 17.] In Washington it was said that General MacArthur had sufficient forces to give the South Koreans air and sea preponderance. [13:3.]

This country's new Far East policy was set at conferences during which the President's positive program and leadership convinced his top aides that his decisions "were both inevitable and right." [1:3-4.] He brought unity to an Administration that had been split on many vital policy issues. [4:6-7.]

Governor Dewey, speaking as head of the Republican party, pledged full support to the President [4:3] and Congress was almost unanimous in its endorsement. [1:7.] The House, 315 to 4, passed a one-year extension of the draft with broad new powers for the President; the Senate will vote today. [1:4.] Senate Republicans, however, blocked a vote today on the foreign arms-aid bill. [14:3.] The National Security Resources Board has ready for introduction a sweeping bill authorizing the President to freeze prices, wages, manpower and materials. [15:2.]

The United Nations Security Council, with Russia absent and Yugoslavia voting no, approved a United States motion to permit member nations to send armed forces to help repel the Korean invasion. [1:2.]

British parties united in supporting President Truman's program. The Labor Government won confidence votes on its refusal to join talks on pooling Europe's heavy industry. [19:4.]

John S. Service, a key figure in Senator McCarthy's charges of communism in the State Department, has been cleared by the department's Loyalty Security Board. [22:3.]

Index to other news appears on Page 28.

Stocks Rally After Big New Losses In War Scare; Sales Near 5 Million

By ROBERT H. FETRIDGE

Securities markets the world over were subjected yesterday to wide fluctuations as the Korean situation approached a crisis of universal concern.

Calmer thinking emerged successful on the New York exchanges, but only after prices encountered terrific battering. Losses that at one time ranged to 5 points and even more in standard issues on the New York Stock Exchange were either trimmed or eliminated. Quotations were definitely on the recovery side at the close, with the final composite rate down only 0.75 point. As pictured by THE NEW YORK TIMES index, the market was midway between the highs and lows of the day at the final bell.

London was the worst sufferer among the major exchanges, while the Canadian markets followed the lead of New York.

It was a wild day on the trading floor of the Stock Exchange. Business almost reached the 5,000,000-share mark, the reporting ticker tape was constantly thrown behind actual transactions and at one time was twenty-seven minutes late. This necessitated "flash" prices on the ticker to keep brokerage offices at least abreast of the price changes in the key stocks.

The trend changed with such rapidity that selling orders were still being executed after the price direction changed for the better.

Continued on Page 41, Column 6

100TH ANNIVERSARY
"All the News That's Fit to Print"
1851 1951

The New York Times.

LATE CITY EDITION
Fair today, increasing cloudiness tomorrow and mild both days.
Temperature Range Today—Max., 60; Min., 45
Temperature Yesterday—Max., 65; Min., 48
Full U. S. Weather Bureau Report, Page 59

VOL. C..No. 34,045. Entered as Second-Class Matter, Post Office, New York, N. Y. NEW YORK, WEDNESDAY, APRIL 11, 1951. Times Square, New York 18, N. Y. Telephone Lackawanna 4-1000 FIVE CENTS

TRUMAN RELIEVES M'ARTHUR OF ALL HIS POSTS; FINDS HIM UNABLE TO BACK U. S.-U. N. POLICIES; RIDGWAY NAMED TO FAR EASTERN COMMANDS

HOUSE VOTES U. M. T. ONLY AS A PROGRAM; MARSHALL WORRIED

Chamber Accepts Compromise Setting Up Commission to Draft Details of Plan

FUTURE LAW IS REQUIRED

Congress' Approval Is Needed to Start Universal Training—General Sees Risk in This

By JOHN D. MORRIS
Special to The New York Times.

WASHINGTON, April 10—Concessions offered by advocates of Universal Military Training to save the program from outright rejection were approved today by the House of Representatives, but it remained to be seen whether the aim had been achieved.

General of the Army George C. Marshall, Secretary of Defense, meanwhile voiced the fear that current maneuvering in the House might "largely emasculate" the training features of the pending draft and training bill.

It was not clear, however, whether he was concerned over the main fight, expected later this week, over a proposal to eliminate all Universal Military Training provisions from the bill.

It was to head this off that the bill's managers headed by Representative Carl Vinson, Democrat of Georgia, offered the concessions that were approved today. The House accepted them on a voice vote.

Further Action Necessary

Consequently, as the bill now stands, little more than the principle of Universal Military Training is retained. A commission to draw up a detailed U. M. T. plan would be created. A "National Security Training Corps" would also be established, at least on paper.

But before anyone could be drafted to serve in the proposed corps, there would have to be another formal act of Congress, subject to Presidential approval or veto like any other bill, authorizing details of the training program.

At the same time, however, the revised bill retains safeguards against future pigeon-holing of U. M. T. in the House Rules Committee or elsewhere. The planning commission, which also would administer the program once Congress had authorized its institution, would be required to submit a detailed training plan to Congress within six months. The House and Senate Armed Services Committees would be required to report out a bill or resolution within forty-five days of receiving the plan. The measure then could be called up at any time.

Opponents Withhold Attack

In the House, bills ordinarily must be cleared by the Rules Committee before they can be considered on the floor. The Rules Committee bottled up a Universal Military Training Bill in the Eightieth Congress.

Opponents of any form of U.M.T. legislation did not fight the concessions approved in the House today, explaining that the proposals would make the bill less obnoxious although still unacceptable to them.

They were still hoping for approval of a substitute sponsored by Representative Graham A. Barden, Democrat of North Carolina, that would retain only what they regard as the "emergency" features of the pending draft measure. These include a three-year extension of authority to draft men 19 through 26 years of age for actual military service.

The Barden bill would eliminate authority to lower the draft age to 18½ as well as all long-range training features of the pending measure.

The Senate has already passed a draft and training bill adhering closely to the Administration's recommendations. It would authorize the drafting of men at the age of 18 and permit the President to put Universal Military Training

Continued on Page 18, Column 4

Tobey Asserts He Recorded R. F. C. Talks With Truman

President Said to Withdraw Fee Accusation—Niles Held Attempting to Aid Dawson

By C. P. TRUSSELL
Special to The New York Times.

WASHINGTON, April 10—Senator Charles W. Tobey, Republican of New Hampshire, was represented tonight as having told the Senate (Fulbright) subcommittee investigating the Reconstruction Finance Corporation that President Truman had charged in a telephone conversation with him that members of Congress had accepted fees for obtaining R. F. C. loans for constituents.

The Senator was said to have reported also that in a later telephonic communication the President had said that he had been mistaken.

Both telephonic conversations were said to have been recorded on disks in Mr. Tobey's possession. The date, or dates, were not made public. The Senator declined to discuss the matter and members of the investigating group also were silent.

In another development in the R. F. C. inquiry, former Senator Burton K. Wheeler, Democrat of

Burton K. Wheeler
Associated Press

Montana, said today that he had asked Senator Tobey to "go easy on" Donald S. Dawson, White House aide, during the Senate investigation of the agency. Mr. Wheeler asserted that he acted at

Continued on Page 25, Column 3

Sterling Hayden Was a Red; 'Stupidest Thing I Ever Did'

Special to The New York Times.

WASHINGTON, April 10—Sterling Hayden, motion picture actor and decorated former United States Marine, told the House Committee on Un-American Activities today that he had been a member of the Communist party from June to December of 1946.

"It was the stupidest and most ignorant thing I ever had done in my life," he said. "I went into it with an emotional and very unsound approach, but I don't mean to imply that I was dragged into it. I went in voluntarily."

Mr. Hayden, a native of Montclair, N. J., said there were thousands of others like him, who should come in and tell their stories.

He added that shortly after the invasion of South Korea his attorney had written to J. Edgar Hoover, director of the Federal Bureau of Investigation, giving his Communist case history and seeking a means of eliminating any prejudice against his recall to the service.

Under questioning for more than three hours, the former husband of Madeleine Carroll, screen star, told of a restless life that started with his quitting high school at the age of fifteen and going to sea, and winding up in Hollywood. A Capt. Warwich Tompkins, described by him as an "open and avowed Communist," ran through his story.

He identified Captain Tompkins as an employ of Amtorg, the of-

Continued on Page 14, Column 5

PRICE AIDE RESIGNS, CONDEMNS DI SALLE

M. E. Thompson, Ex-Governor of Georgia, Hits 'Kansas City Crowd' in Administration

Special to The New York Times.

WASHINGTON, April 10—With bitter words for Price Stabilizer Michael V. DiSalle, and for the "Kansas City crowd" he said was in the saddle in the national Administration, M. E. Thompson, former Governor of Georgia, resigned today as a consultant to the Office of Price Stabilization.

Mr. Thompson, once a power in Georgia politics, and who asserted that he battled successfully against the States Righters there who tried to keep President Truman's name off the ballot in 1948, declared that he would not support the Democratic party in 1952 if the "Kansas City crowd" still held control.

"If this be political treason,

Continued on Page 20, Column 1

Navy Suspends Explosives Expert; State Department Then Bars Wife

Special to The New York Times.

WASHINGTON, April 10—The Navy Department suspended Dr. Stephen Brunauer today as a "security risk," giving the 47-year-old high explosives expert thirty days in which to answer the charges.

The State Department meanwhile, suspended Mrs. Esther Caukin Brunauer, wife of the Navy scientist, pending the outcome of the investigation of her husband. The State Department made it plain in a statement that the action against Mrs. Brunauer was based not on information about her, but only as a result of the Navy suspension.

Both of the Brunauers were named by Senator Joseph R. McCarthy, Republican of Wisconsin, in the course of his charges last year of Communist infiltration of the Government.

The announcement of Dr. Brunauer's suspension, effective immediately, was made while he was on a trip to New England for the Navy. Questioned by reporters at LaGuardia Field, on his way back to the capital, he said:

"I do not know for what reason I was suspended. I think some one made a mistake. I telephoned Washington and a Navy spokesman said he did not know the reason for the suspension. I do not want to comment further on anything."

Mrs. Brunauer issued a stout denial of the McCarthy charges on March 13, 1950, defending herself and her husband against the allegations they were Communists.

The Navy announcement of its suspension of Dr. Brunauer followed the disclosure by the State Department that the action had already taken place. The Navy gave no details of the charges, but said that Dr. Brunauer would have thirty days to answer the charges and request a hearing.

The decision of Francis P. Matthews, Secretary of the Navy will be final, it was said.

Asked whether the suspension of Mrs. Brunauer in response to charges against her husband was

Continued on Page 16, Column 3

RISE IN SALES TAX EXPECTED TO PASS CITY COUNCIL TODAY

Finance Committee Studies Bill at Length—Fight Against Measure Goes On

RUML A FISCAL ADVISER

Mayor Declines Challenge to Debate With Hoving—Joseph Suggests State-Wide Levy

The finance committee of the City Council spent an inconclusive three-hour executive session at City Hall yesterday afternoon weighing the merits of the proposed increase in the retail sales tax from 2 to 3 per cent, but when the meeting ended nothing had changed the prospect that the tax rise would be approved.

It was indicated that today the committee, after further behind-closed-doors deliberations, would favor the sales impost rise by a vote of 8 to 2, or possibly 7 to 3, and that later today the full City Council would adopt the measure by something like 19 to 6.

If the tax bill clears the Council hurdles today, as is indicated, it is expected that the Board of Estimate, whose members are committed to it, will give its approval at tomorrow's regular meeting.

Ruml to Advise Controller

Meanwhile, Controller Lazarus Joseph announced the appointment of Beardsley Ruml, business consultant, financier and economist, as a special deputy controller to advise Mr. Joseph on fiscal matters. Mr. Ruml, whose appointment was for an "indefinite" tenure, will serve without pay.

Mr. Ruml was at one time connected with the Federal Reserve Board and also with the New York Stock Exchange. He is a

Continued on Page 32, Column 4

U. S. PRODS NATIONS

Suggests U. N. Members Send More Troops to Fight in Korea

3 AVENUES ARE LISTED

Contributions Sought From Nations Not Yet Committed

By A. M. ROSENTHAL
Special to The New York Times.

UNITED NATIONS, N. Y., April 10—The United States has been quietly suggesting that members of the United Nations increase, or at least maintain, their contributions of troops for the Korean war effort.

Informed sources here report that for some time the United States has been keeping in touch with members of the world organization to see if non-United States representation in the international army could be increased.

[Chinese Communist troops in Korea clung to their positions along the Hwachon Reservoir in the face of daylong United Nations attacks. Eighth Army headquarters clamped a stringent security blackout on news from the front as a major battle seemed to impend in the reservoir area.]

So far there has been no general appeal to the United Nations members to contribute more troops; it has all been on a country-to-country basis. Diplomats said that there was no indication that a new general request for troops in Korea was in the making for the time being.

But on a longer-range basis, the question of more troops may be considered by the committee set up by the General Assembly on Feb. 1 to plan possible sanctions

Continued on Page 5, Column 3

World News Summarized

WEDNESDAY, APRIL 11, 1951

President Truman relieved General of the Army MacArthur of his command in the Pacific because the United Nations commander had been unable to give his "wholehearted support" to United States and United Nations policies. The Presidential ouster has forced the general from all his commands, including his role in the occupation of Japan. Lieut. Gen. Matthew B. Ridgway has been designated to take over all the Far Eastern commands. [1:8.]

The United States has been asking other United Nations members to increase, or at least maintain, their forces fighting in Korea and asking for troops from countries that have sent none. [1:5.]

Enemy resistance increased in the Hwachon Reservoir area of Korea. The Communists still held the dam although Hwachon itself appeared deserted. [3:1; map P. 2.] Mao Tse-tung was said to have been officially reported ill and Liu Shao-chi was said to be acting in his place at the head of the Chinese Communist regime. [9:2.]

Britain has suggested that the United States invite Communist China to the discussions on a Japanese peace treaty and send Peiping a draft of the proposed pact. The treaty, Britain holds, should include the return of Formosa to China. [1:6-7.]

The days of "easy and automatic" relations between the United States and Canada are over, Canada's External Affairs Minister declared. "There will be frictions" that can be settled easily, he said, if the United States recognizes that Canada's acceptance of Washington leadership does not mean she is "willing to be merely an echo of somebody else's voice." [1:6-7.]

A "severe, but not crippling" budget was presented to Britain by the Labor Government, which chose to increase taxes, already heavy, rather than cut social welfare funds. [1:7.]

The bill giving West German labor equal rights with management in the operation of the steel and coal industries was passed by the lower house. [14:2.]

The House passed and sent to the Senate a supplemental defense money bill 43 per cent below Administration requests [29:1] and cut from the draft bill a provision for Universal Military Training in favor of a Presidential commission to draw detailed plans. [1:1.] Defense Secretary Marshall ordered all three armed services to share equitably draftees of superior standing. [19:3.]

Mobilization Director Wilson called for an end to complacency, selfishness and partisanship if we are to beat down the "dreadful shadow" of history's most "absolute and ruthless" dictatorship. [23:1.] M. E. Thompson resigned as consultant to the Price Stabilizer in protest against "political" control and general wastefulness. [1:2.]

Organized baseball was ordered not to raise players' salaries above a club's 1950 highest. [33:2-3.] The Army halted certain pay rises for nonoperating rail workers until a special panel ruled in the case. [33:1.]

Senator Tobey was said to have disclosed that he had recorded telephone talks with President Truman about the Senate R. F. C. inquiry. [1:2-3.]

The Navy suspended Dr. Stephen Brunauer, a scientist, as a "security risk" and the State Department dropped his wife, Esther, until the husband's case was settled. [1:2-3.]

NEWS BULLETINS FROM THE TIMES
Every hour on the hour
7 A.M. through Midnight
WQXR AM 1560
WQXR FM 96.3

Index to other news appears on last page of this section.

DISMISSED BY THE PRESIDENT

General of the Army Douglas MacArthur

Britain Asks That Red China Have Role in Japanese Pact

By WALTER H. WAGGONER
Special to The New York Times.

WASHINGTON, April 10—Britain has suggested to the United States that Communist China be brought into the negotiations for a Japanese peace treaty. The British proposal also specifically asked that the United States send a copy of its treaty draft to the Peiping regime for its consideration, and, further, that the treaty provide for the ultimate if not immediate return of Formosa to "China."

By "China" the British mean the regime of Mao Tse-tung, since that is the China now recognized by London.

These suggestions have been made in the course of recent conversations between the two Governments. They represent another difference of opinion that has developed between London and Washington on both the procedure for negotiating a Japanese treaty and the form the settlement should have.

The basis for the British request that Peiping be given a look at the United States treaty draft is to enable the Chinese Communists to reject the proposal if they want to, as the Soviet Union is expected to do.

At the same time, it is vigorously denied here that Britain will refuse to sign any treaty draft that Communist China rejects. Reports that such an "or else" position has

Continued on Page 8, Column 5

BUDGET INCREASES BRITONS' TAX LOAD

Income, Profit, Purchase, Auto and Gasoline Imposts Rise —Social Services Uncut

By RAYMOND DANIELL
Special to The New York Times.

LONDON, April 10—The already heavily burdened British people were called upon today to pay even higher taxes to preserve their welfare state. Hugh Gaitskell, Chancellor of the Exchequer, introducing his first budget, told the House of Commons that there were only two ways of meeting the extra cost of rearmament. One, which brought cheers from the Conservative Opposition, was by reducing expenditures for social welfare.

The alternative he offered was a sharp rise in both direct and indirect taxes. This brought cheers

Continued on Page 10, Column 3

Canada Bars a 'Yes' Role to U. S.; Pearson Sees Unity Despite Friction

By The United Press.

TORONTO, April 10—Lester B. Pearson, Canadian Secretary for External Affairs, said today that "easy and automatic" relations between Canada and the United States were a thing of the past.

In a speech apparently aimed at United States consumption, Mr. Pearson said that Canada was not willing to be "merely an echo of somebody else's voice" and reserved the right to criticize "our great friend, the United States."

Mr. Pearson said that Canada intended to prevent the United Nations from becoming "too much the instrument of any one country" and that it was time for the United States to stop telling Canada "that until we do one-twelfth or one-sixteenth, or some other fraction as much as they are doing, we are defaulting."

He said that there might be "angry waves which may weaken the foundation of our friendship" but that Canada would march forward with the United States "in the pursuit of objectives which we share."

"Nevertheless, the days of relatively easy and automatic relations with our neighbor are, I think, over," he added.

Mr. Pearson indicated that one of the "angry waves" that could weaken relations between Canada and the United States was the controversy over General of the Army Douglas MacArthur's statement on the war in Korea.

Later, in a second speech, Mr. Pearson made an indirect reference to General MacArthur when he said that a successful foreign policy must work toward goals accepted by the majority of the people, and it would have a better chance of "reaching these goals if we abandon what has been called 'hoop-la diplomacy' at Lake Success, at Ottawa, or, I hasten to add, at Tokyo."

He said that the free nations stood in danger of "nothing less

Continued on Page 6, Column 3

PRESIDENT MOVES

Van Fleet Is Named to Command 8th Army in Drastic Shift

VIOLATIONS ARE CITED

White House Statement Quotes Directives and Implies Breaches

Texts of statements and orders in MacArthur dispute, Page 8.

By W. H. LAWRENCE
Special to The New York Times.

WASHINGTON, Wednesday, April 11—President Truman early today relieved General of the Army Douglas MacArthur of all his commands in the Far East and appointed Lieut. Gen. Matthew B. Ridgway as his successor.

The President said he had relieved General MacArthur "with deep regret" because he had concluded that the Far Eastern Commander "is unable to give his wholehearted support to the policies of the United States Government and of the United Nations in matters pertaining to his official duties.

General MacArthur, in a message to House Minority Leader Joseph W. Martin Jr. of Massachusetts, made public by Mr. Martin last Thursday, had publicly challenged the President's foreign policy, urging that the United States concentrate on Asia instead of Europe and use Generalissimo Chiang Kai-shek's Formosa-based troops to open a second front on the mainland of China.

The change in command is effective at once. General Ridgway, who has been in command of the Eighth Army in Korea since the death in December of Gen. Walton H. Walker, assumes all of General MacArthur's titles—Supreme Commander, United Nations Forces in Korea, Supreme Commander for Allied Powers, Japan, Commander-in-Chief, Far East, and Commanding General U. S. Army, Far East.

Commanded in Greece

The Eighth Army command will pass to Lieut. Gen. James A. Van Fleet whose most recent important command was as head of the American military mission in Greece, when that country was repelling a Communist-directed guerrilla attack under the Truman doctrine.

In ousting General MacArthur for his public disagreement with American policy designed to localize the Asiatic war, the President said:

"Full and vigorous debate on matters of national policy is a vital element in the Constitutional system of our free democracy.

"It is fundamental, however, that military commanders must be governed by the policies and directives issued to them in the manner provided by our laws and Constitution.

Continued on Page 8, Column 1

News Stuns Tokyo; MacArthur Is Silent

By The Associated Press.

TOKYO, Wednesday, April 11—A small brown envelope with "flash" printed on it in red carried to General MacArthur today the news that he had been discharged from his commands by President Truman.

It was delivered by a senior aide, Col. Sid Huff, who said that the General received the news without comment. Colonel Huff indicated that the General had no forewarning that he was being relieved.

The General announced that he would have no statement immediately.

The message came as a Signal Corps communication about the time and Army radio announced the news.

General MacArthur got the word while at lunch with his wife, Senator Warren G. Mag-

Continued on Page 5, Column 4

"All the News That's Fit to Print"

The New York Times.

Copyright, 1952, by The New York Times Company.

LATE CITY EDITION
Light snow this morning followed by clearing. Fair tomorrow.
Temperature Range Today—Max., 43; Min., 35
Temperatures Yesterday—Max., 45; Min., 33
Full U. S. Weather Bureau Report, Page 55

VOL. CI..No. 34,347. Entered as Second-Class Matter, Post Office, New York, N. Y. NEW YORK, THURSDAY, FEBRUARY 7, 1952. Times Square, New York 36, N. Y. Telephone Lackawanna 4-1000 RAG PAPER EDITION SEVENTY-FIVE CENTS

KING GEORGE VI DIES IN SLEEP AT SANDRINGHAM; ELIZABETH, QUEEN AT 25, FLYING FROM AFRICA; PRESIDENT AMONG WORLD LEADERS IN TRIBUTE

2½% INTEREST RATE FOR SAVINGS BANKS APPROVED BY STATE

85% of Institutions Expected to Adopt 'Permissive' Rule Lifting 17-Year Ceiling

NEW U. S. TAXES A FACTOR

Board Adjusts Payments on Commercial Deposits, Acts to Clear Extra Dividends

By GEORGE A. MOONEY

New York's thrifty received a new incentive yesterday.

Terminating a policy that dates to 1935, the State Banking Board acted to raise its ceiling on interest-dividends paid on savings and thrift deposits from a 2 per cent maximum to 2½ per cent. Eighty-five per cent of the state's 130 savings banks are expected to put the increase in effect at an early date.

Last night the Dime Savings Bank of Brooklyn became the first in this area to announce it would pay 2½ per cent for the current quarter ending March 31.

Trustees of the Roosevelt Savings Bank announced they would meet today to increase the rate from 2 to 2½ per cent on account balances and deposits for the three-month period starting Jan. 1.

Other savings banks and competitive commercial banks, where possible, are likely to take similiar action soon.

Responding to the higher level of prevailing rates, and especially to Federal taxes imposed at the beginning of this year, several savings banks asked permission some weeks ago to pay larger dividends. Under the new tax law, savings institutions are made liable for income taxes at the regular corporate rate on all earnings after surplus and reserves total 12 per cent of deposits.

Regulation Is "Permissive"

William A. Lyon, Superintendent of Banks, in announcing the board's action yesterday said the new 2½ per cent rate was "permissive."

"Banks are permitted under the regulation to pay any rate up to that maximum which directors and trustees believe to be advisable in the light of the earning power and the capital or surplus position of their institutions," he explained.

Two other important amendments also were made in General Regulation No. 3, the dividend and interest rate regulation, Mr. Lyon said. In the first of these, relating to commercial banks' special interest and thrift deposits, the board approved a limit on interest payments at the maximum rate of 2½ per cent on the first $10,000 of any account and setting a ceiling rate of 1½ per cent on that portion of any special and thrift account in excess of $10,000.

The largest individual account that may be accepted by savings banks is $10,000, the maximum

Continued on Page 55, Column 6

Truman 'Shows Off' New White House

By W. H. LAWRENCE
Special to THE NEW YORK TIMES.

WASHINGTON, Feb. 6—Ducking nimbly around and under scaffolding, President Truman today took a few correspondents on a conducted tour of the White House, which is being reconstructed. He said it was still his hope that the First Family would be able to move into it early in April after three and one-half years in Blair House.

Mixing history and comment about the tribulations of a tenant who decides to get a house done over, Mr. Truman led the reporters through the building for forty minutes, answering questions and volunteering observations about nearly every room.

The hum of power saws as workmen went ahead with their jobs sometimes drowned his

Continued on Page 23, Column 1

1-Way Traffic Signs Due Soon in Times Sq.

By JOSEPH C. INGRAHAM

Conversion of Seventh and Eighth Avenues to one-way operation has been decided upon by Acting Traffic Commissioner T. T. Wiley despite objections of the New York City Omnibus Corporation.

Preparations for the new traffic pattern were well under way yesterday, with new guideposts rising in Times Square and the fittings all set to hold the one-way arrows. Work on the other sections of the one-way routes, which extend from Columbus Circle to below Canal Street, also was progressing. Seventh Avenue-Varick Street will handle southbound flow and Hudson Street-Abingdon Square-Eighth

Continued on Page 17, Column 5

CHARGES OF WASTE IN DEFENSE DENIED

Pentagon Aides Tell Senators of Savings—Admiral Calls Himself 'Oyster Fork Fox'

By HAROLD B. HINTON
Special to THE NEW YORK TIMES.

WASHINGTON, Feb. 6—Officials of the Department of Defense underwent a period of criticism before a Senate Appropriations subcommittee today and did not seem to like it. They were appearing in support of defense budget estimates of more than $52,000,000,000.

The principal witness was Vice Admiral Charles W. Fox, Chief of Naval Supplies, who told the Senators of the progress the Navy had made in simplifying the cataloguing of its supplies. When his presentation was interrupted by questions about allegations of waste and extravagance, the Pentagon contingent moved to the counter-offensive.

"I stand before you as Oyster Fork Fox," the admiral asserted, as the Senators and spectators laughed. "I am supposed to have bought 11,000,000 oyster forks for the Navy, and I had nothing more to do with it than you did."

He said that the Navy last

Continued on Page 4, Column 3

RED TRAPS FEARED IN FOE'S PROPOSAL FOR KOREA PARLEY

Communist Demand for Airing of Status of Formosa Viewed as Bar to U. N. Accord

TRUMAN CITED AS A GUIDE

Nam Il Argues Stand Taken by President on Blockading China Widens Issues

Text of Gen. Nam Il's statement is printed on Page 2.

By LINDESAY PARROTT
Special to THE NEW YORK TIMES.

TOKYO, Thursday, Feb. 7—The United Nations Command began today a detailed study of the Communist proposal for a top-level political conference three months after the armistice in the Korean war to deal with related issues in the Far East.

This morning no hint of Allied reaction had come from the advance camp at Munsan, where the United Nations representatives took the Communist program after it had been delivered to them at a plenary session of the truce delegations at Panmunjom, or at the headquarters of the United Nations Commander, Gen. Matthew B. Ridgway, in Tokyo.

The enemy proposal was made by North Korean Gen. Nam Il, head of the Chinese and North Korean delegation, who drove to the meeting place in a big American limousine with whitewall tires. He nodded coldly to the senior United Nations representative, Vice Admiral Charles Turner Joy, and then launched into his prepared introductory remarks — considerably more extensive, it turned out, than the brief formal proposal for a governmental conference for "peaceful settlement of the Korean question and other questions related to peace in Korea."

Before the session adjourned it was agreed that a new plenary sitting should be held by the delegates of both sides after the United Nations study had been com-

Continued on Page 2, Column 6

World News Summarized

THURSDAY, FEBRUARY 7, 1952

King George VI died in his sleep at Sandringham Palace yesterday morning; his daughter was proclaimed Queen Elizabeth II. The King, who seemingly had recovered from an operation for the removal of a growth on his lung, had felt so well he had been out shooting the day before. [1:8.] The British people were stunned by their sudden loss. [1:7.]

King George became the British ruler in 1936 when his brother, King Edward VIII and later Duke of Windsor, abdicated. He saw little peace during his reign. Threats of war, armed conflict and the "cold war" marked his tenure. [10:1.] During the bombing of London he refused to take special precautions or leave Buckingham Palace. [13:7-8.]

The new Queen started for London by plane when she learned of her father's death. She had been touring East Africa with her consort, the Duke of Edinburgh. [1:6-7.] She is the first Queen to ascend Britain's throne since 115 years ago, when Queen Victoria was crowned. [1:5-6.] The Duke of Windsor sails from New York tonight, alone, to attend his brother's funeral. [14:8.]

President Truman, Secretary Acheson and others expressed the sorrow of the United States [1:5] as did former President Hoover, Mayor Impellitteri and others in this city. [14:5.] United Nations flags were flown at half-staff. [15:1.]

The Soviet Union, for the fifth time, vetoed Italy's membership in the United Nations. [1:4.] The Russians did not join forty-seven other countries in pledging funds for expanded technical assistance this year. [3:4.]

Allied officers studied the Communist proposal for a political conference three months after a Korean armistice. [1:3.]

West German leaders were unmoved by American and British pleas to cool their anger over French moves in the Saar and not to endanger plans for West Europe's defense. [6:3.]

A masked witness told a House committee he had seen Russians kill hundreds of Polish officers in Katyn Forest in 1939. [4:3.]

Defense Department heads, testifying on the military budget before a Senate group, vigorously defended their spending. [1:2.] Mobilization heads also were under attack for plans to spread defense contracts to unemployment areas. [39:4.]

The slow-down in the military aircraft production rate will have little immediate effect on consumer goods but will avoid more stringent curbs later, a survey showed. [3:1.]

Governor Byrnes of South Carolina blamed "Negro politicians of the North" for the Democratic party's shift from a State's Rights program. [21:1.]

This state authorized banks to pay up to 2½ per cent on savings and thrift accounts. [1:1.]

Columbia University will increase tuition fees up to 25 per cent next fall and adjust faculty salaries upward. [29:1.]

Index to other news appears on last page of this section.

THE NEW QUEEN AND THE LATE KING

ELIZABETH II — GEORGE VI — Associated Press

SOVIET AGAIN BALKS ITALY'S U. N. ENTRY

Russia for Fifth Time Vetoes Application—Is Beaten on En Bloc Admission Bid

By THOMAS J. HAMILTON
Special to THE NEW YORK TIMES.

PARIS, Feb. 6—Italy's application for membership in the United Nation's was vetoed by the Soviet Union tonight for the fifth time. Ten of the eleven members of the Security Council voted for a French resolution recommending the admission of Italy.

Jacob A. Malik, the Soviet representative, based his action on the refusal of the United States and other Western powers to accept a Soviet proposal for en bloc admission of fourteen applicants, including five Communist governments.

The Soviet resolution afterward was rejected by a vote of six to two. The United States, Brazil, Nationalist China, Greece, the Netherlands and Turkey voted against the resolution, while Pakistan joined the Soviet Union in supporting it. Britain, France and Chile abstained.

Mr. Malik accused the United States of blocking Italy's admission. He declared that "the Italian people will note that it is the United States, with the help of the United Kingdom" that had "provoked" the Soviet veto. He added that if the Western powers had wanted to get Italy admitted, they would have agreed to the Soviet proposal.

Gross Protests "Horsetrade"

Ernest A. Gross, the United States delegate, retorted that on the contrary the Italian people would hardly be grateful for being made a part of the proposed "horsetrade." He asked whether Mr. Malik really believed that Italy should be "put in the same basket" with such "a shadow state" as Outer Mongolia, one of the Communist candidates included in the Soviet resolution.

Mr. Gross also expressed regret that the new state of Libya, which came into existence on Christmas Day, 1951, had been included in the Soviet en bloc proposal—which presumably meant that it likewise would encounter a Soviet veto unless the Western powers agree to the Soviet mass entry proposal.

Mr. Malik replied that Outer Mongolia deserved to be admitted. He said that its participation in the war against Japan "along with that of the Soviet Union" saved 1,000,000 American lives. He said he based his statement on statements by the United States high command.

Reconsideration today of Italy's long-standing application was the result of a General Assembly resolution last fall requesting the Security Council to reconsider it in the light of Italy's responsibilities

Continued on Page 3, Column 5

Ruler Becomes Elizabeth II; Her Son, 3, Is Crown Prince

By CLIFTON DANIEL
Special to THE NEW YORK TIMES.

LONDON, Feb. 6—Britain entered a new Elizabethan era today. Upon the death of King George VI, Princess Elizabeth Alexandra Mary, his elder daughter, automatically became Queen of the United Kingdom and the Dominions Overseas at the age of 25.

Tonight at the first meeting of her Privy Council she was formally styled Queen Elizabeth II.

[Text of the Privy Council's proclamation is on Page 14.]

Thus, for the first time in 115 years, a woman ascended the world's most exalted and stable throne. At the Gloucester Assizes, as in other law courts of the land, the judges marshal closed the court with words not heard since the end of Queen Victoria's sixty-three-year reign in 1901: "God save the Queen and my lords the Queen's justices."

For the first time in British history the sovereign was abroad in the Empire at the moment of accession.

Already bearing the full responsibility of the crown, the new Queen will return here by air from Kenya in Africa tomorrow accompanied by her consort, the Duke of Edinburgh.

They were to have boarded the liner Gothic at Mombasa tomorrow to sail for Ceylon, Australia and New Zealand on a five-month ceremonial tour deputizing for the late King, whose illness prevented him from going.

With the accession of the Queen, her son Prince Charles, three years and two months old, became the Crown Prince and heir to the

Continued on Page 14, Column 3

TRUMAN EXPRESSES SORROW OF NATION

Voices Sympathy for British Over Loss of King—Acheson and Others Pay Tribute

Special to THE NEW YORK TIMES.

WASHINGTON, Feb. 6—President Truman and the nation paid tribute to King George VI today in extending this country's sympathy to the British people on his death.

"He played his part nobly and with full understanding of the responsibility which was his," the President said in a formal statement.

All official Washington responded in kind following the surprise and shock at the news of the monarch's passing early this morning. Highest officials in the Government and leaders of both House of Congress joined in expressions of sympathy and praise for the man who had been a steadfast friend of the United States, and, indeed, had been the first British King to visit the country.

Secretary of State Dean Acheson commented on the courage with which King George had borne his physical suffering and noted: "It is a characteristic English spirit and the King possessed it in abundance."

Envoy Calls on Acheson

Sir Oliver Franks, British Ambassador, accompanied by seven representatives of the British Commonwealth, called on Secretary Acheson shortly after noon to inform him formally of the King's death.

"A world personage who maintained the highest tradition of the English constitutional monarchy passes in the death of His Majesty King George VI," President Truman said in his statement.

"From his accession to the throne through all the ills which beset the world throughout the years of his reign—including the most disastrous war in history—he played his part nobly and with full responsibility which was his. His heroic endurance of pain and suffering during these past few years is a true reflection of the bravery of the British people in adversity.

"The King was ever conscious of his obligations as sovereign of a nation which through centuries has been the champion of personal liberty and those free institu-

Continued on Page 14, Column 5

LONDON IS STILLED AS BRITONS MOURN

All Amusements Closed, Lights Dimmed, Streets Nearly Empty After News Stuns People

By FARNSWORTH FOWLE
Special to THE NEW YORK TIMES.

LONDON, Feb. 6—This was a silent city tonight, with bright lights dimmed and all places of entertainment closed, as Londoners went home shocked by the death of their King.

The news reached most office workers at noon when they went out for lunch and found venders of early editions of afternoon papers shouting "The King is dead!"

"What King?" was a typical first reaction. It was hard to believe that it was indeed their own monarch, even though it had been generally realized since the King's operation last September that he might not have many years to live. Only a week ago tonight he attended a performance of "South Pacific" at the Drury Lane Theatre.

The suddenness of the news contrasted with the memory of how the public had been prepared during the final illness of the King's father, George V, with a broadcast communiqué saying, "The King's life is moving peacefully to its close."

Flags at half-staff appeared on public buildings and many private ones by noon. Theatres, cinemas and night clubs all shut down, as did the Stock Exchange and other markets.

The laughter of London's usually cheerful office girls was muted as

Continued on Page 13, Column 6

Elizabeth Weeps at News of Death, But Is Calm in African Take-Off

By The United Press.

NAIROBI, Kenya, Feb. 6—Young Queen Elizabeth II left hurriedly for home by plane tonight only a few hours after her husband had broken the news to her of her father's death.

The 25-year-old former Princess, after having broken down in tears, was composed when she departed early tonight on the long flight to London.

With Prince Philip she left the hunting lodge where the royal couple had been staying and drove in a closed automobile eight miles to a small airport near the East African town of Nunyuki. She took off in an East African Airways C-47 for Entebbe in Uganda, where the British Overseas Airways craft that had flown her to Africa waited to take her back to Britain.

The royal couple landed at Entebbe airport at 9:10 P. M. (1:10 P. M., Eastern standard time), but news of her arrival was kept from the local populace to spare the new Queen a further ordeal.

A tropical thunderstorm at Entebbe delayed the departure of the Queen's plane for more than two hours, but it finally took off at 11:47 P. M. for Libya as the weather cleared.

[The plane made a stop at the Royal Air Force base at El Adem, Libya, landing there at 1:15 A. M., Thursday, Eastern standard time, The United Press reported.]

At El Adem and Malta the Royal Air Force had planes standing by to escort the Queen's plane over the Mediterranean. It is scheduled to reach London at 4:30 P. M. Thursday, Greenwich time (11:30 A. M., E. S. T.)

Crowds of silent, sorrowful persons of all races lined the main street of Nunyuki as the Queen's party passed through. The Queen, her face showing the strain of the

Continued on Page 13, Column 8

15-YEAR REIGN ENDS

British Monarch's Death at 56 Follows a Lung Operation Last Fall

PARLIAMENT HALTED

Churchill Conveys News to Commons—Attlee Suspends Party Strife

By RAYMOND DANIELL
Special to THE NEW YORK TIMES.

LONDON, Feb. 6—In the early hours of this morning George VI died peacefully in his sleep at the royal estate at Sandringham. As night fell upon this mourning capital of a still great family of nations, his elder daughter was proclaimed Queen of this realm and its dependencies, head of the British Commonwealth and the Defender of the Faith, with the title of Elizabeth II.

She is flying home tonight from her tragically interrupted visit to East Africa with her consort, the Duke of Edinburgh, and is expected back tomorrow to assume her royal duties as the wearer of the crown that somewhat mystically binds the British Commonwealth together.

Like the Elizabeth of England's golden age, she takes the throne at the age of 25.

Operated On 4 Months Ago

The King's death occurred just a little more than four months after an operation for the removal of a growth in his right lung. This operation resulted in the loss of the lung. His recovery seemed assured and in recent days he had been seen publicly at the theatre and at London Airport when he bade good-by to his daughter, now the Queen, as she set out with Prince Philip, her husband, on a journey that was to take her to East Africa, Australia and New Zealand. Only yesterday he was out shooting, his favorite sport.

It was assumed that the King had died as a result of a heart attack, probably caused by coronary thrombosis.

Tributes to the late monarch poured into London from leading world figures and from persons of humbler station.

His death came in his 57th year. It was the beginning of the sixteenth year of an unhappy reign. He never wanted or expected the throne of Britain, but he ascended to it when his brother Edward VIII abdicated to marry "the woman I love," Wallis Simpson.

Six years of his reign were war years when he and Elizabeth, his Queen, who now becomes Queen Mother, endeared themselves to their people by their bravery and devotion to their predestined role.

When he was crowned King on May 12, 1937, he was King Emperor but the title of Emperor went with the granting of independence to India. His reign marked the end of an era of British power.

Parliament Is Suspended

His death also brought to an end this session of Parliament in the midst of a bitter and acrimonious debate on how far this country should go in aligning itself with United States policy in the Far East lest it be dragged into war. That debate, which began yesterday, was left in mid-air as Parliament put aside its controversies to swear allegiance to the new Queen and deferred its partisan arguments on controversial issues until a more seemly time.

At Sandringham when the King died there were his two grandchildren, whom he adored, Prince Charles and Princess Anne; Sir Alan Lascelles, his private secretary; Sir Harold Campbell, his Equerry, and Lady Hyde, Lady-in-Waiting to his Queen. Soon after his death had been discovered by a servant bringing early morning tea, Dr. James Ansell, "Surgeon Apothecary" to the royal household at Sandringham, was called. He said that the King had died in his sleep without pain.

The news of the King's death went out over the news tickers at 10:45 A. M. At 11:15 it was broad-

Continued on Page 13, Column 3

"All the News That's Fit to Print"

The New York Times.

ELECTION EXTRA
Fair, warmer today. Some cloudiness and turning cooler tomorrow.
Temperature Range Today—Max., 62; Min., 38
Temperatures Yesterday—Max., 52; Min., 39
Full U. S. Weather Bureau Report, Page 53

VOL. CII No. 34,619. Entered as Second-Class Matter. Post Office, New York, N. Y. NEW YORK, WEDNESDAY, NOVEMBER 5, 1952. Times Square, New York 36, N. Y. Telephone LAckawanna 4-1000 RAG PAPER EDITION SEVENTY-FIVE CENTS

EISENHOWER WINS IN A LANDSLIDE; TAKES NEW YORK; IVES ELECTED; REPUBLICANS GAIN IN CONGRESS

G.O.P. HOUSE LIKELY

But the Senate Margin Hangs in the Balance of Two Close Races

LODGE TRAILING RIVAL

President Eisenhower May Lack a Working Majority in Congress

By JAMES RESTON

It appeared at 4:30 this morning that control of the United States Senate could be determined by the outcome of the Senatorial races in Michigan and Massachusetts.

At that time the Republicans appeared to have picked up five new seats and lost three others, thus enabling them to wipe out the two-seat advantage held by the Democrats at the end of the Eighty-second Congress.

To assure the power to organize the Senate and place their Republicans at the head of its important committees, however, Senator Henry Cabot Lodge Jr., Republican of Massachusetts, would have to overcome an advantage of more than 75,000 held by Representative John F. Kennedy, his opponent.

And Representative Charles E. Potter, Republican of Michigan had to retain the 47,000 lead he held over the Democratic incumbent, Senator Blair Moody of Michigan.

Morse May Be Vital

So close was the Senate race that there was a possibility that control of the upper chamber could be determined by the decision of Senator Wayne Morse of Oregon, who was elected as a Republican, but who broke with his party during the campaign, and announced that hereafter he was an "independent."

Though it appeared that the Republicans had won control of the House, one thing was certain: that President Dwight D. Eisenhower would not have a comfortable working majority in either house and would require all his gifts of persuasion to win consent for his policies on Capitol Hill.

Several factors in the Senate race were noteworthy:

¶Of the ten so-called isolationist or extremist Republicans who went before the voters yesterday, seven seemed fairly sure of victory. These were Senators Joseph R. McCarthy of Wisconsin; John W. Bricker of Ohio; William E. Jenner of Indiana; Edward Martin of Pennsylvania; Arthur V. Watkins of Utah, George W. Malone of Nevada and Hugh Butler of Nebraska.

Three other Republicans in this same category, however, were in serious trouble if they had not actually been defeated. They were:

Continued on Page 15, Column 1

M'Carthy Is Winner, But Is Last on Ticket

By RICHARD J. H. JOHNSTON
Special to THE NEW YORK TIMES.

MILWAUKEE, Wednesday, Nov. 5—Wisconsin went to the Republicans today for the third time in a national election since 1920.

The predicted Republican sweep of the state and capture of its twelve electoral votes became a certainty a few minutes after midnight.

Gen. Dwight D. Eisenhower, the Republican Presidential nominee ran second on the G. O. P. ticket with Gov. Walter J. Kohler Jr. leading the state in his bid for re-election.

As the returns neared the final count, Gen. Dwight D. Eisenhower's vote indicated he would emerge as leader of the G. O. P. slate in Wisconsin. With 2,036 of the state's 3,224 voting precincts reported, his vote was 554,369 to Gov. Adlai E. Stevenson's 356,218.

Gov. Walter J. Kohler, seeking

Continued on Page 22, Column 6

Electoral Vote by States

	Eisenhower	Stevenson		Eisenhower	Stevenson
Ala.	—	11	Neb.	6	—
Ariz.	4	—	Nev.	3	—
Ark.	—	8	N. H.	4	—
Calif.	32	—	N. J.	16	—
Colo.	6	—	N. M.	4	—
Conn.	8	—	N. Y.	45	—
Del.	3	—	N. C.	—	14
Fla.	10	—	N. D.	4	—
Ga.	—	12	Ohio	25	—
Idaho	4	—	Okla.	8	—
Ill.	27	—	Ore.	6	—
Ind.	13	—	Pa.	32	—
Iowa	10	—	R. Isl.	4	—
Kan.	8	—	S. C.	—	8
*Ky.	—	10	S. D.	4	—
*La.	—	10	*Tenn.	11	—
Me.	5	—	Texas	24	—
Md.	9	—	Utah	4	—
Mass.	16	—	Vt.	3	—
Mich.	20	—	Va.	12	—
Minn.	11	—	Wash.	9	—
Miss.	—	8	W. Va.	—	8
Mo.	13	—	Wisc.	12	—
Mont.	4	—	Wyo.	3	—
			Total	442	89

*Trend.

EISENHOWER TAKES JERSEY BY 300,000

Senator Smith Is Re-elected—Bond Issues Supported in Record Balloting

By RUSSELL PORTER

With more than three-quarters of New Jersey's vote counted early this morning, Gen. Dwight D. Eisenhower appeared headed toward a plurality of close to 300,000 in the state over Gov. Adlai E. Stevenson. This far exceeded Governor Dewey's 1948 plurality of 85,669 over President Truman.

United States Senator H. Alexander Smith, Republican candidate for re-election, won a sweeping victory over his Democratic opponent, Archibald S. Alexander, though Mr. Smith ran behind the head of his ticket. His indicated plurality was about 200,000.

The returns were:

PRESIDENT

3,461 precincts out of 3,840:

Eisenhower	1,203,120
Stevenson	921,375

UNITED STATES SENATOR

3,399 precincts out of 3,840:

Smith	1,089,883
Alexander	903,533

The Republicans appeared to have retained their majority of nine to five in New Jersey's delegation in the House of Representatives.

Both bond issues on the ballot

Continued on Page 23, Column 2

STATE LEAD 850,000

General's Upstate Edge Tops Million—He Loses City by Only 362,674

PROTEST VOTE SEEN

Albany County, Other Areas in Democratic Column Switch

State Presidential Vote

CITY SUMMARY

	Eisenhower (Rep.)	Stevenson (Dem.-Lib.)
Manhattan	300,234	447,877
Bronx	241,545	393,052
Brooklyn	447,148	656,278
Queens	449,505	331,633
Richmond	55,981	28,247
Total	1,494,413	1,837,087
Upstate	2,413,299	1,147,510
Grand total	3,907,712	3,104,597

4,394 election districts out of 4,394 in the city reporting and 5,222 out of 5,954 upstate.

By JAMES A. HAGERTY

Gen. Dwight D. Eisenhower, Republican nominee for President, carried New York State with its forty-five electoral votes with a plurality of landslide proportions that will reach nearly 850,000.

With 33 election districts missing, all outside this city, General Eisenhower led Gov. Adlai E. Stevenson, his Democratic opponent, by an actual plurality of 846,020 and an indicated plurality of 840,034.

To carry his adopted state by this astounding plurality, General Eisenhower held Governor Stevenson down to an actual plurality of 362,674 in this city, far less than the supporters of the Democratic candidate expected.

With the 33 election districts missing, General Eisenhower carried the state outside the city by an actual plurality of 1,265,789 and, assuming that his vote held up in the missing districts, by an indicated plurality of about 1,270,000.

Governor Stevenson carried Manhattan by 147,633, the Bronx by 151,597 and Brooklyn by 209,130, all far below Democratic expectations. General Eisenhower carried Queens by 117,872 and Richmond by 27,834, well above

Continued on Page 24, Column 3

Hill Battle Spurts in Korea; Allies Press 'Triangle' Fight

By LINDESAY PARROTT
Special to THE NEW YORK TIMES.

TOKYO, Wednesday, Nov. 5—The hard-fighting South Korean infantry, driving for the third time in three days up the slopes of the central Korean ridges, drove a penetration today into the Communist lines on the western flank of "Triangle Hill," a strategic position north of Kumhwa.

Early this afternoon, the Republic of Korea (R. O. K.) troops had captured one of the twin peaks that project from "Triangle"—named "Jane Russell Hill." The sharp, indecisive combat continued.

The attack on the twin peaks was tied in with a new drive against the central pyramid of "Triangle Hill." The South Koreans again thrust within yards of the crest.

The Chinese Reds struck again just to the east in a new attempt to capture the summit of "Sniper Ridge," flanking "Triangle" on the United Nations' right.

The crest of "Triangle" had been lost to the Chinese Communists after the United Nations limited objective offensive took it last month. The South Koreans pushed up southern slopes today to within fifty yards of the Reds' lines.

Some reports said the fighting again today was as furious as during the attacks Sunday and Monday, when the South Koreans desperately struggled to regain the positions.

Allied warplanes were out against the enemy guns. About fifty sorties had been flown by Fifth Air Force fighter-bombers before noon against Red artillery on high Papasan Mountain, the Communists' strongpoint just to the north of the central front.

At every opportunity, Allied guns pounded the Reds on the crest of "Triangle."

The Reds' guns dropped 5,000 rounds on the United Nations positions near "Heartbreak Ridge" and the "Punchbowl" in the mountainous eastern watershed, where the heaviest fighting of yesterday occurred. A North Korean battalion hit Allied defense positions on "Heartbreak" on the heels of the barrage, but the enemy failed to make a penetration.

On "Triangle Hill" and the twin peaks to the west of it, contact was light yesterday. At least temporarily, the South Koreans broke off attempts to storm two positions they had lost to the Chinese Reds' counter-attacks, after the United Nations limited objec-

Continued on Page 2, Column 2

New President and Vice President

DWIGHT D. EISENHOWER

RICHARD M. NIXON

The New York Times

IVES IS RE-ELECTED BY RECORD MARGIN

Defeats Cashmore by Biggest Plurality of Any Republican—Harding Mark Topped

Vote for Senator

CITY SUMMARY

	Ives (Rep.)	Cashmore (Dem.)	Counts (Lib.)
Manh'n	303,040	322,157	88,797
Bronx	233,548	277,506	101,014
B'klyn	398,498	522,751	147,370
Queens	429,225	265,812	62,558
Rich'd	51,939	28,742	2,044
Total	1,416,250	1,416,968	401,783
Up-state	2,399,770	1,099,842	52,259
Gr Totl	3,816,020	2,516,810	454,042

4,394 election districts out of 4,394 in the city reporting and 5,854 out of 5,954 up-state.

By LEO EGAN

Senator Irving M. Ives won re-election in a three-cornered race yesterday, by the largest plurality ever obtained by a Republican candidate in New York State, topping President Warren G. Harding's record-setting margin of 1,089,929 in 1920 by more than 200,000 votes.

The former majority leader of the State Assembly and co-sponsor of New York's law against racial discrimination in employment thus became the first Republican Senator to win re-election in New York since the late James W. Wadsworth performed that feat in the Harding landslide of 1920.

Not only did Senator Ives carry the normally Republican upstate area by a plurality that may reach 1,297,972, but he came within 718 votes of capturing normally Democratic New York City as well.

The complete Senate vote in the city gave Senator Ives 1,416,250 to 1,416,968 for Borough President John Cashmore of Brooklyn, the Democratic candidate. Thus Mr. Cashmore's plurality within the city was held to 718 votes.

With 5,854 of the 5,954 districts outside the city totaled, Senator Ives had an actual plurality of 1,299,928. On this basis his final up-state margin should reach 1,300,000.

Dr. George S. Counts, the Liberal party candidate, polled 454,042 votes in the same districts tabulated for Senator Ives and Mr. Cashmore. On this basis his final vote could reach 460,000. Corliss Lamont, the American Labor can-

Continued on Page 21, Column 2

NEW YORK TIMES news bulletins are broadcast over WQXR every hour.

Eisenhower Cracks South, Heads for Victory in Texas

By WILLIAM S. WHITE

Gen. Dwight D. Eisenhower, the Republican Presidential candidate, has smashed the traditionally Democratic Solid South in his national victory over Gov. Adlai E. Stevenson. He has carried outright Florida and Virginia, with their twenty-two electoral votes. This morning unofficial observers gave him the greatest Southern prize of all—Texas and its twenty-four electoral votes, the sixth biggest bloc in the United States.

Confirmation of this indicated loss would involve a Democratic disaster.

Apart from all this and from receiving the greatest popular ballot ever given a Republican in the South, General Eisenhower was first narrowly leading and then narrowly trailing this morning in Tennessee, which has eleven electoral votes. In Tennessee, the position was so close that the result probably will not be known until late this afternoon.

In Louisiana and South Carolina Governor Stevenson had slight leads after trailing often in the early returns.

Only the hardest of the hard core of the Old South has remained wholly faithful to the old Democratic tradition.

Mississippi, Arkansas, North

Continued on Page 22, Column 3

CONNECTICUT G. O. P. SEATS 2 IN SENATE

Benton and Ribicoff Concede to Purtell and Bush While Eisenhower Sweeps State

Special to THE NEW YORK TIMES.

HARTFORD, Conn., Wednesday, Nov. 5—Gen. Dwight D. Eisenhower swept to an amazing landslide victory in Connecticut yesterday, winning by a margin of nearly 130,000 votes over Gov. Adlai E. Stevenson in final returns from the 169 cities and towns in the state.

The victory astounded Republicans as well as Democrats. Prior to the election, Republican leaders had made cautious claims of victory by about 25,000 or 30,000 votes, while Democrats privately thought they had a chance to win the state.

The tremendous Eisenhower sweep carried two Republican United States Senators into office with him. Senator William A. Purtell of West Hartford defeated William Benton, Democrat, for the full six-year term by a margin of 90,286, and Prescott S. Bush, Greenwich banker, defeated Representative Abraham A. Ribicoff of Hartford, Democrat, by 30,373 votes. Mr. Ribicoff made a spectacular uphill run but was edged out by Mr. Bush's lead in the small towns that are traditionally Republican.

Final returns were:

PRESIDENT

169 precincts out of 169:

Eisenhower	610,989
Stevenson	481,482

UNITED STATES SENATOR

(For six-year Term)

169 precincts out of 169:

Purtell (R.)	575,445
Benton (D.)	485,159

(For Four-year Term)

Bush (R.)	559,586
Ribicoff (D)	529,213

The Eisenhower sweep enabled the Republicans to win five of the six seats from Connecticut in the House of Representatives, a gain

Continued on Page 28, Column 3

GENERAL APPEALS FOR UNITED PEOPLE

He Vows Not to Give 'Short Weight' as President—Thanks Rival for Pledge

By WILLIAM R. CONKLIN

A jubilant Gen. Dwight D. Eisenhower accepted his election as President early this morning with a pledge to the American people that he would not give "short weight" in the execution of his new responsibilities in Washington.

With his wife by his side, the Republican President-elect told 2,000 campaign supporters in the grand ballroom of the Commodore Hotel at 2:05 A. M. that it would take the support of a united people to carry his Administration to success in its efforts to build a "better future for America."

His remarks were carried by radio and television to all parts of the country.

He read a message he had sent a few minutes before to his defeated rival, Gov. Adlai E. Stevenson of Illinois, thanking him for his promise of assistance. General Eisenhower expressed hope that Americans of both parties would speedily forget campaign bitter-

Continued on Page 20, Column 2

Stevenson Concedes the Victory As Weeping Backers Cry 'No, No'

By WILLIAM M. BLAIR
Special to THE NEW YORK TIMES.

SPRINGFIELD, Ill., Wednesday, Nov. 5—Gov. Adlai E. Stevenson conceded defeat early today to his Republican opponent, Gen. Dwight D. Eisenhower, and pledged the support "he will need to carry out the great tasks that lie before him."

The Governor came from the Executive Mansion to the Democratic Headquarters in the Leland Hotel to make his announcement before a jammed ballroom of supporters, many of whom broke into tears and cried, "No, no."

Governor Stevenson said:

"General Eisenhower has been a great leader in war. He has been a vigorous and valiant opponent in the campaign. These qualities will now be dedicated to leading us all through the next four years.

"It is traditionally American to fight hard before an election.

"It is equally traditional to close ranks as soon as the people have spoken. From the depths of my heart I thank all of my party, and all of those independents and Republicans who supported Senator Sparkman and me."

The Governor said he had dispatched to General Eisenhower in New York a telegram which he read. It said:

"The people have made their choice and I congratulate you. That you may be the servant and guardian of peace and make the dale of trouble a door of hope is my earnest prayer. Best Wishes.

Adlai E. Stevenson."

Governor Stevenson did have a grin, however, for the crowd and displayed his ever-present humor to reporters. Asked how about 1956, the next presidential election year, he echoed in a loud voice and with mock surprise "56! Examine that man's head."

As for his immediate plans, he

Continued on Page 16, Column 5

RACE IS CONCEDED

Virginia and Florida Go to the General as Do Illinois and Ohio

SWEEP IS NATION-WIDE

Victor Calls for Unity and Thanks Governor for Pledging Support

By ARTHUR KROCK

Gen. Dwight D. Eisenhower was elected President of the United States yesterday in an electoral vote landslide and with an emphatic popular majority that probably will give his party a small margin of control in the House of Representatives but may leave the Senate as it is—forty-nine Democrats, forty-seven Republicans and one independent.

Senator Richard M. Nixon of California was elected Vice President.

The Democratic Presidential candidate, Gov. Adlai E. Stevenson of Illinois, shortly after midnight conceded his defeat by a record turnout of American voters.

At 4 A. M. today the Republican candidate had carried states with a total of 431 electors, or 165 more than the 266 required for the selection of a President. The Democratic candidate seemed sure of 69, with 31 doubtful in Kentucky, Louisiana and Tennessee.

General Eisenhower's landslide victory, both in electoral and popular votes, was nation-wide in its pattern, extending from New England—where Massachusetts and Rhode Island broke their Democratic voting habits of many years—down the Eastern seaboard to Maryland, Virginia and Florida and westward to almost every state between the coasts, including California.

General Wins Illinois

The Republican candidate took Illinois, Governor Stevenson's home state. In South Carolina, though he lost its electors on a technicality, he won a majority of the voters. And, completing the first successful Republican invasion of the States of the former Confederacy, the General carried Texas and broke the one-party system in the South.

The personal popularity that enabled him to defeat Senator Robert A. Taft of Ohio in the Republican primaries in Texas, and present him with the issue on which he defeated the Senator for the Republican nomination, crushed the regular Democratic organization of Texas that was led by Speaker Sam Rayburn of the House of Representatives and had the blessing of former Vice President John N. Garner.

The tide that bore General Eisenhower to the White House, though it did not give him a comfortable working majority in either the national House or the Senate (the Democrats may still nominally control the machinery of that branch), probably increased the number of Republican governors beyond the present twenty-five.

"My fellow citizens have made their choice and I gladly accept it," said Governor Stevenson at 1:46 A. M., Eastern standard time, and he asked all citizens to unite behind the President-elect. The defeated candidate said he had sent a telegram of congratulation to General Eisenhower.

At 2:05 A. M., from the Grand Ballroom of the Commodore Hotel, General Eisenhower said he recognized the weight of his new responsibilities and that he would not give "short weight" in their execution. He also urged "unity" and announced he had sent a telegram of thanks to the Democratic candidate for his promise of support.

The issues of the unusually vigorous campaign that was waged

Continued on Page 14, Column 3

"All the News That's Fit to Print"

The New York Times.

LATE CITY EDITION
Fair, little temperature change today. Mostly fair tomorrow.
Temperature Range Today—Max., 43; Min., 29
Temperatures Yesterday—Max., 44; Min., 33
Full U. S. Weather Bureau Report, Page 41

VOL. CII..No. 34,740. Entered as Second-Class Matter. Post Office, New York, N. Y. NEW YORK, FRIDAY, MARCH 6, 1953. Times Square, New York 36, N. Y. Telephone LAckawanna 4-1000 FIVE CENTS

STALIN DIES AFTER 29-YEAR RULE; HIS SUCCESSOR NOT ANNOUNCED; U.S. WATCHFUL, EISENHOWER SAYS

WORST CITY CRISIS SINCE 1933 IS SEEN IN STATE TAX PLAN

Moore and McGovern Demand Payroll Levy and Transit Unit Mandated to Raise Fares

MAYOR CALLS DEMOCRATS

Estimate Board to Get Report on Views of County Leaders —Bus Reduction Directed

By PAUL CROWELL

The city Government is facing the most serious financial and political crisis to confront any Administration since 1933, when leading banking houses rescued a Democratic regime from fiscal disaster.

This was the consensus last night of top city officials to whom Lieut. Gov. Frank C. Moore and State Controller J. Raymond McGovern had indicated earlier in the day that a sound fiscal program for 1953-54 and succeeding years should include both a city payroll tax and a transit authority with a duty to increase fares to meet operating deficits of the municipal lines.

That the city Administration realized the political dangers inherent in the adoption of the suggested fiscal program was indicated later in the day when Mayor Impellitteri, without consulting the Board of Estimate, asked the five Democratic county leaders to confer with him at noon today at City Hall. Among those invited was Tammany leader Carmine G. DeSapio, the only member of the group who is at loggerheads with the Mayor on matters of patronage.

Leaders' Views Important

After a two-hour conference with Mr. Moore and Mr. McGovern at Mr. McGovern's office, 270 Broadway, the Mayor and Board of Estimate held an even longer closed meeting at City Hall, which will be resumed at 3 o'clock this afternoon. At today's session an important factor will be the attitude of the five Democratic county leaders, as reported by the Mayor, toward the proposals upon which the two state officials apparently are insisting.

In another municipal development, the Mayor's Transit Advisory Commission demanded that the eight privately owned bus companies involved in the recent bus strike and Michael J. Quill's Transport Workers Union, C. I. O., take immediate steps to wipe out excess bus lines and to reduce the number of buses on lines that were needed. City tax relief was made dependent on such action.

The conference with Mr. Moore and Mr. McGovern was a continuation of last Monday's talks at Albany on the city's $218,700,000 fiscal program, which in effect already had been rejected by the two state officials in their joint memorandum of Feb. 22.

At the outset of the meeting the

Continued on Page 19, Column 1

Eisenhower Plans to Pare Policy-Level Civil Service

Directive Will Repeal 2 That Truman Issued Anchoring Some Democrats in Their Jobs —Organization of Administration Object

By PAUL P. KENNEDY
Special to The New York Times.

WASHINGTON, March 5—Several hundred persons face the possibility of losing Civil Service status and probably their Government jobs under an Executive Order to be issued by President Eisenhower next week.

In announcing the forthcoming order, James C. Hagerty, White House press secretary, said that all those affected would not necessarily lose their jobs. The announcement was generally interpreted, however, to mean that the Administration was preparing to clear out holdover Democrats in high policy-making and administrative positions in order to replace them with personnel of the Administration's own choosing.

President Eisenhower's order, which he directed to be drafted immediately, will repeal two Executive Orders of former President Truman in 1947 and 1948 in which certain persons on Schedule A of Civil Service rules would receive Civil Service protection against separation from the Government.

The President's order will emphasize that the rights of veterans, specified in the Veterans Preference Act of 1944 would be respected.

Schedule A is a list of positions to which appointments may be made without reference to Civil Service rules or regulations. The appointees may assume their positions without Civil Service examinations and their classifications are not subject to review by Civil Service Boards.

Mr. Hagerty said the "several hundred" persons to be affected by the order were employed in all departments and agencies of the Government. The order, he said, applied to people who had been put under Civil Service in the last twenty years.

The new Administration, since coming into office Jan. 20, Mr.

Continued on Page 15, Column 2

President May Take a Hand If Inquiries Imperil Amity

By C. P. TRUSSELL
Special to The New York Times.

WASHINGTON, March 5—President Eisenhower indicated today that if the Senate investigation into the Voice of America, being conducted by Senator Joseph R. McCarthy, or other Congressional inquiries, reached a point of inviting international misunderstandings and difficulties he might intervene.

This, he emphasized at a news conference, would mean that he would have to desert his long-held conviction that the Congress had an inherent right to investigate as it pleased. He was still hoping, he said, to avoid a situation in which a spokesman for the Executive Branch of the Government would have to take issue with actions of the coordinate Legislative Branch.

The question that prompted these responses was based upon the hearings being conducted, largely before television, by the Judiciary subcommittee headed by Senator McCarthy, Republican of Wisconsin.

The group is inquiring into the management and personnel of the Voice, the Government's radio program for telling the story of America. Broadcasts are beamed to eighty-seven countries in nearly forty languages.

At yesterday's hearing Reed Harris, deputy director of the State

Continued on Page 14, Column 6

EISENHOWER PRAISES RESTRAINT IN PRICES

Asserts There Has Been Little Evidence of Gouging—More Controls Are Removed

By CHARLES E. EGAN
Special to The New York Times.

WASHINGTON, March 5—President Eisenhower today complimented business for what he termed the admirable restraint it had shown in pricing policies since the removal of most price controls.

General Eisenhower said at his news conference that since the program of removing major segments of the economy from price regulation got under way Feb. 6, there had been little discernible evidence of attempts to gouge consumers.

The President's observations came immediately before an announcement from the Office of Price Stabilization that it had removed price ceilings on another wide range of items, including bread and bakery products, new and used cars, major household appliances, dry cleaning and diaper services.

Hopes for a New Climate

Another development was a Senate committee hearing at which Charles R. Sligh Jr., president of the National Association of Manufacturers, attacked proposals to establish stand-by controls authority. With such authority, the President could declare a ninety-day "freeze" of all prices and wages in event of all-out war or other critical emergency.

About the only major price increase that has occurred since the Office of Price Stabilization began implementing his orders for relaxation of price ceilings, the President said, has been an expected rise of 6 to 7 cents a pound in copper.

The absence of price gouging, the President added, confirms his belief that the American people are ready to be considerate and moderate. He added that he hoped a climate might be established—in labor-management relations, for instance—that would minimize harmful pressures on the economy

Continued on Page 15, Column 3

F.B.I. Agents Depict Rebuff by Monaghan

By LUTHER A. HUSTON
Special to The New York Times

WASHINGTON, March 5—Leland V. Boardman, special agent in charge of the New York office of the Federal Bureau of Investigation, asserted today that Police Commissioner George P. Monaghan had notified him that he would not make New York City policemen available to any Federal law enforcement agency for questioning and that they would respond only to summonses from a Federal grand jury.

This policy, Mr. Boardman said, was founded upon a purported agreement between the New York Police Department and the Criminal Division of the Department of Justice to block out F. B. I. investigators from cases involving police brutality in civil rights cases. Another agent quoted Commis-

Continued on Page 16, Column 3

VISHINSKY LEAVING

Foreign Minister Called to Moscow to Report —Will Sail Today

U. N. TO LOWER FLAG

Lie Praises Premier as Statesman—Pearson Hails Fight on Nazis

By THOMAS J. HAMILTON
Special to The New York Times.

UNITED NATIONS, N. Y., March 5—Soviet Foreign Minister Andrei Y. Vishinsky, who was reported to have been informed of the death of Premier Stalin before the public announcement by the Moscow radio, plans to leave for Moscow tomorrow.

Mr. Vishinsky and a party of Soviet officials are scheduled to sail aboard the French liner Liberté tomorrow at 4 P. M. Plans for the sailing were disclosed at Police Headquarters. The police said they had been informed that the party would travel in seven automobiles from Glen Cove, L. I., where the Soviet delegation to the United Nations has headquarters, to Pier 88, Hudson River at Forty-eighth Street. The liner will call at Plymouth and Le Havre.

Mr. Vishinsky has a heart condition and therefore avoids air travel whenever possible.

Valerian A. Zorin, Soviet representative to the United Nations, revealed this afternoon Mr. Vishinsky's plans to leave tomorrow. Mr. Vishinsky's decision was taken after he had received a telephone call from Moscow earlier in the day.

Disclosure by Consulate

There was no indication whether this telephone call had given any indication of Mr. Stalin's death. The news that Mr. Vishinsky had been informed prior to the public announcement came from a telephone inquiry at the Soviet Consulate at 680 Park Avenue.

Earlier inquiries at the headquarters of the Soviet delegation to the United Nations had brought repeated denials that Mr. Vishinsky was there. The consulate revealed, however, not only that Mr. Vishinsky was actually at the delegation headquarters but also that he had been informed of the news earlier.

According to United Nations protocol, the only flag that will fly at the United Nations flagpole tomorrow is the banner of the United Nations itself, and it will be at half-staff. The same procedure will be followed during the day of the funeral of Premier Stalin.

Informed of the death of Mr.

Continued on Page 13, Column 2

CONDOLENCES SENT

President Orders Terse Formal Note on Stalin Dispatched to Soviet

TRIBUTE IS OMITTED

Eisenhower Still Ready to Confer on Peace With the Kremlin

By JAMES RESTON
Special to The New York Times.

WASHINGTON, March 5—President Eisenhower authorized John Foster Dulles, Secretary of State, tonight to send the United States' "official condolences" to the Soviet Government on the death of Premier Stalin.

Earlier the President had told reporters at his press conference that he could not tell what effect the illness of the Premier would have on the "cold war." A definite watchfulness is our policy for the moment, the President added.

The President announced the statement of condolences less than an hour after he had been informed of Mr. Stalin's death by James C. Hagerty, press secretary, at 6:25 P. M. The statement was as follows:

> The President authorized the Secretary of State to send the following message to the American Embassy in Moscow: The Government of the United States tenders its official condolences to the Government of the Union of Socialist Soviet Republics on the death of Generalissimo Joseph Stalin, Prime Minister of the Soviet Union.

Dulles Informed by Hagerty

Mr. Hagerty notified Mr. Dulles, who was a guest at the British Embassy, immediately after the President had been informed.

The press secretary said the President's message would be transmitted to the Soviet Government by Jacob D. Beam, Chargé d'Affaires in Moscow.

The terse wording of the message was noted here, especially the phrase "official condolences." Diplomatic circles suggested that the wording was about as brief and formal as possible under diplomatic protocol.

They recalled, however, that the President previously had expressed condolences. In the first White House statement issued after word had been received of the serious illness of Mr. Stalin, General Eisenhower directed his words to the Soviet people rather than the Premier or the Government.

Indications were that the President's official condolences would stand in so far as the Government

Continued on Page 12, Column 5

PREMIER JOSEPH STALIN
A portrait released by Sovfoto, Soviet picture agency

Soviet Fear of an Eruption Discerned in Call for Unity

By HARRY SCHWARTZ

The fact that appeals for "monolithic unity" and "vigilance" have now become the main theme of Soviet domestic propaganda appears to be a clear indication that the present Soviet rulers fear Premier Stalin's death may result in an explosive resolution of the major tensions now repressed in the Soviet Union.

The unity theme dominates the official announcement of Stalin's death. It was first voiced in the initial communiqué regarding Stalin's illness issued by the highest Government and Communist party authorities. Unity and vigilance were the central ideas in the long leading editorials that appeared yesterday morning on the front pages of both Pravda and Izvestia.

Yesterday's Pravda editorial may also have given the first hint that Georgi M. Malenkov is leading in the succession race, but this hint seemed far from conclusive. The editorial mentioned by name only Lenin, Premier Stalin, and Mr. Malenkov, quoting the latter's speech last October when he said, "The prospects and ways of our progress are based on the laws of the national economy, on the science of the Communist social structure which have been evolved by Comrade Stalin."

The fact that Moscow has announced that Nikita S. Khrushchev will head the committee preparing

Continued on Page 13, Column 2

AMMUNITION SHORT, VAN FLEET ASSERTS

He Affirms Scarcity in Korea and Byrd Writes to Wilson Demanding Explanation

By HAROLD B. HINTON
Special to The New York Times.

WASHINGTON, March 5—Gen. James A. Van Fleet, former Commander of United Nations ground forces in Korea, told the Senate Armed Services Committee today that he had been handicapped during the entire twenty-two months he had had the command by shortages of ammunition and manpower. He specified hand grenades, and mentioned "other types" of ammunition as having been seriously short all the time and critically short on occasions.

The apparent contradiction of the General's testimony today with that of yesterday, in which he indicated there were no serious shortages of anything in Korea, was unexplained, except for the interpretation that yesterday he had been speaking for the present, whereas today he had been speaking for the past.

Praised by Symington

So much the general said before a public meeting of the committee. Senator Stuart Symington, Democrat of Missouri and former Secretary of the Air Force, praised General Van Fleet for his intelligence and courage in reporting these matters to the public. If other military figures would emulate the example, he declared, "we won't send our youth out to fight with these shortages, even if we have fewer television sets."

[In the Korean war action, Air Force Thunderjet fighter-bombers made a record 1,000-mile raid on a Communist industrial center on the northeast coast sixty miles from Siberia. Navy carrier bombers made heavy attacks in North Korea. Ground action was light.]

In a later closed session with the committee, General Van Fleet apparently amplified his discussion of the shortages. The amplification prompted Senator Harry F. Byrd, Democrat of Virginia, to write a letter to Charles E. Wilson

Continued on Page 5, Column 3

PREMIER ILL 4 DAYS

Announcement of Death Made by Top Soviet and Party Chiefs

STROKE PROVES FATAL

Leaders Issue an Appeal to People for Unity and Vigilance

Text of official announcement of Stalin's death, Page 8.

By HARRISON E. SALISBURY
Special to The New York Times.

MOSCOW, Friday, March 6—Premier Joseph Stalin died at 9:50 P. M. yesterday [1:50 P. M. Thursday, Eastern standard time] in the Kremlin at the age of 73, it was announced officially this morning. He had been in power twenty-nine years.

The announcement was made in the name of the Central Committee of the Communist party, the Council of Ministers and the Presidium of the Supreme Soviet.

Calling on the Soviet people to rally firmly around the party and the Government, the announcement asked them to display unity and the highest political vigilance "in the struggle against internal and external foes." [No announcement was made of a successor to Premier Stalin.]

The Soviet leader's death from general circulatory and respiratory deficiency occurred just short of four days after he had been stricken with a brain hemorrhage in his Kremlin apartment.

Accompanying the death announcement was a final medical certificate issued by a group of ten physicians, headed by Health Minister A. F. Tretyakov, who cared for Mr. Stalin in his last illness under the direct and closest supervision of the Central Committee and the Council of Ministers.

Pulse Rate Was High

The medical certificate revealed that in the last hours Mr. Stalin's condition grew worse rapidly, with repeated heavy and sharp circulatory and heart collapses. His breathing grew superficial and sharply irregular. His pulse rate rose to 140 to 150 a minute and at 9:50 P. M., "because of a growing circulatory and respiratory insufficiency, J. V. Stalin died."

[The news of Mr. Stalin's death was withheld by Soviet officials for more than six hours.]

Pravda appeared this morning with broad black borders around its front page, which was devoted entirely to Mr. Stalin. The layout included a large photograph of the Premier, the announcement by the Government, the medical bulletins and the announcement of the formation of a funeral commission

Continued on Page 3, Column 3

Treaties Manifesto Shelved in Congress

By WILLIAM S. WHITE
Special to The New York Times.

WASHINGTON, March 5—President Eisenhower's proposed United States declaration against "perversion" of the wartime Yalta and Potsdam agreements into instruments for enslaving peoples was put on the shelf in Congress today.

The announced Congressional reason was that the manifesto would be inopportune now in view of Premier Stalin's fatal illness, though the President himself indicated at his news conference that he thought this need not delay action. The Congressional developments came before the announcement of Mr. Stalin's death.

The Republican leaders in Congress could not take the resolution to the floor of either house

Continued on Page 6, Column 4

Pole Flies to Denmark in First Intact Russian MIG-15 to Reach West

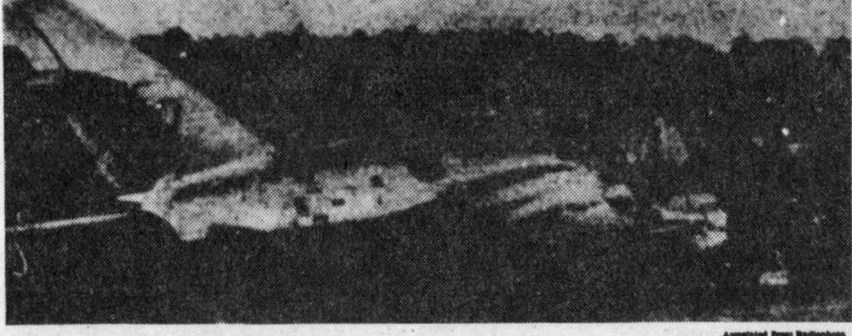

Associated Press Radiophoto

A young Polish pilot seeking political asylum flew this Soviet-made MIG-15 into a Danish airport at Bornholm yesterday, making it the first fighter plane of its type acquired undamaged by the West. Name of pilot (center figure) was withheld.

Special to The New York Times.

COPENHAGEN, Denmark, March 5—The first intact Russian-built MIG-15 jet fighter—the newest known type of Russian jet fighter—to land west of the Iron Curtain came down this morning at Roenne Airport on the Danish island of Bornholm. It came from a Polish Baltic base.

The 21-year-old Polish lieutenant who fled with the fighter gave himself up to Danish authorities as a political refugee and asked for asylum. Very little is known about his story. Danish authorities are keeping it secret for the time being.

The young Pole performed a fantastic maneuver in landing the jet fighter on the grass-covered airstrip at Roenne, only 1,200 meters (3,937 feet) long. Jet fighters normally require a 3,000-meter (9,843 feet) concrete runway to start and land.

At the farther end of the air-

Continued on Page 5, Column 3

"All the News That's Fit to Print"

The New York Times.

LATE CITY EDITION

Warm, humid, showers likely late today. Fair, not so warm tomorrow.
Temperature Range Today—Max., 88; Min., 68
Temperature Yesterday—Max., 79; Min., 62
Full U. S. Weather Bureau Report, Page 35

VOL. CII..No. 34,883. Entered as Second-Class Matter. Post Office, New York, N. Y. NEW YORK, MONDAY, JULY 27, 1953. Times Square, New York 36, N. Y. Telephone Lackawanna 4-1000 FIVE CENTS

TRUCE IS SIGNED, ENDING THE FIGHTING IN KOREA; P.O.W. EXCHANGE NEAR; RHEE GETS U. S. PLEDGE; EISENHOWER BIDS FREE WORLD STAY VIGILANT

GEROSA AND STARK PICKED BY WAGNER TO COMPLETE SLATE

Bronx Contractor to Run for Controller, Brooklyn Clothier for Council President

DESAPIO PRAISES CHOICE

Tammany Head Sees Approval This Week by Party Leaders Opposed to Impellitteri

By PAUL CROWELL

Lawrence E. Gerosa, a Bronx contractor, and Abe Stark, a Brooklyn merchant, were selected as running mates yesterday by Manhattan Borough President Robert F. Wagner Jr., who was chosen last week by the Democratic organizations of Bronx and New York Counties as their candidate for Mayor.

Mr. Gerosa was named as a candidate for Controller and Mr. Stark for President of the City Council. The slate headed by Mr. Wagner will wage a primary contest against the ticket headed by Mayor Impellitteri, whose running mates are City Councilman Charles E. Keegan of the Bronx for Controller and Julius Helfand, assistant district attorney of Kings County, for Council President.

The Impellitteri-Keegan-Helfand ticket has the backing of the Democratic organizations of Brooklyn, Queens and Staten Island.

At the Biltmore Hotel Mr. Wagner said that Mr. Gerosa and Mr. Stark were his personal choices but that he expected the Bronx and Tammany Hall executive committees to approve them without hesitation.

Wagner Voices Confidence

"I was given a free hand in picking my running mates," Mr. Wagner said. "I chose them after consulting with representatives of civic organizations, labor and business and the Bronx and Manhattan county leadership.

"I am confident that the Bronx and New York County executive committees will approve my choices. Speaking for myself and my running mates I am sure that we will win the primary contest next September and go on to win the November election."

Carmine G. DeSapio, the leader of Tammany Hall, expressed confidence that the executive committees of the Bronx and Manhattan organizations would approve Mr. Wagner's selections at a meeting to be held early this week. He described Mr. Gerosa and Mr. Stark as "outstanding representative business men who will make a great contribution to public service."

Mr. Gerosa, who was born in Milan, Italy, Aug. 10, 1894, lives at 615 West 252d Street in the Riverdale section. He is married and has three children.

He was designated in 1945 by four of the five Democratic county leaders as a candidate for Controller on a ticket headed by former Mayor William O'Dwyer, but withdrew in favor of Lazarus Jo-

Continued on Page 20, Column 4

Clark Ready to Start Release Of Red Captives in Few Days

But Allied Commander Says It May Be Two or Three Weeks Before Americans Freed by the Communists Arrive in U. S.

By JAMES RESTON

Special to THE NEW YORK TIMES.

SOMEWHERE IN KOREA, July 26—Gen. Mark W. Clark said tonight he was prepared to start shipping Communist prisoners of war to North Korea and Communist China within a "few days," but he thought it would be two or three weeks before American prisoners would reach the United States.

The United Nations commander told several reporters aboard his plane en route to the signing of the truce agreement at Munsan, Korea, that while the Communists had comparatively few prisoners to send back, United Nations procedures for handling captives were undoubtedly faster.

The United Nations Command now holds 68,000 North Koreans and 5,000 Chinese Communists who want to return to their native lands, and 8,000 North Koreans and about 15,000 Chinese Communists who have refused to return home.

In contrast, the Communists hold only 12,000 United Nations prisoners, of whom 3,000 are Americans.

Nevertheless, General Clark said, he thought it would be unwise for the Americans to expect that United States prisoners would be sent back as fast as the United Nations Command would return the Communists.

He said he expected the Communists to return the American captives at the rate of about fifty daily, while the Allies were in position to return as many as 1,500 Communists every day.

In accordance with plans that are now ready, General Clark asserted, the Communist captives would be put aboard small naval

Continued on Page 9, Column 2

Accord on plans for prisoners of war is on Page 7.

Eisenhower Accepts Aid Cut; Drive to Adjourn Advances

Special to THE NEW YORK TIMES.

WASHINGTON, July 26—The drive for adjournment of Congress by Saturday appeared more certain of success today as the Eisenhower Administration privately indicated it could operate under the $4,562,664,000 foreign aid fund bill approved yesterday by the Senate Appropriations Committee.

The Administration decision, already conveyed to Senate leaders, was said to represent an understanding, reluctantly reached, that little improvement could be hoped for on the committee action, which restored half the $1,115,050,000 reduction made last week in the House of Representatives.

The Administration leaders in the Senate are being asked to do no more than "hold the line" when the Mutual Security money bill comes to the floor for debate, and possibly a vote, on Wednesday.

For the record, the Administration still sought passage before adjournment of the postal rate increase bill, designed to produce an additional $240,500,000 in revenue, but the pressure for the proposal did not seem very great.

Summerfield Is Doubtful

Postmaster General Arthur E. Summerfield, guest on the National Broadcasting Company's "Meet the Press" television interview, said tonight he thought Congress should stay in session to pass the bill but conceded he did not know whether it would.

"I know they've had a busy six months," he said.

The House Post Office and Civil Service Committee, which has been conducting hearings for two weeks, has given no indication when a postal bill will be reported. The House leadership tentatively has scheduled the measure for midweek consideration on the floor. There have been no Senate hearings.

With debate beginning tomorrow, quick Senate approval was forecast for a compromise bill providing for the admission to this country over the next three years of 209,000 refugees, many of them from lands now behind the Iron Curtain. The Administration originally had proposed permitting the entry of 240,000 above-quota immigrants in two years.

The compromise figure, worked out with Senator Pat McCarran, Democrat of Nevada, who will continue to oppose the legislation but will not obstruct its passage, falls below the 220,000 admissions in three years approved by the Senate Judiciary Committee.

House Votes Wednesday

The House will vote Wednesday on its version of the bill in which 240,000 refugees would be admitted over a three-year period. Conferees later will agree to a median figure on entries.

Apart from conference reports, which will be coming up for votes daily, the refugee bill is the last major piece of legislation awaiting

Continued on Page 13, Column 3

55 REPORTED KILLED IN CUBAN REBELLION

Batista Voids Constitutional Guarantees, Hits Partisans of Ex-President Prio

By R. HART PHILLIPS

Special to THE NEW YORK TIMES.

HAVANA, July 26—Fifty-five persons were reported killed and many more wounded in a rebellion today at Santiago de Cuba and near-by Bayamo. Martial law was imposed in Santiago following the uprising and military authorities began to round up members of revolutionary groups.

President Fulgencio Batista and his Cabinet in a special session tonight suspended constitutional guarantees for a period of ninety days, according to an official note from the Presidential Palace. The action was taken to enable the Government to cope with revolutionary activities following the revolt earlier in the day.

"Mercenaries in the service of those who became rich during the regime of Prio [former President Carlos Prio Socarras], in conjunction with Communist elements" were accused of the attacks on the military posts at Santiago and Bayamo in a joint statement signed by the Ministers.

Continued on Page 11, Column 2

Arizona Raids Polygamous Cult; Seeks to Wipe Out Its Community

By GLADWIN HILL

Special to THE NEW YORK TIMES.

SHORT CREEK, Ariz., July 26—Arizona authorities, under an unusual proclamation of insurrection, raided this remote farming hamlet on the state's northern border at dawn today and placed virtually the entire adult population under arrest in an effort to wipe out the nation's last remaining center of organized polygamy.

The defendants, thirty-six men and eighty-six women, constituted the principal membership of a professed Fundamentalist sect — disowned by the Church of Jesus Christ of Latter Day Saints (Mormon) in 1939—that has continued to practice the plural marriage renounced by the Mormon church in 1890.

Separated from the outside world by the towering cliffs and arid gorges of Arizona's wild and inaccessible "Strip" between the Grand Canyon and the Utah border, members of the cult, organized on a communal economic basis, allegedly have been maintaining as many as a half-dozen wives and thirty children, and have fostered child marriages.

In addition to 122 adults and child brides named in warrants held by a raiding force of 120 peace officers, the colony included some 263 children.

The state's avowed objective is to wipe out the community, imprison the adult ringleaders, and find new homes and lives for the children and for the numerous

Continued on Page 36, Column 1

TALK CONDITION SET

U. S. to Boycott Political Parleys After 90 Days if It Finds Foe Stalls

By W. H. LAWRENCE

Special to THE NEW YORK TIMES.

WASHINGTON, July 26—The United States has agreed to join South Korea in walking out of the projected Korean political conference ninety days after it begins if this Government is convinced that the Communists are not negotiating in good faith and that further sessions would be futile.

But this Government has not promised to resume hostilities in Korea at that time, nor has it promised to give South Korea any moral or material support if that Government carries out its threat to attempt to unify divided Korea by military force.

The conditional pledge to quit the Korean political conference after ninety days—if this Government believes it is futile—has been given to Dr. Syngman Rhee, South Korean President, who has already announced publicly that his agreement to cooperate in the armistice extends for only ninety days after the political conference convenes. Under the truce terms the conference will convene within ninety days after the signing of the armistice.

The Communists have not been told heretofore of this American intention to quit the political talks in any specified period if they seem to this Government to be fruitless. The United States contends that a walkout from the political talks would not violate the armistice.

U. S. to Make Decision

This Government is not committed to walk out of the peace talks simply if Dr. Rhee and the South Koreans walk out. The United States will make its own decisions as to whether the political negotiations are being carried on in good faith.

There is not, so far as is known, any agreement by the other principal members of the United Nations to walk out at the same time that the United States might decide to leave the conference.

Observers here did not feel that the assurances given to Dr. Rhee were necessarily in conflict with the guarantee given the Communists by Lieut. Gen. William K. Harrison Jr., chief United Nations negotiator, that there would be no time limit on the political conference.

It was pointed out that the armistice agreement included no time limitation for success or failure of the political conference—but it also imposed no requirement on either the Communists or the Allies to continue negotiations if it

Continued on Page 3, Column 3

PRESIDENT IS HAPPY

But Warns in Broadcast That Global Peace Is Yet to Be Achieved

Texts of Eisenhower and Dulles talks are on Page 4.

Special to THE NEW YORK TIMES.

WASHINGTON, July 26—President Eisenhower greeted the news of the Korean armistice tonight with prayers of thanksgiving but warned the nation that the Allies had won an armistice only on a single battleground and had not achieved peace in the world.

The President spoke over radio and television networks about an hour after the official cease-fire documents had been signed.

General Eisenhower said the United States and all the free world must not relax its guard, or fail to be vigilant against "the possibility of untoward developments."

After the President had spoken, Charles E. Wilson, Secretary of Defense, issued a statement warning against any relaxation in the country's defense program because of the truce. He advised, too, that it would be a "long time" before American troops could be withdrawn from Korea "with safety."

"We must not be misled into the same demobilization which followed World Wars I and II," he said. "Such a demobilization would inevitably again tempt an aggressor."

Dulles Sees U. N. Victory

John Foster Dulles, Secretary of State, described the armistice as a great victory for the United Nations because "for the first time in history an international organization had stood against an aggressor and has marshaled force to meet force."

President Eisenhower spoke from the White House, across Pennsylvania Avenue and about a block east from Blair House, where President Truman decided thirty-seven months ago to commit United States forces to the defense of South Korea, then being overrun by the Communist armies from the north.

The President said he hoped that the coming of peace to Korea would at last convince all nations of the wisdom of composing their differences by negotiation before—rather than after "various resorts to brutal and futile battle."

He closed his brief speech by quoting from the final paragraph of Lincoln's Second Inaugural Address, which he said expressed the resolution and dedication of all Americans, now as in 1865.

These were Lincoln's words: "With malice toward none, with

Continued on Page 4, Column 2

U.N. Assembly Meets Aug. 17 To Plan Post-Truce Parley

Special to THE NEW YORK TIMES.

UNITED NATIONS, N. Y., July 26—Promptly upon receiving formal notification of the signing of the Korean armistice, Lester B. Pearson of Canada, President of the General Assembly, issued a call tonight to member delegations for resumption on Aug. 17 of the suspended seventh Assembly session. The Assembly will decide details of the Far Eastern political conference scheduled to take place within ninety days of the signing of the truce agreement.

Official notification that the truce agreement had been signed was given orally to Secretary General Dag Hammarskjold and to Mr. Pearson by the permanent representative of the United States, former Senator Henry Cabot Lodge Jr., in the same committee room at headquarters here in which the Political and Security Committee held its lengthy debate on the Korean question some months ago.

Mr. Lodge then handed to Mr. Pearson a copy of the text of the communication, addressed to the Secretary General and issued by the United States Mission after word had been flashed from the Pentagon in Washington. It read:

"I have the honor to inform you that an armistice agreement has been entered into between the United Nations Command and the commanders of the Communist forces in Korea, i. e., the Korean People's Army and the Chinese People's Volunteers. The agreement was signed for the United Nations Command at 1000 hours [10 A. M.] on July 27, 1953, Korean time, and becomes effective at 2200 hours [10 P. M.], July 27, 1953, Korean time. [The actual signing was at 10:01 A. M., Korean time, or 9:01 P. M. Sunday, Eastern daylight time.]

"A report of the Unified Command transmitting the official text of the armistice agreement will be sent to you shortly."

Telegrams to the delegates, which had been prepared earlier, were dispatched to the delegations summoning them to report for the reconvened session in mid-August.

In a joint broadcast from the committee room, which followed that of President Eisenhower from Washington, all three of the United Nations principals repeated for radio and television audiences statements issued earlier.

"The whole world is thankful that the negotiations at Panmunjom have brought the fighting in Korea to an end by the signature of an armistice agreement," Mr.

Continued on Page 4, Column 5

The New York Times (by Fred J. Sass)

REPORTS ON TRUCE: President Eisenhower making nation-wide television broadcast from the White House last night.

DEFENSE CHIEFS SEE BILLION CUT IN ARMS

Wilson Tells Quantico Parley Our Gain in Might Makes Any Attack on Us 'Foolhardy'

By AUSTIN STEVENS

Special to THE NEW YORK TIMES.

QUANTICO, Va., July 26—Defense officials attending the high-level defense conference at the Marine Corps base here predicted today that with any kind of "decent" Korean truce defense spending could be trimmed by as much as $1,000,000,000 in the next twelve months.

Secretary of Defense Charles E. Wilson told the conference that "we have attained a strength which should make any attack upon us foolhardy in the extreme, and we are increasing our strength daily."

The previously stated defense spending figure for the fiscal year that started July 1 was $43,200,000,000. Official announcement was made two days ago that W. J. McNeil, Assistant Secretary of Defense in charge of the budget, had told the conference, which included high military leaders, that cuts were expected in that figure. He did not indicate where the cuts were to be made.

In their prediction today the defense officials said that the post-truce reductions would not be greater than $1,000,000,000 in the year because so many fixed costs would continue.

The immediate economies would come in ammunition, trucks and other "consumption items" of war. Over-all military manpower gradually would be cut back from the present 3,500,000 by 200,000, perhaps more. One item mentioned today as an example was the immediate ending of combat pay, which is budgeted at $54,000,000.

However, defense officials stated, some other costs would rise. Assuming, for instance, that large numbers of United States troops would remain in Korea for some time, it was said, it would become necessary to build barracks and other semi-permanent structures.

The three-day highly secret conference called by Secretary Wilson to have the armed services present their situations and problems and also to get members of his new defense "team" to know

Continued on Page 8, Column 1

MARINES STOP REDS IN LAST-HOUR FIGHT

Chinese Foe's Dawn Attacks Hit U. S. Units on West and South Koreans in Center

By The United Press

TOKYO, Monday, July 27 — Chinese Communist troops threw "last hour propaganda" attacks at Allied forces on the central and western fronts of the rain-swept Korean battle line today, only a few hours before the armistice was signed at Panmunjom.

An estimated two enemy companies smashed into United Nations lines at the bend of the Kumsong River on the central front. South Korean forces fought the Reds hand-to-hand for more than an hour.

Allied troops all along the 155-mile line across the peninsula were ordered to hold casualties to a minimum and not to pick fights with the Reds.

The Allied orders were issued as Chinese Red shock troops just before dawn attacked United States Marines on a western front outpost for the fourth consecutive day. The Reds hit the hillpost positions northeast of Panmunjom in forces up to 300 men.

First Marine Division officers said the first wave of the attack was turned off without casualty among the Americans. The marine'

Continued on Page 2, Column 1

CEREMONY IS BRIEF

Halt in 3-Year Conflict for a Political Parley Due at 9 A. M. Today

Armistice text, on Pages 6, 7; Clark and Taylor statements, 9.

By LINDESAY PARROTT

Special to THE NEW YORK TIMES.

TOKYO, Monday, July 27—Communist and United Nations delegates in Panmunjom signed an armistice at 10:01 A. M. today [9:01 P. M., Sunday, Eastern daylight time]. Under the truce terms, hostilities in the three-year-old Korean war are to cease at 10 o'clock tonight [9 A. M., Monday, Eastern daylight time].

[President Syngman Rhee of South Korea promised in a statement at Seoul Monday to observe the armistice "for a limited time" while a political conference tried to unify Korea by peaceful means, The United Press said.]

The historic document was signed in a roadside hall the Communists built specially for the occasion. The ceremony, attended by representatives of sixteen members of the United Nations, took precisely eleven minutes. Then the respective delegations walked from the meeting place without a word or handshake between them.

The matter-of-fact procedure underlined what spokesmen of both sides emphasized: That though the shooting would cease within twelve hours after the signing, only an uneasy armed truce and political difficulties, perhaps even greater than those of the armistice negotiations, were ahead.

Signers Are Expressionless

The representatives of the two sides were expressionless as they put their names to a pile of documents, providing for an exchange of prisoners, establishment of a neutral zone for the cease-fire and a later political conference that would attempt to settle the tragic Korean questions, unsolved by three years of fighting that caused hundreds of thousands of casualties.

According to the latest figures, revealed July 21 by the Department of Defense, the United States has suffered a total of 139,272 casualties. This included 24,965 dead, 101,368 wounded, 2,938 captured, 8,476 missing and 1,525 previously reported captured or missing, but since returned to military control.

Early this afternoon the Allied part in conclusion of the armistice agreement was completed at advance headquarters near Munsan, where Gen. Mark W. Clark, United Nations commander, put his name to the documents previously signed at Panmunjom.

General Clark signed in the presence of some of his high-ranking officers, Vice Admiral Robert P. Briscoe, commander of the naval forces in the Far East; Gen. Otto P. Weyland, head of the Far East Air Forces; Gen. Maxwell D. Taylor, Eighth Army commander; Lieut. Gen. Samuel Anderson of the Fifth Air Force, and Vice Admiral J. J. Clark, heading the Seventh Fleet.

Also present at Munsan was

Continued on Page 2, Column 5

Skeptical G. I.'s Finally Convinced; Most Take News With Little Elation

By GREG MacGREGOR

Special to THE NEW YORK TIMES.

SEOUL, Korea, July 26 — Tonight, on the eve of the armistice, front-line G. I.'s faced their last full night of fighting in the thirty-seven-month-old Korean war. Only a few minor clashes had taken place by early morning, and from all indications the war would be unofficially ended by dawn. No patrols were scheduled for tomorrow.

As news of the armistice filtered down to the men at the front, it left an atmosphere of mingled disbelief and temporary confusion in its wake. In many cases the soldiers flatly refused to accept the word of their own officers and noncommissioned officers. The men had had so many disappointments over cease-fire reports in the past that they were slow to accept the truth.

"It will never happen," a Marine private manning the line on the central front said with a laugh when his sergeant told him the war would end tomorrow.

Not until the Armed Forces Radio broadcast was picked up at 6 P. M. tonight by portable receivers along the front were the men willing to believe the news. Then the announcer's words struck like a bolt of lightning.

Some G. I.'s stared dumbly at each other and others broke out in howls.

"Didja hear that—didja hear that?" one man kept shouting over and over as he ran from his tent.

"Wait'll they sign it—who knows what's going to happen?" a skeptic

Continued on Page 2, Column 7

"All the News That's Fit to Print"

The New York Times.

LATE CITY EDITION
Increasingly cloudy today. Rain tonight and tomorrow.
Temperature Range Today—Max., 45; Min., 31
Temperature Yesterday—Max., 46; Min., 31
Full U. S. Weather Bureau Report, Page 43

VOL. CIII..No. 35,111. Entered as Second-Class Matter, Post Office, New York, N. Y. NEW YORK, FRIDAY, MARCH 12, 1954. Times Square, New York 36, N. Y. Telephone LAckawanna 4-1000 FIVE CENTS

ARMY CHARGES M'CARTHY AND COHN THREATENED IT IN TRYING TO OBTAIN PREFERRED TREATMENT FOR SCHINE

HALF OF DOCKMEN IN BROOKLYN JOIN OUTLAW WALKOUT

Huge Food Cargoes Reported in Danger of Spoiling—Trade Losses Mounting

COURT IS PICKETED AGAIN

Rally Backs a Tie-Up Until I. L. A. Is Certified—Jersey Strikers Pledge Return

By A. H. RASKIN

The outlaw dock strike got worse yesterday.

Half of the longshoremen in Brooklyn, the only section of the port that had been operating normally, joined the week-old walkout.

Importers notified the National Labor Relations Board that millions of dollars worth of fruit and vegetables were in danger of rotting on piers and in the holds of strike-stalled ships.

The tie-up turned into a blockade when Philadelphia locals of the old International Longshoremen's Association refused to unload passenger or cargo vessels diverted from New York. Rank-and-file leaders of the local stoppage sought to make the boycott coast-wide, but received no immediate assurances of help from other ports.

The Commerce and Industry Association reported that the turbulent dock labor situation was causing many large corporations to shunt their import and export schedules to other cities. The group predicted that 10 per cent of the lost trade never would be recovered.

The one bright spot in the waterfront picture was a promise by Jersey City strikers to go back to their jobs this morning. The promise was given by spokesmen for both of the warring dock unions—the I. L. A. and its American Federation of Labor rival—at a conference with Commissioner Lawrence A. Whipple in Jersey City.

Picket Line Is Crossed

The federation union, which has been opposing the walkout, mobilized 100 longshoremen to pierce an I. L. A. picket line at a Manhattan wharf of the United Fruit Company. Ignoring the jeers of several hundred members of the old union, five gangs of A. F. L. dock workers walked onto Pier 3, just north of the Battery, to unload coffee and miscellaneous cargo from Guatemala and Honduras. The cargo was aboard the freighter Lovland.

Two hundred and fifty I. L. A. strikers renewed the picketing of the United States Court House in Foley Square. It was the second time they had marched outside the building in protest against two anti-strike court orders.

One was an injunction forbidding the I. L. A. to strike or to interfere with waterfront truck movements. The other was a $100,000 contempt action against the union and three officers of its West Side locals.

The strike has been carried on in defiance of the two orders and in disregard of back-to-work appeals by Capt. William V. Bradley, president of the I. L. A. Strike leaders say the walkout will continue until the old union is certified as the sole bargaining agent for the port's 24,000 dock workers.

The threat to keep the port tied up for all the months that may

Continued on Page 48, Column 2

Wilson Aide Named Secretary of Navy

Associated Press Wirephoto

Charles S. Thomas, Assistant Secretary of Defense, after he was named the successor to Robert B. Anderson, right.

Special to The New York Times.

WASHINGTON, March 11—Charles Sparks Thomas, Assistant Secretary of Defense, was nominated by President Eisenhower today to be Secretary of the Navy. Mr. Thomas, if confirmed by the Senate, will succeed Robert B. Anderson, who will become Under Secretary of Defense when Roger B. Kyes vacates the post on May 1. A successor to Mr. Thomas has not yet been chosen. The

Continued on Page 3, Column 4

'Direct' Warning to Reds Urged by U. S. at Caracas

By SYDNEY GRUSON

Special to The New York Times.

CARACAS, Venezuela, March 11—The United States called on the Tenth Inter-American Conference today to issue a "simple, clear and direct" warning to the leaders of international communism to keep hands off the Americas.

The best way to do this, John Foster Dulles, United States Secretary of State, said, is to adopt the United States anti-Communist resolution without crippling amendments. These, he said, would "alter the heart" of the proposed denunciation of international communism as a threat to the hemisphere.

After a week of general debate the Communist issue was joined late today in the Political Committee when consideration of the resolution began. The Secretary made his third major speech on the question in an effort to block a series of crippling amendments submitted by Mexico.

Mr. Dulles sought to eliminate the fears of some delegates that the resolution could, in his own words, "be interpreted as intervention or justifying intervention in the genuinely domestic affairs of an American state."

'Natural Historical Fears'

"This concern is, we believe, due to natural historical fears rather than to any language in the United States proposal," the Secretary said.

Delegates of Argentina, Guatemala and Mexico, all of whom spoke in the wind-up of the general debate this morning, had expressed this fear. The spokesmen for Guatemala, where the Communists have won high positions in the Government, have charged that the United States was seeking to cloak interventionist ideas in the guise of collective action against Guatemala.

Mexico's delegate spoke twice today, in the general debate and in answer to Secretary Dulles' rejection of Mexico's amendments. On both occasions Roberto Cordova of Mexico emphasized that his country was not trying to defend international communism but only the right of any people to choose their own form of government and political institutions.

Mexico, he said, would willingly subscribe to the United States proposal if his delegation were convinced that it did not represent a backward step regarding intervention. But later he brushed aside Mr. Dulles' assurances on this point and in fact took no note of the Secretary's announcement that the United States was itself proposing an addition to the declarative portion of the resolution to declare:

"This declaration of foreign policy made by the American republics in relation to the dangers originating outside this hemisphere is designed to protect and not to impair the inalienable right of each American state freely to choose its own form of government and economic system and to live its own social and cultural life."

As the resolution stood before,

Continued on Page 6, Column 4

SCHWABLE TELLS OF P. O. W. ORDEAL

Tells How His Mental Torture by Reds Almost Made Him Believe Germ 'Confession'

By ELIE ABEL

Special to The New York Times.

WASHINGTON, March 11—Col. Frank H. Schwable described today how a mature man could be conditioned to accept as real the fictions he had invented to appease the Communists.

Taking the witness chair for the first time, the lean, nervous Marine aviator talked for six hours before a court of inquiry. He tried to explain how it felt to have his brain washed, how reality became a blur in the mind, how the judgment could be fogged and the will destroyed.

He did not quite believe his own story that the United States had waged bacteriological warfare in Korea, Colonel Schwable told the court, which is investigating his false "confession."

"I was never convinced in my own mind that we in the First Marine Air Wing had used bug warfare," he testified. "I knew we hadn't. But the rest of it [the fraudulent confession] was real to me—the conferences, the planes and how they would go about their missions."

Rear Admiral Thomas J. Cooper, who was questioning the

Continued on Page 5, Column 5

264 Exposed to Atom Radiation After Nuclear Blast in Pacific

By The Associated Press.

WASHINGTON, March 11—The Atomic Energy Commission said tonight that twenty-eight Americans and 236 natives were "unexpectedly" subjected to "some radiation" during the recent atomic test in the Marshall Islands but all those exposed were "reported well."

The commission announced on March 1 that the first of a series of nuclear tests had started in the Pacific proving grounds.

The commission announcement today said:

"During the course of a routine atomic test in the Marshall Islands, twenty-eight United States personnel and 236 residents were transported from neighboring atolls to Kwajalein Island according to plans as a precautionary measure.

"The individuals were unexpectedly exposed to some radiation. There were no burns. All are reported well.

"After completion of the atomic tests, they will be returned to their homes."

The commission made no immediate amplification of this announcement. However, it seemed probably that a "fall-out" of radioactive waste and activated moisture from a cloud drifting from the explosion probably descended on the Americans and natives on the atoll to which they had been moved.

Atomic test officials try to make careful forecasts of wind directions but sometimes miscalculate.

Exposure to mild radiation is not necessarily dangerous. Reporters last spring were within two miles of an atomic explosion at the Nevada proving grounds and later walked to "Ground

Continued on Page 3, Column 4

SENATE COMBINES STATEHOOD PLANS BY VOTE OF 46-43

Ignores Eisenhower's Wishes for Action on Hawaii Alone—Democrats Score Victory

By CLAYTON KNOWLES

Special to The New York Times.

WASHINGTON, March 11—The Senate disregarded Administration wishes in voting today to put Hawaiian and Alaskan statehood proposals into a single bill.

The decision to join the proposals carried by a vote of 46 to 43 and came a day after President Eisenhower had urged separate consideration of the statehood measures. He had asked for immediate statehood for Hawaii alone. This is the Republican party position.

The Senate's vote was mainly along party lines, with the Democrats winning. However, the plan to combine the bills prevailed by the margin of the votes of three Republicans who broke with their party on the question. They were Senators William Langer of North Dakota, John M. Butler of Maryland and George W. Malone of Nevada.

Forty-two Democrats and the Senate's one independent, Wayne Morse of Oregon, cast the other votes for a combined bill.

Forty-one Republicans and two Democrats, Spessard L. Holland of Florida and Russell B. Long of Louisiana, opposed the merger plan.

Knowland to Back Bill

The issue in the three-day debate preceding the vote was whether statehood aspirations of Hawaii and Alaska would be hurt or helped by putting them together. Senator William F. Knowland of California, Republican Senate leader, contended it would hurt. Senator Clinton P. Anderson, Democrat of New Mexico and sponsor of the one-package proposal, asserted it would help.

The vote along party lines stemmed largely from the fact that Hawaii is normally Republican and might be expected to send a Republican delegation to Congress, while Alaska is Democratic at the polls and probably would send Democrats to the Congress.

After the Senate action, Senator Knowland, conceding a chance to pass a combined bill, said he would vote for it. So did other Republicans in opposition on the vote today. Senator Hugh Butler of Nebraska, Interior Committee chairman who fought the Anderson amendment, said the Senate "might fool some people by passing the bill now before us."

The Nebraska Republican alluded to the fact that a group of Southern Democrats, numbering fifteen to twenty, had supported the Anderson amendment in the hope of defeating both statehood proposals. Senator George A. Smathers, Democrat of Florida, frankly conceded during debate

Continued on Page 13, Column 3

SENATOR ATTACKS

Hits Back at Stevenson, Murrow and Flanders in Radio Broadcast

Special to The New York Times.

WASHINGTON, March 11—Senator Joseph R. McCarthy struck back tonight at criticism of him by Adlai E. Stevenson, Edward R. Murrow and Senator Ralph E. Flanders.

The Wisconsin Republican said that Mr. Stevenson's assertion that only one alleged active Communist had been found in the Government in the last year was "absolutely false."

He called Mr. Murrow, Columbia Broadcasting System commentator, one of the "extreme Left Wing bleeding-heart elements of television and radio." He cited an article in The Pittsburgh Sun-Telegraph of Feb. 18, 1935, to charge that Mr. Murrow had been on the advisory council for a summer session of Moscow University, where overthrow of the existing social order was taught.

[Three and a half hours after Mr. McCarthy's broadcast, Mr. Murrow issued a statement in which he said that in 1935, in his capacity as assistant director of the Institute of International Education, he was a member of the advisory committee for a summer school in Moscow. He added, however, that "in actual fact the summer school was canceled by Russian authorities before it began."]

McCarthy Quotes Lincoln

Mr. McCarthy said he would rather stand with Abraham Lincoln, who said during Civil War times the danger to the United States was from within and not from without, rather than with Senator Flanders, a Republican of Vermont, who said the danger today is from without rather than from within.

Appearing on a question and answer radio broadcast with Fulton Lewis Jr., over the Mutual Broadcasting System, Senator McCarthy struck back at Messrs. Stevenson, Murrow and Flanders but made no mention of the implied criticism voiced by President Eisenhower at his news conference yesterday.

He also made no mention of his quarrel with the National Broadcasting Company and the Columbia Broadcasting System because they refused him free time for a reply to Mr. Stevenson and gave it instead to the Republican National Committee, which designated Vice President Nixon to make the official reply Saturday night.

Mr. Murrow had devoted a thir-

Continued on Page 11, Column 1

Cohn Scored When Woman Denies McCarthy's Charges

Mrs. Moss Counters Accusation as Red While Senators Decry 'Innuendo'—Crowd Applauds Hearing Scene

Special to The New York Times.

WASHINGTON, March 11—Mrs. Annie Lee Moss, suspended Army Signal Corps employe, softly but flatly denied all Communist party activities or membership today.

The crowded caucus room of the Senate Office Building, where the Senate Permanent Subcommittee on Investigation was in session, rang with repeated applause as Democratic members struck at "convicting people by rumor and hearsay and innuendo."

The target of Democratic resentment was Roy Cohn, chief counsel for the subcommittee headed by Senator Joseph R. McCarthy, Wisconsin Republican. Mr. Cohn had countered Mrs. Moss' testimony by saying the subcommittee had still secret evidence that she was a Communist.

The Democrats, led by Senator John L. McClellan of Arkansas, demanded that he produce the evidence or refrain from public mention of it.

Senator McCarthy, in the original hearing at which the charges against Mrs. Moss were produced, had suggested she would "run the risk of indictment for perjury" when she appeared before the committee.

Senator McCarthy was absent from the committee room today when the scene over Mrs. Moss' testimony took place. He had gone to his office to prepare for his radio appearance later in which he answered criticism of him and the Republican party by Adlai E. Stevenson, the 1952 Democratic Presidential nominee.

No effort was made by the presiding officer, Senator Karl E. Mundt, South Dakota Republican, to check the crowd's applause or to interfere with the Democrats in their vigorous denunciation of Mr. Cohn's tactics.

Senator Mundt ordered Mr.

Continued on Page 16, Column 2

SENATE UNIT ASKS OUSTER OF CHAVEZ

Cites Election Irregularities in '52 but Does Not Accuse New Mexico Democrat

By WILLIAM S. WHITE

Special to The New York Times.

WASHINGTON, March 11—A Senate showdown on a long-forecast Republican effort to unseat Senator Denis Chavez because of alleged election irregularities in 1952 drew near today. A Republican-controlled Senate subcommittee formally filed its expected report recommending that the New Mexico Democrat's seat be held vacant.

It also urged that the Senate find that "no member was elected from New Mexico in the 1952 general election."

The Republicans asserted that there had been no free expression of the will of the people, in part because of the alleged denial of the right of secret ballot. Senator Chavez nowhere was charged with fraud.

The Republican subcommittee chairman, Senator Frank A. Barrett of Wyoming, said there had been "no intention to cast aspersions" on Mr. Chavez. It simply had been impossible to determine whether Senator Chavez or his Republican opponent, Brig. Gen. Patrick J. Hurley, retired, actually had won, Mr. Barrett said.

Senator Chavez asserted the Republicans had delivered "a tremendous insult to the officials and people of New Mexico."

Democrats Are Confident

The Democrats, who had insisted on clearing the issue without further delay, plainly were confident he would be sustained. Disinterested observation seemed to support their confidence.

If Senator Chavez should be ousted and the Republican Governor of New Mexico, Edwin L. Mechem, should appoint a Republican as temporary successor, the Republican party would gain actual, as distinguished from its present nominal, control of the Senate.

The improbability of such an outcome, however, was reflected by the fact that there now were more Democrats in the Senate than Republicans and in the fact that it was the Democrats who were demanding decisive action.

The Democratic member of the subcommittee, Senator Thomas C. Hennings Jr. of Missouri, gave notice that he would file a dissenting report upholding Mr. Chavez' right to his seat.

The whole issue will go next week, probably on Tuesday, to the full Senate Rules Committee. The universal expectation in the Senate was that the full committee would sustain the Repub-

Continued on Page 14, Column 3

SHOWDOWN NEARS ON TAX EXEMPTION

Martin Admits Some Votes of Democrats Are Needed to Defeat Increase Plan

Special to The New York Times.

WASHINGTON, March 11—The Administration will need the votes of some Democrats to win a showdown battle next week against higher personal income tax exemptions.

This was conceded by the Speaker of the House of Representatives, Joseph W. Martin Jr., Republican of Massachusetts. He said he realized some members of his party would break ranks on the issue but added:

"I am of the opinion that there will be enough responsible members of the Democratic party to more than offset what losses we may have."

His analysis was in response to a prediction by Representative Sam Rayburn of Texas, House minority leader, that the Democrats would win the fight for a $100 increase in present exemptions of $600 each for taxpayers and dependents.

Mr. Rayburn said after a caucus of House Democrats that he knew of none who would vote against the proposal. In that case, defection of half a dozen or so Republicans, depending on the absentee situation when the vote was taken, could bring victory for the Democrats.

Parliamentary preliminaries for the fight were completed this afternoon when the Rules Com-

Continued on Page 3, Column 6

Lasting Prevention of Polio Reported in Vaccine Tests

Dr. Salk Says Discovery Fights Off All 3 Kinds of Crippling Disease

By WILLIAM L. LAURENCE

Special to The New York Times.

NEW ORLEANS, March 11—The latest tests on children with the anti-polio vaccine have revealed that the vaccine provides the body with lasting defensive powers against the three types of viruses causing the disease, it was reported tonight.

This was described as the long-sought answer to a vital question, making it practically certain not only that the vaccine will produce effective immunity against all the three types of polio but also that the immunity will be of the lasting type, possibly for the individual's lifetime.

This could mean that within the next three to five years polio, crippler of young and old alike, will join diphtheria, smallpox, typhoid and other formerly dreaded infectious diseases as plagues finally tamed and conquered by man.

The newest findings were described here tonight before the New Orleans Graduate Medical Assembly by Dr. Jonas E. Salk, of the Virus Research Laboratory, University of Pittsburgh School of Medicine.

Associated Press

Dr. Jonas E. Salk

Dr. Salk developed the vaccine against the three types of polio-producing viruses, using viruses that had been rendered incapable of producing the disease while they still retained their power to produce immunity.

Replying to remarks made this morning in Detroit by Dr. Albert

Continued on Page 23, Column 3

STEVENS A TARGET

Report Quotes Counsel As Saying Secretary Would Be 'Through'

The text of the Army's report is printed on Page 9A.

By W. H. LAWRENCE

Special to The New York Times.

WASHINGTON, March 11—The Army reported today it had been subjected to direct threats by Senator Joseph R. McCarthy and his chief counsel, Roy Cohn.

The threats, the Army said, had been made in an effort to obtain preferential treatment for G. David Schine, now a private in the Army but formerly an investigator for the McCarthy subcommittee.

In a thirty-four-page report sent to each member of Senator McCarthy's Permanent Subcommittee on Investigations and some members of the Armed Services Committee, the Army declared the Wisconsin Republican and Mr. Cohn first had sought a direct commission for Private Schine.

Failing in that, the report said, they had then demanded for him an assignment in the New York area so he could study alleged subversive material in West Point textbooks.

In the period between Oct. 18 and Nov. 3, before Senator McCarthy began his open fight with the Army, John G. Adams, Army Counsel, reported he had told Mr. Cohn that it would not be in the national interest to give preferential treatment to Private Schine.

"Mr. Cohn replied that if the national interest was what the Army wanted, he'd give it a little and then proceeded to outline how he would expose the Army in its worst light and show the country how shabbily it is being run," the report declared.

Threat to Stevens Cited

The report quoted Mr. Cohn as threatening on one occasion to "wreck the Army" and make certain that Robert T. Stevens was "through" as the Secretary of the Army. At another time, the report said, "Mr. Cohn stated to Mr. Adams that he would teach Mr. Adams what it meant to go over his head."

The report is expected to spur growing demands for Mr. Cohn's ouster.

Senator McCarthy made it clear in answer that he would accept battle with "one or two" in the Army high command on the Cohn-Schine case. He said he had instructed his own committee staff to pull out of its files everything bearing on the case and give them to him so they could be "made available to the American public."

"I don't like to do it," he told a New York Times correspondent. "The deeper I get into it, I'm convinced the Army as a whole is damn clean. What some people in the Army do doesn't mean the entire Army."

He said he had sought at a luncheon with Charles E. Wilson, Secretary of Defense, yesterday

Continued on Page 9-B, Col 2

White Meets Backers of Young; Denies Central Compromise Bid

By ROBERT E. BEDINGFIELD

William White, president of the New York Central Railroad Company, had two important visitors in his offices at 230 Park Avenue yesterday: Clint W. Murchison and Sid W. Richardson.

They are the Texas millionaires who bought 800,000 shares of Central stock—one-eighth of the outstanding shares—last month from the Chesapeake and Ohio Railway Company to help their friend Robert R. Young in his attempt to wrest control of the $2,600,000,000 New York Central System from its present management.

Versions of the events leading to the meeting differed sharply.

Mr. White said Mr. Murchison had arranged it on his own motion. But the Texans said it had been requested by John J. McCloy, chairman of the Chase National Bank, of which Percy J. Ebbott is president.

Mr. Ebbott is a Central director. The Chase National Bank was the trustee for the 800,000 shares of Central stock before they were sold by the C. & O.

Mr. McCloy, through a spokesman, said last night that the request for the meeting had originated with Mr. Murchison. But a spokesman for Mr. Young insisted yesterday that the visit had been in response to an appeal from the Central forces for a Young representative to discuss settlement of their differences.

Mr. White branded as a "plain lie" intimations that the Central management might be seeking a compromise with Mr. Young.

Mr. White summoned reporters late yesterday afternoon to deny the "compromise" rumors that had spread through Wall Street and the Grand Central Terminal area after it was dis-

Continued on Page 26, Column 3

"All the News That's Fit to Print"

The New York Times.

LATE CITY EDITION
Fair and cool today. Mostly sunny, continued cool tomorrow.
Temperature Range Today—Max., 68; Min., 52
Temperatures Yesterday—Max., 69; Min., 61
Full U. S. Weather Bureau Report, Page 31

VOL. CIII ... No. 35,178. Entered as Second-Class Matter. Post Office, New York, N. Y. NEW YORK, TUESDAY, MAY 18, 1954. Times Square, New York 36, N. Y. Telephone LAckawanna 4-1000 FIVE CENTS

HIGH COURT BANS SCHOOL SEGREGATION; 9-TO-0 DECISION GRANTS TIME TO COMPLY

McCarthy Hearing Off a Week as Eisenhower Bars Report

SENATOR IS IRATE

President Orders Aides Not to Disclose Details of Top-Level Meeting

President's letter and excerpts from transcript, Pages 24, 25, 26.

By W. H. LAWRENCE
Special to The New York Times.

WASHINGTON, May 17—A secrecy directive by President Eisenhower resulted today in an abrupt recess for at least a week of the Senate's Army-McCarthy hearings.

Democratic and Republican Senators, some publicly and some privately, predicted that the investigation might never resume in earnest. However, there were other Senators who insisted that the investigation would go on to completion.

The recess was voted after Herbert Brownell Jr., the Attorney General, disclosed formally that criminal prosecutions might be instituted against those involved in the "preparation and dissemination" of an altered, condensed but still confidential Federal Bureau of Investigation report. This was offered in evidence last week by Senator Joseph R. McCarthy, Republican of Wisconsin.

Republicans outvoted Democrats 4 to 3 on the Senate Permanent Subcommittee of Investigation to recess the hearings until 10 o'clock next Monday morning. They acted amid charges and denials that the way was being prepared for a "whitewash."

Constitutional Division Cited

President Eisenhower cited the constitutional separation of powers between the Executive and Legislative branches in directing that details and conversations at a "high level" Administration meeting on Jan. 21 must be withheld from the committee.

Testimony already has been given that top White House, Justice and Defense officials had made plans at that conference to deal with Senator McCarthy.

The Presidential order served effectively to seal the lips of John G. Adams, the Army's regular counselor, about what Sherman Adams, the chief Presidential assistant, said to him in advising that a written report be prepared on how Senator McCarthy and his chief counsel, Roy M. Cohn, persistenly sought preferential treatment for Pvt. G. David Schine.

Before his induction, Mr. Schine was an unpaid consultant to the McCarthy subcommittee, the same group that is now conducting the hearings under the temporary chairmanship of Senator Karl E. Mundt, Republican of South Dakota.

Senator McCarthy angrily denounced today's Eisenhower order as "an Iron Curtain." His ire was shared, but in more restrained terms, by all the Republican and Democratic members of the investigating committee.

The week's postponement of

Continued on Page 24, Column 1

Communist Arms Unloaded in Guatemala By Vessel From Polish Port, U. S. Learns

State Department Views News Gravely Because of Red Infiltration

Special to The New York Times.

WASHINGTON, May 17—The State Department said today that it had reliable information that "an important shipment of arms" had been sent from Communist-controlled territory to Guatemala.

It said the arms, now being unloaded at Puerto Barrios, Guatemala, had been shipped from Stettin, a former German Baltic seaport, which has been occupied by Communist Poland since World War II. The Guatemalan regime has been frequently accused of being influenced by Communists.

"Because of the origin of these arms, the point of their embarkation, their destination and the quantity of arms involved, the Department of State considers that this is a development of gravity," the announcement said.

A freighter arrived at Puerto Barrios last Saturday, the State Department reported, carrying a large shipment of armament consigned to the Guatemalan Government.

The New York Times May 18, 1954
Site of arms arrival (cross)

Embassy Says Nation of Central America May Buy Munitions Anywhere

The State Department did not divulge the exact quantity of the arms, their nature or where they had been manufactured.

Reliable sources told The New York Times, however, that ten freight car loads of goods listed in the manifest as "hardware" had been unloaded from this ship and sent to the city of Guatemala since Sunday. Guatemala is 150 miles from Puerto Barrios. The

Continued on Page 10, Column 5

REACTION OF SOUTH

'Breathing Spell' for Adjustment Tempers Region's Feelings

By JOHN N. POPHAM
Special to The New York Times.

CHATTANOOGA, Tenn., May 17—The South's reaction to the Supreme Court's decision outlawing racial segregation in public schools appeared to be tempered considerably today.

The time lag allowed for carrying out the required transitions seemed to be the major factor in that reaction.

Southern leaders of both races in political, educational and community service fields expressed comment that covered a wide range. Some spoke bitter words that verged on defiance. Others ranged from sharp disagreement to predictions of peaceful and successful adjustment in accord with the ruling.

But underneath the surface of much of the comment, it was evident that many Southerners recognized that the decision had laid down the legal principle rejecting segregation in public education facilities.

They also noted that it had left open a challenge to the region to join in working out a program of necessary changes in the present bi-racial school systems.

Three of the most illustrative viewpoints were those expressed by Govs. James F. Byrnes of South Carolina and Herman Talmadge of Georgia, and Harold Fleming, a spokesman for the Southern Regional Council, the most effective interracial organization in the South.

Byrnes Sees Reversal

Governor Byrnes, who has vigorously defended the doctrine of separate but equal facilities in education, said that he was "shocked to learn that the court has reversed itself" with regard to past rulings on that doctrine.

However, Governor Byrnes, a former Associate Justice of the Supreme Court, noted that the tribunal had not yet delivered its final decree setting forth the time and terms for ending segregation in the schools.

Pointing out that South Carolina, a party in the litigation before the court, had until October to present arguments on how the Supreme Court should order the implementation of the decision, Governor Byrnes declared "I urge all of our people, white and colored, to exercise restraint and preserve order."

Governor Talmadge repeatedly has vowed there "will never be mixed schools while I am Governor" and has warned that school integration would lead to "blood-

Continued on Page 20, Column 1

Associated Press Wirephoto
LEADERS IN SEGREGATION FIGHT: Lawyers who led battle before U. S. Supreme Court for abolition of segregation in public schools congratulate one another as they leave court after announcement of decision. Left to right: George E. C. Hayes, Thurgood Marshall and James M. Nabrit.

1896 RULING UPSET

'Separate but Equal' Doctrine Held Out of Place in Education

Text of Supreme Court decision is printed on Page 15.

By LUTHER A. HUSTON
Special to The New York Times.

WASHINGTON, May 17—The Supreme Court unanimously outlawed today racial segregation in public schools.

Chief Justice Earl Warren read two opinions that put the stamp of unconstitutionality on school systems in twenty-one states and the District of Columbia where segregation is permissive or mandatory.

The court, taking cognizance of the problems involved in the integration of the school systems concerned, put over until the next term, beginning in October, the formulation of decrees to effectuate its 9-to-0 decision.

The opinions set aside the "separate but equal" doctrine laid down by the Supreme Court in 1896.

"In the field of public education," Chief Justice Warren said, "the doctrine of 'separate but equal' has no place. Separate educational facilities are inherently unequal."

He stated the question and supplied the answer as follows:

"We come then to the question presented: Does segregation of children in public schools solely on the basis of race, even though physical facilities and other 'tangible' factors may be equal, deprive the children of the minority group of equal educational opportunities? We believe that it does."

States Stressed Rights

The court's opinion does not apply to private schools. It is directed entirely at public schools. It does not affect the "separate but equal doctrine" as applied on railroads and other public carriers entirely within states that have such restrictions.

The principal ruling of the court was in four cases involving state laws. The states' right to operate separated schools had been argued before the court on two occasions by representatives of South Carolina, Virginia, Kansas and Delaware.

In these cases, consolidated in one opinion, the high court held that school segregation deprived Negroes of "the equal protection of the laws guaranteed by the Fourteenth Amendment."

The other opinion involved the District of Columbia. Here schools have been segregated since Civil War days under laws passed by Congress.

"In view of our decision that the Constitution prohibits the states from maintaining racially segregated public schools," the Chief Justice said, "it would be unthinkable that the same Constitution would impose a lesser duty on the Federal Government.

"We hold that racial segregation in the public schools of the District of Columbia is a denial

Continued on Page 14, Column 6

SOVIET BIDS VIENNA CEASE 'INTRIGUES'

Envoy Warns Austrian Chief on Inciting East Zone—Raab Denies Charges

By JOHN MacCORMAC
Special to The New York Times.

VIENNA, May 17—The Soviet Union warned Austria today to put an end to "hostile and subversive intrigues" against the Soviet occupation forces, or Soviet authorities would do it themselves.

Ivan I. Ilyichev, Soviet High Commissioner, reverted to a practice of early post-war days by summoning Chancellor Julius Raab and Vice Chancellor Adolf Schaerf to give them this warning. The Chancellor denied the Soviet charges.

Mr. Ilyichev said the Austrian Government had been guilty of staging actions hostile to the Soviet while the Austrian press had published daily slanderous and inciting announcements about the Soviet Union and Soviet occupation troops.

The cessation of Soviet control over the movement of freight, said the High Commissioner, was abused to smuggle militarist literature and provocative incitements into the Soviet zone with the connivance of the Austrian Minister of Interior.

When Soviet authorities ordered the removal of anti-Soviet placards in their zone, the minister instructed his subordinates to disregard the order and the Government approved his action, said Mr. Ilyichev.

He added that the Government, and particularly the Minister of Interior, had tolerated militarist propaganda by former soldiers' organizations and dissemination of propaganda for another Anschluss (union) with Germany.

The High Commissioner reminded the Government leaders that since Austria had not ob-

Continued on Page 9, Column 3

City Colleges' Board Can't Pick Chairman

The Board of Higher Education was unable to elect a chairman at its annual meeting last night at Hunter College.

A spokesman said it was the first time "within memory of board officials" that such a situation had occurred.

Nineteen of the twenty-one members of the board, which governs the four municipal colleges, attended.

Two members nominated for the one-year-term were unable to attain the required majority of eleven votes. They were Joseph B. Cavallaro, who was up for re-election as chairman, and Dr. Harry J. Carman, who was restored to the board on March 2 by Mayor Wagner.

The election was laid over until June 15.

INDO-CHINA PARLEY WEIGHS TWO PLANS

French and Rebel Peace Bids Will Be Studied Jointly as a Basis for Settlement

By THOMAS J. HAMILTON
Special to The New York Times.

GENEVA, May 17—The Far East conference decided today to take up French and Vietminh proposals jointly as a basis for settlement of the war in Indo-China.

The secret session, which lasted three and a half hours, was generally recognized as the opening round in what may turn out to be a long process of negotiation. Another secret meeting will be held tomorrow.

Western delegates felt that Vyacheslav M. Molotov, Soviet Foreign Minister, was continuing to give the impression that in the end he might throw Moscow's influence on the side of an agreed settlement.

However, the West failed to obtain answers to the two fundamental questions that are expected to determine whether the negotiations here will have any chance of success: Will the Communists agree to a separate settlement for Laos and Cambodia, and will they agree to an armistice in Vietnam without at the same time requiring a political settlement?

The conference will address itself tomorrow to the issue of Laos and Cambodia. The two Indo-Chinese states are relatively free from Communist infiltration, and their leaders contend, with the support of the French, that the only thing that needs to be done is the withdrawal of the Communists.

The Laos-Cambodia and Vietnam issues were discussed inconclusively today after the delegates had devoted the first part of their meeting to the intricate dispute over evacuation of French Union wounded from Dienbienphu, seized by the Communist-

Continued on Page 2, Column 3

2 TAX PROJECTS DIE IN ESTIMATE BOARD

Beer Levy and More Parking Collections Killed—Payroll Impost Still Weighed

By CHARLES G. BENNETT

Two possible new revenue sources were definitely eliminated yesterday by the Board of Estimate in executive session. They were the proposed 1-cent-a-glass tax on beer and the suggestion to extend metered parking into hours now "free."

In a three-hour City Hall parley the board failed once more to decide on a new impost or imposts to balance the 1954-55 budget of $1,639,438,325. Mayor Wagner said after the meeting that the highly controversial 3 per cent sales tax on commercial services was "still one of the taxes at the top of the list."

Saying he felt the Board of Estimate was close to a decision on the knotty tax question, the Mayor added that "there's no decision to discard any tax" except the two mentioned above, and that at the same time "no tax is inevitable."

The board will wrestle with the tax question again in executive session on Thursday at 2:30 P. M. The Mayor said the City Council, which is holding up a bill to impose the sales tax extension, would be invited to send a delegation to the Thursday session.

Mr. Wagner asserted that he would like to see the Board of Estimate decide the tax question

Continued on Page 32, Column 5

MORETTIS' LAWYER MUST BARE TALKS

Jersey Court Orders Counsel to Racketeers in Bergen to Divulge Data to Grand Jury

By GEORGE CABLE WRIGHT
Special to The New York Times.

TRENTON, May 17—The New Jersey Supreme Court today ordered a lawyer who once had represented top Bergen County racketeers to divulge to a grand jury the substance of confidential talks with those clients.

The four-to-three decision reversed the rulings of two lower courts. Involved was the refusal more than a year ago of John E. Selser, Hackensack attorney, to answer four questions put to him by the Bergen County grand jury.

Mr. Selser told the jury that one of his clients, Willie Moretti, slain gambler, had given him the names of persons connected with Walter G. Winne who had received protection money from syndicate gamblers. Mr. Winne, superseded prosecutor of Bergen County, was acquitted last week of nonfeasance in office.

But the attorney balked when asked to reveal these and the names of other persons who, his clients alleged, had been paid protection money or who had received political contributions on the state and county level. He pleaded that his lips were sealed by the duty of "nondisclosure of confidential communications between client and attorney."

Represented Morettis, Others

Mr. Selser had represented Moretti, who was murdered in Cliffside Park in October, 1951, and his brother, the late Salvatore Moretti, for many years. He also was the attorney of record for Joe Adonis, Arthur Longano and James (Piggy) Lynch. The last four were among five men convicted and sent to prison in May, 1952, as the leaders of the Bergen gambling syndicate.

Mr. Selser appeared before the grand jury in February, 1953. The present court action was brought by the state after his refusal to answer the above questions on that occasion and two other questions. The latter pertained to testimony by John J. Dickerson, former Republican state chairman, before the same grand jury.

Mr. Dickerson had testified that Adonis and the two Morettis visited his home in November, 1950, and that Willie told him then that $225,000 in protection money had been paid to Harold

Continued on Page 36, Column 3

RULING TO FIGURE IN '54 CAMPAIGN

Decision Tied to Eisenhower—Russell Leads Southerners in Criticism of Court

By WILLIAM S. WHITE
Special to The New York Times.

WASHINGTON, May 17—Congress as a whole grappled gingerly today with the profound political implications of the Supreme Court's anti-segregation decision.

It became clear at once—and by both parties was accepted in private as inevitable—that the court's action would figure importantly in the coming Congressional election campaigns.

Publicly, however, the Republicans and the non-Southern Democrats, on the whole, maintained silence. The Southerners, all angry or sorrowing in one degree or another, were quickly articulate and split among themselves into at least three factions.

¶One Southern group, by all the indications not a large one, was openly defiant of the court, as typified by the comment of Senator James O. Eastland of Mississippi.

"The South," Mr. Eastland said, "will not abide by nor obey this legislative decision by a political court."

¶A second Southern group, while not openly challenging the court, began to threaten efforts to force an alteration of its view, as illustrated by the comment of

Continued on Page 26, Column 3

Churchill Asks Negotiated Peace With Guarantees for Indo-China

By DREW MIDDLETON
Special to The New York Times.

LONDON, May 17—Britain will seek effective international guarantees for any peace settlement in Indo-China, Prime Minister Churchill declared today.

Negotiation of an "acceptable" settlement at the Geneva conference remains the immediate task of the British Government, Sir Winston emphasized in a statement to the House of Commons.

Until the outcome of that conference is known, he added, "final decisions" cannot be taken by the Government about the establishment of a collective defense system in Southeast Asia and the Western Pacific.

Peace by negotiation emerged from Sir Winston's cautious statement as the only policy that the Cabinet was ready to apply to the problem of Indo-China. Observers were struck by the fact that, aside from the Prime Minister's reference to the necessity of backing a settlement there with guarantees, the British position was substantially the same as when the Geneva conference began.

[Indonesia is considering asking India and Burma to join her in a nonaggression treaty with Communist China as a means of offsetting United States plans for a Southeast Asian alliance.]

Sir Winston's adherence to negotiation is acceptable to both major parties in the Commons.

Continued on Page 4, Column 3

Costello Is Sentenced to 5 Years, Fined $30,000 in U. S. Tax Case

By EDWARD RANZAL

Frank Costello was sentenced yesterday by Federal Judge John F. X. McGohey to five years in jail and fined $30,000 for income tax evasion.

The dapper, 61-year-old gambler was remanded immediately. Later Judge Harold R. Medina in the United States Court of Appeals refused to set bail pending appeal. Costello, who listened to the sentencing in icy-calm manner, was taken to the Federal House of Detention, 427 West Street.

Besides the jail sentence and the fines, Judge McGohey also assessed Costello for court costs. Lloyd F. MacMahon, chief assistant United States Attorney, said the costs would be about $5,000, only a fraction of what it cost the Government in its investigation, which began in earnest in 1952.

Costello was convicted Thursday night by a Federal court jury of five women and seven men of three counts of a four-count indictment. They found the gambler guilty of evading a total of $51,095 in taxes from 1947 through 1949. In 1947 Costello evaded $22,563; in 1948, $13,786, and in 1949, $14,746. He was acquitted of the charge of evading taxes in 1946. Costello's attorney, Leo C. Fennelly, told Judge McGohey that the acquittal on this count meant that the gambler was entitled to a refund for that year.

Before the sentencing Mr. MacMahon said that for years Costello had schemed to cheat the Government out of taxes. He added that the gambler had concealed at least $140,000 of his income from 1947 through 1949, more than half his income.

Mr. MacMahon contended that Costello, by devious means, had concealed the receipt of his income as well as the source by using cash in every transaction where it was possible.

Evidence at the six-week trial, the prosecutor said, showed that from 1937 through 1945 Costello deliberately underestimated his income by at least $202,000. The statute of limitations, he added, bars prosecution for the earlier tax evasions.

"Costello has spent a lifetime making money on the shady side

Continued on Page 56, Column 6

'Voice' Speaks in 34 Languages To Flash Court Ruling to World

Within an hour after the Supreme Court decision on school segregation yesterday afternoon, the Voice of America sent a news broadcast by shortwave to Eastern Europe.

The decision came in time for the regularly scheduled "World-wide English Broadcast" at 3 o'clock. The broadcast was written in English on the Voice's central desk and was sent by teletype to the thirty-four language desks.

There it was translated and sent out in various foreign tongues all over the world as broadcast time arrived for each.

"The Supreme Court has ruled unanimously," the Voice said in its broadcast, "that racial segregation has no place in American public education. It held that separation of students on a racial basis denies equal educational opportunities.

"Chief Justice [Earl] Warren, reading the court's findings, said that the doctrine of providing separate but equal facilities has no place in public education. Separation of children solely because of race, he said, generates feelings in their hearts and minds which might never be undone. * * *

"The ruling in effect outlaws all segregation in public schools throughout the United States. The court held that to separate students is a denial of the due process of law guaranteed by the Fifth Amendment to the Constitution and equal opportunity

Continued on Page 15, Column 4

"All the News That's Fit to Print"

The New York Times.

LATE CITY EDITION
Partly cloudy today. Considerable cloudiness and milder tomorrow.
Temperature Range Today-Max., 41; Min., 30
Temperatures Yesterday—Max., 38; Min., 27
Full U. S. Weather Bureau Report, Page 55

VOL. CIV. No. 35,445. Entered as Second-Class Matter. Post Office, New York, N. Y. NEW YORK, WEDNESDAY, FEBRUARY 9, 1955. Times Square, New York 36, N. Y. Telephone LAckawanna 4-1000 FIVE CENTS

BULGANIN IS PREMIER AS MALENKOV RESIGNS, BUT KHRUSHCHEV IS VIEWED AS REAL LEADER; MOLOTOV, WARNING U. S., CLAIMS H-BOMB LEAD

EISENHOWER ASKS 7 BILLION PROGRAM TO BUILD SCHOOLS

Message to Congress Urges Federal-State-Local Plan for Grants and Loans

DEMOCRATS DECRY SCOPE

Leaders Denounce Proposal as 'Makeshift'—Demand Far Larger Expenditures

Text of the President's message is printed on Page 20.

By W. H. LAWRENCE
Special to The New York Times.

WASHINGTON, Feb. 8—President Eisenhower proposed today a three-year $7,000,000,000 Federal-state-local school construction program.

He asked Congress to make available $220,000,000 in Federal grants and about $900,000,000 in loans to meet a current deficit of more than 300,000 school classrooms.

The message went to a Democratic-controlled Congress. Leaders in the education field in both the Senate and the House called it inadequate and "makeshift."

Some critics declared the Presidential program would be ineffective in about one-fourth of the states, which have constitutional limitations on incurring or increasing debts.

Indirectly, President Eisenhower also suggested higher pay for school teachers, but his message advanced no concrete proposals on this. He said low pay was a factor in the shortage of teachers, which he declared was "less obvious but ultimately more dangerous than the classroom shortage."

"Because of the magnitude of the job, but more fundamentally because of the undeniable importance of free education to a free way of life, the means we take to provide our children with proper classrooms must be weighed most carefully," the President said, continuing:

"The phrase 'free education' is a deliberate choice. For unless education continues to be free—free in its response to local com-

Continued on Page 20, Column 1

A. E. C. WON'T DROP DIXON-YATES PACT

2-1 Vote Disclosed by Board—Congress Plea Rejected

By WILLIAM M. BLAIR
Special to The New York Times.

WASHINGTON, Feb 8—By a 2 to 1 vote, the Atomic Energy Commission has turned down a Democratic demand that the Dixon-Yates private power contract be canceled.

The split vote, taken on Saturday, followed the lead of President Eisenhower, who asserted three days before the vote that he would not withdraw the controversial contract to feed private power into the Tennessee Valley Authority.

Lewis L. Strauss, A. E. C. chairman, and Dr. Willard Frank Libby, a new member, voted to stick by the contract. Thomas E. Murray voted for cancellation.

As Mr. Strauss disclosed the decision today, Mr. Murray went before the Joint Congressional Committee on Atomic Energy to renew his charge that the Dixon-Yates controversy had interfered with the commission's primary job of developing atomic weapons and peacetime uses of the atom.

His main concern, he testified, was "whether we will in the future maintain our present position of world leadership in the nuclear field." He concluded:

"The attention the commission today gives to making policy de-

Continued on Page 37, Column 6

President Appeals For Satellite People

Special to The New York Times.

WASHINGTON, Feb. 8—President Eisenhower urged tonight a continuing effort to "intensify the will for freedom in the satellite countries behind the Iron Curtain."

He spoke from the White House on a closed-circuit television program in behalf of the Crusade for Freedom, which operates Radio Free Europe and the Free Europe Press. The crusade hopes to raise $10,000,000 this year.

He took no cognizance of the resignation of Georgi M. Malenkov as Soviet Premier and his replacement by Marshal Nikolai A. Bulganin. His prepared text was left unchanged after the Moscow developments had become known.

The President emphasized that the masses imprisoned behind the Iron Curtain would remain potential deterrents to

Continued on Page 6, Column 6

HOUSE, 394-4, BACKS DRAFT EXTENSION

Four-Year Continuance Finds the Democrats Unanimous—New Features Added

By C. P. TRUSSELL
Special to The New York Times.

WASHINGTON, Feb. 8—The House of Representatives voted 394 to 4 today to continue the draft for four years.

This extension, the fourth since 1940, was urged by President Eisenhower. The Administration concluded that the international situation generally required the maintenance of the United States armed forces of 2,850,000 officers and men. Such a force, experience had shown, could not be mobilized through voluntary enlistments.

The four who voted against draft extension were Republicans. Democrats supported the move unanimously. The four dissenters were Representatives Noah M. Mason of Illinois, Usher L. Burdick of North Dakota; Clare E. Hoffman of Michigan, and Wint Smith of Kansas.

The extension measure now goes to the Senate. There it is expected to win approval, with its opponents again on the Republican side. No one predicted that the extension would not be approved finally in Congress long before the present draft authorization expires June 30.

In granting the continuance of Selective Service the House added new features to the law. They included:

¶If the selective draft continued it should include all the benefits and allowance given to present draftees to aid their dependents. Also continued for four

Continued on Page 16, Column 4

Private Atom Reactor In This Area Planned

By PETER KIHSS

A plan for the nation's first nuclear reactor entirely owned and operated by private industry was announced here yesterday by the American Machine and Foundry Company. It would use radiations for confidential experiments for co-operating companies.

Gen. Walter Bedell Smith, retired, vice chairman of the foundry concern's board, said invitations to join the scheme had gone to companies in the fields of electronics, petroleum, food, pharmaceutical and chemical products, ceramics, rubber, metals, textiles, agriculture, machinery and others.

The project would occupy 250 acres somewhere in the New York area. A so-called swimming pool reactor would use uranium fuel surrounded by water serving as a moderator, cooler and shield.

The atomic furnace would

Continued on Page 19, Column 3

MIGHT IS STRESSED

Foreign Minister Says Soviet Force Is on Par With West

Excerpts from Molotov speech are printed on Page 6.

Special to The New York Times.

MOSCOW, Feb. 8—Claiming superiority for the Soviet Union in hydrogen weapons, Foreign Minister Vyacheslav M. Molotov delivered to the United States today a warning of the strength of the world Communist forces.

His declaration reiterating the might of the Communist camp was made at a joint session of the Supreme Soviet, the national legislature of the Soviet Union. He spoke immediately following the change in Soviet Premiership that placed Marshal Nikolai A. Bulganin at the head of the Government.

[According to The Associated Press, the Soviet Parliament resumed its joint session at 2 A. M. Wednesday, New York time, and immediately began debating Mr. Molotov's speech.]

Laughter and applause greeted Mr. Molotov's taunts at, and defiance of, the United States, which he singled out as the leader of the "aggressive" Western coalition. He also called on the United States once again to evacuate Formosa.

Balance 'Quite Established'

In one of his most outspoken passages, Mr. Molotov declared that it must be understood that the balance of forces between the Soviet Union and the United States had been "quite established."

Comparing the two and taking into account the vast human and material resources of this country, the strength of its allies, and the justness of its cause, Mr. Molotov declared, "it will become clear that the Soviet Union is no weaker than the United States."

As for atomic strength, he said in an earlier passage that "the aggressive circles of the United States miscalculated again." They thought it would take ten or fifteen years for the Soviet Union to catch up with the United States, he asserted, but "the Soviet people have achieved such success that not the Soviet Union but the United States finds itself in the position of being behind."

In thus belittling and challeng-

Continued on Page 6, Column 4

Associated Press Radiophoto

CHANGE IN HIGH SOVIET COUNCILS: The scene yesterday in Supreme Soviet at Moscow after Marshal Nikolai A. Bulganin was elected to succeed Georgi M. Malenkov. Front row, from left, are Lazar M. Kaganovich, Marshal Bulganin, Nikita S. Khrushchev, Mr. Malenkov and Marshal Kliment E. Voroshilov. At far right in rear is Anastas I. Mikoyan.

SENATE UNIT VOTES FORMOSA TREATY

Committee Ballot Is 11 to 2—Whole Chamber May Adopt Pact by Tomorrow Night

By WILLIAM S. WHITE
Special to The New York Times.

WASHINGTON, Feb. 8—The Senate Foreign Relations Committee approved today the defense treaty with Nationalist China on Formosa. The vote was 11 to 2.

The committee's chairman, Senator Walter F. George, Democrat of Georgia, will take the pact to the Senate tomorrow in the hope that it can be cleared there by Thursday night.

Failing final action by then, there can be none before the week after next.

Beginning Friday, the Senate, by old custom, will have an unofficial holiday from all important business for ten days while Republican speakers celebrate the birthday of Abraham Lincoln.

Mr. George recognized the possibility of delay, though he spoke out against it as undesirable in the light of the changing of com-

Continued on Page 14, Column 2

Khrushchev Comes to Fore In Compromise on Bulganin

The following article is by a member of The Times staff who is a specialist on Soviet affairs.

By HARRY SCHWARTZ

Nikita S. Khrushchev appeared to have emerged yesterday as the most powerful single person in the Soviet Union, the heir to Stalin's mantle.

Stalin ruled the Soviet Union during most of his reign without holding any Government post, content to be general secretary of the Communist party.

It was as first secretary, the new name for general secretary, of the party that Mr. Khrushchev nominated Nikolai A. Bulganin to be Premier. But the largest ovation went to the first secretary, not to the new Premier.

Even before yesterday, Mr. Khrushchev had given abundant testimony that he, not some amorphous "collective leadership," is the leader.

It may be that his power is subject still to the majority of his colleagues in the Presidium of the Central Committee or to the will of the army leaders. But since last December the public image has been of a Mr. Khru-

Continued on Page 4, Column 5

This article is by a reporter of The Times who returned last fall after five years in Moscow.

By HARRISON E. SALISBURY

Marshal Nikolai A. Bulganin almost certainly is a compromise choice as Soviet Premier. He apparently represents a coalition of the party forces of Nikita S. Khrushchev and the army group headed by Marshal Georgi G. Zhukov.

The heralded showdown between Mr. Khrushchev and former Premier Georgi M. Malenkov has occurred more quickly than this observer had expected.

Apparently the army threw its backing to Mr. Khrushchev.

Regardless of the fire and vigor of Foreign Minister Vyacheslav M. Molotov's address yesterday, Soviet power in the international arena will remain weakened for a considerable time. The crisis that resulted in the execution of Deputy Premier Lavrenti P. Beria left little outward signs of cracks in the Kremlin wall. However, it seemed certain the Soviet Government would be a longer time in over-

Continued on Page 4, Column 7

U. S. SEES STRUGGLE AS FAR FROM OVER

Experts on Moscow Conclude It Is Too Early to Decide About Effect of Change

By JAMES RESTON
Special to The New York Times.

WASHINGTON, Feb. 8—The United States Government, concentrating on its plans for blocking Communist expansion, refused to comment today on the battle of the dictators in the Soviet Union.

The capital hummed with speculation all day. But after hours of cooperative guesswork the official experts on the Soviet Union decided to let the events interpret the Moscow changes.

Ambassador Charles E. Bohlen's first official cablegram on the news came in at 7:49 A. M. It was discussed briefly by Secretary of State Dulles at his 9:15 staff conference.

Thereafter the official advisers on the Soviet Union were instructed to analyze the published facts. Their conclusions—far less dogmatic than most opinion in the capital—were as follows:

¶There is trouble in the Soviet "paradise." Premier Georgi M. Malenkov was dismissed not because everything was going well: the dramatic news was a sign, not of Communist strength, but of weakness.

¶Nikita S. Khrushchev, the Communist party boss, is probably the most powerful figure for the moment. But the fierce struggle over succession, always a problem in Russia, even in the time of the czars, is far from over.

¶It is too early to reach any

Continued on Page 7, Column 1

U. S. Plane Downed By Reds in Tachens

By The Associated Press.

WITH UNITED STATES SEVENTH FLEET, in the Tachens, Wednesday, Feb. 9—Red anti-aircraft batteries shot down a United States AD Skyraider plane twenty miles southwest of the Tachen Islands today, the Navy said.

The pilot and two crew members of the carrier-based plane were rescued by the destroyer Isbell, the Navy said.

WASHINGTON, Feb. 8 (AP)—The Navy said tonight that one of its patrol planes received three small holes in one wing from Chinese Communist anti-aircraft fire during the Tachens evacuation today, but returned safely from its mission.

The Navy released a terse message from Vice Admiral Alfred M. Pride:

"Vice Admiral Pride learned during the night that three small holes were discovered in one wing during inspection after returning to base."

All Civilians Off Upper Tachen; First U. S. Ship Returns to Formosa

Associated Press Wirephoto via Radio From Taipei

American and Chinese military personnel, in the foreground, observe the evacuation operation on Upper Tachen Island

Special to The New York Times.

KEELUNG, Formosa, Wednesday, Feb. 9—The first United States Navy ship with Chinese Nationalist civilians evacuated from the Tachen Islands docked here this morning. She was an 8,000-ton transport with 3,816 civilians on board. Vice Admiral Alfred M. Pride, Commander of the United States Seventh Fleet, announced last night that the evacuation of civilians from Upper Tachen Island was completed at 5:17 P. M. yesterday. [In Washington, the Navy announced early Wednesday that the Seventh Fleet had reported that the last "organized group" of civilians had been evacuated from South Tachen Island. The

Continued on Page 14, Column 5

MOSCOW SHAKE-UP

Malenkov Avows Guilt for Shortcomings in Agriculture

Texts of Malenkov statement and Khrushchev speech, Page 2.

By CLIFTON DANIEL
Special to The New York Times.

MOSCOW, Feb. 8—On nomination by Nikita S. Khrushchev, first secretary of the Communist party, Marshal Nikolai A. Bulganin became head of the Soviet Government today. He replaced Georgi M. Malenkov, who had been Premier since the death of Stalin March 5, 1953.

Reproaching himself for inadequate leadership, Mr. Malenkov offered his resignation this afternoon to the Supreme Soviet, national legislature of the Soviet Union.

[News of the resignation was published in a Late City Extra of The New York Times on Tuesday.]

Mr. Malenkov said he would fulfill "with greatest scrupulousness" the duties that would now be assigned to him. Those duties were not stated at once.

In resigning Mr. Malenkov took on himself the "guilt and responsibility" for the present state of Soviet agriculture, which has been roundly criticized by Mr. Khrushchev.

To Support Party Line

Mr. Malenkov also proclaimed his understanding of the Communist party line that forced development of heavy industry must be the basis for increasing agricultural production and all other branches of the Soviet economy. That line has recently been re-emphasized with new firmness by the Central Committee of the party and its propaganda organs.

The Central Committee's decision, taken in the last days of January on the initiative of Mr. Khrushchev, gave orders for still further efforts to increase Soviet agricultural output and Mr. Malenkov said today the decision had revealed to him his shortcomings as an administrator.

The change in the Premiership, accomplished in barely ten minutes of swift political action, left two major questions unanswered for the moment:

What will be Mr. Malenkov's future position and who will be Defense Minister of the Soviet

Continued on Page 2, Column 3

TUNIS LEADER AIDS PINAY ON CABINET

U.S. Bipartisan Idea Adapted by Premier-Designate

By LANSING WARREN
Special to The New York Times.

PARIS, Feb. 8—Premier-designate Antoine Pinay obtained some help today from the Tunisian Premier in his efforts to form a French Cabinet.

After their conference the Tunisian Premier, Tahar ben Ammar, said he had found that he and M. Pinay had similar ideas and that "I hope we shall continue the negotiations that were started with the Government of Mendès-France." M. ben Ammar declared that he was going full of optimism to Tunis to inform the Bey, Sidi Mohammed el Amin, about the consultations.

The statement will be used by M. Pinay in trying to convince the party groups that his Cabinet can handle the crisis in Tunisia.

In dealing with those groups today M. Pinay obtained support from M. Mendès-France's Radical group, but met a rebuff from the Socialists. The Radical executive body voted, 81 to 67, to participate in the Pinay Cabinet. This assures him of about two-thirds of the seventy-six Radical Deputies, who never vote in unison.

The Socialists, through Christian Pineau, former Minister of Finance, declined the invitation to join the Cabinet. M. Pinay had

Continued on Page 11, Column 3

"All the News That's Fit to Print"

The New York Times.

7:30 A. M. EXTRA
Condensation of U. S. Weather Bureau forecast: Mostly sunny and warm today. Mostly fair and warm tomorrow.
Temperature range today: 84—69. Temperature range yesterday: 85.2—67.
Full U. S. Weather Bureau Report, Page 50.

VOL. CV No. 35,978. Entered as Second-Class Matter. Post Office, New York, N. Y. NEW YORK, THURSDAY, JULY 26, 1956. Times Square, New York 36, N. Y. Telephone LAckawanna 4-1000 FIVE CENTS

ANDREA DORIA AND STOCKHOLM COLLIDE; 1,134 PASSENGERS ABANDON ITALIAN SHIP IN FOG AT SEA; ALL SAVED, MANY INJURED

STASSEN SUGGESTS EISENHOWER STATE IF HE IS FOR NIXON

Aide to End Pro-Herter Drive If the President Gives Nod to the Vice President

GETS NO G.O.P. BACKING

Says Hall Tries to Foreclose Choice of Delegates in Advance of Convention

By JAMES RESTON
Special to The New York Times.

WASHINGTON, July 25 — Harold E. Stassen, the loneliest man in Washington, said today he would abandon his anti-Nixon campaign if President Eisenhower personally expressed a preference for Vice President Richard M. Nixon on the 1956 election ticket.

In the absence of such a statement from the President, the White House disarmament aide made it clear that he would continue to advocate the Vice-Presidential nomination of Gov. Christian A. Herter of Massachusetts.

The President has let it be known he was "delighted" that Mr. Nixon was available for the Vice-Presidential nomination. But he has not expressed a clear preference for him over other possible candidates.

Takes Aim at Hall

However, a reliable source informed The New York Times today that Governor Herter agreed to nominate Mr. Nixon for the Vice Presidency yesterday after a telephoned message from the White House saying that it was the President's wish that he do so.

Mr. Stassen was left today without the cooperation of Governor Herter or the public support of a single influential Republican politician.

Nevertheless, he took dead aim both at Mr. Nixon and the chairman of the Republican National Committee, Leonard W. Hall.

The 43-year-old Vice President, Mr. Stassen said, ran last in a private poll he (Stassen) conducted on eight potential Republican Vice-Presidential candidates. He did not say who was polled, or who did the polling, or what questions were asked—only that Mr. Nixon, Governor Herter and Mr. Stassen himself were among the eight.

He also wrote a letter in the middle of last night to Repre-

Continued on Page 8, Column 5

Jordanian Group Attacks U. N. Palestine Truce Unit

Villagers' Fire Wounds One Observer —Burns Scores Incident—Amman Puts the Blame on Israelis

By HOMER BIGART
Special to The New York Times.

JERUSALEM, July 25—Jordanian villagers attacked a team of United Nations military observers today near Jerusalem. Lieut. Col. E. H. Thalin of Sweden was seriously wounded by the Jordanian fire, United Nations sources said.

They reported that the villagers "went berserk" after an exchange of fire with Israelis in which several Jordanians were wounded. During the engagement the Israelis employed mortar fire. There were no Israeli casualties.

[Jordanian sources in Amman said Israeli fire had been responsible. The Amman reports said ten Jordanians were wounded.]

Colonel Thalin was the third United Nations casualty in two days. Yesterday two Canadian officers were seriously wounded in a mine explosion on Mount Scopus.

Maj. Gen. E. L. M. Burns of Canada, United Nations truce supervisor, said tonight that he was "astonished and deeply concerned by the attack by the Jordanian villagers."

He had already made arrangements to confer tomorrow with Maj. Gen. Ali Abu Nuwar, Chief of Staff of the Jordanian Army, on measures to be taken by Jordan to reduce the number of provocative incidents along the Israeli frontier. Israeli's Premier, David Ben-Gurion, has threatened punitive action unless the provocations cease.

The current trouble spot on the frontier is in the Judean hills only five miles from Jerusalem where raw, new houses

Continued on Page 2, Column 3

CRAFT RUSH TO AID

Terse Radio Messages of the Rescue Vessels Depict Operations

Help for the stricken liners Andrea Doria and Stockholm flowed almost instantly from all points of the compass to the spot at which they collided last night.

Ships large and small, Coast Guard vessels, luxury liners, Gloucester fishing boats, coastal steamers, all headed for the spot off Nantucket Lightship where the lives of some 2,500 persons were in danger.

It was 11:22 last night when the ships collided in a dense fog. The Andrea Doria, luxury liner of the Italian Line, shaken dangerously despite a double hull and other special safety features, sent out the first SOS less than a minute later.

The Coast Guard, with stations at Cape Ann, Cape Cod, Boston and other near-by points, sent out every available craft as soon as the position of the crash had been determined. Then came reassuring promises of help from the Ile de France and other craft, within quick reach of the spot.

The Search and Rescue Division of the Coast Guard in New York received its first alert at 11:25 last night. It was then that the Coast Guard radio station at East Moriches, L. I., notified New York headquarters:

"Andrea Doria and Stockholm collided 11:22 local time Lat. 40:30 N., Long. 69:53 W."

Coast Guard Cutters Aid

The East Moriches radio had picked up simultaneous SOS messages from the ships a minute or two before. The next hour was spent verifying positions and notifying all Coast Guard and merchant ships of the disaster and calling on them for help. The Coast Guard sent out ten cutters from New York, Boston and New London, Conn., and diverted three other ships cruising in that area.

The stark drama being played on the open ocean in darkness and fog was pictured in tense, taut radio messages recorded by the wireless room of The New York Times. They read:

12:21 A. M.—S. S. Stockholm says: Badly damaged. The whole bow crushed and No. 1 hold filled with water. Have to stay in our position. If you [Andrea Doria] can lower your lifeboats we can pick them up.

12:21 A. M.—S. S. Andrea Doria replied: You have to row to us.

12:38 A. M.—S. S. Cape Ann reports: Now between the two ships and her boats are ready. Has two lifeboats.

12:45 A. M. Coast Guard boat says: Ten miles away; have eighteen boats.

1:12 A. M. Andrea Doria says: Needs more lifeboats still.

1:13 A. M. Unidentified ship, when queried, says: We have twelve lifeboats.

Stricken Ship's Boats Useless

1:21 A. M. Cape Ann asks Doria: How close do you want our ship to come to you?

1:24 A. M. Cape Ann reports: We have two boats for Andrea. Now proceeding to get close to her.

1:26 A. M. Andrea Doria reports: Danger immediate, need lifeboats, as many as possible. Can't use our lifeboats.

1:30 A. M. Stockholm gives position: Lat. 40:34 N; Long. 69:45 W.

1:33 A. M. Cape Ann asks Andrea: Want Cape Ann to move in any closer than Cape Ann is now?

1:34 A. M. Ile de France says: We are nine miles from you. Will launch as many boats as possible.

1:43 A. M. Doria repeats earlier message: Here danger immediate. Need lifeboats, as many as possible. Can't use our lifeboats.

1:46 A. M. Unidentified ship radios Andrea: Two lifeboats on way over to you.

1:53 A. M. S. S. Manaqui radios both ships: Will arrive yours at 0900 G. M. T. (5 A. M., E. D. T.) Have two lifeboats.

1:54 A. M. Andrea replies: O. K. Thanks.

1:56 A. M. Unidentified Nor-

Continued on Page 15, Column 1

The New York Times

The 29,000-ton Italian Line vessel, the Andrea Doria, which carried 1,134 passengers

The 12,644-ton Swedish American liner Stockholm, largest liner ever built in Sweden

2D VESSEL IS SAFE

Ile de France In Today With Survivors From Crash Off Nantucket

By MAX FRANKEL

The trans-Atlantic liners Andrea Doria and Stockholm collided in a heavy Atlantic fog at 11:22 o'clock last night, forty-five miles south of Nantucket Island.

The Andrea Doria ordered her 1,134 passengers aboard to abandon ship. All were reported to have been rescued at 4:58 A. M. There was no immediate word, however, on the fate of her crew of 575.

At 5:15 A. M. today, however, the Ile de France reported from the scene that no more help was needed.

The French Liner estimated at 7 A. M. that she would arrive in New York shortly after 6 o'clock this afternoon with 1,000 survivors from the Andrea Doria. It was not clear to which ports the other survivors would be taken.

The Stockholm, although it had taken water through a crushed bow, was able to keep her 550 passengers and crew of 200 aboard. She was waiting for an escort to attempt to return to New York at a slow speed.

Many survivors of the Italian ship were said to have been seriously injured. The Stockholm said she had five "critical" cases aboard. Desperate and repeated calls for medical assistance were radioed from the score of rescue vessels in the area.

Deck Dips Into Water

The Andrea Doria lay helpless in the thick fog. The black-and-white ship reported she was listing "very badly." She gave no other indication of the extent or nature of her damage nor was there word whether she could remain afloat.

The Stockholm reported at 6 A. M. that the Andrea Doria's main deck was dipping to the surface of the water.

The 29,000-ton Italian Line vessel apparently was listing so severely that she could launch no more than two of her lifeboats. Her lifeboats can carry 2,000 persons.

The French Ile de France, largest of the rescue vessels on hand, and the Stockholm apparently recovered the bulk of the Andrea Doria's passengers. At one time as many as 100 lifeboats probably were in the area. It was not clear how the passengers were loaded into the lifeboats.

At 4:58, the master of the Ile de France told the Stockholm:

"All passengers rescued.

"Proceeding to New York full speed."

The Ile de France left New York yesterday bound for Le Havre.

Since shortly after the collision, the Andrea Doria had run her lights and radio on emergency power and said she did not how much longer she could keep in touch with rescue craft. Her radio was so weak the Stock-

Continued on Page 14, Column 5

DOWNTOWN TO GET 4TH NEW BUILDING

25-Story Structure Is Slated on Broad Street Site of R. C. A. Communications

By GLENN FOWLER

Another large office building is soon to rise in the downtown Manhattan financial district.

The building, the fourth large structure to be planned in the area within the last two years, will be twenty-five stories high. It will cover the block front on Beaver Street between Broad and New Streets, near Bowling Green.

It will stand on a plot of 48,000 square feet, running back 215 feet along Broad Street and 200 feet along New Street.

To be known as 60 Broad Street, the building will have an aluminum facade and a beacon light atop the roof. It will be fully air-conditioned, will have acoustic ceilings and will be equipped with operatorless elevators. Garage space will be provided in the basement. There will be 650,000 square feet of floor space above the ground floor.

The property on which the structure will be built is owned by R. C. A. Communications,

Continued on Page 41, Column 2

CONFEREES VOTE 3.7 BILLION IN AID

Reappropriated Fund Lifts Total to $4,006,570,000—Curb on Tito Supported

Special to The New York Times.

WASHINGTON, July 25—Conferees from the Senate and House of Representatives agreed today on a compromise foreign aid appropriation of $3,766,570,000.

This sum to carry the Mutual Security Program for another year would be increased by $240,000,000 of reappropriated money to a total of $4,006,570,000.

The bargain struck by the conferees amounted to a substantially even split between the $4,110,920,000 in new money originally allocated by the Senate and the $3,425,120,000 provided originally by the House.

President Eisenhower initially had asked for $4,900,000,000 for the fiscal year that opened July 1, although the appropriation for the fiscal year just ended was only $2,700,000,000.

Retained by the conferees was a rider in the Senate bill directing President Eisenhower not to give new military assistance funds to Communist Yugoslavia except for spare parts and replacements.

This stipulation was primarily the work of the Senate Republican leader, William F. Knowland of California. It did not affect $100,000,000 in military aid to Yugoslavia that already is "in the pipeline," nor did it

Continued on Page 12, Column 3

Eisenhower's Four Years

An Analysis of Agriculture Policy And Steps Taken to Meet Problems

This is the fifth of a series of articles analyzing the record of the Eisenhower Administration at the start of the Presidential election campaign.

By WILLIAM M. BLAIR
Special to The New York Times.

WASHINGTON, July 25—President Eisenhower has faced a number of stubborn dilemmas in the last four years but no other problem on the home front has been comparable to the one on farms.

Like the Communist problem overseas, it has absorbed his attention. From time to time it has been mitigated by his policies. Always, however, it has returned to plague him in one form or another.

In his home town of Abilene, Kan., in mid-1952 the President began formulating his program to reconcile freedom and prosperity for the American farmer. As he put it later, "full parity in the market place" and a minimum of Government regulation were his aims.

It has been a long, perplexing struggle for the President. But despite a notable effort, success has eluded him. The farmer still is tied up in Government controls and has considerably less cash in his pockets.

Every new Administration inherits the past. Thus twenty years of Democratic and often bipartisan farm policies have failed, despite high Federal subsidies, to solve the boom and bust ills that have beset agriculture in the midst of an expanding industrial economy and national prosperity.

Indeed, President Eisenhower and his embattled Secretary of Agriculture, Ezra Taft Benson, have blamed these policies and the last two wars for the surpluses that have resisted their remedies and have depressed farm prices.

From a peak of $15,943,000,000 in 1948, farm income fell to $12,851,000,000 in 1950, before the Korean war. It climbed to $14,801,000,000 in 1951, slipped to $14,051,000,000 in the Presiden-

Continued on Page 13, Column 1

Ailing Millikin Plans To Leave the Senate

By WILLIAM S. WHITE
Special to The New York Times.

WASHINGTON, July 25—Senator Eugene D. Millikin of Colorado, a powerful member of the Republican leadership, said a farewell today in the Senate.

He was compelled by long and agonizing illness to announce that he would not seek re-election in the fall.

The decision was a heavy blow to the Republican party generally, and to its conservative wing in particular.

Mr. Millikin as a well campaigner would have been a formidable favorite to keep his seat safe for the Republicans. Even as an ailing prospective campaigner he had been greatly feared by the Democrats.

His retirement seemed plainly to forward Democratic prospects for retaining control

Continued on Page 10, Column 3

SHIPS' PIERS QUIET IN NEW YORK PORT

Crowds Expected at Andrea Doria's Docks—Relatives Begin Calling Lines

The sea diaster had not early today awakened the pier at West Forty-fourth Street where the Andrea Doria had been scheduled to dock later in the morning.

This pier, as well as the terminal at West Fifty-seventh Street, where the Stockholm had left just before noon yesterday in a gala sailing, remained dark and quiet.

However, unaccustomed night lights began blinking on at the Italian Line's office at 24 State Street before 4 o'clock when members of the company's staff began arriving.

They had been rounded up from their scattered homes around the Metropolitan area by officials of the line under Rosmino Pernigotti, assistant general manager of the company here.

The company officials were making plans to handle expected crowds at West Forty-fourth Street during the morning. Several thousand visitors were expected to begin gathering there by 8 o'clock, some not knowing about the collision.

It is an axiom in the harbor that every arriving passenger attracts five or more relatives and friends as welcomers, and the Italian Line officials were preparing to give them the tragic news and to forestall a rush by worried relatives on the line's downtown office.

Many of the relatives already knew of the crash at sea, and the office and pier of the com-

Continued on Page 14, Column 3

Many Notables Are Listed Aboard the Andrea Doria

Persons prominent in business, the theatre, politics, journalism and government were among the passengers aboard the Andrea Doria when she collided last night with the Stockholm. Two directors of the Standard Oil Company (New Jersey) were on the passenger list. They were Stewart Coleman, traveling with his family, and Marion W. Boyer, accompanied by his wife. Mr. Coleman, 57 years old, lives at 365 Barrett Road, Cedarhurst, L. I. Mr. Boyer, 54, lives in Greenwich, Conn.

Another passenger was Richardson Dilworth, Mayor of Philadelphia, and his wife. Mr. Dilworth, a lawyer by profession, is 57. He served as a Marine in both World Wars, and received the Purple Heart in World War I and the Silver Star in World War II.

Ruth Roman, Hollywood motion picture star, and her son, Richard Hall, were on the Andrea Doria. Miss Roman recently divorced Mortimer Hall, owner of a Los Angeles radio station.

Two refugees from behind the Iron Curtain, the dancers Istvan Rabovsky and his wife Nora Kovach, also were passengers. They are natives of Hungary. In May, 1953, they fled to the West from East Berlin, where they had gone for a dancing engagement. In 1954, they came to this country.

Also on board were Camille M. Cianfarra, Madrid correspondent of The New York Times, and his family. A native of New York, Mr. Cianfarra joined The Times in 1935 in Rome. He became a specialist in Vatican affairs, and has written two books about the Vatican; He became Madrid correspondent in 1951.

Others on board included Ferdinand M. Thieriot, circulation manager of The San Francisco

Continued on Page 15, Column 5

SHIP BUILT TO TAKE COLLISION SAFELY

Andrea Doria Hull Divided to Give Stability—Lifeboats Could Carry 2,000

The Andrea Doria was specially built to give her more stability in case of just such a collision as she had last night with the Stockholm.

The hull was subdivided into eleven watertight compartments extending the entire length of the ship. Bulkheads parallel with her engine rooms were designed to lessen the effect of a collision.

The ship carried lifeboats with a capacity of 2,000 persons. Some of these boats were made of light metal alloy and were hung from davits operated by motor-driven winches. Two of the boats were motor-driven and fitted with radios.

Luxurious to the last detail, the ship was completely fireproofed and radar-equipped.

The ship has two groups of turbines capable of generating 50,000 horsepower to turn its three blade propellors, each weighing sixteen tons. They are nineteen feet in diameter and turn 143 revolutions a minute.

The Andrea Doria and the Stockholm had been the prides of the Italian and Swedish merchant marines.

The Stockholm, when launched in 1948, was the largest passenger vessel ever to have been built in Swedish yards. The Andrea Doria, when launched in 1951, was the last word in modern design and comfort. Each was flagship of its line until supplanted by new vessels a few years later.

When she went into service as flagship of the Swedish American Line, the Stockholm had a capacity of 364 passengers and 150 officers and crew. Alterations in 1953 increased the capacity to nearly 600 passengers with a proportionate increase in the size of the crew.

The Stockholm had an over-all length of 510 feet and a beam of

Continued on Page 15, Column 6

Cause of the Crash Puzzles Radar Men

Experts on radar said today they could not explain how the collision between the Andrea Doria and the Stockholm could have taken place because both vessels were equipped with radar equipment.

They said that even with the "visibility nil" conditions reported in the vicinity each ship should have been able to observe the other for distances up to fifty miles.

The experts declared that, even without knowing precisely what systems the vessels carried, they almost certainly were flexible installations such as are standard on large passenger vessels. They should have been capable of two types of operation—generalized scanning all about the vessel, and a narrower type of observation of a restricted sector of the horizon.

They should also have been

Continued on Page 14, Column 6

The New York Times July 26, 1956

SCENE OF THE COLLISION: The liners Andrea Doria and the Stockholm stricken off Nantucket Island (cross).

"All the News That's Fit to Print"

The New York Times.

LATE CITY EDITION
Scattered showers, warm and humid today and tomorrow.
Temperature Range Today—Max., 79; Min., 65
Temperature Yesterday—Max., 74; Min., 67
Full U.S. Weather Bureau Report, Page 69

VOL. CVI—No. 36,074. Entered as Second-Class Matter, Post Office, New York, N. Y. NEW YORK, TUESDAY, OCTOBER 30, 1956. Times Square, New York 36, N. Y. Telephone Lackawanna 4-1000 FIVE CENTS

ISRAELIS THRUST INTO EGYPT AND NEAR SUEZ; U.S. GOES TO U.N. UNDER ANTI-AGGRESSION PACT

Budapest Rebels Refuse to Yield Until Soviet Troops Leave

EISENHOWER BIDS SOUTH FIGHT BIAS ON A 'LOCAL BASIS'

In Miami He Stresses Roles of States—Hails Byrd in Speech in Virginia

Texts of Eisenhower speeches are on Pages 24 and 25.

By RUSSELL BAKER
Special to The New York Times.

RICHMOND, Va., Oct. 29—President Eisenhower, campaigning in the South today, urged that the problem of achieving racial equality be handled largely "on a local and state basis."

He told a Miami Airport audience he was convinced that progress today in equality of opportunity and equality before the law had "to be achieved finally in the hearts of men rather than in legislative halls."

The President was applauded lightly when he said that "there must be intelligent understanding of the human factors and emotions involved if we are to make steady progress in the matter rather than simply to make political promises never intended to be kept."

In the field of civil rights, he added, he had tried to bring "reason, good sense and good judgment to the performance of clear duty."

Makes 1,800-Mile Trip

Though he delivered three airport speeches in an 1,800-mile aerial campaign in Florida and Virginia, he touched on the civil rights issue only once.

That was in Miami, in the President's first speech today.

In Jacksonville, Fla., and Richmond, Va., where the southern tradition is stronger than in Miami, he did not discuss the racial theme. Nor did he refer directly in any of his speeches to the controversial school integration issue or the Supreme Court decision.

He concentrated instead on three matters: peace, prosperity and attacks on the Democratic ticket.

And at Miami General Eisenhower tried for the first time the handshaking style of campaigning developed to a high art by Senator Estes Kefauver.

Surrounded by several hundred rabid admirers on his way to his plane after speaking, he shook hands by the score with a zest rarely matched by Senator Kefauver and a folksiness as impressive as the Senator's own.

"Hi ya, folks," he said, and

Continued on Page 24, Column 4

Stevenson Says U.S. Gets 'Less Than Truth' on Strife

Charges President Endangered the Nation by 'Good News' From the Mideast—Boston Crowds Hail Candidate

By HARRISON E. SALISBURY
Special to The New York Times.

BOSTON, Oct. 29—Adlai E. Stevenson charged tonight that President Eisenhower had given the nation reassurances about the Middle East that had been "tragically less than the truth."

"The Government has not been telling us the whole truth," Mr. Stevenson said.

Texts of Stevenson statement and speech, Page 28.

The Presidential nominee addressed an overflow Democratic throng of more than 8,000 in Mechanics Hall in the climax of his drive for Massachusetts' sixteen electoral votes.

Mr. Stevenson's address was televised nationally by the American Broadcasting Company. After the telecast was completed, Mr. Stevenson appended one of his sharpest challenges to President Eisenhower's leadership. The Democrat declared:

"I deeply believe that we cannot afford another four years under a part-time leader of a party which will not plan, which will not create, which will not dare to see the vision of a new America and make that vision come true.

"As a campaigning politician there is none better. It is as a performing politician, as a President who knows how to control his own party, who knows how to grasp the reins of Government that he fails."

Several times Mr. Stevenson's partisan audience booed references to the President. The chorus of boos every time he mentioned Vice President Richard M. Nixon started the moment the crowd sensed that Mr.

Continued on Page 29, Column 5

POLAND'S LEADERS BACK HUNGARIANS

Support Demands for Exit of Soviet Troops—Call for End of Strife

By SYDNEY GRUSON
Special to The New York Times.

WARSAW, Oct. 29—The Polish Communist party, differing sharply once again with the Soviet Union, came out formally today in support of Hungarian demands for the withdrawal of Soviet troops from Hungary.

Yesterday the new leadership of the Polish United Workers (Communist) party rejected the Soviet allegation that foreign agents and counter-revolutionaries were responsible for the Hungarian tragedy. Today the Poles stood up again on the side of the Hungarians.

An appeal to those on both sides of the barricades in Hungary to halt fratricidal strife was issued by Wladyslaw Gomulka, the Polish party's First Secretary, and by Premier Jozef Cyrankiewicz.

Emphasizing the growing insistence here for independence in foreign as well as internal affairs, the party statement ignored the Soviet charges of Western interference in Hungary.

For the Poles the statement of solidarity was a means of publicly expressing their appreciation for Hungarian help when Poland was threatened by the Soviet leaders a week ago. Poland escaped Hungary's fate

Continued on Page 22, Column 1

PRESIDENT GIVEN MINNESOTA LEAD

Resurvey Finds Him Moving Ahead in a Close Contest

A Times Team Report

Teams of New York Times reporters have recently surveyed political trends in twenty-seven closely contested states. They are now rechecking the most doubtful states. Following is a resurvey report from Leonard Buder, Donald Janson and W. H. Lawrence.

By DONALD JANSON
Special to The New York Times.

MINNEAPOLIS, Oct. 28—President Eisenhower appears to hold a tenuous lead in the race for Minnesota's eleven electoral votes.

A month ago New York Times reporters found the President and Adlai E. Stevenson running neck and neck in this state. The Eisenhower victory margin of four years ago—155,000 out of 1,379,000 votes cast — had buckled under the impact of defections by farmers who were caught in a cost-price vise.

The farm revolt remains strong today in some areas.

Continued on Page 26, Column 2

Russians Befriend One Hungarian City

By HOMER BIGART
Special to The New York Times.

GYOR, Hungary, Oct. 29—The small Soviet garrison of this industrial city has retired to a near-by wood, giving the townspeople free rein to rally and shout against the Nagy Government and demand democratic national elections.

The Russians here must be credited with sensible behavior. They abandoned their barracks a few days ago under no pressure and took to the wood.

There the Soviet officers are living with their wives and children in tents. They have not shot anyone. The townspeople show their gratitude by taking the Russians eggs and milk.

And although Gyor has

Continued on Page 13, Column 1

FIGHTING PERSISTS

Russians Still Pulling Out, With Hungarian Units Taking Over

Text of editorial in Communist newspaper on Page 10.

By ELIE ABEL
Special to The New York Times.

VIENNA, Tuesday, Oct. 30—Soviet troops remained in control of Budapest this morning while the Government of Imre Nagy pleaded with the stubborn revolutionaries to lay down their arms.

But the rebels refused to give up the fight until Mr. Nagy had made good on his promise that the Soviet forces would evacuate the battered city, monitored reports from the Hungarian capital said.

This morning the Budapest radio broadcast the following communiqué:

"While Soviet forces are being withdrawn from Budapest, Hungarian police and armed youth units are maintaining order. Such armed groups as are still resisting will lay down their arms at 9 A. M. [3 A. M. New York time] and will then take part in maintaining order."

[Up to 5 A. M. New York time there had been no further reports on the situation in Hungary.]

Appeal Is Pressed

Earlier this morning the Budapest radio broadcast an appeal by Karoly Janda, Defense Minister, to the rebels to lay down their arms before 9 A. M.

In spite of the gradual Soviet withdrawal, fighting in Budapest flared up again last night. Soviet tank forces engaged in heavy combat in several parts of the city. Latest reports said artillery fire was heard in Budapest all night.

Rebels from eastern Hungary and from the region of Gyor in the west were understood to have joined the insurgents in the capital.

The rebel-held Miskolc radio in northeast Hungary, in a broadcast monitored here, urged anti-Communists in Budapest not to lay down their arms before the last Soviet soldier had left the country.

A general strike called by the rebel leaders appeared to be continuing in many parts of Hungary for the fifth day. Most factory workers, railroad men and miners stayed away from their jobs again this morning despite pressing appeals from Mr. Nagy's Government to resume work.

Nearly complete was an unofficial school strike. Instead of attending classes many teenagers in Budapest did courier work for the rebels and even

Continued on Page 10, Column 4

Patrols in Budapest Are Trigger-Happy From Propaganda

By JOHN MacCORMAC
Special to The New York Times.

BUDAPEST, Hungary, Oct. 29—The seventh day of the Hungarian revolution has dawned with Soviet soldiers still patrolling the Budapest streets despite a promise by Hungary's new Government that they would be withdrawn. The Government had qualified its announcement yesterday with the condition "as soon as order has been completely restored."

As far as could be learned, armed resistance in Budapest has ceased, even in the Maria Theresa barracks in Ulloi Ut, which was holding out late yesterday. But that order can ever be completely restored in Budapest as long as the Russians are here seems unlikely because of the fears and propaganda with which the Soviet troops seem to be filled.

At 10 o'clock last night, for instance, a Soviet soldier guarding an area known as Szent Istvan Ut shot and seriously wounded Noel Barber, London Daily Mail correspondent. Mr. Barber had been making a tour of inspection to get the public's reaction to Premier Imre Nagy's announcement that there would be no further firing and that the insurrection had been recognized by his Government as

Continued on Page 15, Column 1

1950 PLEDGE CITED

White House Recalls Promise to Assist Victim of Attack

By DANA ADAMS SCHMIDT
Special to The New York Times.

WASHINGTON, Oct. 29—The United States will take the movement of Israeli forces into Egypt to the United Nations Security Council tomorrow morning.

The planned appeal to the United Nations was announced by the White House tonight after President Eisenhower had held an emergency meeting there with Secretary of State Dulles and six other high officials.

[An emergency meeting of the Security Council was set for 11 A. M. Tuesday.]

The White House statement follows:

"At the meeting, the President recalled that the United States under this and prior Administrations has pledged itself to assist the victim of any aggression in the Middle East. We shall honor our pledge.

"The United States is in consultation with the British and French Governments, parties with us to the tripartite declaration of 1950, and the United States plans as contemplated by that declaration that the situation shall be taken to the United Nations Security Council tomorrow morning.

Special Session in Abeyance

"The question of whether and when the President will call a special session of the Congress will be decided in the light of the unfolding situation."

The statement was read by James C. Hagerty, Presidential press secretary. He said it had the full authority of the President and the other conferees.

Others at the meeting, in addition to Mr. Dulles, were Charles E. Wilson, Secretary of Defense; Admiral Arthur W. Radford, Chairman of the Joint Chiefs of Staff; Sherman Adams, Assistant to the President; Herbert Hoover Jr., Under Secretary of State; Allen W. Dulles, director of the Central Intelligence Agency, and Wilton B. Persons, deputy assistant to the President.

The one-and-a-half-hour meeting at the White House took place immediately after the President's return by air from a campaign trip in Florida and Virginia.

The State Department said Americans "not performing essential services" would be asked to leave the Middle East. Among the first to leave was a group that flew from Israel to Athens.

Earlier, Secretary of State Dulles had initiated the joint steps with Britain and France.

The State Department an-

Continued on Page 3, Column 1

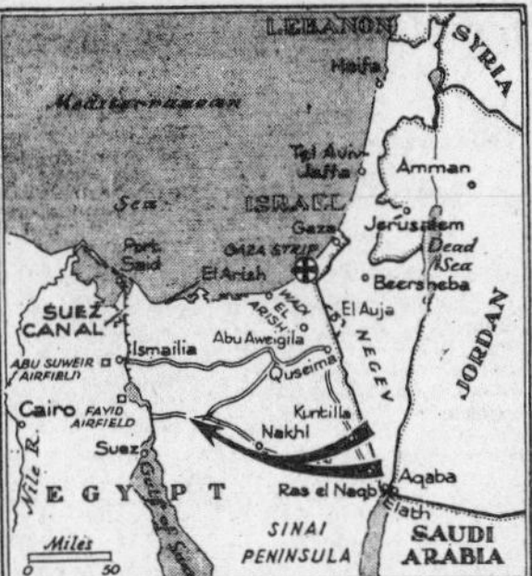

The New York Times Oct. 30, 1956

ISRAELIS OPEN DRIVE: The advance into Egypt was reported made at and below Kuntilla, with a thrust near the Suez Canal. There was a flare-up in Gaza area (cross).

Cairo Says Egyptian Units Have Engaged the Israelis

By The United Press.

CAIRO, Tuesday, Oct. 30—The Egyptian Army said today it had begun "liquidating" an Israeli force that had thrust deep into Egyptian territory toward the Suez Canal. Egyptian army headquarters announced that the Israeli force had suffered "heavy casualties" in the night-long fighting. It gave no precise figures.

"The enemy's plan to penetrate deep inside Egyptian territory failed," the Egyptian communiqué said. "Egyptian armed forces early this morning started liquidating the enemy forces."

[Iraq informed Egypt early Tuesday that Iraqi troops were ready to offer immediate assistance against the Israeli thrust, The Associated Press said. The offer was announced after an urgent morning meeting of Premier Nuri as-Said's Cabinet in Baghdad.]

Leaves Are Canceled

The high command of the Egyptian armed forces recalled all officers and enlisted men on leave to meet the Israeli threat. Orders broadcast by the Cairo radio said all must "report immediately to their units." Reservists were not affected.

The Egyptian communiqué identified the three frontier checkpoints where it said the Israeli raiders had been halted at Kuntilla, Nekhet and El Mimet. All are on the eastern side of the rocky Sinai Peninsula.

[No additional details on the fighting were received up to 5 A. M.]

Suez Canal authorities in Cairo said the situation along the waterway was normal. They said no blackout has been imposed and no emergency alert sounded.

Continued on Page 6, Column 2

FRANCE ACCUSES FIVE OF TREASON

Files Formal Charges Against Algerians Seized in Plane—Sends Aide to Tunisia

By ROBERT C. DOTY
Special to The New York Times.

PARIS, Oct. 29—Five leaders of the Algerian rebellion, seized a week ago, were formally charged today with treason against France. The offense is punishable by death.

The five are Mohammed ben Bella, Mohammed Khider, Mustafa Lachraf, Mohammed Boudiaf and Hossein Ait Ahmed, all members of the Algerian National Liberation Front, which has directed the two-year rebellion against France from headquarters in Cairo.

Their arrest Oct. 22, while aboard a Moroccan plane flying to a conference of North African leaders in Tunis, set off a wave of anti-French protest and violence. Arab anger was based on the theory that the five men were under the protection of Sultan Mohammed V of Morocco, with tacit French consent, at the time of their arrest.

[In the United Nations Security Council, France formally charged Egypt with gun-running for the Algerian rebels.]

As Algerians, the five seized rebel leaders are French citizens, hence subject to a treason

Continued on Page 10, Column 2

Maria Callas Bows At Opening of 'Met'

By ROSS PARMENTER

Bellini's "Norma" has never been notably popular in this country. But last night, when it opened the Metropolitan Opera's seventy-second season, it established a compound record. Never have so many Americans tried to pay so much money to hear an opera.

The actual sum paid by those who managed to crowd into the opera house was $75,510.50. This exceeded by more than $10,000 the previous box-office record of $65,336, which was set with the opening night "Faust" in 1953. The larger sum, though, was not paid by a larger number of persons. After all, sell-outs have been customary on first nights, and fire regulations re-

Continued on Page 42, Column 4

DEEP DRIVE MADE

Tel Aviv Declares Aim Is to Smash Egyptian Commando Bases

Text of Israeli statement will be found on Page 4.

By MOSHE BRILLIANT
Special to The New York Times.

TEL AVIV, Israel, Oct. 29—An Israeli military force thrust into the Sinai Peninsula of Egypt today. It was reported to have reached within twenty miles of the Suez Canal.

Army sources said the Israelis were west of the crossroads where the road to Kuntilla branches off from the Suez-Qusaima highway.

The Israelis were said to have halted there and to have dug in.

A Foreign Ministry statement said the operation had been started "to eliminate the Egyptian fedayeen [commando squad] bases in the Sinai Peninsula."

Army sources said the Israelis had smashed the Egyptian position at Kuntilla and Ras el Naqb at the southern end of the international border. The forces then advanced more than seventy-five miles.

No fighting was reported on the northern end of the border or in the Gaza Strip, which is heavily populated.

'Too Big for a Reprisal'

Reports from the Sinai area described the fighting as "too big for a reprisal and too small for a war." Details of the fighting were not available tonight, but reliable sources said there had been no aerial bombardment of Egyptian positions.

It was not clear tonight whether the Israelis proposed to push on to the Suez Canal or withdraw to Israeli territory, as they have done after reprisal raids. A high official said: "I do not know. It depends on developments."

Yesterday the Israeli Government attributed its decision to call up reserves to what it said was a renewal of commando activities, to the Egyptian-Jordanian-Syrian military alliance negotiated last Wednesday, to Arab declarations that "their principal concern is a war of destruction against Israel" and to the movement of Iraqi forces to Jordan's border.

According to information here, the Egyptians have a considerable part of their Army in the Sinai Peninsula. Their land forces are reported equipped with the

Continued on Page 5, Column 5

CITY SCHOOL AIDES SPUR INTEGRATION

District Lines Are Shifted in Some Brooklyn Areas

By BENJAMIN FINE

Without any public announcement, the Board of Education has quietly begun a program to integrate white and Negro pupils in areas where a segregation pattern has existed in the past.

A score of schools in the Bedford-Stuyvesant area of Brooklyn have become interracial since the fall term opened. Children are taken from the all-Negro schools and put into the formerly all-white schools.

At the same time, fairly large groups of children—ranging from fifty to 200—have been taken from a number of all-white schools and placed in the all-Negro schools. In doing this the board has amended or discarded the old district and school zoning regulations.

This step is part of a "positive program" on integration, Charles H. Silver, Board of Education president, said yesterday. The board has asked its forty assistant superintendents to do everything possible to place Negro and white children in the same schools.

The superintendents not someth

Continued on Page 30, Column

Associated Press Radiophoto

AMERICANS LEAVE ISRAEL: Wives and children of State Department personnel boarding Air Force transport plane last night at Lydda Airport near Jerusalem. They were flown to Athens. More dependents are to follow today.

"All the News That's Fit to Print"

NEWS SUMMARY AND INDEX, PAGE 95

The New York Times.

LATE CITY EDITION
Condensation of U. S. Weather Bureau forecast:
Considerable cloudiness, seasonably cool today and tomorrow.
Temperature range today: 58—49.
Temperature range yesterday: 53.8—48.2.
Full U. S. Weather Bureau Report, Page 95.

SECTION ONE

VOL. CVI . . No. 36,079. Entered as Second-Class Matter, Post Office, New York, N. Y. NEW YORK, SUNDAY, NOVEMBER 4, 1956. Including Magazine and Book Review. TWENTY-FIVE CENTS

SOVIET ATTACKS HUNGARY, SEIZES NAGY; U. S. LEGATION IN BUDAPEST UNDER FIRE; MINDSZENTY IN REFUGE WITH AMERICANS

U. N. Assembly Backs Call to Set Up Mideast Truce Force

STEVENSON HOLDS PRESIDENT LACKS 'ENERGY' FOR JOB

In Last Big Address, He Asks if Nation Is Prepared to Accept Nixon as Leader

Stevenson statement, Page 72; text of speech, Page 73.

By HARRISON E. SALISBURY
Special to The New York Times.

CHICAGO, Nov. 3—Adlai E. Stevenson charged tonight that President Eisenhower "now lacks the energy" to cope with world problems such as the present crisis in the Middle East.

He asked the nation whether it was prepared to accept Richard M. Nixon "as Commander in Chief to exercise power over peace and war."

"Every consideration," Mr. Stevenson said, "the President's age, his health and the fact that he cannot succeed himself make it inevitable that the dominant figure in the Republican party under a second Eisenhower term would be Richard Nixon."

This was the first time that Mr. Stevenson in direct fashion had raised the question of General Eisenhower's health, his physical strength and his ability to survive his full term if reelected.

It placed—on the eve of the election—the question of General Eisenhower's age and his health directly in the forefront of the campaign.

Nixon Draws Boos

Mr. Stevenson's every reference to Mr. Nixon brought forth a hurricane of boos that was equaled only by several waves of boos for General Eisenhower's foreign policy and references to the asserted errors of John Foster Dulles, Secretary of State.

Mr. Stevenson's remarks, which were carried to the nation by television, were cut off the air on a chorus of boos for Mr. Nixon. The conclusion of his address ran over the allotted air time.

General Eisenhower is 66 years old. Mr. Stevenson had foresworn any discussion of the President's health, insisting that this was a matter for each individual voter.

However, in charging tonight that the crisis in world affairs had stemmed directly from the President's "part-time conduct" of his office, Mr. Stevenson took a look into the future.

The fact is, he asserted, General Eisenhower "in the next years would inevitably recede more and more from the picture."

The President, Mr. Stevenson

Continued on Page 73, Column 2

London, Paris Bar Truce; Eden Pledges Israeli Exit

U. N. Occupation Offered

By HAROLD CALLENDER
Special to The New York Times.

PARIS, Nov. 3—Britain and France rejected today the United Nations call for a cease-fire in the Suez area.

At the same time they made a counter-proposal designed to bring their independent military action under the authority of the United Nations. They thus sought to heal the breach between the two powers on the one hand and the United Nations and the United States on the other.

The United Nations General Assembly recommended the cease-fire Thursday by adopting a resolution introduced by the United States.

The two European powers de-

Continued on Page 18, Column 1

Prime Minister Speaks

By DREW MIDDLETON
Special to The New York Times.

LONDON, Nov. 3—The British Government will insure the withdrawal of Israeli forces from Egyptian territory once British and French troops have occupied

Eden's text and Gaitskell excerpts are on Page 28.

key points on the Suez Canal, Sir Anthony Eden declared tonight.

The objective of his policy of intervention in the Middle East is a lasting settlement in the area and a stronger United Nations, able "to act as well as to talk," the Prime Minister told

Continued on Page 28, Column 6

EISENHOWER PLANS TALKS TOMORROW

To Make 2 Short Speeches on TV—Mitchell Reports Advances by Labor

By CHARLES E. EGAN
Special to The New York Times.

WASHINGTON, Nov. 3—Politics held an active, if subordinate, role in White House operations on this Saturday before election.

While the President was closeted with advisers in discussions of events in the Middle East and Europe, his top aides found time:

¶To consult with Leonard W. Hall, chairman of the Republican National Committee, on campaign strategy.

¶To issue a special report by James P. Mitchell, Secretary of Labor, detailing aid given to workers by his department under the present Administration.

¶To give a preliminary outline of the President's two Election Eve television appearances on Monday.

Mr. Hall arrived at the White House at 11:30 this morning. He spent more than an hour there first with Sherman Adams, the Assistant to the President, and later with James C. Hagerty, White House press secretary.

Continued on Page 78, Column 4

DULLES IS GAINING AFTER OPERATION

Part of His Large Intestine Is Removed—He Will Stay in Hospital 2 Weeks

By EDWIN L. DALE Jr.
Special to The New York Times.

WASHINGTON, Nov. 3—John Foster Dulles, Secretary of State, underwent successful surgery today for removal of a perforated portion of his large intestine.

It was announced after the two-and-one-half-hour operation that Mr. Dulles had "left the operating table in good condition" and that he was "resting comfortably."

The announcement was made by a State Department spokesman, Lincoln White, at Walter Reed Army Hospital. It said Mr. Dulles, 68 years old, probably would be in the hospital for two to three weeks and that he "should be able to return to his desk in approximately six weeks." Mr. Dulles' pulse was reported to be 76, his blood pressure 126/75.

The surgery was performed by Maj. Gen. Leonard D. Heaton, commanding officer of Walter Reed, who had operated on President Eisenhower in June for ileitis. He was assisted today by

Continued on Page 78, Column 3

BID TO U. N. CHIEF

Canada's Motion That He Plan Suez Unit Adopted, 59 to 0

Texts of draft resolutions and debate excerpts, Page 29.

By KATHLEEN TELTSCH
Special to The New York Times.

UNITED NATIONS, N. Y., Sunday, Nov. 4—The General Assembly voted early today to ask the Secretary General to submit a plan for creation of a United Nations police force to obtain and supervise a cease-fire in the Middle East.

The policing proposal, sponsored by Canada, was adopted 57 to 0, at 2:17 A. M. at an emergency session of the Assembly.

Nineteen states abstained, among them Israel, France and Britain. The latter two earlier had rejected an Assembly call for a cease-fire and said they would keep on with their "police action" in Egypt to safeguard the Suez Canal.

The proposal, made by Lester B. Pearson, Canada's Secretary for External Affairs, calls on Secretary General Dag Hammarskjold to submit blueprints within forty-eight hours for an "emergency international United Nations force."

New Truce Plan Adopted

No details were suggested by Mr. Pearson, but such a police force presumably would have to include several thousand men. The Canadian spokesman has said he would recommend Canada's participation. His proposal, however, left all arrangements to the Secretary General.

Within minutes, the emergency session adopted a second resolution, co-sponsored by nineteen Asian and African countries. This renewed the cease-fire appeal made two days ago and asked Mr. Hammarskjold to report within twelve hours on whether the states had complied.

The second resolution was approved, 59 to 5, with twelve abstentions. Among the abstainers were France, Britain, Israel, Autralia and New Zealand.

[Washington indicated that the Administration, after initial anger at the British-French and Israeli moves, was taking a more moderate, hopeful and understanding attitude.]

Weary United Nations delegates approved the new proposals at an event-filled emergency session, at which the United States presented a new Middle East plan. This seeks a long-range settlement of the Palestine problem and also of the current Suez Canal dispute.

In warmly supporting the Ca-

Continued on Page 29, Column 8

SOVIET ROAD BLOCK IN HUNGARY: Soviet tank obstructs road near Magyarovar
Associated Press Radiophoto

CAPITAL STORMED

Freedom Radios Fade From Air as Russians Shell Key Centers

By PAUL HOFMANN
Special to The New York Times.

VIENNA, Sunday, Nov. 4—Soviet troops started attacking Budapest and other Hungarian cities, towns and key military installations at dawn today.

At 9 A. M., local time (3 A. M. Eastern standard time) four hours after Budapest had been awakened by Russian artillery fire, overpowering Soviet tanks and infantry forces had stormed the Parliament Building and made Premier Imre Nagy and most members of his government prisoners.

Fighting in Budapest and many other parts of the country was continuing, but the prospects for the free Hungarian Government forces were nearly hopeless in the face of crushing Soviet superiority.

The Budapest radio and other Hungarian freedom stations went off the air one after another.

Before going silent, they directed desperate pleas to the West, especially to the United States, and to the United Nations for help to save the Hungarian people from "annihilation."

Mindszenty in U. S. Legation

Joseph Cardinal Mindszenty, Roman Catholic primate of Hungary, who had been freed from detention last week, and his secretary had taken refuge in the building of the United States Legation.

The United States legation, near the Parliament Building, was under fire at 9:30 A. M.

A fierce battle was raging in the immediate surroundings.

At 7 A. M. "several hundred" Soviet heavy tanks were reported attacking key Hungarian Army positions on the outskirts of Budapest and attempting to penetrate the city. The main thrust of the Soviet forces came apparently from the southeast.

Shortly before 7 A. M. the Budapest radio repeated Premier Nagy's announcement of the Soviet attack. It directed an appeal to Dag Hammarskjold, Secretary General of the United Nations. At the same time the M. T. I. Hungarian news agency reported:

"Russian troops have suddenly attacked Budapest and the entire country. They have opened fire on everyone in Hungary. It is a general attack.

"Janos Kadar [since Oct. 24 secretary of the Hungarian Communist party], Gyorgy Marosan and Sandor Ronai have formed a new Government and started crushing the counter-

Continued on Page 34, Column

ISRAELI PATROLS REACH SUEZ BANK

Penetrate Zone at 3 Points as Delay in British-French Landings Irks Regime

By HOMER BIGART
Special to The New York Times.

TEL AVIV, Israel, Sunday, Nov. 4—Israeli patrols reached the east bank of the Suez Canal yesterday.

A Government spokesman said Israeli columns had penetrated at three places the ten-mile buffer zone east of the canal that Britain and France wanted kept clear of warring Israeli and Egyptian forces.

Meanwhile, the Cabinet of Premier David Ben-Gurion studied reports that Syrian and Iraqi troops had entered Jordan. The developments in Jordan were being followed with "concern and alertness," according to a Foreign Ministry source.

[In Moscow, Marshal Kliment Y. Vorshilov, Soviet chief of state, told President Shukry al-Kuwatly of Syria at a farewell reception that the Soviet Union was prepared to give Syria the "necessary assistance "to reinforce her independence against foreign threats."]

2-Nation Plan Criticized

The Government spokesman offered no reason why the Israelis had entered the proscribed zone. But the Israelis are increasingly disturbed over the slowness of British and French forces in occupying the canal.

The announcement that Israelis were within ten miles of the canal at three points—opposite El Qantara in the north, Ismailia in the center and Suez at the southern terminus—may have been timed to coincide with reports here that the British-French invasion had been put off because of United States pressure.

The British-French proposals for an international police force to occupy the canal zone were regarded here as "unrealistic."

Until its announcement, the Israeli Government had indicated compliance with the British-French ultimatum.

But Israel has insisted that no firm deal was made with the French on where the advance would be halted.

Meanwhile, the Israelis reported, they were rapidly occupying all key points on the conquered Sinai Peninsula.

Lieut. Col. Moshe Pearlman, Government and Army spokesman, said that the whole area was "relatively quiet" and that the "entire peninsula in very short time will be in Israeli hands."

British Embassy sources said

Continued on Page 38, Column 4

British Bomb Raids On Egypt Continued In Landing Prelude

Texts of the communiqués are printed on Page 26.

By LEONARD INGALLS
Special to The New York Times.

LONDON, Nov. 3—British bombers turned their heaviest attack today from airfields in Egypt to ammunition dumps, barracks and armored weapons depots of the Egyptian Army.

There were indications that the landing by British and French forces in the Suez Canal Zone would be made by paratroopers and seaborne invasion units within the next forty-eight hours.

The Beirut radio, quoting an Egyptian communiqué, reported that a British-French force attempted to land at the southern entrance to the canal, but was driven off with heavy losses.

The Egyptians said they had sunk four British naval vessels and captured three troop landing craft at Suez with fire from shore batteries and torpedo boats. One British ship was said by the Egyptians to have been sunk by gunfire, and a British destroyer, a troop carrier and another British naval unit were said to have been sunk by torpedoes.

The Egyptians also reported they had shot down seventeen British-French planes over the Suez Canal area.

[There was little additional information on the military situation in announcements or dispatches from Cairo.]

An Admiralty spokesman said "there is no information in London to support the Egyptian

Continued on Page 17, Column 1

SOVIET VETO BARS ACTION IN COUNCIL

Censure Move in U. N. Over New Attack on Hungary Carried to Assembly

Excerpts from statements in Security Council, Page 35.

By LINDESAY PARROTT
Special to The New York Times.

UNITED NATIONS, N. Y., Sunday, Nov. 4—The Soviet Union early today vetoed a United States resolution proposing Security Council censure of the Russian military attack on Hungary.

Nine nations favored the United States proposal and one abstained, Yugoslavia.

The veto was at 5:15 A. M.

Henry Cabot Lodge Jr., United States representative, immediately moved for an emergency session of the General Assembly to take up the Hungarian crisis. The Assembly already was in permanent special session over the French-British intervention in the Suez Canal area.

Council's Will 'Thwarted'

Angrily, Mr Lodge told the Council that the will of the world organization had been "thwarted" by the Soviet veto and that the eleven-nation body had been prevented from fulfilling its responsibilities. In this "grave situation," he said, Assembly action was required.

The Council adopted the United States resolution for reference to the Assembly by a vote of 10 to 1. This ballot came at 5:21 A. M.

The Assembly meeting was set for 8 o'clock tonight.

The Council adjourned at 5:24 A. M.

The Council's action, marking the Soviet Union's seventy-ninth veto, was taken after the United States had called the group together at 3 A. M. to protest against the reoccupation of Budapest by Soviet troops. According to the latest reports here early today, the Hungarian capital was in the hands of Soviet troops after Russian tanks earlier had ringed the city.

The United States legation was understood to have been under fire. Mr. Lodge also reported that Joseph Cardinal Mindszenty and his staff had taken refuge in the legation.

The Security Council had adjourned shortly after midnight,

Continued on Page 35, Column 6

President Expected to Win; Democratic Congress Seen

New York Times Team Reports

Following are summaries of the apparent voting trends for President and the United States Senate and House of Representatives. They are based on the reports of New York Times teams that have surveyed twenty-seven closely contested states and of correspondents in twenty-one other states.

Presidential Race

By W. H. LAWRENCE

Surveys indicate that President Eisenhower and Vice President Richard M. Nixon will be re-elected on Tuesday by comfortable majorities of both the popular and electoral votes.

Reports from New York Times correspondents who have investigated political sentiment in the forty-eight states indicate these probable results:

For President Eisenhower — A minimum of twenty-seven states with 285 electoral votes, or nineteen votes more than required for a majority of the 531-member Electoral College.

For Adlai E. Stevenson — A minimum of seven states with seventy-six electoral votes.

Leaning toward President Eisenhower — Eight states with ninety-nine electoral votes.

Leaning toward Mr. Steven-

Continued on Page 69, Column 5

Congressional Races

By WILLIAM S. WHITE

The Democrats appear likely to hold Congress in Tuesday's national elections in spite of the prospect that President Eisenhower will retain the White House for the Republicans.

The outlook thus is for a continuation of the divided form of government that has guided the country since 1954.

A landslide for President Eisenhower would, of course, alter every present prospect. The weight of all current evidence suggests clearly, however, these approximate results:

¶The Democrats should at least retain their present thin margin of control in the Senate —49 Democrats to 47 Republicans.

¶There should be a Democratic House of Representatives again with no less than the

Continued on Page 69, Column 3

Major Sports News

FOOTBALL

Yale, Navy, Syracuse, Columbia and Army won major Eastern contests yesterday. Scores of leading games:

Amherst	6	Tufts	0
Army	55	Colgate	46
Columbia	25	Cornell	19
Georgia Tech	7	Duke	0
Illinois	7	Purdue	7
Michigan	17	Iowa	14
Michigan St.	33	Wisconsin	0
Minnesota	9	Pitt	6
Navy	33	Notre Dame	7
Ohio State	6	Northwest'n	2
Oklahoma	27	Colorado	19
Penn	28	Harvard	14
Princeton	21	Brown	7
Rutgers	20	Lafayette	19
Syracuse	13	Penn State	9
Tennessee	20	N. Carolina	0
T. C. U.	7	Baylor	6
U. C. L. A.	14	Stanford	13
W. Virginia	14	G. Wash'gton	0
Yale	19	Dartmouth	0

HORSE RACING

Summer Tan took the Gallant Fox Handicap in track record time at Jamaica.

Details in Section 5.

Mideast Oil Lines Reported Blown Up

By SAM POPE BREWER
Special to The New York Times.

BEIRUT, Lebanon, Nov. 3—Pipelines carrying more than half a million barrels of oil daily from Iraq to the Mediterranean coast have stopped operating as a result of the fighting in Egypt.

Reports circulating here were that the Iraq Petroleum Company's three pumping stations in Syria known as T-2, T-3 and T-4 had been blown up and burned.

[At the United Nations an Egyptian spokesman was quoted by The United Press as having said all oil pipelines in every Middle East country except Saudi Arabia had been blown up or shut down.]

No oil installations in Lebanon were damaged up to tonight. Reports abroad to that effect are incorrect, according

Continued on Page 26, Column 6

Nutting Quits Post; Churchill For Eden

The text of Churchill letter will be found on Page 24.

Special to The New York Times.

LONDON, Nov. 3—Anthony Nutting, Minister of State in the Foreign Office, resigned from the Government tonight because he strongly disagreed with its policy of armed intervention in Egypt.

The blow to the Government represented by the defection of one of its best-known and most effective young ministers at a critical juncture was balanced by a resounding declaration of support from Sir Winston Churchill.

Writing from his lair at Chartwell, the old lion of British politics blamed Egypt for provoking war with Israel, criticized the United States for failing to cooperate fully and

Continued on Page 24, Column 3

This section consists of 140 pages divided into three parts. The news summary and index will be found on Page 95. Society news begins on Page 90 and obituary articles will be found on Pages 86 and 87.

Pravda Denounces Nagy for 'Reaction'

By Reuters.

LONDON, Sunday, Nov. 4—The Soviet Communist party newspaper Pravda attacked Premier Imre Nagy of Hungary today "in strong terms", according to the Moscow radio.

Pravda said: "The task of barring the way to reaction in Hungary has to be carried out without the slightest delay—such is the course dictated by events."

The broadcast quoted Pravda as saying: "Imre Nagy turned out to be, objectively speaking, an accomplice of the reactionary forces. Imre Nagy cannot and does not want to fight the dark forces of reaction."

Pravda asserted that it was Mr. Nagy who had requested bringing Soviet troops into Budapest, "as it was vital for the interests of the Socialist regime."

Continued on Page 15, Column 2

"All the News That's Fit to Print"

The New York Times.

LATE CITY EDITION
Condensation of U. S. Weather Bureau forecast:
Some cloudiness today; cloudy tonight. Clearing, cooler tomorrow.
Temperature range today: 66—50.
Temperature range yesterday: 65.4—52.2.
Full U. S. Weather Bureau Report, Page 63.

VOL. CVI. No. 36,082. Entered as Second-Class Matter, Post Office, New York, N. Y. NEW YORK, WEDNESDAY, NOVEMBER 7, 1956. Times Square, New York 36, N. Y. Telephone LAckawanna 4-1000 FIVE CENTS

EISENHOWER BY A LANDSLIDE; BATTLE FOR CONGRESS CLOSE; JAVITS VICTOR OVER WAGNER

Suez Warfare Stopped Under British-French Cease-Fire

MAYOR CONCEDES

Javits, Swept In With the Eisenhower Tide, Wins Stiff Contest

Vote for Senator
CITY SUMMARY

	Javits (Rep.)	Wagner (Dem.-Lib.)
Manhattan ...	270,146	393,462
Bronx	218,895	374,810
Brooklyn	398,088	605,002
Queens	400,832	372,505
Richmond ...	49,694	32,881
Total	1,337,655	1,778,660
Upstate	2,362,618	1,478,238
Grand total	3,700,273	3,256,898

All E. D.'s of 4,607 in city and 6,522 of 6,525 upstate.

By DOUGLAS DALES

Attorney General Jacob K. Javits was swept to victory yesterday in the Eisenhower Republican landslide in his race against Mayor Wagner for the United States Senate.

Mayor Wagner conceded defeat in a statement at 1:22 A. M. after the trend to Javits' victory became unmistakable.

Mr. Wagner carried three boroughs in the city—Manhattan, Brooklyn and the Bronx—but lost in Queens and Richmond.

The city-wide complete totals gave Mr. Javits 1,337,655 votes to 1,778,660 for Mayor Wagner. The Mayor's total included 233,560 on the Liberal party line. The Liberal line attracted 404,769 votes in the city four years ago, when the party ran its own candidate for the Senate, George S. Counts.

The victor's margin was expected to reach 444,000 with the final results. With all city districts and 6,522 of 6,525 districts upstate reported, Mr. Javits had an edge of 443,375.

Mayor Wagner carried two of the fifty-seven upstate counties, Erie and Albany. Eisenhower carried both.

Everywhere outside the city, Mr. Javits ran substantially behind the President's vote. On the other hand, Mayor Wagner ran well ahead of Adlai E. Stevenson, the Democratic candidate for President.

In view of the size of the

Continued on Page 26, Column 2

PRESIDENT SCORES NEW HIGH IN STATE

Plurality Tops 1,500,000 as He Cuts Rival's City Edge

State Presidential Vote
CITY SUMMARY

	Eisenhower (Rep.)	Stevenson (Dem.-Lib.)
Manhattan ..	299,929	378,018
Bronx	256,909	343,656
Brooklyn ...	459,703	558,187
Queens	471,144	313,311
Richmond ..	64,236	196,653
Total	1,551,921	1,614,825
Upstate	2,766,183	1,127,403
Grand total	4,318,104	2,742,228

All E. D.'s of 4,607 in city and 6,522 of 6,525 upstate.

By LEO EGAN

President Eisenhower swept New York yesterday by a plurality that dwarfed all previous records.

With sixty-one of the state's 11,132 election districts still to report this morning, General Eisenhower's margin exceeded 1,500,000.

The previous record for a Presidential plurality in New York was established in 1920, when the late Warren G. Harding, Republican, defeated James M. Cox, Democrat, by 1,139,927.

All the missing districts are in Republican territory upstate.

Continued on Page 23, Column 1

An International Summary: The Mideast and Hungary

Following are summaries of the leading developments in the Middle East and Europe. The full foreign news report begins on the first page of the second part.

Cease-Fire Is On

Britain and France put a cease-fire into effect and halted their advance in Egypt. Prime Minister Eden told Commons that conditions had been established for an international police force under the United Nations to promote settlement of Middle Eastern issues.

Invaders Hold Canal

The invasion forces claimed control of the Suez Canal Zone. They took Port Said and drove south before the cease-fire became effective.

Egyptians Halt Fight

The Egyptians decided to hold their fire at the deadline in the hope that the United Nations resolution of Nov. 2, providing for withdrawal of all forces behind armistice lines, would be carried out.

Soviet May Send 'Volunteers'

Indications in Moscow were that Soviet "volunteers" who began applying for service with Egyptian forces might go to the Middle East despite the cease-fire. Moscow broadcast a Cairo appeal for aid.

Troop Withdrawal Asked

Asian and Arab states drafted a United Nations resolution calling on Britain, France and Israel to withdraw their troops from Egypt immediately. A special session of the General Assembly called for last night was postponed until this morning.

Hungarian Battle Persists

Stubborn Hungarian revolutionary forces are continuing to fight the Soviet army in Budapest, according to diplomatic reports received in Vienna. Women and children were said to be fighting alongside the men in a house-to-house struggle. The General Assembly scheduled a special session this afternoon to consider Soviet intervention in Hungary.

EISENHOWER SETS RECORD IN JERSEY

Margin of 700,000 Carries All 21 Counties—G. O. P. Wins 2 Hudson Seats

By GEORGE CABLE WRIGHT

President Eisenhower yesterday scored the greatest victory in New Jersey political history.

With most of the state's ballots tallied early this morning, his margin over Adlai E. Stevenson had soared above 700,000, almost double that of 1952. He became the first candidate in modern times to carry all twenty-one counties.

The returns were:

PRESIDENT
4,017 districts out of 4,155.

Eisenhower	1,522,971
Stevenson	821,067

The most startling aspect of his victory was the complete turnabout of Hudson County, for half a century a Democratic stronghold.

This county gave the President a majority of 76,554. In 1952 Mr. Stevenson had carried Hudson by 7,886 votes.

In fact, Republicans swept every county contest. When residents of Hudson awake this morning it is certain that many will find it hard to believe that for the next two years they will be represented in Congress by not one, but two, Republicans. There was no precedent there for that.

A third Democratic incumbent, Representative Harrison A. Williams Jr., went down to defeat in Union County.

Thus, the Democratic representation of six in the House was cut in half. All eight Republican incumbents were re-elected.

President Eisenhower became the first Presidential candidate to carry the solidly Democratic bailiwick of Jersey City since Warren G. Harding did it in 1920. Long the citadel of the late Frank Hague and now of John Kenny, it gave General Eisenhower a majority of 31,527 over Mr. Stevenson. In 1952 the Democratic candidate had carried the city by 8,251.

But the trouncing of the former Illinois Governor was by no means restricted to Hudson. Camden and Mercer Counties, which also went to Mr. Stevenson in 1952, likewise turned their backs to him this year.

Continued on Page 25, Column 5

BUSH RE-ELECTED IN CONNECTICUT

Plurality for Eisenhower of 303,036 Biggest in State in a Presidential Race

By RICHARD H. PARKE
Special to The New York Times.

HARTFORD, Nov 6—President Eisenhower scored an easy victory in Connecticut today. He carried to victory with him Senator Prescott S. Bush, the Republican incumbent.

The President's plurality of 303,036 votes over Adlai E. Stevenson, Democratic candidate, was the greatest margin the State ever has given a Presidential contender. The previous high figure was 136,138 votes, achieved by Prseident Coolidge in 1924.

The President, whose 1952 plurality of 129,363 was considered of landslide proportions, defeated Mr. Stevenson today by 708,995 votes to 405,959, according to complete but unofficial returns.

The Republican sweep was general throughout the state. It carried in Senator Bush by a plurality of 129,544 votes. He defeated his Democratic opponent, Representative Thomas J. Dodd, by 607,330 to 477,876.

The Republicans also retained

Continued on Page 28, Column 5

Coudert Wins in Close Contest; Vote in Queens 7th Rechecked

By CLAYTON KNOWLES

The Republicans emerged from a hard-fought Congressional campaign early today with a possible net gain of one in the state delegation to the House of Representatives.

At 4:20 A. M. a final decision rested on the outcome of the race in the Seventh district of Queens. Here Representative James J. Delaney, Democratic incumbent, claimed victory at 4:15 A. M. by forty votes, but a final tally was unavailable.

An hour and a half earlier, Delaney supporters were conceding the election of Joseph Stockinger, a Republican, but the contest was so close that all 217 districts were being rechecked.

The announced vote for 202 districts was 72,186 for Mr. Stockinger to 72,112 for Mr. Delaney, who ran with Liberal party backing.

The prospect that the Republicans would pick up a House seat in the state, giving them twenty-seven of a total of forty-three, arose when Representative Frederic R. Coudert Jr. staged an eleventh-hour triumph in the Manhattan Seventeenth District.

He prevailed once more over Anthony B. Akers, Democrat-Liberal who had come within 314 votes of defeating him in 1954. This time Mr. Coudert won, 68,862 votes to 66,207.

If Mr. Delaney should go to defeat, the Republicans will have seven of the twenty-two House seats filled in the city.

President Eisenhower's land-

Continued on Page 20, Column 6

SENATE IN DOUBT

Democrats Lag in East on War Issue but Gain in the West

By WILLIAM S. WHITE

The Democrats and Republicans fought along a swaying electoral battle line early today for control of the oncoming Eighty-fifth Congress.

Not all the power of President Eisenhower's landslide victory had been enough to put his Republican Congressional colleagues in front.

The Senate race, in which the Republicans were attempting to overturn a present 49-to-47 Democratic margin of control, was an affair of hairbreadth drama.

Small net Republican gains for the House of Representatives were indicated. But whether these would continue or would be enough remained wholly in doubt.

The Republicans needed a net gain of 15 House seats, and the capture of 2 additional and now vacant seats that had been Republican.

The pattern of the Congressional contest was this: The East, more sensitive than other sections to the last-minute issue involved in the Middle Eastern and Central European war crises, on the whole was hitting the Democrats hard. The appeal of "don't change horses in midstream" was strong in this area. In the interior, however, Democratic organizational strength, farm discontent and other factors were turning up great Democratic strength.

Cooper Wins in Kentucky

The position on the Senate in some critical states was this:

KENTUCKY—A gain of one Republican seat in former Senator John Sherman Cooper's defeat of his Democratic challenger, Lawrence Wetherby, for the seat made vacant by the death of Senator Alben W. Barkley. The possibility of another gain for the Republicans in the fact that the assistant Democratic leader of the Senate, Earle C. Clements, was running behind Thruston B. Morton, a former assistant Secretary of State in the Eisenhower Administration.

NEW YORK—A Republican gain in the victory of Jacob K. Javits over Mayor Wagner for the seat being vacated by Senator Herbert H. Lehman, Democrat-Liberal.

OHIO—A Democratic gain in the defeat by Gov. Frank J. Lausche of Senator George H. Bender.

ILLINOIS—Senator Everett M. Dirksen, Republican, ran ahead of his Democratic opponent, Richard Stengel.

PENNSYLVANIA—Joseph S.

Continued on Page 3, Column 1

PRESIDENT EISENHOWER

VICE PRESIDENT NIXON

G. O. P. MAKES BID TO CAPTURE HOUSE

Picks Up 9 Seats in East, but Drive Eases in West—Midwest to Decide

By JOHN D. MORRIS

Republicans got off to a fast start in their bid to recapture control of the House of Representatives, but appeared to lose steam early today as returns trickled in from the West.

As of 3 A. M., results from yesterday's Congressional races indicated a decided Republican trend, with some major upsets for the Democrats. However, with control of nearly two-thirds of the 435 seats still in doubt, victory for either party was far from certain.

The undecided contests were almost entirely in the Midwest, where the issue of declining farm income was a factor favoring the Democrats, and in the Far West.

G. O. P. Gains in East

Such returns as were available from those areas indicated possible Democratic gains in Iowa, California and South Dakota.

Eastward, where the only decisive tallies were available, Republicans had picked up nine seats held by Democrats in the Eighty-fourth Congress while holding their own in all other contests where returns were conclusive. One, in New York City, was subpect to a recount. Democrats had failed to capture any Republican seat except one that they took in the Maine election on Sept. 10.

Republican incumbents were easy victors in a number of contests that had promised to be close.

The most outstanding upsets were in New Jersey, where the Hudson county Democratic stronghold of the late Mayor Frank Hague of Jersey City unseated its two Democratic Representatives, T. James Tumulty and Alfred D. Sieminski, in the Thirteenth and Fourteenth Congressional Districts.

Mr. Sieminski lost to Norman H. Roth, Republican. Mr. Tumulty, a 300-pound legislator, was defeated by Vincent J. Dellay, Republican.

A third Democratic incumbent in New Jersey, Harrison A. Williams, lost to Florence P. Dwyer, Republican.

Republicans also picked up one Democratic seat in Connecticut, one in Deleware, one in Pennsylvania, one in Indiana and

Continued on Page 3, Column 3

Stevenson Concedes Defeat and Wishes President Success

Stevenson and Kefauver talks appear on Page 13.

By HARRISON E. SALISBURY
Special to The New York Times.

CHICAGO, Wednesday, Nov. 7—Adlai E. Stevenson conceded the election of President Eisenhower in a statement made public at 12:25 A. M. Central standard time today (1:25 Eastern standard time).

In a telegram to President Eisenhower, the Democratic candidate expressed his understanding of "grave difficulties" that the Administration faced and wished all success to General Eisenhower in the years ahead.

Mr. Stevenson coupled his telegram of congratulations to the President with an appeal to his followers to carry forward in the crusade for what he called a "New America."

He called on America's leaders to recognize that the nation "wants to face up squarely to the facts of today's world."

"We don't want to draw back from them," Mr. Stevenson said. "We can't. We are ready for the test that we know history has set for us."

Mr. Stevenson in his statement took note of the troubled conditions of the world.

"Beyond the seas, in much of the world, in Russia, in China, in Hungary, in all the trembling satellites, partisan controversy is forbidden and dissent suppressed," Mr. Stevenson said.

Mr. Stevenson also took note

Continued on Page 13, Column 5

Electoral Vote by States

	Eisenhower	Stev'son		Eisenhower	Stev'son
Ala.	—	11	Nev.	3	—
Ariz.	4	—	N. H.	4	—
Ark.	—	8	N. J.	16	—
Calif.	32	—	N. M.	4	—
Colo.	6	—	N. Y.	45	—
Conn.	8	—	N. C.	—	14
Del.	3	—	N. D.	4	—
Fla.	10	—	Ohio	25	—
Ga.	—	12	Okla.	8	—
Idaho	4	—	Ore.	6	—
Ill.	27	—	Pa.	32	—
Ind.	13	—	R. Isl.	4	—
Iowa	10	—	S. C.	—	8
Kan.	8	—	S. D.	4	—
Ky.	10	—	Tenn.	11	—
La.	10	—	Texas	24	—
Me.	5	—	Utah	4	—
Md.	9	—	Vt.	3	—
Mass.	16	—	Va.	12	—
Mich.	20	—	Wash.	9	—
Minn.	11	—	W. Va.	8	—
Miss.	—	8	Wisc.	12	—
Mo.	—	13	Wyo.	3	—
Mont.	4	—			
Neb.	6	—	Total	457	74

EISENHOWER VOWS TO TOIL FOR PEACE

Hails Landslide Re-election as Proof Nation Wants 'Modern Republicanism'

Texts of the Eisenhower and Nixon talks on Page 12.

By RUSSELL BAKER
Special to The New York Times.

WASHINGTON, Wednesday, Nov. 7—President Eisenhower hailed his landslide re-election victory today as proof that his "modern Republicanism has now proved itself and America has approved of modern Republicanism."

He pledged in a victory statement early this morning to work with "whatever talents the good God has given me for 168,000,000 Americans here at home and for peace in the world."

Addressing a jubilant crowd of party workers at Republican election headquarters here and the nation, over television, the President declared that so long as the G.O.P. pursued the "ideals, the hopes and aspirations" of the people, it would continue to flourish.

"If it is anything less," he said, " it is only a conspiracy to seize power. And the Republican party is not that."

'Looks to the Future'

Thus, in his moment of triumph, General Eisenhower claimed a sweeping triumph for what his Administration's philosophers had styled the "new Republicanism" and what he himself termed this morning "modern Republicanism."

"Modern Republicanism," he said, "looks to the future and this means it will gain constantly new recruits." So long as it continued to remain "modern," he added, it would "continue to increase in power and influence for decades to come."

So long as it clings to its "modern" ideals, the President declared, it would "point the way to peace among nations and prosperity, advancing standards here at home in which everyone will share."

The President delivered his victory statement at 1:45 A. M., about fifteen minutes after this restive crowd gathered in the mammoth ballroom of the Sheraton-Park Hotel had heard Adlai E. Stevenson concede defeat in Chicago.

General Eisenhower had been waiting upstairs in a third-floor suite for three and a half hours,

Continued on Page 13, Column 1

41 STATES TO G.O.P.

President Sweeps All the North and West, Scores in South

By JAMES RESTON

Dwight David Eisenhower won yesterday the most spectacular Presidential election victory since Franklin D. Roosevelt submerged Alfred M. Landon in 1936.

The smiling 66-year-old hero of the Normandy invasion, who was in a Denver hospital recuperating from a heart attack just a year ago today, thus became the first Republican in this century to win two successive Presidential elections. William McKinley did it in 1896 and 1900.

Adlai E. Stevenson of Illinois, who lost to Mr. Eisenhower four years ago, thirty-nine states to nine, conceded defeat at 1:25 this morning.

At 4:45 A. M. President Eisenhower had won forty-one states to seven for Mr. Stevenson. His electoral lead at that time was 457 to 74 for Stevenson, and his popular vote was 25,071,331 to 18,337,434—up 2 per cent over 1952. Two hundred and sixty-six electoral votes are needed for election.

Victory in All Areas

This was a national victory in every conceivable way. It started in Connecticut. It swept every state in New England. It took New York by a plurality of more than 1,500,000. It carried all the Middle Atlantic states, all the Midwest, all the Rocky Mountain states and everything beyond the Rockies.

More than that, the Republican tide swept along the border states and to the South, carried all the states won by the G.O.P. there in 1952—Virginia, Texas, Tennessee and Florida—and even took Louisiana for the first time since the Hayes-Tilden election of 1876.

For the President and his 43-year old Vice Presidential running mate, Richard M. Nixon of California, who carried much of the Republican campaign, it was a more impressive victory than for the Republican party.

So close were many races for

Continued on Page 2, Column 3

CLARK LEADS DUFF IN PENNSYLVANIA

Democrat's Edge Dropping—President Takes State

By WILLIAM G. WEART
Special to The New York Times.

PHILADELPHIA, Wednesday, Nov. 7—Joseph S. Clark Jr., former Mayor of Philadelphia, was running ahead of Senator James H. Duff early today.

But his margin was ebbing as returns from rural areas and small towns began to offset the lead he piled up in large cities.

President Eisenhower won the state's thirty-two electoral votes by a plurality that was steadily mounting.

Mr. Clark expressed disappointment at the defeat of his party's standard-bearer. He attributed General Eisenhower's victory to his "personal popularity." Mr. Clark's campaign manager, Mayor Richardson Dilworth of Philadelphia, said the President's re-election was due to the "emotion caused by the war situation."

In the event the final tally in the Senatorial race is close, an estimated 50,000 absentee votes cast by servicemen and hospitalized veterans may decide the outcome. Under the law, absentee ballots are mailed to county

Continued on Page 13, Column 6

"All the News That's Fit to Print"

The New York Times.

LATE CITY EDITION

U. S. Weather Bureau Report (Page 33) forecasts: Cloudy and cool today and tonight. Mostly fair tomorrow.
Temp. range: 65—53. Yesterday: 62.4—49.2.

VOL. CVII..No. 36,414. NEW YORK, SATURDAY, OCTOBER 5, 1957. 10c beyond 100-mile zone from New York City. FIVE CENTS

SOVIET FIRES EARTH SATELLITE INTO SPACE; IT IS CIRCLING THE GLOBE AT 18,000 M. P. H.; SPHERE TRACKED IN 4 CROSSINGS OVER U. S.

HOFFA IS ELECTED TEAMSTERS' HEAD; WARNS OF BATTLE

Defeats Two Foes 3 to 1 —Says Union Will Fight 'With Every Ounce'

Text of the Hoffa address is printed on Page 6.

By A. H. RASKIN

Special to The New York Times.

MIAMI BEACH, Oct. 4—The scandal-scarred International Brotherhood of Teamsters elected James R. Hoffa as its president today.

He won by a margin of nearly 3 to 1 over the combined vote of two rivals who campaigned on pledges to clean up the nation's biggest union.

Senate rackets investigators and Hoffa critics in the union rank-and-file immediately opened actions to strip the 44-year-old former warehouseman from Detroit of his election victory.

A jubilant Hoffa exhibited, however, greater concern over the possibility that his union might be ousted from the American Federation of Labor and Congress of Industrial Organizations. He appealed for time to prove that he could make the teamsters "a model of trade unionism."

The parent organization has ordered the 1,400,000-member Teamsters Union to get rid of corrupt leadership by Oct. 24 or face suspension. Hoffa said he felt actions by the union at its week-long convention here should satisfy the federation.

Warns Union Will Fight

He made it plain to the 1,700 cheering delegates that he did not intend to go before the convention in the role of suppliant. He said expulsion would not destroy the teamsters. He warned that the union would fight "with every ounce of strength we possess" if it found itself outside.

In such a civil war the teamsters would start with a war-chest of $38,000,000 in the hands of the international union and much more at the disposal of its locals. The teamsters also could count on their strategic power over other unions through their control of trucks and warehouses.

The Hoffa victory brought warnings of repressive legislation from James P. Mitchell, Secretary of Labor, and Senator John L. McClellan, Democrat of Arkansas. The Senator heads the Select Committee on Improper Activities in the Labor or Management Field, which has accused Hoffa of gangster associations and questionable financial practices.

Winner on First Ballot

A three-hour roll-call gave Hoffa the $50,000-a-year union presidency on the first ballot. His machine, in full command of the convention since it opened Monday, registered 1,208 votes for Hoffa.

William A. Lee of Chicago, the union's seventh vice president, was second with 313 votes. Thomas J. Haggerty of Chicago, secretary-treasurer of Milk Wagon Drivers Union, Local 753, trailed with 140 votes.

The Hoffa forces then began providing the new leader a rubber stamp board. It elected five of thirteen vice presidents and would have elected the rest today if time had permitted completion of the cumbersome balloting procedure.

Hoffa repeatedly indicated his irritation that some of the old vice presidents marked for elimination had refused to give up without the formality of a roll-call.

Even before the voting, the McClellan committee subpoenaed the full records of the convention's credentials committee. A United States marshal served the subpoena this morning on Joseph Konowe of New York, the committee secretary. He was directed to turn over all

Continued on Page 6, Column 7

Associated Press Wirephoto

IN TOKEN OF VICTORY: Dave Beck, retiring head of the Teamsters Union, raises hand of James R. Hoffa upon his election as union's president. At right is Mrs. Hoffa.

FAUBUS COMPARES HIS STAND TO LEE'S

Says He Will Remain Loyal to People of Arkansas— All Is Quiet at School

By HOMER BIGART

Special to The New York Times.

LITTLE ROCK, Ark., Oct. 4—Gov. Orval E. Faubus said today that he had made a decision as painfully difficult as the one that had confronted Robert E. Lee at the outset of the Civil War.

"Lee was offered command of the Federal Army in 1861," Governor Faubus recalled. "Lee decided to remain loyal to the people of his state.

"The Democratic party of the North wants me to go along with them on the integration issue. I will remain with the people of Arkansas."

Governor Faubus said he had come under no local pressure to change his stand on integration at Little Rock Central High School. It was a stand that forced President Eisenhower to send Federal troops into this city to uphold Federal Court decisions and to safeguard the nine Negro students registered at Central High.

Winthrop Rockefeller, chairman of the Arkansas Industrial Development Commission, broke silence today on the Little Rock integration crisis, declaring it had "damaged" the state's prospects for economic progress. He called events of the past month "tragic."

It was a quiet day in Little Rock. The nine Negro boys and girls attended school without incident. But no early solution to the crisis seemed likely.

There was no break in the impasse reached Tuesday night when a compromise plan for the

Continued on Page 18, Column 2

Flu Widens in City; 10% Rate Predicted; 200,000 Pupils Out

By ROBERT ALDEN

Asian influenza continued to spread through the city yesterday.

Commissioner of Hospitals Morris A. Jacobs reported that there were ten times more respiratory infections than during the comparable period a year ago.

Attendance in the city's schools fell again. The Board of Education said that close to 200,000 of the city's 941,000 pupils were not in their classrooms yesterday. On Thursday 160,000 pupils were absent.

The attendance estimates were based on a sampling of the schools by the board. The sampling showed that in some schools in the Harlem area—the section hardest hit by the epidemic—more than 50 per cent of the pupils were absent. The board estimated that the overall city absence rate was 20 per cent.

3,000 Teachers Absent

About 3,000 teachers out of about 39,000 were not in their classrooms yesterday, compared with 2,700 absent on Thursday.

The city's acting Health Commissioner, Dr. Roscoe P. Kandle, said he expected that the total number of people affected by the highly infectious disease would run closer to 800,000 rather than 1,600,000 as predicted in some quarters.

It was estimated Thursday that 200,000 persons in New York had contracted the respiratory infection, and the total yesterday was believed to be somewhat higher.

Commissioner Kandle explained that any attempt to project the ultimate number of cases would involve conjecture

Continued on Page 8, Column 1

ARGENTINA TAKES EMERGENCY STEPS

State of Siege Proclaimed in Buenos Aires Region —Arrests Reported

By Reuters.

BUENOS AIRES, Oct. 4—A state of siege, suspending constitutional guarantees, was proclaimed tonight in Buenos Aires city and Province.

The Under Secretary of the Ministry of Interior, Garcia Puente, announced the state of siege at a news conference.

He said the emergency move suspended for thirty days the constitutional guarantees in the capital and the Province of Buenos Aires, but not in the remainder of the nation.

He said the measure was aimed exclusively "at defending the normal development of the Government's political plan, jeopardized through sabotage and social unrest."

The proclamation of the state of siege followed the arrest of scores of labor leaders during the day. The number arrested was estimated by observers as 100 to 300.

Bankers, telephone workers, oilworkers, seamstresses and other unions reported tonight that their leaders had been detained and were taken aboard

Continued on Page 4, Column 5

COURSE RECORDED

Navy Picks Up Radio Signals—4 Report Sighting Device

By WALTER SULLIVAN

Special to The New York Times

WASHINGTON, Saturday, Oct. 5—The Naval Research Laboratory announced early today that it had recorded four crossings of the Soviet earth satellite over the United States.

It said that one had passed near Washington. Two crossings were farther to the west. The location of the fourth was not made available immediately.

It added that tracking would be continued in an attempt to pin down the orbit sufficiently to obtain scientific information of the type sought in the International Geophysical Year.

[Four visual sightings, one of which was in conjunction with a radio contact, were reported by early Saturday morning. Two sightings were made at Columbus, Ohio, and one each from Terre Haute, Ind., and Whittier, Calif.]

Press Reports Noted

Soviet newspapers reported several weeks ago that the Soviet satellites would broadcast on frequencies in the neighborhood of twenty and forty megacycles. More exact frequencies were given by Soviet scientists at a conference on rockets and satellites that took place here this week.

Presumably the Naval Research Laboratory, which is responsible for the United States satellite program under the National Academy of Sciences, immediately set up receivers on those frequencies.

The tracking system established in this country to monitor its own satellites uses 108 megacycles, since much more accurate positions can be obtained with the higher frequencies. The Russians at first agreed to use equipment "compatible" with that of the United States, but then announced the lower frequencies.

Deception Ruled Out

American scientists believe this was because of a shortage of Soviet receivers capable of handling the higher frequency. It was not thought to be designed to hide the satellite since the Soviet signals are within easy reach of American listeners.

This was demonstrated last night as amateur and commercial radio stations, as well as the Naval Research Laboratory, reported hearing them.

Teams of visual observers at 150 stations in the United States and other Western nations were alerted during the

Continued on Page 3, Column 6

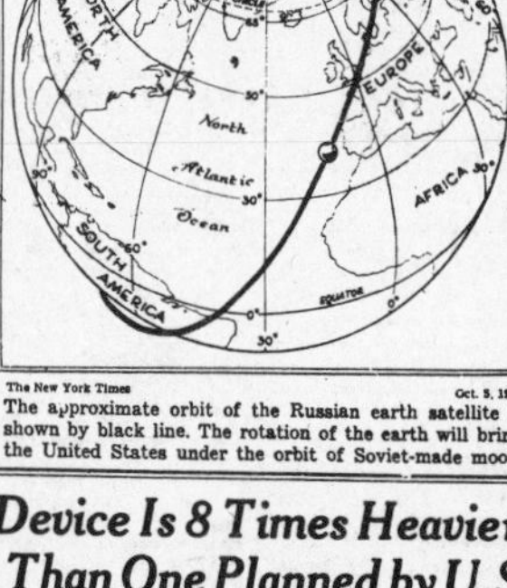

The New York Times Oct. 5, 1957

The approximate orbit of the Russian earth satellite is shown by black line. The rotation of the earth will bring the United States under the orbit of Soviet-made moon.

Device Is 8 Times Heavier Than One Planned by U.S.

Special to The New York Times.

WASHINGTON, Oct. 4—Leaders of the United States earth satellite program were astonished tonight to learn that the Soviet Union had launched a satellite eight times heavier than that contemplated by this country.

Dr. Joseph Kaplan, chairman of the United States program for the International Geophysical Year, described the 184-pound weight as "fantastic." The heaviest American satellites are to weigh twenty-one and a half pounds.

The actual launching, nevertheless, did not take the American scientists by surprise. At the end of working sessions on the International Conference on Rockets and Satellites, which has been taking place here, some said they thought the pitching of a Soviet satellite into the sky was imminent.

The satellite must fly at a speed of about 18,000 miles an hour to counteract the force of gravity at an altitude of 560 miles. The initial announcement in Moscow did not make it clear whether or not the rocket that placed it in orbit was aimed north or south.

Its Direction in Doubt

This would determine whether or not the satellite's initial crossing of the United States was northbound or southbound. Since the earth rotates within the orbit the satellite should in one day traverse almost all nations of the world.

With an orbit inclined 65 degrees to the equator, its sweep would cover virtually the entire region between the Arctic circle and the Antarctic circle.

William A. Holaday, special assistant to the Secretary of Defense for guided missiles, said the launching was not evidence of Soviet technological superiority in missile and rocket developments.

Mr. Holaday noted that Project Vanguard, the United States satellite program, had been an "open" project as part of the International Geophysical year and there has been no

Continued on Page 3, Column 7

SATELLITE SIGNAL BROADCAST HERE

Impulse Carried on Radio and TV—First Reported by Long Island Station

By ROY SILVER

Radio signals from the first satellite launched yesterday by the Russians were broadcast to radio and television audiences here last night.

The first word that the signals had been received in this country was reported by RCA Communication, Inc. It said that its receiving station at Riverhead, L. I., had picked up what it believed to be impulse signals from the Soviet satellite.

The National Broadcasting Company and the Columbia Broadcasting System broke into their radio and television programs to enable their audiences to hear the pinging sound of the "moon's" signal. The British Broadcasting Corporation in London said it had tuned powerful receivers to the Soviet earth satellite frequencies. Reuter's radio station north of London reported hearing the signals.

RCA Communications, a subsidiary of Radio Corporation of America, said the first signal had been received at 8:07 P. M. on a frequency of 20.005 megacycles on the 15-meter wave length.

One hour and twenty-nine minutes later, at 9:36 P. M., the receiving station, situated about eighty miles from the city, reported that the satellite was making another round of the earth. Other approaches by

Continued on Page 2, Column 4

560 MILES HIGH

Visible With Simple Binoculars, Moscow Statement Says

Text of Tass announcement appears on Page 3.

By WILLIAM J. JORDEN

Special to The New York Times.

MOSCOW, Saturday, Oct. 5—The Soviet Union announced this morning that it successfully launched a man-made earth satellite into space yesterday.

The Russians calculated the satellite's orbit at a maximum of 560 miles above the earth and its speed at 18,000 miles an hour.

The official Soviet news agency Tass said the artificial moon, with a diameter of twenty-two inches and a weight of 184 pounds, was circling the earth once every hour and thirty-five minutes. This means more than fifteen times a day.

Two radio tranamitters, Tass said, are sending signals continuously on frequencies of 20.005 and 40.002 megacycles. These signals were said to be strong enough to be picked up by amateur radio operators. The trajectory of the satellite is being tracked by numerous scientific stations.

Due Over Moscow Today

Tass said the satellite was moving at an angle of 65 degrees to the equatorial plane and would pass over the Moscow area twice today.

"Its flight," the announcement added, "will be observed in the rays of the rising and setting sun with the aid of the simplest optical instruments, such as binoculars and spyglasses."

The Soviet Union said the world's first satellite was "successfully launched" yesterday. Thus it asserted that it had put a scientific instrument into space before the United States. Washington has disclosed plans to launch a satellite next spring. Oct. 4."

The Moscow announcement said the Soviet Union planned to send up more and bigger and heavier artificial satellites during the current International Geophysical Year, an eighteen-month period of study of the earth, its crust and the space surrounding it.

Five Miles a Second

The rocket that carried the satellite into space left the earth at a rate of five miles a second, the Tass announcement said. Nothing was revealed, however, concerning the material of which the man-made moon was constructed or the site in the Soviet Union where the sphere was launched.

The Soviet Union said its sphere circling the earth had opened the way to interplanetary travel.

It did not pass up the opportunity to use the launching for propaganda purposes. It said in its announcement that people now could see how "the new socialist society" had turned the boldest dreams of mankind into reality.

Moscow said the satellite was the result of years of study and research on the part of Soviet scientists.

Several Years of Study

Tass said:

"For several years the research and experimental designing work has been under way in the Soviet Union to create artificial satellites of the earth. It has already been reported in the press that the launching of the earth satellites in the U. S. S. R. had been planned in accordance with the program of International Geophysical Year research.

"As a result of intensive work by the research institutes and design bureaus, the first artificial earth satellite in the world has now been created. This first satellite was successfully launched in the U. S. S. R. October four."

The Soviet announcement said that as a result of the tremendous speed at which the satellite was moving it would

Continued on Page 3, Column 8

City Sifts Charge That Schupler, Brooklyn Councilman, Sold a Job

By PAUL CROWELL

The city is investigating a complaint that Councilman Philip J. Schupler accepted a $500 fee last year in exchange for a promise to get a job for a Brooklyn business man.

William R. Peer, executive secretary to Mayor Wagner, said yesterday that the inquiry was started several weeks ago after the complaint had been made by Sol L. Hoffman of 1934 Sixty-third Street, Brooklyn.

At the office of Investigation Commissioner Charles H. Tenney, who is making the investigation, it was said that no findings or conclusions had been reached.

The charge was denied by Mr. Schupler, a Democrat-Liberal, in a telephone interview. He said that he had received a $500 check from Mr. Hoffman in May, 1956, but that it was given to him as a campaign contribution. Mr. Schupler was then a candidate for re-election as a Democratic district leader. He was defeated in the primary election a month later.

Disclosure of the investigation brought from Robert K. Christenberry, the Republican candidate for Mayor, the charge that "corruption and scandal in our City Council is symptomatic of the Wagner administration."

In a formal statement commenting on the Schupler case Mr. Christenberry called upon the city's voters to support his

Continued on Page 16, Column 3

Ex-Premier Mollet Accepts Bid To Form a New French Cabinet

Socialist Leader Agrees With Reluctance and Without Giving Much Hope

By ROBERT C. DOTY

Special to The New York Times.

PARIS, Oct. 4—Former Premier Guy Mollet agreed reluctantly and without much hope today to try to form a new French Cabinet.

M. Mollet's pessimism, shared by many observers here, was based on the fact that both he and his party, the Socialists, still hold strongly to the policies that caused the defeat of the last two Cabinets, M. Mollet's own and that of Premier Maurice Bourgès-Maunoury, a Radical.

Thus the Socialists still support the views on economic and social questions, including the demand for extensive governmental decree powers in those domains, that brought M. Mollet's Government down last May after a record-breaking sixty-eight weeks in office. The average Cabinet's life span has been twenty-nine weeks.

At the same time the Socialists regard as a minimum of reform the program for limited Algerian home rule outlined in the framework law that was defeated in the Assembly Monday.

In both cases, opposition from the Right-wing Independents constituted the margin of defeat.

If M. Mollet should find it impossible to muster a new major-

Continued on Page 5, Column 4

Associated Press

Guy Mollet

Warsaw Crushes New Protest; Clubs, Tear Gas Rout Students

By SYDNEY GRUSON

Special to The New York Times.

WARSAW, Oct. 4—Policemen and students clashed again in the streets of Warsaw tonight.

Security chiefs, seemingly nervous, threw a guard of several hundred workers' militia around the downtown headquarters of the ruling United Workers (Communist) party.

For the second successive night the police broke up demonstrations by firing tear gas and beating students and others with rubber truncheons.

What began last night as a protest against the closing of one newspaper was turning tonight into a general clamor against police brutality and the suppression of free speech. By midnight the city had quieted down and the people had left the streets.

Among those clubbed tonight was Franco Fabiani, permanent correspondent here of the Italian Communist paper L'Unita. He suffered two minor head wounds.

Signor Fabiani was caught in crowds charged by the police after about 3,000 students had met in the Polytechnic and adopted a resolution protesting both the closing of the newspaper Po Prostu and the "brutal interference" of the police at last night's meeting.

Tonight's trouble centered on the Polytechnic, the huge advanced technical school near the heart of Warsaw. It was

Continued on Page 5, Column 2

"All the News That's Fit to Print"

The New York Times.

LATE CITY EDITION
U. S. Weather Bureau Report (Page 62) forecasts: Mostly fair and continued warm today, tonight and tomorrow.
Temp. range: 86—68. Yesterday: 83.2—66.5.

VOL. CVII—No. 36,683 | NEW YORK, TUESDAY, JULY 1, 1958. | 10¢ beyond 100-mile zone from New York City. Higher in air delivery cities. | K | FIVE CENTS

ALASKA TO JOIN UNION AS THE 49TH STATE; FINAL APPROVAL IS VOTED BY SENATE, 64-20; BILL SENT TO EISENHOWER, WHO WILL SIGN IT

2 MORE AMERICANS ABDUCTED IN CUBA BY REBEL FORCES

44 From U. S. and Canada Now Held—Officials of Nickel Plant Latest

Special to The New York Times.

HAVANA, June 30 — Two more Americans were kidnapped today by the Cuban rebels, bringing to forty-four the number of North American servicemen and civilians seized since last Thursday.

Those kidnapped today are officers of the Nicaro nickel plant, on the north coast of Oriente Province.

Oriente is the center of operations of the rebels, led by Fidel Castro and his brother Raul, against the Government of President Fulgencio Batista. The rebels say they have carried out the kidnappings to bring pressure on the United States Government to halt military aid and assistance to the Batista regime.

Among the United States citizens seized — three of the victims are Canadians — are twenty-eight sailors and marines from the United States Naval Base at Guantanamo Bay on the south coast of Oriente.

U. S. Denies Rebel Charge

Replying to a rebel charge that the base had been used by Cuban military planes operating against the insurgents, the United States Ambassador, Earl E. T. Smith, issued a statement yesterday saying that the base was not open to planes on combat operations.

The rebels told a sailor whom they did not abduct that his kidnapped colleagues would be released today.

United States officials have been in contact with the rebels in an attempt to negotiate the release of the naval and marine personnel as well as the ten Americans and two Canadians seized last Thursday. All twelve are employes of the Moa Bay Mining Company, on the north coast of Oriente. Two civilians, an American and a Canadian, were kidnapped last night.

Mine Is Not Guarded

The Americans seized today are Sherman Avery White and J. Andrew Poll, administrator general and assistant administrator general, respectively, of the Nickel Prospecting Company, which leases the Nicaro plant from the United States Government. They were carried off at 8:30 this morning by a group of eight rebels, according to the announcement of the United States Embassy.

No details are available, but it is supposed that the two officials went to the mine, about twelve miles from the small town of Nicaro, where 6,000 workers and officials live, to check on operations. Presumably they were abducted there. The entrance of the town is guarded by an army detach-

Continued on Page 3, Column 6

Russians to Attend Geneva Talk Today

By JOHN W. FINNEY
Special to The New York Times.

GENEVA, June 30—The Soviet Union agreed today to enter into technical talks with the West on the detection of tests of nuclear weapons. As a result, talks between scientists of four Western and four Communist nations will begin here tomorrow afternoon in a conference room in the Old League of Nations headquarters.

The Soviet agreement was announced by Dr. Yevgeni K. Fedorov, head of the Soviet delegation of scientists, following a two-hour conference with Dr. James B. Fisk, chairman of the Western scientific group.

Dr. Fedorov said at a news conference later it had been agreed that the talks would begin tomorrow and that discussions would be limited to

Continued on Page 5, Column 1

BEIRUT USES JETS TO CHECK REBELS

Bombards Force Imperiling Airport—U. N. Questions Suspected Syrians

By United Press International.

BEIRUT, Lebanon, June 30—The Government sent rocket-firing jet fighters against rebels in the hills only seven miles from Beirut International Airport today. At the same time, the Tripoli command reported it had cut the main rebel supply line into that city.

On their side, the rebels declared they had cut the main highway between Beirut and Damascus.

Druse tribesmen under the leadership of rebel chieftain Kamal Jumblatt were in the hills overlooking the airport. Jumblatt's army of 500 to 1,000 men appeared also to be poised for a night attack on Chemlan, fifteen miles southeast of the capital, which had been emptied of civilians.

[At the United Nations, Secretary General Dag Hammarskjold said United Nations observers in Lebanon had begun to question prisoners, "said to be Syrians," on their possible connection with the Lebanese uprising.]

A rebel spokesman said the Druse forces were astride the main highway to Damascus. There was no Government confirmation, but former Premier

Continued on Page 6, Column 3

N. A. ROCKEFELLER ENTERS G.O.P. RACE FOR GOVERNORSHIP

Promises Strong Fight—Mahoney and Hall Top Him in Delegate Votes

Text of Rockefeller statement is printed on Page 36.

By CLAYTON KNOWLES

Nelson A. Rockefeller announced his candidacy for Governor yesterday. He said that if nominated he would "leave no stone unturned" to win election.

The announcement, expected for some weeks, brought the declared candidacies in Republican ranks to two.

Leonard W. Hall of Oyster Bay, L. I., former Republican national chairman, announced his candidacy several weeks ago and has been campaigning vigorously. State Senator Walter J. Mahoney of Buffalo has promised to announce his position "some time in August."

In promising an "aggressive campaign," Mr. Rockefeller declared that New York's status as the Empire State had been put in jeopardy by a "complacent administration" in Albany that evaded, rather than dealt with, serious fiscal and social problems.

New Approach Held Needed

His decision to make the race, he explained, was rooted in the "deep conviction that a new approach to government must be taken in New York State." He said "new energy and efficiency, vision, courage and imagination" would be needed to enable the state "to regain its traditional pre-eminence."

Mr. Rockefeller asserted that "a lifetime spent in administration, both in government and in private and philanthropic activities," qualified him to provide the "progressive, imaginative leadership" that state conditions required.

"If nominated, I will accept the challenge and wage an aggressive campaign on the issues," he said. "If elected, I shall serve with the full awareness of the responsibility such confidence places upon me."

A member of one of America's wealthiest families, the youthful-looking board chairman of Rockefeller Center, Inc., will celebrate his fiftieth birthday next Tuesday. He is the first Rockefeller to seek elective office.

A grandson of the late John D. Rockefeller, who founded the oil dynasty, he said his family

Continued on Page 36, Column 4

The New York Times

ALASKA: Heavy lines define area approved for statehood. The symbols denote its present and potential resources.

July 1, 1958

OPPOSITION WILTS

A Bipartisan Coalition Defeats All Efforts to Amend Plan

By C. P. TRUSSELL
Special to The New York Times.

WASHINGTON, June 30—The Senate approved tonight the admission of Alaska as the forty-ninth state in the Union. The vote was 64 to 20.

Only President Eisenhower's signature, which is assured, and approval in a territorial referendum remain before statehood is formally achieved. Test votes indicate that the issue will carry by an overwhelming majority.

The Senate accepted the statehood bill passed by the House of Representatives word for word, beating down every effort to change it. Thus the bill goes directly to the White House.

Any change in the language would have sent the bill back to the House and invited further delays and possible death.

Final Senate action came after five days and evenings of battle, some of it bitter. The vote crossed party lines. The South fought admission, but not solidly. Senators from other sections of the country were also divided.

Stepovich in Gallery

Thirty-three Republicans and thirty-one Democrats voted in favor of admission. Opposed were seven Republicans and thirteen Democrats.

Gov. Michael A. Stepovich of Alaska sat tensely in the Senate gallery while the vote was being taken. When the result was announced he shouted:

"Thank God."

As well-wishers surrounded him he made a prediction.

"I believe that we will show the United States of America that we will be one of the greatest states in the Union within the next fifty years," he said.

It is expected that Alaska will assume full statehood by autumn or early winter. Its two Senators and one member of the House of Representatives could take their Congressional posts when the Eighty-Sixth Congress convenes next January.

Amendments Defeated

Before the final vote tonight, the Senate rejected by a vote of 62—22 a point of order entered by Senator James O. Eastland, Democrat of Mississippi.

He noted that Alaska Constitution provided that in the election of the first two Senators, one be given a six-year term and the other two or four years, to permit the staggering of Senatorial incumbencies.

Mr. Eastland said that this violated the United States Constitution's provision that all Senators be elected for six years.

But the Senate decided that this was not a valid objection and overrode it.

Senator John Stennis, Democrat of Mississippi, moved that the bill be referred to the Sen-

Continued on Page 16, Column 1

DISMISSAL RULING CURBS PRESIDENT

High Court Holds He Lacks Power to Oust Wiener of War Claims Agency

By RUSSELL BAKER
Special to The New York Times.

WASHINGTON, June 30—The Supreme Court tightened today the limitation on the President's power to remove officials of Federal quasi-judicial bodies.

Where Congress has not defined justifiable causes for dismissal, the court held, it must be assumed that Congress does not want to hang a "Damocles' sword" over these officials by permitting the President to remove them solely to substitute "men of his own choosing."

The opinion, written for a unanimous court by Justice Felix Frankfurter, upheld Myron Wiener's contention that he was wrongfully dismissed from the War Claims Commission in 1953 so that President Eisenhower could administer the agency with personnel of his own selection.

1935 Ruling Recalled

The last significant Supreme Court ruling in the historic debate over Presidential power to dismiss was rendered in 1935. Then, in a case closely paralleling the Wiener case, the court ruled that the President could not dismiss an officer of a Federal regulatory agency for any reason except those stipulated in law.

In the 1935 case, Humphrey's Executor v. United States, President Roosevelt dismissed a member of the Federal Trade Commission on the ground that the "aims and purposes" of his Administration could be "carried out most effectively with personnel of my own selection."

The court overruled him, holding that a President could dismiss only for reasons speci-

Continued on Page 20, Column 2

Alabama Is Denied Access To Rolls of N. A. A. C. P.

Special to The New York Times.

WASHINGTON, June 30—A $100,000 contempt fine imposed by Alabama when the National Association for the Advancement of Colored People refused to disclose its list of members in the state was struck down today by the Supreme Court.

The court held unanimously that compulsory disclosure under the circumstances in Alabama would violate constitutional guarantees of free speech and association, Justice John Marshall Harlan, writing for the court, said:

"Inviolability of privacy in group association may in many circumstances be indispensable to preservation of freedom of

Text of the opinion will be found on Page 18.

association, particularly where a group espouses dissident beliefs.

"Petitioner [the N. A. A. C. P.] has made an uncontroverted showing that on past occasions revelation of the identity of its rank-and-file members has exposed these members to economic reprisal, loss of employment, threat of physical coercion and other manifestations of public hostility."

A Major Victory

The decision was a major victory for the N. A. A. C. P. in a fight to continue operations in the South. Its activities include helping to bring suits to end school segregation.

Seven Southern states have passed legislation aimed at the association or have acted against it through state courts. Included are several statutes to require disclosure of members' names and others to restrict any financial help to Negro plaintiffs in lawsuits.

The organization has carried most of the legal burden of pushing for compliance with the Supreme Court's decision of 1954 holding school segregation unconstitutional.

In 1956 Alabama accused the N. A. A. C. P. of failing to obey a law requiring out-of-

Continued on Page 18, Column 7

HIGH COURT BARS LITTLE ROCK PLEA

Suggests Appeals Bench Set Integration Stay Review Before School Term

Text of the opinion will be found on Page 19.

By ANTHONY LEWIS
Special to The New York Times.

WASHINGTON, June 30—The Supreme Court refused today to review on an emergency basis the order suspending school integration in Little Rock until January, 1961.

But the high court strongly suggested that the case be reviewed by the United States Court of Appeals for the Eighth Circuit before the next school term begins in September. That court has recessed for the summer.

"We have no doubt," the Supreme Court said in a short unsigned order, "that the Court of Appeals will recognize the vital importance of the time element in this litigation, and that it will act upon the application for a stay or the appeal in ample time to permit arrangements to be made for the next school year."

Summer Review Asked

Lawyers of the National Association for the Advancement of Colored People had asked the Supreme Court to by-pass the Eighth Circuit and hear the case this summer to assure early and final review.

A notice of appeal from District Judge Harry J. Lemley's suspension decision has been filed with the Eighth Circuit. So has an application for a stay of the decision pending its appeal. Judge Lemley denied a stay.

If the Eighth Circuit were to grant the stay, the need for speed would be gone, from the N. A. A. C. P.'s viewpoint. Little Rock Central High School would open with a handful of Negro children among the whites, as this last year, while the appeal was argued.

Chief Justice Earl Warren read the order to a packed courtroom at the end of a busy and dramatic day—the last in the high court's 1957-58 term.

Twenty-one cases that had been argued earlier in the term were decided today—with forty opinions. The Chief Justice announced that the court had disposed of all its pending business before recess-

Continued on Page 19, Column 1

ALASKANS APPEAR STUNNED BY NEWS

Civil Defense Whistles in Anchorage Signal Vote to Crowds in the Streets

By LAWRENCE E. DAVIES
Special to The New York Times.

ANCHORAGE, Alaska, June 30—Alaskans were stunned today by the realization that Congress had finally invited them to become "first class citizens."

Here in the territorial metropolis, the center of much of the agitation for statehood, it took them a while to get their bearings.

Long after the civil defense whistles had blown, signaling the Senate's action preparing the way for a forty-ninth star on the flag, unbelieving crowds almost silently walked the streets amid the tooting of automobile horns.

Texas Car Is 'Shot'

Stores did business as usual. A woman traffic policeman rode her motorcycle down Fourth Avenue putting tickets on cars that were parked overtime.

Some amateur photographers gleefully "shot" a passing car bearing a Texas license plate, emblematic of a state that would have to give up its much-loved stories of bigness as Alaska completes the transition to statehood.

Rita Martin, queen of the annual Fur Rendezvous, climbed a fire truck ladder and pinned a huge silver star—the forty-ninth—to a 60-by-40-foot flag hurriedly draped over the front wall of the Federal Building.

Miss Orah Dee Clark, 83 years old, who in 1915 was the first school principal here, stood watching the star-pinning ceremony on an automobile-jammed street.

It was an emotion-packed moment for her. She had come to the territory in 1906, and to

Continued on Page 16, Column 3

Soviet Offers Talk On Yugoslav Credit

By United Press International.

LONDON, Tuesday, July 1—The Soviet Union proposed negotiations with Yugoslavia today on $285,000,000 in credits that the Kremlin had suspended.

The Moscow radio said the proposal was contained in a Soviet note sent to Yugoslavia June 28 and published today in Moscow newspapers.

In the note the Soviet Union said an earlier note to Yugoslavia had suggested revisions in existing economic agreements, including the postponing of one loan for several years. The Soviet Union received no reply to the suggestions, today's note said.

"The Soviet Government suggests that talks of representatives of both Governments should be held as soon as pos-

Continued on Page 2, Column 5

The New York Times

SEEKS NOMINATION: Nelson A. Rockefeller at news conference at which he discussed his candidacy for nomination for Governor of New York on Republican slate.

Narcotics Agent Warns Inquiry Mafia Seeks to Invade Industry

By JOSEPH A. LOFTUS
Special to The New York Times.

WASHINGTON, June 30—An expert on the Mafia told Senators today that the secret criminal organization was making a "concerted effort" to penetrate unions and management.

They are "the same people who are active in the narcotics traffic," Martin F. Pera, a Federal narcotics agent, told the Select Committee on Improper Activities in the Labor or Management Field.

Mr. Pera was the second witness as the committee laid the groundwork for extensive hearings on what the chairman, Senator John L. McClellan said, "appears to be a close-knit, clandestine criminal syndicate."

The Arkansas Democrat, in his opening statement, said the committee "has become convinced that the relationship of the national criminal syndicate with legitimate labor and business is far more critical than has heretofore been revealed."

The first witness was Sgt. Edgar D. Crosswell of the New York State police, who broke up a gangland meeting last Nov. 14 at the home of Joseph Barbara in Apalachin, N. Y. Barbara has a serious heart condition and will not testify.

Mr. Pera had barely touched on the labor-management angle when the committee recessed for the day. Photographs of him were barred because of the nature of his work.

The agent, who has worked on the narcotics problem in several foreign countries, told the committee about the origins of

Continued on Page 14, Column 6

Rayburn Bars G. O. P. Demand For Inquiry on Fox Testimony

By WILLIAM M. BLAIR
Special to The New York Times.

WASHINGTON, June 30—Speaker Sam Rayburn rejected today a Republican attempt to have the House of Representatives investigate the conduct of the subcommittee that has been investigating the relations of Sherman Adams and Bernard Goldfine.

The Democratic Speaker ruled out of order a resolution proposed by Representative Thomas B. Curtis, Republican of Missouri. Mr. Curtis argued that the testimony of John Fox of Boston, a lawyer and business man, should have been taken in executive session, in accordance with House rules.

His move was another effort by Republicans to smother the inquiry, which they contend has developed into a "smear" of Mr. Adams and others and to stem the political fears of Republican candidates up for re-election. Mr. Adams is the assistant to President Eisenhower.

Meanwhile, Mr. Fox announced that he had instructed his lawyers to file libel suits against Mr. Adams and four other persons for what he called "scurrilous" statements about his veracity. He said he would ask $1,000,000 damages from each.

Besides Mr. Adams, he named Roger Robb of Washington and Samuel P. Sears of Boston, lawyers for Mr. Goldfine, New England industrialist; Robert B. Choate, publisher of The Boston Herald and Boston Traveler; William J. Dempsey, counsel for the Boston Herald-Traveler Corporation, and the corporation itself.

As the political atmosphere

Continued on Page 14, Column 6

"All the News That's Fit to Print"

The New York Times.

LATE CITY EDITION
U.S. Weather Bureau Report (Page 57) forecasts: Partly cloudy, warmer today; cloudy milder, chance of rain tomorrow.
Temp. range: 42—25. Yesterday: 35.3—27.9.

VOL. CVIII..No. 36,938. NEW YORK, FRIDAY, MARCH 13, 1959. FIVE CENTS

10 cents beyond 50-mile zone from New York City except on Long Island. Higher in air delivery cities.

HAWAII IS VOTED INTO UNION AS 50TH STATE; HOUSE GRANTS FINAL APPROVAL, 323 TO 89; EISENHOWER'S SIGNATURE OF BILL ASSURED

ADENAUER IS FIRM AGAINST TROOP CUT IN MIDDLE EUROPE

Gets Assurance in Talks With Macmillan That the British Seek No Disengagement

By SYDNEY GRUSON
Special to The New York Times.

BONN, Germany, March 12—Chancellor Konrad Adenauer restated to Prime Minister Harold Macmillan today West Germany's opposition to any reduction of Allied forces in Central Europe except within a general disarmament agreement.

The British leader came to Bonn today to give the Chancellor a personal report on his recent conversations in Moscow and to reassure the West Germans that Britain was not seeking the disengagement of Eastern and Western forces in Germany.

Nor, said a British Foreign Office spokesman, does London favor even a controlled limitation of forces if this would result in disequilibrium between the troops and armaments of East and West in Central Europe.

Trip Is Second of Three

Mr. Macmillan's trip here was the second of his three planned journeys to brief other Western leaders about his talks with Premier Nikita S. Khrushchev of the Soviet Union. Mr. Macmillan was in Paris earlier this week and he will cross the Atlantic for separate meetings with President Eisenhower and Prime Minister John Diefenbaker of Canada next week.

The first session between Mr. Macmillan and Dr. Adenauer, who were accompanied by their foreign ministers and two advisers each, lasted three hours. The talks were resumed tonight after a dinner in Mr. Macmillan's honor. They will continue tomorrow in the Chancellor's Palais Schaumburg offices.

The differences in outlook between the Prime Minister and the Chancellor were evident in their remarks at the airport on Mr. Macmillan's arrival.

Mr. Macmillan said the West was firm and united on the prin-

Continued on Page 3, Column 4

Governor Taking Charge Of Meeting City Tax Needs

Orders Report on Costs and Resources for Conference With Mayor Tomorrow —Wants an Agreement Next Week

By DOUGLAS DALES
Special to The New York Times.

ALBANY, March 12.—With his own program for higher state taxes out of the way, Governor Rockefeller has decided to take personal command of the Albany action needed to help New York City balance its budget for the fiscal year starting July 1.

The decision was made at a meeting with Republican legislative leaders today, called to discuss the conference to be held with Mayor Wagner Saturday morning on the city's budget problem.

The meeting will be held at the Executive Mansion and will be attended by Republican and Democratic legislative leaders.

In preparation for the meeting, Governor Rockefeller hastily named a task force to examine New York City's needs and the resources that might be tapped to meet them. A report has been asked by tomorrow night in time to be digested before the meeting with the Mayor.

The task force was designated at a meeting attended by Mr. Rockefeller, Tax Commissioner Joseph H. Murphy, Budget Director T. Norman Hurd, Majority Leader Walter J. Mahoney of the Senate and Majority Leader Joseph, F. Carlino of

Continued on Page 16, Column 4

Snowfall of 5 to 10 Inches Delays All Transit in Area

By PETER KIHSS

With spring only nine days away, the city got its heaviest snowfall of the season yesterday—5.3 inches. It was perhaps nature's way of marking the seventy-first anniversary of the famous blizzard of '88.

On March 12, 1888, that storm hurled 16.5 inches of snow on the city, and in two more days brought the total to 20.9 inches.

Rockland and Fairfield Counties reported ten inches of snow yesterday; Westchester, seven to nine; Bergen, six to seven; Long Island, five to six; Elizabeth, N. J., 5.4, and New Brunswick, N. J., two to three.

Rain and warming temperatures turned the snow into slush in the city. Temperatures dropped during the night, however, and turned the slush to ice on some roadways. The less heavily traveled roads in the suburbs and upstate were reported especially dangerous.

The forecast for today was for partly cloudy and warmer. The temperature may reach the low forties and cause the ice and snow to melt.

Yesterday's storm was caused by two low-pressure areas moving in from the Midwest and from the Virginia coast. Snow fell throughout the Northeast. Depths ranged up to fourteen inches in Chautauqua County on Lake Erie, the Schoharie Valley west of Albany and in western Maryland.

Seven deaths were attributed to the storm in New York, New Jersey and Ohio.

The city's public schools had only 70 per cent attendance. Radio station WOR, which gathers and broadcasts news of

Continued on Page 22, Column 1

GOVERNOR NAMES COMMERCE HEAD

Appoints McHugh, President of New York Telephone— Utility Picks Successor

Governor Rockefeller completed his Cabinet in Albany yesterday with the appointment of Keith S. McHugh to head the Department of Commerce.

Mr. McHugh, who is 64 years old, will retire as president of the New York Telephone Company on April 30 to accept the appointment.

Governor Rockefeller said he was looking to Mr. McHugh to "invigorate" the department so that its full potential to stimulate business in the state would be realized.

Mr. McHugh is leaving a $150,000-a-year job for one that pays $18,500. However, within a year, he will qualify for a company pension as a forty-year man. A company spokesman said a pension arrangement would be worked out by the board of directors.

Meanwhile, the directors of the telephone company elected Clifton W. Phalen to succeed

Continued on Page 16, Column 2

ROCKEFELLER ASKS A DRIVE ON CRIME

In Message to Legislature, He Urges Tighter Laws

By WARREN WEAVER Jr.
Special to The New York Times.

ALBANY, March 12—Governor Rockefeller called on the Legislature today to join him in prosecuting a war against organized crime "more vigorously than ever before."

The Governor sent a special message to the lawmakers, with a dozen recommendations for tightening the existing criminal law and making law-enforcement organizations more powerful and better trained.

In his election campaign last fall, Mr. Rockefeller was outspoken in his criticism of the increase in criminal activity during the Harriman Administration. He pledged swift action against racketeers and law violators if he should be elected.

Mr. Rockefeller urged today that the Legislature:

¶Make it a misdemeanor to defy a subpoena from the State Commission of Investigation or engage in obstructive or contemptuous conduct before the crime panel.

¶Set up a municipal police training council that would establish minimum training standards for all members of police forces.

¶Increase the statute of limitations for prosecution for tax evasion from two to six years, thus giving the state more time

Continued on Page 16, Column 2

CITY VOTES DEAL ON POWER PLANTS WITH CON EDISON

But Contract Is Changed to Permit New Bids When Final Auction Is Held

By PAUL CROWELL

Contracts for the sale of the city's three rapid-transit power plants to the Consolidated Edison Company at a gross price of $125,840,000 were approved unanimously by the Board of Estimate last night.

The vote was taken after the language of the contracts had been changed slightly to make certain that bidders other than Consolidated Edison could submit offers when the power plants were disposed of at public auction, as required by the City Charter.

The changes were made after Harvey M. Spear, counsel for unidentified "substantial New York interests," had complained that his clients might not be able to submit bids technically admissible under the terms of the agreements.

Clients Not Identified

Mr. Spear declined to tell the board the names of his clients, saying that they would be disclosed when bids were received.

Mr. Spear said his clients, while preferring to submit an offer to purchase the power plants for lease back to the Transit Authority, would also be prepared to submit a bid for purchase and operation.

The contracts approved by the board paved the way for transfer of the plants to Consolidated Edison by July 1, assuming that the company was the successful bidder.

The company's bid was for at least $99,382,871 in cash in addition to concessions that would bring the total minimum purchase price up to $125,840,000. The company also offered to supply the three divisions of the city subway system with power under a ten-year contract at uniform rates.

Company Supplies IND

The company now supplies all power for the IND division. The IRT and BMT divisions obtain power from the three city plants that are on Kent Avenue, Brooklyn, and West Fifty-ninth Street and East Forty-seventh Street in Manhattan.

By its vote the Board of Estimate authorized the Mayor to execute, subject to specified conditions, a contract for selling the three plants and one for purchasing power for the three divisions of the city subway system now operated by the Transit Authority.

The board also authorized the Commissioner of Marine and Aviation, Vincent A. G. O'Connor, to execute waterfront leases in connection with the transfer

Continued on Page 15, Column 2

Associated Press Wirephoto

THE BIG NEWS: Chester Kahapea, 13, offering copies of The Honolulu Star-Bulletin yesterday in the Hawaiian capital. The flag on the front page contains fifty stars.

3 OF JOINT CHIEFS WILL BE RENAMED

Twining, Burke and White Slated for New Terms— Lemnitzer to Get Post

By HANSON W. BALDWIN
Special to The New York Times.

WASHINGTON, March 12—The reappointments of three members of the Joint Chiefs of Staff will be announced soon.

Those who will be reappointed to new two-year terms starting this summer are Gen. Nathan F. Twining, chairman of the Joint Chiefs of Staff; Gen. Thomas D. White, Chief of Staff of the Air Force, and Admiral Arleigh A. Burke, Chief of Naval Operations.

Gen. Lyman L. Lemnitzer, Vice Chief of Staff of the Army, will succeed Gen. Maxwell D. Taylor, present Army Chief of Staff, whose second two-year term ends June 30. General Taylor is expected to retire.

The second two-year term of Gen. Randolph McC. Pate, as Commandant of the Marine Corps, does not expire until next Dec. 31, and as far as is known his successor has not yet been selected. General Pate also expects to retire.

The names of Lieut. Gen. Merrill B. Twining, a brother of the chairman of the Joint Chiefs, and of Lieut. Gen. Edwin A. Pollock have been men-

Continued on Page 4, Column 2

U. S. and Canada List Seaway Tolls, Effective on April 1

By RICHARD E. MOONEY
Special to The New York Times.

WASHINGTON, March 12—The United States and Canada announced St. Lawrence Seaway tolls today, to take effect April 1.

They are identical to those proposed last June after negotiations by committees of both nations. The differences are primarily in definitions, mostly for the types of cargo that would qualify for the low rate applying, to "bulk" shipments.

[Opposition to the toll setup came from port, rail, shipping and civic interests. They called the rates unrealistically low and the estimated revenue too high. The Port of New York Authority feared a loss of 3,500 waterfront jobs because of "unfair competition" resulting from the tolls.]

Railroads Competing

The Seaway links the Great Lakes and the Atlantic for deepwater ships. Part of it was opened last summer, and the full length is scheduled to be working soon.

Interests that would benefit from the new water route and those against whom it would compete had been fighting over the toll issue.

The fight was moving into a new phase. Major railroads are considering a 20 to 25 per cent reduction of rates they charge for transporting grain for export. This would enable them better to compete with the price for shipping via the waterway.

Seaway tolls are intended to

Continued on Page 10, Column 2

HOUSE UNIT CUTS JOBLESS AID BILL

Restricts Extension of U. S. Assistance to 3 Months Instead of One Year

Special to The New York Times.

WASHINGTON, March 12—The House Ways and Means Committee approved today a bill for a three-month tapering-off of emergency Federal aid to the unemployed.

The measure falls far short of earlier plans by Democratic leaders for a year's extension of the program beyond its present expiration date of March 31.

The effect would be to prevent an abrupt cut-off of payments to about 300,000 jobless workers expected to be drawing the emergency benefits at the end of this month.

Instead, these workers would stay on the rolls until they had exhausted the benefits to which they would have been entitled in the absence of a March 31 termination date.

The committee acted in closed session by what was reported as a one-sided voice vote. The House is expected to pass the bill early next week.

Democratic sources reported that the one-year extension plan had been set aside in the interest of assuring quick enactment of a bill. President Eisenhower and House Republican leaders had voiced strong opposition to the earlier Democratic proposal.

Another factor was the apparent lack of enthusiasm with which the proposed one-year

Continued on Page 18, Column 4

Fulton Street Widening Dropped By Jack on Protest of Merchants

The highly controversial proposal to widen part of Fulton Street in lower Manhattan was withdrawn from further consideration yesterday by Borough President Hulan E. Jack of Manhattan.

The action by the Board of Estimate permitting Mr. Jack to drop the project constituted a victory for a group of Fulton Street merchants.

Opponents have fought the proposal as threatening hardship to "hundreds of business men and thousands of their employes." They have also argued that the widening would not materially relieve the area's traffic situation.

Mr. Jack said he favored studies of the possibility of both an eastbound and a westbound artery in lower Manhattan.

Pending such studies, he said, it would be better to withdraw the Fulton Street proposal. In the meantime, he added, he hoped all of those who have been involved in the widening dispute would have a better understanding of the problem.

The proposal that Mr. Jack withdrew called for widening Fulton Street on its south side from Broadway to Water Street. The project was intended as the first stage of an ultimate widening of Fulton Street from South Street to West Street.

Two major slum clearance cooperative housing projects totaling $61,000,000 in cost in the Rockaways, Queens, were approved by the board.

One was Hammels-Rockaway,

Continued on Page 22, Column 6

MEASURE SPEEDED

A Short-Cut Sends It Direct to President, Who Is 'Delighted'

By C. P. TRUSSELL
Special to The New York Times

WASHINGTON, March 12—The Territory of Hawaii was voted into the Union today as its fiftieth state.

The House of Representatives gave its approval by a vote of 323 to 89. Yesterday the Senate approved the Hawaii bill, 76 to 15.

President Eisenhower's approval is assured. The White House said today he was "delighted" and noted that "he has been urging it for some time."

Thus, after one of the fastest actions by Congress in years, only the mechanics of admitting a new state remain before Hawaii joins the Union.

The question arose as to whether the island territory some 2,000 miles from continental United States would seek to put its fiftieth star into the flag July 4 of this year when Alaska adds its forty-ninth. There is barely enough time to do so and island leaders doubted that it would be done.

Governor Gives Word

With the galleries filled, the House started its long roll-call in midafternoon. Among the spectators was the Governor of Hawaii, William F. Quinn. When the roll-call began he quietly left the gallery and went to the office of Sam Rayburn, Speaker of the House.

At the Speaker's office Governor Quinn telephoned Acting Gov. Edward E. Johnston at Honolulu and asked him to hold the line. When he was notified that the roll-call had recorded 219 ayes—a majority of the House—Governor Quinn set off a celebration in the islands by shouting:

"Sound the sirens, close the schools and get going."

A little later he added a note of caution:

"Keep the lid on a little, Ed."

Before Hawaii can attain statehood it must hold a referendum on whether it wants to assume the burdens at this time. Besides agreeing at the polls with provisions of the new law,

Continued on Page 13, Column 3

HAWAIIANS START 2 DAYS' FESTIVITY

Alaska Sends First 'Aloha' to Celebrating Islanders

By LAWRENCE E. DAVIES
Special to The New York Times.

HONOLULU, March 12—The kamaaina and the malihini celebrated today Congressional assurance that the nation was ready to welcome Hawaii as the fiftieth state.

That is to say, the oldtimer—the Hawaiian version of the Alaskan sourdough—joined with the newcomer—the Hawaiian counterpart of the Alaskan cheechako—in opening a two-day demonstration of gratitude over the prospective ending of territorial status for the islands.

The celebration got off to a restrained start. It picked up momentum as the day wore on toward a climax here on the island of Oahu with huge bonfire, aerial and offshore military pyrotechnics and hula dancing.

At the beginning everyone seemed to be waiting for someone else to show the way. Within a half-hour after word came from Washington of the action in the House of Representatives, however, the Waikiki area was clogged with horn-tooting automobiles. Bands and colorfully clad marchers took over at midafternoon.

Colored paper streamers were flung from downtown office buildings along King and Merchant Streets. Hands were thrown forward with a "happy statehood" salutation. Mayor Neal Blaisdell of Honolulu was [illegible]

Continued on Page 13, Column [illegible]

There Are Times When Bad Weather Brings Out the Best in a Man

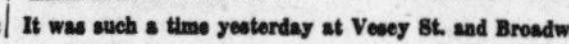

It was such a time yesterday at Vesey St. and Broadway

The New York Times (by Neal Boenzi)

And a man came forward to lend a gallant, helping hand

"All the News That's Fit to Print"

The New York Times.

LATE CITY EDITION
U. S. Weather Bureau Report (Page 93) forecasts:
Cloudy, periods of rain today.
Partly cloudy, colder tomorrow.
Temp. range: 55—41; yesterday: 53.8—40.4.

VOL. CX..No. 37,546. NEW YORK, THURSDAY, NOVEMBER 10, 1960. 10 cents beyond 50-mile zone from New York City except on Long Island. Higher in air delivery cities. FIVE CENTS

KENNEDY'S VICTORY WON BY CLOSE MARGIN; HE PROMISES FIGHT FOR WORLD FREEDOM; EISENHOWER OFFERS 'ORDERLY TRANSITION'

DEMOCRATS HERE SPLIT IN VICTORY; LEHMAN ASSAILED

De Sapio Accepts Challenge for Party Control—Mayor Claims Leadership

Text of De Sapio statement appears on Page 43.

By LEO EGAN

Less than twenty-four hours after the polls closed, the political coalition that gave Senator John F. Kennedy New York's forty-five electoral votes began coming apart at the seams.

Its disintegration was signaled by Carmine G. De Sapio in a statement assailing former Gov. Herbert H. Lehman, key figure in the Democratic reform group, and Alex Rose, Liberal party master of strategy.

The statement accepted Mr. Lehman's election night challenge to a finish fight for control of the party organization in the city and state.

At the same time it appeared to rule out any chance of a Democratic-Liberal party coalition for next year's Mayoral election in New York City and for the Governorship election in the state in 1962 if Mr. De Sapio remains in control of the party machinery.

Kennedy's Delicate Problem

Mr. De Sapio, leader of Tammany and Democratic National Committeeman for New York, consulted Michael H. Prendergast, the Democratic State Chairman, and a number of party leaders in the city and upstate before issuing his statement.

The collapse of the coalition so soon after it achieved its goal gave President-elect Kennedy a delicate political problem before he takes office. At some stage soon he will have to decide whom in New York to consult about appointments for the new Administration.

Thus, in so far as New York is concerned, the election appeared to raise as many questions as it settled. Control of the Democratic party machinery is one of them. Among the others are: What is Mayor Wagner's political future? And what is Governor Rockefeller's?

When told of Mr. De Sapio's statement last night, Mayor Wagner commented that he in-

Continued on Page 43, Column 1

Registration Set-Up Called Faulty Here

By DOUGLAS DALES

Political leaders voiced dissatisfaction yesterday over the way permanent personal registration functioned here Tuesday in its first test in a Presidential election.

Charges were made that thousands of persons had been disfranchised because they were unable to convince election inspectors that they had registered and were eligible to vote.

How many voters may have been so affected was concededly a guess. But a check of the Supreme Courts in the five boroughs indicated that more than 1,300 persons had gone before the justices for orders directing the inspectors to permit them to vote.

"There was a minimum of 10,000 denied the right to vote." Abraham Gellinoff,

Continued on Page 43, Column 5

ASSEMBLY DELAYS U.N. CONGO DEBATE

Postpones It Indefinitely, 48-30, as Soviet Backs Step—U. S. Move Fails

By KATHLEEN TELTSCH
Special to The New York Times.

UNITED NATIONS, N. Y., Nov. 9—The General Assembly voted tonight to postpone the debate on the Congo indefinitely.

The 48-to-30 vote, with eighteen abstentions, was on a surprise move made by Ghana with the help of Guinea and Nigeria and the enthusiastic support of the Soviet bloc.

The United States tried to avoid the adjournment vote by asking for a suspension of the session until delegates could ponder the unexpected request.

Western sources said privately that Ghana's initiative appeared to have been prompted in part by the presence here of President Joseph Kasavubu of the Congo and the likelihood that the Assembly's Credentials Committee would agree to his request for the seating of a Congolese delegation of his supporters.

A Two-Hour Wrangle

Ghana, Guinea, India and five other states have joined in sponsoring a resolution that aims instead at having the Assembly seat a delegation designated by the deposed Congolese Premier, Patrice Lumumba.

The Assembly acted after a two-hour wrangle marked by two table-thumping demonstrations by the Soviet bloc and also by Ghana, both in protest against the efforts of Foreign Minister Pierre Wigny of Belgium to defend his country's position on the Congo issue.

The adjournment request was made by Alex Quaison-Sackey, Ghana's chief delegate. He appealed to the Assembly to hold off any further debate pending the efforts of a fifteen-member Asian-African commission to reconcile the clashing political factions in the Congo and restore some governmental stability.

He said that the commission probably would leave for the Congo in a week and that further acrimonious debate in the Assembly would only hamper the conciliation effort.

However, the adjournment as voted did not stipulate how long the debate should be suspended. United States sources said tonight that they understood this to mean that discussion could

Continued on Page 3, Column 1

ATOM BILL BEATEN IN FRENCH SENATE

Debre to Push Compromise on Nuclear Force Plan

By W. GRANGER BLAIR
Special to The New York Times.

PARIS, Thursday, Nov. 10—The Senate early today rejected President de Gaulle's project for an independent French nuclear striking force.

By a vote of 186 to 83, with seventeen abstentions, this conservative Upper House approved a procedural motion to table the national nuclear deterrent bill that had been passed to it by the National Assembly Oct. 27.

Although the Senate's action was a stinging blow to President de Gaulle and a sharp indication of mounting parliamentary opposition, it did not mean that the Government's measure would not eventually become law.

It was announced after the vote that Premier Michel Debré would call for the creation of a mixed committee of Senators and Deputies to work out a compromise measure. Should this conference committee fail to find a compromise, the Government would resubmit its measure to the Assembly for a second reading and virtually certain approval. The measure would then become law with or without Senate's approval.

The Senate motion to table

Continued on Page 8, Column 1

NEWS INDEX

WINNER'S PLEDGE

Family Is With Him as He Vows to Press Nation's Cause

Text of Kennedy's statement is printed on Page 36.

By HOMER BIGART
Special to The New York Times.

HYANNIS, Mass., Nov. 9—Senator John F. Kennedy accepted in solemn mood today his election as President.

He pledged all his energy to advancing "the long-range interests of the United States and the cause of freedom around the world."

He made this pledge inside the flag-decked Hyannis Armory at 1:45 P. M., an hour after Vice President Nixon, his Republican opponent, had conceded defeat.

His wife, Jacqueline, stood at his side as the 43-year-old President-elect faced 300 newsmen and massed batteries of TV cameras and gave his victory statement to the nation.

Behind him were arrayed the Kennedy family: his father, former Ambassador Joseph P. Kennedy; his mother, three sisters and three brothers.

No Sign of Jubilation

The Kennedys showed no evidence of jubilation. All wore expressions of solemnity. Mr. Kennedy's margin of victory was too slender to stir much elation. Some of his aides acknowledged disappointment over the startlingly narrow gap in the popular vote.

Mr. Kennedy, after responding to applause with a diffident bow and a smile, first read the telegram from Mr. Nixon conceding defeat and extending congratulations. The Senator had stayed up until 3:50 A. M. awaiting this concession and had gone to bed disappointed when the Vice President withheld it.

Replies to Nixon

Mr. Nixon wired the President-elect that all the nation would give him "united support" in the next four years.

Mr. Kennedy replied to Mr. Nixon:

"I know that the nation can continue to count on your unswerving loyalty in whatever effort you undertake, and that you and I can maintain our long-standing cordial relations in the years ahead."

Mr. Kennedy then read a congratulatory message from President Eisenhower.

In his message the President informed Mr. Kennedy that he would shortly receive suggestions from the President as to the change-over of responsibilities for national leadership.

To this Senator Kennedy had replied:

"I am grateful for your wire and good wishes. I look forward to working with you in the near future. The whole country is hopeful that your long ex-

Continued on Page 36, Column 7

United Press International Telephoto

THE MESSAGES WERE CONGRATULATORY: Senator John F. Kennedy displaying telegrams at Hyannis, Mass. With him are Mrs. Kennedy, his parents and Robert F. Kennedy, left, and R. Sargent Shriver, a brother-in-law.

KHRUSHCHEV NOTE SALUTES KENNEDY

Message of Congratulations Asks for Negotiations on Tensions in World

Text of Khrushchev message will be found on Page 42.

By The Associated Press.

MOSCOW, Nov. 9—Soviet Premier Khrushchev congratulated Senator John F. Kennedy today for his Presidential victory.

He expressed hope that Soviet-United States relations would "again follow the line along which they were developing in Franklin Roosevelt's time."

He urged negotiations aimed at easing the international situation.

[In Bonn, Chancellor Konrad Adenauer said he planned to go to Washington early next year for conferences with Mr. Kennedy.]

Mr. Khrushchev's statements in a congratulatory message to Mr. Kennedy coincided with Moscow's insistence that the policies of President Eisenhower had suffered a rebuff in the election.

The Soviet press contended that the election proved "the American people have blackballed the policy of the 'cold war' and the arms race, that they want changes and expect Washington to pursue a reasonable course in international affairs, a course dictated by life and the balance of forces now prevailing in the world." Mr.

Continued on Page 42, Column 4

10 Irish Soldiers Slain in Congo When U.N. Patrol Is Ambushed

By PAUL HOFMANN
Special to The New York Times.

LEOPOLDVILLE, the Congo, Nov. 9 — A patrol of eleven Irish soldiers of the United Nations force in the Congo was ambushed in the northern part of Katanga Province yesterday. The bodies of four men were sighted.

[The United Nations Command said that ten soldiers had been slain in the ambush, Reuters reported. The Irish Army announced in Dublin that one private had survived the attack. Reports received by the United Nations in New York said the surviving soldier was "badly wounded," according to United Press International.]

The patrol belonged to the Irish Thirty-third Battalion, which has headquarters in the industrial city of Albertville. The battalion, with a strength of about 550 men, is responsible for maintaining order in a vast area of North Katanga. The region has been the scene of intertribal warfare and clashes between Baluba tribesmen and the gendarmerie controlled by Moise Tshombe, President of Katanga.

United Nations officials here were unable to say who had attacked the Irish patrol. The ambush occurred south of Niemba, a village between Albertville and Kabalo. The zone is described as "Baluba country," but it is not known whether Baluba tribesmen were responsible for the assault.

Announcing the loss, a United Nations spokesman said it brought the toll of dead in the international force in the Congo to about thirty since the world organization's troops arrived

Continued on Page 2, Column 3

Electoral Vote by States

	Rep.	Dem.		Rep.	Dem.		Rep.	Dem.
Alabama	..	5*	Louisiana	..	10	Ohio	25	..
Alaska	..	..	Maine	5	..	Oklahoma	8	..
Arizona	4	..	Maryland	..	9	Oregon	6	..
Arkansas	..	8	Mass.	..	16	Penna.	..	32
California	..	..	Michigan	..	20	Rhode Island	..	4
Colorado	6	..	Minnesota	..	11	So. Carolina	..	8
Conn.	..	8	Mississippi	**	**	So. Dakota	4	..
Delaware	..	3	Missouri	..	13	Tennessee	11	..
Florida	10	..	Montana	4	..	Texas	..	24
Georgia	..	12	Nebraska	6	..	Utah	4	..
Hawaii	..	..	Nevada	..	3	Vermont	3	..
Idaho	4	..	New Hamp.	4	..	Virginia	12	..
Illinois	..	27	New Jersey	..	16	Washington	9	..
Indiana	13	..	New Mexico	..	4	W. Virginia	..	8
Iowa	10	..	New York	..	45	Wisconsin	12	..
Kansas	8	..	No. Carolina	..	14	Wyoming	3	..
Kentucky	10	..	North Dakota	4	..	Total	185	300

*Five electors are pledged to Kennedy and six unpledged.
**Eight electors not pledged to vote for party candidates.

LIBERALS SUFFER SETBACK IN HOUSE

G. O. P. Picks Up 22 Seats to Aid Conservative Bloc

By JOHN D. MORRIS

The House of Representatives will have a more conservative tinge in the Eighty-seventh Congress.

Inroads into the present House Democratic majority of 283 to 154 scored by the Republicans in Tuesday's elections promised to strengthen their conservative coalition with Southern Democrats.

The liberal legislative program to be submitted early next year by the new Democratic President, John F. Kennedy, may consequently face handicaps in the new Congress, which convenes Jan. 3.

In the Senate, Republicans cut the Democratic margin by two seats, to 64 to 36. That chamber remains predominantly liberal in membership, although conservatives dominate key committee posts.

Gubernatorial Shifts

The Democrats achieved a net gain of one governorship and now control thirty-four of the fifty state houses. In twenty-seven gubernatorial contests the Democrats won fifteen and the Republicans twelve, with an exchange of party control in thirteen.

In the House races, nearly complete unofficial returns showed that the Democrats had elected 257 House candidates and the Republicans 175, with five contests still in doubt.

The Republicans captured twenty-nine seats held by Democrats and lost seven of their own, for a net gain of at least twenty-two. For a bare numerical majority of 219 they would have had to achieve a net gain of sixty-five.

Among the eleven states of the Old Confederacy the Republicans maintained their hold on seven seats of the Eighty-

Continued on Page 38, Column 4

NIXON WIRE GIVES HIS 'BEST WISHES'

Sends Kennedy a Message —500 in Capital Hail Him

By BILL BECKER
Special to The New York Times.

LOS ANGELES, Nov. 9—Vice President Nixon conceded today the Presidential election of his Democratic opponent, Senator John F. Kennedy.

About twelve hours after the polls had closed, the Vice President sent the following telegram to Senator Kennedy at Hyannis Port, Mass.:

"I want to repeat through this wire the congratulations and best wishes I extended to you on television last night. I know that you will have the united support of all Americans as you lead the nation in the cause of peace and freedom in the next four years."

Read by Aide

The telegram was read to newsmen by Mr. Nixon's press secretary, Herbert G. Klein, at 9:45 A. M., Pacific standard time (12:45 P. M., Eastern standard time).

The Vice President did not make a personal appearance. Mr. Klein said Mr. Nixon was resting with Mrs. Nixon and their two daughters in their suite at the Ambassador Hotel.

It was obvious that the Vice President had considered his remarks late on election night a virtual concession.

[A crowd of several hundred greeted Mr. Nixon as he arrived Wednesday night at Andrews Air Base, near Washington, after a flight of four and a half hours from Los Angeles.]

Mr. Nixon remained in seclusion most of the morning although Mr. Klein said he was up about 6 A. M. after little more than three hours of sleep. The secretary said Mr. Nixon

Continued on Page 42, Column 5

RESULTS DELAYED

Popular Vote Almost Even—300-185 Is Electoral Tally

By JAMES RESTON

Senator John F. Kennedy of Massachusetts finally won the 1960 Presidential election from Vice President Nixon by the astonishing margin of less than two votes per voting precinct.

Senator Kennedy's electoral vote total stood yesterday at 300, just thirty-one more than the 269 needed for election. The Vice President's total was 185. Fifty-two additional electoral votes, including California's thirty-two, were still in doubt last night.

But the popular vote was a different story. The two candidates ran virtually even. Senator Kennedy's lead last night was little more than 300,000 in a total tabulated vote of about 66,000,000 cast in 165,826 precincts.

That was a plurality for the Senator of less than one-half of 1 per cent of the total vote—the smallest percentage difference between the popular vote of two Presidential candidates since 1880, when James A. Garfield outran Gen. Winfield Scott Hancock by 7,000 votes in a total of almost 9,000,000.

End Divided Government

Nevertheless, yesterday's voting radically altered the political balance of power in America in favor of the Democrats and put them in a commanding position in the Federal and state capitals unknown since the heyday of Franklin D. Roosevelt.

They regained control of the White House for the first time since 1952 and thus ended divided government in Washington. They retained control of the Senate and the House of Representatives, although with slightly reduced margins. And they increased their hold on the state governorships by one, bringing the Democratic margin to 34—16.

The President-elect is the first Roman Catholic ever to win the nation's highest office. The only other member of his church nominated for President was Alfred E. Smith, who was defeated by Herbert Hoover in 1928.

Faces Difficult Questions

Despite his personal triumph, President-elect Kennedy is confronted by a number of hard questions:

¶In the face of such a narrow victory how can he get through the Congress the liberal program he proposed during the campaign?

¶Can so close an election produce any impetus for loosening the conservative coalition of Republicans and Southern Democrats which has blocked most liberal legislation in the House?

¶Will the new President be able successfully to claim a mandate for legislation such as the $1.25 minimum wage, Fed-

Continued on Page 35, Column 1

PRESIDENT SENDS WIRE TO KENNEDY

He Felicitates Senator and Orders Agency Chiefs to Cooperate With Him

By FELIX BELAIR Jr.
Special to The New York Times.

AUGUSTA, Ga., Nov. 9—President Eisenhower congratulated President-elect John F. Kennedy today on his election and then invited him to designate representatives to participate in all Federal policy discussions to assure an "orderly transition" to the new Administration.

The text of the President's telegram was withheld here at the request of Mr. Kennedy. But President Eisenhower is understood to have told the President-elect that he had instructed all heads of Federal departments and agencies to "cooperate fully" with Mr. Kennedy's representatives.

President Eisenhower arrived here for his customary fall holiday in midafternoon after a two-hour flight from Washington.

The President's message of congratulation to Mr. Kennedy was sent from the White House just before he took off for his favorite vacation retreat here at Augusta National Golf Club.

He also sent messages to the defeated Republican candidate, Vice President Nixon, and his running mate, Henry Cabot Lodge, as well as Vice President-elect Lyndon B. Johnson.

In his telegram to Mr. Nixon

Continued on Page 42, Column 7

Vatican Calls Kennedy Election Proof of American Democracy

By ARNALDO CORTESI
Special to The New York Times.

ROME, Nov. 9—The election of Senator John F. Kennedy, a Roman Catholic, to the Presidency was received with keen satisfaction in the Vatican today.

During the campaign the Vatican remained neutral. Its newspaper, L'Osservatore Romano, abstained from all comment lest it be accused of siding with one candidate against the other.

Today the editor of the newspaper, former Italian Deputy Raimondo Manzini, said:

"Kennedy's victory strengthens the appreciation for the high democratic principles of freedom that guide American public life and assure access to the highest office to every citizen regardless of social class, race, or religion.

"The effective support given by large numbers of Protestant citizens to a Catholic considered suitable for the Presidency has been significant in this respect. Catholics are, of course, satisfied at the solemn confirmation of the principle that the office of President is open to a son of the Catholic Church, which enjoys such large prestige in the United States. Catholics have, however, always admired Nixon's irreproachable attitude of deferential respect for the Catholic hierarchy."

Senator Kennedy's victory was announced under large headlines by the whole morning press in Italy today. In most newspapers it took precedence over the results of the provincial and municipal elections that were held in Italy over the week-end.

Government circles received the news without astonishment

Continued on Page 38, Column 1

"All the News That's Fit to Print"

The New York Times.

LATE CITY EDITION

U. S. Weather Bureau Report (Page 90) forecast: Increasing cloudiness today. Snow, rain tonight. Rain tomorrow. Temp. range: 38—26; yesterday: 37—30.

VOL. CXI . No. 38,014. NEW YORK, WEDNESDAY, FEBRUARY 21, 1962. 10 cents beyond 50-mile zone from New York City except on Long Island. Higher in air delivery cities. FIVE CENTS

GLENN ORBITS EARTH 3 TIMES SAFELY; PICKED UP IN CAPSULE BY DESTROYER; PRESIDENT WILL GREET HIM IN FLORIDA

N.A.S.A. via Associated Press Wirephoto

READY: Lieut. Col. John H. Glenn Jr. walks to the van to take him to the launching site at Cape Canaveral, Fla.

N.A.S.A. via United Press International Telephoto

LIFT-OFF: The Atlas rocket booster bearing the Project Mercury spacecraft roars aloft with 360,000-pound thrust.

N.A.S.A. via Associated Press Wirephoto

RECOVERY: Crewmen of destroyer Noa secure capsule carrying astronaut before lifting it out of the Atlantic.

CARLINO CLEARED IN SHELTER CASE BY ETHICS PANEL

Lane Scored in Unanimous Report, Which He Calls 'Cynical and Callous'

Text of concluding sections of report is on Page 50.

By WARREN WEAVER Jr.
Special to The New York Times.

ALBANY, Feb. 20—The Assembly Committee on Ethics and Guidance exonerated Speaker Joseph F. Carlino today of charges of conflict of interest made by Assemblyman Mark Lane.

In a unanimous report submitted to the Legislature, the bipartisan committee said:

¶Mr. Carlino did not "betray the public trust" by serving as a director of a company manufacturing home fall-out shelters while helping to pass school-shelter legislation last November.

¶He did not draft or support the shelter legislation "in any improper manner" for the benefit of the company, Lancer Industries, Inc.

¶The Speaker was not influenced in his official actions in behalf of the bill by the fact that he was a member of the board of directors of Lancer.

¶He did not receive any special benefit from the passage of the legislation.

Charges Unsubstantiated

"The committee concludes with respect to each and every accusation contained in the charges filed," the report said, "that Assemblyman Lane and those who testified in their support failed to submit credible evidence to substantiate them."

In submitting the report, the Ethics Committee requested that the full 150-member lower house vote "with respect to the conclusions reached herein" in the light of the fact that "the charges were directed against its [the Assembly's] highest ranking official."

Assemblyman Donald A. Campbell, Republican of Amsterdam, who is chairman of the committee, said he would move in the Assembly tomorrow for acceptance of the report. Mr. Carlino is expected to be absent during the debate and vote.

Assemblyman Lane, a Democrat of Manhattan, had charged that the Speaker was guilty of

Continued on Page 50, Column 1

ROCKEFELLER BARS KOREA WAR BONUS

Voices Opposition in Face of Legislators' Backing

By LAYHMOND ROBINSON
Special to The New York Times.

ALBANY, Feb. 20—Governor Rockefeller expressed strong opposition tonight to a state bonus for veterans of the Korean war.

Mr. Rockefeller told the New York State Department of the American Legion that he could not "as a responsible leader of government" support the demand for a bonus. The veterans' group had been campaigning for a $100,000,000 bonus for the 482,000 Korean war veterans or their next-of-kin in the state.

The Governor said his stand was backed "unanimously" by the "Republican leadership of the state." This was a reference to the leaders of the Republican-controlled Legislature.

He said that demands for funds for education, mental health, narcotics control and other state services were too great to permit a diversion of money for a veterans' bonus.

Mr. Rockefeller thus took a position in direct opposition to that of most of the Republican and Democratic members of the Legislature, who have been pushing for the bonus. The issue

Continued on Page 51, Column 1

Jersey Bus Strike Settled; Service Is Due Tomorrow

By PETER KIHSS

An agreement to end the New Jersey bus strike was reached last night. The agreement, subject to ratification by the striking employes, was announced by Gov. Richard J. Hughes. The pact will be submitted to the union members at their garages starting at 7 A. M. today.

Union and management men expressed hope that buses could begin operating tomorrow at 4:30 A. M.

The strike against Public Service Coordinated Transport started at 12:01 A. M. Monday and halted 2,511 buses providing 1,000,000 rides a day. The company's 200 routes serve all of New Jersey's twenty-one counties except Warren and Hunterdon and go into New York City and Philadelphia. The Newark subway system was also shut.

Carlin Gets Credit

Governor Hughes credited Mayor Leo P. Carlin of Newark with having "sparkplugged" the successful negotiations. Mayor Carlin flew back from a Miami Beach vacation yesterday and arranged the talks with both sides and with Daniel F. Fitzpatrick, a Federal mediator, and the Governor and himself. The meeting started in Newark at 8:30 P. M., and the agreement was announced at 11:28 P. M.

Earlier, David L. Yunich, president of Bamberger's New Jersey, had asserted that the strike was having a "devastating * * * almost catastrophic" effect on retail business in Newark and elsewhere in the state. A Camden department store reported sales had fallen nearly 50 per cent on Monday, although not that far yesterday.

Despite the drop in shopping, most commuters managed to get to work by alternate means and with a minimum of confusion.

The agreement reached last night provides for a wage increase of 10 cents an hour retroactive to Feb. 1 and extending to next Feb. 1; 4 cents more an hour from then until Aug. 1, 1963, and another 4 cents an hour from then until

Continued on Page 39, Column 3

ROSENTHAL WINS QUEENS ELECTION

But Democrat-Liberal Has Margin of Only 193 Votes —Machines Guarded

By CLAYTON KNOWLES

Benjamin S. Rosenthal, a Democrat-Liberal backed by President Kennedy, squeaked through to victory last night in a special Congressional election in Queens' Sixth District.

By the slim margin of 193 votes, Mr. Rosenthal, a lanky 38-year-old Elmhurst lawyer, edged past Thomas F. Galvin of Flushing, the Republican candidate, to win a three-way race. Emil Levin of Flushing, a Democrat running as an independent, finished far behind.

The unofficial final tally, delayed as the early vote was hastily rechecked for errors, was: Rosenthal, 16,032; Galvin, 15,839, and Levin, 4,216.

Republicans immediately challenged the result and, while Mr. Galvin did not immediately ask for a recount, he sent a telegram demanding that the voting machines be impounded. All voting machines, normally just

Continued on Page 48, Column 3

McNamara Reports Gains by Vietnamese

By JACK RAYMOND
Special to The New York Times.

WASHINGTON, Feb. 20—Secretary of Defense Robert S. McNamara returned to the capital today and reported improvement in the South Vietnamese effort against Communist insurgents.

He had presided at a meeting of United States military and civilian officials yesterday at the headquarters in Hawaii of Admiral Harry S. Felt, commander of United States forces in the Pacific. The meeting was the third in a series of monthly talks on the hostilities in South Vietnam.

A spokesman for Mr. McNamara said that the forces of South Vietnam, supported by the United States, "are hitting

Continued on Page 8, Column 5

NEWS INDEX

KENNEDY PRAISES 'WONDERFUL JOB'

Tells Glenn Nation Is 'Really Proud of You'—Welcome at White House Planned

By TOM WICKER
Special to The New York Times.

WASHINGTON, Feb. 20—President Kennedy phoned Lieut. Col. John H. Glenn Jr. today immediately after the astronaut's successful orbital flight and arranged to meet him at Cape Canaveral Friday morning.

The President also set in motion plans for bringing Colonel Glenn to Washington on Monday or Tuesday, for receptions at the White House and the Capitol and a parade down Pennsylvania Avenue

A television set in his office and an open telephone line to Cape Canaveral had kept Mr. Kennedy informed of Colonel Glenn's progress all through the day.

The astronaut's three orbits around the earth, Mr. Kennedy said in a statement, have embarked the United States on a "new ocean"—that of space.

"I believe the United States must sail on it and be in a position second to none," the President said within minutes of Colonel Glenn's safe emergence from his Mercury capsule.

Colonel Glenn, he said, is the "kind of American of whom we are most proud." Mr. Kennedy also praised "all those who participated" in making the astronaut's flight successful.

Then, at 4:10 P. M., Mr. Ken-

Continued on Page 23, Column 7

Leaders of Algeria Back Peace Terms

By THOMAS F. BRADY
Special to The New York Times.

TUNIS, Feb. 20—The Algerian nationalist Provisional Government met today and gave full approval to peace accords negotiated with the French by four members of the rebel regime.

One Algerian said afterward: "All twelve members of the Government are in unanimous agreement." This was a reference to five ministers who are prisoners in France, the four negotiators and three ministers who remained in Tunis during the secret talks last week on the French-Swiss border.

The negotiators were Belkacem Krim, M'Hammed Yazid, Saad Dahlab and Lakhdar Ben Tobbal. They met here today

Continued on Page 11, Column 1

The President's Statement

Special to The New York Times.

WASHINGTON, Feb. 20—Following is the text of President Kennedy's statement on Colonel Glenn's flight:

I know that I express the great happiness and thanksgiving of all of us that Colonel Glenn has completed his trip, and I know that this is particularly felt by Mrs. Glenn and his two children.

A few days ago Colonel Glenn came to the White House and visited me, and he is—as are the other astronauts—the kind of American of whom we are most proud.

Some years ago, as a Marine pilot, he raced the sun across this country—and lost. And today he won.

I also want to say a word for all those who participated with Colonel Glenn in Canaveral. They faced many disappointments and delays—the burdens upon them were great—but they kept their heads and they made a judgment, and I think their judgment has been vindicated.

We have a long way to go in this space race. We started late. But this is the new ocean, and I believe the United States must sail on it and be in a position second to none.

Some months ago I said that I hoped every American would serve his country. Today Colonel Glenn served his, and we all express our thanks to him.

ADENAUER WANTS PARLEY ON BERLIN

Suggests Foreign Ministers of Big Four Meet 'Soon'

By SYDNEY GRUSON
Special to The New York Times.

BONN, Germany, Feb. 20—Chancellor Adenauer suggested today that a Big Four foreign ministers' conference on Berlin should be convened "soon." He was speaking to the Parliamentary group of the Christian Democratic Union.

He said that it might be "expedient" to "take a pause" in the Berlin talks now going on between Andrei A. Gromyko, the Soviet Foreign Minister, and Llewellyn E. Thompson Jr., the United States Ambassador to Moscow.

Ambassador Thompson should not continue "negotiating" endlessly, Dr. Adenauer added. There have been four meetings in the last seven weeks between Mr. Gromyko and Mr. Thompson without any advance toward a Berlin settlement.

[A warning by Izvestia, the Soviet Government newspaper, that Moscow was ready to push through a separate peace treaty with East Germany if the United States did not alter its position in the talks raised the possibility of a renewal of the Soviet deadline on a peace pact.]

Dr. Adenauer's advocacy of a new conference of the United States, British, French and Soviet foreign ministers reflected his unhappiness with the course of the Gromyko-Thompson talks.

He is known to believe that Mr. Thompson has made what

Continued on Page 2, Column 2

URBAN PLAN VOTE PUT OFF IN SENATE

Administration Rebuffed on Forcing Issue to Floor

By RUSSELL BAKER
Special to The New York Times.

WASHINGTON, Feb. 20—President Kennedy affronted the Senate's dignity today and got a political rebuff for it.

In a surprising repudiation of the Administration's voting form sheets, the elders turned on the White House and rejected a leadership move to get a quick floor test of the President's urban affairs proposal. The vote was 58 to 42.

Thus, the White House lost its chance to get a favorable Senate vote on the plan before the House could vote to kill it. The Democrats also lost their chance to get the Senate's Republicans clearly on record for or against the plan to create a Cabinet-level Department of Urban Affairs and Housing.

Today's test came on the dusty parliamentary question whether the Senate should take the plan away from the Government Operations Committee and bring it to an immediate floor vote. This is known as "discharging" the committee. It is an extraordinary procedure that is rarely used because it is repugnant to Senate traditions.

Today it became the instrument of the President's defeat.

The move to discharge the Government Operations Committee was undertaken with misgivings yesterday by Mike Mansfield of Montana, Senate Democratic leader. The reason was a sudden threat by the

Continued on Page 16, Column 4

COL. GLENN FLOWN TO ISLE FOR CHECK

He Feels Tired but Elated —Goes to Grand Turk for Report and Examination

By JOHN W. FINNEY
Special to The New York Times.

GRAND TURK ISLAND, Feb. 20—An elated but tired John H. Glenn Jr. returned to earth tonight and reported that he "couldn't feel better."

The 40-year-old astronaut also reported that he had felt no sickness or discomfort during his five-hour, three-orbit flight around the earth, even during the extended period of weightlessness.

Colonel Glenn landed at this small British possession at 9:11 P. M. in a Navy S-2-F submarine patrol plane. He was clad in light blue coveralls. He had co-piloted the plane from the carrier Randolph, where he spent several hours after being retrieved from the Atlantic ocean.

Around his ears were the marks of the earphones that he had worn while piloting a plane that traveled at about one-hundredth the speed of his Friendship 7 space capsule. And on his face was an excited enthusiastic smile.

Asked how he felt, the red-headed marine replied: "Fine, wonderful, I couldn't feel better."

And he was also hungry. His first comment on stepping into the small hospital arranged for him was: "First I want something to eat—I am hungry." A steak dinner was promptly or-

Continued on Page 23, Column 2

Moscow, Unmoved, Gives News of Orbit

By THEODORE SHABAD
Special to The New York Times.

MOSCOW, Feb. 20 — The Russians voiced congratulations tonight on hearing of Lieut. Col. John H. Glenn Jr.'s orbital space flight.

But they showed no enthusiasm on the successful launching and landing of the spacecraft Friendship 7.

These reactions were reported from Moscow University by United States exchange students who had been listening with Russians to radio reports of Colonel Glenn's progress.

"They congratulated us in friendly fashion but were oddly reserved," an American said.

Soviet radio and television were unusually prompt in reporting the flight. The first bul-

Continued on Page 22, Column 5

81,000-MILE TRIP

Flight Aides Feared for the Capsule as It Began Its Re-Entry

Transcript of conversations with Glenn, Pages 25 and 26.

By RICHARD WITKIN
Special to The New York Times.

CAPE CANAVERAL, Fla., Feb. 20—John H. Glenn Jr. orbited three times around the earth today and landed safely to become the first American to make such a flight.

The 40-year-old Marine Corps lieutenant colonel traveled about 81,000 miles in 4 hours 56 minutes before splashing into the Atlantic at 2:43 P. M. Eastern Standard Time.

He had been launched from here at 9:47 A. M.

The astronaut's safe return was no less a relief than a thrill to the Project Mercury team, because there had been real concern that the Friendship 7 capsule might disintegrate as it rammed back into the atmosphere.

There had also been a serious question whether Colonel Glenn could complete three orbits as planned. But despite persistent control problems, he managed to complete the entire flight plan.

Lands in Bahamas Area

The astronaut's landing place was near Grand Turk Island in the Bahamas, about 700 miles southeast of here.

Still in his capsule, he was plucked from the water at 3:01 P. M. with a boom and block and tackle by the destroyer Noa. The capsule was deposited on deck at 3:04.

Colonel Glenn's first words as he stepped out onto the Noa's deck were: "It was hot in there."

He quickly obtained a glass of iced tea.

He was in fine condition except for two skinned knuckles hurt in the process of blowing out the side hatch of the capsule.

The colonel was transferred by helicopter to the carrier Randolph, whose recovery helicopters had raced the Noa for the honor of making the pick-up. After a meal and extensive "de-briefing" aboard the carrier, he was flown to Grand Turk by submarine patrol plane for two days of rest and interviews on technical, medical and other aspects of his flight.

The Noa, nearest ship to the

Continued on Page 20, Column 1

NEW YORK PAUSES TO 'WATCH' GLENN

Millions Rivet Attention on Astronaut in Flight

By NAN ROBERTSON

The thoughts of millions of New Yorkers were riveted for hours yesterday on one man alone in space.

Minute by minute, they followed the orbital flight of Lieut. Col. John H. Glenn Jr. three times around the earth, waiting in agonizing suspense for his safe return. The life of New York almost stood still during the dramatic countdown.

From then on until Colonel Glenn scrambled "hale and hearty" out of his capsule on the destroyer Noa, people carried on absent-mindedly and in spurts. Millions of working hours were lost during the day, but no one could have begrudged this. Employers and the employed alike were drawn irresistibly to radio and television sets.

The most spectacular display of interest occurred in Grand Central Terminal, where throngs of up to 9,000 persons massed before a huge television screen. The police described it as the largest static crowd in the station's history. The terminal manager said those who

Continued on Page 22, Column 6

"All the News That's Fit to Print"

The New York Times.

LATE CITY EDITION
U. S. Weather Bureau Report (Page 74) forecasts: Partly cloudy, breezy, cool today. Fair and cool tonight and tomorrow. Temp. range: 54—45; yesterday: 66—44.

VOL. CXII..No. 38,258. © 1962 by The New York Times Company. Times Square, New York 36, N. Y. NEW YORK, TUESDAY, OCTOBER 23, 1962. 10 cents beyond 50-mile zone from New York City except on Long Island. Higher in air delivery cities. FIVE CENTS

U.S. IMPOSES ARMS BLOCKADE ON CUBA ON FINDING OFFENSIVE-MISSILE SITES; KENNEDY READY FOR SOVIET SHOWDOWN

U. S. JUDGES GIVEN POWER TO REQUIRE VOTE FOR NEGROES

High Court Upholds Order Forcing the Registration of 54 in Alabama County

Special to The New York Times

WASHINGTON, Oct. 22—The Supreme Court held today that Federal judges have the power to make state registrars put specific Negroes on the voting rolls.

Alabama had challenged an order by Federal District Judge Frank M. Johnson Jr. requiring the registration of 54 specific Negroes in Macon County, Ala. The order was upheld by the United States Court of Appeals for the Fifth Circuit.

Today the Supreme Court unanimously affirmed the disputed order. And it did so in a way that indicated once again its mood of impatience with Southern efforts to maintain denials of Negro rights.

One-Sentence Ruling

All that was before the court was an application for review of the Fifth Circuit decision. The usual alternatives would have been to deny the petition or to grant it and hear oral argument later.

Instead, the court granted review and then, summarily, affirmed the lower courts. It did so in a single sentence, with just one citation in the way of explanation.

The citation was to a decision in 1960 upholding a Federal Court order in a Louisiana voting case. There, a district judge had told Louisiana registrars to put back on their books 1,377 Negroes whose names had been removed in a purge by the segregationist Citizens Council.

Action by Congress

The Macon County case was one of the first brought by the Department of Justice under the Civil Rights Act of 1957. It is especially significant because the county is in the so-called Black Belt, with a predominantly Negro population.

In 1958, when the suit was started, virtually all of the 3,000 white persons of voting age in the county were registered. But only about 1,000 of the 12,000 potential Negro voters were actually eligible.

In a further move, the registrars resigned, and this was held to leave no defendants to be sued. Congress in 1960 handled this problem by providing

Continued on Page 24, Column 4

102 SAVED AT SEA AS PLANE DITCHES

Rescue Is Made off Alaska Minutes After Accident

By The Associated Press.

SITKA, Alaska, Oct. 22—A military-charter airliner ditched in the ocean near here today, but all 102 persons aboard were saved in a quick rescue operation.

The plane, a DC-7C of Northwest Airlines, was going from McChord Air Force Base in Washington to Anchorage, Alaska. It carried 95 passengers and a crew of seven.

The rescue was reported by Northwest and the Alaska Coastal-Ellis Airline at Sitka, which also reported that there apparently were no serious injuries.

The plane went down shortly after the Federal Aviation Agency at Anchorage got word that it was being ditched because of propeller trouble.

A Coast Guard plane alighted on the water nearby; the Air Force sent two rescue planes, and small boats from Sitka, about seven miles north of the

Continued on Page 8, Column 3

Chinese Open New Front; Use Tanks Against Indians

Nehru Warns of Peril to Independence —Reds Attack Near Burmese Border and Press Two Other Drives

Special to The New York Times

NEW DELHI, Oct. 22—Prime Minister Jawaharlal Nehru told the people of India tonight that the Chinese Communist attack was a threat to their liberty.

His grave warning followed word that the advancing Chinese had opened a third front in

Excerpts from Nehru's speech will be found on Page 2.

the Himalayas, near the Burmese border, and had used tanks for the first time. Five more Indian posts fell to the Chinese on the third day of savage fighting.

[A bid for negotiations for a peace accord was broadcast by the Chinese Communist radio early Tuesday, The Associated Press reported from Tokyo.]

In a broadcast, Mr. Nehru denounced the Peking regime as "a powerful and unscrupulous opponent, not caring for peace or peaceful methods."

"The time has come," he said, "for us to realize fully this menace that threatens the freedom of our people and the independence of our country."

Prime Minister Nehru said India would not abandon her economic development program and policy of nonalignment with international blocs, but called on the nation to switch "from the slow-moving methods of peacetime to those which produce results quickly."

"We must build up our military strength by all means at our disposal," he said.

The third front in the Himalayan fighting was opened early today when the Chinese attacked an Indian post at Kibitoo, on the border between

Continued on Page 3, Column 1

U.S. Bids U.N. Bar China; Denounces Attack on India

By SAM POPE BREWER

Special to The New York Times

UNITED NATIONS, N. Y., Oct. 22—Adlai E. Stevenson told the General Assembly today that Communist China's "naked aggression" against India was new proof that it was unfit for membership in the United Nations.

The chief United States representative at the United Nations spoke as the Assembly took up the perennial question of admitting Peking.

Mr. Stevenson told the members that by their actions on the Indian frontier the Chinese Communists "again show their scorn for the Charter of this organization."

The Vice President of the Philippines, Emmanuel Pelaez, told the Assembly that there were more than 40,000,000 Chinese living outside China who would become "a Trojan horse" if the United Nations accepted the Communist Government.

Mr. Pelaez said that the Chinese abroad, 1,000,000 of them in the Philippines, would be used for subversion by the Peking Government. He said they could now be controlled because the Communist Government did not have the means to get at them.

On the fighting in India, Mr. Stevenson declared: "Should there be some among us who think that perhaps the whole thing is a mistake that will right itself before long, let me point out that when a nation moves its troops with tanks and armor, it is no mistake. It is a premeditated act. It is naked aggression. And it has been going on with gathering momentum for some three years."

He quoted Prime Minister

Continued on Page 5, Column 3

U. S. SAID TO EASE KATANGA POLICY

Reported Willing to Put Off Any Economic Sanctions —Congolese Disturbed

By LLOYD GARRISON

Special to The New York Times

LEOPOLDVILLE, the Congo, Oct. 22—Authoritative sources said today that the United States was no longer insisting that Katanga Province strictly meet the deadlines of the United Nations plan to end its secession from the Congo.

This has alarmed Congolese officials. They say that the United States shift is reflected in United Nations policy.

The United Nations plan, introduced Aug. 2 by U Thant, Acting Secretary General, was said to have been conceived largely by the United States.

As outlined by Mr. Thant, the plan's first stage called for the following timetable:

Within thirty days a program was to be decided on for the reintegration of Katanga's army into the Congolese National Army. Sixty days were to be allowed for the program to be carried out.

Recall of Missions

All Katangese foreign missions were to be recalled immediately, and all Katanga's foreign currency reserves were to be put under the control of the central Government, with 50 per cent of these reserves rebated to Katanga.

Unification of the Congo's currency was to have begun within 10 days.

Katanga was to have started immediately to share 50 per cent of her tax revenues with the central Government.

Not one of these conditions has been met.

Last week Cyrille Adoula, Premier of the central Government, declared that "the deadline for the first stage has passed." He said that it was time for the United Nations to consider the second stage — economic sanctions.

A shift in United States policy became apparent over the weekend after the departure of George C. McGhee, Under Secretary of State for Political Af-

Continued on Page 3, Column 6

SHIPS MUST STOP

Other Action Planned If Big Rockets Are Not Dismantled

By JAMES RESTON

Special to The New York Times

WASHINGTON, Oct. 22—President Kennedy drew the line tonight, not with Cuba, but with the Soviet Union. After almost a generation of trying to keep the "cold war" from reaching a direct confrontation between United States and Soviet power, a decision has been made to force Soviet missile bases from this hemisphere at the risk of war.

This is the official interpretation of President Kennedy's speech tonight, and the orders to American forces bear it out. On the highest authority, it can be said that these orders include the following:

¶Ships carrying to Cuba weapons capable of striking the continental United States must either turn back or submit to search and seizure, or fight. If they try to run the blockade, a warning shot will be fired across their bows; if they still do not submit, they will be attacked.

¶This applies not only to ships but to any planes suspected of carrying these offensive weapons to Cuba. There is no evidence that there are nuclear warheads in Cuba, but long-range aircraft suspected of carrying these or any other offensive weapons, will be intercepted, and instructions have been issued to do everything possible to check all Communist-bloc planes en route to Cuba via Newfoundland or Africa.

Prepared to Risk War

Even this will not satisfy the new policy announced by President Kennedy. Not only must new offensive weapons be stopped, under the President's orders, but those already in Cuba must be dismantled, or the United States will take whatever additional action is necessary, beginning with a much more rigorous blockade of such things as Cuba's essential oil supplies, to force compliance.

If this leads to Soviet retaliation, such as a counter-blockade of Berlin, the United States is prepared to risk a major war to defend its present position in the former German capital. Accordingly, American forces, not only in Berlin and West Germany but all over the world, have been placed on emergency alert. The new policy has been defined in a private communi-

Continued on Page 19, Column 1

Stocks Plunge Early On Crisis, but Rally

By RICHARD RUTTER

An already badly battered stock market was hit by massive selling yesterday as talk of a new international crisis spread in Wall Street.

The selling was of dimensions reminiscent of late May when the market experienced its worst break in a generation. Yesterday, the tape ran as much as 19 minutes late before a half-hearted recovery set in that cut losses by about one-third.

Both tape lateness and volume were the greatest since July 10. Two million shares were traded in the first two hours.

Stock markets in London, Frankfurt and Brussels, following Wall Street's lead, also took large losses.

The selling was directly ascribed to news in the morning about an air of crisis in Wash-

Continued on Page 49, Column 6

ANNOUNCES HIS ACTION: President Kennedy speaking to the nation last night on radio and television. He told of moves to keep offensive equipment away from Cuba.

Associated Press Wirephoto

TRAFFIC DELAYED AT BERLIN BORDER

Reds Start Intensive Check of Civilian Trucks an Hour Before Kennedy Speech

By SYDNEY GRUSON

Special to The New York Times

BONN, Oct. 22—The East German police began to slow down civilian traffic between West Berlin and West Germany late tonight.

About an hour before President Kennedy announced the United States countermeasures against the Soviet build-up in Cuba, the police started intensive examination of the papers of trucks moving into East German territory.

The connection, if any, between the two actions was not immediately clear. Similar harassment of civilian traffic has occurred periodically over the years. The immediate reaction in West Berlin was to consider tonight's harassment as part of the regular order of things, rather than as an advance countermeasure to the American moves against Cuba.

Nevertheless, there was deep anxiety that the Soviet Union would retaliate by causing trouble on the West's access lines to the city.

The outcome of tomorrow's meetings between Andrei A. Gromyko, the Soviet Foreign Minister, and East German Communist leaders was awaited with concern. Mr. Gromyko

Continued on Page 17, Column 3

Moscow Says U.S. Holds 'Armed Fist' Over Cuba

By SEYMOUR TOPPING

Special to The New York Times

MOSCOW, Tuesday, Oct. 23—In a broadcast before President Kennedy's speech on the missile build-up in Cuba, the Moscow radio said that the unusual activity in Washington indicated that the United States "once again was raising its armed fist over Cuba." The broadcast said there was "real hysteria" in Washington.

A Soviet reply to the United States note on Cuba that was given last night to Anatoly F. Dobrynin, the Soviet Ambassador to Washington, was expected to be delivered in 24 hours. It was expected that the reply would take the form either of a diplomatic communication or a message to President Kennedy from Premier Khrushchev.

Western observers said it appeared inevitable in view of recent Soviet statements that the reply would be a denial of any offensive Soviet intent and a charge of United States aggression against Cuba.

Veracity Questioned

The veracity of the Soviet Government was directly questioned in President Kennedy's speech, which was given after delivery of the note. The President said evidence had been obtained that Moscow was constructing offensive missile bases on Cuban territory.

The Soviet Government statement of Sept. 11, which warned the United States that an attack on Cuba would mean war, contended that the Soviet weapons supplied to Cuba were of a defensive nature.

Western observers said the crisis over Cuba would enter a critical phase when and if United States war vessels sought to halt and search a Soviet ship bound for Cuba.

A number of Soviet vessels carrying civilian goods and pos-

Continued on Page 18, Column 3

BIG FORCE MASSES TO BLOCKADE CUBA

Armada Is Under Orders to Open Fire if Necessary— All Troops Are Alerted

By JACK RAYMOND

Special to The New York Times

WASHINGTON, Oct. 22—American ships and planes began preparing tonight to impose a blockade of Cuba. United States forces are under orders to thwart any attempt to deliver offensive weapons to Havana.

A Defense Department spokesman said that a large force of ships and planes concentrating in the Caribbean area had instructions to use force if necessary, including sinking of ships, to carry out President Kennedy's orders for a "quarantine" of Cuba.

The Pentagon said also that United States military units throughout the world, including the garrison in Berlin and the nuclear-armed Strategic Air Command, had been placed "on alert."

Dependents of servicemen at the Guantánamo Bay Naval Base in Cuba have been evacuated, the department said.

Forces at Base Doubled

It added that the military forces there, which were previously put at 3,300 naval officers and men and several hundred Marines, have been doubled.

Air defense units in the United States, particularly radar warning stations, interceptor aircraft and ground-to-air missiles, "have been redeployed," the department spokesman said.

The orders for additional defense precautions were taken the spokesman continued, on the basis of aerial photographic evidence of long-range ballistic missile bases and the arrival of Soviet Ilyushin-28 bombers in Cuba.

The spokesman displayed some of the aerial photographs and pointed to some missiles sites that, he said, had been established only in the last 10 or 15 days.

He said some of the missile

Continued on Page 20 Column 1

Canada Asks Inspection of Cuba; Britain Supporting Quarantine

Diefenbaker Comments

By RAYMOND DANIELL

Special to The New York Times

OTTAWA, Oct. 22—Prime Minister John Diefenbaker of Canada declared tonight the time had come for an impartial inspection of what is happening in Cuba by eight of the "nonaligned nations."

Interrupting debate of the Canadian economic crisis in the House of Commons, Mr. Diefenbaker described President Kennedy's speech on Cuba as "somber and challenging."

"Naturally," he said, "there has been little time to give consideration to positive action that might be taken. But I suggest that if there is a desire—and I am sure there is on the part of the U.S.S.R.—to have the facts, if a group of nations, perhaps the eight comprising the unaligned members of the 18-nation disarmament committee, were given the opportunity of making an on-site inspection of Cuba to ascertain what the facts are, a major step forward would be taken."

Meanwhile it was disclosed that Canada has barred the use of her airfields, including that

Continued on Page 21, Column 2

British Note Peril

By DREW MIDDLETON

Special to The New York Times

LONDON, Oct. 22—Qualified sources said today that approval for President Kennedy's military quarantine of Cuba could be expected from the British government.

A Foreign Office spokesman declared, "Revelation of the Soviet build-up in Cuba will come as a shock to the whole civilized world."

Official comment cannot be given until after Prime Minister Macmillan and his Cabinet have discussed the President's statement.

Initial reaction among diplomats was that the President had taken the most reasonable course to frustrate what military circles regard as evident danger to the United States: a buildup of Soviet nuclear capacity in Cuba.

The danger that war might result from a Soviet attempt to break what amounts to a military blockade of Cuba is accepted. But one experienced airman expressed the general feeling this way: "War can come from any one of a number of causes,

Continued on Page 21, Column 1

All Military Forces Mobilized by Castro

By The Associated Press

KEY WEST, Tuesday, Oct. 23—All of Cuba's military forces have been mobilized as a result "of the news from the United States," the Havana radio said today.

The broadcast said the order was issued by Premier Fidel Castro, who will address the nation later today.

"Our combat units rapidly placed themselves on a fighting basis," said the Havana broadcast.

"Hundreds of thousands of men were mobilized in the course of a few hours," added the broadcast, which followed by some hours President Kennedy's announcement of a naval blockade against Cuba.

During the evening, Havana appeared slow to react to President Kennedy's broadcast and

Continued on Page 20 Column 5

PRESIDENT GRAVE

Asserts Russians Lied and Put Hemisphere in Great Danger

Text of the President's address is printed on Page 18.

By ANTHONY LEWIS

Special to The New York Times

WASHINGTON, Oct. 22—President Kennedy imposed a naval and air "quarantine" tonight on the shipment of offensive military equipment to Cuba.

In a speech of extraordinary gravity, he told the American people that the Soviet Union, contrary to promises, was building offensive missile and bomber bases in Cuba. He said the bases could handle missiles carrying nuclear warheads up to 2,000 miles.

Thus a critical moment in the cold war was at hand tonight. The President had decided on a direct confrontation with — and challenge to — the power of the Soviet Union.

Direct Thrust at Soviet

Two aspects of the speech were notable. One was its direct thrust at the Soviet Union as the party responsible for the crisis. Mr. Kennedy treated Cuba and the Government of Premier Fidel Castro as a mere pawn in Moscow's hands and drew the issue as one with the Soviet Government.

The President, in language of unusual bluntness, accused the Soviet leaders of deliberately "false statements about their intentions in Cuba."

The other aspect of the speech particularly noted by observers here was its flat commitment by the United States to act alone against the missile threat in Cuba.

Nation Ready to Act

The President made it clear that this country would not stop short of military action to end what he called a "clandestine, reckless and provocative threat to world peace."

Mr. Kennedy said the United States was asking for an emergency meeting of the United Nations Security Council to consider a resolution for "dismantling and withdrawal of all offensive weapons in Cuba."

He said the launching of a nuclear missile from Cuba against any nation in the Western Hemisphere would be regarded as an attack by the Soviet Union against the United States. It would be met, he said, by retaliation against the Soviet Union.

He called on Premier Khrushchev to withdraw the missiles from Cuba and so "move the

Continued on Page 18, Column 1

KENNEDY CANCELS CAMPAIGN TALKS

He and Johnson Take Step to Concentrate on Crisis

By CABELL PHILLIPS

Special to The New York Times

WASHINGTON, Oct. 22—The White House announced tonight that President Kennedy and Vice President Johnson would make no further political appearances in the Congressional campaign because of the Cuban crisis.

The move by the Administration was considered evidence not only of the seriousness of the situation but also of the desire of the President to unify the country behind his blockade order and keep the issue out of partisan politics.

In this connection, the White House said the President personally informed former Republican Presidents Dwight D. Eisenhower and Herbert Hoover, as well as former Democratic President Harry S. Truman, of his decision.

And the White House announced that John J. McCloy, former disarmament adviser to the Kennedy Administration and a Republican, had been as-

Continued on Page 18, Column 7

NEWS INDEX

"All the News That's Fit to Print"

The New York Times.

LATE CITY EDITION

U. S. Weather Bureau Report (Page 58) forecasts: Cloudy, windy, chance of showers today and tonight. Cold tomorrow. Temp. Range: 62—54; yesterday: 64—51.

VOL. CXIII . . . No. 38,654.

NEW YORK, SATURDAY, NOVEMBER 23, 1963.

TEN CENTS

KENNEDY IS KILLED BY SNIPER AS HE RIDES IN CAR IN DALLAS; JOHNSON SWORN IN ON PLANE

TEXAN ASKS UNITY

Congressional Chiefs of Both Parties Promise Aid

By FELIX BELAIR Jr.
Special to The New York Times

WASHINGTON, Nov. 22—Lyndon B. Johnson returned to a stunned capital shortly after 6 P.M. today to assume the duties of the Presidency.

The new President asked for and received from Congressional leaders of both parties their "united support in the face of the tragedy which has befallen our country." He said it was "more essential that ever before that this country be united."

Partisan differences disappeared in the chorus of assurances with which the Congressional leaders responded.

Mr. Johnson was described by those who talked with him as "stunned and shaken" by the assassination of President Kennedy.

Discusses U.S. Security

But he moved quickly from problems of national security and foreign policy to funeral arrangements for Mr. Kennedy.

Across the street from the West Wing of the White House, the President conferred with officials in his old Vice-Presidential offices in the Executive Office Building.

Senator George A. Smathers, Democrat of Florida, a personal friend of the dead President, was one of those who described Mr. Johnson as shaken.

"Everyone is," he added. "But the President is the more so because he was right there when the tragedy occurred."

While flying to Washington aboard the Presidential plane, Mr. Johnson arranged for a meeting with Cabinet members to ask that they remain at their posts. He made the same request of staff members in the executive office.

Meets With Harriman

"Calm and contained" was the way Senator J. W. Fulbright described the President's manner during a discussion of foreign-policy matters with Under Secretary of State W. Averell Harriman. The Arkansas Senator said the President had been working on "what looked like a statement"—presumably an assurance of continuity of the nation's foreign policy.

The new President's first conference was aboard the helicopter that flew him the 15 miles from Andrews Air Force Base

Continued on Page 11, Column 3

Henry Grossman

"This is a sad time for all people. We have suffered a loss that cannot be weighed. For me it is a deep personal tragedy. I know the world shares the sorrow that Mrs. Kennedy and her family bear. I will do my best. That is all I can do. I ask for your help —and God's."—President Lyndon Baines Johnson.

PRESIDENT'S BODY WILL LIE IN STATE

Funeral Mass to Be Monday in Capital After Homage Is Paid by Public

By JACK RAYMOND
Special to The New York Times

WASHINGTON, Nov. 22—The body of John F. Kennedy will lie in state in the rotunda of the Capitol Sunday and then will be borne to St. Matthew's Roman Catholic Cathedral for a pontifical requiem mass at noon Monday.

The President's body was returned to Washington today in the same Air Force jet that carried him to Texas. The airliner, with Mrs. Kennedy, the new President, Lyndon B. Johnson, and Mrs. Johnson aboard, arrived at Andrews Air Force Base at 5:58 P.M.

It was announced later that Mr. Kennedy's body would lie in the White House tomorrow from 10 A.M. to 6 P.M., during which time Government and diplomatic officials will pay their respects.

The coffin will be taken from the White House to the Capitol rotunda Sunday morning, where

Continued on Page 9, Column 3

PARTIES' OUTLOOK FOR '64 CONFUSED

Republican Prospects Rise —Johnson Faces Possible Fight Against Liberals

By WARREN WEAVER Jr.
Special to The New York Times

WASHINGTON, Nov. 22 —President Kennedy's assassination threw the American political scene into turmoil today.

It removed at a single blow the man who would have been renominated for a second term in the White House by acclamation nine months from now.

It elevated into the Presidency and the leadership of the Democratic party an older, more conservative man still emerging from his Southern heritage.

It increased immeasurably for the leaders of the Republican party prospects of electing a President next November.

The shock of the President's death stilled the official voices of politics in the capital, But so profound was the potential effect on the government and leadership that private consideration could not be silenced.

Before, there had been facts and strong probabilities on the

Continued on Page 6, Column 3

LEFTIST ACCUSED

Figure in a Pro-Castro Group Is Charged—Policeman Slain

By GLADWIN HILL
Special to The New York Times

DALLAS, Tex., Nov. 22—The Dallas police and Federal officers issued a charge of murder late tonight in the assassination of President Kennedy.

The accused is Lee Harvey Oswald, a 24-year-old former marine, who went to live in the Soviet Union in 1959 and returned to Texas last year.

Capt. Will Fritz, head of the Dallas police homicide bureau, identified Oswald as an adherent of the left-wing Fair Play for Cuba Committee.

Oswald was arrested about two hours after the shooting, in a movie theater three miles away, shortly after he allegedly shot and killed a policeman on a street nearby.

He was arraigned tonight on a charge of murdering the police officer. The charge related to the Kennedy killing was made later.

Appears in Line-Up

After the arraignment, the suspect, a slight, dark-haired man, was taken downstairs to appear in a line-up, presumably before witnesses of the Kennedy assassination.

While being escorted, handcuffed, through a police building corridor, he shouted: "I haven't shot anybody."

Captain Fritz said Oswald was employed—the exact job was unknown—at the Texas School Book Depository, a warehouse from which the assassin's bullets came. The captain said some witnesses had placed Oswald in the building at the time of the assassination.

The sequence of events leading to his arrest was as follows:

As a citywide manhunt began during the hour following the assassination, an unidentified man notified police headquarters, over a police-car radio, that the car's officer had been

Continued on Page 4, Column 1

NEWS INDEX

Henry Grossman

John Fitzgerald Kennedy
1917-1963

Why America Weeps

Kennedy Victim of Violent Streak He Sought to Curb in the Nation

By JAMES RESTON
Special to The New York Times

WASHINGTON, Nov. 22—America wept tonight, not alone for its dead young President, but for itself. The grief was general, for somehow the worst in the nation had prevailed over the best. The indictment extended beyond the assassin, for something in the nation itself, some strain of madness and violence, had destroyed the highest symbol of law and order.

Speaker John McCormack, now 71 and, by the peculiarities of our politics, next in line of succession after the Vice President, expressed this sense of national dismay and self-criticism:

"My God! My God! What are we coming to?"

The irony of the President's death is that his short Administration was devoted almost entirely to various attempts to curb this very streak of violence in the American character.

When the historians get around to assessing his three years in office, it is very likely that they will be impressed with just this: his efforts to restrain those who wanted to be more violent in the cold war overseas and those who wanted to be

Continued on Page 7, Column 6

The City Goes Dark

By ROBERT C. DOTY

The center of New York, the restless night city, wore darkness and went in near silence after the murder of President Kennedy last night.

In and around Times Square, the normal, frenetic Friday night pulse slowed as near to a halt as it ever comes. Most legitimate and movie theaters, night clubs and dance halls closed their doors and darkened their marquees.

As dusk came, automatic devices turned on the huge, gaudy display signs that normally blot out the night. Then, one by one, the lights blinked out, turning the great carnival strip into what was almost a mourning band.

There were exceptions, of course. Restaurants, by decision of their trade associations, remained lighted and open as a

Continued on Page 5, Column 2

Gov. Connally Shot; Mrs. Kennedy Safe

President Is Struck Down by a Rifle Shot From Building on Motorcade Route—Johnson, Riding Behind, Is Unhurt

By TOM WICKER
Special to The New York Times

DALLAS, Nov. 22—President John Fitzgerald Kennedy was shot and killed by an assassin today.

He died of a wound in the brain caused by a rifle bullet that was fired at him as he was riding through downtown Dallas in a motorcade.

Vice President Lyndon Baines Johnson, who was riding in the third car behind Mr. Kennedy's, was sworn in as the 36th President of the United States 99 minutes after Mr. Kennedy's death.

Mr. Johnson is 55 years old; Mr. Kennedy was 46.

Shortly after the assassination, Lee H. Oswald, described as a one-time defector to the Soviet Union, active in the Fair Play for Cuba Committee, was arrested by the Dallas police. Tonight he was accused of the killing.

Suspect Captured After Scuffle

Oswald, 24 years old, was also accused of slaying a policeman who had approached him in the street. Oswald was subdued after a scuffle with a second policeman in a nearby theater.

The shooting took place at 12:30 P.M., Central standard time (1:30 P.M., New York time). Mr. Kennedy was pronounced dead at 1 P.M. and Mr. Johnson was sworn in at 2:39 P.M.

Mr. Johnson, who was uninjured in the shooting, took his oath in the Presidential jet plane as it stood on the runway at Love Field. The body of the President was aboard. Immediately after the oath-taking, the plane took off for Washington.

Standing beside the new President as Mr. Johnson took the oath of office was Mrs. John F. Kennedy. Her stocking was saturated with her husband's blood.

Gov. John B. Connally Jr. of Texas, who was riding in the same car with Mr. Kennedy, was severely wounded in the chest, ribs and arm. His condition was serious, but not critical.

The killer fired the rifle from a building just off the motorcade route. Mr. Kennedy,

Continued on Page 2,

Capt. Cecil Stoughton via United Press International

THE NEW PRESIDENT: Lyndon B. Johnson takes oath before Judge Sarah T. Hughes in plane at Dallas. Mrs. Kennedy and Representative Jack Brooks are at right. To left are Mrs. Johnson and Representative Albert Thomas.

Associated Press

WHEN THE BULLETS STRUCK: Mrs. Kennedy moving to the aid of the President after he was hit by a sniper yesterday in Dallas. A guard mounts rear bumper. Gov. John B. Connally Jr. of Texas, also in the car, was wounded.

"All the News That's Fit to Print"

The New York Times.

LATE CITY EDITION
U. S. Weather Bureau Report (Page 45) forecasts: Cloudy, then fair today; fair and cooler tonight. Fair tomorrow. Temp. Range: 70—55; yesterday: 73—59.

VOL. CXIV. No. 38,964. | © 1964 by The New York Times Company. Times Square, New York, N. Y. 10036 | NEW YORK, MONDAY, SEPTEMBER 28, 1964. | Today's Issue Contains 96 Pages in Two Sections | TEN CENTS

WARREN COMMISSION FINDS OSWALD GUILTY AND SAYS ASSASSIN AND RUBY ACTED ALONE; REBUKES SECRET SERVICE, ASKS REVAMPING

F.B.I. IS CRITICIZED

Security Steps Taken by Secret Service Held Inadequate

By FELIX BELAIR Jr.
Special to The New York Times

WASHINGTON, Sept. 27—A sweeping revision of the organization and basic operating practices of the United States Secret Service was recommended today by the Warren Commission.

The commission sharply rebuked the Secret Service for failure to make adequate preparation for the visit of President Kennedy to Dallas last November. It reprimanded the Federal Bureau of Investigation for failure to supply the Secret Service with information concerning the presence of Lee Harvey Oswald in Dallas.

The commission deplored the fact that "there was no fully adequate liaison" between the F.B.I. and the Secret Service before the Dallas trip. It noted that some improvements had occurred since then but it insisted that, ultimately, Presidential protection required improvement in working arrangements of all Federal agencies concerned, including the Central Intelligence Agency, the State Department and the military intelligence branches.

Scrutiny Is Urged

The State Department was admonished to scrutinize more carefully requests for return to the United States of defectors

The report's appendix on Presidential protection will be printed in tomorrow's Times.

like Oswald "who have evidenced disloyalty or hostility to this country or who have expressed a desire to renounce their citizenship."

The brunt of the commission's indictment was directed at the century-old agency responsible for the safety of the President and his family. Its chief charge was that the Secret Service had not checked buildings along the route of the Presidential motorcade in Dallas nor asked the local police to do so.

The commission called for the appointment of a new special assistant to the Secretary of the Treasury with general supervisory authority over the Secret Service.

The commission found, however, that the conduct of the Secret Service agents in the Presidential motorcade "demonstrates that the President and the nation can expect courage and devotion to duty from agents of the Secret Service."

It acknowledged that whatever the human and material resources at the command of the Secret Service, a President can only be made as safe as he wants to be.

The report declared that its recommendations were "compelled by the facts disclosed in this investigation." It noted that

Continued on Page 15, Column 1

Harris & Ewing

THE WARREN COMMISSION: President's Commission on the Assassination of President Kennedy at commission offices at Veterans of Foreign Wars Building, Washington. From left: Representative Gerald R. Ford, Representative Hale Boggs, Senator Richard B. Russell, Chief Justice Earl Warren, Senator John Sherman Cooper, John J. McCloy, Allen W. Dulles, and J. Lee Rankin, commission counsel. Portraits are of President Johnson, President Kennedy and Joseph J. Lombardo, head of Veterans of Foreign Wars.

PANEL UNANIMOUS

Theory of Conspiracy by Left or Right Is Rejected

The text of the report begins on the first page of the second section.

By ANTHONY LEWIS
Special to The New York Times

WASHINGTON, Sept. 27—The assassination of President Kennedy was the work of one man, Lee Harvey Oswald. There was no conspiracy, foreign or domestic.

That was the central finding in the Warren Commission report, made public this evening. Chief Justice Earl Warren and the six other members of the President's Commission on the Assassination of President John F. Kennedy were unanimous on this and all questions.

The commission found that Jack Ruby was on his own in killing Oswald. It rejected all theories that the two men were in some way connected. It said that neither rightists nor Communists bore responsibility for the murder of the President in Dallas last Nov. 22.

Why did Oswald do it? To this most important and most mysterious question the commission had no certain answer. It suggested that Oswald had no rational purpose, no motive adequate if "judged by the standards of reasonable men."

A Product of His Life

Rather, the commission saw Oswald's terrible act as the product of his entire life—a life "characterized by isolation, frustration and failure." He was just 24 years old at the time of the assassination.

"Oswald was profoundly alienated from the world in which he lived," the report said. "He had very few, if any, close relationships with other people and he appeared to have had great difficulty in finding a meaningful place in the world.

"He was never satisfied with anything.

"When he was in the United States, he resented the capitalist system. When he was in the Soviet Union, he apparently resented the Communist party members, who were accorded special privileges and who he thought were betraying Communism, and he spoke well of the United States."

The commission found that Oswald shot at former Maj. Gen. Edwin A. Walker in Dallas on April 10, 1963, narrowly missing him. It cited this as evidence of his capacity for violence.

It listed as factors that might have led Oswald to the assassination "his deep-rooted resentment of all authority, which was expressed in a hostility toward every society in which he lived," his "urge to try to find a place in history" and his "avowed commitment to Marx-

Continued on Page 14, Column 1

JOHNSON NAMES 4 TO ACT ON REPORT

Commission Calls for Action to Increase the Security of the Presidency

By The Associated Press

JOHNSON CITY, Tex., Sept. 27—President Johnson appointed a four-man committee today to advise him "on the execution of the recommendations of the Warren Commission."

The commission, which investigated the assassination of President Kennedy, recommended action to tighten the protection of Presidents and to make the killing of a President or a Vice President a Federal crime.

[Mike Mansfield of Montana, the Senate majority leader, said in Washington that Congress, which has been aiming at adjournment at the end of this week, "should stay here and act, if the President sends us any recommendations."]

Members of the committee are Secretary of the Treasury Douglas Dillon, Acting Attorney General Nicholas deB. Katzenbach, John A. McCone, director of the Central Intelligence Agency, and McGeorge Bundy, Special Assistant to the President for National Security Affairs.

The President named no chairman for the committee, but it was understood that Secretary Dillon, as ranking member, would have general supervision over the group.

The group will presumably

Continued on Page 17, Column 3

A New Chapter Unfolds in the Kennedy Legend

By JAMES RESTON
Special to The New York Times

News Analysis

WASHINGTON, Sept. 27—The Warren Commission has fulfilled its primary assignment. It has tried, as a servant of history, to discover truth. But the assassination of President Kennedy was so symbolic of human irony and tragedy, and so involved in the complicated and elemental conflicts of the age, that many vital questions remain, and the philosophers, novelists and dramatists will have to take it from here.

The commission has not concluded the Kennedy mystery so much as it has opened up a whole new chapter in the Kennedy legend.

It has provided the greatest repository of Presidential political history, drama and fiction since the murder of Mr. Lincoln and since legend is often more powerful than history, this may be the commission's most significant achievement.

Now the central mystery of who killed the President has been answered by the commission only in the process of raising a new catalogue of mysteries. Now the main characters in the play have been surrounded by a host of new characters, each of whom appears briefly at a critical moment with some vital testimony, only to disappear without our really knowing much about who they are.

The whole story is full of the mystery of life. Lee Harvey Oswald's motive for murdering the President remains obscure. The distinguished members of the commission and their staff obviously gave up on it.

The "might-have-beens" are maddening. If only he had been given that visa to go to Cuba and thence to the Soviet Union just before the assassination! If he had not been allowed to come back from there in the first place! Who was "the neighbor" who got him the job in the Texas Book Depository, from where he shot the President? And what were the details of Oswald's attempted suicide in Moscow?

The wild accidents are equally intriguing. There is, for example, the case of Mrs. Bledsoe, who rented Oswald a room in Dallas and then, on a 10,000-to-1 chance, just happened to be on the bus he boarded when he was running away from the crime.

Then there are the consoling yearnings and kindnesses in the midst of tragedy: Ruth Paine, who was also "alienated" and "isolated," and frustrated like Oswald, but who nevertheless "befriended" Marina Oswald in her time of

Continued on Page 15, Column 6

'MYTHS' OF CASE DENIED IN DETAIL

Panel Says Misinformation on the Assassination Led to 'Distorted' Views

By PETER KIHSS

The Warren Commission rejected in detail yesterday a number of charges suggesting that Lee Harvey Oswald had not acted alone in the assassination of President Kennedy.

The commission said that "publicizing of unchecked information" had led to "myths" and "distorted" interpretations. While each inaccuracy could be explained, it went on, "the number and variety of misstatements issued by the police" in Dallas would have "greatly assisted a skillful defense attorney."

On the other hand, Mark Lane, chairman of a Citizens Committee of Inquiry here, contended that if the report contained all the available evidence, "Oswald would have been acquitted" of both the President's assassination and the murder of the Dallas patrolman, J. D. Tippit.

In a news conference, Mr. Lane, a former Assemblyman, said his group would continue its efforts to "answer the unanswered questions." He said it had more than 250 workers here, with other committees in England, France and Denmark, and interested groups on 20 college campuses. His group estimated that it had raised and

Continued on Page 16, Column 4

High Clerics to Ask Stronger Statement By Council on Jews

Special to The New York Times

ROME, Sept. 27—A powerful array of Roman Catholic prelates, including at least three American Cardinals, are preparing to speak out for a strong statement by the Ecumenical Council on the Jews, clerical sources said today.

The sources said that Richard James Cardinal Cushing, Archbishop of Boston, is known to have prepared an address to be given at the Council when the issue is debated.

The draft of the declaration was introduced last Friday by Augustin Cardinal Bea, the German Jesuit, who heads the Council's Secretariat for the Promotion of Christian Unity. It is considered by many Council Fathers—the voting prelates—and observers to be a "watered down" version of an earlier draft.

Other Cardinals Named

The earlier statement, among other things, made plain that the Jews of Christ's time and of today bore no responsibility for the Crucifixion. The weakened declaration declares only that Jews of today cannot be blamed.

Among those expected to attack the newer version are two other American Cardinals—Joseph Elmer Ritter, Archbishop of St. Louis, and Albert Gregory Meyer, Archbishop of Chicago.

Cardinal Spellman of New York has also said that he favors the more forceful state-

Continued on Page 7, Column 1

2 CITIES DENY REIN ON POLICE IN RIOTS

Civilian Review Units Hold F.B.I. Criticism Unfounded

By FRED POWLEDGE

Officials of civilian police advisory boards in Rochester and Philadelphia disagreed yesterday with a statement by the Federal Bureau of Investigation that boards such as theirs had "virtually paralyzed" the police during the summer riots.

The Rev. William H. Gray Jr., executive secretary of Philadelphia's eight-member review board, said: "It's over-simplifying the situation to say that the board has an effect on the rioting or the police behavior."

Ross J. Guglielmino, the executive director and legal counsel of the Rochester board, said he did not feel the F.B.I. criticism applied to Rochester.

What the F.B.I. Found

The two men commented in telephone interviews on a report released Saturday by President Johnson. The President had asked the F.B.I. to collect its investigations of summer riots in New York City, Rochester, Dixmoor, Ill.; Philadelphia, Seaside, Ore., Hampton Beach, N. H., and Jersey City, Paterson, and Elizabeth, N. J., and advise him if there were any pattern in the outbreaks.

The report, submitted by F.B.I. Director J. Edgar Hoover, concluded that the riots were not basically racial, although large numbers of Negroes took part; that they were not organized on a national basis, and that none of them was planned by any one group or individual.

Among the several points

Continued on Page 48, Column 1

Congress Will Act On Appalachia Aid And Medical Care

Special to The New York Times

WASHINGTON, Sept. 27—The fate of two key Administration programs—health insurance for the aged and aid to Appalachia—may be decided this week as Congress pushes toward adjournment.

"We could finish up Saturday; that's my most optimistic guess," Senator Mike Mansfield of Montana, the majority leader, said today. "But I have my fingers crossed."

The health insurance issue, currently in House-Senate conference, could delay adjournment until the following week, some legislative leaders believe.

Prospects for conference approval of some form of health insurance for the aged under Social Security have ranged from bright to gloomy in recent days.

The House passed a bill this summer to increase Social Security taxes as well as cash

Continued on Page 18, Column 4

NEWS INDEX

CAMPAIGN IMPACT BELIEVED LIKELY

'Kennedy Legacy' Could Aid Democrats at the Polls

By TOM WICKER
Special to The New York Times

WASHINGTON, Sept. 27—The effects of the Warren Commission's report are sure to extend far beyond its conclusion that Lee Harvey Oswald, acting alone, killed President Kennedy last Nov. 22.

The massive document could have repercussions in the 1964 elections, on the present conduct of President Johnson, and ultimately on the availability to the public of Mr. Johnson and future Presidents.

It may produce major changes for the Secret Service, the agency now assigned to protect the President.

Other Agencies Affected

The assignments and powers of other agencies such as the Federal Bureau of Investigation and even the Central Intelligence Agency might be revamped and independent review of their activities and efficiency might be increased.

In the field of legislation, the report might produce—as recommended by the commission—a law making it a Federal crime to kill or attempt to kill a President, a Vice President or any officer next in line to the Presidency and the President-elect and Vice President-elect. Other legislation, particularly relating to security and investigative agencies and to the protection of Presidents, could also grow from the report.

Although the State Department was generally cleared of

Continued on Page 15, Column 5

G.I.'s Rescue Vietnam Captives; Uprising Stirs Mistrust of U.S.

By PETER GROSE
Special to The New York Times

SAIGON, South Vietnam, Sept. 27 — United States Army helicopters rescued 60 Vietnamese hostages today from a camp of rebel tribesmen in the central highlands.

The release of the prisoners met a Government condition for negotiations with the armed mountain tribesmen. It appeared to reduce the danger of a violent clash.

Nevertheless the revolt is having serious political consequences, involving growing suspicion between the United States mission and the Premier, Maj. Gen. Nguyen Khanh. The rebellion has intensified Saigon's feeling that the United States, which has supported General Khanh, is undergoing a change of policy.

[About five persons were reported shot dead when security forces fired on a crowd in Quinhon, 270 miles northeast of Saigon. Later a mob stormed a radio station and troops were called in to evict the demonstrators, Reuters reported.]

Officials around General Khanh say he no longer believes he can count on American help to stay in power and he feels he must seek firmer support from

Continued on Page 2, Column 1

Scientific Police Work Traced Bullets to Rifle Oswald Owned

By JOHN W. FINNEY
Special to The New York Times

WASHINGTON, Sept. 27—The Warren Commission's conclusion that Lee Harvey Oswald killed President Kennedy rests in large part on scientific evidence painstakingly established through modern technology.

On the basis of the scientific evidence alone it was possible to establish that the shots were fired by a rifle owned and possessed by Oswald, that the shots were fired from the sixth-floor window of a building in which Oswald worked, and that the fatal wound could have been caused by the bullets from the high-powered rifle.

These crucial points were established through scientific detective work that combined the techniques of handwriting, ballistics, and fiber and wounds analysis. Among the devices used were microscopes, spectroscopes, X-rays, surveying instruments and skulls filled with gelatin.

Even nuclear science was employed. Paraffin casts from Oswald's hands and face were put into a nuclear reactor at the Oak Ridge (Tenn.) National Laboratory in an unsuccessful attempt to see if radiation would show up traces of gunpowder. One major question left

Continued on Page 16, Column 5

"All the News That's Fit to Print"

The New York Times.

LATE CITY EDITION

U. S. Weather Bureau Report (Page 94) forecasts: Light rain and snow, then clearing today; becoming cloudy tomorrow. Temp. range: 46—37; yesterday: 48—42.

VOL. CXV..No. 39,408. | NEW YORK, THURSDAY, DECEMBER 16, 1965. | TEN CENTS

TWO GEMINIS FLY 6 TO 10 FEET APART IN MAN'S FIRST SPACE RENDEZVOUS; CREWS, FACE TO FACE, TALK BY RADIO

U.S. JETS SMASH BIG POWER PLANT OUTSIDE HAIPHONG

Cut Nation's Current 15%—Generators Supported Industries in Hanoi

By NEIL SHEEHAN
Special to The New York Times

SAIGON, South Vietnam, Dec. 15—United States jet fighter-bombers destroyed a large power plant today 14 miles from Haiphong, North Vietnam's chief port, in the first American air strike against a North Vietnamese target of major industrial importance.

A military spokesman said the planes, flown by Air Force pilots, had struck the Uongbi thermal power plant, northeast of Haiphong. The plant has a capacity of 24,000 kilowatts, about 15 per cent of North Vietnam's total electric-power output. It supplies some of the power needs of both Hanoi and Haiphong.

The center of the plant, housing steam turbines, generators and other sensitive equipment, was smashed at 11 A.M. with 12 tons of 3,000-pound bombs. A single flight of F-105 Thunderchief fighter-bombers—apparently four to six craft—made the raid.

Secondary Blasts Sighted

A spokesman said that the pilots had encountered bad weather and heavy antiaircraft fire but reported having destroyed the plant. Several secondary explosions—detonations of explosives on the ground—were observed during the raid.

This was the first time United States aircraft had struck so close to North Vietnam's two major cities—Hanoi and Haiphong. The closest previous strike was a recent raid against a firing site for Soviet-made surface-to-air missiles, 22 miles from Hanoi.

[Secretary of Defense McNamara, who arrived back in Washington shortly after midnight from the North Atlantic Alliance meeting in Paris, said the bombing of the power plant near Haiphong "is representative of the type of attack we have carried out and will continue to carry out," The Associated Press reported Thursday. Page 3.]

Many Homes Darkened

According to military spokesmen here, the destruction of the power plant was certain to affect North Vietnamese civilians much more directly than have previous strikes, almost all of which have been aimed at road, rail and river networks and military installations.

The power-station raid will probably cut off electricity in large numbers of civilian homes as well as significantly reduce the amount of power available for industries in the Hai-

Continued on Page 3, Column 1

U.S. Said to Caution Latins on Moscow

By HENRY RAYMONT
Special to The New York Times

MONTEVIDEO, Uruguay, Dec. 15—The United States is warning Uruguay and other Latin-American countries against underestimating the continued aggressiveness and subversive potential of Soviet Communism, qualified sources said today.

The diplomatic initiative is directed against what United States authorities consider to be undue complacency among Latin-American leaders.

These authorities think that the split between Moscow and Peking has led to the assumption among Latins that pro-Soviet Communists no longer threaten republican institutions in the Western Hemisphere.

According to United States officials, this assumption ignores the deterioration in East-West

Continued on Page 17, Column 1

Gemini 7 Crew

Lieut. Col. Frank Borman

Comdr. James A. Lovell Jr.

Major Steps From Launching to Rendezvous

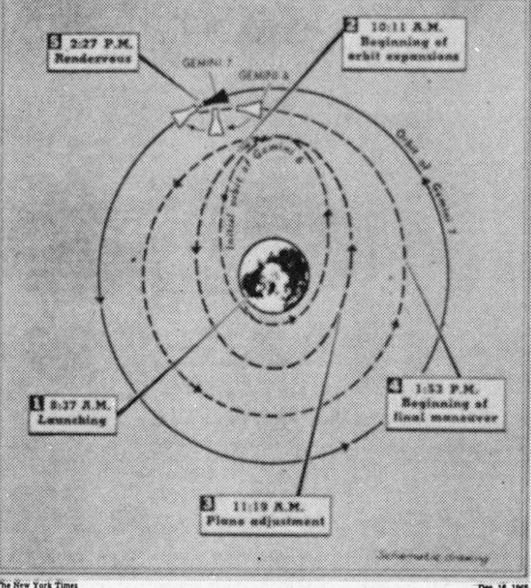

The New York Times — Dec. 16, 1965

Major steps of yesterday's rendezvous of the Gemini 6 and Gemini 7 spacecraft are shown, from the launching of Gemini 6 to its meeting with Gemini 7, orbiting about 185 miles above the earth. At rendezvous two craft were nose to nose within 10 feet of each other.

Gemini 6 Crew

Capt. Walter M. Schirra Jr.

Maj. Thomas P. Stafford

Craft in Formation Orbit 185 Miles Up

Officials of Space Agency Are Jubilant at Success—Maneuver Is Vital to a Manned Landing on Moon

By JOHN NOBLE WILFORD
Special to The New York Times

HOUSTON, Dec. 15—Four American astronauts steered Gemini 6 and Gemini 7 today to man's first rendezvous in the vastness of outer space.

In a spectacular performance of space navigation, the astronauts brought their craft within six to ten feet of each other about 185 miles above the earth. The two capsules then circled the earth nearly two times on a four-hour formation flight before Gemini 6 broke away to a lower orbit.

The pilots of the pursuing Gemini 6 were Capt. Walter M. Schirra Jr. of the Navy and Maj. Thomas P. Stafford of the Air Force. Pilots of the Gemini 7 target ship were Lieut. Col. Frank Borman of the Air Force and Comdr. James A. Lovell Jr. of the Navy.

The crews came close enough to see into each other's cabins, trade gibes and inspect details on the exteriors of their funnel-shaped spacecraft. The Gemini 6 astronauts could see Commander Lovell's beard and could tell that Colonel Borman was chewing gum.

"We have company tonight!" radioed Colonel Borman from Gemini 7, which has been in orbit 11 days of its record 14-day mission. Gemini 6, launched from Cape Kennedy at 8:37 A.M., Eastern standard time, today, is expected to splash down near the Bahamas at 10:29 A.M. tomorrow.

Officials Jubilant

The success of the mission brought jubilation at the space center here.

"It's the biggest milestone since the flight of John Glenn," Christopher C. Kraft Jr., the flight director, said.

Colonel Glenn's Mercury flight, on Feb. 20, 1962, was the first orbital mission by an American.

The two Geminis today proved that two spacecraft can find each other, rendezvous and presumably link up.

Such a maneuver is necessary if astronauts are to land on the moon and then return to their mother ship, which would be circling in a lunar orbit. Space officials are aiming for such a manned landing in 1969.

Today's rendezvous also opens the way to operations in which men and supplies can be ferried out to orbiting stations, such as the Air Force's planned Manned Orbiting Laboratory.

'Made It Look Easy'

"These crews made it look easy," said Dr. Robert Gilruth, director of the Manned Spacecraft Center here, praising all those who had made the mission a success.

Just before final rendezvous, there was an anxious moment of silence. Radio contact between the craft and the ground was lost. Then a relay tracking station off Hawaii reported in. The two Gemini had drawn within 120 feet of each other.

"There just seems to be a lot of traffic up here," Captain Schirra commented.

"Call a policeman," Colonel

Continued on Page 28, Column 1

AT LAST, GEMINI 6 HAS A PERFECT DAY

Even Sun Comes Out in Time to Dispel Last Doubt of Jubilant Ground Staff

By EVERT CLARK
Special to The New York Times

CAPE KENNEDY, Fla., Dec. 15—After twice having had its wings clipped by failure, the Gemini 6 finally climbed to its space rendezvous today in a most spectacular way.

For 15 years, missiles have flown from this sandy point of land. But no one today could recall a flight of greater beauty.

It left behind a sense of exhilaration missing since Mercury capsules took the first American astronauts into space four years ago.

On top of the triumph, plans were quickly made to have Gemini 6 splash down about 800 miles east of here at 10:29 o'clock tomorrow morning. The pilots will return here on Friday for the first of many days of debriefings.

A splendid sunrise had created the perfect backdrop and set the mood for the day. It dispelled a worrisome ground fog that had clung to the scrubby palmetto like the doubts that had hung over Gemini 6 in recent days.

Attitude Was Cautious

Through last night the memory of two recent false starts was so fresh that the attitude was one of caution and crossed fingers.

Yet today, from the beginning, a cockiness and almost a jubilance seemed to run through the pilots, the overworked ground crews and official observers.

It was typified by the reaction of James S. McDonnell, the 67-year-old engineer whose factory in Missouri makes the Gemini capsules.

He overslept. Awakened at 6:30 A.M., as the sun began to turn the high, scattered clouds the color of a tea rose, he looked at the sky and cried out:

"You see! I told them I'd bring them good weather from St. Louis!"

It became a day for enthusiasm.

"She looks like a dream," Navy Capt. Walter M. Schirra

Continued on Page 28, Column 8

McNamara Warns NATO Of Chinese Atom Threat

By PETER BRAESTRUP
Special to The New York Times

PARIS, Dec. 15—Defense Secretary Robert S. McNamara urged the United States' Western European allies today to start worrying now about the threat posed by Communist China's growing nuclear strength.

At the same time, he pledged that the mounting United States effort in Vietnam would not require the withdrawal of "major combat units" from American forces in Western Europe.

Mr. McNamara addressed ministers of the 15-nation North Atlantic Treaty Organization in their year-end meeting, which began yesterday.

Behind Closed Doors

The Defense Secretary spoke behind closed doors. His remarks, like those of other speakers, were summarized by a delegation spokesman.

Mr. McNamara said that the Chinese Communists, having already detonated two test nuclear devices, would produce enough fissionable material in the next two years to start a small stockpile of atomic weapons.

Moreover, he continued, the Chinese, despite a "near-famine" economy, are spending 10 per cent of their gross national product on defense.

He said Peking's new mili-

Continued on Page 8, Column 3

JOHNSON AND AYUB CALL PEACE VITAL

Say Dispute With India Must Cease So Efforts Can Be Turned to Key Problems

By JOHN D. POMFRET
Special to The New York Times

WASHINGTON, Dec. 15—President Johnson and President Mohammad Ayub Khan of Pakistan said today that they agreed on the need for a peaceful resolution of all outstanding differences between India and Pakistan.

This is necessary, they said, "so that the energies and resources of the peoples of the subcontinent would not be wastefully diverted from their efforts to meet their vitally important social and economic problems."

The two leaders issued a joint communiqué at the conclusion of two days of meetings at the White House. It described the discussions as "frank, wide-ranging and productive."

Kashmir Main Issue

The main dispute between India and Pakistan is over Kashmir. This dispute led to a short war last summer.

There was no expressed agreement between the two Presidents on the specific lines along which the dispute over Kashmir should be settled.

They both were said to believe that the working out of such specific arrangements must await the outcome of further conferences that already have been scheduled.

President Ayub and India's Prime Minister, Lal Bahadur Shastri, are to meet Jan. 4 at the invitation of the Soviet Union to discuss their differences. They will confer at the Soviet Central Asian city of Tashkent.

Prime Minister Shastri and President Johnson will meet in Washington Feb. 1 and 2.

The United States cut off military aid and new economic

Continued on Page 6, Column 3

47-CENT FARE SEEN IN QUILL DEMANDS

Transit Authority Warns It Would Be Needed to Meet Union Pay Proposals

By EMANUEL PERLMUTTER

The Transit Authority said yesterday that if it granted the contract demands of its unions it would have to raise the 15-cent fare to 47 cents.

It asserted that a fare increase that great would lead to such a loss of riders that "the reduced use of the system would be financially catastrophic."

The authority has estimated that demands of the Transport Workers Union would cost it $680 million in a two-year contract.

"Adding an increased labor cost of $340 million annually to the T.A. budget would, in the absence of other sources of revenue, increase the present 3-cent deficit incurred for each passenger carried by 19 cents, creating a 22-cent operating deficit per ride," the authority asserted. "The fare would have to be increased to not less than 47 cents."

The authority said that granting the demands would also result in increasing the "basic wage rate per hour alone

Continued on Page 58, Column 4

Staggered Working Hours Urged to Cut Transit Jam

By JOSEPH C. INGRAHAM

The chronic morning and evening subway crushes can be eliminated by staggering working hours, according to a plan made public by Mayor Wagner yesterday. The success of the proposal hinges on whether employers and employes can be persuaded to alter their traditional 9-to-5 work pattern, the Mayor said.

Only the conclusions of the eight-volume, 200,000-word report, based on a six-year study that cost $200,000, were released by the Mayor. The study was directed by Prof. Lawrence B. Cohen of the department of industrial engineering of Columbia University.

Principal Finding

The principal finding was that "work staggering is a feasible way of relieving subway congestion into and out of Manhattan's central business district during the rush hours so that standing passengers might be reasonably comfortable."

Professor Cohen held that the idea was technically and economically feasible and, within limits, which he defined very generally, was sociologically acceptable to management and labor.

In Professor Cohen's view, rush-hour crowding would be markedly alleviated if a 25 per cent spread of the peak loads

Continued on Page 58, Column 3

NASA CUTS BACK SCIENCE PROGRAM

Orbiting Solar Observatory Canceled in Move to Hold Down Expanding Budget

Special to The New York Times

WASHINGTON, Dec. 15—The National Aeronautics and Space Administration, caught in a tight budgetary squeeze, canceled today one of its most ambitious scientific projects.

"Budgetary considerations" were cited by the agency in explaining a halt in further work on the Advanced Orbiting Solar Observatory. The observatory, capable of making detailed observations of the sun, had been planned for launching in 1969.

Behind the cryptic explanation was the deliberately unpublicized fact that the agency was faced with a budgetary dilemma. It has been attempting to finance its expanding program and still heed White House directives to hold down nonmilitary spending.

Some Delays Foreseen

The present expectation is that the civilian space budget for the fiscal year 1967, beginning next July 1, will be held by the White House to about $5.17 billion, equal to the appropriation for this year, and perhaps even less. This would be about $500 million less than the space agency considered necessary to maintain the momentum of its expanding program and sought from the White House.

Enough money will be provided in the budget next year to keep Project Apollo on its schedule of landing a manned expedition on the moon before 1970. But to keep within the budgetary confines imposed by the White House, there will have to be some curtailment in the

Continued on Page 30, Column 4

Somerset Maugham Is Dead at 91

Novelist, Short Story Writer, Playwright Succumbs in Nice

By The Associated Press

NICE, France, Thursday, Dec. 16—W. Somerset Maugham died early today at his Riviera villa, La Mauresque. The world-famous novelist, playwright and short-story writer was 91 years old.

Maugham fell last Friday and then suffered a stroke. He was taken to the British-American Hospital Saturday. After a medical consultation on Sunday, physicians gave him only hours to live.

He rallied slightly but weakened yesterday. When all hope was gone, he was taken from the hospital to die in his Moorish-style villa at nearby Cap Ferrat, his secretary and companion of many years, Alan Searle, said in announcing Maugham's death.

Pictorial Parade

W. Somerset Maugham

A prolific author, Maugham turned out 30 plays, 21 novels and 120 short stories. His masterpiece was "Of Human Bondage," published in 1915 when he was 41 years old. It centered

Continued on Page 50, Column 1

Johnson Calls Feat Step Toward Moon

By JACK RAYMOND
Special to The New York Times

WASHINGTON, Dec. 15—President Johnson hailed the Gemini satellite rendezvous today as a step toward the moon.

The President congratulated the astronauts and all those who had anything to do with the space feat.

"You have all moved us one step higher on the stairway to the moon," he said exuberantly.

The President conveyed his feelings in a message to James E. Webb, administrator of the National Aeronautics and Space Administration. He had watched the progress of the launching and flight anxiously throughout the day.

Bill D. Moyers, the President's press secretary, said Mr. Johnson watched the Gemini 6 launching over his bedroom television set. Then, throughout the

Continued on Page 29, Column 4

NEWS INDEX

"All the News That's Fit to Print"

The New York Times

LATE CITY EDITION

Weather: Fair and warm today and tonight. Partly cloudy tomorrow. Temp. range: today 85-63; Wed. 81-62. Temp.-Hum. Index: mid-70's; Wed. 72. Full report on Page 93.

VOL. CXVI. No. 39,947 — NEW YORK, THURSDAY, JUNE 8, 1967 — 10 CENTS

ISRAELIS ROUT THE ARABS, APPROACH SUEZ, BREAK BLOCKADE, OCCUPY OLD JERUSALEM; AGREE TO U.N. CEASE-FIRE; U.A.R. REJECTS IT

JOHNSON WILL USE CABINET TO COURT STATES' OFFICIALS

Aides Will Seek to Tighten Ties Between Governors and the White House

By WARREN WEAVER Jr.
Special to The New York Times

WASHINGTON, June 7—President Johnson has decided to use the members of his Cabinet as diplomatic agents in his campaign to improve relations between the Administration and state governments.

The President has approved a plan under which each member of the Cabinet would be assigned four or five states as his personal responsibility, with instructions to maintain personal contact between the Governors and the White House.

As part of the same effort, each of the 50 states will be given a "day" in Washington next fall and winter, when a planeload of its key officials will fly here to hold conferences all over the capital, capped by a meeting of the Governors with the President.

Bryant's Work Continued

Both projects reflect Mr. Johnson's continuing determination to build domestic as well as foreign bridges by working to sort out the tangled Federal-state relations that have been increasingly complicated by the administration of the Great Society programs.

Both are attempts to give some permanency to the contacts established during the last four months by Farris Bryant, the President's envoy to the states, on visits to 40 capitals with a squad of Federal experts.

Mr. Bryant, a former Governor of Florida who is now the director of the Office of Emergency Planning, plans to leave his White House post this summer, possibly to return to politics in his home state, and he is eager to help establish more permanent lines of communication before his departure.

As now envisioned, each Cabinet officer would visit all of

Continued on Page 29, Column 2

Rise in Debt Ceiling Rejected in House; Johnson Rebuffed

Special to The New York Times

WASHINGTON, June 7—The House of Representatives dealt the Johnson Administration a sharp setback today by rejecting a bill to increase the ceiling on the national debt $29-billion, to $365-billion.

The vote against passage was 210 to 197, with Republicans voting solidly to kill the bill. Enough Democrats, mostly Southerners, voted with them to turn the tide.

About six Northern Democratic "doves"—opponents of the war in Vietnam—also joined the opposition.

In all, 34 Democrats joined with 176 Republicans to defeat the measure.

Today's action raised the possibility—though a slim one—of financial chaos after June 30. At that time the debt limit reverts to its "permanent" ceiling of $285-billion, though the debt, at $330-billion, is already far above that level. The legal authority of the Treasury to pay its bills would be in doubt.

However, the Ways and

Continued on Page 30, Column 4

U.S. VOWS TO SEEK A DURABLE PEACE

Johnson Recalls Bundy for New Mideast Planning Unit —'Real Chance' Is Seen

By MAX FRANKEL
Special to The New York Times

WASHINGTON, June 7 — President Johnson pledged today to do his best to help translate the new Middle Eastern situation into a more lasting settlement between Israel and her Arab neighbors.

Apparently hoping to exploit Israel's lightning military success—which has surprised but not displeased the White House—Mr. Johnson ordered the drafting of special policies for a "new peace" and set up new machinery to deal with the situation.

The President said that the United States, which had worked hard to avoid the war, felt that "there is now a real chance" to turn from "the frustrations of the past to the hopes of a peaceful future."

But Mr. Johnson said the handling of the crisis and the preparations for a lasting settlement would require the most careful consideration in the United States Government. To organize that effort he recalled McGeorge Bundy to temporary duty at the White House as executive secretary to a special subcommittee of the National Security Council.

Mr. Bundy will seek a temporary leave from the presidency of the Ford Foundation, which he assumed last year after serving as special assistant for

Continued on Page 19, Column 1

EBAN SEES THANT

Says Acceptance Is Based on Enemy's Reciprocal Action

Excerpts from debate at U.N. are printed on Page 18.

By DREW MIDDLETON
Special to The New York Times

UNITED NATIONS, N. Y., June 7—The Security Council unanimously adopted a Soviet resolution today calling on the combatants in the Middle East to "cease fire and all military activities" at 4 P.M., New York time today.

The Government of Israel shortly thereafter announced that she had accepted the call of the Council for a cease-fire, provided her Arab foes agreed.

In the evening, reports from the Middle East indicated rejection of the call by the United Arab Republic, Syria, Iraq, Saudi Arabia, Algeria and Kuwait. Jordan told Secretary General Thant that she would abide by the cease-fire, except in self-defense.

Says It's in Effect

Abba Eban, the Foreign Minister of Israel, told the Secretary General that a cease-fire was already in effect between Jordan and Israel.

In presenting the resolution, the Soviet delegate, Nikolai T. Fedorenko, made it clear that if Israel failed to heed the Security Council's demands, Moscow would consider severing diplomatic relations. The original Security Council resolution, adopted yesterday, simply called for a cease-fire.

But the reports from the Arab capitals indicate, diplomatic sources here said, that military operations will continue.

According to diplomats, the best hope lies in a draft resolution presented by George Ignatieff, the Canadian delegate. This proposes that the President of the Security Council and the Secretary General take measures to insure compliance with the resolutions.

Today's resolution demanded that the combatants "cease fire and all military activities on 7 June 1967 by 2000 hours Greenwich mean time." The resolution was adopted less than an hour before this time, which is 4 P.M. New York time, 10 P.M. in Jordan and Israel and 11 P.M. in the United Arab Republic and Syria.

The Council adjourned without voting on the Canadian draft largely because Milko Ta-

Continued on Page 18, Column 2

United Press International Radiophoto

OLD JERUSALEM IS NOW IN ISRAELI HANDS: Israeli soldiers in prayer at the Wailing Wall yesterday

Major Mideast Developments

On the Battlefronts

Israel claimed victory in the Sinai Desert after three days of fighting. Sharm el Sheik, guarding the entrance to the Gulf of Aqaba, fell after a paratroop attack, and the Israelis said the blockade of the gulf was broken. Other Israeli units were within 20 miles of the Suez Canal, and one Israeli report placed them in the eastern section of Ismailia, on the canal itself.

In Jerusalem, for the first time in 19 years, Israeli Jews prayed at the Wailing Wall as their troops occupied the Old City. Israeli troops captured Jericho, in Jordan, and sped northward to take Nablus, giving them control of the west bank of the Jordan.

The Egyptian High Command reported that its forces had fallen back from first-line positions in the Sinai Peninsula and were fighting fiercely from unspecified secondary positions. It announced that Egyptian troops had pulled back from Sharm el Sheik to join main defense units.

In the Capitals

In the United Nations, Israel accepted the call for a cease-fire, provided the Arabs complied. Jordan announced that she would accept and ordered her troops to fire only in self-defense. But Baghdad declared that Iraq had refused. There were indications that Syria, Algeria and Kuwait were also opposed.

In Cairo, an Egyptian official said the United Arab Republic would fight on.

In Moscow, the Soviet Union threatened to break diplomatic relations with Israel if she did not observe the cease-fire.

In Paris, the French proposed an international agreement for free passage in the Gulf of Aqaba similar to the one governing the Dardanelles in Turkey.

In Washington, President Johnson promised to seek a settlement that would assure lasting peace in the Mideast.

In London, the British urged the Israelis to halt before they aroused more turmoil in the Arab world and diminished the chances for a settlement.

Israelis Weep and Pray Beside the Wailing Wall

By TERENCE SMITH
Special to The New York Times

JERUSALEM, June 7—Israeli troops wept and prayed today at the foot of the Wailing Wall—the last remnant of Solomon's Second Temple and the object of pilgrimage by Jews through the centuries.

In battle dress and still carrying their weapons, they gathered at the base of the sand-colored wall and sang Hallel, a series of prayers reserved for occasions of great joy.

They were repeating a tradition that goes back 2,000 years but has been denied Israeli Jews since 1948, when the first of three wars with the Arabs ended in this area.

The wall is all that remains of the Second Temple, built in the 10th century before Christ and destroyed by the Romans in A.D. 70.

The Israelis, trembling with emotion, bowed vigorously from the waist as they chanted psalms in a lusty chorus. Most had submachine guns slung over their shoulders and several held bazookas as they prayed.

Among the leaders to pray at the wall was Maj. Gen. Moshe Dayan, the new Defense Minister. He told the troops:

"We have returned to the holiest of our holy places, never to depart from it again."

General Dayan, who was ap-

Continued on Page 17, Column 1

CAIRO ANNOUNCES A SINAI PULLBACK

Blames Foreign Aid to Foe, but Says Troops Fight On in Secondary Positions

By ERIC PACE
Special to The New York Times

CAIRO, June 7—An Egyptian military communiqué reported today that forces of the United Arab Republic had fallen back from some first-line positions on the Sinai Peninsula and were engaged in fierce fighting against Israeli troops from secondary positions.

Another statement of the High Command, broadcast four hours later by the Cairo radio, said Egyptian troops at Sharm el Sheik, guarding the entrance to the Gulf of Aqaba, had joined other Egyptian forces "now concentrated in the Sinai Peninsula."

There was no elaboration, but the communiqué, broadcast about 5:30 P.M., appeared to confirm Israeli reports that the Egyptians had been forced to retreat from Sharm el Sheik.

At night, the High Command reported that Israeli paratroops had dropped over the "second-line Egyptian front" but had been "completely wiped out."

The communiqué also said the Israelis had tried another drop at Sharm el Sheik after the

Continued on Page 17, Column 6

AQABA GULF OPEN

Dayan Asserts Israel Does Not Intend to Capture the Canal

By The Associated Press

TEL AVIV, June 7—Israel proclaimed victory tonight in the Sinai Peninsula campaign against the United Arab Republic. On the eastern front, both the Old City of Jerusalem and Bethlehem were captured from the Jordanians.

"The Egyptians are defeated," said Maj. Gen. Itzhak Rabin, the Israeli Chief of Staff.

"All their efforts are aimed at withdrawing behind the Suez Canal, and we are taking care of that. The whole area is in our hands. The main effort of the Egyptians is to save themselves."

Israel Losses 'Not Great'

Describing the developments through the third day of this third Arab-Israeli war in 19 years, General Rabin made these claims:

¶Sinai, the Egyptian territory between Israel's Negev Desert and the Suez Canal, is taken.

¶Most of the Jordanian territory on the west bank of the Jordan River, including Jericho, is in Israeli hands, and most of Jordan's army has been captured.

¶Relative to what was done, the number of Israelis casualties was "not great."

The Israelis were reported to have swept to the Suez Canal.

[An Israeli delegation source at the United Nations said Israeli troops had seized that part of the canal city of Ismailia that is on the eastern side of the waterway. But this was denied by an army source in Tel Aviv, who said, according to Reuters, that the Israelis had not taken any point along the canal.

[Maj. Gen. Moshe Dayan, the Israeli Defense Minister, declared that there was "no intention" of taking the canal, United Press International reported.]

'Never to Depart'

After the fall of the Old City of Jerusalem, Defense Minister Moshe Dayan said there that the Israelis had reunited their capital and would never "depart from it again."

Israel reported that paratroops aided by naval units had captured Sharm el Sheik, commanding the entrance to the Gulf of Aqaba, and said the blockade that the Egyptians had mounted from that position had been broken.

"The Strait of Tiran is now open," General Rabin said.

Israel's chief of staff said his men had taken on the United Arab Republic, Jordan, Syria and Iraq, knocked out their air forces and overrun their armor and infantry.

"All this the armed forces of Israel did alone," he declared.

The general then turned over the briefing to Brig. Mordechai Hod, commander of the air force, who announced 441 Arab

Continued on Page 16, Column 1

CONFEREES BLOCK A DRAFT LOTTERY

Compromise Bill Continues Deferment of Students

By United Press International

WASHINGTON, June 7 — Senate and House negotiators reached agreement today on a new military draft bill that rules out, for the present, any lottery-like random selection system to determine the order of induction.

The bill was a compromise of differing bills that the Senate and House had passed. It would guarantee the continuance of educational deferments for college undergraduates and students enrolled in apprentice and job training programs.

Senator Richard B. Russell, Democrat of Georgia, who is chairman of the Senate conferees, said the Senate might act on the four-year draft extension bill tomorrow. House action must await approval by the Senate.

Congressional action will clear the way for President Johnson, under current discretionary powers, to reverse the order of induction and take 19-year-olds first from the Selec-

Continued on Page 3, Column 1

NEWS INDEX

News Summary and Index, Page 49

Dorothy Parker, 73, Literary Wit, Dies

By ALDEN WHITMAN

Dorothy Parker, the sardonic humorist who purveyed her wit in conversation, short stories, verse and criticism, died of a heart attack yesterday afternoon in her suite at the Volney Hotel, 23 East 74th Street. She was 73 years old and had been in frail health in recent years.

In print and in person, Miss Parker sparkled with a word or a phrase, for she honed her humor to its most economical size. Her rapier wit, much of it spontaneous, gained its early renown from her membership in the Algonquin Round Table, an informal luncheon club at the Algonquin Hotel in the nineteen-twenties, where some of

Continued on Page 38, Column 1

The New York Times — June 8, 1967

CONQUEST IN THE MIDEAST: Israeli troops took Sharm el Sheik (1), drove on to the Suez Canal (2) and seized control of the Old City in Jerusalem (3). Photo was taken in September, 1966, during the flight of Gemini II.

Pentagon Believes Israeli Jets Struck From Sea, Eluded Radar

By WILLIAM BEECHER
Special to The New York Times

WASHINGTON, June 7 — At least a part of the Israeli Air Force that caught large numbers of Egyptian aircraft on the ground in the early hours of the war may have slipped through gaps in the United Arab Republic's radar net by flying in over the Mediterranean.

This possibility was raised today by Pentagon analysts. If correct, it would help to explain how Israeli pilots were able to surprise so many Egyptian jets before they could get into the air.

It might also serve to provide part of the explanation behind insistent Arab assertions that carrier-based United States and British jets participated in the raids.

The early blows to Arab, and especially Egyptian, air strength is credited by most military analysts as having been a decisive factor in the Israeli successes on land that followed.

"We know that some of the Israeli planes returned to their bases by way of the sea," one ranking officer said, "and we assume they may have approached from the seaward too."

The officer said it was obvious that Israel had excellent intelligence on weaknesses in the Egyptian radar system and exploited them.

Shortly after the raids, he went on, the Jordanian radio charged that Jordanian radar

Continued on Page 18, Column 8

"All the News That's Fit to Print"

The New York Times

LATE CITY EDITION

Weather: Clearing today, turning cold tonight. Fair, cool tomorrow. Temp. range: today 62-44; Thurs. 73-52. Full U.S. report on Page 92.

VOL. CXVII. No. 40,249 — NEW YORK, FRIDAY, APRIL 5, 1968 — 10 CENTS

MARTIN LUTHER KING IS SLAIN IN MEMPHIS; A WHITE IS SUSPECTED; JOHNSON URGES CALM

JOHNSON DELAYS TRIP TO HAWAII; MAY LEAVE TODAY

President Spends a Hectic Day Here and in Capital —Sees Thant at the U.N.

By MAX FRANKEL
Special to The New York Times

WASHINGTON, April 4 — President Johnson postponed his trip to Hawaii at least until tomorrow after he heard of the death of the Rev. Dr. Martin Luther King Jr. tonight.

The news, which visibly shocked the President, came at the end of one of the most extraordinary days in perhaps the most extraordinary week of his Administration.

Mr. Johnson was to have flown from Washington at about midnight for a weekend of strategy conferences with his military and diplomatic leaders stationed in South Vietnam. On the way, he had planned a breakfast meeting in California with former President Dwight D. Eisenhower.

Instead, the President telephoned Mrs. King in Atlanta, made a brief appeal for calm on television and went to his office to follow the reports of unrest and disturbance given him periodically by Attorney General Ramsey Clark.

Cancels Dinner Appearance

Mr. Johnson also canceled an appearance before a Democratic party fund-raising dinner here —the final event of a hectic schedule that became ever more hectic as the day unfolded.

The President began the day by making final arrangements for the Hawaii meeting. It had been tentatively planned before his order Sunday to curtail the bombing of North Vietnam and the news yesterday that Hanoi was interested in establishing direct contact.

[The new United States peace moves are producing a quiet but bitter reaction in the South Vietnamese Government that is causing increasing concern among United States officials in Saigon. Page 14.]

But the diplomatic development, though not the principal subject of the Honolulu meetings, added special weight to his conversations with Gen. Wiliam C. Westmoreland, the American commander in South Vietnam, and other officials.

Mr. Johnson was careful not to arouse false hopes of peace, but he appeared encouraged and in buoyant spirt as he decided before noon to fly first to New York to attend the investiture of the Most Rev. Terence J. Cooke as Archbishop of New York.

Then, while in New York,

Continued on Page 12, Column 1

Hanoi Charges U.S. Raid Far North of 20th Parallel

By EVERT CLARK
Special to The New York Times

WASHINGTON, April 4 — North Vietnam charged in a broadcast today that United States planes had bombed a "populated area" in northwestern Vietnam far north of the 20th parallel. The Defense Department said it knew of no such raid but was investigating.

President Johnson has ordered that there be no attacks on North Vietnam north of the 20th Parallel as a step toward de-escalating the war.

[In South Vietnam, United States marines beat off an attack by about 400 North Vietnamese soldiers charging up a hill near Khesanh, killing 93, The Associated Press reported. Meanwhile, an American relief column was nearing the besieged base. Page 15.]

The Hanoi radio, in a broadcast monitored and translated here, said three waves of United States planes dropped more than 50 bombs on a "populated area" about 30 miles west of Laichau, capital of Laichau Province, this morning.

The nearest village to that

Continued on Page 15, Column 1

The New York Times April 5, 1968

Hanoi said that area near Laichau (cross) was target.

HUMPHREY HINTS HE'LL ENTER RACE

Tells Unionists in Pittsburgh He Will Act Soon—Abel and Wirtz Back Him

By ROY REED
Special to The New York Times

PITTSBURGH, April 4—Two thousand labor representatives, including the head of the United Steel Workers union, clamorously urged Vice President Humphrey today to run for President.

The Vice President left little doubt that he would oblige them, but he indicated that he would wait until President Johnson returned from his Hawaii conference before making an announcement.

"I know what your request is, and I know what your thoughts are," he told the delegates to the Pennsylvania A.F.L.-C.I.O. convention. "I am most grateful. I am not one to walk away from a decision, and a decision will come in due time."

But nothing he does should interfere with President Johnson's peace mission, he said.

Several other political leaders urged Mr. Humphrey today to enter the race for the Democratic Presidential nomination. The most prominent among them was Secretary of Labor W. Willard Wirtz, who was addressing a union convention at Miami Beach.

I. W. Abel, president of the steelworkers Union, rose as Mr.

Continued on Page 32, Column 1

Johnson Shuns Role Of '68 'Lame Duck,' Kennedy Was Told

By JOHN HERBERS
Special to The New York Times

WASHINGTON, April 4—In his meeting with Senator Robert F. Kennedy yesterday President Johnson said he would remain out of the political fight this year because he did not believe it was appropriate for a "lame duck" President to try to pick his successor.

This and other details of the Johnson-Kennedy meeting were learned today from knowledgeable sources.

The meeting, which Senator Kennedy had requested in the interest of "national unity," was described as an extraordinarily friendly one, with both the Senator and the President speaking in a conciliatory manner.

President Johnson was pictured as the "elder statesman" of the party who had decided to remain aloof from this year's scramble for the Presidency in an effort to keep the party as strong as possible and retain his own dignity and effectiveness as President.

At one point, it was reported, the President said he did not want to make a spectacle of himself as a lame duck President attempting to dictate to the party who should be nominated at the national convention.

In this regard, he pointed out that in 1956 former President Harry S. Truman went to the

Continued on Page 31, Column 4

DISMAY IN NATION

Negroes Urge Others to Carry on Spirit of Nonviolence

By LAWRENCE VAN GELDER

Dismay, shame, anger and foreboding marked the nation's reaction last night to the Rev. Dr. Martin Luther King Jr.'s murder.

From the high offices of state to the man in the street, news of the moderate civil rights leader's violent death in Memphis yesterday drew, for the most part, stunned and sober statements.

Most major Negro organizations and Negro leaders, lamenting Dr. King's death, expressed hope that it serve as a spur to others to carry on in his spirit of nonviolence. But some Negro militants responded with bitterness and anger.

Roy Wilkins, executive director of the National Association for the Advancement of Colored People, said his organization was "shocked and deeply grieved by the dastardly murder of Dr. Martin Luther King."

"His murderer or murderers must be promptly apprehended and brought to justice," Mr. Wilkins said.

'A Man of Peace'

"Dr. King was a symbol of the nonviolent civil rights protest movement. He was a man of peace, of dedication, of great courage. His senseless assassination solves nothing. It will not stay the civil rights movement; it will instead spur it to greater activity."

Whitney M. Young Jr., executive director of the National Urban League, said:

"We are unspeakably shocked by the murder of Martin Luther King, one of the greatest leaders of our time. This is a bitter reflection on America. We fear for our country.

"The only possible answer now is for the nation to act immediately on what Dr. King has been fighting for—passage of the civil rights and anti-poverty bills and a true and just equality for all men. Those of us who have remained loyal to his concept of nonviolence have been dealt a mortal blow."

Mayor Richard G. Hatcher of Gary, Ind., a Negro, termed the death of Dr. King "every man's loss."

"Men who care for humankind and struggle for its salvation through reason and faith have lost a leader of monumental stature," he said. "A man of his magnitude will not soon pass this way again."

At his home in Stamford, Conn., the former baseball star Jackie Robinson called the

Continued on Page 26, Column 1

PRESIDENT'S PLEA

On TV, He Deplores 'Brutal' Murder of Negro Leader

Statements by Johnson and Humphrey are on Page 24.

Special to The New York Times

WASHINGTON, April 4— President Johnson deplored tonight in a brief television address to the nation the "brutal slaying" of the Rev. Dr. Martin Luther King Jr.

He asked "every citizen to reject the blind violence that has struck Dr. King, who lived by nonviolence."

Mr. Johnson said he was postponing his scheduled departure tonight for a Honolulu conference on Vietnam and that instead he would leave tomorrow.

The President spoke from the White House. At the Washington Hilton Hotel, where Democratic members of Congress had gathered to honor the President and the Vice President, Mr. Humphrey, his voice strained with emotion, said:

"Martin Luther King stands with our other American martyrs in the cause of freedom and justice. His death is a terrible tragedy."

The dinner was canceled 10 to 15 minutes after the Vice President spoke. Mr. Johnson, who was scheduled to appear at the dinner, canceled his plans to attend.

F.B.I. Inquiry Ordered

Attorney General Ramsey Clark ordered an immediate inquiry by the Federal Bureau of Investigation into the shooting of Dr. King in Memphis.

He said the purpose of the investigation would be to determine whether any Federal law had been violated.

One provision of the law that could be invoked makes it a crime to engage in a conspiracy to deprive a person of his civil rights.

In addition to F.B.I. agents, Department of Justice civil rights representatives were on the scene in Memphis and were in touch with the Attorney General.

Military sources said that no National Guard units had yet been Federalized and no Regular Army troops had been alerted yet for possible movement to cities where violence had broken out.

National Guard troops, such as the 4,000 men who have been called into Memphis, remain under state control until the responsible Governor requests help and the President

Continued on Page 24, Column 7

Associated Press

THE REV. DR. MARTIN LUTHER KING Jr.

Scattered Violence Occurs In Harlem and Brooklyn

12 Are Arrested Here

By THOMAS A. JOHNSON

Sporadic violence erupted in Harlem and Brooklyn's Bedford-Stuyvesant section last night after news of Dr. Martin Luther King's assassination spread in the two predominantly Negro communities.

Mayor Lindsay, who went to Harlem in an effort to quiet the outbreaks, was caught in the midst of an unruly crowd and had to be hustled into a limousine by bodyguards.

Police reinforcements, including elements of the riot-trained Tactical Patrol Force, were rushed into both communities.

Two arrests were reported in Brooklyn and 10 in Harlem. A television crewman was said to have been injured by flying glass.

There were numerous instances of rock-throwing, looting and arson reported both in Brooklyn and in Harlem, starting around 11 P.M. and continuing early today.

Gangs of youth in both areas were reported roaming through the streets, now and then taunting policemen and firemen on duty.

The police fired several volleys of shots in the air to disperse crowds along Brooklyn's Fulton Street and Harlem's

Continued on Page 26, Column 2

Widespread Disorders

Disorders broke out in scattered parts of the nation last night after the slaying of the Rev. Dr. Martin Luther King Jr. The National Guard was called out or alerted in several cities.

In Washington, scattered but persistent looting and vandalism erupted, led for a time by Stokely Carmichael, former head of the Student Nonviolent Coordinating Commitee. All available policemen were being called to duty.

About 4,000 Tennessee National Guardsmen were ordered to duty in Nashville because of disorders.

In North Carolina, Gov. Dan K. Moore alerted the Guard in Greensboro at the request of Mayor Carson Bain. State Highway patrolmen were dispatched to Raleigh.

There were riotous outbursts

Continued on Page 26, Column 5

NEWS INDEX

GUARD CALLED OUT

Curfew Is Ordered in Memphis, but Fires and Looting Erupt

By EARL CALDWELL
Special to The New York Times

MEMPHIS, Friday, April 5— The Rev. Dr. Martin Luther King Jr., who preached nonviolence and racial brotherhood, was fatally shot here last night by a distant gunman who then raced away and escaped.

Four thousand National Guard troops were ordered into Memphis by Gov. Buford Ellington after the 39-year-old Nobel Prize-winning civil rights leader died.

A curfew was imposed on the shocked city of 550,000 inhabitants, 40 per cent of whom are Negro.

But the police said the tragedy had been followed by incidents that included sporadic shooting, fires, bricks and bottles thrown at policemen, and looting that started in Negro districts and then spread over the city.

White Car Sought

Police Director Frank Holloman said the assassin might have been a white man who was "50 to 100 yards away in a flophouse."

Chief of Detectives W. P. Huston said a late model white Mustang was believed to have been the killer's getaway car. Its occupant was described as a bareheaded white man in his 30's, wearing a black suit and black tie.

The detective chief said the police had chased two cars near the motel where Dr. King was shot and had halted one that had two out-of-town men as occupants. The men were questioned but seemed to have nothing to do with the killing, he said.

Rifle Found Nearby

A high-powered 30.06-caliber rifle was found about a block from the scene of the shooting, on South Main Street. "We think it's the gun," Chief Huston said, reporting it would be turned over to the Federal Bureau of Investigation.

Dr. King was shot while he leaned over a second-floor railing outside his room at the Lorraine Motel. He was chatting with two friends just before starting for dinner.

One of the friends was a musician, and Dr. King had just asked him to play a Negro spiritual, "Precious Lord, Take My Hand," at a rally that was to have been held two hours later in support of striking Memphis sanitationmen.

Paul Hess, assistant adminis-

Continued on Page 24, Column 1

Archbishop Cooke Installed; President Looks On

By EDWARD B. FISKE

The Most Rev. Terence J. Cooke was installed as the seventh Roman Catholic Archbishop of New York yesterday in a historic pageant attended by the President of the United States and highlighted by prayers for the success of his peace efforts in Vietnam.

"Let us pray with all our hearts that God will inspire our President," the 47-year-old Archbishop said in his homily at St. Patrick's Cathedral.

"In the last few days, we have all admired his heroic efforts in the search for peace in Vietnam. We ask God to bless his efforts with success. May God inspire not only our President, but also other leaders and the leaders of all nations of the world to find a way to peace."

Then the Archbishop, speaking from a white marble pulpit and surrounded by a blaze of purple, gold and scarlet robes, addressed himself directly to Mr. Johnson, who sat below him in a front pew.

The President, sitting with his hands clasped and his legs crossed, listened with obvious intensity to the Archbishop's words.

"Mr. President," he said, "our hearts, our hopes, our continued prayers go with you."

Mr. Johnson, accompanied by his daughter, Mrs. Patrick J. Nugent, led a festive congregation of about 5,000 cardinals, bishops, priests, laymen, nuns, civic leaders

Continued on Page 38, Column 1

The New York Times (by Neal Boenzi)

President Johnson and his daughter, Mrs. Patrick J. Nugent, right, listening during yesterday's ceremonies. At left are Mrs. John F. Kennedy and Lieut. Gov. Malcolm Wilson. Security personnel are in the row between them.

Archbishop Luigi Raimondi, Apostolic Delegate to the U.S., speaking after Archbishop Terence J. Cooke was enthroned

"All the News That's Fit to Print"

The New York Times

LATE CITY EDITION

Weather: Sunny, warm today; fair, continued warm tonight, tomorrow. Temp. range: today 88-62; Wed. 83-59. Temp.-Hum. Index 75; Wed. 74. Full U.S. report on Page 94.

VOL. CXVII..No. 40,311 NEW YORK, THURSDAY, JUNE 6, 1968 10 CENTS

KENNEDY IS DEAD, VICTIM OF ASSASSIN; SUSPECT, ARAB IMMIGRANT, ARRAIGNED; JOHNSON APPOINTS PANEL ON VIOLENCE

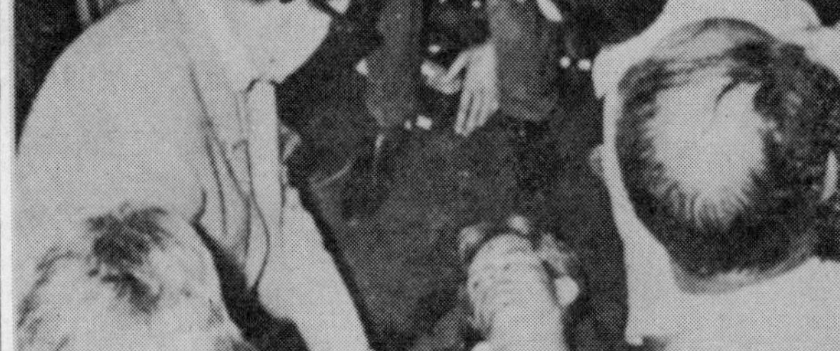

AFTER THE SHOOTING: Senator Kennedy's wife, Ethel, bends over him as a man checks pulse to determine condition

SURGERY IN VAIN

President Calls Death Tragedy, Proclaims a Day of Mourning

Texts of the medical reports appear on Page 22.

By GLADWIN HILL

Special to The New York Times

LOS ANGELES, Thursday, June 6—Senator Robert F. Kennedy, the brother of a murdered President, died at 1:44 A.M. today of an assassin's shots.

The New York Senator was wounded more than 20 hours earlier, moments after he had made his victory statement in the California primary.

At his side when he died today in Good Samaritan Hospital were his wife, Ethel; his sisters, Mrs. Stephen Smith and Mrs. Patricia Lawford; his brother-in-law, Stephen Smith; and his sister-in-law, Mrs. John F. Kennedy, whose husband was assassinated 4½ years ago in Dallas.

In Washington, President Johnson issued a statement calling the death a tragedy. He proclaimed next Sunday a national day of mourning.

The Final Report

Hopes had risen slightly when more than eight hours went by without a new medical bulletin on the stricken Senator, but the grimness of the final announcement was signaled when Frank Mankiewicz, Mr. Kennedy's press secretary, walked slowly down the street in front of the hospital toward the littered gymnasium that served as press headquarters.

Mr. Mankiewicz bit his lip. His shoulders slumped.

He stepped to a lectern in front of a green-tinted chalkboard and bowed his head for a moment while the television lights snapped on.

Then, at one minute before 2 A.M., he told of the death of Mr. Kennedy.

Following is the text of the statement from Mr. Mankiewicz:

"I have a short announcement to read which I will read at this time. Senator Robert Francis Kennedy died at 1:44 A.M. today, June 6, 1968. With

Continued on Page 20, Column 1

MARCUS TESTIFIES DE SAPIO HAD ROLE IN A CON ED DEAL

Says Itkin Sought Delay of Permit to Aid Own Scheme With Ex-Tammany Head

By BARNARD L. COLLIER

Former Water Commissioner James L. Marcus testified yesterday that he had been asked to delay approval of a permit to Consolidated Edison while the former Tammany Hall leader, Carmine G. De Sapio, was trying to make a deal with the utility company.

Marcus testified that the request came last September from his business partner, Herbert Itkin, who was in turn trying to negotiate a deal with Mr. De Sapio.

The testimony was elicited from Marcus under cross-examination on the third day of a Federal bribery conspiracy trial that has been marked by the mention in Marcus's testimony of several prominent members of both the Republican and Democratic parties.

Marcus was asked if there was a time when he, as Commissioner of Water Supply, Gas and Electricity, had "done business" with Con Edison. His answer was yes.

Says Itkin Asked Delay

"Itkin came to me," he said, "and said that Con Ed wanted a permit to increase the voltage on one of their power lines for 20 miles." He added that his approval as Commissioner was needed.

"Itkin said I should hold up for a while because he was negotiating with Carmine De Sapio, who was negotiating with Con Ed."

Marcus said that Mr. Itkin asked him to delay the approval for "a few weeks."

At that point in the trial, which came at about 4:40 P.M., Herman Zoloto, a lawyer representing Henry Fried, a contractor, and Mr. Fried's company, S. T. Grand, Inc., shouted:

"You're way ahead of your story, Mr. Marcus!"

Judge Edward Weinfeld broke in and scolded Mr. Zoloto for "a highly improper re-

Continued on Page 41, Column 1

TRANSIT PACKAGE SUBMITTED TO CITY

M.T.A. Seeks Approval of 8 New Subway Routes

By EMANUEL PERLMUTTER

A $1.27-billion package of subway and commuter railroad additions and improvements was submitted to the Board of Estimate and Mayor Lindsay yesterday.

The program was presented by the Metropolitan Transportation Authority and the New York City Transit Authority with a request for speedy city agreement on the new routes and engineering designs.

The over-all plan, which would take 10 years to complete, consists of eight new subway routes, including a Second Avenue subway, and Long Island Rail Road connections to the East Side of Manhattan and to Kennedy International Airport.

City approval of the routes and designs is a first step before application can be made for $60-million set aside by the Legislature for the engineering design of the mass transportation program presented by the Metropolitan Transportation

Continued on Page 55, Column 1

France Will Meet Tariff Deadline; Strikes Dwindling

By HENRY TANNER

Special to The New York Times

PARIS, June 5 — Maurice Couve de Murville told France's partners in the Common Market today that despite the nationwide strike now coming to a close, the Government would honor the July 1 deadline for the abolition of remaining tariffs in the European trade bloc.

Today workers in the nationalized railroad company, the Paris transit system, the post and telegraph offices and other public administrations voted to go back to work. Trains are expected to start running tomorrow on several major national lines and the Paris subways.

By the end of the week, it is expected, the nationwide strike, now in its 18th day, will be all but ended.

Mr. Couve de Murville, who is the new Minister of Economy and Finance, also reassured his countrymen

Continued on Page 15, Column 1

JERUSALEM POLICE CLASH WITH ARABS

Israelis Halt Procession on Anniversary of War—U.N. Council Meets on Fighting

Special to The New York Times

JERUSALEM, June 5—A silent Arab procession commemorating the first anniversary of the Arab-Israeli war erupted into a violent clash today when Isareli policemen intercepted the marchers at the edge of the walled Old City of Jerusalem.

The clash was the most violent aspect of a widespread protest in which Arabs shuttered shops and other businesses here and elsewhere on the west bank of the Jordan and in the occupied Gaza Strip. It came after a day-long battle yesterday across the Jordan between the Israelis and Jordanians, in which aircraft and artillery were used.

[The United Nations Security Council met Wednesday at the urgent request of Israel and Jordan to consider recurrent hostilities along their cease-fire line. It postponed debate, probably until Thursday. Page 3.]

In the west-bank towns of Nablus, Jenin and Tulkarm, all centers of Arab nationalism, the general strike was 100 per cent effective. All stores, cafes and offices were closed, public transportation ceased and the streets were virtually devoid of traffic and pedestrians.

Schools throughout the west bank and Gaza Strip had no

Continued on Page 2, Column 4

Italy's Cabinet Quits As Parliament Opens

By ROBERT C. DOTY

Special to The New York Times

ROME, June 5—Premier Aldo Moro and his center-left coalition Government, which has ruled Italy for four and a half years, resigned tonight with the convening of the new parliament, the fifth since World War II.

President Giuseppe Saragat asked Mr. Moro and his ministers to remain in office as a caretaker government while the search for a new government, which may be arduous, goes on.

Resignation of the government with the convening of a new parliament is automatic. But any hope that the Moro

Continued on Page 14, Column 3

6 IN RACE GUARDED

Secret Service Given Campaign Security Task by President

Text of the Johnson speech is printed on Page 23.

By MAX FRANKEL

Special to The New York Times

WASHINGTON, June 5—For the second time in five years, Lyndon B. Johnson undertook today, amid national shock and outrage, to offer protection, prayer, comfort and assistance to his political rivals in the Kennedy family and then to try to heal the country's political and psychological wounds.

The President's first reaction to the shooting of Senator Robert F. Kennedy this morning was that "there are no words equal to the horror of this tragedy."

But tonight, in an emotional and at times even angry statement on television, he pleaded with all Americans to end the violence in their midst once and for all, to tolerate neither hatred nor the preaching of violence and to resolve to live under the law.

A Guard for Candidates

Mr. Johnson said he was appointing a commission of distinguished citizens to investigate both the circumstances and the causes of physical violence of all kinds in the United States, in the hope that the nation can learn "how we can stop it".

Earlier he had moved swiftly to provide protective Secret Service details to the six announced Presidential candidates of major parties, other than Vice President Humphrey, who already has such protection because of his office.

Meanwhile, in the House of Representatives, a vote of 317 to 60 cleared the way for the House to accept the Senate version of an anticrime bill, including controls over the interstate sale of hand guns. The vote rejected a move to send the legislation to a Senate-House conference.

Members of Commission

To the commission Mr. Johnson named Milton Eisenhower, former president of Johns Hopkins University; Archbishop Terence J. Cooke of New York; Albert Jenner, Chicago lawyer who worked for the commission that investigated the assassination of President Kennedy; former Ambassador Patricia Harris; Eric Hoffer, the longshoreman-turned-philosopher; Senators Philip Hart, Democrat of Michigan, and Roman L. Hruska, Republican of Nebraska; Representative Hale Boggs, Democrat of Louisiana, majority whip in the House; Representative William M. McCulloch, Republican of Ohio, and Federal Judge Leon Higginbotham of Philadelphia.

The President described himself as shocked, dismayed and deeply disturbed, as he knew all Americans were, by the shooting, which he described as the "latest spectacular example" of lawlessness and violence.

"So let us, for God's sake, re-

Continued on Page 23, Column 1

NEWS INDEX

HANOI INSISTS U.S. HALT ITS BOMBING

Aides Call Talks Response to Johnson—Suspicion Voiced of a Plot Against Kennedy

By HEDRICK SMITH

Special to The New York Times

PARIS, June 5—North Vietnamese negotiators contended today that Hanoi had responded to President Johnson's restriction of American air attacks on the north by entering official talks here. They asserted that the next move, a total halt in bombing, was up to the United States.

The North Vietnamese argument, put forward in the seventh negotiating session between the two sides since May 13, produced one of the sharpest exchanges since the Vietnam talks began here.

The North Vietnamese made no direct comment on the shooting of Senator Robert F. Kennedy, but circles close to the delegation voiced suspicions in private, asking if the attack was not part of a conspiracy by the Johnson Administration. [Page 33.]

Near the end of today's session at the former Majestic Hotel, Hanoi's chief representative, Xuan Thuy, leaned across the negotiating table and asked the American delegates bluntly:

"When will the United States unconditionally cease the bombing and all other acts of war against the Democratic Republic of Vietnam so that other questions can be discussed?"

In response, W. Averell Har-

Continued on Page 8, Column 4

Big Board Weighs 4 Special Closings

By VARTANIG G. VARTAN

A securities industry panel recommended yesterday that the New York Stock Exchange, the American Stock Exchange and the over-the-counter market close down for four days over the next month to cope with the deluge of paperwork in brokerage offices.

The panel proposed closing the securities markets for three Wednesdays—June 12, 19 and 26—as well as Friday, July 5.

The board of governors of the New York Stock Exchange will meet this afternoon to consider the proposal. Wall Street sources said that in view of the critical situation the governors are expected to accept the pro-

Continued on Page 73, Column 1

The New York Times (by George Tames)

ROBERT F. KENNEDY

A Pall Over Politics

Murder Raises Grave Questions for Presidency Races Now and in Future

By TOM WICKER

Special to The New York Times

News Analysis

WASHINGTON, Thursday, June 6—The murder of Robert F. Kennedy shattered the 1968 Presidential campaign and lowered a pall of uncertainty over American politics now and in the years to come. For the immediate future, it may well have assured the nominations by the Democrats and Republicans of the present front-running candidates — Vice President Humphrey and Richard Nixon. It raised grave questions, however, about the personal dangers of political campaigning in the United States. It added a tragic new dimension to the near-martyrdom of the Kennedy family, which has now lost two sons to assassins' bullets.

It removed forever one of the most promising young political leaders in recent American history, one with particular appeal for the poor, the downtrodden and the alienated inhabitants of the Negro slums. That appeal had been proved in all of Robert Kennedy's primary victories this year.

These elements of society also revered the Senator's brother, President Kennedy, who was assassinated on Nov. 22, 1963. How they would react to Robert Kennedy's murder—both in the immediate future and for the long political pull—was a crucial question.

The murder added sorrowful emphasis to one of Robert Kennedy's major political themes—the necessity for orderly and just redress of grievances, in place of violent action.

Ultimately, Mr. Kennedy's death—the first assassination of an American Presidential candidate—might lead to changes in campaigning practices, even to the fundamental manner in which the nation chooses its President.

The most immediate effect, however, was that for the third—and most harrowing—time a shock wave of unexpected events had completely altered the shape of the 1968 campaign.

The first came on March 12 when Senator Eugene J. McCarthy of Minnesota won 42 per cent of the Democratic vote in the New Hampshire primary, and Mr. Kennedy immediately thereafter became an active candidate.

The second transformation

Continued on Page 25, Column 6

NOTES ON KENNEDY IN SUSPECT'S HOME

Cite 'Necessity' to Murder Senator Before June 5, Anniversary of War

By PETER KIHSS

A notebook found in the Pasadena home of Sirhan Bishara Sirhan had "a direct reference to the necessity to assassinate Senator Kennedy before June 5, 1968," Mayor Samuel W. Yorty of Los Angeles said last night.

The date was the first anniversary of the six-day war, in which Israeli forces smashed those of the United Arab Republic, Syria and Jordan.

Sirhan, a 24-year-old Christian Arab, who has described himself as a Jerusalem-born Jordanian, is being held in the shooting of the New York Senator.

Justice Department records indicated that Sirhan came to the United States with his family in January of 1957 as immigrants, less than three months after the Suez war in 1956. Sirhan was 12 at the time.

The family quickly broke up in discord, the father staying in New York to work as a plumber and then going back to their former Palestine home, the mother taking five children to California, where a sixth child immigrated later.

Sirhan was described yesterday by Police Chief Thomas Reddin of Los Angeles as "very cool, very calm, very stable and quite lucid."

He was quoted as having said,

Continued on Page 21, Column 6

Father of Suspect 'Sickened' by News

By TERENCE SMITH

Special to The New York Times

ET TAIYIBA, Israeli-Occupied Jordan, Thursday, June 6—Bishara Sirhan's hands trembled as he talked about his son Sirhan Bishara Sirhan, the accused assailant of Senator Robert F. Kennedy.

Mr. Sirhan dwelled on the tragedy of the shooting. He became angry as he talked, and finally said: "This news made me sick when I heard it. If my son has done this dirty thing, then let them hang him."

Mr. Sirhan's memories of his five sons are those of 10 years ago, when he last saw them and their mother. After years of fierce family quarrels, Bishara

Continued on Page 21, Column 4

KUCHEL UNSEATED AS RAFFERTY WINS

Conservative Beats Senator in California's Primary

By LAWRENCE E. DAVIES

Special to The New York Times

LOS ANGELES, June 5—Dr. Max Rafferty, State Superintendent of Public Instruction, defeated Senator Thomas H. Kuchel in the Republican Senatorial primary in California yesterday, cutting short Mr. Kuchel's 15-year career in the Senate.

Returns from 20,714 of 21,301 precincts gave:

Rafferty	1,056,038	50%
Kuchel	985,097	47%

As the vote count continued today, it became apparent that the conservative Republicanism of Southern California had carried Dr. Rafferty to victory over the heretofore unbeatable Republican whip in the Senate.

Mr. Kuchel, an outspoken liberal-moderate who had made political extremists such as John Birch Society members his targets in recent years, was beaten by the voters in Los Angeles, San Diego and Orange Counties, after having led Dr. Rafferty last night and early today.

Dr. Rafferty, who has become

Continued on Page 28, Column 3

"All the News That's Fit to Print"

The New York Times

LATE CITY EDITION

Weather: Sunny, warm today; fair, seasonable tonight and tomorrow. Temp. range: today 89-73; Tuesday 91-72. Temp.-Hum. Index yesterday 81. Complete U.S. report on Page 90.

VOL. CXVII . No. 40,387 | NEW YORK, WEDNESDAY, AUGUST 21, 1968 | 10 CENTS

CZECHOSLOVAKIA INVADED BY RUSSIANS AND FOUR OTHER WARSAW PACT FORCES; THEY OPEN FIRE ON CROWDS IN PRAGUE

13 INDICTED HERE IN RIGGING OF BIDS ON UTILITY WORK

Contracts Worth 49-Million Involved—14 Construction Companies Also Named

By MARTIN TOLCHIN

Fourteen major construction companies, 12 top corporate executives and one employe were indicted here yesterday on charges of rigging bids on utilities contracts totaling $49.8-million.

The defendants were accused of deciding among themselves who would be low bidder in the contracts with Consolidated Edison, the Brooklyn Union Gas Company, and the Empire City Subway Company—the latter a subsidiary of the New York Telephone Company.

The indictments charge that the defendants then accommodated the selected low bidder by submitting higher bids.

The companies included such important contractors as Lipsett, Inc., a leading demolition company that razed Pennsylvania Station, the Savoy Plaza Hotel and the Third Avenue El; the Slattery Contracting Company, which held the general contract for excavating the site of United Nations Headquarters and built subway spurs and the Lincoln Center reflecting pool, and the Thomas Crimmins Contracting Company, which did the excavation for numerous skyscrapers.

1959 Activities Covered

The companies received contracts to dig trenches for electrical conduits and gas mains and for paving work. The contracts totaled $49,788,165.

The four indictments, with a total of 28 counts, were an outgrowth of the investigation of James L. Marcus, former City Water Commissioner, who pleaded guilty in Federal court to receiving a $40,000 kickback on a city reservoir cleaning contract.

"Our interest in Marcus and [Herbert] Itkin led us to the inquiry that led to these indictments," Frank S. Hogan, New York County District Attorney, said.

He noted that the indictments alleged activities that began in 1959, "before the community at large was aware of Marcus and Itkin," and

Continued on Page 35, Column 3

Democrats Debate Position on the War in Vietnam

The New York Times

Secretary of State Rusk defended the Administration's policies at the hearing.

Associated Press

Senator George S. McGovern of South Dakota was critical of the Administration.

The New York Times (by George Tames)

Kenneth P. O'Donnell, left, who was an aide to President Kennedy, talks with Senator J. W. Fulbright, standing right, at the platform hearing. The Senator spoke against the war.

SOVIET EXPLAINS

Says Its Troops Moved at the Request of Czechoslovaks

By RAYMOND H. ANDERSON
Special to The New York Times

MOSCOW, Wednesday, Aug. 21 — Moscow announced this morning that troops from the Soviet Union and four other Communist countries had invaded Czechoslovakia at the request of the "party and Government leaders of the Czechoslovak Socialist Republic."

The announcement followed unofficial information here that Alexander Dubcek, the reform leader of the Czechoslovak party Presidium, had been overthrown.

In a statement authorized by the Soviet Government, the official press agency, Tass, declared at 7:30 A.M. Moscow time (12:30 A.M., New York time) that Czechoslovakia had come under a threat from "counterrevolutionary forces" involved in a collusion with foreign forces hostile to socialism.

Friendship Stressed

Tass said that troops from Bulgaria. East Germany, Hungary, Poland and the Soviet Union, acting from motivations of "inseverable friendship and cooperation," entered Czechoslovakia early this morning.

The troops will be withdrawn as soon as the threat to Czechoslovakia and neighboring Communist countries has been eliminated, according to Tass.

"The actions that are being taken are not directed against any state and in no measure infringe state interests of anybody," the statement said. "They serve the purpose of peace and have been prompted by concern for its consolidation."

"The fraternal countries firmly and resolutely counterpose their unbreakable solidarity to any threat from outside," the Soviet explanation continued. "Nobody will ever be allowed to wrest a single link from the community of Socialist states."

Polemics Resumed

The handwriting was on the wall for the Czechoslovak reform regime last Friday when the Soviet press abruptly resumed its bitter polemics against the country.

Czechoslovakia's seven-month-old experiment with democracy under Communist rule was explicitly doomed yesterday when the Soviet Communist party warned in an editorial that imperial intrigues must be "nipped in the bud."

Rumors swept Moscow yesterday that the Soviet party's Central Committee had met in secret session, presumably to endorse intervention. Official sources insisted, however, that

Continued on Page 14, Column 6

Baltic Sea · Berlin · EAST GERMANY · Warsaw · POLAND · SOVIET UNION · Kiev · Prague · CZECHOSLOVAKIA · WEST GERMANY · Bratislava · Vienna · Budapest · AUSTRIA · HUNGARY · RUMANIA · Bucharest · Belgrade · YUGOSLAVIA · ITALY · Adriatic Sea · BULGARIA · Sofia · Rome · Tirane · ALBANIA · GREECE · 100 · 200 · 300 mi.

The New York Times Aug. 21, 1968

FIVE-POWER INVASION: Soviet planes carried troops into Prague (cross). Ground forces of bloc crossed Czechoslovak borders that are indicated by heavy line.

Versions of the Two Sides

Following are the texts of the Prague radio announcement of the Soviet-bloc invasion of Czechoslovakia, as monitored in Washington, and of a Soviet statement distributed in New York by Tass, the Soviet press agency.

Czechoslovak Radio Broadcast

To the entire people of the Czechoslovak Socialist Republic:

Yesterday, on 20 August, around 2300 [11 P.M.], troops of the Soviet Union, Polish People's Republic, the G.D.R. [East Germany], the Hungarian People's Republic and the Bulgarian People's Republic crossed the frontiers of the Czechoslovak Socialist Republic.

This happened without the knowledge of the President of the Republic, the Chairman of the National Assembly, the Premier, or the First Secretary of the Czechoslovak Communist party Central Committee.

In the evening hours the Presidium of the Czechoslovak Communist party Central Committee [had] held a session and discussed preparations for the 14th Czechoslovak Communist party congress.

The Czechoslovak Communist party Central Committee Presidium appeals to all citizens of our republic to maintain calm and not to offer resistance to the troops on the march. Our army, security corps and people's militia have not received the command to defend the country.

The Czechoslovak Communist party Central Committee Presidium regard this act as contrary not only to the fundamental principles of relations between Socialist states but also as contrary to the principles of international law.

All leading functionaries of the state, the Communist party and the National Front: Remain in your functions as representatives of the state, elected to the laws of the Czechoslovak Socialist Republic.

Constitutional functionaries are immediately convening a session of the National Assembly of our republic, and the Presidium is at the same time convening a plenum of the Central Committee to discuss the situation that has arisen.

PRESIDIUM OF THE CZECHOSLOVAK COMMUNIST PARTY CENTRAL COMMITTEE.

Announcement by Moscow

Tass is authorized to state that party and Government leaders of the Czechoslovak Socialist Republic have asked the Soviet Union and other allied states to render the fraternal Czechoslovak people urgent assistance, including assistance with armed forces. This request was brought about by the threat which has arisen to the Socialist system existing in Czechoslovakia and to the statehood established by the Con-

Continued on Page 14, Column 2

TANKS ENTER CITY

Deaths Are Reported —Troops Surround Offices of Party

By TAD SZULC
Special to The New York Times

PRAGUE, Wednesday, Aug. 21—Czechoslovakia was occupied early today by troops of the Soviet Union and four of its Warsaw Pact allies in a series of swift land and air movements.

Airborne Soviet troops and paratroopers surrounded the building of the Communist party Central Committee, along with five tanks. At least 25 tanks were seen in the city.

Several persons were reported killed early this morning. Unconfirmed reports said that two Czechoslovak soldiers and a woman were killed by Bulgarian tank fire in front of the Prague radio building shortly before the station was captured and went off the air.

[Soviet troops began shooting at Czechoslovak demonstrators outside the Prague radio building at 7:25 A.M., Reuters reported. C.T.K., the Czechoslovak press agency, was quoted by United Press International as having said that citizens were throwing themselves in front of the tanks in an attempt to block the seizure of the city.]

Move a Surprise

The Soviet move caught Czechoslovaks by surprise, although all day yesterday there were indications of new tensions.

Confusion was caused in the capital by leaflets dropped from unidentified aircraft asserting that Antonin Novotny, the President of Czechoslovakia who was deposed in March by the Communist liberals, had been pushed out by a "clique." The leaflets said that Mr. Novotny remained the country's legal President.

At 5 A.M. the Prague radio, still in the hands of adherents of the Communist liberals, broadcast a dramatic appeal to the population in the name of Alexander Dubcek, the party

Continued on Page 14, Column 1

OUTLOOK GUARDED FOR EISENHOWER

His Condition Still Critical Despite 'Favorable Trend'

By FELIX BELAIR Jr.
Special to The New York Times

WASHINGTON, Aug. 20 — Former President Dwight D. Eisenhower clung resolutely to life today, but with a fragile grip that his doctors acknowledged could loosen at any time.

The condition of the 77-year-old General of the Army still was listed as "critical" and the outlook for his survival as "guarded." His doctors have used this term to mean uncertain or unpredictable.

A bulletin issued at Walter Reed Army Medical Center about 11 A.M. mentioned the development of a "favorable trend" in the pattern of abnormal heart rhythm.

The episodes of rapid irregularity in the heartbeat persisted, the doctors reported, but they were isolated and did not involve the sustained fibrillating, or fluttering, reported prior to last night.

At the time of the morning

Continued on Page 13, Column 1

NIXON INCREASES GALLUP POLL LEAD

Tops Humphrey, 45% to 29, and Maintains His Margin Over McCarthy, 42 to 37

Special to The New York Times

PRINCETON, N. J., Aug. 20—Richard M. Nixon stretched a slim mid-July edge over Vice President Humphrey to a 45-to-29 per cent lead in voter preference immediately following the Republican National Convention, according to the latest Gallup Poll.

Against Senator Eugene J. McCarthy—Mr. Humphrey's chief rival for the Democratic Presidential nomination—Mr. Nixon held a 42-to-37 per cent lead, almost the same margin he had in the previous test in mid-July.

Mr. Nixon's improved advantage over the Vice President was caused more by Mr. Humphrey's losses than by gains by Mr. Nixon. The Republican nominee was 5 percentage points higher than the preconvention survey, while Mr. Humphrey was 9 points lower.

Support for the independent candidacy of George A. Wallace of Alabama held up. He polled 18 per cent in the Nixon-Humphrey-Wallace test and 16 per cent in the Nixon-McCarthy-Wallace post-convention survey.

In interviewing between Aug. 8 and 11, the following question was asked of a representative sample of 1,526 adults in over 320 localities:

"Suppose the Presidential election were being held today. If Hubert Humphrey were the Democratic candidate, running against Richard Nixon, the Republican candidate, and George Wallace of Alabama were the candidate of a third party, which would you like to see

Continued on Page 34, Column 2

Guard Is Called Up To Protect Chicago During Convention

By DONALD JANSON
Special to The New York Times

CHICAGO, Aug. 20—Gov. Samuel H. Shapiro called up the National Guard today to keep order in the city during the Democratic National Convention.

At the request of Mayor Richard J. Daley, the Governor ordered 5,649 Illinois National Guardsmen to round-the-clock duty in Chicago beginning Friday to head off threats of "tumult, riot or mob disorder."

Meanwhile, an Army spokesman in Washington confirmed in a telephone interview that about 6,000 regular Army troops received rigorous riot-control training at Fort Hood, Tex., last week as a precautionary measure.

That exercise, he said, was called Operation Jackson Park, after the park in Chicago

Continued on Page 32, Column 2

Democrats to Seat Mississippi Rebels

By MAX FRANKEL
Special to The New York Times

CHICAGO, Aug. 20—Mississippi's regular delegation to the Democratic National Convention was barred from its seats tonight by an overwhelming vote of the Credentials Committee on the ground that it had failed to meet national standards to assure the full participation of Negroes in the political process.

A biracial delegation including many members who have fought many years for this moment will be seated in place of the regulars.

At the same time, the Credentials Committee rejected by various votes the delegate

Continued on Page 32, Column 6

KENNEDY BACKERS OFFER WAR PLANK

But McCarthy Group Balks at Compromise—Rusk Is for General Statement

Text of plank and excerpts from statement, Page 33.

By JOHN W. FINNEY
Special to The New York Times

WASHINGTON, Aug. 20—Supporters of the late Senator Robert F. Kennedy circulated in the Democratic platform committee today a compromise dovish plan on Vietnam calling for a halt in the bombing of North Vietnam, a cease-fire and negotiations between the Saigon Government and the National Liberation Front, the political arm of the Vietcong.

In the bitter fight developing within the platform committee, the proposed plank is designed to provide a common front for supporters of Senator Eugene J. McCarthy, Senator George S. McGovern and Senator Kennedy.

For the moment, however, some difficulty was being encountered in winning the approval of some McCarthy partisans, who were holding out for a plank that would be more critical of the Administration.

As the doves began to mount a concerted attack on the Administration's Vietnam policy, Secretary of State Dean Rusk was called in to defend the Administration position. Mr. Rusk,

Continued on Page 33, Column 2

NEWS INDEX

13 Points in Delta Are Shelled by Foe

By JOSEPH B. TREASTER
Special to The New York Times

SAIGON, South Vietnam, Wednesday, Aug. 21 — The Vietcong shelled 13 cities and military installations in the Mekong Delta this morning, extending their latest wave of attacks into South Vietnam's southern-most region.

Seven of the shellings were followed by ground attacks.

Initial reports were sketchy, but a United States military spokesman said that allied casualties and damage in all of the attacks appeared to be light.

To the north, allied troops are making an increasing number of forays into the southern

Continued on Page 4, Column 3

Soviet Turns Back Clock

By JAMES RESTON

News Analysis

The Soviet invasion of Czechoslovakia has transformed world and American politics.

It occurred in the middle of the American Presidential election of 1968, as the Soviet invasion of Hungary took place during the Eisenhower-Stevenson Presidential election of 1956. The Soviet Union moved on Prague while the United States was preoccupied in Vietnam, as they moved on Budapest in 1956 while the British and French were preoccupied with the invasion of Suez. The latest move by Moscow startled Washington just as officials there were convening on new moves to reach an understanding with the Soviet Union on Vietnam.

Washington was prepared for a dramatic move by the Soviet Union against the new liberal regime in Prague, but not for anything quite so bold as an invasion by the Red Army.

It had been observing closely the increasingly violent attacks on the Czechoslovak Government in the Soviet press, and Under Secretary of State Charles E. Bohlen, former United States Ambassador to the Soviet Union and France, had warned of the possibility of a coup d'état, followed by Soviet military intervention in Czechoslovakia. But a direct invasion at this time was discounted.

In fact, the Johnson Administration, under attack on its Vietnam policy just before the Democratic Presidential nominating convention next week in Chicago, was discussing new moves to enlist the help of the Soviet Union for a compromise in Vietnam when the Red Army moved.

The first impression of the crisis was that this Soviet intervention in Czechoslovakia, like the first one at the end of World War II, would increase

Continued on Page 15, Column 1

JOHNSON SUMMONS SECURITY COUNCIL

Calls Emergency Session After Seeing Soviet Envoy

By B. DRUMMOND AYRES JR.
Special to The New York Times

WASHINGTON, Aug. 20—President Johnson met with the National Security Council in an emergency session tonight to discuss developments in Czechoslovakia after he received a visit from the Soviet Ambassador.

The Council meeting, which was held in the Cabinet Room in the West Wing of the White House, began at 10:15 P.M. and lasted for 55 minutes.

It was followed by a 15-minute meeting at the State Department between the Soviet Ambassador, Anatoly F. Dobrynen, and Secretary of State Dean Rusk.

There was no indication after either of the meetings of what course the United States would take in the crisis, which clearly came as a stunning surprise here.

During the recent weeks of tension around Czechoslovakia, the Administration has insistently maintained a hand-off attitude, arguing that any gestures of support from Washington would only complicate the Prague regime's status in the Communist camp. Any move to exploit the Soviet di-

Continued on Page 15, Column 1

"All the News That's Fit to Print"

The New York Times

LATE CITY EDITION

Weather: Rain, warm today; clear tonight. Sunny, pleasant tomorrow. Temp. range: today 80-66; Sunday 71-66. Temp.-Hum. Index yesterday 69. Complete U.S. report on P. 50.

VOL. CXVIII . No. 40,721

NEW YORK, MONDAY, JULY 21, 1969

10 CENTS

MEN WALK ON MOON

ASTRONAUTS LAND ON PLAIN; COLLECT ROCKS. PLANT FLAG

Voice From Moon: 'Eagle Has Landed'

EAGLE (the lunar module): Houston, Tranquility Base here. The Eagle has landed.

HOUSTON: Roger, Tranquility, we copy you on the ground. You've got a bunch of guys about to turn blue. We're breathing again. Thanks a lot.

TRANQUILITY BASE: Thank you.

HOUSTON: You're looking good here.

TRANQUILITY BASE: A very smooth touchdown.

HOUSTON: Eagle, you are stay for T1. [The first step in the lunar operation.] Over.

TRANQUILITY BASE: Roger. Stay for T1.

HOUSTON: Roger and we see you venting the ox.

TRANQUILITY BASE: Roger.

COLUMBIA (the command and service module): How do you read me?

HOUSTON: Columbia, he has landed Tranquility Base. Eagle is at Tranquility. I read you five by. Over.

COLUMBIA: Yes, I heard the whole thing.

HOUSTON: Well, it's a good show.

COLUMBIA: Fantastic.

TRANQUILITY BASE: I'll second that.

APOLLO CONTROL: The next major stay-no stay will be for the T2 event. That is at 21 minutes 26 seconds after initiation of power descent.

COLUMBIA: Up telemetry command reset to reacquire on high gain.

HOUSTON: Copy. Out.

APOLLO CONTROL: We have an unofficial time for that touchdown of 102 hours, 45 minutes, 42 seconds and we will update that.

HOUSTON: Eagle, you loaded R2 wrong. We want 10254.

TRANQUILITY BASE: Roger. Do you want the horizontal 55 15.2?

HOUSTON: That's affirmative.

APOLLO CONTROL: We're now less than four minutes from our next stay-no stay. It will be for one complete revolution of the command module.

One of the first things that Armstrong and Aldrin will do after getting their next stay-no stay will be to remove their helmets and gloves.

HOUSTON: Eagle, you are stay for T2. Over.

Continued on Page 4, Col. 1

VOYAGE TO THE MOON

By Archibald MacLeish

PRESENCE among us,

wanderer in our skies,

dazzle of silver in our leaves and on our
waters silver,

silver evasion in our farthest thought—
"the visiting moon" . . . "the glimpses of the moon" . . .

and we have touched you!

From the first of time,
before the first of time, before the
first men tasted time, we thought of you.
You were a wonder to us, unattainable,
a longing past the reach of longing,
a light beyond our light, our lives—perhaps
a meaning to us . . .

Now
our hands have touched you in your depth of night.

Three days and three nights we journeyed,
steered by farthest stars, climbed outward,
crossed the invisible tide-rip where the floating dust
falls one way or the other in the void between,
followed that other down, encountered
cold, faced death—unfathomable emptiness . . .

Then, the fourth day evening, we descended,
made fast, set foot at dawn upon your beaches,
sifted between our fingers your cold sand.

We stand here in the dusk, the cold, the silence . . .

and here, as at the first of time, we lift our heads.
Over us, more beautiful than the moon, a
moon, a wonder to us, unattainable,
a longing past the reach of longing,
a light beyond our light, our lives—perhaps
a meaning to us . . .

O, a meaning!

over us on these, silent beaches the bright
earth,
presence among us

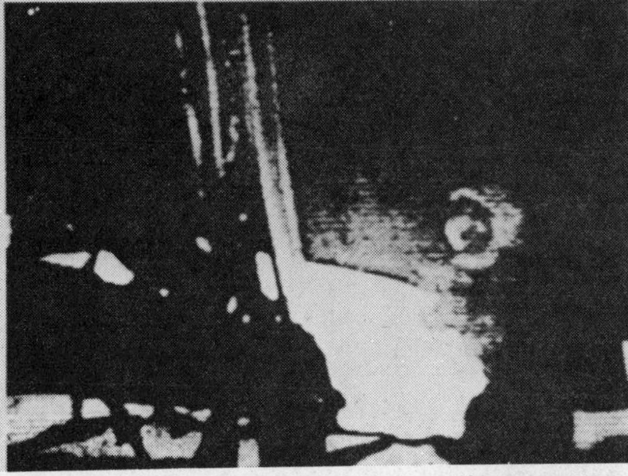

Neil A. Armstrong moves away from the leg of the landing craft after taking the first step on the surface of the moon

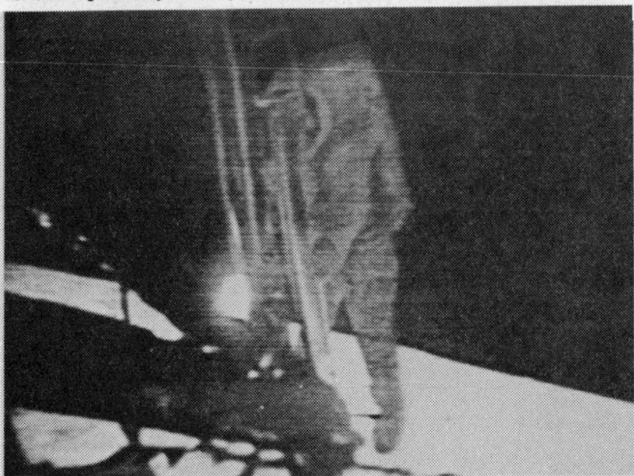

The New York Times from C.B.S. News

Col. Edwin E. Aldrin Jr. climbing down the ladder. The television camera was attached to a side of the lunar module.

Associated Press

Mr. Armstrong, right, and Colonel Aldrin raise the U.S. flag. A metal rod at right angles to the mast keeps flag unfurled.

A Powdery Surface Is Closely Explored

By JOHN NOBLE WILFORD

Special to The New York Times

HOUSTON, Monday, July 21—Men have landed and walked on the moon.

Two Americans, astronauts of Apollo 11, steered their fragile four-legged lunar module safely and smoothly to the historic landing yesterday at 4:17:40 P.M., Eastern daylight time.

Neil A. Armstrong, the 38-year-old civilian commander, radioed to earth and the mission control room here:

"Houston, Tranquility Base here. The Eagle has landed."

The first men to reach the moon—Mr. Armstrong and his co-pilot, Col. Edwin E. Aldrin Jr. of the Air Force—brought their ship to rest on a level, rock-strewn plain near the southwestern shore of the arid Sea of Tranquility.

About six and a half hours later, Mr. Armstrong opened the landing craft's hatch, stepped slowly down the ladder and declared as he planted the first human footprint on the lunar crust:

"That's one small step for man, one giant leap for mankind."

His first step on the moon came at 10:56:20 P.M., as a television camera outside the craft transmitted his every move to an awed and excited audience of hundreds of millions of people on earth.

Tentative Steps Test Soil

Mr. Armstrong's initial steps were tentative tests of the lunar soil's firmness and of his ability to move about easily in his bulky white spacesuit and backpacks and under the influence of lunar gravity, which is one-sixth that of the earth.

"The surface is fine and powdery," the astronaut reported. "I can pick it up loosely with my toe. It does adhere in fine layers like powdered charcoal to the sole and sides of my boots. I only go in a small fraction of an inch, maybe an eighth of an inch. But I can see the footprints of my boots in the treads in the fine sandy particles.

After 19 minutes of Mr. Armstrong's testing, Colonel Aldrin joined him outside the craft.

The two men got busy setting up another television camera out from the lunar module, planting an American flag into the ground, scooping up soil and rock samples, deploying scientific experiments and hopping and loping about in a demonstration of their lunar agility.

They found walking and working on the moon less taxing than had been forecast. Mr. Armstrong once reported he was "very comfortable."

And people back on earth found the black-and-white television pictures of the bug-shaped lunar module and the men tramping about it so sharp and clear as to seem unreal, more like a toy and toy-like figures than human beings on the most daring and far-reaching expedition thus far undertaken.

Nixon Telephones Congratulations

During one break in the astronauts' work, President Nixon congratulated them from the White House in what, he said, "certainly has to be the most historic telephone call ever made."

"Because of what you have done," the President told the astronauts, "the heavens have become a part of man's world. And as you talk to us from the Sea of Tranquility it requires us to redouble our efforts to bring peace and tranquility to earth.

"For one priceless moment in the whole history of man all the people on this earth are truly one—one in their pride in what you have done and one in our prayers that you will return safely to earth."

Mr. Armstrong replied:

"Thank you Mr. President. It's a great honor and privilege for us to be here representing not only the United States but men of peace of all nations, men with interests and a curiosity and men with a vision for the future."

Mr. Armstrong and Colonel Aldrin returned to their landing craft and closed the hatch at 1:12 A.M., 2 hours 21 minutes after opening the hatch on the moon. While the third member of the crew, Lieut. Col. Michael Collins of the Air Force, kept his orbital vigil overhead in the command ship, the two moon explorers settled down to sleep.

Outside their vehicle the astronauts had found a bleak

Continued on Pages 2, Col. 1

Today's 4-Part Issue of The Times

This morning's issue of The New York Times is divided into four parts. The first part is devoted to news of Apollo 11. and includes Editorials and letters to the Editor (Page 16). Poems on the landing on the moon appear on Page 17.

General news begins on the first page of the second part. The News Summary and Index is on the first page of the third part, which includes sports news, obituaries (Page 51) and transportation news and weather reports (Pages 50 and 52).

Financial and business news begins on the first page of the fourth part.

Following is the News Index for today's issue:

News Summary and Index, Page 35

"All the News That's Fit to Print"

The New York Times

LATE CITY EDITION

Weather: Rain today; mostly cloudy tonight. Fair and milder tomorrow. Temp. range: today 51-55; Monday 53-66. Full U.S. report on Page 82.

VOL. CXXI . . No. 41,744 NEW YORK, TUESDAY, MAY 9, 1972 15 CENTS

NIXON ORDERS ENEMY'S PORTS MINED; SAYS MATERIEL WILL BE DENIED HANOI UNTIL IT FREES P.O.W.'S AND HALTS WAR

Governor Reported Irked By Nixon's Abortion Views

Rockefeller Indicates Plan to Veto Bill Stands Despite President's Support for Repeal of Present State Law

By JAMES F. CLARITY
Special to The New York Times

ALBANY, May 8 — Governor Rockefeller was reliably reported today to be angered by President Nixon's intervention in the issue of elective abortions, now pending in the Legislature.

One of the highest elected Republican officials in the state described Mr. Rockefeller as "very upset" about the President's action.

The Governor's office said that despite the President's announced support for repeal of the state's liberal abortion law, Mr. Rockefeller would veto the repeal if it was approved by the Legislature. Relations between the Governor and the President, which had improved greatly in the last several months, with Mr. Rockefeller agreeing to serve as the President's campaign manager in the state, now seem strained, at least on this one issue.

The Assembly was expected to debate the repeal legislation tomorrow.

Evidence of the Governor's pique was clear in the statement his office issued in response to requests for comments on the President's action: "We are referring all calls to the White House on this."

Mr. Nixon intervened in the state issue in a letter to Cardinal Cooke. The letter, made public Saturday, made clear the President's support for repeal of the New York law, which permits elective abortions through the 24th week of pregnancy.

The day before the letter was made public, Mr. Nixon had rejected recommendations for lib-

Continued on Page 26, Column 2

PAY BOARD TRIMS EAST COAST RAISE OF LONGSHOREMEN

Votes, 6-1, to Permit Rises of 9.8 to 12% Instead of 15 —Fitzsimmons Dissents

By EDWARD COWAN
Special to The New York Times

WASHINGTON, May 8—The Pay Board directed East and Gulf Coast shippers and longshoremen tonight to roll back their agreed wage increase of 70 cents an hour to 55 cents.

About 49,000 longshoremen will be allowed increases ranging from 9.8 per cent to 12 per cent under the decision, which scaled back an agreement that had contemplated an increase calculated by the board at 15 per cent.

George H. Boldt, chairman of the seven-member board, said that he expected the International Longshoremen's Association "to look it over, be disappointed and go along with what's now the law of the land."

Boldt Declines to Predict

However, Judge Boldt, in a brief corridor meeting with newsmen, declined to prognosticate when asked if he thought the dock workers would strike.

Judge Boldt issued a brief summary of the decision after a difficult four-hour board meeting that ended with a vote of 6 to 1. The dissenter was Frank E. Fitzsimmons, president of the International Brotherhood of Teamsters, who is the only labor leader still on the board.

Four other union leaders quit the board in March after it scaled back the longshore settlement on the West Coast to 14.9 per cent from a proposed 20.9 per cent. Only Mr. Fitzsimmons remained.

President Nixon then reconstituted what had been a 15-member tripartite group as a panel of seven public members.

In New York, Thomas G. Gleason, president of the Inter-

Continued on Page 17, Column 1

Associated Press
VIETNAM ADDRESS: President Nixon speaking last night

The New York Times/May 9, 1972
NEW TARGETS: Ports (underlined), rail lines from China

SPEAKS TO NATION

He Gives the Ships of Other Countries 3 Days to Leave

By ROBERT B. SEMPLE Jr.
Special to The New York Times

WASHINGTON, May 8 — President Nixon announced tonight that he had ordered the mining of all North Vietnamese ports and other measures to prevent the flow of arms and other military supplies to the enemy.

Mr. Nixon told a nationwide television and radio audience

The text of Nixon's speech is printed on Page 18.

that his orders were being executed as he spoke.

From the President's somber and stern speech and from explanations by other Administration officials, the following picture of the American action emerged:

¶All major North Vietnamese ports would be mined, ships of other countries in the harbors, most of which are Russian, would have three "daylight periods" in which to leave. After that the mines will become active and ships coming or going will move at their own peril.

¶United States naval vessels will not search or seize ships of other countries entering or leaving North Vietnamese ports, thus avoiding a direct confrontation with the Russians.

¶American and South Vietnamese ships and planes would take "appropriate measures" to stop North Vietnam from unloading matériel on beaches from unmined waters.

¶United States and South Vietnamese forces would interdict, presumably by bombing, the movement of matériel in North Vietnam over rail lines originating in China.

There was much confusion tonight about whether the United States and South Vietnam had proclaimed a blockade. The President did not use the word and Pentagon spokesmen denied that a blockade existed in the technical sense. But some observers felt that the practical effect on North Vietnam of the President's actions would be the same as a blockade.

[In Saigon, the United States command announced Tuesday that Navy planes had completed the initial phases of the mining operations in North Vietnamese harbors ordered by President Nixon.]

Two Basic Conditions

Mr. Nixon said the mining, the attacks on the rail lines within North Vietnam, and the efforts to interdict the movement of supplies by water would cease the moment the enemy agreed to two basic conditions: the return of American prisoners of war, and an internationally supervised cease-fire.

"Then," he said, "we will stop all acts of force throughout Indochina and proceed with the complete withdrawal of all forces within four months."

The White House would not say tonight whether, in these words, Mr. Nixon was in effect making the North Vietnamese a new peace proposal.

But observers here noted that he mentioned no political requirements for American withdrawal. Until now he has always insisted on some form of

Continued on Page 18, Column 5

HIGH MEAT PRICES LAID TO RACKETS

City Consumers Squeezed by 15% Inflation of Costs, Law Officials Report

By LACEY FOSBURGH

The infiltration of organized crime into key positions in the New York City meat industry has artificially inflated the retail prices for fresh meat in supermarkets by 15 per cent, according to information developed by the Manhattan District Attorney's Office and other law-enforcement agencies here and in Washington.

Consumers buying meat in the New York-New Jersey area, they say, are putting at least a million dollars a week directly into the coffers of organized crime.

Years of Collusion Alleged

Racketeers — both in the industry and in the unions that service it — have reportedly been in collusion for at least two years "systematically" extorting "week by week, month by month," as one source put it, "vast sums of money" from the supermarket chains and the wholesale suppliers.

"This is the price they pay to stay in business," another source said, "the price of labor peace."

This picture of extortion, bribery and the ultimate victimization of the consumer

Continued on Page 66, Column 1

State Senate Votes To Liberalize Curbs In Rape Testimony

By ALFONSO A. NARVAEZ
Special to The New York Times

ALBANY, May 8—The Senate gave overwhelming approval today to a bill modifying the extent to which a rape victim's testimony must be corroborated to convict an alleged attacker.

The measure, which passed by a vote of 56 to 1, removes the need for testimony corroborating the identity of the alleged assailant and the fact that penetration actually took place. The bill, passed with no debate, now goes to the Governor, who is expected to sign it.

In other action today as the Legislature continued its push for adjournment:

¶Three city officials—Controller Abraham D. Beame, City Council Majority Leader Thomas J. Cuite and the Council's finance chairman, Mario Merola—met here with state budget officials on legislation affecting the city's proposed $9.9-billion budget. The meet-

Continued on Page 27, Column 1

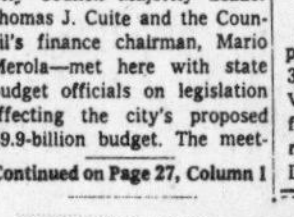

New Vega Recall

The General Motors Corporation yesterday recalled 350,000 of its 1971 and 1972 Vegas to correct a safety defect. It was the second major recall of Vegas in a month. Details on Page 16.

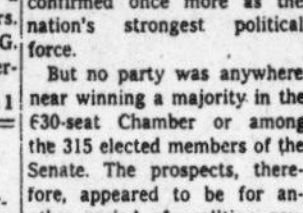

Ruling Party Leads In Italian Election; Neo-Fascists Gain

By PAUL HOFMANN
Special to The New York Times

ROME, Tuesday, May 9—The governing Christian Democrats achieved a remarkable comeback in Italy's general elections Sunday and yesterday, receiving a clear mandate to continue leading the Government as they have been doing since 1945.

At the same time, however, the neo-Fascists advanced and the Communists won gains in the Chamber of Deputies and suffered losses in the Senate. With most of the votes counted early today, increasing polarization between left and right in Italian politics became apparent.

The Christian Democrats apparently raised their share of the total popular vote close to 40 per cent again and were confirmed once more as the nation's strongest political force.

But no party was anywhere near winning a majority in the 630-seat Chamber or among the 315 elected members of the Senate. The prospects, therefore, appeared to be for another period of coalition governments and, possibly, protracted instability.

Italian commentators attributed the rightist gains and

Continued on Page 3, Column 1

CONGRESS IS SPLIT ON NIXON'S ACTION

Republicans Acclaim His Leadership—Democrats Call Him Reckless

By JOHN W. FINNEY
Special to The New York Times

WASHINGTON, May 8—President Nixon was alternately praised tonight by members of Congress for his firm leadership and accused of setting the nation on a dangerous confrontation with the Soviet Union that could lead to world war.

Republicans praised him on both political and military grounds for his decision to mine North Vietnam's harbors.

Representative Gerald R. Ford, the House Republican leader, described Mr. Nixon as "generous in his bid for peace but firm in his determination that we will not surrender."

"The only way left to end the Vietnam war is to deprive the enemy of the supplies he needs to continue the invasion," Mr. Ford said.

Senator Robert P. Griffin of Michigan, the assistant Republican leader in the Senate, said "it was strong medicine but necessary."

Democrats, however, used

Continued on Page 19, Column 1

President Urges Soviet To Avoid Confrontation

By BERNARD GWERTZMAN
Special to The New York Times

WASHINGTON, May 8—President Nixon's speech tonight appealed to the Soviet Union not to let its support of Hanoi lead it to a confrontation with the United States over his decision to try to cut off supplies to North Vietnam.

In carefully chosen language, Mr. Nixon appeared anxious to avoid turning the Vietnam war into a direct Soviet-American clash.

But some diplomats feel the mining of North Vietnam's ports has raised the possibility of cancellation of Mr. Nixon's scheduled trip to Moscow two weeks from today and even of a military confrontation if Soviet naval forces try to thwart Mr. Nixon's actions.

Dobrynin Informed

Officially, the Nixon Administration said tonight that plans for Mr. Nixon's visit to the Soviet Union were still going ahead. But a high official added that the chances that it would take place had sharply lessened because of the tensions sure to be raised as the result of the effort to prevent supplies from arriving in North Vietnam.

Anatoly F. Dobrynin, the Soviet Ambassador to the United States, was informed of Mr. Nixon's speech about an hour beforehand at a White House meeting with Henry A. Kissinger, President Nixon's adviser on national security.

Mr. Dobrynin was also the Soviet envoy in October, 1962, when President John F. Kennedy ordered a quarantine of offensive Soviet weapons being shipped to Cuba. This led to the so-called Cuban missile crisis,

Continued on Page 19, Column 5

HANOI SAYS RAIDS STRUCK AT DIKES

But U.S. Asserts Military Installations Were Hit in Attacks on North

By CRAIG R. WHITNEY
Special to The New York Times

SAIGON, South Vietnam, Tuesday, May 9—United States Navy fighter-bombers struck at North Vietnamese storage facilities, barracks and training facilities in an area about 15 miles west of Hanoi yesterday in the closest strikes to the North Vietnamese capital since April 16, the American command announced.

The command's announcement said the planes attacked "military heartland targets" that "are helping to support the Communist invasion" of South Vietnam.

The Hanoi radio, in a broadcast at noon, said American planes "deliberately struck at the dike system in Namha Province" southeast of Hanoi.

[The United States command denied that American jets had bombed the dikes, United Press International reported.]

The dikes support an elaborate system of irrigation and

Continued on Page 19, Column 7

4 Armed Arab Hijackers Hold Jet and 101 Hostages in Israel

By The Associated Press

TEL AVIV, May 8—Despite a tip-off and a security search, four armed Arabs hijacked an Israel-bound Belgian Sabena jetliner carrying 101 persons today.

After landing in Tel Aviv, they threatened to blow up the plane and its passengers unless Israel freed 300 Palestinian guerrilla prisoners and flew them to Cairo. A senior Israeli Army officer told the hijackers that freeing hundreds of prisoners within a few hours was impossible.

The Israelis, speaking to the hijackers by radio, were reported to have offered to free 15 or 20 military prisoners of war "as a gesture of goodwill."

The gunmen, who seized the plane after it left Vienna, set a deadline of 10 P.M. Tel Aviv time to make a deal, but the deadline passed with no explosion or other evident action.

As negotiations were being carried on by radio, the pilot, Captain Reginald Levy, said that the plane was unfit to take off. The hijackers said that it must be made ready to leave at 5:30 A.M. or that it would be blown up. They later extended the deadline again but stipulated no time.

The Arabs also demanded to talk with a representative of the International Committee of the Red Cross.

"If the plane is not refueled I think they will blow it up," Captain Levy said by radio. "They are serious."

The police in Brussels said that they had been told by tele-

Continued on Page 7, Column 1

Local School Units Defended by Mayor

By LEONARD BUDER

Mayor Lindsay declared yesterday that the city's decentralized school boards had brought "a new vigor to the whole process of achieving quality public education."

Mr. Lindsay said that while it is "much too soon to make a final judgment on decentralization" he felt that "the community school boards have made important advances since the inception of decentralization a little less than two years ago."

The Mayor made the statement in commenting on the assertion Sunday by Dr. Kenneth B. Clark, a member of the State Board of Regents, that school

Continued on Page 53, Column 5

The New York Times/William E. Sauro

CITY OFFICIALS IN ALBANY: Foreground, from left: Controller Abraham D. Beame and Councilmen Thomas J. Cuite, majority leader, and Mario Merola, finance committee chairman. City budget was topic. Rear, from right, State Senator John J. Marchi, Assemblyman Alexander Chananau, almost hidden; Senator Warren M. Anderson.

NEWS INDEX

"All the News That's Fit to Print"

The New York Times

LATE CITY EDITION

Weather: Cloudy, mild with chance of showers today, tonight, tomorrow. Temp. range: today 59-73; Monday 57-74. Full U.S. report on Page 86.

VOL. CXXI . No. 41,751 · NEW YORK, TUESDAY, MAY 16, 1972 · 15 CENTS

WALLACE IS SHOT; CONDITION SERIOUS; A SUSPECT SEIZED AT MARYLAND RALLY

Associated Press

AFTER SPEECH: Gov. George C. Wallace takes off jacket and goes to shake hands. At front is Secret Service agent.

C.B.S. News via United Press International

DURING SHOOTING: Man at right with light hair and sun glasses holds gun as person in crowd tries to shake his arm

Saigon's Forces Reoccupy Bastogne Base Near Hue

By MALCOLM W. BROWNE
Special to The New York Times

SAIGON, South Vietnam, Tuesday, May 16 — South Vietnamese troops, led by a platoon of 30 soldiers flown in by helicopters, reoccupied Fire Base Bastogne yesterday on the southwesterly approaches to Hue.

The five helicopters carrying the soldiers reportedly encountered no enemy fire as they landed at the base, which the South Vietnamese abandoned April 28 under heavy attack. The base had fallen after the North Vietnamese who had besieged it for more than three weeks sent commandos storming in to penetrate the barbed-wire defenses.

But after routing the defenders at the end of April, the North Vietnamese did not move their long-range 130-mm. artillery into Bastogne to shell Hue, the former imperial capital of Vietnam on the coast 15 miles away.

[The United States command announced the arrival of the carrier Saratoga off the Vietnamese coast Monday, bringing to six the number of attack carriers there. United Press International reported. The United States Seventh Fleet was now said to have 60 ships in the area.]

[In Washington, Secretary of State William P. Rogers angrily defended the mining of North Vietnam's harbors and said that if the Johnson Administration had taken the step earlier, the war might have ended long ago. Page 14.]

Allied officers in the Hue area said that if the re-entry into Fire Base Bastogne appeared to have been easy, this was only because it had capped more than a week of slow, hard fighting and several more days of heavy air and artillery bombardment.

South Vietnamese spokes-

Continued on Page 14, Column 3

Court Exempts the Amish From Going to High School

By FRED P. GRAHAM
Special to The New York Times

WASHINGTON, May 15—The Supreme Court ruled 7 to 0 today that the Amish religious sect is exempt from state compulsory education laws that require children to attend school beyond the eighth grade.

The Amish—the rural "plain people" who cling to a horse-and-buggy way of life—believe that education beyond the eighth grade teaches worldly values at odds with the simple life required by their creed.

With this in mind, the Court held that state laws requiring children to attend school until they are 16 years of age violate the constitutional rights of the Amish to free exercise of religion.

The decision specifically applied to Wisconsin, but it was written in terms broad enough to apply to all states that require attendance in public or private schools beyond the eighth grade. Mississippi and South Carolina are the only states that do not have compulsory school attendance laws.

The opinion, written by Chief Justice Warren E. Burger, was the first by the Court holding a religious group immune from compulsory attendance requirements.

The Court stressed the 300-year resistance of the Amish to modern influences and served notice that faddish new sects or communes that reject formal education would probably not be granted similar exemptions.

"It cannot be overemphasized," Justice Burger wrote, "that we are not dealing with a way of life and mode of education by a group claiming to have recently discovered some 'progressive' or more en-

Continued on Page 20, Column 1

NEWS INDEX

PRESSURE GROUPS ANGER ROCKEFELLER

He Asserts Judges Blocked Court Reform and Lawyers Stymied 'No-Fault' Bill

By JAMES F. CLARITY
Special to The New York Times

ALBANY, May 15—Governor Rockefeller charged today that "inordinate pressures" placed on legislators by judges and lawyers had blocked two of his "vital programs"—court reform and no-fault insurance—in the 1972 Legislature.

Mr. Rockefeller, commenting on the action of the Legislature three days after it had adjourned for the year, said the judges had stymied most of his court-reform program. The lawyers, Mr. Rockefeller said, had blocked the no-fault automobile accident insurance bill he had supported.

The no-fault insurance bill was defeated through the lobbying efforts of one small group of men—the New York State Trial Lawyers Association. Article on Page 31.

The Governor pledged to continue to fight for passage of the two programs next year. He said undue pressure had also been exerted on the legislators to repeal the state's liberalized abortion law. The Governor vetoed the repeal measure Saturday.

"My pledge is to make an all-out fight for no-fault automobile insurance and court reform in 1973," Mr. Rockefeller said at a news conference in the Red Room of the Capitol. "Some headlines have interpreted the failure of the Legislature to enact these two vital programs as a setback for me. The truth is that they marked a setback for the people of New York State.

"At no time," the Governor

Continued on Page 30, Column 3

Hogan Drops Jay Kriegel Case; Reports He Can't Prove Perjury

By DAVID BURNHAM

The question of whether one of Mayor Lindsay's closest aides, Jay L. Kriegel, committed perjury during his testimony before the Knapp Commission will not be presented to a grand jury, District Attorney Frank S. Hogan announced yesterday.

Mr. Hogan said his office was dropping the case because "the people would not be able to establish beyond a reasonable doubt that there was a willful, irreconcilable inconsistency" between Mr. Kriegel's testimony before the Knapp Commission on June 17, 1971, and Dec. 20, 1971.

The commission was created by Mayor Lindsay—on the recommendation of a special committee that included Mr. Hogan—to investigate allegations of widespread police corruption and of failure by officials in the Lindsay administration to follow up on information about cases of corruption brought to their attention.

Mr. Hogan, in a two-and-a-half-page statement, said another reason for not proceeding with the case was that "there is substantial doubt concerning the authority of the Knapp commission to administer the oath" at the December hearings.

Whitman Knapp, the chairman of the commission, said in

Continued on Page 28, Column 3

C.B.S. News via Associated Press

KNEELING OVER HUSBAND: Mrs. Cornelia Wallace bending over the Governor after he was shot at close range

3 MORE WOUNDED

Legs of Governor Are Paralyzed but Hope Is Voiced by Doctor

By R. W. APPLE Jr.
Special to The New York Times

LAUREL, Md., Tuesday, May 16—Gov. George C. Wallace of Alabama, seemingly on the verge of his greatest electoral triumphs, was shot and gravely wounded yesterday afternoon as he campaigned for President at a shopping center in this suburb of Washington.

Late last night, after the 52-year-old Governor emerged from almost five hours of emergency surgery at the Holy Cross Hospital in nearby Silver Spring, Md., one of his surgeons said that he expected Mr. Wallace "to make a full recovery."

The surgeon, Dr. Joseph Schanno, said that Mr. Wallace had suffered at least four wounds and the doctors had removed one bullet. He said that another bullet was lodged near the spine and that the Governor's legs were paralyzed as a result.

Will Continue Campaign

The Governor's wife, Cornelia, said she was "very happy that he's alive and has a sound heart and a sound brain." Billy Joe Camp, his press secretary, reported this morning, after Mrs. Wallace had talked with the Governor, that he would continue his Presidential campaign and "will be at the Democratic convention as a strong, viable candidate."

The state and local police arrested a suspect, who was identified by the Justice Department as Arthur Herman Bremer, a 21-year-old white man from Milwaukee. The department said that the Secret Service had taken custody of a .38-caliber, snub-nosed, five-shot revolver allegedly used by Mr. Bremer in the shooting. Later, Federal and state charges were filed against him.

Held in $200,000 Bond

Mr. Bremer was taken before United States Magistrate Clarence Goetz in Baltimore last night and was ordered held under $200,000 bond.

Three persons who were with Governor Wallace as he plunged into the crowd at the Laurel Shopping Center were also hit by the four or five bullets fired by the attacker.

The shooting occurred after the Governor, having finished a speech here, shed his coat and stepped from behind the protection of his bullet-proof speaking stand.

A young man wearing sungasses and a red, white and blue shirt bedecked with Wallace buttons thrust his right hand between two other people

Continued on Page 34, Column 1

GUNMAN'S ATTACK CLOUDS CAMPAIGN

Uncertainty Created Both by Wallace's Status and Impact of Shooting

By MAX FRANKEL
Special to The New York Times

WASHINGTON, May 15—The bullets that felled George C. Wallace on the eve of his greatest achievements in national politics will also upset both the conduct and the calculations of the 1972 Presidential campaign.

If he could recover in time to resume some form of campaigning, and his press secretary says he will, the Alabama Governor may find an even more aroused constituency rallying to his cause. And some degree of sympathy vote may further swell his expected victories tomorrow in the Democratic primaries of Michigan and Maryland.

The Governor had 210 delegate votes of the 1,509 needed for nomination when he was struck down.

If he is forced out of the campaign, there is no one now in sight to pick up the banner of populism, tinged with an overtone of segregation, that brought the Governor 9.9 million votes, or 13.5 per cent of the total cast for President, in 1968 and seemed to promise him an equally strong following this year.

No one has ever quite

Continued on Page 34, Column 7

Shooting Suspect Shouted: 'Hey, George! Over Here!'

By WARREN WEAVER Jr.
Special to The New York Times

LAUREL, Md., May 15 — George C. Wallace was shot while standing at the new crossroads of middle America today, between the drive-in bank and variety store of a suburban shopping center.

The suspected assailant, a young white man, called the Alabama Governor over to him after Mr. Wallace had stepped from behind his bullet-proof speaking stand and came down to shake hands with the crowd of about 1,000.

"Hey, George! Hey, George! Come over here! Come over here!" the man shouted insistently, according to several witnesses. The man had been standing against the ropes that cleared a space for security guards and reporters between the crowd and the small parking lot speaking stand.

Mr. Wallace heard the shouts and veered to his left, working his way down the line of admirers. He came first to Mrs. Brigitte Howkins of Hyattsville, a plump matron, who reached over a man, took Mr. Wallace's hand and said: "Good luck, Governor Wallace."

"He smiled at me," Mrs. Howkins recalled later, "dropped my hand and reached out for another when the man who had been standing on my right lifted his right arm and suddenly there were shots."

Mr. Wallace fell to the asphalt parking surface and lay on his back in the brilliant sunshine. Witnesses said he was bleeding from the chest and appeared also to have been struck in the right arm.

Val Hymes, a columnist for several Maryland newspapers, saw the Governor sprawled on the pavement, a large red splotch spreading across his shirt front. "I thought at first he was dead," she said.

Mrs. Wallace ran to his side,

Continued on Page 34, Column 4

Kennedy Guarded By Secret Service

By BEN A. FRANKLIN
Special to The New York Times

WASHINGTON, May 15—Shortly after Gov. George C. Wallace of Alabama was shot today, President Nixon ordered Secret Service protection for Senator Edward M. Kennedy of Massachusetts, Representative Shirley Chisholm of Brooklyn and Representative Wilbur D. Mills of Arkansas.

Senator Kennedy, who has declared repeatedly that he is not a candidate for President, accepted the offer, and an unspecified number of agents were guarding his home tonight in nearby McLean, Va. Agents joined Mrs. Chisholm in Detroit, where she was stay-

Continued on Page 35, Column 1

MILWAUKEE MAN HELD AS SUSPECT

Seized on Weapons Charge Last October in Wisconsin —Many Paradoxes Seen

By JAMES T. WOOTEN
Special to The New York Times

WASHINGTON, May 15—The young white man arrested as a suspect today in the shooting of Gov. George C. Wallace is a 21-year-old resident of Milwaukee who pasted Wallace bumper stickers on his car and his apartment door and was exuberantly cheering the Democratic Presidential candidate only moments before the shots rang out.

Those apparent contradictions are but a small part of the paradoxical picture now being sketched of Arthur Herman Bremer, the man accused by Federal authorities today of having tried to kill the Alabama Governor at a shopping center in Laurel, Md.

It was reported that he was arrested on a charge of carrying a concealed weapon last Oct. 18 and was subsequently convicted of disorderly conduct.

A Justice Department spokesman said that the .38-caliber snub-nosed revolver allegedly used at Laurel had been purchased in Milwaukee Jan. 13 and fired five times today.

From descriptions supplied

Continued on Page 34, Column 3

"All the News That's Fit to Print"

The New York Times

LATE CITY EDITION

Weather: Sunny and milder today; fair and mild tonight, tomorrow. Temp. range: today 58-77; Tuesday 57-74. Temp.-Hum. Index yesterday 67. Full U.S. report on Page 90.

VOL. CXXI... No. 41,864 · NEW YORK, WEDNESDAY, SEPTEMBER 6, 1972 · 15 CENTS

9 ISRAELIS ON OLYMPIC TEAM KILLED WITH 4 ARAB CAPTORS AS POLICE FIGHT BAND THAT DISRUPTED MUNICH GAMES

United Press International

A copter making a test run before picking up Arabs involved in the attack on Israelis. At rear is the Olympic Tower. Sign in German says, "Olympic Village, Gate 6."

MRS. MEIR SPEAKS

A Hushed Parliament Hears Her Assail 'Lunatic Acts'

By TERENCE SMITH
Special to The New York Times

JERUSALEM, Sept. 5—Her voice heavy and trembling with emotion, Premier Golda Meir today denounced "these lunatic acts of terrorism, abduction and blackmail, which tear asunder the web of international life."

Speaking to a hushed and somber parliament before the fate of the Israeli hostages held captive in Munich was known, she said, "It is inconceivable that the Olympic events should continue as long as our citizens are under the threat of being murdered in the Olympic Village."

She called on all the nations participating in the Olympics to do "whatever is necessary" to rescue the nine Israelis taken hostage by Arab guerrillas in an early-morning attack in which two other Israelis were killed.

[Official sources in Jerusalem said early Wednesday that the Cabinet would meet later in the morning and that there would be no statement on the deaths of the hostages until then.]

Cabinet Still Firm

Although she was not explicit, Mrs. Meir left the impression that Israel would continue to refuse the guerrillas' demands for the release of 200 Palestinian commandos held in this country. Cabinet sources said the Government remained committed to its hard-line policy of neither dealing with nor making concessions to the guerrillas.

Most Israelis seemed stunned by the news of the bizarre attack on the Israeli athletes, which was first reported here on a radio broadcast at 9 A.M. (3 A.M. Tuesday, New York time). Although Israeli citizens traveling abroad have been attacked by Palestinian guerrillas before, the Olympics seemed to many an unlikely setting.

"The games were going so well," one Jerusalem news dealer said, "and now this."

In parliament, where the members had gathered in an extraordinary session to confirm the Justice Minister, the attack was the sole topic of conversation.

Cabinet Ministers and members of parliament sat in the building's modern, sun-washed dining room waiting for additional news from Munich. Each hour on the hour, the large room grew silent and the ministers gathered four deep around a radio as the Israeli radio summarized the developments.

The tension was greatest at

Continued on Page 20, Column 2

West German policemen talking with a spokesman, right, for Arabs who invaded Israeli quarters at Olympic Village

Associated Press

A West German Army ambulance passing through the heavily guarded gate at the military airfield in Fürstenfeldbruck, near Munich, after the commandos and the hostages landed in three helicopters.

A 23-HOUR DRAMA

2 Others Are Slain in Their Quarters in Guerrilla Raid

By DAVID BINDER
Special to The New York Times

MUNICH, West Germany, Wednesday, Sept. 6—Eleven members of Israel's Olympic team and four Arab terrorists were killed yesterday in a 23-hour drama that began with an invasion of the Olympic Village by the Arabs. It ended in a shootout at a military airport some 15 miles away as the Arabs were preparing to fly to Cairo with their Israeli hostages.

The first two Israelis were killed early yesterday morning when Arab commandos, armed with automatic rifles, broke into the quarters of the Israeli team and seized nine others as hostages. The hostages were killed in the airport shootout between the Arabs and German policemen and soldiers.

The bloodshed brought the suspension of the Olympic Games and there was doubt if they would be resumed. Willi Daume, president of the West German Organizing Committee, announced early today that he would ask the International Olympic Committee to meet tomorrow to decide whether they should continue.

Policeman Killed

In addition to the slain Israelis and Arabs, a German policeman was killed and a helicopter pilot was critically wounded. Three Arabs were wounded.

There were some reports that two of the hostages said to have been killed might still be alive. "It is a dim hope," said Dr. Bruno Merk, the Interior Minister of Bavaria, "but I am skeptical on this point."

The bloodbath at the airport that ended at 1 A.M. today, came after long hours of negotiaton between German and Arabs at the Israeli quarters in the Olympic Village where the Arabs demanded the release of 200 Arab commandos imprisoned in Israel.

Finally the West German armed forces supplied three helicopters to transport the Arabs and their Israeli hostages to the airport at Fürstenfeldbruck. From there all were to be flown to Cairo.

A Boeing-707 provided by the Lufthansa German Airlines was waiting.

Two of the terrorists, carrying their automatic rifles, walked about 170 yards from the helicopters to the plane. And then they started back to pick up the other Arabs and the hostages.

Positions Cited

As the Arabs were returning, German sharpshooters reportedly opened fire from the darkness beyond the pools of light at the airport. The Arabs returned fire.

The torment of the entire event was heightened by confusion created in the public mind by contradictory reports from German and Olympic officials after the gunfire erupted at the airport.

Dr. Merk, in a press conference at 3 o'clock this morning said:

"In this situation our task and goal to free the hostages was made more difficult by the lack of agreement from Israel to free prisoners or to get guarantees from the Arabs not to take action against the hos-

Continued on Page 18, Column 1

752 Air-Conditioned Cars Ordered for City Subways

By EDWARD RANZAL

Mayor Lindsay announced yesterday that 752 new air-conditioned subway cars had been ordered for $210.5-million. He said the contract was the largest ever signed in the country for the purchase of passenger railroad cars.

The first group of cars, which will be manufactured by the Pullman - Standard Company, are to be delivered by 1973

The cars will provide a quieter ride than present equipment, according to Dr. William J. Ronan, chairman of the Metropolitan Transportation Authority.

The new equipment, which will be used on the IND and BMT lines, will enable the authority to phase out more than 1,200 pre-World War II cars, which are smaller than the new ones. A study is being made, Dr. Ronan said, to produce an air-conditioned unit that can be used in cars in the smaller tunnels of the IRT system.

20% of Fleet by '75

Each car will cost more than $273,000. The city will provide one-third of the total funds—the money has been provided in the city's 1972-73 capital budget—and the Federal Urban Mass Transportation Administration will supply the rest.

By 1975 more than 20 per cent of the city's fleet of nearly 7,000 subway cars will consist of new air-conditioned cars.

The first order under the contract will be for 454 cars at a cost of $127.4-million. Some of them will be delivered in

Continued on Page 91, Column 2

Berrigan and a Nun Get Prison Terms In Letter Smuggling

By JOHN KIFNER
Special to The New York Times

HARRISBURG, Pa., Sept. 5—The Rev. Philip F. Berrigan—cleared of charges that he led a plot to kidnap President Nixon's adviser on national security affairs, Henry A. Kissinger—was sentenced in Federal District Court here today to four concurrent two-year terms for smuggling letters out of the Lewisburg Penitentiary.

Sister Elizabeth McAlister, also cleared of the plot charges, was sentenced to one year in jail and three years' probation for smuggling letters.

Moments after the sentences were announced, Government attorneys moved to dismiss the first three substantive counts of their indictment, confirming that the Justice Department would not seek a retrial of the controversial "Harrisburg Seven" case.

The Government charged Father Berrigan, Sister Elizabeth, two other Roman Catholic priests, a former priest, a former nun and a Pakistani scholar with conspiracy to kidnap Mr. Kissinger as ransom to force a halt to the bombing in Viet-

Continued on Page 16, Column 1

PARLEY REJECTS HIJACKING TREATY

U.S.-Canadian Project for Penalizing Nations Aiding Air Pirates Rebuffed

By ROBERT LINDSEY
Special to The New York Times

WASHINGTON, Sept. 5—Delegates to a 17-nation conference here rejected today United States-Canadian efforts to negotiate an international anti-hijacking treaty based on a draft proposed by the two nations.

The move for nonacceptance was led by France and Britain and supported by the Soviet Union and Egypt.

Faced with what appeared to be certain defeat of the proposed treaty if it came to a vote, the two North American nations acquiesced in a French proposal to start writing a new treaty from scratch, after debates on what "principles" should be included.

The delegates have eight working days left before the conference is scheduled to end.

Today's rejection was a significant setback for the United

Continued on Page 91, Column 2

Nixon Tightens Security In U.S. Against 'Outlaws'

By TAD SZULC
Special to The New York Times

WASHINGTON, Sept. 5 — President Nixon said today that "extra security measures" would be taken in the United States to protect American citizens as well as visiting Israelis from possible attacks by Palestinian guerrillas.

Mr. Nixon, speaking to newsmen in San Francisco, left it unclear, however, whether he meant that this new protection would cover prominent American Jews or only those whom he described as "Americans of Israeli background, American citizens."

Speaking before the gunfight at a military airport in Munich, in which the Israeli hostages were killed, Mr. Nixon discussed the capture of Israeli Olympic team members by Palestinian guerrillas and the slaying of two Israelis. He said:

"Since we are dealing with international outlaws who are unpredictable, we have to take extra security measures to protect those who might be the targets of this kind of activity in the future. That might include Americans of Israeli background, American citizens."

Late tonight, after word was received in Washington of the death of the Israeli hostages and West German policemen, Secretary of State William P. Rogers issued this statement on behalf of the Administration:

"There are no words which can fully express our reaction to today's tragedy at the Olympic Games. I know I speak for all Americans in extending the deepest sympathies of the

Continued on Page 18, Column 4

Reports First Said Israelis Were Safe

Contradictory reports last night about the fate of the Israeli hostages seized by Arab terrorists in the Olympic Village threw the public into confusion all over the world.

Throughout the day, as the tragedy in Munich unfolded, millions of viewers throughout the world watched on live television, which employed circuits that had been intended for the Games. But in the evening, when the events reached their climax, viewers could get no definitive word for hours on how the hostages fared.

At first the West German Government's official spokesman, Conrad Ahlers, announced

Continued on Page 20, Column 1

GAMES SUSPENDED; RITES IN ARENA SET

Halt Is the First Since 1896, When the Classic Resumed —Egypt Team in Forfeit

By NEIL AMDUR
Special to The New York Times

MUNICH, West Germany, Wednesday, Sept. 6 — The Olympic Games were suspended yesterday for the first time since competition in the modern era began in 1896.

Late-afternoon and evening events were called off in the wake of an attack staged by Arab guerrillas before dawn on the Olympic Village in which two Israelis were killed and nine others taken hostage. The hostages were later killed.

After the attack, Mark Spitz, the American swimmer who won seven gold medals at the Munich Olympics and who is Jewish, flew hurriedly to London on his way back to the United States. There were fears before his departure that he too might become a victim. [Page 20.]

The announcement of the suspension, made by the International Olympic Committee, also said that a memorial service would be held for the victims

Continued on Page 18, Column 7

Elizabeth City Hall Under Investigation

By RONALD SULLIVAN
Special to The New York Times

TRENTON, Sept. 5—Law enforcement authorities reported here today that the administration of Mayor Thomas J. Dunn of Elizabeth was the target of a Union County grand jury investigation of alleged municipal corruption.

Mayor Dunn, a Democrat running for a third term, said in an interview that he had "no knowledge of any investigation involving me or my administration." But he said he volunteered last spring to go before a Union County grand jury.

According to official sources, the grand jury is investigating charges of payoffs and kickbacks involving city officials, contracts and businessmen. City license officials have already been subpoenaed, as have a number of city records and contracts.

Karl Asch, the county prosecutor, refused to comment on the nature of the reported investigation. He did say his staff had been instructed to seek indictments before the Nov. 7 elections.

Last week two of Mr. Dunn's three mayoral opponents were indicted in separate matters by a Union County grand jury.

Matthew J. Nilsen, a Republican freeholder in the county, was indicted on charges of atrocious assault in August in a case involving an alleged extortion.

In the other indictment, Michael J. DeMartino, a Democratic City Councilman in Elizabeth, was charged with misconduct in office in a case involving a $3,000 bribe in 1968.

Mayor Dunn recently endorsed President Nixon for re-election. Political observers in Union County noted that the indictments of two of his opponents were sought by a Republican prosecutor, and were seen as aiding the Mayor's re-election chances.

However, Mr. Asch, who has obtained indictments against prominent Union County political figures in recent months, contended today that his anti-corruption drive was "absolutely nonpolitical" and that the investigation of the Dunn

Continued on Page 49, Column 6

NEWS INDEX

"All the News That's Fit to Print"

The New York Times

LATE CITY EDITION
Weather: Rain late today, tonight becoming light snow early tomorrow. Temp. range: today 40-45; Saturday 40-44. Full U.S. report on Page 19.

SECTION ONE

VOL. CXXII . . No. 42,008 — NEW YORK, SUNDAY, JANUARY 28, 1973 — 50 CENTS

VIETNAM PEACE PACTS SIGNED; AMERICA'S LONGEST WAR HALTS

Nation Ends Draft, Turns to Volunteers

Change Is Ordered Six Months Early—Youths Must Still Kegister

By DAVID E. ROSENBAUM
Special to The New York Times

WASHINGTON, Jan. 27—Defense Secretary Melvin R. Laird announced today that the military draft had ended.

As a result of the announcement, men born in 1953 and afterward will not be subject to conscription, and men born before 1953 but not yet drafted will have no further liability to the draft.

These men will be the first in two generations to have no prospect of being drafted. Except for a brief hiatus in 1947 and 1948, men have been conscripted regularly since 1940.

President Nixon's authority to conscript troops into the military expires June 30. Since no one has been drafted since December, the President achieved his goal of turning the military into an all-volunteer force six months ahead of the deadline.

The President and Mr. Laird had promised repeatedly that the June 30 deadline would be met. But Mr. Laird had held out the possibility that as many as 5,000 men would be drafted this year from March through June.

Message From Laird

But, in a message to senior defense officials that was made public today, Mr. Laird said:

"With the signing of the peace agreement in Paris today, and, after receiving a report from the Secretary of the Army that he foresees no need for further inductions, I wish to inform you that the armed forces henceforth will depend exclusively on volunteer soldiers, sailors, airmen and marines.

"The use of the draft has ended."

Although no one will be drafted, the Selective Service machinery will most likely remain on the books for standby use in an emergency. Men will continue to have to register for the draft when they turn 18, and young men will still be assigned lottery numbers based on their birthdays.

Congress has mandated, however, that the Government call up Reserves and National Guardsmen before it turns to a reinstatement of the draft to meet future emergencies.

A spokesman for the Selective Service System said that men who had refused to report for induction would still be subject to criminal prosecution. But, he said, men with induction postponements that were due to expire before June 30 will not be drafted.

"We will draft nobody," the spokesman said.

Hopes Senate Will Act

Mr. Laird's single qualification about ending the draft applied to doctors and dentists. The Nixon Administration has asked Congress to approve sizable bonuses for doctors and dentists in an effort to attract enough volunteers in those professions.

The House of Representatives passed such legislation last year, and Mr. Laird said in his message today:

"I am particularly hopeful that the Senate will promptly follow the lead of the House and enact legislation giving added incentives for service from members of the health professions, so that the requirements for health services personnel can also be put on a volunteer basis."

The House is almost certainly willing to pass the bill again this year, but Representative F. Edward Hébert, chairman of the House Armed Services Committee, has said that his committee will not act until the Senate passes the legislation.

Mr. Laird also urged Congress to approve bonuses to attract men to the National Guard and

Continued on Page 28, Column 1

In the morning ceremony at the Hotel Majestic in Paris were, from the left, the Vietcong, North Vietnamese, South Vietnamese and U.S. delegations

Associated Press, United Press International and C.B.S. News

Signing, from left, William P. Rogers for U.S., Nguyen Duy Trinh for Hanoi, Mrs. Nguyen Thi Binh for the Vietcong, Tran Van Lam for Saigon

CEREMONIES COOL

Two Sessions in Paris Formally Conclude the Agreement

By FLORA LEWIS
Special to The New York Times

PARIS, Jan. 27—The Vietnam cease-fire agreement was signed here today in eerie silence, without a word or a gesture to express the world's relief that the years of war were officially ending.

The accord was effective at 7 P.M. Eastern standard time.

Secretary of State William P. Rogers wrote his name 62 times on the documents providing—after 12 years—a settlement of the longest, most divisive foreign war in America's history.

The official title of the text was "Agreement on Ending the War and Restoring Peace in Vietnam." But the cold, almost gloomy atmosphere at two separate signing ceremonies reflected the uncertainties of whether peace is now assured.

The conflict, which has raged in one way or another for over a quarter of a century, had been inconclusive, without clear victory or defeat for either side.

Involvement Gradually Grew

After a gradually increasing involvement that began even before France left Indochina in 1954, the United States entered into a full-scale combat role in 1965. The United States considers Jan. 1, 1961, as the war's starting date and casualties are counted from then.

By 1968, when the build-up was stopped and then reversed, there were 529,000 Americans fighting in Vietnam. United States dead passed 45,000 by the end of the war.

The peace agreements were as ambiguous as the conflict, which many of America's friends first saw as generous aid to a weak and threatened ally, but which many came to consider an exercise of brute power against a tiny nation.

Built on Compromises

The peace agreements signed today were built of compromises that permit the two Vietnamese sides to give them contradictory meanings and, they clearly hope, to continue their unfinished struggle in the political arena without continuing the slaughter.

The signing took place in two ceremonies. In the morning, the participants were the United States, North Vietnam, South Vietnam and the Vietcong. Because the Saigon Government does not wish to imply recognition of the Vietcong's Provisional Revolutionary Government, all references to that government were confined to a second set of documents. That set was signed in the afternoon,

Continued on Page 24, Column 7

Hanoi Lists of P.O.W.'s Are Made Public by U.S.

By BERNARD GWERTZMAN
Special to The New York Times

WASHINGTON, Jan. 27—The State Department tonight released the list of American civilians acknowledged by North Vietnam as having been captured in South Vietnam during the Vietnam war. The list lef. about half the 51 American civilians believed missing or captured unaccounted for.

The list that the North Vietnamese turned over to American officials in Paris today named 27 American civilians as prisoners of the Vietcong, and listed seven other Americans as having died in captivity.

At the same time, the Defense Department began releasing, in batches, the names of the military prisoners in Communist hands who were on the list turned over in Paris along with the civilians.

2 Diplomats Listed

The United States, in Paris, provided a list of 26,000 Communist prisoners held by South Vietnam in exchange. The lists were turned over following the formal signing of the Vietnam cease-fire agreement.

Frank A. Sieverts, the State Department official charged with prisoner affairs, said that Hanoi apparently did not in-

Continued on Page 26, Column 1

The Toll: 12 Years of War

Military

United States—45,933 killed, 303,616 wounded, 587 captured, 1,335 missing (up to Jan. 13, 1973).
South Vietnam—183,528 killed and 499,026 wounded.
North Vietnam and Vietcong—924,048 (an estimate by Saigon; figures on wounded not available.)

Civilian

415,000 South Vietnamese killed and 935,000 wounded in combat (1965 through 1972).
31,463 South Vietnamese killed and 49,000 abducted as result of Vietcong actions against civilians.
20,587 killed by Saigon actions against civilian Vietcong.
North Vietnamese—Casualties not known.

BATTLES CONTINUE AFTER CEASE-FIRE

U.S. Copter Sent to Pick Up Vietcong Officers Said to Have Been Shot Down

By FOX BUTTERFIELD
Special to The New York Times

SAIGON, South Vietnam, Sunday, Jan. 28—A cease-fire officially went into effect throughout Vietnam at 8 A.M. today, but widespread fighting continued and there were reports that an unarmed American helicopter sent to pick up a Vietcong delegation and bring it to Saigon had been shot down over Tay Nin Ninh Province.

The helicopter, which was painted white and which is normally used for medical evacuation flight, was to bring the Vietcong's delegation to the four-power Joint Military Commission that will oversee the cease-fire. There was no immediate word on the fate of the crew.

[North Vietnam issued a statement Sunday informing its people of the cease-fire, saying, "Today, the 28th of January, war completely ends in both zones of our country," Reuters reported from Hong Kong.]

334 Incidents Reported

The South Vietnamese command reported this morning that in the 24 hours ending at dawn, North Vietnamese and Vietcong troops initiated 334 incidents throughout the country. According to Government officers, that is the highest number since they began keeping a record. However, more Communist troops were probably involved during the 1968 Tet offensive, they said.

Only an hour and a half before the cease-fire began, Communist gunners struck Tan Son Nhut airport on the outskirts

Continued on Page 18, Column 1

A Reluctant G.I.'s Life and Death

By JON NORDHEIMER
Special to The New York Times

ST. JOSEPH, Mo.—The house on Penn Street where Charley Stockbauer used to live sits near a historic crossroads of America.

It was from St. Joseph that the pioneers who won the West a century ago set out across the prairie in rough wagons drawn by mules and oxen and gritty conviction.

They came here by railroad and steamboat in the waning days of winter and huddled in muddy encampments on the gray bluffs above the Missouri River, waiting with mounting excitement for the floodwaters to recede from the Kansas plain.

As with most American school children, the seeds of patriotism were planted deep in Charley Stockbauer, and he grew to manhood in St. Joseph surrounded by the ghosts of 19th-century heroes and the legends of the days when men strode boldly toward an uncertain horizon, enduring hardship and fear on the impulse of duty or national destiny.

Values Questioned

These values are still enshrined, but they have been questioned as never before by Charley Stockbauer's generation during the turbulent years when the vagaries of the war in Vietnam challenged traditional American attitudes about sacred abstractions such as patriotism.

Charley Stockbauer was a confused and reluctant warrior in a conflict that almost nobody fully understands, and that confusion and reluctance are mirrored here in the town that was his home before he died in Vietnam. Patriotism has not died in St. Joseph, but here, as elsewhere across the country in these days when the war has at last come to an end, there is a reticence about it all, a nervous hesitance about parading the flag.

The myths and the legends persist. Buffalo Bill and Wild Bill Hickok were raw-boned riders from the Overland Pony Express, and the mail they carried westward started out from a brick building that still stands on Penn Street. Indian fighters purchased, with leather pouches

Continued on Page 24, Column 2

Today's Sections

Index to Subjects

*Included in all copies distributed in New York City and the suburban area.

Nation Celebrates Peace In Prayer and Muted Joy

By MICHAEL KNIGHT

President Nixon, like millions of other Americans, watched the signing of the Vietnam cease-fire agreement on television yesterday and then, like many others, took part in a modest and somber celebration of the end of a tragic war.

The President, relaxing in his home at Key Biscayne, Fla., had proclaimed 7 P.M. yesterday as a "national moment of prayer and thanksgiving" and the 24-hour period thereafter as a day of prayer.

Throughout the country, in cities and in hamlets, church bells tolled, fire companies sounded their horns, and small, quiet gatherings were held in homes and in public places.

Some Voice Caution

Some of those who celebrated the end of the American war did so cautiously. The executive secretary of the Washington, D. C., Council of Churches said, "The reason many of us are not throwing our hats in the air is that we are just so stunned and ashamed because the war went on so long, so needlessly."

In Elmira, N. Y., Mrs. Lucielle Cesari did not turn on the lights of a Christmas tree in her yard, lights she had lit every night for five years in a "vigil" remembering the war.

In Longmeadow, Mass., a bell forged by Paul Revere, the silversmith and patriot, was sounded in its steeple at the First Church of Christ. The bell was first sounded to signal the end of the War of 1812.

In Key Biscayne, the President attended a special service at the Key Biscayne Presbyterian Church about a mile from his home.

The minister, the Rev. John A. Huffman, Jr., borrowed from a song by two antiwar activists,

Continued on Page 20, Column 3

United Press International

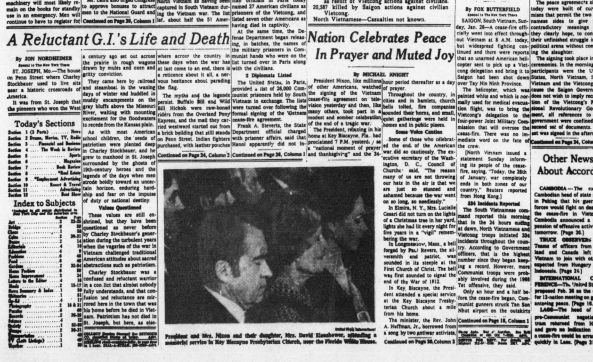

President and Mrs. Nixon and their daughter, Mrs. David Eisenhower, attending a memorial service in Key Biscayne Presbyterian Church, near the Florida White House.

Other News About Accords

CAMBODIA—The exiled Cambodian head of state said in Peking that his guerrilla forces would fight on despite the cease-fire in Vietnam. Cambodia announced a suspension of offensive activities tomorrow. [Page 26.]

TRUCE OBSERVERS—Teams of officers from Poland and Canada left for Vietnam to join with others expected from Hungary and Indonesia. [Page 24.]

INTERNATIONAL CONFERENCE—The United States proposed Feb. 26 as the date for 12-nation meeting on guaranteeing peace. [Page 16.]

LAOS—The head of the pro-Communist negotiating team returned from Hanoi and gave no indication that a cease-fire could be arranged quickly in Laos. [Page 21.]

"All the News That's Fit to Print"

The New York Times

LATE CITY EDITION

Weather: Mostly sunny, mild today; cloudy, chance of rain tonight. Temp. range: today 56-73. Friday 51-71. Additional details on Page 70.

VOL.CXXIII....No.42,266

NEW YORK, SATURDAY, OCTOBER 13, 1973

15 CENTS

GERALD FORD NAMED BY NIXON AS THE SUCCESSOR TO AGNEW

Appeals Court Agrees President Should Give Up Tapes

Israelis Drive Syrians Back Within 18 Miles of Damascus

Capture of Capital Thought Unlikely

By CHARLES MOHR

Special to The New York Times

EL QUNEITRA, on the Golan Heights, Oct. 12—Parts of the Syrian Army appeared to be in full retreat today as the Israeli Army advanced to within 18 miles of the Syrian capital of Damascus.

But an Israeli officer said: "We won't be having dinner together tomorrow in Damascus."

[In Tel Aviv, a well-informed Israeli source said that "the latest thinking is that we will not capture Damascus, which would be a terrible headache." An Israeli military spokesman said that Israeli forces had encountered Iraqi troops in the Golan heights for the first time.]

In at least one area of the Syrian front, northeast of the town of El Quneitra, it was apparent that Syrian forces were in retreat, although still fighting delaying actions.

Reporters following the Israeli Army—and clocking distances on the odometers of their rented sedans—could see that the Israeli forward elements were at least 30 kilometers, or 18 miles, past the old 1967 cease-fire line—and thus about 30 kilometers from Damascus.

It was apparent to neutral foreign observers that, in this one area at least, the main Syrian line of resistance had been smashed. The heavy fortifications constructed by Syria on the 1967 cease-fire line were abandoned and many of its bunkers damaged or destroyed.

Great plumes of brown dust rose in the air as Israeli tank companies moved forward over the rolling, hill-dotted terrain east of the cease-fire line.

A heavy Syrian artillery barrage came in on an area about four miles within Syria this afternoon, but journalists had no clear idea what was happening at the spearhead of the Israeli advance and how determined Syrian resistance was in the most forward areas.

On a brief visit to what is now the Israeli rear area on the route of advance, there were

Continued on Page 14, Column 5

3 Freighters Sunk

By JUAN de ONIS

Special to The New York Times

DAMASCUS, Syria, Oct. 12—Syrian air defenses today shot down 35 Israeli planes that attacked military air bases around this capital and other targets, according to a military spokesman.

Three freighters, one Soviet, one Japanese and one Greek, were sunk during attacks by Israeli missile boats on the ports of Latakia and Tartus, an official announcment said today. The Syrian spokesman said eight of the attacking Israeli craft were sunk by Syrian missile boats.

[In Cairo, military communiqués said that Egyptian forces were continuing to pour across the Suez Canal. Page 15.]

On the ground, "fierce fighting" continued all along the Syrian front, said the spokesman. He said more than 40 Israeli tanks and 20 armored vehicles had been destroyed. There was no figure on Syrian losses.

The front, along the occupied Golan Heights, was 24 miles southeast of this city of 840,000 people, which was calm tonight under a nearly full moon.

Traffic in the blacked-out streets consisted mainly of

Continued on Page 15, Column 1

To Our Readers

Distribution of this issue of The New York Times was delayed by work stoppages by the printers' union in defiance of a court order. The stoppages also made it necessary to reduce coverage of the news. Details, Page 24.

United Press International

Fumes and smoke rise as Israeli artillerymen, on the Syrian border, fire 155-mm. guns

Israel Is Accused in U.N. Of Sinking a Soviet Ship

By ROBERT ALDEN

Special to The New York Times

UNITED NATIONS, N. Y., Oct. 12—The Soviet Union accused Israel today of "barbarous" attacks on nonmilitary targets and demanded that they be stopped at once.

Yakov A. Malik, the Soviet delegate, read to the Security Council a dispatch from Tass, the Soviet press agency, that said the Soviet merchant ship Ilya Mechnikov had been sunk in Tartus, a Syrian port, by an Israeli attack.

Tass demanded "an immediate stop to the bombings of peaceful towns in Syria and Egypt, and the strict observance by Israel of the norms of international law."

"The continuation of criminal acts by Israel will lead to grave consequences for Israel itself," the Tass article added.

Yosef Tekoah, the Israeli representative, said his information on the basis of a news dispatch was that the Soviet merchant ship had been damaged as a result of a naval battle that took place between Syrian and Israeli naval vessels outside the port. He termed the damage "unfortunate."

Reports from Damascus said that the ship had subsequently been sunk, as had a Greek and a Japanese merchant ship during attacks made by Israeli missile boats on the ports of Tartus and Latakia.

"We regret the sinking of

Continued on Page 14, Column 2

Rival Stadium Plans Stir a Bistate Furor

By FRANK LYNN

A bitter behind-the-scenes struggle has developed between New York and New Jersey over a proposed Sunnyside, Queens, sport complex that has the strong backing of Governor Rockefeller and that could effectively kill a similar New Jersey race track and football stadium.

High New York State sources said that the Governor had approved the announcement of the Queens sports complex last Saturday that forced postponement of the sale of a $280-million bond issue to finance the New Jersey race track and stadium for the New York Football Giants in the Hackensack Meadows.

"We were signaling investors of New York's interest in its

Continued on Page 24, Column 5

JUDGES RULE 5-2

Historic Decision Finds President Not Above Law's Commands

By LESLEY OELSNER

Special to The New York Times

WASHINGTON, Oct. 12—In what it called an "unavoidable" and "extraordinary" ruling, the United States Court of Appeals held tonight that President Nixon must turn over to the Federal District Court here the disputed White House tape recordings possibly bearing on Watergate crimes.

By a 5-to-2 vote, the appeals court said that the District

Excerpts from court opinions will be found on Page 21.

Court could then give the Watergate grand jury any relevant material, unless it felt that there was some public interest to be served by withholding "particular" statements or information.

"Though the President is elected by nationwide ballot, and is often said to represent all the people, he does not embody the nation's sovereignty," the court said. "He is not above the law's commands."

Order Is Upheld

Participants in today's decision were David L. Bazelon, chief judge, and J. Skelly Wright, Carl McGowan, Harold Leventhal, Spottswood W. Robinson, 3d, George E. MacKinnon and Malcolm R. Wilkey.

The court's ruling, issued at 6 P.M. through the clerk's office on the fifth floor of the Federal Courthouse here, thus substantially upheld the order last August of Federal District Judge John J. Sirica, although it appeared to take an even tougher stance against the President than Judge Sirica had.

The appellate court made its ruling in response to requests by both Mr. Nixon and Archibald Cox, the special Watergate prosecutor, to reverse Judge Sirica. Mr. Cox, who had initiated the proceedings when he had a subpoena issued for the tapes, asked the appeals court to order that the tapes be turned over directly to the grand jury.

Mr. Nixon, for his part, asked

Continued on Page 20, Column 4

United Press International

Gerald R. Ford with President, after Mr. Nixon nominated him for Vice President

MOVE IS SURPRISE

House G.O.P. Leader Would Be the 40th Vice President

By JOHN HERBERS

Special to The New York Times

WASHINGTON, Oct. 12—Gerald Rudolph Ford of Michigan, the 60-year-old minority leader of the House of Representatives, was nominated by President Nixon tonight to be the 40th Vice President of the United States.

Mr. Nixon, making the surprise announcement on national television and radio shortly after 9 P.M., said that he would

Texts of Nixon and Ford remarks are on Page 19.

send the nomination to Congress tomorrow. Because of Mr. Ford's long service in that body, 25 years, he was expected to be easily confirmed.

Under the 25th Amendment, ratified in 1967 and never used before tonight, the nomination must be approved by simple majorities of both the House and the Senate before he can take office.

Mr. Ford's selection came two days after Spiro T. Agnew, who had served in the office almost five years, resigned, pleaded no contest to income tax evasion, was fined $10,000 and was placed on probation for three years.

Move Toward Unity

In a brief announcement speech in the East Room of the White House, Mr. Nixon made it clear that he had chosen a respected member of Congress for the post because he considered it essential for national unity to select a person who would not be the subject of a protracted and bitter fight in Congress.

It was learned that Mr. Nixon had given strong consideration to former Treasury Secretary John B. Connally but that leaders in the Democratic-controlled Congress had served notice they would oppose him. They opposed Mr. Connally because he recently switched to the Republican party and because it would have appeared that Mr. Nixon was setting him up for the Presidency in the 1976 elections.

Mr. Ford, the President said, "has earned the respect of both Democrats and Republicans."

'Unwavering' on Vietnam

"He is a man also who has been unwavering in his support of the policies that brought peace with honor for America in Vietnam and in support of the policies for a strong national defense," Mr. Nixon said.

Several score Congressional leaders, Cabinet members and other high Government officials burst into cheers and surrounded the baldish, tanned Republican and offered congratulations even before Mr. Nixon uttered his name. They knew he was the nominee when Mr. Nixon said his choice "is a man who has served for 25 years in the House of Representatives with great distinction."

Mr. Ford, the President said, met the three criteria he had set for the nominee—that "the

Continued on Page 19, Column 1

Amtrak Will Double Fleet Of 'Corridor' Metroliners

By EDWARD C. BURKS

Amtrak, the nationwide rail passenger system, announced yesterday that it would virtually double its fleet of Metroliner cars and extend high-speed Metroliner service from New York to Boston.

It signed contracts in Washington for new equipment valued at $63.5-million including the following:

¶Fifty-seven new Metroliner-type coaches, capable of operation in trains pulled by either electric or diesel locomotives, for service in the Washington-New York-Boston "Northeast Corridor."

¶Eleven new 6,000-horsepower electric locomotives (added to 15 ordered earlier this year) to replace the famed but ancient Penn Central GG-1 electrics that have operated in the corridor since the nineteen-thirties.

¶Seventy new diesel passenger locomotives for other Amtrak routes around the nation.

In Philadelphia, Judge John P. Fullam, who is in charge of the Penn Central Railroad's bankruptcy case in Federal District Court, said he believed there was no immediate need for the carrier to cease its operations. [Details Page 47.]

With the award of yesterday's contracts, Amtrak has now committed more than $110-million this year to new locomotives and passenger cars.

Started in 1969, the high-speed Metroliner service between New York and Washington has been expanded to a train every hour in each direction from early morning until evening on weekdays.

There are somewhat fewer services on the weekends. In addition, some Metroliners go on through New York as far as New Haven.

Although very-high speed service on the New York-Boston line must await the day of extensive track realignment on the curving route, new equipment ordered yesterday can substantially reduce present running times, according to Amtrak.

Bryan Duff, Amtrak's news director, said that the first of the new Metroliner-type coaches with airliner interiors should be delivered in 15 months. They are to be built by the Budd Company at Red Lion, Pa.

The 61 Metroliner cars now in operation are self-propelled and equipped with pantographs on the roof. Their use is thus limited to the relatively short stretches in this country with overhead catenary installations.

The new cars will have the

Continued on Page 70, Column 5

CHOICE IS PRAISED BY BOTH PARTIES

Widespread Enthusiasm Is Expressed in Congress—Fast Confirmation Seen

By RICHARD L. MADDEN

Special to The New York Times

WASHINGTON, Oct. 12—Congressional Democrats and Republicans received President Nixon's choice of Gerald R. Ford to be Vice President with widespread enthusiasm tonight.

The reaction indicated that the nomination of Mr. Ford of Michigan, who has been the House Republican leader since 1965, would be confirmed relatively quickly by both houses, barring some unforeseen development.

However, it was expected that the Senate would take more time than the House in considering the nomination.

"My own feeling is Gerry will probably be confirmed," said Speaker Carl Albert of Oklahoma, he added:

"I think I was the first in Congress to tell the President that Gerry would be the easiest candidate to sell to the House. He's a very fine man to work with. I think he earned this."

Senator Robert C. Byrd of West Virginia, the Democratic majority whip and member of the Senate Rules Committee, which will probably handle Mr. Ford's nomination, said he did not think it would be proper

Continued on Page 19, Column 5

P.S.C. Certifies Shortage Of Fuel Oil on Long Island

First in the State

By DAVID A. ANDELMAN

The State Public Service Commission certified yesterday that a major shortage in home and industrial fuel oils existed for Long Island—the first region in the state to be declared an "oil insufficient area."

According to the certification, between now and Jan. 15 Long Island will face a shortage of at least 150.1 million gallons of No. 2 home heating oil and 39.5 million gallons of Nos. 4 and 6 industrial fuel oils.

The certification was made to Henry L. Diamond, the State Environmental Conservation Commissioner, who must now decide whether to lift the regulations prohibiting use of high-sulphur fuel oil to ease the anticipated shortage.

Yesterday's certification applies only to fuels distributed through Northville Industries, the largest distributor on Long Island, but reportedly not the only one finding supplies short.

As a result, a senior official of the Public Service Commission noted, "there may be other

Continued on Page 36, Column 3

Federal Controls Ordered

By The Associated Press

WASHINGTON, Oct. 12—The Nixon Administration reluctantly adopted today a mandatory allocation program governing the wholesale distribution of home heating oil.

At the same time, Congress moved steadily closer to forcing a mandatory program for all petroleum products.

The Administration's limited program, which will take effect Nov. 1, requires suppliers to distribute home heating oil, jet fuel, kerosene, diesel fuel, range oil, stove oil and gas oil to their customers in proportion to purchases made in the calendar year 1972.

On Oct. 2, the Administration imposed a similar allocation program on propane gas, but so far there is no Government control over the distribution of crude oil or of gasoline and other petroleum products.

Legislation now before Congress would require mandatory allocation of all petroleum products and crude oil.

The House Rules Committee

Continued on Page 36, Column 8

Agnew Prosecution Took Pains To Prepare a 'Locked-Up Case'

By AGIS SALPUKAS

Special to The New York Times

BALTIMORE, Oct. 12—It started modestly.

When George Beall, the United States Attorney for Maryland, asked that a grand jury be impaneled last Dec. 4, he recalled in an interview today, the thought was: "If we ended up bringing criminal charges against a couple of building inspectors in Baltimore it would have been justified."

And the inquiry remained focused on lesser political figures, with no hint that it would lead higher, until the beginning of June when several key witnesses began to seek favored treatment from the prosecutors by telling them what they knew about making payments to the then Vice President Agnew.

By the beginning of July, Mr. Beall was convinced that the case against the Vice President was serious and on July 3 he called Attorney General Elliot L. Richardson to inform him of the explosive turn of events.

Mr. Beall comes from a long line of prominent Republicans in Maryland. He is the son of J. Glenn Beall, the former Republican United States Senator, and the brother of J. Glenn Beall Jr., who won election to the Senate in 1970. Today he recalled his feelings at that point last summer when he realized the implication of the inquiry.

"I was turning somersaults," he said as he sat at his neat

Continued on Page 18, Column 2

NEWS INDEX

News Summary and Index, Page 37

"All the News That's Fit to Print"

The New York Times

LATE CITY EDITION

North: Partly cloudy, mild today; fair and cool tonight. Temp range 65-78. South: Mild, chance of a few showers today and tonight. Temp. range 67-80. Details on Page 66.

VOL. CXXIII . . . . No. 42,566 — © 1974 The New York Times Company — NEW YORK, FRIDAY, AUGUST 9, 1974 — 20¢ beyond 50-mile radius of New York City except Long Island. Higher in air delivery cities — 15 CENTS

NIXON RESIGNS

HE URGES A TIME OF 'HEALING'; FORD WILL TAKE OFFICE TODAY

'Sacrifice' Is Praised; Kissinger to Remain

By ANTHONY RIPLEY

Special to The New York Times

WASHINGTON, Aug. 8—Vice President Ford praised President Nixon tonight for "one of the greatest personal sacrifices for the country and one of the finest personal decisions on behalf of all of us as Americans."

Mr. Ford, who will take office as the 38th President at noon tomorrow, vowed to continue Mr. Nixon's foreign policy and announced that Secretary of State Kissinger had agreed to stay on in the new Administration.

"I pledge to you tonight, as I will pledge to you tomorrow and in the future, my best efforts in cooperation, leadership and dedication to what's good for America and good for the world," he said.

The Vice President, who never sought the nation's highest office and disclaimed any intention of seeking it after Mr. Nixon's term, will be sworn in in a private ceremony at the White House.

Thus will be become the first man to serve as President without being chosen by the American people in an election. Tomorrow night he will address the nation on radio and television. It is expected that he will speak at 6 P.M.

All day today the signs of the historic change were in the air, sensed by the crowds that gathered along Pennsylvania

Text of Mr. Ford's remarks appears on Page 2.

Avenue near the White House. Applause rang out from the crowds when Mr. Ford appeared briefly.

After watching Mr. Nixon on television tonight with his family, the Vice President stepped outside into a slight drizzle at his suburban split-level home in nearby Alexandria, Va., to face television cameras and photographers assembled in the street and about 100 cheering neighbors.

'A Very Great Man'

Speaking without notes or a prepared text, Mr. Ford pledged to continue the Nixon foreign policy and called the Secretary of State "a very great man" whom he has known for many years.

On domestic policy, he said that he had been "very fortunate in my lifetime" to have adversaries in Congress but said that he did not think he had "a single enemy" there.

President Nixon had cited in his resignation address his lack of support in Congress as one of the major reasons for his resignation.

Mr. Ford said, "The net result is that I think tomorrow I can start out working with Democrats and with Republi-

Continued on Page 4, Column 3

Associated Press

Vice President Ford meeting with newsmen last night

United Press International

President Nixon on TV as he announced his resignation

SPECULATION RIFE ON VICE PRESIDENT

Some Ford Associates Say Selecting a Successor Could Take Weeks

By CHRISTOPHER LYDON

Special to The New York Times

WASHINGTON, Aug. 8 — Potentially the most revealing and most important decision of Gerald R. Ford's Presidential debut — his choice of a successor in the Vice Presidency — was a much-discussed mystery here today.

Close friends of Mr. Ford continued to feed speculation about more than a dozen possible candidates. But none of the friends claimed to have discussed the Vice-Presidential question with Mr. Ford or to be speaking for him on it. A number of Ford associates thought he might hold off the decision for days or even weeks.

"Eveybody's on tenterhooks up here," a Senator remarked this afternoon in a telephone interview from the Republican cloakroom, "but I think they're wasting their time. It's going to be a week or two. So far I'd say he's a loner on this issue."

Former Defense Secretary Melvin R. Laird, a Ford counselor in the House for more than a decade, was being quoted again today as saying he believes that Nelson A. Rocke-

Continued on Page 4, Column 1

POLITICAL SCENE SHARPLY ALTERED

G.O.P. Prospects Improved, Ford in Good Spot for '76 and Watergate Fades

By R. W. APPLE Jr.

Special to The New York Times

WASHINGTON, Aug. 8—President Nixon's resignation drastically altered the American political landscape.

It improved Republican prospects for the Congressional elections in November, thrust Vice President Ford into the favorite's role for the 1976 Presidential election, ended the Watergate agony that has served to bind together the heterogeneous Democratic party and removed from the political stage the man who was the dominant Republican for the last 15 years.

In a larger sense, it seemed to presage an era of more open government, of more cooperation and less antagonism between Capitol Hill and the White House and of decline of the White House staff as an independent power center.

Lives Are Altered

A kind of "honeymoon" between the executive and legislative branches was widely predicted by Congressional leaders today. Congressmen who knew Mr. Ford for years as a Capitol Hill colleague said that they expected to work closely with him.

At least in the beginning, pragmatic conservatism is expected to remain the dominant ideological tone in the executive branch.

How that will be translated into policies, and how those policies will shape the political dialogue, will not be clear for weeks. But experts in the two fields forecast an essentially unchanged foreign policy and a similar, but more carefully and consistently applied, economic policy.

By his decision, Mr. Nixon

Continued on Page 6, Column 4

Rise and Fall

Appraisal of Nixon Career

By ROBERT B. SEMPLE Jr.

The central question is how a man who won so much could have lost so much. How could a public figure who so well perceived the instincts of the majority of his countrymen have misused the powers and duties those same countrymen so eagerly ceded him?

The historians will be kept busy on these questions, but for those who spent their time observing Mr. Nixon for the last six years the answer may well be found in a phrase he often applied to himself. "At bottom," he used to say, "I am a political man."

By his own description, he was a man of action rather than contemplation, a tactician rather than a theologian, a student of technique who seemed always impatient with substance, a figure whose exceptional antennae seemed to dwarf and even hide what lay at the core.

To his enemies, he was both manipulative and synthetic; to his friends, a pragmatist unencumbered by inflexible principles; to those who watched him, a man who learned to run before he had learned to walk and who, on reaching his destination, was not always certain what to do when he got there—except, perhaps, to keep going.

That image has only been reinforced and deepened by the transcripts of three conversations with H. R. Haldeman on June 23, 1972, six days after the Watergate break-in, which were released on Aug. 5, and the edited transcripts of White House conversations published April 30. Whatever history's judgment of those tapes, this much was clear: Faced with mounting evidence of deception and wrongdoing in his own official family, he sought not to confront the issue but to manipulate it until he himself became part of the deception.

Mr. Nixon used the words "I am a political man" proudly, as if to challenge the moralists, but in the end they became his epitaph—a possible explanation for both his success and failure.

For if the words implied the presence of a talent for finding opportunities for political prof-

Continued on Page 11, Column 1

JAWORSKI ASSERTS NO DEAL WAS MADE

Says Nixon Did Not Ask for and Was Not Given a Way to Avoid Prosecution

By RICHARD D. LYONS

Special to The New York Times

WASHINGTON, Aug. 8—Leon Jaworski, the special Watergate prosecutor, said tonight after President Nixon's resignation speech that no deals had been either made or offered that would have given Mr. Nixon immunity from prosecution on any charges that might stem from the Watergate scandal.

"There has been no agreement or understanding of any sort between the President or his representatives and the special prosecutor relating in any way to the President's resignation," Mr. Jaworski said in a statement issued by his office.

Mr. Jaworski's words, plus the fact that the President made no mention of the immunity issue in his address to the nation, left open the possibility, at least for the moment, that Mr. Nixon might be charged and stand trial.

No Immunity Sought

Mr. Nixon did not ask for any immunity assurances from Mr. Jaworski before the resignation speech, the prosecutor said, adding that none had been offered.

As Mr. Jaworski put it, "The special prosecutor's office was not asked for any such agreement or understanding and offered none."

"Although I was informed of the President's decision this afternoon, my office did not participate in any way in the President's decision to resign," the statement concluded.

Mr. Jaworski met earlier today with Gen. Alexander M. Haig Jr., the White House chief of staff, but that meeting was said to have been only for the purpose of informing the special prosecutor of what the President would say later in the evening.

The meeting did not take place in the White House, presumably because Mr. Jaworski would have been recognized there, and his visit would have excited speculation.

Earlier today, there were moves in both houses of Congress to grant Mr. Nixon immunity from prosecution, but

Continued on Page 2, Column 4

The 37th President Is First to Quit Post

By JOHN HERBERS

Special to The New York Times

WASHINGTON, Aug. 8—Richard Milhous Nixon, the 37th President of the United States, announced tonight that he had given up his long and arduous fight to remain in office and would resign, effective at noon tomorrow.

Gerald Rudolph Ford, whom Mr. Nixon nominated for Vice President last Oct. 12, will be sworn in tomorrow at the same hour as the 38th President, to serve out the 895 days remaining in Mr. Nixon's second term.

Less that two years after his landslide re-election victory, Mr. Nixon, in a conciliatory address on national

Text of the address will be found on Page 2.

television, said that he was leaving not with a sense of bitterness but with a hope that his departure would start a "process of healing that is so desperately needed in America."

He spoke of regret for any "injuries" done "in the course of the events that led to this decision." He acknowledged that some of his judgments had been wrong.

The 61-year-old Mr. Nixon, appearing calm and resigned to his fate as a victim of the Watergate scandal, became the first President in the history of the Republic to resign from office. Only 10 months earlier his first Vice President, Spiro T. Agnew, became the first man to resign the Vice Presidency.

Contrast in Tone and Content

Mr. Nixon, speaking from the Oval Office, where his successor will be sworn in tomorrow, may well have delivered his most effective speech since the Watergate scandals began to swamp his Administration in early 1973.

In tone and content, the 15-minute address was in sharp contrast to his frequently combative language of the past, especially his first "farewell" appearance—that of 1962, when he announced he was retiring from politics after losing the California governorship race and declared that the news media would not have "Nixon to kick around" anymore.

Yet he spoke tonight of how painful it was for him to give up the office.

"I would have preferred to carry through to the finish whatever the personal agony it would have involved, and my family unanimously urged me to do so," he said.

Puts 'Interests of America First'

"I have never been a quitter," he said. "To leave office before my term is completed is opposed to every instinct in my body." But he said that he had decided to put "the interests of America first."

Conceding that he did not have the votes in Congress to escape impeachment in the House and conviction in the Senate, Mr. Nixon said, "To continue to fight through the months ahead for my personal vindication would almost totally absorb the time and attention of the President and the Congress in a period when our entire focus should be on the great issues of peace abroad and prosperity without inflation at home."

"Therefore," he continued, "I shall resign the Presidency effective at noon tomorrow. Vice President Ford will be

Continued on Page 3, Column 1

The Other Major News

Wholesale Prices Up

A new upward surge of farm prices joined a big jump in industrial prices to produce the year's largest monthly increase in the wholesale price index. The rise for July was 3.7 per cent, seasonally adjusted, and 3.9 per cent before adjustment. Page 45.

Election Bill Voted

The House approved by a vote of 355 to 48 a broad campaign-finance reform bill. The measure would set limits on political contributions, restrict candidate spending and provide subsidies for Presidential primaries, conventions and elections. The bill now goes to a House-Senate conference committee. Page 36.

Cyprus Talks Open

The foreign ministers of Greece, Turkey and Britain met in Geneva to try to work out an effective cease-fire on Cyprus and to tackle the political problems behind the fighting there. Page 16.

On Cyprus, acting President Glafkos Clerides named a moderate Cabinet stripped of any militant proponents of union with Greece.

Mr. Clerides, who will occupy the key posts of Foreign Affairs and Interior, left for Athens on his way to Geneva for the talks on a political settlement. Page 16.

10 Police Accused

Ten New York City police sergeants were arrested for allegedly participating in a "club" that collected more than $250,000 over a decade from legitimate businesses and illegal rackets operations in Queens. Page 68.

Meskill Named Judge

Gov. Thomas J. Meskill of Connecticut was nominated by President Nixon to a seat on the Federal bench. Mr. Meskill, a Republican, stunned the state Republican party earlier this year by declining to run for a second term amid reports that he had been offered a judgeship. Page 38.

NEWS INDEX

A Tiny G.O.P. Bastion Feels Loss and Relief

By PRANAY GUPTE

Special to The New York Times

SHELTER ISLAND, L.I., Aug. 8—Six years after he put it on his car, Evans K. Griffing sadly stripped off his bold, red-lettered bumper sticker today — the one that said "NIXON."

Mr. Griffing felt a sense of loss. So did hundreds of people in this conservative community 100 miles east of New York City.

In 1968 and 1972, Suffolk County gave Richard M. Nixon the largest single election plurality of any county in the United States. Today all that had changed on Shelter Island.

As the hour of the President's resignation announcement approached, many islanders expressed both a feeling of hurt at having been "betrayed" by Mr. Nixon and relief that he was leaving office.

"We tried to stay by him till the very end," said Thomas L. Jernick, the Town Supervisor. "But when he disclosed on Monday that he had covered up his role in Watergate, we couldn't support him any more. He lied to us, and for a President of the United States to lie is inexcusable."

"We really believed in Mr. Nixon" was a phrase used again and again by dozens of islanders today.

At the same time they spoke hopefully of the Ford Administration and of moving urgently to tasks long neglected—ending the nation's political turmoil and easing its economic distress.

Shelter Island has 1,800 year-round residents, most of whom are registered Republicans.

Only last June interviews with islanders indicated that whatever else Watergate had done, it apparently had not diluted Shelter Island's faith in Mr. Nixon. People said at the time that they felt the President was being vilified by the media

Continued on Page 7, Column 6

Only Nixon Is Serene At Sad White House

By PHILIP SHABECOFF

Special to The New York Times

WASHINGTON, Aug. 8—On his 2,027th and penultimate day as President of the United States, with his staff and family unable to conceal their anguish, Richard M. Nixon went composedly through the schedule of a busy President.

He met with his Vice President and the bipartisan leadership of Congress. He appointed Federal judges, accepted resignations from executive agencies and signed several laws.

He vetoed as inflationary an appropriation bill for the Department of Agriculture and the Environmental Protection Agency.

He also announced, over national television, that tomorrow he would resign his high office.

Mr. Nixon did not loosen his self control even when he talked of his "regret" and his "sadness" at leaving the Presidency. His delivery, with its familiar half-smiles, did not reflect the momentous message he had for his audience: that at noon tomorrow he would become the first healthy, living American President to leave office before his term expired.

At 12:30 this afternoon, the White House press secretary, Ronald L. Ziegler, announced that the President would address the nation at 9 P.M.

Mr. Ziegler did not say what the speech would be about. He did not have to. He choked on his words several times and was struggling visibly to keep himself under control as he left the rostrum of the packed but hushed briefing room at the White House.

The young women who work in the press office went through the motions of their jobs while tears streamed down their faces.

But the President himself, according to his appointments

Continued on Page 2, Column 6

"All the News That's Fit to Print"

The New York Times

LATE CITY EDITION

Weather: Continued mostly cloudy, cool today, tonight and tomorrow. Temperature range: today 46-58; Tuesday 45-53. Details on Page 81.

VOL. CXXIV.. No. 42,830 — NEW YORK, WEDNESDAY, APRIL 30, 1975 — Price higher in air delivery cities. — 20 CENTS

MINH SURRENDERS, VIETCONG IN SAIGON; 1,000 AMERICANS AND 5,500 VIETNAMESE EVACUATED BY COPTER TO U.S. CARRIERS

U.S., GREECE AGREE TO END HOME PORT FOR THE 6TH FLEET

Air Base of Americans at Athens Is Also Closed, but Some Facilities Remain

By United Press International

ATHENS, April 29—United States and Greek officials announced today the termination of the home-port arrangement for Sixth Fleet ships at the port of Eleusis near Athens and the closing of the American air base at Athens airport.

The announcement came in a joint statement at the end of a second round of talks on the status of United States military facilities in Greece.

The Greek Government threatened to close all United States bases and it withdrew from the North Atlantic Treaty Organization's military command after the invasion of Cyprus by Turkey last July.

"Certain United States facilities which contribute to Greek defense needs will continue to operate on the Greek Air Force base at Hellenikon," today's statement said.

The statement said that the second phase of the talks, held April 7 to 29 by the two delegations under the United States Embassy Minister, Monteagle Stearns, and Ambassador Petros Kalogeras of Greece also discussed the status of other facilities.

"Agreement is also expected on the elimination, reduction and conservation of other United States facilities in Greece," it said.

The two delegations said that they made progress on the review of the privileges, immunities and exemptions of American personnel in Greece.

The two Governments said

Continued on Page 4, Column 4

G.M.'s Profits Fall

First-quarter profits of General Motors declined 50.8 per cent from the depressed 1974 quarter. Page 53.

HEAVY USERS FACE CON ED INCREASE

P.S.C. Also Orders Cuts for Smaller Consumers

By WILL LISSNER

The state's Public Service Commission ordered the Consolidated Edison Company yesterday to raise its rates for those customers who accounted for the heaviest summer power demands and to cut the rates for customers whose usage did not create excess power demand.

The change — technically a revision of the rate structure approved last November to give the utility $338.7-million more a year — will not mean any extra revenue for the company. Nor will it affect the rates for the great majority of customers, the 2.5 million small residential and commercial users.

Instead, yesterday's order makes revisions in bills that will take less than $20-million from some customers and give it to others, a relatively small amount compared with its total annual billings for electricity of $2.10-billion. It affected less than 500,000 of its 2.9 million customers in New York City, Westchester County and part of Nassau County.

But the order was significant because it introduced into energy ratemaking the philosophy that the customers who are responsible for excess costs should be required to bear more

Continued on Page 34, Column 5

United Press International

A crewman from an American helicopter helping evacuees to the top of a building in Saigon for flight to a U.S. carrier

Abram Offers Bills To Curtail Abuses Of Nursing Homes

By ALFONSO A. NARVAEZ
Special to The New York Times

ALBANY, April 29—Morris B. Abram proposed today a series of changes in the laws governing nursing homes to "deal with the most serious immediate problems" uncovered during his month-long investigation.

The proposals were contained in a package of 11 bills submitted to Governor Carey and legislative leaders by Mr. Abram, head of the Moreland Act Commission investigating the nursing-home industry.

Among other things, they would authorize nursing-home residents to file class-action suits for deprivation of their rights and would entitle them to receive a minimum of 25 per cent of the daily reimbursement rate paid by government regulations for each day of a violation.

[In Washington, Senator Frank Moss, Democrat of Utah and chairman of the long-term care subcommittee of the Special Committee on Aging, introduced a package of 36 bills for nursing home reform. Among them were measures to make long-term care more readily available to all older Americans, improve inspection and enforcement procedures and provide training for nursing-home physicians, nurses,

Continued on Page 81, Column 3

CAMBODIA ORDERS FOREIGNERS OUT

Planned 250-Mile Road Trip to Border Is Protested by Paris as Debilitating

By FLORA LEWIS
Special to The New York Times

PARIS, April 29—The French Government said today that the people who have been isolated in its Phnom Penh embassy since the Cambodian Communists took over two weeks ago had been ordered expelled "in the worst possible conditions."

There are 610 refugees in the embassy. They are to be sent out by truck to the town of Poipet on the Thailand border, beginning tomorrow.

Foreign Minister Jean Sauvagnargues told newsmen after having conferred with President Valéry Giscard d'Estaing:

"We fear these extremely precarious evacuation conditions will be beyond the strength of some whose health is poor."

"We continue to insist that the plane that we have held in Vientiane for evacuation of the ill be allowed to land in Phnom Penh."

However, a Foreign Ministry spokesman said that so far there has been no response to

Continued on Page 17, Column 6

74 Saigon Planes Fly 2,000 to Thailand

By DAVID A. ANDELMAN
Special to The New York Times

BANGKOK, Thailand, April 29—At least 74 South Vietnamese Air Force planes fleeing the country streamed into U Taphao air base in southern Thailand without warning this afternoon.

The pilots and passengers—2,000 people—requested asylum, American and Thai Foreign Ministry officials said.

About 30 of the planes were F-5 jet fighters and there were reports that at least one had crashed on a highway near the base as it was making its approach.

The planes began arriving at the huge naval and air base on the Gulf of Siam at about the time that the American evacuation of South Vietnam was ending and the planes were still landing as night fell.

The aircraft were said to include C-47 transports and the C-130 cargo planes that the American military has been using to ferry refugees from South Vietnam to Guam and the Philippines. However, all the aircraft were understood to be Vietnam Air Force planes, originally supplied by the United States.

A Thai Foreign Ministry spokesman said that American authorities at U Taphao had been asked to turn over the aircraft to the Thai Government, which would return them to "the new South Vietnamese government." The pilots and passengers, the Thai spokesman said, "must leave Thailand."

"They just landed first and asked permission afterwards," said an astounded Thai Foreign Ministry official. Other Government sources said that apparently no efforts were made to prevent the planes from landing and no aircraft went up to intercept the fighters as they roared in.

American Embassy officials in Bangkok declined to comment on the Thai request that the planes be returned and their status was unclear. An unresolved question here appeared to be whether the planes were still American property or belonged to whatever government continued in Saigon. The planes could be worth $200-million, one official said.

No details were available on the status of the refugees or

Continued on Page 16, Column 6

United Press International

President Ford and Secretary of State Kissinger returning to White House to resume talks on Vietnam. They had just said good-by to King Hussein of Jordan after visit.

2d Key Met Museum Aide Quits In Dispute Over Hoving Methods

By GRACE GLUECK

With an attack on Thomas P. F. Hoving's administration at the Metropolitan Museum of Art alleging its inability to function "in any way that creates or preserves trust, confidence and decency," Anthony M. Clark, chairman of the museum's department of European paintings, has resigned.

Mr. Clark's resignation, one of several that have occurred among senior curatorial personnel at the museum in recent years, represents the first open challenge to Mr. Hoving's administration.

The resignation, effective June 30, follows that of John Walsh, the vice chairman and curator of this key department a month ago. Mr. Clark would not speak for Mr. Walsh, who is abroad, but it is understood that their basic grievances are similar.

"I can't work with or for the present administration at the Met," said Mr. Clark, who had been director of the Minneapolis Institute of Arts for 10 years before his appointment to the Metropolitan in 1973. "I believe that its relation to art has become incidental, wrong and even risky. It's also hell on professionals."

In a statement last night, Mr. Hoving said that he was

Continued on Page 24, Column 1

NEWS INDEX

FORD UNITY PLEA

President Says That Departure 'Closes a Chapter' for U.S.

By JOHN W. FINNEY
Special to The New York Times

WASHINGTON, April 29—The United States ended two decades of military involvement in Vietnam today with the evacuation of about 1,000 Americans from Saigon as well as more than 5,500 South Vietnamese.

The emergency helicopter evacuation was ordered last night by President Ford after the Saigon airport was closed

Ford statement and excerpts from Kissinger's, Page 17.

because of Communist rocket and artillery fire. The 1,000 Americans were the last contingent of a force that once numbered more than 500,000.

They were carried by a fleet of 81 American helicopters to carriers in the South China Sea.

The helicopters removed the 5,500 South Vietnamese citizens because their lives were presumed to be in danger with a Communist take-over of South Vietnam. Over the last two weeks, a total of about 55,000 South Vietnamese have been removed. Most of them will come to the United States. The helicopter flights ended the United States evacuation of South Vietnamese.

Last Marines Evacuated

The final withdrawal of Americans was completed at 7:52 P.M., about two hours after the White House had announced the evacuation was completed, when 11 marines were taken by helicopter from the roof of the American Embassy in Saigon. Officials said that the marines, the last of a security guard sent in to protect the evacuation, were safely removed although small-arms fire had broken out around the deserted embassy.

President Ford, in a statement issued by the White House, said the evacuation "closes a chapter in the American experience." In a plea for national unity in the post-Vietnam period, the President said:

"I ask all Americans to close ranks, to avoid recrimination about the past, to look ahead to the many goals we share and to work together on the great tasks that remain to be accomplished."

Appeal by Kissinger

At a news conference, Secretary of State Kissinger appealed to North Vietnam not to storm Saigon by force because the United States believed the new South Vietnamese Govern-

Continued on Page 17, Column 1

END OF DEFENSE

Troops Leave Posts in Capital and Turn in Their Weapons

By The Associated Press

SAIGON, South Vietnam, Wednesday, April 30—President Duong Van Minh announced today the unconditional surrender of the Saigon Government and its military forces to the Vietcong.

Columns of South Vietnamese troops pulled out of their defensive positions in the capital and marched to central points to turn in their weapons.

[In Washington, the White House said that President Ford had "no comment" on the surrender of Saigon, but a White House spokesman said the surrender was considered "inevitable." Page 16]

Troops Move In

Within two hours, Communist forces began moving into Saigon, and a jeep flying the Vietcong flag and carrying eight cheering men in civilian

The text of President Minh's statement is on Page 16.

clothes armed with an assortment of weapons could be seen driving near the United States Embassy compound.

The Vietcong flag was raised over the presidential palace at 12:15 P.M. (12:15 A.M. Wednesday, New York time), and soon after a detachment of Communist troops in a jeep arrived at the palace and asked General Minh to accompany them. He drove off with them, but their destination was not immediately disclosed.

Vietcong flags materialized on other buildings as well, and Vietcong soldiers soon walked along the main streets shaking hands with Saigon residents. The red, yellow-starred flag of North Vietnam could also be seen on trucks carrying soldiers in green helmets and uniforms.

Bursts of Fire

Sporadic bursts of firing could be heard, but the only resistance to the Communist take-over was reported to be from marines stationed at the zoo and public gardens.

The take-over followed by hours the ending of the American involvement in Vietnam through the evacuation of most of the approximately 1,000 Americans still here yesterday.

The surrender announcement, made in a broadcast to the nation, signaled the end of three decades of fighting. It came 21 years after the 1954 Geneva accords divided Vietnam into North and South and a little more than two years after the Vietnam cease-fire

Continued on Page 16, Column 1

Saigon Copter Lands on Another In Stampede to U.S. Ship's Deck

By The Associated Press

ABOARD U.S.S. BLUE RIDGE, in South China Sea, April 29—Scores of South Vietnamese helicopters filled with military men and civilians fled Saigon today and headed out to sea to search for the carriers of the United States Seventh Fleet.

Seven of the helicopters arrived unexpectedly above this vessel carrying Americans and Vietnamese evacuated from South Vietnam. The seven copters made a dash for the helipad at the rear of the ship.

One pilot dropped his helicopter on the blades of another that had just landed and chunks of metal ripped through the air. The top helicopter, with its load of women and children, nearly toppled into the sea, but they were rescued and there were no injuries.

United States sailors heaved the two damaged choppers overboard to clear the landing pad. For the Vietnamese it was a last-ditch chance to survive.

As other Vietnamese helicopters landed their passengers were pulled free. American sailors ripped the doors off the craft to make them sink and the pilots then jettisoned them in the sea to make room for other arrivals circling overhead. Two small craft rescued the swimming pilots.

The American evacuation was reported orderly, although it was delayed several times because of weather and pilot fatigue.

The Blue Ridge is the command and communications vessel of the 40-ship Seventh Fleet armada waiting off the coast of South Vietnam to evacuate Americans and other foreigners

Continued on Page 17, Column 2

"All the News That's Fit to Print"

The New York Times

LATE CITY EDITION

Weather: Partly cloudy, warm and humid today, tonight and tomorrow. Temperature range: today 73-88; Thursday 73-83. Details on Page 60.

VOL. CXXIV . . No. 42,909

NEW YORK, FRIDAY, JULY 18, 1975

Price higher in air delivery cities.

20 CENTS

U.S. AND SOVIET ASTRONAUTS UNITE SHIPS AND THEN JOIN IN HISTORIC HANDSHAKES

City Will Dismiss 1,434 In Sanitation Force Today

Beame Says Union Fund Is Running Out —Tells M.A.C. He'll Do 'Whatever Is Necessary' to Open Bond Market

By RONALD SMOTHERS

Mayor Beame said late yesterday that 1,434 sanitationmen would be dismissed this afternoon, and that 750 others would have to be laid off at the end of the month because the unusual $1.6-million fund pledged by their union to pay their wages was running out.

John J. DeLury, president of the Uniformed Sanitationmen's Association, urged all union members who still had jobs to report to work as scheduled, and not repeat the wildcat walkout of two weeks ago.

He noted that the union was in State Supreme Court pressing its challenge of any layoffs of garbagemen. "Let the courts decide it," he said.

The layoff announcement was the most concrete development of a day in which municipal officials and outside fiscal experts struggled with the city's seemingly endless financial crisis. Among the other actions yesterday were the following:

¶Officials of the Municipal Assistance Corporation suggested to Mayor Beame that, in addition to a proposed wage freeze, he might have to consider pay cuts for city workers, increased transit fares, and tuition at the City University to restore investor confidence in the corporation's bonds. The Mayor pledged to do "whatever is necessary" to regain access to money-lending markets. [Page 10.]

¶Leaders of municipal unions angrily denounced the proposal to freeze or roll back the 6 per cent raise that went into effect July 1, saying it would be illegal contract-breaking. And lawyers for the politically divided Legislature differed on whether the city or state would have the authority to suspend the raises. [Page 7.]

¶The Mayor said he would announce today the dismissal of more than 30 appointees in "high-level positions," drawing salaries ranging from $18,000 to $33,000 a year. He did not give the names of those to be dismissed, but said the action might save the city $750,000 a year.

The announcement of the layoff of sanitationmen signaled the loss of a gamble taken by the sanitation union on July 3.

Sanitationmen had gone on a two-day wildcat strike to protest the scheduled dismissal

Continued on Page 9, Column 1

ISRAEL GIVES U.S. NEW PROPOSALS FOR SINAI ACCORD

Plan, to Be Relayed to Cairo, Said to Include an Offer to Pull Back in Passes

Special to The New York Times

WASHINGTON, July 17 — Ambassador Simcha Dinitz of Israel today gave Secretary of State Kissinger the latest Israeli proposals for breaking the deadlocked talks with Egypt on a new Sinai agreement. Americans and Israelis said later that "progress" had been made toward an accord.

The 90-minute session was reported to have covered all major geographic and political points of an accord.

Despite an Egyptian threat not to renew the mandate of the United Nations peace-keeping force in Sinai, a cause of concern here and in Israel, the American mediation efforts still appear to be on the course that seemed charted last week when the first signs of definite progress emerged.

If the Egyptians refuse to allow the United Nations force to be extended, however, the current negotiations are expected to collapse. At this time, this is not anticipated.

Talks Depend on Mandate

Senior officials in Israel said today that the future of the negotiations hinged on whether a way could be found to extend the mandate, which expires next Thursday. An Israeli policy-maker said that the negotiations were "still on track" but frozen.

The official Egyptian view appears to be that Cairo has instilled a sense of urgency into the search for a settlement, but has closed no door that had previously been opened. [Page 3.]

Mr. Dinitz and Mr. Kissinger will meet again tomorrow morning for further clarification of the Israeli position. The new Israeli ideas will then be given to Hermann F. Eilts, Ambassador to Cairo, for relay to Egypt over the weekend.

It is hoped by Americans and Israelis that the latest ideas will be sufficient to persuade the Egyptians to accept a new mandate for the United Nations force, and thereby forestall a bitter debate next week in the United Nations Security Council.

Mr. Dinitz, who brought the

Continued on Page 3, Column 5

United Press International

Inside the Soyuz spacecraft, astronauts listen to message from President Ford. From left: Valery N. Kubasov, Col. Aleksei A. Leonov, Brig. Gen. Thomas P. Stafford and Donald K. Slayton. Vance D. Brand remained in the Apollo craft.

'GLAD TO SEE YOU'

Crewmen Eat Lunch— Brezhnev and Ford Praise Link-Up

By JOHN NOBLE WILFORD

Special to The New York Times

HOUSTON, July 17—Astronauts of the United States and the Soviet Union united spaceships today and then joined hands in the first international meeting away from earth, a symbolic gesture of the two nations' expressed desire to cooperate in the exploration of space.

The American Apollo made physical contact with the Soviet Soyuz at 12:09 P.M., Eastern daylight time, about 140 miles over the Atlantic Ocean, 620 miles west of Portugal. Then, three and a half minutes later, the two ships achieved a firm link-up.

"We have capture," Brig. Gen. Thomas P. Stafford of the Air Force, the Apollo commander, radioed in Russian to the Soyuz commander, Col. Aleksei A. Leonov.

'Well Done, Tom'

"Well done, Tom, it was a good show," Colonel Leonov responded in English. The two crews, when speaking to each other, use the listener's language.

The Soviet and American crews met face to face more than three hours and two orbits of earth later. The linked spaceships were passing over Amsterdam at the moment.

Peering through the opened hatches into the Apollo's connecting module, Colonel Leonov welcomed General Stafford with the English words, "Glad to see you."

General Stafford, replying in Russian, said:

"A, zdravstvuite, ochen rad vas videt" ("Ah, hello, very glad to see you.")

Commanders Shake Hands

The two astronauts then shook hands through the hatches, an event that would have been all but unthinkable a few years ago when the two nations were rivals in space, as in most other affairs.

General Stafford and Donald K. Slayton crawled into the Soyuz where they presented a gift of flags to the Soviet astronauts, listened to messages from the leaders of their two countries and ate lunch together.

The 16-ton Apollo and $7\frac{1}{2}$-ton Soyuz are scheduled to remain docked for two days, until Saturday morning. During that time, the astronauts will exchange gifts, share meals and conduct some scientific experiments.

The other member of the Soyuz crew is Valery N. Kubasov. The third member of the Apollo crew is Vance D. Brand, who remained in the Apollo during the first crew transfer.

Back on earth, in Moscow and Washington and at the Johnson Space Center here, officials of both nations offered

Continued on Page 12, Column 1

LEVELING IS FOUND IN NATION'S OUTPUT

G.N.P.'s Total in 2d Quarter Seen as Further Evidence of a Waning Recession

By EDWIN L. DALE Jr.

Special to The New York Times

WASHINGTON, July 17—The nation's total output of goods and services was essentially flat in the second quarter, providing further evidence that the recession has hit bottom, the Commerce Department reported today.

Preliminary figures showed that the gross national product, the broadest measure of the total economy, declined at an annual rate of three-tenths of 1 per cent in the April-June quarter, after adjusting for higher prices. This nominal drop in the "real" G.N.P. is within the range of statistical error and means basically that the total output went neither up nor down. The G.N.P. plummeted at a rate of 11.4 per cent in the first quarter and had declined in every quarter since the end of 1973.

There would have been a rise in the second quarter but for a

Continued on Page 41, Column 1

Destruction of LSD Data Laid to C.I.A. Aide in '73

By NICHOLAS M. HORROCK

Special to The New York Times

WASHINGTON, July 17 — The staff of the Rockefeller commission concluded that the chief of the Central Intelligence Agency's testing of LSD destroyed the drug program's records in 1973 to hide the details of possibly illegal actions, commission sources said today.

These sources said that the chief of the program, Dr. Sidney Gottlieb, a 57-year-old biochemist, was personally involved in a fatal experiment in November, 1953, in which the commission has said a researcher was surreptitiously given LSD, a potent mind-altering drug. The researcher, Frank R. Olson, jumped to his death from a New York City hotel room less than two weeks later after reportedly showing symptoms of anxiety.

The Rockefeller commission staff, on the basis of its investigation, concluded that 20 years after Mr. Olson's death, and 10 years after the LSD experiments were purportedly halted, Dr. Gottlieb ordered the destruction of all the records of the program, including a total of 152 separate files, commission sources said.

The record destruction came shortly after other records had been destroyed by Richard Helms, then director of Central Intelligence, these sources said.

Dr. Gottlieb retired from the agency a few months after Mr. Helms left in January, 1973, they said.

The Rockefeller commission previously reported the destruction of records on the LSD experiments, but did not mention Dr. Gottlieb by name. It also reported a program through the Federal Bureau of Drug Abuse Control in which the C.I.A. had arranged to test LSD on "unsuspecting volunteers" in two programs, one in the West and the other along the East Coast.

Staff sources on the Rockefeller commission said this program was also commanded by Dr. Gottlieb.

For a short time after he resigned from the C.I.A., Dr.

Continued on Page 6, Column 1

LSD Report Disputed

Robert V. Lashbrook, a former employe of the Central Intelligence Agency, said he believed Frank R. Olson, a scientist who committed suicide in 1953, had knowingly participated in an experiment with LSD. The statement appeared to contradict the Rockefeller commission's finding that Mr. Olson had been given the drug surreptitiously. Page 6.

A.T.&T. DISCLOSES SAUDI FINANCING

$100-Million, Six-Year Note, Bearing Rate of 8.40%, Is Placed With OPEC Nation

By REGINALD STUART

The American Telephone and Telegraph Company has placed a $100-million note issue with the Government of Saudi Arabia, the giant telecommunications company said yesterday.

The six-year note, bearing a 8.40 per cent interest rate, is the first such financing of its type by A.T.&T., which has traditionally restricted its borrowings to domestic financial markets.

"The private placement relieves some of the demand on the domestic capital market and should make it easier to raise the remainder of the year's financing by Bell operating companies," said a brief A.T.&T. statement that quoted Charles L. Brown, the company's executive vice president and chief financial officer.

Although Mr. Brown's statement made no reference beyond his assertion that the Saudi deal would ease the domestic capital-market situation, A. T. & T. itself has had some problems in the money market. The most recent example was its inability to raise more than $160-million through the exercise of 31.3 million stock-purchase warrants in May. Had they all been exercised, A. T. & T. would have realized about $1.6-billion.

Negotiations for the loan were underway since April, the company said, with the interest rate set on April 29. A.T.&T.

Continued on Page 41, Column 1

Estimate Board Assuming Sharper Role With Mayor

By STEVEN R. WEISMAN

A week ago Mayor Beame was assuring his fellow political leaders that the city's "crisis" had lifted, at least for a while. But within the last 48 hours he has found himself in something approaching a state of siege, faced with demands for drastic steps to bring the city, for the second time in a month, back from the brink of possible default.

For the first time in the history of his mayoralty, Mr. Beame was dealing with a Board of Estimate—long-accustomed to docility—acting independently, taking the initiative and to even criticizing the Mayor to his face. Some members of the board questioned, in private, whether Mr. Beame had been sufficiently aware recently of the seriousness of the city's weakening fiscal position.

The focus of the new moves by the Board of Estimate yesterday and the day before was the suggestion—long discussed at City Hall, but never really taken seriously—of freezing municipal wages as a step to impress investors who are refusing to lend money either to the city or to the Municipal Assistance Corporation.

The idea of the freeze emerged Wednesday morning at a sometimes heated breakfast meeting between the Board of Estimate and Mr. Beame. It was later discussed at an informal session held

Continued on Page 8, Column 3

United Press International

ROYAL COUPLE ATTACKED IN OKINAWA: Crown Prince Akihito of Japan and Princess Michiko, left, leap back as a fire bomb hurled by a radical explodes before them. The couple were laying flowers at a monument to the war dead, near Naha, when the incident took place. Both escaped unhurt. Two men were arrested. Page 4.

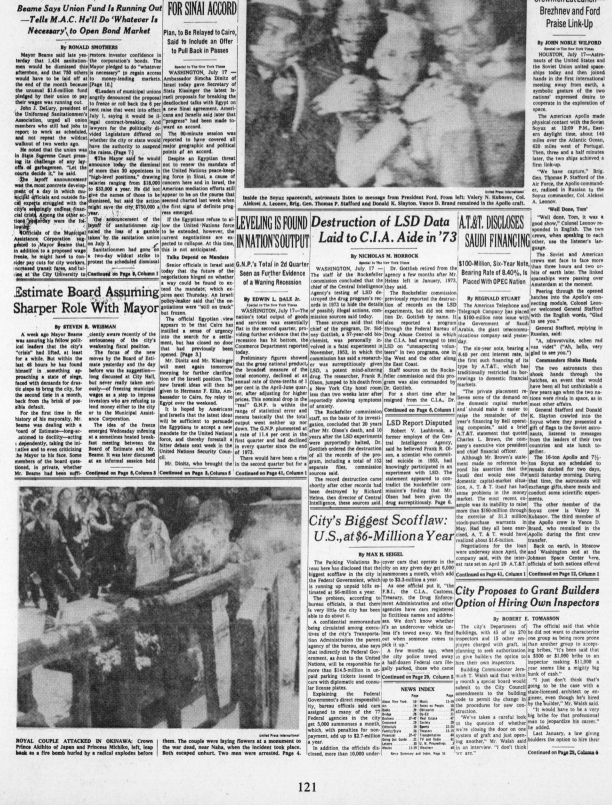

City's Biggest Scofflaw: U.S., at $6-Million a Year

By MAX H. SEIGEL

The Parking Violations Bureau here has disclosed that the biggest scofflaw in the city is the Federal Government, which is running up unpaid bills estimated at $6-million a year.

The problem, according to bureau officials, is that there is very little the city has been able to do about it.

A confidential memorandum being circulated among executives of the city's Transportation Administration the parent agency of the bureau, also says that indirectly the Federal Government, as host to the United Nations, will be responsible for more than $14.5-million in unpaid parking tickets issued to cars with diplomatic and consular license plates.

Explaining the Federal Government's direct responsibility, bureau officals said cars assigned to many of the 77 Federal agencies in the city get 5,000 summonses a month, which, with penalties for nonpayment, add up to $2.7-million a year.

In addition, the officials disclosed, more than 10,000 undercover cars that operate in the city on any given day get 6,000 summonses a month, which add up to $3.3-million a year.

As one official put it, "the F.B.I., the C.I.A., Customs, Treasury, the Drug Enforcement Administration and other agencies have cars registered to fictitious names and addresses. We don't know whether it's an undercover vehicle unless it's towed away. We find out when someone comes to pick it up."

A few months ago, when the city police towed away a half-dozen Federal cars illegally parked, those who came

Continued on Page 29, Column 5

NEWS INDEX

City Proposes to Grant Builders Option of Hiring Own Inspectors

By ROBERT E. TOMASSON

The city's Department of Buildings, with 45 of its 270 inspectors and 15 other employes charged with graft, is planning to seek authorization to give builders the option to hire their own inspectors.

Building Commissioner Jeremiah T. Walsh said that within a month a special board would submit to the City Council amendments to the building code to permit the change in the procedures for new construction.

'We've taken a careful look at the question of whether we're closing the door on one system of graft and just opening another," Mr. Walsh said in an interview. "I don't think we are."

The official said that while he did not want to characterize one group as being more prone than another group to accepting bribes, "it's been said that a $500 or $1,000 bribe to an inspector making $11,000 a year seems like a mighty big hunk of cash."

"I just don't think that's going to be the case with a state-licensed architect or engineer, even though he's hired by the builder," Mr. Walsh said.

"It would have to be a very big bribe for that professional man to jeopardize his career," he added.

Last January, a law giving biulders the option to hire their

Continued on Page 29, Column 4

"All the News That's Fit to Print"

The New York Times

LATE CITY EDITION

Weather: Cooler, rain likely today, tonight. Partly cloudy tomorrow. Temperature range: today 56-68; Monday 54-72. Details on Page 73.

VOL. CXXV.. No. 42,976

NEW YORK TUESDAY, SEPTEMBER 23, 1975

25 cents beyond 50-mile zone from New York City, except Long Island. Higher in air delivery cities.

20 CENTS

FORD ESCAPES HARM AS SHOT IS DEFLECTED; WOMAN SEIZED WITH GUN IN SAN FRANCISCO

Associated Press

President Ford doubling over near his limousine as a shot was fired when he stepped out of the St. Francis Hotel in San Francisco

2D COAST EPISODE

The Suspect Had Been Queried but Freed by Secret Service

By PHILIP SHABECOFF

Special to The New York Times

SAN FRANCISCO, Sept. 22—A shot was fired at President Ford as he stepped out of a downtown hotel here today, but a civilian bystander deflected the gun just as it went off and the President was not hit. A woman suspect was arrested immediately.

The bullet struck the pavement, ricocheted up and slightly wounded a man in the crowd of more than 3,000 that had gathered outside the St. Francis Hotel for a glimpse of the President.

Police officers and Oliver Sipple, a 30-year-old former marine who had deflected the weapon, seized the .38-caliber revolver from the assailant. She was later identified by the authorities as Sara Jane Moore, a 45-year-old activist who had been questioned by the Secret Service here last night but not detained.

Screams and pandemonium erupted from the crowd at the crack of gunfire. Mr. Ford, stunned momentarily, doubled over and was immediately shielded and hustled by Secret Service agents into his limousine at the curb, several feet away.

Taxi Driver Wounded

In the confusion, many thought the crouching President had been hit. But the ricocheting bullet—a flat-nosed, .38-caliber slug designed to splatter upon impact—struck a taxi driver, inflicting what was later described as a slight wound.

The assailant was said to have fired the single shot from across the street—a distance of about 40 feet from the President.

While the police reported that Mr. Sipple had deflected the gun just as it went off, one policeman on the scene gave a different acount that suggested that Mrs. Moore had fired an unobstructed shot before the gun was deflected.

Officer Tim Hettrich recalled: "I was five or seven feet away from the suspect. I looked to my left and saw her raise her arm holding the gun, and I saw her fire a round. Then I saw Sipple's hand reach out and push her hand down. I grabbed the cylinder of the gun, took it away."

113 Bullets Found

After being disarmed and wrestled to the ground by Mr. Sipple and Officers Hettrich and Gary Lemos, Mrs. Moore was dragged across Post Street and into the hotel as Mr. Ford's limousine pulled away and sped toward San Francisco International Airport.

The President's plane left almost immediately and arrived at Andrews Air Force Base near Washington at 11:26 P.M.

The police said that Mrs. Moore had been arrested yesterday and cited for carrying an illegal handgun, which was confiscated along with 13 bullets found in her purse and 100 more found in her car. She also was questioned by the Secret Service as a potential threat to the President, but was released.

According to an affidavit signed by Parks H. Sterns Jr., special agent for the Federal Bureau of Investigation, Mrs.

Continued on Page 26, Column 1

Kissinger, at U.N., Asks Freer Forum on Mideast

By BERNARD GWERTZMAN

Special to The New York Times

UNITED NATIONS, N.Y., Sept. 22—Secretary of State Kissinger proposed today an informal meeting of key nations as a possible new approach for clearing the way to further diplomatic progress in the Middle East.

This tentative new concept was described by American officials as an effort to spur peace moves either through direct Arab-Israeli talks or through a reconvened Geneva conference, not as a substitute.

An "informal" meeting, the American officials said, might

Excerpts from Kissinger's speech are on Page 16.

give Israel and the Arabs a forum to discuss possible next steps without being bogged down by such issues as the seating of a Palestinian delegation.

'Every Feasible Step'

The suggestion was unveiled by Mr. Kissinger in a wide-ranging 50-minute speech to the 30th General Assembly. He lauded the interim Egyptian-Israeli accord on Sinai that he recently helped to conclude, and stressed that Washington was determined to press ahead with "every feasible step" to promote further progress.

In the interests of further progress, he said, the United States will support "any promising initiative." He cited the old approaches of direct Syrian-Israeli negotiations and a reconvened Geneva conference, and appended the new proposal—for "a more informal multilateral meeting to assess conditions and to discuss the future."

In his address Mr. Kissinger also touched upon the following issues:

¶Following up an earlier American-South Korean proposal, Mr. Kissinger called for a new conference of the United

Continued on Page 16, Column 1

TAPE GAP DENIAL BY NIXON IS CITED

Lawyer Says Ex-President Disclaimed Under Oath Any 'Responsibility'

By LESLEY OELSNER

Special to The New York Times

WASHINGTON, Sept. 22—Former President Richard M. Nixon has denied under oath "responsibility" for the 18½-minute gap in a key White House tape recording, one of his attorneys said today.

Mr. Nixon made his denial, according to the attorney's statement, when he gave 11 hours of grand jury testimony in California last June under questioning by lawyers from the office of the special Watergate prosecutor. Until today, both Mr. Nixon's lawyers and the prosecutors have refused to disclose any of Mr. Nixon's testimony.

Mr. Nixon's attorney, Herbert J. Miller Jr., brought up the subject of the denial during oral arguments in Federal Court here over the constitutionality of a new statute that gives the Government control over Mr. Nixon's Presidential papers and tape recordings.

Mr. Nixon is challenging the statute as unconstitutional. He contends, among other things, that it violates the principle of separation of powers and that it provides for a "wholesale, unreasonable seizure" in

Continued on Page 12, Column 1

PRESIDENT SEEKS BIG ENERGY DRIVE

Backs $100-Billion Program for U.S. Self-Sufficiency in a Decade or Less

Special to The New York Times

SAN FRANCISCO, Sept. 22—President Ford said today that next week he would ask Congress for authority to begin a $100-billion program to give the United States "energy independence in 10 years or less."

Mr. Ford plans to create a new Government cooperation called the Energy Independence Authority, which would cooperate with private industry in providing the massive financing that he said was required to develop energy resources.

Mr. Ford said that the new energy authority would be a "dramatic crash program." He likened it to the Manhattan Project, which developed the atom bomb in World War II, and to the program to put an American on the moon.

An unlikely coalition of environmentalists and oil-state conservatives is expected to seek to scuttle President Ford's plan on the ground that the new agency would have unusual power that would be subject to little Congressional review. [Page 15.]

Telephoned Nixon

The new agency would "have the power to take any appropriate financial action—to borrow and to lend—in order to get energy action," the President said. "It will serve as a catalyst and stimulant, working through—not in place of—American industry."

He announced the plan in a speech to a meeting of the Building and Construction Trades Department of the American Federation of Labor and Congress of Industrial Organizations at the Hyatt House Hotel here.

Mr. Ford's address on the

Continued on Page 15, Column 1

United Press International

Sara Jane Moore at an interview last spring

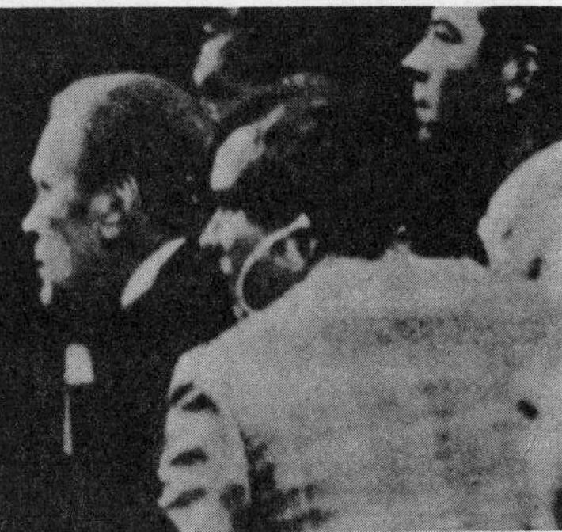

Associated Press

Mr. Ford being hustled into his car by Secret Service agents

Four More Beame Aides May Lose Their Positions

By FRED FERRETTI

Four more Beame administration officials, including the heads of two of the city's superagencies, face the possible loss of their jobs in the coming reorganization of the city's governmental structure, sources at City Hall said yesterday.

The four who face either dismissal, demotion or transfer are reported to be Michael J. Lazar, Transportation Administrator; Robert Low, Environmental Protection Administrator; Jerome Hornblass, Commissioner of the Addiction Services Agency, and Edgar C. Fabber, Commissioner of Ports and Terminals.

Reports of further administration shake-ups followed in the wake of weekend resignations by Sanitation Commissioner Robert T. Groh and Edwin L. Weisl Jr., Administrator of Parks, Recreation and Cultural Affairs—resignations that continued to leave a trail of acrimony.

Mr. Weisl denounced Mr. Beame as a "political hack clinging to power when power is gone," and as a superior who had tried to force him to take "political hacks" into his department.

At a City Hall news conference, Mr. Beame smiled thinly when advised of Mr. Weisl's statement, and when asked to react to it dismissed Mr. Weisl as an "ex-commissioner."

He said "I don't bother with people who were in my administration," and added that Mr. Weisl's attack was "a graceless and bitter way to end one's relationships."

Mr. Groh, on the other hand, had served with "dedication and integrity," Mr. Beame said.

Reorganization of the city government has been a recurring demand of the banking and

Continued on Page 33, Column 5

SUSPECT ASSERTED SHE HELPED F.B.I.

Also Volunteered for Civil Rights and Leftist Groups and Worked for Hearst

By HENRY WEINSTEIN

Special to The New York Times

SAN FRANCISCO, Sept. 22—Sara Jane Moore, the woman arrested here today after a gun was fired near President Ford, recently contended that she once was an informant for the Federal Bureau of Investigation and a volunteer worker among several civil rights and leftist groups.

She was a volunteer for the People-In-Need free food program that Randolph A. Hearst set up in an attempt to gain the freedom of his daughter, Patricia. She also worked for a time as a bookkeeper for Mr. Hearst's San Francisco Examiner.

Mrs. Moore discussed her background after presenting herself to The New York Times for an interview last May. Her language reflected the upper-middle-class Virginia background she described. But she appeared to be confused and disturbed as she discussed her activities for hours at a health-food restaurant and in a park.

She said she was concerned for her own safety and that of her 8-year-old son, with whom she lived in a Mission District apartment in San Francisco. She said she suspected that she was under surveillance by both the F.B.I. and persons of the political left whom she would not identify.

She wanted to talk about

Continued on Page 27, Column 1

Cheers, Then a Shot, And Crowd Screams

By LACEY FOSBURGH

Special to The New York Times

SAN FRANCISCO, Sept. 22—The corner of Post and Powell is usually quiet and sedate. Here, just a few yards in on Post Street from Union Square, is the side entrance to the elegant St. Francis Hotel.

This is the spot where the Rolls-Royces and Cadillacs wait, the place where chauffeurs walk the toy poodles, and the place where, if necessary, a President can come and go with a minimum of trouble.

Today, about 3:30 P.M., the corner of Post and Powell was a madhouse. Hundreds, probably thousands, of people had wedged their way toward this place hoping to catch a glimpse of Gerald R. Ford. The President was inside the hotel, they knew, and some even had heard he was speaking to the World Affairs Council there.

They lined the streets, and for two, almost three, blocks the sidewalks were dense with people, pushing and shoving, hoping to see Mr. Ford.

Then, a wave of excitement began to move across the crowd.

Ken Fisher remembers it. He was directly across the street from the hotel entrance and he knew, he said, that the President had to be coming because, first, he saw the tall muscular men, the Secret Service, he thought to himself.

John Alexander, an accountant, was there, too, near the United Airlines office, and he had just started to count the number of black limousines when Mr. Ford pushed through the swinging glass door.

"He was smiling," Laura

Continued on Page 26, Column 7

FORD WON'T STOP SEEING THE PUBLIC

Says at the White House He Will Not 'Capitulate' to Would-Be Killers

Special to The New York Times

WASHINGTON, Tuesday Sept. 23—President Ford pledged today that despite the second attempt on his life in 17 days he would not "capitulate" to would-be attackers by altering his personalized, hand-shaking style of meeting the public.

In an appearance at the White House minutes after his arrival in Washington from San Francisco, where the latest assassination attempt took place yesterday afternoon, Mr. Ford declared that if a President could not walk among the American people, then "something has gone wrong in our society."

He said: "The American people are good people. And under no circumstances will I—and I hope no others—capitulate to those who want to undercut what's good in America."

California Invitation

Mr. Ford's remarks seemed to indicate that despite yesterday's occurrence — in which, unlike an incident on Sept. 5 in Sacramento, Calif., a bullet was actually fired—he would continue his journeys across the country seeking support for his policies and meeting prospective political backers.

The White House said there was no change in the President's plans to visit the Middle West early next month but that he had not decided whether to accept an invitation by California Republicans to address two fund-raising events there late next month.

Vice President Rockefeller, reached at his Washington home last night and asked for his reaction to the San Fran-

Continued on Page 26, Column 3

F.B.I. Focus of Inquiry on Oswald Note

By JOHN M. CREWDSON

Special to The New York Times

WASHINGTON, Sept. 22—The Justice Department has begun a criminal investigation of the circumstances surrounding the destruction of a letter threatening the Dallas police that was delivered by Lee Harvey Oswald to the Dallas office of the Federal Bureau of Investigation shortly before the assassination of John F. Kennedy.

The investigation, which is being conducted by lawyers in the department's Criminal Division, was said by authoritative sources to be focusing on "conflicting statements" given by present and former F.B.I. agents and officials about their roles in, or knowledge of, the decision to destroy the letter following President Kennedy's murder on Nov. 22, 1963.

The letter reportedly contained a threat by Oswald, the accused assassin of the President, to "blow up" a Dallas police station unless the F.B.I. ceased its efforts to find and interview him and to stop what he described as its harassment of his Russian-born wife, Marina.

According to several sources familiar with the results of a recently ordered administrative inquiry by the bureau into the incident, the Oswald letter made no mention of any intention to commit a murder or of any animosity toward Mr. Kennedy.

The F.B.I.'s efforts to find Oswald before the assassination were prompted by security interests and were based upon suspicion aroused because Oswald had taken up residence in the Soviet Union, renounced his American citizenship and then returned to the United States married to a Russian native.

The letter was delivered by Oswald to the bureau's Dallas field office in early November, 1973, after a special agent there, James P. Hosty Jr., had made two visits to a home where Oswald's wife was staying with a friend.

Despite the threatening language it contained, the letter

Continued on Page 23, Column 1

A Torrent of Questions

By CLIFTON DANIEL

Special to The New York Times

News Analysis

WASHINGTON, Sept. 22—It was raining torrents in Washington tonight, and there were torrents of questions about the personal safety of the President of the United States and about people who want to be President.

The central question was whether the President, chosen for his job or fallen heir to it, can move among the people, talk to them, shake their hands, commune with them and come out alive.

In a democracy, that would seem to be a crucial issue, and it was an issue that was opened again by what happened today in San Francisco.

It was an issue that was opened not only for President Ford, the incumbent in the White House, but also for all those who might want to contend for the White House in 1976. All of them have to consider what happened to the President today.

Here was Gerald Ford, a well-meaning man trying to do his job, and suddenly, for the second time in less than three weeks, he was exposed to the threat of assassination.

Just 17 days ago in Sacramento, Calif., a young woman named Lynette Alice Fromme, a follower of Charles M. Man-

Continued on Page 26, Column 7

St.-John Perse Dies

St.-John Perse, the romantic poet who won the Nobel Prize for literature in 1960, died at the age of 88. Page 38.

NEWS INDEX

"All the News That's Fit to Print"

The New York Times

LATE CITY EDITION

Weather: Showers today, ending tonight. Partly sunny tomorrow. Temperature range: today 52-66; Saturday 51-72. Details on page 55.

SECTION ONE

VOL. CXXV .... No. 43,156

NEW YORK, SUNDAY, MARCH 21, 1976

$1.00 beyond 50-mile zone from New York City, except Long Island. Higher in air delivery cities.

75 CENTS

The New York Times/Tyrone Dukes

Rubin Carter rushes past newsmen and spectators outside the Passaic Sheriff's office after being released.

Carter and Artis Released on Bail After Nine Years

By SELWYN RAAB

Special to The New York Times

PATERSON, N. J., March 20—Rubin (Hurricane) Carter, 45472, and John Artis, 45473, exchanged their prison numbers for freedom here today.

Following a 15-minute hearing in Passaic County Court, their status instantly changed from murder convicts to murder suspects. Both are now presumed innocent pending a new trial on a charge of triple murder.

Mr. Carter, the former middleweight boxer, and Mr. Artis had each served nine years of life sentences before their convictions were overturned last Wednesday by the New Jersey Supreme Court. A second trial has been granted in the stormy, greatly publicized case and may be held this spring or next fall.

Mr. Carter, 38 years old and a leading prizefighter before his arrest for the 1966 homicide here, said he planned to fly to Florida tonight with his wife and daughter. His wife, Mae Thelma, and their daughter, Theodora, 13, were not in Paterson for the official release,

Continued on Page 35, Column 1

The New York Times/Keith Meyers

John Artis leaving Leesburg State Prison on his way to the hearing in Paterson, N.J., where he was set free.

THAILAND ORDERS LAST U.S. FORCES TO LEAVE BY JULY

Talks Stalled Over Extent of Bangkok's Control—270 Advisers to Stay

By DAVID A. ANDELMAN

Special to The New York Times

BANGKOK, Thailand, March 20—The Government tonight ordered the United States to close its remaining military installations in Thailand and withdraw all its military personnel, except 270 military aid advisers, in the next four months.

The decision came after a nearly two-hour meeting of the Cabinet following a deadlock in year-old negotiations on the future of the United States military presence in Thailand. The troops are the last American forces remaining in Southeast Asia.

Last March 19 Prime Minister Kukrit Pramoj told reporters that "within one year, all American troops will be gone from Thailand." The ultimatum was later modified to mean "combat forces," and these, according to American officials, were withdrawn by Dec. 20.

Envoy Is Given Decision

The 4,000 American personnel now in Thailand are noncombat personnel, and the United States had been negotiationg in hope of keeping about 3,000 to operate certain installations.

After last night's Cabinet meeting Prime Minister Kukrit summoned the Ambassador, Charles S. Whitehouse, to Government House to hand him the decision, which would end a 26-year American military presence in Thailand.

There were conflicting reports whether the Thai Government had ordered the shutdown of all American base operations at midnight tonight, but such a demand was not contained in any official government order.

While the ambassador was on his way to Government

Continued on Page 15, Column 1

MISS HEARST IS CONVICTED ON BANK ROBBERY CHARGES; FACES SENTENCE APRIL 19

United Press International

Patricia Hearst arriving at Federal courthouse yesterday

SHE TURNS ASHEN

Maximum Penalty on Two Counts Is 35 Years in Prison

By WALLACE TURNER

Special to The New York Times

SAN FRANCISCO, March 20—Patricia Hearst was convicted by a Federal Court jury this afternoon of armed bank robbery and the use of a gun to commit a felony.

Miss Hearst had testified that she had helped a revolutionary group rob the Sunset branch of the Hibernia Bank on April 15, 1974. But she said that she had done so only under threat of death.

After hearing 66 witnesses, viewing almost 1,000 exhibits and measuring that evidence against the instructions of Federal District Judge Oliver J. Carter, the jurors refused to accept Miss Hearst's claim.

Face Turns Ashen

Miss Heart seemed to shrink and her pale face became ashen as the verdict was read. Her parents, Mr. and Mrs. Randolph A. Hearst, sat 10 feet away. She did not look at them.

Mrs. Hearst, who left the court in tears yesterday, dropped her gaze to the floor. Mr. Hearst rubbed his forehead and stared into space.

Their daughter Anne, 20, seated beside them, broke into tears. Two other sisters, Vickie and Mrs. Virginia Bosworth, were in court. A fourth, Catherine, was not present.

After the verdict was announced, Miss Hearst leaned toward her chief lawyer, F. Lee Bailey, and said, "I wonder if I ever had a chance."

Judge Carter set April 19 for sentencing. The maximum sentence for armed robbery is 25 years in prison. For use of a firearm to commit a felony it is 10 years.

The 22-year-old defendant still faces a number of felony counts in state court in Los Angeles, as a result of an incident on May 16, 1974, when she fired an automatic carbine into a street and storefront as she sought to help two members of the revolutionary group, the self-styled Symbionese Liberation Army. The two were about to be seized by store clerks who suspected them of shoplifting.

The Symbionese group had kidnapped Miss Hearst on Feb. 4, 1974.

Jury Is Polled

As the jury filed into its box at 4:27 P.M., Miss Hearst's chief defense counsel, F. Lee Bailey, put his arm around her and leaned his heavy shoulder as if to support her upright, slender form.

Mr. Bailey's partner, Albert Johnson, sat on the other side of Miss Hearst. The prosecution team, led by United States Attorney James L. Browning Jr., sat beyond them at another table.

Mr. Bailey asked that the jury be polled—that is, asked individually if they supported the verdict, which had to be unanimous in this case.

As the court clerk, Gene F. Driscoll, read their names, each of the seven women and five

Continued on Page 46, Column 1

Briefly, a Half-Smile, And Then the Verdict

By LACEY FOSBURGH

Special to The New York Times

SAN FRANCISCO, March 20—She looked tiny, fragile, pale, more than a bit too small to be the focus of so much attention, and for a moment late this afternoon she even wore that now familiar half-smile that some have called haunting and mysterious.

Patricia Campbell Hearst walked into the Federal courtroom here in San Francisco at 4:27 P.M. today and for perhaps less than half a minute she looked happier and younger than she has in a long time.

She looked serious, but not nervous, not frightened, and it was as if, perhaps, she found the moment of the approaching verdict a relief.

The room was hot, crowded and tense.

Miss Hearst looked straight ahead with that smile on her face. She did not look at her parents, as she usually does on entering court, and she did not look about her. She sat down almost primly, as if at tea, and then moved in close to her chief attorney, F. Lee Bailey, as if to seek comfort through the touching of their shoulders.

And then she, too, waited.

Continued on Page 46, Column 4

2-YEAR COLLEGES UNDER PRESSURES

Aides of Schools Concerned by Funding Problems and Choices on Priorities

By GENE I. MAEROFF

Special to The New York Times

WASHINGTON, March 20—Officials of the nation's 1,000 two-year community colleges, long the portal to higher education for the academically underprepared and the economically disadvantaged, are concerned that the doors are slowly closing.

Financial pressures and hardening attitudes about the functions of postsecondary education are threatening the policies of nonselective admissions and low tuition that are the cornerstones of the community colleges, which have grown to include 3.8 million of the nation's 11.1 million college students.

The future of open access was a dominant theme at the annual meeting of the American Association of Junior and Community Colleges, which ended yesterday at the Washington Hilton Hotel.

A Choice of Missions

"We acknowledge the problems of finance in our present economy," the association said in a resolution. "But we cannot support solutions that simply propose a return to past priorities. Society's needs have changed, especially with regard to preparation for work, retraining and retirement."

Community college leaders feel that circumstances are forcing them to choose between what have become their two major missions—the traditional

Continued on Page 37, Column 1

Today's Sections

Index to Subjects

Five Mafia Families Open Rosters to New Members

By NICHOLAS GAGE

For the first time since 1957, New York's five Mafia "families" have been authorized by the national Mafia commission to initiate new members, according to law enforcement officials.

The officials said that each family had been given permission to initiate 10 new members, but had been told to select them from men who were already moneymakers in the rackets, had no legal problems facing them and were of proved loyalty.

The membership books were closed in 1957 to prevent gangsters who were informers for law enforcement agencies from gaining entry into Mafia families. One Mafia informer, Joseph Valachi, testified in 1962 that the move followed a series of arrests of high-level leaders, including Vito Genovese, then the most powerful Mafia boss in the country.

But about six weeks ago the commission met in the Greater New York area and approved the opening of the books on a limited scale, the officials said.

The change has been confirmed both by the police and Federal officials through informants and court-authorized electronic surveillance.

'Oaths of Silence'

"There's no doubt they've opened the books again on a tightly controlled basis," said a Justice Department official. "They've been holding initiation ceremonies in New York for the past month."

He said the ceremonies had been held in the homes of under-bosses and selected fami-

Continued on Page 40, Column 3

REAGAN, WALLACE FACING KEY TESTS

North Carolina Primary on Tuesday May Decide the Fate of Both

By R. W. APPLE Jr.

Special to The New York Times

CHARLOTTE, N. C., March 20—North Carolina, one of the nation's dozen largest states, has seldom exercised national political clout, but it may determine on Tuesday the fate of two conservative Presidential hopefuls.

Ronald Reagan, Republican, the former Governor of California, and George C. Wallace, Democrat, the present Governor of Alabama, have run as independent-minded outsiders in this year of presumed public impatience with the status quo in Washington.

Both have been damaged, however, in the early primaries; in three major tests, each has lost three times. Next week, on what each considers favorable ground, each will try to recoup, with the knowledge that another loss could be fatal.

Public-opinion polls indicate that Mr. Reagan is likely to lose to President Ford and Mr. Wallace to former Gov. Jimmy Carter of Georgia in the North Carolina primary. If the polls are borne out, senior advisers

Continued on Page 43, Column 3

Flu Experts Soon to Rule On Need of New Vaccine

By HAROLD M. SCHMECK Jr.

Special to The New York Times

WASHINGTON, March 20—It was as though they heard a single scream in the night and then silence.

It was a single aberrant outbreak of flu at Fort Dix, N.J., first detected last month. It startled public health experts because it was a new virus—possibly a harbinger of a new worldwide strain, a warning of serious danger next winter.

The outbreak may have affected 500 or more men. There was one death. For public health specialists it has been a dilemma because they have searched the nation and found no other outbreak with the same virus. Yet a decision must be made, probably within days, on whether the Fort Dix episode means that an entirely new influenza vaccine must be developed for next winter's flu season.

In recent days, top Federal health experts here have been discussing possible unprecedented action against flu. Apparently no recommendation has yet been sent to F. David Matthews, Secretary of Health, Education and Welfare, but a decision is expected next week.

$180 Million Cost Estimate

Some public health leaders, both within and outside the Federal ranks, expect the decision will be to request from Congress enough money to provide flu vaccine for all Americans next winter. The probable cost has been estimated by one expert at $180 million to $200 million.

At a meeting in Atlanta about a week ago, a group of leading advisers on vaccine policy to the Federal Government spent

Continued on Page 39, Column 1

Cuban Influence in Caribbean Rises, Worrying U.S. Officials

By DAVID BINDER

Special to The New York Times

WASHINGTON, March 20—In the last two years Cuba has gained considerable influence among the small republics of the Caribbean and is now enjoying some regional support for its military ventures in Africa, in the assessment of top-ranking United States policymakers.

The principal friends in the region of the Government of Prime Minister Fidel Castro are Guyana and Jamaica, both of which endorsed Cuba's intervention on behalf of the Marxist Popular Movement for the Liberation of Angola, which won the civil war in Angola.

In addition, Administration officials believe that the younger generation of political leaders throughout the Caribbean view Cuba as the most successful model of social and economic development in their experience. "The young leaders are very radical," one official observed, adding that they are "sympathetic to Castro."

As a result, the Ford Administration recently began to examine the implications for United States security posed by expanding Cuban influence in what had largely been a

Continued on Page 6, Column 1

Rhodesia Hints at Restoring British Tie

By HENRY KAMM

Special to The New York Times

JOHANNESBURG, South Africa, March 20—Prime Minister Ian D. Smith held out the possibility today that he might be prepared to abandon Rhodesia's 11-year-old declaration of independence from Britain in the search for a solution of the country's constitutional crisis.

Experienced observers in Salisbury and here could recall no precedent for such an expression of willingness to go back on Rhodesia's act of defiance, however circumspectly Mr. Smith phrased it.

The Prime Minister addressed a news conference called a day after the breakoff of constitutional talks between the Smith Government and Joshua Nkomo, leader of one faction of the divided African National Council.

In reply to a question, Mr. Smith declared that his Government had explored the possibility of revoking the declaration of independence, in the framework of the search for a constitutional settlement.

"If I am satisfied and it could be shown to me that this, or any other decision, is necessary in the interests of Rhodesia," he continued, "I will lend my support to carrying out that decision."

The Prime Minister said that his sole motivation was the interest of his country.

"If anybody thinks that be-

Continued on Page 20, Column 1

United Press International

MY LAI MASSACRE REMEMBERED: South Vietnamese villagers gather at the place where large numbers of people—347 according to Washington, 504 according to Saigon—were killed by American soldiers in 1968. Banners under protrait of Ho Chi Minh proclaim "Hatred for American Imperialism" and "My Lai Massacre, Never Forgotten." Vietnamese photographer who works for an American agency was allowed to take photo. Page 6.

Rutgers Five Gains

Undefeated Rutgers gained the semifinals of the National Collegiate basketball championships yesterday by beating Virginia Military Institute, 91-75. Rutgers, which has won 31 games this season, next plays Michigan, a 95-88 victor over Missouri. Indiana's undefeated and top-ranked team beat Marquette, 65-56, and will play U.C.L.A., which beat Arizona, 82-66. Details in Section 5.

"All the News That's Fit to Print"

The New York Times

LATE CITY EDITION

Weather: Partly sunny today; cold tonight. Sunny and cool tomorrow. Temperature range: today 40-60; Monday 35-59. Details on page 69.

VOL. CXXV . . No. 43,172 — NEW YORK, TUESDAY, APRIL 6, 1976 — 20 CENTS

25 cents beyond 50-mile zone from New York City, except Long Island. Higher in air delivery cities.

Howard Hughes Dies at 70 On Flight to Texas Hospital

Stroke Given as Cause of Billionaire's Death —Security Is Tight

By JAMES P. STERBA

Special to The New York Times

HOUSTON, April 5—Howard R. Hughes died today as mysteriously as he had lived.

United Press International

Howard Hughes years ago

The reclusive 70-year-old billionaire was on the way from Acapulco, Mexico, to the Methodist Hospital here for emergency medical treatment. A physician accompanying him told hospital officials that Mr. Hughes died at 1:27 P.M. in a chartered Lear jet flying over south Texas.

The body was taken by ambulance to the hospital, where tight security was imposed. Four armed Houston policemen stood guard outside the hospital's pathology laboratory, in the basement, where the body lay.

Hospital officials declined to discuss any medical details. They referred all questions to a Hughes spokesman in Los Angeles.

A spokesman for the Summa Corporation, the heart of the Hughes empire, said tonight, "Howard R. Hughes is dead."

A Hughes spokesman in Los Angeles said the cause of death was a "cerebral vascular accident." This is otherwise known as a stroke.

Mr. Hughes left an estate estimated to be worth $1.5 billion or more.

Mr. Hughes's wishes for the disposition of his holdings were as completely shrouded in secrecy as his life had been in recent years. His movements were always the subject of rumors but the rumors were rarely confirmed.

Larry Mathis, a Methodist Hospital vice president, reported that a Hughes aide telephoned hospital officials about 9 A.M. and said Mr. Hughes would be arriving this afternoon.

"We were aware it was an emergency, but we did not know what the nature of the problem was and we still don't know," Mr. Mathis said at 7:30 tonight.

The Harris County medical examiner, Dr. Joseph A. Jachimczyk, consulted with hospital officials tonight but refused to be interviewed afterward.

A spokesman for the Baylor College of Medicine, of which Methodist Hospital is a teaching affiliate, said that a Hughes aide telephoned Dr. Henry D. MacIntosh, the chairman of its department of internal medicine, this morning and requested that arrangements be made for an examination and treat-

Continued on Page 59, Column 4

DEMOCRATS SEEK NEW YORK BACKING IN PRIMARY TODAY

Jackson, Udall and Carter Wind Up Campaigning— Wisconsin Also Voting

By FRANK LYNN

The three major candidates for the Democratic Presidential nomination wound up their drives for today's New York primary with diverse campaigning yesterday that reflected their political priorities and strategy.

Senator Henry M. Jackson of Washington, who must win decisively here to regain momentum in the Presidential race, campaigned across the state from Buffalo to Staten Island.

Representative Morris K. Udall of Arizona, who has tried to divide his effort between New York and Wisconsin, which also votes today, made a perfunctory appearance designed to attract as much news attention as possible.

Jimmy Carter, former Governor of Georgia, who spent the day in Wisconsin, campaigned in absentia in New York with mimeographed announcements of endorsements.

Wisconsin Campaigning

Meanwhile, in Wisconsin, Mr. Carter and Representative Udall were tying up loose ends in their campaigns. The two men, who are considered the front runners in Wisconsin, scurried across the state in a last-minute hunt for support.

Former Senator Fred R. Harris of Oklahoma, who had virtually abandoned his campaign here, made rare appearances in the city and upstate to try to salvage some delegates.

The polls in New York City will be open from 6 A.M. to 9 P.M. and outside the city from noon to 9 P.M. A total of 856 Democrats are vying for 206 national convention delegate berths in the state's 39 Congressional districts.

9 Percent of Delegates

The district delegates and 68 delegates at large to be appointed by the Democratic state committee and apportioned to each candidate on the basis of his showing today represent 9 percent of the 3,008 delegates who will convene July 12 at Madison Square Garden.

Senator Jackson has repeatedly predicted—and he did so again yesterday—that he will win a majority of the delegates. He has also made a major commitment of manpower, money and his own

Continued on Page 22, Column 1

Callaghan, Party's Choice, Is Prime Minister of Britain

Associated Press

James Callaghan, Britain's Foreign Secretary, arrives at Labor Party headquarters in London with his wife, Audrey.

Special to The New York Times

LONDON, April 5—James Callaghan, the Foreign Secretary, was chosen today as Britain's new Prime Minister. He promptly called on the divided factions of his party to unify behind efforts to rescue Britain from its long-term economic decline.

The Labor Party members of the House of Commons gave Mr. Callaghan, 64 years old, the party's leadership and this country's top government post by a comfortable margin in the third round of a balloting process that began on March 16, when Harold Wilson unexpectedly announced his resignation from office.

Mr. Callaghan received 176 votes today. Michael Foot, the Secretary of State for Employment and champion of the party's left wing, won 137 votes. They were the only nominees to survive the earlier rounds.

Technically, the most the members could confer on Mr. Callaghan was the leadership of the Labor Party. But since Mr. Wilson resigned as Prime Minister midway through the Labor Party Government's five-year term of office, his successor as party leader automatically became Prime Minister.

Although the vote made Mr. Callaghan's succession certain, he observed the time-honored ritual of presenting himself to Queen Elizabeth II before formally taking office.

Mr. Wilson arrived at Buckingham Palace at 5:26 to hand in his resignation and told the Queen of his and his party's "advice." Mr. Callaghan arrived

Continued on Page 16, Column 3

PEKING IS RACKED BY A DAY OF RIOTS; MILITIA STEPS IN

Crowds, Put at 30,000, Set Cars on Fire and Try to Storm the Great Hall

BACKING FOR CHOU SEEN

Demonstrations Appear to Be Backlash to Campaign Against 'Rightists'

By Reuters

PEKING, Tuesday, April 6 — Violent demonstrations, apparently in support of former Prime Minister Chou En-lai and his associates, were staged through the day yesterday in Peking's Tien An Men Square, and few attempts were made to stop them.

After a day of incidents in which demonstrators estimated to total 30,000 tried to break into the Great Hall of the People and many set cars and a nearby building afire, militiamen armed with wooden staves cleared the area. Long orderly lines of militamen were seen escorting people, apparently demonstrators, into the ancient Forbidden City, and late last night quiet appeared to have been restored.

Struggle for Power

The demonstrations appeared to be a backlash against the so-called antirightist campaign begun as part of the power struggle in the Chinese leadership after Mr. Chou died in January.

Peking's Mayor, Wu Teh, linked the demonstrations to that struggle as he appealed in late afternoon for the crowds to disperse. In a message broadcast through loudspeakers, he charged that the riots were aimed at Chairman Mao Tse-tung and the Central Committee of the Chinese Communist Party and that behind them were persons who supported the "capitalist road."

This was an allusion principally to Deputy Prime Minister Teng Hsiao-ping, an associate of Mr. Chou who had been expected to become Prime Minister and who has been main target of the antirightist campaign.

Teng Had Been in Disgrace

Mr. Teng, who was denounced during the Cultural Revolution of the late 1960's, was brought back from disgrace by Mr. Chou and given the posts of senior Deputy Prime Minister, Deputy Chairman of the party and acting Chief of Staff of the army in apparent preparation for taking over as head of the government. He has not appeared in public since the Chou funeral and has been increasingly accused of stressing material incentives over political awareness and thus trying to bring back capitalism.

The post of Acting Prime Minister that he was expected to get went instead to Hua Kuo-féng, a Deputy Prime Minister and Minister of Public Security.

Yesterday, throughout the day in Tien An Men Square, unarmed troops and militiamen tried to maintain order but were careful to avoid clashes. Authorities made no attempt to break up the crowds and appeared to

Continued on Page 8, Column 4

A Modified Soviet Bloc Is Avowed as U.S. Policy

By DAVID BINDER

Special to The New York Times

WASHINGTON, April 5—Helmut Sonnenfeldt, Secretary of State Henry A. Kissinger's chief adviser, told American ambassadors in Europe that it is in the long-term interest of the United States to encourage East European countries to develop "a more natural and organic" relationship with the Soviet Union, according to an official but nonverbatim summary of his remarks.

The summary, made available today to The New York Times, has been the subject of controversy for two weeks as a result of various versions disclosed by the press.

Summary of the Sonnenfeldt remarks is on Page 14.

It was drafted when Mr. Sonnenfeldt, the State Department counselor, addressed a London meeting of ambassadors in mid-December and was distributed to them in the form of a cablegram from Washington as a memorandum last Feb. 12.

"With regard to Eastern Europe," the memorandum says, "it must be in our long-term interest to influence events in this area—because of the present unnatural relationship with the Soviet Union—so that they will not sooner or later explode, causing World War III. This inorganic, unnatural relationship is a far greater danger to world peace than the conflict between East and West."

He then entered a qualification, saying that if Western Europe turned inward in preoccupation with economic and social problems, it could cause a shift in the power balance inimical to American interests. Continuing on the East European theme, the summary said:

"So, our policy must be a policy of responding to the clearly visible aspirations in Eastern Europe for a more autonomous existence within

Continued on Page 14, Column 4

Seaver Accepts Pact

Tom Seaver agreed last night to a three-year contract with the New York Mets that will pay the pitcher more than $200,000 a year. Seaver had two meetings with the Mets' board chairman, M. Donald Grant, before agreeing to terms. Details, Page 43.

City U. Board Acts To Save John Jay; Students in Protest

By JUDITH CUMMINGS

Acting on its controversial austerity program to restructure the City University, the Board of Higher Education voted last night to close or merge several of its colleges but accepted a modification that would allow John Jay College to remain open with a diminished enrollment.

At the end of a seven-hour meeting in which the board's vice chancellor resigned to protest the cuts, Alfred A. Giardino, the board's chairman, declared that the board would not impose tuition.

The board voted, 6 to 1 with one abstention, to eliminate liberal arts majors from John Jay's curriculum, but to retain its criminal justice and "fire science" courses, effective Sept. 1, 1976.

On the Medgar Evers issue, the board voted, 6 to 3, to downgrade the curriculum, effective in June, 1978.

Earlier, the board approved plans to merge Richmond College with Staten Island Community College and to join Hostos Community College with Bronx Community College.

The board acted after a day in which student demonstrations erupted briefly into fights between the police and supporters of the colleges.

Some demonstrators marched to the East River Drive at 77th

Continued on Page 69, Column 1

HIGH COURT DENIES APPEAL BY CALLEY

Refuses, Without Comment, to Review His Conviction in 22 Slayings at My Lai

By LESLEY OELSNER

Special to The New York Times

WASHINGTON, April 5—The Supreme Court refused today to review the court-martial conviction of former Army Lieut. William L. Calley Jr. for the murder of 22 civilians in the South Vietnamese hamlet of My Lai in 1968.

The Court's action, announced without comment or explanation, closes one of the most bitter chapters of the Vietnam War.

It ends for all practical purposes the long legal aftermath of the My Lai episode, in which 25 Army officers and enlisted personnel were charged with various offenses growing out of the slayings; only six of those 25 were tried, and only Mr. Calley was convicted.

Mr. Calley, who has been free on bail pending appeal since late 1974, after serving a little more than three years of what was originally a life sentence, will not be returned to confinement.

The Army announced this afternoon that, in accord with earlier Army decisions and pronouncements on the case,

Continued on Page 25, Column 1

U.S. Assays Peking Strife As Move Against Radicals

By BERNARD GWERTZMAN

Special to The New York Times

WASHINGTON, April 5 — United States Government officials said today that the violent demonstrations in Peking appeared to represent a major counterattack by supporters of a moderate political policy against radicals who had appeared in the ascendency in China since Prime Minister Chou En-lai's death in January.

Because of the importance of the months-long political struggle in China, the demonstrations have received close attention here. Specialists in various agencies are comparing notes and reading the latest news dispatches and cables from the United States Liaison Office in Peking.

There was disagreement among the China-watchers on the degree of spontaneity of the demonstrations that followed the discovery that wreaths laid in Mr. Chou's honor had been removed. But even those who gave more weight to the spontaneity agreed that there had to be direction and manipulation from influential figures in Peking sympathetic to the moderate cause.

According to a view in top Government circles here, Mr. Chou's death prompted the radicals to make a significant effort to seize as much power as they could.

They were able to prevent Mr. Chou's hand-picked successor, Teng Hsiao-ping, from tak-

Continued on Page 9, Column 1

Hair Codes for Policemen Upheld by Supreme Court

By PRANAY GUPTE

The United States Supreme Court ruled yesterday that police departments had the right to order police officers to wear their hair short and not to wear beards.

In a 6-to-2 vote, the Court reversed a decision by the United States Court of Appeals in New York that said policemen had the constitutional right to wear their hair any way they wished and also to be hirsute if they so chose.

Delivering the majority opinion, Associate Justice William H. Rehnquist said that people who worked for government agencies had "no absolute constitutional right" to wear any hair style. Police departments, he said, could enforce grooming codes if there was a "rational basis" for such regulations.

The Supreme Court's ruling was on a case involving the Suffolk County Police Department and the Suffolk Patrolmen's Benevolent Association, in which police officers of the Long Island county had protested against their department's regulation concerning beards and hair lengths.

Although there is temporarily no grooming code in the Suffolk Police Department, policemen were forbidden to wear beards and maintain hair that touched the ears or shirt collar when the class-action suit first went to Federal Court in 1972.

The majority opinion of the

Continued on Page 25, Column 1

The New York Times/Don Hogan Charles

Students from Medgar Evers College of City University block traffic on the East River Drive at 77th Street as part of their protest

Oil Prospects Off Jersey 'Encouraging'

By MARTIN WALDRON

The prospect of finding oil and gas under offshore sites in the Atlantic Ocean is "very encouraging," according to the first reports from an exploratory well sunk by a consortium of petroleum companies 80 miles off the New Jersey coast.

The companies have declined to comment on the results, citing their proprietary interests, but New Jersey officials yesterday confirmed that core samples brought up in the test drilling suggest the presence of large oil and natural-gas deposits.

The test well was drilled three miles deep on the edge of the Baltimore Canyon, a trough that stretches from just south of Long Island to the Delaware-Maryland state line.

Initial tests, which ended on March 28, found "core samplings which followed exactly what could be expected from the indications of earlier seismic tests," a state official with access to the reports said.

On the basis of seismic tests and geologic studies, the Interior Department has estimated that two to four billion barrels of oil and five to 14 trillion cubic feet of gas lie under the Continental Shelf from Maine to Florida.

No offshore wells have been sunk to substantiate the presence of oil and gas reserves under the Continental Shelf.

The exploratory well was drilled to test the geological strata of what was believed to be a promising site. The mud, sand and rock brought up by the rig at the site suggested only that conditions for oil pooling and gas accumula-

Continued on Page 32, Column 6

NEWS INDEX

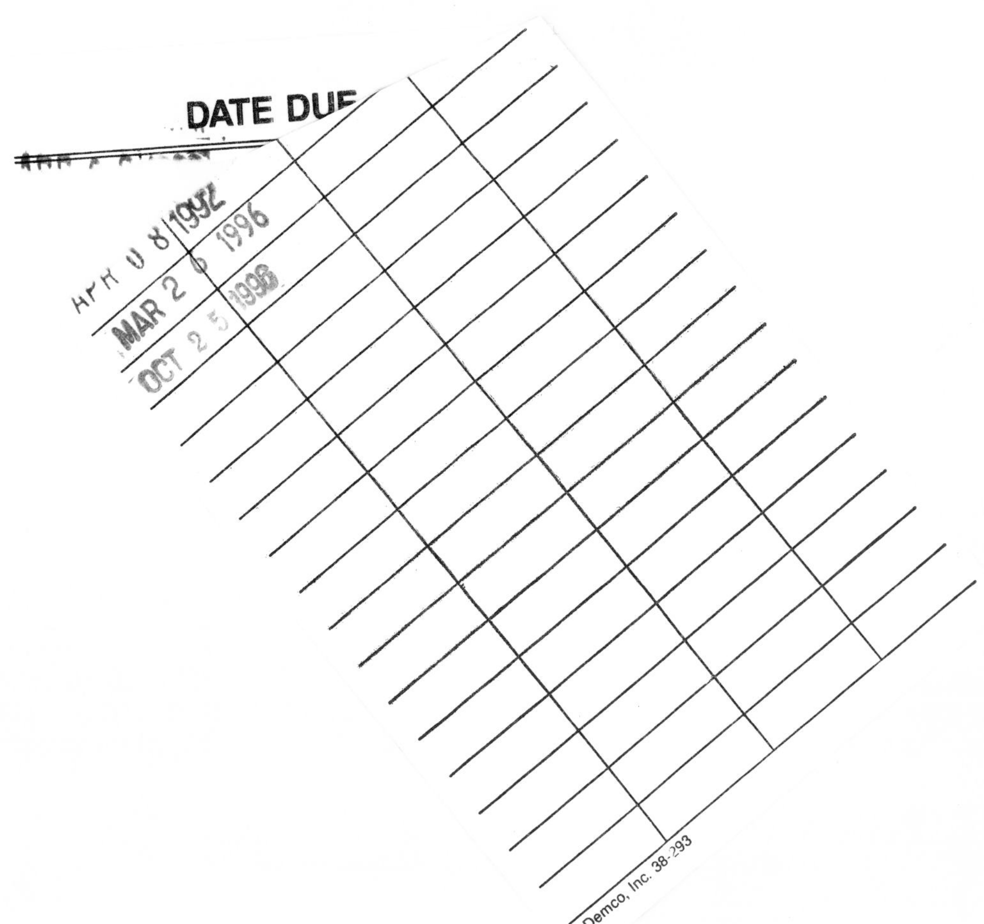
DATE DUE
APR 0 8 1992
MAR 2 6 1996
OCT 2 5 1998
Demco, Inc. 38-293